CLASSICAL
AND MEDIEVAL
LITERATURE
CRITICISM

Guide to Gale Literary Criticism Series

For criticism on	Consult these Gale series
Authors now living or who died after December 31, 1999	*CONTEMPORARY LITERARY CRITICISM (CLC)*
Authors who died between 1900 and 1999	*TWENTIETH-CENTURY LITERARY CRITICISM (TCLC)*
Authors who died between 1800 and 1899	*NINETEENTH-CENTURY LITERATURE CRITICISM (NCLC)*
Authors who died between 1400 and 1799	*LITERATURE CRITICISM FROM 1400 TO 1800 (LC)* *SHAKESPEAREAN CRITICISM (SC)*
Authors who died before 1400	*CLASSICAL AND MEDIEVAL LITERATURE CRITICISM (CMLC)*
Authors of books for children and young adults	*CHILDREN'S LITERATURE REVIEW (CLR)*
Dramatists	*DRAMA CRITICISM (DC)*
Poets	*POETRY CRITICISM (PC)*
Short story writers	*SHORT STORY CRITICISM (SSC)*
Black writers of the past two hundred years	*BLACK LITERATURE CRITICISM (BLC)* *BLACK LITERATURE CRITICISM SUPPLEMENT (BLCS)*
Hispanic writers of the late nineteenth and twentieth centuries	*HISPANIC LITERATURE CRITICISM (HLC)* *HISPANIC LITERATURE CRITICISM SUPPLEMENT (HLCS)*
Native North American writers and orators of the eighteenth, nineteenth, and twentieth centuries	*NATIVE NORTH AMERICAN LITERATURE (NNAL)*
Major authors from the Renaissance to the present	*WORLD LITERATURE CRITICISM, 1500 TO THE PRESENT (WLC)* *WORLD LITERATURE CRITICISM SUPPLEMENT (WLCS)*

ISSN 0896-0011

Volume 44

CLASSICAL AND MEDIEVAL LITERATURE CRITICISM

Excerpts from Criticism of the Works of World
Authors from Classical Antiquity through the
Fourteenth Century, from the First Appraisals
to Current Evaluations

Elisabeth Gellert
Jelena O. Krstović
Editors

GALE GROUP

Detroit
New York
San Francisco
London
Boston
Woodbridge, CT

STAFF

Lynn M. Spampinato, Janet Witalec, *Managing Editors, Literature Product*
Kathy D. Darrow, *Product Liaison*
Elisabeth Gellert, Jelena Krstović, *Editors*
Mark W. Scott, *Publisher, Literature Product*

Jenny Cromie, Mary Ruby, *Technical Training Specialists*
Deborah J. Morad, Kathleen Lopez Nolan, *Managing Editors, Literature Content*
Susan M. Trosky, *Director, Literature Content*

Maria L. Franklin, *Permissions Manager*
Edna Hedblad, *Permissions Specialist*

Victoria B. Cariappa, *Research Manager*
Tracie A. Richardson, *Project Coordinator*
Andrew Guy Malonis, Barbara McNeil, Gary J. Oudersluys, Maureen Richards, Cheryl L. Warnock, *Research Specialists*
Tamara C. Nott, *Research Associate*

Dorothy Maki, *Manufacturing Manager*
Stacy L. Melson, *Buyer*

Mary Beth Trimper, *Composition and Prepress Manager*
Carolyn Roney, *Composition Specialist*

Randy Bassett, *Image Database Supervisor*
Robert Duncan, *Imaging Specialist*
Mike Logusz, *Graphic Artist*
Pamela A. Reed, *Imaging Coordinator*
Kelly A. Quin, *Imaging Editor*

Library of Congress Catalog Card Number 88-658021
ISBN 0-7876-5060-9
ISSN 0896-0011
Printed in the United States of America

10 9 8 7 6 5 4 3 2 1

Contents

Preface vii

Acknowledgments xi

Preface

Since its inception in 1988, *Classical and Medieval Literature Criticism* (*CMLC*) has been a valuable resource for students and librarians seeking critical commentary on the works and authors of antiquity through the fourteenth century. The great poets, prose writers, dramatists, and philosophers of this period form the basis of most humanities curricula, so that virtually every student will encounter many of these works during the course of a high school and college education. Reviewers have found *CMLC* "useful" and "extremely convenient," noting that it "adds to our understanding of the rich legacy left by the ancient period and the Middle Ages," and praising its "general excellence in the presentation of an inherently interesting subject." No other single reference source has surveyed the critical reaction to classical and medieval literature as thoroughly as *CMLC*.

Scope of the Series

CMLC provides an introduction to classical and medieval authors, works, and topics that represent a variety of genres, time periods, and nationalities. By organizing and reprinting an enormous amount of critical commentary written on authors and works of this period in world history, *CMLC* helps students develop valuable insight into literary history, promotes a better understanding of the texts, and sparks ideas for papers and assignments.

Each entry in *CMLC* presents a comprehensive survey of an author's career, an individual work of literature, or a literary topic, and provides the user with a multiplicity of interpretations and assessments. Such variety allows students to pursue their own interests; furthermore, it fosters an awareness that literature is dynamic and responsive to many different opinions. Early commentary is offered to indicate initial responses, later selections document changes in literary reputations, and retrospective analyses provide the reader with modern views. The size of each author entry is a relative reflection of the scope of the criticism available in English.

An author may appear more than once in the series if his or her writings have been the subject of a substantial amount of criticism; in these instances, specific works or groups of works by the author will be covered in separate entries. For example, Homer will be represented by three entries, one devoted to the *Iliad,* one to the *Odyssey,* and one to the Homeric Hymns.

CMLC continues the survey of criticism of world literature begun by Gale's *Contemporary Literary Criticism* (*CLC*), *Twentieth-Century Literary Criticism* (*TCLC*), *Nineteenth-Century Literature Criticism* (*NCLC*), *Literature Criticism from 1400 to 1800* (*LC*), and *Shakespearean Criticism* (*SC*).

Organization of the Book

A *CMLC* entry consists of the following elements:

- The **Author Heading** cites the name under which the author most commonly wrote, followed by birth and death dates. Also located here are any name variations under which an author wrote, including transliterated forms for authors whose native languages use nonroman alphabets. If the author wrote consistently under a pseudonym, the pseudonym will be listed in the author heading and the author's actual name given in parenthesis on the first line of the biographical and critical information. Uncertain birth or death dates are indicated by question marks. Single-work entries are preceded by a heading that consists of the most common form of the title in English translation (if applicable) and the original date of composition.

- The **Introduction** contains background information that introduces the reader to the author, work, or topic that is the subject of the entry.

- A **Portrait of the Author** is included when available.

- The list of **Principal Works** is ordered chronologically by date of first publication and lists the most important works by the author. The genre and publication date of each work is given. In the case of foreign authors whose works have been translated into English, the list will focus primarily on twentieth-century translations, selecting those works most commonly considered the best by critics. Unless otherwise indicated, dramas are dated by first performance, not first publication. Lists of **Representative Works** by different authors appear with topic entries.

- Reprinted **Criticism** is arranged chronologically in each entry to provide a useful perspective on changes in critical evaluation over time. The critic's name and the date of composition or publication of the critical work are given at the beginning of each piece of criticism. Unsigned criticism is preceded by the title of the source in which it appeared. All titles by the author featured in the text are printed in boldface type. Footnotes are reprinted at the end of each essay or excerpt. In the case of excerpted criticism, only those footnotes that pertain to the excerpted texts are included. Criticism in topic entries is arranged chronologically under a variety of subheadings to facilitate the study of different aspects of the topic.

- A complete **Bibliographical Citation** of the original essay or book precedes each piece of criticism.

- Critical essays are prefaced by brief **Annotations** explicating each piece.

- An annotated bibliography of **Further Reading** appears at the end of each entry and suggests resources for additional study. In some cases, significant essays for which the editors could not obtain reprint rights are included here. Boxed material following the further reading list provides references to other biographical and critical sources on the author in series published by Gale.

Cumulative Indexes

A **Cumulative Author Index** lists all of the authors that appear in a wide variety of reference sources published by the Gale Group, including *CMLC*. A complete list of these sources is found facing the first page of the Author Index. The index also includes birth and death dates and cross references between pseudonyms and actual names.

Beginning with the second volume, a **Cumulative Nationality Index** lists all authors featured in *CMLC* by nationality, followed by the number of the *CMLC* volume in which their entry appears.

Beginning with the tenth volume, a **Cumulative Topic Index** lists the literary themes and topics treated in the series as well as in *Nineteenth-Century Literature Criticism, Twentieth-Century Literary Criticism,* and the *Contemporary Literary Criticism* Yearbook, which was discontinued in 1998.

A **Cumulative Title Index** lists in alphabetical order all of the works discussed in the series. Each title listing includes the corresponding volume and page numbers where criticism may be located. Foreign-language titles that have been translated into English are followed by the titles of the translation—for example, *Slovo o polku Igorove (The Song of Igor's Campaign)*. Page numbers following these translated titles refer to all pages on which any form of the titles, either foreign-language or translated, appear. Titles of novels, dramas, nonfiction books, and poetry, short story, or essay collections are printed in italics, while individual poems, short stories, and essays are printed in roman type within quotation marks.

Citing *Classical and Medieval Literature Criticism*

When writing papers, students who quote directly from any volume in the Literary Criticism Series may use the following general format to footnote reprinted criticism. The first example pertains to material drawn from periodicals, the second to material reprinted from books.

T. P. Malnati, "Juvenal and Martial on Social Mobility," *The Classical Journal* 83, no. 2 (December-January 1988): 134-41; reprinted in *Classical and Medieval Literature Criticism,* vol. 35, ed. Jelena Krstović (Farmington Hills, Mich.: The Gale Group, 2000), 366-71.

J. P. Sullivan, "Humanity and Humour; Imagery and Wit," in *Martial: An Unexpected Classic* (Cambridge University Press, 1991), 211-51; excerpted and reprinted in *Classical and Medieval Literature Criticism,* vol. 35, ed. Jelena Krstović (Farmington Hills, Mich.: The Gale Group, 2000), 371-95.

Suggestions are Welcome

Readers who wish to suggest new features, topics, or authors to appear in future volumes, or who have other suggestions or comments are cordially invited to call, write, or fax the Managing Editor:

Managing Editor, Literary Criticism Series
The Gale Group
27500 Drake Road
Farmington Hills, MI 48331-3535
1-800-347-4253 (GALE)
Fax: 248-699-8054

Acknowledgments

The editors wish to thank the copyright holders of the excerpted criticism included in this volume and the permissions managers of many book and magazine publishing companies for assisting us in securing reproduction rights. We are also grateful to the staffs of the Detroit Public Library, the Library of Congress, the University of Detroit Mercy Library, Wayne State University Purdy/Kresge Library Complex, and the University of Michigan Libraries for making their resources available to us. Following is a list of the copyright holders who have granted us permission to reproduce material in this volume of *CMLC*. Every effort has been made to trace copyright, but if omissions have been made, please let us know.

COPYRIGHTED EXCERPTS IN *CMLC*, VOLUME 44, WERE REPRODUCED FROM THE FOLLOWING PERIODICALS:

COPYRIGHTED EXCERPTS IN *CMLC*, VOLUME 44, WERE REPRODUCED FROM THE FOLLOWING BOOKS:

PHOTOGRAPHS APPEARING IN *CMLC*, VOLUME 44, WERE RECEIVED FROM THE FOLLOWING SOURCES:

Archilochus
fl. mid-7th century B.C.

(Also spelled Archilochos) Greek poet.

INTRODUCTION

In antiquity revered as the finest poet next to Homer, Archilochus is chiefly remembered as the poet of abuse. Credited by the ancients with creating iambics, satire, and elegiac couplets, Archilochus wrote fierce, direct, innovative verses which greatly influenced many poets and dramatists who followed him. Although it is doubtful that he truly originated iambics, his iambs are the earliest extant examples of satire and they indisputably demonstrate his mastery of the mode. While Archilochus's bitter attacks, which survive today only in fragments, have made his name endure, his innovative emphasis on self-expression has endeared him to the modern world.

BIOGRAPHICAL INFORMATION

It is difficult to separate facts from fiction concerning the life of Archilochus since myths came to be fashioned as the poet attained legendary status. Some sources indicate that Archilochus was the illegitimate son of a noble father, Telesicles, and that he was born in Paros, Greece. According to one often-repeated report, his mother was a slave named Enipo. His planned marriage to Neobule, also according to legend, was denied by her father, Lycambes. Bitter, Archilochus composed slanderous lyrics concerning Lycambes, Neobule, and her sisters that so defamed them that they killed themselves. Although the story of their suicides is the most famous concerning Archilochus, it may not have much basis in truth, for it was the highest of praise to have it said that one's satire was so cruel that it caused the subject of the verses to kill himself. Archilochus was also important in instilling Bacchic worship at Paros, for which he composed lewd songs to Dionysus. He left his birthplace to live in the remote island of Thasos, which was founded by his father. There he served as a noble soldier and wrote war poetry. According to legend, Archilochus was killed in battle by a man named Crow; this too may be more myth than substance. Although many historians have done so, critics point out that it is inadvisable to draw factual conclusions from fragments of Archilochus's poetry because lines that appear to be autobiographical may actually be instances of the poet's adopting a persona. Dates concerning Archilochus have been the source of much dispute among scholars; attempts to narrow the time line of his life, beyond that of placing him in the middle of the seventh century B.C., have been made but have not gained wide critical acceptance.

MAJOR WORKS

No complete works of Archilochus survive and the fragments that do exist are often scattered and mangled. There is enough extant, however, to conclusively show he was a master of many styles and that, if he did not actually originate the iamb and the elegiac couplet, he made them his own through his skill and brilliance. He appears to have worked within tradition in some respects, for he strictly adheres to certain rules. His depictions of war are generally more realistic and less glorified in tone than are found in treatments by other poets. Sometimes his war poems are ironic, sometimes disillusioning, and often ambiguous. This ambiguity has fostered different interpretations of his intent and has helped to make his poetry enjoyable in sharp translations for modern readers. His city songs urged citizens to have faith in the midst of fortune's frequent reversals and during times of shifting circumstance. A renewal of enthusiasm in Archilochus studies was caused by the discovery of a lengthy fragment, first published in 1974, rife with examples of Archilochus's "scorpion tongue."

CRITICAL RECEPTION

Archilochus was the recipient of great praise for centuries, mentioned alongside Homer and Hesiod and perceived as being divinely inspired. He nevertheless had some detractors, including Critias, an aristocratic writer and politician, who criticized him for attacking friends as well as foes, and for not hiding his own personality defects. Roman poets regarded Archilochus as a major force, and Horace particularly, in his epodes, pays tribute to him. In discussing his reputation among early Church Fathers, H. D. Rankin explains that they "knew the two main elements of the tradition: that he was a talented poet; and that his work was biased toward sinister and morally less edifying subjects." Rankin states that Archilochus was "regarded by the great writers of the Christians as an outstandingly bad example of character and conduct," but that they nevertheless appeared to be "unwillingly fascinated by his wildness." Frederic Will writes that, because Archilochus "stands much more nakedly than Homer before the perceivable and interpretable world," he is in that sense "the first modern man." Will credits Bruno Snell with noticing "the 'despair of love' creeping, for the first time in western literature, into the poetry of Archilochos (and Sappho)." Will also cites Hermann Fränkel's pointing out Archilochus's concern with the "immediate data of personal experience." Instead of dealing with poetic matter retrospectively, Archilochus effortlessly brings his readers to the here-and-now. In modern times Archilochus is commonly celebrated for being, in Anne Pippin Burnett's words, "a figure of full-bodied, romantic realism—a bastard and a mercenary, a bitter pragmatist who hated tradition and sang with the lewd voice of revolt and poverty, a drunkard who fought with both friend and enemy, a rebel against worn-out values, a debunker of aristocratic ideals, a brawling upstart with a vein of music in him." But Burnett is skeptical of such mythologizing, which she does not find supported by archaeological evidence. Rankin sees Archilochus representing in his poems "two extreme and persistent pressures upon the lives of the Greek individual citizens: that of social duty and that of competitive self-realization." Contemporary critics agree that Archilochus's poems are powerful and original and largely break free from heroic formulas.

PRINCIPAL WORKS

Principal English Translations

Greek Lyrics [translated by Richmond Lattimore] 1960
Carmina Archilochi: The Fragments of Archilochus [translated by Guy Davenport] 1964
Archilochos [translated by Frederic Will] 1969
The Soldier and the Lady: Poems of Archilochos and Sappho [translated by Barriss Mills] 1975
Archilochus of Paros [translated by H. D. Rankin] 1977
Three Archaic Poets: Archilochus, Alcaeus, Sappho [translated by Anne Pippin Burnett] 1983

CRITICISM

John Addington Symonds (essay date 1873)

SOURCE: "The Satirists," in *Studies of the Greek Poets*, Smith, Elder, & Co., 1873, pp. 98-109.

[*In the following excerpt, Symonds provides a brief overview on Archilochus's life, reputation, and accomplishments.*]

The Greeks displayed their æsthetic instinct in nothing more remarkably than in their exact adaptation of the forms of art to the nature of the subjects which they undertook to treat. The Hexameter had sufficed for the needs of the Epic. The Elegiac had fulfilled the requirements of pathetic or contemplative meditation. But with the development of the national genius a separate vehicle for satire was demanded. Archilochus of Paros created a new style, and presented in the Iambic metre a new instrument to the

poets of his race. The circumstances of the birth and parentage of Archilochus are significant. He was the son of Telesicles, a noble Ionian, and of Enipo, a slave-woman. Thus from the very first there were inequalities in his circumstances which may have sufficed to sour his temper. His birth, which may be fixed about 729 B.C., was predicted, according to old tradition, by the oracle at Delphi. The same oracle busied itself at a later period with his death, by cursing the Naxian soldier Calondas, who had killed him in battle, because he had "slain the servant of the Muses." As the fragments which we possess of Archilochus render it difficult to understand the very high estimation in which he was held by the Greeks, and which these stories indicate, it may be well to preface this account of him with some quotations from the ancient critics. Longinus,[1] to begin with, explains the incongruities of his poetry by saying that he "dragged disorderly elements into his verse under the impulse of divine inspiration." Plato[2] calls him . . . the prince of sages, which, in the mouth of a philosopher, is the highest panegyric. The Alexandrian critic Aristophanes, when asked which of the poems of Archilochus he liked best, answered with laconic brevity, "the longest." Hadrian,[3] in an epigram, says that the Muses turned the attention of Archilochus to mad Iambics, in order that their darling Homer might not have so dangerous a rival in the field of the Epic. All antiquity agreed in naming him second only to Homer: "Maximus poeta aut certe summo proximus," says Valerius Maximus. The birthdays of Homer and Archilochus were celebrated on the same day; their busts were joined in Janus fashion—two faces and one head: Hippodromus the Sophist[4] called Homer the Voice, Archilochus the Breath or Soul, of the students of wisdom. The epithet [*kállistos*] was ascribed to him because of his perfect style, though the subjects of his poetry were anything but beautiful. Of this style Quintilian[5] says that it excelled in "powerful as well as short and quivering sentences," that it contained "the greatest possible amount of blood and sinews." The highest praise which Gorgias could pronounce on Plato when he published his dilaogues upon the Sophists, was to say that Athens had produced a new Archilochus. To multiply these panegyrics would be easy. But enough has been adduced to prove that the ancients looked on Archilochus as a worthy rival of Homer, as a poet supreme in his own department, as the creator of a new kingdom in poetry, as the sire of a long line of mighty artists. What remains of the verse of Archilochus and what we know of his life are curiously at variance with this enthusiasm. Nothing proves the difference between ancient and modern views of art more strongly than the fact that all antiquity concurred in regarding as a divinely inspired benefactor of the human race, a man who in the present day would have been hunted from society with execrations. This son of the slave-woman, born in an Ionian island, where license was more tolerated than in a Dorian state, devoted himself to satire, making his genius the instrument of private hate, and turning the golden gifts of the Muses to the service of his selfish spite. A greater contrast cannot be conceived than that which exists between Homer, the priest of Gods and Heroes, the poet of high actions and lofty passions, whose own life is buried in sacred and sublime mystery, and this satirist who saw the world with jaundiced eyes, prying about for subjects of his wrath and bitterness and scorn, whose themes were the passions of his own black heart, the sordid misadventures of his vulgar personality. It was this contrast between Archilochus and Homer that gave the former a right in the estimation of the Greeks to take equal rank with the Father of the Epos. He, the greatest poet next in date to Homer, by virtue of a divine originality of genius, exercised his art in exactly the opposite field to that which Homer ruled as his demesne. Clearer sign than this of inspiration could not be demanded; and how should posterity withhold its gratitude from the poet who had unlocked a new chamber of the treasure-house of art? This was how the ancients reasoned, instead of measuring their poets, as the moderns try to do, by moral standards and conventional conceptions of propriety.

The facts of the life of Archilochus are briefly these. He was engaged to be married to Neobulé, daughter of Lycambes. Her father retracted his consent to the marriage, having possibly discovered that the temper of his proposed son-in-law was a mixture of gall, wormwood, vinegar, verjuice, vitriol, and nitric acid. Thereupon, as Horace says:—

"Archilochum proprio rabies armavit iambo."

He made the Iambic metre his own, and sharpened it into a terrible weapon of attack. Each verse he wrote was polished and pointed like an arrow-head. Each line was steeped in the poison of hideous charges against his sweetheart, her sisters, and her father. The set of poems which he produced, and, as it would appear, recited publicly at the festival of Demeter, were so charged with wit and fire, that the country rang with them. The daughters of Lycambes, tradition avers, went straightway and hanged themselves—unable to endure the flight of fiery serpents that had fallen on them: for, to quote the words of Browning, Archilochus had the art of writing verse that "bit into the live man's flesh like parchment," that sent him wandering, branded and for ever shamed, about his native streets and fields. After this murderous exhibition of his power Archilochus left Paros.[6]

"Away with Paros! her figs and fishy life!"

He removed to Thasos, where the Parians founded a colony But Thasos was worse than Paros:[7] "Like the backbone of an ass it stood bristling with wild wood; for, in sooth it is not a fair land, or pleasant, or delightful, like that which spreads by Siris' stream." It was here he threw his shield away in a battle with the Thracians, and gave Horace and Alcæus a precedent by writing a poem on his want of prowess. The remainder of his life was spent in wandering. He visited Sparta, where, however, he was not suffered to remain an hour. The Ephors judged rightly that this runaway soldier and foul-mouthed Ionian satirist might corrupt the Spartan youth, or sow dissension in the State. The publication of his works was forbidden in this, the most conservative of all Greek States. Finally Archilochus

returned to Paros, and was killed in battle by a native of Naxos. A more unhappy existence, wretched in itself and the cause of wretchedness to others, can scarcely be imagined, if the tale of the life of Archilochus be true. Dishonoured by the inequality of his parentage, slighted in the matter of his marriage, discontented at home, restless and rejected abroad, he seems to have been formed by the facts of his biography for the creation of Satire. And this is his greatest title to fame.

It is possible that the Iambic metre existed before the date of Archilochus. An old myth connects it with the festivals of Demeter. Demeter, it is said, could not be made to laugh after her daughter's loss, until a nymph, Iambé, by her jests and sarcasms, raised a smile upon her lips. This legend proves that the Greeks referred the origin of the Iambic to those jokes and gibes which were common in the feasts of Demeter, and from the licentious mirth of which the satiric element of Comedy was developed. The Iambic is nearest in cadence to the language of common life; it is therefore the fit vehicle for dialogue, and for all poetry that deals with common and domestic topics. Again, it is essentially rapid in movement: Horace speaks of *celeres Iambi* . . . : this rapidity fitted them for sharp attack and swift satiric pungency. Admitting then that the metre may have been employed in early attempts at colloquial satire, Archilochus, perceiving its capacities, fashioned it to suit the purpose of his own consummate art. He was celebrated among the ancients for having perfected the metres belonging to . . . the Iambic and Trochaic rhythms, in which either the arsis or the thesis has twice the time of the other. In a trochee the first syllable equals two of the same time as the second; in an iamb this order is reversed; whereas the dactyl and the spondee, on which the hexameter and elegiac metres are based, are feet, each member of which has the same time, the two shorts of the dactyl being equivalent to the second long of the spondee. Archilochus, if not absolutely the inventor, was the creator of these two metres, the Iambic and Trochaic, as truly as Homer was the creator of the heroic measure. No proof of the power of his genius can be greater than the fact that, whatever changes may have been subsequently wrought in the Iambic and Trochaic metres, they remained substantially the same as those which Archilochus employed, whether afterwards adapted to Satire, Tragedy, or Comedy. While speaking of Archilochus as a technical artist, it ought to be mentioned that he gave further proof of his originality by elaborating the metrical systems which the Greeks called Asynartêtes, or unconnected. These consisted of a mixture of dactylic and anapæstic with trochaic feet. The Ithyphallic, which was marked by a succession of three trochees at the end of the line, was the most distinguished.

To translate Archilochus is almost impossible. His merit is the perfection of style, which will admit of no transplantation. His language is the language of common life, exquisitely chosen, and kept within the most exact limits, with a view to the production of a carefully studied effect. It is hopeless to render such fragments as we possess without making them seem coarse or prosy, the poet's supremacy having been achieved by his artistic handling of vernacular Greek. When we compare its pithy terseness with the flowing grandeur of the Epic—a grandeur which had already become conventional in Greece, a fluency which poetasters abused—it is easy to understand that the racy epigrams of Archilochus, in which the subject was set forth with exquisite point and without circumlocution, must have been an acceptable novelty to his audience. . . .

Notes

1. *On the Sublime,* xxxiii. 5.

2. *Rep.,* 365, c.

3. *Anth. Pal.,* vii. 674.

4. *Philostr. Bioi Soph.,* 620.

5. x. 1. 60.

6. Bergk, *Poetæ Lyrici,* p. 696.

7. *Ib.* p. 689.

T. Hudson-Williams (essay date 1926)

SOURCE: "Archilochus and Callinus," in *Early Greek Elegy: The Elegiac Fragments of Callinus, Archilochus, Mimnermus, Tyrtaeus, Solon, Xenophanes, & Others,* The University of Wales Press Board, 1926, pp. 9-12.

[*In the following excerpt, Hudson-Williams outlines some of the problems scholars face in trying to determine accurate dates in the life of Archilochus.*]

I

ARCHILOCHUS AND CALLINUS; CHRONOLOGY

Ever since the dawn of literary criticism there has been much wordy warfare over the rival claims of Archilochus and Callinus to be regarded as 'the Father of Greek Elegy'. . . .

We have really no fixed date in the history of Archilochus; he certainly lived in the seventh century B. C., and heard of Gyges and his wealth (see *infra,* p. 12). No definite information can be extracted from the famous description of the noonday eclipse (Arch. 74); the words with which Aristotle introduces his quotation (Rhet. 3. 17) are of some significance. As Hauvette (*Archiloque,* p. 14) has pointed out, they at least make it unnecessary to suppose that the poet was describing an event which he himself, or indeed any of his contemporaries, had witnessed; however vivid the verses may appear to us, we have no right to assume that Archilochus was relating a personal experience. He might be referring to an ancient tradition about the eclipse of 763 B. C., or perhaps to the eclipse visible to the east of Rhodes in 657 B. C.; it is of course still more likely that the eclipse was the one seen at Thasos in 648 B. C.; but the fragment certainly does not justify us in assuming that Archilochus must therefore have been at Thasos in 648 B.

c., still less in regarding 6 April 648 B. C. as 'the first exact date we have bearing on the history of Greece' (Bury, *History of Greece,* p. 119).

The ancient chronologists could not agree about the date of Archilochus; Eusebius sets his floruit about 665 B. C., others (including Eusebius himself on another occasion) give 688 B. C.; Cicero reproduces a tradition which made him a contemporary of Romulus (i. e. 753-716 B. C., Tusc. 1. 1. 3), while Cornelius Nepos is said by Gellius (17, 21) to have mentioned Archilochus as a poet famous in the reign of Tullus Hostilius (672-640 B. C.).

Hauvette in his brilliant monograph on Archilochus (Paris, 1905) has sought to place our chronology on a more solid basis by utilizing an inscription discovered at Paros and first published by Hiller von Gärtringen in 1900; he claims to have refuted a view regarded as self-evident by many modern critics, viz. that the ancients had no traditional data for a life of Archilochus. A careful consideration of his arguments has not convinced me that a hitherto unknown historian, Demeas of Paros, wrote about the middle of the fourth century B. C. a treatise on Archilochus from which the literary historians of Greece derived their information regarding the Parian poet; for a full discussion see my review of Hauvette's *Archiloque* in the *Classical Review* for August 1907. It will be seen from the passages cited that even for Strabo and Clement the priority of Callinus to Archilochus was only something to be inferred from a comparison of the two poets' writings, and their chief argument is drawn from a line of very doubtful interpretation. . . . If Strabo has a sound basis for his statement about the reference made by Callinus to the prosperity of Magnesia and its success in the war against its neighbour Ephesus, then we must admit a similar soundness of information for his remark about the connexion of Callinus 3 . . . with the taking of Sardis, an event which occurred about 655-652 B. C. Our evidence would then come to this; Callinus mentions an incident that happened about 655-652 B. C. and other events of previous date; Archilochus perhaps refers to an eclipse which he saw in 648 B. C., and perhaps also to an occurrence that cannot be dated much later than 650 B. C. (the fall of Magnesia), an event that, assuming Strabo to have all the requisite data at his disposal, was not mentioned by Callinus.

Strabo was probably not sufficiently acquainted with the poetry of Callinus to justify him in drawing any conclusion from the apparent absence of a reference to the destruction of Magnesia. Further, it is by no means certain, to judge from the extant fragments, that Archilochus ever did refer to the destruction of Magnesia; 'the woes of the Thasians', of which he preferred to sing (if the amended text can be taken as correct), did not include the destruction of their state; and finally it should be remembered that we know far too little about the history of the period or the writings of Callinus to justify us in altogether ignoring the remarks of Athenaeus. . . .

In any case the mention or failure to mention the fall of Magnesia can give us no clue. We may safely regard the two poets as contemporaries; further than that it would be risky to go; we must leave this quarrel of the ages still unsettled and be content to say with the cautious Roman:

> quis tamen exiguos elegos emiserit auctor
> grammatici certant et adhuc sub iudice lis est.

> (Horace, A. P. 77, 78.) . . .

C. M. Bowra (lecture date 1935)

SOURCE: "Origins and Beginnings," in *Early Greek Elegists,* Barnes & Noble Inc., 1960, pp. 3-36.

[*In the following essay, originally delivered as a lecture in 1935, Bowra discusses the flute-song origins of the elegy and the significance of Archilochus's use of Homeric language in his verses concerning war.*]

Few forms of verse can have had so long a history as the Greek elegiac couplet. It first appears, so far as we know, in the eighth century before Christ, and it was still vital in the tenth century after Christ. It is the aim of these lectures to give a sketch of this form and of its users in its early days and to mention some of its chief characteristics in a period when it was the vehicle not only for passing emotions but for considered ideas. In the centuries from the eighth to the fifth before Christ the elegiac existed by the side of lyric poetry and was to some extent an appanage of it, but it kept its own kind of language and subject and may well be studied by itself.

The elegiac couplet has been called "a variation upon the heroic hexameter in the direction of lyric poetry."[1] It consists of two lines which form, so to speak, a verse or stanza. The first line is the familiar hexameter of the epic and differs little from it in structure. But the second line is more peculiar; it is usually called a pentameter, but only mathematically can it be said to have five feet. For when we scan a so-called pentameter such as William Watson's

> Man and his glory survive, lost in the greatness of God,

we find that we have not five successive dactyls but two and a half dactyls followed by another two and a half. . . .

So the alleged pentameter is really made out of two separate metrical units, which were in practice kept distinct from each other by the simple rule that a word could not be carried over from the first to the second. By attaching the so-called pentameter in this way to the hexameter the Greeks created a new metrical unit for poetry. The elegiac couplet differed on the one hand from the epic hexameter which was operated as a single line and never built into regular stanzas, and on the other from the varying stanzas of lyric verse in which different metrical units were formed into an endless variety of patterns. The couplet had the advantage of being both regular and melodious; it provided a

set form for the poet to compose in, but inside this there were many possible harmonies, especially as the Greeks, unlike their Roman imitators, did not insist that a sentence should be confined to a single couplet but freely allowed it to flow over into the next. It is, then, not surprising that a form so free and musical was much used.

The origin of this form is a matter of some dispute. The word [*élegeion*], from which the modern word "elegy" is ultimately derived, first occurs in a fragment of Critias, the friend of Socrates, written at the end of the fifth century.[2] The word must be connected with [*élegos*], which is freely used by Euripides and later writers to mean "lament." Moreover, long before this Echembrotus won the contest for the flute at Delphi about 586 B.C. by singing . . . elegiac verses. It is therefore not surprising that Hellenistic and Roman writers regarded the elegiac as a mournful measure—Ovid's "flebilis Elegeia." But to this view of the nature of the elegiac there is an insuperable objection,—that the oldest types of elegiac verse have little or nothing to do with lamentation.[3] They seem in the main to be either military or convivial, and such grief as they express is seldom concerned with the dead. Even the early and frequent use of the elegiac for inscriptions on tombs can hardly be described as a form of lamentation, since it seldom expresses grief and is usually put in the form of words spoken by the dead about themselves. It is, in fact, fairly certain that the use of the elegiac for laments was an old Peloponnesian custom practiced by Echembrotus, Sacadas and Clonas. It survives in the elegiac lament of Euripides' *Andromache* 103-116, and a late example may be seen in Callimachus' *Bath of Pallas.* But all earlier examples of such elegy are now lost, and this Peloponnesian use, whatever it once was, does not concern us. It was isolated and no doubt had its own characteristics. But it had little to do with early elegy as we know it.

In practice the elegiac couplet seems to have been a song sung to the accompaniment of the flute, just as lyric poetry was sung to the lyre. This conclusion emerges from a statement of Archilochus,[4] from a tradition that Mimnermus was a fluteplayer,[5] and from passages in the *Theognidea* where the poet says that he sings to the flute and refers to his elegiacs.[6] It was also known to ancient authorities such as Plutarch[7] and Pausanias.[8] Moreover it gets support from a simple fact. The earliest known elegiac pieces are either military like those of Callinus and Tyrtaeus or convivial like those of Mimnermus, and it happens that the flute was a favorite instrument for both soldiers and feasters. Homer illustrates both uses. He names "flutes and pipes" among the musical instruments heard by Agamemnon in the Trojan encampment at night,[9] and he makes flutes an important element of noise in the scene of feasting on the Shield of Achilles.[10] There seems, then, little reason to doubt the simple theory that the elegiac was originally a flute-song. The word may be of Asiatic origin, and some have recognized a collateral descendant in the Armenian root *elegn-.* The names of Greek musical instruments are usually of foreign origin, and since the first pieces of elegiac verse come from Asia Minor and the adjacent islands, an Asiatic influence, whether Phrygian or Lydian or the like, is easy to understand. In any case the flute was an instrument in ancient Babylon and was certainly not invented in Greece.

The elegiac, then, came into existence as a flute-song, and such it remained for some three or four centuries. Who first invented it is a mystery. The Greeks seem to have hesitated between Archilochus, Callinus, and Tyrtaeus,[11] but since these are the earliest known elegists, it looks as if the Alexandrian scholars knew no more than we do and assigned the invention to the first elegists known to them. Of these three Archilochus has perhaps the greatest claims, if not to the invention of the elegiac, at least to its improvement and adaptation to different uses. Blakeway showed that Archilochus lived between about 735 B.C. and 665 B.C.[12] A man of surpassing power and originality, he polished for Greek poetry some of its most enduring forms of verse and wrote poems of an astonishing directness and strength. His poetry was the reflection of his wandering, unsuccessful, and unhappy life. A bastard, poverty-stricken and crossed in love, he could not help bursting into words of bitter hate against his enemies, so that for later generations he was the type of the harsh-spoken man, and Pindar referred to him as "fattening his leanness with hate and heavy words."[13] But his hatreds are to be found more in his iambic than in his elegiac verses, and he shows a truly Greek sense of appropriateness in keeping the subject matter of the two kinds apart.

So far as we can tell from the scanty fragments, Archilochus' elegiacs were often written in moments of relaxation when he was leading an active life on campaign. In Thasos, which he helped to colonize about 708, he had trouble from Thracian barbarians, and his war experiences were not confined to this. He may have taken a part in the Lelantine War in which Chalcis fought Eretria and strong powers were ranged on either side; tradition tells that he died fighting.[14] Against this background of active life we may set his elegiac verses, which are, so to speak, his own candid and disarming comments on it. He saw himself as passing his life under arms and wrote: . . .

> My spear wins bread, my spear wins Thracian wine:
> To drink it, on my spear-head I recline.[15]

But in spite of this he did not see himself as nothing but a soldier. He was also a poet, and proud of it: . . .

> I am the servant of the Lord of War,
> And I know too the Muses' lovely gift.[16]

Such simple couplets were probably improvised and sung in the intervals of fighting, when someone had a flute and the poet was called upon for a song. They are eminently topical, and yet they are so concentrated, so careful to state only the essential facts, that this topical origin is left behind. They have become verses suitable to any soldier-poet. Crisply and firmly they state some aspect of Archilochus' life, and nothing can be added to their brief directness.

Archilochus knew many sides of war, and had many different feelings and views on the subject. He did not stage himself as a hero and had the true soldier's dislike for any kind of heroics. He liked to show his realistic attitude towards war by a lighthearted cynicism and contempt for appearances. Twice at least he wrote verses which would not please a sergeant-major. In one he is concerned with the boredom of keeping watch, and his solution is to drink wine: . . .

> Come, pass a cup along the swift ship's benches:
>   Draw the drinks off from the hollow tuns.
> Drain red wine to the lees. No more than others
>   Can we keep sobriety on guard.[17]

This is bad enough by all military rules, but what are we to think of the following? . . .

> A perfect shield bedecks some Thracian now;
>   I had no choice: I left it in a wood.
> Ah, well, I saved my skin, so let it go!
>   A new one's just as good.[18]

The delightful insouciance of these lines presents a marked contrast to the way in which Homer makes his heroes fight over armor, as if to lose a weapon were an appalling dishonor. Archilochus, with years of military experience, had no such illusions, and started a fashion which was copied by Alcaeus, Anacreon, and Horace,[19] as if Archilochus had made the loss of a shield respectable, at least for a poet.

These poems come from the lighter side of war, and if a soldier is to keep sane, he must see things as Archilochus saw them. This does not mean that he was dulled to war's horrors and sorrows: rather, he steeled himself to endure them and not to complain about the inevitable. In some verses to a friend, Pericles, he shows a philosophic spirit about suffering and loss, but it is based on genuine sympathy and understanding: . . .

> Of lamentable miseries complaining
>   Neither man nor town enjoys the feast:
> These men, 'tis true, the sea's wave loud-resounding
>   Overwhelmed, and our hearts swell with grief.
> And yet for cureless ills in staunch endurance,
>   Friend, the Gods have given us a drug.
> To-day this man may suffer, that to-morrow:
>   Now our turn to weep a bloody wound:
> Soon will it pass to others. Lay aside, then,
>   Quickly woman's sorrow and endure.[20]

The circumstances in which these lines were sung are fairly clear. The poet is at a feast, and his companion cannot help weeping because of some friends who have been lost in a disaster at sea. Archilochus knows what Pericles suffers, but feels that it is better to cheer and console him than to sympathize too tenderly. He preaches the doctrine of "staunch endurance," and calls such grief womanish. His apparent sternness is due not to hardness of heart but to a lesson which he has learned from experience, to face adversity without complaining and to accept disaster with an almost Stoic calm.

These small pieces of poetry throw some light on Archilochus' life and character, but they have also a technical interest. They are the earliest elegiacs we possess, and they may well have had an influence on later work. In any case they show at least one characteristic which was to persist in the elegiac until the Alexandrian poets changed its style. In these pieces Archilochus uses definitely Homeric language. We may note the familiar epithets, the "swift" ship, the "loudly-resounding" sea, the "red" wine, the "kneaded" bread, the traditional phrases like "the War-god's mellay" and "the end of death," the archaic genitive in [-*oio*] which did not belong to Archilochus' own spoken tongue. Archilochus, it is clear, wrote elegiacs with his mind full of Homer and the epic vocabulary. And this is easily understood. The epic was preëminently the poetry of martial men, and it was only natural to use its phrases when writing about war. Moreover its vocabulary was too rich and too appropriate for an elegiac poet to neglect it; it lay there for his taking and fell at once into his dactylic couplets. But Archilochus showed his sense of form and style by excluding these epic phrases from his other forms of verse.[21] When he wrote in iambic and trochaic meters, he not only avoided them but used a more homely language which included words too colloquial for epic dignity. The distinction which he made is important; for others observed it. All the early elegists used the epic language, not, indeed, slavishly, but with ease and discernment. But the iambic poets allowed themselves considerably more freedom and nearness to the speech of every day. The elegiac at its very beginning was dignified with the rich vocabulary of Homer.

The elegiacs of Archilochus belong to the camp. Hence their brightness and briskness, their touch with life and their absence of trimmings. This was the kind of poetry that soldiers liked. But in different circumstances, especially in Ionian cities where elegiac poems were sung over the wine in select company, there was a natural tendency to spread oneself, to make a poem of some length if the subject was important enough. The result was an art less concentrated than that of Archilochus, but still undeniably impressive. In the first half of the seventh century the whole of Asia Minor was ravaged by barbarian hordes of Cimmerians.[22] Among other places, they attacked Ephesus about 650 B.C. but failed to take it, though they burned the temple of Artemis outside the town. The crisis of this invasion inspired a poet of whom hardly anything else is known, the Ephesian Callinus. That he feared the invasion of the Cimmerians is shown by his splendid lone line:
. . .

Now comes the murderous Cimmerian army.[23]

Notes

1. W. R. Hardie, *Res Metrica*, p. 49.

2. Fr. 2, 3 Diehl.

3. The whole question is discussed with great ability and fullness by D. L. Page in *Greek Poetry and Life*, pp. 206-217.

4. Fr. 123 Bergk.

5. Strab. xiv. 643.

6. 241, 533, 825, 943, 1041.

7. *Mus.* 8.

8. x. 7, 5.

9. *Il.* x. 13.

10. *Il.* xviii. 495.

11. Didymus, quoted by Orion, p. 58, 7 ff.

12. *Greek Poetry and Life,* pp. 34-55.

13. *Pyth.* ii. 54-6.

14. Plut. *de Ser. Num. Vind.* 17, Aelian fr. 80.

15. Fr. 2 Diehl.

16. Fr. 1.

17. Fr. 5.

18. Fr. 6b. Tr. Sir William Marris.

19. Cf. *Greek Lyric Poetry*, p. 152.

20. Fr. 7.

21. Cf. A. Hauvette, *Archiloque,* pp. 232-245.

22. Cf. T. Hudson-Williams, *Early Greek Elegy*, pp. 12-19.

23. Fr. 3 Diehl.

A. A. Blakeway (essay date 1936)

SOURCE: "The Date of Archilochus," in *Greek Poetry and Life: Essays Presented to Gilbert Murray,* Oxford at the Clarendon Press, 1936, pp. 34-55.

[*In the following excerpt, Blakeway argues that certain conclusions about the chronology of Archilochus are erroneous because they are based on the solar eclipse of 648 B.C. rather than the solar eclipse of 711 B.C.*]

I. THE ASTRONOMICAL EVIDENCE

The external literary evidence for the chronology of Archilochus is as follows:

Cicero places him in the lifetime of Romulus. (Traditionally 753-716 B.C.)

Clement, arguing from the foundation date of Thasos, dates his fame from *c.* 700 B.C.

Eusebius, in the *Praeparatio Evangelica,* Tatian, Cyril place his *floruit* about the Twenty-third Olympiad, 688-685 B.C.

Nepos places his fame in the reign of Tullus Hostilius. (Traditionally 671-640 B.C.)

Eusebius, in Jerome's version of the *Chronici Canones,* notices him against the first year of the Twenty-ninth Olympiad, 664-663 B.C. (665-664 B.C. Armenian version.)

Herodotus makes him the contemporary of Gyges. (? *c.* 652 B.C. according to the Assyrian Chronology.)

Since the identification of the eclipse of Archilochus with that which was total in Paros on April 6th, 648 B.C., much of this evidence has been disregarded as valueless. With a fixed point so firmly established by an exact science, Hellenistic, Roman, and early Christian chronologies could be treated with the scant respect they deserved. The 648 B.C. date stood firm on a fourfold foundation; Astronomy, the inscription of Assurbanipal, Herodotus, and Archilochus himself. It was one of the few certain dates of the eighth and seventh centuries, and to it all reconstructions of that period had to conform.

This creed I found fairly satisfying until I was forced into scepticism by (i) a study of Greek Colonization of the West and the dates of the Sicilian colonies, (ii) a study of the so-called 'Lelantine War', (iii) the date of the colonization of Thasos as given by Xanthus and the close connexion of Archilochus with that colonization implied by Clement of Alexandria and Oenomaus of Gadara.

I shall return to these points later. For the moment it is only necessary to state that in all three inquiries the 648 B.C. date for Archilochus seemed to me inconsistent with the majority of the best evidence, and that all three seemed to demand that part of Archilochus' lifetime should fall within the eighth century.

For this last there was indeed fairly good literary evidence, and further, with the exception of the reference to the eclipse, there was nothing in the extant fragments of Archilochus inconsistent with such a date. The eclipse, however, was not to be denied, and for long I thought that the 648 B.C. date must be retained even at the cost of discarding some of the most reliable dates in Thucydides. It was only when I found that the area of totality of the eclipse of 711 B.C. had last been calculated before the computations of Fotheringham, Schoch, and Neugebauer that I considered the possibility of the eclipse of that year being the eclipse of Archilochus and appealed to Dr. Fotheringham[1] to make the necessary calculations in my behalf.

I quote from two letters written to me in the summer of 1933.

I

'I have now computed with the latest elements, i.e. Schoch's last published elements with the correction to the Moon's node which he sent me in a letter shortly before his death, the total eclipse of the sun of 711 B.C. March 14th.

'But I find that this last small correction does not affect the result. I have in fact worked through the computation for the elements and the details for Thasos, substituting the last published corrections wherever they affect it. So the final result is not dependent on any unpublished figures.

'I find that the eclipse was total in Thasos. I have computed for 40° 40' N. 24° 20' E., but it would be total throughout Thasos. I find for the middle of totality 10:16 a.m. local solar time, which is rather nearer to mid-day than the time when the eclipse of 648 B.C. April 6th was total at Paros.

'I find that the eclipse of 711 B.C. March 14th attained a magnitude of 11·46 digits at Paros.

'Totality is reckoned at 12 digits. This means that 95.5 per cent. of the sun's diameter was eclipsed. The uneclipsed crescent would have a width amounting to 4.5 per cent. of the sun's diameter—a thin crescent.

'So if you have other reasons for regarding 711 B.C. March 14 at Thasos as a possible time and place, the astronomy supports you.'

II

'I find that the last printed corrections to the position of the Moon's node at which I arrived by so curious an accident, and which were issued by Schoch on a flysheet and afterwards published by Neugebauer, most fully in his *Astronomische Chronologie* (1929) I, 133, give as magnitude of the solar eclipse of 711 B.C. March 14 for Paros (37° 2' N. 25° 11' E.) 11·47 digits and for Thasos (40° 40' N. 24° 20' E.) 12·15 digits, where anything amounting to 12·00 or over is total. The small correction which Schoch communicated to me in a letter, but which he did not live to publish, changes these to 11·46 and 12·14 respectively. These elements were verified by Schoch over a long series of eclipses, but he did not live to publish the verification. The elements, as printed, were also verified by Neugebauer in *Astronomische Nachrichten*, Band 8, Nr. 2 (1930), pp. B 24-B 32.'

The eclipse of 648 B.C. was total at Paros, that of 711 B.C. total at Thasos and not far from total at Paros.

At the least there is nothing to choose between the two eclipses astronomically. In the words of Dr. Fotheringham, 'It is rather distressing that in spite of all our refinements astronomy should still offer this dual solution'. At the most the eclipse of 711 B.C. approaches more nearly to the description of Archilochus than that of 648 B.C. To quote Dr. Fotheringham again, 'I find for the middle of totality at Thasos in 711 B.C., 10.16 a.m. local solar time, which is rather nearer to mid-day than the time when the eclipse of 648 B.C. April 6th was total at Paros.' If anything astronomy supports the 711 B.C. date. 648 B.C. can no longer be regarded as a certain and fixed point in the lifetime of Archilochus. Ultimately our choice between the two can only be determined by an examination of the extant evidence, internal and external, for the period of his life. The majority of this evidence seems to me to point to the earlier date, but I propose to examine it in detail before attempting a reconstruction. . . .

X. CONCLUSION

We are now in a position to put forward a tentative reconstruction of the chronology of Archilochus' life.

c. 740-730 B.C. Conjectural date of Archilochus' birth.

734 B.C. Colonization of Syracuse (Episode in the Colonization mentioned by Archilochus, *Athenaeus,* iv. 167 *d*).

c. 720 B.C. Colonization of Thasos, Dionysius (Clem. Alex. *Strom.* i, p. 333 B).

716 B.C. Traditional date of end of reign of Romulus (752-716 B.C.), Cicero, *Tuscul. Quaest.* i. i. 3, refers Archilochus to his reign. Archilochus would be aged 14-24 in 716 B.C.

711 B.C. Total Eclipse of the Sun throughout Thasos. Archilochus aged 19-29.

c. 708 B.C. Colonization of Thasos, Xanthus (Clem. Alex. *Strom.* i, p. 333 B). Archilochus aged 22-32.

Archilochus' share in the colonization stated by Oenomaus ap. Euseb. *Ev. Praep.* vi. 7, and implied by Clem. Alex. *Strom.* i, p. 333 B. Both authors used a lost poem of Archilochus?

c. 700 B.C. *Floruit* of Archilochus according to Clem. Alex. *Strom.* i, p. 333 B. Archilochus aged 30-40.

c. 700 B.C.? 'Lelantine War' mentioned by Archilochus with indication that it was in progress or about to take place. Fragment 3, Diehl.

c. 700-*c.* 690 B.C. Fall of Magnesia. Dated to soon after *c.* 700 B.C. by Clem. Alex. *Strom.* i, p. 333 B, and to well before the accession of Gyges by Pliny, *N. H.* XXXV. 8 and vii. 38. Fragment 19, Diehl.

688-685 B.C. *Floruit* of Archilochus. Euseb. *Ev. Praep.* x. 11. 4; Cyril, *c. Jul.* i. 12; Tatian, *Ad Graecos* 122. Archilochus aged 42/5-52/5.

687 B.C. Conjectural date of accession of Gyges.

Before *c.* 670 - *c.*660 B.C. Archilochus slain in battle.[2]

The date chosen for Archilochus' death needs some further explanation.

According to a tradition preserved in Heracleides, Plutarch, and Dio Chrysostom,[2] Archilochus was slain in battle. If this is accepted he cannot have been an old man, say more than sixty-five, at the time, and in accordance with the evidence we have so far considered his death would fall before the decade 670-660 B.C.

This involves the rejection of the date given for Archilochus by Cornelius Nepos,[3] who refers him to the reign of Tullus Hostilius—671-640 B.C. according to the traditional chronology—and the mention of him in Jerome's version of Eusebius under the year 664-663 B.C. (665-664 B.C. Armenian Version). The rejection of these two authorities, Nepos especially, is undoubtedly a serious matter and not to be undertaken lightly, but it is a far smaller sacrifice of

evidence than that which is involved in the acceptance of the 648 B.C. eclipse. If 648 B.C. is the date of the eclipse of Archilochus we must discard the evidence of Cicero, Tatian, Cyril, Oenomaus of Gadara (probably based on Archilochus himself), and Clement of Alexandria (based on Xanthus, Dionysius, and possibly Archilochus himself). We must assume that Archilochus' reference to Aithiops the Corinthian was to a story at least sixty to seventy years old, that Clement was mistaken in his dating of Archilochus' reference to the fall of Magnesia, and that Pliny's story of Candaules and Bularchus' picture of that event is a hopeless chronological confusion, that Archilochus played no part in the colonization of Thasos, that indeed he was not born at that time, and that his reference to the 'Lelantine War' is to a struggle in the second half of the seventh century.

The difficulties involved in such a wholesale sacrifice seem to me enormous—in spite of the fact that it has so frequently been made. As long as we were forced to accept the 648 B.C. eclipse as the eclipse of Archilochus this sacrifice was necessary. Now, thanks to Dr. Fotheringham, it is no longer so. The literary evidence must be examined again without that unconscious bias in favour of the 648 B.C. eclipse which has so far influenced it.[4]

It may be that I have stated the case for 711 B.C. too emphatically. If that is so I can only plead that the case for 648 B.C. is habitually overstated and much of the relevant evidence tacitly omitted. I ask for a further examination of the evidence in the light of Dr. Fotheringham's computation.

Notes

1. I am indebted to Dr. Fotheringham for the information which follows, which in itself contains whatever value this discussion may possess, and also for much kindness and interest in my approach to the problem.

2. Heracleides, *Pol.* viii; Plut. *Ser. Num. Vind.* 17; Dio Chrysostom, 33, p. 397 M.

3. Cornelius Nepos ap. *Aul. Gell.* xvii. 21. 6 'Postea Pythagoras Samius in Italiam venit, Tarquini filio regnum optinente, cui cognomentum Superbus fuit, isdemque temporibus occisus est Athenis ab Harmodio et Aristogitone Hipparchus, Pisistrati filius, Hippiae tyranni frater. Archilochum autem Nepos Cornelius tradit Tullio Hostilio Romae regnante iam tum fuisse poematis clarum et nobilem.'

   Nepos' statement is logically capable of two interpretations. Archilochus was already famous before 640 B.C. or he was already famous in 671 B.C. (or soon after). Historically the second interpretation is far more probable. The first interpretation would mean that Nepos, alone among ancient writers, placed the greater part of the life of Archilochus after 640 B.C. The context in Aulus Gellius gives no help. It merely indicates a time very much earlier than the last-mentioned event.

4. The 'modernity' of Archilochus, the individual character of his poetry and its stylistic development, may

appeal to some people as evidence for the later rather than the earlier date. To this I can only reply that Archilochus was a genius whatever his date, and that, to me, an innovating literary genius at the end of the eighth and in the first quarter of the seventh centuries is no more than what I should expect from the efflorescence of Greek Art in Corinth, Crete, and Ionia at that time.

Henry Osborn Taylor (essay date 1939)

SOURCE: "Soul of Archilochus," in *A Historian's Creed*, Kennikat Press, 1939, pp. 87-115.

[*In the following essay, Taylor offers an imaginary autobiography of Archilochus, with emphasis on his philosophy.*]

I

On Paros, island of the gleaming rock, my eyes first caught the light of Helios. Fathered by an impetuous man, my mother a slave, childhood with me was passionate and my youth a storm. Our city's walls held more hate than love. Breaking away from some fierce dispute, an angry clique might take ship and look for a new home. I, long called a maligner, would speak truth. Our men were united against foes. In peace common prejudices and like pursuits fostered a working fellowship. There was comradeship among those of us who had shared danger together. Strong impulse as well as ingenious thought marked our Ionian towns. Life was eager with each man and with the people when assembled in the market place.

My own life, now mirrored in memory, is no longer distracted as when in the flesh. It was cast on circumstance. I recall its rancors and can measure its violence. I can still laugh, as once I jested, at my shield thrown away in flight—a deadly shame in Sparta, where they drove me out with jeers. No shame was felt by one who chose to live, knowing how to lose as well as win and raise his head again above the waves. My nature is put best in those iambics spoken to my soul: "Soul, soul! stricken with overwhelming troubles, bear up! Thrust back the onslaught and the ambushed danger, breast to foe. And neither, conquering, foolishly exult, nor, conquered, wail and cry. But in joys rejoice and in evils grieve not overmuch. So learn what rhythm holds men."

I could endure as well as another. Speaking from myself, I counseled a friend that for irreparable ills the gods had given the medicine of steadfastness. I fought and hated. My verse tore those who thwarted the fevered eros that was loosening my limbs. Yet throughout the anger and violence of my life consideration knocked at the door. I could praise valor in a foe, and heeded Odysseus' chiding of the old nurse not to exult over the dead. The unforeseen might descend on any man, like the darkening of the sun at noon. But Zeus gave mind and mood to meet what might befall, and toil brought forth things useful for mortals. I

knew that Father Zeus beheld men's knavish as well as lawful deeds, and could raise from the black earth those struck down by ills.

The best was that I ever followed, cherished, and increased within me, the Muses' lovely and mighty gift of verse. Knowing and chanting Homer's poems, I was no imitator. Of myself, above all other men, I moulded those quick iambics to pithy form, made them to sting and bite; made them beautiful in their power to tell the passions and the fates of men. The poet Homer spoke from himself, out of his nature. How else could he? Yet his chant was of what all men might wish for or would shun, with no word of his own chequered lot. I had no song of Zeus-born kings. My verse was of myself—voicing my hates and longings, the passions of the men about me, which often touched me sore: men like myself entangled, driven, reaching a brief success. It was myself, my setting, my needs, often my own dire lot, I sang.

Verse brought me renown in life and fame thereafter. That man called Korax, whose spear let out my breath, might not purify himself before the Pythian priestess, swearing that he killed me fairly. As having slain one sacred to the Muses, he was driven out till he should appease my ghost. I am praised by men in the far times to come; in my island city is set my monument, and men are still bidden to pause before one whose fame had flown from the rising to the setting sun.

I am a mind reflecting and absorbing: doing nothing, I experience. The lusting, fighting body, which was part of me, could endure its present, look back regretfully, or ahead, dreading yet hopeful of the future. But now occurrences no longer succeed each other. Thought carries what once had seemed to go before, and points to what shall be disclosed more clearly. Though a temporal sequence may order events which feed my mind, past and future are manifested in each other. It is all actualization, a flowering rather than succession.

The exertions and endeavors, the turmoil, struggle, and killing that went on through the Ionian islands and coast cities when I was in the body, and the dire times that saw the barbarians enslave our peoples—this complex of struggling or despairing life, the panorama of it all, is in my thought. Alas! there seems always to have been some clever Ionian whose grasping selfishness wrecked the fortunes of his city, and ruined those civic liberties which are a springboard for intellectual achievement. But my thought swells proudly as it turns to the victory of our Athenians over the Persian foe. And what a flowering followed of civic fullness, and art and drama and philosophy. The mind which now is me takes in the far event and sees the measureless import of Athens for mankind.

There is no rancor in me, and scarcely regret for ill fortune; what seems the past opens to me its why and wherefore reassuringly. Reminiscence as well as thought's fair prospect brings a genial expansion of spirit. Genial, I say, because, while violence and sense-riot do not enter, I am interested and often moved. Discrimination brings desire for whatever discloses itself as truth.

There are sequences in the visible world; also in human knowledge. I have been turning to the thoughts of men who were unborn when I was in the flesh. Then the gods were often on my tongue; I have since queried as to the source of things and their ways of action—the causes, so to speak. There is a Milesian who foretold that on a given day a shadow would push across the sun. Such a shadowing, once seen by me, seemed to overtop all other wonders. Is it such a wonder if a man can foretell it? Its cause lies not in my old gods whose action none could guess. This same Milesian says all things come from water, while a friend of his finds a more unlimited and total source. Heat and cold, and the wet and dry things, separate themselves out of this, while living animals are born of moisture and its warm evaporations. This seems to me real thinking and not just accepting what we used to put in poetry and daily speech.

I see that men will answer such questions in many ways, which shall show their progress in thinking. For myself I mark that these Milesian schemes take no account of that which *I am,* [*Thumós*]—soul, mind, will, purpose. So their insufficiency appears. Other thinkers offer me other thoughts. A certain sage makes over this basic matter into numbers and their relationships. He applies like thoughts to human conduct, hoping that through them men will learn to adapt their lives to social needs, eschew violence and gain moderation. I am with him here, little as my bodily life conformed. But as yet my own experience does not agree with his idea of souls passing from a dead body to a live one.

This man lives far to the west, where there are others who are showing how insecure is man's reliance on what his eyes and ears and fingers tell him of the world. One must have thinking, thinking to purge such evidence from contradiction and reach a thought of stable and sure being. I too am drawn to realize how little we can trust the quick message of our senses till thought has gone over and over it, and sifted what they have told us.

But what do I hear from Ephesus of still one who denies that there is any stable being to be tested by thought? He thinks nothing abides; indeed that nothing *is,* but only *becomes.* All is ceaseless change and flux. He calls it fire, and sees it kin to the human soul and the rational principle of the Kosmos. Out of this change and strife comes harmony! Dark are his words; but perhaps a new name for his thought comes echoing dimly from the future—process. From still another I hear there is a power outside the whirl; a thing of might: he calls it [*nous*], or mind. And still another younger man will solve the dispute between the Ephesian and the western sages, by cutting up matter into an infinitude of infinitesimals moving eternally throughout the void.

II

Surely my mind has grown thinking these pregnant thoughts of younger men. They shall be called philosophers. Yet all wisdom is not with them. I might have known this while still in the rioting body. For I was myself a poet; and I knew the wisdom of the epics; how they fitted life to the ways of things, and the ways of things to life, and called it fate. Fate might be hard, but it had fitness, as it moved along paths made by the man's temper and conduct, bringing him to a terminus not unforeseen. There was wisdom too in that plodding poet of the *Works and Days,* who died before I was born. Surely the poet has his share of wisdom from the Muse. His inspiration may be a glimpse of the divine ordering, and his verse carry a fuller round of life and truth than the reasonings of my good philosophers.

I am thinking of a great choral poet whose songs are sought and well rewarded by the victors in the games. It is given him above other men to show the golden truth of meaning in these triumphs. Magnificent his odes in words and thought, as they sing how men win in the games as in life by the favor of Zeus, themselves not lacking in valor. God and man's hero nature bring him to the goal of fame, immortalizing him in his passing deed. I am stirred by the lyric wisdom of this great Theban, whose city at this time is far from glorious, to his pain.

I am soon to learn a deeper lesson of life's sure retributions—still under Zeus. Fate had been suitable and fit with my first epic teacher. Its justice and righteousness were now to be revealed. From the Attic stage come the words: "It is the impious act that begets its kind: righteous houses are blest with fair children. The ancient Insolence engenders an offspring of insolence in evil men, an avenging dæmon not to be put off."

I hear the complement and crown of this dread principle: for the man not wholly bad, enlightenment follows retribution; from suffering, wisdom. First among men an Athenian makes clear the web of crime and punishment held in an old story: "He is wise who sings in praise of Zeus, Zeus who leads mortals to be wise: whose law it is that suffering shall teach. Mindfulness of past woes drops on the heart in sleep and makes men wise against their will." Those fixed unwritten laws of Zeus—let no man-sprung edict attempt to override them, sings another poet. From this younger man I gain the subtle principle that intent makes the crime; he whose will deeds were sufferings, rather than acts, may gain acquittance in the end—win through to expiation.

Drawing wisdom from these men, I became sentient and perceptive through their minds. With them I moved through those great days when we fought off Persia and slavery. In these experiences human life became weightier and gained a new significance. The need was more insistent to understand the good and ill of it, the worth of its perceptions; also the reasons of its fateful courses. Insistence upon man himself began to vitalize and humanize the thinking of men I call philosophers. Those who found ultimate being in the atoms tried to draw the principles of human conduct within the atomic whirl; the ideal of knowledge must include the ideal of life. Philosophy turns to the doer and thinker. I seem to discern man the thinker as henceforth the pivot of his thought, though it embrace the world he lives in—immense, fate-driven, or God-created. The unity of man's nature will insist that what is best for man must be at one with what is true. Philosophy becomes a test, a consistency of thought.

A snub-nosed Athenian goes up and down the city streets, pursues men to the nooks and crannies of their business, questioning, arguing on names and words, seeking meanings that will stand sifting. Some men, and I among them, see the foolishness of current talk as well as the pitfalls in the thinking of the old philosophers. We are nearing new heights, and I perceive that the way up is not merely a path but verily a part of whatever height is reached. Now I see that earlier thoughts, and experience from decade to decade enlarging, still work in the conduct of later men, and in later thought become springs of energy and light. I feel around me a careful weighing of conduct, discernment and skill in sculpture, deepened significance in drama and lyric. New verses are sung in music made for them. Music and line and strophe spring from old, still living, forms. My own iambics, bold and new in their time—no one had used them so cunningly before—have made the drama's dialogue, and more. I am part of it all, and men recite my verses still.

And now I listen to the drastic thinking of men moving in our world. Old opinions are sifted, some thrown aside, but more of them given new form and life. Well-thumbed ideas jostle each other and take on a second youth with our philosophers here at Athens, which is my spirit's home. Above them soars, and sometimes gambols, one who dwells in the conviction that the supreme reality is mind. I possess the proof of this in my own enduring life of thought. Yet I marvel at this philosopher as he fuses the thoughts of former men and of some still living in the flesh. He wields the reasoning power of such as upheld the scheme of being, one and absolute. They are perhaps the springs of his own spiritual truths. But his mind holds also the counter-reasons of the keen Ephesian, so destructive of everything except modes of change. Although repugnant, the atomic doctrines are well understood. Fully appreciating the sense-perceptive and relative nature of knowledge, his reason is steadied by its training in analytic definition from the good snub-nosed teacher. He raises his concepts to principles of life; would win through to a grasp of the supreme good as the surest reality. The impulse is love, purged of lust, straining on to beauty absolute and unchanging.

Alas, perhaps, all of these thoughts are not for me. I have heard the wonderful song of the *Phaedrus* which, in language almost beyond words, tells the passion of the soul divinely maddened by its yearning to fly upward to the

beauty from which it fell at birth. I have also in the *Symposium* followed this passion from its genesis in lusts, up through the desire for the better, unto the yearning for the best. It loves souls rather than bodies, and seeks the beauty of laws, institutions, sciences, and that broadest knowledge, which is knowledge of the beautiful—the beauty which is not fair in one respect and foul in another, which neither waxes nor wanes, is neither a becoming nor a perishing: beauty absolute in which perishing beauties share without affecting it.

This is the ideal beauty, or the beauty of the ideal. All reverence for the soaring thought that has conceived and reached it. But I am still a poet and my thought of beauty lives and moves in poetry, in all art, if one will. In beauty, as I think it, there is [dúnamis], which is power; and [dúnamis] is always in action. A mighty thinker, pupil of this high philosopher, opens his talk on Poetry with the words, "Let us speak of poetry and its kinds and the [dunamin] of each." He discusses the excellence of poetry, the drama especially. Such excellence falls in with the methods of the poets and the best forms of conduct. Without using the word "beauty," he discloses the qualities of tragedy so as to make clear what is its ideal excellence. My great Theban poet had shown the beauty of the success won by noble striving. Looking further back, I recall the dynamic modes of beauty in the Trojan epic. Helen is most fair to look on and her words are beautiful; but her beauty is not unmoving and her words speak thought that moves so fitly. My great Athenian would agree that fitness, temperance, and the golden mean of self-control are elements of beauty; and one must ascribe the quality of power to his changeless beauty, even as this quality is held in the Unmoved Mover, the conception of his pupil.

Such thoughts as mine concerning beauty find form and life in the supreme trilogy of the master of tragedy. The story of Agamemnon is in everyone's memory. That is the [muthos], by some called the plot, of the tragedy. It forms and controls the drama. Each incident is held to the measure of its contribution to the action. The personages act and speak in and for the drama. They are sheer agents. Every line they speak reflects the situation and is portentous of what must come. The roots and causes of the tragedy are given in veiled allusion and forebodings understood by all of us. This drama is not invented or composed by the dramatist, but is *revealed* by him in its causal setting to show how it came to pass. In the energy of its language and the suggestions of its images, in the fitness and right functioning of every incident, the play called *Agamemnon* possesses the excellence of power . . .—and so is beautiful. Its beauty is manifested in its dynamic being and the action of its qualities. I find the same beauty in the second play of the trilogy, which brings the over-vengeful murderous queen to her fit and proper death. The third play frees Orestes from the horrors of matricide by proving that his deed was guiltless under the prompting and promise of the gods.

This trilogy may justify my halting criticism of the Athenian philosopher. Doubtless our minds pass upward, as in his *Symposium,* from lower to higher beauties or conceived excellences or powers . . . , and thus may reach perhaps a highest thought of beauty. Still, all beauty is dynamic, an activity working in power. At all events, such seems to me the beauty of art and poetry. The structure of a poem sets its dynamic quality, and meter, rhythm, rhyme, are elements of power. Yet no formula can exhaust the depth and riches of fact—of our perception or experience of anything. The recognition of this throughout the talks of that great Athenian is one of the sure proofs of his greatness. To say that beauty is power does not exhaust our experience of beauty. If this dictum applies to drama or to oratory or to the epic, does it touch our feeling for an acanthus leaf or the significance of any deed or human form? Much remains untold, perhaps ineffable.

III

If an immortal spirit, freed from the rancors of the flesh, could be torn by the anguish of those who are near and dear in mortal kinship, immortality would be intolerable. Yet my sympathies are sadly moved by the long war in which Greeks will not give over destroying each other. From the courses of events I foresaw how internecine rivalry was leading to an insatiable war. My grand Athenians need not have been overthrown had they been prudent. Folly in the people and selfish vanity in those who misled them brought on the fatal Sicilian venture. Alas for temperance lost and self-control!

I foresee no end of wars to come: no end to pseudo-patriotism and valor misdirected, all masking cupidity. Foolish mankind will continue even as I was once. Fighting is in the blood; keen minds do not perceive its futility. Yet people are becoming concerned with feeling, interested in the softer as well as the more violent emotions. Love's passion and its counterpart of hate are displayed in tragic drama. The art of sculpture is sensitized in statues showing human moods and emotions; it has abandoned the old calm.

The age of Macedon's semi-barbarian dominance in Greece is here. Hellenism is no longer free. Neither will it liberate itself through Alexander's conquests, nor in his genial effort to make East and West absorb each other. His overarching might and the warring dynasties succeeding him make Greeks feel their powerlessness. Doubtless they were never quite masters of their destinies; now they are conscious of their impotence. The more thoughtful are trying to establish their souls in a self-determined freedom. Prevailing ways of thinking are looking to the welfare of the man within himself. The impelling mood, if not the constructive thought, of these systems enters into me. Not that I am oppressed by any resistless mortal power, seeing that I am all soul and subject to no assault. Am I free? I feel free and yet am a market for whatever human experience comes to my consciousness. I am most deeply affected by what seems truth.

It may be that I reflect the minds of men in every passing present. But I am also a growing soul, and feel growing pains. I have needs and yearnings for a larger adjustment

with the universe than had touched my immaturity. If aforetime I tried to propitiate sundry gods, that is now too casual. I must reach accord with the universal and infinite Godhead. For I need to think within the compass of his power. I would yearn and think and act in accordance with his will. I am no mere thinker, but a yearner too.

So I have nought in common with a certain Epicurus who will have it that the gods take no part in men's affairs. They are contented and supine and deaf to prayer. Let men also keep to the least disturbing pleasures, leaving the rest to pass undesired. Then there is no place for fear. Such thoughts suit godless men who scarcely look beyond comforts alike ignoble whether of the mind or body.

The other system has many reasonings that do not appeal to me; otherwise with its ideals. It sets man's peace, even content and happiness, within the conduct of his will, but views his will as part of universal law. With limping arguments it makes that law divine, to wit the will of God—for men an all-ruling providence. It even looks to God as a helpmate within each soul. So it would turn to Him in prayer, but with slight rational assurance of response.

A sense of human impotence seems to move both these systems. They lack the energy which lifted the thought of the Athenian philosopher to an assured spiritual reality. Not for long will these systems give strength and gladness to their advocates. Even now do do they help men widely? If stronger souls can make a fortress of the human will, that is an empty notion for the masses who have little strength and many fears. They need outer aid and comfort, say from the gods and daemons touching whom they are anxious day and night. Men and women are making a careful stepping anent the gods. They see omens everywhere, and watch the turning of a feather to find what fortune or misfortune awaits their acts. More than formerly they seek their fortunes in the inexorable stars. It is all an anxious stepping.

Yet Stoicism, the better one of these two systems, has raised the thought of God. Looking back upon my fellows in the flesh, I recall how all of us feared the gods and would buy their favor by silly acts and gifts. We imagined the gods to be like our own grasping or groveling selves, only secure from mischance. There was too much of man and of the unaccountable ways of nature in our religion. Even Zeus in Homer was far from fixed and righteous, and could be deceived, lured by his own whims or lusts. There was too much of *me,* Archilochus, and too little of the divine in Zeus. Only afterwards Aeschylus made him a righteous dispenser of justice. Probably my own thoughts of God are broader still.

In these many years after Alexander's death we Greeks go here and there among the peoples less disdainfully. Stoicism expresses the new feeling that there is something of the same in men everywhere. It even teaches that all men are brothers—a shaky kinship, as it still seems to me. The rule of Alexander and his successors is being replaced by the power of a great republic in the west, soon to become imperial. If these mighty kingdoms and their supplanter have made men know the individual's impotence, the Empire begins to make its subjects behave as citizens of a world. They are governed by a single ruler and a central ministration of law. There is a state religion, somewhat thin. Under its aegis various religious practices and many curious superstitions minister to the prejudices of races and the wants or weaknesses of men and women. All people borrow religion and rites and superstitions. What is thoughtful blends with the absurd. Religion flourishes through the common need of protection in an all too chancy world. This need reaches out beyond the life of the present body, looking for some ghostly safety for the shade. Hope plots the ways and means of its fulfillment.

Our Greek religion gave scanty aid beyond the funeral pyre, only certain "mysteries" lending a rather particular support. Roman religion has nothing more. So we Greeks and dumbly Hellenized Romans, finding our own cults wanting, are willing to try out assurances from the stocks of other nations. The choice is wide indeed.

IV

A certain restless Jewish people pushes about the world. They are unsocial and uncomfortable, not like other men. They call the rest of the world gentiles, just as we Greeks used to call them all barbarians. They pull back their skirts as from defilement with gentile touch, and yet seek converts for their faith. For religion is a faith with them; there is passion in their relation to their god. I am a Hellene and never cared for Jewish views. They have no thought of natural law; everything hangs on the will of their Jehovah-god. Reading their books, I find his will was frequently violent and cruel. This people was carried captive into Asia, and suffered dire discipline of body and spirit. Their captivity may have brought new thoughts, possibly some notion of a future life and a conviction that they had a mission in the world. It would seem that the sins of the Jews and their calamities inspired their prophets to elevate Jehovah from a jealous God of one small people to a righteous ruler of all the peoples of the earth. He is made a universal god, and yet is still a person with a will and character having no kinship with natural law.

Here was something new for me: that a god should become God universal and supreme and yet continue sheer personality and not a symbol or element or phase of law, into which the Stoic god was always turning. With all his righteousness and might, Jehovah had also love, at least for his own people. Elements of like thoughts had harbored in my own Greek self, but had never formed a convincing personality. It seems to me that personality is needed in a ruler over human destinies and for the purposeful creation of the world.

Renovation and new life for the Jewish faith are emerging out of Judaism itself in its old home of Palestine; no building out of ceremonies, but a flowering of the spirit likely to burst the old bonds of the Jewish law. Righteousness had lain in its strict fulfillment. Now a man arises, a prophet or perhaps more than a prophet, who declares that he comes to fulfill the law, but in a way that destroys its letter. He teaches that righteousness does not lie in doing or refraining, but in the spirit of the obedient man and the reason of his conduct. I can look back to a similar spiritualizing of our old Greek morality as stress was laid on the intent with which an act was done. But this man lifts such principles above mere ethics, sees them as final forms of the divine command. He draws two precepts from the Jewish law: "Thou shalt love the Lord thy God with all thy heart, and with all thy soul, and with all thy mind. This is the first and great commandment; And the second is like unto it, Thou shalt love thy neighbor as thyself. On these two commandments hang all the law and the prophets." This is indeed a spiritualizing of righteousness—of the entire contents of human conduct. He shows its application among men: "All things therefore whatsoever ye would that men should do unto you, even so do ye also unto them; for this is the law and the prophets." Our Stoicism was groping towards the love of God and man; but it lagged far behind the inspiration and command of these living words, which set the spirit of man's life and filled it with acts of love.

Then this man declared the outcome of such living and its reward to be life eternal—which is what men are looking for with all mortality's yearnings. *If only they could believe it!* As a disembodied spirit I could speak to them: but that is barred. Only I will here set down—is it for me? for whom is it?—how this doctrine was presented at its best and highest, and how it touched myself.

The man wrote nothing, but was always speaking to those about him; to his followers or to individuals, or to multitudes. When not angrily rejected, his teaching was accepted and afterwards recorded according to the tempers, spiritual aptitudes, and intelligence of his hearers. It survives in different forms. One is that of the kingdom of heaven for those who will believe and follow Christ—which he proclaimed himself to be. The Kingdom is set forth in images—parables, as they are called. These represent ways of God's redeeming love and the manner of man's acceptance of the Kingdom or failure to enter in. They are phases of the relationship between man and God, a relationship that may comprise the sum of human life. The teacher points to himself as the embodiment of the Kingdom of God and as the way to it.

Another record gives a profoundly complementary disclosure of the nature of life eternal. Its problems or dilemmas are put in statements that appeal to an educated and intellectual Greek, because of linkages with his philosophy. Such a one had learned that the life of mind is most desirable and that luxury and wealth might well be abandoned for it. We Greeks could understand the words: "Love not the world, neither the things that are in the world." Also the command laid on the disciples to love one another as the master had loved them, or even as God loved them.

We who knew the great Athenian's philosophy could understand this. Now the discourse becomes profounder, esoteric perhaps, showing some likeness to what was taught in our own "mysteries." The Son of God was sent as an offer of eternal life: "For God so loved the world, that he gave his only begotten Son, that whosoever believeth on him should not perish, but have eternal life." Belief begins as the Father draws the man to Christ; it strengthens through the believer's love. Life is set forth as knowledge of the truth that frees man from bondage to sin and death; in fine, as knowing God and him whom He has sent. "This is life eternal, that they might know thee the only true God, and Jesus Christ whom thou has sent." The record contains further revelation of the believer's life in Christ and God: "That they may be one, even as we are one; I in them, and thou in me, that they may be perfected into one."

As I consider the tendencies of thought and feeling in the years before and those which followed the appearance of this man, I see how his teaching—the Gospel, as it came to be called—carried an answer and fulfillment to prevailing religious yearning. I who am a mind and soul reflecting men's fervent thoughts find my own religious feeling responded to and satisfied. The Stoic god was vague and material, and the thoughts on the divine held by the Athenian philosopher never quite reached a living focus. I needed personality in God, even though one built out of human aspirations. No living divine personality had ever been conceived such as was revealed in this Gospel set upon Jewish thought but reaching so far beyond. Besides this, some kind of imperishable existence is desired by all sorts of mortals. The Gospel promised it in promises snatched at and understood in many ways.

But the reasoning mind continued in Greeks and Greek-taught Romans—certainly in me. The Greek philosophic reason could not be so Judaized as to accept the Gospel as at first set forth. Its statements had to be made over in terms acceptable to Hellenic thought. So in my case. I followed sympathetically the disputes and labors of the Christian Fathers to make the relations between the divine Son and Father and mankind thinkable. These modes of Hellenized Christianity appealed to me and satisfied my philosophic nature.

What a fortune lay before these dogmas, in which the Gospel core lived on through its appeal to the hearts of men and women. Yet I, who feel the stirrings of what history would call the future time, already know that the reasonings of the Hellenic setting of the Gospel and the arguments of the mighty Apostle to the Gentiles will eventually lose the power to convince. For they will cease to correspond with any sense of reality present in men's minds.

V

For the time my religious feeling is satisfied by the Gospel of the Saviour Jesus Christ, and I accept its dogmatic rendering. My reason, unimpaired perhaps, is redirected by a faith that has made me introspective and furnished new matter to be fitted into an intellectual frame. I would never admit that we Greeks lacked the faculty of observing nature as well as man. The promptings of mathematics pushed us to discovery. Personally I have always been drawn to poetry and art and have done my thinking along the ways of reasoning rather than through observation. In my present state observation does not interest me. Mythology and religion find symbols and look for allegorical meanings in history. I may come to recognize that these images turn us from reality. But allegory will dominate the period into which our peoples are passing.

The turning of the world to Christianity is affecting intellectual taste as well as mood and feeling in another way. One would hardly call the Greeks unemotional. Passion inspired our art and swayed our history. But we never deified emotion, and looked always to its control. That it might be without limit and absolutely righteous did not occur to us. The Christian love of God is bringing a change. It is an overmastering emotion with those who feel it, and is deemed the essence of righteousness. No temperance . . . here. The devoted soul cannot have too much of that which should embrace its entire nature. This boundless intellectual passion inspires the writings of the bishop of Hippo, whose genius I revere. I foresee the same passion moulding poetry and art. Our old Greek measures imposed emotional limit and control. They are dropped. The Christian hymn is taking on rhythms and rhymes which will gather power to express limitless yearning. Christian prose also will become emotional. Emotion will give new forms to poetry and new qualities to sculpture and painting.

Nevertheless, in these earlier centuries of conversion the masses of mankind go on much the same. They have merely redirected their superstitions. Is it not always so? The intellectually and spiritually chosen are sensitive to the impact of ideals originating in unique individuals or arising from human growth. From the first, such men were reinspired by the Gospel and gained in mental and emotional power. They reached new heights of righteousness—of intolerance, perhaps. Creative in thought and feeling, they are the great Fathers of the Church and saints as well. I feel their power. But I see that common men, with affections and desires good and bad, are unchanged. Wars go on, and internecine struggles among Christians still grasping at the Empire. The birth throes of dogma are violent enough, and bring forth subjects of rancorous dispute. Men hate each other still. I fail to see that bishops and their shouting factions are any better than pagans used to be. They are certainly less pleasant. Yet the tough old world may be about to receive a novel impress.

I am thinking of another aspect of this problem. Our antique world held much strength and life when Jesus was born. Its energies seemed to sink while his teachings, more or less altered, were reaching general acceptance. My own experience through this period of spiritual intermingling and renovation impresses me with the impossibility of distinguishing the causes of these two phenomena or even the phenomena themselves—to wit, the apparent weakening of Greco-Roman civilization and the Gospel's spread. Men are evincing new susceptibilities and capacities of feeling, which tend to develop into creative faculty, thus making amends for what is lost. The antique Greek and Roman character, although subject to superstitions, was strong and self-reliant. The staunchness relaxed under a deepening need of religious solace and support. This need brought forth the means of consolation. The times of the Church Fathers were creative of Christian art as well as Christian dogma. The Fathers themselves in the fourth century after Christ were not mentally inferior to Epicurus and the founders of Stoicism in the fourth century before his birth. Christian art was less skillful than the art of our Skopas and Praxiteles, but more original in its accomplishment of the novel task of presenting the Christian epic.

Thus I saw new elements of faculty and character replacing the antique strength. One hesitates to speak of a human deterioration. But disasters press upon my thought. I see the resources and population of the Empire wasted by war, disorder, and disease. The impact of barbarian peoples is now a calamity rather than a renewal of strength. Our civilization is no longer able to assimilate and fashion them.

VI

I am moved by the tendencies of each passing time, and yet consider them detachedly. This is my freedom. I see the world entering a period of downfall and ignorance to be followed by a gradual recovery rich in possibilities. The course of disruption and recovery passes across my vision. Through the centuries I hear the beat of thought and feel the gathering passion of the Faith. I think in terms of the *Summa theologiae* and almost gain the gift of tears. Then I become aware of a dawning freedom struggling through the need of the antique heritage. Eyes are opening to the natural world. Observation becomes active and experimental, prying into movement and growth. Religion holds a smaller part of human interest. Man's earthly life bounds forward as if unfettered. There is delight in art; and the passionately human world asserts itself with glorious violence in Shakespearean plays.

Moving on to what seems the present, I am dizzied by the novel facilities of daily life and intercourse. In the whirl of opportunity it is humanity that stays the same. What though men talk across the ocean if they have but small things to say? Inventions are a fool's test of progress. The cry is for application and utility. But applied science is baneful as well as beneficial: neutral between good and ill. Easement and facility are well when leading to broader purpose and the uplifting of the mind. It is an insult to knowledge to accept surface utility as a criterion of its worth. We Greeks kept the balance between philosophy and science. Now the efficiency of rational thinking is denied. Men forget that in sifting nature perception is fashioned by the perceiving mind with the concurrence of its

reasoning faculties. The gain is valid when harmonized with the background of well-considered thought. This court of last resort passes on every fact. Natural knowledge broadens the basis of that ultimate rational consideration which is philosophy.

Though the world perplexes me, I know whither I have come. A touch of the divine in the liberated soul enables it to see all things in the light of eternity. I can also view my own experiences as successive. With the passing of mortal breath, the distraction and contentions of composite existence gave way to quietude and gentle tolerance. I became hospitable to others' thoughts, would consider novel opinions and recognize new drifts of feeling. I absorbed the early philosophers and the laws of conduct declared by the Theban poet and our Athenian drama. Having soared with Plato, my thoughts were sobered as man's helplessness appeared in the times of Stoicism. The pathos of mortality brought home the need of divine deliverance. I gained a new intelligence from the conviction that God, once the All-mover, now the Father, held human qualities in the divine harmony of his nature. He had made us unto himself. There was scope along that path for human energies, and content and peace. Thus I fared onward. Insistence upon living within the divine purpose remains unshaken. I, Archilochus, have found the peace of God which passeth understanding. And I also am an allegory.

Frederic Will (essay date 1962)

SOURCE: "Archilochus and His Senses," in *The Classical Journal*, Vol. 57, No. 7, 1962, pp. 289-96.

[*In the following essay, Will analyzes Archilochus's method of conveying his sensory experiences through the metre and diction of his poetry.*]

The immediacy of Archilochus' sense-experience to his poetry strikes us first in meter. This is something new. We never feel, with Homer or Hesiod, that the lived texture of the poet's experience is directly translating itself into the sound of his verse. Rather we seem always, in those two writers and throughout the epic cycle, to be hearing an impersonal, "epic" voice. Those creators address us from the end of an "epic" culture, the Mycenaean, and though Hesiod (fl. 730) may have been no more than three generations older than Archilochus (fl. 660), his aural tone *sounds* far older.[1] It is deeply embedded in the past. Archilochus, as a person, reaches us immediately, and from his own present, through sound.

It is significant, then, that he expressed himself through sensuous, heavily rhythmic, quickly oscillating meters.[2] The ancients, who admired Archilochus greatly—often classing him with Homer, in fact—considered him the inventor of the iamb; thus of one of the most "heavily sensuous" Greek meters. Certainly he is the first *extant* Greek poet to offer us this meter. (What other poets may be lost, we can not even begin to guess.) He used the iamb pre-eminently in his satires (the verb *iambo* means "to assail"), where it reinforces and grows from the meaning of his feelings. For example (Frag. 31):

> Old woman that she was, she failed to bathe,

(Translation, here and throughout this article, mine unless otherwise indicated. Textual references are to Bergk, *Poetae lyrici Graeci,* Leipzig 1915, vol. 2.)

Or (Frag. 33):

> An awful racket roamed the house.

This is the meter of many of his erotic poems, too, where aural sensuousness interweaves with sensuous meaning. In those erotic poems Archilochus also, frequently, combines trochees with iambs, letting the two meters vacillate in a potent counterpoint. Even the trochee, as Archilochus manipulates it, is sensuous. Occasionally, as in some of his tetrameters, he writes purely trochaic verse. Fragment 50 reads:

> Homeless, fellow-citizens, now grasp my words . . .

Or (Frag. 52):

> So the wretchedness of all the Greeks had come to Thasos . . .

In Archilochus both of these chief meters rely on abrupt and sensuous rhythmic emphases, by contrast, say, with the epic dectyl, which is more monotonous, and less tense.

In conjuring up the sensuous qualities of the iamb and the trochee in this early lyric poet, it is useful to remember certain conditions of the production of his verse. Unfortunately, little is known. The way in which Archilochus composed his works is not clear. No doubt, in the first half of the seventh century, he could write. But did he compose in that way? Or did he compose by singing? In any case he does speak of reciting to the flute (Frags. 76, 123), and that alone proves that he must have been highly conscious, as creator, of the pitch and key of his prosody, as well as of its simpler stress pattern. Here, then, we have a kind of index of the sensuous subtlety of his work. This index becomes more meaningful when we remember that Archilochus' verse, with its musical accompaniment, was intended for public recital, like Homer's and Pindar's poetry. On such occasions, Archilochus' poetry may have sounded more like musical recitative than like poetry as we know it. We can only insist, in reconstructing that atmosphere, that the innate sensuousness of his meter, as we read it now, must have been created *into* an originally all-embracing sensuous context. In trying to grasp this situation, we must make the same kind of effort as in assessing the overall sensuous creation of the Greek temple, with its organic interfunctioning of shape, medium, and color.

Nor is it enough just to appreciate the immediate social-sensuous context of Archilochus' verse: we must also remind ourselves of the sensuous-historical background of that verse. We must recall that although Archilochus was the *literary* founder of the iamb, and although he is the first *extant* Greek poet to offer us trochees, there was a communal choral-religious origin for both meters which reached far into the past. For one thing, the exchanging of insults and obscenities in iambic meter was an approved part of early Greek religious ceremonies.[3] But there is a further explanation for the early use of those meters. Both iambs and trochees are appropriate to rapid dances: dactyls by contrast are not. It is assumed that dances in those meters took place in festivals of Demeter and Dionysus, that is in religious fertility ceremonies. The name *ithyphallic,* given to one of the oldest trochaic forms, points to this origin. There is a passage in Aristophanes' *Frogs* (386 ff.) in which a rural celebration of Demeter is recited in hopping iambic dimeters, in the way that we can well imagine it was done long before Archilochus. The sensuousness of these meters in Archilochus, then, has a sensuous-historical context. His importance is not lessened when we know that context. These meters rise directly from inside him, not from any subservience to tradition. He used his prosodic tradition, we may assume, because it suited his aesthetic needs. His inner sense-experiences found appropriate form in such meters.

Discussion of the qualities of meter, despite all appeals to historical context, runs a particular danger of appealing solely to private taste. Let us turn to the question of the kind of experience Archilochus seems to embody in meter; to the experiential content of his poetry. It may be asked, in view of Archilochus' reputation as the first Western lyric poet, whether his content is not simply "himself." It is a truism that the lyric is an expression of the self. But this is a great simplification. Even the Homeric epic, in a sense, is an expression of self. That epic is simply a more oblique expression of the self, one conditioned by more "external" factors, such as contemporary social conventions, verbal traditions, or inherited stories. The ancient lyric, in distinction to the later "romantic" lyric, was also seriously bound by "external" conditions, was in many ways cut off from spontaneous self-expression. In this it was a characteristically Hellenic product; the ancient lyric must be seen in the context of the whole Greek poetic atmosphere. Archilochus, for instance, made no effort to "express himself," at least in the sense we customarily give to that phrase. He had neither desire nor possibility to express some ineffable, disembodied essence, "himself," and thus to be freed of the inner oppressiveness of selfhood. Neither did other Greek lyric poets—Solon or Sappho—attempt such a radical, modern act. Werner Jaeger put the Greek situation well, when he wrote:

> . . . Greek expressions of personal emotion and thought have nothing purely and exclusively subjective in them: it might rather be said that a poet like Archilochus has learnt how to express in his own personality the whole objective world and its laws—to represent them in himself.[4]

Archilochus, as poet, is particularly anxious to register the sense-events, or feelings, of his own being—the intersections of himself with the experienceable world—rather than to reach to the immovable, and soul-like, within. In this he and his contemporaries distinguish themselves from the mystic in search of his soul, as well as from the Symbolist poet, a Mallarmé or Verlaine, in search of sufficiently attenuated imagery to translate the ineffable within.

Both chronologically and in degree of importance, the first sense-origin of events for Archilochus is his body, that gross and beautiful first boundary with what-is. If we wish to think of Greek lyric poetry as a step in the growing awareness, by the human being, of himself, as part of the *Selbstentdeckung des Menschen,* we need not be surprised by the major importance played by body in this discovery. A child becomes aware of and through his body first, and only much later grows aware of the mind "inside" it. Some of the early Greek lyric poets are like children in this respect. Archilochus himself is not merely preoccupied with the elements of the life of his body, but primarily with its sexual responsiveness: preoccupied "psychologically," that is, as well as in the texture of his meter, which, as we have noticed, itself often has a transparently erotic rhythm.

A few of Archilochus' fragments concern his reproductive organs (Frags. 47, 136). It is important to notice these passages, because they help us to see on what an intimate level Archilochus is prepared to confront and transcribe personal experience. They also show us how little pruient this poet—like his contemporaries—was; by these simple, direct, unembarrassed utterances we are transported to the pre-prurient age of Greece, to that first stage of self-discovery, in the eighth and seventh centuries, when sexual repression was relatively slight, when poetry was not yet, as it would be in the fifth century, a compensation for loss, but was still continuous with "real life." Much of the earlier attitude is to be found in Archilochus' erotic poetry. He translates it through such lines as (Frag. 72):

> Just to fall upon her swelling womb
> Meeting her thigh to thigh.

The physical is alleviated of grossness, turned into an accomplishment. When it came to poetry, Archilochus was in artistic control of his passion. He could also translate tenderness with a strange tangible line (Frag. 71):

> If only I could touch my loved-one's hand.

The sensual excitement is here very light, but it breathes over the line and leaves a simple finality. In these lines in which the basic sense-life of the body is brought into poetry—scarce lines, as everything connected with Archilochus is scarce[5]—we read the controlled closeness of that poetry to the poet's sense-life. That particular life—so differently from the lives of Homer or Hesiod—is providing the raw material of his poetry.

The *personae* of his body—for to certain poets the inner organs may become virtually that, as though they were actors in a drama—sometimes take the stage metaphorically as well as in person in Archilochus' poetry. The following lines (Frag. 103) are an example:

> Such is the passion for love that has twisted its way beneath my heartstrings
> and closed deep mist across my eyes
> stealing the soft heart from inside my body . . .

> (Trans. Lattimore)

At first one is reminded, almost, of the formulaic death of an Homeric hero. The physical picture looks comparable. In fact, though, we have here an originally worked, and thoroughly unheroic, expression of refined sense-experience. (Archilochus never disappoints us with facile language.) The "heart" seems to be felt half-physically, half-symbolically. So do the "mist," and the "body." We are not yet in the language-world—of romantic "heart," "bosom," and "hand"—which tends to translate the physical into *purely* non-physical terms. "Heart" and "eyes" are by no means simply metaphors here. Nor, on the other hand, do the physical terms in our passage refer to anything *merely* physical. Archilochus is clearly not considering the same heart that a physician considers. We are here in a language-world which retains the physical object, but in a volatilized, and lightened, condition.

A similarly intermediate physical-spiritual inner event is translated in the following lines (Frag. 84):

> Wretchedly I lie desiring,
> Soulless, with an anguish from the gods
> Transfixed, clear through the bones.

The last words, "transfixed (or stuck), clear through the bones," are more than a conventional, sentimental lover's outcry, although they are partly that. They seem to translate pain through evoking a physical experience which never "really" happened, yet one which could not be described in any but physical terms. The "bones" in this fragment are not real bones, any more than they are whatever might be merely symbolized by the notion of "bones." They are real-unreal bones.

The chief source of sense-experience for Archilochus, as for most poets, is neither his inner sexual tensions nor his spiritual-physical romantic feelings. It is the events of his eye. He treats us to many fresh visual experiences in his language. In one of his finest iambs he gives us a pure vision of the eye, undisturbed by reflection (Frag. 29):

> She held a branch of myrtle and
> Flowering rose and down her back
> And shoulders flowed her hair.[6]

A beautifully simple fidelity to sense-experience is the source of the poem's purity and stillness; the poem has a pellucid, sensuous surface, which reminds one of the "innocence" of some of Archilochus' most erotic fragments (Frags. 47, 72, 136). That is not to say, here or in any fragments previously considered, that Archilochus' verse is, in a passive way, simply an "imitation" of inner events. Even in this fragment his symbolical translation of experience is oblique. Yet we can feel that some limpid visual image or images generated this small poem. The border between art and life is distinct but narrow here.

The eye could not often be, for Archilochus, even as passive a part of the body as it appears in this poem. Not only sexual and romantic-pathetic awarenesses, but also visual awareness tended toward mental awareness with Archilochus. In the following fragment (Frag. 21) we see comment appended to vision, and emerging from it:

> Like the spine of an ass this island
> Stands, with timber for a crown.
> Not a lovely or a wanted place,
> Or charmed, as one upon the banks of Siris.

Here the poet describes the rough island of Thasos, contrasting it to the beauty of South Italy. Unlike the vision of the last fragment, this one—the first two lines, that is—contains an image, a simile, and in that loses something of its purely visual sense-character. Vision is tinged. But even this vision is not permitted to stand alone. It is merged into an evaluation which it, itself, seemed to point toward. With the second pair of lines added, the mood of the first two is transformed. We are made to experience the completion of the implication of the first two lines—as we learn that Thasos *is* a grim island. Vision has proven continuous with attitude.

The fusion of vision with reflection, their simultaneous expression, is not common in Archilochus, because he is so radically a poet of the senses. That is one way of explaining what is unusual in the following often-discussed fragment (Frag. 58):

> I don't like the towering captain with the spraddly length of leg,
> one who swaggers in his lovelocks and cleanshaves beneath the chin.
> Give me a man short and squarely set upon his legs, a man
> full of heart, not to be shaken from the place he plants his feet.

> (Trans. Lattimore)

The sensual images of the two kinds of men described—"towering," "spraddly," "squarely"—contain the relevant reasons for such men being likable or not. The very way the men are being seen is the source of the attitude with which they are being seen. The participles and adjectives describing the men, through which they are made visible, are also vehicles of Archilochus' attitude toward them. The kind of half-sensuous translation of experience, as we find it here, is related to the kind of metaphorical language of "heart" and "mist" which we noticed above (Frags. 84, 103). It is the language of sense-experience penetrated with attitude and understanding.

In these characteristic ways in which Archilochus deploys his visual experience in his poetry, we see various stages of the lyric transcription of sense-experience. We have noticed above, too, that Archilochus refines more or less on pure sexual, or on romantic, sense-awareness. Man's life needs constantly to be caught up in progressively more "spiritual" layers of awareness, to be released and lightened with metaphor. Archilochus responds to this demand in a series of intermodulated efforts, through which we see the integrity of his effort to be true to his sense-experience. By contrast with this effort, in fact, Archilochus' attempts to *think* through his verse are paltry.

We must ask ourselves whether Archilochus had a poetic philosophy, whether a small universe of responses, in all its completeness, reflects itself from the body of his verse. As some of the preceding quotations have illustrated, Archilochus had a point of view, an angle of vision. It emerges more or less directly from his sense-experience. It was neither a consistent point of view, nor a reflective one: but it *was* a consistent mood in which his senses happened to transact aesthetically with the outer world. There is more than this, though. There are persistent conceptual themes in Archilochus' poetry, and though they add up to very little, as a testimony to abstract thought, or even as poetically integrated thought, it is worth considering those concepts if only to gain negative evidence that Archilochus was a poet of the senses. As it is, many of his "ideas" seem to be simply reflexes from his sense-experience. He writes (Frag. 65):

> One main thing I understand,
> to come back with deadly evil at the man who does me wrong.

> (Trans. Lattimore)

This "idea" in Archilochus is hardly more than a nagging animal reflex, and it recurs often in his poetry, as we might expect. It is dominant in those scattered and furious iambs which he hurled at the man, Lykambes, who refused him his daughter in marriage, iambs which reputedly drove both father and daughter to hang themselves. In those attacks, Archilochus seems to have written directly out of the turbulence of his sense-life. On a more reflective level, he offers prudent statements based on his direct experience of the world. We read (Frag. 56):

> To the gods all things are easy. Many times from circumstance.
> of disaster they set upright those who have been sprawled at length
> on the ground, but often again when men stand planted on firm feet,
> these same gods will knock them on their backs, and then the evils come,
> so that a man wanders homeless, destitute, at his wit's end.

> (Trans. Lattimore)

It is interesting to see here, in a different guise, the images of uprightness, and square-stance, which we saw above (Frag. 58) in the lines describing two kinds of soldiers. In our present passage, the images have been heightened almost entirely into metaphor and as a result—in *this* poem—virtually stripped of their poetic power. What we have here, rather, is the minimal effort of a man who wants to generalize his experience. These are lines of folk-wisdom, the outcome of experience of practical life. From his experience Archilochus draws a private rule of life (Frag. 66):

. . . and if you beat them, do not brag in open show,
nor, if they beat you, run home and lie down on your
bed and cry.
Keep some measure in the joy you take in luck, and
the degree
you give way to sorrow. All our life is up-and-down
like this.

(Trans. Lattimore).

The tough mercenary soldier, who in another fragment insisted that pleasure could make nothing worse, agrees here that it is wise not to tempt the variable gods with displays of extreme feeling. Such practical wisdom is the summit of Archilochus' philosophy. Concepts were not, for him, either continuous with his poetic sensibility, or generative ways into poetry.

Do we see in Archilochus, the first consequential lyric poet in the western tradition, a new awareness of the self, or an expression of greater subjectivity after the relatively impersonal—or at least highly "projected"—age of the Homeric epic? After the rather schizophrenic verbal world of Hesiod, torn between its epic form and the demand for personal intervention? The answer is "yes," but, as has been suggested already, it needs to be qualified. Certainly the ego is prominent in Archilochus' poetry. He tells us what he feels, what he sees, what he thinks he should do. He represents "his own" inner life openly and fully. What is more, and what is more significant, he does this with ease. His ease, particularly, differentiates him from Hesiod, the first European poet to name himself in his work. When Hesiod tells us that the Muses of Helikon addressed him, or that he once travelled to Chalkis in order to participate in a singing-contest, he introduces himself awkwardly. He finds it hard to "be in" his poetry, and is obviously ill at ease there. Archilochus is perfectly at ease in his own poetic illusion.

Yet though he handles himself successfully, as an ingredient of his poetry, it is worth repeating the earlier remark that Archilochus implicitly looks on himself as closely related to the outer world. His best poetry emerges from the point of contact between sense-impressions and his self. That point of contact is crucial to his artistic success. Archilochus is only incidentally concerned with the self in a metaphysical sense. He is not plumbing his own depths. Perhaps we should rather say, as Jaeger implies in the lines already cited, that Archilochus is interested in himself as subject, that his poetic stance is one of relative subjectivity, and yet that Archilochus, as subject, always requires an object, an experience in terms of which to exist.

What, looking more closely, seems to be the character of Archilochus' subjectivity? The double meaning of the word "subject" may help us to develop an answer. Not only does Archilochus appear in his poetry as a grammatical subject, an "I"—that is, as subject of various sense-experiences, the person who "has" those experiences—but he appears also in *subjection* to those experiences. This is the more significant aspect of his poetic being, and the as-pect which deserves more attention. Archilochus is basically a center of awareness which is impinged on by a multitude of sense-impressions which are the basic level of his world, which to a great extent simply *are* his world. To this extent, one might say, he is almost the victim of his sense-impressions. The point is important; turning it into more philosophical language, we might say that sense-impressions are accidents of Archilochus' substance, that they happen to him. This subjective situation can be put into a wider context by an historical comment.

In modern times many thinkers—Goethe, Schiller, or Kant, for instance—have analyzed the aspects of man's being through which he is sensually aware, that is, the sensuous aspects of his being. Each of those three thinkers asserted, in his way, that mankind, through its senses, is a part of nature. The sensuous part of the human being is antirational, essentially without intelligible form. This part of our natures, they held, is fate, weight, matter. It is true that these same thinkers also insisted that man has supersensuous powers. Reason (*Vernunft*), in various meanings of the word, was the one of those powers they most admired. But they felt that sense-experience is cut off from reason. This description and "location" of sense-experience helps toward understanding the subjectivity of Archilochus in its second, passive meaning. A good part of Archilochus' mode of being did belong to nature.

Yet there is another relevant historical point here, one made especially by Kant, in his reflections on the relation of art to sensuous experience. Kant argued that aesthetic creativity is one way in which mere sensuous experience can be removed from the realm of nature toward, though never quite to, the realm of Reason. Through form, Kant believed, man can virtually rescue, that is universalize, certain of his fleeting sense-experiences. Kant was only one of many modern thinkers who considered art an effort to intermediate between "lower" and "higher" human faculties. But Kant's own thought, in particular, is relevant to the present point. Just as his thinking might help us to locate and understand Archilochus' sense-experience, so it might help us also to see the context of Archilochus' rescuing of that experience through form. Archilochus was struggling against mere subjection to the sense-world. In this he was in the major tradition of the Greek lyric.

In fact, with Archilochus' subjection to sense-experience went a distinctive and eternal lyrical motive. That motive is the urge to conquer the mere particularity of the sense-event, the sensual accident which happens to the self.[7] Essentially the self is hostile to the accidental, to luck. A lyric poet, it seems, wants to translate the here-and-now limitation of sense-experience into a formal expression, art, which confers some exemption from place and time, and thus gives the self momentary power over "the accidental." Archilochus' disciplined, clear poems prove that this motive was powerful in him. It operated, as we can judge, not to control any ordinary sense-world, but to control the particularly intense world of his own senses. That was the world which he struggled to universalize. Exercising this control cannot have been an easy battle even for a tough Parian mercenary. Yet he won, and we are grateful.

Notes

1. For a recent effort both to date those writers, and to characterize their rapidly changing social environment. cf. A. R. Burn, *The lyric age of Greece* (New York 1960).

2. For general discussions of Archilochus' prosody, cf. Amédée Hauvette, *Archiloque* (Paris 1905) pp.132-162; and, more recently, the treatment in *Archiloque: fragments* (Paris 1958) pp. lxii-lxix, by François Lasserre.

3. Cf. Hauvette, *op. cit.,* pp.140 ff. The social-religious origins of the lampooning iambic spirit, as well as of the verse-form itself, are taken up by Werner Jaeger, *Paideia* I (trans. Highet, New York 1939) pp.119-121. He shows that we *need* not consider Archilochus' lampoons products of strong spite: they could have been traditional releases of communal emotion.

4. Jaeger, *op. cit.,* p.114.

5. But constantly less scarce. There have been numerous discoveries, in recent years, which have added both to our knowledge about Archilochus' life, and to the body of his poetry. For a recent survey of the additions, cf. A. Giannini, "Archiloco alla luce dei nuovi ritrovamenti," *Acme* 11 (1958) 41-96.

6. It is interesting and surprising to read the comment on this fragment by J. A. Symonds, *Studies of the Greek poets,* 1 (New York 1901) p.280:

   Greek sculpture is not more pure in outline than the following fragment, which sets before our eyes the figure of a girl embossed on marble or engraved in chalcedony . . .

   Does Symonds think that the poem is describing a work of art? Probably the girl is a prostitute.

7. Hermann Fränkel, *Dichtung und Philosophie des frühen Griechentums* (New York 1951) p.191, writes of Archilochus:

   Die Weltgeschichte verblasst gegenüber dem was sich im eignen Umkreis begibt.

   Fränkel's whole chapter on Archilochus, pp.182-207, explores the poetic mentality of the lyric poet ingeniously and from many angles.

Frederic Will (essay date 1969)

SOURCE: "From Sense to Attitude," "Ideas," "A Gathering of Fragments," "Archilochos and Classical Antiquity," and "Archilochos and Our Day," in *Archilochos,* Twayne's World Authors Series, Twayne Publishers, Inc., 1969, pp. 39-91.

[In the following excerpt, Will examines Archilochus's point-of-view, ideas, and critical reputation both in his own and in modern times.]

FROM SENSE TO ATTITUDE

Thus we believe that a certain intelligibility mixed with a certain obscurity exists in every true work of poetry.

Jacques and Raïssa Maritain, Situation de la Póesie

Sense-experience as an ingredient in Archilochos' poetry makes a subtle topic. There are some preserved instances of limpid sense-experience in which the sensuous flavor of meter speaks into the texture of an expressed world, the world of the girl with the myrtle, of the columnar young men, and of the dedicatory Alcibie. But even in those cases meter works against sensuous density, toward the more refined sensuousness of *récitatif,* where the world of things has been carried far toward pure poetry. The subjects themselves have been lightened, turned toward play by wit—as in the column epigram: "Mighty those columns, Aristophoon, Megatimon: / Columns, my great mother earth, held in your bosom today"—or by innuendo. (It is at least possibly implied that the girl who "held a branch of myrtle" is a whore.)

I pushed the initial point, that of Archilochos' kind of sensuousness, to suggest that as a man of the new post-epic world, he was literarily operative as a whole human being, more so than Hesiod or, in one sense, Homer. It is no contradiction of this point to say that Archilochos assumes his new position also on a more complex level. The thrust, at the center of his sensuousness, was toward alleviation. In a larger sense it was toward attitude. The distance from seeing to point-of-view is not great. What ultimately compels us in Homer is his lack of point-of-view, or his control over what Schiller might have called the "divine" point-of-view. In Archilochos, we admire the coming into being of the first recorded secular, individual, Hellenic point-of-view.

Operations of sight are the point in Archilochos where we can best notice his seeing turning into, fusing with, or earning, his point-of-view. We begin, though, with a pair of more elementary examples, in which dark, half-tactile experience interweaves with attitude. (Attitude is essentially self-reflexive, thus the poems, in a way, are onanistic; they turn in on themselves.)

The first poem is:

> Wretchedly, I lie desiring,
> Soulless, with an anguish from the gods
> Transfixed, clear through the bones.

(Fr. 84)

This is sensuousness without things. Even bones are dissolved into incarnate feelings. On the other hand, feelings are sensuous and sensible. Longing has become a sickness which infects bones, and which lays all flat and lifeless about it. This is a perfect dramatization of the physical-unphysical hypnosis of the lover who can't find his way out of love into action. The second poem is comparable:

> Such is the passion for love that has twisted its way
> beneath my heartstrings

and closed deep mist across my eyes
stealing the soft heart from inside my body . . .

(Fr. 103) (Translation by Richmond Lattimore)

Like the first poem, this one may perhaps not be incomplete. (It is a characteristic of the early Greek lyric—alive wherever you touch it—that even its fragments seem entire). Like the first poem, this also preserves a sensuous-spiritual balance, even fusion, which is rare. We are used to poems about longing, the things longed for, and the feelings in the one who is longing; but we are unused to locating the feelings among the organs of the body. The heart is present as an organ, not as the metaphoric rhetoric-organ of which later languages, even later Greek, speak: as in our "take my heart," or "I give you my heart."[1] The mist poured over the eyes of the one who longs seems to bring its physical reality into the body of the poem.

When the breast is opened up, for the wits to be snatched from it, we suffer softly. There is no effect closer to this than that of Sappho's famous poem, imitated by Catullus and read by experienced lovers ever since: the poem on her jealousy at another person's calmness in enduring the presence of her (Sappho's) lover. That person, who can endure such proximity, seems to her like a god: it would drive the poet's heart into her breast, strangle her voice. Her tongue would freeze, a light fire would run just under the surface of her skin, her eyes and ears would stop functioning, sweat (*idros,* a sweaty word) would run down her body; trembling would seize all of her, as she grows paler than sedge-grass. The effects described compel the reader to a physical projection which is rare in great poetry; and the more surprising in this, because the language is so highly formed. Being pre-Christian and unashamedly pagan, Archilochos and Sappho were somehow able to project physical awareness into language without softening the awareness into sentiment or straining it into prurience. Here we think of the undiscussable, self-adequate, self-equal presence of the human body in fifth-century Greek sculpture.[2]

I. SHIFT TO ATTITUDE

In the two poems discussed above, sense-awareness and spiritual state were fused. In poems of scene, where the eye translates the I, Archilochos can be watched passing from sense-perception to attitude. We begin with a simple, fragmentary example:

Ptossoúsan hóste pérdiká

(Fr. 106) (And crouching like a partridge there)

and then ask, for a second of academic privilege, to have the three words considered in themselves, as if they were a whole. They translate not only a position of the body, but a mood. The body is half-seen, half-felt where it is, through these words. Their vowelly sibilance holds, inexplicably, the secret of small, crouching animals; they are lonely but ready to skitter. The sensuously neutral is restless for a meaning which was no doubt directly at hand in the original whole.

In the following poem, statement mates syntactically with described sense:

With incensed tresses and a breast
that even an old man would have loved.[3]

(Fr. 30)

Again the activated sense is only partially sight. We see, smell, and feel the being, whereas earlier we only saw the girl with the myrtle. Next, "that" operates, quietly and grammatically proper, as both relative pronoun and introduction to a result clause, to show us one of the consequences possible to that sense-feast. The elected consequence is an expression of a minimal attitude toward the sexiness.

In the following poem, the same simple but poetically important progress is found in a different form:

Like the spine of an ass this island
Stands, with timber for a crown.
Not a lovely or a wanted place,
Or charmed, as one upon the banks of Siris.

(Fr. 21)

First we see, and that as clearly as possible. Again we notice how convincingly the external world existed for Archilochos. Many memories of harsh Greek spine-hills have been in the recipe for this language. It is impelled, prosodically, by a highly orchestrated gravity. (In Archilochos iambs do much besides assailing.) Then the poem, like a syllogism with middle term suppressed, moves to its conclusion. The logic of feelings takes on the guise of necessary logic. The guise is more illusory than in the preceding poem, because the "not," *ou gar,* in the island poem alone, does not introduce a consequence, but a state which is concomitant and reinforces that announced in the first two lines. It does not follow, from the look of mule-spined Thasos, that it is uncharming, that it is unlike the Siris river in Southern Italy. It is simply a fact, made sensuous and felt in the first two lines, and explicit in the last two. Attitude is implicit in the whole piece, but it is made more explicit by the last part.

In this light two more poems should be discussed, chosen because they present a different technique of organizing visual material for attitude. There is no longer the poetic syllogism of the "so that" kind; hardly even of the second, concomitance-stating kind. The first example:

Glaukos behold, the heavy sea is shaken
by waves and a vertical cloud stands
straight at the summit of Gyrae;
a signal of winter; dread from
the unexpected arrives.

(Fr. 54)

Greek fear of the storm and sea is known. This poem appears at first sight simply to arrange powerful observed symbols for that fear. Then, at the word "winter," it repeats itself in more pregnant (though more abstract) language. There is no syllogistic development as the poem passes from what is seen to an attitude toward what is seen. Nor is there the kind of syllogism by concomitance found at the end of the poem on Thasos where "the wretchedness of all the Greeks had come to Thasos." Here we have a repetition of the point of the first two and a half lines which puts that point in a different, possibly even self-transcending, way. It is a mysterious accounting for a meteorological situation. If there is logical progression in this poem, we might call it a liturgical logic.

The last sight for the moment is this:

> I don't like the towering captain with the spraddly
> length of leg,
> one who swaggers in his lovelocks and cleanshaves
> beneath the chin.
> Give me a man short and squarely set upon his legs, a
> man
> full of heart, not to be shaken from the place he plants
> his feet.

> (Fr. 58) (Translation by Richmond Lattimore)

For the first time in these examples, attitude and perception are almost totally interwoven. (The poem is, in this respect, one of a small class.) True, the "I don't like," and the "give me a man short . . ." in the third line, make the author's evaluation explicit. He parades his prejudice.

Suppose those two clarifying remarks were missing and replaced by descriptive introductions to lines one and three? The poem would be almost unchanged; much less significantly changed than the preceding sight-poems would be changed by removal of their explicitness. In each of those, the explicitness—"even an old man would have loved," "no beautiful place like those near Siris", "fear comes from the unknown"—adds a great deal: either by limiting the possibilities for conclusion through expanding the reference of the poem's sensuous detail, or by drawing an awful pregnancy out of that detail. In the present poem, all point is carried by the sensuous detail. The adjectives used to describe the two kinds of captain express, in their respective combinations, the characters of the two men, the author's attitude in each instance having been part of his way of seeing.

II. Narrative Poetry

All of Archilochos' poetry draws attention to its sound, and must have done so far more compellingly in the ancient sense-context. Furthermore, as we have already seen, a number of his poems use sense-material, things seen or felt, as their raw stuff. Yet, by one strategy or another, these poems turn themselves into expressions of attitude. It may be that Archilochos is not unusual, but simply human, in this thrust to leaven the sense-weight of language.[4] (What else, really, is the whole tendency toward idea in individual human development?) What is of interest here is the *particular way* in which Archilochos performs his trick.

We can follow his projection of attitude from a different mode of poetry, from narrative or rhetorical pieces, with their bases only loosely sunk into a sense-foundation. For the first, we choose a tiny example:

> Seven men fallen dead, whom we hammered with
> feet,
> a thousand killers we.

> (Fr. 59)

This is a piece of story which at first seems harmless. The trochaic meter runs unselfconsciously, not winking. Only a second later, in this fragment of the original whole, do we get the heavy irony. The attitude is a bitter laugh.

A little tale is often Archilochos' way into attitude. Take this example:

> No great number of arrows will fly or rapid
> slings, when Ares crashes his war
> on the plain; the muchgroaned labor of swords will
> rage.
> Of such a war they are masters,
> The spearfamed lords of Euboea.

> (Fr. 3)

The story, propelled by regular distichs, is foremost and easy. Perhaps it was weighted with some implication which could be known only in context of the missing parts of the poem. However, as it stands, it is not without implication, it is not merely an account. The second line carefully dresses the War God in his most ominous role. Then the language, in the third line, grows densely cruel: the labor of swords will be "muchgroaned" (*polystonos*). The adjective is rare in early Greek. (Though of course we inherit only a fragment of early Greek literature and, in any case, have no way to judge the character of the period's spoken language, against which supposed oddities of written language must be measured in order to determine the total effect of any word.)[5] A sinister pressure is given back by the *daimones,* translated here as "masters," of the fifth line: the lords of Euboea are uncannily knowing, even demons at this kind of fighting. The poem began as a flat indication of what kind of weapon would or would not be used in a certain battle, but the thrust was toward the sinister weapon actually to be used. And the conclusion, as we have it, brought us into the hearts of the ones who will use the weapon.

What I call the rhetorical-narrative manner in Archilochos rarely reaches us so free of explicit comment as in the last poem. This situation may be only the accident of preservation. To the end of the third line, the following poem resembles the preceding in offering weighted but uncommented narrative:

> Come on, on the seats of the rapid ship
> come on and draw from the giant vats
> drink scarlet wine from the bung; who's about
> to stay alert on guard this night?

> (Fr. 4)

There is a sense pervading the first three lines that the occasion of wine drawing is soon to be explained; even a feeling that it may be a strange or powerful occasion. In this, the drinking and fighting poems are comparable; we see in each the development of tension. In the present poem, attitude is not quite what emerges. Explanation, though, adds a kind of abandon which reinforces the earlier exhortations and becomes almost a way of looking at them.

My last two examples in the category also tell brief stories, but this time more meaningfully autobiographical. In the first, attitude is near the surface at every point:

> By spear my kneaded bread, by spear my wine
> of Ismaros, I drink leaned on that spear.
>
> (Fr. 2)

This is a dazzling self-revelation: no tone can be imagined more conclusively announcing the end of the epic voice. It is rapid narrative, moving over three poses, each struck briefly, kaleidoscopically, and the maker himself swaggering. Attitude seems so much part of the poem that it is hard to imagine separation between sense-material and elaborated point of view. The world of syllogistic poetry is sharply excluded. Something new in Archilochos replaces it: a relation of the poet as maker, outside the poem, to the poem he has made.

There is an irony in the present distich. We are forced back to the kind of awareness Jean Giono elaborated in *La naissance de L'Odyssée*. Poets are generally not soldiers of the soldierly sort, even when they can fight. The poetic effort, to make self-sufficient presented objects, is totally different from the out-turning, practical movement of the soldier into his world. This limitation to poetic stance may not have existed in Archilochos. (I don't propose psycho-analysis here any more than in the first chapter.) But, undoubtedly, Archilochos the poet was aware (and especially in his poetry) of a tension between the poetic and military attitudes. He has embodied this tangible sense of strain: the orderly tightness of prosody tenses off against the poet's flip ascription to himself of the military way. This embodied sense of tension is Archilochos' attitude toward his poem. It is attitude only in a slightly new sense.

I have been concerned with a kind of evolution of attitudes, from the fairly flat poem, on Megatimon and Aristophoon, or on Alcibie, through more implicatory poems, "Glaukos see . . . ," to somewhat direct statements of attitude, within the poem, as in "Like the spine of an ass . . ." In the present distich, which still moves out from sense, there is attitude, even swaggering attitude, in the language. But the author's self-consciousness is also present as attitude and works as a hidden ingredient in the language.

Something similarly complex holds for the next piece, which has suffered equally for its invitation that we should consider it only as an extraordinary document in Greek cultural history:

> A certain Saian delights in my shield
> which I left in a bush, not caring.
> I'm still alive thank god; to hell
> with the shield; I'll find me a better one soon.
>
> (Fr. 6)

We are so possessed by the fluency of the offhand language that a close look is difficult. We stop with the obvious and the important: Archilochos throws away the heroic code with his shield. Homer and Hesiod do not even write about such characters or character. Although Homer is never guilty of a stylized heroic attitude, and Hesiod is in many ways simply a prudent farmer, still neither epic maker could imagine a flip and mercenary attitude toward a situation drawn from the heroic context. To refuse the game, in Archilochos' suggested way, had been impossible (at least in epic literature).[6]

The poem that works this wonder is again narrative, and puts us once more in the realm of syllogistic attitude. The tale is told, as elsewhere in these two-distich pieces, by the first two and three-quarter lines. Then an attitude is adopted toward the tale. It continues the tale which had at least potentially implied such a conclusion. (Though the vagueness of that potency is one of the poem's charms, giving the decisiveness of *erreto*, "let it go to hell," great and added punch.)

Again in this poem, as in the last one, attitude seems to be shed from outside upon both the narrative and the attitude within the poem. The narrator comes closer to us at the end of the poem. He addresses an unspecified audience, the neutral but presumably sympathetic and even intimate audience generally posited by the lyric voice. Strictly speaking, this was also the audience in the beginning, in the first two lines. But if we read and reread these lines, we realize that Archilochos is speaking to himself, perhaps breathlessly, in a kind of private retrospection. However, at the end, he is facing his audience. Archilochos the maker is, of course, larger than both these personae, than both these guises of distinctive address toward the audience. By introducing a break in the direction and tenor of his two assumed personae, Archilochos openly manipulates the poem in which he is acting. This experienced manipulation is essentially an attitude of Archilochos toward the attitude which he expresses in his poem.

III. FUSION OF SENSE AND ATTITUDE

The question of attitude has been introduced as a line along which to guide a systematic analysis of Archilochos' poems. I will want, finally, to give some sense of the spectrum of his self-expressions, of the wholeness of his language-self. In analyzing Archilochos, the main job is getting off the ground; showing with some finesse, if possible, just how he himself moved from the expression and experience of sense-realities to a view of those realities; how, in other words, he leavened his poetry. This is no analysis of temporal development, of the evolution, in time, of Archilochos' control over language. As I have said, too little is known of Archilochos for that kind of inquiry to be worthwhile. My interest has been rather in the essential character of Archilochos' poetry, not in its history. I have aimed at the ontology or original structure of the work.[7]

Visual (and other) descriptions, and narrative-rhetoric poems have been the chief specimens in this chapter. In each of these types I have shown the emergence of attitude which, in the last two pieces considered, seemed an increasingly complex concept. I want to close the chapter by considering a small category of sense-poem.

I am thinking of a kind of optative poem in which a wish for sense-pleasure is expressed, and which shows, in perfect fusion, the meeting of sense and attitude.

> If only I could touch Neoboule's hand.
>
> (Fr. 71)

The soft, sensuous finality of the prosody and vowel qualities carries the sadness of feeling. The feeling itself is erotic-romantic, intense but sublimated, in a way unparalleled elsewhere in Archilochos. (It is closer, by far, to a frequent mood in Sappho.) The sensuous, really the sensual, is here leavened not by attitude, and certainly not by idea, but simply by longing. Archilochos is generally willing, as he says moralistically in a few of his idea-poems, to restrict his hopes to reality. Such optative poetry as the present line is therefore rare. When it occurs, it can evidently turn sense into sense plus longing and create a romantic poem.

Such longing, in Archilochos, is not only rare, but it gives a delicacy of aspiration, as distinct from one of prosody and craftsmanship, which has led some classicists to substitute other imaginable words for the *cheira* ("hand") in Archilochos' line. Such scholars have fewer textual temptations with this second optative poem:

> And to fall upon her, belly on belly
> Meeting her thigh to thigh.
>
> (Fr. 72)[8]

It is possible that Neoboule, lost temporarily or permanently, was also the object of this wish.

The sensuousness of portrayal is heavy and forceful (in the Greek, almost brutal). The general prosodic point holds: that these trochees, lengthened and emphasized at their outsets, force and drive the language ahead. They control the reader. But in addition there is an extraordinary adjustment of the sensuous in words to its achieved reason, to its prose sense. I mean through the immediate repetitions of "belly," though (in Greek) in different cases, and of "thighs," though (in Greek) in different cases. The desired falling of belly on belly, and the desired heaving of thigh on thigh, are dramatized by the immediate, slashing proximity of the words for those two parts of the body. The slashing force is strengthened by the use of datives

for the particular "thigh" and "belly" moved against. (I may be relying too heavily on the exciting strangeness of such an inflected language. Perhaps dative usage here, grammatically controlled in the Greek by the prefix of *prosbalein,* to "meet" or "cast upon," would have struck the ancient Greek ear as only neutrally natural.) The dative seems to function as receptacle; "motion toward" seeming, therefore, to imply a further, more desired, motion continuous with it.

Whether or not this grammatical point holds, the little piece returns us to a starting point. From here it is worth thinking back to certain poems discussed earlier: again to those on Aristophoon or Alcibie, which, on the whole, seemed placidly visual; or to those in which Archilochos was, as I said, onanistically bent over the moods of his own viscera; to those poems, in short, in which Archilochos seemed least to adopt an attitude toward his poetic stuff. The second of the two optative poems achieves just this kind of neutrality, but in a different way. It expresses a wish so mutely (and eloquently) physical, and through language so adequate, that it leaves no interstices for attitude.

. . . . .

IDEAS

Idea is the form of things recollected by the imagination. . . .

Émile Bernard

The status of ideas in poetry is hard to describe. We realize that the discussion of poetry in terms of form and content is dangerous, and that the discussion of content largely in terms of ideas or of the poet's beliefs is even more dangerous; in fact, it makes a joke of criticism. It leaves the always essential sensuous substratum (and middle stratum) out of consideration. It turns criticism into freshman philosophy.[9]

To this point consideration has been given to the character of Archilochos' poetry from the ground up, from his most sensuous awareness, and presentations, to those poems, the matter of this chapter, in which he most nearly troubled himself about what we might call ideas. A weakness in method has followed me all the way. I considered prosody in the beginning chapter, and have continued to wave my hat at the topic. But increasingly, and even more in the present chapter, I talk about poems as though they were not, in part, radically mere sound, or sense-material, and as though they were not part of an immediate, or rational historical context. I have tried thus far to avoid referring to ideas, but I have slipped into much talk about content.

This unavoidable violence done by the language of criticism to that of poetry can be mitigated by an effort to see what I called the spectrum of a poet's expression, and how it ranges from the most to the least sensuous aspects of that expression. Insisting on the sensuous ground of the things said, in poetry, is at least a kind of running atonement for ignoring the sounds in which the meaning is said.

I. POETRY OF IDEA

I begin this chapter, atoningly, with poetry of idea which best recalls the closeness of all Archilochos' poetry to the life of the senses. The poem tells a story and draws a conclusion:

> Nothing impossible is such
> no thing miraculous, since father Zeus
> sent out of noon a night, and shut the light
> of the brilliant sun; a wretched fear came down on
> men.
> Since then all seems credible to men, and hopeable.
> None of you now be startled, watching
> when beasts change nature with dolphins
> and fall in love with echoing waves of the sea
> and mountains are the sweetest home for fish.
>
> (Fr. 74)

Except for a strangely grave tone in the first three and a half lines, this poem starts off with a familiar promise: to move from the particular to the general, to argue, as we saw earlier in the following two poems:

> Glaukos behold, the heavy sea is shaken
> by waves and a vertical cloud stands
> straight at the summit of Gyrae;
> a signal of winter; dread from
> the unexpected arrives.
>
> A certain Saian delights in my shield
> which I left in a bush, not caring.
> I'm still alive thank god; to hell
> with the shield; I'll find me a better one soon.

Yet, a caveat has been entered at the beginning of the eclipse piece; the puzzling suggestion that anything now is possible; a suggestion which, at this point, looks like stage-setting, while, in fact, it proves to be a wedge of the sureality which conquers at the end. Not only is personal attitude not being anticipated, as it is in the other two poems, but a strange heightening of the narrative events is from the beginning acquired in the present poem. The heightening, perhaps slightly ironical but still high style, prepares us for the final talk of a topsy-turvy world.

The final vision of inverted natures may (or may not) be taken as a move into the precinct of ideas. At its simplest level it is a conceit; and I see no reason to deny early Greek lyric poets a sense of word play; we are usually too strict with them.[10] Play words, like the "echoing waves" or the "sweet" in the last line, bear out such an interpretation. I prefer a slightly heavier view; and for this reason consider this as a poem of ideas.

The Greek word *nomos,* at the end of line seven, "when beasts change nature with dolphins," is a clue. Broadly, that word means "law" or "principle of order." In application to a genus of beings it will mean something approaching *telos,* "end" or "final cause." This is apparently what it means here. We are to expect a universe in which the appointed natures of creatures may be changed, even traded

off. Genera will overflow those boundaries in terms of which they have their meaning. Meaning itself will flow loosely and as uselessly as spilled water through the universe.

The other poems to which I attend in this chapter are more direct in presenting the ideas they treat; they lie farther from purely presentational language. I begin, for the sake of clarity only, with two one-line gnomic examples. The first:

> All things labor achieves for man, labor and mortal study.
>
> (Fr. 15)

and the second:

> All things luck and fate, O Perikles, present to man.
>
> (Fr. 16)

These are perfect dactylic hexameters, each cast in a strangely Ur-epigrammatical form. I feel, here, the plausibility of a theory: that the lyric may originally and then later in the early Renaissance have grown from the epigram, or in close affiliation with it. Epigrams are all the same in felt-form. The stunning difference between these two pieces is made almost unnoticeable by their similar surface radiances.

Neither poem arrests itself for specific sense-detail or for elaboration; yet the thrusts are forceful and opposite. The first poem ascribes all good fortune to human effort; the second, to luck and fate. Considering the two lines, for the moment, as philosophy, not as philosophy in poetry: is there a possible reconciliation between the two lines?

Archilochos is a philosopher close to nature; close especially to the violence of one expression of external nature, the sea; and to one internal expression, passion and rage. As he works with these two forces he becomes, at least as a personage in his poetry, increasingly aware of the degrees and ways in which men are unable to control their own destinies. (We may assume that the rage at losing Neoboule gradually converted itself into resigned acceptance of the exigency in life.) Fate and luck will have deified themselves slowly through experience. There will remain, at the same time, a sense of the importance of human effort. Men close to the sea or to their passions are likely to feel this too with the growth of their experience; they will feel that they must do all in their power to anticipate and control nature. On the other side of that prudence lies fatalism. This may not be the philosophy of the schools, but it is often the philosophy of philosophers in poetry. (Poetry and labor come close together here.)

I have no desire to prove Archilochos a philosopher or to build unimagined bridges among his often widely separated thoughts. The lines quoted above have in any case an unrepresentative, tantalizing relation to one another. Between them, though, they do suggest a range of concerns which embrace most of the extant philosophical remnants of Archilochos: that suggestiveness is our chief profit from the two lines.

At their center lies a concern with what I loosely termed nature, meaning to stress a force which puts man in mind of his limitations and of certain necessary controls. Harsh outer nature usually means the sea. Archilochos was born on an island, lived on islands; as always in the Aegean, those islands were small, shaven, and forever opening up prospects of ocean. Ships were only fairly strong, storms were frequent, and the sea was often a killer. We have one brief testimony from Archilochos:

> Let's hide the unholy gifts of the lord Poseidon.
>
> (Fr. 10)

The "gifts" are the drowned bodies.

II. A Bridge Between Physics and Metaphysics

The theme of drowned bodies is picked up much more elaborately in the following:

> The funeral groans, Perikles, no one of the citizens,
> not one small city can know in rejoicing;
> such are the men whom the wave of the echoing
> ocean had buried, leaving us pressure of pain
> at our hearts; but the gods, my friend,
> have given us mighty endurance of pain,
> medicament; now one, now another is struck.
> We groan with the bloody wound today
> in turn to be others': instantly
> push your effeminate pain away, and endure.
>
> (Fr. 9)

At the center lies the sensed cruelty of the sea. As often, the sea itself is not described; as often, the natural world existed for the Greek poet—Sappho, Alcaeus, Solon, too—as a genesis of human feelings. Archilochos' voice is very differently related to the world from the voice he assumed in "She held a branch," or "Wretchedly I lie desiring. . . ." The luck of text preservation may partly account for this feeling. In the present poem much is preserved, and perhaps the entire poem.

The whole esthetic structure—prosody, imagery—appears and, as always, somewhat interposes itself between the things experienced and the person who experiences them. But there is an irony in the tone of narration which does much to put the narrator's person in the foreground, in the front of what he is talking about. In the second line the "know in rejoicing," the "pain at our hearts" (literally, at our "lungs"), the exquisite placing of the word (in Greek) for medicament: all these studied turnings not only bring the author's persona into firm relief, but they suggest bitterness toward the sea, which is of more poetic interest than the sea itself. It is no surprise to find that in what is the end, apparently, the poet pulls out a familiar Stoic slo-

gan. Archilochos is playing the soldier in his best manner. A caesura intervenes artfully, and with careful distributive power, between "effeminate" and "pain" in the last line.

Stoicism is an attitude in the face of both external and internal nature. It is a universal refuge of the instinctively unphilosophical mind when it is driven by personal experience to adopt some attitude toward life which will absorb shock. Nature forces that solution on Archilochos.[11]

Holding out is the core of Archilochos' Stoicism: the principle is defended on simple grounds, that human affairs change, and that man, unhappy today, will be happy tomorrow. We saw this argument before, and find it more prominent here:

> Leave all things to the gods; for often from evil
> they raise up men laid flat on the cobalt land,
> and often they trip the steady and firm
> on their backs; when evils in number arrive
> a man is beside himself, in lack of life.
>
> (Fr. 56)

The feeling of holding out is dwelt on, but simply.

I have discussed ways in which the sensuous texture and objects of Archilochos' poetry are refined toward the more abstract exigencies of pure poetry. A new kind of example presents itself in the preceding poem where Archilochos works through a central, and almost mathematically demanding, equation. Upright stance is equated to being in prosperity, and proneness is equated to being in adversity.[12] Such metaphors, drawn from the physical world, are poetic commonplaces; but the metaphor in this case is so boldly, even baldly, equivalencing (I think of the rapid bodily ups and downs of slap-stick comedians) that the role of the physical world in the construction of the metaphor is forgotten. The precariousness of human affairs is so sharply dramatized that a move into theology earns its place at the beginning of the poem. This is not the only scrap of explicit theology in Archilochos, as we shall soon see.[13]

First, however, another example of Stoicism based on sense of flux, on a sense which the philosophers of Asia Minor were to examine metaphysically no more than a century later. The next poem courageously, but in purely poetic terms, sketches plans for a bridge between ethics and metaphysics:

> My heart, my heart stirred up by blocking griefs
> rise up, and cast your chest to block them
> bravely, and near your foes be safe
> and neither in victory boast out open
> nor beaten fall in weeping at home:
> take joy in joys, and give in not
> too much to evils: knowing what rhythm holds all
> men.
>
> (Fr. 66)

The last line is justly famous and has deserved much of the discussion dedicated to it. The chief question has been: what is *rhysmos,* "rhythm"? The question is important because the idea of flux in human affairs is generally important in Archilochos—as in the poems discussed above. It is also important because in some way Archilochos seems to be pioneering or attempting for the first time in the West to abstract from a wide variety of daily experiences to a notion of the nature of things. "Rhythm" is surely *not* only the ups and downs of human life, sadness followed by joy, followed by sadness. It is partly that. But, as in the previous poems, we feel that those ups and downs are caused by the interaction of the outer world with the subject. Archilochos, the persona of these poems, is no manic-depressive: he reacts to details of the outer world, sometimes to the sea, sometimes to his passions, sometimes to what he collectively calls, as in this poem, the "blocking griefs," sufferings for which no strategy of solution seems to be at hand. Rhythm is the way the world goes where world is the intersection of man, as subject, with the objects outside him. Archilochos here achieves a philosophical statement, backed by the described texture of his own experience, which moves out from passion, but testifies to an untroubled belief in the existence of the real world. The special success of formulation in this poem conforms to its especially delicate perception of the ethical situation, which follows from living in a rhythmic world. There is some of the earlier and easier response found in the previous poem: know that your estate will change. But there is a new turn: one should not give in to excessive sorrow, or to good fortune: he should simply know that these conditions will *not* last.

A kind of equanimity is finally preached, in the impressive words "neither in victory boast out open." An evenness of understanding and temper is needed in order to conform to the rhythm of what-is. This is perhaps a strange argument. Certainly it looks forward to the Stoics, properly so-called, to men like Zeno and Chrysippos, who occupied a firm world view in terms of which to iron out such wrinkles of paradox. Archilochos is simply translating his own experience. His bridge between ethics and metaphysics is thus all the more remarkable. He sees quite nakedly, and perhaps mainly through the thought-prompting stringencies of his own art, the way in which what a man *does* is related to the nature of the world in which a man *is*. It is the deepest achievement in Archilochos.

. . . . .

A GATHERING OF FRAGMENTS

Much, not many.

Greek proverb

A picture has emerged from the analysis of the poems in the last two chapters, which, though incomplete at many points, makes Archilochos appear more than usually versatile in lyric-poetic terms. What he is saying in prosodic language varies from the thickly (or rather violently) sensuous, through the subtly, often ironically attitudinal, toward the metaphysical, a highly refined and general perception, as in the last poem discussed, into the character of being. The range is wide, even rather balanced. But the

balance can be deceptive in one particular way. The language which displays this wide range is itself highly sensuous and must have been far more sensuous, as I have argued, when it was surrounded by music and tones. (This is not to mention the living context of production, which was probably public, and so, like a play, introduced the living scene of life into itself as an ingredient of the esthetic experience.)

Such a picture, furthermore, has acquired some of the idiosyncratic features that make an individual. The Archilochos whom Archilochos writes into his poetry, as far as we have considered it, is a complex man. There is a strong military-poetic attitude at the center of what remains. We see here the attitude in fragment 1, for instance, where the War God and Muses are cited as twin patrons, and again in fragment 2, which praises the life of the spear in neat, almost effete, lines. So smooth, even swaggering, is the attitude, that flipness hardly surprises us, as it does in fragment 6, which talks about the lost shield. From fragments 1 and 2 we had supposed Archilochos to be a tough and competent soldier, but no idealist; he sounded like a man who could say "to hell with it." But wasn't there something shrill about the way he said the words in making this world-historical utterance? Probably not. War was a serious matter for him, and he resented its cruelties. He hated the war lords of Euboea (fragment 3). He hated himself as a murderer, that is, as a soldier (fragment 59). He was, in fact, easily unbalanced from his sense of personal well-being: unbalanced by a sense of strangeness and numinousness in nature. Even more, it seems, he was unbalanced by a countering of his own erotic need, by the brutal rupture of his marriage plans. There are many Stoic poems, cautious and prudent, in which Archilochos tells himself that it all comes out the same in the end. And in the direction of sensuous hypersensitivity, and of vulnerability to the world, there are also rich and full testimonies to the character of his longing (fragments 84, 78), to the delight of an untroubled eye (fragments 29, 17), to the pleasures of speech almost for its own sake (fragment 17). At the other end of the spectrum, near the other kind of vulnerability to ideas, Archilochos proves himself a Stoic reaching out for a much more than soldierly consolation. He touches metaphysics with a deftness we could just barely expect from the man who threw his shield to the Saians.

The purpose of the present chapter is to bring in some of the many remaining fragments of Archilochos, in order, as far as possible, to complete the present portrait.

I. POEMS OF SARCASM

Many of the remaining fragments are small or so hopelessly cut off from their contexts that they cannot be discussed properly; they deserve to be left in their semi-articulate peace. But the poems which bear analysis confirm, and in some ways sharpen, my character sketch of the Archilochos who is to be found in his poems.

There is very little more of what I described above as a swaggering pose, or the pose of the casual poet-soldier. In discussing prosody, I have already referred to the first couplet, in which Archilochos calls himself the servant of the War God and the Muses. The brisk perspective of this piece affiliates itself with the kind of brisk Stoicism whiffed here:

> Nothing will I improve by weeping or make
> the worse by rejoicing and kicking my heels.
>
> (Fr. 13)

Why do such expressions seem to speak out from Archilochos' core persona? Perhaps it is that the confidence of his prosody, which catches its sentiments in seemingly unchangeable phrase, makes confidence and energy seem to be the chief attitude translated there.

The remaining fragments include those in which Archilochos most turns from casual virility, and *virtù,* to openly expressed pugnacity. We come on some of those poems, so famous in antiquity, from which Archilochos derived his main reputation as a sarcastic reviler, as a man who worked in iambs so harsh that they drove Lykambes and his family to commit suicide. For prelude, I choose a line in which Archilochos takes his complaint to Zeus:

> Paternal Zeus, I shared no marriage then . . .
>
> (Fr. 99)

Of the attack on Lykambes, the cause of this loss, only the following is left:

> Father Lykambes, what did you utter then?
> Who robbed you of the brains
> which you had once; you're now
> the city's lovely laughing stock.
>
> (Fr. 94)

Even when we put this together with the other fragments, like the poem on the eclipse (fragment 74), which may have been gibes at Lykambes, we are left finding this stuff tame. Aristophanes or, for that matter, Theognis or Hipponax, season us to tougher attacks than we have in this poem. Was there enough in what is said above to make the victim commit suicide?

The iamb had been associated, before Archilochos, with personal assault. In early religious ceremonies for Demeter, hopping iambic dimeters, scurrilously directed at men present, alternated with sacred rites: a certain awefulness of the sacred seems, as it does in gargoyles, to have been preserved in this art form. Though by the time of Archilochos the form had probably been largely divorced from its religious context, yet the iamb, energetic and ready for a fight as it is by phonetic nature, was still surrounded by an aura. It acquired especially forceful meanings for the argument it conveyed. Lykambes may have felt that force. He may also, as a seventh-century Greek, inheritor of a world which was still in many ways epic-heroic, have had a strong sense of his own *timē* ("honor"), his worth in public estimation. To be called "the city's lovely laughing

stock" may have carved him through; especially if, when the poem was written, Archilochos had already come into some part of the great fame he won during his life time.[14]

The assault on Lykambes gains some strength when we add to the present fragment a famous and sadly butchered fragment on the fox and the eagle. The story seems a close replica of one by Aesop, who was probably a contemporary of Sappho, and whose work on folk-oral sources was known to Archilochos. The basic line of the tale in both Aesop and Archilochos concerns breach of contract. An eagle and a fox have made a friendship pact. When the fox has to leave his lair, however, the eagle flies down and steals the cubs, takes them to its nest, and devours them. Returning, the fox is outraged, and even more enraged at his own helplessness. Finally, in the Aesopic version, a strong wind blows up, knocks the eagle's young to the ground, and the fox devours them. Friendship has been converted into double savagery. Archilochos' fragment 95, quite plausibly the conclusion of his telling, reads something like:

> a great oath you have broken, deny
> me salt and your table's company . . .
>
> (Fr. 95)

It is tempting to assume that fragment 89, about the monkey and the fox, continues the attack:

> I tell you a fable, Kerux's son,
> a herald's staff, a bitter message.
> A monkey wandered, far
> from all animals, alone
> on a set-apart field.
> Toward him advanced a wily fox,
> with a clever thought in his head.
>
> (Fr. 89)

The "fox" presumably is Archilochos. His victim, a projected hope, is the monkey, as comic a figure to the seventh century Greek as it is to us.

Whatever the explanation for the presumed effectiveness of these attacks on Lykambes, Archilochos seems to have been serious, or at least to have been posing seriously, in these poems of bitter disappointment over lost love. (The distance between pose and actual attitude grows infinitesimal at this point.)

Another line comes out of his longing for Neoboule and argues the same involvement with Eros:

> But limbloosing longing, friend, subdues me.
>
> (Fr. 85)

His hatred for Lykambes may have been so strong only because his longing and desire for Neoboule had been so strong.

His capacity for hatred receives more general expression in the following:

One great thing I know,
to answer him who hurts me with hardcutting blows.

(Fr. 65)

But so does his gift for faithful friendship, above all for piety toward man:

But one man warms another's heart,

(Fr. 36)

and, better:

No noble thing to blame a dying man.

(Fr. 64)

Love, even in a larger sense, does not conquer all. But a sense of the ultimate equality of all men translates itself into an understanding of what it is to be man.

Sensitivity to human relations, too, is kin to an intense awareness of nature, that other large form of "the other." Two sharp little poems remain to say:

Beseeching a sweet return through the waves
of the foam-coiffed silver sea . . .

(Fr. 55)

The statement is plaintive. A "sweet return" through the "foam-coiffed sea" apparently is nothing to be counted on. It was the kind of occurrence Archilochos might pray for. The other fragment is bitter:

Of fifty men the gentle Poseidon has left us Koiranon.

(Fr. 114)

Play and bitterness seem almost to meet. The internal rhyming, between the endings of the Greek words "men" and "Poseidon," joins with the playing, though bitterly playing spirit of the "gentle" Poseidon. We know from above how much suppressed feeling is likely to be latent in this gamey assault.

This sensitivity convenes naturally, of course, with the precautionary Stoicism: the self-protective movement seen earlier, and, in Archilochos, instinctively internalizing, self-disciplining. A single well-known piece will illustrate:

Moneybag Gyges no interest to me
not jealous of him, not jealous of
works of the gods, not asking for splendor
of rule; things far from my eyes.

(Fr. 25)

Gyges was a contemporary, it seems, and already proverbially famous not only for his wealth, but for that fascination with money for its own sake which made his *Weltanschauung* famous. Archilochos is not jealous. Why? Perhaps because he is too deeply aware, or one part of him is aware, that pleasures dependent on external conditions are precarious. An external world as threatened and

kinetic as that which Archilochos allowed himself to endure, contained many quiet warnings that only what a man is can nourish him.

It is worth considering a last fragment in which Archilochos turns to God in a way distinctive of him and of early Greek experience. The poet seeks understanding more than peace.

Glaukos, Leptines' son, a man
has so much heart as Zeus
provides him day by day,
and for . . .

(Fr. 70)

Our spirit and courage are measured out to us by Zeus. The careful measuring out of the language says this too. Regular trochees capture the careful gravity of the argument. Archilochos makes us feel, while we are learning, that he has found a place in which to convert life-distress into life-understanding.

. . . . .

ARCHILOCHOS AND CLASSICAL ANTIQUITY

Stand and behold Archilochos that ancient poet
Whose iambs and multifold fame have spread from the
dawn to the setting sun.

Theocritus, Epigram XXI

Some foreign cultures are opaque to us; the Greek, among those cultures which are at all close to us, is probably the most opaque. We understand, of course, its general point of view. It assumes the importance of the human; more specifically, the value of effort in time, the clear distinctness between subject and object in knowing; the qualified concern with the possibility of overcoming time. Given such broad features, however, often surprisingly little remains for our understanding.

What the Greeks made well, what *was* significantly theirs, enjoyed great autonomy. Vases, iambs, temples, were well-made wholes so realized that they left no obvious blemish for critical feeling to wedge into; they left little room for our critical understanding, as distinct from our admiration or appreciation. It is almost impossible for us to discuss the best made of these creations.

A Homeric simile drawn from human relations may help to show us one kind of past into understanding the Hellenic path. We can imagine a man whose conversation, through its brilliance or perfect adequacy to himself, relegates our responses to astonishment; yet heard in dialogue, he is far more intelligible. So works of Greek culture, which are opaque to us through their self-completeness, may be better understood when they enter into dialogue. I mean, when they are criticized, or talked about by other Greeks. We may not only learn much about the Greeks, and about Archilochos, by reviewing the Greek attitude to that poet; but we may learn certain things about Archilochos which in any other way would be impenetrable to us.

I. EARLY CRITICS OF ARCHILOCHOS

The influence of Archilochos on the Greeks cannot be the title of this chapter, for the man followed through this book never influenced his fellow countrymen. He was a concern to them, a demanding block or mass in what to the later Greeks became their own literary history; but with a few exceptions, as far as I can see, he did not enter into and mold the writings of other authors.[15]

The first recorded comment on Archilochos, attributed to Heraclitus, runs as follows:

> Heraclitus used to say that Homer deserves to be thrown out of the musical contests and to be whipped, and Archilochos too.[16]

I suspect that the attack on Homer, which comes to us in this passage without immediate context, is prompted by hatred of myth, by a metaphysician's impatience with narrative means of explaining what is. This argument was urgently strong among the first Milesians, who, in the western world, were just discovering the delights of knowing and discussing being. They were apostles of a new vision. But why did they attack Archilochos, whose lyric directness must have seemed to them much less mythical than Homer's language?

We are perhaps touching the quarrel between *mythos* and *logos,* the former an attempt to persuade through sense-presentation, the latter through discursive compulsion. By this argument, also familiar to the Milesians, Homer and Archilochos might have appeared equally objectionable. In that case, they would have appeared chiefly as examples of poem-makers. In their exemplary function they would remind us of the curious Greek custom of reference to Archilochos and Homer as though they were comparable and equally great poets.[17] The Greek assumption, in this instance, is one more indication of our distance from the Greek standpoint.

Or can one speculate that Heraclitus might have been angry at the immorality of Homer and Archilochos? Could this have been an early form of that moralistic attack which rages in Plato and which often recurs in the tradition of comment on Archilochos? Such an interpretation is not out of the question, but it hardly suits the general thrust of Heraclitus. He was not, as far as we can tell from the fragments, an ethically pious author; his physics directly attacked the poetic theology of the epic world. He was a pioneer. It hardly seems that Heraclitus would have shared Plato's conservative sentiments.[18]

The second recorded critique, from Pindar, may follow the interpretation suggested above (though presumably only by accident):

> I must flee
> the furious bite of slanders.
> From far I have seen Archilochos,

> assailer himself, assailed
> and at loss from enmity,
> deep-bite language.[19]

The tenor of the poem and the wider context in Pindar suggest a broad intention, a desire to stand apart from the arena of confused human passions in order to maintain a certain proud proximity to the Olympian. Perhaps this attitude is closer to that of Heraclitus, and less idiosyncratically Pindaric than at first appears. Naturally, Pindar, prince of images and prosodic magician, is not speaking against poetry here; but he may be attacking what is too personal in poetry, that in it which achieves the opposite of abstract presentation. In Pindar, as in the Ionians, there is a drive towards essence. Compare the elemental passions of the Ionians, their metaphors of fire, air, water, with Pindar's love of water, metallic radiance, and pure deep hues. This drive may have made Archilochos seem petty to Pindar. (It is worth noting that none of these critics takes much interest in Archilochos' historical importance as the first lyricist, an importance which is of the highest meaning to us now.)

The third significant criticism of the work of Archilochos before 400 B.C. is ascribed to Critias the Sophist, politician during the Peloponnesian Wars and a figure in some of the Platonic dialogues. It reads:

> Critias raises the objection, against Archilochos, that he was his own worst slanderer. "If," as he says, "Archilochos had not spread this opinion of himself among the Greeks, we would never have known that he was the son of Enipo, a slave woman, nor that he left Paros from poverty and indigence, and so went to Thasos, nor that upon arrival there he alienated himself from *those* people, making light of friend and foe." "Furthermore," he says, "we wouldn't even know that he was an adulterer, if we didn't have it from him, nor that he was unbridledly, even indecently, sensuous, and, worst of all, that he threw his shield away. Archilochos was no good testimony to himself, leaving that sort of slander and scuttlebutt behind him." Reproaches raised not by me, notice, but by Critias.[20]

Whatever the motive, the attack is related to those of Heraclitus and Pindar; the baseness of Archilochos is the target. The perspective is no longer that of metaphysics or of the noble in poetry. Baseness is charged on far less radical grounds and from the typically social Stoic position.

Critias seems to be saying that Archilochos projected a bad image of himself and that this was his weakness, society's judgment being the chief criterion of value in human negotiations. On the other hand, as with Heraclitus and Pindar, we cannot be sure. We know too little about Critias, and far too little about the context of this passage, which is here only quoted from another source. Critias may well have been criticizing this bad image because it was bad, rather than simply because it was poor image projection. In either case, the indictment is the same. Archilochos is accused of complicity with those lower human instincts for one aspect of which Pindar had attacked him, and for which, on a higher level of generality, where poetry became the realm of the sensuous, Heraclitus also attacked him.

The three criticisms gathered here are few but precious, for they are the only significant early evidences left to us on the matter. They may have been selected for us chiefly by time and chance, not by human plan. Such unintentioned factors restrict our body of classical literary criticism even more ruthlessly than they choose our classical literature. Yet there is a representative quality, to preserved classical criticism, which repeats itself; it almost seems to imply more than chance in its formation. The remarks in Pindar, Heraclitus, and Critias offer us that representative quality. They offer, to mention the obvious first, no close criticism, no criticism directed to literature as esthetic construction. It was a long time, apparently, before the Greeks learned to take that kind of explicit interest in literature. Aristotle had already begun to take such interest in the *Poetics*. In many places he considered the devices of the word-maker, tropes, inversions, aspects of logic in syntax, and at all times he remained concerned with such basic elements as character and plot. His *Rhetoric* proves his interest in the strategies of verbal persuasion. But none of this is literary criticism working out from the texts; or even, in the most general way, out from language. It is all prescriptive argument, glancing at texts en route toward conclusive and predetermined convictions about literature.

Not before Longinus' *On the Sublime* do we reach a more genuinely literary criticism. There details of expression are closely surveyed and authoritatively assessed; the magic of language is wrestled with. But the perspective remains deductive and rhetorical. We are still concerned with the bag of tricks available to the author in order to make his point, or to persuade. It is one of the puzzles of Greek literary culture that the power to create vastly outdistanced the power to discuss creations. This mystery may relate to its sister mystery: that the Hellenic literary sense of the fullness of personality and character never translated itself into anything like a systematic psychology. The very word for personality was lacking throughout all the great centuries.[21]

Longinus, however, is already far from Aristotle in approach to verbal criticism, and much farther from the three critics of Archilochos whom I have discussed. It would be too much to say that their concern is chiefly biographical. On the other hand, it is much too little to say that Heraclitus, Pindar, and Critias are not interested in verbal criticism. They strike in between in a way which deserves mention because it is representative of extant earlier Greek criticism. They concern themselves with the attitudes of Archilochos which realize themselves in his poetry.

II. LATER CLASSICAL CRITICS OF ARCHILOCHOS

Among subsequent mention of Archilochos in Greek literature, most is still to be learned from the strangely offhand uses of his name. From these we see, as in offhand references today to Shakespeare as "bard," or to Shelley as "skylark" or "pure spirit," just how deeply Archilochos had insinuated himself into Greek feeling. A few of these fairly random pieces of evidence add up to something more than a fragmentary picture.

Plato gives us a little evidence, naming (*Ion* 531a) Homer, Hesiod, and Archilochos together as a naturally joined trio. We have seen above the readiness of Heraclitus to consider Homer and Archilochos together. Later references to Archilochos show a similar readiness of such marginal authors as Heracleides Ponticus and Antipater of Salonika. The former, a student of Plato, is credited with a work, *Concerning Homer and Archilochos;* while Aristotle, in a probably reliable catalogue of his own work, lists *Sayings of Archilochos, Euripides, and Choerilos,* a title in which our poet finds himself in new but still great company. He also appears a little later when Antipater of Salonika (around the time of Christ) concludes an epigram with:

> To Archilochos today let us drink, and to Homer the man.
> The mixing bowl sickens of drinkers of water.[22]

Two other references indicate, through indirection rather than through a recording of lists of names, how well known Archilochos was. The first example was verbal. By the time of New Comedy, during the age of Menander, a common expression, "you tread Archilochos," had developed. The idiom stressed Archilochos' own supposed roughness and was sufficiently current that we understand the poet's remarkable entrance into casual thought. The second example, roughly contemporaneous, is from Theophrastus' work on meteorology, *De Signis Tempestatum* ("On the Signs of Storms"), and refers to Archilochos' poem on the rising of storm and fear (above, p. 51). Theophrastus writes:

> . . . if the oaks bear good fruit, often many storms come. If a vertical cloud stands over the peak of a mountain, it means a storm, for which reason Archilochos wrote:

> Glaukos behold, the heavy sea is shaken
> by waves and a vertical cloud stands
> straight at the summit of Gyrae;
> a signal of winter . . .[23]

True, science and poetry were considered closer by the Greeks than they are by us. The perceptions of the poet and of the natural scientist like Theophrastus were thought particularly close. But even in Greek terms the passage deserves attention. It suggests Archilochos' peculiarly authoritative aura. Nothing less could have brought him and his passage into such context, which at this point seemingly showed no concern at all for poetry.

On the one hand, then, Archilochos is becoming a commonplace of speech and reference. On the other hand, a myth or exaggerated habit of reference about Archilochos is growing up through these centuries after the fifth. I mean the tale about Archilochos' cruelty, and his savage iambic assaults, a tale picking up part of the energy in the earlier critiques by Heraclitus, Pindar, and Critias, but extending them much farther in the direction of personal assault, even of gossip. (It is clear, ultimately, that the tradition of Greek criticism of Archilochos, like that of other Greek heroes, has few edifying moments. A big squabbling family seems to have been at work here.)

The move into harshness often passes through grotesquerie, a direction taken, we suppose, in a strange play by Diphilus, a contemporary of Menander. The play was called *Sappho,* and seems to have shown, "as lovers of Sappho, Archilochos and Hipponax," poets who lived a century apart and cannot possibly have shared a single year of life. (Characteristic Greek indifference to positive history is shown here, as A. von Blumenthal is right to say.) What can these three *characters* have done together in a single play? It was domestic comedy, if we are right in guessing from what we know of Diphilus, and probably verged on farce: the two male leads gnashing their iambic teeth, while Sappho watched the moon.

By the time of Callimachus the myth and its tone were hardening. Callimachus himself seems to have left us:

> His the dog's black bile
> and the sting of a wasp;
> from both, the poison of his tongue,[24]

and thereby to have opened floodgates of poetic eloquence on the sting and bile of Archilochos. Bad-biled and wasp-tongued, Archilochos was to float down this current of cultural history. He was to be ferried by a host of wordmen. The most famous was Horace, but the company is varied. Some warn about the descent of Archilochos into Hades. Julian the Egyptian, who lived under Justinian, addressed Cerberus:

> Now more than before observe the portals
> of mighty hell with your sleepless eyes, now hound,
> be guard. When Lykambes' moaning daughters arrive,
> cut off from the light, pursued
> by Archilochos' iambs,
> then will not every corpse take heel
> and depart from your bitter halls
> to escape the attack?[25]

This is a developed, and really astoundingly strong, statement, as far as any of our textual evidence indicates, and suggests what a long operation of mythologizing Archilochos had undergone by that time.

The imputation about his mistreatment of the daughters of Lykambes is picked up often, as in the assault by Gaetulius (at the time of Caligula):

> This is the seaside grave of Archilochos, the first
> to baptize a Muse with bitter venom and gall,
> make blood on peaceful Helikon.
> Lykambes mourns three daughters hanged . . .[26]

The end of the poem reveals the wasps sitting on Archilochos' gravestone, to which the poet adds, as a warning to the passerby, that he should tread lightly, not to avoid troubling the dead, but to avoid stirring the wasps. These commonplaces multiply rapidly.

The tradition of literary hostility to Archilochos persists, though it is continually expressed in terms that suggest underlying respect. Besides the hostility, we still find the use of the poet's name as one of the great poets, as a companion to Homer. Such habit of reference supports the impression that the hostility to Archilochos, expressed by Callimachus and others, had become a turn of phrase rather than a felt attitude. Certainly the hostility was no longer based on knowledge.

III. CHANGING CRITICAL ATTITUDES

A number of more penetrating, and even more interesting, critiques are being made around the later margins of this history. It has been suggested already in the epigraph from Theocritus cited at the beginning of this chapter that Archilochos was recognized as a poet of great value. Recognition of this value showed itself in the later literature in a new attitude, that of taking the poet seriously. The first example, from Dio Chrysostom, deserves to be quoted in full:

> There have been only two poets with whom none of the earlier can reasonably be compared: Homer and Archilochos. Homer was master of almost everything, animals and plants and oceans and land and weapons and horses . . . but Archilochos took the opposite direction, that of reproach [*to psegein*], because, as I see it, he knew that men need this more, and his first object of attack is himself. Therefore he alone, both after his death and before his birth, received the greatest divine confirmation . . . which all shows that the person capable of assailing, in language, who can grasp and show up other people's faults in his writing, is better than those who are used to praising.[27]

This is already a distant perspective on to Archilochos. We are in the fourth century after Christ, and Archilochos is far in the past. He was even more distant for Chrysostom, in the use of the Greek language, than Bede is for us in the use of English. (This is one more evidence of the amazing conservatism of Greek, which had changed relatively little in those eleven centuries.) Distance seems to have favored good sense. The remark on Homer is fine, though not so unusual. But the understanding of Archilochos, even if still impressionistic and morally centered, is impressive. We have not heard, before, the good caution that Archilochos is as severe with himself as he is with others. Critias had remarked in a totally different spirit that Archilochos had given all the evidence against himself, evidence of nonheroism, of adultery, of blasphemy, of hatred. There is no trace of self-justification in his poetry. And Chrysostom mentions the usefulness of such critical poetry, thus lifting the argument to an important concern: the function of poetry in society. Archilochos is here understood, unusually we now know, as a moral critic.

One of the last echoes of ancient secular comment on Archilochos, this time from the Emperor Julian the Apostate, carries this perception farther. Because his point is potentially powerful, it also requires full hearing:

> To Alcaeus and Archilochos of Paros the Muse was no longer given in order to turn their thoughts toward happiness and pleasure. Obliged as they both were to suffer in various ways, they used their Muse in this connection, making the different gifts of fate more endurable to themselves, by attacking men who had done them wrong.[28]

There is nothing in this passage to indicate that Archilochos had attacked himself foremost, but there is perhaps a cognate awareness of the kind of purity and relief which can be experienced in poetry. Dio realized that poetic self-attack provides poetry with a kind of reflexive dimension which raises poetic attack against others to a generally meaningful level. Attack is given meaning as commentary on the human situation. To Julian, Archilochos similarly seems to have found personal meaning through poetic assault. One senses, between the lines, that assault is not only psychologically gratifying as a kind of revenge but is an effort at equilibrium. It is as though by assaulting a hostile world, one were somehow enabled to reacquire ontological evenness with that world.

As a final example of this somewhat fresher kind of perspective on to Archilochos, we can glance at the last preserved ancient testimony on the matter, from Synesius' *De Insomnia* ("On Insomnia"):

> . . . as Alcaeus and Archilochos, both of whom expended their poetic gifts on their private life. For that reason a record is preserved, for all times, of what they suffered and enjoyed. For they didn't just shoot the breeze or declaim emptily on outworn themes like the present generation, nor did they put their gifts to the service of other people, as did Homer and Stesichorus, who through their verses so increased the reputation of the race of heroes.[29]

This point includes the others. Somehow, Archilochos' fidelity to private experience was the source of his psychological achievements, of his verbal energy, of his engaging power of assault. Not that he was peculiarly realistic, even in prosody, where he tried to speak with a fully human voice, but that he hewed his awareness closer to the individuality of human experience than did his predecessors, and all but a few of his successors, in Greek literature. The remark of Synesius, in fact, seems to be what we had expected to hear long before in Greek assessments of Archilochos. We have had to wait until the early fifth century after Christ, over a millennium, to hear a Greek expatiate on the individual voice of Archilochos. That voice, which would seem to us perhaps the distinctively important trait in the poet, was of no apparent concern to early Greek critics.

There is little evidence that the ancient Greeks were concerned with their own process of coming into self-awareness as a people. The historical viewpoints of men like Herodotus, Thucydides, or Polybius do not stop at phenomena but constantly pierce to the causes and patterns of human events. However, there is always some shallowness in their conception of the genetic. Causes are understood as prior events with effects, never really as pressures with textures through which the new is laboriously brought to birth. This weakness transfers itself *a fortiori* to literary criticism, in which, as the present chapter shows, the underside of the argument rarely interested the ancients. The sense of literature as problem or as density is almost totally lacking.

The examples of ancient criticism, seen here applied to Archilochos, suggest a series of other ancient critical interests: of interest, only implicitly critical, in the canon of the great poets, say of Archilochos and Homer paired; of interest in the moral dimension, as we saw it measured by Heraclitus, Pindar, and Critias; of merely topos-like or turn-of-phrase interest in the moral, as reflected in the verses about Archilochos' poetic savagery; finally, of interest in the general world-perspective of Archilochos, the poetic assaulter. There was no room for concern with Archilochos' poetry itself in purely (or even mainly) literary terms. To the ancient critic the maker of the poem seemed to stand directly and transparently behind the made work. Thus he occupied, or preoccupied, the field of critical vision.

IV. THE INDEBTEDNESS OF HORACE TO ARCHILOCHOS

For examples of closer criticism we would have needed to look at created literature itself, in which the Greek writer, far more than the modern, carried on a dialogue of resonances with earlier works. We would have done much more with those passages, properly understandable only in the original, where nuance, even slighter than irony, shows the affiliation of a later writer to an earlier. We would have seen Alcaeus reflecting Archilochos's episode of the "lost shield"; Anacreon repeatedly, and slightly, imitating Archilochos; a line of Cratinus, the fifth-century comedian, parodying a line of Archilochos; Aristophanes, in the *Frogs,* picking up strong Archilochean resonances in a pair of iambic dimeters as they were recited during a country festival; Callimachus, in his *Aetia,* clearly taking off from verbal springboards provided by Archilochos. Fortunately, we have a clearer and firmer single example of all this in Horace, and we can turn to him.[30]

First, Horace makes two open statements of indebtedness or awareness. He is quite clear on the importance of Archilochos to him, though he qualifies carefully by writing:

> . . . Parios ego primus iambos
> ostendi Latio, numeros animosque secutus
> Archilochi, non res et agentia verba Lycamben.
>
> (I first gave Parian
> iambs to Latium, followed the meters and mood
> of Archilochos, but not the matter and words
> that assailed Lycambes.)[31]

He goes on, even beyond the qualification in the last line, to assure us that he did not hesitate to modify the character of Archilochos' poetry (*mutare modos et carminis artem,* "to change the modes and kind of his song"). Lest you consider me too servile, he assures, remember that in my poetry:

> temperat Archilochi musam pede mascula Sappho,
> temperat Alcaeus, sed rebus et ordine dispar,
> nec socerum quaerit quem versibus oblinat atris,
> nec sponsae laqueum famoso carmine nectit.

> (Sappho tempers Archilochos with a steady meter,
> so does Alcaeus, though different in structure and meter,
> and seeks no father-in-law to slander with language
> and ties no noose of illustrious song for his bride
> . . .)

However, the strong first impression of debt to Archilochos clings. Though the acknowledged debt is mainly technical, we know that the best of Horace is itself, in large part, technique.[32]

The second passage, lodged in the middle of the *Ars Poetica,* shows awareness of that technical ancestry while taking a bow toward the Archilochean myth. Homer, says Horace, was the master of meters appropriate to *res gestae regum,* ("great affairs of kings") and *ducumque tristia bella,* ("sad, huge wars of rulers"). But there is great dispute among grammarians about who was the first author of those later verses, *impariter junctis* ("of unequal lengths"), like the elegiac. The dispute continues, but one thing is certain in that early history:

> Archilochum proprio rabies armavit iambo;
> hunc socci cepere pedem grandesque cothurni,
> alternis aptum sermonibus et popularis
> vincentem strepitus et natum rebus agendis.[33]

> (Fury equipped Archilochos with his iambics:
> The foot slipped into the comic sock as neatly
> As into the tragic boot, so dramatists used it
> To make their dialogue heard, even over the noise
> The audience was making, the rhythm of purposeful action.)

>   (Translation by Palmer Bovie)

Anger lay behind Archilochos' own prosodic inventiveness, and the result of it, the iamb, was to flow into a long historical tradition, making much newness possible in poetry.

The presence of that influence in Horace's own poetry is far more often felt than provably active; yet it is felt so persistently that it drives even a major positivistic classicist like Eduard Fränkel to continuous heights of intuition. He refers to Leo's paper, *De Horatio et Archilocho,* in which the bond between those two poets was first clearly revealed, as having set much of Horatian scholarship on the right track.

Horace's elaborate use of iambs, in what scholarship has come to call the first, second, third, and fourth Archilochean meters, developed combinations of dactyl with iamb, reflects a medley of lyric experimentations once carried out by Archilochos. It is in fact simply the concern with mixing lines of different meter that most generally and most powerfully shows Horace's debt to the first known Greek lyric poet. Horace's book of epodes, reflecting his student experiences with Greek literature in Athens, is in that connection a decisive moment in Latin literature, showing it unsuspected prosodic possibilities.

More detailed echoes of Archilochos seem to be widely, though only half certainly, scattered here. Fränkel is a useful guide through such mysteries. Behind Epode XVI, Horace's harangue to the Roman people on the dangers of civil strife in 41 B.C., Archilochos is heard singing out his "Homeless fellow citizens, now grasp my words . . ." and assailing ignorance and public folly as Horace is, rather uncharacteristically, also doing. Behind Horace's *beatus ille* poem, Epode II, lies some deeply digested experience of Archilochos' Gyges poem with its similar protest against the mercenary life, yet also, we guess, some similarly urbane disclaimer tucked away in a surprise ending. Or, finally for our purposes, lines in Horace (Epode V) like

> At o deorum quidquid in caelo regit
> terras et humanum genus[34]

> (Whatever divine controls, in heaven,
> lands and the race of men . . .)

seem to recall Archilochean prayer parallels like

> Zeus, o Father Zeus,
> the strength of heaven is yours,
> you see what men do here
> misdeeds, impossible deeds.
> You notice the hybris of beasts . . .[35]

Yet no matter how far the last sentence, here uncompleted, is supposed to extend, we will not, in these Horatian reminiscences, be meeting literary criticism. Instead, we will find a subtle but not rationalized response to the understanding of an earlier poet. We cannot hope for much more. At this point, we simply touch the act in which the ancient critic was best able to meet his predecessors, the act of integration, a dense-textured reworking of the earlier text.

. . . . .

ARCHILOCHOS AND OUR DAY

With clear determination Archilochos grasps the first, the immediate, data of personal experience: the Now, the Here, and the I.

> Fränkel, Dichtung und Philosophie

There may be good reasons, as this last point suggests, for the ineptitude and relative indifference of the Greeks to the explicit literary skills which we have come, especially in this century, to value highly. Of course in assessing the Greeks we must, first of all, allow for the dreariness dominant in the entire history of literary critical activity. Until our century, I believe, there has never been an extended period of high criticism. Our own advances are the consequence of a laborious historical preparation in which techniques of scholarship, earned respect for "art for art's sake," and fatigue with emotional or doctrinal criticism culminated in special fidelity to the esthetic structure. But we were separating ourselves off, in this activity, no more from the Greeks and Romans than from the rhetorical analyzers of *topoi* in the Middle Ages, from the hairsplitting Renaissance Aristotelians, or from the Romantic generalizers about the language of common men. The Greek literary theorists take a decent place in this company, especially when we consider what a peripheral thrust theirs was in the development of Greek literary culture.[36]

There is another way of looking at the relative indifference of the Greeks to critical skills, a reason suggested directly by survey of the ancient criticism of Archilochos. The Greeks were accustomed to another and far more direct kind of criticism than that which interests us; to criticism emerging from direct reworking of texts. Greek culture, much more than ours, was attuned to heard language, sensitive knowledge acquired through the ear. The printing press, and all that it signifies, has in this respect changed our sensibilities vastly, making us far more intellectual and abstract than the pre-Renaissance man.[37] The Greek poet, particularly among his people, was at any rate a specialist in the balancing of sounds and seems to have known all the meaningful sounds made by his predecessors. When Aristophanes wanted to mimic, attack, or merely recall Archilochos, he could do it deftly by inserting a wedge of dithyramb-like iambs into a choral ode. The tragic poets are forever carrying on this kind of dialogue among themselves. It constitutes—which is my point here—the most refined method of criticism which the Greeks ever made available to themselves. It is the way in which they were best able to say what they thought of their own literary history.

As far as explicit, rationalized literary criticism is concerned, Archilochos inspired little of this; by the nature of his poetic persona he collected around his work much that was most naively biographical, or philosophical-biographical, in the ancient critical manner. This continued to be so after the end of classical criticism and up to the threshold of our own moment. That is, it continued to be so to the extent that Archilochos in any way was experienced between the end of classical antiquity and our own century.

Already in later antiquity an ideological, and not a literary, interest in this poet was starting to make itself felt. It was something different from the moral judgments passed by Critias or Pindar, or from the protestations of shock in the later epigrammatists. Philostratus, in his *Lives of the Sophists,* says that the philosopher Hippodramus

> was very enthusiastic about Archilochos, calling Homer the "voice of the Sophists," while Archilochos was their very breath . . .[38]

A mysterious assertion, unless it was intended to suggest Archilochos' aggressive, untraditional freedom of spirit.

The passage looks forward to a harsher view, to that of certain Church Fathers who attacked precisely this open freedom of Archilochos.

Clement of Alexandria, in his *Stromata* (late second century), includes Archilochos among a group of reproachable "ancients." He asks:

> . . . then must we permit Theopompus and Timaeus to write fables [*mythous*] and blasphemies: must we allow Epicurus, founder of atheism, and Hipponax and Archilochos to continue writing shamelessly; while we hinder the writer who proclaims the truth, from leaving his useful message to men of later ages?[39]

Archilochos is accused of writing *aischrōs,* or "without a sense of honor." It is easy for us to see how much interpretation had gone into this accusation. Eusebius writes similarly, but more fully, in his *Praeparatio evangelica* ("Evangelical Preparation").

During the earlier Christian centuries, ideological interest in Archilochos is largely confined to observations like these. After such critics, and after those late ancient critics like Julian and Synesius sampled in the previous chapter, little more is heard about Archilochos for some centuries. (Or little more is heard by us, at any rate, though we can never be sure what languid literary perceptions may have crossed the minds of copying monks as the sunrays filtered in through their scriptorium windows.)

Texts of Archilochos in the Higher Middle Ages must have been hard to find. A scholiast of the period makes this observation, on being unable to find exact references to the poet:

> the proverb is this: "Not even Heracles against two"; but what Archilochos' statement really is, we don't know; perhaps it might be this very one.[40]

In the tenth century Constantine of Rhodes prides himself, in the words of Ferdinand Lasserre,

> on knowing Archilochos, but in fact cannot remember more than a few quotations from him drawn directly from lexicons.[41]

Similar pretensions, it seems, find themselves in a couple of thirteenth century Byzantine scholars, Michael Psellus and Nicetas Choniates, whose claims to expertise in the matter have long been exploded. As Lasserre again puts it:

> As for the pompous assertions of Nicetas Choniates and Psellus, who are supposed to have commented on Archilochos in their literary lectures, their assertions no longer fool anybody.[42]

Archilochos next surfaces, importantly, in the huge reengagement with antiquity which we call the Renaissance. He owes the beginning of his new life to Henri Estienne, the great, the indefatigable, imaginative, and scholarly sixteenth century printer. Estienne's *Carminum Poetarum novem . . . fragmenta* ("Fragments of Nine Poets' Songs") was published in Paris in 1560. It brought the early Greek lyric poets with it. This edition of Archilochos was not superseded until the appearance of Richard Brunck's *Analecta veterum Poetarum Graecorum* ("Selections of Ancient Greek Poets"), Strasbourg, 1785. By that time, Archilochos was a possession of the age of scholarship.

I. TWENTIETH CENTURY CRITICS

Closer to our time, his work becomes again the kind of intensely demanding document which, we sense, it was to many ancient poets. The ages of scholarship, we have seen, brought him back to the learned eye; but more than eyes, whole persons were soon to meet him.

It will suit our purpose to consider the contribution made by some of these whole, and in this case twentieth-century, persons to the reviving experience of Archilochos. Doing so, we will be learning more about the tradition of understanding of the poet, and at the same time practising for a final assessment of what Archilochos can mean to all of us, existentially, presently, virtually outside time.

All these scholars were tending toward such an encounter, at least in the sense that they were committing themselves to a faith; the faith that Greek antiquity had, in fact, once existed, and that we must therefore meet it from the center of our own existence.

It is on the surface remarkable that almost all of these significantly committed scholars of Archilochos were (or are) German. But it is only surprising on the surface. Werner Jaeger, Hermann Fränkel, Bruno Snell, Emil Staiger, and Max Treu have all been trained in a German philological tradition, which, at its best, sinks its deepest roots among the great German Hellenists of the eighteenth century, in Winckelmann, Schiller, Herder, Goethe. That tradition makes itself felt still today in the distinguished, humane scholarship of a Wolfgang Schadewaldt or Bernhard Schweitzer, and it did so far more generally early in this century. The faith in man, the complex but wholehearted humanism of eighteenth-century German Hellenism, made itself deeply realized among all the scholars listed here.

The relevant works of Jaeger, Snell, and Fränkel constitute a somehow internally coherent group of contributions. Snell's best work on Archilochos is found in his article "The Rise of the Individual in the Early Greek Lyric," published (in German) in 1941 in *Antike und Abenland.* But the argument, especially the kind of argument found there, makes large sense only in terms of Snell's perspective onto Greek culture in general; that is, only in the context of *The Discovery of the Mind,* the large and imaginative collection of essays in which our present piece is reprinted. The even more ambitious and more systematic studies of Archilochos by Jaeger and Fränkel surround Snell's book chronologically. Jaeger discussed Archilochos in *Paideia* (first edition, 1934), at the point where the book's argument shifted from the epic to the individual lyric world. The whole thrust of that huge treatise must be

somewhat understood before the analysis of Archilochos is clear. The same is true in the case of Fränkel's *Dichtung und Philosophie des frühen Griechentums,* ("Poetry and Philosophy of Early Hellenism"), published in 1950.

It would be wrong to suppose, among three so different works, closer interrelations than those I suggested when I mentioned the humanistic tradition of such scholars. Each of these scholars, well equipped though he is with the weapons of classical inquiry, comes upon a hugely (and somehow demandingly) living picture of Archilochos. I have the inescapable feeling from these three works that Archilochos has here, probably for the first time since he wrote, been adequately encountered by criticism.

In each man's work humanism is made viable, and preserved from the sentimentality which usually corrupts it, by being incorporated into a larger cultural-historical perspective through which human events are understood as parts of an organic process; understood both horizontally in their own time and vertically in their temporal sequence. These three bodies of work stand in a tradition of systematic insight into the unity of the classical world, a tradition deeply impelled already by men like Giambattista Vico and Johann Winckelmann, and brought triumphantly through the nineteenth century by scholars like Fustel de Coulanges and Erwin Rohde.

Many of Snell's best insights have been inspired by an awareness of linguistic growth. (He is a professional and learned student of the history of language.) In his finest classical essay, "Homer's View of Man" (1939), he examines the ways in which Homer's view of reality was defined by the ways in which he was able to talk about reality.[43] The most telling examples concern Homer's words for *ways of seeing* and for *describing the body.* In each case the points were similar; that in such descriptions details prevailed over general grasp; that this was so because the level of experience was still limited by the concrete forms of experience. "To see," an act normally expressible in fifth-century Greek in only two or three ways, was commonly expressed by nine verbs in Homeric Greek, verbs whose meaning ranged through the niceties of "to have a particular look in one's eyes," "to look about inquisitively," "to look with one's mouth wide open," "to be a spectator."

It is not that any of these meanings were excluded in the fifth century; only that few of them were used, and the others rarely; and that the general word *horao* had, for most purposes, absorbed the more precise words. The spiritual laboring from specific to general is also shown in the long process by which a notion of personality was worked on, though never finally achieved, in the Greek language. Stated briefly, the Homeric mind conceives readily of the *different parts* of the personality, from the specific organs to the more general notions of *psyche* ("soul"), *thymos* ("spirit," "anger"), or *noos* ("seat of intelligence"). However, it has no success in appreciating or naming the idea of personality itself, and little in understanding what *psyche,* as a single, unifying, kinetic principle, might be. Ultimately, as Snell is helped by this last material to see, Homer had little specifically linguistic perception of quality. It seems suddenly of the highest importance that in Homer one thinks "much" or of "many things," but not "deeply." Or even, by extension, that inner conflict is described by Homer in terms of formal debate, rather than of qualitative tensions. Interior agony can be shown, but not described.

II. ARCHILOCHOS AS A MODERN MAN

It remained, as textbook language goes, for a student of Snell to carry this linguistic analysis into the center of the lyric age, thus to suggest at close range some of the distinctive characteristics of that new age. In Max Treu's *Von Homer zur Lyrik* ("From Homer to the Lyric" [1955]) Archilochos is repeatedly mentioned, each time as object of useful *aperçus.* A couple of luminous pages on Archilochos show how much is still worth doing in the effort to acquire a fresh viewpoint onto the breakdown of the Greek epic world and the emergence of a new sensibility.

Treu presses further with the question of quality, which he sees in "a pronounced feeling for spatial depths, spatial thicknesses and outlines" ("*räumliche Tiefe, räumliche Dichte und Profilierung . . .*"). He finds this expressed in the totally un-Homeric "vertical cloud stands straight" in Archilochos' comparison of the island of Thasos to "an ass's spine," or in the shading of hair, which we have seen in:

> She held a branch of myrtle and
> flowering rose and down her back
> and shoulders flowed shadowing hair.

Connected to this, among other awarenesses, is a new tactile feeling, what Hermann Fränkel calls *Hautsinn* ("flesh-sense"). One form of it is *pathologische Anschauung* ("pathological perception"), a sense (erotically or neurotically colored) of the curious mood emitted by tactile awareness, as in "transfixed, clear through the bones" and in "love that has twisted its way beneath my heartstrings." Such perceptions are part of another new understanding: that surfaces seen are not merely surfaces, and, by extension, that virtue (or meaning, or value) may lurk where it appears not to be. An example of such perception is found in the soldier who is tough, short, stout, without heroic attributes, without being towering, cleanshaven, or swaggering. Treu, like Snell, readies us linguistically for a new grasp of the lyric ethic.

Snell's contribution, in fact, is decisive for the whole new tradition of insights which Jaeger and Fränkel have inaugurated. Snell himself continued out some distance from these linguistic points. Above all, he noticed the "despair of love" creeping, for the first time in western literature, into the poetry of Archilochos (and Sappho). He discussed the way in which a *sense of justice,* in Archilochos, emerges simply as an extension of his personal will. All this probes, but it is subservient to the main, bold, discov-

ery: that Archilochos, like the lyric poets generally, stands much more nakedly than Homer before the perceivable and interpretable world. In that sense, more than in any other, Archilochos is the first modern man.[44]

Jaeger, as much as Snell, is influenced by Archilochos in the process of discussing him, which is only to say that Jaeger takes the poet seriously, accepting the existential demand ready to spring from the poet's works.

Jaeger's enormous work, *Paideia* (1934-47), examines the Greek conception of education in the widest sense; in reality it examines the conception of culture. Within the development of that conception Archilochos "speaks for a freer world" (Vol. I, p. 117), as Jaeger shows again and again.

Yet his meeting with Archilochos acquires its greatest meaning at another point. The originality of Archilochos is obvious, even if not easy to show, even if its obviousness needs to be understood, as it was by Snell, through all the trained resources of philology. We moderns have at least a first, a very easy and probably very accurate, sense that Archilochos belongs to our world. What we need, as students of the matter, is some sense of the traditional atmosphere in which Archilochos' revolution is taking place. Jaeger is at his best in suggesting this involved sense.

He is eloquent about the religious origins and spirit of the lampoon; the kind of bond, between obscenity and assault, and belief, which seems to reveal itself in many early cultural stages, and to have been conspicuous in Greece. The free play of aggression in Demeter and Dionysus festivals (in both of which Archilochos says he took part) has its later parallels in the Fastnachtspiele, Narrensprünge, and other ritual spring releases of western Europe. Without forgetting that Archilochos was a poet, Jaeger reminds us of the special character of Archilochos' poetic milieu.

At his best he brings this perception to the nature of subjectivity in Archilochos, and in Greek lyric poetry generally. It might have seemed, from the work done by Snell, Fränkel, or Bowra, that the Greek lyric was the product of relatively untended emotional expression. These scholars did not say it that way; indeed they were, I suppose, careful not to discuss the Greek lyric as Romantic lyric. Nevertheless, their collective emphasis on Greek lyric individuality, as when they wrote of the Lyric Age, had seemed to point in that direction; had seemed to stress the *revolutionären Bruch* from the old world, the break which Fränkel names and assesses with such skill.

But Jaeger takes pains to put this point fully:

> Although the Greek poet, in exploring the new world of individuality, expresses ideas and emotions which are truly personal, he is still somehow bound by universal standards, and recognizes the law which rules his fellow men. . . . Certainly it [the Greek notion of "individuality"] was not the Christian ideal of personality, by which every soul feels its own individual value. . . . Greek expressions of personal emotion and

thought have nothing purely and exclusively subjective in them: it might rather be said that a poet like Archilochos has learnt how to express in his own personality the whole objective world and its laws, to represent them in himself . . .[45]

This is a difficult and profound series of notes, worth extended quotation because of their uniquely probing contribution to an understanding of the early Greek experience. Do they fit Archilochos?

Earlier I contrasted the tangibility of things, as felt in poems by Wallace Stevens and Marianne Moore, with something far more perspicuous in Archilochos' depiction of the external world. Even though that external world existed for Archilochos, it existed as diaphanously as the girl with the myrtle-sprig in her hand. (Treu's discussions of *Hautsinn* and *Räumlichkeit* in Archilochos help to qualify and deepen this interpretation, but they do not make Archilochos' perceived world into a modern world of "trumpet vine, / fox-glove, giant snap-dragon, a salpiglossis that has / spots and stripes . . .") Similarly, preserving the same, rather imprecise, vocabulary, we might say that Archilochos' revelations of himself in his poetry lack the sense of self, lack anything corresponding to the tangibility of the outer world. The uniqueness of feelings is absent in:

> How I wish I could touch Neoboule's hand

or

> I'm still alive thank god; to hell
> with the shield; I'll find me a better one soon . . .

or

> Wretchedly I lie desiring,
> Soulless, with an anguish from the gods
> Transfixed, clear through the bones,

where we feel in touch with what Treu called *pathologische Anschauung* ("pathological perception"), and where the intimacy of personal presence is intense. In each of these examples the generally human seems somehow to have embodied itself. There is of course no trace of symbolic technique, in the modern sense; simply, perhaps, a full realization of the generally human powers of response. It may replace much analysis here to contrast these lines of Archilochos with Dante's lament, in the *Vita Nuova*:

> Alas! By influence of many sighs
> Born of the thoughts that are within my heart,
> The eyes are overcome and have no strength
> To gaze at anyone who looks at them.
> They have become what seems like twin desires,
> The one to weep, the other to show pain,
> And many times they mourn so much that love
> Encircles them with martyrdom's red crown.
> These meditations and the sighs I breathe
> Become so torturing with the heart
> That love, who dwells there, faints, it pains him so;

> For they have on themselves, these grieving ones,
> The sweet name of my lady-superscribed,
> And many words relating to her death.[46]

The point of meeting between Fränkel and Archilochos forms perhaps the most meaningful node in the growth of the re-experience of Archilochos. (Although Snell's encounter, rooted as it is in a growing branch of science, linguistics, may prove the most fertile in positive learning.)

At certain points Fränkel picks up, clarifies, and adds nuances to suggestions made already by Snell or Jaeger. Such continuations are worth mentioning here, partly because they show the self-confirmation of an imposing new tradition of understanding Archilochos. Building out from Snell, or from Treu, into the concern with surface and depth, Fränkel observes that in Archilochos

> there is no "discrete" politeness, no mild toning down, no play of half-lights: absolutely lacking is any depth from the background. Everything plays itself off under the same intense light on one and the same level.[47]

The point, of course, is not the same as that made by Snell, or Treu, on the question of Archilochean surface; or rather the points do not meet squarely, though in dialectic they can be induced to reinforce each other. What matters is that a habit of useful concern has been achieved. With similar obliquity, Fränkel picks up Jaeger's qualifications about the individualism of Archilochos. He claims that Archilochos' subjectivity does not reveal

> an individually formed and colored life picture [*Lebensbild*] . . . [but] what Archilochos communicates is in essence typical.[48]

Or, a little later,

> The judging I [*das urteilende Ich*] in archaic literature is always intended representatively.[49]

The angle of perspective is different, and the directions of continuation numerous.

The distinctive awareness of Fränkel, into Archilochos' world of experience, concerns that poet's relation to his world. With these words, Fränkel launches a profound inquiry into that relation. First, he cites Archilochos'

> The fox knows many tricks, the hedgehog one great trick—one great trick know I:
> to pay back with double interest
> the wrong another does me . . .
>
> (Fr. 65, 118)

then adds that

> Through this bizarre but drastic image of the hedgehog the I, the first person pronoun, establishes itself—for the first time in European literature—as the opposite pole of the Not-I, the other.[50]

We suddenly realize how bored we had grown with all the old talk about the new individualism of the lyric age. Or rather, we had wanted to continue considering the matter, but in terms, finally, that explored what it meant to be a representative of that new individualism. One thing meant was a new relation of subject to object, a defining of subject in terms of object. Perceptions of nature as well as awarenesses of personal differences, as in this poem, equally show the new clarity of Archilochos' perceptual world. Hatred, love, or simply the perspicuousness of a perceived island or girl all illustrate this point. Homer's world was certainly not indistinct or unclear. It shares much clarity with the Archilochean vision. But the direction of personal address or of perception which justifies Fränkel's use of the notion of polarity is lacking in Homer.

Fränkel develops another point, which is also concerned with the phenomenology of Archilochos' way of perception, and also drives toward a deeper account of what takes the place of the epic *Denkweise.* The crucial sentence, which crystallizes the argument, is this:

> With clear determination Archilochos grasps the first, the immediate data of personal experience: the Now, the Here, and the I.[51]

Wars are experienced in terms of a lost shield; islands in terms of resemblance to ass-spines; generals of a certain kind in terms of idiosyncratic gait. The impinging personal impression leaves its mark on the poet. To a degree, it victimizes the poet, leading him through the vagaries of its occurrence. Yet only the poet, by his perceptual willingness, makes the occurrence possible. Only he is responsible for the existence of a Now, a Here, or even an I.

III. CONTEMPORARY REAPPRAISAL OF ARCHILOCHOS

Emil Staiger, one of the finest contemporary German literary critics and, perhaps not accidentally, a former professional student of classics, has for some time been working with the same perceptions that we see here in Fränkel. So had Benedetto Croce, long before his death; and so, in America, had Irving Babbitt, as early as his *New Laokoon,* which was concerned with the nature of the generic in literature. The thought, emergent here, will also help carry us toward a final confronting with Archilochos, toward the question of Archilochos and our day.

Staiger's *Grundbegriffe der Poetik* examines the three chief generic forms of literature: epic, lyric, drama. His great achievement, for our purpose, is to have isolated the peculiar relation of the lyric both to time and to effort. Drama, he believes, is full of tension toward the future; a sense of *the impending.* One feels that in every scene. Epic, on the other hand, is retrospective; it not only deals with material of a chronologically distant past, but its mood is that of recall and retrospection, of a survey of *res gestae.* The lyric, by contrast, is pure and immediate presence: what Theodor Vischer called

> the instantaneous illumination of the world in the lyrical subject.[52]

The lyric demands attention for itself, in its presence. It reflects immediacy of production and presentation, conditions of it which Staiger illustrates but for which Croce, in his *Aesthetic,* has given an elaborate phenomenological account. That hyper-romantic account, stressing the identity of conception and expression, goes even further to make clear Staiger's main point: that the existence of the lyric poem is instantaneous. (This, however, only faintly helps us to reach that stranger and harder point, that the lyric has a way of existing outside of time altogether.)

Staiger's coordinate emphasis on the effortlessness of the lyric poet, thus also of his poem, completes the analysis. He makes his point especially well through analyzing Goethe's "Wanderers Nachtlied," in which, as he says:

> It is not the case that here, on the one hand, is the *Abendstimmung* ["evening mood"], and there language with sounds at its disposal, which can be used on this particular object. But rather the evening, in and of itself, "sounds like language"; the poet accomplishes [*leistet*] nothing.[53]

The result is a product which shows *no* signs of force or stress. In this, lyric poetry contrasts sharply with "epic" and "dramatic," where effortless immediacy is no longer— and really need no longer be—the central awareness; where strategically planned organization of time is essential, and leaves its mark.

Fränkel had interested us in Archilochos' concern with the "immediate data of personal experience," and had thus taken us closer than either Snell or Jaeger—not to mention other scholars—to the essential originality of Archilochos. He had begun the suggestion that there was, in Archilochos, not simply a new relation to history but a new relation in history, a paradigmatically new stance, at least as far as man's esthetic experience goes. Now Staiger helps us further to see what might be radically original in this stance. He helps us to understand the deep sense in which the lyric poet is not manipulating time in his work.

Archilochos is very precisely not manipulating time. And by understanding this about him we acquire a key to understanding the peculiar meaning which he, as the first extant western lyric poet, acquires for us. In re-experiencing his work, as accurately and fully as we can, we reawaken in ourselves one of our own primal tropes of verbal achievement, as fellow members of the verbal tradition which constitutes world literature. It is not simply that we duplicate his effort, and that he was one of the first, if not the first, to make that effort. It is that in making that effort when he did, Archilochos the lyric poet "stood outside time," and to a degree simply met the world, as it was and is, at a burning but effortless middle-point: his own versed language. Where that language exists, incandesced to its nature, we literally continue to meet Archilochos as though no time separated him from us. And because he is our first-father, in this western achievement, we stand through him at the source of the western lyric.

Notes

1. Cf. various works by Bruno Snell and Max Treu for discussion of the simultaneous developments in *linguistic* and *cultural* history.

2. The issue touched here is far too ambitious for my present text, yet certainly one of the most important to arise directly and legitimately from it. Archilochos, I think, had a perfectly pre-Christian temper: of a natural goodness, capable of love, lacking the guidance of grace. For a phenomenology of that temper, in terms of cultural history, we still have nothing better than C. N. Cochrane's *From Christianity to Classical Culture* (Oxford, 1940).

3. Echoes, which even we can hear, abound in the lyric poets. Isn't it likely that a contemporary of Archilochos, hearing these lines, would have thought of Helen at the Skaian gates and her effect on the old men there? Thinking of what we do hear, like this, makes us doubly conscious of what we must miss.

4. I have tried, in "From Naming to Fiction-Making," *Giornale di Metafisica,* V (1958), 569-83, to develop this idea; that language inevitably moves away from what it names into the world of idea, or at least, a beginning of such "spiritualization" into that of syntax. Some attention should also be paid to the purely demonstrative function of language, even in its early stages of growth.

5. Max Treu's *Von Homer zur Lyrik* (Munich, 1955), makes a skillful assault on these problems in linguistic history. It is sometimes appaling to realize how little we know, not only about frequency of vocabulary in ancient Greek, but also about the ironies and levels of words, that is, in what kinds of mouth, and in what ways, they would have sounded appropriate.

6. I have steered away from the literary-historical meaning of this fragment, but there, obviously, its chief importance is lodged. Werner Jaeger, in *Paideia* (trans. Oxford, 1939-44), does fullest and most imaginative justice to the revolutionary implications.

7. A special advantage to the study of ancient literature is just this: that we are repeatedly forced to ignore chronology and to take a chance on essence. Obviously we lose something, a kind of intelligibility, in this way. But we gain immediacy and a new sense, which scholarship is forever trying to quell, of the pressure on us of the very existence of a literary work.

8. These erotic fragments are so wholehearted and clean. It is hard to decide when prurience got into Greek literature. We find virtually none in Homer or Hesiod and very little in the lyric poets. It is similarly lacking in archaic sculpture, of course. It makes perhaps its first literary appearance in Euripides: certainly in the *Bacchae* or *Hippolytus* it is obvious. But there is none in the remains (and copies) of fifth-century sculpture, in the Parthenon or Bassae figures, or in the finest Apolline statues. Archilochos seems far prior to whatever larger cultural neuroses expressed themselves in the fifth century.

9. About as close as we can come to useful discussion of "literary ideas" is to be found in Yvor Winters' *In Defence of Reason* (Denver, 1947). Winters, I think, finds that literature "immoral" which does not develop at least some meaningfully isolatable ideas; and he would certainly be right to claim Plato as a partial ally. There is an excellent discussion of this point in Wellek and Warren, *The Theory of Literature* (New York, 1949), in the chapter on "Literature and Ideas."

10. Not always, fortunately; as there are fine studies like W. B. Stanford's *Ambiguity in Greek Literature* (Oxford, 1939) and *Greek Metaphor* (Oxford, 1936); or H. A. Musurillo's literary *Symbol and Myth in Ancient Poetry* (New York, 1961). Almost always, though, the critic must stop short of wit as it turns toward humor or play. That realm is always, it seems, the best-guarded sanctum of a language, though it is also, perhaps, the lair of a language's true genius.

11. It had best be reminded, here, that the Greeks of the time had no single word for "nature," in any of the senses we give it. We do translate their *physis* as "nature"; but its meaning was abstract, referring simply to "things which grow."

12. An equation reminding us of the very useful work which could be done on the idiom of metaphor in the Greek lyric poets; that is, a study of the physical symbols habitually chosen to bring out inner states.

13. Or as has been shown by R. Pfeiffer in an important article on divinity and the individual, *Philologus,* LXXXIV (1929).

14. Dodds, on *The Greeks and the Irrational* (Berkeley, 1951), is vastly useful on the remnants of epic, face-saving ethic in the later world of Greek lyric.

15. The topic of ancient literary influences, the influences of one ancient author on another, is extremely delicate, partly because so much has been lost, so that we must miss most of the resonances, but mainly because literary property in antiquity was much more public than it is today, indeed than it has been since the Renaissance, so that what might strike us as plagiarism is in fact, generally, the result of legitimate emulation, what Milton called *aemulatio*. On this ancient perspective, cf. Fiske, *Lucilius and Horace* (Madison, 1920), and my "Publica Materies," *Arion,* II (1963).

16. Heraclitus, fr. 42 (I, 160, Diels-Kranz edition).

17. Treu prints, as the first of the "new discoveries" in his *Archilochos* (Munich, 1959), the text of a fictional debate between Homer and Archilochos, made up of quotations from the two authors, and taken from a third century B.C. papyrus. In his notes on the debate, pp. 174 ff., he assembles the other considerable evidence for pairing Homer with Archilochos.

18. Cf., for more analysis of the evidence, Philip Wheelwright, *Heraclitus* (Princeton, 1959).

19. *Pythian.* 2. 52 ff.

20. Critias, fr. 44, in Aelian, *Varia Historia,* X, 13.

21. This is one subject, for the classicist, which has been little touched, and should be further explored, for it goes to the heart of the way in which ancient Greece was an esthetic culture. On the definition of the *I,* in Greek culture, the best study is still J. Böhme, *Die Seele und das Ich bei Homer* (Göttingen, 1929); while my "The Concept of *Character* in Euripides," *Glotta,* XXIX (1960-61), looks at a particular, and important, feature of the question. The larger topic, of Greek literary self-awareness, comes up for occasional study in J. W. H. Atkins' *Literary Criticism in Antiquity* (Cambridge, 1934).

22. *Anthologia Palatina,* XI, 20.

23. *De Signis Temp.* 45.

24. Fr. 37 (Schneider's edition).

25. *Anthologia Palatina,* VII, 70.

26. *Anthologia Palatina,* VIII, 71.

27. First Tarsian speech: XXXIII, Vol. I, 330, 9 ff., ed. Arn.

28. *Imp. Misop.,* p. 433, ed. Hertlein.

29. Synesius, *De Insomnia* xx.

30. For more of the Greek evidence, see the careful résumé in Schmid-Stählin, *Geschichte der griechischen Literatur* (Munich, 1929), I, 1, 396.

31. *Epistula* i. 19. 22 ff. For more comments on Horace's indebtedness, see Fraenkel, *Horace* (Oxford, 1957).

32. Lasserre, *Les Épodes d'Archiloque* (Paris, 1950), makes an effort to show a detailed dependence of Horace on Archilochos.

33. *Ars Poetica* 79-82.

34. Epode V, 1-2.

35. Fr. 94 D (Treu).

36. This point is essentially confirmed in Brooks and Wimsatt, *Literary Criticism: A Short History* (New York, 1957).

37. Point powerfully elaborated by Marshall McLuhan in *The Gutenberg Galaxy,* cited above, Chapter 2, note 2.

38. *Vitae* ii. 27. 10.

39. Clement of Alexandria, *Stromata* i. 316.

40. Scholiast on Archilochos, fr. 275; cited in Lasserre, *Les Épodes d'Archiloque* (Paris, 1950), at relevant point in fragment list.

41. Lasserre, *Les Épodes,* lxxxvii.

42. *Ibid.*

43. This kind of linguistic-philosophic insight has been most satisfactorily developed for the English speaking and reading world by B. L. Whorff in his *Language, Thought and Reality* (Cambridge, 1956). His viewpoint has been elaborated into a major weapon both of literary criticism and of philosophical analysis.

44. For an exemplary study of such poetic nakedness, in modern verse specifically, but with wide extension, see Geoffrey Hartman, *The Unmediated Vision* (New Haven, 1954).

45. Jaeger, *Paideia* (Oxford, 1939), I, 114.

46. *Vita Nuova,* Canto XXXIX, translated by Mark Musa.

47. Fränkel, *Dichtung und Philosophie* (New York, 1951), p. 169. My translations.

48. *Ibid.*

49. *Ibid.,* note 240.

50. *Ibid.,* p. 156.

51. *Ibid.,* p. 191.

52. Cited by Staiger, *Grundbegriffe* (Zürich, 1946), p. 24.

53. *Ibid.,* p. 16.

H. D. Rankin (essay date 1977)

SOURCE: "The Fate of the Lycambids," in *Archilochus of Paros,* Noyes Press, 1977, pp. 47-56.

[*In the following essay, Rankin investigates the merits of the tradition that the Lycambid family members were driven to suicide over attacks on them in verse by Archilochus.*]

There is a tradition, widespread in the first few centuries of our era, that Archilochus killed Lycambes and his daughters by means of his satires. The motive attributed to him was revenge for his rejection as a suitor of Neoboule. Various versions agree that his words drove the family to suicide, and that their method of self-destruction was hanging. Horace is our earliest authority for this catastrophic event, and he mentions Archilochus' revenge four times,[1] referring obliquely but surely to the means whereby Neoboule made away with herself,[2] and he speaks of Archilochus' words 'hunting' or 'driving' Lycambes.[3] Scholiasts fill out Horace's allusions with detail which clearly is drawn from a general tradition. Ovid shows himself acquainted with the story, including its suicidal aspect; and he speaks of Archilochus' poetic weapons being dyed with 'Lycambean blood'.[4] We cannot use this as indicating that Lycambes was a separate victim apart from his daughters; for the adjective is capable of a general, familial connotation, and the reference is of a vague allusive kind.

Ovid's remarks are supplemented by various scholiastic comments, some of them so imaginatively illogical as to give comfort to sceptics about the whole tradition by their very coexistence with the more frequently occurring elements of the story.[5] Martial echoes Ovid's phrase about

'Lycambean blood'. There are a number of treatments of the theme in the Greek Anthology, most of which concern the pathetic fate of the two daughters[6] who are victims of that species of poetic fury which Horace disclaims in himself,[7] glad though he is to acknowledge his imitation of Archilochus' poetic and metrical forms exclusive of their ferocious contents.

The poets of the Anthology who mention the affair include Dioskorides, whose poem in which the girls defend their honourable reputation against Archilochus' slurs is important in discussions of this theme.[8] Oenomaus finds it strange that Apollo should so enthusiastically give his patronage to an abusive and disreputable character like Archilochus, who, amongst other misdeeds, pours ridicule upon women who refuse him marriage.[9] I take it that Oenomaus plural 'women' is a general reference to Neoboule rather than an actual plurality, although it remains possible that the poet courted others.[10] Also, the emperor Julian forbade priests to read Archilochus.[11] No doubt he feared that the poet's outrageous works might injure the repute of the reformed paganism which he essayed; and he may well have had in mind the avoidance of the kind of criticism of Archilochus which we find in the philosopher Oenomaus. But it is clear that he knew Archilochus' works thoroughly, and that they were available to read in his time.[12] From a fragment of his letters, it is evident that he believed Archilochus to have spoken falsehoods against Lycambes.[13]

Horace and these others evidently derive support for their remarks from Archilochus' poetry itself, and not merely from a parallel tradition, though such no doubt existed. Certainly the Lycambids were important in Archilochus' life and consciousness: as we have seen, there are comparatively numerous references to them even in the scattered fragments of his work that survive.[14] Even if we allow a certain preference for scandalous material on the part of those who quote and preserve his words on the subject, this in itself indicates the striking and prominent character of his references to Lycambes and his family as well as the general currency of the story.[15]

The Lycambidae were an actual family of Paros, and probably of some importance in the politics of the island.[16] They are not merely concocted extrapolations from the poems or simple accretions by a mythopoeic process like that which represents Sappho in love with Phaon;[17] or the notion, which had considerable comic possibilities, and was used (indeed possibly invented) by poets of Athenian comedy, that Archilochus and Hipponax were both lovers of Sappho.[18] Without discounting the element of popular fantasy that no doubt influences the story as we have it, it is reasonable to believe that we are dealing with a version or versions of some real events, at least until evidence is forthcoming to disprove this. I agree with G. W. Bond's view that the onus of proof lies upon those[19] who reject completely the tradition about the Lycambids. The story fits well with the references to the Lycambids which survive and, though not one of these unquestionably refers to

the event, it is sufficient that the fragments refer with criticism, hostility and opprobrium to members of the family. Nor need we be surprised not to find it included in the inscription together with the hagiographically respectable story of the Muses and the cow. If the Cologne fragment is genuine,[20] it contributes important evidence to our attempts at reconstructing the armoury of weapons used against Lycambes and his daughters; for the poem is of such a character that would make it difficult, if it gained popular currency, for a family to continue an honoured and self-respecting life on a small island. Thus there is something to be said in favour of an attempt to look once more at the story; for if it is true, it represents Archilochus' most ruthless achievement and one which is unique in our records of Greek life and experience.

Horace's authority as a self-confessed student of Archilochus and his reputation as a man of acknowledged good sense cannot easily be disregarded. If we had nothing but his allusions to the story together with our present fragments of the poet, we would still be obliged to consider the question seriously. As it is, the tradition which fans out from Horace's time provides still stronger support for it. Evidence for its availability before Horace is much slighter, and nowhere entirely unequivocal. In the fifth century B.C. Cratinus . . . indicates that the poet could expect his audience to know who Lycambes was. This might suggest that they knew, or might be expected to know, something about the bad relationship between Archilochus and Lycambes, knowledge which they would obtain from his poems or a contemporary tradition associated with them and his name. This 'fragment' does not entitle us to infer that the story of the suicides was known in fifth century Athens; but we cannot be sure that it was not.

Critias is said not to have known of it either;[21] otherwise he could hardly have failed to include a mention of the Lycambids amongst his hostile comments on Archilochus. . . . We cannot tell whether Critias knew of the Lycambids or not, since he confines his comments about Archilochus' sexual life to these three disobliging words, and from the way in which the passage of his prose runs, it seems probable that he decided not to go into more detail, or did not have any more detail to produce.[22] Critias' chosen 'brief' was to point out that the poet was in the habit of revealing discreditable facts about himself in his poetry. Archilochus' attacks upon the Lycambids would not fall into this category (apart from their possible inclusion in the insults mentioned above), for in his assault upon them Archilochus shows himself to be a terrifyingly effective defender of his own honour; and Critias would not wish to represent him in this role. However, it must be conceded that Critias gives us no reason to believe that he was especially interested in the matter.

If we recall Alcidamas' remark that the Parians honoured Archilochus although he was [*blásphiemos*] we may be provided with a clue to the source of the tradition about Lycambes and his daughters. Archilochus' memory was revered by the later generations of his countrymen, as is evidenced by the *Archilocheion* and its associated inscriptions. But the inscription[23] tells us that Archilochus was banished by his contemporary Parians for being excessively abusive; it is possible this alludes to attacks upon an important family of the island which had tragic consequences for some of its members.

This does not exclude the possibility that Archilochus' conflict with the Lycambid family had political overtones which are lost beneath the personal emphasis of the tradition associated with Archilochus' subsequent cult. The tendency of Alcidamas' brief comment and the evidence about the poet's temporary banishment from Paros suggest that the Lycambid story, with other details of his life, may be of distinctly Parian origin, and may not have become widely known outside the island in the fifth century B.C. In the fourth century B.C. Alcidamas possibly has heard something of it; and for the third century B.C. a papyrus poem provides our first discernible testimony about the suicides.[24]

We do not know whether Archilochus actually wished to kill Lycambes and his daughters. We do not know what his particular intentions were, but there is no doubt that he gave this family warning that he knew how to hurt those who injured him.[25] He also knew how to wield poetic curses, but the surviving examples of his art in this sphere are probably not directed against Lycambes and his family.[26] The 'Strasbourg' epode, which is generally accepted as being genuinely his work, contains a powerful curse;[27] and if we can accept the idea that there is a close relationship between Horace's *Epodes* and the epodes of Archilochus without committing ourselves entirely to M. Lasserre's interesting theory of a precise correspondence between the two sets of poems,[28] we may observe that curses are not infrequent in Horace's book; perhaps we may also infer a correlative frequency for them in Archilochus' epodes.

One fragment of the poet has been interpreted as referring to the self-destruction of this family: . . . 'hanging [?] they spewed out all their arrogant pride'.[29] The use of the verb κυπτειν to signify 'hanging' (i.e. by a rope so as to cause death) is authenticated only by a late interpretation[30] which itself may be influenced by the tradition of the Lycambids' suicide. It may be an attempt to read the story of their self-destruction into a text where it has no place; since the verb could more easily mean 'hanging their heads in shame'.[31] The masculine plural of the aorist participle . . . shows that the group to which it refers could have a masculine element in it, since the masculine can be used to designate a group of both genders. If these words refer to the Lycambid daughters, they must also include Lycambes himself. There is no reason to suppose that Archilochus' fragment which echoes the Homeric sentiment that 'it is not righteous to quarrel with the dead' necessarily indicates his unwillingness to gloat over the death of those who had dishonoured him.[32] Even Achilles abused the dead Hector, and in any case, the context of this fragment is lost and we have no idea of its purpose. However, all that we can properly deduce from the . . . fragment is

the likelihood that Archilochus observed, noted (or even perhaps hopefully anticipated) some effects, deadly or otherwise, of his poetic campaign against Lycambes and his family.

I suggest that the traditional story is too strongly established to be laughed off as a piece of mythopeia at folk level, or as an invention of comic poets in Athens, and that probably Lycambes and his daughters did commit suicide. The other point upon which the tradition hinges seems assured: namely that Archilochus attacked them in his verse.[33] Archilochus attacked them; and they, sooner or later afterwards, committed suicide. What is the real connection between these two propositions which the tradition regards as cause and effect?

Let us look first at the theory, supported by the analogy of Irish and Arabic satirists' alleged powers, that it was by some magical operation, some spell, that Archilochus brought his victims to suicide.[34] It would be understandable enough if such a view of his powers prevailed on his native island of Paros in the folk-tradition: it was the centre of his hero-cult, and he seems to have been regarded there as a kind of 'holy man', who had a special relationship with the gods.[35] His bitter tongue earned him exile, as we are told in the inscription; but it was the oracle of the god Apollo that secured his recall,[36] and it was the god Dionysus who inflicted the males of Paros with impotence for having sent him away.[37] This would appear to be a fertile ground for legends of his 'magic' powers as a satirist to take root, but in fact we have no specific account of how this vengeful power was supposed to operate. Its 'mechanics' are quite obscure to us, and as far as his own attitude is concerned, we simply have the evidence of his warning verses that told how he could hurt his enemies, and the poetic curses which we have mentioned. Even these may be claims in which he himself wished to believe, rather than confident assertions of his powers; they may be the whistlings in the dark of a man who feels wronged, but who is powerless to obtain his rights; mere fantasies of supernatural ability; the delusions of grandeur with which a loser sought to comfort his isolation and poverty.[38] Or else it is a question of a poet who, as Piccolomini soberly put it in 1883, naturally wishes to increase the influence and power of his profession, and speaks accordingly.[39]

Poetic abusiveness no doubt had its representatives before Archilochus, although we can name no examples. The ceremony of outrageous insult and flyting is perhaps to be seen, in some traces at least, in the Homeric poems. Achilles insults Agamemnon; Agamemnon insults Achilles and Calchas; we hear Paris being heaped with insults, almost in a ritual manner, by Hector: . . . 'Foul Paris, fairest in form, woman-crazy, talker of nonsense',[40] has the ring of some possible predecessor of Archilochus in the art of poetic abuse; and it also has a repetitive, emphatic character that is not unreminiscent of a magical spell.[41] But there is no indication that any magic was intended, either in Homer, or in Hesiod, with his obsessive abuse of the judges whom he nominates as 'bribe-devouring',[42] nor indeed as far as we can see, in Archilochus.

But the analogy of the powers of Irish and Arabian satirists has been put forward to explain how Archilochus drove his enemy and his two daughters to their death. And so, before we go further, we had better consider this suggestion, confining ourselves to the Irish parallel, which involves a community of substantially Indo-European character, like that of Greece. The common lore from at least the sixteenth century onwards,[43] had it that Irish bards could 'rhyme rats to death'.[44] Little detail is known about this procedure, although the last recorded instance of it relates to the eighteenth century. A poetic 'spell' or satire seems to have been used. The poets of Ireland claimed some human victims also; not merely from their own people, but including a relatively sophisticated Anglo-Irish state official,[45] who nevertheless was no less superstitious than those whom he affected to rule,[46] and no doubt the more susceptible to spells on that account. Even in the twilit time of Gaelic social decline, in the later seventeenth and early eighteenth centuries, poets retained their ability to kill. Eoghan O'Rahilly is supposed to have killed a man with his poetry, though as his editor points out, most of the satire of contemporary Irish poets was little more than 'rhythmical barging';[47] a sad genre which we also see exemplified in David O Bruadair's fierce poem against a barmaid who would not allow him any more credit; this is a powerful piece of invective, worthy in many ways of Archilochus, and expressing, again like Archilochus, miserable personal circumstances with indignation rather than shame.[48]

This is the end of a long Irish tradition in which poets were honoured, as they were in Greece,[49] and feared, as they do not seem to have been in Greece. Satire was a more important constituent of poetic activity in Ireland than in Greece, and it was organized into a number of different kinds, appropriate to different purposes.[50] In its very early form, Irish poetic satire had a spell-like character, seeking to inflict wounds by the homoeopathic power of words descriptive of them, and not yet paying much attention to the delineation of personal characteristics or individual vices.

This simple magic by innate power of words themselves was a fearful weapon. Coipre Mac Etain's attack upon the king Brés, which is mentioned in an account of the second battle of Moytura, simply compares his condition to starvation, isolation, loneliness and misery of spirit, and in this way, according to the story, irrecoverably robs him of his vitality and confidence.[51] The story is preserved in a manuscript of the tenth century B.C., but it clearly refers to pre-Christian times. Clearly the bard wished to impose a certain physical condition by his curse, which in its comprehensive exclusion of its victims from the society of men and human comforts of every kind resembles the traditional curse of the Bouzyges[52] which the Athenians ceremonially directed against offenders of its city and its laws. The infliction of shame does not seem to be an emphatic element in the Coipre's intention, although any unfavourable thing said about a king or any other man in a high position in ancient society inevitably brought some shame and dishonour to him.

In later satires an acrid note of personal ridicule and sarcastic comment, comparable to that of Archilochus, becomes the dominant element; but the characteristics of the ancient spell do not entirely disappear, and in the seventeenth century we find Feardocha O Dalaigh with spell-like insistence and comprehensiveness calling down the curses of God, the Virgin, Apostles, Pope, priests, monks, widows and orphans upon the party whom he wishes to assail.[53]

A manuscript of the fourteenth century tells how Athirne and his sons made satires about a beautiful woman called Luaine, because she would not sleep with them; and as a result of their satires her face was blemished and she died of shame.[54] Here we have an interesting link between the earlier type of poetic spell, like that from which Brés suffered, and the later more 'satirical' type which induces shame. Shame, or a quite literal 'loss of face' in the case of Luaine, arose from something quite obvious and simple, a beautiful woman's loss of the beauty which brought her honour in her society. She was not merely disfigured by the three blisters of Reproach, Ill-fame and Shame, represented by their corresponding colours of unjust judgments, black, red and white; she was also degraded and, in spite of their injustice and her innocence, could not survive.

Such are the ways of the 'shame' culture, in which honour is more significant than innocence, and disgrace can drive out and overwhelm consciousness of right. Such was the fate of Lucretia, in Roman tradition, who proved herself innocent by the self-imposed trial of death; and such also, perhaps, were the fates of the daughters of Lycambes. And in both Greek and Irish cultures, underneath the complex mathematics of honour and shame, there persisted the magical superstition of simple souls, like the girl described by Theocritus, attempting by the aid of the wryneck on its wheel, to bring back her lover;[55] or in nineteenth century Ireland, the persistence of a belief that to have a poem, even in fulsome praise, made about one was an unlucky thing and likely to bring death. This attitude is well summed up by a countrywoman whose words are quoted by Douglas Hyde. Talking about the dreadful fate of Mary Hines, a beautiful girl celebrated in the poetry of the nineteenth century Irish poet Anthony Raftery, she said: 'Divil long does a person live who has a poem made on them.'[56]

Greek poetry that is known to us has none of this true primitive magic about it. It has been secularized of magic—even the hymns to the gods have a secular flavour. We cannot deny that there may have been earlier, more magical forms, but they are not available to us.[57] The process of rationalization and the adoption of a laic attitude has already gone a considerable distance in the time of Hesiod, whose *Theogonia* does not reproduce the sacral character of the Asianic poems which were amongst its models.[58] Hesiod wishes to teach and persuade, rather than cast spells, in spite of his characteristic fear of ill omens. His wish, like that of any Greek, is not to offend the gods.

Archilochus' connections with the cults of the gods on Paros and his enjoyment of the special patronage of Apollo did not confer upon him the powers of a wizard; but he had a genius for poetry which he and others regarded as a gift of the gods, and this faculty enabled him to deploy his words most hurtfully. He is far off from the world of Coipre, and from that of Athirne, even though we observe a comparable element of 'shame' culture involved in the case of Luaine.

Outside the legend of Orpheus, whose art had physical 'magic' effects, Greek poets did not wield supernatural power, but left that to the gods whom they served. Assertion of such powers would savour of υβρις. Nothing in Archilochus' fragments suggests that he regarded himself as a 'magical' person capable of inflicting injury by his words. This did not prevent him from praying down curses on his enemies in his verses, or asserting his power to hurt: the former is what anyone, poet or not, would do to enemies; the latter is part confidence in his satirical genius, part intense hatred, and part a sense of being unjustly treated. If he killed Lycambes and his daughters, it was by shaming them rather than rhyming them to death like Irish rats.

We know from the observation of other cultures than the Greek that shame can kill, and that death can seem preferable to dragging out an ungrateful existence bereft not merely of all the honourable opinion of one's fellow men,[59] but so degraded that the victim can no longer be regarded or be capable of regarding himself as a member of the community. This state of mind is not 'guilt' in the sense of a consciousness of having done wrong or acted against the ethos of society intentionally. It has nothing to do with the 'guilt' culture of Christianity and modern Western society. It is more comparable to a deep sense of social contamination; of being stained or polluted by the onslaught of evil, vice, or injustice. 'Shame' in this sense is not merely superficial, or imposed from without; it arises irrespective of the justice or otherwise of its causation. Life can become unendurable for those who are shamed, afflicted as they are by a self-hatred that cannot be rationalized away by arguing the essential innocence of the sufferer.[60] It is only in the time of Plato that we find it explicitly argued by his Socrates in the first book of the *Republic* that it is less happy or advantageous to commit injustice than endure it.

The suicide of a person irredeemably shamed may be observed in the case of Iokasta (Epikaste in Homer). Homer's version simply relates that she kills herself for shame,[61] as a result of finding out the nature of her relationship to Oedipus; Sophocles' Iokasta only decides to kill herself when it becomes apparent to her that the incestuous relationship is inevitably going to be published at large.[62] The story of Phaedra and Hippolytus is more complex: in her decision to kill herself and leave a message alleging her dishonour at the hands of Hippolytus, thereby implicating him in the shame which she herself has suffered as a result of his rejection of her love, she certainly utilizes the ethical equipment of the kind of society that emphasizes shame and honour as standards of its members. Whether she also feels 'guilt' in addition to shame, is arguable; but her action can be interpreted in terms of 'shame' or honour, and probably many Athenians of the fifth century who witnessed Euripides' Hippolytus plays simply understood it in that way.

Further, there is evidence that the Greeks feared the dead, especially the spirits of those who had been unjustly killed. J. G. Frazer points out an interesting survival in Greece of a very primitive way of driving such spirits away, when he mentions in the course of his general discussion of fear of the dead in many cultures, the example of Aigisthus in Euripides' *Electra*[63] throwing stones at the tomb of Agamemnon, whom he has murdered. He mentions elsewhere our one piece of evidence for the fear of the spirits of suicides in Greece: a reference in Aeschines to the custom of burying a suicide's hand separate from the corpse—so that the dead man cannot use the hand against others which he has used so mercilessly against himself.[64]

I do not suggest that these points represent the most important part of the Lycambids' motivation in killing themselves; but the idea of suicide as an act of revenge may very well have been familiar enough.[65] By killing themselves, they vanquish the person who has driven them to do the deed; it is he who, being left behind, must justify himself before the world, and their ghosts persist to do him harm amongst his fellow citizens.

The most pressing motive for Lycambes and his daughters to seek their own deaths would hardly be this desire for revenge, but more probably a conviction that for all practical purposes they were already dead because their honour had been killed. It is probable that the process whereby they were brought to the state of mind in which they killed themselves lasted over a period in which, possibly for years, they endured the fury of Archilochus' poetic attacks upon them.[66] Some climax of vexation could be inferred finally to have made life intolerable for them. If this is a reasonable hypothesis, have we in the remains of Archilochus' poetry any fragment which seems to be a suitable candidate for the part of final detonator of the family's misery? Of the number of fragments which have an insulting character and refer to women, there are some that probably do not apply to the Lycambids at all, or at least are in doubt. None of these smaller fragments seems, in the present state of our knowledge, to fit this role. But the power and ferocity, the ingenuity of scurrilous description and sexual allusion in the Cologne fragment strongly favour its claims for this honour. Who, even now, could endure without anguish the singing of such a song against themselves in the streets? It and presumably others like it which are lost could be used as hammer-blows to shatter the position of the Lycambids in their society.

Notes

1. Horace *Epode* 6, 11; *Serm.* 2, 3 11; *Epist.* 1, 19, 23; *Ars Poet.* 79 (Tarditi, *Archil.* 84, 85, 86, 87); cf. chapter 2 note 87 above.

2. *Epist.* 1, 19, 31; *nec sponsae laqueum famoso carmine nectit.*

3. *Epist.* 1, 19, 2315: *Parios ego primus iambos ostendi Latio / numeros animosque secutus /Archilochi non res et agentia verba Lycamben.*

4. Ovid *Ibis* 54.

5. However, Ovid's scholiast is positive that Lycambes hanged himself, so also are the scholiasts on the Ovidian passage. The latter is certain of the statement that Archilochus was pursued by the friends of Lycambes, and himself eventually committed suicide—a story for which there is no other evidence whatever. The scholia also contain a disquieting reference to Hipponax, which may be derived from the plot of a comic play in which Archilochus confronts this other great satirist: cf. chapter 2 note 168 above.

6. Gaetulicus, *AP,* 7 71 is our only authority for three rather than two daughters.

7. See note 3 above.

8. E.g., it has a third century B.C. predecessor, the theme of which it follows: Bond, pp. 1-11, see chapter 2 note 91.

9. Eusebius *Praep. Ev.* 5, 32.

10. Another Lycambid, a sister of Neoboule if the Cologne Papyrus is authentic; the fragment *Pap Ox* 2310 is addressed to a woman who very probably is Neoboule, though F. R. Adrados has reservations about this: *PP* 41 (1955-56) 38-48; see also chapter 2 note 88.

11. Nor Hipponax either, nor any other composer of like material: Julian *Epist.* 89 b 300 C.

12. Julian *Misopog.* 1. 337 a.

13. Julian *Epist.* 80.

14. Chapter 2 notes 84, 85.

15. Chapter 2 note 86.

16. *Mnes. Inscr.* E 1, col II, 45.

17. V. Grassmann, *Die Erotischen Epoden des Horaz, Literarischer Hintergrund und Sprachliche Tradition* (Munich 1966), p. 4.

18. In a play of Diphilus (Athenaeus 599 d).

19. Bond, p. 11.

20. See the discussion in chapter 5, also the appendix.

21. Hauvette, p. 69; Wolf, pp. 62-63.

22. It is impossible to be quite certain of this in view of the brevity of the extract, but the intention of Critias seems to have been to emphasize Archilochus' self-destructive tendencies rather than the analytical one of comprehending all the facts about his relationship with other people. He is propounding a case—as apparently Alcidamas also is—not writing biography.

23. The occurrence . . . is probably to be translated as 'rather too satirically' in its context of A's exile: *Mnes. Inscr.* E, col III, 37; Ovid's scholiast on *Ibis* 521 seems to know the story about his exile for satirical acerbity.

24. Bond, p. 11.

25. Fgs 54 T 10-11; 104 T; 109 T.

26. E.g., 30 T, in which he asks Apollo to curse some person or persons, has no apparent connection with the Lycambid family.

27. 193 T.

28. Lasserre, *Les Epodes* etc.

29. 36 T.

30. Piccolomini, pp. 264 ff.; Bond, p. 10 n. 11; M. Treu, pp. 251-52.

31. Piccolomini, pp. 264 ff.; Hauvette, p. 69.

32. 103 T. The phrase follows a Homeric model: *Odyssey* 22, 412, and is also echoed by Cratinus (see Tarditi's comments on the fragment); for a different view, Grassmann, pp. 4-5.

33. The most palpable attack in the fragments themselves is 166 T (see chapter 2 note 91) . . . ; other fragments less certain nevertheless suggest strongly the reputation of the beauty and virtue of the daughter: Rankin, *GB.* The Cologne Papyrus also is a fierce attack upon Neoboule; for the rest, there is the secondary tradition discussed above.

34. For references to recent articles, etc., propounding this view see Rankin, *Eos,* p. 1; the best known proponents of the 'magic' theory are Hendrickson, pp. 101-27; Elliott, *Power,* pp. 1-15; *Antaios* 4 (1963) 313-26. Also Vendryes, pp. 94-96.

35. Chapter 2 note 74.

36. For an attempted reconstruction of this oracle, see Parke, p. 93.

37. Kontoleon, *Arkh. Eph.* pp. 80 f.; Rankin, *Eos,* footnotes 79-85.

38. 54 T (*Pap Ox* 2310): Rankin, *Eranos,* p. 7.

39. Piccolomini, p. 266.

40. *Iliad* 3, 39; 13, 769. . . .

41. A repetitive element can be seen in the refrain of Theocritus *Idyll* 2, which is about a magic spell; also perhaps in Catullus' *Poem* 5, and certainly in *Patrick's Hymn,* W. Stokes and J. Strachan, *Thesaurus Palaeohibernicus,* vol. 2 (Cambridge 1903), p. 357.

42. Hesiod *Works and Days* 39, 221, 264.

43. As far as I know, Ben Jonson is the first modern to have made the comparison between Archilochus and the Irish poets in his *Poetaster,* 160-65.

44. W. Shakespeare, *As You Like It*, III, 2; it is also mentioned by Sir Philip Sidney, John Donne and others.

45. As recorded in the *Annals of the Four Masters*: D. Plunket Barton, *Links between Ireland and Shakespeare* (Dublin/London 1919), p. 64.

46. E.g., G. L. Kitteredge describes how in the sixteenth and seventeenth century educated men in England, including the most distinguished jurists, accepted easily the notion of witchcraft: 'English Witchcraft and James the First', in *Toy,* pp. 1-65.

47. *Danta Aodhagain Ui Rathaille,* Irish Texts Soc. (1911) XXX: he is said to have killed a man by his satire, but it is clear that much of his poetry of attack left his enemies unmoved.

48. *Duanaire Dhaibhidh Ui Bhruadair,* edited by J. Mac-Erlean, Irish Texts Soc. (1913), XXXI.

49. *Odyssey* 6, 184-85; 471-81.

50. Diodorus V, 31.2; Vendryes 95; Mercier, p. 109.

51. The spell-like character can clearly be seen:

> cen colt crib [cerníne]
> cen gert ferrba fora n-assa athirni
> cen adba fir fer druba diserche
> cen dil dami resi rob sen Brisi

> without food quickly in a dish
> without a cow's milk whereon a calf grows
> without a man's abode under the gloom of night
> without paying a company of story tellers, let that be Bres' condition!

'and there was nothing but lassitude on that man from that time' from W. Stokes, *Revue Celtique* 12 (1891) 52-130; cf. Elliot, *Power,* p. 38; Hendrickson, pp. 124-25; J. Travis, *PMLA* 57 (1942) 909-915.

52. E. Ziebarth, *RE* s.v. 'Fluch'; J. H. Mozley, 'On Cursing in Ancient Times', appendix to Ovid, *The Art of Love and Other Poems* (Loeb Classical Library, London 1947).

53. Quoted by Mercier, pp. 148 f.

54. W. Stokes, 'The Wooing of Luaine and the Death of Athirne', *Revue Celtique* 24 (1903) 270-87; Elliott, *Power,* p. 27.

55. *Idyll* 2.

56. D. Hyde, *Abhráin atá leagtha ar an Reachtuíre* (Dublin 1903), p. 16.

57. F. N. Robinson, 'Satirists and Enchanters in Early Irish Literature' in *Toy,* p. 99.

58. M. L. West, *Hesiod, Theogony* (Oxford 1966), pp. 9-10; 14-15.

59. Julio Caro Baroja, 'Honour and Shame, A Historical Account of Several Conflicts', translated by R. Johnson, in *Honour and Shame,* pp. 79-137 (esp pp. 85 f.).

60. Sophocles shows Ajax (*Aias* 666-90) attempting to rationalize away his sense of dishonour by means of the characteristically Greek argument from the balance and rhythm of the natural world's changes. The argument fails to help him and his self-destructive desire prevails.

61. *Odyssey* 11, 271-80: she hanged herself for grief: Eustathius in *Od* 1684.

62. Sophocles, *Oedipus Tyrannus* 1060-61.

63. J. G. Frazer, *The Golden Bough,* Part IX, p. 19 referring to Euripides *El* 327.

64. Ibid., Part IV, pp. 44-49, 141, 220; Aeschines *In Ctesiphontem* 244.

65. B. Bohannan, *African Homicide and Suicide* (Princeton 1960), p. xxx mentions the custom of the injured person killing himself before the door of his offender. For suicide in the ancient world see Thalheim, *RE* s.v. Selbstmord: R. Hirzel, *Der Selbstmord* (Darmstadt 1968, reprint), who, significantly for our theme, quotes (p. 16 n. 2) a number of examples of Greek women who killed themselves on account of shame.

66. Chapter 2, the section on Neoboule.

List of Abbreviations

AP: Anthologia Palatina

Bond: G. W. Bond, 'Archilochus and the Lycambides, A New Literary Fragment', *Hermathena* 80 (1952) 1-11

Diels-Kranz: H. Diels, *Die Fragmente der Vorsokratiker, Griechisch und Deutsch, herausgegeben von Walther Kranz* (Berlin 1972)

Elliott, *Power:* R. C. Elliott, *The Power of Satire* (Princeton 1960)

Elliott, *Satire:* R. C. Elliott, 'Satire und Magie', *Antaios* 4 (1962) 313-26

Frazer: J. G. Frazer, *The Golden Bough, A Study in Magic and Religion*

Hauvette: A. Hauvette, *Archiloque, sa vie et ses poésies* (Paris 1905)

Hendrickson: G. L. Hendrickson 'Archilochus and the victims of his Iambics', *AJP* 46 (1925) 101-27

Honour and Shame: Honour and Shame, The Values of Mediterranean Society, edited by J. G. Peristiany (Nature of Human Society Series, London 1965)

Kontoleon, *Arkh Eph:* N. Kontoleon, 'Neai Epigraphai peri tou Arkhilokhou ek Parou', *Arkh Eph* 91 (1952) 32-95

Lasserre: F. Lasserre, *Les Épodes d'Archiloque* (Paris 1950)

Mnes. Inscr.: Mnesiepis Inscriptio, Tarditi, *Archilochus,* p. 4 ff

Parke: H. W. Parke, 'The Newly Discovered Delphic Responses from Paros', *CQ* 8 (1958) 90-94

Piccolomini: A. Piccolomini, 'Quaestionum de Archilocho capita tria', *Hermes* 18 (1883) 264 ff

PP: *La Parola del Passato, Rivista di Studi Classici*

Rankin, *Eos:* H. D. Rankin, 'Archilochus was no magician', *Eos* 19 (1974) 5-21

Rankin, *Eranos:* H. D. Rankin, 'Archilochus (*Pap. Ox.* 2310 Fr 1 Col 1)', *Eranos* 72 (1974) 1-15

Rankin, *GB:* H. D. Rankin, . . . Critias and his criticism of Archilochus', *Grazer Beiträge* 3 (1975) 323-34

RE: Pauly-Wissowa, *Real-Encyclopädie der Classischen Altertumswissenschaft*

Travis: J. Travis, 'A Druidic Prophecy, the First Irish Satire and a Poem to Raise Blisters', *PMLA* 57 4, 1 (December 1942), 901-15

West, *CQ:* M. L. West, 'Greek Poetry 2000 B.C.-700 B.C.', *CQ* 23 (1974) 179-92

Wolf: F. Wolf, *Untersuchungen zu Archilochos' Epoden,* Dissertation, Halle-Wittenburg 1966

Anne Pippin Burnett (essay date 1983)

SOURCE: "Archilochus: Blame," in *Three Archaic Poets: Archilochus, Alcaeus, Sappho,* Harvard University Press, 1983, pp. 55-76.

[*In the following essay, Burnett examines Archilochus's fables, particularly their element of anger that led to his reputation as the poet of abuse.*]

The Parians who made a hero of Archilochus remembered his patriotic poems and his cult songs, but the rest of the ancient world honoured him primarily as a poet of abuse, the first and best, and one whose evil tongue could kill. He was at once the inventor and the most perfect practitioner of blame (Vell. Pat. 1.5) and his loud verses were 'filled with rage and the venom of dread scurrility' (*AP* 9.185), because he had 'sprinkled his harsh Muse with Echidna's bile' (*AP* 7.71).[1] Teachers recommended the study of his modes of attack,[2] and Plutarch records the moment when Cato 'angrily and impetuously turned his energies to the writing of iambics, in which he made a violent attack upon Scipio, using the bitter style of Archilochus and allowing himself to exaggerate and make childish jokes' (*vit. Caton. min.* 7). The tale of Lycambes and his daughters, hounded to death by obscene libels, was repeated again and again to prove the force of the Archilochean genius, and ugly though it was it did not seem to contradict other stories about Apollo's patronage of the poet, for according to later antiquity men had more need of blame than of praise in their poetry (Dio Chrys. *or.* 33.11f.). Archilochus' old calumnies were thus music

to the ears of Rome's cynical politicians and dilettanti, but in their own time they had served a far deeper purpose, for the archaic poetry of blame was an instrument of social health, as necessary to a sound community as those complementary songs that put splendour in the air. Abuse was one of the two poetic practices essential to social life, and as such it had its history, its rationale and, in Momus, even its presiding divinity.

Momus, in the time of Callimachus, was a mere personification of envy. His voice was that of sterile criticism[3], and with that voice he passed into the Renaissance as the jealous colleague who tried to destroy the sublime work of Apelles.[4] Originally, however, Momus had been a creature much more powerful and more ambivalent than this, for according to Hesiod he was a child of Night, the brother of Grief, and one of a host of dark *daimones* who were both harmful and beneficent (*Theog.* 214). Momus was the natural companion of Death, since blame was associated with silence and forgetfulness, but he was as well the friend of Sleep, the Moirai, and the maids of paradise, who were all forces of order and health. This allegorised blame-figure defined himself in action in the stories of the epic cycle, for it was he who strongly urged Zeus to prosecute the Trojan War, that the pressures of human population might be reduced (Schol. at *Il.*1.5 = *Cypr.*1).[5] Momus had always a very low opinion of the value of mankind, which he saw as the worst section of the animal creation (Babrius, *Fab.* 59),[6] and in Stoic diatribe he blamed now Prometheus, now Hermes, for ever having devised such a species.[7] In this respect he was a peculiarly archaic deity, for it was his apportioned task to remind men always of their ungodlike qualities, and so to check their growing audacity and pride.

On earth, the work of Momus was done by abusive song, which was thought of as being almost as old as music itself.[8] Combined with obscenity, poetic attack had become a magical weapon for driving out demons, and the apotropaic effects of the filthy insult were borrowed from superstition for use in rites of fertility and in certain rituals of Dionysus and Demeter.[9] Momus, however, was interested in men, not gods, and blame found its widest uses in the secular world, where it was employed in the self-regulation of the primitive community.[10] Individual behaviour was monitored only by the pressure of the group, and opinion had to assume a form that would actually inhibit or encourage those who were censured or approved. Blame and praise not only had to be expressed, they had to be invested with the power of wounding and rewarding, and the magic of metre and melody was exploited to this end. Praise adopted the same choral music that was used for magnifying gods, and eventually it produced that strangely atavistic form, epinician song, while blame chose the monodic forms that belonged to the witch, the healer and the itinerant dealer in purification. It had need of some such magic, since it had to bind and control those absurd and bestial parts of men that Momus scorned from above.

In theory blame was the natural companion of praise, but in the practical world of composition and performance the two sorts of song were inevitably rivals, since they were opposite in spirit as well as in technique. Successful praise magnified its subject; it made use of sweetness, looked only for the noble, and roused a sense of emulating pride in its listener.[11] Blame, on the other hand, made its object small: 'chew', 'chop fine', is probably the meaning of its major verb, *psegein* (though some have supposed that it activates the disgusted exclamation, *pso*).[12] Successful blame was bitter and degrading; it searched out what was shameful, obscene, deformed or grotesque, and it roused a laughing scorn,[13] but also a covert questioning of self, within its audience. Ideally, praise created a sense of unity as it mixed one man's virtue into the virtue of the group that had produced him, but blame was necessarily divisive, since it separated the base or unsound man from his fellows and ejected him, almost as if he were a *pharmakos*.[14] Blame was, thus, in the vulgar sense, more political than praise, for its legitimate abuse kept alive the spirit of contention that made cities prosper, and it also acted as a kind of popular review, a *dokimasia* that any man who gained prominence would have to undergo. Its power could even be projected into the future with an inhibitory effect, for the poetry of blame acted, in its potential form, as an effective threat. It was an obvious truth that, in a small city, 'no one who felt the people's scorn as a burden could find much to enjoy' (14W),[15] and this meant that the mere presence of a master of calumny ensured an increase in propriety among the citizens.

The praise poets of a later time equated blame with slander,[16] and Pindar pictured the blame-singer as an ugly creature who manipulated envy and courted the dregs of society. For him, Archilochus was the perfect emblem of everything that song should never stoop to, and he called him by name in his great ode on ingratitude (*P*2.52-6):

> I for my part
> must avoid the bitter gall of calumny
> for from a distance I observe Archilochus,
> futile and abusive, growing fat[17]
> on heavy words of scorn.

Such superb abuse from a poet who insists that he is above the practice is the fairest crown that Archilochus could win,[18] but this passage not only fixes Archilochus' reputation, it also provides a reverse description of his profession. Blame is not richly rewarded, according to Pindar, which means that its poet is not the servant of a wealthy patron. Blame fawns upon the populace, by this report, which means that it does not flatter the rich and powerful. Blame is like an ape who pleases children, says the Theban,[19] which means that its poet is a citizen among citizens and understood by all, not a prophet whose deep meaning can be taken only by the few. Blame, then, is an art that is independent,[20] popular and even in the fifth century still so powerful that a Pindar must scorn it, still so reputable that he can do so without spoiling his own dignity.[21]

Blame addressed the bestial part of man because its function was to keep that part from controlling society and offending gods who were ready to blame. The singer of

defamatory song kept off the lesser demons of presumption and self-satisfaction, and also the greater ones of corruption, pride and injustice, and so in his own view he was as important as any priest or magistrate. He practised an art that was conscious and traditional, one that maintained the health of the community, and consequently it will be egregiously wrong to take the slanders of Archilochus as the mere raw outbursts of an angry man who happened to have a lyre in his hands. Archilochus is fond of saying that anger is a part of his nature, but the statement is meant to validate his professional vocation, proving that his blame is as honest as other poets' praise and that, coming from his *thumos*, it is not for sale.

The three most prominent characteristics of Archilochean blame turn out to be a distance from the object, a consciousness of function, and a manipulation of convention, all of which are evident in the poet's descriptions of himself as a singer of abuse. Standing back to observe the cleanness of his own passion, he can say, 'One important thing I understand—how to answer wrong with wrongs' (126W), or 'I love a fight with you as I love a drink when I'm thirsty' (125W).[22] Anger is generalised and the audience is reminded that attack is a form of artistic activity and also a form of wisdom—the expression of a hard, popular instinct for communal self-defence. 'The fox knows many tricks, the hedgehog just one—but his is a good one!' (201W) is not the boast of a privately angry man. It is instead a programmatic statement from a poet of anger,[23] a very different creature indeed, and it can be found amusingly repeated by another professional, the seventeenth-century Englishman Joseph Hall, who wrote, 'The Satyre should be like the Porcupine / That shoots sharpe qwils out in each angry line' (*Virgidemiarum*, Sat.3.1-2).[24] With his hedgehog, Archilochus announces that his verse is meant to wound, but that it will do so with an Aesopic justice and also with an Aesopic consciousness that its singer shares in the common bestiality of all.

The animal tale was in fact one of Archilochus' favourite weapons when he wished to be abusive, for by the mere choice of the form he could announce that his anger was exemplary. The beast fable was exotic, being an import from Asia Minor,[25] and it was also anachronistic, since it had been invented long ago by people who needed to laugh at creatures more miserable than themselves. Such stories were cruel survival aids that taught men to be proud that they were not animals, while they laughed at themselves because the difference was so slight, and in their primary form they were subversive of all morality since they admired nothing beyond raw success.[26] When they were repeated among more fortunate peoples, certain ethical suggestions sometimes crept into these harsh Near Eastern tales, but as far as one can tell there is still very little of ordinary morality in the fable poems of Archilochus. Instead, the original tendency towards vilification of the entire human race is caught in a very elegant metrical arrangement, and the result is a curious mode in which the singer, his own passion artfully disguised or dissipated, elicits a joyous and almost abstract scorn from his audience.

The fable was a mannerly though vulgar means of attack, for by telling an old beast tale (or what pretended to be one) the poet necessarily muted all emotion and assumed the sardonic calm of the raconteur. He announced, in effect, that his song was an artifact, not a vehicle for personal rage, and Archilochus at these times liked to employ a special two-line stanza whose mixed iambic and dactylic elements reflected his own mixture of insult and narrative.[27] Balance and contrivance were the outstanding characteristics of this epode form, and evidently the same characteristics marked the poems as wholes, for the fables were developed according to proclaimed programmes, and they were introduced by prefaces that stamped them as pieces of dispassionate wit. One begins with a challenge that is positively good-humoured in its confident superiority (172W): . . .

> Father Lycambes, what was this plan of yours?
>   Your wits were sound; who's
> fuddled them? You're going to be
>   a joke around this town!

The next formal element seems to have been a passage in which the poet described himself as a terrible adversary, but with obvious self-irony. 'Why did you want to provoke a garrulous poet like me, one who's always ready to make more iambics?' is Lucian's parody of one such transitional phrase (*Pseudol.* 1).[28] After this the victim's 'crime' might be specified, perhaps with lines like, 'You went back on your oath and betrayed table and salt', though these words (173W) have an unwonted earnestness about them. Finally the fable would be given its official introduction, much as the mythic example is officially proposed in the victory ode,[29] though these stories were far from splendid (174W): . . .

> People tell the tale, you know,
> of how the eagle and the fox
> went into partnership . . .

In another fragment, the announcement of the fable stands at the beginning of the song, where it mingles with a challenge built on the victim's name (185W): . . .

> I'll tell you a story, Kerykides,
>   but you won't like my message much . . .
> The ape was sent in banishment by his
>   companion beasts, once, and went alone
> into the wilderness and there the cunning fox
>   pursued, because he had a clever plan.

The stories that followed these introductions can only be guessed at. Even their length is problematical, though apparently the tale told in the song addressed to Lycambes stretched out for about thirty lines (172-181W, if all these fragments do in fact belong together). One thing, however, is certain, and that is that these fables, again like the

mythic examples of epinician, were dramatic in form and could contain passages of direct speech.[30] A fragment from the Lycambes song preserves the voice of the fox, whose friend the eagle has stolen his cubs and destroyed them (177W). . . .

> 'O Zeus, Father Zeus, yours is heaven's rule!
>   You supervise the deeds of men,
> their crimes and villainies; you care as well
>   about the beasts, and whether they are rough
> or just . . .'

'Come to my aid now, for I have been wronged' is the obvious burden of the fox's prayer, and in the story his call was answered, for the eagle soon set fire to his own nest with a bit of stolen altar meat. The eaglets fell from their flaming bed and were eaten by the fox in a compensatory feast (179, 180W).[31]

But how did a fable like this one function as abuse? Presumably the audience recognised the poet in this fox, and the target Lycambes in this punished bird, but as far as one can tell from the poem's remains, the Lycambes-eagle was never actually slandered. Instead he seems to have flown off at the end, childless but still swift and free (181.10-11W). Lycambes was thus warned that if he enriched his own household by raiding those of his friends he would eventually harm himself, but this is hardly damaging to his reputation, nor would it have provoked scorn on the part of the listener. Further, since according to the ancient explanation the actual Lycambes did not take anything from Archilochus but offended in the opposite way, by refusing to give, the story seems to be no more apt than it is devastating.[32] If we use the ancient gossip and press hard for meaning, the tale can be made to yield a slightly stronger paraphrase, since it may be saying that, just as Lycambes took the fiancée of Archilochus, so Archilochus will in return devour (i.e. slander) the child of Lycambes, who happens to be that same fiancée. Even in these terms, however, the fable does no more than repeat the opening threat of the song, while it postpones the very defamation that it promises.

Instead of conveying anger, the fable in this case deflects anger from a song that in itself attaches no shame to its victim, and the only possible conclusion is that direct personal abuse was never a part of the poet's true purpose here. He seems rather to be engaged in creating a double fable, wherein a typical poet and a typical Lycambes reduplicate the typical fox and eagle, and where the listener is asked to scorn, not a particular man, but a general trait that may even be one of his own. Probably the real aim of the song was achieved through its satire of humanity, for this is the impulse most evident in the animal prayer that was cited above.[33] As a suppliant, the Archilochus-fox shows an obvious touch of Xenophanes' later scepticism as he calls upon a god who is concerned about beasts exactly as the gods of Homer and Hesiod were about men, and yet it is not the gods who suffer *meiōsis* here. The poet-fox, in spite of his grief, employs the rules of rhetoric and, proceeding Aristotle-fashion, he divides all of creation into its human and its bestial species, allowing to each a double set of characteristics. Beasts, it seems, may behave either with violence or justice, while men's deeds likewise fall into one or the other of two classes—the Villainous or the Unlawful!

The fable that was addressed to Kerykides (perhaps a punning name since it means 'herald's son') concerned the fox and the ape (185W), and if its contents were like those of Aesop's tale of the same pair (Chambry 31) it must have been a bit more insulting than the Lycambes fable was. The later story, at any rate, tells of an ambitious ape who had attempted to rule over the other animals but had been rejected by them. The fox went to him in his exile and promised to reinstate him,[34] but he was a creature of wily plans and he did just the opposite. He played upon the greed of the ape, got him into a trap, and displayed him to the others in a posture that showed him to peculiar disadvantage, calling out, 'And you thought you were somebody, with a bare ass like that!' (187W). Perhaps Kerykides was a striving power-seeker, perhaps he was a private enemy (or friend) lampooned with a charge of effeminacy, but in either case one notable fact remains the same. The fable does not itself make a genuine attack upon him, but instead it depicts the poet in the act of attack, describing a blame-maker who does not devour this time but instead denudes the object of his scorn.

Animal fables paradoxically allowed the poet to maintain a tone of cool superiority even as he descended to the bestial level assigned to his victim; it was as if he said, 'In crudeness too I can outdo you!' They also gave his abuse a mark of conscious and traditional artistry that set it apart from mere ephemeral rage. The fable, however, was not the only instrument for achieving these ends, and in two fragments we find Archilochus using the wise-man's gnomic manner so as to get exactly the same effects of coolness, irony, and generality. In an iambic trimeter that starts out like an old saw, the poet says (25W): . . .

> Man's nature is [a various thing;]
> each takes his pleasure in his different way.
> . . . Melesander, for example, loves a cock
> just as Phalonius, the bumpkin [likes a bit of ass.]
> No minor prophet tells you this
> but I, [endowed with Zeus' sacred gift . . .]
> so well-renowned a seer
> even old Eurymas couldn't fault me.

Exactly what Phalonius prefers to the *sathē* favoured by Melesander is not clear (the translation follows a suggestion of West's), but his choice is obviously indecent, for the trick of these lines lies in their substitution of a list of sexual practices for the list of vocations or values usually proposed by poets in the priamel.[35] The time-honoured pattern, 'One man chooses wealth, another power, but I . . .' as a rule produced a final term of elevated importance—courage, health or beauty—but this priamel seems to be an Aristophanic joke. After the singer's overblown self-validation—probably a jibe at the praise-poet's habitual boast of inspiration—a last term will be produced and, though it

may swerve from the sexual realm, we can guess that it will be triumphantly base.[36] The singer's favourite pleasure will surpass those of Melesander and Phalonius, but it cannot, after such a start as this, offer them any solemn correction. The blame that attaches to them is only incidental, anyway, for the central purpose here seems to be to ridicule a pompous way of thinking. In effect what the poet apparently says is that those laudable values so often discovered by singers are not in fact the ones that shape men's lives. Man's nature *is* everywhere the same in that it is everywhere absurd and obscene, and this is why all stand in need of the poetry of blame.

Four iambic lines survive from another poem that likewise parodied the priamel. Aristotle says that the poet here put his lines into the mouth of a fictitious person, a carpenter called Charon, because he did not want to take their excesses upon himself, but we do not know what the imaginary situation was, why the poet made his speaker an artisan, or how the sequence came to an end. All we have is a voice that mimics a common man in order to say (19W): . . .

> 'Gyges' gold[37] is no affair of mine—
> I don't want it, and I don't envy gods
> their deeds, or dream of tyrants' thrones:
> that's further than I look . . .'

Wealth, eternal life, and worldly powers are all rejected for a final object which is what the speaker emphatically *does* care for. We have no clue as to what this ultimate value was; it may have been public or private, political or erotic, decent or obscene. Possibly this 'carpenter' announced with rude exactitude just what he and his tools would like to do to an enemy whom the audience could easily identify, but however that may be two things at least are sure. One is that the fourth term was extremely shocking, since otherwise the mask of Charon need not have been assumed. And the second is that the mask was in no way an actual disguise, but was instead an announcement of intention. By speaking as Charon, Archilochus said to his audience: This is the kind of song that one pretends to disown!

There was a second song that followed the same convention, according to Aristotle (*Rhet.* 1418b28) and likewise put its blame into the mouth of another. This time a fairly elaborate fiction was set up and the remaining fragment shows that the singer's formal distance from his target was actually established thrice over: by impersonation, by irony, and by the employment of a showy figure of speech. The imaginary situation is extremely obscure, but seemingly a father is speaking about a daughter whose hand is being sought in marriage,[38] though she is either ugly or lewd. In his astonishment he addresses her suitor with these sarcastic words (122W): . . .

> 'Nothing is too odd or wonderful,
> nothing is beyond belief since Father Zeus
> made night from noon, hid away the sun
> and laid a shrinking fear on men.

> From that time all things were possible
> and so no man should marvel if
> the forest beasts remove to dolphins'
> salty fields, finding roaring waves
> a sweeter home than land, while fishes plunge
> high up on wooded mountain slopes.'

'Nothing is too odd', he seems about to conclude, 'and yet this is indeed a wonder—a man who wants a girl like mine!'

One's heart goes out to the creature whose own father is made to scorn her—whose wedding can only be explained as a reversal of all of nature's laws—and yet the arresting thing about these lines is their freedom from explicit calumny. Perhaps there was a direct attack in some other part of the song, but here at least the famous Archilochean poison is entirely contained within a fastidious form of ridicule. As the song descends from misplaced planets[39] to misplaced beasts, and then with exquisite bathos lights upon the man who intends to misplace himself in this young person's bed, no further syllable is needed, for the girl has been beautifully rendered hideous.[40]

In the song of the ugly girl, the direct speech that embellished the fables appears with a new function, for here, instead of merely supporting a narrative, it is itself the substance of the song. In this particular case we don't know whether or not the suitor also spoke, exciting the old man's answer, but there are other Archilochean songs in which two-way exchanges do certainly occur. In recognising these it would be pleasant to hail Archilochus as the first writer of non-epic dialogue, were it not for the fact that the ubiquitous question-and-answer rhyme of children's games existed in early Greece[41] and was common enough in Sappho's time to be exploited in her song for two players, the bride and her maidenhood (114V).[42] There are in truth conversational songs in most folk repertoires, and so Archilochus must not be thought of as an inventor because he sometimes gave his songs this shape. He was, however, as far as one can tell, the first to expand the simple challenge and response ditty into a discrete scene[43] something like those of his later imitator, Theocritus.[44]

In the true game songs no words are uttered outside the direct speeches, but in Archilochus' archaic idylls the singer employs epic formulae to mark a change of speaker ('So he spoke. I answered . . .'), and one such poem displays a narrative close. The Hellenistic imitations suggest that there were sometimes brief introductions as well, either in the third person or in the poet's first person, with perhaps an address to a friend.[45] (Something of the sort can be seen at the opening of a banquet anecdote that is offered to Glaucus for his amusement, 48W). The expository frame was evidently minimal, however, leaving the body of the poem to voices that were still typical—not to the eagle and the fox, now, but to human creatures who were generalised by a very formal mode.

No Archilochean dialogue poem survives in full, but two long papyrus fragments represent the mode, one in trimeters and the other an epode. In the trimeter song only the

last speech can be read, but nevertheless it is clear that a small but complete scene is being played, one in which an action (that of persuasion) is depicted not in narrative but in dramatic form. The purpose of the song is not, however, simple entertainment, for three familiar elements mark it as an exercise in the art of blame: an Aesopic touch, an extended figure of speech, and a plain statement of injurious intent. A man and a woman have been set in conversation, and the woman has just ceased speaking when the song becomes legible (23W):[46] . . .

> I answered her:
> 'Madame, do not let this vulgar calumny
> distress you. Pleasure is my care
> so make your heart propitious . . .
> Did you think I'd sunk to such a state
> of wretchedness—did I seem so cowardly?
> I'm not that kind, nor were my ancestors!
> This I understand—how to love my love
> and how to hate my enemy and do him harm,
> for I'm an Ant—*that* tale at least is true!
> This city that you now explore
> men have never sacked; you have taken it
> by storm and you shall have its fame.
> Rule it now, as tyrant of the place;
> be envied by that multitude of men!'

Because of the disappearance of the poem's opening, the fictional situation is painfully opaque. The speaker's simplest assertion seems to be that a city is open to the woman's rule because it has not fallen to others, but this fairly plain statement is preceded by a balancing but seemingly irrelevant claim of personal innocence, and the two passages are joined (or divided) by an exclamation about an ant![47] The sequence is so bizarre that it has inspired at least a half-dozen different reconstructions of the inner drama that is here proposed, some of them quite elaborate. Certain scholars, struggling with a conviction that city-sacking is not a proper pastime for a woman (and also with the fact that the adjective 'envied' in the final line shows a masculine form),[48] have supposed that actually there was a cast of three, so that the present speaker may turn from his female companion to a male soldier or regent in the course of his remarks. Others suggest a conversation between two men in which our speaker is reporting to his masculine friend yet *another* conversation which he had at another time with a woman. Still others have insisted that the speaker's companion is not the mistress that she seems to be[49] but instead a female potentate from the Near East,[50] the wife of a friend named Ant,[51] or a male acquaintance whose predilections cause him to be called 'Madame' in derision.[52] Those who do not wish to face this wealth of suggestion prudently set both the fiction and the fragment aside and call them both 'baffling'.[53]

Baffling it certainly is, but there are nevertheless two important observations to be made. First, these lines contain, not an attack but its counterpart, a complete speech of defence made in response to slanders that have probably been recounted by the previous speaker. And secondly, since this defence ends the poem and cannot be amended or contradicted, its final reassurance must fix the emotion which is the abiding achievement of the song. With this speech the speaker refutes his enemies and wins a verbal victory, and so his triumph under attack, mixed with that warmth of heart that he asks the lady for, is what is left behind when the song is done. This one speech is preserved in full; it is short and it was successful, which means that every one of its elements must have had a clear and vital significance, both as poetic matter and as persuasive rhetoric. Its two parts—its argument from character and its assertion about the city—must therefore be closely bound together in the service of the single end of refutation. In short, these fourteen lines must contain within themselves the calumny that they would resist, and consequently it should be possible to elicit from them the substance of the attack that provides the imaginary occasion for the song.

The first point in the defence is pleasure or well-being, and this suggests that the defamatory rumour had somehow denied the speaker's interest in, or power to provide, joy and satisfaction. 'On the contrary', he insists, 'that is all I care about.' His enemies' denial of his hedonism would, if believed, trouble the woman and cause her to harden her heart towards her friend, but under the influence of his opposite assertion she is to become warm and gracious. She too is therefore interested in pleasure.

The next point is that whatever the speaker was accused of is something that one might be brought to if one were wretched, or cowardly, or of a certain 'sort'. In dealing with these suggestions, the speaker is at first realistic—'I was never that hard up'—and then proud—'I'm not that sort, nor is anyone in my family'.[54] As further evidence that he is not the kind who would behave as charged, he claims to be one who (like the abusive poet) deals in sincere and appropriate hatred and love. The slander is false because he knows how to pleasure his friends and give real pain to his enemies.

Once he has established himself as a man of just emotions, the speaker turns to a city which he says is open to the woman's rule. The evil gossip evidently reported that it had been sacked and was therefore worthless, but this he simply denies. The woman is its single conqueror, and yet he offers it to her as if it were his own, marking his proprietary sense with a touch of complacency. It has never fallen, but many have coveted it and when she takes possession she will be envied by a multitude of men. Under the influence of the evil report, the woman has evidently refused the city as unworthy of her, but with his reassurance she will change her mind and accept it, for the song ends with a prospective vision of her happy tyranny in the unspoiled stronghold where her friend will place her.

The two sections of the song thus in effect duplicate each other, for in each of them the woman is persuaded to receive something of value that the speaker has to give: first pleasure and then dominion. These two offerings have both been smirched by a single slander, then cleared by a single defence, as the speaker's claim to justice in his loves and hatreds worked a simultaneous enhancement on them both. In a passage as short as this, such perfect parallelism necessarily brings the two parts of the speech into conflation as the woman is begged to make her heart receptive to delight and then straightaway begged again to receive the rule of an envied place. Delight and rule overlap and mingle in their close similarity, and in consequence the lover is heard to urge just one action to which, like a psalmist, he has given two consecutive descriptions. 'Oh take pleasure in your friend, exercise power over your town' is the pattern of his plea, and when it is recognised the song loses its incoherence. It is plain that the city the lady is to rule is identical with the friend—no political community but her lover's body—and that the pleasure she is asked to take is identical with a power that is not military but erotic.[55]

Once the metaphor of the city is recognised, the nature of the rejected slander becomes apparent. The rumour that disturbed the woman and made her ungracious asserted that this man who would be her lover, being poor and a coward, interested in money rather than pleasure, and unable to discriminate between friend and enemy, has allowed his 'city' to be sacked. His enemies have been saying, in other words, that he has sold himself, their accusation being not unlike that of Archilochus himself when he says elsewhere, of female prostitutes, that their sexual parts are 'places of no pleasure' because they work for hire (263W). Presumably he has been slandered as one who served men (it would be difficult for a man to sell himself in any other way, where women had no money and no freedom) and this suits the standard *topos* of abuse for effeminacy. Archilochus had made that charge against Melesander, though with tongue in cheek, in the Eurymas song, and again with friendly derision in the line 'Sing Glaucus of the sculptured curl' (117W).[56] He had given it the ruder form of the ape fable as well, if the point there had to do with shaving the body, and later antiquity knew songs of his aimed at a certain flute-player whom the poet presented (by means of the epithet 'blower of horns') as a kind of eponymous hero of male homosexuality (270W).[57] When the occasion arose, Archilochus was perfectly ready to lay a charge of perversion upon an enemy, but in the present case he has chosen another stance and has pretended to repulse such an attack, as if he himself were the victim of calumny.[58]

Such indirection suggests that this song was meant for friends, not enemies—that it was a piece of that childish banquet raillery that Hermes' original singing had ordained. Its riddling dialogue supposes an initiated audience that knows the history, or pseudo-history, of this and many another battle of abuse. The song has more than this to offer, however, and its larger meanings likewise address a group of companions to whom the poet presents, not an enemy for scorn, but himself, for approbation. In the fiction a lover, attacked as a male whore, persuades his mistress to reject the slanders of his enemies and receive him; in the speaker's metaphor, a city rumoured to have been sacked persuades its conqueror to take it as unspoiled. The little drama is consistent and complete, and yet there is obviously another level to the poet's intentions, for the speaker is portrayed not just as a lover but also as an artist in blame. 'I am an ant!' he announces in a moment of high rhetoric, and this homely insect, standing alone and unexpected at the beginning of line 16, almost destroys the dramatic illusion. The ant doesn't suit a plea to a disdainful mistress, and yet he has obviously been carefully chosen, since he brings into the defence a true *logos* that will outweigh the lying *phatis* of the speaker's enemies.[59] People were wont to say, 'There's wrath, even in an ant' (schol. Ar. *Birds* 82), and when they did they referred to a fable in which Ant bit a bird-catcher who was about to entrap his friend Dove (Aesop, Chambry 242). The doughty little ant thus provides an illustrative commentary upon the words that have just been uttered ('I understand how to love and hate . . .') and in addition, by specifying the harm done to enemies as a bite, the work of his mouth, the insect turns the speaker's boast into a motto for the profession of blame.

The ant of this poem thus joins the cicada, the fox and the hedgehog as one more animal figure for the poet of abuse, and with his bite (and his ability to love) he is perhaps the most telling of the four. He proves that the male speaker here is a version of Archilochus, and he likewise proves that, to the fable's announcement, 'I am dreadful when I attack others', this song now adds the complementary claim, 'When others attack *me*, I am impervious'. On this level, the blame-poet, slandered as having been for sale, persuades his audience to listen to him as the very best of his kind, indeed a prince of blame. Nevertheless, because his service is to Momus, his own claims must be deflated and deprived of any tendency towards pomposity, and here again the ant is useful to him. The ant has allowed the lover to refute the charge that he sold his love, while he let the poet deny that his hate was for sale; he has in addition allowed the singer-speaker to threaten his slanderers with retaliation, and yet no one can deny (and the singer least of all) that when this poet-ant is set beside his other self, the lover-city, the resulting disproportion is desperately ridiculous. Because of the ant, the man who views himself as an acropolis faces his conquering mistress on the field of eros, where no one should suffer *meiōsis*, as an insect of the smallest sort.

Archilochus thus uses his two metaphors to laugh at himself more artfully than ever his enemies could, and in so doing he refutes other more serious charges that might have been brought against his profession of calumny. The woman is mere *staffage*, a mouth-piece for slander which likewise becomes incidental as the poet promises his fellow citizens that they will be gratified by his unbought anger, just as the lady will be by his unbought love. He fully understands (*epistamai*, 14) how to honour and how to scorn because he has none of the self-righteousness or hypocrisy that might have turned his biting blame into spite or jealousy, and in demonstration of this fact he sets his own ant to attack his own citadel. Both of them in consequence suffer from absurdity, for Archilochus is here prac-

tising the self-satire that is for the abusive singer what self-praise is for the maker of epinician odes—a proof of the infallible precision of his song.

Notes

1. Cf. *AP* 7.69, where Archilochus is said to have used 'fierce iambics brought to birth by a tongue of bitter gall'. Callim. fr. 380Pf. has him mix the bitterness of dog's bile with the sharpness of a wasp's sting to make the poison of his tongue.

2. Students of rhetoric were urged not to neglect their study of Archilochus, that they too might know how to treat enemies (Menander, *Rhet. epideict.* ii 393 (p. 122 Russell and Wilson) = Lasserre test. 35; cf. Hermogenes, 319R).

3. Swift, with the same antipathy, makes the critic the offspring of Hybris and Momus, in *The Tale of the Tub*.

4. R. Foerster, 'Die Verleumdung des Apelles in der Renaissance', *Jahrb. der König. pr. Kunstsammlungen* (1887) traces the Apelles story from Pliny to Alberti's *Trattato della Pittura* of 1435. However, the Veronese at the National Gallery in London shows that the renaissance notion of Momus was not confined to this incident, since it included the erotic blame of jealousy.

5. Compare the role of Mummu in the Enuma Elish (Tablet 1), the god who counsels Apsu to destroy the noisy lesser gods (A. Heidel, *The Babylonian Genesis,* Chicago 1942, 19). . . .

6. Athena, Poseidon and Zeus have a contest to see who can make the best thing and Momus is their judge. Of Athena's house he says, 'Why hasn't it wheels?' of Poseidon's bull, 'Why aren't its horns under its eyes?' and of Zeus' man, 'Why doesn't his chest open, that his thoughts may be evident?'

7. *Stobaei Hermetica Exc.* 23.44-6 (Scott, Oxford 1924); cf. Ferguson, *Hermetica* iv 455-61 and Eustathius 1574-.16; see R. Reitzenstein, 'Die Göttin Psyche', *SB Heidelberg,* PhH K1. 8 (1917) 10. Abh., 76ff. The argument is that man, unfettered, is prone to excessive *spoudē* and wants to explore the secrets of the gods and even to storm the heavens . . . . Earlier expressions of the dangers of *spoudē* are found in Solon 13; cf. Soph. fr.257. . . . This stoic scene between Momus and a divine friend of man may have as its source the lost Sophoclean satyr-play called *Momus* (frr. 419-24 Radt).

8. At *h.Herm.* 54-5 Hermes invents the lyre and at once begins to sing mocking taunts . . . as boys do at feasts.

9. For obscenity in the Athenian Thesmophoria, Apollod. 1.5.1; in the Demeter cult at Syracuse, Diod. 5.4.6; at Pellene, Paus. 8.27.9; and in the cult of Damia and Auxesia at Aegina, Hdt. 5.83. Aristotle, *Pol.* 7.1336b17 testifies to scurrilous abuse called *tōthasmos* as part of the cult practice of his own

time. Nilsson believed he could distinguish a divergence in primitive Greek practice, by which phallic reference became appropriate to fertility magic, while gestures and symbols relative to female parts were used to ward off evil spirits (*Gesch. der gr. Rel.* I³, Munich 1967, 118f). In general, see H. Fluck, *Scurrile Riten in gr. Kulten* (Diss. Freiburg 1931).

10. At *Od.*2.86, just, true and inspired reproaches are meant to fasten blame upon those who have behaved shamefully, but the poetry of attack more usually employed the childishness and exaggeration that Cato copied. . . . On praise and blame in epic contexts see G. Nagy, *The Best of the Achaeans,* 222-42; in general, see M. Detienne, *Les Maîtres de la Vérité* (Paris 1967) 21ff.

11. The bee of praise fed on *aretē* (*P.P.*10.53) but the momus-bee avoids the honey-lady of Semonides (7.83) and so by implication feeds on rottenness, being the opposite of the normal insect. . . .

12. Menander (*Rhet. epideict.* ii 3 93, 9f. (p. 122 Russell and Wilson) = LB test. 35). . . .

13. Compare the distinctions made by Dio of Prusa (33; I.300.9ff. Arn.). . . . Cf. Plato, *Laws* 11.935 where poets are not to make a man laughable. In that it made its object worse than he was to start with, blame had an obvious connection with the battlefield insult that was meant to make an opponent weak, cowardly, ignoble and womanish; see E. Vermeule, *Aspects of Death,* 101ff.

14. The idea of the *pharmakos* is explicit in the abusive songs of Hipponax; see 5-10W.

15. Archil. 14W. This fragment is usually interpreted as a defiance, on the part of the singer, announcing his own superiority to mere public opinion, but the commentator's explanation . . . shows that he had in mind the particular, painful, poet-formed scorn of professional abuse. He could, of course, be proclaiming his imperviousness to attacks from rival calumniators, but it is at least equally likely that he is here boasting of his own power, as a poet of abuse, to make any man's life miserable.

16. Simonides reads Scopas a lesson . . . (37/542.33 *PMG*); note also Bacchylides 13 (12) 199ff., where *mōmos* is ready to attack all of men's deeds, but is defeated by an *alatheia* that seems to be identified with sung praise. The ambiguity and innuendo of abuse no doubt contributed to its classification as the reverse of truth. . . . Pindar recognised blame as valuable in certain circumstances—when it justly attached itself to excess (*I.* 2.20-1) and when it followed upon a betrayal of honour (*O.*10. 7ff.). Once he even imagined the scattering of blame upon sinners as part of his own responsibility (*N.* 8. 37-9), and once also he demonstrated the effectiveness of potential blame in ensuring virtuous action, for at *P.* 1.82 he counselled himself to work in the way that would minimise surfeit and consequently would minimise blame. At other times, however, he found a mutually exclusive opposition between praise and blame (e.g. *N.* 7. 61-3; fr. 181S).

17. At *P.* 2. 56, . . . Pindar may be playing upon Archilochus' boast that a fight was to him better than a drink (125W), but he doubtless also has in mind the general ancient association made among the concepts of stomach, idleness, parasitism and lies. . . .

18. Pindar in fact pays Archilochus the compliment of imitation, for though he suggests (with his reference to the ape) that animal fables are low, he nevertheless, towards the end of his ode, poses himself as a wolf beside the fox of blame. His word for foxes . . . is the one that Babrius later used, and for his choice of the wolf as his own beast, compare Babrius 53, where the wolf plays Hades to the fox's Sisyphus. Archilochus identified himself as a fox at 174W and 185W, and the later popularity of the notion is reflected at Pl. *Rep.* 365c: . . . (of those who would be sly).

19. *P. P.* 2.73-4. . . . This phrase effects the song's return to the subject of calumny. One of the Archilochean epodes concerned an ape (185-7W) who was excessively eager for power, and this Pindar's audience would remember. Nevertheless, the present ape is probably meant more generally, as a figure for lowness, indecency and the imitation of one's betters.

20. Freedom is the claim of the Archilochus that Lucian pictured; he sings like a cicada, because it is his nature and because he is full of words . . . (*Pseudol.* 1).

21. To appreciate the essential nobility of Pindar's abuse, one has only to compare Sir Car Scrope, abusing Rochester for the same sort of satiric activities:

Sit swelling in thy hole, like a vext toad
And full of pox and malice spit abroad . . .

22. Sir George Etherege, in *The Man of Mode or Sir Fopling Flutter* made his hero (Rochester thinly disguised) say, 'Next to coming to a good understanding with a new mistress, I love a quarrel with an old one'. . . .

23. A programmatic statement of a different sort occurs at 134W, where 'It is not honourable to scold the dead', read positively, yields 'It is an honourable thing to scold the living'.

24. Ed. A. Davenport (Liverpool 1949) 83.

25. For the derivation of the fable from Ionia, see Morten Nojgaard, *La fable antique* I (Copenhagen 1964) 150 and the bibliography cited there. For the larger Near Eastern background, see W. G. Lambert, *Babylonian Wisdom Literature* (Oxford 1960), 217f. which reports an eighth-century Assyrian tablet with anecdotes containing animal speakers (cited by M. West, 'Near Eastern materials in Hellenistic and Roman literature', *HSCP* 73, 1969, 113ff.).

26. Cf. Nojgaard, op. cit., 517: 'un raisonnement qui sape de l'intérieur les bases de la morale de la société officielle.'

27. On the development of these epodic metres, see L. E. Rossi, 'Asynarteta', *Arethusa* 9 (1976), 207ff.

28. Compare Odysseus at *Od.* 9.494. . . .

29. Compare another offering, addressed ostensibly at least to a friend (168W):

'Charilaus, son of Erasmonides,
    I'm going to tell
a funny tale, O best of friends
    —one that you'll like to hear.'

Cf. also Pl. *Gorgias* 523A . . . (introducing a mythic example). F. R. Adrados, 'Nouveaux fragments d'Archiloque', *Rev. de Phil.* 30 (1956) 30f. discusses the formulaic nature of phrases . . . (174W).

30. This use of direct speech within the narrative (not just for the triumphant quip or résumé at the end) is unlike the usual Aesopic form, and may have influenced the later Babrius; see Nojgaard, op. cit., 451.

31. The development of events in the tale of the fox and the eagle can be reconstructed from the Aesopic fable (1 Hausrath and Perry = 3 Chambry); there is full bibliography at West *Studies,* p. 132, note 4.

32. K. Latte, 'Zeitgeschichtliches . . .' *Hermes* 92 (1964) 387, note 2, concluded that the fable of the fox and the eagle could not belong to a song attacking Lycambes: 'Die fable wäre schlecht gewählt, da Lykambes dem Archilochos nichts geraubt, sondern nur etwas nicht gegeben hatte.' He noted that the papyrus versions show no traces of Lycambes' name and that it was in fact Diehl who attached the fable fragments to the lines addressed to Lycambes.

33. Prayers offered by animals also occur in a Sumerian proverb and a Babylonian tale (Ebeling 22.1.14), both cited by Nojgaard, op. cit., 452. . . .

34. The formula 'two beasts, having become friends . . .' is typically Aesopic, as is also this praxis, by which whatever the fable-world finds anomalous is expelled; see Nojgaard, op. cit., p. 452. . . .

35. The interpretation of this song is obviously highly conjectural, but it was known in antiquity as a parody of the *topos* familiar from *Od.*14.228 . . . and E. *Oeneus* (fr. 560N²), to which examples the long sequence beginning at Solon 3.39, Pindar. *O.*1.113 and E.*Ba.*905ff. are the most obvious additions. See the discussion of the priamel, pp. 281ff. below.

36. K. Latte, op. cit., 387, restored . . . at the beginning of line 6 and in line 7. . . . He paraphrased the resulting poem as being something like the Strasburg curse (Hipp. 115W), a reproach to a faithless friend: 'Was selbst Eurymas nicht fertig gebracht hatte, das hat ein Zwischenträger oder irgendwelche Umstände erreicht. Zeus hat den Bund gestiftet, weil der Eid bei ihm bekräftigt hat. So erscheint der Bruch des

Vertrauens als Vergehen gegen den Gott.' What this would have to do with the opening of the song is not clear. West, *Studies,* 122, recognised Archilochus' essential statement as, 'There's no accounting for tastes', but supposed that the singer went on to describe his own father's love for a slave girl (though elsewhere he doubts the reality of Enipo)! He would . . . read, 'but I, whose father Zeus established as noble and good in social terms'. It is obvious, however, that the strong emphasis upon 'I' in line 5 is not meant to be thrown away on someone else; this 'I' is going now to speak about himself, not his father or his friend, and he is probably going to specify his own favourite pleasure as that of slandering. This, at any rate, is the strong suggestion of the heavily emphasised name 'Eurymas'; in Homer (*Od.*9.509) Eurymas was the ur-mantic, the father of all prophecy, but Pherecydes reported him as a master of blame, one who tried to stir up trouble between the Dioscuri with his slanders (fr.164 Jac = FGH³; see Latte, *Gnomon* 27, 1955, 493). . . .

37. A late Roman metrician, Juba, reported a poem about Gyges composed by Archilochus but this is the only mention of him in the surviving fragments; see O. Crusius *RE* sv 'Archilochus', 489.

38. The scholiast at Ar. *Rhet.* 1418b28 attempts to explain the fictional situation of this song in various ways. According to one of his theories the father is answering someone who has said that his girl is evil and ugly by saying, 'Considering that anything can happen, what is surprising about my having an ugly daughter?' According to another theory, the father speaks to an impoverished suitor, encouraging him to hope, either for money or for the girl. Since the abuse, according to Aristotle, ought to be in the mouth of this 'disguised' speaker, the first of these theories is discredited, and since it ought to be as excessive as possible, the second seems very unlikely.

39. The eclipse referred to is generally thought to be that of 648 BC; see F. Jacoby, 'The date of Archilochus', *CQ* 35 (1941) 97ff.

40. It has been frequently asserted that this father is Lycambes, this daughter Neobule, as if no other father and daughter existed in Paros or Thasos; F. Lasserre, 'Le fr.74', *MH* 4 (1947) 5ff. believed them to be the father and sister of Archilochus! The appearance of the name Archenaktides in line 10 does nothing either to support or to destroy either identification, though Treu (op. cit., p. 223) is convinced that this unknown must be the rival to whom Neobule was given. For a contrary argument, see S. Luria, 'Zu Archilochos', *Philolog.* 105 (1961) 183.

41. For Greek songs of play . . . (Athen. 14.629E = 19B) and the Tortoise (Pollux 9.125, Eust. 1914 = 21 B); see the discussion of T. B. L. Webster, *The Greek Chorus* (London 1970) pp. 60-1). For elegiac dialogue, note Theognis, 577-8, and see West, *Studies,* 17-18. In Egypt and the Near East there was a genre

of poetic debate that produced exchanges between Winter and Summer, Olive and Laurel, Stomach and Head, which seem to have influenced the Aesopian debates; see M. West, 'Near Eastern materials in Hellenistic and Roman literature', *HSCP* 73 (1969) 119 note 21. Compare also the Babylonian satiric dialogue between master and slave reported by Lambert, *Babylonian Wisdom Literature,* 139ff.

42. Another example is the song for the voices of Sappho and Alcaeus that survives in the Sapphic corpus (137V); cf. S.102V and Alc. 10V. Alcman 107 *PMG* apparently represents an exchange for bride and groom: see T. Nissen, 'Zu Alkman frgm, 95D', *Philol.* 91 (1936-7) 470ff. At Hipp. 25W a man and woman exchange curses; cf. Hipp. 92W, which seems to be an anecdote with direct speech reported. West would classify Archil. 33W as a dialogue song, too, but there is no proof that the voice of the daughter of Lycambes was there presented directly.

43. Sappho used almost the same structure in her fr. 94; see below, pp. 290ff.

44. Compare especially Theocritus 27. Their Hellenistic imitations have caused some scholars to doubt the authenticity of the Archilochean dialogues; see Gelzer and Theiler, 'Ein wiedergefundenes Archilochos-Gedicht?' *Poetica* (1974) 490.

45. Cf. Theoc. 6, 8, 13, 18, 20, 23 for third person; Theoc. 2, 11, [21] for first person; Theoc. 6, 11, 13, [21] for address to friend; the exx. of Theoc. 11, 13 and [21] suggest that these songs could also begin with a gnome, to which the dialogue was appended as a demonstration.

46. In spite of language, metre and a typical piece of abusive self-identification, the Archilochean authorship of these lines has been doubted; see C. Gallavotti, 'P.Oxy.2310', *Philol.*119 (1975) 153-62. K. Latte (*Gnomon* 27, 1955, 494) reported a single song that continued through 24W (as did LB and Treu) and resumed the situation as follows: someone has gone on a pirate expedition to Crete and has brought back a treasure, but the city to which he has returned is full of rumours against him, perhaps because the treasure originally belonged to it; a woman has also been brought back from Crete.

47. Line 16 has been read in various ways. . . . Like Theognis at 347 . . . , the speaker is making an animal boast with this single nominative; see R. D. Murray, 'Theognis 341-50', *TAPA* 96 (1965) 277ff.

48. It should be noted that Euripides twice uses this same masculine adjective for a woman, at *Androm.*5 and *Med.*1035.

49. F. Adrados, 'Sobre algunos papiros de Arquiloco', *PP* (1965) 38-41, identified the woman as the poet's mistress, as did also F. Lasserre, 'Un nouveau poème d'Archiloque', *MH* 13 (1956) 226-35, who went on to assert that she is Neobule. According to the interpretation here proposed, she is imagined as the speaker's mistress.

50. Treu, *Arch.* 181ff. proposed a woman ruler who would take an actual city but is afraid she will be criticised; to her the speaker says (like Clytemnestra to Agamemnon): 'Go ahead. You will never be envied if you do not dare'. See also J. C. Kamerbeek, 'Archilochea', *Mnem.* 14 (1961) 9ff., and Kirkwood, *EGM,* 29.

51. See W. Peek and O. Lendle, *Sammelband Politeia und ResPublica,* Palingenesia iv (Wiesbaden 1969) 47, and G. Schiassi, 'De novo Archilocho', *RFIC* 85 (1957) 151-66.

52. See D. L. Page, 'Various conjectures', *PCPS* 187 (1961) 68-9 and K. Latte, loc. cit.

53. Kirkwood, *EGM,* 29: 'Little more than chaos has issued from the study of this baffling fragment.' . . .

54. Cf. West, *Studies* 120: 'So you take me for a low person and mistake the true class of the man before you and of his background . . .'

55. Adrados, op. cit., suggested that the city might be an erotic metaphor, but he was covered with scorn by Kamerbeek, op. cit., 11: 'Archiloque n'est pas un poète de basse époque. Il est libidineux, obscène même à ses heures, mais jamais poète ne fût plus exempt de mièvrerie et d'autre part de gongorisme que lui.' Kamerbeek of course did not know of the garden = pubis, gateway = vagina figures that appear in the Cologne fragment, but he might have remembered the woman = field of 188W, the fig-tree = prostitute of 331W, or the hose and pail of 46W. To such a list West would add woman = mountain landscape, in 190W, but nothing makes this expression necessarily metaphorical or if metaphorical necessarily sexual in its application. (W. pretends that unless it is metaphorical the line would express an un-archaic delight in mountain-walking, but there is no explicit delight here, and the line at any rate may have come from a speech in a fable). The idea that the city represents the body of the speaker is accepted by West (*Studies,* 119), who adduces Theognis 951 (=1278c) as a parallel metaphorical conquest, though there the city is not erotic. . . .

56. Unless the more correct translation is 'Sing Glaucus the horn-moulder', in which case the line is explicitly obscene; cf. 239W and 240W, both comic words apparently applied to effeminate hair styles, and 217W and 265W, references to bodies shaved to make them more elegant (like the unfortunate ape of the fable for Kerykides).

57. According to ancient report, Archilochus attacked homosexuals as 'the lowest of the low', (294W) and Julian (*epist.* 80, 97, 19B-C) claimed to know an Archilochean work in which Laius was abused, presumably on the score of Chrysippus (see Wilamowitz, *Kl. Schr.* iv 363). In addition, two Renaissance forgeries (327 and 328W) prove that such attacks were later thought to be typical of his work; see G. Tarditi, 'Due carmi giambici di uno ps. Archiloco',

RCCM 3 (1961) 311-16 and A. Garzya, 'Varia Phil. IV.5', *BPEC* 9 (1961) 44-5. Compare also Hipp. 148W.

58. Note that there is an attack upon himself by an imaginary enemy among Solon's tetrameters (33W), and that the song of Alcaeus contained in P.Oxy. 2506, fr. 77, likewise seems to be a poetic rebuttal of a piece of slander; see below, p. 169.

59. West, *Studies,* 119, supposes that this *logos* is contrasted with another *logos* of the speaker's which the woman has rejected as untrustworthy. For *logos* in the sense of a proverb, cf. Aesch. fr. 235N; *Sept.* 225; Pindar *O.*7.21 (of the received version of the Tlepolemos tradition) and *P.*1.35 (of the proverb about fair beginnings and fair ends). . . .

FURTHER READING

Criticism

Bowra, C. M. "Origins and Beginnings." In *Early Greek Elegists,* pp. 3-36. New York, Barnes & Noble, 1960.

    Discusses the flute-song origins of the elegy and the significance of Archilochus's use of Homeric language in his verses concerning war.

Bremer, J. M., *et al.* "Archilochus." In *Some Recently Found Greek Poems: Text and Commentary,* pp. 1-69. Leiden, The Netherlands: E. J. Brill, 1987.

    Text and full commentary for three recently discovered fragments of poems by Archilochus.

Davison, J. A. "Archilochus Fr. 2 Diehl [7 LB]." In *From Archilochus to Pindar: Papers on Greek Literature of the Archaic Period,* pp. 141-45. London: Macmillan, 1968.

    Offers a new interpretation of a famous couplet composed by Archilochus.

Fraenkel, Eduard. "Epistle XIX." In *Horace,* pp. 339-50. Oxford: Clarendon Press, 1957.

    Examines a statement by Horace that Sappho had used, but changed, the metrical form of Archilochus.

Marcovich, Miroslav. "Archilochus Fr. 122 West (Ap. Stob. 4.46.10)." *Rheinisches Museum für Philologie* 121 (1978): 101-02.

    Advances alternate readings of specific Greek words in this corrupted fragment.

Rankin, H. D. *Archilochus of Paros.* Park Ridge, N.J.: Noyes Press, 1977, 142p.

    Provides an overview on Archilochus's surviving fragments and explores his politics and his use of sexuality in his poems. An excerpt from this book is found above.

Geoffrey of Monmouth
c. 1100-c. 1155

(Also known as Gaufridus Monemutensis and Geoffrey Arthur) English historian, prose writer, and poet.

INTRODUCTION

Geoffrey is best known for his *Historia Regum Britanniae* (c. 1138; *The History of the Kings of Britain*), a formal and cohesive mythical history of Britain and ninety-nine of its rulers spanning approximately eighteen hundred years, and ending with the death of Cadwallader in 689. Geoffrey ventured further into the past (all the way to the fall of Troy) than had yet been attempted by any other British historian, sometimes drawing on mere fragments of documents and greatly expanding upon the writings of such earlier chroniclers as Gildas, Nennius, and Bede. Britons had fared badly compared to Romans in previous accounts; Geoffrey turned this situation upside-down, giving his people heretofore undreamt of pride in their past. *The History of the Kings of Britain* was one of the most popular books of the Middle Ages, generally accepted as true, revered by the public, and translated into Anglo-Norman, French, and English. For centuries many writers freely borrowed from or paraphrased it, and it inspired many works—notably *Sir Gawain and the Green Knight*—and led to the spread of Arthurian material throughout the continent. William Shakespeare based his *King Lear* (1606) on the story of Leir as told by Geoffrey, and John Milton used his story of Sabrina in *Comus* in 1637. Through the inspired invention of Merlin, Geoffrey immortalized the legends of King Arthur; and many of the other characters he launched—Guinevere and Gawain, Bedivere and Modred, and Kay and Morgan le Fay—have earned him recognition as a superlative creator of imaginative literature.

BIOGRAPHICAL INFORMATION

Geoffrey was born around 1100, possibly in Monmouth in what is now Wales. As is the case with many matters concerning Geoffrey, there is considerable controversy regarding whether he was indeed born in Monmouth or whether he merely resided there, and whether he attended a Benedictine priory located in the area. Some biographers contend that he was of mixed Norman- or Breton-Welsh origin. Based on signatures he placed as witness to six different charters connected with religious houses at or near Oxford, it is possible to construct a likely history of Geoffrey's early career. He probably was a secular canon at the College of Saint George's, which he had joined in 1129 and where he may have taught (although Oxford was not yet a university). The provost was Archdeacon Walter, from whom Geoffrey claimed to have received both written and verbal sources for *The History of the Kings of Britain*. Another of Geoffrey's works, the *Prophetie Merlini* (before 1135; *The Prophecies of Merlin*), was dedicated to Robert de Chesney, who served as canon of Saint George's. Geoffrey's last known work, the *Vita Merlini* (before 1151; *Life of Merlin*) is also believed to have been a product of his Oxford period. Geoffrey was made bishop-elect of Saint Asaph's in 1151 and ordained priest at Westminster in February 1152; eight days later he was consecrated bishop at Lambeth, although he apparently never visited his see. He probably resided in London during the last four years of his life. He reportedly died in 1155, in Llandaff, Wales, according to some accounts.

MAJOR WORKS

The Prophecies of Merlin was eventually published as book seven of *The History of the Kings of Britain*. Geoffrey claimed to have translated the work "from the British tongue into Latin," a claim he would repeat for the larger work. Merlin was conflated from the "marvelous boy" depicted in Ambrosius of Nennius's *Historia Britonum* and the wild man Myrddin of Welsh legend. His prophecies result from a seizure induced by his explanation of the red (British) and white (Saxon) dragons beneath Vortigern's collapsing tower. Merlin offers a panoramic history of Britain through a dense series of political prophecies, grounded in animal symbolism, which serve to ratify the subsequent contents of *The History*. The popularity of *The Prophecies of Merlin* is attested to by the survival of nearly eighty independent manuscripts and its inclusion in almost a dozen others. Geoffrey claimed he translated *The History of the Kings of Britain* into Latin from a "most ancient book in the British tongue," but scholars routinely dismiss this claim as an attempt to lend authority to the work. Instead they credit Geoffrey as an author of a virtuosic imagination and narrative skill. The book which Geoffrey claimed he copied is not mentioned by any other historian and thus widely believed to have been invented by him. It begins with Brutus, either grandson or great-grandson to Priam of Troy, as he gathers up colonies of Trojans with whom he founds Britain. Geoffrey includes lists of kings punctuated by tales of love, war, and daring adventures. In addition to Brutus, other main characters include Belinus, said to have captured and sacked Rome, and Arthur, the greatest British king. Much of the book is devoted to Arthur's history and the recounting of his victories in battle. Before Geoffrey, Arthur was a minor hero known only in limited areas. Geoffrey completely reworked the character, lending him a vitality which endures to the present. *The History of the Kings of Britain* survives in well over two hundred Latin manuscripts, separable into versions known as the Vulgate and the Variant. Which of the versions came first has long been a matter of great debate among Geoffrey scholars, as has whether Wace's *Roman de Brut* (1155) inspired the Variant, or whether the Variant inspired Wace's work. Neil Wright criticizes previous efforts to determine the answers to such questions as inadequate exercises. He has published a definitive comparison of the versions and concludes that the Vulgate was written first, that the Variant is a redaction of the Vulgate made by an unknown contemporary of Geoffrey's, and that Wace used the Variant in *Roman de Brut*. *Life of Merlin*, a hexameter poem, appears to have been intended for a learned audience familiar with Geoffrey's scholarly and hagiographic sources. It is founded on Celtic, postclassical, and what Basil Clarke in his edition of the poem calls exotic sources. Merlin takes to the Caledonian forest out of grief at the death of his companions in battle. Wooed out of the woods by music, he reveals his queen's adultery and, giving his wife permission to remarry, moves once again to the forest. Returning with deer as a wedding present for her, he kills her new husband on a whim. Taken captive, he spouts prophecies, which are ratified as true, and then returns to the forest, where his sister Ganieda at his request builds him a dwelling with a large staff of astronomers. He again prophesies, this time of Britain's fate. The work survives in only one complete manuscript, and as extracts in various others. It was not published until 1830.

CRITICAL RECEPTION

Although *The History of the Kings of Britain* was denigrated by a few historians as a fake even in Geoffrey's time, it was accepted as genuine by almost everyone else. The work was tremendously successful from the beginning, satisfying a need of the people of Britain for a heroic national history heretofore undocumented. Although today little of the work is believed to be historically accurate, Geoffrey's reputation has continued to grow. Scholars are quick to explain that the practice of historians has changed radically over the centuries and that aspects now deemed unacceptable were standard in the Middle Ages; students of medieval historical writing find Geoffrey to be a fascinating and invaluable source for study. Robert W. Hanning, for example, contends that Geoffrey's work helped popularize secular accounts of history, breaking from religious historiographical notions best exemplified in the works of Bede. Hanning points out what he calls a remarkable feature of *The History*: "a narrative technique whereby [Geoffrey] addresses himself to the crucial and concrete problem of personal fulfillment within the march of history." Christopher Brooke views Geoffrey as a parodist who enjoys poking fun at laws and the church. Valerie I. J. Flint agrees and contends that Geoffrey's purpose in writing was not chiefly to express his literary talents but, through parody and ridicule, "to diminish the authority"

with which certain exponents of literature spoke, and "to call into question the position held and hoped for in twelfth-century Anglo-Norman society by literate and celibate canons regular and monks." Because of the recognition of the masterly quality of *The History*, relatively little attention has been paid to *Life of Merlin*, which Brooke calls "a strange and horrifying fairy-story." Until very recent times critically authoritative texts of Geoffrey's works were not available, but now that that situation has been corrected, scholars are demonstrating a keen interest in Geoffrey's accomplishments.

PRINCIPAL WORKS

Prophetie Merlini [*The Prophecies of Merlin*] (fiction) before 1135

Historia Regum Britanniae [*The History of the Kings of Britain*] (historical fiction) Vulgate version circa 1138, Variant version before 1155

Vita Merlini [*Life of Merlin*] (poetry) before 1151

Principal English Translations

The Vita Merlini (edited and translated by John Jay Parry) 1925

The Historia Regum Britanniae of Geoffrey of Monmouth (Vulgate version; edited by Acton Griscom and R. E. Jones) 1929

Geoffrey of Monmouth: Historia Regum Britanniae: A Variant Version (Variant version; edited by Jacob Hammer) 1951

Life of Merlin (edited by Basil Clarke) 1973

The Historia Regum Britannie of Geoffrey of Monmouth. Vol. 1 (Vulgate version; edited by Neil Wright) 1985

The Historia Regum Britannie of Geoffrey of Monmouth: The First Variant Version; A Critical Edition. Vol. 2 (Variant version; edited by Neil Wright) 1988

CRITICISM

Robert A. Caldwell (essay date 1963)

SOURCE: "Geoffrey Monmouth, Prince of Liars," *The North Dakota Quarterly*, Vol. 31, Nos. 1 & 2, Winter-Spring, 1963, pp. 46-51.

[*In the following essay, Caldwell argues that the original work from which the Variant version of* The History of the Kings of Britain *stemmed was compiled by Archdeacon Walter and was not in the British language, but in Latin.*]

Probably in 1135 or 1136 A.D. Geoffrey of Monmouth, or Geoffrey Arthur as he sometimes called himself, a member of the house of Augustinian canons at Osney near Oxford, released to the world his *Historia Regum Brittaniae,* or *The History of the Kings of Britain.* That his work created something of a sensation and was immediately a success seems certain, though not all the reviews, if there had been book reviews in those days, would have been favorable.

Thus, a sober, serious chronicler William of Newburg, writing a *History of the English* about 1196, doubted the authenticity of Geoffrey of Monmouth's work, largely because the Latin and continental historians made no mention of Geoffrey's principal figure, King Arthur. William charged that Geoffrey made Arthur's little finger larger than Alexander the Great's back, and that he perpetuated the British fable that Arthur, after he was mortally wounded, was taken to Avalon where he still lived. William expressed himself as not certain whether Geoffrey did this through fear of the British or for love of lying.

And Gerald of Wales, who wrote a history of the English conquest of Ireland, was even more subtly devastating. In his *Itinerary of Wales,* written about 1191, Gerald tells about a certain Meilerius, who lived in the neighborhood of Caerlon, near Monmouth, and was a familiar of evil spirits. Through the aid of these, Meilerius could predict the future, distinguish truth from falsehood, and even though he was himself illiterate, could pick out false passages in a book. When this Meilerius,

> Was being abused beyond measure by foul spirits . . . the Gospel of John was placed on his breast; the spirits vanished completely, at once flying away like birds. When the Gospel was later removed and *The History of the Kings of Britain* by Geoffrey Arthur was substituted for it, by way of experiment, they settled down again, not only on his entire body, but also on the book itself, for a longer time than they were accustomed to, in greater numbers, and more loathsomely.

But in fairness to Geoffrey, and in candor toward Gerald, it should be added that elsewhere in his works Gerald of Wales cites Geoffrey of Monmouth's *History* as an authoritative work and as interesting reading.

About the life of Geoffrey of Monmouth, we know little, and that little does almost nothing to explain his work. We have the text of the *History* itself, though not everything about it seems as certain as it did until about twelve years ago. It is now known, for example, that there were at least three distinct versions of it, instead of the one previously known to scholars, and which I call the Vulgate. In 1951 Jacob Hammer published a *Variant Version* from four manuscripts. And a second variant, found in some fourteen manuscripts, on which Hammer was working at the time of his death, is still unpublished. We know nothing about it except the fact of its existence. Hammer's study had probably gone far enough to justify the conclusion that the rest of the more than two hundred manuscripts contain essentially the Vulgate text.

Geoffrey's own account of his book is given in his Preface, where he says that while he was wondering why Gildas and Bede had nothing to say of the Kings of Britain before the Incarnation, or of King Arthur, or of his successors, a certain Walter, Archdeacon of Oxford, "a man learned not only in the art of eloquence, but in the histories of foreign lands," offered him a book. And this "certain most ancient book in the British language . . . set forth the doings of them all in due succession and order from Brute, the first king of the Britons, onward to Cadwallader, the son of Cadwallo, all told in stories of exceeding beauty." Geoffrey claims, then, simply to have translated this book.

That there ever was such a book in the British language, is so certainly to be doubted that Geoffrey's claim can be dismissed as pure camouflage. Whether or not Walter gave him a Latin book which he revised and embellished is a matter to which I shall return later. In the meantime, I shall refer to Geoffrey as the sole responsible author of the *History* that goes under his name.

Geoffrey certainly made use of the works of Gildas and Bede. He also made excellent use of the account of the founding of Britain, of Arthur's battles, of the wonders of Britain, and of other materials that he found in a *History of the Britains,* probably put together in its final form in the ninth century by a writer conventionally known as Nennius. He also made good use of the Old Testament, of Virgil's *Aeneid,* of Livy, of St. Jerome's *Epitome,* of Eusebius and the later continuations of the *Epitome,* as well as of many other Latin writers and historians, both classical and early medieval. He was extremely skillful at inventing characters and stories to account for well-known names of places, and he must have made large use of orally transmitted Welsh tradition, even folklore, though many eminent scholars would flatly deny this. The evidence is accumulating slowly and cannot be finally evaluated until we have a better text of the *Historia* than is now available.

But in spite of the fact that Geoffrey wove his *Historia* from a multitude of sources, so that there is scarcely a detail that cannot be traced to an earlier writer or paralleled from Welsh or Irish folklore and tradition, he creatively combined what he had borrowed. Certainly not as great a poet or creator as Chaucer or Shakespeare, he was a greater narrator of story than either. Indeed, the earliest known version of the story used by Shakespeare in *King Lear* is found in Geoffrey's *Historia,* from which Shakespeare got it by way of an Elizabethan translation.

But the high point of his work as a creator of story, the part of his *Historia* seized on by his contemporaries and of crucial importance to scholars today, is the story of King Arthur. It is an account in the manner of a chronicle rather than in the manner of the later romances.

Arthur's father was Uther Pendragon, whose name *Pendragon* signifies something like "chief leader in war" or "leader of battles," though it can also be interpreted as "chief dragon" or perhaps as "dragon head." His mother Igerna was at the time of his conception married to Gorlois of Cornwall, who was conveniently killed in battle the next morning so that Uther could marry the widow and make the future king at least quasi-legitimate. After Uther's death—Geoffrey does not say how long after—the assembled barons prevailed on Dubricius, archbishop of Caerlon, the City of Legions, to crown Arthur as king, and the glorious reign, rather certainly designed to give the Norman rulers of England a counter-weight to the prestige of Charlemagne, began.

Arthur's first task was to free the land of the Saxon armies, which after Uther's death had been doing as they pleased in Britain. With the aid of his nephew Hoel of Armorica, Arthur succeeded in this task, though not quickly or easily nor, it would seem, without the aid of the Virgin Mary, whom he invoked in his final victory over the Saxons at Mount Badon. It was in this battle that Geoffrey credits Arthur and his sword Caliburn with the death of four hundred and seventy men, whom he killed single handed.

After Mount Badon, Arthur turned to Scotland, the affairs of which he effectively settled, something none of his English successors would be able to do until as late as the eighteenth century. Then "he took unto him a wife born of a noble Roman family, Guenevere, who, brought up and nurtured in the household of Duke Cador, did surpass in beauty all the other dames of the island." Actually, as my teachers, Professors Cross and Nitze, amply demonstrated in their book *Lancelot and Guenevere,* Guenevere's ancestry is to be found not among the Romans but in Irish myth and legend, where her habit of being abducted by others than her husband was so well established that neither Geoffrey nor Arthur could well be expected to have broken it.

During the twelve years of peace that followed, we may, if we wish, imagine that the incidents told about in the Arthurian romances occurred—that Lancelot (who is never mentioned by Geoffrey) came to court, won the love of Guenevere, and rescued her from the abductor Meleagrance; that Arthur and his Round Table were asked to preside over the ordeal of Iseult, accused of adultery with Tristan; and that the quest of the Holy Graal was undertaken and achieved. But Geoffrey says nothing of these things, not even of the Round Table, which is first mentioned in a French translation of Geoffrey's work completed in 1155.

After twelve years of peace, during which the same French translation says that the marvels of Britain occurred, Arthur conquered Norway and the Roman province of France. In this campaign, he was first joined by his nephew Gawain, who had been reared and knighted by Pope Sulpicius. The complete subjugation of France, however, required nine years, after which Arthur returned home to celebrate his victories. At this time, Geoffrey says, Britain was:

> Exalted unto so high a pitch of dignity as that it did surpass all the other kingdoms in plenty of riches, in luxury of adornment, and in the courteous wit of them that dwelt therein. Whatsoever knight of the land was renowned for his prowess did wear his clothes and his arms all of one same color. And the dames, no less witty, would apparel them in like manner in a single color, nor would they deign to have the love of none save he had thrice approved him in the wars. Wherefore at that time did dames wax chaste and knights the nobler for their love.

These details are motifs of the courtly Arthurian romances, all of which are later in date than Geoffrey's work. Whether the romances are borrowed from Geoffrey or he borrowed from earlier romances now lost is something Arthurian scholars argue about hotly and inconclusively.

Ordered by Rome to give up France, which he had taken wrongfully, and to pay the tribute which Britain had owed since Julius Caesar's conquest of the island, Arthur defied the Emperor and sailed to the Continent with a large army. After a series of skirmishes, he defeated the Romans in a pitched battle where Kai, Bedevere and Gawain distinguished themselves. Arthur was prevented by winter from following up his victory, but laid plans for marching on Rome itself the next Spring.

This proposed expedition had to be called off, however, because news came that Modred, Arthur's nephew, had usurped both Guenevere and the throne of Britain. At Richborough Arthur defeated Modred; but Gawain was killed. Arthur then pursued Modred to Winchester, and then finally caught up with him at the river Camel in Cornwall. In the great battle there Arthur, Modred and nearly all their followers were killed. The throne passed to Arthur's kinsman, Constantine, in "the year of the Incarnation of our Lord five hundred and forty two."

The rest of the *Historia* can be passed over briefly. After alternate successes and failures, the Britons (now become the *Welsh,* a word from the Old English *wielisc* meaning "foreign") were finally warned by the voice of an angel to desist from trying to regain Britain. More than decimated by pestilence, they withdrew to Wales, and their history closed. "Howbeit, their kings who from that time have succeeded in Wales," says Geoffrey of Monmouth. "I hand over in the matter of writing to Karadoc of Llancarvon, my contemporary, as I do those of the Saxons unto William of Malmesbury and Henry of Huntingdon, whom I bid be silent as to the Kings of the Britons, seeing that they have not that book in the British speech which Walter, Archdeacon of Oxford, did convey hither out of Brittany, the which being truly issued in honour of the aforesaid princes, I have on this wise been at the pains of translating into the Latin speech."

The question of the historicity of Arthur is outside the scope of this paper. There is sound historical and archaeological reason for believing that at about the time Nennius and Geoffrey represent Arthur as winning his victories over the Saxons, some British leader inflicted on the Saxon invaders a defeat in the southwest from which it took them nearly half a century to recover. This question and that of

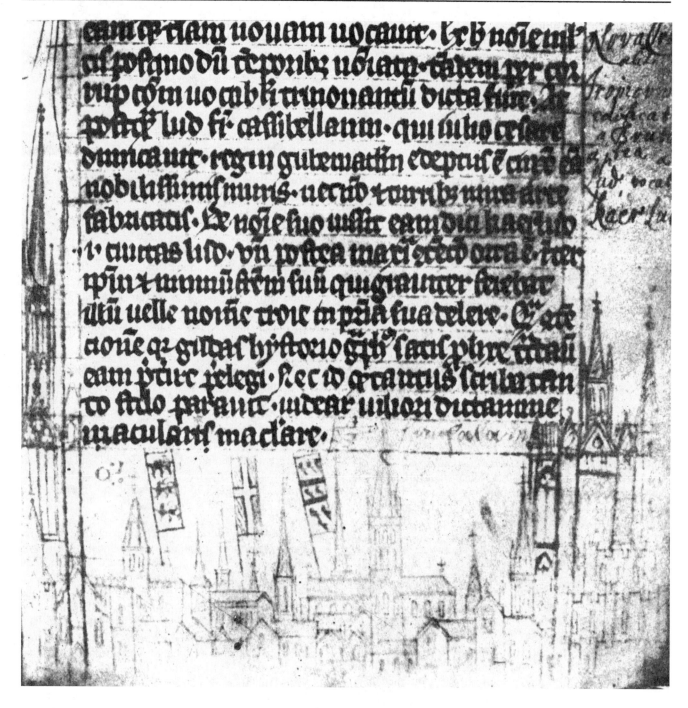

Page from an early 14th century manuscript of Geoffrey of Monmouth, with a contemporary pencil sketch of London.

the most ancient book in the British tongue which Geoffrey said he received from Walter of Oxford, are bound together. The answers to both questions depend on the solution of the textual problems. If we had a satisfactory edition of the *Historia,* in which the relations of the manuscripts and the history of the text were clearly laid out, we would be able to work out the history of composition and then arrive at some reasonably certain answers. Since we do not have such an edition, much of what follows can be only tentative and conjectural.

Hammer's edition of the *Variant* is for the most part accurate and dependable. Because he worked from a photostat without, apparently, examining the manuscript itself in its entirety, he made at least one slip in his description of the manuscript in Exeter Cathedral, but this does not affect his presentation of the text. Unfortunately, he followed in his edition a manuscript which combines the *Variant* and the *Vulgate,* with the result that it is extremely difficult to use his edition for the study of the *Variant* itself. The two modern editions of the *Vulgate,* that by Edmond Faral, published in the "Bibliothèque de l'École des Hautes Études" in Paris, and that by the Reverend Acton Griscom published in New York, appeared in the same year, 1929. They are usable and valuable up to a point, but neither is fully satisfactory for the simple reason that neither was based on a full enough study of the manuscripts. Neither makes all the necessary evidence available.

In the preface and the conclusion to the *Historia* Geoffrey says that Archdeacon Walter gave him a book, written in the British language, relating the deeds of the British kings. At the opening of Book XI, as he enters on the story of Modred's treachery, he again refers to this book, and also, it seems, to orally transmitted stories that he had heard from Walter. All that can at present be said of Walter is what Geoffrey says of him in the *Historia,* and that his name occurs, along with Geoffrey's, among the witnesses to certain legal documents. There may be more to be discovered, but the discoveries have not been made. As for the book in the British tongue, there is not the slightest reason for believing that any such book ever existed. There is no reference to it any place outside Geoffrey, and it is difficult to believe that no one else ever saw it or mentioned it, if it did exist. Geoffrey's reputation for veracity is not sufficiently good to justify our believing in the book's existence on his word alone. And it is altogether unlikely that such a book was written down; for the Welsh then used writing only for verse, and transmitted prose by word of mouth.

There may have been, however—and I am very much inclined to believe there was—a book in Latin. If there was, it can probably be identified. It would have to contain the same materials, put together in the same way, from the same sources, as the *Vulgate* text in which, as we have seen, Geoffrey names himself four times as author. If such a Latin book possibly existed, then scholarship should consider that possibility in the light of the available facts.

Many years ago, in his *Catalogue* of the romances in the Department of Manuscripts of the British Museum, H. L. D. Ward made the suggestion that Walter did give Geoffrey a book, but a compilation which Walter himself had put together, which for some reason he was not able to put in final form for publication. Geoffrey then took these materials, revised and polished them, and said that what he had been given was a book written in the British language. That was, of course, a lie; but it was swallowed, along with the other 'veracities' of Geoffrey's *Historia,* by nearly all English historians until well into the seventeenth century. And certainly it was no worse a lie to claim a British source that was actually in Latin than to claim a British source that never existed.

Here then I would suggest that the original from which the four manuscripts published by Hammer as the *Variant Version,* and to which I have referred, was the book that Walter gave to Geoffrey. I cannot, I admit freely, prove that it was, but the probability seems great.

In 1932 Professor John J. Parry at the University of Illinois called attention to a manuscript written by a Welsh antiquarian in the eighteenth century. In this manuscript were excerpts of a version of the *Historia Regum Brittaniae* obviously different from the *Vulgate* text hitherto known. Parry, who was at work on the Welsh translations of the *Historia* and editing one of them at the time, seems to have assumed without question that these excerpts were from a late recension or reworking of the *Vulgate.* He conjectured this version of the excerpts, if it were recovered in its entirety, would turn out to be closer than the *Vulgate* to the Welsh translations.

The excerpts, however, turned out to be from the *Variant Version* that I have mentioned, of which Hammer found four manuscripts, and which he published in 1951. And my own comparison of this *Variant* with the *Vulgate* and the Welsh versions available to me in translation did not reveal anything to confirm Parry's conjecture that the *Variant* lay between the Vulgate and the Welsh translations.

Hammer also considered the *Variant Version* to be a late recension of the *Vulgate,* but he felt called upon to say as well: "There is no doubt that the *Variant Version* often preserves Geoffrey's phraseology. The divergence, however, . . . is both qualitatively and quantitatively such as to rule out a hypothesis that we have here a recension from the pen of the author." Hammer did not argue this latter point, nor marshall detailed evidence to support it; but as the opinion of an extremely competent Latinist who had spent twenty-five years in study of the manuscripts of the *Historia* it commands respect, and in the light of my own comparison of the two versions, I am very much inclined to accept it.

It may be noted that the writer of the *Vulgate* refers to himself as Geoffrey of Monmouth four times—in his Preface, in a dedicatory epistle to **"The Prophecies of Merlin,"** in the story of Modred's treason as a disclaimer of responsibility, and in the ironic colophon leaving Arthur's successors to Karadoc of Llancarvon, William of Malmesbury and Henry of Huntingdon. These references found in all the manuscripts of the *Vulgate* that I have seen do not occur in the *Variant Version.*

There is, however, a brief colophon to the *Variant,* which, while omitting the *Vulgate*'s references to Karadoc of Llancarvon, William of Malmesbury and Henry of Huntingdon, does read: "I, Geoffrey Arthur of Monmouth, who undertook the translation of this history of the Britons from their language into ours, leave the writing of the acts and fortunes of the kings who succeeded from that time in Wales to my successors." Admitting that I would rather like to explain this colophon away, there are three points to make about it. First, the four manuscripts of the *Variant Version* are all late, and a colophon being a particularly vulnerable part of a text, this one might have been added to the *Variant* at some point in the transmission by a scribe familiar with the *Vulgate* text tradition. Second Geoffrey styles himself either Geoffrey of Monmouth as in the *Vulgate* or in a colophon to the *Vita Merlini* (*Life of Merlin*), or Geoffrey Arthur as witness to certain charters. Nowhere that I know of does he style himself Geoffrey Arthur of

Monmouth. Third there is a considerable body of references, which have never been seriously considered except possibly by Ward, to Walter of Oxford as the translator of the work from British to Latin. In some of the Welsh translations in fact the work is said to have been retranslated back from Latin into Welsh.

Within twenty years of the publication in 1135 or 1136 of Geoffrey's Latin *Historia,* there were at least two translations of it into French verse. One of these was made by a French poet Geoffrey Gaimar working in the northeast of England probably about the middle of the 1140's. No copies of his translation exist today, but in a later work which is preserved he speaks of his earlier work, and seems to say that he then had two versions of the *Historia* to translate from. At least he says that he had two copies. One, he says, came from Robert of Gloucester, to whom the *Vulgate* is dedicated in the earlier manuscripts. The other might well have been the *Variant.*

Gaimars' translation was probably lost because it was replaced by a more popular translation of a Norman writer of Caen named Wace. Wace was undoubtedly a smoother, more competent, more pleasing versifier. He made some additions to what he found in the *Historia,* most notably the first recorded reference to Arthur's round table. He tells us that he completed his translation in 1155, which would have been within no more than a year of Geoffrey of Monmouth's death.

In a paper published in *Speculum,* I showed that Wace used both the *Vulgate* and the *Variant* versions of the *Historia.* The evidence consisted in the fact that where the two versions differ Wace sometimes translated one and sometimes the other. Now we do not know how early in 1154 Geoffrey of Monmouth died, nor how early or late in 1155 Wace completed his translation. The maximum time between the two events was hardly enough, however, to allow for the production of both the *Variant Version* and Wace's translation in succession. Clearly the *Variant Version* must have been in existence during Geoffrey's lifetime.

It was obviously in order next to try to determine which of the two versions was the earlier. I attacked this problem in two papers, one read at the Fifth Congress of the International Arthurian Society, meeting in Bangor, Wales, in 1957, and the other at the Modern Language Association meeting in the same year in Madison, Wisconsin. In the papers, I concluded that the direction of revision must have been from the *Variant* to the *Vulgate.*

The evidence was of a kind that it would be tedious and pedantic to repeat. In general, it was more frequently and more easily possible to explain the divergences between the two versions as resulting from revision of the *Variant* into what appears in the *Vulgate* than the contrary. The *Variant* has more direct quotation from literary or historical sources, while in the *Vulgate* these quotations are either dropped completely or paraphrased. Contradictions of

known history and self-contradictions found in the *Variant* are often, though not always, covered over or removed in the *Vulgate.* The *Variant* is also much less rhetorical than the *Vulgate.* What appears in the *Variant* as a paraphrased summary of a speech is elaborated in the *Vulgate* into a fully developed speech itself, quoted as it was imagined to have been delivered. And in at least one major instance, confusion in the narrative, understandable in a first draft but not in a revision, is found in the *Variant* but is then cleared up in the *Vulgate.*

If the *Variant* was revised into the *Vulgate*; and if the *Variant* and the *Vulgate* were not written by the same man—and I am convinced with Hammer that they were not—then obviously the *Variant* was not written by Geoffrey of Monmouth, but was used by him in preparing the *Vulgate* which he certainly did write. If this is so, what is the *Variant*? And who was responsible for it? In the light of the available evidence, the most reasonable answer seems to be that Walter, Archdeacon of Oxford, put the *Variant* together. And having done this, he turned the work over to Geoffrey, for reasons we can only guess, to revise and polish and publish.

Robert W. Hanning (essay date 1966)

SOURCE: "Geoffrey of Monmouth's *Historia regum Britanniae*: Great Men on a Great Wheel," in *The Vision of History in Early Britain,* Columbia University Press, 1966, pp. 121-72.

[*In the following essay, Hanning discusses the impact of the Normans on the more secular attitude toward historical study in the twelfth century. He focuses on how Geoffrey demonstrated this new approach through his accounts of outstanding individuals and the cyclical nature of history.*]

The secular interpretation of British history brought to birth by at least one of the authors of the *Historia Brittonum* can be said only to have reached a promising youth in that work. Its potential remained unrealized for over three hundred years, until Geoffrey of Monmouth's *Historia regum Britanniae,* appearing suddenly in twelfth-century England, offered to its first, amazed readers a comprehensive and spectacular vision of the British past largely free of Christian assumptions.[1] The work's remarkable reception occupies a special place in the history of medieval literature: almost at once the story and the heroes of the rise and fall of Britain became matters of excitement and controversy, not only on the island itself, but throughout much of western Europe as well. Furthermore, the duration of Geoffrey's success was to equal its magnitude, for his account of British history exercised an enormous influence over historians and chroniclers for centuries to come.[2]

Geoffrey, who lived *ca.* 1100-1155, and spent most of his life as an Augustinian canon in Oxford,[3] must be considered a major literary figure of his day and of the entire medieval period. That he has not always been accorded such recognition is due not so much to his limited output—his only known work besides the *Historia* is the *Vita Merlini,* a poem of 1500 Latin hexameter verses on the legendary Welsh prophet-bard who also figures in *Historia regum Britanniae*[4]—as to the unfortunate treatment he has received at the hands of many critics through the centuries, beginning practically in his own day.[5] To his detractors, Geoffrey has always seemed a liar pure and simple, the unscrupulous fabricator of a legendary British past, and as such deserving of no serious consideration whatsoever. Happily, contemporary criticism has succeeded almost entirely in abdicating the office of censor with regard to Geoffrey;[6] he remains, however, often misjudged if not condemned, and as controversial as ever.

In this century, scholarly disputes over Geoffrey can generally be classified under one of two headings: the relationship of the *Historia regum Britanniae* to its sources, and Geoffrey's purpose in writing it. The first of these questions lies outside the scope of this study and need not detain us; suffice it to say that the eye of the storm is a passage at the beginning of the *Historia,* where Geoffrey claims that his account of Britain is a translation of an old British book ("britannici sermonis librum vetustissimum") given him by his friend, the archdeacon Walter.[7] Many and varied have been the attempts to deduce, discover, or defend the existence of Geoffrey's *vetustissimus liber,* or, as has been the case more recently, to delineate the nature and extent of the Welsh traditions, vouched for in works of Geoffrey's contemporaries, which were available to him.[8] While the search has unearthed much interesting material and prompted attractive conjecture, it must still be considered very much in progress, with the issue in doubt. Several scholars, preferring not to involve themselves in it, have simply dismissed the idea of Geoffrey's single source or coherent tradition, recognized the great originality of the *Historia,* and explained that its author was actually a romancer, an historical novelist, a shrewd propagandist for both the Welsh and the Normans, or the writer of a political tract.[9]

This brings us to the larger question of Geoffrey's purpose in writing the *Historia regum Britanniae.* I have already remarked that a gap of more than three centuries separates the *Historia Brittonum* and Geoffrey's *Historia,*[10] and that the latter takes up the secular strain of the former, systematically amplifying it to dominate the narrative exposition of the British past while reducing to a few scattered references the Christian, ecclesiastical view of history. Geoffrey's specific relationship to the earlier fall of Britain texts will shortly be considered in some detail; however, it is readily that a major change has taken place in the historical imagination of a writer who deliberately removes national history from its traditional context, the history of salvation.[11] The reasons for such a change in historical outlook—and historical writing—may forever be lost in the mists of time, but it is worth the attempt to reconstruct them, however tentatively. Accordingly, the main intention of this, the last chapter of the present study, is to anato-

mize Geoffrey's historiography, and thereby to lay bare his ultimate aim in reinterpreting the fall of Britain tradition at a point so distant in time from the events (be they true or fictitious) he is narrating.

As the latest, longest, and most celebrated early medieval treatment of the British past, *Historia regum Britanniae* has many obvious claims on our attention. Even more important than these attributes, however, is the fact that Geoffrey's *Historia* captures uniquely the spirit of a major evolution—one might almost say revolution—in historiography which occurred in twelfth-century England and Normandy, and which remains one of the most remarkable landmarks of a century rich in striking cultural and intellectual developments. The Anglo-Norman historians who reexamined and recounted the national pasts of the English and Norman peoples introduced into the tradition of Christian, early medieval historiography new methods, new interests, and new concepts; they approached the human condition, the national past, and divine providence in novel and sometimes startling ways. Without consciously wishing to break with the historical vision of the past centuries—indeed they shared a tremendous admiration for Bede the historian[12]—they modified, and in some respects undermined, that vision fundamentally, if not irrevocably. And what they did unconsciously, even perhaps unwillingly, in treating the recorded history of the Anglo-Norman national past, Geoffrey imitated, or rather parodied with considerable consciousness and purpose, working not with historical material but with legends and with his own fertile imagination, in filling out the great unrecorded gaps in the British past. In his work we have a valuable and absorbing document, a controlled and self-aware testimony to a momentous change in the early medieval historical imagination.

To understand Geoffrey's achievement we must therefore: (1) recapitulate, from a point of view slightly different from any taken so far, the early medieval Christian historiography which Geoffrey is rejecting; (2) outline briefly the new historiography which he parodies in *Historia regum Britanniae*;[13] and (3) examine his relationship to the Gildas tradition which, as we have seen, dominated the fall of Britain literature up to Geoffrey.

With regard first to the national histories of barbarian nations written in the centuries before Geoffrey:[14] the facet of this genre which has here been under scrutiny is its general tendency to treat barbarian history at least in part as ecclesiastical history. The extent to which a nation's heroic traditions and postimperial career were interpreted in terms of the history of salvation varied widely from writer to writer, but it is generally true that an early medieval historian who wished to make the past serve a moral purpose presented it in an identifiably Christian context. In so doing, he was reiterating the conviction, as old as historical writing, that the past is in its very nature instructive to the man who cares to profit from it. I have already mentioned the early appearance among classical historians of the exemplary view of history, and remarked that it was primarily a rhetorical device.[15] But rhetoric, the science of effective expression, must always express something. The oft-repeated dictum, therefore, that history provides us with examples to be imitated and others to be eschewed, and the presentation of history in order to support the dictum, are the rhetorical consequences of the conviction that history is moral.

How is history moral? Rhetoric cannot by itself answer that question; only ideology or belief can. History is moral, and historiography exemplary, in one way for a Stoic, in quite another for a Christian, in yet a third for a Marxist. To put it more concretely, the fact that Livy and Bede, in the prefaces to their histories, declare in practically identical words that history provides good and bad (or paradigmatic and cautionary) *exempla* in no way means that Livy and Bede share similar views on the meaning of history. Rather, the continuous use of such an exemplary formula[16] would seem to indicate that the tradition of historical rhetoric has protected historians from realizing fully how greatly and how distinctively their historical methods and writings have been colored by their ideologies. This should not surprise us; the dominant moral view of a period tends always to be taken for granted, and it is harder to put one's own bias—especially when it is held in common with most of one's contemporaries—in perspective than it is to distinguish the prejudices of the past.[17]

The early medieval Christian historian constantly revealed his moral commitment in his exemplary attitude toward history. Passages in national-ecclesiastical histories that we would call stylized or conventional were inserted specifically for their exemplary value.[18] It is largely these passages which I have analyzed in this study, showing that the ideological beliefs which control the form of the *exempla* were specifically Christian, and operated within the context of the history of salvation, as clarified by scriptural exegesis. The twelfth-century Anglo-Norman historians inherited and propagated the tradition of the exemplary value of history, but we should not automatically assume, as many critics have, that they preserved intact the Christian view of history and providence which has occupied us until now in this study. The rhetoric remained the same,[19] but its flowers now sprang from the rich soil of a new historical outlook. The providential view of history was subtly modified to allow a larger role for purely human causation, and to reflect a lively interest in psychological motivation; complementarily, divine providence was impersonalized to a certain extent, and even at times replaced by the concept of fortune's ruling the affairs of men. Traces of a cyclical view of history appeared, although situated within a larger framework that remained Christian. Most importantly, the exegetical parallel between personal and national levels of history grew markedly weaker, implying a conscious or unconscious revaluation on the part of the historian of the link between the history of salvation and national history. While these changes cannot here be studied in detail, they demand some attention if we are to understand the milieu from which Geoffrey of Monmouth's highly imaginative historiography sprang.

The twelfth century was a period of brisk historiographical revival within the boundaries of the Anglo-Norman empire established in 1066 by William, Duke of Normandy, and inherited after his death in 1087 by his descendants and successors, William Rufus (1087-1100) and Henry I (1100-1135).[20] The main figures of the "new" historiography were Eadmer, who was a monk of Anglo-Saxon origin and a follower of Anselm, archbishop of Canterbury, and who completed his *Historia novorum in Anglia* by 1115;[21] Ordericus Vitalis, an English-born monk of the monastery of St. Evroul in Normandy, where his *Historia ecclesiastica* was written in several recensions from some time after 1109 until 1141;[22] Henry, archdeacon of Huntingdon, whose *Historia Anglorum* was published in successive editions between 1129 and 1154;[23] and William of Malmesbury, a Benedictine monk whose *Gesta regum Anglorum* covered English history until 1125, and was brought up to date by a continuation, the *Historia novella,* in 1135 and 1140.[24] No brief consideration of the large and varied output of these historians can begin to do their work justice; however, some attempt to account for their near-simultaneous activity and to generalize about their historical vision or visions is worth making.

In considering the twelfth-century revival of literary interest in the past, we must locate historiography within a larger context of cultural expansion and renewed intellectual activity, the so-called "twelfth-century renaissance." In its early maturity, this period of European intellectual aggressiveness was marked by a great fascination with the political and literary achievements of the classical past.[25] Evidence of this fascination is especially apparent in the works of the Anglo-Norman historians, and takes a variety of forms: intoxication with the heroes and events of classical literature;[26] awe at the success of classical institutions, especially the political achievements of Rome;[27] and a willingness to apply to new narrative situations the traditional techniques of classical rhetoric.[28] In short, the routine early medieval dependence upon the legacy of Rome has given way in these histories to a fresh awareness of the extent of that legacy, and to an engaging, almost naive eagerness to effect a massive transfusion of classical blood into the veins of a vigorous and exciting, but still culturally anemic civilization.[29]

The factor which more than any other had impressed upon the civilization of the Anglo-Norman historians its peculiar form was the phenomenon of the Normans themselves. These last pagan, barbarian invaders of northern Europe had won control in the tenth century of the part of France which still bears their name; by the middle of the eleventh century their dukes had taken their place among the continent's most powerful rulers, and had established within their domains an ecclesiastical hierarchy and organization that rivaled the wealthiest and best organized of Europe.[30] In 1035, the large and tightly controlled duchy devolved upon William, the bastard son of Duke Robert I, who was to prove himself worthy of his inheritance. When Duke William, already an innovator within his ancestral domain,[31] decided to extend his power by claiming the English throne after the death of Edward the Confessor in January 1066, he embarked upon an undertaking which culminated in his coronation on Christmas day of that year as King of the English, and confirmed him as the greatest political and military figure of his day in Europe.

The remarkable career of the Normans, still fascinating today, enthralled contemporaries as well, and it is certainly the expansion of Norman power, and specifically the spectacle of the Anglo-Norman monarchy established by William, that prompted the rash of historical works now under consideration. William, Henry, and Orderic devote whole sections in their histories to a minute consideration of the reigns of the Anglo-Norman kings.[32] In so doing, they reveal basic assumptions of their views of history. First of all, as Christians, they feel that the phenomenal rise to splendor of the Normans, and especially of William, is a clear indication of God's providence.[33] In keeping with this judgment, they attempt to explain the Norman Conquest in terms reminiscent of those used by Gildas to interpret the ruin of Britain, i.e., as the work of God operating figurally in history to punish sinful men and nations.[34] (Henry even draws a parallel between the Saxon conquest of the Britons and the Norman conquest of the Saxons, an important point to which I shall return shortly.)[35] From one point of view, then, the Normans are God's chosen people—the latest heirs of Israel, and the successors in national-ecclesiastical history of Gregory's Franks, Paul's Langobards, and Bede's Saxons. But this is only one side of the story. From another point of view, one provided by classical history and rhetoric, the Normans are imperial repressors of English liberty.[36] The juxtaposition of this theme to the first creates a tension within the historiography of the Anglo-Norman historians, and reflects the coexistence in the minds of the writers of two mutually distinct views of the past, the legacies of two different moral and rhetorical traditions.

Nor do these two approaches exhaust the Anglo-Norman historians' complicated understanding of their immediate past. The Norman barons, a colorful and tempestuous lot, were continually at war with each other and with their feudal lords. The Anglo-Norman historians present the barons as men of tremendous ambition, bravery, and greed, who are also capable of great cruelty and treachery.[37] Their shortcomings and sins repeatedly result in social disturbance and misery for Normans and English, in the form of national disasters which the historians brand now as punishments inflicted by God, now as exemplary proof of the classical dictum that internal disorder ruins national greatness.[38]

The political world of the Anglo-Norman historians was therefore one of greater complexity than they could compress into one consistent historiographical vision or system. Although any age presents enormous complexities to its chroniclers, in this case the genuine uniqueness of the Norman experience and the divided interests of the Christian but antiquity-loving historians combined to render impossible a unified approach to the past. Nor was this am-

bivalence the result of conscious choice. In an intriguing and, I think, highly indicative passage of his ecclesiastical history, Orderic complains that in the past history has been full of miracles, examples of God's power among men, but that in this evil age such manifestations of divine intervention are hard if not impossible to find.[39] The historian here reveals, in effect, that despite his allegiance to the tradition of Christian ecclesiastical history (signified by the "old-fashioned" title and overt aim of his work),[40] his sense of the present no longer corresponds to the norms of that tradition.[41] Orderic claims literally to be looking about him for miracles; this procedure, I submit, is essentially foreign to the writers of early medieval ecclesiastical history or hagiography, who sought their miraculous material not in literal experience, but in the norms of the history of salvation (i.e., in the facts which gave real meaning to all history, but which were fully visible only in the revelation of holy scripture).[42]

In addition to political complexity and the coexistence of traditional Christian interpretations with revivals of classical values, there are still other noteworthy features of Anglo-Norman historiography in the twelfth century. Further common traits which strike the modern reader's eye are an interest in new, wider realms of human experience and possibilities (including extremes of behavior and ability), an attempt to give psychological insight into the lives and characters of important men, and an increased awareness of the role played by fortune in the lives of men and nations. The historians are constantly drawn beyond the boundaries of their homeland by events whose oddity or symbolic qualities fascinate them and demand inclusion in even a national history. William describes the occult arts practiced by Pope Sylvester II, and adds stories of visits by magicians to fabulous hidden worlds;[43] he is attracted by stories of men who returned from journeys to hell and told of their experiences;[44] he reports that in Normandy two women shared one body from the waist down, and uses the prodigy as an occasion to lament the union of England and Normandy, which has cost the English their liberty.[45] In addition, William and Henry both describe at length the exploits of the crusaders.[46]

Amid the welter of human activities and experiences, the figures of the Anglo-Norman kings rise like great beacons surveying the world of little men which lies about them. The historian is as sensitive to the ways in which William the Conqueror and his successors tower over their age and kingdom—ordering its life, bringing it misery or prosperity—as he is to the relentless movement of history, which, through fortune, ultimately rules the rulers themselves. In order to provide relief, as it were, from the self-imposed burden of explaining the stature of great leaders and the events which determine their fate, the Anglo-Norman historians appeal to the complexity of life as lived at a less exalted level, or long ago and far away. The introduction of anecdotes and extraneous matter into the histories resembles the opening of a safety valve in order to prevent the pressure of history from weighing too heavily on the life and destiny of the ordinary man;[47] for the individual is no longer the architect of his own salvation within a national context responsive to and dependent upon the aspirations of each Christian. The divergence of the history of kings and nations from the history of human experience as a continuing, self-justifying phenomenon marks a sharp break in the development of medieval historiography. Analogous in part to the contrast between Christian and classical interpretations of political and national history described above, this new distinction separates the work of the Anglo-Norman historians from the tradition of Christian historical writing, in which personal and national history run on parallel tracks under God's guidance and toward his chosen end.[48]

We must finally consider the attitude of the Anglo-Norman historians toward the monarchs who had controlled recent national history, and toward those forces which in turn had controlled the monarchs. I mentioned above that the lives of the Anglo-Norman kings occupied much of the attention of William, Henry, and Orderic. The historians consciously attempted to present balanced pictures of those great men which, while stressing their virtues, did not hide their vices.[49] The portraits are rich in detail, utilizing characteristic gestures, encounters, and acts, as well as describing circumstantially the physical and mental peculiarities of the monarchs.[50] In short, the Anglo-Norman kings are presented as individuals, not simply as royal types or ideal Christian monarchs. Unlike Bede's Oswald or Eusebius' Constantine, the man behind the office matters to the historian, who probes for precisely those characteristics which separate one man and one king from another, and which may therefore help to explain the character of each reign.

Although the Anglo-Norman kings and other great men of the kingdom emerge as individuals, they do not, however, exist beyond the control of external forces. Beside the Christian tradition of a divine providence still embraced by the historians, the new force of fortune comes into play—Dame Fortune who strikes down the mighty at the summit of their achievement.[51] Of course, blind fortune and Christian providence make strange bed-fellows; nowhere do we see more clearly the peculiar duality of this new historiography than in Orderic's description of the death of William the Conqueror in the seventh book of his *Historia ecclesiastica.*[52] The dying monarch, bedridden at Mantes, is seen justifying his reign and repenting for his sins at great length in a rhetorical, set speech. The Conqueror's words are, on the one hand, full of conventional piety;[53] on the other, they provide a political resumé of English and Norman history during the twenty-one years of his reign in England. The speech betrays William's (and Orderic's) vital and articulate sense of the Normans as a people:

> The Normans, when under the rule of a kind but firm master, are a most valiant people, excelling all others in the invincible courage with which they meet difficulties, and strive to conquer every enemy. But under other circumstances they rend in pieces and ruin each other. They are eager for rebellion, ripe for tumults, and ready for every sort of crime. They must therefore

be restrained by the strong hand of justice, and compelled to walk in the right way by the reins of discipline. But if they are allowed to take their own course without any yoke and like an untamed colt, they and their princes will be overwhelmed with poverty, shame, and confusion. I have learnt this by much experience. My nearest friends, my own kindred, who ought to have defended me at all hazards against the whole world, have formed conspiracies, and rebelling against me, nearly stripped me of the inheritance of my fathers.

The beleaguered greatness which was William's is communicated with noble intensity in this passage, as is the historian's response to a mighty and turbulent nation.

In confessing his sins, William reveals eloquently many extremes of human behavior such as fascinated the Anglo-Norman historians. "I was bred to arms from my childhood, and am stained with the rivers of blood I have shed. . . . I wrested [the crown of England] from the perjured king Harold in a desperate battle, with much effusion of human blood, and it was by slaughter and banishment of his adherents, that I have subjugated England to my rule. I have persecuted its native inhabitants beyond all reason. . . . These events inflamed me to the highest pitch of resentment, and I fell on the English of the northern counties like a raving lion." The great, strident voice booms on, alternately imploring and accusing.

Meanwhile, the king's sons are seen to react to their father's dying behavior in highly individual ways. William Rufus, promised the throne of England, rides away at once to secure the crown. Henry, to his chagrin given no land but only five thousand pounds of silver, "was equally prompt in securing the money allotted to him. He had it carefully weighed that there might be no deficiency, and, summoning his intimate friends in whom he could confide, sought a place of safety in which to deposit his treasure."

Finally the king expires, "suddenly and unexpectedly," throwing all the courtiers and retainers present into great confusion. All ride away to look after their own interests in the face of an anarchic interregnum, while "the inferior attendants, observing that their masters had disappeared, laid hands on the arms, the plate, the robes, the linen, and all the royal furniture, and leaving the corpse almost naked on the floor of the house hastened away."

Orderic then describes the funeral services, at which the bishop of Evreux eulogizes "William's having extended by his valour the bounds of the Norman dominion, and raised his people to a pitch of greatness surpassing the times of any of his predecessors." However, an old enemy of William steps forward dramatically to claim the land on which the church lies and in which William is to be buried. He must be bribed into agreeing to the burial; then, as the body is being placed into the stone sepulchre, its bowels burst and a terrible stench fills the church. "The priests therefore hurried the conclusion of the funeral service and retired as soon as possible, in great alarm, to their respective abodes." Orderic adds passionately,

A king once potent, and warlike, and the terror of the numberless inhabitants of many provinces, lay naked on the floor, deserted by those who owed him their birth, and those he had fed and enriched. He needed the money of a stranger for the cost of his funeral, and a coffin and bearers were provided, at the expense of an ordinary person, for him, who till then had been in the enjoyment of enormous wealth. He was carried to the church, amidst flaming houses, by trembling crowds, and a spot of freehold land was wanting for the grave of one whose princely sway had extended over so many cities, and towns, and villages. His corpulent stomach, fattened with so many delicacies, shamefully burst, to give a lesson, both to the prudent and the thoughtless, on what is the end of fleshly glory. Beholding the corruption of that foul corpse, men were taught to strive earnestly, by the rules of a salutary temperance, after better things than the delights of the flesh, which is dust, and must return to dust.

It is impossible not to be struck by the air of disillusionment, decay, and horror which repeatedly intrudes into the narrative of the Conqueror's death and burial. The ephemeral nature of worldly glory and the slenderness of the bonds between a ruler and his subjects fascinate the historian and are obviously associated in his mind with the insufficiency of human achievement in the face of malignant fortune. The lesson to be drawn from this is that all earthly triumph fades and sours. "His corpulent stomach, fattened with so many delicacies, shamefully burst, to give a lesson, both to the prudent and the thoughtless, on what is the end of fleshly glory."[54]

Having exposed so graphically the pessimistic, visionary strain of Anglo-Norman historiography, Orderic then hastens to remark on the need to "turn over the pages of the Old and New Testament, and take from thence numberless examples which will instruct you what to avoid and what to desire." In so doing, he reveals his desire to save his highly dramatic vision of the Conqueror's death for the Christian view of history, according to which he has merely been recounting "manifestations of God's providence at the duke's death." But the attempt is not convincing; the Christian theology of history accords ill with Orderic's morbid reflections on the fate of all human achievement. The purely human greatness of the central figure—his violence, his control over an unruly people, and their attainment under him of new heights of glory—impress us more than the historian's overtly Christian reflection on the deathbed and funeral scenes. Orderic is no Bede; his interest is clearly divided, and his narrative at this point vibrates with the tension between his human involvement and his Christian detachment.

Having arrived at a minimal appreciation of the twelfth-century Anglo-Norman historiographical achievement, its complexities and its internal tensions, we are now ready to examine the relationship to this achievement of Geoffrey of Monmouth's *Historia regum Britanniae.* Critical investigations have already demonstrated that the structure of the *Historia* is basically a copy of that of the histories of William and Henry; starting with smaller notices of events in the distant past, the narrative pace broadens as the "present" is reached (the reigns of William, William Rufus, and Henry I in the actual histories, the reign of Arthur in the legendary history), and is followed by a more disconnected, less circumstantial chronicle form (as in the post-Arthurian period of Geoffrey's work) as the historian adds later recensions to bring his work up to date.[55] The difference between Geoffrey and his structural "sources" lies in his independence of factual record, which enables him to integrate into his narrative greatly expanded key incidents whenever his artistic conscience dictates. The resultant effect—alternate sections of tersely recounted, quickly moving events and of thoroughly explored crises—has often been remarked as the chief artistic virtue of the *Historia regum Britanniae.*[56]

To what end, however, has Geoffrey carefully elaborated such a structure? The answer, I think, insofar as one can ever be given, is that he felt impelled to create a work in which the interests of the new historiography of his day could have free play—in which, that is, the innovations in thought and expression of the Anglo-Norman historical vision, isolated from the Christian traditions with which they clashed in the works of William, Henry, and Orderic, could regulate a complete and self-consistent narrative of the past. If this was Geoffrey's intention, then it may seem singularly odd that he should choose the history of Britain as his vehicle, for, as I have attempted to show, the Gildas tradition exerted all its weight on the side of a strictly Christian interpretation of the fall of Britain. The key to this paradox lies in certain passages of Henry of Huntingdon, already described, in which the historian perceives a divine plan in the successive rule of Britons, Saxons, and Normans in Britain.[57] Like so many other judgments by the Anglo-Norman historians, this one cuts in more ways than Henry perhaps intended. If the overt regulating factor in the succession of reigns in Britain is God's providence, there is nonetheless a covert, even unconscious recognition of a cyclic pattern in history, a pattern which remorselessly regulates the life and death of realms in a manner analogous to fortune's regulation of the lives and deaths of great men.

It was this imprecisely articulated perception of Henry's which, I think, intrigued Geoffrey, and led him to retreat to the more remote past to reconstruct the *rise and fall* of Britain—an earlier phase still of history's endlessly recurring cycle—as the ideal context within which to work out the implications of the new historiography. The traditional interpretations of Bede and Gildas exercised an honorable tyranny over the end of British history and the beginnings and early maturity of English history, from which no later writer could hope to escape. By leaping backward beyond the fall of Britain, Geoffrey partially avoided the Gildas tradition and landed in *terra incognita* with only the origin stories of the *Historia Brittonum* to guide him. The remaining problem, i.e., Gildas' interpretation of the actual fall of Britain, Geoffrey solved by "translating" a key passage of *De excidio Britanniae* from the prophetic, religious language of Gildas into a stylistically similar, yet thoroughly secular language and inserting it toward the end of his narrative, thereby preserving what we might call the "Gildas tone" and insuring the plausibility of his work, while making a very different point.[58]

In one sense, then, Geoffrey was the first historian of the fall of Britain to escape completely from the Gildas tradition—but in another sense his *Historia* merely testifies to the lasting influence of Gildas. For, while muting the intensely religious voice of the British monk, the Anglo-Welsh canon preserved intact the tradition of a self-caused, catastrophic climax to British history. Even the inventive Geoffrey felt the accumulated weight of the interpretation of British history bequeathed him by Gildas; he could secularize the legacy, but not ignore it.

Geoffrey's carefully constructed historical account makes use of all the fall of Britain texts in ways which continually support the hypothesis that he intended to produce a thoroughly original and primarily secular account of the rise and fall of a nation.[59] He modifies Gildas in other passages besides the one just mentioned,[60] and does even more violence to Bede; where the latter described justifiable English victories over the obstinate Britons, the *Historia* presents the same episodes in precisely the opposite sense, making the Britons heroes and the Saxons villains.[61] The best example of this technique is Cadwaladrus, the last British king, who goes to Rome after fleeing Britain and dies there in the odor of sanctity. The inspiration for this character is partly Bede's portrait of the holy Cadwallo, a Saxon king![62]

If Geoffrey's rehandling of Bede and Gildas is revealing, equally revealing is his decision to expand certain source material without reinterpreting it. The best examples of this procedure are the Brutus origin story, the advent of Caesar and the Romans, and the encounter between Vortigern and Merlin, culminating in Merlin's prophecies.[63] Each of these episodes is crucial in the structure of *Historia regum Britanniae*. Brutus' adventures state themes which appear throughout the work; the Roman victory over the Britons defines Geoffrey's concept of Roman power and begins a narrative movement toward Arthur's battle with Rome, the climax of British history, and his sudden downfall; and Merlin's entrance into the story marks the beginning of Britain's finest hours, while his prophecies clearly establish a link between the events of the *Historia* and Geoffrey's own day.[64]

Now, it is noteworthy that these three episodes which Geoffrey borrows from *Historia Brittonum*—expanding them greatly, as I have said, but without altering their essential character from the earlier text—are precisely those which were singled out in the last chapter as indicative of the secular strain of national history present in that ninth-century compilation of British historical texts. Comparison with Geoffrey's wholesale reinterpretation of Bede and Gildas leads us to a conclusion which is reinforced by the fact that Geoffrey omits certain Christian features of the *Historia Brittonum* narrative—all the St. Germanus por-

tions of the Vortigern story, for example[65]—viz., that Geoffrey, having found a way to neutralize the Gildas tradition, actually set about constructing a narrative on the basis of the secular chapters of *Historia Brittonum*, adapting his other main sources to conform to this skeletal scheme.

Within this structural and narrative framework Geoffrey also considered separately and in combination themes which he borrowed from the historical works of his contemporaries, and which we may now summarize before examining the *Historia regum Britanniae* in some detail.

One of his central preoccupations is the spectacle of human greatness. In Brutus, Cassibelanus, Ambrosius, Uther, and especially Arthur and his court, Geoffrey presents a cavalcade of national heroes whose careers and achievements he elaborates with obvious pleasure. The inspiration for Geoffrey's concern with secular greatness was undoubtedly the Anglo-Norman historians' presentation of William the Conqueror and other Anglo-Norman monarchs and barons.[66] The same pride in accomplishment, ease in wearing the mantle of authority, and potentiality for a violent greatness, demonstrated continually by these rulers in the pages of William or Orderic, appear as well in Geoffrey's presentation of Brutus, the liberator-founder of his nation, and of Arthur, who, like William the Conqueror, "extended by his valour the bounds of the [British] dominion, and raised his people to a pitch of greatness surpassing the times of any of his predecessors."[67]

Against this near-intoxication with the human greatness of national leaders must be set the cyclical view of history which I have already suggested was extracted by Geoffrey from Henry of Huntingdon. For, if the heroic deeds of men emphasize human control of history, the view of history as an endless series of cycles emphasizes the power of history over men. Operating through Fortune, the inexplicable and fickle force which raises man on her wheel and then throws him off, history tyrannizes over man and mocks his efforts to control his fate and that of his nation.[68] Arthur's career provides the prime instance of Geoffrey's dual historical vision. His reign illustrates the pinnacle of human greatness and at the same time serves as a mighty *exemplum* of Fortune's thrusting greatness down to sudden destruction. The ultimate consequence of Arthur's fall is the fall of Britain and the rise of the Saxons. Personal fortune here mirrors and affects national fortune; the two levels interact in a manner which we may call the secular equivalent of the Christian theology of history working itself out at personal and national levels of exegesis.

Geoffrey elaborately develops and repeatedly underscores the cyclical nature of history. The British nation arises from the ashes of Troy: the first Britons are Trojan captives of the Greeks who unite under Brutus and free themselves from Grecian bondage. Arriving in Britain, the Britons grow strong and prosperous, and, having reached maturity, must face two national enemies, the Romans and the Saxons. In treating the relations among the three nations, Geoffrey establishes the cyclical nature of history by showing the similar effects of recurrent national crises upon each of the three as they pass through the stages of their political existence.[69] Finally, when Britain reaches the end of her cycle and succumbs to the Saxon invaders,[70] Geoffrey invents a vision in which an angel appears to Cadwaladrus, last king of the Britons.[71] The angelic voice tells the king, who is in exile in Brittany, not to contemplate a return to the island of Britain, for God has willed that the Britons will only regain their homeland at some time in the indeterminate future when certain specific (and primarily religious) conditions are met.[72] Cadwaladrus, convinced by the voice, abandons his planned return and goes to Rome, where he dies a holy death. The import of this episode is clearly that the fall of Britain is but another phase in the eternal cycle. At some point, the Britons' turn will come again to mount Fortune's wheel, just as they rose at the beginning of the story from the ruined remnants of a previously prosperous nation.

Beyond all these indications of the cyclic nature of history, Geoffrey also hit upon a rhetorical organization for his narrative which reinforces his cyclic theory at the same time that it fills British history with exciting incidents. In recounting the successive reigns of the British monarchs, he repeatedly inserted variants of several basic situations— feuds among brothers, British expeditions to Rome, the illicit loves of kings, etc.—which have far-reaching national consequences. The inevitable effect upon the reader of this repetition of incidents at various points in British history is a semiconscious realization that "this has happened before"—i.e., that history continually repeats itself. In evoking such a response to his creation, Geoffrey brilliantly gives credence to one of his basic historical theses.

Geoffrey's twin concern with human greatness and historical recurrence (one could almost say determinism), reminiscent as it is of the duality not only of the Anglo-Norman historians but of the historiography of classical antiquity as well,[73] can serve as a transition to other aspects of his historical vision: the use of classical rhetorical themes and the formation of a general outlook more in harmony with classical than with Christian assumptions about history. The constant motivation of the Britons in their dealings with other nations is the desire for liberty and the escape from tyranny. This traditional theme of ancient historiography[74] states rhetorically the way in which history is moral or at least meaningful: when a nation impairs the freedom of others, it encounters resistance and arouses its would-be subjects to great deeds in defense of liberty. Not the least of Geoffrey's achievements is the deftness and plausibility with which he integrates this *topos* into the context of Britain's rise and fall. Like the theory of rise and fall, or of human greatness versus fortune, freedom versus tyranny is an historical abstraction of the kind which the Oxford canon proves himself to be a master at handling and interweaving with other such abstractions.

But is *Historia regum Britanniae* simply a *jeu d'esprit* involving the juggling of historical abstractions? I think not. Geoffrey's profound interest in the human condition can

be deduced not only from his keen appreciation of human greatness but also from what is perhaps the most remarkable feature of the *Historia*: a narrative technique whereby he addresses himself to the crucial and concrete problem of personal fulfillment within the march of history. Here Geoffrey seizes upon yet another feature of the historiography of his contemporaries: its division of interest between the great men and events of history and the complexity of human life considered in itself.

I have suggested that the latter fascination resulted in the digressive character of Anglo-Norman historiography, and in its willingness to include stories and reports of prodigies, supernatural experience, and the like. Geoffrey's approach is much more sophisticated, and, as we might expect, carefully integrated into the larger patterns of his historiography. It grows out of his technique, already noted, of casting microcosmic incidents into reiterated narrative patterns whereby similar characters undergo similar crises at various stages of national history. Geoffrey thereby ingeniously supports his cyclical view of history.

This rhetorical device, however, sometimes dramatizes a new and serious tension between individual desires and national welfare, especially when Geoffrey employs it to set at odds the individual's search for happiness (a secular equivalent of salvation) and national order, the keystone of national prosperity.[75] The protagonist of a thematic episode, in other words, seeks a personal *desideratum*—Assaracus the Greek his patrimony,[76] Androgeus the Briton justice for his nephew,[77] Brennius his rightful share of the kingdom,[78] etc.—and in the process brings chaos to his society. In some of these episodes the protagonist is clearly in the wrong: he is a traitor, or an overreacher.[79] But in other cases it is not possible to decide on the guilt or innocence of the destroyer of civil order; the structure or circumstances of the particular incident do not provide criteria. A typical example is the treason of the Greek Anacletus,[80] which ruins his brother Pandrasus, king of the Greeks, but allows the Trojans to escape from slavery and to settle Britain.[81] Anacletus acts to save his life, betrays his nation, and yet strikes a timely, albeit unwilling, blow for the cause of British freedom. How is he to be judged?

In many cases where tension exists in the *Historia regum Britanniae* between personal needs or desires and national stability, the crux of the situation is a special relationship of some kind, i.e., between two brothers, or cousins, or even between father and daughter. Again and again Geoffrey constructs episodes in which one relative is given the diadem of Britain, while the other, convinced he has been cheated, becomes disaffected from the king and the national good. A common development underlies and relates all these fabricated crises: the individual begins to emerge as a person from the pattern of history, a person moreover whose extrapolitical relationships, especially kindred ones, determine his actions, even if the result is national chaos.[82] Again, the duality of history and the resultant historical tension press in upon Geoffrey and upon his reader. The synthetic historical imagination of earlier centuries, when

Christian world views determined a harmonious vision of providential history, has vanished and been replaced by an analytic approach leading consistently to the stone wall of irreconcilable tendencies by which history is surrounded.

Far from ignoring the individual in history, then, Geoffrey exalted him to new stature, distinguishing him as a creature with a destiny and desires potentially different from those of his nation, and as an individual involved in a range of relationships not integral to, and even at odds with, the political relationships which determine national history.[83] In the process, Geoffrey opened a Pandora's box which had remained closed during the centuries when Christian thought dominated historical writing, and wrote a final chapter to the literary history of the fall of Britain which contains developments hardly imaginable in the light of what had gone before it. . . .

Notes

1. All references to *Historia regum Britanniae (HRB)* are to the edition of Acton Griscom. Translations are my own, though I have consulted the rendering of Sebastian Evans. The complete surprise of Geoffrey's contemporary, the historian Henry of Huntingdon, on discovering a MS of *HRB* (reported in a letter of 1139 as quoted in E. K. Chambers, *Arthur of Britain,* pp. 251-52) may fairly be called representative of the effect Geoffrey's work must have had on the learned, courtly-clerical audience among whom it was first circulated, despite T. D. Kendrick's reference (*British Antiquity,* p. 11) to "a background of antiquarian expectancy" in Geoffrey's day, and to his "waiting public." As I shall point out later, the interests of the Anglo-Norman historians whose works prompted *HRB* were historical, psychological, and philosophical rather than "antiquarian."

2. A number of works on Geoffrey's influence have been written including H. Brandenburg, *Galfrid von Monmouth und die frühmittelenglischen Chronisten* and L. Keeler, *Geoffrey of Monmouth and the Late Latin Chroniclers.* See also the relevant sections of R. H. Fletcher, *Arthurian Material in the Chronicles,* pp. 116 ff., and of the works mentioned in note 5, below.

3. See J. S. P. Tatlock, *The Legendary History of Britain,* p. 439; Edmond Faral, *La légende arthurienne,* II, 1-38; J. E. Lloyd, "Geoffrey of Monmouth," *EHR,* LVII (1942), 460-68; and J. J. Parry and R. A. Caldwell, "Geoffrey of Monmouth," *ALMA,* pp. 72-75, for summaries and varying interpretations of the available information about Geoffrey's antecedents and activities. Geoffrey's signatures on charters establish his residence in Oxford at least from 1129 to 1151.

4. *Vita Merlini* was edited by J. J. Parry (*Illinois Studies,* X, 243-380), who established beyond doubt the previously disputed attribution of the work to Geoffrey.

5. The vicissitudes of Geoffrey's reputation have proven a popular topic with students of history and of Brit-

ish *Kulturgeschichte.* See, for example, R. F. Brinkley, *Arthurian Legend in the Seventeenth Century,* pp. 60-88, and E. Jones, *Geoffrey of Monmouth, 1640-1800.* Kendrick, pp. 78-104, describes "the battle over the British History" (and therefore over Geoffrey's credibility) in the sixteenth and seventeenth centuries; he also outlines, on pp. 11-13, the earliest doubt concerning, and opposition to, the presentation of the British past in *HRB.* The two famous twelfth-century denunciations of Geoffrey as a fraudulent historian (by William of Newburgh, in the *proemium* of *Historia rerum Anglicarum,* and Giraldus Cambrensis, *Itinerarium Kambriae,* i. 5) are printed by Chambers, *Arthur,* pp. 268, 284.

6. Almost, but not quite. There are still those who, like R. S. Loomis, prefer the language of pejoration when speaking of *HRB.* See *The Development of Arthurian Romance,* p. 35: ". . . Geoffrey was quite unscrupulous, for the *History of the Kings of Britain,* which he claimed to have translated from an ancient book imported from Brittany, was one of the world's most brazen and successful frauds."

7. *HRB,* i. 1. In xii. 20 Geoffrey adds that Walter brought the book "ex britannia"; scholarly opinion is divided over a correct translation of *britannia* as Wales or Brittany. See Griscom, Introduction, p. 22, n. 1; W. F. Schirmer, *Die frühen Darstellungen des Arthurstoffes,* p. 35, "Exkurs I"; Tatlock, *Legendary History,* pp. 422-23; A. W. Wade-Evans, tr., *Nennius's "History of the Britons,"* p. 17; and G. H. Gerould, "King Arthur and Politics," *Speculum,* II (1927), 37.

8. See Griscom's introduction to his edition, and R. S. Loomis' writings on the subject in *Speculum,* including "Geoffrey of Monmouth and Arthurian Origins," III (1928), 16-33, and a review of Schirmer's book, XXXIV (1959), 677-82.

9. The leading opponents of the "Celtic tradition" theory have been Faral, Chambers, and Tatlock. W. L. Jones, in "Latin Chroniclers from the Eleventh to the Thirteenth Centuries," *CHEL,* I, 169-71, exonerated Geoffrey as a harmless romancer whose "*History* can be adequately explained only as the response of a British writer, keenly observant of the literary tendencies of the day, to the growing demand for romance." H. Pilch, "Galfrid's *Historia.* Studie zu ihrer Stellung in der Literaturgeschichte," *Romanische Monatsschrift,* N.F. VII (1957), pp. 254-73, thinks of Geoffrey as an historical novelist, while Kendrick, p. 10, proposes that "he may after all have been doing no more than write a book of antiquarian interest for fellow antiquaries. . . ." Gerould and Tatlock incline toward divergent interpretations of *HRB* as propaganda, while Schirmer insists that the work was intended as a topical political warning.

10. *HRB* was most probably written somewhere between the years 1135 and 1138. Griscom, comparing the content of the various dedications which Geoffrey

wrote to public figures of his day, opts for a date nearer the beginning of this period, while Schirmer's theories of the work's meaning are best supported by the latest possible date. Tatlock, pp. 433-37, cautiously suggests 1130 and 1138 as outer limits.

11. Geoffrey's systematic secularization of British history in a work of literary polish and pretensions is to be distinguished from the political and nationalistic developments which, as we have seen in the preceding chapter, led to the appearance of the secular episodes of the *Historia Brittonum*. The appeal to the *vetustissimus liber,* of which he is but the translator, is very possibly an indication that Geoffrey was aware of the radical nature of his departure from the fall of Britain tradition and sought to soften the impact of his approach by giving it a pedigree of its own.

12. See H. Richter, *Englische Geschichtschreiber des 12. Jahrhunderts,* pp. 170-71.

13. I do not mean to impute frivolity to Geoffrey in calling his work a parody; rather, I refer to the process whereby he took certain models, distorted them significantly, heightened and emphasized their nontraditional features, and produced thereby a fictional copy in which all lines are more sharply etched than those of the "originals"—and in which, consequently, the genius of the genre is isolated and magnified.

14. I exclude from this section any account of early medieval universal chronicles or rehandlings of Roman history. There is some discussion of these works and of Geoffrey's relationship to them in two unpublished University of California dissertations: F. P. Colligan, "The Historiography of Geoffrey of Monmouth," pp. 82-88, and L. M. Myers, "Universal Histories in the Early Middle Ages."

15. See above, Chapter I, notes 35-38 and corresponding text.

16. The practice continued on into the Tudor period and beyond, a famous case being the introduction to Sir Walter Raleigh's history of the world. In fact, it can be argued that Collingwood's statement on the uses of history (quoted above, Chapter I, note 1) is itself exemplary, and that it proposes to regard history as a storehouse of metaphysical rather than moral *exempla.*

17. One is constantly made aware of this difficulty in attempting to make students realize that today's "scientific" and "critical" history, or social and intellectual history, far from being "objective," reflect the humanistic, sociological, psychological, and psychoanalytical insights and preoccupatons of contemporary society.

18. This is also true of those sections in which the historian's aims were not specifically Christian. The unhorsing of the "little Greek" by a Langobardic warrior in Paul's *Historia Langobardorum* is patently exemplary (see above, Chapter IV, note 27 and corresponding text).

19. The prefaces of the histories of William of Malmesbury, Henry of Huntingdon, and Ordericus Vitalis contain conventional references to the exemplary uses of history, and Orderic again takes up the theme in the first chapter of his sixth book: "It is every man's duty to be daily learning how he ought to live, by having the examples of ancient worthies ever present before his eyes, and profiting thereby."

20. The efflorescence may be studied in Richter, and in H. Lamprecht, *Untersuchungen über einige englische Chronisten des 12. und beginnenden 13. Jahrhunderts,* and set within the context of twelfth-century historiography generally in C. H. Haskins, *The Renaissance of the Twelfth Century,* pp. 224-78, and F. Heer, *The Medieval World,* pp. 227-38.

21. On the dating of the work's successive stages, see R. W. Southern, *St. Anselm and his Biographer,* pp. 298-300. Eadmer's work covers a shorter period of time than the other histories here under consideration, and poses certain special problems to the investigator as well; I have therefore reluctantly decided to exclude it from the present discussion. See Richter, pp. 20-53.

22. The dating of the various parts and reworkings of Orderic's work is an extremely complicated process. See the masterful summary in H. Wolter, *Ordericus Vitalis,* pp. 65-71. References to Orderic follow the edition of A. Le Prevost; translations are based on that of Thomas Forester.

23. References are to the edition of T. Arnold (*R.S.*), and the translation is once again Forester's.

24. References are to the text of *Gesta Regum Anglorum* edited by W. Stubbs (*R.S.*); translations are based on J. A. Giles' revision of the Sharpe rendering. The *Historia Novella* has been edited with a translation by K. R. Potter.

25. See Haskins, pp. 93-126, 193-223.

26. Orderic is especially exemplary of this intoxication; a perfect example is the speech of Robert of Normandy to his father, the Conqueror (*Hist. Eccl.,* v. 10), in which he says he will undertake the life of a voluntary exile and become a mercenary soldier, thereby imitating Polyneices the Theban. Cf. Henry's preface, in which he proves the great exemplary value of history by adducing the Homeric heroes as great examples of virtue and vice. The historians' knowledge of Greek literature was all secondhand, of course.

27. Orderic compares the Norman barons to the Roman senate (*Ibid.,* iii. 11); he and Henry, borrowing from early medieval chronicles, recapitulate the complete series of Roman emperors in the west, which Henry prefaces with a word of praise for the emperors (*Hist. Eccl.,* i. 23; *Hist. Ang.,* i. 15 ff.).

28. There are many examples of the traditional patriotic exhortation, notably Caesar's to his troops when they invade Britain (*Hist. Ang.,* i. 13); also traditional is

the speech of Tostig, who in his complaint to the king of Norway (*Hist. Eccl.,* iii. 11), excoriates his brother Harold, king of England, for his tyranny; on the other hand, the confrontation of Robert and William, mentioned in note 26, and William's deathbed speech (*Hist. Eccl.,* vii. 15; see below, pp. 132 ff.) are innovations and striking indications of Orderic's art.

29. William speaks in his preface of his desire to "season the crude materials" of his history "with Roman salt" ("exarata barbarice Romano sale condire").

30. Norman Cantor, *Medieval History,* p. 255, feels that "the . . . most decisive stage in the emergence of Normandy was involved in the relationship between the Norman dukes and the church in their territory." To D. C. Douglas, "the ecclesiastical development of Normandy during the earlier half of the eleventh century was almost as remarkable as the growth at the same time of its secular strength . . ." (*William the Conqueror,* p. 105).

31. See Douglas, pp. 83-155, esp. "The Duke in his Duchy," p. 155, for a penetrating assessment of William's preconquest achievements, which Douglas considers were "among the most remarkable political phenomena of eleventh-century Europe, . . . [and] the basis of . . . [William's] establishment of the Anglo-Norman kingdom."

32. Heinrich Pähler, *Strukturuntersuchungen zur Historia Regum Britanniae des Geoffrey of Monmouth,* p. 58, shows how the histories of William and Henry are constructed around the central, elaborate sections dealing with the Anglo-Norman monarchs.

33. See, for example, *Hist. Eccl.,* iii. 8, v. 2; Orderic stresses the great virtues of William which make him beloved of God. Henry, on the other hand (*Hist. Ang.,* vi. 27, 38) sees the Normans primarily as the instrument chosen by God "because he perceived that they were more fierce than any other people." They carry out God's revenge on the sinful English, whom God gives up "to destruction by the fierce and crafty race of the Normans." William of Malmesbury (*Gesta,* iii. 238, 244) speaks of "the prudence of William, seconded by the providence of God," and thinks that God especially protected the Conqueror in the battle of Hastings.

34. William especially paints a gloomy picture of the decadence of the English, one which has too frequently been taken literally, even until the present century. See *Gesta,* iii. 245. Henry (*Hist. Ang.,* vi. 38) sees the English defeat to be the result of "the righteous will of God." Orderic is more impartially providential, and says of Hastings (*Hist. Eccl.,* iii. 14), "Thus did Almighty God . . . punish in various ways the innumerable sinners in both armies."

35. *Hist. Ang.,* vi. 1; in vii. 1, he says further that God, having punished the Saxons, "now began to afflict the Normans themselves, the instruments of his will, with various calamities."

36. See *Hist. Eccl.,* iv. 3, 4, 8; vi. 2; Orderic says that "Under [William's rule] the native inhabitants were crushed, imprisoned, disinherited, banished and scattered beyond the limits of their own country"; he tells frequently how "the English deeply lamented the loss of their freedom" and, "sighing for their ancient liberties," were "provoked to rebellion by every sort of oppression on the part of the Normans" who "had crushed the English and were overwhelming them with intolerable oppression." Cf. *Gesta,* ii. 207; and *Hist. Ang.,* vi. 38, where Henry characterizes the Normans as a people who fight until they have "so crushed their enemies that they can reduce them no lower," at which point they turn against each other.

37. Orderic says of the barons that they are "always restless [and] longing for some disturbance" (v. 10); describes one as "a brave soldier, lavish in his liberalities, [taking] great delight in riotous sports, in jesters, horses, and dogs, with other vanities of that sort" (vi. 2); and, when an Anglo-Norman party sets out for Italy, remarks, "The Normans are ever given to change and desirous of visiting foreign lands, and they therefore readily joined themselves to the aspiring prelate whose ambition was not satisfied by the dominion of England and Normandy" (vii. 8). Like William (see *Gesta,* ii. 227), Henry stresses the great greed of the Norman lords (vii. 19) as well as their rebelliousness (vii. 2), and tells us that when the Conqueror was exhorting his forces to victory before the battle of Hastings, "all the squadrons, inflamed with rage, rushed on the enemy with indescribable impetuosity, and left the duke speaking to himself!" (vi. 30). On the cruelty of the Normans, see the preceding note.

38. Henry of Huntingdon inclines more toward the former view (vii. 1-2), Orderic the latter. See for example *Hist. Eccl.,* v. 10: "Thus Normandy had more to suffer from her own people than from strangers, and was ruined by intestine disorders."

39. *Eccl. Hist.,* v. 1; Orderic returns to this point again in vi. 1.

40. Preface: "I shall search out and give to the world the modern history of Christendom, venturing to call my unpretending work 'An Ecclesiastical History.'"

41. See another important passage, *Hist. Eccl.,* viii. 15, where Orderic notes, "I see many passages in the sacred writings which are so adapted to the circumstances of the present times, that they seem parallel. But I leave to studious persons the task of inquiry into these allegorical quotations [allegoricas allegationes] and the interpretations applicable to the state of mankind, and will endeavor to continue the history of Norman affairs a little further in all simplicity." Here the writer overtly disassociates himself from the methods, if not the beliefs, of national-ecclesiastical historiography, preferring a record of the present human condition not overtly organized around the history of salvation.

42. See the section headed "Vera lex historiae" in C. W. Jones, *Saints' Lives and Chronicles in Early England*, pp. 81-85, for a brief analysis of the historical method of the early medieval historian.

43. *Gesta*, ii. 167 ff.

44. *Ibid.*, iii. 237, 268. Cf. *Hist. Eccl.*, viii. 17 (a vision of purgatory).

45. *Gesta*, ii. 207.

46. *Ibid.*, iv. 343 ff.; *Hist. Ang.*, vii. 5 ff.

47. As Richter (p. 65), puts it, "[William] berichtet von den grossen Menschen, die Geschichte machten, denn sie erlebten die Möglichkeiten des Daseins tiefer und voller als die Masse der Unbekannten; aber er erzählt auch von denen, denen sich irgendwie einmal das Tor zu der anderen Welt auftat."

48. An amusing and perhaps significant example of the historians' awareness of the problem of reconciling national and personal desires is Orderic's mention (*Hist. Eccl.*, iv. 4) of the perplexity of Norman barons in England whose wives insisted that they return to Normandy or risk conjugal infidelity, while William urged them to remain in England and become his lieutenants in ruling and controlling the newly conquered nation.

49. See William's preface to the third book of *Gesta* where, speaking of the Conqueror, he says, "where I am certified of his good deeds, I shall openly proclaim them; his bad conduct I shall touch upon lightly and sparingly [leviter et quasi transeunter], just enough that it may be known."

50. See especially William of Malmesbury on William Rufus, *Gesta*, iv. 312-14, 333.

51. See *Gesta*, iv. 333 (of William Rufus): "He formed mighty plans, which he would have brought to effect, could he have spun out the tissue of fate or broken through, and disengaged himself from, the violence of fortune." See Henry's similar reflections on the death of Ralph, the powerful and unscrupulous bishop of Salisbury, *Hist. Ang.*, viii. 11, in which the *rota volubilis* of fortune is specifically mentioned, and Orderic's comment on the Norman Conquest, iii. 14: "Inconstant fortune frequently causes adverse and unexpected changes in human affairs; some persons being lifted from the dust to the height of great power, while others, suddenly falling from their high estate, groan in extreme distress."

52. See vii. 15.

53. Orderic, *Hist. Eccl.*, vii. 15. Note the almost psalmic quality of William's confession that "I became . . . an object of jealousy to all my neighbours, but by His aid in whom I have always put my trust, none of them were able to prevail against me."

54. Henry of Huntingdon strives briefly for the same effect in describing the death of Henry I, *Hist. Ang.*, viii. 2; the account stresses the stench exuded by the corpse, and Henry counsels his readers, "Observe, I say, what horrible decay, to what a loathsome state, his body was reduced . . . and learn to despise what so perishes and comes to nothing."

55. See Pähler, pp. 58-60.

56. See Tatlock, pp. 392-95; Colligan, pp. 22-24, and, most thoroughly, Pähler, pp. 87-126.

57. See above, note 35 and corresponding text.

58. W. F. Schirmer first noted this important passage and correctly interpreted it. See Schirmer, pp. 25-27, and *Exkurs IV,* "Geoffrey und Gildas," pp. 38-39. Where Gildas' words condemned his nation for its sins, Geoffrey interrupts the narrative to upbraid the Britons for the political strife which is leading them to national catastrophe. He could have found many models for this interruption and its point of view in the Anglo-Norman historians; see above, note 38.

59. Pähler, pp. 95 ff., demonstrates the structural importance for *HRB* of the "Wechsel von Aufstieg und Niedergang" in the narrative, but never completely subscribes to the idea that the entire work is organized around the rise and fall of the Britons.

60. E.g., *HRB*, vi. 2, when the Romans leave Britain for the last time. The basis for this scene is Gildas (cf. *De exc.*, 18), but Geoffrey inserts a long speech by Guethelin, bishop of London, who urges the inhabitants to fight for their freedom. The insertion effectively modifies the pathos which the scene has in *De exc.*, and takes away from the Romans the prominence given them in the older narrative.

61. See *HRB*, xi. 12, 13 (the destruction of the British monks by the Saxons under Ethelfrid after the Britons refuse to cooperate with St. Augustine; cf. Bede, *HE*, ii. 2 ff.); etc.

62. Cf. *HRB*, xii. 14 ff. and *HE*, iv. 15; v. 7. With typical self-assurance, Geoffrey remarks of Cadwaladrus, "quem beda clieduallam iuvenem vocavit" without mentioning, of course, his metamorphosis in nationality.

63. HB, 10-11, 19-30, 40-42.

64. Schirmer, p. 29, sees in Geoffrey's placement and use of the prophecies the influence of Anchises' prophecies in the sixth book of the *Aeneid* which connect the story of Aeneas directly to the greatness of the Augustan present. On Geoffrey's reasons for wanting to establish a line between the story of the Britons and the present, see below, p. 171.

65. The arrival and *gesta* of St. Germanus in Britain are mentioned in *HRB*, vi. 13, but not recounted. In the narrative of Vortigern's destruction (*HRB*, viii. 2), Geoffrey adapts the violent, "religious" tradition of *HB*, 47, but removes St. Germanus from the story and replaces the fire that descends from heaven by fires set by the Britons who have besieged the sinful monarch in his castle.

66. William of Malmesbury prefaces his history with an epistle to Robert, Earl of Gloucester (also a dedicatee

of *HRB*) which begins by extolling "the virtue of celebrated men" ("virtus clarorum virorum") and their "great actions."

67. In *HRB,* ix. 13 Geoffrey apostrophizes the Britons under Arthur's rule in an analogous fashion. See Arthur's speech to his army before the battle with the Romans at Siesia (x. 7), Brutus' threats to Anacletus (i. 8), and the cruelty of Arthur's Britons in ravaging Normandy (ix. 11) for further examples of "Norman" pride, vigor, and cruelty as adapted by Geoffrey.

68. It may be precisely the arbitrariness and inexplicability of Fortune to which Geoffrey alludes when he interrupts the narrative of *HRB* immediately following the announcement of Modred's treason, which forces Arthur to turn back from Rome and go to his death in Britain; addressing his words to his patron (xi. 1) Geoffrey says that he will not comment on this turn of events ("De hoc Galfridis munomotensis tacebit") but will confine himself to rendering his source as briefly as possible.

69. Geoffrey includes a fourth nation, Brittany, in the cycle; see below, p. 167.

70. In recounting the final destruction of the kingdom of the Britons, Geoffrey borrows from Gildas an account of plagues which ravage the nation (cf. *De exc.,* 22). Once again his treatment of his source is revealing: in Gildas, the plagues are sent by God as warnings to the sinful Britons before the final punishment, the Saxon invaders; in *HRB* the plagues, coming after the Saxon arrival and not sent by God, represent the final fury of amoral nature, stamping out the doomed nation of the Britons who have reached the end of their cycle.

71. *HRB,* xii. 17.

72. Among them is the return to Britain of relics of the saints carried off during the Saxon invasions. Before this can happen, however, a fated time must come ("postquam fatale tempus supervenisset . . .").

73. See above, Chapter I, pp. 17-20.

74. It is as old as Herodotus' portrayal of the struggle between Persian might and Greek freedom in the seventh and eighth books of his history. See M. Ritter, "Studien über die Entwicklung der Geschichtswissenschaft. I: Die antike Geschichtsschreibung," *Hist. Zeit.,* LIV (1885), pp. 1-41.

75. See Schirmer, pp. 26-28, and Pähler, pp. 92-107, *passim.*

76. *HRB,* i. 3.

77. *Ibid.,* iv. 8-10.

78. *Ibid.,* iii. 1-7.

79. E.g., Porrex (*ibid.,* ii. 16); Maximianus (v. 9-16); etc.

80. On the topical import of the name, see Tatlock, "Contemporary Matters in Geoffrey of Monmouth's *Historia Regum Britanniae,*" *Speculum,* VI (1931),

206-23: Anacletus II was the name taken by an antipope who "reigned" from 1130-1138.

81. *HRB,* i. 8-9.

82. There is a striking parallel between this development in *HRB* and the *Chanson de Roland,* where a relationship between godfather and godson (Ganelon and Roland) leads to the former's treason and consequent national disaster. In the *chanson,* Charlemagne represents the nation and its historical destiny and, like Britain in *HRB,* undergoes rise and fall dependent upon the behavior of his vassals. Charles is on the threshold of great national triumph in his Spanish campaign when Ganelon's treason brings about the loss of Roland and the twelve peers and raises for Charles the specter of future national hardships and defeats (see *Roland,* lines 2887 ff., Charles' lament for Roland and for his own power).

83. Of course, the range of relationships is very limited; again we may cite as a parallel the nonfeudal relationships of the *chanson de geste.* It remained for the romance to discover a new world of interpersonal relationships by its exaltation of love to a new level of psychological and narrative importance. To Geoffrey, as we shall see, love is still primarily the madness it was to the ancients. . . .

Abbreviations

ALMA: Arthurian Literature in the Middle Ages

CHEL: Cambridge History of English Literature

De civ.: Augustine, *De civitate Dei*

De exc.: Gildas, *De excidio et conquestu Britanniae*

De gub.: Salvian, *De gubernatione Dei*

EH: Eusebius, *Ecclesiastical History*

EHR: English Historical Review

HB: Historia Brittonum

HE: Bede, *Historia ecclesiastica*

HRB: Geoffrey of Monmouth, *Historia regum Britanniae*

Hist. Zeit.: Historische Zeitschrift

MGH: Monumenta Germaniae historica

PQ: Philological Quarterly

Proc. Brit. Acad.: Proceedings of the British Academy

RS: Rolls Series (Chronicles and Memorials of Great Britain and Ireland during the Middle Ages)

TRHS: Transactions of the Royal Historical Society

Z.f.d.Ph.: Zeitschrift für deutsche Philologie

Brynley F. Roberts (essay date 1976)

SOURCE: "Geoffrey of Monmouth and Welsh Historical Tradition," *Nottingham Mediaeval Studies,* Vol. 20, 1976, pp. 29-40.

[*In the following essay, Roberts contends that Geoffrey's historical view was influenced by the teachings of native Welsh historians.*]

Former generations of readers, who accepted Geoffrey's claim to have translated a "British" book, naturally regarded the **Historia Regum Britanniae** as an authentic and valuable source for early Welsh or British history. Even after the eclipse of the book as an acceptable account of genuine history, there remained a belief in its value as a source of Welsh legend and tradition. If Geoffrey had in fact concocted a largely imaginary history of Britain, it was assumed that he had drawn on early Welsh legendary lore and that the book, therefore, could be used as evidence of Welsh story. When the reaction to Geoffrey became more pronounced, when the "ancient book" was held to be merely another example of an appeal to a fictitious authority, and when the careful dissecting of the work revealed not only literary borrowings, verbal reminiscences, contemporary fashions and modes of thought, but a thoughtful design and structure also, it seemed right to regard Geoffrey as a creative Anglo-Norman author drawing on contemporary and classical literary sources and moving in Norman society, rather than as a conserver of Welsh tradition. It seemed fruitless, therefore, to expect to find any genuine, or at least uncontaminated, fragments of native tradition in his work. Geoffrey's statements tend to be dismissed, and any agreement with Welsh stories has too often been explained away as the **Historia**'s influence. However, the last word on Geoffrey, his aims and methods, and particularly his sources, including the "ancient book", has not yet been said, and like those seventeenth-century defenders of the British History, we would be wise to steer a middle course, neither accepting the **Historia** as being wholly, or even mainly, true to Welsh tradition in the majority of its episodes, nor yet rejecting Geoffrey's work as the fruits of a lively imagination, able to combine diverse sources in a new pattern, playing upon the reading of an educated man. There are signs that there is now greater readiness to regard Geoffrey as a serious writer, neither the tongue-in-cheek rogue that has been sometimes portrayed rather censoriously, nor the ambitious climber imposing his fraud on a gullible public, and to believe that he can tell us something about the aims and ideals of twelfth-century historical writing. That, however, is not the aim of this paper, which will attempt to examine some points of contact between Geoffrey of Monmouth and what native Welsh historians taught as the accepted history of Britain.

"Native Welsh historians" is a term which needs some explanation, for there are no historical treatises in Middle Welsh other than those which are translations of Latin works, the versions of the **Historia** and of Dares Phrygius, and of some few chronicles, in particular the Chronicle of the Princes which in its final form is later than Geoffrey. Nor is there extant in Latin anything other than some annals, sometimes showing Geoffrey's influence, and of course Gildas and Nennius. By native historians is meant here the conservers of traditional historical material or of the accepted myth of the Welsh past, transmitted and controlled by a learned class. This class was probably the poets, whose duties and learning exceeded what the word implies for us. The poet was a court official, highly trained in his art and standing in a close relationship with his lord whom he praised, eulogized, congratulated and mourned as the representative of his people.[1] Eulogy and elegy in a formal courtly setting cannot be separated from the subject's lineage, and throughout history the bards have been poets and genealogists; but apart from the emotive appeal of ancestors' names, genealogies have to be clothed in the memories of deeds and exploits to become meaningful. Behind the written record of a name lies an extensive oral context.

The conserving of historical tradition has always been one of the poet's functions in Wales, as in other courtly settings.[2] The mediaeval poetic triads refer to the three features which give amplitude to a poet, poetics, old verse and knowledge of histories, "the History of the Notable Acts of the Kings and princes of this land" that a late poetic treatise speaks of.[3] The poets sometimes refer to themselves as historians, and in one or two poems we have a portrait of the poet and his patron reading history together.[4] This traditional learning underlies much of the corpus of bardic knowledge known as the Triads of the Island of Britain, the dominant themes of which have been described by Dr Rachel Bromwich as mythological, historical and heroic. The Stanzas of the Graves are based on the same historical learning, but here more closely associated, perhaps, with topographical features and antiquarian speculations.[5] The history was probably transmitted in narrative forms which we would regard as story. "Considerable sections of the people have never risen to the appreciation of history proper, but have remained in the stage of saga, or what in modern times is analogous to saga", and we may compare Jan Vansina's description, "History is told in proverbs and in songs, and above all in tales, which the Rundi do not distinguish from tales and fables with non-historical themes".[6] D. A. Binchy has summarized the duties of the Irish learned class, the *filid,* "Besides the praise-poems and the elegies, the learned men also had the task of conserving the genealogies of the powerful families, the tribal lore, the stories of conquest or migration and so on. I should think that it was from this storehouse of tribal memory that the sagas originated".[7] The corpus of Welsh learning was *cyfarwyddyd,* and though this frequently means no more than a tale in Middle Welsh, and *cyfarwydd* is the normal word for story-teller, its original denotion was much wider. It is related to Latin *video; cyfarwyddyd* is "guidance, information, knowledge".

Knowledge, learned lore, here would comprise origins, history, genealogies, the heroic age, geography, topography and onomastics, the detritus of older mythology, and tales.[8] This culture, which was, for the most part, oral, comes to us second, even third, hand, as allusions and references in poems, stories and triads, and at a stage farther removed from its source, in Latin, as in Nennius's tale of Vortigern which, it has been claimed, derives very largely from a typical Welsh *cyfarwyddyd.*[9] Enough remains, however, for us to attempt to sketch the outlines of the traditional British history or the myth of the British past, using myth in Vansina's meaning, "the collective representation of past events," (*Oral Tradition,* 12), that is, what men believed had happened in the past, and which illuminated and gave direction to their lives.

The physical area covered by the traditional history and geography is not merely Wales but the Island of Britain. The corpus of learning preserved by the poets as a source of reference is called the Triads of the Island of Britain, and when the king prepared for battle, the law books, none of which is earlier than the late twelfth century in its present form, state that it was the duty of the poet of the body-guard (*comitatus*) to sing "the poem called the Monarchy of Britain". The terms of geographical reference were not Anglesey to Monmouth as for modern Welshmen, but from Caithness to Cornwall, and Anglesey to Kent, or from the North Sea to the Irish Sea.[10] Britain had three adjacent islands and twenty-seven minor islands, three chief estuaries and 140 minor ones, 34 chief ports, 33 chief cities. Although this information is preserved in a fairly late mediaeval copy,[11] Nennius's description of Britain, with its *tres magnas insulas, . . . Sic in proverbio antiquo dicitur, quando de iudicibus vel regibus sermo fit, 'iudicavit Britanniam cum tribus insulis'*, chap.8, its *duo flumina praeclariora ceteris fluminibus, . . . quasi duo brachiatoria Britanniae*, chap.9, and its twenty-eight cities, chap.7, is obviously derived from a similar body of learning. There are frequent references in mediaeval texts to the three realms of Britain, which seem to have been Wales, Cornwall and the North, and this would imply an ethnic unity which existed before the advent of the Saxons and which may derive from the idea of Roman Britain, inherited by Brythonic peoples from the lowlands of Scotland to Cornwall. This concept of a unified Britain has some validity and the distinction between North Britons, Welsh and South Britons is acceptable in linguistic terms. Nevertheless, the simple homogeneity of Britain was not the whole of the myth, for even more important was the political unity of the island. "No one had a right to this Island except only the Cymry, the remnants of the Britons", claims the tract, *The Names of the Island of Britain,* a concept found also in Nennius, "Brittones olim implentes eam [Britanniam] a mari usque ad mare iudicaverunt", chap.9. The symbol of sovereignty was the Crown of London, a term used in the tales and in the laws; this implied concept of a single king is made explicit when Arthur is called *rex totius maioris Britanniae, rex universalis Britanniae, pen teyrnedd yr ynys hon.*[12] No doubt there is an element of rhetoric in these titles, (as is suggested in *Studia Hibernica,* XI, pp. 181-2), but it is the rhetoric of the ideal, for the same title was borne by historical Welsh kings who, although having no political right to it, claimed it as representatives of "the remnants of the Britons". Thus Taliesin calls his lord Urien of Rheged in the sixth-century Lord of Britain (Ud Prydein) and in the following century Cadwallon of Gwynedd was termed leader of Britain (Lluydawc Prydein) by his poet.[13] The Island of Britain was one, there was one crown, and at any one time, a single king.

In such a tradition as this, one might expect to find an emphasis on a succession of kings and although one must admit that this is not a feature of the texts which have come down to us, Peter Bartrum (*Bull. Board of Celtic Studies,* XXIII, pp.1-6) has suggested, on the basis of his study of mediaeval Welsh genealogies, that there may have existed a king-list, "the genealogical skeleton of an early connected 'History'."[14] It is this conception of a succession of single kings which underlines the rhetoric of the titles bestowed on British kings of the sixth and seventh centuries. It was not a meaningless rhetoric, for the battles of the seventh century were the battles for the overlordship of Britain, and these titles were full of significance for those who used them. Adomnán, *Life of St Columba,* tells of the defeat of Catlon (Cadwallon) at the hands of Oswald of Northumbria in the mid seventh century, "victor post bellum reversus postea *totius Brittanniae imperator* a deo ordinatus est'; Sir Frank Stenton has explained Bretwalda as an abbreviated form of Bretenanwealda, 'only ruler of Britain'.[15]

Myth and history coalesce here, for the traditional history sought to explain how the Britons, or the Welsh, lost their sovereignty and saw their unity shattered. The old divisions, Wales, Cornwall, the North, lacked any political reality and they were re-expressed in a later triad, England, Wales, Scotland. Thus the second strand which runs through Welsh history is the theme of loss. Dr Bromwich (*Trioedd,* 84-6), has remarked on the term *gormesoedd* used to denote foreign oppressors. In the tale of Lludd and Llefelys, which occurs first in Welsh versions of the ***Historia,*** one of these *gormesoedd* is a race called Coraniaid, clearly supernatural beings, and we may have here the remnants of a truly mythological story, similar to the Irish tale of the Battle of Mag Tuired, which recounted the winning or the defence of Britain against Otherworld enemies;[16] but in historical terms, the primary invaders who had threatened British sovereignty were the Romans.

The theme of Wales and Rome was a fruitful one, for it had two aspects. On the one hand, the Romans represented one of the waves of invaders who had assailed Britain and had settled there. Though they had abandoned the island, leaving the sovereignty in British hands, more than one general had been proclaimed Emperor by his troops in Britain, and the constant denuding of Britain of her fighting men had so weakened her that she had been left open to the attacks of new marauders, Irish, Picts and Saxons. These Romano-British emperors linked Britain with the remnants of the Empire. The Britons were the heirs of Rome and new dynasties were not slow in tracing their descent from these Roman emperors.[17] The relationship could be expressed in more imaginative terms. Caswallawn (Cassivellaunus), the British leader who opposed Julius Caesar, was a natural figure around whom stories could develop.[18] There appears to have been a tradition that he had repulsed Caesar and had driven him from the island, a tradition which is referred to in Triad 35, the men who went across the sea with Caswallawn in pursuit of the men of Caesar, and which is suggested in Ieuan ap Sulien's poem to his father (*Studia Celtica,* VIII/IX, 81, 56). Geoffrey may also reflect this tradition in IV. 3, 9. Another triad may suggest that the Roman conquest, like the Saxon, was due to trickery.[19] Triads 67 and 71 refer to Caswallawn's love for Fflur and his seeking her in Rome, which may be an allusion to a lost tale of a dynastic marriage not unlike the story of the Emperor Maxen who sought a British wife. Geoffrey's account of Octavius, Maximianus and the succession of the British crown (V.9-16) is obviously closely related to this latter story, *The Dream of Maxen.* This is the historical Magnus Maximus who was proclaimed Emperor in Britain in 383 A.D., and who led his troops to the continent where he ruled until his death in 388. In both Geoffrey and *The Dream* the marriage motif is linked with another theme, the association of Maxen and Cynan (Conanus Meriadocus) and the founding of Brittany by their troops. Both authors have preserved related, though not identical, versions of a traditional account of the establishment of Brittany. This legend may be as old as Gildas's day, as N. K. Chadwick has suggested, *Early Brittany,* Cardiff, 1969, pp.163-4, and is therefore to be regarded as part of the common traditional history of both Welsh and Bretons.[20]

Stories arising from the Roman conquest represent one aspect of the Roman-Welsh relationship; another was the common and equal descent of both nations from the heroes of Troy. This Trojan origin, however, seems to be a learned development which was not part of the origin myth of the Britons. In the older tradition Prydein son of Aedd, who is no more than a name to us, may have been the eponymous hero, though the tract *The Names of the Island of Britain, Trioedd,* 228, refers to the "first name" Clas Merdin, subsequently superseded by Y Vel Ynys when the island had been taken and settled, and further states that it was called Britain only when it was conquered by Prydein vab Aed Mavr.

After the Saxon settlements the theme of loss is a dominant thread in Welsh history. Gildas is the first to give full expression to it in his moral explanation of the Saxon conquests which were due to British perfidy and laxity. The British had proved themselves unfaithful to Rome and to God, and had opened the way for Barbaria, the heathen Saxons who are the instruments of God's justice. The coming of the Saxons was the turning-point in Welsh history and psychologically it was, indeed is, one of the deepest events in the Welsh consciousness. The predominant element here is the loss of sovereignty, not simply the loss of unity. The historical myth could accommodate the partition of Britain and even the idea of subreguli: as *The Names of the Island of Britain* puts it, "There should be therein a Crown and Three Coronets".[21] What gave cohesion to the three realms of Britain was the basic concept of unity expressed in a single overlordship. Early English history is the story of attempts to create unity and establish sovereignty: Welsh history recounts the loss of sovereignty and consequent fragmentation.[22]

Gildas was writing in the throes of battle. By the time Nennius was putting together the *Historia Brittonum,* the political scene was clearer and the Saxon conquest in its main outlines was over. The loss was a fact, but the en-counter could now be related in imaginative terms, and the myth could be developed to meet the new situation.[23] Gildas's "proud tyrant" who had invited Saxon mercenaries, becomes Vortigern, the foolish king who is duped by Saxon exiles, and thus history becomes fable.[24] However one might explain the arrival of the Saxons, their dominance was undeniable. God's judgement, the Romans' fault, says Nennius, but he has also the story of the fighting dragons, revealed to Vortigern by the boy Ambrosius, and he relates how the red dragon, *gens nostra,* finally drives the white, *gentem Anglorum,* from the scene. By the ninth century, therefore, the theme of loss had produced its emotional, national, reaction, the hope of renewal and the re-establishment of British sovereignty, expressed by means of prophecies and vaticinations. The day would come when the Britons would rise up under an age-old hero and regain what was rightfully theirs. Arthur and Owain both play this role, but the earliest deliverers are Cynan and Cadwaladr who appear to be representatives of the Breton and Welsh peoples. Cynan Meiriadoc seems to have been regarded as the leader of British troops who settled in Brittany and who were the first colonizers, so that his role as the returning deliverer is explicable. Cadwaladr, however, is almost unknown except as King of Gwynedd towards the end of the seventh century. His father, Cadwallon, is far better known and is the natural figure around whom legends could have grown. It is not clear why Cadwaladr should be cast as the deliverer, unless we assume either some degree of confusion with his father or that accounts of his exploits have not come down to us. Whatever may be the explanation, Cadwaladr's role as saviour is older than Geoffrey of Monmouth. Political prophecies in verse are a feature of Welsh literature throughout the Middle Ages.[25] One of the earliest extant examples is *Armes Prydein Vawr,* (The Great Prophecy of Britain), written about 930, which prophesies the return of Cynan and Cadwaladr at the head of a confederation of all the peoples of Britain and Ireland, Irish, the Dublin Danes, Welsh, men of Strathclyde, Cornishmen, and even Bretons, who will drive out the Saxons and their High King, presumably Athelstan, whose arrogance and taxes had became unbearable. This stirring poem reveals that the themes we have been discussing were established in a coherent, unified pattern of thought by *c.*930. The poem is an appeal to "history", a call to re-establish the British entity, from the Scottish lowlands to Brittany, from Dyfed to Thanet, and to regain the crown now "worn by slaves".[26] The poem was composed as a response to a particular political situation in the tenth century, the preparations for the alliance of the Danes of Dublin, the Scots and men of Strathclyde, which the Welsh did not join and which was defeated by Athelstan at Brunanburh in 937;[27] but it derives its strength not merely from a reading of political possibilities and options, but from an emotional appeal to an accepted myth. There was small hope of either Cornish or Bretons joining such a coalition and the poet must have known this, but no appeal to the myth, which he was using in an attempt to influence Welsh policy, could omit them. *Armes Prydein* is an example of the use of the Welsh historical myth in a specific contemporary context.

How relevant is this myth of unity, loss and renewal,[28] to a reading of the *Historia Regum Britanniae*? Little is known about Geoffrey's life and career, although some well-founded deductions can be made. It is assumed that he was of Breton or Welsh extraction, perhaps a Normanized Breton, and that during the period of the writing of the *Historia* he was living at Oxford as a secular canon at St George's. The *Historia* was written by one who was an outsider to British tradition, one with sympathy and interest but one for whom the tradition was not an integral part of his cultural make-up, and who was living far removed from the living waters of that tradition. It is not surprising that Geoffrey sometimes misunderstood native material and that the majority of the episodes which he recounts in the *Historia* is not based on traditional tales. The pieces of genuine tradition found here are insertions rather than the basic content of the work; but that there are genuine pieces cannot be doubted and in his attitude to British history it may well be that Geoffrey is not only true to the myth but that it has meaning for him.

The theme of Wales and Rome is a recurrent one in the *Historia,* and structurally it is the one which gives cohesion to the work. Geoffrey seems to have built his narrative around three kings whose relations with Rome reflect the jealousy of two ancient nations sprung from the same stock, or the conflict in the Welsh mind between the bitterness of a Roman conquest and pride in a Roman descent. Rome is a constant unwelcome presence in the *Historia,* but there are three peaks in the relationship. If we disregard Geoffrey's introductory chapters and his epilogue, the *Historia* seems to be made up of three similar sections, (*a*) a period of civil wars culminating in the stability of the reign of Belinus and Brennius and their sacking of Rome: (*b*) the Roman Conquest, preceded by a statement of British moral ideals and brought about more by British dissension than by Roman superiority. The Roman period ends in civil discord and with Constantinus's return to regain his rule in Rome: (*c*) another period of decay is ended with Arthur's coronation, and though Arthur's immediate enemies are the Saxons, the culmination of his reign is his march on Rome. He sees himself as the heir of Brennius and Constantinus (IX.16-17), but the measure of the decline of the Britons is that he fails where his predecessors had succeeded. In romance terms, Arthur fails the hero's quest, and it is this failure which symbolizes and foreshadows the end of British sovereignty.

The sovereignty of Britain is the thread which runs through the whole book. Geoffrey accepted both the unity of Britain and its traditional divisions. The first king is Brutus and his sons are the eponymous founders of the three realms of Britain, England, Wales, Scotland (Locrinus of Lloegr, Camber of Cymru and Albanactus of yr Alban), but there is also a suggestion that Cornwall was a recognized province, as in the older division, and it is given its own founder, Corineus.[29] He also makes it clear that though there are three regions, there is only one Kingdom. The eldest son Locrinus is the chief ruler (II.1), and the supremacy of the crown of London is formally expressed

later (III.1) when the elder Belinus is crowned King of the island and rules Lloegr, Wales and Cornwall, leaving the North to the younger Brennius. Cassivellaunus rules the whole island, though he has subordinate kings and powerful regional earls. Geoffrey stresses the unity and single kingship of Britain. In his first three books he presents pictures of the anarchy which stems from the denial of this concept. The jealousy of Ferrex and Porrex leads to civil war which is ended only by Dunvallo's accession, but history begins to repeat itself when his sons fall into the same snare and civil war is averted only by their mother's appeal. Geoffrey returns to this theme at the end of the *Historia,* for the final irrevocable breach between English and Welsh occurs when Edwin seeks permission to wear a crown in his own region.[30] Cadwallo's advisers are indignant, "it was contrary to law and to the customs of their ancestors that an island with one crown should be placed under the sway of two crowned heads", XII.3.[31] It is the upholding of this principle which leads to the final catastrophe, for the crown passes to Athelstan "who was the first among them to be crowned King", XII.19.

The concept of a succession of single kings which is at the root of Geoffrey's view of British history is wholly traditional. It poses, however, a question regarding the book which he claimed was his source. He describes it as an ancient book written in Breton (or Welsh) relating the acts of the kings of Britain in succession, in an ornate style: it was brought out of Brittany (or Wales), and given to Geoffrey to translate by Walter of Oxford. The only improbable features here are the references to an ornate style, to a single source, and the claim of translation. Professor Dominica Legge[32] has stressed the links between the "Lincoln circle" and Caen, and has reminded us that the earliest specific reference to a copy of the *Historia* comes from Bec in 1139. A Breton manuscript, of early British history,[33] at Oxford seems quite possible. Moreover, a book, if not of the acts, certainly of the names, of successive kings is wholly in keeping with the British historical tradition and has been suggested from a study of the genealogies. That such information was available in a written form is suggested by Gerald of Wales, who tells us that the poets of the twelfth century had books of genealogies, *Descriptio Kambriae,* I.3.

The idea of unity is implicit in the theme of loss and cannot be separated from it. This theme pervades the whole of the *Historia,* which is an account of the rise to greatness of a favoured people and their decline and loss of sovereignty. However glowing specific reigns may be, in Welsh eyes it is a rather sombre book in its final effect. Although Geoffrey makes some attempt to explain the English conquest in terms of the wisdom and good sense of the Saxons, his recurrent explanation is the moral one, that wickedness and unfaithfulness incur the wrath of a patient Providence. The book opens with this statement, "The Britons once occupied the land from sea to sea, before the others came. Then the vengeance of God overtook them because of their arrogance and they submitted to the Picts and Saxons", I.2; the reader is allowed to view the working out of this vengeance but Geoffrey again states his theme clearly (XI.9, XII.6-7, 10, 12, 15, 17) as the book draws to an end.

The theme of loss is deepened by the place Geoffrey gives to prophecy, which is used carefully to introduce significant characters and to point to the idea of greatness and loss. The representatives of the nation are introduced by prophecies, Brutus before his birth by Ascanius's magi, the greatness of his line by Diana. Arthur is first mentioned in Merlin's Prophecy and the final stages of the history are revealed by the Angelic Voice. Merlin's Prophecy, therefore, is not simply a virtuoso performance of abstruse nonsense. It is placed exactly in the centre of the book, immediately after that most significant event, the arrival of the Saxons who are the instruments of God's vengeance. History stands still for a moment while we seek its significance. We look ahead past Arthur, beyond the end of the *Historia,* to the very end of time. Merlin prophesies the greatness of Arthur, his victories against the Saxons and Romans. The spectre of civil war is revealed as the Red Dragon tears itself and the Saxons win sovereignty. The new conquerors are themselves bound in everlasting captivity by people in wood and iron suits, and so on to contemporary history. But the tone changes. Britons will arise, and Cadwallader shall call Conanus; Welsh, Cornish, Bretons will drive out the foreigners and "The island shall be called by the name of Brutus". Geoffrey surely derived this from Welsh prophecies,[34] and here he has the themes of British unity and restitution at their simplest, the British alliance which even for the author of *Armes Prydein* had been "long prophesied", and which Geoffrey was to use again in *Vita Merlini.* The Prophecy changes its tone again and from here to the end it makes use of animal symbolism and celestial portents, but it seems significant that the last clear, intelligible reference in this Prophecy which sets out the meaning of history, is to the restoration of British rule, sometime in an undefined future.

Gerald of Wales, in *De Vaticiniis,* the Preface to the lost Book III of the *Expugnatio Hibernica, Opera,* Rolls Series, V, 402, provides evidence for the existence of written prophecies in Welsh attributed to Myrddin (Merlin) in the twelfth century, and a fragment of one is quoted in the twelfth-century *Life of Gruffudd ap Cynan* (ed. Arthur Jones, Manchester, 1910, pp. 110-111). Even an early critic of Geoffrey, William of Newburgh, accepted his claim to have translated the prophecies. In this context the version of Merlin's Prophecy prepared, with a Commentary, by John of Cornwall about 1154 is important. This prophecy goes over much of the ground covered in the version in the *Historia* but more concisely. It refers to the return of Conanus and Kavaladro and makes it more explicit than either the *Historia* or the *Armes,* that Conanus, who "navigat undas", represents the Bretons, (cf. *Vita Merlini,* l. 967, *donec ab Armorica veniet temone Conanus*). This version is more direct in its appeal and ends on the note of restitution, *Posteritas magni tollet diadema Britanni,* without Geoffrey's celestial upheavals. Rupert Taylor's view[35] was that "John of Cornwall was not versifying Geoffrey's

book . . . It is assumed on the strength of his own statement that he had a Welsh original"; but the sentences in the commentary believed to be Welsh are in fact Cornish,[36] so that there can be little doubt that for John *in Britannico* was Cornish. If this prophecy is translated *iuxta nostrum Britannicum,* it would appear that these hopes of British restitution, and therefore the traditions of unity and loss, were common to Wales and Cornwall and not unknown in Brittany. The historical myth outlined here was a common British tradition.[37]

What, therefore, is the *Historia Regum Britanniae,* a fairly light-hearted fraud by a clever writer of few principles and some ambitions, or a genuine imaginative response to the meaning of history, in this case the legendary history of Britain? Geoffrey follows contemporary historical thought, in his views of "the destiny of a nation", and of the working out of fate or Providence; he has his contemporaries' fears and abhorrence of civil war; but he found these ideas incipient and ready for him in traditional British history and he uses them to express his own historical ideals. What raises the *Historia* from being no more than an entertaining chronicle of the rise and fall of a succession of imaginary kings is the eschatalogical view of history which he took from the traditional history with its interweave of loss and renewal, of history and prophecy. The period of the *Historia,* Troy to Saxon Conquest, is well-defined, but the significance of the narrative is left open-ended. Geoffrey leaves his readers with the question: has Providence completed her purpose for the Britons? Geoffrey, as always, is ambiguous: but, as he pondered "about the history of the kings of Britain" and as he considered the myth of loss and restitution, did Geoffrey, like others after him, find his mixed loyalties, emotions and hopes rather a problem? The way we resolve the ambiguities he has left us may be no more than a reflection of our own problems, hopes and fears.

Notes

1. For court poetry in Ireland and Wales see J. E. Caerwyn Williams, "The Court Poet in Medieval Ireland", Sir John Rhŷs Lecture, *Proc. British Academy,* LVII, pp.85-135; id., "Beirdd y Tywysogion: Arolwg", *Llên Cymru,* XI, pp. 3-94.

2. Myles Dillon, "The Archaism of Irish Tradition", Sir John Rhŷs Lecture, *Proc. British Academy,* XXXIII, pp.261-2; Seán mac Airt, '*Filidecht* and *Coimgne*', *Ériu,* XVIII, pp. 139-52.

3. *Llên Cymru,* III, pp.234-9, "Y Tri Chof" (the three Memorials, history, language, genealogies). For the survival of oral history see Ifor Williams, *Hen Chwedlau,* Caerdydd, 1949, pp.3-4.

4. "Ystoria", *Bull. Board of Celtic Studies,* XXVI, pp.13-20, I. Williams & T. Roberts, *Cywyddau Dafydd ap Gwilym a'i Gyfoeswyr,* Caerdydd, 1935, p.159. The history these poets read was the Brut which had been absorbed into the poetic tradition by the XVth century. Even in the following century some of the major poets wrote or compiled histories.

5. Rachel Bromwich, *Trioedd Ynys Prydein,* Cardiff, 1961, lxvii-iii; Thomas Jones, "The Black Book of Carmarthen 'Stanzas of the Graves'," Sir John Rhys Lecture, *Proc. British Academy,* LIII, pp.97-137.

6. H. Gunkel, *The Legends of Genesis,* 1-2 (quoted in *Llên Cymru,* XI, p.45); Jan Vansina, *Oral Tradition,* Penguin, 1973, p.49.

7. "The Background of Early Irish Literature", *Studia Hibernica,* I, pp.11-12; cf. Gerard Murphy, *Saga and Myth in Ancient Ireland,* Dublin, 1961, 12: "the *fili,* who as well as being a learned poet, master of *senchus* (history) and *dinnshenchus* (placelore), had been trained to narrate 'the chief stories of Ireland to kings, lords, and noblemen'."

8. See further Gerard Murphy, *op. cit.;* T. F. O'Rahilly, *Early Irish History and Mythology,* Dublin, 1946; Brian Ó Cuív, "Literary Creation and Irish Historical Tradition", Sir John Rhŷs Lecture, *Proc. British Academy,* XLIX, pp.233-62; A. & B. Rees, *Celtic Heritage,* London, 1961; Rachel Bromwich, "The Character of the early Welsh Tradition", N. K. Chadwick, ed., *Studies in Early British History,* Cambridge, 1959, pp.83-136.

9. *Hen Chwedlau,* pp.14-15.

10. See, e.g., *Trioedd Ynys Prydein,* 229, or the tale *The Dream of Maxen.*

11. "The Names of the Island of Britain", *Trioedd,* 228, cxxiii-vii.

12. *Life of St Gildas, Culhwch and Olwen.* A. W. Wade-Evans, *Archaeologia Cambrensis,* 95, pp.249-50, and Saunders Lewis, *Meistri'r Canrifoedd,* Caerdydd, 1973, pp.6-9, argue that the "crown of London" concept is derived from Geoffrey of Monmouth; Wade-Evans attributes the idea of the unity of Britain to Gildas. For contrary arguments see Thomas Charles-Edwards, *Trans. Cymmrodorion Society,* 1970, p.290.

13. I for Williams and J. E. Caerwyn Williams, *The Poems of Taliesin,* Dublin, 1968, VII, 1. 31; *Bull. Board Celtic Studies,* VII, 23.

14. Cf. T. M. Chotzen, *Etudes Celtiques,* IV, pp. 252-3, who suggests evidence for 'la généalogie des premiers rois de la Grande-Bretagne' and 'la lignée de plus anciens rois' as elements in Geoffrey's source material.

15. A. O. and M. O. Anderson, *Adomnán's Life of Columba,* Edinburgh, 1961, p.200; F. M. Stenton, *Anglo-Saxon England,* Oxford, 1943, pp.34-6. Cf. Leslie Alcock, *Arthur's Britain,* Penguin, 1973, pp.320-2; N. K. Chadwick, *Bull. Board Celtic Studies,* XIX, pp.225-30.

16. Brynley F. Roberts, *Cyfranc Lludd a Llefelys,* Dublin, 1975, xix.

17. For these genealogies and dynastic origins see P. C. Bartrum, *Early Welsh Genealogical Tracts,* Cardiff, 1966, 2, 10, (nos 2,4), 11 (no. 16); Rachel Bromwich,

"Character of Early Welsh Tradition", *op. cit.,* pp.107-9, 135-6. Nennius has a long section on the Romano-British emperors, chaps 19-30, a sign of the interest this period in their history held for the Welsh.

18. Lludd, son of Beli Mawr, is a mythological king who may have had a traditional role as a defender of Britain, as is suggested in *Cyfranc, op. cit.* xii-xx. Caswallawn played a similar part in the historical tradition. It is not surprising, therefore, to find the two associated in mediaeval legend, and that the historical Caswallawn is listed as Lludd's brother, one of Beli's other sons. For Caswallawn see *Trioedd,* pp.300-3, "Character . . .", *op. cit.,* pp.132-3.

19. *Hen Chwedlau,* p.17, *Trioedd,* pp.159-60.

20. For the view that Geoffrey's source for this story, or a version of it, is extant in Breton historical material see Gw. Le Duc, "L'Historia Britannica avant Geoffroy de Monmouth", *Annales de Bretagne,* LXXIX, pp.819-35. On the Dream of Maxen see "Character . . .", *op. cit.,* pp.107-9; Susan M. Pearce, "The Traditions of the Royal King List of Dumnonia", *Trans. Cymmrodorion Society,* 1971, pp.128-9.

21. *Trioedd,* 228. Cf. again R. W. Hanning, *The Vision of History in Early Britain,* Columbia, 1966.

22. Attitudes towards the Edwardian conquest of 1282 reveal the two viewpoints in a later period. For English annalists this was a triumph of unification, *Hic monarcha effectus et totius insulae dominus, Wallenses saepius rebellantes devicit, Scotos subvenit,* and referring to the Scottish defeats of 1296, *Unde ex Anglia, Scocia, et Wallia monarchiam quondam tocius Britannie per multa tempora decisam et truncatam occupavit,* quoted by Robert Stepsis, *Medievalia et Humanistica,* n.s., no. 3, 73; but for the anonymous Aberconwy chronicler (*Register and Chronicle of the Abbey of Aberconway, The Camden Miscellany,* I, 1847, 12), recording the death of Llewelyn the Last, *Reddiderunt etiam Coronam famosissimi Arthuri quondam regis Britanniae; et sic gloria Walliae et etiam Wallencium regibus et magnatibus Angliae translata est.*

23. Cf. Vansina, *Oral Tradition,* 51, "A number of myths are exclusively aimed at providing an explanation of the creation of the world and of society as it exists, and their function is to justify the existing political structure". For the adaptation of Irish origin myths see *Etudes Celtiques,* XIII, 109-10. A late example of a Welsh political explanatory story is the account of the founding of the Lordship of Glamorgan by the twelve knights, *Glamorgan Historian,* III, pp.153-69.

24. For the historicity of early references to Hors, Hengist and Vortigern see *Bull. Board Celtic Studies,* XXIII, pp37-59.

25. Enid M. Griffiths, *Early Vaticination in Welsh,* Cardiff, 1937; Glanmor Williams, "Proffwydoliaeth, Prydyddiaeth a Pholitics yn yr Oesoedd Canol", *Taliesin,* XVI, pp.31-9; Basil Clarke, *Life of Merlin,* Cardiff, 1973; *Et. Celt.,* XIII, pp.73-4.

26. See line 34, *keith y mynuer.*

27. The poem is edited by Ifor Williams, trans. Rachel Bromwich, *Armes Prydein,* Dublin, 1972.

28. Psychological aspects of the theme are discussed by R. F. Hobson, *The King who will return,* Guild of Pastoral Psychology, Lecture 130, 1965, pp.31-41.

29. Cf. again Geoffrey's three bishoprics, London, York, Caerleon, with those of the tract "The Names of the Island of Britain", London, York, Menevia, *Trioedd,* 228.

30. For Edwin see *Trioedd,* 339; Alcock, *op. cit.,* 322, 353; Stenton, *op. cit.,* 80.

31. Trans. taken from Lewis Thorpe, *History of the Kings of Britain,* Penguin Classics.

32. "L'influence littéraire de la cour d'Henri Beauclerc", *Mélanges offerts à Rita Lejeune,* Gembloux, 1969, pp.679-87.

33. Down to the period of the emigration and for some centuries afterwards, Welsh, Cornish and Bretons shared common historical traditions and common genealogies: see Susan M. Pearce, *Trans. Cymmrodorion Society* 1971, pp.128-39; L. Fleuriot, "Old Breton Genealogies and Early British Traditions", *Bull. Board Celtic Studies,* XXVI, pp.1-6; Myles Dillon and N. K. Chadwick, *The Celtic Realms,* London, 1967, pp.88-9. For connections in later periods, see Jean Marx, "Monde Brittonique et Matière de Bretagne", *Et. Celt.,* X, pp.478-88; L. Fleuriot, "Breton et Cornique à la fin du Moyen-Age", *Annales de Bretagne,* LXXVI, pp. 706-21. Cf. n.20.

34. E.g. *Armes Prydein,* lines 171-5: 'Wise men foretell all that will happen: they will possess all from Manaw to Brittany, from Dyfed to Thanet, it will be theirs: from the Wall to the Forth, along their estuaries, their dominion will spread over Yr Echwydd', trans. taken from Williams and Bromwich, *op. cit.*

35. *The Political Prophecy in England,* New York, 1911, p.20. For the contrary view, see Paul Zumthor, *Merlin le Prophète,* 1943, p.79.

36. The Prophecy has now been edited and translated by P. Flobert, *Et. Celt.,* XIV, pp.31-41. L. Fleuriot, *ibid.,* pp.43-56., discusses these "British" phrases and sentences, and holds that they are proto-Cornish. On John of Cornwall see Eleanor Rathbone, *Recherches de Théologie anc. et mod.,* XVII, pp.46-60.

37. Arthur's role as the returning deliverer is a later development than the Cynan-Cadwaladr traditions, as is pointed out in *Medium Aevum,* XLIII, 183. Basil Clarke, *op. cit.,* pp.162-3, suggests that Arthur first appears clearly as a "deliverer figure *c.*1168 in Etienne de Rouen's *Draco Normannicus*", and that this was a Breton development. That all three British peoples subsequently regarded Arthur in this light is shown by a commentary on Merlin's Prophecy, *Speculum,* XV, pp.141-5, *omnium scilicet haec est superstitio, Britonum, Guallorum et Cornubiensium.*

Christopher Brooke (essay date 1976)

SOURCE: "Geoffrey of Monmouth as a Historian," in *Church and Government in the Middle Ages,* edited by C. N. L. Brooke *et al.,* Cambridge University Press, 1976, pp. 77-91.

[*In the following essay, Brooke explores some possible motives and intentions of Geoffrey in writing* The History of the Kings of Britain.]

Geoffrey of Monmouth's ***History of the Kings of Britain***[1] purports to be a history of the rulers of Britain from the foundation of the British race by Brutus, great-gradson of Aeneas, in the second half of the second millennium B.C. to Cadwalader in the seventh century A.D. It is a shapely, well-conceived book, written in Latin in the style of contemporary histories; its climax and centrepiece is the account of King Arthur, the greatest of the British Kings; its comparatively matter-of-fact approach is only once set aside for more than a moment, in the ***Prophecies of Merlin.*** It purported to be history, and history it was taken to be: with only a few dissentient voices the Latin world immediately accepted it as genuine, and gave it a tremendous reception. And this is remarkable, since we now know that hardly a word of it is true, that there has scarcely, if ever, been a historian more mendacious than Geoffrey of Monmouth.

His achievement was essentially literary; he produced one of the most popular of medieval Latin histories, and he floated Arthur as matter for serious historical enquiry, thus playing a crucial role in making him respectable throughout western Europe, and the centre of the Matter of Britain. Geoffrey's interest as a historian is that he reveals the aims and methods of one of the most flourishing schools of historical writing in the middle ages—that of southern and western Britain in the early twelfth century—untrammelled by the limitations and exigencies of evidence and source. No modern scholar would look for reliable historical evidence about early Britain in Geoffrey, even though all acknowledge that he has access to sources now lost.[2] In fact it may matter little for our enquiry whether he was a serious student troubled, like a number of other chroniclers of the tenth, eleventh and twelfth centuries, by an incurable incapacity to distinguish truth from fiction; or a deliberate 'liar', to use a contemporary word intended to distinguish 'history' in the sense used by Bede or William of Malmesbury, from the fiction of the courtly romance.[3] Indeed, it is not clear to some modern scholars that Geoffrey would entirely have understood the distinction. Yet for his interpretation it seems to me fundamental to establish at the outset whether he designed his book to read like history out of serious purpose or a desire to parody. Nor shall we expect to find a simple answer to a question from which all ambiguity cannot be removed; for parody may be as serious as imitation.

There are certain passages in Geoffrey's ***History*** which can hardly be based on anything but bravado. The Laws of Molmutius, he alleges, were established by Dunuuallo

Molmutius in some remote period B.C. (a generation or so after the death of King Lear) and 'are famous among the English to this day'; and Geoffrey proceeds to specify some of them.[4] Later he observes that Belinus, one of Molmutius's sons, confirmed the laws, 'and if anyone is curious to know what he decreed concerning them [the highways] let him read the Molmutine laws, which Gildas the historian translated from British into Latin, and King Alfred into English'.[5] This passage is very characteristic of Geoffrey. He takes famous names and genuine authors, thus lending to an implausible tale a certain verisimilitude, and uses them out of context.[6] There has been much argument as to how much he invented, and this will never be concluded, for no one doubts that some of his sources are lost.[7] What the patient researches of Tatlock and others have made abundantly clear is that he liked to create, as it were, a mosaic pattern in which most of the pieces had some existence in his material, some of the pieces were recognisably historical, but most of the pattern was invention.

Another characteristic of this passage is the use of the *topos* of translation. This was to have a great future; in numerous courtly romances and similar works the author claims that his work is simply based on a translation—from a Latin original discovered by Walter Map, from an Arabic version by Kyot the Provençal, to name only two of the most famous.[8] In the majority of cases the point of these *topoi* is that the statement, though significant, is obviously false. It seems rarely to have been intended to deceive contemporaries as it has often deceived modern critics. The most important use of this *topos* for our purpose is Geoffrey's claim that his whole work is a translation from a book in the 'British' tongue discovered by Walter, archdeacon of Oxford;[9] and to this we shall return. For the moment, let us observe that it sits on the face of the passages we have just inspected that Geoffrey can hardly have expected serious belief in the Laws of Dunuuallo Molmutius.

This passage, then, is evidently a literary adventure; but whether the intent was wholly frivolous cannot be established from one part of the book alone. The most revealing passage elsewhere is the famous account of Arthur's court and crown-wearing at Caerleon-on-Usk, which is the climax of the whole book. It contains a long list of lesser worthies, which is now known simply to be an extract from a Welsh genealogy.[10] It is doubtful if a Welsh audience would have been deceived, likely enough that an English or Anglo-Norman audience would have believed that this was a genuine list of names. The greater magnates included 'the three archbishops of the three metropolitan sees, London, York, and Dubricius of the City of Legions. This prelate, who was primate of Britain (*Britannie primus*), and legate of the apostolic see, was so eminent for his piety that he could cure any sick persons by his prayers . . .'[11] There follows the crown-wearing over which Dubricius (St Dyfrig), as bishop of the see of Caerleon, presided, and all the panoply of a royal court; finally, the business of the day and ecclesiastical appointments.

'St Dubricius, from a pious desire of leading a hermit's life, made a voluntary resignation of his archiepiscopal dignity; and in his room was consecrated David, the king's uncle, whose life was a perfect example of that goodness to those whom he had taught.' This and other passages imply some knowledge of the ecclesiastical organisation of Roman Britain in the fourth century: how much we cannot say, for this had been the subject of much speculation in the early twelfth century by supporters of the claims of London and St Davids against Canterbury in the primacy disputes of the age. What is clearer is Geoffrey's interest in these contemporary controversies. We know of four which flickered or flared between the Norman Conquest of England and the composition of the *History* in the 1130s. First, the controversy of Canterbury and York, opened in 1070 by Lanfranc's claim to be primate of all Britain, a title used by his successors when receiving the professions of their suffragans, and naturally attributed by Geoffrey to Dubricius. When Geoffrey wrote it was dormant, for in spite of the Canterbury Forgeries the popes had recently supported York in its claim not to be subject to Canterbury.[12] Next there was the claim based partly on ancient history, partly on the declared intentions of Gregory the Great and partly on obscure passages in eighth-century history, that London should be the seat of the archbishopric—or at least that the bishop should have a pallium. This claim is echoed not only in the reference to London in this passage, but also in the *Prophecies of Merlin,* where it is forecast that the pallium of Canterbury shall adorn London. Both passages gave heart to Gilbert Foliot in his fight against Thomas Becket in the 1160s;[13] but long before Foliot's accession, Bishop Richard de Belmeis I had tried to revive such a claim in 1108.[14] Next there was the struggle of the Welsh and Scottish Churches for independence of the English metropolitans. In this the Scots were successful; the Welsh failed. But the claim that St David himself had been an archbishop and that his see should be archiepiscopal was still very active in the early twelfth century, and its major protagonist, Bishop Bernard (1115-48), still very much alive when Geoffrey wrote.[15] It had not, however, commended itself to the founders of the diocese of Llandaff, who raised what appears to be a counter-claim, that their own founders—Teilo, Euddogwy (Oudoceus), and Dyfrig (Dubricius) himself—had been archbishops.[16] Finally, soon after Geoffrey's book had been issued, Henry of Blois, bishop of Winchester, was to demand a pallium and an independent province.[17]

It cannot be supposed that Geoffrey wrote this passage in support of any contemporary cause. Of Canterbury he naturally makes no mention, since he is writing of an epoch earlier than Augustine; but if his story was taken as literal truth, it could deal a deadly blow at Canterbury, as Foliot saw. Against St Davids and Llandaff he strikes impartially, since he makes Caerleon the metropolitan see of Wales and enthrones there in succession Dubricius and David himself. Nor could York or London gain much comfort from being made subject to a Welsh primate (as they would have understood it); and in any case when Geoffrey wrote London and Llandaff were vacant, as was Canterbury. Thus he declared a plague on all their houses, and can have intended nothing but mockery and mischief.

There is curious confirmation of his mischievous intent in the manner in which the book was issued. Early copies were dedicated to King Stephen, the earl of Worcester, the earl of Gloucester, and to the bishop of Lincoln:[18] it is evident that Geoffrey wished it to circulate widely among possible patrons (as was shortly to be shown) of varying political complexion in the disputes of Stephen's reign, soon to flare into civil war. But the first recorded reader was Henry, archdeacon of Huntingdon, who was a colleague of Geoffrey in the diocese of Lincoln, fellow-archdeacon of Geoffrey's accomplice Walter of Oxford, and one of the best known chroniclers of the day.[19] It would have been natural for Geoffrey to take Henry into his confidence and to consult him in the process of compiling his history. Yet Henry was left to discover it in peculiar and, one might have supposed, suspicious circumstances. For early in 1139 Henry visited the Norman abbey of Le Bec in company with Archbishop Theobald, en route for the papal curia.[20] At Le Bec Henry's attention was drawn to Geoffrey's book by their fellow-chronicler, Robert of Torigny, as he himself tells us in a letter he wrote to Warin Brito, full of the excitement of his discovery, which both Henry and Robert entered in their chronicles.

Henry is directly referred to in the epilogue to Geoffrey's *History,* which is known to be missing from two early manuscripts and may be an afterthought, but bears all the marks of authenticity.[21]

> The kings who have ruled in Wales from that time I leave as a theme for Caradoc of Llancarvan, my contemporary, and those of the Saxons for William of Malmesbury and Henry of Huntingdon: but I forbid them to say anything of the kings of the Britons, since they have not that book *britannici sermonis* which Walter archdeacon of Oxford brought out of *Brittania*; which is a true account of their history; and which I have thus in these princes' honour taken pains to translate into Latin.

Caradog was author of saints' lives of little substance—the word *contemporaneus* may or may not hint that Caradog was a historian of Geoffrey's ilk;[22] William and Henry were the best known English historians of the day. In the light of the passages we have inspected, we may surely take the last two clauses quite literally and presume that Geoffrey's confidence that William and Henry could not have access to the Welsh book was based on his knowledge that it did not exist.[23] But it is so couched, as with the translation of the Molmutine laws, to disguise the implication from a gullible reader—and modern interpreters very far from credulous have failed to draw the conclusion. Since we know that no Welsh book could have contained more than a tiny portion of Geoffrey's narrative, and that his only other use of the *topos* of translation is a palpable fiction, it would in any case seem reasonable to conclude that Geoffrey, like later writers, used the *topos,* to hide a fiction. For myself, I think his success as a historian was

beyond his expectation and that the epilogue expresses the daring of a man who cannot believe that he will continue to be taken seriously.

In any case he took elaborate pains to make his book seem like history. Although the materials are rich and varied, his idea of how history should read seems to owe most to William. For at its best it consists of a string of narrative reconstructed with great ingenuity from tenuous evidence, embellished and turned into readable narrative by frequent recourse to stories beautifully told. The difference is that William's ingenuity was exercised in genuine historical research, in fitting annals and charters and stories into a single whole; but the effect on a credulous reader is much the same. The long stretches of fairly jejune succession stories are also reminiscent of Henry of Huntingdon, and Geoffrey shared the interest which both William and Henry showed in antiquities. He follows Henry in describing the making of Roman roads, and he seems to have created a whole romantic chapter on the basis of a Roman inscription in Carlisle, already noted and mildly misinterpreted by William.[24] His method and his fancy enabled him to carry this interest further, and out of Caerleon and its Roman remains he created the chief city of Arthur's empire. Yet through most of the *History* the tone is tolerably matter of fact; there is a little magic, a few references in the christian epoch to miracles; but much less of the marvellous than in other contrived narratives of the early or central middle ages. Even the making of Stonehenge is attributed to technology of a kind rather than to magic.[25]

To the comparatively rational tone of the history there is one notable exception. Outside the seventh book there is comparatively little mystification; in the seventh book there is little else. King Vortigern built a tower, and the more he added to the top, the more the foundations sank into the ground. His magicians declared that the only solution was to sprinkle the foundations with the blood of a child born without a father. After elaborate search, such a child was found. But Merlin (for such was the child's name)[26] turned the tables on his persecutors: he not only knew what was in the minds of the magicians, but he was able to explain the mystery of the tower, in a highly rational way. Under the foundations was a pond: the tower was sinking into the mud. His predictions continued. At the bottom of the pond were two stones and under the stones two dragons. The pond was cleared at Vortigern's command, and the dragons were duly found; they came out of their lair and proceeded to fight with one another. The king enquired of Merlin what these dragons signified and so compelled the sage to tell Vortigern of the fate of his people. The dragons were symbols of the British and the English—and thus we are launched on a lengthy prophecy, in symbolic language stretching far into the future. The first section carries the story to the reign of Henry I—that is, to Geoffrey's own day—and most of the details can be interpreted after a fashion.[27] But this only accounts for less than a quarter of the whole. The next section is also comparatively clear: it represents the messianic hope of a pan-Celtic revival, although there is no suggestion that Arthur is to be the messiah. 'Cadwalader shall call upon Conan and take Albania into alliance' seems to mean that Wales (or South Britain as a whole) shall join with Scotland and make common cause, to expel the foreigner and set up a native Celtic or British kingdom again.[28] A little over half the prophecy remains, and it has been from that day to this utterly unintelligible. The idiom is much the same as before, but no sort of interpretation can be made of it and no picture emerges of the prophet's intention. The final passage is apocalyptic and astrological.

There was plenty of precedent for planting political prophecy into a historical narrative; and also for the kind of prophecy which gives itself plausibility by opening with an account of recent events put into the mouth of a great figure of the past. Both, for instance, occur in the Book of Daniel[29] From Daniel and the Psalms come the animal symbolism, the composite animals, and the rhythm and style of the prophecies. The opening story and start of the prophecy come from the *Historia Brittonum*, into which Geoffrey has inserted the name Merlin; the astrological catastrophe at the end comes, in garbled form, from Lucan's *Pharsalia*.[30] There seems little doubt that the inspiration of the piece is Celtic, that it owes a great deal to a type of prophecy popular among contemporary Celts. But in detail it is Geoffrey's composition, and it is as difficult to find precise Celtic elements here as elsewhere in the *History*.[31] It has been suggested that the unintelligible sections of the Prophecies were taken over from a Celtic source more or less wholesale; and it is reasonably certain that they were as unintelligible to Geoffrey as to us. But this kind of jigsaw puzzle of nonsense is dangerously easy to compose, and the only satisfactory explanation is that when the original purpose of the prophecy was fulfilled the parodist's pen carried on. In the summary of this prophecy which Geoffrey gave in his other work, the *Life of Merlin,* the later part is wholly omitted.[32]

Geoffrey followed his *History* after about ten years, or a little more, with the *Life of Merlin,* a strange and horrifying fairy-story, in which the portrait of Merlin is in some ways quite different from that in the *History*.[33] It serves to show that Geoffrey had an abiding interest in prophecy, for he repeats in summary form the intelligible part of the earlier prophecies, adds a supplement to bring it up to date and yet another account of the messianic hope. But in the main it underlines by an extraordinary contrast the comparatively matter-of-fact tone of the *History.*

Some students of medieval historical writing are inclined always to search for political motives and political bias and to see these as a force more powerful in the historian's mind than an interest in the past or the love of historical truth; to others, disciples of the school of *Geistesgeschichte,* chronicles are primarily expressions of a world of ideas. Both approaches explain too little and too much. When Bede, after a lifetime spent in other work, came in his grey hairs to write the *Historia Ecclesiastica,* he revealed a profound curiosity in the story of the conversion of the English people as well as an extraordinary gift for fitting scattered and disparate materials into a flowing narrative.[34] When Bede wrote, there was no fashion and little precedent, save in ancient narratives, for writing history. Geoffrey of Monmouth wrote in a milieu in which history flourished—in the wake of Eadmer, William of Malmesbury, John of Worcester and Henry of Huntingdon.[35] We may discount the love of historical truth as a motive for his work; but it is well to explore for a moment the possibility of political bias and a fascination with historical reconstruction and historical storytelling as possible motives; and his place in a *Geistesgeschichtliches* scheme.

The Prophecies and the *Life* were dedicated to successive bishops of Lincoln;[36] the *History* to various secular potentates, including both Robert, earl of Gloucester, and King Stephen. This does not suggest any particular predilection for one side or the other in the civil wars of Stephen's reign—rather, perhaps, an inclination to hedge his bets. But if we are right in thinking that the book was completed in 1138, a year before the Empress entered England, it may not have been clear even to an intelligent observer that civil war was on the way.[37] The dedications suggest that the narrative of the narrative of the *History* was expected to appeal to men who liked good secular narratives, the Prophecies to men of a more learned and sophisticated turn of mind. None of them is known to have had Celtic ancestors in the recent past, although the chief recipient, Robert of Gloucester, was a great marcher lord with much Welsh territory under his rule.[38]

The *History* gives the British element in the island's past a massive boost, and the Prophecies obscurely hint at a pan-Celtic revival.[39] But neither is calculated to bring this home to any audience likely to pay attention: we have no reason to suppose that any of the dedicatees would have viewed such a movement with sympathy—quite the reverse—and any wish to stir such a movement might have been better expressed, less obscurely, in Welsh. It is much more likely that Geoffrey was deliberately obscure in presenting expressions of sympathy for his fellow-Celts.

More substantially, he portrays a golden age in British monarchy in the past, in the reign of Arthur; he makes Arthur appear in all his lineaments like a very grandiose version of Henry I; and the prophecies of the future might be read as referring to the Angevin empire rather than to a Celtic revival. The glorification of British, or Anglo-Norman, monarchy seems strangely ill-timed: by 1138 it can hardly have seemed that Stephen would be a worthy successor to Arthur; yet it would have required considerable prescience to foresee the triumph of Henry II, then a small boy of five. But it is in the nature of the monarchy in the middle ages that it most needed propaganda when it was weak, and there is nothing impossible in Geoffrey conceiving in the 1130s that it was an acceptable time to boost the monarchy by setting beside Edward the Confessor as the source of monarchical legend—and in rivalry to Charlemagne[40]—the heroic figure of Arthur.

Such an idea may or may not have entered Geoffrey's head; it can hardly in any case have accounted for most of the book which we know. This is a literary work of remarkable skill, above all, a skill in storytelling and in re-constructing the past out of fragmentary materials. It is in this sense that he takes his place both among the major literary figures and among the most ingenious historians of the age. He was perhaps the most popular of all historical writers of the middle ages: over two hundred manuscripts testify to his success; even Bede, with a four-hundred-year start, cannot quite muster 150.[41] More than that, he played a substantial part in creating one of the great literary fashions of the middle ages. Even those scholars who have been most concerned to belittle his role in the creation of the Matter of Britain could hardly deny him that.

Equally striking to a modern reader is the way in which he has created out of genealogies, king-lists, and such documents as lay to hand, as well as out of a copious imagination, the kind of reconstruction of history which impresses the modern scholar in William of Malmesbury and the authors of *Liber Landauensis*. It has long been known that William of Malmesbury attempted to reconstruct lists of kings, bishops and abbots by fitting together succession-lists, annals and charters; above all, that he understood in principle—even if he floundered in practice—how charters could reveal the relative epochs of kings and ecclesiastics.[42] It has been argued that a similar technique, even more brilliantly though less truthfully applied, explains the lists of bishops in the Book of Llandaff.[43] In recent years Wendy Davies has accumulated formidable evidence to suggest that this was much over-stated: that in fact the authors had authentic charters or *notitiae* of some kind to work on and failed effectively to unite them with the genealogies.[44] Even so, it seems clear that they knew and attempted to use, however inadequately, William of Malmesbury's techniques. Essentially, it was a kind of jigsaw they were constructing; and in piecing together a convincing history out of often tiny fragments commonly belonging to quite a different context Geoffrey was imitating their technique. In this way he reflects contemporary fascination with history as a reconstruction of obscure past events.

Geoffrey also owed a debt to one greater than William of Malmesbury; and his technique appears at its most refined and effective when he is closest to Bede.[45] The early to mid-seventh century was the last British heroic age in his eyes, and he understandably closes his **History** with Cadwallon and Cadwalader, for the former was a major figure in history as well as in legend. But it was also a notable age in English history, and the closing section had to encompass two of Bede's heroes, Edwin and Oswald, as well as the rise of Mercia under Penda. There is plenty of other evidence that there was a Welsh literary tradition of this epoch with different emphasis from Bede's; and details, such as the story that Edwin was nurtured in Wales, and Cadwallon's flight to Ireland,[46] seem almost certainly to prove that Geoffrey knew and used these traditions. Doubtless he realised that there were divergences between his sources; and this provided the need, and the challenge, for a measure of novelty. The result is calculated to appeal to a Welsh audience and to seem not too out of line to one

acquainted with Bede; and yet there are stings for both. Readers of Bede were and are surprised to find the whole scene dominated by Cadwallon, to whom Penda is a mere satellite Cadwallon survives his defeat by Oswald to preside over Oswald's later destruction and to participate in the battle of Oswestry (though Geoffrey follows Bede in making Penda destroy Oswald) and to die a natural death in the time of Oswiu. To bemuse his Welsh audience, after his account of how Cadwalader, Cadwallon's son, had made an edifying end (borrowed from the English Caedwalla),[47] Geoffrey unkindly associates the decline in British power with the change of name to Welsh, tries out one or two etymologies of the word, but concludes that it may just refer to their barbarity. Thus the whole section reveals Geoffrey at his most characteristic, piecing together genuine sources and ancient legends, twisting them a little to his purpose, improving a notable saga; save in skill and inventiveness little different at first sight to the *Historia Britonum,* or Dudo on Norman origins, or much twelfth-century hagiography, in honourable fudging. Yet there is an edge to Geoffrey's work rarely evident among his rivals; and when he introduces Cadwalader he covers over the fact that Bede never refers to the last great British king by boldly asserting that Bede called him Chedwalda,[48] a characteristic touch of bravado, in some sense preparing us for the deliberate confusion with Caedwalla which follows. There is little in this to suggest a substantial political or 'patriotic' motive, although it is a fitting tail-piece to a wonderful vision of the British past. But the motive most in evidence is the desire to display the literary gifts of a historian.

Thus at the end of the day it is the more purely literary achievement, the construction of a history enshrining heroic legend, which most impresses us. If the Celtic hope was uppermost in his mind, or the Norman empire, he could easily have made his interest much clearer. The adventure of Henry of Huntingdon may suggest personal spite on Geoffrey's part or just anxiety about his book's reception. None of this can be taken very seriously. The conversion of Arthur from a minor hero in one small part of Europe into the central figure in the most popular legendary cycle of the French- and German-speaking world is quite another matter. We must not attribute everything to Geoffrey. But the basic achievement is his. The Latin chronicles connected with the Charlemagne cycle had helped to foster the legends of Saint-Denis and Roland, but hardly to make Charlemagne respectable, for that he was preeminently before. In Arthur's case this was not so. William of Malmesbury had seen the possibility. 'Arthur is he of whom the Breton ditties today still burble; but he was worthy not to be dreamt of in bogus legends but to be described in a genuine history, since he long sustained his failing country and urged the unbroken spirit of his fellow-countrymen to war.'[49] It was just such a 'genuine' history which Geoffrey purported to provide, and this remarkable sentence may well in a measure have inspired him.

Notes

1. There is no critically constructed text of the *Historia Regum Britanniae,* although a project to remedy that

deficiency now exists: for its first fruit, see Wright, *The Historia.* My citations refer to the chapter numbers of Wright's single-manuscript edition (which are also those of Faral, *La Légende,* III.63–303). The English version is generally my own, although I have made some use of Giles, *Six Old English Chronicles,* pp. 87–292, and I have derived much pleasure and profit from the translation and notes by Thorpe, *Geoffrey.* The fullest commentary is that of Tatlock, *The Legendary History* for a useful general study see also Parry & Caldwell, 'Geoffrey'. Interesting recent studies include Pähler, *Strukturuntersuchungen*; Schirmer, *Die frühen Darstellungen* pp. 7–40; Hanning, *The Vision* pp. 121–72 and 221–47; Flint, 'The *Historia*'; Leckie, *The Passage.* For a list of manuscripts see Dumville, 'The manuscripts' (wtih supplements, now continued by J. Crick). The status of the (First) Variant Version (ed. Wright, The Historia, II), shorter that the vulgate text, is still under discussion. On the whole it is probably a rewritten abbreviation, albeit one made in Geoffrey's lifetime but not by Geoffrey himself. But if it were to become clear that it is a draft, only minor modifications of my argument would be needed. (For further complications see Huws & Roberts, 'Another manuscipt', and Dumville, 'The origin'). Also important is the so-called Second Variant Version (as yet unedited), on which see Emanuel, 'Geoffrey of Monmouth's *Historia*'. On Geoffrey in his context as a historian, see also Gransden, *Historical Writing in England* c. 550 to c. 1307, especially pp. 200–9; for his historical impact, see Ullmann, 'On the influence'. In the notes which follow, bibliographical references have been kept to a minimum, since the full literature on this, as on every aspect of the Arthurian tradition, is immense; it is listed annually in the *Bibliographical Bulletin of the International Arthurian Society.*

2. See Tatlock, *The Legendary History, passim*; and for his use of Welsh sources, some now lost (whose contribution Tatlock tended to minimise), see especially the penetrating paper by Piggott, 'The sources', as well as Bromwich, 'The character', pp. 125–8, and Roberts, 'Geoffrey of Monmouth and Welsh historical tradition'. Piggott doubted whether the 'prehistoric' parts of the historia-narrative could be entirely of Geoffrey's invention, since the use of materials is sometimes clumsy; but the effect of this is always to enhance his likeness to other historical writers, and he is never so clumsy as his most substantial earlier Welsh source, the *Historia Brittonum* (ed. Dumville); nor does any serious scholar doubt that his work is a mosaic rather than pure invention.

3. For a rather different view from mine, briefly expounded but with great penetration, see Southern, 'Aspects', especially pp. 193-6 (also pp. 191-2 on the Norman Dudo). Walter Map described himself as 'a foolish and dull poet—yet not a writer of lies; for he does not lie who repeats a tale, but he who makes it' (*De nugis curialium,* I. 25; the text is ed. & transl.

James, *Walter Map,* pp. 84–113—see aespecially 112–13), perhaps answering Hugh of Rotelande's accusation that he was an expert in the art of lying, and—more remotely—taking up Bede's famous definition of *uera lex historiae* (on which see Ray 'Bede's *Vera lex*'); cf. Webster, 'Walter Map's French things'.

4. § 34.

5. § 35.

6. Good examples of his misuse of authors are his references to Homer and Gildas in §§ 19 and 22. On his use of *De excidio Britanniae* see Wright, 'Geoffrey of Monmouth and Gildas' and 'Geoffrey of Monmouth and Gildas revisited'. For his use of classical names, see especially Tatlock, *The Legendary History,* pp. 116–70.

7. See especially Bromwich, 'The character', and Roberts, 'Goeffrey of Monmouth and Welsh historical tradition'.

8. Map is named in the *Queste del Saint Graal* and the *Mort Artu* of the prose Lancelot cycle; Kyot is named in Wolfram von Eschenbach's *Parzival.* See further Bäuml, 'Varieties'.

9. Walter was archdeacon from *ca* 1111/12, or earlier, to his death in 1151, and a friend of Geoffrey (see Greenway, *John le Neve: Fasti Ecclesiae Aglicanae 1066–1300,* III. 35; Morey and Brooke *The Letters* p. 537 and references given there, especially to Salter, 'Geoffrey') 'British' has been variously interpreted as Breton and Welsh; in fact, the ambiguity could well be deliberate.

10. Piggott, 'The sources', pp. 281-2.

11. § 156

12. See especially Southern, 'The Canterbury Forgeries'.

13. Morey & Brooke, *Gilbert Foliot* pp. 151-62.

14. *Ibid.* p. 151 and n. For the earlier history of this claim, see Whitelock, *Some Anglo-Saxon bishops of* especially p. 14; Brooke & Keir, *London 800–1216,* pp. 119–21.

15. See above, pp. 28–30. See also work of Richter 'The *Life*' and 'Professions'.

16. See above chapter II, especially pp. 18–21. Among more recent studies of *Liber Landauensis* and its context, see especially Davies, 'St Mary's Worcester and 'The consecration'. For another possible approach to its sources, see Davies, 'The orthography'.

17. John of Salisbury, *Historia Pontificalis,* § 40 (ed. and transl. Chibnall, p. 78); cf. Morey & Brooke, *Gilbert Foliot* pp. 158-9.

18. The 'Prophecies of Merlin' (*Historia,* §§ 109–117) have a separate dedication (§§ 109–110) to Alexander, bishop of Lincoln (for its own seperate transmissions see Eckhardt, 'The *Prophetia*'); one surviving manuscript of the *Historia,* carries a dedication

to King Stephen and Robert, earl of Gloucester (See Dumville, 'An early text'); several bear a double dedication to Earl Robert and Waleran, count of Meulan and earl of Worcester; the large majority carries a dedication to Earl Robert alone. See Thorpe, *Geoffrey*, p. 39(-40), n. 7, and especially Parry & Caldwell, 'Geoffrey', p. 80, n. 2.

19. A new edition and translation of Henry of Huntingdon in his preparation by D. E. Greenway for the series 'Oxford Medieval Text'. On Henry, see Gransden *Historical Writing in England c. 550 to c. 1307*, pp. 193-200. The edition by Arnold (*Henrici Archidiaconi Huntendunensis Historia Anglorum*) is incomplete, since it includes onnly one of the letters which are an integral part of the book, and gives a very inadequate account of the complex and interesting MS tradition.

20. Henry's letter is given most fully in Robert of Torigny's, Chronicle (ed. Delisle I. 97-111); see now also Wright, 'The place'. For the context of this journey, see Saltman, *Theobald*, pp. 14-15.

21. § 208; cf. above, pp. 43–4.

22. For brief discussion, see above, p. 43.

23. The contrary view is expressed by Southern, 'Aspects', part 1, p. 194: 'Personally I am convinced that the source which he claimed to have received from Walter, archdeacon of Oxford, really existed. But when we observe the freedom with which other historians in the same tradition treated their sources, we shall not expect any exact correspondence between Geoffrey's source and the "translation" which he made of it.'

24. *Gesta Pontificum Aglorum*, III. 99 (ed. Hamilton, RS pp. 208-9); cf. Tatlock, *The Legendary History*, p. 20; Dumville, 'Celtic-Latin texts', pp. 26–8.

25. §§ 128–130

26. §§ 106–117, *passim*. On Merlin, see especially the references given by Parry, the *Vita Merlini*, introduction; Bromwich, 'The character', pp. 125–6; Jarman, *The Legend*; Clarke, *Life of Merlin*; Tolstoy, *The Quest* (a book to be used with considerable caution: see the review by D. N. Dumville in *Nottingham Medieval Studies*).

27. There is no full modern attempt to follow the medieval commentaries of the twelfth to sixteenth centuries into the 'that Serbonian bog, interpretation of the Prophecies' (Tatlock, *The Legendary History*, p. 403), but Tatlock's own account (*ibid.*, pp. 403–21) is extremely useful, with references to earlier, respectable literature. See also the editions of Hammer listed in the bibliography, below; cf. Eckhardt, 'The date'. There is new work by Eckhardt, *The Prophetia Merlini*. For 'findetur forma commercii: dimidium rotundum erit' (*Historia* § 113 [11]), cf. Grierson & Brooke, 'Round Halfpennies'. I am grateful to Dr Marjorie Chibnall for reminding me of the conclusive evidence of Orderic Vitalis, *Historia Ecclesias-*

tica (ed. and transl. Chibnall, VI. 380–9), that the Prophecies were known 1135: cf. Fletcher, 'Two notes', p. 468; Thorpe, 'Orderic'; Wright, *The Historia*, I. x-x11.

28. For discussion of Geoffrey's political interests, see Tatlock, The Legendary History pp. 284–304 and 425–30; the interesting paper (suggesting glorification of the Norman dynasty) by Gerould, 'King Arthur and politics', especially 48-9. Dumville 'An early text', pp. 18–27. Doubtless there are obscure hints here and elsewhere of sympathy with Celtic aspirations (cf. Padel, 'Geoffrey'); but Geoffrey's chief patron was a great marcher lord, and this section of the Prophecies can equally be read as a glorification of the Norman dynasty—was early read, not unnaturally, as prophecy of the Angevin empire. On Celtic political prophetic poetry, see most recently Dumville, 'Brittany and "Amres Prydein Vawr"'.

29. Cf. Heaton, *The Book*, especially pp. 57-8, on Daniel 7.

30. *Historia*, § 117 (73). On the influence of Lucan see Tatlock, *The Legendary History*, pp. 405–6 (and his references).

31. But see above, n. 2. See also Taylor, *The Political Prophecy*.

32. Lines 580-688.

33. In the *Historia*, Merlin is essentially the Ambrosius (Emrys) of Nennius; in the *Historia Brittonum*; in *Vita Merlini* 'he has many of the traits of the Celtic Myrddin' (Parry, *The Vita Merlini*, p. 13). Cf. n. 26, above..

34. This is well brought out by Kirby, 'Bede's native sources'.

35. See Southern, 'Aspects', part 4, pp. 246–56; Brooke *The Twelfth Century Renaissance* pp. 166–9; Gransden, *Historical Writing in England, c. 550-c. 1307*.

36. See above, n. 18; Parry, *The Vita Merlini*, pp. 30-1 and 119.

37. On the date, see above, p. 43. n. 103. The evidence of the dedications has sometimes been used to suggest a date as early as 1136; and the combination in one MS of Stephen and the Empress's half-brother Robert of Gloucester makes a date as late as 1139/40 difficult to accept. But the fact that Henry of Huntingdon could 'discover' the work in Normandy early in 1139 makes it almost incredible that the work was circulating more than a few months earlier than this. For Stephen's reign in general, see Davis, *King Stephen*, and Cronne, *The Reign*.

38. On Robert of Gloucester as a patron, see Cokayne, *The Complete Peerage*, v. 683–6.

39. See n. 28. above.

40. See Barlow, *Edward the Confessor*, pp. 256–88; Folz, *Le souvenir*.

41. On Geoffrey-manuscripts, see above, n. 1. For Bede, see Mynors *apud* Colgrave & Mynors, *Bede's Ecclesiastical History*, pp. xxxix-lxx and lxxv-lxxvi.

42. See especially Robinson, *Somerset*, pp. 1–53; Southern, 'Aspects', part 4, pp. 253–6 (and the context, pp. 249–56, emphasising the wider interest in charters and documents of many kinds in the late eleventh– and twelfth–century England); Scott, *The Early History*.

43. See above pp. 46–8.

44. See above, n. 16.

45. On Geoffrey's use of Bede, see Faral, *La Légende*, II. 314–40; and on this section, Tatlock, *The Legendary History*, pp. 251-3. The essential passages are Geoffrey, *Historia*, §§ 190–208, and Bede, *Historia Ecclesiastica*, II.20, III (especially III. 1-3, 6, 9).

46. For these details and the other sources, see Lloyd, *A History*, I. 182–6 (especially 183 and 185); see now the fuller account by Bromwich, *Trioedd*, pp. 293–6, 546.

47. Bede, *Historia Ecclesiastica*, v.7; see also n. 48 below. The names Cadwallon (Welsh) and Cædwalla (Old English) are of course one and the same.

48. Faral's reading: § 202 (*La Légende*, III. 299); and something of the kind must be intended, although in the present state of knowledge of the manuscripts Geoffrey's spelling cannot be confidently affirmed. Clearly, as Tatlock pointed out (*The Legendary History*, p. 253, n. 102), it is 'a reminiscence of Bede's "Caedualla, iuuenis strenuissimus de regio genere Geuissorum"' (*Historia Ecclesiastica*, IV.15 [13]). This serves to underline Geoffrey's bravado.

49. *Gesta Regum Anglorum*, I. 8 (ed. Stubbs I. 11); cf. above, p. 43 and n. 104, and Brooke, *The Twelfth Century Renaissance*, p. 166.

Valerie I. J. Flint (essay date 1979)

SOURCE: "The *Historia Britanniae* of Geoffrey of Monmouth: Parody and Its Purpose—A Suggestion," *Speculum*, Vol. LIV, No. 3, July, 1979, pp. 447-68.

[*In the following essay, Flint presents evidence that* The History of the Kings of Britain *was intended to make fun of other histories and ultimately to advance the cause of worldly society over monastic society.*]

The *Historia Regum Britanniae* of Geoffrey of Monmouth has enjoyed an enormous amount of attention. In the first place, the work itself was extraordinarily popular. The most recent edition of the text, by Acton Griscom, lists almost 200 surviving Latin manuscripts, 48 of the twelfth century,[1] and more have been added and will be added.[2] In the second, it was and is a puzzle. It was found difficult to interpret as soon as it appeared. Henry of Huntingdon was frankly surprised by the work, which he found at Bec in 1139. Gerald of Wales claimed that it had been exposed as a fraud; William of Newburgh would have it so exposed. Alfred of Beverley thought it worthy of at least some serious attention by historians.[3] Gerald's claim is good-natured and softened by a story. William's is not; indeed his accusation that Geoffrey attempted to give historical falsehood the color of truth by turning it into Latin forms one of the most vitriolic of his passages.[4]

This full range of responses, from bewilderment through amusement and exasperation to serious attention, is still to be found in the works of twentieth-century commentators. Griscom collects opinions on Geoffrey as a romancer.[5] Griscom is himself perhaps the most earnest modern defender of Geoffrey as a sober historian. Here the matter was for a long time allowed to stand. Those inclined to be indulgent saw Geoffrey's "romanticism" as forgivable by reason of artistic license and the popularity of the work. Those not so inclined, from William of Newburgh onwards, supported their indignation by reference to a veracity and moderation which are the foundations of all historical literature deserving of the name, foundations of which Geoffrey was ignorant, or for which, still worse, he did not care. Geoffrey was either an historian who fell short of a full expertise at his craft or a writer of fiction occasionally curiously mired in fact.

I say for a long time. The magisterial study of the *Historia* by J. S. P. Tatlock, published in 1950,[6] far from furnishing the last word on the subject became the herald of a new effort to understand Geoffrey's work. A few examples of this effort may be mentioned. In 1958, two scholars paid tribute to the skill and close knowledge, especially of contemporary writing and events, that went into the construction of the work.[7] In 1966, in a study of many aspects of historical writing in early Britain, a long chapter devoted to Geoffrey stressed the growing complexity of the histories produced in Anglo-Norman England and, in particular, the "secular strain" to be found in them.[8] The *Historia Regum Britanniae* emerged from this analysis as a heightened and artistic form of a developed historiographical movement. It gained in dignity accordingly. The anger of its opponents and the anxiety of its defenders began to dissolve before these demonstrations of the sophistication of the treatise. Geoffrey's *Historia* became a "superbly" audacious piece of writing[9] and a "mirror of his own times" of considerable craftsmanship.[10] More recently still Geoffrey has himself been given fresh dignity as an historian, imaginative certainly, but in essence reliant upon, and faithful to, Welsh historiographical tradition.[11]

Then, in 1976, Professor Christopher Brooke pushed the question one stage further.[12] Geoffrey was a writer of parody, a poker of fun at contemporary society. He laughed at the laws, at the church, even, perhaps, at pressing national ambitions. His aim, and his success, in this exercise remained, however, literary: "This is a literary work of remarkable skill: a skill in story-telling above all, and in reconstructing the past out of fragmentary materials. It is in this sense that he takes his place both among the major literary figures and among the most ingenious historians of the age." "The motive most in evidence is the desire to display the literary gifts of the historian."[13] Fun, fiction, and fact are all means to this end. The conflict between "romance" and "history" disappears again but does so beneath this sharper purpose of mockery and satire.

I have only admiration for interpretations of Geoffrey's work that would expose him as an artist and a parodist of enormous skill; Geoffrey's desire to display his literary gifts is indeed the motive most in evidence in the ***Historia.*** But this was not, I hope to argue, his primary motive. Geoffrey was in appearance historian and littérateur because he was expert in both arts and could show himself to be so. Yet he did not use history purely in the service of parody or primarily to demonstrate higher standards of literary achievement. His purpose was more profound. If he displayed "the literary gifts of the historian," if, as well, he exaggerated certain trends in historical writing, it was to mock that literature and confound its authors. He meant to make telling points about the quality of the literature and to diminish the authority with which some of its exponents spoke. He meant, ultimately, to call into question the position held and hoped for in twelfth-century Anglo-Norman society by literate and celibate canons regular and monks.

. . . . .

The ***Historia,*** the story, reign by reign, of ninety-nine kings of Britain from Brutus to Cadwallader with that of Arthur as the centerpiece, was written at or near Oxford in the 1130s, completed by 1138.[14] The early twelfth century produced in England a quite extraordinary amount of written material in Latin. We are confronted, first of all, with the physical stocking of abbey and cathedral libraries after the Conquest (those, for example, of Malmesbury, Canterbury, Abingdon, Lincoln, Salisbury, Rochester, Hereford, Worcester, Durham, Exeter, St. Albans, Bury) and the enthusiasm with which these collections were used and extended.[15] Secondly there was an increase in the records of government and, with it, in the demand for the services of those literate in Latin. The recent edition of the *Regesta Regum Anglo-Normannorum* bears witness to the great growth in quantity of writs and charters in the reigns of Henry I and Stephen, and in the *Constitutio Domus Regis* the Chancellor and the Master of the Writing Office are officials of considerable importance who are named first.[16] Thirdly there was literature newly translated in England from languages other than Latin or newly composed in Latin there. These three divisions comprehend an enormous variety of materials: patristics, lives of saints, legal compilations, instruments of bureaucracy and argument secular and ecclesiastical, histories.

A striking aspect of this enormous effort at copying, collecting, arguing, recording—all in Latin—is that it took on a special intensity in the third and fourth decades of the twelfth century, that is, in the years just before Geoffrey began to write. William of Malmesbury wrote his Latin life of St. Wulstan, based in part upon the Anglo-Saxon life by Coleman, between 1124 and 1140,[17] and his life of St. Dunstan probably towards the end of that period.[18] Caradoc of Llancarfan perhaps began to write his lives of

St. Gildas and St. Cadoc shortly after 1120, and the life of St. Dubricius, found in British Library MS Cotton Vespasian A.xiv and in the *Liber Landavensis,* seems to have been written then also.[19] So too, perhaps, was an edition of the life of St. Teilo.[20] The *Leis Willelme* is traceable in the French form and most probably therefore in the Latin to the later part of the reign of Henry I, and the *Consiliatio Cnuti* may only have been completed in 1130. The *Leges Edwardi Confessoris,* a curiously titled collection of current and earlier law, in Latin, seems to have been put together between 1130 and 1135.[21]

Materials for the support of bureaucratic government and argument poured forth. The *Canterbury Forgeries* seem to spring from the years 1121-1123,[22] and a part of the *Liber Eliensis* was begun soon after 1131.[23] The core of the *Liber Landavensis* was almost certainly compiled in the years 1120-1129 and completed by 1140.[24] The *Constitutio Domus Regis* was itself written between 1135 and 1139, most probably in 1136.[25]

Of the nameable writers of histories John of Worcester attended to his part of the Worcester *Chronicon ex Chronicis* between 1124 and 1140,[26] and Hugh the Chanter's work was finished in 1127.[27] William of Malmesbury produced the *Gesta Pontificum* in 1125 and revised it thereafter, and the *Gesta Regum* by 1125, again with revisions between the years 1135 and 1140. Between 1129 and 1139 he wrote his *De Antiquitate Glastoniense Ecclesiae,* and between then and c. 1143 the *Historia Novella.*[28] Henry of Huntingdon began to write the *Historia Anglorum* between 1129 and 1133 and worked at it in the following years, perhaps adding a prologue, and certainly making changes, between then and 1135.[29] Of the unattributable histories and annals, the *Annales de Regnis et Ecclesiis* was written in the early 1130s and perhaps completed in 1137.[30] The third section of the Durham *Historia Regum* was written soon after 1129, and an abridgement of a part of this was made, again, in the last years of the reign of Henry I.[31] During the 1120s and 1130s copying too seems to have quickened.[32] The world of the literate, in short, was in these years very greatly expanded. Saints' lives and histories, especially histories of Anglo-Saxon England and its church, constitute a large part of this accumulation. Advocates of the regular religious life are heavily involved. Finally, the composition and copying of books, especially in Benedictine scriptoria, seems to have been undertaken with particular vigor in a region of England very close to that in which Geoffrey spent the major part of his career.[33]

. . . . .

Geoffrey refers to contemporary writers in the epilogue that is attached to what I take to be the earliest form of his work.[34] He names William of Malmesbury, Henry of Huntingdon, and Caradoc of Llancarfan. William and Henry are warned not to attempt to write about the kings of the Britons because of their own linguistic inadequacies—William and Henry do not possess a certain book in the "British" language which has been Geoffrey's strength and which he claims to have translated. Caradoc, on the other hand, is invited to continue where Geoffrey leaves off, and to write of the kings of Wales.[35] I shall return to him and to the book. For the moment there is a great wealth to be explored in Geoffrey's reference to the other two historians alone. This reference has long been regarded by some as a joke.[36] A closer look at Geoffrey's use of William and Henry, whose major works he certainly knew and drew upon, suggests that it was not just one joke but the end of a whole series of jokes. This has not generally been recognized.

The jokes begin, appropriately, at the beginning. In their prefaces both William and Henry lay stress upon the quantity and breadth of their reading. William, for example, in the preface to the *Gesta Pontificum,* speaks of his sources: "et hic et alibi traxi stilum per latebrosissimas historias, quanquam mihi non hic affluat eadem copia scientiae quae in Gestis Regum."[37] Henry explains that he used Bede: "nonnulla etiam ex aliis excerpens auctoribus, inde chronica in antiquis reservata librariis compilans."[38] Henry especially, and still in the preface, makes a great show of the profit he has derived from his readings in Horace, Homer, and the Old Testament, of his capacity to write prose and verse, and of his view of the high calling of the historian and of history in general, "quod ipsa maxime distinguat a brutis rationabiles." Geoffrey, in words not too far removed from those of William, sounds in his own preface a first clear note of discord: "infra alienos ortulos falerata verba non collegerim, agresti tamen stilo propriis calamis contentus." He is a simple man; he must content himself with little. For his history he has only one book (though one, he must remark, inaccessible to William and to Henry), to the translation of which he applies his rustic style.

We must return to the rustic style later. For the present: those offended by Geoffrey's "romantic" approach to history have long found vindication in, those who loyally support Geoffrey as an historian have long found their case hampered by, his use of his sources. To the second, save for "corrupt texts" or "oral tradition," unaccountably; to the first all too understandably—he makes mistakes. The works of William and Henry suffer directly and especially severely from these "mistakes." Take for instance the section in *Historia* 4.17 in which Geoffrey speaks of the British king Marius, grandfather of king Lucius, who beats the Picts and has an inscription commemorating his victory. The only known source for this is William's *Gesta Pontificum,* in which he describes a triclinium at Carlisle that bears the inscription "Marii Victoriae."[39] To William the work is Roman from Roman Carlisle and commemorates a Roman victory; to Geoffrey this is British work (as was, of course, 2.9, the foundation of Carlisle). Again in the *Gesta Pontificum* William earnestly attributes the construction of the hot baths in Bath to Julius Caesar.[40] Geoffrey (2.10) insists that they were the work of King Bladud, an extraordinary figure who met his death upon the temple of Apollo in London after an unsuccessful attempt to fly.[41] William in his works is fond of topography and monuments, and frequently allows them to support, even form,

his historical narrative. Geoffrey too has frequent recourse to them; but he uses them to support "romance."[42]

Geoffrey's story of Estrildis seems to be taken from the *Gesta Pontificum,* but the name and country are changed and so is William's edifying ending.[43] Geoffrey does not use William as a source of edification for his readers; quite the reverse. A case in point is Geoffrey's now famous account (4.19) of the mission to Britain of Faganus and Duvianus. William's *De Antiquitate* contains plenteous reference to the missionaries Phaganus and Deruvianus, but in the revision of the *Gesta Regum* that he made between 1135-1140, which uses the *De Antiquitate,* William omits these names and declares, indeed, that the names of the missionaries have been forgotten.[44] The suggestion has been made that William expressed resentment against Geoffrey in this passage.[45] The problem of the Lucius legend is more complex than was then generally supposed,[46] as is the problem of the exact relationship between the *Gesta Regum,* in its revisions, and the *De Antiquitate.* However, an expression on William's part of resentment against Geoffrey between 1135 and 1140 would not have been wholly without justification. Early in the *Gesta Regum* William declared a generous belief that Arthur was worthy of a good history: ". . . Artur de quo Britonum nugae hodieque delirant; dignus plane quem non fallaces somniarent fabulae, sed veraces praedicarent historiae. . . ."[47] He followed this passage with an account of Arthur's victory at Mons Badonicus. In *Historia* 4.20, following his own account of the mission of Faganus and Duvianus Geoffrey cites a supposed book by the monk Gildas, Bede's famous precursor, as his source—the *De Victoria Aurelii Ambrosii.* According to William the victory was Arthur's; Geoffrey's source was spurious and so, it seems William later thought, were Faganus and Duvianus. If it was deliberate, then Geoffrey's mischief becomes outrage in the context of William's expressed hope for a "true" history of Arthur—especially if William's idea stood, as has been thought,[48] behind Geoffrey's work.

There is much more. William's treasured Glastonbury, for example, is ignored by Geoffrey, though the Giants' Dance built at Geoffrey's imaginary abbey of Amesbury by Merlin may be an echo of William's solemn description of its pyramid tombs.[49] William associates St. Patrick with Glastonbury in a passage very close to that in which he speaks of St. David's praise of the abbey. Geoffrey mentions Patrick only to rob St. David of the credit for founding the abbey of Menevia.[50] Behind Geoffrey's famous reference (12.14) to Bede's Chedwalda (according to Bede, of course, an Anglo-Saxon king) as the source for his own very different British Cadwaladrus stands the shadow of William's Cadwalla, who is very clearly Bede's.[51] Behind Geoffrey's wizard-consulting Edwin stands again the very different Christian convert of William and Bede. In short, William of Malmesbury's work was used by Geoffrey in a manner that closely resembles deliberate teasing abuse, and teasing abuse directed at least in part at William's monastic sources and treasured monastic foundations.

Geoffrey's opening chapters of his first book are startlingly like those of Henry of Huntingdon. The two are alike in their praise of Britain, even to the measurement of the island with its twenty-eight cities, in their accounts of the Trojan origins of the Britons and the circumstances of the birth, exile, and early journeys of Brutus, in the mentions of kings Belinus and Cassivellaunus. Some of the resemblances, indeed all those I have mentioned, could have sprung from an independent use of versions of Gildas and "Nennius."[52] Other, closer resemblances, however, cannot be explained in this way. Henry and Geoffrey draw especially near to one another in three places: in their accounts of the death of Constantius and of the derivation of Helen, in the mention of Maxentius, and in their words on the roads of England. The problems of exactly when and in what ways Henry extended and revised the *Historia Anglorum* are far from being resolved, but it does seem clear that the first edition had appeared before Geoffrey began to write, and that the close similarities between the two works are to be found in this edition.[53] If we are right to assume that there was borrowing, then Geoffrey was the borrower.

In a way that is becoming familiar, the borrowing seems to be muddled and distorted. According to Henry, Coel of Colchester was a king, the father of Helen and grandfather of Constantine the Great. Helen was a saint; her husband, Constantius, a ruler of great stature. Geoffrey's Coel was a duke who seized the kingdom and made a pact with Constantius, a senator. Constantius married Helen to make sure of the kingdom. Henry's Maxentius is the son of the emperor Maximianus, against whom Constantine is directed by God. Geoffrey's is a tyrant against whom Constantine is directed by the suffering Britons. Henry's Constantine goes on to build churches and suppress heresy; Geoffrey's (4.8) to promote Helen's British relations, one of whom loses the kingdom to another duke. When he speaks of the roads, Henry involves no particular king and is accurate in his general description of the four major ones. Geoffrey attributes the building of the roads to the British king Belinus and is inventive in his description of one of them. This road, quite unknown to history, begins at St. David's and ends at Southampton. All Geoffrey's roads, moreover, are protected by the equally unknown Molmutine Laws. The Molmutine Laws first make their appearance in *Historia* 2.17. The work, according to Geoffrey, of the British king Dunwallo Molmutius, they guarantee the sanctuary of temples, cities, ploughs, and roads. Geoffrey concludes his chapter on the roads with another reference to Gildas: "Si quis autem scire voluerit omnia quae de ipsis statuerit, legat molmutinas leges quas gildas hystoricus de britannico in latinum, rex vero aluredus de latino in anglicum sermonem transtulit."

In each of these cases the distortion has consequences.[54] In the first, Geoffrey provides a Helen who is musical, beautiful, and learned but not a saint, and a Coel, Constantius, and Constantine who are not of royal blood. The aura of sanctity, royalty, and divine direction conjured up by Henry has disappeared and been replaced by individual and family ambition. We have here a subtle but quite relentless substitution of images. A similar substitution, but one directed towards a different object, occurs in the case of Belinus and the roads. In the case of the Molmutine Laws and the roads, Geoffrey may have had a second source also in mind, the *Leges Edwardi Confessoris.*[55] This compilation purported to translate and, through translation, to record and defend the efforts of Anglo-Saxon lawgivers, especially those of the well-known and saintly founder of Westminster Abbey. This compilation, and behind it those of King Alfred the Great, are here reduced by Geoffrey to the role of mere translations into Latin of laws essentially British. In another part of his history (3.13) he attributes the laws of Mercia to a British queen, Marcia, and has Alfred, again, the mere translator into Saxon of her efforts. The insults would not have been lost upon a learned contemporary,[56] still less upon those who cared for the Anglo-Saxon monastic past with its reverence for its kings and for their protection of sanctuary law. And once again the insult is driven home by a reference to Gildas. Geoffrey makes six open and supposedly serious references in the *Historia* to Gildas as his source.[57] In the case of the first three references (1.17, Lud and Kaerlud; 2.17, the Molmutine Laws; 3.5, Belinus and the roads) at least one of his sources seems to have been Henry. The fourth, I suggested, may have been meant to express something of Geoffrey's attitude to William of Malmesbury. None of these four references can be traced in fact to Gildas.[58] The names of both Gildas and of Bede were dear to William and to Henry. When used by Geoffrey they seem to be meant on occasion to express not respect for the writing of the past but a profound lack of respect for the writing of the present. The two are used not primarily as sources but as scapegoats in a highly complex exercise in contemporary criticism.

Before turning to the larger scene, we may perhaps note one more sting that awaits contemporary historians in general and perhaps Henry in particular. At points in his narrative Henry inserts cross references to world history, a habit based perhaps on Jerome-Eusebius and pursued at length in the Worcester *Chronicon ex Chronicis.* Geoffrey does this too, for example in 1.18, 2.6 (twice), 9, 10, 15, 4.11, 15. The cross references inserted by Henry and the Worcester Chronicler are always, of course, seriously meant as a means of placing verified events within a wider context. Each of the cross references I have noted in Geoffrey's *Historia* follows a totally, in some cases glaringly, fictional passage. The first, for example, follows the section on Lud, Kaerlud, and the first source citation of Gildas. The second two follow the imaginary account of the rule of a woman, Gwendolen, and that of an equally imaginary tyrant supposedly modelled on William Rufus. The third follows the passage in which Geoffrey associates the founding of William of Malmesbury's Roman Carlisle with the British king Leil, and the fourth the attribution of the hot baths in Bath to Bladud and not to Caesar. It is hard to imagine that any of this was accidental.

The third person Geoffrey mentions in his epilogue is Caradoc of Llancarfan. After barring William of Malmesbury and Henry of Huntingdon, Geoffrey actively invites him to continue his history for him. This invitation has often been taken seriously. Now, we know little about Caradoc of Llancarfan, but the little we do know is an encouragement to suspect, not to trust, Geoffrey's invitation.[59] There is nothing in the accepted writings of Caradoc that have come down to us, the lives of Sts. Gildas, Cyngar, and Cadoc, to suggest that he was interested in the history of kings. The evidence points wholly to the contrary. Caradoc was one of a company of professionals who dealt in the lives not of seculars but of saints. Put at their simplest, the interests of Caradoc and his circle were not in the triumph but in the humiliation of kings. These humiliations were to be brought about preferably by ascetics exceptionally learned, endowed with powers far above the natural, and associated with distinguished monastic communities. Caradoc's Life of St. Cadoc is a good example of these preoccupations. It describes the saint admiringly in this way: "quamvis regis proles, regii cultus despiciebat pompam, sub vili habitu singulis horis frequentando ecclesiam."[60] In the face of his parents' desire for him to conduct himself properly as their firstborn and heir and become a soldier, Cadoc takes to learning, then to miracles (often at the expense of royal pride) and to the leadership of a large religious community. He is then instructed by an angel to end his life in exile from his homeland, and does so.

Some of the lives written by Caradoc's companions are to be found in the famous collection in British Library MS Cotton Vespasian A.xiv, apparently based on a collection made at St. Peter's abbey, Gloucester, in the 1130s.[61] Three of the lives in this collection have a special bearing upon Geoffrey's history because all deal in a particular way with Geoffrey's hero, Arthur.[62] They are, the *Vita Cadoci,* the *Vita Carantoci,* and the *Vita Paterni.* All of them diminish the stature of, even to the point of vilifying, Arthur. In the *Vita Cadoci* Arthur is represented as a young man whose libidinous desires are much in need of correction; "Arthurus . . . libidine in amorem adolescentulae nimium successus, ac iniqua cogitatione plenus. . . ." These are restrained only by Kay and Bedevere. Later in the narrative Arthur's vengeful search for the slayer of three of his knights is stilled only by the intervention of the saint, who, with the help of others, among them St. David, protects Arthur's victim. Arthur's demands are shown to be unreasonable and a resort to "divine spells" is justified by the intensity of Arthur's rage and greed. This story is repeated in Caradoc's life of the saint. In the *Vita Carantoci* Arthur needs the saint's assistance in the domestication of a dragon. In the *Vita Paterni,* Arthur's greed reappears. "Confossus zelo avaritiae" he tries to steal the saint's tunic, only to be threatened with a display of the saint's power over nature. He is humbled and repents. Caradoc, though more gently, had portrayed a repentant Arthur in his life of St. Gildas.

Neither Caradoc nor his companions emerge from this as writers about Welsh kings of the stamp of Geoffrey. The likelihood is, I think, that Geoffrey knew this well, and

that he set himself quite deliberately to mock their known propensities, not merely in the epilogue but in the text also. In *Historia* 9.1, for example, when Arthur is crowned king, the virtues Geoffrey gives him are the antithesis of the vices mentioned in the lives. Arthur is "iuvenis inaudite virtutis et largitatis in quo tantum gratiam innata bonitas prestiterat ut a cunctis fere populis amaretur." Such aggression as he showed was never prompted by greed, still less by lust, but was the result of a courageous disposition and a laudable desire to distribute largesse. Arthur is never humbled before bishops and clergy. They are humbled before him (9.6), though not by magic but by his prowess in battle. When Arthur appears in Geoffrey's *Historia* as an avenger (10.3), he is avenging the cruel death of a woman, and Kay and Bedevere appear not as his keepers but as his helpers in this just cause. Arthur has no cause to domesticate the dragon which appears to him in 10.2; he is, on the contrary, to treasure the symbol in his just conflict with Lucius Hiberius. The invitation to Caradoc seems to have sprung, in short, from the same spirit as the banning of William and Henry. The latter were not to write because they lacked a source; the former was to write, but upon a subject utterly opposed to his known interests. The animating spirit was once again the desire to ridicule contemporary literary pundits in the most devastating way possible; to ridicule them individually and severally through a reversal some of the claims and features of the sources that had been their supports.

With Caradoc, I had said we should return to that "liber vetustissimus" which Geoffrey claimed to have translated in rustic style and for lack of which William and Henry were excluded from British history. The mention of the *liber* evokes as great a variety of responses as did the appearance of the *Historia.* This is Geoffrey's story. While musing about the singular lack of a history of the kings of Britain he was offered an ancient book in the "British" language—"quendam britannici sermonis librum vetustissimum." The book was offered to him by Walter, archdeacon of Oxford, "vir in oratoria arte atque in exoticis hystoriis eruditus." The work which follows, says Geoffrey, is a translation of this book. He refers to the book again in 11.1, as the authority for his account of the battles between Arthur and Modred. In the epilogue he refers to it once more. He adds that Archdeacon Walter brought it "ex britannia." To the first two references to the book he adds self-deprecatory remarks upon his own rustic style. The problem of whether this ancient Welsh or Breton book existed cannot be adequately explored by one not versed in those languages. Alfred of Beverley and Gaimar believed in the ancient book, but then they believed in Geoffrey. Archdeacon Walter certainly existed. As well as being an archdeacon, he was provost of the college of secular canons of St. Georges at Oxford of which it is almost certain that Geoffrey too was a member. He was canon of Warwick, and he was witness with Geoffrey at Oxford to charters dated between 1125 and 1139. Henry of Huntingdon describes Walter as "superlative rhetoricus," a description which is like Geoffrey's.[63] But was he sober helper or mischievous collaborator in Geoffrey's venture? That we cannot say for certain, though the balance of probabilities lies in favor of the latter.

We can say something about Geoffrey's "rusticity," though. This was pretence. For all its apparent simplicity, the *Historia* is a work of considerable learning and elaboration.[64] For example, Geoffrey refers openly to Juvenal, Lucan, and Apuleius. He writes eloquent speeches which on at least one occasion (9.17) he takes care to have described as Ciceronian. Names and places are borrowed from Ovid, Juvenal, Virgil, and possibly Livy.[65] The journeys of Brutus before his arrival in Albion owe much to the *Aeneid* and *Thebaid*,[66] and Geoffrey borrows the closing words in the preface containing the double dedication from Virgil's first *Eclogue*.[67] The last section of *Historia* 7.4 is certainly an adaptation, perhaps a parody, of Lucan's *Pharsalia* 1, 643-665. Geoffrey's "rusticity" was a joke. Was the idea of a translation of a "liber vetustissimus" a joke too? If we attribute even some degree of truth to his statement, several very recent books are inherently more probable than one very old one as sources. But a joke is far more probable. As Latin literature was accumulating round him when Geoffrey was writing, so too was anxiety about translation.[68] As he made fun of the literature, so too it is extremely likely that he chose to make fun of this as well. There is an element of pure delight in the thought that the single source which Geoffrey claimed his learned contemporaries lacked, and for lack of which, in apparent deference to their professional standards, he barred them from exercising their craft in the history of Britain, was, all the time, make-believe.[69]

. . . . .

In this attempt to suggest that Geoffrey meant not to make one history book but to mock many, attention has been focussed upon the three contemporary authors he named. The quest becomes even more rewarding when we widen its scope. Though history was his means, historians qua historians were not his only prey. We may see this by turning to some of the most arresting parts of Geoffrey's work—those parts in which he deals with the church in Britain.

In 4.19, 20 and 9.12, 13, 15, Geoffrey devotes attention to the organisation of this church. He divides it into three secular metropolitan sees: London, York, and Caerleon. London commands England and Cornwall, York everything north of the Humber, Caerleon Wales. He ignores in this, of course, the monastic see of Canterbury at a time of peculiar sensitivity.[70] He gives prominence to York and to its control over Scotland when York's duty of subservience to Canterbury had only recently and with pain been relaxed.[71] He supports the dreams of London and he invents in Glamorgan a Welsh metropolitan see in the face once again of metropolitan ambitions very recently disappointed—those of St. David's and Llandaff.[72] Some named archbishops are assigned to Geoffrey's sees: Dubricius, then David, to Caerleon, Samson to York, Guithelinus to London (6.2). We know that this is mischief.[73] Less stressed, however, is the fact that once again behind this

mischief is a *recent* accumulation of Latin literature of propaganda, especially of propaganda in the cause of religious communities of regular life. Dubricius of Caerleon who crowns Geoffrey's Arthur (a choice reflecting harshly upon the claims of Canterbury) is the namesake of the saintly founder of the hopeful see of Llandaff. His life forms a part of the *Liber Landavensis*. He is also the namesake of the predecessor claimed at St. David's for St. David himself. Geoffrey gives Dubricius the titles of primate and legate (9.12), titles which William of Corbeil had claimed for Canterbury. Three archbishops of England in the time of King Lucius and twenty-seven of Geoffrey's twenty-eight flamens are also to be found in a recent letter from St. David's to Pope Honorius, though of course not the see of Caerleon, the appearance of which distorts the whole.[74]

In reaching back to St. Patrick as the founder of the abbey of Menevia yet excluding St. David's from his sees (11.3), Geoffrey makes play both with the traditional association of Dyfed with the Dessi of Leinster (as represented, for example, in the Welsh genealogies in MSS B.L. Harley 3859 and Jesus College Oxford XX) and with inner conflicts present in recent supports for St. David's pretensions, the letter to Honorius and the life of St. David. The late-eleventh-century life of St. David by Rhigyfarch meant to leave no doubt in the minds of its readers that St. David's was a metropolitan see, that the abbey was its strong support, and that David and not Patrick was its founder. The letter to Honorius, on the other hand, shows sympathy with Patrick as David's subordinate and as subordinate too to direction from Rome. We are here in the deep difficulties of contemporary divisions within the Irish Church;[75] Geoffrey's iconoclasm seems easily to comprehend these too. His own David, archbishop of the secular see of Caerleon, drawn in affection to the abbey of Menevia that St. Patrick had founded and in which David was buried by order of the king, and all while Rome was Britain's enemy, makes nonsense of it all. William, Henry, and Caradoc are, it might be noted, included in this nonsense; Henry allows St. David's at least a brief period of metropolitan status in succession to Caerleon and William has St. David uncompromisingly at St. David's itself and Patrick associated with him only in his praise of Glastonbury.[76] Caradoc may have lent his skill to the forging of the *Liber Landavensis*.[77] The nonsenses accumulate. The letter from the chapter of St. David's to Honorius, for instance, names a certain Samson, later archbishop of Dol, as St. David's successor as archbishop of St. David's. Geoffrey has an Archbishop Samson—but of the secular see of York. He mentions Samson of Dol (9.15) only to point out that he was succeeded at Dol by a certain Teilo, priest of Llandaff. The *Liber Landavensis* is familiar with Teilo and connects him, indeed, with Dol; but Teilo there is one of the founders of the metropolitan see of Llandaff and not just a priest.[78] To top it all, in 4.20 Geoffrey cites the familiar *De Victoria Aurelii Ambrosii* of Gildas as his authority for his metropolitan dispositions. He adds, as an excuse for shortening his own account: "Quod autem ipse tam lucido tractatu paraverat, nullatenus opus fuit ut inferiori stilo renovaretur." Neither the inferior penmanship nor the lucid exposition existed. Again we have the paradox of invented literary authority given the appearance of antiquity, combined with real inventive mockery of current literature. Mockery of the written supports of current metropolitan claims, through a spurious source, furthermore, had special point in the context of the many spurious compilations involved. Finally if Caradoc of Llancarfan, writer of a recent life of Gildas, did indeed help to forge the *Liber Landavensis,* Geoffrey's invocation of the authority of Gildas within this context for his own arrangements, turns again into outrage.

. . . . .

So far, we have been concentrating upon the immediate causes and objects of Geoffrey's mischief-making. I have attempted to show that the enormous accumulation of Latin literature and especially the literature with which he found himself surrounded formed his chief provocation, and that he constructed and directed his history to make fun of it. He made fun by parodying its sources and its method, by distorting its message, by directing known and named experts to tasks they hated or banning them on the most specious of grounds from tasks they loved, and by pretending throughout to a simplicity which, it must have been all too clear even to the semi-learned, he did not possess. On occasion, it seems, in addition, that he ridiculed, through literature, many of the principal motives behind its composition. Works that supported certain known ecclesiastical policies fell in ruins before Geoffrey's dispositions, and Geoffrey's apparently slipshod use of legal and historical compilations brought about subtle but quite devastating changes of emphasis and national sympathy. The supports and pretensions of some of the greater monastic sees and houses suffered especially severely from Geoffrey's teasing.

I have no doubt at all that there are many more hidden literary parodies in the *Historia* waiting to be discovered. Contemporary authors other than those he named may have suffered from the same treatment. Rather than pursue this line of investigation, however, I should prefer to end with a suggestion. The suggestion is tentative and cannot be resolved into a conclusion, but it calls upon evidence which has not, to my knowledge, previously been applied to an understanding of Geoffrey's work. For that reason alone it may claim attention. The evidence is of two kinds: that derived from an examination of the contents of the *Historia* as a whole, and that derived from an examination of the immediate social context within which Geoffrey lived. I wish to suggest that Geoffrey, through both his ridicule and his serious literary creation, held to one overriding purpose. By both mocking and writing Latin literature, he meant to exalt certain virtues he felt currently to be diminished both by the literature and by those supporters and exponents of the celibate and cenobitic life which were in the forefront of its production. He meant also to exalt certain of the ways of life that monasticism threatened. The virtues he meant to exalt were the physical bravery of men, the judicious influence of women, and the

power for good in society of family care and pride. The way of life he meant to exalt was that of responsible rulership and marriage.

In the *Historia Regum Britanniae* Geoffrey seems to diverge from that Latin literature to which he was close in his treatment of three major (and interrelated) subjects: lay rulers, women, and churchmen. I have said something of his divergence from the views of contemporary hagiographers in the matter of Arthur. He diverges, too, from the kings of William and Henry. Geoffrey's hero has a greater moral stature than any of theirs, stature that comes from a revision of opinion about the relative status of specific virtues and vices. Put simply, qualities dismissed by certain of Geoffrey's contemporaries as vices become, for Geoffrey, virtues. Pride becomes prowess, covetousness the necessary forerunner to largesse, anger the righting of cruel wrong, lust the laudable will to beget and provide for heirs. Arthur's right to rule is hereditary and his virtue "innata" (9.1), not of grace, but of birth. His conquests are justified by his need to provide for those close to him: "Arturus ergo quia in illo probitas largitionem comitabatur, statuit saxones inquietare, ut eorum opibus que ei famulabatur ditaret familiam. Commonebat etiam id rectitudo, cum tocius insule monarchiam debuerat hereditario iure obtinere." He provides accordingly, but especially for his own family (9.9), and these efforts clearly govern the dignity of a known terrestrial realm and the happiness of its inhabitants. Similar though less exalted instances of just such a collection of virtues may be found in Arthur's royal predecessors: Cassivellaunus, for example. Conversely family discord and the consequent breakdown of such efforts are the most frequent heralds of vice and failure (2.6, 15).

In Geoffrey's accounts of royal celebrations wives play an important part.[79] Though the crown passes through the male line, women are frequently given by him a vital role in the government of the kingdom.[80] The conflict of the brothers Brennius and Belinus is ended by their mother, and that between Arviragus and Vespasian by Queen Genuissa.[81] In these cases too we have the same concern for family prosperity. We have also the pattern of virtues and failings definable as such not according to an abstract terminology but according to the measure of happiness they give or refuse to groups of blood relations and the measure of prosperity they secure or fail to secure for the countries to which these are tied by birth and by affection. I have mentioned Geoffrey's changes to the story of Helen. A much more striking example of such changes is to be found in his version of the legend of St. Ursula. The previous versions have these points in common. Ursula is a British virgin desired in marriage by the son of a continental tyrant. Urged by a divine vision and accompanied by eleven thousand other virgins, she goes. She refuses a barbarian marriage, however, and all are slaughtered by the Huns as virgin martyrs; rousing stuff, with a very clear message. Geoffrey distorts it. According to him (5.15-16) Ursula goes not to a tyrant but to a man built much on the Arthurian model, Conan of Britanny, who "commissam patriam viriliter defendebat," and, after his victory, "voluit commilitonibus suis coniuges dare ut eis nasceretur heredes, qui terram illam perpetuo possiderent." The accompanying eleven thousand, therefore, are to be wives for a meritorious army, and Geoffrey never describes either them or Ursula as virgins, but as "filias" or "mulieres." The majority of those who hesitate do so because they love their kinsmen and country. A few prefer chastity or even death, but not, it seems, to the loss of virginity as such, but to marrying for money. The company resists not marriage but the barbarians' wish "lascivire cum eis."

The modifications look slight. They are in fact fundamental. All the inessentials of the story are retained in the guise of essentials. The true essential of the original, the "virtuous" opposition between virginity and marriage is quite destroyed and replaced by a far more complex story about desirable and undesirable human motives and affections. Meritorious warfare and the desire to beget heirs are reconcilable and praiseworthy. It is not marriage itself but its abuse which leads to disaster. Virginity as a virtue seems to have no part.[82]

Finally we return to Geoffrey's ecclesiastical dispositions. I have mentioned that all his metropolitan sees are secular sees. There is no monk-bishop to be found in the whole work. Gloucester is lauded as a bishopric, which, when Geoffrey wrote, it was not, and not as an abbey, and a peculiarly important one, which it was.[83] Moreover, Eldod, the bishop of Gloucester, is a warrior who like Guithelinus of London and Dubricius of Caerleon stirs soldiers to meritorious warfare. Geoffrey never invokes that supernatural power which, according to Caradoc and his circle, comes of physical and mental asceticism, never directly exalts the regular religious life as such, and does much indirectly to diminish its place. King Elidur, for example (3.17), does not retire to a monastery in the Anglo-Saxon manner when he gives up his crown to his brother. The reign of the monk-king Constans is an unrelieved disaster to which the monastic life contributes materially: ". . . debilitas sensus ipsius id faciebat, nam infra claustra aliud quam regnum tractare dedicerat" (6.6). Geoffrey pays tribute (9.15) to the pious wish of Archbishop Dubricius to become a hermit, but makes it clear that Dubricius's successor to the archbishopric, David, the king's uncle and appointed by the king, is a model of goodness. And the life of the hermit, of course, is by no means synonymous with the regular cenobitic life. There is a pleasantly perverse touch in a previous chapter (9.13). Habits of a single color are the badges of knights of prowess and of ladies who are appropriately demanding in their love. The abbey of which Geoffrey speaks most often, Amesbury, is praised primarily as a mausoleum for kings and faithful warriors. Geoffrey's abbeys are always, indeed, subject to kings, and his monks, when he does allow them a place, are devoted to a life of withdrawn and penitential prayer. I have said how marked, in context, is Geoffrey's omission of Glastonbury. The omission was in part pure fun at William's expense, but it had, I think, a deeper side too. To omit Glastonbury which claimed his bones while making

so much of Arthur, and to invent a purely imaginary monastic mausoleum when real ones stood at Westminster and Reading, struck hard at monastic claims upon kings. Glastonbury may well have laid claim too to relics of St. Ursula and her ten chief companions.[84]

It is a singular fact that the later years of the reign of Henry I were occupied by a particularly intensive debate about clerical continence. Ecclesiastical councils legislated for clerical celibacy,[85] but strong legislation is often a measure of the strength of the opposition to it. In this case Henry I, in both condemning clerical marriage and ensuring that it was in practice possible, played a masterly dual role[86] and made certain that, in precisely those years in which Geoffrey began to write his *Historia,* the debate was far from being resolved. The claims of monks and canons regular to the priesthood and through that to episcopal office are of course reconcilable with and supported by a successful drive for celibacy; other claims not perhaps so easily so.

It is a still more singular fact that the Oxford in which Geoffrey lived and wrote yields, from a time still closer to his time of writing, independent evidence of an entry into this particular fray. In about 1132 Archbishop Thurstan of York asked one Master Theobald, then teaching at Oxford, whether monks should have pastoral care. His reply was unambiguous. They should have neither pastoral care nor tithes, for they had no rights to the public priesthood and to public clerical status and its rewards.[87] Monks were to withdraw from public power and revenues and to live of their own a life of penitence. This reply had perhaps been predicted, for Theobald had expressed himself equally unambiguously upon related matters earlier in his career.[88] He had earlier declared his belief that priests' sons were eligible for the priesthood and had made some very direct remarks about the pride which often lay in open chastity. There is some suggestion that Theobald was himself the son of a priest and that he held and expressed, though indirectly, to his friend Philip, views favorable to the marriages of priests.[89]

Theobald was probably a secular canon of St. Georges in Oxford. Geoffrey almost certainly was. Geoffrey's friend, Archdeacon Walter, to whose generosity Geoffrey attributed the provision of the "liber vetustissimus" was provost of St. Georges. Walter, moreover, was almost certainly married.[90] St. Georges began to succumb to the claims of celibate, regular clergy in 1129, when the regular house of Osney was founded in part on its revenues.[91] It was closed in 1149. Theobald's virulence is understandable in the light of, and is very likely to have been prompted by, this threat to his origins and livelihood. If my description of at least some of Geoffrey's preoccupations is a correct one, then the two are most firmly allied. Both sought to defend the rights in public life of the virtues of the family from its enemy—aggressive monasticism equally anxious for public rights. The difference is that Geoffrey tried in addition to defend the delights of Latin literature, and largely from that same enemy, and did so with the most consummate skill.[92]

. . . . .

There are many levels to Geoffrey's achievement. I have tried to single out four. I have agreed that Geoffrey was primarily a parodist, and that he parodied the postures of sections of contemporary society. I have suggested in addition that he parodied in particular the literature which supported these sections of society in their laughable state, and that he tried to do so by using the same literature but in a very different way. Most important, however, are the third and fourth levels, those which rest upon Geoffrey's immediate surroundings and which provide help towards an understanding of his ultimate purpose. The last years of the reign of Henry I and the first years of the reign of Stephen were years in which the position in England of the secular and married clergy came under serious threat at the hands of a still powerful and celibate monastic church. The threat from canons regular and monks was felt with great intensity at Oxford. Perhaps from this fact, surely from the expressed position of his colleague Theobald, Geoffrey took the opportunity to devise a defence. The desire to defend the virtues of secular society and to rebut the claims of the celibate played a vital part in the composition of the *Historia* and perhaps in its success. Geoffrey constructed in it a powerful alternative to monastic literature and to monastic society. His work is literate, polished, learned, but, above all, amusing. And in the world he creates it is not celibates and monks but kings and queens with heirs to care for, a country to love, and the courage and imagination to provide for them who rule the land and church of Britain. The recommendation of these essentially human values in the face of increasingly vigorous and articulate threats to them guided, perhaps prompted, Geoffrey's deeply artistic creation. I do not wish to deny the existence of other interests and other ends. The work is far too complex for that. But most of these other interests need this perspective for their proper understanding. The friendship expressed in Geoffrey's dedications for Robert of Gloucester and, apparently, for the cause of Mathilda[93] is compatible, for example, with the purpose I have ascribed to him, and is perhaps explained by it. The exaltation of the virtues of the family cuts two ways of course; the too free suffer with the too severe (though not perhaps as much).[94] It may also cut across the bounds of recent national allegiances.[95] This fact may explain the irresolution with which attempts to define Geoffrey's larger political sympathies end.

Parody is not in general the stuff of which histories are made; and, if it is good, the target or targets of parody are concealed. In both cases, if I am right, Geoffrey's inventiveness and skill were very great. So too, though, was his restraint. The *Historia Regum Britanniae* was a work of the gentlest counterpropaganda; it was perhaps all the more telling for that reason. It deserves to be given a far more important place than it has hitherto received in the literature of the twelfth-century monastic reform.

Notes

1. Acton Griscom, *The Historia Regum Britanniae of Geoffrey of Monmouth* (New York, 1929), pp. 551-582. References in this paper are to the book and chapter divisions of this edition. This paper was completed with the help of a Visiting Fellowship at the Humanities Research Centre, ANU, Canberra, for which I am most grateful.

2. J. Hammer, "Some Additional Manuscripts of Geoffrey of Monmouth's *Historia Regum Britanniae,*" *Modern Language Quarterly* 3 (1942), 235-242. Hammer cites an additional four manuscripts of the thirteenth and fourteenth centuries in his edition of the variant version: Jacob Hammer, *Geoffrey of Monmouth's Historia Regum Britanniae: A Variant Version* (Cambridge, Mass., 1951), pp. 5-8. See also W. Levison, "A Combined Manuscript of Geoffrey of Monmouth and Henry of Huntingdon," *English Historical Review* 58 (1943), 41-51, H. D. Emanuel, "Geoffrey of Monmouth's *Historia Regum Britanniae*: A Second Variant Version," *Medium Aevum* 35 (1966), 103-110; D. Huws and B. F. Roberts, "Another Manuscript of the Variant Version of the 'Historia Regum Britanniae'," *Bibliographical Bulletin of the International Arthurian Society* 25 (1973), 147-153; and W. G. East, "Manuscripts of Geoffrey of Monmouth," *Notes and Queries* 220 (1975), 483-484.

3. The relevant passages from their works are conveniently collected in Edmund K. Chambers, *Arthur of Britain* (Cambridge, 1927), pp. 251-2, 260, 268, 274-5.

4. "Quidam nostris temporibus, pro expiandis his Britonum maculis, scriptor emersit, ridicula de eisdam figmenta contexens, eosque longe supra virtutem Macedonum et Romanorum impudenti vanitate attollens. Gaufridus hic dictus est, agnomen habens Arturi, pro eo quod fabulas de Arturo, ex priscis Britonum figmentis sumptas et ex proprio auctas, per superductum Latini sermonis colorem honesto historiae nomine palliavit: qui etiam maiori ausu cuiusdam Merlini divinationes fallacissimas, quibus utique de proprio plurimum adiecit, dum eas in Latinum transfunderet, tanquam authenticas et immobili veritate subnixas prophetias, vulgavit . . ." (Chambers, *Arthur*, pp. 274-5). William of Newburgh's attitude to Geoffrey is discussed by N. Partner, *Serious Entertainments* (Chicago and London, 1977), pp. 62-68.

5. Griscom, *Historia*, pp. 109-110. "Geoffrey's manipulation of his material, where its nature is apparent to us, makes it impossible to believe that he was a completely veracious chronicler, even where due allowance is made for what he might reasonably consider as legitimate rhetorical embroidery." Chambers, *Arthur*, p. 56. See also Robert W. Hanning, *The Vision of History in Early Britain* (New York, 1966), p. 122 and notes.

6. John S. P. Tatlock, *The Legendary History of Britain: Geoffrey of Monmouth's Historia Regum Britanniae and Its Early Vernacular Versions* (Berkeley, 1950).

7. Heinrich Pähler, *Strukturuntersuchungen zur Historia Regum Britanniae des Geoffrey of Monmouth* (Bonn, 1958), especially pp. 58-60 and 92-134, and Walter F. Schirmer, *Die frühen Darstellungen des Arthurstoffes* (Cologne, 1958).

8. Hanning, *Vision,* pp. 121-172, especially pp. 126-130, 135-136, 142, 171.

9. Reginald F. Treharne, *The Glastonbury Legends* (London, 1967), p. 66. Treharne also draws attention to the lack, in the *Historia,* of Christian spirit and feeling. Ibid., pp. 69-70.

10. Antonia Gransden, *Historical Writing in England c. 550-c. 1307* (London, 1974), p. 206. Pp. 207-208 of the same work emphasize again Geoffrey's un-Christian, even sadistic, attitudes. The few pages devoted here to Geoffrey are full of insights.

11. B. F. Roberts, "Geoffrey of Monmouth and Welsh Historical Tradition," *Nottingham Medieval Studies* 20 (1976), 29-40.

12. Christopher Brooke, "Geoffrey of Monmouth as a Historian," in *Church and Government in the Middle Ages,* ed. Christopher Brooke, D. Luscombe, G. Martin, D. Owen (Cambridge, 1976), pp. 77-91. Professor Brooke supplies in his first footnote further directions on Arthurian bibliography.

13. Ibid., pp. 88, 90.

14. Christopher Brooke, "The Archbishops of St. David's, Llandaff and Caerleon on Usk," in *Studies in the Early British Church,* ed. Nora K. Chadwick (Cambridge, 1958), p. 231 n.2. For a long and careful discussion of the bearing of the dedications upon the date see Griscom, *Historia,* pp. 53-85. The prophecies of Merlin were known to Orderic Vitalis in 1134/5 when the work as a whole was in the course of composition.

15. For the collections added to Abbot Godfrey's library by William of Malmesbury see H. Farmer, "William of Malmesbury's Life and Works," *Journal of Ecclesiastical History* 13 (1962), 47-51, 54. At Abingdon between 1100 and 1117 Abbot Faricius had six *scriptores* copy manuscripts of the Fathers: *Chronicon Monasterii de Abingdon,* 2 (RS, London, 1858), 289. Many of the surviving manuscripts from this period are named and discussed by Neil R. Ker, *English Manuscripts in the Century after the Conquest* (Oxford, 1960), pp. 22-34.

16. C. Johnson, ed., *Dialogus de Scaccario* (Nelson, London, 1950), p. 129.

17. D. H. Farmer, "Two Biographies by William of Malmesbury," in *Latin Biography,* ed. T. A. Dorey (London, 1967), p. 166.

18. This is suggested by the epilogue in which William speaks as though the better part of his own life is

over. W. Stubbs, ed., *Memorials of St. Dunstan* (RS, London, 1874), p. 324.

19. K. Hughes, "British Museum Ms. Cotton Vespasian A.xiv ('Vitae Sanctorum Wallensium'): Its Purpose and Provenance," in *Studies in the Early British Church* ed. Nora K. Chadwick, (Cambridge, 1958), p. 193.

20. Gilbert H. Doble, *St. Teilo* (Lampeter, 1942), pp. 10 ff.

21. Felix Liebermann, *Die Gesetze der Angelsachsen,* 3 (Halle, 1903-16), 340.

22. R. W. Southern, "The Canterbury Forgeries," *English Historical Review* 73 (1958), 224. For different views on the date and purpose of these documents, however, see Margaret Gibson, *Lanfranc of Bec* (Oxford, 1978), pp. 231-237 (Appendix C).

23. E. O. Blake, ed., *Liber Eliensis* (London, 1962), p. xlviii.

24. W. Davies, "Liber Landavensis: Its Construction and Credibility," *English Historical Review* 88 (1973), 350.

25. Johnson, *Dialogus,* p. 1.

26. Reginald R. Darlington, *Anglo-Norman Historians* (London, 1947), p. 14.

27. C. Johnson, ed., *Hugh the Chanter: the History of the Church of York 1066-1127* (Nelson, London, 1961), p. x.

28. Gransden, *Historical Writing,* pp. 168, 181-183.

29. Ibid., p. 194.

30. Felix Liebermann, *Ungedruckte Anglo-Normanische Geschichtsquellen* (Strassbourg, 1879), pp. 15-24. We might ascribe a part of the *Annales Plymptonenses* to this period too: ibid., pp. 24-30.

31. Hilary S. Offler, *Medieval Historians of Durham* (Durham, 1958), pp. 9-11; P. Hunter Blair, "Some Observations on the Historia Regum Attributed to Symeon of Durham," in *Celt and Saxon: Studies in the Early British Border,* ed. Nora K. Chadwick (Cambridge, 1963), pp. 63-118; S. T. O. d'Ardenne, "A Neglected Manuscript of British History," in *English and Medieval Studies presented to J. R. R. Tolkein,* ed. Norman Davis and C. L. Wrenn (London, 1966), p. 88. I am grateful to Professor Offler for this last reference and for generously sending me offprints of his own work.

32. "Existing books suggest that in many of the great Benedictine abbeys the scriptorium was an its best in the second quarter of the twelfth century." Ker, *English Manuscripts,* p. 8.

33. Ker speaks of "that region of the West of England centering on Gloucester which was, we can still dimly realize, one of the great regions of book production in the twelfth century." Ibid., p. 7.

34. Griscom lists seven manuscripts which contain that double dedication to Robert of Gloucester and Wale-

ran of Meulan which, for him, designates the earliest recension. Only one of these omits the epilogue. The remaining six, together with scores of others, both early and late, contain it. Griscom's preferences for this single manuscript (Cambridge University Library II, i, 14) is one of the least comprehensible of his editorial idiosyncracies. Griscom, *Historia*, pp. 31-33, 42-43.

35. Griscom, *Historia*, p. 536.

36. See Griscom's fierce and unconvincing defence of its seriousness, ibid., p. 52.

37. William of Malmesbury, *Gesta Pontificum*, ed. N. E. S. A. Hamilton, *Willelmi Malmesbiriensis Monachi De Gestis Pontificum Anglorum* (RS, London, 1870), p. 4.

38. Henry of Huntingdon, *Historia Anglorum*, ed. T. Arnold, *Henrici Archidiaconi Huntendunensis Historia Anglorum* (RS, London, 1879), pp. 1-3.

39. William of Malmesbury, *Gesta Pontificum*, pp. 208-209.

40. Ibid., p. 194.

41. It is difficult not to see behind Bladud the shadow of another Malmesbury figure, aviator Eilmer, who made a similar attempt though happily without the same fatal result. L. White, "Eilmer of Malmesbury, An Eleventh Century Aviator," *Technology and Culture* 2 (1961), 97-111.

42. Examples of Geoffrey's fanciful use of monuments, apart from those I have mentioned, may be found in 1.16, 6.17, 8.10-12, 10.3.

43. Geoffrey, 2.2-5; William of Malmesbury, *Gesta Pontificum*, pp. 412-415.

44. William of Malmesbury, *Gesta Regum*, ed. W. Stubbs, *Willelmi Malmesbiriensis Monachi de Gestis Regum Anglorum Libri Quinque*, 1 (RS, London, 1887-9), 23.

45. Tatlock, *Legendary History*, p. 233.

46. See the remarks on it, and the appendix of texts given, in Christopher Brooke, "The Archbishops," pp. 207, 240-242. The Abingdon Chronicler, writing early the reign of Henry II, still accepted the story of Faganus and Duvianus.

47. William of Malmesbury, *Gesta Regum*, p. 11.

48. Christopher Brooke, "The Archbishops," p. 232.

49. Geoffrey, 8.9-12; William of Malmesbury, *Gesta Regum*, pp. 25-26.

50. Geoffrey, 11.3; William of Malmesbury, *Gesta Regum*, p. 26.

51. William of Malmesbury, *Gesta Regum*, p. 33; Bede, *Historia Ecclesiastica Gentis Anglorum* 4.15-16, 5.7, ed. B. Colgrave and R. A. B. Mynors (Oxford, 1969), pp. 381-385, 469-473.

52. Ferdinand Lot, *Nennius et l'Historia Brittonum* (Paris, 1934), pp. 151, 153-155, 228.

53. T. Arnold, ed., *Henrici Archidiaconi Huntendunensis Historia Anglorum* (RS, London, 1879), p. liii. A chapter is devoted to Henry's attitude to history in Partner, *Serious Entertainments*, pp. 11-48.

54. Tatlock, *Legendary History*, p. 31 n.1, doubts whether Geoffrey borrowed King Lud from Henry. This doubt cannot be resolved until we know more about the text of the *Historia Anglorum*, but if Geoffrey did borrow, then there is distortion here too, for Geoffrey fathers the "Kairlundene" of Henry and Nennius onto Lud, and declares, indeed, as they do not, that Kaerlunden is a corruption of Kaerlud.

55. Liebermann, *Gesetze*, 1:637-638. A similar passage is found, too, in the *Leis Willelme*.

56. The author of the *Leges Henrici Primi* and *Quadripartitus* also was greatly interested in West Saxon law: L. J. Downer, ed., *Leges Henrici Primi* (Oxford, 1972), p. 45.

57. The references are in 1.17, 2.17, 3.5, 4.20, 6.13, 12.6.

58. And on the free play Geoffrey makes with Gildas when he does use him see Schirmer, *Darstellungen*, pp. 25-27 and 38-39.

59. On Caradoc see J. S. P. Tatlock, "Caradoc of Llancarfan, SPECULUM 13 (1938), 139-152, expanded and corrected by P. Grosjean, "Vie de S. Cadoc par Caradoc de Llancarfan," *Analecta Bollandiana* 60 (1942), 35-45, and Brooke, "The Archbishops," pp. 228-236. Le Père Grosjean edits the Life of St. Cadoc, "Vie," pp. 45-67. Caradoc's Life of St. Gildas is edited by Th. Mommsen, MGH AA 13 (Berlin, 1898), 107-110.

60. Grosjean, "Vie," p. 48.

61. The Vespasian manuscript itself, interestingly enough, was possibly compiled at Monmouth Priory. K. Hughes, "British Museum Ms. Cotton Vespasian A.xiv," p. 197.

62. The extracts are conveniently set out in Chambers, *Arthur*, pp. 243-249.

63. H. E. Salter, "Geoffrey of Monmouth and Oxford," *English Historical Review* 34 (1919), 382-385, and "The Medieval University of Oxford," *History* 14 (1929), 57-58. Henry of Huntingdon, *Epistola de Contemptu Mundi*, p. 302. There is testimony to Walter's involvement in the process of translation in the late-fourteenth-century Red Book of Hergest and the late-fifteenth-century manuscript of Welsh materials, Jesus College, Oxford, MS LXI. Griscom, *Historia*, pp. 149-150, would have it that the latter reference was taken from an earlier version, but there is no earlier record and a muddled memory of Geoffrey's words could also be its source.

64. Hammer's index of authors cited demonstrates this beyond doubt for the variant version: *Variant Version*, pp. 267-269.

65. Other examples of Geoffrey's learned associations are to be found in Tatlock, *Legendary History*, pp. 379-380.

66. Edmond Faral, *La Légende Arthurienne,* 2 (Paris, 1929), 79-81. M. Faral's commentary on the *Historia* is particularly rich in information about Geoffrey's classical sources.

67. "Tityre, tu patulae recubans," *Eclogue,* I, 1; ". . . recipias ut sub tegmine tam patulae arboris recubans," Griscom, *Historia,* p. 220. In that same preface, of course, Geoffrey, in pointed contrast to Henry, had declared he would not gather flowers from other men's gardens.

68. The old Cornish glossary in British Library MS Cotton Vespasian A.xiv, the manuscript already mentioned as the source of many of the saints' lives of the circle of Caradoc, seems to have been made in the early twelfth century from a Latin-Anglo-Saxon glossary drawn up at Cerne. Kenneth H. Jackson, *Language and History in Early Britain* (Edinburgh, 1953), pp. 60-61. Another surviving list, this time of Anglo-Saxon law terms, was perhaps made for Alexander of Lincoln, dedicatee of Geoffrey's work on the prophecies of Merlin. H. Hall, ed., *Red Book of the Exchequer,* 3 (RS, London, 1896). cclvi-lxv, 1032-9. The translator Adelard of Bath was active in England in the 1130s, was connected with the Anglo-Norman court, and may have dedicated one work to a son of Robert of Gloucester. Charles H. Haskins, *Studies in the History of Medieval Science* (Boston, 1924), pp. 26-27, 34. I have mentioned the translation into Latin of the Anglo-Saxon Laws, and also William of Malmesbury's translation and adaptation of Coleman's Life of Wulfstan. We have in the Canterbury version (F) (London, British Library MS Cotton Domitian A viii) a bilingual Anglo-Saxon Chronicle made again at this time.

69. It now seems certain that Geoffrey called upon authentic Welsh and even Breton sources, and that he did so with the contemporary concerns of these nations in mind. Roberts, "Geoffrey of Monmouth," pp. 34, 37-40. To suggest, as I do, that Geoffrey used the idea of the single "liber vetustissimus" as a multiple means of poking fun is not to deny that he also used genuine material nor to deny him knowledge of contemporary Welsh or Breton hopes. But did he use this material and this knowledge as others used it? This I doubt. If he was capable of using Latin sources and their topoi as a means of making mischief in one context, it is not impossible that he used his knowledge of sources in other languages to make similar mischief in another. In the single case of the "liber vetustissimus," if Welsh or Cornish or Breton historical materials were, in the early twelfth century, in as complex and fragmentary a state as one is led to believe, then the thought that they could be contained within a single book was perhaps as ludicrous to those who did have access to them as it was infuriating to those who did not.

70. Canterbury finds mention in Geoffrey as a place the wicked Vortigern liked to visit (6.10), and as Merlin's prophesied successor to London (7.3).

71. Donald Nicholl, *Thurstan, Archbishop of York (1114-1140)* (York, 1964), pp. 99-103.

72. The canons of St. David's claimed metropolitan status for the see in the pontificate of Honorius II (1124-1130): J. Conway Davies, ed., *Episcopal Acts and Cognate Documents relating to Welsh Dioceses,* 1 (Historical Society of the Church in Wales, 1946), no. 80. For further information on the metropolitan claims of the see of St. David's and their fate later in the century see M. Richter, "The Life of St. David by Giraldus Cambrensis," *Welsh History Review* 4 (1968-69), 381-386, and "Professions of Obedience and the Metropolitan Claim of St. David's," *National Library of Wales Journal* 15 (1967-68), 197-214. Urban of Glamorgan's ambitions for Llandaff had only died with him in 1134: Martin Brett, *The English Church under Henry I* (Oxford, 1975), pp. 52-53.

73. Christopher Brooke, "Geoffrey of Monmouth," pp. 80-82.

74. Christopher Brooke, "The Archbishops," pp. 203-210.

75. For a careful discussion of the literary aspects of these conflicts see N. K. Chadwick, "Intellectual Life in West Wales in the Last Days of the Celtic Church," in *Studies in the Early British Church,* ed. Nora K. Chadwick (Cambridge, 1958), especially pp. 136-142, 145-146.

76. William of Malmesbury, *Gesta Regum,* pp. 26-27.

77. Brooke, "The Archbishops," pp. 229-231.

78. Ibid., pp. 204-206.

79. For example 2.2-6, 4.8, 5.15, 16, 6.5, 12, 14, 15, 7.19-20, 9.13, 10.13. 2.8 is perhaps an excessive demonstration of the point.

80. 2.6, Gwendolen reigns for fifteen years and concedes the throne to her son Maddan only when she considers him of age. 2.15, Cordelia reigns for at least five years. 3.13, Marcia writes the laws which King Alfred merely translates, then rules for her son until he comes of age. 5.6, Helen is instructed to succeed her father. In placing such an emphasis upon the role of women it may be that he used his knowledge of Welsh tradition here to serious effect.

81. 4.16.

82. The modifications become all the more important in view of the especially wide currency the legend had in early-twelfth-century England. Wilhelm Levison, *Das Werden der Ursula-Legende* (Cologne, 1928), pp. 91-96.

83. K. Hughes, "British Museum MS Cotton Vespasian A.xiv," pp. 190-192, 197. On the aggressive part played by the abbey of Gloucester in monastic politics in both England and Wales in the period in question see also Christopher Brooke, "St. Peter of Gloucester and St. Cadoc of Llancarfan," in *Celt and Saxon, Studies in the Early British Border,* ed. Nora

K. Chadwick (Cambridge, 1963), pp. 258-283. The comparatively recent acquisition of Welsh properties, especially the church of St. Cadoc at Llancarfan, by St. Peters, the likelihood that the collection of Welsh saints' lives, later copied into the Vespasian manuscript, was originally made at the abbey partly from Llandaff materials, and the possibility, mentioned by Ker, that the scriptorium at Gloucester was an important one, all of course give an extra edge to Geoffrey's mockery of the Welsh hagiographers and propagandists and to his omission of St. Peters. So does the fact that Robert, earl of Gloucester, was Geoffrey's main dedicatee.

84. *De Antiquitate,* PL 179:1964. Gransden, *Historical Writing,* pp. 207-208, notes Geoffrey's use of the legend of St. Ursula and his attitude to monasticism, but suggests that his object was principally to amuse.

85. We have some record of two of the last three councils of William of Corbeil, the councils of Westminster and London, 1127 and 1129. In both, clerical continence was the principal object of concern. In the first, of which we have versions of the canons themselves, clerical marriage and concubinage were very strongly condemned. Brett, *English Church,* pp. 81-82.

86. Ibid., p. 220. See also the interesting remarks on Gratian's own ambivalence towards this question in J. Gaudemet, "Gratian et le célibat écclésiastique," *Studia Gratiana* 13 (1967), 341-369.

87. R. Foreville and J. Leclercq, "Un débat sur le sacerdoce des moines au XII siècle," *Studia Anselmiana* 41 (1957), 52-53.

88. Nicholl, *Thurstan,* p. 188.

89. Pl 163:767-70; Foreville and Leclercq, "Un débat," pp. 10-11, 21.

90. F. M. Powicke and A. B. Emden, eds., Hastings Rashdall, *The Universities of Europe in the Middle Ages,* 3 (Oxford, 1936), 17, notes 1 and 2. Archdeacon Walter passed on one of his prebends to his son. H. E. Salter, ed., *Cartulary of Osney Abbey* (Oxford, 1934), no. 20, p. 31.

91. Geoffrey witnessed the foundation charter of 1129, in company with Archdeacon Walter. H. E. Salter, "Geoffrey of Monmouth," p. 385.

92. An able demonstration of the effect of the 1127-1129 pressure for clerical celibacy upon the historical work of no less a person than Henry of Huntingdon is to be found in N. Partner, "Clerical Celibacy and the Writing of History," *Church History* 42 (1973), 467-475. I owe this reference to Ms. Jan Foote. Henry too regarded the pressure with distaste, a distaste made the more explicable by the possibility that he was married (Partner, *Serious Entertainments,* pp. 14-15). He expressed his displeasure, however, in a far less skillful way than, if I am right, did Geoffrey. He was wholly without Geoffrey's lightness of touch. This similarity of opinion, yet deep difference in

style, may in part explain Geoffrey's open teasing and private neglect of Henry.

93. On Geoffrey's probable support of Mathilda see Tatlock, *Legendary History,* pp. 286-288, 426-427.

94. Hanning, *Vision,* pp. 150-152.

95. Though we know little about the conduct of Anglo-Norman crown wearings it is hard to see Geoffrey's account of the company at Arthur's coronation feast (9.13), with its careful separation of the sexes and its devotion to musical appreciation, as anything but a parody of them. As Brooke points out, the previous chapter has stings too for the Welsh at the Norman court. Brooke, "The Archbishops," p. 80.

R. William Leckie, Jr. (essay date 1981)

SOURCE: "New Light on a Shadowed Past," in *The Passage of Dominion: Geoffrey of Monmouth and the Periodization of Insular History in the Twelfth Century,* University of Toronto Press, 1981, pp. 29-54.

[*In the following excerpt, Leckie discusses the many problems faced by medieval historians in chronicling Britain's past and traces the reaction to and impact of Geoffrey's effort.*]

Prior to the second quarter of the twelfth century information on pre-Saxon Britain was sparse and largely discontinuous. The deeds of the island's early Celtic inhabitants had left few traces in extant sources. Scattered entries afforded brief glimpses of isolated events, but no coherent account of British rule had survived. In fact, the period of Roman domination constituted the first discernible epoch in Insular history. For Bede and the annalists of the *Anglo-Saxon Chronicle,* the record of events began with Caesar's expeditions (HE, 1.2, pp 20-2; ASC, pp 5-6). Of the island's history before the coming of the Romans virtually nothing could be reported. The prefatory descriptions of Britain serve in lieu of a historical survey, but these sections contain mostly geographic data.[1] In the ninth century the *Historia Brittonum* added a store of legendary materials, but these did not fundamentally alter the fact that recorded history started abruptly with the events of 55-4 BC (HB, cc 7-19, pp 147-62). The principal guides to what little remained of Britain's pre-Saxon past were Latin historians with a decidedly Imperial bias.

Had Insular accounts once been available, then Gildas, a Briton by birth, might be expected to have knowledge of such records. But he too begins with Roman Britain and must rely heavily on Continental historiographers. Before surveying the course of events, Gildas comments on the source problem. Circumstance has forced him to draw not from local records, but from the 'transmarina relatione, quae crebris inrupta intercapedinibus non satis claret' (DEB, c 4, p 29). If British historical documents ever existed ('si qua fuerint'), then the texts must either have been destroyed by fire or removed by exiles.

Gildas was right to cast doubt on the existence of local historical records, if only parenthetically. His scepticism would seem based on empirical evidence, but the inference drawn, regarding the probable cause of this lamentable circumstance, misses an essential point. Gildas lived at a time when British culture remained largely pre-literate where the keeping of historical records was concerned. Prolonged contact with Roman civilization had not altered the Britons' dependence upon oral transmission for preserving noteworthy items from the past. Indeed, these traditional means would continue to be a major factor in the survival of materials bearing on Celtic history for centuries to come.

Although the lack of written British sources posed insuperable difficulties, Gildas did have access to oral traditions and drew on this repository of information. The recovery of pertinent detail from the available body of historical or quasi-historical lore would remain an integral part of the historian's craft throughout the Middle Ages. Gildas begins with events of Claudius' reign,[2] and consequently all the items presumed to be of traditional provenience bear on matters which fall after the invasion of AD 43. Pre-Roman Insular history is not included. Gildas freely admits to the selectivity of his approach and states that for didactic reasons he has passed in silence over the exploits of the valiant (DEB, c 1, p 25). Clearly Gildas knew another side to British history, but whether his information extended back into pre-Roman times is unclear. When the *Historia Brittonum* was compiled in the ninth century, no event directly involving the Britons could be assigned to the thousand-year period which separated Brutus' settlement of the island from Caesar's expeditions.[3] Gildas was familiar with Orosius and could have begun with the events of 55-4 BC had he so desired.[4] But how extensive his knowledge of earlier periods might have been remains obscure. Although many traditions current in Gildas' day probably did not survive into the ninth century, some caution would seem advisable in assessing the likely content of oral lore available to him.[5]

Whatever memories of events and personages the Britons might once have preserved, there is no indication that such oral traditions ever reached the written cultures of the non-Celtic world. The Romans perforce drew on materials which they themselves compiled, and these data would form the basis for all subsequent treatments of pre-Saxon British history by both Insular and Continental writers down to the appearance of the *Historia regum Britanniae.* As Gildas states in the passage cited above (DEB, c 4, p 29), the surviving record from across the Channel was filled with gaps. The character and distribution of the available written materials mirrored the history of Roman involvement in Insular affairs.

Except for the data on Roman Britain, classical and postclassical authors possessed very little information on the Insular Celts. Continental sources did not record a single event which antedated Caesar's expeditions. Britain had, to be sure, attracted some geographic and ethnographic interest earlier, but only of a very general nature. Little was known beyond the location of the island and the Celtic make-up of its populace.[6] Caesar hesitated to undertake military operations in Britain on the basis of such meagre information and sought to remedy the situation before crossing the Channel with his expeditionary forces. When the interrogation of Gaulish traders failed to yield sufficient specific data, Volusenus was dispatched to reconnoitre by ship.[7] Before the Roman landings Britain's isolation from recorded history was virtually complete, and even after the island had become the object of military concern, the historical background of its inhabitants remained obscure.

Down to the first century BC historians had little reason to turn their attentions to so remote an island. British affairs did not impinge upon the politics of the Mediterranean basin. For all practical purposes, the Britons generated history in a realm apart. The ramifications of events exhausted themselves within this sphere and required no systematic treatment by writers to the southeast. Toward the close of the second century BC the influx of Germanic tribes into Transalpine Gaul inaugurated an era of Roman military involvement in this relatively new province. The forces set in motion would eventually bring the legions to Britain's shores, but for many years the Belgic tribes served as a buffer between the Insular Celts and hostile interests, whether Roman or Germanic. In 57 BC, however, Caesar conquered the Belgae piecemeal, and the new threat posed by Roman control of the maritime regions prompted British intervention on the Continent of a kind which could not be ignored. The uprisings of 56 BC found Insular levies being used as reinforcements. According to Caesar, the Britons' support of the Celtic cause made invasion of the island a necessity (DBG, 4.20, p 112). A stable peace could hardly be achieved if Rome suffered the supplying of insurgents by an independent Britain. The long period of comparative isolation ended when the conduct of Insular affairs interfered with Roman aspirations.

The initial encounters between the Romans and the Britons followed a pattern which would become all too familiar in Insular history. When Britain attracted the attention of a Continental power, the island's isolation proved illusory. Caesar's expeditions produced neither lasting military results nor sustained historiographic interest. The information gathered over two successive summers of campaigning remained isolated. It was not until the Claudian Invasion inaugurated a period of Roman occupation and administration that certain kinds of data received fairly consistent notice by Continental writers. Physical presence made possible the accumulation of material on contemporary affairs, and gave at least some events immediate relevance for the Empire's historians.

With the Claudian Invasion Britain became the most northerly appurtenance of a far-flung Empire which dominated historical perceptions in late antiquity. During the period of Roman rule several kinds of historical writing flourished on the Continent, but where remote territories were concerned, historiographers tended to view events from an Imperial perspective. Regional history was not important in its own right, a fact which severely limited the amount of detailed information recorded. The available data were evaluated and culled with an eye to their impact on Imperial politics. British history possessed no intrinsic value, and, generally speaking, only local matters which directly affected the Empire were noted. The participation of an illustrious Roman in Insular affairs might prompt the recording of somewhat greater detail, but only because his career figured prominently in Imperial history. Despite the growing importance of the historical monograph, no citizen of the Empire treated the years of dominion over Britain as a separate subject. When compared with the preceding epoch, the period of Roman dominion produced a wealth of historical materials, but of a special kind. The writers in question were not concerned with providing a comprehensive survey of provincial history, nor did they select their data from the standpoint of importance to the Britons. Consequently, the surviving material on Britain's membership in the Roman Empire could never provide a real substitute for local records.

During the Roman occupation Latin became the language of administration, major commerce, and—to an extent more difficult to determine—everyday communication between Britons.[8] Although linguistic competence certainly does not presuppose formal training, provincial schools were established in Britain and seem to have had a considerable influence.[9] There can be little doubt that at least in the lowland urban areas the process of acculturation reached a very advanced stage, accompanied by a rising literacy rate. These developments, however, do not appear to have resulted in Celtic-Latin historical writing, and some possible reasons suggest themselves. History was not taught in Roman schools, and without specific instruction even an educated Briton could hardly be expected to perceive the long-term advantages for his own culture of transmitting historical data in written form. The inherent weaknesses of oral-traditional methods become obvious only in retrospect, and only when some basis for comparison exists. I think it unlikely that substantial numbers of Britons were even familiar with this particular use of writing. No Roman historian is known to have composed his account in Britain, and in all probability none did. As a result, only the keeping of daily administrative and commercial records would have been apparent to the local populace. Detailed ethnological information is lacking for the Britons, but Continental Celtic peoples had long employed writing for specific applications, while preservation of the cultural heritage was carried on orally.[10] If the Romans were judged solely on the basis of the observable uses of writing, then a similar division might reasonably have been postulated for them. Be that as it may, Insular historiographic activity was not one of the immediate byproducts of Romanization.

Data bearing on many aspects of contemporary Insular history were gathered by the Romans in the normal course of provincial administration. Official records and personal observations greatly increased the store of available knowledge, but the writing of history took place far from Britain's shores. Information flowed from this remote province toward the centre of the Empire, and quite probably both the quantity and the quality of the data suffered as a result. Despite the problems inherent in purveying the materials of history across any considerable distance, events would prove that the point of greatest vulnerability lay at the source. The acquisition of Insular data for use in historical writing depended upon the Roman presence. When the legions departed and the administration collapsed, information was cut off at the point of origin.

In the fifth century, Roman writers found much to occupy their attention and paid little heed to a distant former province. Contemporary or near-contemporary references to Insular occurrences became exceedingly rare on the Continent, while the Britons themselves still kept no written historical records. In Gaul writers did note some items bearing on Insular history, but not to the extent which might have been expected. During the fourth and fifth centuries the intellectual contacts between Britain and Gaul seem to have been fairly extensive.[11] Yet despite the documented travels of British churchmen and the presumed transit of British pilgrims, the information in Gaulish sources remains disappointingly meagre.[12] Bede did, to be sure, draw on Prosper Tiro's *Epitoma chronicon* and Constantius' *Vita Germani*. But where fifth-century Insular history is concerned, the information culled from these two works bears only on the career of St Germanus.

During the first half of the fifth century the teachings of the British heresiarch Pelagius attracted the attention of Western Christendom's leading churchmen. When Pelagianism continued to flourish in Britain, Prosper reports that Celestine, the bishop of Rome, asked Germanus' help in suppressing this heretical doctrine.[13] The bishop of Auxerre is said to have visited britain in 429, but Prosper seems poorly informed as to what actually transpired on the other side of the Channel.[14] He knows nothing of a second visit, nor does he note the advent of Anglo-Saxon rule. By the middle of the century, however, Prosper Tiro had moved from Gaul, and it is distinctly possible that news of Insular developments simply failed to reach him.[15] Constantius does provide a fairly full account of Germanus' activities in Britain, but there is a notable absence of detail.[16] None of the incidents recounted is assigned to a specific locale and date. Hagiographers exhibit a notorious lack of concern for chronological precision; indeed, most of the miracles reported by Constantius can be found with minor variations in countless other saints' lives. Only the Alleluia Victory has the feel of an event with some basis in historical fact.[17]

The sequence of events leading to written notice of Germanus' Insular career reveals a great deal about the concerns of Continental authors in the fifth century. Pelagius probably arrived in Rome not long after the year 400. Nothing is known of his background or of his earlier activities; indeed, had he not spread heretical teachings on the Continent, Pelagius might have left no trace. Prosper remarks that Celestine was the first bishop of Rome to take an active interest in Insular affairs.[18] The statement may not be completely accurate, but certainly within living memory Britain had never attracted such interest.[19] The controversy ignited by Pelagius on the Continent drew the attention of Celestine and others to the island which had spawned this heresiarch. The discovery that Pelagianism flourished in Britain prompted the request to Germanus. If allowed to go unchecked, there would be nothing to prevent a steady stream of heretics from spreading a doctrine which struck at the very heart of Roman orthodoxy. Germanus intervened in Insular affairs to protect the interests of the Continental Church. His visit to Britain attracted written notice because Pelagianism was a matter of major concern to the Continent. What governed the selection of data in fifth-century Gaul was exactly the same standard of relevance which underlay the materials included by earlier, more secularly minded Roman historians.

The inference drawn from Prosper and Constantius receives confirmation from the other two writers who provide near-contemporary testimony on fifth-century Britain. Zosimus, probably quoting Olympiodorus, reports that under the usurper Magnus Maximus the Britons seceded from the Roman Empire and were forced to defend themselves against foreign incursion.[20] Procopius describes a practice brought about by the rapid population growth of the Frisians and the Anglo-Saxons in Britain. Every year large numbers of people are said to have been sent to the Franks, who provided Continental lands for settlement.[21] The accuracy of Procopius' account is not at issue, any more than the historicity of incidents reported by Constantius. Important is the pattern of inclusions: only items which bear in some way on Britain's relationship to the Continent receive notice.

How widespread knowledge of the Germanic invasions may have been is difficult to say. The Anglo-Saxon ascendancy did not affect Continental policy-making, and for the most part contemporary historians seem to have regarded the governance of the island as a matter of strictly internal interest. On the other hand, the struggle for control of Britain would tend to militate against the transmission of detailed information across the Channel. The landings by Germanic tribesmen took place along the coastline facing Gaul, and these incursions must have affected normal intercourse. Despite the evidence of strong traditional ties between Britain and Gaul, the records for the fifth century are notoriously spotty, and the gaps could easily conceal a major interruption in Channel traffic. Be that as it may, the Britons and the Anglo-Saxons were far too absorbed in their own struggles to provide the kind of stimulus which would have attracted notice by Continental historiographers. During the fifth century Insular affairs seem to constitute essentially a closed system.

The advent of Anglo-Saxon rule did not fundamentally alter Continental attitudes toward Britain's history. Bede became well known on the other side of the Channel, and

the spread of his works provided a considerable store of previously unknown materials. From the second half of the eighth century onwards Continental writers were much better informed regarding Insular affairs, but this produced no significant advances in the depiction of British and early English history. The greater availability of data prompted neither detailed consideration of Britain's past nor interest in current developments. Bede's principal importance for the history of Continental historiography lay in his system of chronology.[22] Writers did, to be sure, mine the chronicles appended to his computistical tracts, and the *Historia ecclesiastica* also enjoyed wide circulation. Such statistics must be interpreted with care. Historians on the Continent included only a small amount of the material bearing specifically on Insular affairs, and these data are reported from a perspective quite unlike Bede's.[23]

One feature of eighth- and ninth-century Continental depictions does merit discussion. Among the materials regularly selected for use was Bede's account of the barbarian incursions which plagued sub-Roman Britain, culminating in the Anglo-Saxon conquest. Unlike Gildas and Bede, Continental writers placed these events in the larger context of the Germanic migrations and the fall of the Roman Empire.[24] The Insular data provided a useful addendum to what were already regarded as developments crucial to an understanding of the fifth and sixth centuries. English writers doubtless would have benefited from this broader perspective, but the Carolingian histories in question do not appear to have exerted any influence across the Channel, whether direct or indirect. Even in the twelfth century, when compendious surveys formed such a large part of the contemporary historiographic activity, writers in England turned to much earlier sources for their information on the Empire.

Carolingian historians exhibit complete disinterest in recent Anglo-Saxon developments. Their attitude is rather surprising, given the prominence of Englishmen in the Kingdom of the Franks during the eighth and ninth centuries. Boniface, of course, receives historiographic notice for his contribution to the spread of the faith on the Continent, but neither such missionary work nor the scholarly activity of Alcuin and others draws attention to the history of the island whence these men came. Carolingian writers treat them as Continental figures whose accomplishments can be understood without reference to Insular developments.[25] To judge from the silence of the *Anglo-Saxon Chronicle*, English annalists also regarded men like Boniface and Alcuin as important only to the Continent.[26] The extraordinarily heavy cross-Channel traffic between centres of learning left few historiographic traces,[27] but other types of evidence, particularly the surviving letters, attest to how well-informed at least the leading figures of the day actually were.

The history of relations between England and the Continent during the Carolingian era simply cannot be written from contemporary chronicles. Indeed, down to the Norman Conquest it would be well-nigh impossible to distinguish periods of Anglo-Saxon influence from periods of comparative isolation using only historiographic witnesses. On the basis of the data supplied, one might be tempted to conclude that England's relationship to the Continent was the same during the reign of Charlemagne, as it was at the height of the Danish invasions, when the forces of history actually threatened for a time to sunder the island's ties with non-Scandinavian Europe. Chronicle entries on both sides of the Channel bespeak the fairly rigorous exclusion of information which did not bear directly on regional developments, whether temporal or ecclesiastical. In many cases the Continental perspective was significantly broader than the Insular, but, generally speaking, writers took notice only when one history impinged upon the other. The Battle of Hastings was just such a juncture, and by the twelfth century its aftermath had brought about significant changes in the prevailing attitudes toward Britain's past.

The Norman Conquest drew England into the mainstream of European politics to an extent unparalleled since the Claudian Invasion over a millennium earlier.[28] As part of a steadily expanding Norman domain, the island assumed a new importance for the balance of power on the Continent. William's successors were not always able to style themselves both Duke of Normandy and King of England, but the impact on historical perceptions was great nonetheless. Just as the Britons once regarded themselves as citizens of Rome, so now the island's inhabitants saw themselves and their history in a European context, a view shared at least in some Continental circles. Unlike the Roman period, when the Britons kept no historical records of their own, the historiographic response to the Norman Conquest must be traced on both sides of the Channel.

Although few Continental writers pass in silence over Hastings, physical proximity and perceptions of historical relevance continue to govern the selection of data. The level of interest in Anglo-Norman affairs, as reflected in the number of entries, tends to decrease with geographic remove. Historians in traditionally Imperial lands betray a decidedly Mediterranean orientation and do not report developments to the northwest with any consistency.[29] This distribution pattern is important for an understanding of where historiographic interest in Britain's past first manifests itself on the Continent following the Norman Conquest.

Within a half-century of Hastings, Sigebert of Gembloux provides a clear indication of the change in Continental attitudes. His universal chronicle continued the work of Eusebius and Jerome, but Sigebert numbered the Insular peoples among those whose histories merited tracing down through the ages.[30] There can be little doubt that his view of the contemporary balance of political power prompted this decision. In Jerome's day the inclusion of a separate column for the kings of Britain had not seemed warranted,[31] but after centuries of comparative neglect on the part of Continental writers the Norman Conquest sparked new interest in the contours of Insular history. The significance of Hastings made some consideration of the background essential, but Sigebert did not stop with the succession problems following the death of Edward the Confessor, as so many did. Within the limits of the available sources Sigebert extended this line of historical inquiry back across the entire time-span covered by his depiction, producing the first systematic consideration of Insular history by a Continental writer.[32]

Throughout the twelfth century Sigebert of Gembloux served as an important link between the large-scale survey of Continental tradition and historiographic developments in the Anglo-Norman domain. By incorporating Britain's past into the framework of universal history, Sigebert ensured that his chronicle would be used by English and Norman writers who sought to place Insular developments in a larger context. Sigebert's work was supplemented and continued by numerous historians during the twelfth century.

Like the Carolingian writers before him, Sigebert knew only Bede's *Chronica majora* and *Historia ecclesiastica*. A much higher percentage of the Insular data found in these works was included by him, but he could not move beyond his sources for the earliest periods. As a direct result of Sigebert's total dependence on Bede, pre-Saxon British history remained essentially a blank. Furthermore, Sigebert seriously distorted the already compressed chronology of Bede's depiction of the fifth and sixth centuries. A single annal encompasses the events from Germanus' first visit through the Battle of Mount Badon (SG, a 446, p 309).[33] In England a highly differentiated picture of at least the Germanic take-over was available in the *Anglo-Saxon Chronicle,* but the language of composition undoubtedly precluded use of this source by Continental historians. Certainly there is no evidence of its dissemination on the other side of the Channel in Sigebert's day.[34]

Advances in the depiction of early Insular history had to come from England. A Continental writer with Sigebert's interests could do little but content himself with Bede while awaiting further historiographic developments. In the second and third decades of the twelfth century Insular historians set to work systematizing the available data with an eye toward producing a comprehensive overview in Latin. William of Malmesbury took the first step in this direction and established what was to become the prevalent pattern in the use of English sources. The *Anglo-Saxon Chronicle* provided William with the underlying chronological framework, and supplementary materials from Bede were then intercalated to produce a coherent account.

The *Worcester Chronicle* exhibits the same combination, even though the compilation process was rather different. The Worcester chronicler began with Marianus Scotus, thereby providing evidence of the importance of Continental models for what Insular writers sought to accomplish. Unlike Sigebert, Marianus was primarily concerned with problems of chronology, but his scant treatment of Britain's past did derive from Bede.[35] At Worcester the *Anglo-Saxon Chronicle* was interpolated into Marianus' framework. Although additional material from Bede does not appear to have been added, the two constituent elements in the depiction of early English history remain essentially the same as in William's *Gesta regum Anglorum*.

By whatever means, the combining of Bede with the *Anglo-Saxon Chronicle* resulted in the virtual exclusion of the Britons from any consideration. Neither William of Malmesbury nor the Worcester chronicler has anything of substance to report on the Insular Celts. The omission, however, is not as noticeable as might be expected. William expressly limits himself to English history and seems to have considered the Britons a negligible force after the first Saxon landing. In the *Worcester Chronicle* the much broader scope of the depiction tends to obscure the loss of the entire pre-Saxon era. The account sketches the familiar contours of universal history, and in the absence of evidence to suggest the Britons' importance for an understanding of the standard paradigms, their omission would attract little attention. No attempt was made either in the *Gesta regum Anglorum* or in the *Worcester Chronicle* to incorporate British history into the overview. Henry of Huntingdon's *Historia Anglorum* marked the first effort in this direction, but when the pre-Saxon materials were assembled, the paucity of data became painfully evident. The problem with the available information emerged only when serious consideration was given to the Britons. Henry's depiction of British history was seriously limited by both the quantity and coherence of the material.[36]

The composition of the pre-Saxon segment of the *Historia Anglorum* (Book 1) antedates Henry's first glimpse of the **Historia regum Britanniae** at Bec in 1139.[37] Subsequent revisions were made, including minor additions from Geoffrey, but the depiction remained essentially pre-Galfridian.[38] For Henry, as for his predecessors, the systematic portion of the account could begin only with Caesar (HA, 1.12, p 16). Even after the first recorded contacts with Rome, the dearth of Insular materials necessitated heavy reliance on what were ultimately Roman sources. Indeed, from the arrival of Caesar's expeditionary forces (55 BC) through the Britons' appeal to Aetius (446-50 AD) Henry employs the Roman succession as the only viable framework for a chronology (HA, 1.12-46, pp 16-35). Much of the data bears more directly on Imperial politics than on Insular concerns, but Henry could do little else. A well-structured account was possible only from a Roman perspective. With the departure of the legions came total dependence on local materials and a concomitant loss in clarity of outline. The situation improved gradually after the arrival of Hengist and Horsa, because from this point forward Henry was able to combine Bede with the *Anglo-Saxon Chronicle* to produce a coherent, if not always detailed account.

Henry's skilful handling of the Roman materials obfuscated some difficulties, but certainly not all. As Warin the Briton was quick to point out, the combination of available sources actually underscored the existence of a major lacuna. Henry's epistolary summary of the **Historia regum Britanniae** came in response to Warin's question regarding this gap: 'Quæris a me, Warine Brito, vir comis et facete, cur patriæ nostræ gesta narrans, a temporibus Julii Cæsaris inceperim, et florentissima regna, quæ a Bruto usque ad Julium fuerunt, omiserim.'[39]

Warin had perceived what was a major weakness in the *Historia Anglorum*. Following a preliminary descriptive section (HA, 1.1-8, pp 5-13), Henry took up the settlement of Britain and recounted the story of Brutus from the *Historia Brittonum* (HA, 1.9, p 13; HB, c 10, pp 149-53). The reign of this eponymous hero was dated by means of a synchronism which derived from the same source: 'Dicunt autem illi auctores, quod quando Bruto regnabat in Britannia, Hely sacerdos judicabat in Israel, et Posthumus sive Silvius filius Æneæ regnabat apud Latinos, cujus nepos erat Bruto' (HA, 1.9, p 13; cf HB, c 11, p 153). The origins of the Irish and the Picts were then discussed, before Henry turned to Julius Caesar.[40] Between Eli's judgeship (c 1100 BC) and Caesar's expeditions (55-4 BC) lay more than a thousand years; yet not a single historical occurrence was assigned to this period. By way of explanation Henry described his fruitless search for information: 'Respondeo igitur tibi quod nec voce nec scripto horum temporum sæpissime notitiam quærens invenire potui' (RT, 1:97). Now, to his amazement, he had found a work which filled the lacuna.

The distribution of materials on early Insular history has long been seen as a key factor in the success of Geoffrey's imaginative depiction. A medieval historian's ability to render critical judgments on the reliability of his sources is a function of the availability of data. Only in cases where a basis for comparison exists, can a writer exercise some modicum of control. Geoffrey of Monmouth undoubtedly traded on this fact. That his stunning achievement represented a gross violation and wilful manipulation of accepted historiographic practice was often suspected, but difficult to prove. The extent to which his account overlaps with standard authorities is exceedingly small. Geoffrey is the only source for most of what he reports. Even when he treats well-attested matters, Geoffrey of Monmouth offers a British point of view not to be found elsewhere. His approach is seemingly orthodox, the events endowed with surpassing verisimilitude. In the absence of controlling data it was inordinately difficult to catch him in a lie.

Medieval historiographers lacked reliable means for determining what should and should not become part of the canon of history. For the distant past the historicity of the preponderance of data was established by simple reference to authority. Information concerning remote eras had passed through the hands of men whose veracity was not open to question. The odd crux might remain, but a preselection process operated which largely obviated the necessity for critical judgments. This method of evaluating data from the distant past proved vulnerable long before Geoffrey of Monmouth. Erroneous and pseudonymous attributions were commonplace in the Middle Ages, and Geoffrey most assuredly did not invent the old-book topos. Indeed, the **Historia** was pseudo-history of a kind found in every medieval founding story. For the most part, such historical fictions could not be sustained over any considerable time-span. Geoffrey's *Historia* differed from other examples in scope and skill of execution, but not in underlying assumption. Scores of writers, both before and after, exploited the same weakness in the methods employed for screening historical data. The age placed great stock in authority, because the means of verification were so limited. The likelihood that a specific item could be and would be compared with a putative source was exceedingly small. The very practices instituted to guarantee accuracy provided the favourite devices for justifying the spurious.

The physical location of writers and sources remained an important consideration throughout the Middle Ages. Generally speaking, monastic chroniclers found themselves limited to materials available in a relatively small geographic area. Religious communities situated close to courts or along pilgrimage routes enjoyed a natural advantage over more isolated monasteries. A few writers were able to travel extensively in conjunction with their offices, thereby gaining wider access to sources of information. But even for individuals fortunate enough to undertake such journeys, chance encounter played a significant role. Henry of Huntingdon discovered the *Historia regum Britanniae* at Bec; yet Geoffrey resided in the diocese of Lincoln, where Henry was an archdeacon.[41] The willingness to believe that certain materials survived in a rare, even unique copy of a work, available only to another writer, was not merely a sign of credulousness. The historiographic holdings of medieval libraries varied enormously, and chroniclers could not hope to check every entry of their predecessors or contemporaries. Trust in an author's veracity might turn out to be misplaced, but some measure of reliance on the testimony of others was absolutely unavoidable.

Geoffrey wrote in an age when early Insular history was still being given shape. Efforts to produce a coherent overview of the island's past dominated contemporary historiography. For William of Malmesbury, the Worcester chronicler, and Henry of Huntingdon, the systematization of history was not motivated by a sudden infusion of new data. Each writer endeavoured to impose order on a store of information which had gone largely unchanged for centuries. Not only had the size of the corpus remained static, but earlier attempts to systematize the data were few in number. Since the passing of Bede, only Æthelweard had undertaken the task, and William of Malmesbury found much to criticize in the style of this late tenth-century chronicle.[42] Writers regarded the materials of Insular history as essentially unordered; yet the *Anglo-Saxon Chronicle* provided a chronological framework for a major segment of the past. At issue was the use of the available information to delineate major developments and, by so doing, to identify the forces which had shaped Insular history. Systematizers in the first half of the twelfth century perceived a need to render the course of events comprehensible. The order sought by these men went beyond the chronological arrangement of data to the interpretation of history.

In addition to the uneven distribution of materials, two major obstacles impeded the progress toward a coherent overview. The first was Britain's long, disjunctive history. The welter of events, punctuated by foreign incursion, largely exceeded human understanding. For this reason the view was widely held that the many vicissitudes constituted divine retribution visited on a sinful populace. The difficulties inherent in the data were compounded by the almost total lack of historiographic conventions bearing specifically on the shape of Britain's history. No patterning devices had evolved from which writers in the twelfth century might extrapolate. For Bede the progress of the apostolic faith served as a unifying principle, especially in the early sections of the account. But the further he moved from Augustine's mission, the more difficult it became to organize the material around this single thread. The loose structure of the closing books in the *Historia ecclesiastica* bears witness to the problem. Æthelweard's attempt to impute universal significance to Anglo-Saxon history resulted only in a gross disparity between the frame and the data. He lacked an effective contact point with the larger structures of history, and therefore could not tap the dynamism of the standard paradigms. Given both the character of Insular history and the dearth of conventions, it is hardly surprising that the efforts to systematize the materials fell far short of consistent interpretation.

Despite the difficulties, the first decades of the twelfth century witnessed considerable progress, at least where the Anglo-Saxon and Norman periods were concerned. Writers drew on a comparatively small number of sources and quickly approached consensus on the outlines, if not on matters of interpretation. The first substantial block of new data to require incorporation into this emerging overview was the *Historia regum Britanniae.* Geoffrey filled the notorious pre-Saxon lacuna with an essentially discrete block of history. The account treated the period from the settlement of the island to the passing of British rule. Although Merlin's prophecies spanned the later epochs, no attempt was made to depict the subsequent course of events in systematic fashion. Geoffrey presupposed the historiographic activity of his own day, a fact which would seem to be confirmed by the epilogue to the *Historia.* Here it is stated that anyone interested in the kings who reigned after the close of the seventh century should consult Caradog of Llancarfan for Wales and William of Malmesbury or Henry of Huntingdon for England.[43] Geoffrey's contemporaries and near-contemporaries had obviated the necessity of extending the account to include more recent history, be it Welsh or Anglo-Saxon.

Although Geoffrey depicted a discrete and largely unknown segment of Insular history, he clearly regarded his account as compatible with the prevailing view of subsequent events. Were this not the case, Geoffrey of Monmouth could hardly have relied on Merlin's prophecies to bridge the chronological gap between the end of the *Historia* and twelfth-century England. The vatic utterances evoked what he correctly presumed to be familiar historical contours.[44] Merlin offered a preview which agreed in general outline with the accounts of Geoffrey's contemporaries. The seer did what no medieval chronicler could do before, namely he surveyed the entire course of Britain's history from a consistently Insular perspective. The series of prophecies reveals a highly significant advantage which accrued to historiographers using the *Historia regum Britanniae.* Geoffrey's account permitted a continuity of viewpoint which transcended the interruptions produced by foreign invasion.

Despite the usefulness and seeming orthodoxy of the *Historia,* twelfth-century historiographers exhibit considerable ambivalence toward this new source. After centuries of ignorance regarding pre-Saxon history, the very brilliance of Geoffrey's depiction elicited caution. To discover so much material for so distant an era was unusual. That anecdotes and other minor items might have escaped the notice of earlier writers was plausible, even expected, but the timely recovery of an entire age struck contemporaries as less likely. On the other hand, the existence of such a huge lacuna was itself puzzling. Continental sources for the period in question left much to be desired, but the record of events was significantly better than the Insular survivals. The twelfth century saw no obvious reason for this discrepancy, and the difficulties inherent in historical research only compounded the uncertainty. It must be assumed that Henry of Huntingdon embarked upon his search for pre-Saxon materials in the very real hope of finding additional information.[45] The early history of more than one people owed its survival to chance preservation in a single source.

Historians responded to Geoffrey's depiction by scouring standard authorities for corroborating testimony. Some supporting evidence was deemed necessary for an account which so radically altered the prevailing view of the Britons. Geoffrey of Monmouth, however, insinuated his portrayal into the numerous gaps left by previous writers. He seemed to anticipate the response of his contemporaries and successfully avoided factual contradictions throughout much of the *Historia.* Although Geoffrey displayed extraordinary skill, difficulties did occur. The problems in the post-Arthurian segment differed substantially from those in earlier portions of the text. The two sections must be kept separate in any discussion of the factors influencing Geoffrey's reception.

Down to the reign of Arthur, the *Historia regum Britanniae* agreed in general outline with what little could be surmised regarding the shape of British history. This framework imposed few restrictions on Geoffrey; indeed, there was no surviving record of Insular occurrence for the millennium which separated Brutus from Cassibellaunus. Geoffrey supplied a regnal list for the pre-Roman era and far beyond, interspersing brief characterizations with rather lengthy royal biographies.[46] In his account the Britons emerged as a people with a rich past, one filled with examples of human greatness and human folly.

So far as Geoffrey and his contemporaries were concerned, only Rome boasted a coherent record of events for the period in question. Britain's early isolation had long been proverbial, and local occurrences would hardly be expected to attract the notice of historians in the Mediterranean basin. Consequently, Geoffrey of Monmouth enjoyed complete freedom in depicting matters of strictly Insular concern. Care had to be taken only with points of contact between British and Roman history. Geoffrey appears fully cognizant of this limitation. It is surely not by accident that Brutus demonstrates his worth far from the environs of Rome (**HRB,** cc 6-20, pp 73-90). On the other hand, Britain's eponym is the great-grandson of Aeneas, and can be seen retracing the peregrinations of his illustrious ancestor. Geoffrey even elaborates the parallels with extensive borrowings from Virgil.[47] Roman historiography might represent the sole potential control on the depiction, but the City's past also possessed paradigmatic value.

Rome serves as the standard against which British achievement is measured. Geoffrey's depiction of the Britons' early potential does not hinge solely on Brutus' ancestry. The founding story gives impetus to the narration, but the thrust would quickly dissipate without comparison of a more direct kind. Geoffrey gauges the Britons' strengths and weaknesses through military encounters with Rome. The standard authorities record no such armed conflicts prior to Caesar's expeditions, but the *Historia* offers a different picture. During the post-settlement period the Britons demonstrate a capacity for real greatness and actually conquer Rome over three centuries before Caesar's arrival. The care taken in handling this episode attests to Geoffrey's awareness that Roman historiography provided the only check on the early sections of the *Historia.*

The conquest of Rome is attributed to the leadership of Belinus and Brennius. Acting in concert, the two brothers defeat first the Gauls and then the Romans (**HRB,** cc 42-4, pp 115-18).[48] Belinus returns to Britain after the fall of the City and rules in peace for the rest of his life. Brennius remains in Italy, where he treats the populace with extreme severity. Geoffrey characterizes Brennius' subsequent career only briefly. The interested reader is invited to consult Roman histories for additional information: 'Habita ergo victoria, remansit Brennius in Italia, populum inaudita tyrannide afficiens. Cujus ceteros actus et exitum, quia romanae historiae declarant, nequaquam tractare curavi, cum et nimiam prolixitatem huic operi ingessissem et, id quod alii tractaverunt perarans, a proposito meo divertissem' (**HRB,** c 44, p 118). This statement follows a familiar pattern, but further research would indeed yield more data. Geoffrey has appropriate Brennus, commander of the Senonian Gauls who sacked Rome in 390 BC.[49] A Continental Celt has been transformed into a Briton, but Geoffrey knew full well that the background of the historical Brennus was obscure. Rather than serving as a control, the Roman testimony actually seemed to confirm Geoffrey's account.[50]

This pattern of usage recurs in the depiction of Caesar's invasions and throughout the sections dealing with the period of Roman domination. Whenever possible, Geoffrey employs well-attested matters to lend credence to the account. Through the addition of countless details, familiar events are recounted from a decidedly Insular perspective, but the basic elements admit of ready corroboration. Previous accounts contained little more than a sparse outline, making refutation of Geoffrey's depiction inordinately difficult. The twelfth century simply could not adduce any hard evidence to the contrary. There was only the silence of standard authorities to gainsay the level of attainment depicted in the *Historia.* For writers accustomed to relying on Continental sources for their knowledge concerning Roman Britain, the omission of so much material did raise questions. The character of the corroborating testimony was merely puzzling for the early sections, but a major problem for the reign of Arthur.

The first man to comment on the absence of supporting evidence is Alfred of Beverley.[51] Approximately half of his modest and highly derivative history is given over to a depiction of British rule. Geoffrey's regnal list provides the underlying framework, but Alfred is openly distrustful of his principal source. Four criteria are cited as forming a basis for the selection of data from the *Historia.* Alfred promises to recount only such matters as 1/ are credible, 2/ make good reading, 3/ will stick in readers' minds, and 4/ can be corroborated by the testimony of other authorities (AB, pp 2-3). These criteria apply exclusively to the selection of data from Geoffrey's account. Alfred of Beverley did not apply the four tests with any rigour, nor could he.[52] But the practicability of such a selection process does not alter the fact that Alfred perceived a need to establish the scrupulousness with which the *Historia regum Britanniae* had been handled. He remarks the lack of corroboration on two occasions, but only after he has included the materials in question.

Book 1 of the *Annales* treats the lengthy period of independent British rule from Brutus through Lud (AB, pp 10-23).[53] At the start of Book 2 Alfred describes how he scoured Pompeius Trogus, Suetonius, Eutropius, and Orosius for some mention of the sovereigns who so dominate the first epoch in Britain's history. Gildas and Bede were also consulted (AB, p 24). This extensive research failed to yield information on the British monarchs who ruled prior to Caesar's arrival. Despite the care taken by Geoffrey, Alfred apparently did not identify Brennius with Brennus the Gaul.[54] No further comment is offered, but what prompted the observation can perhaps be inferred. Alfred is about to depict the centuries of Roman domination, a period for which there is a comparative abundance of supporting data. The account in fact ceases to be an epitome of the *Historia* and becomes a compilation of familiar sources, including Geoffrey. It is the contrast with the preceding epoch which has elicited the comment. Alfred signals a change in the availability of corroborating testimony, but he does not call attention to any particular problems raised by the distribution of data.

In the second instance Alfred is more explicit. At the close of his depiction of British history he wonders aloud that 'de inclito rege Arturo nichil Romana, nichil Anglorum hystoria meminerit, cum tamen ipse non solum in Britan-

nia contra paganos, sed et in Galliis contra Romanos res præclaras ingenii audacia miraque probitate gesserit' (AB, p 76). Alfred follows Geoffrey closely in depicting King Arthur's career (AB, pp 58-73). The fabled sovereign rules over a far-flung domain and even challenges the authority of Rome. Indeed, Arthur doubtless would have triumphed, had he not been betrayed at home. That Continental exploits of this magnitude should have left no trace in other sources is disquieting. The gaps in Insular accounts were notorious, but Alfred apparently regarded the situation on the other side of the Channel as sufficiently better for the period in question to make Arthur's omission problematic.

Although clearly troubled, Alfred has not felt that the lack of supporting evidence warranted complete rejection of Geoffrey's account. The circumstances have, however, affected Alfred's ability to deal critically with Arthur's exploits: 'Quas [res] ego hystoricæ fidei derogare non audens, studio brevitatis ista de Britonum hystoria excerpere curavi, ut quæ incredibilia a quibusdam viderentur prætermitterem, et tamen virtuti nichil detraherem' (AB, p 76). What applies in the case of King Arthur also holds true for the rest of British history: without a second source which treats the same events, Alfred has no effective basis for rendering critical judgments on the accuracy of Geoffrey's account.

Alfred of Beverley inserted a substantial portion of Geoffrey's account into what was essentially a historical vacuum. The problems were rather different when the data had to be interpolated into a pre-existent frame. A case in point is Robert of Torigni, who grappled with the problems attendant upon incorporating materials from the *Historia regum Britanniae* into the universal chronicle of Sigebert of Gembloux.[55]

Geoffrey of Monmouth's account is notable for its remove from the standard paradigms of Christian history.[56] Robert's undertaking, however, did not entail the imposition of a schema on the data. Sigebert had continued the work of Eusebius and Jerome. Like his illustrious predecessors, Sigebert had correlated a series of essentially discrete chronologies. Such activity was an expression of belief in an underlying providential design, but did not involve the patterning of material. Sigebert's information on the Britons, the Anglo-Saxons, and the Normans was sketchy (RT, 1:94). Robert planned to interpolate data not known to Sigebert and then to continue the universal chronicle from the year 1100 (RT, 1:96). To include the *Historia regum Britanniae* would have necessitated only inserting notice of British rulers and important events into the entry for the appropriate year. Dating problems were, of course, inevitable, but Geoffrey did employ a system of synchronisms which could have facilitated the positioning of blocks of material, if not always the fixing of specific items.[57] Yet Robert of Torigni did not handle Geoffrey's account as he did other sources.

The material contained in the *Historia regum Britanniae* posed a special problem which Robert discusses in the prologue to his work. Some of the events recounted by

Geoffrey were of great antiquity; indeed, Brutus was the great-grandson of Aeneas. If Robert were to include Geoffrey's entire regnal list, the names of British sovereigns would have to be interpolated not only into Sigebert's frame, but into the chronologies of Jerome and even Eusebius: 'Sed quia Brutus pronepos æneæ, a quo et insula Britannia vocata est, primus ibi regnavit, si vellem omnes reges sibi succedentes ordine congruo ponere, necesse esset michi non solum per librum Sigisberti, verum etiam per totum corpus chronicorum Jeronimi, et per magnam partem chronographiæ Eusebii, eadem nomina spargere' (RT, 1:95-6). Robert is loath to intercalate the chronological framework of the ***Historia regum Britanniae.*** He regards as unseemly (*indecens*) the interpolation of outside data into the writings of men of such authority as Eusebius and Jerome (RT, 1:96). To satisfy the interested reader, he has included Henry of Huntingdon's letter to Warin (RT, 1:97-111).

That Robert of Torigni should voice his respect for Eusebius and Jerome is hardly surprising. The combined efforts of the two Fathers formed the chronological basis for the writing of universal history in medieval Christendom. Robert viewed his own work in the context of this historiographic tradition, as had Sigebert before him. Sigebert of Gembloux may have added Insular history to the framework, but he had not extended the line back through the time period covered by Eusebius and Jerome. The last event reported by Jerome is the death of Valens in 378. Sigebert begins his compilation with the year 381, 'quo anno post mortem Valentis Valentinianus minor et Gratianus, filii maioris Valentiniani, incipientes simul regnare, regnaverunt annis 6' (SG, p 302). The choice of this starting point obviously depends upon Jerome, and Robert's reverence would also seem highly conventional.

Robert of Torigni's chronicle is found in manuscripts together with both Eusebius-Jerome and Sigebert[58] An examination of the interpolations made by Robert for the period before 1100 reveals a discrepancy between his avowed respect for the inviolability of Eusebius-Jerome and his actual practice. Although few in number and rather inconsequential, he did add materials bearing on events prior to 381.[59] It would seem reasonable to conclude that Robert of Torigni harboured misgivings about the *Historia* which go beyond the posturing of the prologue. I am persuaded, however, that his comments do hold the key to the handling of Geoffrey's account, and that even the interpolations made in Eusebius-Jerome are important for an understanding of Robert's attitude.

In discussing the ***Historia regum Britanniae,*** Robert of Torigni alludes both to the antiquity of events and to the large number of British kings. Although the first point raises the entire question of Eusebius and Jerome, I believe that the second touches the area of real concern. Robert's comments betray uneasiness over the quantitative impact of Geoffrey's account, and these fears can hardly be considered unjustified. In the second half of the twelfth century the situation with regard to the availability of data on the Britons differed dramatically from what it had been in Sigebert's day. Given his dependence on Bede, Robert's predecessor could have known little more than the name of Cassibellaunus for the period before 381, and the effect of interpolating such meagre data into Eusebius-Jerome would have been negligible. Robert, on the other hand, had an enormous amount of information at his disposal, so much that the deeds of the Britons might eclipse the accomplishments of other ancient peoples at least at scattered junctures. Geoffrey had succeeded in rectifying the earlier quantitative imbalance, but by so doing he had created a new problem.

Underlying the selection of material for any universal chronicle is the assumption that peoples should receive notice in proportion to their importance for the larger structures of history. Specific choices frequently reflect other factors, including a desire on the part of the writer to force reassessment of a regional history within the universal framework.[60] Such propagandistic motives notwithstanding, a correlation can be said to exist between perceived historical significance and the quantity of data supplied. To interpolate Geoffrey's entire regnal list, together with some indication of key events, would have substantially altered prevailing notions of the relative importance of peoples in antiquity, and Robert appears troubled by the implications. He never intended to undertake a major revision of traditional views as reflected in Eusebius-Jerome. That would seem to be the sense of his comments in the prologue, and the few minor interpolations made for events prior to 381 are not inconsistent with this approach. Indeed, the additions can be seen as reflecting Robert's conception of what constitutes the extent of change permissible in the work of two such venerable authorities.

Robert's attitude toward Sigebert was entirely different, but this fact did not have practical consequences for the handling of Geoffrey's *Historia.* Sigebert of Gembloux had begun his chronicle with the joint rule of Valentinianus and Gratianus, but lacked much of the material available to Robert on Insular and Norman history. Robert of Torigni systematically went back over the centuries treated by Sigebert, adding data previously unknown outside a small geographic area. The number of interpolations increases steadily, as Robert approaches the twelfth century, and he takes over the account completely with the annal for 1100. It was Sigebert, not Eusebius and Jerome, who incorporated Insular history into the universal chronicle, and Robert of Torigni exhibits no reluctance to interpolate substantial amounts of material on Britain's past into Sigebert's frame. Geoffrey of Monmouth also notes the accession of Valentinianus and Gratianus (**HRB,** c 80, p 154). Beginning at this point, Robert could have picked up Geoffrey's account without any significant change in his handling of Sigebert; in fact the ***Historia*** would seem to offer precisely the kind of supplementary data required. Between 381 and Cadwaladr's death in 689 lay over three centuries of British history, including the reign of Arthur. Robert made numerous additions to Sigebert for the period in question; yet none came from the ***Historia regum Brit-***

anniae.[61] It is difficult to know what importance should be attached to the exclusion of Galfridian materials for the years from 381 to 689. By Robert's day the *Historia* had gained such popularity that to include only the latter part of Geoffrey's account might have raised more problems than it solved. I am inclined to think that such restricted usage probably was not a real possibility.

Robert of Torigni clearly regarded any effort to incorporate the early sections of Geoffrey's *Historia* into Eusebius-Jerome as inherently problematic. His hesitancy would seem to stem from the quantitative impact of the Galfridian materials on traditional conceptions of history, and I think that more cannot be read into the evidence. Robert voices no distrust of Geoffrey's factual accuracy and includes the whole of Henry of Huntingdon's epistolary summary without caveat. The contents of the *Historia* were worth reporting, but the data could not be accommodated in the account proper for fear of distorting traditional perceptions.

The bulk of the Insular data interpolated into Sigebert's chronicle derives from Henry of Huntingdon. Robert knew the full text of Geoffrey's *Historia*; indeed in 1139, while a monk at Bec, he had revealed the existence of this startling account to Henry and must have witnessed the burst of enthusiasm recorded in the letter to Warin. There can be no doubt that Robert of Torigni held Henry in very high esteem. At Bec, Robert had a copy of the *Historia Anglorum,* perhaps brought by Henry himself, which covered the years down to 1135. Later, when Robert (now abbot of Mont-Saint-Michel) compiled his chronicle, he used the version extended to 1147.[62] Henry may not have incorporated any substantial amount of Galfridian material into Books 1-3, but one feature of the expanded edition was a new Book 8 which contained the epilogue to the first edition and three epistles, including the letter to Warin.[63] Robert explicitly states that he took Henry's epistolary summary of Geoffrey's account directly from the *Historia Anglorum* (RT, 1:111-12). In other words, it was Henry of Huntingdon who led the way providing a simple expedient for avoiding the difficulties posed by the Galfridian data. Both the letter and the preponderance of the Insular material used by Robert derived from the same unimpeachable source, and it is not reasonable to assume that he doubted the accuracy of one, but not the other.

To some extent the usability of the *Historia regum Britanniae* must be regarded as inversely proportional to the strength of the prevailing views with which the materials were to be integrated. On the other hand, the weight of historical tradition and personal authority had little to do with the quantity or quality of the data reported. There was no reason to believe that a standard source defined the limits of what could be known about the past. Eusebius-Jerome had to be supplemented with regional histories, Bede with the *Anglo-Saxon Chronicle,* and so forth. The traditional overviews of antiquity and the earlier Middle Ages were highly composite and filled with gaps. Both the amount and the coherence of the data in the *Historia*

regum Britanniae surpassed the established authorities. As is clear from Robert of Torigni, such superiority could create difficulties, but not all writers assessed the *Historia* in the same way. Although the force of tradition was an important limiting factor in Geoffrey's reception, other considerations tended to complicate matters for twelfth-century historiographers.

Geoffrey of Monmouth offered a plausible explanation for the wealth of new material which he reported. Initially Geoffrey himself could only marvel at the absence of information on early British rule. Gildas and Bede knew nothing of the kings who had reigned before the birth of Christ and even omitted Arthur. The deeds of these men, however, had survived, transmitted orally from generation to generation. The materials of pre-Saxon history had been handed down through a succession of individuals whose memories were as accurate as written record (**HRB**, c 1, p 71). Ultimately, the data had found inclusion in an extremely old book in the British tongue which Walter, archdeacon of Oxford, asked Geoffrey to translate into Latin (**HRB**, c 2, p 71).

The ancient book may be a convenient fiction,[64] but Geoffrey's explanation of the potential value of oral tradition is perfectly valid. To suit his own purposes, he credits this mode of transmission with the capacity for preserving historical data intact. Geoffrey claims that his account forms part of a chain of narration which extended unbroken back over Walter's book and various intermediaries to actual events. Other twelfth-century writers were more critical in assessing the accuracy of such lore, but no one doubted that certain oral traditions had historical underpinnings.

If Geoffrey's premise is accepted, then the superiority of his data over Continental survivals can be easily rationalized. The traditional, non-Insular view may rest upon unshakeable authority, but, except for Caesar, the writers in question neither witnessed the actual events nor drew on local sources. The historiographic consequences of such remove were familiar to the Middle Ages. Many a work underwent revision and interpolation for precisely this reason. Jerome added material on Roman history to Eusebius' chronicle, in part because more information was available regionally.[65] Robert of Torigni possessed data on Insular and Norman affairs which had been unknown to Sigebert of Gembloux. The number of examples can be multiplied at will. Indeed, it would be difficult to find a medieval chronicle which did not in some way reflect the advantages of local records and local traditions.

The examples cited make clear that physical location influences a writer's perceptions of history, as well as the availability of data. Jerome's view is Romano-centric, Eusebius' was not. Similarly, Robert concentrates on Anglo-Norman affairs to an extent which Sigebert probably would have found unjustified. Sigebert of Gembloux, however, did regard Insular history as an important component in a much larger framework. He imputed an intrinsic value to Britain's past which earlier Continental writers and particularly the Romans had not done. Nevertheless, the traditional view of the pre-Saxon era depended largely on the conquerors' records, and even a medieval author might reasonably be expected to conclude that the Britons must have viewed their own history through very different eyes. The prevailing notions of British history obviously needed a corrective, one which only local sources could supply. Geoffrey of Monmouth offered just such an Insular viewpoint, purportedly drawn from traditions which rested ultimately on firsthand information.

The appeal of the *Historia regum Britanniae* owes a great deal to Geoffrey's consistently Insular perspective, but despite this unity of viewpoint, not all sections of the account would be handled in the same way by subsequent historians. The mode and incidence of usage vary depending on the presence, strength, and nature of prior views. For the pre-Roman period Geoffrey was the only source of information on Insular affairs, but the situation became more complex in later sections where Geoffrey's perspective was adopted, modified, and even rejected. The factors governing such decisions change with the character of the competing traditions.

Despite the comparative wealth of Continental data on Roman Britain, Geoffrey's version of events enjoyed considerable success. His account was taken as an important corrective to the essentially hostile view of the conquering Romans. The *Historia* offered new insight into the Britons' conduct, but did not deviate from the traditional outline of the epoch's notable occurrences. The two perspectives seemed to complement each other. As a result, Continental authorities and their derivatives, notably Bede, could be used to buttress Geoffrey's account. Corroboration was supplied for the major events and inevitably lent verisimilitude to the Galfridian details. Alfred of Beverley offers an instructive example of such complementary usage.[66] The distribution of Continental materials, however, limited the applicability of this approach to the period of Roman domination.

Beginning with events of the mid-fifth century, local data became available, data which bore directly on the passage of dominion to the Anglo-Saxons. From the appeal to Aetius onwards, Geoffrey no longer represented a counterpoise to a foreign viewpoint but rather an alternative to a parallel Insular tradition. Two competing peoples would be expected to view the same events from different perspectives, but clearly the situation was changing. For the first hundred years of the Anglo-Saxon presence Geoffrey continued to be extraordinarily successful in what he had undertaken. It must be remembered that the only specific event reported by Bede between the Germanic landings and Augustine's mission was the Battle of Mount Badon. The fact that Bede attested to a British resurgence at the close of the fifth century could hardly be considered a problem. The *Anglo-Saxon Chronicle* did convey the impression of a steadily rising curve of Germanic influence, but for writers who drew on Geoffrey, the sparse information contained in these annals could not compete with what the *Historia* recounted about the hero of Mount Badon, the legendary Arthur.

In the *Historia regum Britanniae* the century following the appeal to Aetius is dominated by the rise of the house of Constantine and the reign of Arthur. After the Roman consul has dashed any hope of further military assistance against the Irish and the Picts (**HRB,** c 91, pp 167-8), the Britons are said to have dispatched Archbishop Guithelinus to Brittany. There he reminds King Aldroenus that the earlier colonization of Armorica with British soldiers is one of the roots of their current dilemma. They are all Britons, and Guithelinus implores the sovereign to accept the British crown and undertake the protection of the island which Rome has abandoned to the barbarians. Aldroenus himself declines, but agrees to send his brother Constantine who does in fact restore the British monarchy (**HRB,** c 92, pp 168-9).

Constantine's marriage to an unnamed noblewoman is blessed with three sons: Constans, Aurelius Ambrosius, and Utherpendragon—in the order of their birth (**HRB,** c 93, p 170). When King Constantine is assassinated by a Pict, a dispute develops over the succession. Constans the first-born has entered a monastery, and some favour Aurelius Ambrosius, others Utherpendragon, even though both of the eligible brothers are still only children. While the arguments rage, Vortigern, the *consul Gewisseorum* (**HRB,** c 94, p 170), persuades Constans to leave the religious life and accept elevation to the throne. When no prelate can be found to anoint Constans, Vortigern, functioning *vice episcopi* (**HRB,** c 94, p 171), crowns the former monk in a highly irregular ceremony. Not satisfied with simply manipulating the puppet king, Vortigern eventually has Constans killed and assumes the throne himself. Aurelius Ambrosius and Utherpendragon, however, escape to Brittany (**HRB,** cc 95-6, pp 171-4). Fearing both a campaign on behalf of the rightful heirs and renewed attacks by the Picts, Vortigern turns to the Saxons for help. He does not actually invite Hengist and Horsa, but rather attempts to use the fortuitous arrival of a band of warriors to his own advantage (**HRB,** cc 97-8, pp 174-6). The hapless Vortigern, however, proves no match for the wily Hengist.[67]

Geoffrey sets the first Germanic landings against a rather different background than did his predecessors. The threat of incursions from the north is still there, but the emphasis has shifted dramatically. Vortigern sits uneasily on the British throne primarily because he is a usurper. His fears over the possible return of the brothers are a much more important factor in determining his actions than are the Picts. Vortigern later finds himself completely unable to restrain the Saxons, and in desperation he attempts to build an impregnable tower. It is in conjunction with this construction that Merlin enters the *Historia.*[68]

The presence of Aurelius Ambrosius and Utherpendragon in Brittany has already created a tendency to look beyond Vortigern, and the prophecies of Merlin reinforce this feature of the account (**HRB,** cc 109-18, pp 189-203). Following the usurper's death, Aurelius Ambrosius and then Utherpendragon drive back the Britons' foes. Both kings succumb to Saxon treachery, but by this time the *Historia* is moving inexorably toward the reign of Arthur. The dynamics of the Galfridian narrative are such that interrupting the account for a discussion of the early English settlements becomes a virtual impossibility. Writers who drew on Geoffrey simply could not regard the Britons as a negligible force after the arrival of Hengist and Horsa, because to do so would be to discount the deeds of King Arthur.

Geoffrey's portrayal of King Arthur seems to have enhanced what was already a considerable popular reputation. The legendary sovereign gained a new respectability by virtue of his inclusion in the *Historia,* a fact which poets and historians alike would exploit for centuries to come. Despite the existence of contradictory Anglo-Saxon traditions, the *Historia* would prove a potent force in shaping conceptions of British potential and British achievement during the period from the mid-fifth to the mid-sixth century. Geoffrey of Monmouth places Arthur's demise in 542 (**HRB**, c 178, p 278), some ninety-three years after the date normally assigned to the arrival of Hengist and Horsa.[69] Writers found room for the fabled monarch in an age previously thought to have witnessed only the emergence of the Anglo-Saxon kingdoms. The chronological difficulties posed by conflicting English tradition should not be underestimated, but Arthur's appeal prompted attempts at historiographic compromise of a kind which these selfsame writers were unwilling to make for the post-Arthurian segments.

Beyond the reign of Arthur the attractiveness of the account was not a significant factor. The tenor of British rule deteriorated and the island's future clearly belonged to the Anglo-Saxons. This loss of appeal was not the only significant change with which Geoffrey had to cope. From the sixth century onwards the materials of Insular history improved steadily. Although gaps persisted and uncertainties continued to abound, local record did possess clarity of outline. The *Historia regum Britanniae* entered a period for which the Insular data were better and conventions stronger. Despite the many breaks and frequent confusion, Geoffrey of Monmouth no longer enjoyed the latitude he once did.

At that point where Geoffrey began to concern himself with fixing the chronological limits of British rule, he also had to contend with circumstances far different from those which obtained for earlier sections. Determining the juncture at which dominion passed to the Anglo-Saxons would become a crux, because Geoffrey attempted to exploit what he took to be the vulnerability of contemporary notions regarding the contours of sixth- and even seventh-century Insular history. Geoffrey of Monmouth drew his readers well past the arrival of Hengist and Horsa, and then continued to insinuate a radical British view into the many gaps left by his predecessors, while at the same time paving the way for eventual Anglo-Saxon ascendancy. The

undertaking was fraught with difficulties, not all of which he successfully avoided. Geoffrey forced hard choices on twelfth-century writers, and where the post-Arthurian era was concerned, the age and familiarity of Anglo-Saxon tradition came to the fore.

Notes

1. See Gildas, DEB, c 3, pp 28-9; and Bede, HE, 1. 1, pp 14-20. The D, E, and F manuscripts of the *Anglo-Saxon Chronicle* begin in similar fashion: ASC, p 5.

2. A very plausible explanation of what may lie behind Gildas' choice of a starting point has been offered by Stevens, 'Gildas Sapiens,' 355-6.

3. The *Historia Brittonum* dates Brutus' reign by means of a synchronism: 'quando regnabat Britto in Brittannia, Heli sacerdos iudicabat in Israhel et tunc arca testamenti ab alienigenis possidebatur, Postumus frater eius apud Latinos regnabat' (HB, c 11, p 153). Eli's judgeship probably should be placed c 1100 BC, approximately a thousand years before Caesar's expeditions of 55-4 BC (HB, c 19, p 162). The intervening chapters in the *Historia Brittonum* supply legendary materials on the other peoples who inhabit the British Isles. The migration of the Irish out of Scythia is said to have begun at the same time that the children of Israel crossed the Red Sea (HB, c 15, pp 156-7), but such data do not alter the fact that the compiler knows nothing of the Britons' activities between the settlement of the island and Caesar's campaigns. On the importance of the synchronizing tendencies in the *Historia Brittonum* see Dumville, 'On the North British Section of the *Historia Brittonum*,' 349 and 353-4. Dumville has shown conclusively that authorship of this highly composite text can no longer be attributed to Nennius: '"Nennius" and the *Historia Brittonum*,' 78-95. The compilation of the *Historia Brittonum* can be dated with considerable precision to 829-30: Dumville, 'Some Aspects of the Chronology of the *Historia Brittonum*,' 439-40.

4. On the possible reason for passing over Caesar see Stevens, 'Gildas Sapiens,' 355.

5. Molly Miller has contrasted the apparent situation in Britain with that in Herodotus' Greece. The first writers to deal with early Insular history do not seem able to draw upon a comparable corpus of historical and quasi-historical narrative traditions: 'Starting to Write History: Gildas, Bede and Nennius,' 458-9.

6. The tin trade attracted early interest to the area, but little more than rumours appear to have reached writers in the Mediterranean basin: Thomson, *History of Ancient Geography,* 53-6. No eyewitness accounts which antedate Caesar's expeditions have survived, but Pytheas of Marseilles probably journeyed to Britain as much as three centuries earlier. Some of the data gathered on Pytheas' voyage may have found inclusion in later sources: Bunbury, *A History of Ancient Geography,* 1:590-601. See also Thomson, *History of Ancient Geography,* 143-51.

7. Caesar, DBG, 4.20-1, pp 112-14. Despite this precaution, Caesar's lack of familiarity with the coastline and local water conditions resulted in a sizable loss of ships on both expeditions.

8. Jackson, *Language and History in Early Britain,* 96-106.

9. Jackson has shown that a high percentage of the Latin loanwords in Brittonic came from speakers trained in Roman schools: 'On the Vulgar Latin of Roman Britain,' 83-103; and *Language and History in Early Britain,* 107-12. On Gildas' Latin see Kerlouégan, 'Le Latin du *De excidio Britanniae de Gildas,*' 151-76.

10. Caesar is the most important witness to the uses of writing and oral transmission on the Continent: DBG, 6.14, pp 185-6. See Tierney, 'The Celtic Ethnography of Posidonius,' 189-275. Daphne Nash has offered some well-reasoned criticism of Tierney, and sees Caesar as a much more independent authority: 'Reconstructing Poseidonios' Celtic Ethnography: Some Considerations,' 111-26.

11. Chadwick, 'Intellectual Contacts between Britain and Gaul in the Fifth Century,' 189-253.

12. An anonymous 'Gaulish' chronicle was long thought to provide roughly contemporary testimony on the passage of dominion from the Britons to the Anglo-Saxons: *Chronica Gallica,* ed Mommsen, p 660 (a 441-2). This entry, however, has now been shown to be part of a Carolingian continuation of Jerome: Miller, 'The Last British Entry in the "Gallic Chronicles",' 315-18.

13. *Epitoma chronicon,* p 472.

14. Nothing is reported beyond the fact that Celestine sent Germanus to Britain. Prosper even leaves the duration of the visit open. Chadwick, however, has pointed out the likelihood that Prosper learned of Germanus' mission in Rome. He is known to have visited the city in 430 and again in 431: Chadwick, *Poetry and Letters in Early Christian Gaul,* 172. If Prosper did hear news of this campaign against British Pelagians from Roman sources, that would explain the character of the entry and particularly the lack of Insular detail. The possibility also exists that Germanus was still in Britain in 430 and 431, thereby accounting for the absence of any information on how long the mission lasted.

15. Prosper apparently followed Leo I to Rome in 440 immediately following the papal election. Thereafter, Prosper seems to have held a secretarial post in the papal chancellery: Chadwick, *Poetry and Letters in Early Christian Gaul,* 172-3.

16. Constantius, *Vita Germani episcopi Autissiodorensis,* ed Levison, cc 12-18, pp 259-65 (first visit); cc 25-7, pp 269-71 (second visit).

17. *Vita Germani,* cc 17-18, pp 263-5. Levison rightly points out that historical fact has been overlaid with a considerable amount of legend in Constantius' account of the Alleluia Victory: Levison, 'Bischof Germanus von Auxerre und die Quellen zu seiner Geschichte,' 123-4. For a general discussion of Germanus' visits to Britain see de Plinval, 'Les campagnes de saint Germain en Grande-Bretagne contre les Pélagiens,' 135-49.

18. *Liber contra collatorem,* PL, 51, c 21, col 271.

19. The British Church was, of course, represented at major councils on the Continent during this period. What Prosper appears to mean is direct papal intervention in local ecclesiastical matters.

20. Zosimus, *Historia nova,* ed Mendelssohn, 6.1-6, pp 282-7. See Thompson, 'Zosimus on the End of Roman Britain,' 163-7.

21. *De bello Gothico,* ed Haury, 4.20, pp 589-91.

22. See von den Brincken, *Studien zur lateinischen Weltchronistik bis in das Zeitalter Ottos von Freising,* 108-13.

23. For example, Frechulf of Lisieux treats Augustine's mission as an accomplishment of Gregory's papacy, but no attempt is made to define the conversion's importance for English history: *Chronicon,* PL, 106, col 1256 (2.5.24). Regino of Prüm handles the material in identical fashion: *Chronicon,* ed Kurze, a 517-37, p 25. Both writers mention Æthelberht's conversion, but no other Anglo-Saxon king receives notice. The pattern carries through the period and beyond. England's rulers are noted only when their actions have a bearing on major ecclesiastical matters.

24. See for example Frechulf of Lisieux, *Chronicon,* 2.5.13, cols 1244-5; and Ado of Vienne, *Chronicon,* PL, 123, cols 101-2 and 105.

25. Only Boniface receives notice in the major histories. His activities as a Continental churchman and his martyrdom among the Frisians are described in brief. For example, see Ado of Vienne, *Chronicon,* col. 123.

26. The A-text (Parker ms) sporadically includes items bearing on papal history, but beyond these entries only the death of Charlemagne is reported: ASC, a 814, p 39. The E- and F-manuscripts, which contain a great deal of information on Continental affairs, date from after the Norman Conquest.

27. On the intellectual commerce during this period see Levison, *England and the Continent in the Eighth Century,* 132-73.

28. Norman writers did not miss the Roman analogy, but the comparison is with Caesar, not Claudius. Guy of Amiens terms William *Iulius alter: Carmen de Hastingae proelio,* ed Morton and Muntz, line 32, p 4. See also lines 345-54, pp 22-4. William of Poitiers draws an extended parallel with Caesar's expeditions: *Histoire de Guillaume le Conquérant,* ed Foreville, 2.39-40, pp 246-54. William is exceedingly fond of classical analogues. The relationship between

Guy's *Carmen* and William's *Gesta Guillelmi* remains unclear.

29. Frutolf of Michelsberg offers perhaps the most extreme example. See his comments on the Norman Conquest: *Chronica,* ed Schmale and Schmale-Ott, p 78. Frutolf provides no other information on post-Conquest Insular affairs. Otto of Freising selects his data using the same criterion of immediate relevance seen earlier. Matilda's marriage to the emperor gives Otto reason to enter some items on Henry I: *Chronica sive Historia de duabus civitatibus,* ed Hofmeister, 7.15, p 329; 7.16, pp 332-3; and 7.21, p 341.

30. Sigebert begins his *Chronographia* with an introductory paragraph on each of the nine peoples whose histories will be traced. He lists the *Angli* as number five, but apparently finds it impossible to treat English history in isolation. The introductory statement begins with the Britons and sketches the events which led up to the Anglo-Saxon conquest: SG, pp 300-1. In the account proper Sigebert regularly includes available data bearing on pre-Saxon Britain. For a discussion of Sigebert's work see von den Brincken, *Studien zur lateinischen Weltchronistik,* 182-7.

31. Jerome omits Caesar's expeditions, and supplies only information bearing directly on Imperial affairs from the Claudian Invasion onwards: *Chronicon,* ed Helm, p 179.

32. Sigebert's entries on Insular affairs reflect the distribution of data in Bede. Though selective, Sigebert does include notices on Anglo-Saxon kings with a consistency not found among earlier Continental writers. See for example (down to Edwin's accession): SG, a 491, p 313; a 561, p 318; a 599, p 320; a 604, p 321; a 615, p 322; and a 616, p 322. This pattern continues until just after the entry on Bede's death (SG, a 731, p 330), when Sigebert states: 'Abhinc regnum Anglorum annotare supersedeo, quia hystorias maiorum, quas sequar, non habeo' (SG, a 735, p 331). The extent of Sigebert's dependence on Bede becomes clear as the account continues. Although items pertaining to English history do not disappear entirely, Sigebert has lost the ability to trace Insular developments.

33. It is difficult to account for Sigebert's handling of these materials, especially since he states that Ambrosius Aurelianus led the British resistance for forty-five years. He has compressed well over a century of Insular history into a single entry. Cf Bede, HE, 1.16, p 54.

34. The encyclopedist Lambert of Saint-Omer would seem to be the first Continental writer to draw on the *Chronicle.* He includes a sizable section on English history in his monumental work completed in 1120: *Liber Floridus,* ed Albert Derolez, fols 68^r-76^r, pp 137-55. Albert Derolez provides a convenient review of the dating evidence in the introduction to the edition, pp vii-viii. The information on English history is drawn in substantial measure from the F-text of the *Anglo-Saxon Chronicle.* For a discussion of Lambert's handling of the sources available to him see René Derolez, 'British and English History in the *Liber Floridus,'* 59-70.

35. Marianus was Irish, but his interest in Bede had nothing to do with this background. From 1056 until his death in 1082 or 1083, Marianus lived on the Continent. The purpose of his universal chronicle was primarily computistical, and he took exception with Bede's system of chronology which had long held sway among Continental writers. The Insular data borrowed from Bede are largely incidental to the discussion of theoretical matters. For an excellent review of Marianus' life and work see von den Brincken, 'Marianus Scottus,' 191-208.

36. Indicative of the problem is the manner in which Lambert of Saint-Omer found it necessary to divide up materials from the *Historia Brittonum,* placing them in several sections of his work. On Lambert's handling of the data see Dumville, 'The *Liber Floridus* of Lambert of Saint-Omer and the *Historia Brittonum,'* 103-22.

37. Henry of Huntingdon set to work compiling the *Historia Anglorum* shortly before 1133. The first edition reached to the year 1129, and a second brought the account down to 1135. This was accomplished by simply extending the final book. No further changes appear to have been made prior to the visit to Bec. In all likelihood it was Henry himself who provided Robert of Torigni with a copy of the *Historia Anglorum* to 1135, presumably the most up-to-date version available at the time. See Gransden, pp 194 and 200.

38. For the later editions and particularly the expanded version (to 1147) see Gransden, p 194; and Partner, pp 17-18.

39. RT, 1:97. The *Epistola ad Warinum* was included by Robert of Torigni in his chronicle, cited here from Delisle's edition. Though extant, Henry of Huntingdon's own text of the letter has not been edited.

40. The information on the origins of the Irish and the Picts is also drawn from the *Historia Brittonum:* HA, 1.9-11, pp 13-16; HB, cc 12-15, pp 154-8.

41. Henry's ignorance of Geoffrey's activities is very puzzling: Tatlock, p 434. The *Historia Anglorum* was written at the behest of Alexander bishop of Lincoln (HA, prologus, p 3), the same man for whom Geoffrey of Monmouth translated the *Prophecies of Merlin* (HRB, cc 109-10, pp 189-90). The two authors obviously moved in similar circles, and Geoffrey certainly knew the *Historia Anglorum.* These curious circumstances prompted Brooke's contention that Henry of Huntingdon was 'evidently singled out to be one of the first and most considerable victims of the fraud:' Brooke, 'The Archbishops of St David's, Llandaff and Caerleon-on-Usk,' 231. Although I can see no reason for such trickery, Brooke's view is a possibility. Even if Geoffrey did purposely conceal

the existence of his work from Henry, the success of this deception only underscores the importance of chance, where historical research in the twelfth century was concerned. For the context of Henry's visit to Bec see Saltmann, *Theobald, Archbishop of Canterbury,* 14-15.

42. GRA, prologus, 1:1-3. Æthelweard was not widely known; indeed, no other writer can be shown to have had firsthand familiarity with the text until the sixteenth century: Campbell, ÆC, pix. William of Malmesbury boasts that he is the first since Bede to treat the whole of English history in Latin, thereby discounting Æthelweard entirely: GRA, prologus, 1:1. On the date of Æthelweard's chronicle see Campbell, ÆC, pp xii-xvi.

43. HRB, c 208, p 303. The Second Variant also contains the full epilogue: CUL, ms Mm. 5.29, fol. 107^r and BL, ms Royal 4.C.XI, fol. 248^v. The First Variant has a much shorter version which omits the names of the three historians: 'Regum autem acta qui ab illo tempore in Gwaliis successerunt et fortunas successoribus meis scribendas dimitto, ego Galfridus Arturus Monemuthensis, qui hanc historiam Britonum de eorum lingua in nostram transferre curavi' (FV, 11.18, p 264). On the use made of Caradog's name in the epilogue see Tatlock, p 5.

44. The fact that so many later writers saw Merlin's prophecies fulfilled in events of their own day bears witness to the correctness of Geoffrey's supposition. On the structure and function of the vaticinations see Pähler, *Strukturuntersuchungen zur 'Historia regum Britanniae' des Geoffrey of Monmouth,* 127-49.

45. Henry describes his efforts in the *Epistola ad Warinum,* RT, 1:97.

46. On the rhythm of the narrative see Pähler, *Strukturuntersuchungen,* 87-126.

47. See Faral, 2:70-81.

48. Prior to their Continental campaign Belinus and Brennius, the sons of Dunvallo Molmutius, wage war against each other until a reconciliation is brought about by their mother: HRB, cc 35-41, pp 108-15.

49. Brennus' campaign is reported in many sources. For example, see Orosius, HAP, 2.19, pp 130-1.

50. Faral is persuaded that Geoffrey altered the name slightly from Brennus to Brennius in order to mask the borrowing of such a well-attested figure (Faral, 2:135). Tatlock, on the other hand, feels that Geoffrey wanted to demonstrate the superiority of his knowledge (Tatlock, p 169, fn 279). Although Tatlock is undoubtedly much closer to the truth, he misses the importance which attaches to providing partial corroboration for such a crucial juncture in British history.

51. The *Annales* were begun in 1143 (Tatlock, pp 210-11, and Gransden, p 212). The completion date can-

not be fixed with any certainty because Alfred does not carry the account down to his own day. The last events recorded are those for the year 1129. Hearne added the title *Annales* (AB, p 1, fn 1), which is something of a misnomer. Strictly speaking, the arrangement of materials does not become annalistic until rather late in the account (AB, p 99).

52. Remarking Alfred's inconsistency on the question of corroborating testimony, Tatlock terms him a 'dullard' (Tatlock, p 210). This judgment is excessively harsh and betrays a lack of understanding for the problems faced by Alfred. The beginnings of a more just evaluation have been provided by Hammer, 'Note on a Manuscript of Geoffrey of Monmouth's *Historia regum Britanniae,*' 225-34.

53. Alfred divides his account of British rule into five unequal sections, the *quinque status regni.* Each of the first five books treats a separate *status.* Use of this structural device ends with the passage of dominion.

54. Alfred remarks: 'Horum gesta tam Romana quam Britania narrat hystoria, de quibus hic aliqua sunt memoranda' (AB, p 16). Belinus' deeds, however, are not recounted in Roman sources, and this statement must be regarded as an empty formula.

55. On Robert's life and historiographic activity see Gransden, pp 261-3.

56. This feature of Geoffrey's *Historia* is emphasized by Hanning, *The Vision of History in Early Britain,* 123.

57. Geoffrey inserts ten synchronisms into his account: HRB, c 22, p 92; c 25, p 96; c 26, p 96; c 27, p 97; c 28, p 98; c 29, p 98; c 30, pp 98-9; c 32, p 106; c 64, p 138; c 68, p 141. See the discussion of the first eight synchronisms in Parry, 'The Chronology of Geoffrey of Monmouth's *Historia,* Books I and II,' 316-22.

58. See Delisle's discussion of the manuscript transmission: RT, 1:iii-liii.

59. Delisle prints separately all the interpolations made by Robert in Eusebius-Jerome and Sigebert. For the period before 381 see RT, 1:1-3.

60. Æthelweard's chronicle is a case in point. By treating the Anglo-Saxons in this context, he implies their importance for the larger structures of history. Æthelweard dedicated the chronicle to his relative Matilda of Essen: ÆC, p 1. She was the granddaughter of the Emperor Otto I and his wife Edith, Athelstan's sister. Æthelweard obviously intended his approach to instil in Matilda a sense of pride in her Anglo-Saxon heritage.

61. These interpolations are printed separately by Delisle, RT, 1:3-6.

62. See Gransden, pp 195-200.

63. See Gransden, p 194; and Partner, pp 17-18.

64. I regard Geoffrey's old book as a topos, although the tantalizing possibility that such a source once existed

continues to attract believers. For example, see Southern, 'Aspects of the European Tradition of Historical Writing, 1. The Classical Tradition from Einhard to Geoffrey of Monmouth,' 194.

65. In the prologue to his chronicle Jerome comments on the need to add Roman data to Eusebius' account: *Chronicon*, p 6.

66. In Books 2-4 (from Caesar to the appeal to Aetius) Alfred's style becomes that of the compiler, not the epitomist: AB, pp 24-46. Material from other sources, principally Bede, is inserted wherever available; indeed, for some sections the *Historia ecclesiastica* provides the underlying framework, Geoffrey the supplemental data.

67. Hengist has his daughter Renwein brought over from the Continent. She blinds Vortigern with passion, and Hengist receives Kent in return for his consent to their marriage: HRB, c 100, pp 178-9.

68. Geoffrey derived the nucleus of the story from the *Historia Brittonum* (HB, cc 40-2, pp 181-6).

69. Geoffrey does not date the first landing with any precision. After describing Vortigern's fear that both the Picts and the rightful heirs might launch attacks, it is simply stated: 'Interea applicuerunt tres ciullae, quas longas naves dicimus, in partibus Cantiae, plenae armatis militibus, quibus duo fratres, Horsus et Hengistus, ducatum praestabant' (HRB, c 98, p 175).

Abbreviations

AB: Alfred of Beverley *Annales, sive Historia de gestis regum Britanniae* ed Thomas Hearne (Oxford 1716)

ÆC: Æthelweard *Chronicon* ed A. Campbell Nelson's Medieval Texts (Edinburgh 1962)

ASC: *The Anglo-Saxon Chronicle: A Revised Translation* ed Dorothy Whitelock with David C. Douglas and Susie I. Tucker (London 1961)

DBG: C. Julius Caesar *De bello Gallico* ed Otto Seel *Commentarii rerum gestarum* 1 (Leipzig 1961)

DEB: Gildas *De excidio et conquestu Britanniae* ed Theodor Mommsen MGH:AA,: 13 (Berlin 1898) 25-85

EdE: Geffrei Gaimar *L'Estoire des Engleis* ed Alexander Bell Anglo-Norman Texts, 14-16 (Oxford 1960)

Faral Edmond Faral *La légende arthurienne*: 3 vols Bibliothèque de l'École des Hautes Études, Sciences historiques et philologiques, 255-7 (Paris 1929)

FV: First Variant *Geoffrey of Monmouth, Historia regum Britanniae: A Variant Version* ed Jacob Hammer Publications of the Mediaeval Academy of America, 57 (Cambridge Mass. 1951)

GC: Gervase of Canterbury *The Historical Works* ed William Stubbs 2 vols Rolls Series (London 1879-80)

GRA: William of Malmesbury *Gesta regum Anglorum* ed William Stubbs 2 vols Rolls Series (London 1887-9)

Gransden Antonia Gransden *Historical Writing in England c 550 to c 1307* (London 1974)

Griscom Geoffrey of Monmouth: *Historia regum Britanniae* ed Acton Griscom (London, New York, and Toronto 1929)

HA: Henry of Huntingdon *Historia Anglorum* ed Thomas Arnold Rolls Series (London 1879)

HAP: Paulus Orosius *Historiarum adversum paganos libri* VII: ed C. Zangemeister CSEL,: 5 (1882; repr Hildesheim 1967)

HB: *Historia Brittonum* ed Theodor Mommsen MGH:AA,: 13 (Berlin 1898) 111-222

HE: Bede *Ecclesiastical History of the English People* ed Bertram Colgrave and R.A.B. Mynors Oxford Medieval Texts (Oxford 1969)

HRA: William of Newburgh *Historia rerum Anglicarum* ed Richard Howlett 2 vols *Chronicles of the Reigns of Stephen, Henry* II.: *and richard* I.,: 1-2 Rolls Series (London 1884-5)

HRB: Geoffrey of Monmouth *Historia regum Britanniae* Faral, 3: 64-303

LB: Layamon *Brut* ed G.L. Brook and R.F. Leslie 2 vols EETS,: 250, 277 (Oxford 1963-78)

O'Sullivan: Thomas D. O'Sullivan *The 'De excidio' of Gildas: Its Authenticity and Date* Columbia Studies in the Classical Tradition, 7 (Leiden 1978)

Partner: Nancy F. Partner *Serious Entertainments: The Writing of History in Twelfth-Century England* (Chicago and London 1977)

RD: Ralph Diceto *The Historical Works* ed William Stubbs 2 vols Rolls Series (London 1876)

RdB: Wace *Le Roman de Brut* ed Ivor Arnold 2 vols SATF (Paris 1938-40)

RT: Robert of Torigni *Chronique* ed Léopold Delisle 2 vols (Rouen 1872-3)

RW: Roger of Wendover *Chronica, sive Flores historiarum* ed H.O. Coxe 4 vols (London 1841-2)

SG: Sigebert of Gembloux *Chronographia* ed L.C. Bethmann MGH:SS,: 6 (1844; repr Leipzig 1925) 268-374

Tatlock: J.S.P. Tatlock *The Legendary History of Britain: Geoffrey of Monmouth's 'Historia regum Britanniae' and Its Early Vernacular Versions* (Berkeley and Los Angeles 1950)

T. D. Crawford (essay date 1982)

SOURCE: "On the Linguistic Competence of Geoffrey of Monmouth," *Medium Aevum*, Vol. 51, No. 2, 1982, pp. 152-62.

[In the following essay, Crawford examines evidence indicating that Geoffrey did not read Welsh and was unfamil-

iar with Breton, but that, rather, his history was based on remembered oral tales, embellished with imagination.]

There is a striking disagreement among students of the work of Geoffrey of Monmouth about his ability to speak the Welsh language. *A propos* of his breaking off the composition of the *Historia Regum Britanniae* in order to translate the **'Prophecies of Merlin'**, Parry and Caldwell declare, 'There is no evidence that at this time he had any command of that language [Welsh], but he would have had little difficulty in learning the style and something of the substance of this material from those who did'.[1] This amounts to claiming that Geoffrey composed the *Historia* up to this point (i.e. as far as the end of Book VI) without the help of any 'very ancient book in the British language', which *ex hypothesi* he could not have understood,[2] and that this book is therefore a figment of his imagination. If there were agreement upon Geoffrey's ignorance of Welsh, the question of his sources would be greatly simplified; but Tatlock states equally firmly, 'There is proof that he knew at least some Welsh',[3] and cites various sections of the *Historia,* including three references to Books I-VI. It seems worthwhile, therefore, to look at the whole question of Geoffrey's linguistic attainments insofar as his work allows us to judge of them.

We will begin with his knowledge of Latin and Norman-French, taking the two together for the sake of convenience. To the quality of his Latin the *Historia* bears witness: '. . . he writes very well indeed', says Tatlock, 'competently, picturesquely and above all tersely, but of course in the medieval manner, which did not pretend to be classical'.[4] Geoffrey himself, however, appears to invite comparison with writers of classical Latin by making Hoel refer to one of Arthur's speeches as 'tua deliberatio Tulliano liquore lita'[5]—but then of course his ancient British source was supposed to relate these happenings 'perpulchris orationibus'![6] Thorpe is no doubt right in saying, '. . . one senses that his modesty is assumed and that in effect he was pleased with what he had written', and in quoting the Hoel reference in support of that view.[7] Geoffrey writes the Latin of his day with remarkable fluency, and there is no reason to doubt his competence in it as a spoken language also.

What is particularly interesting is to find him referring to Latin as 'lingua nostra'. This occurs once in the main body of the text ('Albanactus junior possedit patriam quae lingua nostra his temporibus appellatur Scotia . . .')[8] and once in the DEH Variant Version of the *explicit* ('. . . ego Galfridus Arturus Monemuthensis, qui hanc historiam Britonum de eorum lingua in nostram transferre curavi').[9] Now Latin, though the *lingua franca* of educated men in Geoffrey's time, was no longer anyone's everyday language. Geoffrey himself must have had a different mother-tongue, either Breton brought over by his family after the Norman Conquest,[10] a possibility suggested by Tatlock,[11] or the Norman-French general among the post-Conquest aristocracy. His references to Latin as 'lingua nostra' tilt the balance very decidedly in favour of Norman-French. For a native speaker of Breton, Latin would be an entirely foreign language, but Welsh a rather similar one to his own and largely intelligible without undue effort. It is therefore psychologically improbable that a Breton-speaking Geoffrey would have written '. . . de eorum lingua in nostram transferre curavi' after supposedly translating from Welsh or Breton into Latin. On the other hand, an educated native speaker of Norman-French could not fail to be aware that his everyday speech was historically a descendant of Latin and might well regard the former as no more than a degenerate version of the latter. If Geoffrey's mother-tongue was Norman-French, it would be quite natural for him to think of Latin as a refined form of his own language.

Before considering Geoffrey's knowledge of Celtic languages we may glance briefly at his English. This, as Tatlock observes, he would have learned at Oxford, not in Monmouth[12]—as an adult, therefore. To what extent it would be essential for him to learn the vernacular of Oxford is not easy to determine; conceivably he could have existed there comfortably knowing nothing but Latin and Norman-French. The question loses significance when we consider his references to the English language in the *Historia.* He gives 'etymologies' for the Mercian Law,[13] for *Guallenses,*[14] and for various place-names, including Ludgate,[15] Walbrook,[16] 'Thancastre',[17] and 'Cunungeburg'.[18] He translates the name of Shaftesbury by the curious Latin-Welsh hybrid 'Oppidum montis Paladur',[19] and converts Bede's 'Hefenfelth' into 'Hevenefeld' which he then glosses as 'Caelestis Campus'.[20] He makes Hengist explain the origin of the words 'Wednesday' and 'Friday',[21] and accounts for the custom of saying 'Was hail!' and 'Drinc hail!'.[22] After all this it comes as something of a surprise that he speaks of the Saxons as 'nefandus populus'[23] and refers to 'British' and Latin as the two languages of Britain as if English did not exist.[24] But Geoffrey no doubt thought of himself as a Norman and might be expected therefore to look down on the people whom the Normans had conquered, and, by extension, on their language. That this in no way precluded a keen interest in English speech and customs is adequately demonstrated by the examples quoted. They are not the work of a man whose acquaintance with English was a grudging one forced upon him by the circumstance of his moving to an English-speaking town. Rather, they bespeak a lively, if condescending, interest in the people among whom his career had chanced to place him.

But to take an interest in a language does not automatically bestow total competence in it, and we cannot be sure how thorough was Geoffrey's knowledge of English. Tatlock points out that his etymology of 'Thancastre' is the earliest record we have of the word 'thong' with initial /θ/ instead of /θw/.[25] It may indeed be that this change was under way and that Geoffrey happens to have been the first to leave us a record of it, but some caution is necessary. Geoffrey would be familiar with the sound /θ/ if, as we shall see is virtually certain, he also knew Welsh; but nothing in Latin, Norman-French, Welsh, or even Breton would prepare him to recognize the initial combination /θw/. It is notorious that the learner of a language tends to misinterpret unfamiliar sounds and sound groups as similar sounds and sound groups in languages with which he is already familiar, and in all probability that is what Geoffrey has done here. Of course if he heard /θw/ as /θ/, he himself would pronounce it as /θ/, but this would not have caused significant difficulties in comprehension, and in an age which adopted a cavalier attitude towards vernacular languages it is unlikely that anyone would have bothered to correct him.

This presupposes that Geoffrey did not *read* English, for in the script of the time he would have found the initial combination /θw/ in various guises.[26] The point is an interesting one in relation to the more basic question of whether he could really read 'British' as he claims, and some supporting evidence is worth quoting. As Tatlock observes, Geoffrey's conversion of the Saxon name 'Cerdic' into 'Cherdic' reflects the southern and central English move from /κ/ to /tʃ/ in such cases, 'and points to Geoffrey's knowledge of English'.[27] But if Geoffrey were at all familiar with historical records in English he would have known the correct spelling, even if he failed to realize that a change of pronunciation had taken place. This is the sort of material which one might expect a man of Geoffrey's historical interests to read if he read English at all. Moreover, he would not have to go to documents very much before his own time to discover the old form of 'king', i.e. *cyning,* and to realize the true origin of the name 'Cunungeburg'.[28] This is very inconclusive evidence, but the balance of probability is that Geoffrey, although he spoke English, did not read it to any significant extent.

Let us turn now to the question of Geoffrey's knowledge of Welsh. We may begin by observing the improbability that a man who moved to Oxford and learned the vernacular there should not have troubled to learn the language commonly used in his native region. Fortunately, however, we are not dependent upon argument from probability. The text of the *Historia* makes it quite plain that Geoffrey had a certain competence in Welsh. We have already noticed how he translates the 'Shaft-' of 'Shaftesbury' by *paladur.* Tatlock discounts the possibility that this could be a genuinely ancient Celtic name for the town: 'The place being unimportant, and in his [Geoffrey's] day far from Welsh territory, it is not likely to have retained a Celtic name . . .'.[29] We can probably go further. The Latin name 'Sephtonia' does not appear to be on record before the Middle Ages, but the 'Sepht-' is too similar to the 'Shaft-' of 'Shaftesbury' for the names to be independent of each other. Since *Sepht* is not meaningful in Latin whereas 'Shaft' is meaningful in English, it is extremely probable that an original latinized name was taken over and modified by the invading Saxons to whom it suggested a familiar word in their own language. Geoffrey's 'oppidum montis Paladur' would then have to date from later than the Saxon occupation of Shaftesbury and could not be the original Celtic name of the town. We can be fairly certain, therefore, that Geoffrey knew that *paladr* was Welsh for

'shaft'. We can similarly infer from some of his other coinages that he knew *caer* 'fort' and *porth* 'gate',[30] though it would be difficult to live for long in Wales without grasping the meaning of these. More interesting is his cryptic account of how the 'British' language came to be so called:

> Denique Brutus de nomine suo insulam Britanniam appellat sociosque suos Britones: volebat enim ex derivatione nominis memoriam habere perpetuam. Unde postmodum loquela gentis, quae prius Trojana sive curvum Graecum nuncupabatur, dicta fuit Britannica.[31]

Roberts is undoubtedly right in asserting that 'curvum Graecum' is an attempt at etymology;[32] 'curvum Graecum' in Welsh is *cam Roeg,* and the Welsh world for the Welsh language is *Cymraeg.* It is possible in theory that Geoffrey could have borrowed this etymology from a source now no longer extant without having himself any command of Welsh, but the way in which he inserts it into his text militates against this. The point of his 'curvum Graecum' is necessarily lost on any reader of the *Historia* who does not know Welsh,[33] and this can scarcely have been Geoffrey's intention, for his work is aimed at an audience which could not be expected to have such knowledge. Yet if Geoffrey himself had no knowledge of Welsh he would surely have been conscious of the difficulty which the passage would cause his readers. The casual introduction of this etymology rather suggests a considerable degree of facility in the language, which he momentarily forgot that his audience did not share. Again we may recur to the case of Shaftesbury; the significance of 'oppidum montis Paladur' is lost on any reader who does not know that (1) 'Sephtonia' in English is 'Shaftesbury', and (2) 'shaft' means the same as *paladur.* Geoffrey's original audience perhaps knew the first, but how many knew the second? We might suspect a scribal omission did not the two cases confirm each other. As it stands, they furnish the best evidence we have for Geoffrey's familiarity with both English and Welsh.[34]

We come to the crucial question of whether, in the case of Welsh, this familiarity extended to the written language. Is there any evidence that Geoffrey had experience of reading in Welsh the sort of material from which he claims to derive his history?[35] We need not doubt that he could have done so had he wished; the orthography of Welsh would have posed no insuperable problem to a man accustomed to that of mediaeval Latin. There was, however, a considerable degree of variation, as in the orthography of all vernaculars of the period. If the Vulgate Version of the *Historia* preserves anything approaching Geoffrey's original spelling of Celtic place-names, then he was giving the letters of the alphabet values not too far removed from those of Latin, e.g., his 'Kaerliudcoit',[36] with which compare Variant Version C's 'Kaerlwydcoed',[37] much closer to the modern Welsh 'Caerlwytgoed'. Given the variability of mediaeval Welsh orthography combined with the likelihood of scribal errors, it would be rash to try to infer anything about Geoffrey's reading habits from spellings unsupported by other internal evidence. But Geoffrey's persistent etymologizing gives us such evidence in two crucial cases.

Kamber autem [possedit] partem illam quae est ultra Sabrinum flumen, quae nunc Gualia vocatur, quae de nomine ipsius postmodum Kambria multo tempore dicta fuit: unde adhuc gens patriae lingua britannica sese Kambro appellat . . .

(Faral, p. 93; II, i).

Consider this together with Geoffrey's derivation of *Cymraeg* (/kʌmraɛg/) from *cam Roeg* (/kam reig/) and the fact that in Welsh the word for a Welshman is *Cymro* (/kʌmro/), plural *Cymry* (/kʌmri/). The two cases confirm each other and eliminate any possibility of scribal interference. Geoffrey is obviously representing the Welsh /ʌ/ as an 'a', and this is a practice not found in extant Welsh orthography of the period in question. The usual representation is 'y', as today; 'i' is sometimes used, and occasionally 'e'; but not 'a'. On the other hand, for a speaker of mediaeval Welsh who was trying to transcribe Welsh words on the basis of *Latin* alphabetic usage, 'a' is a perfectly sensible choice. In mediaeval Latin it represents two sounds, /a/ and /ɑ/, open front and open back vowels respectively. The vowel /ʌ/ is almost open, and central (i.e. between /a/ and /ɑ/). Therefore to anyone judging by ear alone, 'a' would be the closest available representation of /ʌ/,[38] much closer than 'e' or 'o', let alone 'i'. We need not assume in this instance that Geoffrey would actually have mispronounced Welsh /ʌ/ as /a/ or /ɑ/, although as with /θw/ and /θ/ in mediaeval English the failure to differentiate might not be a serious obstacle to comprehension. But, familiar as he was with using 'a' for two quite distinct sounds, /a/ and /ɑ/, in Latin, he would have no reason to hesitate about extending it to /ʌ/ in Welsh, especially as the existence of Latin *Cambria* would point in the same direction. Indeed, we may see Latin influence in the epenthetic 'b' of his 'Kambro' (for *Cymro*). The combination of a nasal consonant + /r/ is rare in Latin and the Romance languages (and in English, for that matter), and where it does occur there is a tendency to insert the voiced stop consonant corresponding to the nasal consonant between the latter and the /r/. Thus /mr/ becomes /mbr/, and /nr/ becomes /ndr/. Welsh has no such tendency, and the sequences /mr/ and /nr/ are quite common. Geoffrey is inconsistent in his practice; when etymologizing *Cymraeg* from *cam Roeg* he remembers that the sequence is /mr/, but when he has a free hand to create the eponym, as with 'Kamber', he slips into the Latin-Romance pattern. Which he would have used in speech we cannot be sure; using /mbr/ for /mr/ would have had no appreciable effect on his comprehensibility.

But if Geoffrey had before him a 'very ancient book in the British language' he would have known that the normal orthography for /ʌ/ was not 'a'; in fact the most limited inspection of any Welsh text would furnish this knowledge. Similarly he ought to have known that *Cymro* and *Cymraeg* were spelt with <mr>, not <mbr>. On the other hand, if we assume that Geoffrey read no Welsh, what becomes of his 'very ancient book'? Could it have been in Breton? It seems that this possibility can be disregarded. All the Celtic in the **Historia** is found in Welsh except for the *huel* in *Kaerpenhuelgoit,* the name Geoffrey gives to Exeter.[39] *Huelgoat* is a place-name in Brittany, but *wheal* (a later form) is extremely common in Cornwall and Devon also as a place-name element,[40] and Tatlock is no doubt right in regarding the name *Kaerpenhuelgoit* as 'clearly authentic' and the correct version of a name found much distorted in surviving MSS of Nennius.[41] Geoffrey therefore had some source of information about Exeter which is lost to us, but this is not surprising, as the **Historia** shows that he took a particular interest in Devon and Cornwall.

Moreover, some of Geoffrey's Celtic is definitely Welsh and not Breton. No Breton word for 'shaft' resembling *paladur* is recorded; *Loegria* for 'England'[42] is close to Welsh *Lloegr* but to no Breton equivalent; and 'curvum Graecum' in Breton would give nothing similar to *cam Roeg.* Furthermore, the Breton equivalents of *Cymraeg* and *Cymro* are *kembraeg* and *Kembread* with a /b/. It appears that this too may be an epenthetic /b/, not a relic of the Brythonic sources *Combrogica* and *Combrogos,* for the group /mb/ was reducing to /m/ before the separation of the Brythonic languages;[43] but if so, the /b/ had been re-inserted before Geoffrey's time, for it appears in Breton cartularies of the xi and xii centuries.[44] Geoffrey's 'curvum Graecum' makes sense only if we assume that he is etymologizing the *Welsh* form *Cymraeg,* not the Breton *kembraeg,* and that 'curvum Graecum' is meant to be translated into its Welsh equivalent.

The one pointer to Breton rather than Welsh as Geoffrey's 'British' language is his statement that 'loquela gentis, quae *prius* Trojana sive curvum Graecum nuncupabatur, dicta fuit britannica'.[45] This suggests that in Geoffrey's own day the language was called 'British' or something resembling this. There is no evidence that Welsh at that time was ever known as 'British' in the Welsh language itself; the term is always *Cymraeg,* not *Brythoneg.* But Breton appears always to have been known in Breton as *brezhoneg, kembraeg* being reserved for Welsh. The probable explanation is that Geoffrey was thinking in Latin terms, and in Latin *any* Brythonic language would be *lingua britannica.* Of course Welsh had never been known as *Cymraeg* in Latin, but Geoffrey was scarcely the man to worry about such a detail, assuming that he was even conscious of it.

The preference for Brittany rather than Wales as the origin of Geoffrey's 'very ancient book' has arisen largely from his bearing an apparently Breton name and speaking more favourably in the **Historia** of the Bretons than of the Welsh. As regards his name, there must have been at least two generations between Geoffrey and the Breton followers of William the Conqueror, plenty of time for the family to have become thoroughly Normanized. Any intermarriage with a Norman family would inevitably result in the offspring speaking Norman-French, not Breton. Moreover, as Roberts points out, there is no certainty that because a follower of William bore a Breton name, he therefore spoke Breton, for French had already made inroads into Basse-Bretagne.[46] The linguistic evidence, as we have seen, suggests that Geoffrey was thoroughly Norman. But he would be conscious of his Breton origins, and praise of the Bretons was politically very acceptable in his day; the Geoffrey who wrote those fawning addresses to Robert, Waleran and Alexander[47] would need no further urging. On the other hand the Welsh were sporadically at war with the Normans; too much sympathy for them, especially as the *Historia* moved towards more recent times, might be taken amiss. Geoffrey might speak Welsh, but he was no Welshman, and we have seen in considering his command of English how he could combine an interest in a culture with a thoroughly jaundiced view of the people whose culture it was. His criticisms of the Welsh, despite some rhetoric *à la* Gildas, are cool and detached—the voice of an outsider, a Norman pleasing a Norman audience.

We return therefore to our previous question: if Geoffrey read no Welsh and knew no Breton, what becomes of his 'very ancient book in the British language'? Clearly there could be no such source for the *Historia,* and one is led to wonder what gave him the idea for this strange fiction. Roberts has indicated the difficulty of supposing that there was no book of any kind, and that Walter, Archdeacon of Oxford, and possibly also the canons of the College of Saint George, were parties to a simple deception.[48] Without placing too much faith in the veracity of such functionaries in an era when religious establishments regularly forged their own charters, we may agree that the circumstances are peculiar. Furthermore, Tatlock observes that the **'Prophecies of Merlin'** can scarcely be in their entirety the invention of Geoffrey.[49] We have seen reason to doubt that Geoffrey had a written 'British' source for the *Historia* as a whole; but could he have had one for the **'Prophecies of Merlin'**? The material that cast doubt upon his familiarity with written Welsh comes from Books I and II of the *Historia.* Geoffrey inserts the **'Prophecies'** after Book VI, and intimates that interest in them began to be aroused *after* he had begun the *Historia,* though before the completion of Book VI.[50] All the indications are that, apart from the prefatory dedications, Geoffrey wrote the *Historia* in the order in which we have it. It looks as though rumour had spread that he was competent in Welsh and either Walter or Alexander, Bishop of Lincoln, or both, took advantage of his knowledge in order to obtain a 'translation' of a tract in which there was current interest. Geoffrey broke off the *Historia* to comply with their request, handling the material fairly freely either from inclination or because he found it difficult to read, inserted the **'Prophecies'** very abruptly into the *Historia,* and then continued with his original plan.[51] It is worth noting that the only references to the 'very ancient book' are in the preface (which would be written last), Book XI, and the *explicit* (not in all MSS). It seems quite possible, therefore, that the 'very ancient book' was an afterthought, inspired by Geoffrey's acquaintance with the source of the **'Prophecies of Merlin'** and designed to lend authority to the larger work which Geoffrey was concocting with the utmost artistic licence out of purely oral traditions.

If we set aside the question of the 'very ancient book', Geoffrey's preface gives a strong hint as to the true nature of his sources: '. . . gesta . . . quia a multis populis quasi jocunde inscripta et memoriter praedicarentur'.[52] For once we can actually support what he says from a 'British' source: 'Ynteu Wydyon goreu kyuarwyd yn y byt oed. A'r nos honno, didanu y llys a wnaeth ar ymdidaneu digrif a chyuarwydyt, yny oed hoff gan paub o'r llys . . .' ('Now Gwydyon was the best story-teller in the world. And that night he entertained the court with delightful conversation and storytelling, so that he was beloved of every member of the court . . .').[53] This quotation is itself from a story which Geoffrey might actually have heard, for the collection of tales in which it comes down to us had been assembled by his time, if not earlier,[54] although our oldest MS dates from about 1225.[55] The *cyfarwydd* or story-teller was a familiar and valued figure in mediaeval Welsh society, and Geoffrey could hardly have lived in Monmouth and known the Welsh language without becoming acquainted with his art. The tales which survive are a remarkable medley; pre-Christian myth and magic, romanticized history (with etymologies in abundance!), folklore, satire—and some of it, in its present form, undoubtedly written 'perpulchris orationibus'.[56] Nothing like an ordered history, of course; but here was oral material which a man of active imagination and not so active conscience could weave into a tapestry that would not be out of place alongside the histories of Greece and Rome and post-Celtic Britain. Geoffrey must have heard these tales in his youth, before moving to Oxford,[57] so that in writing the *Historia* he would be relying purely on his memory, which, even had he been intent on accuracy, was certain to lead him into error. Thus to the inconsistencies of the original stories and Geoffrey's deliberate remodelling[58] are added accidental misappropriations, by which 'Caerlwytgoed', the Welsh name of Lichfield, becomes attached to Lincoln,[59] and 'Caerweir', that of Durham, to Warwick,[60] and cases where we can no longer be sure how the confusion arose, as when Dumngual Moilmut, a northern British prince of around A.D. 500, becomes a Cornishman and famous lawgiver of the later V and early IV centuries B.C.,[61] and Llŷr, lifted from a Welsh legendary past to provide an eponym for Leicester, gets involved in a folk-tale about a king and his three daughters, and is later taken up by an anonymous writer for the Elizabethan theatre and eventually immortalized by Shakespeare as 'King Lear'.[62] And at the end of it all we have a history which is fairly credible (except for Bladud's flying and the occasional giant or dragon, which would strain mediaeval credulity less than they do ours), and Geoffrey is safe from all but the most learned of critics because, as he knows full well, there is no 'very ancient book in the British language' to gainsay him, the true 'History of the Kings of Britain' will never be known, and the average reader of his day prefers a good story (history or not) to a blank in the record. So the *Historia* is sprung upon a receptive world, to feed the growing appetite for *matière de Bretagne* and win its author an audience beyond the wildest dreams of any *cyfarwydd*, until 'the whirligig of time brings in his revenges' and Geoffrey's own biography falls into the hands of another arch-fabricator, Iolo Morgannwg, from whose attentions only the thoroughness of modern scholarship and the availability of the original sources have succeeded in rescuing it.[63]

Notes

1. J. Parry and R. Caldwell, 'Geoffrey of Monmouth', in *Arthurian Literature in the Middle Ages,* ed. by R. Loomis (Oxford, 1959), p. 76.

2. Parry and Caldwell assume that when Geoffrey says the book was brought *ex Britannia* he means Wales (*op. cit.,* p. 81).

3. J. Tatlock, *The Legendary History of Britain* (Berkeley, 1950), p. 445.

4. *Op. cit.,* p. 445.

5. E. Faral, *La Légende arthurienne. 1ere partie: Les plus anciens textes; Tome 3: Documents* (Paris, 1929), p. 250. This is the so-called Vulgate Version of the *Historia.* According to Commelin's division of the *Historia* into twelve books, which Faral does not retain, this passage occurs at IX, xvii.

6. Faral, p. 71 (I, i).

7. In the introduction to his translation of the *Historia* (Harmondsworth, 1966), pp. 24-5.

8. Faral, p. 93 (II, i).

9. J. Hammer, *Geoffrey of Monmouth: 'Historia Regum Britanniae'; a Variant Version Edited from Manuscripts* (Cambridge, Mass., 1951), p. 264 (XII, xx).

10. For the sake of the present discussion I accept Tatlock's arguments in favour of a Breton origin for Geoffrey (*op. cit.,* p. 443).

11. '. . . whether or not he spoke Breton with his nearest and dearest . . .' (*op. cit.,* p. 445).

12. *Op. cit.,* p. 445.

13. Faral, p. 120 (III, xiii).

14. '. . . Guallenses, vocabulum sive a Guallone, duce eorum, sive a Gualaes regina, sive a barbarie trahentes' (Faral, p. 303; XII, xix); *barbarie* because *wylisc* in the English of Geoffrey's time still signified both 'Welsh' and 'foreign'.

15. Faral, p. 125 (III, xx).

16. Faral, p. 150 (v, iv).

17. Faral, p. 178 (VI, xi).

18. Faral, p. 207 (VIII, v); location uncertain.

19. Without actually giving the English name (Faral, p. 98; II, ix); *paladur* (*paladr* in the modern orthography) is Welsh for 'shaft'.

20. Faral, p. 296 (XII, x); and compare Bede, *Historia Ecclesiastica Gentis Anglorum,* III, ii.

21. Faral, p. 176 (VI, x).

22. Faral, pp. 178-9 (VI, xii).

23. Faral, p. 301 (XII, xvi).

24. '. . . usque in hunc diem appellatum est flumen britannica lingua Habren, quod per corruptionem nominis alia lingua Sabrina vocatur' (Faral p. 95; II,v). No doubt Thorpe is correct in translating *alia* as 'the other' rather than 'another' (*op. cit.,* p. 77); Latin is much too prominent in Geoffrey's outlook for him to refer to it as just 'another' language. It is not significant that English was introduced into Britain after the period that Geoffrey is here describing; this is true of Latin also, and moreover the passage on names is in the present tense and must refer to the time of writing, which (whether or not we assume that Geoffrey is seriously trying to pass the work off as an accurate translation from an ancient book) is certainly later than the coming of the English.

25. *Op. cit.,* p. 24, n. 84.

26. *OED* gives examples of 'ðw', 'þw', and 'þu'.

27. *Op. cit.,* p. 147.

28. Unless, of course, he preferred his own fictitious etymology in any case, which with Geoffrey is not inconceivable. *OED* gives the form *cynincges* as late as 1001 in the Old English Chronicle.

29. *Op. cit.,* pp. 43-4.

30. The first occurs too often to require references; the second in *Porthlud* (Faral, p. 125; III, xx), which is assuredly Geoffrey's creation.

31. Faral, pp. 90-1 (I, xvi).

32. B. Roberts, 'Sylwadau ar Sieffre o Fynwy a'r *Historia Regum Britanniae', Llên Cymru,* XII (1972/3), 137, n. 45.

33. Including the composer of the Variant Version, who omits the words 'sive curvum Graecum' (Hammer, p. 40). To the reasons already published for regarding this as later than the Vulgate Version (P. Gallais, 'La *Variant Version* de l'*Historia Regum Britanniae* et le *Brut* de Wace', *Romania,* LXXXVII (1966), 1-32) I would add the following. The composer of the Variant Version changes 'Troia Nova' to 'Nova Troia', thereby losing the point of the etymology: 'Condidit itaque civitatem ibidem eamque Trojam Novam vocavit. Ex hoc nomine multis postmodum temporibus appellata, tandem per corruptionem vocabuli Trinovantum dicta fuit' (Faral, p. 92; I, xvii); 'Condidit itaque ibidem civitatem eamque Novam Troiam vocavit, quae postmodum per corruptionem vocabuli Trinovantum dicta est' (Hammer, pp. 40-1).

34. This is not to imply that he had a complete command of spoken Welsh. Apart from possible oddities of pronunciation, to which we shall refer later, he mistakes *Kaerleil* (modern 'Carlisle') as a current Welsh form and 'etymologizes' it accordingly (Faral, p. 98; II, ix). In fact Carlisle in Welsh is *Caerliwelydd,* and appears as *Caer Lliwelyt* in the poetry of Geoffrey's younger contemporary Hywel ab Owain Gwynedd (J. Morris-Jones and T. Parry-Williams (eds), *Llawysgrif Hendregadredd* (Cardiff, 1933), p.

316). It appears that this came from an original *Lu-guvălíum,* and that a variant form *Luguválium* arose to give the *Karleil* which was adopted by the invading English. The question is discussed in more detail in A. Armstrong *et. al., The Place-Names of Cumberland: Part I* (Cambridge, 1950), pp. 40-2.

35. Scholars have sometimes assumed that Geoffrey claims to be *translating* the British book (Parry and Caldwell, *op. cit.,* p. 81; B. Roberts, 'Geoffrey of Monmouth and Welsh historical tradition', *Nottingham Medieval Studies,* XX (1976), 38), but this is to interpret too narrowly the word *transferre.* In fact Geoffrey makes no attempt to pass the work off as a mere translation. His introductory remark '. . . tametsi infra alienos hortulos phalerata verba non collegerim, agresti tamen stylo propriisque calamis contentus . . .' (Faral, p. 71; I, i) is scarcely appropriate unless he is handling his material fairly freely. Three times he intrudes into the text in the first person (Faral, p. 118; III, x; Faral, p. 283; XI, x; and Faral, p. 93; II, i, the reference to Latin as *lingua nostra* to which we have already alluded). He cannot have expected his readers to believe that it was the author of his ancient British source to whom the first person referred. Moreover, '. . . Kamber [possedit] . . . partem illam quae est *ultra* Sabrinum flumen, quae nunc Gualia vocatur . . .' (Faral, p. 93; II, i)'. The writer is looking at Wales from the *English* side of the Severn (from Oxford, no doubt, and therefore Geoffrey was not at Bec when he wrote this part of the *Historia* at least, *pace* Tatlock, *op. cit.,* p. 444, n. 36). Lastly, the Normans are listed as inhabitants of Britain (Faral, p. 73; II, ii) and *Lundres* is given as the most recent name for London, 'applicantibus alienigenis, qui patriam sibi submittebant' (Faral, p. 125; III, xx). If Geoffrey is merely translating, therefore, his 'very ancient book' is no more than 70 years old!

36. Faral, p. 231 (IX, iii).

37. Hammer, p. 153.

38. /Λ/, /a/, and /ɑ/ are actually dialectal variants for the vowel of modern English 'but'; /Λ/ in R.P., /a/ in Cockney, and /ɑ/ in parts of Ireland.

39. *Caer-wysg* is the accepted Welsh name for Exeter.

40. According to William Pryce's *Archaeologia Cornu-Britannica* of 1790, there was a village called 'Wheal-an-Coats'. If correct, this would be equivalent to Breton *Huelgoat.*

41. *Op. cit.,* pp. 50-1.

42. Faral, p. 93 (II, i).

43. K. Jackson, *Language and History in Early Britain* (Edinburgh, 1953), pp. 508-11.

44. J. Loth, *Chrestomathie Bretonne* (Paris, 1890), p. 115, s.v. *Cembre.*

45. Faral, pp. 90-1 (I, xvi).

46. 'Sylwadau', p. 128, n. 9.

47. Faral, p. 72 (I, i); Faral, pp. 189-90 (VII, ii).

48. 'Sylwadau', pp. 134-5.

49. *Op. cit.,* pp. 414-18.

50. Faral, p. 189 (VII, i).

51. *Ex hypothesi* he would by now be familiar with Welsh orthography, but one may doubt his inclination to go back and make corrections in matters of minor detail. Only an edition of the *Historia* based on all available MSS could permit us to ascertain whether his orthography of British names changed in the course of composition. The existing editions depend on too few sources, and place us at the mercy of scribal vagaries. It does not help that Geoffrey virtually loses interest in etymology about half-way through the *Historia.*

52. Faral, p. 71 (I, i). The Variant Version has the more natural order '. . . quasi inscripta iocunde et memoriter . . .' (Hammer, p. 22).

53. I. Williams, *Pedeir Keinc y Mabinogi* (Cardiff, 1930), p. 69 (with my own translation).

54. *Op. cit.,* p. xli.

55. *Op. cit.,* pp. vii-viii.

56. Though we may share Tatlock's doubts as to whether the Latin-loving Geoffrey would have appreciated them (*op. cit.,* p. 423).

57. He cannot *both* have been familiar with the British oral tradition, as he claims in the preface, *and* have known nothing of its content until receiving the 'very ancient book', as he also claims (Faral, p. 71; I, i).

58. In particular the element of the supernatural is much less prominent in Geoffrey than in the old Welsh stories.

59. Faral, p. 231 (IX, iii); Tatlock, *op. cit.,* p. 26; T. Jones: review of Tatlock, *op. cit., Llên Cymru,* I (1950/51), 193 (in Welsh).

60. Faral, p. 243 (IX, xii); Tatlock, *op. cit.,* p. 28; Jones, *op. cit.,* p. 193.

61. J. Lloyd, *A History of Wales,* 3rd edn (London, 1948), I, 318; Faral, pp. 107-8 (II, xvii).

62. Faral, pp. 99-105 (II, xi-xiv); S. Lee (ed.), *The Chronicle History of King Leir* (London, 1909).

63. Tatlock, *op. cit.,* pp. 446-8.

Hugh A. MacDougall (essay date 1982)

SOURCE: "The Britains as Trojans: The Legendary World of Geoffrey of Monmouth," in *Racial Myth in English History: Trojans, Teutons, and Anglo-Saxons,* Harvest House Ltd., 1982, pp. 7-27.

[*In the following excerpt, MacDougall discusses the significance of* The History of the Kings of Britain, *the controversy surrounding its authenticity, and its reception.*]

In the history of myths of national origin few have been as influential and have had such a curious development as those popularized by Geoffrey of Monmouth in his ***History of the Kings of Britain.*** His writing, appearing about 1136, was destined to become "the most famous work of nationalistic historiography in the Middle Ages."[1] It had a marked influence in subduing the social animosities of the Bretons, Anglo-Saxons, and Normans and drawing them together into a single nation. Geoffrey's fanciful account was used by early Plantagenet monarchs to support their regal claims and for both Tudors and Stuarts it came to constitute a useful prop to their dynastic ones. Though confidence in its historical reliability had almost evaporated by the eighteenth century, as the chief source of the Arthurian legend its influence carried on into the nineteenth century and as a spur to Celtic imagination continues into our own day.

The author of the famous ***History*** was a Welsh cleric, probably of Breton descent, who a few years before his death became Bishop of St. Asaph. At the outset of his book Geoffrey acknowledged his debt to Walter, Archdeacon of Oxford, who had provided him with "a very ancient book written in the British language" which related the actions of the British kings "from Brutus, the first king of the Britons, down to Cadwallader" the last.[2] At Archdeacon Walter's request, so writes Geoffrey, a Latin translation of the ancient book is offered the reader.

Since no corroborating evidence for the existence of Walter's *"vetustissimus liber"* has ever come to light, one may credit Geoffrey's colorful ***History*** to a fertile imagination fed by contemporary oral traditions and accounts by earlier scribes like Gildas and Nennius.[3] Geoffrey's motivation in writing his book no doubt was a desire to provide an heroic epic on the origin and exploits of a people subdued successively by Romans, Saxons, Danes, and Normans. By portraying the British as a once great people with extensive dominions he could at once raise their status in the eyes of their new Norman overlords and suggest a precedent to the Norman kings in their imperialistic ambitions. Geoffrey's success can be measured by the gradual acceptance of his account as a great national myth supporting a developing people moving toward nationhood.

In locating the origin of British history in ancient Troy Geoffrey was following an accepted tradition. The dignifying of one's own history by associating its beginnings with an earlier civilization or even with the gods was a practice well known to classical writers. Rome provided a model ready at hand. Its patriotic writers, admiring Greek civilization though disliking the Greeks, chose as their mythical hero Aeneas, son of Venus, a chief defender of Troy. Vergil in his great Latin epic, the *Aeneid,* portrayed him after various heroic exploits as the founder of *Lavinium,* the parent city of Rome. The Gallo-Romans as well as the Franks in Gaul drew on the tradition of Trojan origins, as, in time, did the Normans. Geoffrey in his ***History*** simply exploited an existing myth which was guaranteed to sit well with the Norman masters of England.[4]

The ***History*** begins with an account of the birth and upbringing of Brutus, grandson of Aeneas of Troy, son of Venus. Held responsible for his mother's death in childbirth and the accidental killing of his father, the fifteen-year-old boy was banished from his country. After many wanderings and heroic exploits, Brutus arrived with his faithful followers in the land *Albion,* to which he gave his own name, Britain. The land had fine rivers and forests and was inhabited only by a few giants. The giants were conquered, the land occupied and a city called New Troy (*Trinoventum*) founded. After their leader, the new inhabitants were called Britons and their language British.

Twenty years following his arrival on the island Brutus died, leaving Britain divided among his three sons—the eldest holding England, the second son Scotland, and the youngest Wales. Upon the death of the younger sons the entire land reverted to the eldest, Locrinus. The ***History*** continues with the heroic exploits of a long line of kings including the famous account of King Leir and his three daughters—a romantic tale subsequently retold by at least fifty writers before Shakespeare immortalized it.

Among some of the more notable British kings descended from the original Trojans were Belinus and Brennius who shared a divided kingdom and together conquered Gaul. Brennius occupied Rome and exercised there an unheard of tyranny, such was his might. Another, King Lud, rebuilt the walls of New Troy and gave it his name, which through the corruption of language became known as London. During the reign of Lud's successor, King Cassivelaunus, Julius Caesar turned his gaze on Britain. Caesar recognized the common descent from the Trojans of both Romans and Britons but the latter he judged degenerate, knowing nothing of the art of war and separated from the rest of the world. He accordingly demanded tribute and submission to Rome, a demand stoutly resisted by the Britons.

The next king, Arviragus, was reconciled with the Romans and married the daughter of the Emperor Claudius. The reign of his grandson, Lucius, was notable for the conversion of his kingdom, making Britain the first of all nations publicly to profess Christianity. He was buried in Gloucester Cathedral in A.D. 156—the first precise date given by Geoffrey.

Constantine I was another luminary in the ranks of the British kings. With the support of Roman exiles he captured Rome, overthrew the tyrant Maxentius and was made overlord of the whole world. Upon Constantine's death the treacherous Vortigern became king. Instead of resisting the incursions of the infidel Saxons he accepted their offer of service. Infatuated by Renwein, the beautiful daughter of the Saxon leader Hengist, he came to love the Saxons above all other peoples. The influx of Saxons became so great that the Britons overthrew Vortigern in favor of his son Vortimer who forced the Saxon warriors back to Germany. But following the death of Vortimer, his father once more became king and invited the Saxons to return. Hengist landed with an army of 300,000 men and a great massacre of Britons ensued.

Confronted with a ravaged kingdom, Vortigern sought counsel from magicians. Geoffrey relates at length the king's association with the magician Merlin and the seer's predictions concerning the future history of Britain. The prophecies are filled with imagery of dragons in conflict—the white dragon (Saxons) is initially victorious, but ultimately vanquished by the red dragon (Britons) through the assistance of a people dressed in wood and in iron corselets (Normans in their ships and coats of mail).

As foretold by Merlin, a champion of British and Roman ancestry, Aurelius Ambrosius, appeared to overthrow Vortigern and reduce the Saxons. Upon his death the work of restoration was continued by his brother, Utherpendragon, until he was poisoned by the Saxons. The climax of Geoffrey's entire *History* is reached with the ascendancy of Utherpendragon's illegitimate son, Arthur. King Arthur is clearly Geoffrey's hero. The remarkable success and continuing influence of his *British History* is due in no small measure to his brilliant portrayal of a British king with qualities well beyond the ordinary human—the stuff of which great myths are born.

Crowned king at the age of fifteen, Arthur was a youth of unparalleled courage and generosity. In time he subdued the Saxons—in one battle killing 470 with his own hand—forced the Scots and Picts to make peace, conquered Ireland, Iceland, the Orkneys, Sweden, Norway, Denmark, Aquitaine, and Normandy. The fame of his valor spread over the whole world. The splendor of his court was unrivaled and he eventually ruled over a kingdom that led the entire world in civilization.

In the meantime Rome grew alarmed at Arthur's growing power and his refusal to pay tribute. The Roman Procurator, Lucius Tiberius, demanded that Arthur report to Rome under the threat of his bringing the sword to Britain. Arthur refused and after consultation with his allies prepared for war. Lucius called upon the eastern kings for support. A host of kings with their generals and nobles—up to the number of forty thousand one hundred and sixty—pledged him support. Arthur then led his great army to Gaul to confront the Romans, leaving the government of his kingdom to his nephew Modred. In a great battle Lucius Tiberius was killed and the Britons were victorious. Many Romans subsequently offered themselves as slaves. Arthur then made preparations to march on Rome. As he approached the Alps news came that Modred had treacherously seized the Crown and taken Queen Guinevere as his wife. Arthur returned to Britain and in a resulting civil war Modred was killed. Arthur in the final battle was mortally wounded and carried to the magical isle of Avalon to be healed. He surrendered his crown to his kinsman Constantine, son of the duke of Cornwall, and passed out of the story. Geoffrey notes that the year was 542.

The reign of Constantine and his successors was beset with dissension and vice and the Saxons, aided by Gormund, King of the Africans, again overran the country. There was a brief revival of the hope of the Britons under the rule of the last British king, Cadwallader, but pestilence and famine forced them to leave the island altogether and take refuge in Brittany. Britain was now destitute of its ancient inhabitants except for a remnant in Wales. The Angles and Saxons had finally triumphed.

Cadwallader made plans to revive his kingdom, but was commanded by an angel to desist. He was instructed to go to Rome where, after penance, he would be enrolled among the saints. The Britons, so spoke the heavenly voice, would not recover their land until the time foretold by Merlin and decreed by God was come. Cadwallader, the last of the British kings, died in Rome on 12 May 689.

Geoffrey shrewdly ended his *History* with a warning to others to be silent concerning the British kings since they were not privy to the ancient book from Walter, Archdeacon of Oxford.

As a work of creative imagination Geoffrey's *History* was a superb achievement. Its heroic account of great deeds and dramatic failures salted with romantic intrigue and supernatural intervention was well designed to capture the medieval reader. By the time of his death in 1154 his account had been related so often that to be unfamiliar with it was, in the words of a contemporary, "to incur a mark of rusticity."[5] Paraphrases and translations abounded, among the most noteworthy of the early versions being *Geste des Bretons* (1155) by the poet Maistre Wace, dedicated to Eleanor, the wife of Henry II, and the *Brut* (c. 1200) by the English priest Layamon. Even Welsh writers, who possessed an Arthurian tradition predating Geoffrey, came to borrow much from him. Gradually his *History* became the foundation of a great historical myth which supported racial and dynastic aspirations for over five hundred years.

Still, several of the earliest critics were sceptical of the *History*'s authenticity. Alfred of Beverly (fl. 1143), a chronicler who was initially drawn to history through reading Geoffrey and had borrowed heavily from him in his own writings, was puzzled by the lack of corroboration for the *History* in writers outside of Britain.[6] Giraldus Cambrensis, a contentious Welsh historian, treated Geoffrey's account with disdain.[7] He told the tale of a Welshman who was beset by unclean spirits. When the spirits oppressed him the gospel of St. John was placed on his tormented breast, and they departed; but when Geoffrey's *History* was substituted for the gospel, the evil spirits returned to torment him in greater numbers than ever. The most categorical rejection, however, was made by William of Newburgh. In a preface to his *Historium Rerum Anglicarum* he dismissed Geoffrey's *History* as made up of "the most ridiculous fictions." "Whatever Geoffrey has written," he acidly comments, "is a fiction invented either by himself or by others, and promulgated either through an unchecked propensity to falsehood, or a desire to please the Britons, of whom vast numbers are said to be so stupid as to assert that Arthur is yet to come, and cannot bear to hear of his death." Newburgh noted that ancient historians were silent on the alleged Arthurian exploits: "It is plain that whatever this man published of Arthur and Merlin are mendacious fictions, invented to gratify the curiosity of the undiscerning." There was no doubt in William of Newburgh's mind how Geoffrey and his *History* should be treated: "Let this fabler, with his fictions, be instantly rejected by all."[8]

In spite of initial criticism, the *History* went on to triumph and came to be generally accepted until the Renaissance. Apart from the inherent attraction of a well-told tale dealing with origins, Geoffrey's *History* held special political appeal. A history presenting the extraordinary achievements of past British kings was calculated to please Norman conquerors (in Geoffrey's account also descended from Trojan exiles) who could now see themselves as inheritors of a kingdom with a proud past and notable achievements. Lacking any historical figure of heroic stature comparable to Charlemagne, the Norman and Angevin kings were in an inferior position to their continental French rivals. In Arthur, Geoffrey provided such a figure. Arthur in time served an additional function: more than Brutus or Cadwallader, he came to be seen as a hero of a composite people, uniting Britons, Saxons and Normans.[9]

From its beginnings Geoffrey's *History* was closely associated with the monarchy. One of the original manuscripts carried a dedication to Stephen who succeeded to the throne in 1135. Most of the manuscripts also included a dedication to Robert, Earl of Gloucester, a natural son of Henry I, who was to contribute much to the success of Henry II. The latter king was closely associated with the "discovery" of Arthur's body at the famous Benedictine monastery at Glastonbury. This renowned religious center, probably through the efforts of zealous monks who wished to increase its prestige, came to be identified as the mysterious isle of Avalon. King Henry, the chroniclers report, initiated the investigation which resulted in the discovery of the tomb and a subsequent magnificent reinterment.[10] Henry's motive in "arranging" the discovery need not have gone beyond his desire to put an end to the legend that Arthur was still alive and would return, a belief kept current by rebellious Welsh who dreamed of recovering national leadership. In 1187 King Henry had his grandson christened Arthur, the intended identification being obvious.

It was Edward I more than any of his predecessors who turned the *History* to his own advantage. He liked to cast himself in the role of "Arthurus redivivus."[11] In 1278, along with Queen Eleanor, he visited Glastonbury and ordered the opening of Arthur's tomb. A contemporary account tells of the extraordinary occasion: "The lord Edward . . . with his consort, the Lady Eleanor, came to Glastonbury . . . to celebrate Easter. . . . The following Tuesday . . . at dusk, the lord king had the tomb of the famous King Arthur opened. Wherein, in two caskets painted with their pictures and arms, were found separately, the bones of the said king, which were of great size, and those of Queen Guinevere, which were of marvellous beauty. . . . On the following day . . . the lord

king replaced the bones of the king, and the queen those of the queen, each in their own casket, having wrapped them in costly silk. When they had been sealed they ordered the tomb to be placed forthwith in front of the high altar, after the removal of the skulls for the veneration of the people."[12]

Thus Edward succeeded magnificently in linking his own royal house with the most renowned of the ancient British kings and at the same time helped promote Glastonbury as a religious center to rival the fame of French abbeys like Cluny. Another Arthurian-Glastonbury association brought even further prestige and was appropriately exploited. The incorporation of St. Joseph of Arimathea through the Grail legend as the founder of a church in Glastonbury in A.D. 63 sanctioned the claim of an English church established in Apostolic times, a claim useful in the promotion of a national church less subject to the control of Rome.[13]

The advantage to Edward of the British connection was further demonstrated in 1301 in a jurisdictional dispute which the Scots brought to the court of Rome. In a letter to Boniface VIII, countersigned by a hundred English barons, Edward presented evidence to support the rights of the English crown over Scotland. Most of the evidence was drawn from Geoffrey's *History*.[14]

The young Edward III was no less enthusiastic for his British heritage. He contemplated reestablishing the Round Table and around 1348 founded the illustrious Order of the Garter, reviving the tradition of Arthurian knighthood.[15] He heavily patronized Glastonbury Abbey. Accompanied by his queen, he paid it a state visit in 1331. It has been suggested that his attempts to conquer France were influenced by the accounts of Arthur's continental conquests related in the *History*.[16] The reign of his namesake, Edward IV, a hundred years later, showed the enduring quality of the British legend. Genealogical authorities of his time traced his descent back to Cadwallader, the last of the British kings, and he was hailed by his supporters as the British Messiah, the Red Dragon foretold by Merlin who would once again rule England, Scotland and Wales.[17]

In the ninth year of Edward IV's reign (1469), Thomas Malory completed his epic work on Arthur. Derived more from twelfth-century French prose romances and a fourteenth-century English poem than from Geoffrey's *History* itself, it was published by William Caxton with considerable editorial liberty. Under the title *Morte d'Arthur* it became the best-known Arthurian account in English.[18] Interestingly, Caxton in his preface felt compelled to level sharp criticism at those who "holde oppynon that there was no suche Arthur and that alle suche bookes as bein maad of hym ben but fayned and fables."[19] Caxton had no time for Renaissance scepticism which led men like John Whethamstede, Abbot of St. Albans, to consider "the whole discourse of Brutus" to be "rather poeticall than historicall."[20] It is worth noting that the first printed book in the English tongue was *The Recuyell of the Historyes of Troye*, a translation from the French of

Raoul Le Fèvrè's work. In 1480 Caxton printed the popular medieval account based on Geoffrey's *History, Chronicle of the Brut,* under the title *The Chronicles of England.* By the end of the century this work alone had appeared in six editions. Caxton, as well, printed Ranulf Higden's *Polychronicon,* a "universal history" containing much material on British history derived from Geoffrey. The *Polychronicon* and the *Brut* came to be by far the most widely read history books in fifteenth-century England.

The accession of Henry Tudor in 1485 was interpreted by many as the long awaited return of a British king in fulfillment of the ancient promise. It was under the banner of the Red Dragon that he had overthrown Richard III. In a welcoming pageant planned, but never actually held, for the new king at Worcester in 1486 an actor was to speak the following lines:

> Cadwalader Blodde lynyally descending,
> Long hath bee towlde of such a Prince comyng,
> Wherfor Frends, if that I shal not lye,
> This same is the Fulfiller of the Profesye.[21]

The Welsh were particularly enthusiastic, for their bards had frequently written of the coming of a great Welsh leader who would restore their ancient position.[22] But the most impressive testimony of Henry VII's special lineage came from the pen of Bernardus Andreas, the official historian of the new king. Andreas was an Augustinian friar from Toulouse who had come to England at the beginning of Henry's reign. He became the king's poet-laureate and historiographer, a useful combination from the regal point of view. In his *History of Henry VII* Andreas underlined Henry's British origins, tracing his royal descent from Cadwallader and portraying him as the fulfillment in his person of the ancient prophecy.[23] It appeared highly appropriate for the new king in 1486 to have named his first-born son after the great Arthur and thus heighten the promise of a new golden age. In 1548 the chronicler Edward Hall expressed what was still a popular sentiment when he wrote of Prince Arthur's christening at Winchester, a place noted for its Arthurian associations: "of whiche name Englishemen no more rejoysed than outwarde nacions and foreyne prynces trymbled and quaked, so muche was the name to all nacions terrible and formidable."[24] Writing in 1622, Francis Bacon noted the naming of Arthur, "according to the Name of that ancient worthy King of the Brittaines."[25]

In Tudor days belief in Trojan origins and reverence of King Arthur was by no means restricted to those who might justly claim British descent. Englishmen in general were heartened by tales of the legendary achievements of past British kings and, as T. D. Kendrick has written, "often extremely unwilling to acknowledge the barbaric Saxons as their ancestors, saw in the heroes and conquests of the Brut an obvious source of their country's pride and valiant heart."[26]

Henry VII's successor, Henry VIII, was at first far too concerned with establishing himself as a great monarch in his own right to be preoccupied with ancient tales of heroic achievements whose historicity his humanist friends were coming to question. (Humanists brought a more self-conscious approach to the study of political institutions, and the state gradually came to be seen as a formal structure distinct from any particular ruler.) Still the pageantry which Henry carried to the Field of the Cloth of Gold in 1520 spoke vividly of Arthur, the intrepid warrior of world renown.[27] Later in his reign when the great question of the divorce arose, a deliberate attempt was made to exploit Geoffrey's *History* to the King's advantage. In seeking to convince Charles V's ambassador of the justice of the king's plan for divorce, the duke of Norfolk, Henry's diplomatic spokesman, argued that his king held supreme imperial jurisdiction in his realm, a jurisdiction derived from ancient beginnings. The incredulous Chapuys was informed that Brennius, an Englishman, had conquered Rome, that Constantine had reigned in England and that, as well, his mother was English. In addition, an English monarch, Arthur (of whom Chapuys had never heard), had been Emperor of Britain, Gaul and Germany.[28] The ambassador's sardonic response that he regretted Arthur was not also called Emperor of Asia is understandable. The bold language in the preamble to the famous Act in Restraint of Appeals (1533), asserting that England was an empire "governed by one Supreme Head and King having dignity and royal estate of the imperial Crown," was dependent upon the tradition that Henry through the British kings was descended from the Emperor Constantine who was himself of half British origin and "had united British kinship with Roman emperorship."[29]

Ironically, the historian Polydore Vergil, whose work ultimately led to the destruction of the credibility of Geoffrey's entire history, undertook to write his history under the patronage of the first Tudor king and completed it under the second. Polydore Vergil was born at Urbino in the Romagna. He entered papal service and by the time he came to England in 1502 as a collector of Peter's Pence, he already had a reputation as a scholar. A friend of Erasmus, his world was that of the Renaissance, a movement barely beginning to make itself felt in England. He was not long there when, on the king's request, he began to work on a history of England. Henry VII, desirous of gaining European recognition of his dynasty, saw a new history designed for a continental readership and written in the best humanistic style as an asset which would enhance the king's reputation.[30]

From the beginning of his study, Vergil showed a complete disdain for Geoffrey's *History.* Though dutifully presenting a brief account of it for the sake of sensitive English readers ("They seem to be in heaven," he wrote, "where with good will I leave them,"), he approvingly cited William of Newburgh's characterization of it as "impudent lyeing."[31] He summarily dismissed the vaunted Trojan descent of the British through Brutus, the cornerstone of Geoffrey's *History*: "But yet neither Livie, neither Dionisius Halicarnaseus, who writt diligentlie of the Roman antiquities, nor divers other writers, did ever once make rehersall of this Brutus. . . ."[32] On the invasion of Rome by Brennius he noted that if the reference in the *History* was to the actual historical attack then in Geoffrey's version Brennius "lived 310 years before the battayle was taken in hande."[33] He devoted a single barbed paragraph to Arthur, presenting him as a mysterious man of romance and legend akin to Roland, a presentation certain to outrage Arthurian enthusiasts. He lightly rejected the claim that Arthur was buried in Glastonbury Abbey: "whereas in the dayse of Arthure this abbaye was not builded."[34]

Vergil's *Anglica Historia* was completed in 1513, but, despite the customary dedication to the king, twenty years were to elapse before it was published. (In the meantime in 1525 he had published an account of British history written in Anglo-Saxon times by Gildas in which King Arthur was not even mentioned.) Vergil's rejection of the British tradition could not help but displease the King. Henry's annoyance, it has been plausibly suggested, explains the long delay in its publication.[35] Its appearance in 1534 may be attributed to Henry's new situation. Having broken with Rome over the divorce issue Henry found it more important than ever to establish the imperial (and thus independent) nature of his crown in the eyes of continental rivals. The *Anglica Historia* in Renaissance fashion stressed the imperial nature of kingship and thus its appearance in 1534 served the king's purposes well. Significantly, Vergil's published version had a revised dedication and ending, both emphasizing, more than the original manuscript, Henry's imperial status.

Vergil's *Anglica Historia* was a work of impressive scholarship and could not be ignored. But his irreverent chiding of Englishmen on their view of the past evoked bitter hostility and mistrust among many scholars. His opponents tended to see him as an alien enemy set on furthering Rome's interests. The most impassioned attack came from the pen of the antiquarian John Leland.[36] He denounced "Polydorus the Italian" for his sceptical interpretation of Geoffrey's *History*, which he noted was "filled with Italian bitterness."[37] Especially worthy of reprobation was Vergil's presentation of Arthur who for Leland was "the chiefest ornament of Brittayne."[38] While admitting some absurdities had crept into the Arthurian account, he saw no reason why the presence of a few flaws weakened its overall credibility. So complete was Leland's commitment to the general line of Geoffrey's *History* that he offered a stout defense of Merlin—"a man even miraculously learned in knowledge of thinges naturall"—against the criticism "of any cowled or loytering grosseheaded Moncke" (a reference to William of Newburgh, whose authority Vergil had cited).[39] In concluding his defense Leland anticipated that "most mighty enemies will affaulte my doings," but he was confident that in the end, "the light of Brittish Antiquitie shall shine forth."[40] Another leading antiquarian and friend of Leland, Bishop John Bale, believed even more passionately in the authority of Geoffrey's *History*. Once a member of the Carmelite monastic order, he had joined the Protestant reformers and became violently anti-Roman.

Bale charged Vergil with "polluting our English Chronicles most shamefully with his Romish lies and other Italian beggarys."[41] A more sober criticism came from Sir John Price, a Welsh lawyer, in his *Historiae Brytannicae Defensio.*[42] While recognizing Vergil's learning, he did not believe that the humanist had shaken Geoffrey's account. Other Welsh antiquarians like Humphrey Lhuyd and David Powel were far less restrained in their condemnation of Vergil.[43]

By the last quarter of the century the popular image of Vergil was that of a scheming Italian papist who had insinuated himself into England by devious means and had proceeded to attack her most venerable traditions. "Polydore Vergil that most rascall dogge knave in the worlde," one angry commentator summed him up.[44] But the serious scholarship underlying Vergil's *Anglicana Historia* could not but impress conscientious readers. His scholarly method was in advance of any previous English historian. A scepticism born of the Renaissance prompted him to weigh authorities far more carefully than any contemporary English historical writer. The stimulus he provided for a more critical approach to sources was immense. His influence on the work of men like Edward Hall, Francis Bacon, and a whole range of later historians was considerable.[45]

Despite the vociferous defense of the British tradition by most English antiquarians there were a growing number of doubters. Five years before Vergil's history appeared, John Rastell, the antiquarian brother-in-law of Thomas More, commented that for some men of his day the story of Brutus was but "feyned fable."[46] For Rastell it was highly significant that Bede "spekyth nothyng of Arthur."[47] Though he went on to present in *The Pastyme of People* a brief version of Geoffrey's *History,* he would not vouch for its truth. Neither the antiquarians, John Twyne and George Lily, contemporaries of Leland, accepted the Trojan origin of the British, and the chronicler Thomas Lanquet was of the opinion that Geoffrey's *History* was full of errors.[48] There is no evidence that English humanists like Colet and More gave it credence.

During the Elizabethan age it was common to relate the English monarch to British antiquity, and pageantry and drama were filled with Arthurian imagery.[49] Spenser's *Faerie Queene,* linking Elizabeth to Arthur and heralding the advent of a new Golden Age, was an outstanding example of the continuing attraction the ancient British legend held for literate Englishmen.

It was the great Elizabethan and Jacobean antiquarian, William Camden, who did more than any other native English writer to weaken the authority of Geoffrey's *History.* His *Britannia,* the first comprehensive topographical survey of Britain, appeared in 1586. It immediately established his reputation as an outstanding scholar and came to be recognized "as the crowning achievement of Tudor and early Stuart antiquarianism."[50] Within his lifetime six London editions of his history were published. In beginning his discussion of the origin of the British people, Camden dealt delicately with Geoffrey's *History.* He assured his readers that he did not seek "to discredit that history," but on the contrary sought to maintain it: "I have often strained my invention to the utmost to support it. Absolutely to reject it, would be to wage war against time, and to fight against a received opinion." But the cautious Camden went on at length to give reasons why so many "very learned and judicious men" rejected it.[51] His gentle attempt to appease the admirers of Geoffrey's *History* ill-concealed his scepticism. Since for Camden the origins of the name of Britain and its first inhabitants were so uncertain, and despite the efforts of scholars would probably remain so, he concluded he might justly treat Geoffrey's version as irrelevant.[52] Drawing on linguistic similarities, he was inclined to the opinion that the ancient Britons were of the same stock as the Gauls.[53] Yet he was not prepared to jettison Arthur, that "mighty bulwark of the British Government," and lamented that the age had not afforded "a panegyrist equal to his virtues."[54]

The latter years of Elizabeth's reign were marked by a growing anxiety over the question of succession. As it became apparent that Elizabeth would produce no heir, hopes for an orderly succession turned more and more on James VI of Scotland. His pedigree had much to offer Arthurian enthusiasts eager to herald a new Golden Age. It could be shown that he was of the line Brut, first through his grandmother, Margaret Tudor, but also through the male Stuart line reaching back to Llewelyn, the last native Prince of Wales. James, well acquainted with ancient British lore, accepted his role as fulfiller of Merlin's prophecy. He saw himself as a second Arthur who would restore the ancient unity of England and Scotland established by Brutus. James's accession was greeted with tumultuous joy in England and pageants joyously proclaimed his Arthurian ancestry.[55] Significantly, without the consent of parliament, he assumed the title of King of Great Britain—no mention being made of the separate kingdoms of Scotland and England.

The most eloquent champion of British antiquity and its continuity in the Stuart dynasty was the poet Michael Drayton. In his ardent work, *Poly-olbion* (1613), he defended "the long traduced Brute," as well as the seer Merlin and other notable figures out of the British tradition.[56] Geoffrey of Monmouth's stories, he protested, were not "idle tales . . . nor fabulous, like those devised by the Greeks."[57] Drayton took his stand as a fierce supporter of their literal truth: "I would restore Antiquity to Britain, and Britain to his Antiquity."[58] Though Drayton had the historian John Speed add historical notes to the *Poly-olbion,* the scepticism of the latter about much of Geoffrey's *History* did little to strengthen the poet's advocacy.

In spite of the new life given the *History* by James I and his supporters, doubts continued to be raised by antiquarians. Writing in 1607, Edward Ayscu discussed the origins of the first inhabitants of Britain and passed over Brutus and the Trojans as a fabrication "coyned in some Monkish

mint about foure hundred years agone."[59] Drawing on Caesar and Tacitus he asserted "that the Britaines tooke beginning from their next neighbours the Gaules."[60] Ayscu's doubts about the *History* were more than matched by Peter Scriverius of Haarlem, who fervently pronounced it: "a great, heavy, long, thick, palpable and most impudent lie, and that so manifest as to need no refutation."[61]

In 1614 John Speed dedicated his *History of Great Britaine* to the new king as "Inlarger and Uniter of the British Empire. Restorer of the British name." Yet, after a careful assessment of the arguments for and against the theory of Trojan origins, he concluded with a call to Britons to, "disclaime their Brute, that bringeth no honour to so renowned a Nation, but rather cloudeth their glorie in the murder of his parents, and imbaseth their descents, as sprung from Venus, that lascivious adulteress."[62] If, Speed continues, "we will needs have our descents from the Trojans, may we not then more truly derive our blood from them through the Romans, who for the space of four hundred three score and six years were planted amongst us?" On Arthur he was more cautious, being prepared to "let Monmouth the Writer, Newberry the Resister and Leland the Retainer" speak for him.[63] But he believed Geoffrey's exaggerations deprived Arthur of "truly deserved honours."[64]

Sir Walter Raleigh, who brought out *The History of the World* in the same year as Speed's *History,* dealt more radically with early British history. Wishing to start where the facts were certain he began his outline with the Norman Conquest.[65]

In 1615 a stout defense of the Brut and Geoffrey's *History* was presented in John Stow's *The Annales.* In Stow's mind those who cast doubts on the *History* had much to answer for: "And the impugners of this ancient Historie must not with so light a breath, as they doe, seeme to blow away the authoritie of so many grave testimonies, the succession of so many Princes, the founders of so many monuments, and Lawes, and the ancient honors of the nation, that first with publike authoritie received Christianitie."[66] The chief villain for Stow was Polydore Vergil, who, "with one dash at a pen cashireth threescore Princes together, with all their histories and historians, yea and some ancient Lawes also."[67] Edmund Bolton in his *Hypercritica* (1618) was even more concerned about the consequences of sweeping away the *History*: "Nevertheless out of that very Story (let it be what it will) have Titles been framed in open Parliament, both in England, and Ireland, for the Rights of the Crown of England, even to entire Kingdoms. . . . If that Work be quite abolished there is a vast Blanck upon the Times of our Country, from the Creation of the World till the coming of Julius Caesar."[68] Bolton went on to calculate the positive support for the *History* against the opposition and concluded, "if the cause were to be try'd, or carried by Voices, the affirmative would have the fuller Cry."[69] His criteria for historical authenticity were broad indeed: "For my part I incline very strongly to have so much of every Historical Monument, or Historical Tradition maintain'd, as may well be holden without open absurdity."[70]

The concerns of men like Stow and Bolton that a challenge to traditional accounts of one's past represented a threat to the English system of government reflected the growing conflict between crown and parliament which was to reach its climax in the Civil War. In the main, Geoffrian enthusiasts sided with the King, while those who were cool to the ancient British accounts stressed parliamentary privileges. The latter turned more to Germanic sources for the fount of their traditional freedoms. Still, in spite of the emerging Saxon challenge, the vitality of the Geoffrian legend was far from spent and was to receive new life with the Restoration.

Charles II, a Stuart, who with as much right as his predecessors might claim to be a second Arthur, had learned to tread cautiously in asserting ancient prerogatives. Yet there were those who throughout his reign showed no reticence in trumpeting the cause of British antiquity. The antiquary Silas Taylor, in the course of establishing that, "Our English Laws are for the most part those that were used by the Antient Brytains," went out of his way to attack the "vulgar opinions" begun by Polydore Vergil that Geoffrey's *History* was fictitious. Geoffrey, Taylor triumphantly observed, "was the translator only of such a Language as Polydore did not understand."[71] That the Geoffrian account had popular appeal is suggested by the presentation of the play *The Destruction of Troy*. The author, the prolific dramatist John Bankes, anticipated that the specators, who were addressed as "London Trojans," would identify with events surrounding the fall of Troy. In the prologue it was noted that when Troy fell "its Remnant here did plant. And built this Place call'd it Troy-novant."[72]

It was the figure of Arthur that specially attracted Restoration writers. Perhaps the most spirited defense of his historicity was presented in Nathaniel Crouch's *The History of the Nine Worthies of the World* (1687). Arthur, it was recalled, was the seventh worthy in a line which included Hector of Troy, Alexander the Great, Julius Caesar, Joshua, David, Judas Maccabeus, Charlemagne and Godfrey of Bouillon. Of his many heroic deeds his most noteworthy was his conquering of the Saxons for Christianity. Crouch scornfully dismissed those who expressed disbelief in Arthur: "As it may be judged folly to affirm there never was any Alexander, Julius Caesar, Godfrey of Bullen, or Charlemagne, so may we be thought guilty of incredulity and ingratitude to deny or doubt the honourable Acts of our Victorious Arthur."[73] Crouch's work was well received and ran to three further editions by 1700.

The most significant writer to show an interest in Arthurian history as it related to the Stuart monarchy was John Dryden. (On Milton, see pp. 67-68.) He had the ambition to write a supreme epic poem. His theme would center on Arthur and as a poem of triumph would celebrate the descent of Charles II from Arthur, the greatest of the British kings. Other demands on his time prevented him from

ever realizing his goal, but in conjunction with Henry Purcell he completed the dramatic opera, *King Arthur,* in 1684. However, it was not produced until 1691 and in the interval dramatic political changes had occurred that could be ignored at an author's peril. With the Stuarts deposed, Dryden was compelled to alter his text radically, dropping anything that might be interpreted as political allegory bearing on contemporary events. As he wrote to the Marquis of Halifax: "Not to offend the present time, nor a government which has hitherto protected me, I have been obliged so much to alter the first design, and to take away so many beauties from the writing, that it is now no more what it was formerly than the present ship of the Royal Sovereign, after so often taking down and altering, is the vessel it was at the first building."[74]

A bizarre adaptation of the Arthurian legend came at the end of the century in Sir R. D. Blackmore's epic poems *Prince Arthur* (1695) and *King Arthur* (1700). Hardly ever was political allegory made more obvious than in Blackmore's attempt to cast the events of the Glorious Revolution in an heroic mold. William of Orange, portrayed as the Christian Arthur, emerged as the bold champion of political freedom and true religion (Protestantism) against heathen Saxons (Catholics!). The Arthurian legend was suitably altered to accommodate all the major achievements of the Prince of Orange from his early career in the Netherlands, to his victory in England and his championing of the Protestant cause against Louis XIV.

Blackmore's poems represented a final effort by an English writer to make the ancient British legend serve a political purpose. Though interest in it continued well into the Augustan age—Alexander Pope toward the end of his life contemplated writing an epic on Brutus as the Trojan hero who established a great empire in Britain—the ancient myth had spent itself.[75] The seventeenth century had seen England moving from a monarchically based society with a Crown claiming an absolute authority derived from ancient prerogatives to a self-conscious nation dominated by landed and rising commercial interests with parliament seen as the principal center of political power. Old myths of origin stressing achievements of kings no longer served the interests of dominant groups and were pushed more and more into the realm of poetic fancy. The series of events which in the first half of the century culminated in the Civil War and in the second half in the Glorious Revolution amply demonstrated that a myth of origin more rooted in historical reality was required. There was one ready to hand that had taken form in the latter decades of the sixteenth century. The freedoms of Englishmen and past achievements in which they all might glory came more and more to be seen as proceeding along a path that led back not to Brutus, Troy, and the British kings, but rather to Saxon England and the forests of Germany. Anglo-Saxonism, born in the sixteenth century in response to a need to demonstrate an historical continuity for the national church, and nourished in the seventeenth in debates over royal supremacy, finally triumphed and became the dominant myth that fired the national imagination. The social utility of the legendary history of Geoffrey of Monmouth had expired.

Geoffrey's remarkable account of the Trojan origins of the British nation served Englishmen well for over five hundred years. Though finally rejected by an historically-conscious people, its influence carried into the nineteenth century in the writings of Wordsworth and Tennyson. The founding in our own century of the International Arthurian Society, with membership in thirty-three countries, attests to its continuing fascination for the modern reader.

Notes

Where unspecified, London is the place of publication.

1. Halvdan Koht, "The Dawn of Nationalism in Europe," *American Historical Review,* 52 (Jan., 1947), p. 271.

2. *The History of the British Kings,* trans., Lewis Thorpe (Harmondsworth, Penguin, 1966), p. 51.

3. Gildas in his *De Excidio et Conquesta Britanniae* (c. 550) presented a condensed and sometimes incoherent reconstruction of the Roman and Anglo-Saxon conquests. The *Historia Brittonum* (c. 900), generally assigned to Nennius, is a very brief, semi-legendary account of the Britons. Both works are cited by Geoffrey. The far more reliable *Historia Ecclesiastica Gentes Anglorum* (731) by Bede was used by Geoffrey but it has little on the Britons. In a recent article in *Speculum,* Geoffrey Ashe argues with some cogency that "an unknown source of some kind remains possible." ("A Certain Very Ancient Book," April, 1981), p. 301.

4. Bede makes no mention of Trojan origins, suggesting that the tradition was not accepted in Britain in his time.

5. *Aluredi Beverlacensis Annales,* ed., Thomas Hearne (Oxford, 1716), p. 2.

6. *Annales,* p. 76.

7. *Itinerarium Cambrensis,* VI Rolls Series, Book I, Ch. v, ed., J. F. Dimock (1868), 58-59.

8. *The History of William of Newburgh,* trans., J. Stevenson, *The Church Historians of England,* IV, part I, Preface (1856).

9. See G. H. Gerould, "King Arthur and Politics," *Speculum,* II (Jan., 1927), 33-51.

10. See R. H. Fletcher, *The Arthurian Material in the Chronicles* (New York, 1966), pp. 191ff., 279ff.

11. R. S. Loomis, "Edward I, Arthurian Enthusiast," *Speculum,* XXVIII (Jan., 1953), 114-27.

12. *The Annals of Waverly,* cited in G. Ashe, *The Quest for Arthur's Britain* (1968), pp. 99-100.

13. See V. M. Lagorio, "The Evolving Legend of St. Joseph of Glastonbury," *Speculum,* XLVI, 1971.

14. Loomis, pp. 121-22.

15. See Arthur Jocelyn, *Awards of Honour* (1956), p. 17.

16. Ashe, *Arthur's Britain,* p. 12.

17. See Sydney Anglo, "The British History in Early Tudor Propaganda," *Bulletin of the Johns Rylands Library,* 44 (1961-62), 21-44.

18. See Eugene Vinaver, "Sir Thomas Malory," *Arthurian Literature in the Middle Ages,* ed. R. S. Loomis (Oxford, 1959).

19. *The Works of Sir Thomas Malory,* ed. E. Vinaver (1954), Preface, p. xvi.

20. Cited in John Speed, *The History of Great Britain* (1614), p. 164.

21. Cited in John Leland, *De Rebus Britannicis Collectanea,* ed., T. Hearne (1770), p. 196.

22. See Howell T. Evans, *Wales and the War of the Roses* (1915), p. 7.

23. *Historia Regis Henrici Septimi,* ed., James Gairdner, *Memorials of King Henry VII* (1858), pp. 9-11.

24. *Chronicles* (1809), p. 428.

25. *The Historie of the Raigne of King Henry the Seventh,* (1622), p. 18.

26. T. D. Kendrick, *British Antiquity* (1970), p. 38.

27. See E. A. Greenlaw, *Studies in Spenser's Historical Allegories* (1932), p. 40.

28. R. Koebner, "'The Imperial Crown of this Realm': Henry VIII, Constantine The Great and Polydore Vergil," *Bulletin of the Institute for Historical Research,* XXVI (1953), 40.

29. Koebner, p. 31.

30. See Denys Hay, *Polydore Vergil* (Oxford, 1952), p. 9.

31. *Polydore Vergil's English History,* from an early 16th century translation, ed., Sir Henry Ellis (1846), pp. 29, 33.

32. Vergil, p. 30.

33. Vergil, p. 38.

34. Vergil, p. 122.

35. Koebner, p. 36.

36. In 1536 Leland wrote a brief response entitled *Antiquarii Codrus, Sive Laus et Defensio Gallofridi Arturii Monumetensus contra Polydorum Virgilium.* This was expanded in 1544 in *Assertio Inclytissmii Arturii, Regis Britanniae.*

37. *The Assertion of K. Arthure,* a sixteenth century translation by Richard Robinson, ed., Christopher Middleton, in *The Famous Historie of Chinon of England* (1925), p. 53.

38. Leland, p. 17.

39. Leland, p. 86.

40. Leland, pp. 89-90.

41. *Select Works of John Bale* (Parker Society, 1849), p. 8.

42. The *Defensio* was written c. 1553 but not published until 1573.

43. See Kendrick, pp. 87-89.

44. Cited in Hay, p. 159.

45. See Hay, Ch. V; McKisack, *Medieval History in the Tudor Age* (Oxford, 1971), pp. 98-102. For his general influence see C. L. Kingsford, *English Historical Literature in the 15th Century* (1913).

46. *The Pastyme of People* (1811), p. 7.

47. Rastell, p. 106.

48. Kendrick, p. 41.

49. See Greenlaw, pp. 42-50.

50. McKisack, p. 152.

51. *Britannia*, trans., Edmund Gibson (1722), pp. 4-6.

52. See F. J. Levy, "The Making of Camden's Britannia," *Bibliotheque d'humanisme et Renaissance* XXVI (1964).

53. *Britannia*, p. 15.

54. *Britannia*, p. 183.

55. See R. F. Brinkley, *Arthurian Legend in the Seventeenth Century* (1932), Ch. 1; A. E. Parsons, "The Trojan Legend in England," *Modern Language Review*, XXIV (July, 1929), 402ff.

56. *Works*, ed., J. Hebel, IV, song X (1903), 206.

57. *Works*, p. 207.

58. Cited in Oliver Elton, *Michael Drayton* (New York, 1966), p. 112.

59. *A Historie of the Warres* (1607), p. 3.

60. Ayscu, p. 4.

61. Cited in George S. Gordon, *The Discipline of Letters* (Oxford, 1946).

62. *The History of Great Britaine under the Conquests of Ye Romans, Saxons, Danes and Normans* (1614), p. 166. Venus, as mother of Aeneas, was accordingly great-grandmother of Brutus.

63. Speed, p. 316.

64. Speed, p. 317.

65. *The History of the World* (1614).

66. *The Annales or General Chronicle of England* (1615), p. 6.

67. Cited in C. H. Firth, *Essays Historical and Literary* (Oxford, 1938), p. 70.

68. *Hypercritica: or a rule of Judgement, for Writing or Reading our History* (1722), pp. 205-06.

69. Bolton, p. 206.

70. Bolton, p. 212.

71. Silas, Taylor, *The History of Gavel-kind* (1663), p. 83.

72. *The Destruction of Troy,* "Prologue," (1679).

73. *The History of the Nine Worthies of the World* (1687), pp. 146-47.

74. Cited in C. E. Ward, *The Life of John Dryden* (1961), p. 250.

75. See Ian R. Jack, *Augustan Satire* (Oxford, 1942), p. 5.

Neil Wright (essay date 1984)

SOURCE: An introduction to The *"Historia Regum Britannie" of Geoffrey of Monmouth: I. Bern, Burgerbibliothek, MS. 568,* edited by Neil Wright, D. S. Brewer, 1985, pp. ix-lix.

[*In the following excerpt, Wright discusses the merits and shortcomings of various editions of* The History of the Kings of Britain.]

. . . THE PRESENT EDITION

It is surprising that a work as important and influential as the *Historia Regum Britannie* has previously been edited on only eight occasions; in view of the plethora of surviving manuscripts, it is less surprising that none of these editions can be considered to fulfill the needs of modern scholarship.[1]

Geoffrey's *Historia* was edited twice in the sixteenth century. The *editio princeps* was prepared by Ivo Cavellatus, a professor of the College of Quimper in Paris, and printed in Paris by Josse Bade of Asche in 1508.[2] In his introduction Cavellatus stated that he used four Paris manuscripts for his edition; but, as none of these manuscripts has yet been identified, it is difficult to assess the accuracy of the edition. Cavellatus's text is, however, marred by arbitrary and silent corrections, typical of Renaissance editorial practice, which severely limit its usefulness and reliability;[3] these deficiencies are rendered all the more serious because Cavellatus's text directly or indirectly influenced all subsequent editions until the present century. A second edition was printed in Paris by Josse Bade in 1517, but this differed from the the first only in point of some minor corrections.

The next edition of the *Historia* appeared near the end of the same century. It was the work of Hieronymus Commelin and was printed in Heidelberg in 1587.[4] Commelin knew and used the text of Cavellatus, but claimed to have improved it by collation with a manuscript belonging to his friend Paul Knibbe;[5] again this manuscript has not so far been identified. Thus, while Commelin's edition corrects some of the obvious errors of Cavellatus's, it too rests on uncertain manuscript authority. It is clear, then, that we cannot begin to assess the true value of these early editions until we have a clearer understanding of their relationship to the complicated text-history of the *Historia Regum Britannie.*

It was over two hundred and fifty years before Geoffrey's work was re-edited by J. A. Giles, whose text was published in England in 1844. According to Giles himself, his text represented a great advance, since it was based on a collation of no fewer than nine manuscripts. But Griscom has shown that this claim was without foundation.[6] The first three of Giles's 'manuscripts' comprise Commelin's printed text, the marginal notes of one Petreius—'uir doctus, nuper defunctus'[7]—to his copy of Commelin, and a printed text of the *Prophetie Merlini.*[8] The remaining six of Giles's sources were indeed manuscripts, but he collated only one of these in its entirety; this manuscript has not been identified.[9] Of the other five manuscripts, one was incomplete, while Giles collated the remaining four only in part. Moreover, where these known manuscripts vary from Commelin's text, Giles does not record their variant readings. Giles's edition, then, is completely uncritical and of very little value.

Ten years later Giles's text was reprinted by 'San Marte' (the nom-de-plume of a German scholar, Albert Schulz). Apart from the addition of a useful commentary, Schulz's only contribution to the text was to report some variant readings drawn from the editions of Cavellatus and Commelin.

In the present century, 1929 was something of a red-letter year for Galfridian studies, since it witnessed the publication of the editions by Acton Griscom and Edmond Faral. Both were marked improvements on the previously published texts; however, both also had limitations, chiefly caused by their failure to deal adequately with the complicated textual history of Geoffrey's work. Griscom's text consisted of a diplomatic edition of Cambridge, University Library, MS. Ii. 1. 14 (1706). He collated this manuscript with two others, the important Bern, Burgerbibliothek, MS. 568 and a late and indifferent manuscript, Aberystwyth, National Library of Wales, MS. Porkington 17, recording their variant readings in a double apparatus. While Griscom's transcription was generally accurate (at least in as far as it can be judged by his reporting of Bern 568),[10] the major drawback of this edition was his reliance on the Cambridge manuscript as the chief witness. On the strength of its double dedication, Griscom thought that not merely the version of the text contained in the manuscript but also the manuscript itself could be dated to 1136; not only was this hypothesis, as we have seen, misguided,[11] but the Cambridge manuscript is demonstrably corrupt.[12] Griscom's diplomatic text therefore leaves the reader to edit the Latin as he reads, while the apparatus of variant readings from the Bern and Aberystwyth manuscripts serves no particularly useful purpose.

Faral's edition was on a far more ambitious scale than that of Griscom; it was more broadly based on ten manuscripts, the most important of these being Cambridge, Trinity College, MS. 0.2.21 (1125), Bern, Burgerbibilothek, MS. 568, Leiden, Bibliotheek der Rijkuniversiteit, MS. B.P.L.20, and Paris, Bibliothèque nationale, MS. lat. 6233.[13] Relying on these manuscripts, Faral attempted to produce a heavily edited critical edition—an aim which was self-defeating without a thorough understanding of the text-history in all its ramifications. Moreover, Faral's repeated changes of policy in constructing his text are bewildering; this and the lamentable inaccuracy of his apparatus,[14] combined with the reader's uncertainty as to the manuscript-source or sources of any given word in the text, contrive to render Faral's otherwise useful edition significantly less satisfactory, although nonetheless more helpful to the reader than Griscom's eccentric work.

Finally, in 1951 there appeared the edition of Jacob Hammer. Hammer's extensive studies of Galfridian manuscripts enabled him to print a version of the *Historia Regum Britannie* significantly different from any previously published. Despite its obvious importance, Hammer's edition also had alarming deficiencies; but they and this text, the so-called First Variant Version of the *Historia Regum Britannie,* need not concern us here, since a re-edition of the latter will be the subject of one of the volumes to be published shortly in this series.

Embarking on the present programme for the re-edition of Geoffrey's *Historia* at once meant that certain basic choices had to be made. The immediate requirement is that a simple, readable text of the *Historia Regum Britannie* be made readily available so that students may once again routinely consult and familiarise themselves with this complex and important work. Since the rich and variegated textual history of Geoffrey's *magnum opus,* which exists in at least 210 copies, is at present quite unknown, the only decision possible at this stage is to edit the text of a single manuscript.

Given that present ignorance of Galfridian textual history, severe limits are automatically placed on the choice of source for a one-manuscript edition. Many early copies of Geoffrey's *Historia* survive, but the rule *ulteriores non deteriores* inhibits the use of any one of them without compelling reason. There is no point in reproducing Griscom's chosen manuscript—for the reasons already stated. The only other manuscripts which have impressed themselves on modern scholarship are Leiden, Bibliotheek der Rijksuniversiteit, MS. B.P.L.20, part 2, written at Le Bec in Normandy in the 1140s or 1150s, and Bern, Burgerbibliothek, MS. 568, of uncertain origin, but probably Norman, and possibly from Fécamp, and probably written in the last quarter of the twelfth century. The reputations of both have suffered at the hands of modern scholars. The Leiden manuscript was once thought to have been the copy of Geoffrey's *Historia* which Robert of Torigni showed to the astonished Henry of Huntingdon at Le Bec in January 1139. But that is scarcely possible and a number of pointers suggest that this Le Bec scriptorium-product embodies a recension which owes something to the hand of Robert of Torigni himself.[15] The Bern manuscript has exercised a fascination over students of Geoffrey since Madden first wrote about it in 1858.[16] But extravagant claims were made for it in 1926 by Acton Griscom who allowed his enthusiasm for its text to colour his judgment as to the date of its writing. The subsequent realisation that the manuscript was written later in the twelfth century has allowed it and its text to pass further from view than is merited. In neither state of mind have scholars properly allowed the ever necessary distinction between date of text and date of manuscript.

Jacob Hammer recognised that Bern 568 formed part of a group of manuscripts associable by their texts. Of these he named only London, British Library, MS. Arundel 237. It has recently been shown that Rouen, Bibliothèque municipale, MS. U.74 (1177) is another member of this group.[17] Possibly others remain to be discovered among the innumerable unclassified copies of the *Historia,* thus leading to amplification of the textual history. This is the version which Hammer unconvincingly labelled as an 'attempt to whitewash the Saxons'.[18]

Recently this group has been studied by David Dumville[19] who has displayed a textual history which can convincingly be carried back into the reign of King Stephen, which is at least of equal authority with the Leiden manuscript, and which may also owe its diffusion to the influence of Le Bec. Its version too becomes a candidate for identification with that shown to Henry of Huntingdon at Le Bec in 1139. Indeed, in so far as it cannot be proved that the Leiden book was that seen by Henry, its claim to consideration rests solely on its later Le Bec origin; yet in 1164 the Le Bec library possessed at least one other copy of the *Historia,* and the exchange of manuscripts among the Norman Benedictine abbeys during the preceding twenty-five years inhibits any general assumptions about the circulation of the text. Only a reconstructed text-history can be the basis for firm assertions about the circulation of this or that version of the *Historia.* Dumville has provided what is, to date, the only scholarly history of such a text. To the extent that the pedigree of this version is now known, back to Stephen's reign, it has seemed wisest to adopt it as the source of the present edition. No claim is made thereby for its originality; we can say merely that we are dealing with with a known quantity. To the extent that the dedicatory preface, unique to this manuscript, shows signs of being a revised version of that to Robert of Gloucester and Waleran of Meulan,[20] that part, at least, of the Bern text cannot represent Geoffrey's first edition of the work. But no version of the text with the Robert-Waleran preface has been studied in print, and Hammer's comments suggest that great textual variety among the eight manuscripts now containing it inhibits description of them as constituting a group or representing a version of the text;[21] until they have a history, choice of one manuscript would in these circumstances be misleading.

No attempt has been made here to present a critical edition based on the Bern, Arundel, and Rouen manuscripts. The labour expended would be wasted, for it would have to be redone when other copies of this version are identified (as they surely will be) during reconstruction of the total text-history. The present edition, therefore, presents a semi-diplomatic text which reproduces the Bern manuscript faithfully except where its Latin will not construe. Any emendations which have been considered necessary are indicated within the text by the use of angle-brackets; in all such cases, the readings of the manuscript are also reported. All abbreviations have been silently expanded.[22] I have not considered it wise to follow the editions of Faral and Hammer in introducing Classical Latin orthography into the text, since this system was foreign to Geoffrey and to the scribes who copied his work.[23] Accordingly, I have reproduced the orthography of the Bern manuscript closely; although this policy occasionally results in slightly unfamiliar forms, it is dictated by the need for editorial consistency. I have also refrained from correcting the spelling of the Bern manuscript, except in a very few cases where it was unintelligible or where serious ambiguity might have arisen. Similarly, I have made no attempt to 'normalise' the spelling of proper names (except in the case of a few very obvious scribal errors), since we cannot begin to understand how Geoffrey himself spelt these names, many of which are latinisations of vernacular forms, until the evidence of all the extant manuscripts has been gathered and assessed.[24] When the Bern manuscript employs more than one form of a name, all the spellings have been reproduced; for ease of reference, all variant forms have duly been recorded in the indices of names and places.

Modern punctuation has been introduced to allow the reader to follow the text with the minimum of difficulty, but I have, as far as possible, retained the sentence-structure of the Bern manuscript. The question of the internal division of the text on a larger scale raises some difficulties. In Bern MS. 568 the text is simply subdivided into paragraphs, each with a prominent initial. In this respect, the Bern manuscript reflects the practice of the majority of surviving manuscripts, but some exhibit instead more complex divisions into various numbers of books, often themselves internally divided into chapters. Only a complete investigation of the text-history of the *Historia* will enable us to ascertain the origin of these various systems of internal division and, indeed, whether any of them are due to Geoffrey himself, which is perhaps unlikely. Nevertheless, despite the uncertainty surrounding their genesis, the book- and chapter-divisions of these manuscripts in turn influenced the printed editions. Cavellatus's *editio princeps* was divided into nine books. Commelin introduced a division into twelve books, each subdivided into a number of chapters; this division became standard, being reproduced by Giles and San Marte. Even Griscom's diplomatic edition, which followed the paragraphing of the Cambridge manuscript, retained Commelin's book- and chapter-division in its margins. These editors' adoption of this system is, however, far from satisfactory, since, as Griscom himself conceded,[25] none of the early manuscripts contains the division into twelve books. Faral's answer to this problem was to divide the text arbitrarily into two hundred and eight chapters in his edition. Given our present total ignorance of the origins and development of the manuscript book-divisions, Faral's system seems the most sensible solution. In the present semi-diplomatic edition, I have reproduced the paragraphs of Bern MS. 568 exactly as they appear in the manuscript; however, in order to avoid the introduction of yet another system of internal division by numbering these paragraphs, I have employed Faral's chapter-numbers which are indicated in the text by the use of bold type. This arrangement permits immediate comparison of the division found in Bern MS. 568 with that introduced by Faral, while at the same time allowing the text to be cited conveniently by chapter-number. Faral's chapter-numbers will moreover be employed consistently in future editions to appear in this series so that all versions of the **Historia** can be readily compared.[26]

At one point only have I chosen not to follow the paragraphing of the Bern manuscript—that is, in the body of the **Prophetie Merlini** (**Historia Regum Britannie** Ch. 112-17) which by their very nature constitute a special case. I have subdivided the **Prophetie** into smaller and more manageable subsections, numbered 1-74, each representing—as far as the obscure subject-matter permits this to be determined—a discrete prophecy dealing with a single event or closely related group of events; my intention is to allow these arcane oracular pronouncements to be more easily referred to and cited than has thus far been possible.

At a few points the text of Geoffrey's **Historia** found in Bern MS. 568 diverges from that printed by Faral, in that some words found in Faral's edition are not present in the Bern manuscript. In such passages, my policy has been to restore words to the text only when the Latin cannot be understood or easily construed; these additions have always been clearly indicated by the use of angle-brackets. In the majority of cases only a single word is needed to restore sense, but in some few passages clauses are missing. This raises a problem: do the clauses absent from Bern MS. 568 represent omissions caused by careless copying or have they been deliberately supressed? Conversely, it might be argued that they are interpolations, witnessed by other manuscripts but not by Bern 568. This problem can be solved only by close analysis of the passages in question. I set them out for consideration here with the clauses taken from Faral's edition placed in angle-brackets. . . .

Notes

1. Griscom, *The Historia*, pp. 10-18, and Hammer, 'Remarks', pp. 522-5, discuss the deficiencies of previous editions.

2. See Renouard, *Bibliographie*, II.460-62.

3. Griscom, *The Historia*, pp. 11-12; Hammer, 'Remarks', p. 523.

4. See Port, *Hieronymus Commelinus*, p. 55.

5. Knibbe also provided a manuscript of another text edited in the same volume; on this, and on Knibbe

himself, see Stubbs, *Willelmi Malmesbiriensis Monachi de Gestis Regum Anglorum*, I.xcix-c.

6. Griscom, *The Historia*, pp. 15-18.

7. Giles, *Galfridi Monemutensis Historia Britonum*, p. 240.

8. Michel & Wright, *Galfridi de Monemuta Vita Merlini*, pp. 63–76.

9. Hammer, 'Remarks', p. 524.

10. Griscom's errors are very rare; to give two examples, at *Historia Regum Britannie* Ch. 41 he fails to note the dittography 'cum illo illo', and at Ch. 90 mistakenly reports 'omni assidui itineris' for 'assidui itineris'.

11. See above pp. xv-xvi.

12. Given our present ignorance of the text-history of the *Historia,* it is not easy to establish any manuscript's degree of corruption. An external control, however, is afforded by Geoffrey's extended borrowings from other authors. Examination of the passages in which he uses Gildas (Wright, 'Geoffrey of Monmouth and Gildas', pp. 34-40) reveals clearly that Griscom's Cambridge manuscript is corrupt.

13. Faral also used Cambridge, University Library MSS. Ii.1.14 (1706) and Ii.4.4 (1801), Oxford, Bodleian Library, MSS. Add. A.61 (*S.C.* 28843) and Bodley 514 (*S.C.* 2184), Paris, Bibliothèque nationale, MS. lat. 6040, and Roma, Biblioteca Apostolica Vaticana, MS. Vat. lat. 2005.

14. Faral's errors in reporting Bern MS. 568, for example, are too numerous to record in detail. In *Historia Regum Britannie* Ch. 15 alone there are four: he reports *permanere* for *commanere, affectu* for *effectu, et omni* for *omni,* and *excelsa puppi* for *in excelsa pupi* (indeed, such variant spellings as *pupi* are generally corrected silently).

15. Dumville, 'An early text', pp. 2-6.

16. 'The Historia Britonum'.

17. Dumville, 'An early text', pp. 16-17.

18. 'Remarks', pp. 525-6; see further below, pp. lvi-lix.

19. Dumville, 'An early text', pp. 16-29.

20. See above pp. xiv-xv.

21. 'Remarks', p. 525.

22. An anomaly must be noted here. Scribe 1 (see p. xlv, above) very often employs the abbreviation for *gra,* as opposed to *gre,* in the past tense of the verb *gradior* and its compounds (*e.g. supergrassus,* fo 18r, line 29); once only he uses it in the word *grex* (*grages,* fo 50v, line 17). Since this appears to be a personal quirk rather than a simple error, I have in these cases accordingly transcribed the abbreviation as *gre.*

23. See the review of Hammer's edition by Parry, pp. 239-40.

24. Arthur's queen is named four times in the *Historia* and on each occasion the name is spelt differently (Ganhumara, Ganhumera, Guenhumara, Guenhuuara) in the Bern manuscript; how are we to decide which is the correct form? See also Roberts, 'The treatment'.

25. Griscom, *The Historia*, p. 28.

26. The only problem is that Thorpe's translation, based on Griscom's text, retains the traditional division into twelve books. I have therefore included, as an appendix, a conversion-table for Faral's chapter- and Commelin's book-numbers so that the present edition can be more easily used in conjunction with Thorpe's English version.

Bibliography

DUMVILLE, D. N. 'An early text of Geoffrey of Monmouth's *Historia Regum Britanniae* and the circulation of some Latin histories in twelfth-century Normandy', *Arthurian Literature* 4 (1984) 1-33

FARAL, Edmond (ed.) *La Légende arthurienne* (3 vols, Paris 1929)

GILES, J. A. (ed.) *Galfridi Monemutensis Historia Britonum* (London 1844)

GRISCOM, Acton & JONES, R. E. (edd.) *The Historia Regum Britanniae of Geoffrey of Monmouth with Contributions to the Study of its Place in Early British History* (New York 1929)

HAMMER, J. 'Remarks on the sources and textual history of Geoffrey of Monmouth's *Historia Regum Britanniae*', *Bulletin of the Polish Institute of Arts and Sciences in America* 2 (1943/4) 501-64

MICHEL, Francisque & WRIGHT, T. *Galfridi de Monemuta Vita Merlini . . . suivie des prophécies de ce barde, tirés du IVe livre de l'Histoire des Bretons* (Paris 1837)

PARRY, J. J. [review of Jacob Hammer (ed.), *Geoffrey of Monmouth: Historia Regum Britanniae—A Variant Version*], *Journal of English and Germanic Philology* 51 (1952) 237-42

PORT, Wilhelm *Hieronymus Commelinus 1550-97. Leben und Werk eines Heidelberger Drucker-Verlegers* (Leipzig 1938)

RENOUARD, Phillippe *Bibliographie des impressions et des ouevres de Josse Badius Ascensius, imprimeur et humaniste 1462-1535* (3 vols, Paris 1908)

ROBERTS, B. F. 'The treatment of personal names in the early Welsh versions of the *Historia Regum Britanniae*', *Bulletin of the Board of Celtic Studies* 25 (1972-4), 274-90

STUBBS, William (ed.) *Willelmi Malmesbiriensis Monachi de Gestis Regum Anglorum: Historiae Novellae Libri tres* (2 vols, London 1887-9)

WRIGHT, N. 'Geoffrey of Monmouth and Gildas' *Arthurian Literature* 2 (1982) 1-40

Sheila Delany (essay date 1987)

SOURCE: "Geoffrey of Monmouth and Chaucer's *Legend of Good Women*," *The Chaucer Review*, Vol. 22, No. 2, 1987, pp. 170-74.

[*In the following essay, Delany discusses Chaucer's use of* The History of the Kings of Britain *for a line in his* Legend of Good Women.]

Chaucer took much of the material in his *Legend of Good Women* from Ovid's *Metamorphoses,* and this text, supplemented with the *Ovide Moralisé,* was his primary source for the legend of Thisbe.[1] However, one curious and unforgettable line from the legend occurs neither in Ovid nor in the *OM*: it is the oddly farcical phrase describing Piramus's death, when Thisbe finds him "Betynge with his heles on the grounde" (863).

The image is not original with Chaucer, but is found in Geoffrey of Monmouth's ***Historia Regum Britanniae*** (1136), a source not hitherto noticed in connection with this Chaucerian *locus.* In narrating the death of the tribune Frollo at Arthur's hands, Geoffrey says the following: "Quo vulnere cecidit Frollo, tellurem calcaneis pulsans, et spiritum in auras emisit" (IX, xi).[2] [With this wound Frollo fell, beating the ground with his heels, and sent his spirit out to the winds.] (My translation.) Translating this line, the Anglo-Norman Wace (1155) retains a feeble echo of the striking (as it were) image in his original, while Layamon (1205) omits the heel-beating altogether.[3] Chaucer's version, by contrast, reads like a close translation of the Latin original. It retains the present participle of the verb, specifies heels, and retains earth or ground as object of the heels' action.

This borrowed detail thus confirms the conclusion that to date has rested solely on Chaucer's use of the Celtic name "Arvirargus" in the *Franklin's Tale,* and on certain motifs in that same tale perhaps drawn from Geoffrey's story of Merlin and the giants' ring.[4] The fourteenth-century poet did indeed know Geoffrey of Monmouth's romanticized history of England. In browsing through the Arthurian section, he would doubtless have savored the phrase about Frollo's demise precisely because it evokes an image so comically inappropriate to the high patriotic seriousness supposedly at stake. He must have treasured it up and inserted it into his reworking of the Ovidian tale in order to underscore his burlesque treatment of the Piramus and Thisbe material—indeed to serve his ironic intention in the *Legend* as a whole.[5] Coincidentally too, there is a Piramus in the Arthurian section of the ***Historia,*** and only a few pages before the death of Frollo: it is Arthur's chaplain, appointed Archbishop of York (IX, viii). Without leaning unduly on this coincidence, I believe that the name Piramus would seem as inappropriate in context as does the manner of Frollo's dying. It must surely seem to the medieval reader, as to the modern one, an oddly classical and an oddly romantic name for a bishop: Tatlock calls it "ludicrously unfitting."[6] Whether the juxtaposition of these two salient and problematic details was deliberately repeated by Chaucer in the legend of Thisbe, no one can know. However, that it is repeated does suggest that Chaucer found more significant material in the *Historia* than a Celtic name and a curious poetic formula. What he found there might have contributed a good deal to the project embodied in the *Legend of Good Women.*

To begin at the beginning: The dedication[7] of Geoffrey's work addresses the same general topic broached in the opening lines (F and G, 1-15) of the Prologue to the *Legend of Good Women:* historical tradition and the modes of its transmission. Both authors then move to assess their place in the tradition to which they aspire; both assume the role of mere translators, and plain translators at that (G, 85-88). Both avail themselves of the modesty topos to demonstrate, somewhat paradoxically, their familiarity with the great rhetorical and literary tradition that precedes them. Finally, in at least seven manuscripts, Geoffrey concludes his dedication with a pastoral scene (imitated, as Griscom notes, from Virgil's *Eclogue* I, i) not unlike the setting of Chaucer's *Prologue:*

> Fidelis itaque protectio tuorum existens me tuum vatem codicemque ad oblectamentum tui editum sub tutela tua recipias ut sub tegmine tam patulae arboris recubans, calamum musae tue coram invidis atque improbis tuto modulamine resonare queam
>
> (Griscom, p. 220).

> p[And so, being the faithful protector of your own, receive into your care me your poet and this treatise published for your pleasure, so that, reclining in the shade of such a spreading tree and safe despite envious and dishonest men, I may be able to make melodious music on the reed of your muse.]
>
> (My translation.)

What strikes one about this self-defining image, this mythic projection of author and work, is what it is not: it is not the image of library or monastic cell that one might expect at the opening of a historical translation. Indeed the little allegorical scene seems rather blatantly to subvert the previously declared intention of strict translation, for what translator ever worked with muse and panpipes under the shade of a tree? This is the iconography of poetic invention, not of scholarship. Thus Geoffrey asserts himself as it were in opposition to his stated intention, rendering the nature of his project ambiguous from the start. That ambiguity intensifies as we move through the work, for here is a history which includes obvious fantasy (for example, the Merlin chapters) as well as plenty of rhetorical exaggeration, contradiction and improbability, authorial interjection, and (perhaps) unintentional humor.[8]

An essentially similar, and similarly ambiguous, self-assertion takes place in Chaucer's *Prologue,* where the narrator's continual display of his poetic wares quite thoroughly subverts his professed modesty, the strictures of Amor, and our expectation of a bare-bones translation. In much the same way, the legends that follow ironically subvert the god-critic's demand for iconic representations of womanhood. Thus in both texts there is a constant tension between writerly self-assertion and the demands or conventions of the subject matter.

One wonders whether, in perusing the *Historia,* Chaucer might not have felt a kindred spirit at work, for his own engagement with the Latin literary classics ("history" of a less political kind than Geoffrey's) surely parallels that of Geoffrey with the history of England. In general terms we might say that the two Geoffreys confront the same task: to integrate British experience with classical legend. Geoffrey of Monmouth aims to graft British "history" onto the cycle of Troy and Rome as represented in the *Aeneid*; Chaucer, more subtly, to retell classical tales for an up-to-date courtly and urban English audience.

I don't intend to imply that Chaucer drew his inspiration for the *Legend of Good Women* from Geoffrey of Monmouth's *Historia.* After all, the question of truth in human communication was one that Chaucer struggled with throughout his creative life, and the issues posed in the *Legend*—whether tacitly or overtly—were not uncommon among medieval classicizing authors. Still, the *Historia* would feed into those issues in a fairly direct way as a text which simultaneously transmits and problematizes tradition. Such was its mixed reception from the start.[9] Such indeed it remains, for as Griscom reminds us, "It is too commonly overlooked, as it should not be, that Geoffrey has preserved for us many native Welsh and Breton traditions, which he gathered together at a time when they were still familiar, and before Saxon, Danish, and Norman invaders had destroyed the written native records" (p. 3). It is one of those books "That tellen of these olde appreved stories" (I, F 21) which we may neither prove nor disprove and to which, according to the Chaucerian narrator, we must therefore grant "feyth and ful credence" (F, 31).

Or must we? "If you believe that, you'll believe anything" is the response that comes to mind when the book in question is the *Historia.* It is a terribly naïve profession of faith that the Chaucerian narrator makes here, not least because it skirts the troublesome phenomenon of contradictory authoritative texts. Virgil's and Ovid's versions of Dido and Aeneas offer an instance of that phenomenon, which Chaucer had already confronted in the *House of Fame* and which he would again confront in the *Legend.* I suspect, therefore, that Chaucer encountered Geoffrey's *Historia* with a healthy skepticism, as many readers had done before him. And the line he lifted from it to enhance his version of the romance of Piramus and Thisbe ought to lead us to suspect such skepticism as the informing spirit of the *Legend of Good Women.*

Notes

1. *Metamorphoses* IV, 55-166. On Chaucer's use of the twelfth-century *lai* of Thisbe inserted into the early fourteenth-century *Ovide Moralisé,* see Sheila Delany, "The Naked Text: Chaucer's Thisbe, the

Ovide Moralisé and the Problem of *Translatio Studii* in the *Legend of Good Women,* to appear in *Ovid in the Middle Ages,* ed. Marilyn Desmond. All Chaucer quotations are from F. N. Robinson, ed., *The Works of Geoffrey Chaucer,* 2nd ed. (Boston, 1957).

2. *The Historia Regum Britanniae of Geoffrey of Monmouth,* ed. Acton Griscom (New York, 1929), p. 450. The edition also contains a translation by R. E. Jones of a Welsh text, the *brut* (chronicle) *Tysilio,* which Griscom claims represents the type that might have been Geoffrey's source (Griscom, Chapter 9), but which, according to Tatlock, is an adaptation of the *Historia:* J. S. P. Tatlock, *The Legendary History of Britain* (Berkeley, 1950), p. 6n. I have supplemented Griscom with the Penguin Classics translation by Lewis Thorpe (1966), based on the same manuscript that Griscom uses: Cambridge University Library 1706. The edition by J. A. Giles, *Galfredi Monumetensis Historia Britonum* (London, 1844; repr. New York, 1967) is sharply criticized by Griscom (pp. 15-18). Although Griscom is concerned to convince us of the reliability of Geoffrey's account, and especially of the existence of the source-book which Geoffrey claims to be translating, Tatlock describes the *Historia* as "an almost wholly imaginary history of the Briton kings" (p. 3), while John J. Parry claims "the evidence is all against" the existence of a source-book: "Geoffrey of Monmouth," in *Arthurian Literature in the Middle Ages,* ed. R. S. Loomis (Oxford, 1959), p. 81. See Tatlock's discussion in Chapter 18.

3. Wace has "Des piez un poi eschaucirra, / Illec murut, mot ne suna" (10091-92) in *Le Roman de Brut de Wace,* ed. Ivor Arnold, SATF (Paris, 1938), 2: 530. Layamon has "Þa feol Frolle / folde to grune. uppen þan gras-bedde / his gost he bi-laefde" (23983-86) in *Layamon's Brut,* ed. F. Madden (1847; repr. Osnabruck, 1967), 2: 585. According to Jones's translation, the Tysilio has "digging up the ground with his heels" (Griscom, p. 450), while another Welsh chronicle has the same phrase as in the *Historia: Brut y Brenhinedd,* trans. John J. Parry (Cambridge, Mass., 1937), p. 166. The earliest manuscript of this *brut* (not the one printed in the volume) is the late twelfth-century Dingestow Court MS, and again it is unclear whether the text is a possible source or an adaptation of the *Historia.*

4. *Sources and Analogues of Chaucer's Canterbury Tales,* ed. W. F. Bryan and Germaine Dempster (New York, 1941; repr. 1958), pp. 383-85. There is also a reference to Geoffrey of Monmouth in the *House of Fame* III, 1470 ("Englyssh Gaufride") as one of those who bear up the fame of Troy; but this does not necessarily imply direct familiarity with the text.

5. On ironic intention in the *Legend of Good Women* see Elaine T. Hansen, "Irony and the Antifeminist Narrator in Chaucer's *Legend of Good Women,*" *JEGP* 82 (1983): 11-31. Also Sheila Delany, "The Logic of Obscenity in Chaucer's *Legend of Good Women,*" *Florilegium* 7 (1985): 189-205.

6. Tatlock, p. 167. The original, Tatlock suggests, could be the sixth-century Irish bishop St. Pieranus (p. 244).

7. There are three different dedications represented in 190 manuscripts: one to Robert only (in the majority of manuscripts), a double dedication to Robert and King Stephen (in a single manuscript, the Bern), and a double dedication to Robert and Waleran (in the Cambridge and six other manuscripts). There is also a fourth group or edition without any dedication. See Griscom's study of the dedications, Chapter 6. According to Griscom, the double dedication to Robert and Waleran is the earliest, but see Tatlock, Chapter 19, for other opinions. Giles has the dedication to Robert alone, which therefore lacks the pastoral coda addressed to the second patron. It is interesting to note that two features combined in the Cambridge group of manuscripts and in the Bern manuscript are also combined in the *Legend of Good Women*: dual sponsorship (Amor and Alceste in the *Legend*) and the pastoral setting with attention to the muse.

8. One might read the Frollo section as a deliberate study in anti-heroism, intended to glorify Arthur at the expense of his enemies. Although its narrative inconsistencies and rhetorical absurdities are not so blatant as those in Chaucer's *Tale of Thopas,* there are nonetheless certain similarities in method or at least in effect.

9. See Laura Keeler, *Geoffrey of Monmouth and the Late Latin Chroniclers, 1300-1500* (Berkeley, 1946; repr. Pennsylvania, 1974).

Mary L. H. Thompson (essay date 1988)

SOURCE: "A Possible Source of Geoffrey's Roman War?" in *The Arthurian Tradition: Essays in Convergence,* edited by Mary Flowers Braswell and John Bugge, The University of Alabama Press, 1988, pp. 43-53.

[In the following essay, Thompson presents evidence that Geoffrey used Caesar's Commentary on the Gallic Wars *as a source for his own* History.*]*

Arthur's campaigns in Gaul, here collectively termed his Roman War, make up a part of Geoffrey of Monmouth's ***Historia Regum Britanniae*** for which almost no historical evidence has been forthcoming and which has thus been considered exclusively fictional. After his pacification of the region and a period of nine years of peace, the king holds court at Paris; no significant amount of time appears to intervene between that court and the one held later in Caerleon at Whitsuntide. Since Geoffrey (XI, ii, 501) dates the fatal battle between Arthur and Mordred as occurring in 542, for Geoffrey, all the events of Arthur's war in Gaul seem to have taken place in the second quarter of the sixth century. History, however, offers no evidence of troop movements from Britain to the Continent during this period. Geoffrey Ashe has suggested a historical basis for such movements in the crossing of British forces into Gaul in about 470, but the particulars of that expedition offer little correspondence with the persons and events described in the *Historia*. Nevertheless, it is my contention that many points of resemblance exist between Geoffrey's narration and a much earlier account of an invasion of Gaul and of warfare between Celt and Roman: Julius Caesar's *Commentarius de bello Gallico*. These similarities indicate that events of Caesar's campaign, in 58-50 B.C., might have been included in an intermediary Celtic account that became Geoffrey's source for this part of the *Historia*. This hypothesis, that Caesar's Gallic campaigns underlie Geoffrey's account, is well worth exploring, for it might help refute charges that certain parts of Geoffrey's account, like the battle at Siesia—or, indeed, this entire section of the *Historia*—are purely imaginary. It would help substantiate Lewis Thorpe's brave conclusion that "Geoffrey did not invent it."

Opinion differs whether Geoffrey might have known Caesar's *Commentary*. J. S. P. Tatlock feels that he must have, and Hans Keller agrees, on the basis of Tatlock's assertion that a certain "Gesta Caesaris" appears in many medieval library catalogues. Still, as astute a critic as Edmond Faral thought Geoffrey could have had no direct knowledge of Caesar because, in describing military actions between Langres and Autun, the *Historia* gives place names not found in the *Commentary*.

I have examined carefully the language of both Caesar and Geoffrey of Monmouth in the several cases of correspondence to be discussed in this essay. In none of them does Geoffrey appear to have borrowed phraseology from the *Commentary,* as he seems to have done when using Bede as a source. A typical example is the incident of the felling of trees for use as military fortification. Not one word of Geoffrey's Latin (including even prepositions and conjunctions) duplicates anything found in Caesar. To illustrate, the passage from the *Commentary* reads: "Caesar silvas caedere instituit, et ne quis inermibus imprudentibusque militibus ab latere impetus fieri posset, omnem eam materiam quae erat caesa conversam ad hostem conlocabat et pro vallo ad utrumque latus extruebat" (III, 29). In contrast, Geoffrey writes: "Quod arturus intuens iussit arbores circa illam partem nemoris indici et truncos ita in circuitu locari, ut egressus eis abnegaretur. Uolebat namque ipsos inclusos tamdiu obsidere donec fame interirent" (IX, iii, 436). Judging from a comparison of all such relevant passages, there seems to be no stylistic evidence that Geoffrey knew Caesar's account in the original.

Nevertheless, Geoffrey definitely seems to have known of the events of Caesar's campaign. The idea proposed here—that Geoffrey may have had access to a Celtic version of these same events—leads me to conclude that Arthur's exploits are based in part on those of Gallic chieftains who resisted Caesar's advance.

There is an obvious objection to this theory: history records the Romans, not the Celts, as victors. Against this argument must be placed the argument that a Celtic tale would have preserved a somewhat different emphasis—at the least, a focus on both the virtues and the vices of Caesar's opponents. It should be remembered that the conquest of Gaul was neither quick nor easy. Caesar faced a series of revolts during his nine years in Gaul. During hostilities he was briefly a captive, and in 52 B.C. he was nearly defeated by an alliance of tribes under their best-known leader, Vercingetorix. Sporadic resistance to Roman rule continued for years, even under the empire. Caesar had, of course, written his self-laudatory commentary to establish his claim to military skill, but this aim did not preclude his mention of temporary Gallic successes or of the difficulties he faced owing to the valor of his opponents. Moreover, it is clear that Caesar's eventual victory was due not only to his own ability and to better Roman organization and discipline but to the lack of steadfastness of the Celts and especially to the long-standing enmity among the various tribes as well.

Aulus Hirtius notes (VIII, 25 and 48) that defeated Gallic chieftains (for example, Ambiorix, Commius) sometimes escaped and moved away from the expanding Roman sphere of influence. Others may have sought refuge in Britain. No matter where they went, migrating survivors no doubt took with them their own version of what had happened in Gaul in the first century B.C., probably emphasizing, as had Caesar for himself in his turn, their own successes and discounting their own defeats. Further, it is not unlikely that in later centuries, Gauls and Britons might have edited what they may have heard (or even read) of the Roman version of the conflict, in the process presenting a far more favorable picture of Celtic resistance—even to the point, perhaps, of turning defeat into stalemate or into something more favorable.

Because both the section in Geoffrey's *Historia* on Arthur's Gallic wars and Caesar's entire *Commentary* are about warfare, it is to be expected that certain verbal conventions in describing battle produced similarities. Nevertheless, the two accounts share so many details that, on balance, it is difficult to believe that Geoffrey did not draw on some version of Caesar's account. In another essay, I note how the two works seem to agree in certain particulars—the geographical locations of battles and the size of armies involved. Here, the subject will be limited first to noteworthy parallels between Geoffrey and Caesar in the nature of military incidents, and second, to similarities in the names of principals involved. These are discussed in the order in which they occur in the *Historia.*

In Arthur's first expedition to Gaul (XI, xi, 446-51), four elements in Geoffrey have clear parallels in Caesar (Book VII of the *Commentary*) writing about Celtic resistance under the Gallic chieftain Vercingetorix: Arthur's ambition to secure dominion over a vast region; his laying waste of the countryside; his strategy of giving gifts to secure the cooperation of Gauls against Romans; and his ordering of a military action to the south under the command of a subordinate. Geoffrey says that Arthur's invasion of Gaul grew out of his ambition to conquer the whole of Europe.

In like fashion, Caesar reports that Vercingetorix encouraged his supporters by declaring that, after winning over other Gallic tribes not yet in agreement with their aims, "he would create a single policy for the whole of Gaul. . . . With Gaul thus united, the whole world could not stand against them" (VII, 29). Arthur is described as laying waste the countryside; Vercingetorix, unsuccessful in halting Roman attacks on Gallic towns, proposes to his council that now "the war must be waged in a quite different way than hitherto." To prevent the enemy from gathering food from barns and granaries, he declares that "all villages and isolated buildings must be set on fire in every direction from the Romans' line of march as far as foragers seemed likely to be able to reach" (VII, 14). A third parallel involves the use of gifts to gain allies. Geoffrey says that Frollo is unable to resist Arthur's invasion successfully, in part because the better part of the army of the Gauls was already in Arthur's service: he had bought them over by gifts (IX, xi, 448). Caesar also finds that tribes formerly loyal to Rome desert to join Vercingetorix, who used "every means he could think of to bring the other tribes into the alliance, even trying to seduce them with bribes and promises" (VII, 31). Finally, after his victory over Frollo, Arthur sends Hoel to Aquitania to force the Poitevins and Gascons to surrender (IX, xi, 450-51). Similar is the dispatch by Vercingetorix of a subordinate, Lucterius the Carducan, to induce or compel tribes in the south of Gaul to join the alliance (VII, 5 and 7). In each instance, Arthur's motives or actions strongly resemble those of the most renowned of the Celtic warlords of Caesar's account.

It seems possible that two of Caesar's campaigns provide elements used in Geoffrey's story of the battles between Arthur and the fictional Roman emperor Lucius. Especially important are Caesar's account of the revolt of the Eburones under Ambiorix (Book V) and that of the resistance of Vercingetorix two years later (Book VII). In Geoffrey's story of the skirmish at Autun (X, iv, 474-79), Arthur comes upon the Roman forces near the Aube and sends a delegation, including Gawain, to Lucius, demanding that the Romans either withdraw or meet the British in battle. For its part, the *Commentary* tells of a parley called by the Eburones, who have surrounded a Roman winter camp and who offer the garrison, in the person of its envoy, Gaius Arpineius, similar terms—either safe conduct to another camp or renewed attacks (V, 26-37). In Geoffrey's account, Gawain is angered by a slur made by a Gaius Quintillianus and beheads him; according to Caesar, the great Gallic revolt of 52 B.C. was initiated by an uprising in which several Romans were killed, including a Gaius Fufius Cita (VII, 3).

At this point in the *Historia,* Geoffrey is as uncomplimentary of the fighting spirit of these Britons as Caesar is about that of the Gauls in his *Commentary.* Geoffrey reports that, while the Britons yearned for a fight with all their heart and soul, once they began it, they did not care much whether they won or lost (X, iv, 477). This sounds like the references to the "fickleness" of the Gauls in the *Commentary* and to their "delight in fighting." Caesar says that "while the Gauls are quick and eager to start wars, they lack the determination and strength of character needed to carry on when things go against them" (III, 19). When consent has been given for an attack, they are "exultant; it was almost as if the victory was already theirs" (III, 18). Similarly, both authors praise the Romans for their cool professionalism under attack. When Geoffrey shows the Romans making a stand, he is careful to praise the Roman commander, saying that the Romans were carefully instructed by Petreius Cocta, good captain (X, iv, 477). Caesar's statement about the legate Lucius Cotta, who was in charge of the defense against the Eburones (note the similarity in names), has the same ring: "He did everything possible to save the army, calling on the men and encouraging them as a commander-in-chief would, and fighting in the line like an ordinary soldier" (V, 33).

In Geoffrey, entrapment of the Romans results in a victory for the Britons; he says the Romans were enfeebled and dispirited and ready to show their backs, for they had lost their captain (X, iv, 478). In Caesar's account of the Roman fight against the Eburones, Romans who had left their camp in a kind of panic nevertheless stand firm against Gallic ambush from dawn until mid-afternoon (V, 32-36). Then Sabinus, one of the Roman legates, goes to Ambiorix, chief of the Eburones, to ask for quarter and is treacherously killed. Having lost their commander, the Romans retreat to their camp at nightfall where, all hope gone, the survivors commit suicide (V, 37).

The largest part of the confrontation between Arthur and Lucius in Geoffrey's *Historia* is the battle of Siesia (Saussy?) (X, vi-xiii, 481-96). Arthur's tactics there approximate those chosen by Gallic chieftains in Caesar's account. Arthur occupies the valley, waiting for Lucius as he marches out of Langres. The advantage lies with the Britons, who descend from the heights on the Roman column; Morvid, Earl of Gloucester, who had been stationed higher up in the hills, attacks the Romans in the rear when they least expect it (X, xi, 494). In Caesar's account, in anticipation of the evacuation of the Roman camp, Ambiorix's men are positioned in a double ambush in the woods: "When the greater part of our column had descended into a deep defile the Gauls suddenly appeared at each end of it and began to harrass the rear-guard and stop the head of the column climbing the hill to get out" (V, 32). Arthur's speech to his troops in Geoffrey includes these words: "You have put the Romans to flight. . . . They have had to withdraw. . . . They must come through this valley on their way to Autun, where you will be able to fall upon them when they least expect it" (X, vii, 484). In Caesar's *Commentary,* Vercingetorix has a similar rallying speech: "The Romans are leaving Gaul . . . and fleeing to the Province. . . . [We] must attack them now, while they are on the march and encumbered by their baggage" (VII, 66). The two situations are similar in several respects—the Roman retreat, the surprise ambush from an elevated position, the urgency felt by the Celtic commanders to annihilate the Roman threat while they have the chance.

If Arthur seems modeled on the character of Vercingetorix, even the British king's last defeat bears some resemblance to the final failure of that Gallic leader. The key element is treachery, betrayal. Geoffrey recounts how, on his triumphant way to Rome, Arthur learns that Modred has made himself king. Modred is condemned in the strongest possible language: "treacherous tyrant," "traitor," "perjurer," and so on (XI, i, 496-98). In the story told by Caesar, Vercingetorix, like Arthur, is unable to attain his final goal—in this case, elimination of Roman influence from Gaul—and there is reason to believe that treachery on the part of his subordinates is responsible. For example, it is difficult to understand why the huge Gallic army raised to relieve the Roman siege of Alesia was not able to break through, unless it was because the disaffected Gauls failed to support Vercingetorix. A tribe called the Bellovaci, for instance, do not send their full quota of men, declaring they will fight only at their own discretion and not under the command of anyone else (VII, 75). Caesar notes as well that another tribe, the Aedui, bitterly resented being rejected from the leadership of the Gallic campaign and that two of their cavalry commanders, Eporedorix and Viridomarus, "took orders from Vercingetorix" but "much against their will" (VII, 63). These and other glimpses of dissension among the Gauls could have given Geoffrey a key to help explain Arthur's lack of success against the Romans.

Whereas military motives, strategy, and tactics are always somewhat conventional, the foregoing account shows that the activities of the Gallic forces against the Romans (and, more particularly, of the main Gallic leaders Ambiorix and Vercingetorix) in many respects run parallel to those of Arthur and the British, who were fighting the same enemy in the same theater of operations. Such parallels become more convincing when the names of some of the principals in Geoffrey's *Historia* are compared with those in Caesar's account. In general, enough close resemblances occur to suggest that Geoffrey's cast of characters is roughly patterned after Caesar's.

The first Roman that Arthur encounters in Gaul is the tribune Frollo (IX, xi, 448). In the *Commentary,* the nearest equivalent is "Ollovico" (VII, 31), the name of a Gallic chieftain, not a Roman official. Yet Caesar reports that the Senate had granted him the honor of being called "friend of the Roman people." Although *tribunus* under the Republic denoted either an aide attached to a legion or an elected official at Rome, the word originally meant chieftain of a tribe. Possibly, Geoffrey uses *tribunus* in the latter sense when applying it to Frollo, for the last syllables of Ollovico, -vico, are found in the titles of other Gallic chieftains. Had the name used by Caesar also included a standard Gallic honorific prefix vor-, ver- in a Celtic source known to Geoffrey, the result would have been "Vorollovico" ([*Vor*]-*ollo-vico*), or, with the ending clipped, simply V[o]rollo.

While Geoffrey is thought merely to have invented Latin-sounding names for his Roman generals, we find names in Caesar's *Commentary* that could be the basis for several.

According to Geoffrey, the Roman general killed in the skirmish at Autun was Vulteius Catellus (X, v, 474); the name could be the result of the faulty transmission, oral or written, of Caesar's "(Gaius) Volcatius Tullus" (VI, 29). Geoffrey's fight between Britons and Romans near the Aube, discussed above, is similar to the attack Caesar describes against the retreating Romans led by Lucius Arunculeius Cotta (V, 24-37); in the same battle died the standard-bearer Lucius Petrosidius. It is possible Geoffrey's Senator "Petrius Cocta" (X, iv, 477) is a conflation of these two Romans in Caesar's account.

Geoffrey's Roman emperor Lucius Hiberius is not found in history. The praenomen was a common Roman one; in Caesar's *Commentary* are ten persons of that name who play active roles. Among them are senior centurions, who would have taken a prominent part in battles; *legati* in command of legions; and one Lucius Caesar, who nevertheless appears only in command of forces in the Province (Gallia Narbonensis, in the south of France) (VII, 65). In addition, there are three consuls named Lucius, and Caesar refers to four Romans with this first name who were defeated by the Gauls in wars before 58 B.C. Any negotiations between the Gauls and the Romans would have featured prominently the names of the consuls, chief officers of the Republic.

The only person described by Caesar as a Spaniard (*hiberus*) is Quintus Junius, a negotiator sent by Sabinus and Cotta to meet with attacking Gauls under Ambiorix (V, 27). There is no indication of his fate, but one assumes that in the subsequent ambush he perished along with Lucius Petrosidius, Lucius Aurunculeius Cotta, and a Quintus Lucanius. It is possible that attempts to simplify confusion among these names of similar sound and spelling may have led to the creation of Geoffrey's "Lucius Hiberius," who is described first as procurator, then as emperor.

In Caesar's time, a procurator was simply an agent or deputy, but in the imperial period the term came to mean an official of the government. *Imperator* was the title of a general in charge of two or more legions, the designation indicating at basis the distinction of command as opposed to the duties of a soldier. The title was conferred on a general after an important victory and later was one of the titles of the successors of Julius Caesar as head of state—hence, also, the source of our meaning of "emperor." Thus it may be that "general" is a better translation of the title held by Geoffrey's "Lucius Hiberius."

Following the same line of argument, certain Celtic names in the *Historia* can be matched with those in Caesar's work. The name Dubricius, belonging to the bishop at the plenary court at Caerleon (*Historia,* IX, i, 432), recalls Diviacus (or Divitiacus), chief of the Aedui at the time of Caesar (I, 3). Gorbonian map Goit, listed among those in attendance at Caerleon (IX, xii, 454), is reminiscent of that of the uncle of Vercingetorix, Gorbannitio (VII, 4). And a Briton killed at Siesia, Riddomarcus (*Historia,* X, x, 491) could easily be based—onomastically—on the Aeduan cavalry commander Viridomarcus (VII, 38).

The most interesting connection between Galfridian and Caesarian nomenclature, however, may lie outside those names actually listed in the *Historia.* The meaning of the title by which the chief opponent of the Romans was known may bear particular importance for Geoffrey's understanding of the role of Arthur. Three of the Celtic chieftains appearing in Caesar's account provide a close connection with a title that must have been known to Geoffrey. Two are named Cingetorix, and the third is, of course, the illustrious Vercingetorix. Some Celtic scholars suggest that the meaning of *cing* is "people" or, alternatively, "champion." The root *get* (or *cat*) means "battle" or "warrior," while *rix* clearly is "chief" or "leader." (The prefix *ver-* [or *vor-*], as above, retains its honorific value of "great.") Thus the actual meaning of *Vercingetorix* was something like "great leader of the people in battle" or, indeed, something close to the title Nennius says King Arthur himself bore—*dux bellorum.*

To conclude, reading Geoffrey's *Historia* after Caesar's *Commentary* is much like looking at the underside of a brightly woven cloth, where the patterns and figures seem oddly duplicated, though the design may be somewhat blurred and the colors grown faint. The congruence between the two works over "the war in Gaul" is never exact, but certain similarities are sufficiently intriguing to suggest the possibility that one "source" Geoffrey had access to for his account of King Arthur's exploits on the Continent—in no matter how distorted and attenuated a form it had come to him through more than ten centuries of transmission—was Caesar's *Gallic Wars.*

Neil Wright (essay date 1988)

SOURCE: An introduction to *The "Historia Regum Britannie" of Geoffrey of Monmouth: II, The First Variant Version: A Critical Edition*, edited by Neil Wright, D. S. Brewer, 1988, pp. xi-cxvi.

[*In the following excerpt, Wright provides an overview of the First Variant version of* The History of the Kings of Britain.]

The First Variant Version of the *Historia Regum Britannie*: Contents, Date, and Authorship

In 1951 Jacob Hammer published—albeit in seriously mangled form—a text of the **Historia Regum Britannie** which differed considerably from that hitherto regarded as the standard version of Geoffrey's **Historia**.[1] Hammer referred to the former as the First Variant version[2] and to the latter as the vulgate, terms which have since gained general acceptance among Galfridian scholars. Yet despite this agreement, basic questions concerning the genesis of the First Variant version have, since the appearance of Hammer's edition, elicited widely divergent responses from his critics. There has thus far been no consensus of opinion on such fundamental issues as exactly how the text of this

Variant relates to that of the vulgate, when and with what motives the Variant was composed, and who was responsible for it. Indeed, so diverse have been the various hypotheses advanced in answer to these questions that it will be necessary to summarize them here before attempting to resolve the problems which they raise.

Hammer himself, in the introduction to his edition, devoted some space to an examination of the relationship of the First Variant text to the vulgate. He catalogued, giving a few examples in each case, the following details as characteristic of the Variant: additional material, sometimes drawn from older sources; a fondness for biblical phraseology; some speeches abbreviated or omitted, or, conversely, paraphrased or completely altered in form and content; and a tendency to tone down or omit unpleasant details.[3] Hammer nowhere explicitly discussed the question of the priority of the Variant or vulgate text or of the dating of the Variant, but it is clear that he considered the latter to be a reworking (of the vulgate) for which Geoffrey of Monmouth was not responsible; he referred to the Variant's 'author' as an 'unknown Welsh redactor' (this merely on the strength of parallels between the Variant and Welsh versions of the **Historia**) and as a 'chronicler who, though inspired by Geoffrey, refused to reproduce him slavishly'.[4] The view that the First Variant postdated the vulgate is implicit in these statements, and it may be concluded that Hammer saw the Variant as a later—probably considerably later—redaction of the **Historia.**

The first scholar to address the question of the date of the Variant version directly was Robert Caldwell, who devoted two articles to this problem. The first of these was primarily concerned with the interrelationship of the Variant with the *Roman de Brut* of Wace.[5] While it had long been recognised that Wace's poem was essentially a vernacular version of Geoffrey's **Historia**,[6] Caldwell maintained that there were clear indications that the *Roman de Brut* had closer links with the Variant version than with the vulgate. He showed first that the 'additional material' in the Variant, cited by Hammer to illustrate the differences between it and the vulgate, was also present in the *Roman de Brut*; and secondly that some of the additions which (Margaret Houck had argued)[7] were made by Wace to his source could in fact also be found in the Variant. Further comparison of the *Roman de Brut* with the Variant version led Caldwell to conclude that Wace had drawn principally on the Variant (but not exclusively, as some passages in the second half of the poem, especially that part dealing with the reign of Arthur, were clearly derived from material found solely in the vulgate).[8] This conclusion provided evidence for the date of the Variant, since the *Roman de Brut* was completed in 1155.[9] According to Caldwell, therefore, the Variant version must have been written before that date and, indeed, within the lifetime of Geoffrey himself (who died probably in 1155).[10] As to the question of authorship, Caldwell accepted Hammer's inference that the Variant was not produced by Geoffrey, while rejecting—rightly in my view—Hammer's ill-founded assertion that it was demonstrably the work of a Welshman.

In a second article,[11] Caldwell refined his approach to the dating of the Variant version. Turning his attention to its relationship with the vulgate, he argued that the absence from the vulgate of some material found in the Variant and the inclusion in the Variant alone of some passages drawn directly from prior sources (Bede and Landolfus Sagax) could best be explained if the vulgate were regarded as a reworking of the Variant. Elsewhere, Caldwell stated that the Variant 'looks like an early draft put together from original sources' and the vulgate 'like a deliberate revision'.[12] In his opinion, then, the Variant version antedated not only Wace's *Roman de Brut,* but also the vulgate **Historia Regum Britannie** itself, probably published in 1138.[13] However, Caldwell apparently did not modify his acceptance of Hammer's view that the Variant could not be the work of Geoffrey. His hypothesis therefore involved the difficulty of maintaining that the Variant represented a version of the **Historia** composed by an unknown author at some time before Geoffrey compiled the vulgate text—a difficulty which Caldwell made no attempt to resolve.

Caldwell's arguments were vigorously countered by Pierre Gallais.[14] The latter regarded Caldwell's claim that the Variant version preceded the *Roman de Brut* as a serious challenge to Wace's originality, since it threatened to reduce the status of the romance poet to that of a 'compilateur'.[15] Gallais accepted that, by reason of its style, the Variant could not have been written by Geoffrey himself, but he rejected the proposition that an unknown author could have produced such a version prior to the appearance of the vulgate text; accordingly, the Variant must have been composed after 1138 and, if Caldwell were right in seeing it as Wace's prime source, before the latter began work on the *Roman de Brut* (viz, Gallais suggested, around 1150). However this seemed too short a time to Gallais, who thought it unlikely that a revision of the **Historia** by an author other than Geoffrey would have been made so soon after the publication of the vulgate text or, for that matter, in Geoffrey's lifetime. Furthermore, a painstaking comparison of that part of the *Roman de Brut* concerned with Arthur and the corresponding sections of the vulgate and First Variant texts[16] led Gallais to a conclusion diametrically opposed to that of Caldwell: namely that the Variant version drew on Wace's *Roman de Brut* and was, therefore, composed after 1155. While Gallais made no attempt to date the Variant version more precisely, he tentatively suggested that stylistic comparison with the works of late twelfth- and early thirteenth-century writers (such as Gerald of Wales, Walter Map, or Gervase of Tilbury) might produce interesting results.

Gallais's arguments were themselves attacked by Hans-Erich Keller,[17] who advocated a return to the position adopted by Caldwell, though in a qualified form. Keller held that comparison of the treatment of the proper and place-names in the Variant and the *Roman de Brut* indicated that Caldwell had been right to suppose that Wace had used the Variant. He also accepted Caldwell's contention that the Variant, though not written by Geoffrey, antedated the vulgate text. Elaborating another suggestion made by Caldwell,[18] Keller identified the two versions of the **Historia** (viz vulgate and Variant) with two sources (supposedly in Latin) mentioned by Geffrei Gaimar who compiled, probably shortly before 1140, the *Estoire des Engleis,* another vernacular verse work based in part on Geoffrey of Monmouth's **Historia.**[19] Keller maintained that Gaimar referred to the vulgate as 'le livere Walter Espac', and to the Variant version as 'le bon livere de Oxenforde / Ki fust Walter l'arcediaen'.[20] On the strength of this latter identification, Keller concluded that the source of the **Historia Regum Britannie** was not, as Geoffrey alleged, an ancient Welsh- or Breton-language book in the possession of Walter archdeacon of Oxford,[21] but rather the Variant, composed before 1138 and possibly, Keller suggested, written by Archdeacon Walter himself.

Caldwell's position also finds support from R. William Leckie, Jr., who has devoted an important study to the impact of Geoffrey's **Historia** on twelfth-century littérateurs and historians.[22] Leckie highlighted Geoffrey's innovative treatment of the transfer of power from the native British to their English foes; since Geoffrey's account directly contradicted those of accepted authorities such as Bede, it inevitably drew from contemporary and near-contemporary authors various attempts to resolve this problem or to reach a compromise solution. In the course of examining these responses to Geoffrey's narrative, Leckie maintained that the Variant version at several points manifested a concern to deal with the problems raised by the vulgate text and must, therefore, have postdated the **Historia.**[23] Furthermore, he argued that the *Roman de Brut* also exhibited a similar, yet distinct, approach which, according to Leckie, could not have arisen independently but must represent an attempt to modify the Variant.[24] Leckie, then, upheld Caldwell's conclusion that the Variant was composed before 1155. Since he had rejected Caldwell's argument that the Variant was earlier than the vulgate, Leckie preferred to view the First Variant as a later recension compiled by an unknown redactor (working at some time between 1138 and the early 1150s).

The diverse and contradictory nature of these various hypotheses serves to underline the great difficulties with which questions about the date, authorship, and purpose of the First Variant version present us. Indeed, none of the views set out above is beyond criticism. Hammer's comparison of the vulgate and Variant texts was far from comprehensive, while his pronouncements—such as they were—on the date and authorship of the Variant were nowhere supported by rigorous argument. Caldwell's comparison of the Variant with the *Roman de Brut* was more thorough, but he offered no real evidence for his assertion that the undeniable parallels between the two texts demonstrated that Wace had relied on the Variant version, rather than vice versa. Similarly, his arguments in favour of the priority of the Variant over the vulgate fell far short—at least in the form in which they were published—of conclusive proof; furthermore, Caldwell made no attempt to resolve the serious difficulties which this theory engendered. Gallais, on the other hand, compared vulgate, Variant, and the *Roman de Brut* with great care, but his examination was nevertheless incomplete, being based only on the Arthurian section of the texts (which is precisely the part of Wace's poem which makes most use of the vulgate ***Historia*** and thus considerably clouds the exact nature of the relationship of the *Roman de Brut* and the Variant text). The suspicion must also be entertained that Gallais's investigation may have been prejudiced by the desire to safeguard Wace's claims to literary originality. Keller's comparison of the *Roman de Brut* and the Variant was also incomplete, since in his case it was limited to their treatment of names—an area of notorious difficulty because of the vagaries of mediaeval scribal practice. Further, his identification of Gaimar's 'bon livere de Oxenforde' with the Variant version and his assertion that the latter, compiled by Archdeacon Walter, represents Geoffrey's source is wild speculation. Even Leckie's careful and otherwise cogent arguments about the literary-historical relationship of the vulgate, the Variant, and Wace's *Roman de Brut* are based only on parts of those texts, rather than on their entirety.

The paramount objection is that none of the critics has examined all aspects of the problem comprehensively in order to achieve a solution compatible with all the available evidence. Such a comprehensive approach must be directed to answering three crucial questions. Was the Variant version composed before or after the vulgate? Was the Variant written by Geoffrey himself or by another author? And was the Variant used by Wace, or does it rather reflect the influence of the *Roman de Brut* and consequently post-date that text? Clearly, the first two questions can, since conclusive external evidence is lacking, only be addressed after the Variant and vulgate texts have been compared more carefully than has so far been the case; moreover, the results of such a comparison may also provide additional important evidence, useful in conducting a much needed reinvestigation of the relationship of the Variant to Wace's *Roman de Brut*.

With these aims in view, the vulgate and Variant texts have been compared systematically and the results set out in Table I. However, before these results and their broader implications can be examined, a number of definitions must be made. Let us begin with the terms 'vulgate' and 'Variant' themselves. 'Vulgate' is here used to denote that version of the ***Historia Regum Britannie*** found in all editions prior to that of Hammer (irrespective, that is, of minor variations in the dedication of the ***Historia***); in the present work, the vulgate is quoted from the text of the Bern manuscript, already edited in this series, which is, except in point of some small details, essentially a representative of the standard version of the ***Historia***.[25] By the term 'Variant version' is meant the uncontaminated text printed here, as opposed to that of Hammer's edition which drew heavily on a manuscript interpolated with the vulgate.[26] In the present edition, as in that of the Bern manuscript which preceded it, the text has been divided into the two hundred and eight chapters first used in the edition of Edmond Faral;[27] this permits a close, chapter-by-chapter comparison of the vulgate and Variant texts. . . .

Notes

1. *Geoffrey of Monmouth: Historia Regum Britanniae. A Variant Version* (henceforth referred to as *Variant Version*).

2. Hammer used this term because he had discovered another variant version, which he was editing at the time of his death; see Emanuel, 'Geoffrey of Monmouth's *Historia Regum Britanniae:* a Second Variant Version'.

3. Hammer, *Variant Version*, pp. 8-12.

4. *Ibid.*, p. 19.

5. Caldwell, 'Wace's *Roman de Brut*'; Wace's poem is edited by Arnold, *Roman de Brut.*

6. Ulbrich, 'Über das Verhältnis'; Waldner, *Waces Brut;* Arnold, 'Wace et l'*Historia Regum Britanniae*'.

7. Houck, *Sources*, pp. 215-60 (especially 228-37).

8. 'Wace's *Roman de Brut*', pp. 680-81.

9. *Roman de Brut,* lines 14863-6, 'Puis que Deus incarnatiun / Prist pur nostre redemptiun / Mil e cent cinquante e cinc anz / Fist mestre Wace cest romanz'.

10. Wright, *Historia Regum Britannie,* I.x.

11. 'The use of sources'; it is regrettable that Caldwell's paper was published in abstract form which did not set out his arguments in full.

12. Parry and Caldwell, 'Geoffrey of Monmouth', p. 87.

13. Wright, *Historia Regum Britannie,* I.xii-xvi.

14. 'La *Variant Version*'.

15. *Ibid.*, p. 4.

16. *Ibid.*, pp. 4-30.

17. 'Wace et Geoffrey de Monmouth'.

18. 'Wace's *Roman de Brut*', p. 682.

19. Edited by Bell, *L'Estoire* (see pp. li-lii on the date of Gaimar's poem).

20. *L'Estoire,* lines 6442 and 6458-9. The problems posed by Gaimar's two sources are discussed by Bell, pp. liii-liv; for a counter-argument that Gaimar refers very imprecisely to only one source (Geoffrey's *Historia*), see Tatlock, *The Legendary History,* pp. 453-5.

21. Wright, *Historia Regum Britannie,* I.xvii-viii.

22. *The Passage.*

23. *Ibid.*, pp. 102-9 (also 25-8).

24. *Ibid.*, pp. 109-17.

25. For a discussion of the points of difference, see Wright, *Historia Regum Britannie,* I. liv-ix.

26. See below, p. xcii.

27. *La Légende,* III.63-301.

Antonio L. Furtado (essay date 1991)

SOURCE: "Geoffrey of Monmouth: A Source of the Grail Stories," *Quondam et Futurus*, Vol. 1, No. 1, Spring, 1991, pp. 1-14.

[*In the following essay, Furtado concludes that the Elidurus episode in Geoffrey's narrative, or at least a related document or tradition, served as the source for later versions of the legend of the Holy Grail.*]

The most influential version of the Grail story, the first to introduce the term "grail" (a deep wide dish, a platter), is the *Perceval—li Contes del Graal* of Chrétien de Troyes. Chrétien died before concluding the work, and one can only conjecture the kind of ending he had in mind. Nor did he have the chance to review what he had written, in order to eliminate inconsistencies. To make these matters even more controversial, he declared at the outset: "That is the Story of the Grail, found in the book the count [Philip of Alsace, Count of Flanders] gave him" (Chrétien 375). Although the identity of this book is not known, one possibility is the Welsh *Peredur* in *The Mabinogion* (217-57), in which case the name Perceval would be a form of Peredur, freely adapted to French diction. But Perceval dates from the twelfth century while Peredur was not put in written form until the thirteenth century.

Several authors, although agreeing that the two works are related, find that there was also an influence of a different sort, whereby *Peredur* incorporated elements extracted from *Perceval.* The prevailing opinion is that both might come from a common previous source, a "proto-*Peredur.*" There is a strong possibility that this "proto-*Peredur*" can be identified as the Elidurus episode found in Geoffrey of Monmouth's twelfth century **Historia regum Britanniae,** a work which predates Chrétien's *Perceval.*

Because Geoffrey was the author who initiated (or at least gave a decisive impetus to) the literary body which comprises the Arthurian legend, the hypothesis seems rather natural. The plausibility of the hypothesis increases when one recalls that a character by the name of Peredurus participates in the episode, which would have occurred before the Roman invasion. The transposition of the story to the time of Arthur may have been encouraged by the fact that both Peredurus and several other participants in the same episode are in a sense "resurrected" by Geoffrey, with their names altered to a larger or lesser degree, to appear in a plenary court called by King Arthur. Of course, Chrétien knew Latin, for he states at the beginning of *Cligès* that he translated certain works of Ovid; perhaps he also read Wace's French adaptation of the material which Geoffrey wrote.

Although a detailed discussion of the texts of Chrétien and the Welsh *Peredur* proves interesting, a comparison of the basic schema of the most important scene of the Grail story with the episode from Geoffrey's book suffices to indicate the corresponding features of the two works. The fundamental scene of the Grail story, considering elements common to both versions (Chrétien's and the Welsh *Peredur*) can be summarized as follows:

> A knight is invited by a king to visit his castle. As the knight enters, he is attended by the king's servants and later led to the king's presence. The king appears to be ill. In the castle, there is a mystery whose manifestations are two objects that pass by in front of the guest as they are being taken to a room—a bleeding spear and a platter (grail). Attached to this mystery there is a question on which the fortune of the kingdom depends, "Who is served from the grail?" Another related question is "Why does the spear bleed?" The guest fails to ask the questions.

In each of the two versions there is an element that is missing in the other one. In Chrétien, the first question is answered later in the story: *the grail serves a second king, who is kept hidden in the room whereto the objects are carried.* In the same part of the text is the information that the contents of the platter is a consecrated wafer. In the Welsh *Peredur,* the contents of the platter is a severed head, in which case the second question has an obvious answer: *the spear bleeds because it was used to kill the knight whose head is carried in the platter.*

However, the theme of the severed head is not altogether absent from Chrétien's version. As he leaves the castle, Perceval meets a damsel holding the decapitated body of a knight. The damsel reproaches Perceval for his failure to ask the questions, saying that had he asked them the king would be healed, the kingdom would not suffer a series of calamities, and Perceval himself would reap a large profit. Another damsel, of ugly appearance, explains later what such calamities are:

> And do you know the fate of the king who will hold no land or be healed of his wounds? Through him ladies will lose their husbands, lands will be laid waste, maidens left orphaned and helpless, and many knights will perish. . . .
>
> (Chrétien 436)

In addition, Chrétien has a carving dish which passes after the grail, which some critics see as the instrument of decapitation. These two elements, the hidden king and the severed head, are essential components of the basic schema of the castle scene. Most texts, of course, refer to the king who appears to be ill as the maimed king.

In the **Historia regum Britanniae,** Geoffrey of Monmouth tells the following story which happened before the Roman invasion.

> When Elidurus had been king for some five years, he came upon his deposed brother when he was hunting in the Forest of Calaterium. Archgallo (the deposed brother, who had reigned before Elidurus) had wandered about through certain of the neighboring kingdoms, seeking help so that he might recover his lost honor. He had found no support there and, coming to the point where he could no longer bear the poverty which had overtaken him, he had returned to Britain with a retinue reduced to ten knights. He was travelling through the above-named forest, seeking those whom he had in earlier times called friends, when his brother Elidurus came upon him unexpectedly. The moment he saw him, Elidurus ran up to him, embraced him, and kissed him repeatedly. When he had spent some time lamenting the misery to which Archgallo was reduced, Elidurus took him to one of his cities called Alclud and

there *he hid him in his own bedroom.* He *pretended to be ill* and sent messengers through the kingdom for a whole year to request the princes under his jurisdiction to come to visit him. They all assembled in the town where he lay and he ordered them each in turn to come into his bedroom, saying that if they came in a crowd the noise of so many voices would make his head ache. Each believed his story and obeyed his order, entering his house one after the other. Elidurus ordered his servants to seize each man as he came in and *to cut off his head if he would not swear allegiance* a second time to his brother Archgallo. Elidurus submitted them all in turn to this treatment and by *playing on their terror* reconciled them all to Archgallo. When this oath had been ratified, Elidurus led Archgallo to York and there he took the crown from his own head and placed it on that of his brother. It was for this reason that he was called the Dutiful (*pius* in the Latin original), because of the brotherly love which he had shown towards Archgallo.

(Geoffrey 103-04; Faral 3:122-23 [italics mine])

This closely corresponds to the basic schema, besides offering an explanation of the mystery. What is missing is the "dramatization" of the scene, in which the bleeding spear and the severed head pass by in front of a guest. One can readily imagine that this would be a most efficient way to intimidate each knight, showing him what had happened with one of his companions. This solemn procession occurs in one form or another in all versions of the Grail story and any reader would consider it indispensable to establish the fairy atmosphere that pervades the tale, even though one may say that its lack is not surprising in Geoffrey, intent on keeping the sober style of a chronicler (but see the Cadwallo episode later in this text).

Of even greater significance, one notes, is the origin of the fundamental question on which the future of the kingdom depends. "Whom swears the grail to serve?" later becomes "Who is served from the grail?" And as it was in the basic schema, the expected answer is the king hidden in the room. In the Welsh story the guest is Peredur, later revealed to be a nephew of the king. In Geoffrey, Peredurus is a brother of Elidurus and Archgallo. Though at first glance Geoffrey's episode and the Welsh tale seem to have more points of contact—the name of the hero itself, the severed head—one should note that some aspects seem to have been absorbed in Chrétien's story without going through the Welsh *Peredur,* especially the existence of the hidden king who should be (somehow) served.

But there is another rather curious point of contact. Chrétien does not name the kings but he names another character whom Perceval had met before visiting the castle, who had, acting as some kind of tutor to the hero, advised him against asking questions. His name is Gornement de Gohort. On the other hand, Gorbonianus is in Geoffrey the name of a deceased brother of Peredurus; also in Geoffrey, a Gorbonian map Goit is mentioned as one of the knights who come to King Arthur's plenary court. The similarity of their names is clear; still more significant is the similarity of their roles as models of wisdom and virtue.

This plenary court occasions the gathering of several other characters involved in the same episode, which probably facilitated the transposition of the story to Arthurian times. Besides Gorbonianus, other names that appear, with rather simple alterations, are Peredur map Peridur (or map Eridur in Faral's edition), Arthgualchar (Arthgal) of Gueirensis (now Warwick), Jugein of Leicester, and Morvid of Gloucester. Jugein is probably Ingenius, another brother of Peredurus (there were five brothers altogether). Morvid is Morvidus, father of the five brothers and descendant of Ebraucus (Evrawc, founder of York, Alclud, and the castle of Mount Agned, also called—by Geoffrey—the Maidens' Castle and the Dolorous Mountain).

The names examined here are even more ancient than Geoffrey's work, for they already appear in a part of the *Historia Britonum* assigned to the tenth century (cf. Eugein, Arthgal, Garbaniaun, Peretur together with Eleuther, and Moriud in Faral 3:52-55, lists 3, 5, 10, 12, and 20). However, most of these persons belong to separate genealogies and the episode itself does not appear anywhere in the book, which suggests that Geoffrey may have fabricated it. In addition, these names appear again in later Grail stories, with greater or lesser alterations. Among such versions must be mentioned, besides the "continuations" to Chrétien's *Perceval,* the cycle of Robert de Boron, the vast *Prose Lancelot* compilation which includes a *Quest of the Holy Grail,* the *Perlesvaus,* the *Parzival* of Wolfram von Eschenbach, and *Le Morte Darthur* of Sir Thomas Malory (see Marx, especially the Appendix [317-88]), for well presented summaries of the relevant part. In some versions, Mordrain (Morvid?) is one of the characters involved in a fight against an ogre by the Irish Sea. Garlon (Archgallo?), remaining "invisible" (hidden), kills several knights; Garlon is a brother of Pelles or Pellam or Pellinor (Pius Elidurus?), the maimed king. The name Eliezer, a son of Pelles in one story, may also be related to Elidurus. In all versions the character corresponding to Perceval has some kind of family relationship with almost all the others, who are in turn related among themselves in different and often confusing ways.

An additional set of names was introduced in these post-Chrétien stories, perhaps borrowed from Geoffrey's account of Cadwallo's reign. The main addition is Pellitus (Pellit or Pelliz in Wace), a Spanish magician serving the Saxon King Edwin. Pellitus is killed by Brian, Cadwallo's nephew, with "an iron rod . . . with a point at the end" (Geoffrey 275), an object quite similar to a spear. Besides, in this death scene an object similar to a platter is also paraded, namely a basin (*pelvis,* in Latin) where Brian's sister carries water to a queen. All this is very closely reproduced by the episode, found in Malory and in his French sources, in which Balin wounds Pellam with a "dolorous stroke"; furthermore Balin is accompanied by a damsel who offers her blood in a silver dish to cure the lady of the castle. Then Brian and Pellitus would correspond to Balin and Pellam. The genealogy of Cadwallo and of Brittany's King Salomon may also be significant, including for instance Belin (nearly identical to the name Balin) and

Alan, which recalls Alain, the hero's father in the *Perlesvaus*. The presence of a "Salomon" is itself significant, it we remember that the hero of the *Quest of the Holy Grail,* Galahad, was believed to descend from the biblical King Solomon.

Both Chrétien and some writers after him use the denomination "rich fisher king" which, in Chrétien, clearly refers to the maimed king, to whom as said before he never assigns a proper name. In fact, there is at least one rich fisher king in Celtic tradition: Gwyddno, who—in the story of Taliesin—was a king and owed his wealth to a fishing net that was one of the wonders of Britain (Markale). But what Chrétien tells to justify calling the maimed king a fisher looks rather contrived. In Geoffrey we find that Morvidus (like Mordrain) had tried to kill a monster coming from the Irish Sea but, after using his weapons in vain against the monster, it had devoured him as if he were a little fish—*velut pisciculum devoravit* (Faral 3:121). Would this episode explain, quite ironically indeed, the strange denomination passed to his son?

A perhaps more acceptable (but still not entirely convincing) explanation is brought to mind by one of the many forms of the maimed king's name used elsewhere: *Pellinor* (Marx 132; *La Queste* 288 n209). On the one hand Pellinor recalls Pius Elidurus (or *Peridur*); on the other hand it recalls *pescheor* the old French word for fisher. If this is true, Chrétien's fisher king denomination may be simply a misunderstanding caused by some variant spelling. In addition, tracing its origin to the name Pellitus would imply that Chrétien also took elements from Cadwallo's episode to compose his tale.

A brief digression: Cadwallo's episode was almost certainly borrowed from Bede (85, 116, 135). According to Bede, King Edwin had no Spanish magician in his court, but he did have a Christian bishop, Paulinus. This Paulinus had come to England together with the future archbishop Mellitus. It is more than likely that the sinister Pellitus resulted from the combination of these saintly men: *Paulinus + Mellitus,* motivated by Geoffrey's hatred of the Saxons. Moreover, Bede also reports an attempt to kill King Edwin himself (not his "magician," therefore), which did not entirely fail, since two of his men died and Edwin remained ill for some time, having been wounded with a poisoned dagger. All this, except the poisoned dagger, is confirmed in *The Anglo-Saxon Chronicle* (25).

Let us recall that according to Geoffrey the five sons of Morvidus are Gorbonianus, Archgallo, Elidurus, Peredurus, and Ingenius. Attention has been given here to each of them except Ingenius, who plays an important role in what follows. Allowing the imagination to complement Geoffrey's tale, one might suggest that Peredurus would have been one of the guests of the two kings in the Grail castle. Perhaps because he did not pose the expected questions, he was spared both being sacrificed and swearing obedience to Archgallo. With this interpretation, the advice of staying silent, given by Gornemant, would have the pur-

pose of protecting the hero, whose mother had kept him ignorant not only of the risks of chivalry but, above all, of his being a candidate for such a dangerous throne. Returning to Geoffrey:

> After a time he [Archgallo] fell into a coma; and when he died he was buried in the town of Leicester. Thereupon Elidurus was restored to his former honour and made King once more; but while he was following virtuously in the footsteps of his eldest brother Gorbonianus, his two remaining brothers, *Ingenius and Peredurus, collected an army* together from all sides and marched forward to do battle with him. The two were victorious; they seized Elidurus and shut him up in a tower in the town of Trinovantum (now London), setting a guard to watch over him. Then *they divided his kingdom in two.*
>
> (104)

In other words: after the first visit to the Grail castle, done when he was not sufficiently prepared, Peredurus returns once more. And now he comes in the company of a brother—Ingenius—bringing an army with them.

Looking at the Welsh *Peredur* and at the *Perceval,* we see that this brother has been replaced by one of Arthur's chief knights: Gawain (Gwalchmei, in the Welsh *Peredur*). The story gains interest with the substitution, but loses the obvious motive for the participation of this second character in the fight—the desire of the two brothers to share the kingdom to which they are entitled as members of the royal family. With this motive reestablished, we understand the existence of two heroes in the story and can abandon the supposition of a few critics that the long section reserved by Chrétien for Gawain was a separate story unduly incorporated later. The greater importance of Peredur/Perceval might come from Peredurus's having assumed the whole kingdom with the death of Ingenius.

In the Welsh *Peredur*, the army called by Peredur and Gwalchmei consists of King Arthur and his men, and the fight is against the witches of Gloucester, who were responsible for the king's illness and for the death of one of his sons (whose head was that one shown on the platter). Those interested in the anthropological point of view will note that the primitive mentality associates the potency of the king with the fertility of the land and is accustomed to regard witches as maleficent spirits which must be destroyed to free the reproductive powers of plants and animals (Frazer 753), so as to magically heal the king and regenerate the "waste land." The story ends abruptly with the defeat of the witches.

Chrétien died leaving the *Perceval* unfinished. But almost at the end of his work he includes a call to an army, consisting of Arthur and his knights, made by Gawain simply to have them watch Gawain's single combat against the knight Guiromelant. Chrétien's continuators added an outcome where Perceval kills the knight who wounded the maimed king (causing his infirmity, which could be healed only through vengeance), and assumes the kingdom after his death. This enemy—Partinal—might have been created from a character named Partholoim, reported in Geoffrey to have started to populate Ireland as ordered by an ancestor of Morvidus. In versions coming after Chrétien, the maimed king does not die, retiring instead to a monastery, thus reminding us of the fate of Elidurus who is confined in a tower after his defeat.

The culmination of the evolution of the Grail legend was Chrétien's decision not to place the severed head on the platter (grail). In the empty grail one could then introduce different things, satisfying different interpretations. The contents could be a consecrated wafer to be taken to the hidden king, as indicated by a hermit later in Chrétien's tale itself. Or it could be Christ's blood, in versions with a deeper Christian orientation. Instead of a platter or a cup, the grail could be a stone, as in the *Parzival* of Wolfram von Eschenbach, or one of the famous Celtic cauldrons, which magically nourish the guests or resurrect the dead.

The omission of the severed head seems motivated by the more refined tastes and costumes of the place and time when Chrétien wrote. Also he may have regarded as "barbarous" the attitude of the Pius Elidurus in his bloody ruse to force the princes to submit, as well as the struggle for power by Peredurus and Ingenius leading to the imprisonment of the same Elidurus, their own brother. The pretended illness of Elidurus was thus transformed into an authentic one (though the trick with simulated wounds curiously emerges in the confrontation of Gawain with Greoreas) and one of the missions of Perceval is now to relieve the sufferings of the maimed king, not only by healing his wounds but even by assuming the power in his stead.

The persistent nobility of Geoffrey's narrative, echoed in other versions, came from the generous loyalty of the brothers, which appears as a silent solidarity between the maimed king and the hidden king. This feeling contrasts with the theme of ingratitude that characterizes the episode of King Leir in the same book. Both episodes reappear in later literature, with *King Lear* in Shakespeare and *Artegal and Elidure* in Wordsworth. As the legend evolved, the medieval theme of the chivalric quest became dominant. The quest may be a pagan search for a talisman or a more spiritual strife towards self-improvement, a notion greatly moving to the religious mind, a concept amply recognized by modern psychology (Jung).

Into this framework of the story, represented by the basic schema and the outcome, various other "adventures" have been assimilated. Most of them are in defense of ladies and damsels left helpless by the mysterious calamity that devastates the country, causing the death of many knights whose fault was, if we are right, to have refused their allegiance to the hidden king. Though they enliven the tale, these adventures do not always seem well integrated into the main thread of the narrative. In general, they mark the preparation (or initiation or purification) of the two heroes—Perceval and Gawain—so that they may succeed in their second visit to the castle.

The basic ingredients of the Grail story, then, correspond to an episode recounted in the pseudo-history of Britain by Geoffrey of Monmouth. The authors of the various subsequent versions either based their narratives directly on this episode or had access to some related oral tradition or document apart from Geoffrey's work.

The strongest argument to associate the episode with the Grail story is, of course, the presence of a leading character with the same name—Peredur(us)—which occurs in the Welsh story. A comparison of the episode with what is here termed the basic schema, along with attention to the outcome of the story in Geoffrey, reinforces the association. The major missing element—the solemn procession where the grail and the bleeding lance are shown—is implicit in the episode as it appears in Geoffrey; but another episode in the ***Historia*** may have inspired it, namely that of Brian and his sister displaying an iron rod and a basin throughout King Edwin's court.

However, even if the hypothesis is true, many problems about the genesis and transformation of the story remain unsolved. In particular, what was the origin of the episode told by Geoffrey? On the other hand, if the episode is of his invention, was his source of inspiration what was happening in England amidst the anarchy of the period during which the book was written? One recalls that Geoffrey dedicated his work to Robert of Gloucester who chose to support claimants to the succession after Henry I (first Stephen and later Matilda) rather than assert his own claim, just as Elidurus demanded that the princes swear allegiance to his brother Archgallo rather than to Elidurus himself. Although too late to influence Geoffrey's ***Historia,*** the accession of Henry II, who like the Grail hero attempted to obtain the throne twice (the first time when he was only fourteen years old, and, on his second victorious attempt, was merely made Stephen's heir instead of immediately replacing him), was crucial to later redactions of the Grail narrative (Warren 33). Ultimately, the Elidurus episode in Geoffrey constitutes the basic narrative which later inspired a broad spectrum of symbolic meaning and archetypal themes: the legend of the Holy Grail.

Works Cited

The Anglo Saxon Chronicle. Trans. G. N. Garmonsway. London: Dent, 1978.

Bede. *Historia ecclesiastica gentis Anglorum.* Trans. Leo Sherley-Price. Harmondsworth: Penguin, 1986.

Chrétien de Troyes. *Arthurian Romances.* Trans. D. D. R. Owen. London: Dent, 1987.

Faral, Edmond. "La Légende arthurienne." Librairie Ancienne Honore Champion. Paris: Champion, 1929.

Frazer, James G. *The Golden Bough.* New York: Macmillan, 1956.

Geoffrey of Monmouth. *Historia regum Britanniae.* Trans. Lewis Thorpe. Harmondsworth: Penguin, 1984.

Jung, Emma, and Marie-Louise von Franz. *The Grail Legend.* Trans. Andrea Dykes. London: Hodder and Stoughton, 1972.

The Mabinogion. Ed. Jeffrey Gantz. Harmondsworth: Penguin, 1987.

Markale, Jean. *L'Épopee celtique en Bretagne.* Paris: Payot, 1975.

Marx, Jean. *La Légende arthurienne et le Graal.* Paris: Presses Universitaires de France, 1952.

La Queste del Saint Graal. Ed. Albert Pauphilet. Paris: Librairie Ancienne Honore Champion. Paris: Champion, 1923.

Wace, Robert. *Le Roman de Brut.* Ed. Ivor Arnold. Société des anciens textes Français. Paris, 1938.

Warren, W. L. *Henry II.* Berkeley: U of California P. 1983.

Acknowledgement: I am grateful to Henry H. Peyton, III, whose careful editing has considerably improved the text.

Brynley F. Roberts (essay date 1991)

SOURCE: "Geoffrey of Monmouth, *Historia Regum Britanniae* and *Brut y Brenhinedd,*" in *The Arthur of the Welsh: The Arthurian Legend in Medieval Welsh Literature,* edited by Rachel Bromwich *et al.,* University of Wales Press, 1991, pp. 97-116.

[*In the following essay, Roberts considers the conception, planning, and design of* The History of the Kings of Britain.]

The early history of the Britons appears to have been Geoffrey of Monmouth's sole literary or 'scholarly' interest, inasmuch that the two, perhaps three, works associated with his name are narratives of pre-Saxon Britain and of the English conquest. His earliest book was probably the *Prophetiae Merlini* which seems to have been issued a few years before his major work, *Historia Regum Britanniae.* The *Prophetiae* are incorporated into the *Historia* as Book VII, but as this section retains its own dedication to Alexander, Bishop of Lincoln, to whom no copies of the complete *Historia* are dedicated, it would appear to have had its own separate identity. The *Prophetiae* do not refer to the death of Henry I in 1135 but that the text was known about that date is shown by Ordericus Vitalis's quotations from it, referred to as a certain 'libellus Merlini', in his *Historia Ecclesiastica, c.* 1135-6. Nevertheless, it is clear that the *Prophetiae,* which Geoffrey claimed to have translated from the British tongue, were intended to be part of the complete *Historia.* This section has its own development and refers to events in the *Historia,* but the way in which it is placed at the central point in Geoffrey's narrative suggests strongly that it was part of his original literary conception (see below p. 103). Geoffrey says as much in his Preface and Dedication, for after describing Vorti-

gern's flight to Wales and Merlin Ambrosius's explanation of the sinking foundations of his new fortress, he claims that he had not yet reached this point in his narrative when he realized that the prophet Merlin was the object of a great deal of general curiosity and a number of acquaintances, including Bishop Alexander, urged him to interrupt his work to prepare a Latin translation of the *Prophecies.* This 'libellus Merlini' was in circulation *c.* 1135 but it is such an integral part of the *Historia* that there is little doubt that the latter had been well mapped-out and was in the process of being written by then. *Historia Regum Britanniae*[1] had appeared by January 1139, for in his *Epistola ad Warinum* Henry of Huntingdon says that Robert of Torigni showed him a copy at the Abbey of Bec at that time.[2] Henry's evident surprise and his unexpected pleasure at coming across 'librum grandem Gaufridi Arturi' which gave him the information on the pre-Roman British kings which he had sought, suggest that the book had been newly published, sometime late in 1138.[3] Geoffrey's last work, *c.* 1150, was a hexameter poem *Vita Merlini* which claims to continue the story of Merlin and to relate some of his other prophecies. In spite of Geoffrey's attempts to harmonize the portraits of the two Merlins—that of the *Historia* and the later figure of the *Vita*—what becomes clear is that the latter corresponds most closely to the Welsh Myrddin[4] and that the former, while owing much to Ambrosius, the fatherless boy of the *Historia Brittonum,* is largely Geoffrey's creation.

Geoffrey's work, in its overt subject matter and orientation, can be claimed to be Welsh, but there is little or no evidence that he himself is to be regarded as Welsh or Cambro-Norman, in contrast with, for example, Giraldus Cambrensis whom one may regard as being Welsh not simply by domicile but also partly by descent. Geoffrey was known to his contemporaries as Galfridus Artur(us), two names said to be more common amongst Bretons than Welsh in the twelfth century.[5] In the *Historia* he refers to himself as Galfridus Monemutensis, 'of Monmouth'.

The castle and lordship of Monmouth had been established in 1067 by William FitzOsbern, Earl of Hereford. In 1075 they passed to Wihenoc, from Dol in Brittany, who left the castle to his nephew William FitzBaderon while he established at Monmouth a priory under the jurisdiction of the Abbey of St Florent de Saumur.[6] Geoffrey shows some familiarity in his work with the topography of this part of the March, and the role of Caerleon both as an episcopal seat and as Arthur's court in the *Historia* may be the fruits of a lively historical imagination playing upon the visible remains of an imposing Roman city. It is possible that Geoffrey's family were among those Bretons who had been such a significant element in William I's forces, many of whom settled in south-east Wales.[7] Geoffrey's subject was the early history of the Britons who were the ancestors not only of the Welsh but also of Cornishmen and Bretons. But the later history of the Welsh, though the essential theme of the *Historia,* was held in scant respect by him. For when Maximianus and his noble troops had emigrated to Armorica, there to establish Little Britain, there was left in Britain a mere remnant of frightened, ineffectual soldiery, so despised that the crown of Britain could be refused by the Breton king even when offered as a gift. The greatest of all the kings of Britain has a Breton ancestry and Arthur's most glorious soldiers are the Bretons. Hoelus, King of Brittany, alone comes to Arthur's Whitsun crown-wearing ceremony with his own sub-kings and throughout the latter part of the *Historia* Brittany is portrayed as a refuge where is to be found the true essence of Britain's former glory. Geoffrey's 'racial sympathies'[8] may be inferred from his work, but nevertheless there is no direct evidence of his Breton antecedents. The place given to south-west Britain and Brittany in the *Historia* may reflect the orientation of some of Geoffrey's source material rather than a personal predilection;[9] nor must it be forgotten that contemporary political considerations would have made it difficult for any author to present a favourable view of Welsh skill-at-arms and nobility to a Norman audience and to patrons at court. That branch of the ancient Britons who had aligned themselves so firmly with the Normans were better placed to express old British virtues. To what degree these Breton families might have been channels of Breton culture and traditions is open to question. From the tenth century the Breton aristocracy, even in Basse-Bretagne, had been strongly influenced by French culture and were bilingual French-Breton, or even monolingual French.[10] The bearing of a Breton name might frequently cloak a Normanized family.

Nothing is known of Geoffrey's early career. He signed as a witness in six charters in Oxford between 1129 and 1151. Some of these suggest an association with the secular College of St George and as Geoffrey twice uses the title *magister* he may have been a canon of the college and a teacher there. Three of these charters also name Walter, Archdeacon of Oxford, who was Provost of the college, and it is significant that the last of these charters also names Robert de Chesney, Bishop of Lincoln, a former canon of St George's to whom Geoffrey dedicated his *Vita Merlini.* The College of St George came to an end in 1148. In February 1152 Geoffrey was ordained priest at Westminster and consecrated Bishop of St Asaph a week later. There is no evidence that he ever visited his diocese. In 1153 he was a witness to the agreement between Stephen and Henry and the Welsh Chronicle of the Princes records his death in 1154, *recte* 1155.[11] It would appear, therefore, that he was born towards the end of the eleventh century, presumably in Monmouth, that the greater part of his life was spent at Oxford, and that preferment came to him only late in life.

At Oxford Geoffrey would have been in the mainstream of the intellectual and cultural life of the day. The university had not yet developed but colleges like St George's were already centres of learning and education and the city itself was an important crossroads which attracted learned visitors and political figures. Oxford was a centre of historical enquiry and writing, in the life of which Geoffrey would have shared. Alexander, Bishop of Lincoln (Oxford lay within his diocese) had already proved himself an in-

telligent and active patron of Henry of Huntingdon, and he was later to request from Geoffrey a version of the *Prophecies of Merlin.* Another of Geoffrey's patrons was Robert, Earl of Gloucester, who had supported William of Malmesbury and would continue to do so. Geoffrey dedicated his *Historia* to men who were both politically powerful and proven patrons of historical works, and there is little doubt that Oxford was an important element in his literary development.[12] Geoffrey's awareness of the gaps in British history which previous historians had failed to fill is one element in the motivation for the writing of the *Historia,* as he himself suggests in his epilogue where he leaves the kings of the Saxons to Henry and to William but warns them to say nothing of the later princes of Wales (a task which he leaves to Caradog of Llancarfan) as they did not have his unique source. By the twelfth century the Anglo-Normans, no longer conquerors in a strange land, had acquired an interest in the history of their new country and they had become conscious of the gap in their knowledge of the inheritance into which they were beginning to enter. Their claim to an English inheritance had from the first been given historical justification, but it was generally accepted that Angles and Saxons were themselves comparatively recent—and indeed pagan—newcomers to Britain whose claim to sovereignty was that of conquest.[13] The period of British, pre-Saxon rule was truly a dark age as far as historical evidence was in the question. Henry of Huntingdon's explanation in the letter to Warinus of the reason that he begins his account with Julius Caesar omitting what may have lain before,

> Respondeo igitur tibi quod nec voce nec scripto hortum temporum saepissime notitiam quaerens invenire potui
>
> *(My reply is therefore that in spite of very frequent enquiries I have not been able to obtain any information on these times either orally or in writing)*

is echoed by Geoffrey in his Preface

> in mirum contuli quod . . . nichil de regibus qui ante incarnationem Christi inhabitauerant, nichil etiam de Arturo ceterisque compluribus qui post incarnationem successerunt repperissem.
>
> *(It seems remarkable to me that I have not found anything about the kings who dwelt here before the Incarnation of Christ, nor anything even about Arthur and the many others who succeeded him after the Incarnation.)*

The lack of historical evidence for pre-Saxon Britain was an old problem which had been addressed in the ninth-century *Historia Brittonum* and by twelfth-century writers, and Geoffrey of Monmouth, cogitating on a possible theme which would be attractive to patrons, may have resolved, with an audacity too blatant to be doubted, to overcome the problem by claiming for himself a unique source which made good the deficiencies in the narratives of Gildas, Bede, and 'Nennius' of the early history of the Island of Britain. Geoffrey provided the book which his audience, lay and learned, had long wished to read. At the root of the popularity of the *Historia* is not only its lively narration of events but Geoffrey's recognition of the demands of his contemporaries and compatriots.[14]

He claimed for the *Historia* a privileged status in that his source which he had simply translated, he said in his Preface, was a certain

> Britannici sermonis librum uetustissimum qui a Bruto primo rege Britonum usque ad Cadualadrum filium Caduallonis actus omnium continue et ex ordine perpulcris orationibus proponebat.
>
> (*very ancient book in the British language which set out in a consecutive and orderly fashion the acts of all (the kings) from Brutus, the first king of the Britons, down to Cadwaladrus, the son of Cadwallo, in a style of great beauty.*)

In his epilogue he referred again to this book presented to him by Walter, Archdeacon of Oxford, and which had been brought by him *ex Britannia.*

The *Historia,* however, cannot be a mere translation, even in the extended medieval sense. Almost every study of the work reveals its imaginative and creative use of a range of literary sources, the majority of which are in Latin, and it becomes increasingly clear that one of Geoffrey's most fruitful talents was his ability to create episodes and characters from a variety of disparate and unconnected elements. The firm narrative structure of the *Historia* and a developed authorial view of British history further mark this as an individually composed narrative.[15] The reference to the authoritative source may, therefore, be regarded as an example of the 'old book' topos, but Walter, Archdeacon of Oxford, Provost of St George's, the *uir in oratoria arte atque in exoticis historiis eruditus,* and *in multis historiis peritissimo uiro* described by Geoffrey, whose words recall those of Henry of Huntingdon, *superlative rethoricus,* was real enough. Stripped of its status as the sole source and of the description of its style as *perpulcris orationibus,* there is nothing inherently impossible in the suggestion that Walter should have brought from Brittany a manuscript which contained native historical material relating to Brittany and south-west Britain. Genealogies and traditional history were the common stock of Breton and south-west British culture[16] and king-lists, annals, genealogies and the like may be what is intended by Geoffrey's *actus omnium [regum] continue et ex ordine.* The *liber uetustissimus* may have had a real existence as a source used by Geoffrey, not perhaps a major one in terms of its contribution to the complete *Historia* but significant, nevertheless, as a source of information on British traditional history and as one of the seeds from which sprang the concept of an *Historia Regum Brittaniae.*[17]

British traditional history, however, involved more than knowledge of a collection of 'facts', names and documents. The learned classes of medieval Wales, responsible for the organization and transmission of traditional learning in all its varied aspects, seem to have developed a coherent historiography of the Britons, the major themes of

which are central to the *Historia Regum Britanniae.* These are the myths (properly so-called) of the unity of the Island of Britain, symbolized by the Crown of London, the sign of a single kingship, of the loss of sovereignty to the English, and of national renewal and the restoration of British hegemony, expressed in prophetic terms. The concept of a succession of single kings, sovereigns of Britain, is at the root of Geoffrey's view of the path of British history. He accepted both the unity of Britain and the traditional divisions of the whole. The first king is Brutus and his sons are the eponymous founders of the three realms of Britain, England, Wales, Scotland (Locrinus of *Lloegr,* Kamber of *Cymru* and Albanactus of *yr Alban*), but there is also a suggestion that Cornwall was a recognized province, as in the older division found in the native tract *The Names of the Island of Britain,*[18] and it is given its own founder, Corineus. He also makes it clear that though there are three regions, there is only one kingdom. The eldest son Locrinus is the chief ruler (II.1), and the supremacy of the Crown of London is formally expressed later (II.1) when the elder Belinus is crowned King of the Island and rules England, Wales and Cornwall, leaving the North to the younger Brennius. Cassibellanus rules the whole island, though he has subordinate kings and powerful regional earls. Geoffrey stresses the unity and single kingship of Britain. In his first three books he presents pictures of the anarchy which stems from the denial of this concept. The jealousy of Ferreux and Porrex leads to civil war which is ended only by Dunuallo's accession, but history begins to repeat itself when his sons fall into the same snare and civil war is averted only by their mother's appeal. Geoffrey returns to this theme at the end of the *Historia,* for the final irrevocable breach between English and Welsh occurs when Edwin seeks permission to wear a crown in his own region. Caduallo's advisers are indignant: 'it was contrary to law and to the customs of their ancestors that an Island with one crown should be placed under the sway of two crowned heads' (XII.3). It is the upholding of this principle which leads to the final catastrophe, for the crown passes to Athelstan 'who was the first among them to be crowned King' (XII.19).

The idea of unity is implicit in the theme of loss and cannot be separated from it. This theme pervades the whole of the *Historia,* which is an account of the rise to greatness of a favoured people and their decline and loss of sovereignty. However glowing specific reigns may be, in Welsh eyes it is a rather sombre book in its final effect. The book opens with this statement: 'The Britons once occupied the land from sea to sea, before the others came. Then the vengeance of God overtook them because of their arrogance and they submitted to the Picts and Saxons' (I.2); the reader is allowed to view the working out of this vengeance but Geoffrey again states his theme clearly (XI.9, XII.6-7, 10, 12, 15, 17) as the book draws to an end. The theme of loss is deepened by the place Geoffrey gives to prophecy, which is used carefully to introduce significant characters and to point to the idea of greatness and loss. The representatives of the nation are introduced by prophecies, Brutus before his birth by Ascanius's magi, the greatness of his line by Diana. Arthur is first mentioned in Merlin's Prophecies and the final stages of the history are revealed by the Angelic Voice. ***Prophetiae Merlini,*** therefore, is not simply a virtuoso performance of abstruse nonsense. It is placed exactly in the centre of the book, immediately after that most significant event, the arrival of the Saxons who are the instruments of God's vengeance. History stands still for a moment while we seek its significance. We look ahead past Arthur, beyond the end of the ***Historia,*** to the very end of time. Merlin prophesies the greatness of Arthur, his victories against the Saxons and Romans. The spectre of civil war is revealed as the Red Dragon tears itself and the Saxons win sovereignty. The new conquerors are themselves bound in everlasting captivity by people in wood and iron suits, and so on to contemporary history. But the tone changes. Britons will arise, and Cadualadrus shall call Conanus; Welsh, Cornish, Bretons will drive out the foreigners and 'The Island shall be called by the name of Brutus'. Geoffrey derived this from Welsh prophecies, and here he has the themes of British unity and restitution at their simplest, the British alliance which even for the author of the tenth-century Welsh political prophecy, the poem *Armes Prydein,* had been 'long prophesied',[19] and which Geoffrey was to use again in ***Vita Merlini.*** The ***Prophetiae*** change their tone again and from here to the end they make use of animal symbolism and celestial portents, but it seems significant that the last clear, intelligible reference in these ***Prophetiae*** which set out the meaning of history, is to the restoration of British rule, sometime in an undefined future.[20]

The interweaving of these strands gives the narrative its thematic structure and confirms how integral to that structure is the section ***Prophetiae Merlini*** which must therefore have been conceived as part of the ***Historia*** though published earlier. The work achieves its cohesion in these themes, and through them Geoffrey invites his readers to discover the pattern of history and its significance for them. In this lies the paradox of the composition, for where contemporary historians had regretted the loss of material which would enable them to write the early history of Britain, Geoffrey resolved the problem by creating a spurious body of evidence but in so doing put on the mantle of a real historian. He learned to adopt (rather than to parody[21]) the methods of his contemporaries and he manipulated his sources effectively, but at a deeper level he perceived that history narrated and unfolded the fate of nations and that the historian laid before the people warnings from the past which they should heed. What binds the chronicle of events into a history is the moral principle that a nation reaps what is sown in past ages. Sometimes Geoffrey regards the righteous king and the rule of justice as the basis of national prosperity; in other sections he sees history in humanist terms as a progress of natural causes and consequences. The Britons are ruined by a combination of natural disasters and innate degeneracy, while the English, living more prudently, inevitably flourish. Geoffrey's final verdict (XII.19) is:

> Supradicta namque moralitas et fames atque consuetudinarium discidium in tantum coegerat populum super-

bum degenerare quod hostes longius arcere nequiuerant . . . At Saxones sapientius agentes, pacem et concordiam inter se habentes, agros colentes, ciuitates et opida aedificantes et sic abiecto dominio Britonum, iam toti Loegriae imperauerant duce Adelstano qui primus inter eos diadema portauit.

> (*Indeed, the plague about which I have told you, the famine and their own inveterate habit of civil discord had caused this proud people to degenerate so much that they were no longer able to keep their foes at bay. The Saxons, on the other hand, behaved more wisely. They kept peace and concord among themselves, they cultivated the fields, and they rebuilt the cities and castles. They threw off completely the dominion of the Britons and under their leader Adelstan, who was the first among them to be crowned King, they ruled over the whole of Loegria.*)

Discordia, treachery, plague and famine are all governed by Providence, and although Geoffrey reflects views of the civic virtues of the just ruler and the practical value of sensible husbandry, his underlying theme is that history is providential and that its pattern is part of God's purpose.[22] The Britons were called to high favour but they retain their position only to the extent that they are faithful to their calling. When they reject moral law and follow the paths of jealousy, arrogance and laxity, they suffer defeat and loss; and if they continue on this path they must forgo their lordship of the Island of Britain. This is the note struck in I.2 where the loss of British sovereignty is attributed to *ultione diuina propter ipsorum superueniente superbiam.* It recurs constantly, it is stated explicitly as the interpretation of history in XI.9, and is proven consistently for the reader in a series of examples throughout Book XII.

Geoffrey has planned his ***Historia*** on a broad canvas. He is equally attentive to the detail of the structure of his narrative. Crucial episodes are used to point towards later developments and significant characters are introduced unobtrusively but insistently. Modredus and Guenhuuara are casually named for the first time in the same paragraph in IX.9, linked in X.2, and their unfaithfulness to Arthur is reported immediately before the Battle of Camlan in X.12. Gorlois, the respected warrior, appears in VIII.6, he is a wise leader in VIII.18, and in the following chapter as the husband of Igerna he is the crucial figure, already established in a sympathetic light, in the account of the begetting of Arthur. The clearest example of the preparing of the ground before the significant appearance of an important character is Arthur himself. He is consistently introduced in a prophetic context—the Boar of Cornwall in Merlin's Prophecies, the shaft of light over Gaul (VIII.15), and named at his strange begetting as a future hero (VIII.19). Throughout the latter part of the ***Historia*** Geoffrey provides summaries of the history in a series of speeches or monologues (Ambrosius VIII.2, Eldol VIII.5, Brianus XII.2, Salomon and Caduallo XII.5-6) which serve to tighten the narrative and to summarize the meaning of the history.

Geoffrey sets out in the Preface the parameters of his history which will run from Brutus, the first king, who gave his name to the Island and to his descendants, to Caduala-drus, son of Caduallo, that is he will trace the history of this people from their origins to what he regards as the crucial change in their status, the loss of sovereignty to Athelstan which is reflected in the change of the name of the Britons to Welsh (XII.19). The *Historia* has seven chronological sections: 1. Origins and the journey to Albion. 2. The settlement in Britain. 3. The Romans in Britain. 4. The decline of the Britons and the Breton deliverance. 5. Vortigern and the advent of the Saxons (the section includes Merlin's Prophecies). 6. King Arthur. 7. The Saxon supremacy. The 'plot' narrative, however, is thematically constructed around three characters who represent three peaks in British history viewed as the relationship of Britain and Rome, one of the most meaningful themes of traditional British historiography.[23] Following an introduction describing the Trojan descent of Brutus, section I narrates the history of the kings of the Britons which ends in periods of civil strife until Belinus and his brother Brennius attack Rome: II, Julius Caesar formally sets out the relationship of the two nations in IV.1. The moral superiority of the Britons is made clear in Cassibellanus's response that his people have ever sought the dignity of freedom in preference to the imposition of the yoke of servitude upon others, and the Roman conquest is achieved not by force of arms but by British discord and then by agreement. Periods of civil war again ensue until Constantinus returns to conquer Rome. In III the years of Roman rule are seen to have had a debilitating effect on the British character for their native love of freedom and their moral strength are now to be found in Brittany. Britain faces a new threat in the *adventus Saxonum* and Arthur emerges as the new hero. But though he succeeds in defeating the Saxons and establishing long periods of peace, the culmination of his reign is his meeting of the Emperor's challenge and his march upon Rome. He sees himself as the heir of Belinus and of Constantinus, but the measure of the decline of the Britons is that he fails where his predecessors had succeeded, a failure which symbolizes and foreshadows the end of British sovereignty. Characteristically it is brought about by treachery, disloyalty and civil war. Following Arthur's return from Rome and the Battle of Camlan there is little to relate and the *Historia* moves quickly to its close.

Arthur's role is central to the *Historia.* Geoffrey's theme is the loss of sovereignty. The change of orientation from Troy and Rome with their connotations of *British* dignity and status in the classical world to the contemporary reality of Saxon and Norman domination over the *Welsh* required a powerful focus, while, equally, the vaticination of renewal which Geoffrey regarded as an important element in his view of British history also needed a strong emotional symbol.[24] Arthur is the final flicker of the flame of British sovereignty but in his ambiguous passing he becomes the hope for renewal. Arthur is a personification of British history. He is the king of all Britain, who fails the hero's quest but who is nevertheless the king who will return. Arthur's centrality in Geoffrey's structure is reflected in the space given to his antecedents and to his reign.

About a quarter of the *Historia* (a little more than a quarter if the *Prophetiae* are included) deals with the House of Constantine and the wars of Aurelius and Uther Pendragon against the Saxons up to the birth of Arthur: just under another quarter of the book is taken up with the account of Arthur's reign and final defeat. When these proportions are considered in the context of the careful structuring of the complete narrative, then the significance of Arthurian Britain for Geoffrey becomes even more marked. This preoccupation with the figure of Arthur may have given rise, over the long period of the gestation of the *Historia,* to the nickname Galfridus *Artur(us).*[25] The Arthurian section dominates the structure of the *Historia.* The long introduction to Arthur's appearance is necessary as a bridge from the end of Roman Britain to the beginnings of Saxon supremacy, but it is also a means of reintroducing from Brittany the old British virtues which give credence to the revival under Arthur. The king, even before his first appearance, is established in a genealogical and dynastic context which justifies his throne while at the same time distancing him from the Britons.[26]

It is clear that Geoffrey has designed his narrative of Arthur's reign so that it can achieve a dramatic epic quality which makes it an entity in its own right, separate from the rest of the book. Taking the historical context from 'Nennius' he makes Arthur come to the throne at a time of Saxon advance and the young king's first campaigns are structured around the battle-list of the *Historia Brittonum.* Douglas, (York), Kaerluidcoit i.e. Lincoln, Caledon Wood, culminate in the Battle of Badon (Bath), obviously a significant landmark as is shown by the description of the ritualistic arming of the hero with his personal weapons—the shield Pridwen, the spear Ron, and the sword forged in Avalon, Caliburnus. Arthur then turns against the Scots and the Picts, at Alclud, Moray and Loch Lomond (Geoffrey uses some of the Nennian *mirabilia* for his locations), with such ferocity that 'all the bishops of this pitiful country with all the clergy under their command, their feet bare and in their hands the relics of their saints and the treasures of their churches, assembled to beg pity', an episode reminiscent of the appeal of the Irish saints to Arthur in *Culhwch ac Olwen.* This second group of victories is necessary to justify his claim to be king of all Britain, Arthur's traditional title in *Culhwch ac Olwen* and the *Vitae* and a symbol of the unity of British sovereignty, so important in the historical myth. Arthur exercises his kingship at York, where he re-establishes the privileges of the princes, the brothers Urianus and Anguselus, and Loth of Lodonesia, who had married Arthur's sister Anna and was the father of Gualguanus and Modredus. He himself marries Guenhuuara. The conquest of the neighbouring countries and islands follows and during the ensuing twelve years Arthur's court becomes the model of courtly behaviour. The king's ambitions grow broader and the scene is set for his development over the next nine years into the world (i.e. European) emperor and the acknowledgement of his court as the epitome of chivalry. Geoffrey is attempting to give historical expression to ideas which were already fruitful in Welsh tradition. The speech of the legendary figure of Glewlwyd Gafaelfawr and the court and Arthurian entourage at Celli Wig are the seeds from which grew the Galfridian account of the Whitsun crown-wearing at Caerleon with which Arthur celebrates his conquest of Europe from Ireland and Norway to Gaul and the borders of Rome and to which come all his subject kings and nobles. The chivalric connotations of Caerleon were to be more potent than the heroic features of Celli Wig and one of Geoffrey's most enduring gifts to Arthurian literature was to be this transformed court and its central regal figure.

To this great celebration come, uninvited, the envoys of Lucius Hiberius, procurator, who accuse Arthur of offering an insult to Rome in the presumption which he displayed in his conquests and they call upon him to make amends before the Senate. Though his nobles gladly accept the challenge, Arthur immediately sees it in historical terms comparing himself with Belinus, Maximianus and Constantinus. The scene soon acquires an epic quality as each noble pledges loyalty to the king in long formal speeches. The reader is being prepared for a climax as the roll-call of kings and allies, the exchange of letters, of charge and counter-charge, lead to the battle preparations. The defence of Britain is left to Modredus and Guenhuuara, and Arthur sets sail for Normandy. Though the unexpected scene in which Arthur fights with the giant of Mont St Michel intervenes, the narrative of the campaign is soon taken up again and the reader is left in no doubt that he is approaching the end of the reign. Skirmishes develop into the final battle, preceded by rhetorical speeches, and the king's closest companions are slain. Arthur is victorious in his efforts, but as he sets out to subdue Rome the news reaches him of his betrayal by his nephew and his wife. Geoffrey will not pursue the story of the betrayal, he says, but will describe the Battle of Camlan as he has read of it in his source and heard of it from Walter. Modredus allies himself with the Saxons (Geoffrey has been careful to underline the fact that both the Roman and Saxon conquests owe more to British treachery than foreign superiority of arms) but this is the greatest civil war of all. Having established Arthur as the most favoured of kings, his fall cannot but be final. He is mortally wounded and taken to the (unlocated) Isle of Avalon where his sword had been forged, for the healing of his wounds. His crown passes to his cousin Constantinus of Cornwall, but Arthur's end is uncertain.

Geoffrey aspired to present Arthur as a credible historical figure, acceptable in contemporary terms, both literary and realistic. He is the epic, *chanson de geste,* hero who engages in single combat, who leads by personal example, has personal arms and who wages his wars in real geographical areas. He is the Norman king ambitious to extend his realms, rewarding his most faithful companions with important dukedoms—Kaius of Anjou who is buried at Chinon, Bederus of Normandy who is buried at Bayeux, and asserting his authority in crown-wearing ceremonies.[27] Geoffrey was not above using some of the Nennian *mirabilia* to provide Arthurian locations or to supply inter-

esting comments on the wonders of natural history, but it is significant that he rejects the Arthurian wonder-tales found in the same source, the hunt of *porcum Troy(n)t,* the Twrch Trwyth of *Culhwch ac Olwen,* and the account of the grave of Arthur's son. Traditional material is transmuted by Geoffrey into contemporary literary terms, but the historical realism comes closest to slipping in the episode of the giant of Mont St Michel which may be a traditional onomastic story given a new Arthurian context.[28] Though this helps to prepare the reader for Arthur's later personal heroic exploits in the battles with the Romans and at Camlan, the source of the role fulfilled here is reflected in the comment that men crowded around to gape at the head of the giant 'and to praise the man who had freed the country from such a voracious monster', for freeing the land from giants and monsters was a characteristic Arthurian exploit in Welsh tradition.[29] Geoffrey uses this episode as a peg upon which to hang another giant story which appears to be a genuine and unadapted piece of Welsh tradition. This is the account of the fight between Arthur and Ritho *in Arauio monte*; Ritho had demanded Arthur's beard so that it might be given pride of place on the cloak which he had made of kings' beards. It is difficult to judge how independent of the story in the *Historia* later recordings of 'Ritta gawr' may be, but it has clear affinities with stories like that of Dillus Farfawg in *Culhwch ac Olwen.*[30]

The Arthurian section is Geoffrey's literary creation and it owes nothing to a prior narrative, but elements here as throughout the book appear to be drawn from Welsh—or British—tradition. In the *Historia* Geoffrey had access to some written Welsh sources. In Books II and III he has a series of king-lists in which names are reproduced with a minimum of comment. These lists derive from a collection of Welsh genealogies which have been manipulated and combined to produce chronological lists, while in Book IX.12 a similar type of source is employed to create a list of guests at Arthur's court.[31] Other personal names, betraying their origin in the Old Welsh (or early Middle Welsh) orthography in which they appear, are taken at random and applied to new characters who are Geoffrey's creations, or are back formations derived from collections of city names similar to that which appears in the *Historia Brittonum.*[32] Other place-names, cities, rivers, are also in Welsh orthography. More important, however, were oral sources, by whatever means these may have been made available to Geoffrey. His knowledge of Welsh cannot be assumed to have been extensive[33] and the *Historia* seems to have been largely composed while he was in Oxford. Nevertheless he may well have retained some connection with Wales, and that he was cognizant with work, not unlike his own in character, being undertaken in south Wales during these years is suggested by the similarity of some of the features of the ecclesiastical pseudo-history of the 'archbishoprics' of Llandaf and of Caerleon and the accounts of saints Dubricius, Teilo and Samson given in the Book of Llandaf and the *Historia.*[34]

Some episodes and statements found in the *Historia* reflect extant Welsh traditional legend and story. Geoffrey knows of the triadic geographical division of Britain and uses it to create the eponymous sons of Brutus. His Dunuallo Molmutius owes something to the Dyfnwal Moel Mut of medieval Welsh legal legend, and Geoffrey has heard of the fame in battle of Owain ab Urien, *Hiwenus filius Uriani,* the hero of poems by the sixth-century poet Taliesin. At times Geoffrey gives a version of a narrative which is similar to, but not identical with, that found in native (vernacular or Latin) sources and these are best regarded as cognate versions deriving from the same body of tradition. His account of the relationship of Edwinus and Caduallo (Edwin and Cadwallawn) and the Battle of Chester is one example, while the more extended narrative of Maximianus, his British wife and the settlement of Brittany offers a number of points of comparison with the Welsh *Dream of Maxen* and with Breton Latin texts.[35] Geoffrey's knowledge of Welsh (and possibly Breton) legendary and historical tradition is not insignificant but although he has understood the nature of the myth, in the developed narrative history which he produced from a multiplicity of sources—classical, Biblical, British, contemporary—the native material is one, but not a predominant, feature. Geoffrey appears to have restricted his use of Welsh/Breton material to what might be regarded as historical, rather than folkloric, but the manipulation of his sources, which is his most characteristic literary skill, makes retrieving that material a hazardous task.

This is equally true of the Arthurian section. Geoffrey has learned the names and the roles of the king's closest companions, Kaius and Beduerus (Cai, Bedwyr), the nephew Gualguanus (Gwalchmai), the queen Guenhuuara (Gwenhwyfar); he knows of three of Arthur's possessions (but *Prydwen* is his ship in the poem *Preiddeu Annwn* and in *Culhwch ac Olwen,* and his lance Ron is Rongomynyat, his sword Caliburnus is Caletuwlch in *Culhwch ac Olwen*). Utherpendragon may have been Arthur's father, or if not, could have been deduced to be so, but Arthur has no genealogy in early Welsh tradition (though he has sons and uncles not mentioned by Geoffrey), nor is there a tale of his birth; though Geoffrey's narrative has folkloric features there is nothing to show whether it is his creation or not. *Culhwch ac Olwen,* the *Vitae* and early Arthurian poetry portray an Arthur who is a great king, whose court is a centre for suitors seeking a boon, and who frees the land from the terror of monsters. Geoffrey gives this portrait a historical context and composes around the king a structured narrative, transforming into his own terms the image of Arthur and his court found in the Welsh tradition. But the account of Arthur's end appears to have a progression which may derive from an established coherent narrative. It is significant that Geoffrey's sole explicit reference to an oral source is made in connection with this part of his account of Arthur's reign (XI.1):

> . . . nuntiatur ei Modredum nepotem suum cuius tutele permiserat Britanniam eiusdem diademate per tyrannidem et proditionem insignitum esse reginamque Ganhumeram uiolato iure priorum nuptiarum eidem nephanda uenere copulatam fuisse.

Nec hoc quidem, consul auguste, Galfridus Monemutensis tacebit sed, ut in prefato Britannico sermone inuenit et a Gwaltero Oxenefordensi in multis historiis peritissimo uiro audiuit, uili licet stilo breuiter propalabit que prelia inclitus ille rex post uictoriam istam in Britanniam reuersus cum nepote suo commiserit.

(the news was brought to him that his nephew Mordred, in whose care he had left Britain, had placed the crown upon his own head. What is more, this treacherous tyrant was living adulterously and out of wedlock with Queen Guinevere, who had broken the vows of her earlier marriage.

About this particular matter, most noble Duke, Geoffrey of Monmouth prefers to say nothing. He will, however, in his own poor style and without wasting words, describe the battle which our most famous King fought against his nephew, once he had returned to Britain after his victory; for that he found in the British treatise already referred to. He heard it, too, from Walter of Oxford, a man most learned in all branches of history).

To some degree, that these are episodes in an established narrative is confirmed by the existence of an account in *Vita Gildae* of the abduction of the queen by Melwas and also by a number of references to Camlan in the Triads and elsewhere which suggest that the account of this last battle was a focus for the development of associated minor episodes.[36] The significance of the passing of the king to *Auallonis insula* is not developed by Geoffrey but the very ambiguity of his account suggests strongly that he was aware of it and chose to ignore it for political reasons.[37] In the **Vita Merlini,** however, the story is recounted far more clearly, lines 929-40, 954-7.

Geoffrey's knowledge of Welsh tradition was sometimes confused, although he invariably made the best possible use of what he had. The example of Merlin is familiar (see below p. 135), and what he has on Beli and two of his sons, Lludd and Caswallawn (Heli, Lud, Cassibellanus) and their part in a saga of the Roman conquest is obviously incomplete,[38] but such was the authority which the **Historia** swiftly gained in medieval Wales that the translators and guardians of native tradition were more ready to attempt to adapt and harmonize than to correct inconsistencies between the Galfridian history and their own version. The **Historia** was translated into Welsh more than once (in texts often known as *Brut y Brenhinedd,* 'the *Brut* of the Kings') and some three versions of the **Prophetiae Merlini** were also produced. Three translations of the **Historia** appeared in the thirteenth century, two, possibly the three, of them from the same environment. Two other translations were made in the fourteenth century and amalgams of versions or combinations of texts were made up to the eighteenth century so that these Welsh *brutiau,* some sixty in number, are, with the Welsh laws, the most frequently copied texts in Welsh manuscript literature.[39]

These are for the most part translations, more in the modern than in the common medieval sense. They do not alter the shape of the narrative nor do they change its nature, though they normally omit Geoffrey's dedications. In general they are content to relate specific statements in the *Historia* to Welsh tradition or to confirm the identity of certain characters when this could be accomplished with minimum effort or change. The Cleopatra *Brut* (*CBB*) is the most individual of all the translations but the borrowings and harmonization here reflect the translator's knowledge not only of Welsh tradition but also of other texts in Latin and perhaps Wace (or Laymon). Most of the Welsh translators recognized the names of Geoffrey's characters and gave them their Welsh equivalents or restored the Old Welsh names more or less successfully to their contemporary Middle Welsh forms. In a few cases the Welsh texts add patronymics or epithets which are found in native sources. Eygyr (Eigr), a name apparently not attested in a pre-Galfridian source, is used for Igerna, Arthur's mother. She is claimed, in the Dingestow *Brut,* to be a daughter of Amlawdd Wledig, a shadowy figure whose daughters are the mothers of heroes, his only role in extant Welsh texts and a device which allows heroes like Culhwch, Gorau and St Illtud to be Arthur's cousins.[40] Whether Eygyr daughter of Amlawdd is traditional is, however, not clear. The Breton *Hoelus . . . filius sororis Arthuri ex Budicio rege Armoricae* consistently appears as Howel son of Emhyr Llydav. *Emyr* is a common noun, 'leader, prince', and *emyr Llydaw* must originally have been a description, 'king of Brittany'. In the *brutiau* it becomes a personal name, displacing Budicius, and as an Arthurian character he finds his way into the lists in *Breuddwyd Rhonabwy* and *Geraint,* but not that in *Culhwch ac Olwen.*

Where Geoffrey was dealing with characters established and familiar in Welsh tradition, the translators naturally used native forms of names and occasionally attempted a synthesis of the *Historia* and their own knowledge.[41] At its simplest this might involve no more than the use of a Welsh name or a traditional epithet, but in other cases even a simple substitution might reveal inconsistencies between the *Historia* and traditions associated with the 'restored' characters. One such example is Heli son of Cligueillus, father of Lud. Lud was an established figure in Welsh tradition and the names could easily be 'corrected' to Beli Mawr son of Manogan, father of Lludd. But having made the substitution, the Llanstephan I translator (followed by all later writers of the Welsh *brutiau*) felt obliged to insert into his version the tale of Lludd and his brother Llefelys, which he prefaced (III.20), 'Beli had three sons, Lludd, Caswallawn and Nynnyav, *and as some of the story-tellers say, he had a fourth son, Llefelys*'.[42]

Geoffrey refers in V.6 to Coel's daughter Helena, who married Constantius, the Roman senator, and who was the mother of Constantinus. He obviously has in mind St Helena, mother of Constantine the Great, and the discoverer of the Cross. The translators duly rendered the passage, using the names of Coel, Constans, and Cystennyn. Both the Dingestow *Brut* and Llanstephan I identified her with an already existing figure in Welsh tradition, Elen Luyddawg, using this epithet for Helen daughter of Coel. Elen Luyddawg, however, appears in a different context in the tale *The Dream of Maxen Wledig,* where she is the daugh-

ter of Eudaf and is the British princess whom the Emperor Maxen (Maximianus) had seen in his dream. Geoffrey has a variant form of this tradition in V.9. Octavius, ruling in Britain, is persuaded to give his daughter (unnamed), with the crown, to Maximianus senator, to the chagrin of her cousin Conanus Meriadocus (named as her brother in the *Dream*). The translators follow the tradition of the *Dream* in the names, changing Octavius (which might have been suggested by the Old Welsh form, Oudam) to Eudaf, Maximianus to Maxen and call the unnamed daughter 'Helen', but they were unable to use the epithet *Luyddawg* as it had already been applied to (St) Helena.

The names of the chief figures in the Arthurian section were traditional, and Utherpendragon, Guenhuuara, Beduerus, Kaius, caused no difficulty as there was identification here of character and name. Modredus was, apparently, a little different. The form may be Cornish and the translators substituted for it the cognate Welsh name Medrawt. This led to a change in the latter's status in Welsh, for traditionally Gwenhwyfar's abductor had been Melwas, and Medrawd who fell with Arthur at the Battle of Camlan according to the annal, was an acceptable heroic character, though not claimed to be Arthur's nephew, in the poetic tradition.[43] By the fifteenth century, however, Geoffrey's identification had been accepted together with a deterioration in the character's role. 'Gualguanus filius Loth' also caused some difficulty. Loth had been rendered Llev vap Kynvarch by the translators, and Gwalchmai and Gualguanus had already been accepted as equivalents. Gwalchmei vap Llev, therefore, was acceptable. But Geoffrey, having to explain the relationship with Arthur, claims that Arthur's sister Anna was the mother of Gualguanus and Modredus, in Welsh, Anna mother of Gwalchmai and Medrawd. But Gwalchmai was already firmly known in Welsh tradition as Gwalchmei vap Gwyar, and the two statements regarding his mother had to be reconciled. Llanstephan I did not attempt to reconcile them but the translator, nevertheless, seems aware of the difficulty when he refers to 'Anna, and she was the mother of Gwalchmey and Medrawt and was wife to Llev vap Kynvarch, *according to the truth of the Historia*', which may be taken as an indication of his uncertainty. Peniarth 44 resolved the difficulty quite simply by claiming for Anna that 'she was also called Gwyar and was the mother of Gwalchmey and Medravt', though there were no grounds for connecting Gwyar and Medrawd. The Dingestow *Brut* accepted Geoffrey's account and refers to Gwalchmai son of Lleu and Anna in IX.9, 11, but when this character begins to play a prominent role (X.4 etc.), the earlier statments are ignored and he appears consistently as Gwalchmei vap Gwyar.

There are comparatively few examples of inconsistencies of this kind between Geoffrey and his Welsh translators. The *Historia* seems to use existing Welsh tradition directly in only a few sections and consequently these were the only opportunities for differences between the two to arise. By replacing the proper names by genuine Welsh forms, sometimes related to the Latin forms, frequently not, they made the *Historia* even more acceptable to a Welsh audience. The scribes did occasionally note discrepancies between their own knowledge and statements in the **Historia,** and they sometimes refer to Welsh or other traditions,[44] but viewed as a whole, the **Historia** and the Welsh versions were quickly accepted in Wales as the authoritative account of the early history of Britain. The 'traditional history' was to remain a potent element in Welsh national consciousness until the end of the eighteenth century, such was the pride engendered by Geoffrey in a glorious past and the hope sustained in a restored future. If the most surprising gloss in the medieval Welsh translations is the explanation in the Peniarth 44 text that the translator omits Merlin's Prophecies because 'they are difficult for people to believe', the most intriguing is the comment made by the translator of the Dingestow *Brut* after he has translated Geoffrey's ambiguous description of the passing of Arthur: 'And the book does not say anything more certain or clearer than that about him.'

Notes

1. This is the usual title given to the work since it was first used in the Commelin edition of 1587. It does not have MS authority but it is now too well established to be replaced. Commelin too is responsible for the division of the text into twelve books which I have followed here.

2. For the text see E. K. Chambers, *Arthur of Britain* (Cambridge, 1964), 251-2, and cf. *HRB* xii.

3. See further *HRB*(T) x-xxi. The *Historia* is found in a 'vulgate' version but a number of variant versions also exist. The most important of these is edited in *HRB*(V) where it is shown to be an abbreviated revision of Geoffrey's text.

4. See A. O. H. Jarman, below pp. 131-2, and *VM.*

5. J. E. Lloyd, 'Geoffrey of Monmouth', *EHR,* 57 (1942), 460-8.

6. Silas M. Harries, The Kalendar of the *Vitae Sanctorum Wallensium', Journal of the Historical Society of the Church in Wales,* 3 (1953), 3-25, 10-16.

7. See, e.g. F. M. Stenton, *The First Century of English Feudalism* (Oxford, 1961), 25-9. Cf. p. 259 below.

8. This is Tatlock's phrase: see ch.16 of Leg. Hist.

9. The fullest discussion of this matter is O. J. Padel, 'Geoffrey of Monmouth and Cornwall', *CMCS,* 8 (1984), 1-27.

10. Roparz Hemon, *La langue bretonne et ses combats* (La Baule, 1947), 46; Henri Waquet, *Histoire de la Bretagne* (Paris, 1958), 33-4; J. Loth, 'Les langues romane et bretonne en Armorique', *RC,* 28 (1907), 378-403. See J. E. C. Williams below, p. 259.

11. For accounts of Geoffrey's life and interpretations of the evidence, see Lloyd, art. cit., E. Faral, 'Geoffroy de Monmouth, les faits et les dates de sa biographie', *Romania,* 53 (1927), 1-42; *VM* 26-35, *HRB* ix-xi; *HRB*(T) 10-14.

12. See further M. Dominica Legge, 'L'influence littéraire de la cour d'Henri Beauclerc', in *Melanges offerts à Rita Lejeune* (Gembloux, 1969), 679-87; H. E. Salter, *Medieval Oxford,* Oxford Hist. Soc., 100 (1935), 90-2. For Geoffrey's dedications see A. Griscom, 'The Date of Composition of Geoffrey of Monmouth's *Historia:* New Manuscript Evidence', *Speculum,* 1 (1926), 129-56; *HRB* xii-xvi.

13. See comments by R. W. Southern, 'The Place of England in the Twelfth Century Renaissance', *History,* 45 (1960), 201-16, 208; H. V. Galbraith, *Historical Research in Medieval England* (London, 1951).

14. For comparisons of the *Historia* with the works of contemporary historians see LA, ii, 386-401, Leg. Hist. 428-30, Myra J. Rosenhaus, 'Britain between Myth and Reality', (unpublished Ph.D. dissertation, University of Indiana, 1983), Nancy F. Partner, *Serious Entertainments: the Writing of History in Twelfth Century England* (Chicago, 1977). For Geoffrey's influence on British historiography see Robert W. Hanning, *The Vision of History in Early Britain from Gildas to Geoffrey of Monmouth* (New York, 1966), R. William Leckie, Jr., *The Passage of Dominion: Geoffrey of Monmouth and the Periodization of Insular History in the Twelfth Century* (Toronto, 1981). See also references in TRh 280-2.

15. Studies are LA, Leg. Hist., W. F. Schirmer, *Die frühen Darstellungen der Arthurstoffes* (Köln, 1958), 7-40, *HRB,* ALMA ch.8, B. F. Roberts, 'Sylwadau ar Sieffre o Fynwy a'r *Historia Regum Britanniae*', *LlC,* 12 (1973), 127-45.

16. For such common material see Susan Pearce, 'The Traditions of the Royal King-list of Dumnonia', *THSC,* 1971, 128-39; Léon Fleuriot, 'Old Breton Genealogies and Early British Traditions', *B,* 26 (1974), 1-6; Gwenael Le Duc, 'L'Historia Brittanica avant Geoffrey de Monmouth', *AB,* 79 (1972), 819-35; HLCB 98-102, 116-18; Caroline Brett, 'Breton Latin Literature as Evidence for Literature in the Vernacular, AD 800-1300', *CMCS,* 18 (1989), 1-26, discusses the fragmented nature of Breton historiography and reviews the extant texts.

17. Most modern scholarship is sceptical of Geoffrey's claim, but cf. R. W. Southern, 'Aspects of the European Tradition of Historical Writing, 1 The Classical Tradition from Einhard to Geoffrey of Monmouth', *Trans. Royal. Hist. Soc.,* 5S, 20 (1970), 173-96, p. 194: 'Personally I am convinced that the source which he claimed to have received from Walter, archdeacon of Oxford, really existed.'

18. For the text and discussion see *TYP* 228-37, cxxiii-vii.

19. *AP* 1. 13. Cf. p. 136 below.

20. See further 'Geoffrey of Monmouth and Welsh historical tradition', *NMS,* 20 (1976), 29-40. I am grateful to the editor for permission to reproduce here portions of my article.

21. V. I. J. Flint, 'The *Historia Regum Brittaniae* of Geoffrey of Monmouth: Parody and its Purpose. A

suggestion', *Speculum,* 54 (1979), 447-68. See also C. N. L. Brooke, 'Geoffrey of Monmouth as a Historian' in C. N. L. Brooke *et al., Church and Government in the Middle Ages* (Cambridge, 1976), 77-91 (repr. in C. N. L. Brooke, *The Church and the Welsh Border in the Central Middle Ages,* ch.9), and n.14 above.

22. This moral view of history is, of course, not unique to Geoffrey nor is it specifically Welsh. Deriving from the Old Testament prophets and St Augustine it is a common medieval interpretation. For a study of Geoffrey in this context see S. M. Schwartz, 'The Founding and Self-betrayal of Britain: an Augustinian Approach to Geoffrey of Monmouth's *Historia Regum Britanniae*', *Medievalia et Humanistica,* 10 (1981), 33-58.

23. For this theme see *NMS,* 20 (1976), 33-4 and references cited there; also G. Goetinck, 'The Blessed Heroes', *SC,* 20/21 (1985-6), 87-109.

24. Geoffrey refers to the hope of Arthur's return obliquely in XI.2, 'letaliter uulneratus est; qui illinc ad sananda uulnera sua in insulam Auallonis euectus'.

25. For the suggestion that this is a nickname see Padel, art. cit., 2. William of Newburgh claimed that 'Gaufridus . . . agnomen habens Arturi, pro eo quod fabulas de Arturo, ex priscis Britonum figmentis sumptas et ex proprio auctas, per superductum Latini sermonis colorem honesto historiae nomine palliavit', E. K. Chambers, *Arthur of Britain,* 274-5.

26. For an ideological interpretation of Geoffrey's Arthurian section see Stephen Knight, *Arthurian Literature and Society* (London, 1983), ch.2.

27. Cai is referred to as *swyddwr* in *Culhwch ac Olwen,* with which compare *BD* 156, *pen swyddwr,* 'dapifer'. For the Whitsun crown-wearing see Leg. Hist. p. 271-4.

28. See LA ii, 284-9. For a view which ascribes the episode to Geoffrey see Lewis Thorpe, 'Le Mont Saint-Michel et Geoffrei de Monmouth', in *Millénaire du Mont Saint Michel,* ii (Paris, 1967), 377-82.

29. *CO*(1) lxxxvi-vii, and cf. above p. 84.

30. *CO*(1) lvi-viii.

31. S. Piggott, 'The Sources of Geoffrey of Monmouth: I The "pre-Roman" King-list', *Antiquity,* 15 (1941), 269-86. The text of the genealogies from London, British Library MS Harleian 3859, a text very similar to, or identical with, that used by Geoffrey, is given in *EWGT* 9-13. See also P. C. Bartrum, 'Was there a British Book of Conquests?', *B,* 23 (1968), 2-5.

32. *Historia Brittonum* was one of the sources for Geoffrey's account of Merlin and his story of Vortigern and the *adventus Saxonum.* For lists of city names see above, ch.3, n.45.

33. Views differ on the extent of Geoffrey's knowledge of Welsh. Tatlock, Leg. Hist. 445, believed that his ability to translate some epithets and his use of some place and personal names revealed some real knowledge and T. D. Crawford, 'On the Linguistic Competence of Geoffrey of Monmouth', *Medium Aevum,* 51 (1982), 152-62, suggests that Geoffrey had a better knowledge of spoken than of written Welsh. The evidence remains inconclusive. Geoffrey's derivation of 'loquela gentis que prius Troiana siue curum Grecum nuncupabatur dicta fuit Britannica' (I:16) is academic folk etymology which explains *Cymraeg* as *camroeg,* and which is repeated by Giraldus Cambrensis, *Descriptio Kambriae* I.7.

34. Christopher Brooke, 'The Archbishops of St David's, Llandaff and Caerleon-on-Usk', *SEBC* 201-42 (rev. version in ch. 2, *The Church and the Welsh Border*).

35. For these examples see *TYP* cxxv-vi, xcv-viii, 480-1; CS 150-1; SEBH 107-9, 126-8; *LlC,* 12, 138. For Breton narrative material similar to Geoffrey's accounts see n.16 above, J. E. C. Williams below p. 265, *HRB* xvii-viii; C Sterckx and G. Le Duc, 'Les fragments inédits de la Vie de saint Goëznou', *AB,* 78 (1971), 277-85, C. Brett, *CMCS,* 18 (1989), 15-17.

36. See above pp. 81, 85.

37. See J. E. Lloyd, 'The Death of Arthur', *B,* 11 (1941), 158-60.

38. *CLlLl* xiii-xv.

39. The three thirteenth-century translations are, referring only to the oldest MS in each group, Aberystwyth NLW MS Llanstephan I, NLW MS Peniarth 44, and the Dingestow *Brut* (*BD*), the two former are in the same hand. Fourteenth-century versions are NLW MSS Peniarth 21 and 23, and the Cleopatra *Brut* (*CBB*). For fuller discussions on the Welsh *brutiau* see Edmund Reis, 'The Welsh Versions of Geoffrey of Monmouth's *Historia*', *WHR,* 4 (1968), 97-127; *BB* xxiv-xxxvi; Brynley F. Roberts, 'Testunau Hanes Cymraeg Canol'; TRh 274-301, 'Historical Writing', Guide, 244-7. For the so-called *Brut Tysilio* see Brynley F. Roberts, *Brut Tysilio* (Abertawe, 1980); and for Geoffrey's influence in Wales see *BB,* Appendix, 55-74; 'Ymagweddau at *Brut y Brenhinedd* hyd 1890', *B,* 24 (1971), 122-38.

40. *TYP* 365-7. See also p. 82, and ch.3, n.31 above.

41. On the Welsh personal names see Brynley F. Roberts, 'The Treatment of Personal Names in the Early Welsh Versions of *Historia Regum Britanniae*', *B,* 25 (1973), 274-90.

42. Cf. *CLlLl* 1.

43. *TYP* 454.

44. Examples are the circumstances of the death of Malgo, quotations from triads, Dubricius's exile in Bardsey, and the name 'given by the poets' to Severus's wall. See also TRh 291-2, *BB* xxxiii-iv.

Abbreviations

AB: *Annales de Bretagne.*

ALMA: *Arthurian Literature in the Middle Ages,* ed. R. S. Loomis (Oxford, 1959).

AP: *Armes Prydein: 'The Prophecy of Britain',* ed. Ifor Williams. English edition translated by Rachel Bromwich, DIAS Medieval and Modern Welsh Series VI (Dublin, 1972, 1982).

B: *Bulletin of the Board of Celtic Studies.*

BB: *Brut y Brenhinedd* (Llanstephan I Version), ed. B. F. Roberts (DIAS 1971).

BD: *Brut Dingestow,* ed. Henry Lewis (Cardiff, 1942).

CBB: John Jay Parry, *Brut y Brenhinedd: Cotton Cleopatra Version* (Cambridge, Mass., 1937).

CLlLl: *Cyfranc Lludd a Llefelys,* ed. B. F. Roberts, DIAS Medieval and Modern Welsh Series VII (Dublin, 1975).

CMCS: *Cambridge Medieval Celtic Studies.*

CO/CO(1): *Culhwch ac Olwen: Testun Syr Idris Foster,* ed. and completed by Rachel Bromwich and D. Simon Evans (Cardiff, 1988) (*CO*(1)). An enlarged English edition with new introduction and notes is in the Press: references to line numbers in the text of the tale will correspond in the two editions.

EHR: *English Historical Review.*

EWGT: *Early Welsh Genealogical Tracts,* ed. P. C. Bartrum (Cardiff, 1966).

HLCB: *Histoire littéraire et culturelle de la Bretagne,* ed. Jean Balcou et Yves le Gallo (Paris-Geneva, 1987).

HRB: *Historia Regum Britanniae,* I: Bern Burgerbibliothek MS 568, ed. Neil Wright (Cambridge, 1984).

HRB(T): *Historia Regum Britanniae,* trans. Lewis Thorpe, *The History of the Kings of Britain* (Harmondsworth, 1966).

HRB(V): *Historia Regum Britanniae,* II: The First Variant Version, ed. Neil Wright, (Cambridge, 1988).

LA: E. Faral, *La Légende arthurienne,* 3 vols. (Paris, 1929).

LlC: *Llên Cymru.*

NMS: *Nottingham Medieval Studies.*

RC: *Revue Celtique.*

SC: *Studia Celtica.*

SEBC: *Studies in the Early British Church,* ed. N. K. Chadwick (Cambridge, 1958).

THSC: *Transactions of the Honourable Society of Cymmrodorion.*

TRh: *Y Traddodiad Rhyddiaith yn yr Oesau Canol,* ed. Geraint Bowen (Llandysul, 1974).

TYP: *Trioedd Ynys Prydein,* ed. and trans. Rachel Bromwich (Cardiff, 1961, 1978, 1991).

VM: *The Life of Merlin* (Geoffrey of Monmouth's *Vita Merlini*), ed. and trans. Basil Clarke (Cardiff, 1971).

WHR: Welsh History Review.

Julia C. Crick (essay date 1991)

SOURCE: "Reception," in The *"Historia Regum Britannie" of Geoffrey of Monmouth: IV, Dissemination and Reception in the Later Middle Ages,* D. S. Brewer, 1991, pp. 218-26.

[*In the following excerpt, Crick credits* The History of the Kings of Britain *with inspiring the composition of other histories and argues that Geoffrey's work circulated widely not because it was accepted as historical fact, but because it served the needs of its readers.*]

So far this study has largely been concerned with the immediate circumstances in which Geoffrey's History was transmitted, a subject hardly separable from the broader question of how the *Historia* was regarded and used, which will now be addressed. Works associated with the History provide a starting point for such an investigation.

Thanks to the evidence of test-collations, the original list of associated contents presented in Chapter II can now be sorted: material which was evidently transmitted together with the *Historia* can be distinguished from repeated patterns of association not explained by the filiation of Geoffrey's History. The apparently non-inherited or rather repeatedly observed connections suggest the natural affinity of certain subject-areas with Geoffrey's History. This is indisputable when different works of similar nature accompany Geoffrey's History.

Such apparently non-inherited associations are of various kinds (a list may be found in Appendix III). There are numerous histories dealing with Troy, Alexander, the Crusades, the East, Britain, not to mention Universal histories, local and monastic chronicles from England and the Continent, chronologies, genealogies, and origin-stories. Texts concerning the geography (often marvellous) of Britain, the East, and the World as a whole also appear. Legal texts are found in *Historia*-manuscripts. Less obviously apposite texts include well circulated devotional literature (including hagiography) and a significant quantity of apocrypha and apocalyptic. Prophecy and wisdom literature are also associated with the *Historia.*

These associations must be handled with caution. Works could become associated purely by chance. Even when a scribe or compiler deliberately selected the contents of a manuscript, his choice may have been determined not by the works' compatibility but by convenience or availability. On the other hand, association which is repeated without textual explanation is unlikely to be purely accidental; the quantity of material available for Geoffrey permits some degree of confidence. To be made to yield their full results, the associated classes just described must be compared with profiles of the works accompanying other histories, information which is as yet unavailable. A few associations are sufficiently marked, nevertheless, to deserve comment, however one-dimensional.

Many *Historia*-manuscripts (from the twelfth century to the fifteenth) contain serious histories, both Insular and Continental, and sometimes historical collections.[1] Although this association cannot be interpreted as suggesting that the *Historia* was accepted wholeheartedly as historical,[2] it does imply that the work was considered to have some factual foundation and value as a source. We may note that even Geoffrey's critics were sometimes prepared to make limited use of his material.[3]

Stronger indications of Geoffrey's historical credibility may be inferred from the association of the *Historia* with texts relating to the debate about the lordship of Scotland.[4] Walter Ullmann noted twenty-five years ago the indebtedness to Geoffrey of the letter of Edward I to Pope Boniface VIII (1301) in which he laid out his claim to Scotland.[5] This formed the second phase of a royal propaganda campaign: the first had been launched in 1291 when Edward had appealed to religious houses for information relevant to his case.[6] The *Historia* had been conspicuously absent on this occasion perhaps, it has been suggested, because of historical scruples.[7] The inclusion of Edward's letter in two *Historia*-manuscripts, in the original hand in one instance,[8] and of other documents relating to the claim,[9] seems to suggest that, although the propagandists did not cite Geoffrey by name, the work was not generally considered entirely disreputable.

The *Historia* evidently had an affinity with crusading histories. This perhaps reflects audience. One would imagine that crusading material particularly appealed to the laity—many members of noble families, especially in France and Flanders, had taken the Cross. 'An enthusiasm for the crusading exploits of Charlemagne', 'at first restricted to a small group of uneducated knights', has been identified by Ian Short as one element in the success of the *Historia Turpini* in twelfth-century France.[10] Short's discussion focussed on the vernacular Turpin, however. As with Arthurian literature, there were in addition to the vernacular works various Latin texts in circulation which may have attracted an audience of a different sort. Little work seems to have been done on the readership of such literature.[11]

Classical pseudo-histories, especially those of Troy and Alexander, may be found in English and Continental *Historia*-manuscripts, primarily of the fourteenth century or earlier. The degree of historical credence attached to Classical pseudo-histories in the Middle Ages remains an open question[12] but it was probably not inconsiderable. Alexander was a historical figure, after all; the medieval reader had few means of detecting that the legend of Troy was not also based on historical fact.[13]

It is noticeable that *Historia*-manuscripts containing Histories such as those of Bede, Henry of Huntingdon, William of Malmesbury, and Higden rarely include Classical pseudo-histories,[14] but this may reflect their Insular subject-matter rather than their perceived historical authority. French historians had claimed Trojan origins for their nation from the time of Fredegar.[15] The myth was still potent in the fifteenth century, when French propagandists aimed to score political points by claiming that the Britons had forfeited their Trojan lineage and their hegemony when the Saxons invaded.[16] It has even been suggested that French sympathy with Scotland and Ireland was founded not only on a community of interest but on a perceived common descent.[17] Even the descendants of the Scandinavian settlers of Normandy claimed Trojan ancestry.[18] Geoffrey had given the Anglo-Normans a stake in an increasingly important game: legitimation of political power by appeal to the heritage of Antiquity.[19] To avoid suggestions of past subjection to Rome, one appealed directly to the ancestors of the Romans, the Trojans.[20] Lee Patterson has noted the popularity at Henry II's court of vernacular epics on Classical themes.[21] The Trojans feature in genealogies and origin-legends which travel with *Historia*-manuscripts, a genre stoked by the *Historia* itself.[22]

The Alexander-legend was put to a number of uses. Cary's study of the legend concentrated on its moral and didactic value: how, much like certain Roman histories, the subject-matter provided a theatre for the portrayal of moral issues,[23] especially those concerning the exercise of power. It is possible that Geoffrey's History served a similar purpose. It is associated with wisdom literature, including the textbook for kingship, *Secreta Secretorum*; G. R. Owst's study of preaching *exempla* provides two instances of the use of Arthurian material, one quite possibly taken from Geoffrey.[24] The text evidently reached appropriate circles: MS. 124 belonged to a priest, and a document concerning the rector of a Scottish parish is copied into MS. 87.

Alexander was more than a figure of historical myth. He presented a supreme model of power and empire, extending even to the eschatological: the Alexander who confines Gog and Magog until the Last Times. We have already seen how Alexander-texts are often accompanied by the Pseudo-Methodian Revelations and stories of Antichrist (above, II). While there is evidently considerable justice in setting side by side the stories of two secular heroes[25]—Geoffrey's Arthur may anyway be modelled on Alexander[26]—it is not impossible that the apocalyptic resonances of Alexander's story extended to Geoffrey's work.[27] Non-Galfridian narratives about Arthur attribute to him a messianic function. Perhaps the presence of Merlin in the *Historia* imparts a similar atmosphere. Whatever the explanation, association with widely maintained eschatological stories suggests that that work was regarded as far from frivolous.

Prophecy, which often carried a comparable apocalyptic message—the Sibylline material, for example[28]—, forms another well represented class of associated material. This is not unexpected. The figure of Merlin was too compelling to be ignored. His mysterious prophecies gain validity within the **Historia** by the ancient technique of masking history as prophecy,[29] but at the same time they remained largely open to interpretation, a challenge undertaken from time to time by commentators, professional and amateur (above, III: Commentaries). This material constituted 'matter of grave concern to serious and practical men', deriving cogency and intellectual respectability from its Biblical roots[30] and from its interpretation by charismatic public figures such as Joachim of Fiore. Prophecy impinged on large and vital issues—the threat of Islam after the fall of Jerusalem in 1187[31] and, later, the Black Death.[32]

Prophetic and apocalyptic texts suggest a certain milieu. According to R. W. Southern, 'The keenest students of Merlin . . . were University men with intellectual aspirations'.[33] Similarly, it was the 'well-educated and well-situated clerical intelligentsia' who were able to exploit prophecy and apocalyptic for political and religious purposes:[34] the political commentary which passed as the prophecy of John of Bridlington was composed by an Augustinian canon. Vaticination was a convenient vehicle for political messages. Sibylline prophecies were being exploited in thirteenth-century France to boost the royal prestige of Philip Augustus.[35] The figure of Merlin, which gained widespread acceptance in Europe,[36] acquired an increasingly political importance. The Galfridian Merlin-prophecies appeared on an English dynastic roll *c.* 1250.[37] Merlin became a pawn in the propaganda war between England and France in the fifteenth century. Christine de Pisan claimed that Merlin had predicted the success of Joan of Arc; Jean Brehal turned prophecies found 'in historia Bruti' to a similar purpose.[38]

Alexander-stories have another facet: Alexander's journeys to the East. Tatlock suggested that the marvellous geography of the East supplied by Alexander-texts inspired the *mirabilia* found in Geoffrey.[39] This may be an over-simplification—the *Historia Brittonum* is a more obvious source—but certainly Geoffrey's History was frequently copied with the *Epistola Alexandri* and a variety of other geographies besides, often mythical, particularly concerning the East.

Legal texts constitute a final class of material whose association with the **Historia** suggests that it was regarded seriously. Geoffrey's occasional allusions to law-making, for example the Molmutine code, are entirely spurious historically but, as Tatlock noted, strikingly relevant to early twelfth-century legal issues.[40]

Lee Patterson has recently stressed the instability and uncertain status of material about the remote past of Britain, both Trojan[41] and British: the **Historia** is, in his view, 'a myth of origins that deconstructs the origin', a '*Gründungssage* that undermines the very ground upon which it rests'.[42] Although the evidence presented here cannot be taken to represent the whole reception of the text, there is nothing to imply that this perceived subversiveness and

ambiguity was communicated to the work's audience. It certainly did not impede the use of the **Historia** as a historical source and the present discussion indicates that the work was lent sufficient credence for it to be associated with documents and ideologically important material—eschatological and prophetic. This last association displaces any connotations the **Historia** may have of elegant courtly badinage with a different image—the work as carrier of potent prophetic material.

These observations about how and why the **Historia** circulated offer promising material to test a contentious statement made recently by Per Nykrog: 'Writing is costly and rare, and it seems that civilizations have to reach a certain level of technology and productivity before downright and avowedly first-hand fiction can be put into writing'.[43] Taking this proposition at face value, where does Geoffrey's work belong on Nykrog's scale of cultural sophistication?

Much of the answer depends on an issue hardly considered here, Geoffrey's use of sources. How much of the **Historia** is his invention? If Geoffrey's narrative was dictated by oral Celtic stories, then his fiction is not first-hand but 'consecrated as truth' by long oral transmission.[44] Published studies provide ample evidence of Geoffrey's creative exploitation of material. Geoffrey took sources perceived as factual—histories, chronologies, and genealogies[45]—and moulded them to his own design. Even viewed from the surface, Geoffrey's work betrays its artificiality: it is free from the unevennesses and parataxis typical of medieval chronicles,[46] it is too elegant, well structured, smoothly crafted. When the **Historia** is set against the poverty of written materials available to its author, the imaginative input is undeniable.

Geoffrey's manipulation of the past in the cause of contemporary concerns has precedents, some related to vernacular, oral literature. Such material had occasionally crossed into Latin. The Latin History of Dudo of Saint-Quentin has been described by Eleanor Searle as deriving inspiration and direction from Norse saga; Dudo's aim was to legitimate the ruling dynasty of Normandy.[47] David Dumville has identified elements of the Celtic synchronising history in the ninth-century *Historia Brittonum*.[48] Indeed, Celtic conceptions of history provide a convincing background for Geoffrey's historical mythologizing, as Patrick Sims-Williams has shown.[49]

Although Geoffrey may have composed rather than compiled, imaginative expression was not his primary motivation, as is especially clear when his work is viewed in the Celtic tradition. Nykrog, pointing out the historical trappings of Geoffrey's work—the use of histories as models, the historical framework—, classified it as a transitional work, belonging to the period before 'avowedly first-hand' written fiction emerged a generation later.[50] Geoffrey was not inventing freely but picking the spoils from the post-Conquest degeneration of the Celtic epic tradition, a process which Nykrog has called 'secondary, creative recomposition'.[51]

Nykrog's definition of fiction requires that both author and public acknowledge the narrative as the product of creative imagination. If Geoffrey's position in this equation is ambiguous, that of his audience certainly is not. The reception of the *Historia* suggests that, despite the work's potential as an entertaining narrative, it circulated, both in and outside Britain, by virtue of its functional value. Interest often concentrated in regions of historiographical activity. The work served as a historical source, accompanying legal and historical documents. Association with geographical, prophetic, and apocalyptic literature indicates too that it was read primarily for information. This is not to claim that it was not enjoyed by some nor that it was unreservedly approved by others. As, by the thirteenth century, the Galfridian early history of Britain appears to have been consecrated as historical truth (albeit decorated), we cannot take the observation that the work was not regarded as fictional literature as an index of the 'level of technology and productivity' in later generations. But even in the twelfth century, when the work's status was disputed by some, its great popularity apparently depended on its informational rather than a recreational or even edifying value.[52]

If, on both counts, the *Historia* fits better into the realm of history than of literature, should we regard its success as a monument of medieval gullibility and lack of sophistication? I see reason to reject this idea. The opposition between history and literature which it implies is crudely anachronistic. A professional, technical record of the past was provided by annalistic chronicles; but history proper was expected by its patrons 'to arrest the attention and divert the imagination' and was valued for 'information, morality, amusement, and beauty of language'.[53] As a branch of rhetoric,[54] history-writing required considerable imaginative power in order to arrange and embellish the materials available. The result can be paradoxical, as Southern has noted in one case: 'The more successful Einhard is in handling his subject, the less reliable he is as a source for modern historians'.[55] If the aim was to divert and entertain and if the noblest theme available was the destiny of nations,[56] then Geoffrey was an exceptionally accomplished historian. The skeleton of the narrative, admittedly disarticulated and reconstituted by Geoffrey, could be found in genealogies, chronologies, and especially the *Historia Brittonum*. The story Geoffrey tells is of a kingdom unified from the first, but we cannot accuse him of propagandizing. His sources described a succession of kings, not a tribal polity; the models of government available to him were overwhelmingly monarchic—even Roman consuls are king-like in Geoffrey's portrayal.

Viewed in these terms, the *Historia*'s success does not prove an indictment of the powers of discrimination of Geoffrey's contemporaries. Readers could and did cull information from the book, while acknowledging that the account was embellished. History, as Nancy Partner has shown, tended in any case to imitate the conventions of narrative fiction besides enjoying 'many of the freedoms of fiction; and fiction, in turn, conventionally masqueraded

as fact—no serious deception was intended by either'.[57] The peculiarity of the *Historia* lies in its subject matter—a lost, essentially irrecoverable, past. Here Geoffrey's audience could be accused of gullibility: they accepted that, under the imaginatively crafted surface, Geoffrey's material was fundamentally historical. But, apart from the absence of corroborating sources (except for the *Historia Brittonum,* that is) and the initial novelty of the material, Geoffrey's History was no less plausible than others circulating at the time. Other areas of knowledge were accessible through a single work. Criticism of parallel accounts was a luxury available to very few professional historians, let alone their readers.

But no direct connection can be drawn between the success of Geoffrey's work as a history and a presumed paucity of information which impaired the judgment of medieval readers. The historical writing popular even in a sophisticated, highly literate community such as the educated élite of Imperial Rome and the Hellenistic Empire (where histories are known to have been available in public libraries)[58] is likewise often concerned with remote origins; it too deals with the past with unabashed creativity, whether or not sources existed.[59] In fact technical rhetorical training encouraged such authors in their manipulation of the facts.[60] So what were the conditions which should have produced comparable treatments of the past in two such apparently different societies? Propaganda was of course a constant motivation: political circumstances in the fourth and third centuries B.C. made it expedient for Messenia to acquire a (pseudo-) historical past.[61] There was also literary interest: the past provided moral lessons which found expression in the composition of both history and poetry.[62] The potency of the past was such that it could hardly be treated with detachment.

Secondly, in the medieval and Classical periods, history was not a free-standing discipline but an auxiliary one;[63] it was used to grind the axes of men whose concerns were moral, political, theological, and occasionally personal, but rarely those of professional scholarship. Lacking a niche in the academic world, historians in both periods had to catch their audience in a way that writers of technical literature generally did not. One recent critic has noted how Classical historians

> 'had continuously to repeat the claim that their histories were either instructive or pleasurable or both, because the word "history" did not by itself suggest either instruction or pleasure'.[64]

In such a market content, style, and general appeal to the reader were essential to a work's success.

I should contend that Geoffrey did not perpetrate one of the best hoaxes of the Middle Ages but that he was an exceptional artist fully governing and not governed by his material. His choice of subject was a brilliant success. The remote past of Britain held the attention not only of later inheritors of the island kingdom (to borrow Galfridian sentiments) but of readers outside Britain. Geoffrey portrayed an ordered and rational world beginning not with the Romans or even the coming of Christ but with the first pagan inhabitants of Britain; his heroes were secular figures with whose human rather than Christian virtues the reader could identify.

Notes

1. See MS. 200.

2. Compare Gerritsen, 'L'Episode', pp. 344-45. It was also the subject of parody by Walter Map (*De Nugis curialium,* ii.17): see Brooke, *apud* James, *Walter Map,* pp. xxxix-xli.

3. Fletcher, *The Arthurian Material,* pp. 179-82 and 185-91. see also Crick, 'Geoffrey'.

4. See Appendix IV.

5. 'On the Influence', p. 267.

6. Gransden, *Historical Writing,* I.441-42; Guenée, 'L'Enquête'.

7. Stones & Simpson, *Edward I,* I.138 and 148; Guenée, 'L'Enquête', p. 579.

8. MS. 133; in MS. 24 in a fourteenth-century collection appended to an earlier manuscript.

9. MSS 135 and 150.

10. Short, 'The Pseudo-Turpin', p. 19.

11. Tatlock noted Geoffrey's own interest in the Crusades: 'Certain contemporaneous matters'.

12. Chronicles and histories hardly feature in the main study of the medieval attitude to Alexander: Cary, *The Medieval Alexander.* See, however, Bunt, 'Alexander'.

13. Compare Crick, 'Geoffrey'.

14. Only in MSS 32, 70, 83, 92, 163. A similar trend emerges when the early circulation of the *Historia* is compared with that of the histories of Henry of Huntingdon and William of Malmesbury.

15. And onwards: see Bossuat, 'Les Origines troyennes'.

16. Curley, 'Fifteenth-century Glosses', pp. 336-37; Bossuat, 'Les Origines troyennes'.

17. Bossuat, *ibid.,* p. 197.

18. Searle, 'Fact', p. 125.

19. Compare the revival of the Roman senate in the twelfth century: Benson, 'Political *Renouatio*', pp. 340-59.

20. On the rationale of such appeals to the Classical and Trojan past see Southern, 'Aspects . . . 3', pp. 189-90.

21. *Negotiating the Past,* pp. 158-59, 202.

22. Compare Matter, *Englische Gründungssagen,* pp. 234-47.

23. Compare Smalley on Sallust: *Historians,* pp. 19-20.

24. The depiction of the Virgin on Arthur's shield (compare §147) is mentioned in a vernacular sermon; a Latin work describes the story of Vortigern's tower, beginning 'Lego in gestis Britonum': *Literature and Pulpit,* p. 161 and n. 2. For *Gesta Britonum* as a title for the *Historia,* see above, VI.

25. Nykrog, 'The Rise', pp. 596-97; for later associations see Matthews, *The Tragedy,* pp. 33-39, 66-67. Compare the association with material about Charlemagne (*Historia Turpini,* Einhard).

26. Compare Tatlock, *The Legendary History,* pp. 312-14.

27. On the apocalyptic element in Geoffrey's History itself, see Roberts, 'Geoffrey of Monmouth', p. 40.

28. Southern, 'Aspects . . . 3', pp. 166-68.

29. Compare McGinn, *Visions,* p. 7.

30. Southern, 'Aspects . . . 3', pp. 168 and 162-77.

31. *Ibid.,* pp. 174-75.

32. Lerner, 'Western European Eschatological Mentalities', p. 78.

33. 'Aspects . . . 3', p. 168.

34. McGinn, *Visions,* p. 32.

35. Brown, 'La Notion', pp. 78, 89-93.

36. See Zumthor, *Merlin,* pp. 76-78, 85-87, 97-113.

37. Gerould, 'A Text'.

38. Curley, 'Fifteenth-century Glosses', pp. 335-36.

39. *The Legendary History,* p. 319.

40. *Ibid.,* p. 283; compare pp. 278-83. For a different view see Williams, 'Geoffrey of Monmouth'.

41. *Negotiating the Past,* pp. 203-4.

42. *Ibid.,* p. 202.

43. Nykrog, 'The Rise', pp. 593-94.

44. *Ibid.,* p. 594.

45. Compare Wright, 'Geoffrey of Monmouth and Bede', p. 53; Miller, 'Geoffrey's Early Royal Synchronisms', Piggott, 'The Sources', pp. 275-76.

46. Compare Partner, *Serious Entertainments,* pp. 197-200 and 'The New Cornificius', p. 18; Spiegel, 'Genealogy', p. 44; Fleischmann, 'On the Representation', pp. 291-92.

47. 'Fact', pp. 121, 137.

48. 'The Historical Value', pp. 5-7. Compare Sims-Williams, 'Some Functions', pp. 97-98, 105-6.

49. *Ibid.,* especially pp. 97-98, 114, 117-19. The process is not of course a Celtic preserve: contemporary concerns naturally tend to influence, sometimes benignly, or to motivate the investigation of the past.

50. Nykrog, 'The Rise', pp. 594-96. Compare Olson, *Literature as Recreation,* p. 230; Shepherd, 'The Emancipation', especially p. 50.

51. Nykrog, 'The Rise', p. 595.

52. Compare Olson, *Literature as Recreation,* pp. 229-31.

53. Partner, *Serious Entertainments,* pp. 2-3.

54. Southern, 'Aspects . . . 1', p. 181.

55. *Ibid.,* p. 184.

56. *Ibid.,* p. 188.

57. *Serious Entertainments,* p. 195.

58. Momigliano, 'The Historians', p. 68.

59. Wiseman, *Clio's Cosmetics,* especially pp. 9-10, 31-37. Wiseman notes the analogy with Geoffrey: *ibid.,* pp. 21-22.

60. *Ibid.,* pp. 31-37.

61. *Ibid.,* p. 23; Pearson, 'The Pseudo-History', p. 402.

62. Wiseman, *Clio's Cosmetics,* pp. 38, 144-46.

63. Compare Guenée, 'Y-a-t-il une historiographie médiévale?', pp. 264-65; Momigliano, 'The Historians', p. 60.

64. *Ibid.,* p. 61.

Neil Wright (essay date 1991)

SOURCE: An introduction to *The "Historia Regum Britannie" of Geoffrey of Monmouth: V, Gesta Regum Britannie,* edited and translated by Neil Wright, D. S. Brewer, 1991, pp. ix-cxiii.

[*In the following excerpt, Wright considers the date of composition and the author of the* Gesta Regum Britannie, *a 5000-line hexameter version of* The History of the Kings of Britain.]

I. DATE AND AUTHORSHIP

The *Gesta Regum Britannie* can be dated, though not exactly, through its addressee. In the prologue of the poem (I.16), the dedicatee is referred to as *presul Uenetensis* or bishop of Vannes; and in the last line of the work (X.501), he is named as Chadiocus. His name, in the form Chadioccus, is also found as an acrostic, set out below, which is spelled out by the opening letters of the ten books of the poem (viz. excluding the short introductory *capitula* which precede each book):

Caliope referas ut te referente renarrem;
Hiis ita dispositis Brutus sibi construit urbem;
Architenens uix Romuleum compleuerat annum;
Dum Kibelino subiecta Britannia seruit;
Innumeris uero collectis Maximianus;
Omnia Merlinus intenta colligit aure;
Candida Caliope, cetu comitante sororum;
Continuis sollempne tribus celebrare diebus;
Uisibus humanis premissa nocte cometes;
Spes regni reditusque sui rerumque relinquit.

Cadioc (or Chadiocus) was elected bishop of Vannes in 1235 and was consecrated in the following year; he died in 1254.[1] The poem must therefore have been written between those dates.

Michel, the first editor of the *Gesta Regum Britannie,* suggested that the poem belongs to the earlier part of Cadioc's episcopate because it may contain a reference to an event of recent Breton history.[2] In a highly rhetorical apostrophe to Conanus Meriadocus, legendary founder of Brittany, the poet, having described the bloody takeover of Armorica by the Britons, their extermination of the existing Gallic population, and the elevation of Conanus as the first king, prophesies dire repercussions for the future Bretons (*Gesta Regum Britannie,* IV.480-509):

O regnum minime felix! O sanguine fuso
Optentum regale decus! Conane, resigna
Hoc ius iniustum! Prescripcio nulla tueri
Te poterit quoniam dum uixeris intus habebis
Accusatricem que teque tuosque nepotes
Semper mordebit. Non debet predo reatum
Dum tenet ablatum? Res semper erit uiciosa
Que uenit ex rapto, dum raptam predo tenebit;
Predonisque heres, postquam rem nouit ademptam,
In uicium succedit ei. Tecum tua proles
Uerget in interitum penam luitura perhennem,
Dum sic possideat iniuste res alienas;
In sobolem peccata patrum de iure redundant,
Dum soboles effrena patrum peccata sequatur.
Quis putet intrusos Britones uel semen eorum
In male quesitis cum pace quiescere terris?
Euentus quis habere bonos se credat in illis
Que male parta tenet? Meritis Deus equa rependit.
Stirps homicidarum totis homicidia uotis
Perpetrare studens reputat dispendia pacem.
Cortinam cortina trahit, sanguisque cruorem.
Inconstans Britonum populus constanter in ipsa
Mobilitate uiget; numquam Ranusia uirgo
Mobiliore rota fertur quam spiritus eius.
O regio, tibi nunc rex presidet; ante ducatus
Aut comitatus eras. Non regnum siue ducatus
Sed comitatus eris; tu, que ducibus dominaris,
Cum seruis domino continget te dominari.
Ecce dies uenient quibus ad sua iura reducti
Tristia sub pedibus Galli tua colla tenebunt.

According to the poet, the kingdom born in blood will never prosper; the Gauls will regain their rights and hold the Bretons in subjugation; Brittany, formerly a kingdom, will be neither kingdom nor duchy, but merely a French county. Michel argued that this passage refers specifically to the homage paid by the recently defeated Pierre Mauclerc, Duke of Brittany (1213-37), to Louis IX of France in 1234;[3] and thus that the poem was written shortly after Pierre's submission. Allowing for poetic hyperbole, this interpretation is not implausible, although it should be noted that the homage rendered on that occasion by Mauclerc was personal rather than offered on behalf of the Bretons as a whole. However, the intended historical reference may not be as precise as Michel maintained. Mauclerc had also previously done homage to Philippe-Augustus of France on becoming duke in 1213 (although that homage was again personal).[4] Indeed, the very elevation of the Capetian Pierre Mauclerc as Duke of Brittany might, with rhetorical exaggeration, be viewed as exactly the kind of humiliation described by the poet. Moreover, Mauclerc's son, Jean le Roux, also did homage to Louis IX on his succession as duke in 1237.[5] This event could therefore equally well be seen as the humbling to which the poet alludes; in that case the poem may have been composed after 1237. Similarly, the allusion to Brittany being treated as a county rather than duchy could, if it is anything more than rhetorical, apply equally well to Mauclerc or to his son since both termed themselves duke but were regarded as counts by the French court.[6] Thus the passage cannot conclusively be shown to refer to the events of 1234, as Michel claimed; rather, given due latitude for the pessimistic tone evident within the poem as a whole, it fits well enough with the political situation which obtained in Brittany after 1213 and need not necessarily refer in particular to the homages of 1234 or 1237.

The identity of the author of the poem is more difficult to determine. Three different attributions are found in the surviving manuscripts, but two can swiftly be discounted. The ascription to the sixth-century British writer Gildas found in Cotton Julius D.xi need not detain us since it is no older than the seventeenth century.[7] In addition to having no mediaeval authority, this attribution is patently irreconcilable with the date of the poem (1236-54), its reliance on Geoffrey of Monmouth's *Historia Regum Britannie* (published c. 1138), and its extensive borrowings from the *Alexandreid* of Walter of Châtillon (c. 1176-82). A second attribution, to Alexander Neckam, is found in Valenciennes 792, where the poem is introduced by the rubric 'Sequitur de eadem materia historia Britonum uersificata et magistro Alexandro Nequam compilata, ut credo, et scripta ad dominum Cadiocum episcopum Uenetensem' (fo 54v). This appears to be an example of the arbitrary attribution of works to famous authors; for, as Michel pointed out, the ascription is a guess on the part of the scribe (as is indicated by his use of the phrase *ut credo*); the poem is nowhere else assigned to Neckam, who, moreover, died at the latest in 1227, almost ten years before Cadioc became bishop of Vannes.[8] The author of the poem cannot therefore have been Neckam.

There remains a third attribution, found in Paris, BN lat. 8491, where the poem ends with the following colophon 'Explicit decimus liber gestorum regum Britannie per manum Guillelmi dicti de Redonis monachi' (fo 60v). Michel suggested that this 'Guillelmus dictus de Redonis monachus' might be identical with the known contemporary author, William of Rennes.[9] He was a Dominican, born in Thorigné, two miles from Rennes. Educated at Dinan around 1250, he proceeded from there to Paris. He composed a gloss or *apparatus* on the *Summa de Poenitentia et Matrimonio* of Raimond of Peñafort, who was apparently his teacher, and 'un questionnaire sur les cas de conscience' which also draws on Raimond's *Summa*, both gloss and questionnaire being transmitted with that text; in addition to these works, William is also supposed to have written many books on canon and civil law ('multa in utroque iure'), which have not survived.[10]

Michel's suggestion seems plausible at first sight, and the attribution of the poem to William of Rennes, along presumably with Michel's identification of the author, has been accepted without question by Rosemary Morris.[11] Indeed, in favour of Michel's identification it could be argued that William, as a Breton born in Thorigné, might well have been responsible for a verse paraphrase of the *Historia Regum Britannie* which was of evident relevance to contemporary Breton politics and addressed to a Breton bishop. Moreover, the poet of the *Gesta Regum Britannie* occasionally evinces an interest in legal vocabulary and questions of law.[12] This too might arguably conform with the known interests of the Dominican William of Rennes.

On closer inspection, however, a number of difficulties arise. First, we may wonder how likely it is that a serious-minded Dominican friar and jurist would have produced a metrical paraphrase of Geoffrey's pseudo-history. And, even if we conclude, like Michel, that William might have cultivated poetry as a diversion,[13] or that the paraphrase may be a product of William's youth written during his education at Dinan, there remains the problem that such a poem is nowhere recorded amongst William's writings. Second, there is the question of why William, if he were the author of the *Gesta Regum Britannie*, should have dedicated the poem to Cadioc, bishop of Vannes. The chronology of William's life is far from certain, but, if he composed the poem during the time of his education by the Dominicans at Dinan (c. 1250) and before he left for Paris (as would seem likely since Cadioc died in 1254), why should he have sent the poem to a southern bishopric rather than, for example, to his local bishop at Dol? That William should have dedicated the poem to Cadioc is made all the more unlikely by the fact that the Dominicans had no house in Vannes during the 1250s; the first mendicant house in Vannes, which belonged to the Franciscans, was not founded until the 1260s, after Cadioc's death.[14]

A further difficulty is raised by the use of the words *per manum* in the colophon of the Paris manuscript. As Michel rightly observes, these words 'seem to point out the amanuensis rather than the author.'[15] Michel found it difficult to believe that a man of the standing of William of Rennes 'could lower himself to the humble office of an amanuensis.'[16] Nevertheless Michel did not consider the possibility that, if the phrase 'per manum' does, as it appears, denote the role of copyist, William not only composed the *Gesta Regum Britannie* but was also the scribe of the Paris manuscript. That hypothesis can, however, be ruled out because the level of textual corruption found in the Paris manuscript makes it extremely unlikely that it is the author's autograph.[17] If, then, the colophon of the Paris manuscript, as Michel suspected, names the copyist rather than the author of the poem and if it does indeed refer to the Dominican William of Rennes, he did no more than copy the poem.

It is, therefore, important to stress that in the final analysis Michel felt it was more likely that 'a William of Rennes, different from the jurisconsult, was merely the transcriber of the metrical History of the Britons.'[18] Even if the phrase 'per manum' were to denote the author rather than the copyist, which seems unlikely, there is no guarantee that 'Guillelmus dictus de Redonis monachus' is identical with the Dominican William of Rennes. It is safest to conclude provisionally that the authorship of the poem remains uncertain, and that even if a William of Rennes composed the poem rather than, as is more likely, merely copied it, we cannot be sure that this William is the same as the Dominican friar and jurist.

One final problem needs to be considered. Despite the poem's dedication to a Breton bishop and the poet's evident interest in Breton affairs, Ward and Herbert nevertheless questioned whether the author was himself Breton; although, on the strength of the dedication, they concede that the poet was resident in Brittany, they state that it is 'difficult to decide whether he speaks as a Breton or a Welshman.'[19] Their doubts stem from the following lines in the epilogue of the poem (*Gesta Regum Britannie,* X.490-8):

> Saxones hinc abeant; lateant mea scripta Quirites;
> Nec pateant Gallis, quos nostra Britannia uictrix
> Sepe molestauit. Solis hec scribo Britannis,
> Ut memores ueteris patrie iurisque paterni
> Exiliique patrum propriique pudoris, anhelent
> Uocibus et uotis ut regnum restituatur
> Antiquo iuri, quod possidet Anglicus hostis;
> Neue male fidei possessor predia nostra
> Prescribat sumatque bonas a tempore causas.

For Ward and Herbert, the problem is whether these lines are addressed to the Bretons or to the Welsh, as descendents of the original Britons. Does *nostra Britannia* refer simply to Brittany, which has frequently harried the French, or in a broader sense to Britain, foe of English, Romans and Gauls alike? Is the homeland to be recovered by the Bretons, the Welsh or both? Like Ward and Herbert, Michel felt that this passage could be related as well, if not better, to Welsh aspirations to drive out the English as to an implausible appeal to the Continental Bretons to recover their lost homeland.[20] In a sense, of course, this is right. The poet, following the lead of the *Historia Regum Britannie,* is here writing as a greater Briton, and one of his aims is to foster Breton memories of former British glory; but be that as it may, his impractical dream of restoring the ancient kingdom of Britain need not be literally interpreted as evidence that he was a Welshman rather than a Breton.[21]

Two further pieces of evidence bear on the poet's nationality. The first occurs in a passage which describes a battle between the British king Aurelius and Hengist, which, according to Geoffrey of Monmouth, takes place on a plain called Maisbeli (*Historia Regum Britannie,* §121, 'campo qui dicitur Maisbeli').[22] The name of this plain, which has not been identified, means in Welsh 'the field of Beli', a name very probably invented by Geoffrey.[23] In the poem, this place-name is correctly explained by the author: 'Cam-

pus erat Beli de nomine nomen adeptus' (*Gesta Regum Britannie* VI.131). However, the poet's correct latinisation of the place-name Maisbeli need not mean that he was himself a Welshman, since at that time the Welsh and Breton languages were not dissimilar and Welsh may well have been largely comprehensible to a Breton-speaker. Indeed, an error earlier in the same passage strongly suggests that the poet was not Welsh. Before the battle of Maisbeli, Hengist had crossed the Humber and gathered troops from the far north. In *Historia Regum Britannie,* §120, these northern troops are specified as being drawn from the 'Pictis, Scotis, Dacis, Norguegensibus'. In the Breton poem, only the Scoti and Daci are retained, the Picti and Norguegenses being incongruously replaced by the Uenedoti (*Gesta Regum Britannie* VI.119-20):

> Ex aquilonali plaga Dacos, Uenedotos
> Congregat et Scotos.

Unless 'ex aquilonali plaga' is here understood to refer only to the Daci, which seems impossible as it applies equally well to the Scoti,[24] the poet appears to be locating the Uenedoti, or northern Welsh, far to the north of the Humber. Such an error is extremely unlikely to have been made by a Welshman and so points strongly in favour of the author of the poem having been a Breton.

Notes

1. *Gallia christiana,* XIV, cols 926-7.

2. *Gesta,* p. xiv.

3. La Borderie, *Histoire,* III.324-5; Poisson, *Histoire,* p. 102.

4. La Borderie, *Histoire,* III.301-2; Poisson, *Histoire,* p. 99.

5. La Borderie, *Histoire,* III.329 and 336; Leguay & Martin, *Fastes,* p. 34.

6. Montigny, *Essai,* p. 22.

7. See p. xcix below.

8. Michel, *Gesta,* p. viii.

9. *Ibid.,* pp. ix-x.

10. On William of Rennes and his works, see *Histoire littéraire,* XVIII.403-6 and XXIX.602-6; and Martin, *Les ordres,* pp. 127, 159 and 164.

11. 'The *Gesta*', p. 61.

12. See, for example: I.331 (Corineus's invocation of the *lex ueterum*); IV.193-8 (use of legal metaphors); IV.481-99 (illegality of the foundation of Brittany); VIII.53-71 and 93-106 (rejection of Rome's rights over Britain); X.470-1 and 492-8 (illegality of English occupation of Britain; cf. also X.354-5).

13. *Gesta,* pp. ix-x.

14. Martin, *Les ordres,* p. 12.

15. *Gesta,* p. ix.

16. *ibid.,* p. ix.

17. See p. cv below.

18. *Gesta*, p. x.

19. *Catalogue*, p. 274.

20. *Gesta*, p. xvi.

21. Cf. Morris, 'The *Gesta*', pp. 110-12, who, reading the passage similarly, regards the author as a Breton pessimistic about Breton independence, but who saw in the Welsh resurgence of the 1230s a chance of recovering 'British' greatness.

22. Bern 568 here reads *Maubeti* (Wright, *The Historia*, I.87), but the correct form *Maisbeli* is found in the majority of the manuscripts.

23. See Tatlock, *The Legendary History*, pp. 21 and 39. On Geoffrey's knowledge of Welsh, see Crawford, 'Linguistic competence'.

24. A number of passages (especially *Gesta Regum Britannie*, VI.257 and IX.501-2) make it clear that the Breton poet uses Scoti to denote the Scots (as opposed to the Irish), as indeed does Geoffrey of Monmouth; see Tatlock, *The Legendary History*, pp. 8-9.

Alison André (essay date 1993)

SOURCE: "Geoffrey of Monmouth's Portrayal of the Arrival of Christianity in Britain: Fact or Fiction?" *Reading Medieval Studies,* Vol. 19, 1993, pp. 3-13.

[*In the following essay, André argues that Geoffrey's writings concerning Christianity are in part historically authentic and in part politically-motivated propaganda.*]

William of Newborough described Geoffrey of Monmouth as 'effrenta mentiendi libidine' (that is, as an imposter writing from an inordinate love of lying). In more modern times, Geoffrey has fared little better in the hands of R. W. Hanning, who calls him 'an unscrupulous fabricator of a legendary British past'.[1] However, I would like to suggest that an open-minded approach to a reading of the *Historia Regum Britanniae* shows that Geoffrey does not entirely deserve his reputation. By examining his portrayal of the structure of the pagan church, the arrival of Christianity in Britain, and the subsequent progress of the Christian faith, I hope to go some way towards redeeming Geoffrey's reputation, and suggest that the work does not entirely spring from his lively imagination. Instead, I maintain that, there is evidence not only that he has made use of source material, but that there is, in fact, some truth in what he has written.

Let us begin by briefly summarising what Geoffrey says on the arrival of Christianity in Britain. He describes the pagan church as it existed in Britain before the coming of Christianity with flamens presiding over territorial districts. These in turn were answerable to arch-flamens. He then goes on to discuss how Christianity was brought to Britain during the reign of King Lucius in the second cen-

tury. According to Geoffrey, the Christian religion then flourished until the days of Asclepiodotus, when the Diocletian persecutions began. During this time churches were destroyed, copies of the Holy Scriptures were burnt in market places and priests were butchered. However, the heroism of the martyrs ensured that Christianity did not die out completely.

Geoffrey mentions Christianity again when he talks of the Pelagian hersey and the way that the true faith was restored by Germanus, Bishop of Auxerre, and Lupus, Bishop of Troyes. However progress is by no means smooth, and during the reign of Vortigern, the Saxons drive him out of his kingdom, lay waste the countryside and virtually destroy Christianity once more. Even after the church was restored by Aurelius, the faith was tainted by corruption, and Pope Gregory sent Augustine to Britain to preach Christianity to the Angles who had lapsed back into paganism.

It has to be admitted that there are occasions when Geoffrey uses his descriptions of religion to reveal his own political sympathies. One example of this occurs earlier in the *Historia,* before the coming of Christianity. Geoffrey describes the war between the Greeks and the Trojans, and Antigonus and his comrade Anacletus are captured. Anacletus is persuaded by Brutus to act as a traitor and deceive his own countrymen. A. J. P. Tatlock points out in 1931 that this episode is a piece of political propaganda on Geoffrey's part.[2] Anacletus' name is almost certainly an allusion to Petrus Petri Leonis, who came to England as Cardinal Legate in 1121 and visited the king in Wales, and the convent in Canterbury. He travelled in great pomp, gained a large amount of loot, and then left the country, having made promises to Canterbury that he could not keep. He was then elected pope and changed his name to Anacletus. Innocent II however, was elected by another group, and he was ultimately successful in gaining the papacy, so, by giving a traitor the name of Anacletus, Geoffrey is showing loyalty to the 'right' pope.

Geoffrey also tends to place bishoprics in towns where we have no historical proof of their existence, for propaganda reasons. For example, the passage:

> Post hec conuocatis ducibus decernere precepit quid de Hengisto ageretur. Aderat Eldalus Claudiocestris episcopus, frater Eldol, uir summe prudentie et religionis.

> [Next he called his leaders together and ordered them to decide what should be done with Hengist. Among those present was Eldadus, Bishop of Gloucester, the brother of Eldol, and a man of the greatest wisdom and piety.][3]

shows us that Eldadus, the monk who says the last rites over the Britons treacherously murdered by Hengist, and who is renowned for wisdom and piety, is bishop of Gloucester—11 years before one existed historically. As Robert of Gloucester was Geoffrey's patron, it seems likely that Geoffrey was indulging in some flattery.

It is even more significant that Geoffrey almost completely ignores Canterbury, and instead, Caerleon appears as the pre-eminent see with the most distinguished incumbents. Its archbishop carries out the important task of crowning Arthur in Silchester, and again at the Whitsun court at Caerleon. Some scholars believe that Geoffrey, as a Welshman, was asserting claims that the Welsh church should be free from the jurisdiction of Canterbury. But it has also been pointed out that Geoffrey does not devote a great deal of attention to St David's, which would have been the logical head of a Welsh Church. It is therefore quite likely that we are seeing an example of Geoffrey's sense of humour here, and he is actually making fun of contemporary Welsh ecclesiastical interests.

Geoffrey has also been criticised for neglecting to write of Glastonbury and the great religious houses at Durham and Westminster, and for omitting to mention the important part that monks played in the life of the country. His reference to monastic learning is somewhat cynical. In order to poison Aurelius, Eopa the pagan Saxon disguises himself as a monk learned in medicine with cropped hair and shaved beard.

Valerie Flint pointed out in 1979 that anti-monastic views would not have been uncommon in Geoffrey's time.[4] Theobald, who taught at Oxford, and who could well have known Geoffrey, was asked by Archbishop Thurston of York whether monks should have pastoral care. He replied that they should have neither pastoral care nor tithes, as they had no rights to the public priesthood nor to public clerical status, and its rewards. He maintained that monks should withdraw from public power and revenues and live a life of self-supporting penitence. He also made some direct remarks about the pride that often lay in open charity. If Geoffrey was indeed aware of these views and agreed with them, it is not surprising that members of monastic orders do not feature highly in his work.

Up to this point, I have been discussing examples of where Geoffrey's work is influenced more by propaganda than by the truth. Let us now turn to some examples of where he makes use of source material and is more concerned with historical truth.

The following passage is taken from Book IV of the *Historia* and shows Geoffrey's description of a pagan church in Britain which was established before the arrival of Christianity.

> Hos etiam ex precepto apostolici ydolatriam eriperunt et ubi erant flamines episcopos, ubi archiflamines archiepiscopos posuerunt. Sedes autem archiflaminum in nobilibus tribus ciuitatibus fuerant, Lundoniis uidelicet atque Eboraci et in Urbe Legionum.
>
> [At the Pope's bidding, the missionaries converted these men from their idolatry. Where there were flamens, they placed bishops, and where there were archflamens they appointed archbishops. The seats of the archflamens had been in three noble cities, London, York and the City of Legions.][5]

The country was divided into twenty eight territorial divisions, each of these being presided over by a flamen. Over these flamens were 3 archflamens. S. Williams points out in 1952 that the *False Decretals of Pseudo-Isidore* show that the pagan church had consisted of a carefully organised territorial state with powerful hierarchies.[6] This work had been written in the 9th century to prove that the pagans had a fully-fledged ecclesiastical organisation before the birth of Christ. Likewise, Anselm's *Collectio Canonum* provides the same picture, and Williams believes that Geoffrey could well have had access to this work. So we can see in this instance that Geoffrey was not merely using his own imagination but was using source material.

Geoffrey describes the coming of Christianity to Britain in the reign of King Lucius in the second century. We can see that Lucius was inspired with a desire for the true faith after having seen the miracles that had been performed by young Christian missionaries. He therefore wrote to Pope Eleutherius and asked to be received into the Christian faith. The pope sent Faganus and Duvianus, two learned religious men, who baptised Lucius and the people of the neighbouring tribes. In Geoffrey's words:

> Exitum quoque suum preferre uolens principio epistulas suas Eleutero pape direxit petens ut ab eo christianitatem reciperet . . . Siquidem beatus pontifex comperta eius deuotione duos religiosos doctores Faganum et Duuianum . . . abluerunt ipsum babtismate sacro et ad Christum conuerterunt.
>
> [(Lucius) sent a letter to Pope Eleutherius to ask that he might be received by him in the Christian faith . . . The holy father, when he heard of the devotion of Lucius sent him two learned doctors, Faganus and Duvianus . . . who converted Lucius and washed him clean in holy baptism.][7]

The pagan temples were dedicated to God and the saints, and the flamens were replaced by bishops and the archflamens by archbishops. There were 28 bishops who were under the jurisdiction of 3 archbishops who had seats in London, York and Caerleon.

We have to admit that, historically, much of this account is probably untrue, although the exact date and circumstances of the introduction of Christianity to Britain are agreed to be unknown, and it is therefore always possible that Geoffrey may have more facts behind him than we are giving him credit for. Indeed, Petrie, writing in 1917, suggests that there is some plausibility in Geoffrey's account.[8] He asserts that a certain Bran was a hostage in Rome for 7 years in Caesar's household before the reign of Lucius. As the *Epistle to the Romans* was written in 58 AD, Christianity would have been a strong element in Caesar's household and it is not improbable that Bran would have been converted. Lleury, Bran's great great grandson gave lands and the privileges of freemen to those who dedicated themselves to the faith of Christ. The description of Lucius' reign follows this episode, and it is therefore plausible that Lucius gained his knowledge of miracles performed by Christian missionaries from those areas of Britain. Modern historians tend to disagree with Petrie's account, and it is generally believed that Christianity was an idea introduced by traders. However, this does not mean that the episode was merely from Geoffrey's imagination.

The story of the Lucian conversion is found in both Bede and Nennius. In Chapter 4 of Bede's *Historia Ecclesiastica* we learn that Lucius wrote to the holy Eleutherius and asked to be made a Christian under his direction. This request was quickly granted and the Britons received the faith, maintaining it undisturbed until the persecutions during the reign of the Emperor Diocletian. Other scholars have suggested that Geoffrey's sources for these events might also include the Latin *Annales Cambriae,* some Welsh royal genealogies, the *Life of St David,* and other *Lives* of 6th century Celtic saints.

C. N. L. Brooke provides us with further evidence for the existence of Duvianus and Faganus.[9] He tells us that between 1125 and 1130, the Chapter of St Andrew and St David addressed a letter to Pope Honorius II asserting that their church had been metropolitan since the days of Pope Eleutherius who sent Fagan and Duvian and founded bishoprics and three archbishoprics. It is possible that Geoffrey knew this letter and used it as one of his sources. More evidence for their existence is found in the Welsh *Brut Tysilio* in which they appear as Dyvan and Fagan, and churches dedicated to them were known in Geoffrey's time and in his district, within eight miles south and west of Llandaff.

Geoffrey's account of the Diocletian persecutions also deserves notice. In section 77 of the **Historia** we read:

> Superuenerat Maximianus Herculius, princeps milicie perdicti tyranni, cuius imperio omnes subuerse sunt ecclesie et cuncte sacre scripture que inueniri poterant . . . Inter ceteros utriusque sexus summa magnanimitate in acie Christi perstantes passus est Albanus Uerolamius, Iulius quoque et Aaron Urbis Legionis ciues . . . martyrii tropheo conuolauerunt.

> [Maximinianus Herculius, the general commanding the tyrant's armies, came over to Britain. By his orders all the churches were knocked down, and all copies of the Holy Scriptures which they could discover were burnt . . . Among the people of either sex, who with the greatest possible courage, stood firm in the battle-line for Christ were Albanus who suffered at St Albans, and Julius and Aaron, two of the townsfolk of the city of the Legions . . . bearing with them the crown of martyrdom.][10]

There is some authenticity in this account. The marytrdom of Saint Alban is accepted as fact, and both Gildas and Bede discuss the Diocletian persecutions. Bede tells us that Diocletian ordered that all churches must be destroyed and all Christians hunted out and killed. These orders were carried out without respite for ten years, with churches being burnt, innocent people outlawed, and martyrs slaughtered.

Geoffrey goes on to describe the restoration of the true faith during the reign of Vortigern:

> In tempore illo uenit sanctus Germanus Altissiodorensis episcopus et Lupus Trecacensis ut uerbum Dei Britonibus predicarent. Corrupta namque fuerat christianitas eorum tum propter paganos tum propter Pelagianam heresim cuius uenenum ipsos multis diebus affecerat. Beatorum igitur uirorum predicatione restituta est inter eos uere fidei religio quia multis miraculis cotidie preclarebant.

> [It was at this time that St Germanus, the Bishop of Auxerre, came, and Lupus, Bishop of Troyes, with him to preach the word of God to the Britons: for their Christian faith had been corrupted not only by the pagans but also by the Pelagian heresy, the poison of which had infected them for many a long day. However, the religion of the true faith was restored to them by the preaching of these saintly men. This they made clear almost daily by frequent miracles.][11]

We can see that the true faith was restored successfully because of the miracles performed by these men.

Both Bede and Augustine testify that Pelagius came to Britain. He preached that there was no moral difference between the clergy and the laity, and the true Christian way of life lay in the renunciation of riches. Three things should be found in the character of every Christian—knowledge, faith and obedience. By knowledge we recognise God, by faith we believe in Him, and by obedience we serve Him. Pelagius was more concerned with Christian living than with abstract problems of theology. The main dispute between Pelagius and Augustine arose over sin. Pelagius maintained that sin was a quality to be discerned in individual actions when a human being is imitating Adam, rather than a 'substance' which could be handed on to act upon human nature. The opponents of Pelagius argued that these views denied the necessity of the Cross, because if mankind's sin was not solid, but atomic, there could be no single solid act of redemption for mankind as a whole. It was certainly true that the Cross was not central to Pelagius' teaching. He saw Jesus as an example of human perfection, providing Christians with an example of how life should be lived, rather than God confronting sin. Pope Celestine regarded Britain as a stronghold of this heresy, and in 429 he sent Saint Germanus, Bishop of Auxerre as his own representative, to uproot the evil.[12] So here again, we find that Geoffrey's account bears some resemblance to the truth.

Section 188 of the **Historia** concerns Geoffrey's mention of Augustine's mission:

> Postquam ergo uenit Augustinus, inuenit in eorum prouintia vii episcopatus et archiepiscopatum religiosissimis presulibus munitos et abatias complures in quibus grex Domini rectum ordinem tenebat.

> [When Augustine arrived he found seven bishoprics and an archbishopric in the Britons' territory, all of them occupied by most devout prelates. There were also seven abbeys and in them God's flock observed a seemly rule.][13]

Geoffrey's narrative goes on to concentrate on the war between the Bishop of Bangor, who refused to co-operate with Augustine, and Ethelbert of Kent and his followers. Augustine's mission is given no further discussion.

It is accepted as historically true that Augustine landed in Britain on the Isle of Thanet in Kent in the year 597, and in 601 was consecrated Archbishop of Canterbury. This centralised order was to supersede the Celtic order, and it was the duty of the Canterbury church to establish unity throughout the British church and convert the Saxon kingdoms that remained heathen. This event is mentioned in the Anglo Saxon Chronicle for 596, which states 'in this year Pope Gregory sent Augustine to Britain with a good number of monks, who preached God's word to the English people'.[14]

The fact that Geoffrey often refers to paganism remaining in the British church is also born out by historical evidence. In 601, Mellitus brought a letter from the Pope to St Augustine saying that Pagan temples should not be destroyed, but only the idols which they housed. The buildings themselves were to be purified and altered to be made fit for the service of God. Sacrifices of animals could be continued as a means of providing good cheer for Christian festivals. A generation later, similar instructions were given by Pope Boniface to Edwin of Northumbria, and even then Paganism was not entirely destroyed. The first formal edict ordering the destruction of idols throughout the Kentish realm was not issued until nearly the middle of the seventh century.

Dubricius is the most important Welsh saint to feature in the Historia. In Section 130, Geoffrey says of him:

> (Aurelius) concessi[t] Eboracum Sansoni, illustri uiro summaque religione famoso; Urbem uero Legionum Dubritio quem diuina prouidentia in eodem loco profuturum elegerat.
>
> [(Aurelius) gave York to Samson, a most distinguished man, who was famous for his great piety. The City of the Legions he bestowed upon Dubricius, whom divine providence had already singled out as one suitable for promotion there.][15]

He later appears as Archbishop of Urbs Legionum and the primate of the land. He crowns Arthur, and makes a rousing speech to the Britons before the Battle of Bath, telling them that whoever dies for the sake of his brothers and his countrymen is following in the footsteps of Christ Himself. He is said to be so pious that his prayers were sufficient in themselves to cure any sick man. After Arthur's crowning at Caerleon, Dubricius resigns from his office as Archbishop to live as a hermit.

R. H. Fletcher explains in 1966 that this material is from Welsh tradition, and Dubricius features in the Vita Samsonis, which is the earliest surviving life of a Celtic saint.[16] Geoffrey indeed mentions Samson as Archbishop of Dol, which is in accordance with Breton tradition, as he is regarded as the patron saint of Brittany and the first archbishop of Dol. Samson's successor at Dol is Teliaus, and it has been suggested that this is the Latin form of Teilo,

who appears in the Life of Teilo, which is part of the Book of Llan Dav. Here is is said that when the Saxons were devastating the island, Teilo went to Armorica, and was joyfully received there by Samson.

Other characters Geoffrey mentions in passing who have some historical authenticity, include Piramus, Arthur's chaplain, who is made Archbishop of York. It is believed that Piramus is a mistaken spelling for Piranus, to whom Cornish chapels were dedicated. Geoffrey would have known of him as a fairly important saint in the Celtic church. St Helen is also mentioned, although Geoffrey presents her as a beautiful and accomplished British princess, and he ignores the most celebrated event in her history, which is her discovery of the True Cross in Jerusalem.

To conclude this paper, I would admit that we cannot take Geoffrey too seriously as a historian, and we have seen that much of what he says is written with a political motive. However, Julia Crick is perhaps being a little unfair when she describes the **Historia** as 'a pseudo-history in historical clothing'.[17] There is, in fact, a surprising amount of evidence that, in his depiction of the coming of Christianity, Geoffrey makes use of a considerable amount of source material, and does not merely make use of his own imagination. Furthermore, his writing does contain an unexpected degree of accuracy. Geoffrey only mentions religion occasionally, and rarely goes into great detail, and I believe that it is possible that he should be taken more seriously when he does mention religion, as at such times he is more at pains to write what he considers to be the truth. His reputation throughout history as a liar, is therefore not always justified, and his account of the arrival of Christianity shows both fact and fiction.

Notes

1. R. W. Hanning, *The Vision of History in Early Britain: from Gildas to Geoffrey of Monmouth*, (New York 1966), p.122.

2. A. J. P. Tatlock, 'Certain Contemporaneous Matters in Geoffrey of Monmouth', *Speculum*, VI (1931), 221-223.

3. Geoffrey of Monmouth, *Historia Regum Britannie*, ed. N. Wright, (Cambridge 1985), p.88, section 125. Hereafter cited as *HRB*. Geoffrey of Monmouth, *The History of the Kings of Britain*, trans. L. Thorpe, (Harmondsworth 1966), p.193, section viii. Hereafter cited as Thorpe.

4. V. J. Flint, 'The *Historia Regum Britanniae* of Geoffrey of Monmouth: Parody and its Purpose, a Suggestion', *Speculum*, LIV (1979), 466-467.

5. *HRB*, p.46, section 72. Thorpe, p.125, section iv.

6. S. Williams, 'Geoffrey of Monmouth and the Canon Law', *Speculum*, XXVII (1952), 186-187.

7. *HRB*, p.46, section 72. Thorpe, pp.124-125, section iv.

8. F. Petrie, 'Neglected British History', *Proceedings of the British Academy*, VIII (1917-1918), 216 ff.

9. C. N. L. Brooke, *Studies in the Early British Church* (Cambridge 1958), pp.207 ff.

10. *HRB,* p.50, section 77. Thorpe, pp.130-131, section v.

11. *HRB,* p.68, section 100. Thorpe, p.160, section v.

12. J. Ferguson, *Pelagius* (Cambridge 1956), pp.145 ff.

13. *HRB,* p.135, section 188. Thorpe, p.266, section vi.

14. *The Anglo-Saxon Chronicle,* ed. and trans. D. Whitlock et al (London 1961), p.14.

15. *HRB,* p.92, section 130. Thorpe, p.198, section viii.

16. R. H. Fletcher, *The Arthurian Material in the Chronicles* (Boston 1966), p.77.

17. Julia C. Crick, *The Historia Regum Britannie of Geoffrey of Monmouth. IV. Dissemination and Reception in the later Middle Ages* (Woodbridge 1991), p.196.

Kellie Robertson (essay date 1998)

SOURCE: "Geoffrey of Monmouth and the Translation of Insular Historiography," *Arthuriana,* Vol. 8, No. 4, Winter, 1998, pp. 42-57.

[*In the following essay, Robertson explains how Geoffrey distanced himself from rhetorical historians and the prevailing practices of historiography by asserting that his chronicle was a translation. Robertson also discusses the problem posed by Geoffrey's writing in Latin, a language associated in the Middle Ages with conveying the truth.*]

> In claiming to translate his Latin history from a Celtic source, Geoffrey attempts to disrupt the received Anglo-Latin historical tradition. The divergent responses of monastic writers and secular rulers to the *HRB* later in the twelfth-century attest the success of his project.
>
> (KR)

The Trojan vernacular was the most influential language never spoken in the British Isles during the Middle Ages. As one of the first (and most conspicuous) promoters of this hitherto undocumented language, Geoffrey of Monmouth has attained an ascendancy among the practitioners of so-called 'rhetorical historiography.' Attached to many twelfth-century chronicles by later historians, this designation acts as a kind of *caveat lector,* alerting the modern reader to the partial views and factual infelicities (such as a preoccupation with Trojan origins) that characterize many of these writings. And yet most twelfth-century historians were not coy about the overtly rhetorical nature of their writings. Since history was seen as a branch of literature, the task of the historian was to marry historical truth with rhetoric. In the preface to his *Gesta regum Anglorum* (ca. 1125), William of Malmesbury explains that the writing of history requires an author 'to season rough materials with Roman wit' ['exarata barbarice Romano sale condire'] (1:2). Later in this same work, William praises

Bede as a writer whose true stories were conveyed in an eloquent idiom, finding in him a model for later writers to follow.[1] These comments document a belief shared by many early twelfth-century historians: textual truth did not exist in spite of rhetoric but rather was only fully revealed through its agency. Classical rhetorical figures were not mere stylistic affectation for these historians; this manner of speaking was seen to be the appropriate literary counterpart to the ceremonies and symbolic events which these writers described. Rhetorical writing thus had a social dimension, for, as John Ward has pointed out, it 'functioned, like liturgy, to close out doubt and encourage and create certainty: it was practiced by the technical leaders of society, many of whom were linked with the best families: the bishops, the abbots' (148).

If Geoffrey of Monmouth is often included among this group of rhetorical historians, by his own account he does not belong in such company. In the preface to his *HRB,* Geoffrey describes the genesis and methodology of his history, an ostensible translation from a certain 'britannici sermonis librum vetustissimum':

> Rogatu itaque illius ductus, tametsi infra alienos ortulos falerata uerba non collegerim, agresti tamen stilo propriisque calamis contentus codicem illum in Latinum sermonem transferre curaui. Nam si ampullosis dictionibus pagin<a>m illinissem, tedium legentibus ingererem, dum magis in exponendis uerbis quam in historia intelligenda ipsos commorari oporteret.
>
> (2:6-12)

> [Guided by the request of that man [i.e. Walter, Archdeacon of Oxford], I have taken care to translate the book into the Latin language, though in doing so, I have not gathered ornamental words from other gardens, but have instead been content with a simple style and my own reed pens. If I had covered the page with bombastic figures, I would have bored my readers, for it would have been necessary for them to spend more time in expounding the words than in understanding the story.][2]

In contradistinction to William, Geoffrey claims that rhetorical prose works against the historian's desire to craft smoothly flowing narrative. Note that this is not an apology (a conventional instance of the humility topos) but a renunciation (a rejection of the norms of rhetorical history altogether); he does not say that he has done it badly, but rather that he has not done it at all. Geoffrey's wholesale rejection of rhetoric is odd for several reasons. First, the *HRB*'s narrative, loaded as it is with circumstantial detail and direct dialogue, tends to be more rhetorical than contemporary histories that explicitly embraced a rhetorical view of the past. Second, Geoffrey claims to disdain rhetorical figures within the narrative, while he adopts the topos of *translatio* as a legitimate place from which to narrate his history. I will argue that Geoffrey's announced rejection of rhetorical prose can be seen as symptomatic of his rejection of a particular strain of historical certainty, and his substitution of translation for rhetoric attests the ideological differences that mark out his own work from the works of historians like William of Malmesbury and Bede. If these writers viewed rhetorical prose as a necessary means of legitimating historical truth, Geoffrey asserted that his work could claim an authority from its status as a translation rather than from its dependence on the tradition of classical eloquence. In this way, Geoffrey's *HRB* opposes an ostensibly 'British' historiographical tradition to an Anglo-Latin one. Indeed, the *HRB* actively resists the tacit Anglo-Latin alliance that was Bede's legacy and that had governed the writing of history on the island since the ninth century.

THE TRANSLATION OF TROY

In the well-known colophon found in several manuscripts of the *HRB,* Geoffrey differentiates his own project from those of contemporary historians like William of Malmesbury and Henry of Huntingdon, whom he advises to occupy themselves with historical writings that do not demand a knowledge of the island's British pre-history. William and other early twelfth-century historians (following Bede) saw the history of Britain as a continuation of the history of classical Rome, a past transmitted solely via the act of *translatio studii*; Geoffrey emphasized the island's Trojan origins, a lineage communicated to the present through the Welsh people and their language in Walter's old book.

Geoffrey refashions the classical past emphasizing the Trojan rather than the Roman past of the island, the British rather than the exclusively Saxon. His narrative foregrounds disruptions to the historical continuum established by Bede (and then embraced by later historians): Britain was founded by Brutus who came to the island via Troy rather than directly from Rome; Caerleon (where Arthur holds his plenary court) is said to be Rome's rival in imperial splendor; the British defeat the Roman general Lucius Hiberius and nearly capture Rome itself. If Rome was for writers like William the emblem of learning and civilization from which contemporary Britain was regretfully alienated, for Geoffrey such alienation was inseparable from the island's origins and reinforced by the continual British struggle against Roman *imperium.* The *HRB*'s narrative thus poses an unusual critique of Roman history, disarming this historical model not as Augustinian historians did the Virgilian one—that is, by suppressing secular history in favor of salvational—but rather preferring an alternative model of secular history to the Virgilian one. Geoffrey's resistance to the centrality of Rome in insular history allows him to differentiate a British historiographical space distinct from an English one. In this way, Geoffrey's resistance to a rhetorical classicism expressing itself as 'Roman nostalgia' witnesses his opposition to the tacit alignment of the Anglo-Saxon with the Roman that prevailed in insular historiography more generally.

Moreover, Geoffrey claims to reverse the tide of *translatio studii* in which Bede and William participate. In asserting that his work is a translation from an old British book, Geoffrey moves knowledge from west to east, from ver-

nacular into Latin instead of the other way around. Geoffrey returns to this unusual claim at several points in the work, and he is the first writer to explore the potential of such a topos in Anglo-Latin writing (though he was not, of course, the first historian to translate such materials).[3] Geoffrey announces in the *HRB*'s preface that his translation was necessary to fill in the gaps left by Bede with reference to British history; he says, in effect, that his translation arose out of a disjunction within the tradition of insular historiography. Yet history writing in the twelfth century (as today) occurred primarily through acts of affiliation (for example, both William of Malmesbury and Henry Huntingdon say that they follow Bede and merely continue where he has left off). The gesture of disaffiliation with which the *HRB* begins is reinforced by Geoffrey's introduction of the translation topos into twelfth-century historiography as well as his elaboration upon the Trojan origins of the British people.

In the first section of the *HRB,* Brutus names the capital of his new-found land, 'Troia Nova,' the name by which, Geoffrey tells us, it was known for a long time until through corruption it came to be called Trinovantum. This etymology inscribes Trojan origins on the insular landscape, a rhetorical conversion of the existing Roman topography that gives a new past to the Welsh people.[4] 'Trinovantum' does not actually denote an ancient Roman town (as earlier historians tell us), but only appears that way because of the corrupting influence of time. In this way, the *HRB* repeatedly shows how rhetoric can constitute, and not merely describe, historical events. To claim Trojan origins is to set yourself up as the rival of Rome, rather than its descendant (and indeed this competition unfolds in the narrative as Arthur first challenges and then defeats the Roman forces). The emergence of the new nation coincides with the emergence of a new language, for what used to be called 'Trojan or Crooked Greek' is now called 'British' (21:11-13). If Trojan origins offer resistance to Roman ones, similarly, a Trojan-derived vernacular will offer resistance to Latin (as it does in Geoffrey's preface).

But what does Geoffrey's narrative, written in Latin, gain from a staged resistance to Rome and its language? Why claim to be a translator at all? The answer lies partly in the relation of Latin to the other languages spoken on the island in the twelfth century and partly in the received tradition of insular historiography out of which Geoffrey was writing. It is a commonplace that Latin conveyed the authority of both the patristic and academic past; as the public discourse, it stood against an essentially private and parochial vernacular culture. A passage taken from the opening of Bede's *Historia Ecclesiastica* attests this view of the relations among the various languages spoken on the island:

> Haec in praesenti, iuxta numerum librorum quibus Lex Divina scripta est, quinque gentium linguis, unam eandemque summae veritatis et verae sublimitatis scien-

tiam scrutatur et confitetur, Anglorum videlicet, Brettonum, Scottorum, Pictorum et Latinorum, quae meditatione Scripturarum ceteris omnibus est facta communis.

(1:16)

[This island at this present, with five sundry languages equal to the number of the books in which Divine Law hath been written, doth study and set forth one and the same knowledge of the highest truth and true majesty, that is, with the language of the English, the Britons, the Scots, the Redshanks [i.e., the Picts], and the Latin, which last by study of the Scriptures is made common to all the rest (trans. King)].

Latin has a kind of 'transparency' in relation to the other languages, a transparency that comes from the fact that Latin is not connected to a particular nationality but rather unites them all. If Bede's comment witnesses the cultural (and epistemological) priority assumed by Latin, at the same time, it claims to witness Latin's impartial communality in relation to the insular vernaculars. Latin was not shared equally among the speakers of all the languages on the island, however. Writers like Bede positioned the English people and their Anglo-Saxon language as the natural heirs both to the Roman empire and its church as well as to the Latin learning that accompanied them.

Geoffrey's project, in opposition to Bede's, was to make Latin 'visible' in insular historiography. By giving the British language Trojan roots and foregrounding the agency of *translatio* in his narrative, Geoffrey is able to approach the issues of language and nation as categories worthy of scrutiny rather than merely historical givens. Geoffrey is attempting something new, to establish what Deleuze and Guattari (in their discussion of Kafka) call somewhat ambiguously a 'minor literature'—a label that describes a work's perspective rather than its quality. This term refers to a literature composed in a 'major' language but from a peripheral place (for example, the kind of writing produced by Kafka as a Czech Jew writing in German).[5] Writing in the dominant discourse, but from a different perspective, allows a writer to 'deterritorialize' language; in Deleuze and Guattari's phrase, such deterritorialization makes it possible for a writer to enter into his language 'as if he were a stranger' ['entre dans sa propre langue comme un étranger'] (48). Geoffrey's claim that he is translating from Trojan-derived Welsh challenges not only the authority of an Anglo-Saxon that is privileged in its relation to Latin, but also the Anglo-Latin historiographical tradition in which the Welsh were seen as morally corrupt and their subjugation to the Saxons read as the appropriate corollary to *translatio imperii*. Bede portrayed the British as recalcitrant first in the face of Roman missionaries and later in the face of the ecclesiastic hierarchy that was Rome's legacy. Bede's narrative continually conflates English and Roman history so that Latin was neither impartial nor transparent in the way that Bede had described, but was instead aligned with one of the insular vernaculars. If for Bede (as for more recent writers like Homi Bhabha) nation is narration, for Geoffrey of Monmouth nation originates in translation. In order to write a history that could address the past of the whole island, Geoffrey had to resurrect the British language as a viable historical medium, one on a par with Latin, which he does by giving it Trojan origins within his narrative.

'CICERONIAN ELOQUENCE': MODELS OF SECULAR AUTHORITY

If Geoffrey resists the view of Rome common in Anglo-Latin insular historiography, that does not mean he has no use for the Roman writers found so frequently in the works of contemporaries like William of Malmesbury. This classical past authorizes a particularly British model of speech within the narrative. The defining moment of Britain's relationship to Rome occurs when messengers from Rome arrive at Arthur's plenary court in Caerleon and demand the payment of tribute withheld by Arthur as well as the return of lands seized from the empire. This challenge is interpreted directly by Cador, Duke of Cornwall, as a sign from God that the Britons have succumbed to sloth and that divine intervention has provided them this opportunity to redeem themselves and restore their former reputation for virtue and bravery (158:27-36). His response echoes religious arguments frequently marshalled behind the notion of *translatio imperii,* a concept originating in the Bible (Ecclesiastes 10:8) and amplified in patristic writings that tried to make sense of Rome's decline. Writers like Jerome portrayed a Rome needing purification of its sins in order to regain the paths of both heavenly salvation and earthly dominion.[6] The British response to the Roman challenge calls into play the rhetoric of *translatio imperii*; but rather than casting itself in the role of fit receptacle for an imminent transfer of Roman *dominium,* Britain feels the impending threat of *dominium* passing away. In Geoffrey's **HRB,** the conflict between Rome and Britain stems from the fact that each believes that it occupies the same historical position.

More importantly, however, this confusion over the correct site of empire masks Geoffrey's transfer of *translatio imperii* from the religious to the secular realm. Arthur stigmatizes Rome's claims as illegal rather than immoral:

'Nichil enim quod ui et uiolentia adquiritur iuste ab ullo possidetur. Qui uiolentiam intulit irrationabilem ergo causam pretendit qua nos iure sibi tributarios esse arbitratur. Quoniam autem id quod iniustum est a nobis presumpsit exigere, consimili ratione petamus ab illo tributum Rome'.

(159:17-21)

['Nothing that is acquired by force and violence can ever be held legally by him who has done the violence. Therefore he pleads an unreasonable case in so far as he maintains that we are his tributaries by law. Since he presumes to demand something illegal from us, let us by similar reasoning seek from him the tribute of Rome.']

In biblical and Hieronymian accounts, the historical movement of *translatio imperii* was the result of moral iniquity, rather than political transgression. In Geoffrey, the movement of power between countries is not so much redemptive as retributive: Britain will not redeem the injustices perpetrated by Rome but will rather reenact them just as we have seen in the narration of Arthur's brutal campaigns in Gaul and Ireland that precedes the description of his plenary court. In effect, Arthur's rhetoric witnesses Geoffrey's 'translation' of *translatio imperii,* not only from Rome to Britain, but from the religious sphere into the political and legal realm.

Arthur's response to the Roman challenge prompts Hoel, leader of the Armorican Britons, to declare that Arthur's speech "'adorned with Ciceronian eloquence'" ["'tua deliberatio Tulliano liquore lita'"] has inspired them to defend their liberty against Rome (160:6-7). Hoel's seemingly fatuous comment points to the fact that Arthur uses the rhetorical tools of the very power he opposes. To employ the rhetoric of Rome is to occupy the imperial position of Rome. This 'Ciceronian eloquence' attests the model of kingship which Arthur embodies in the *HRB,* one based not only on the assumption of the rhetoric of *dominium* but also on the appropriation of Latin rhetoric more generally. The rhetoric rejected by Geoffrey of Monmouth in his preface is here employed by the character of Arthur, and its appearance raises the question of what precisely 'Ciceronian eloquence' comes to signify in the *HRB.* In addition to his numerous rhetorical treatises, Cicero had come down to the Middle Ages as the advocate for a *res publica* in which a citizen's primary duty was not to religion, but to his country. Arthur's response to the Roman challenge paints him as an inheritor of this type of *pro patria* language. *Patria* was a word frequently employed by Arthur, but we also see it in the speech of Dubricius, Bishop of Caerleon. In exhorting Arthur's troops to bravery in the coming battle, he urges them: "'Fight for your fatherland, and endure death willingly for it if you should be killed'" ["'Pugnate pro patria uestra et mortem si superuenerit ultro pro eadem patimini'"] (147:6-7). This *patria* coincides with the entire island in Geoffrey's account, for, after the death of Utherpendragon, Arthur is said to inherit by rightful claim, 'totius insule monarchiam' ['rulership of the whole island'] (143:18-19). This sense of a unified *patria,* defined geographically as the entire island, is found in neither Bede nor William of Malmesbury. Neither of these histories admit common ground in the political and religious divisions that rule the island; the only common ground shared among the various racial groups in these accounts is the legacy of Rome. If *patria* was originally a term defined on the basis of a Roman 'us' versus a foreign 'them,' Geoffrey changes the referents. In turning the Roman idea of *patria* against Rome, he uses it as a national rallying cry to repel Roman threats to British empire. Arthur becomes a kind of cultural heretic: he is a Briton who speaks with Roman eloquence against the Romans, the embodiment of the cultural difference Geoffrey stages throughout his history. Arthur's speech, like the Trojan origins of the British people, opens up a new space in insular historiography.

THE RECEPTION OF GEOFFREY AND ARTHUR

If Arthur's speech detailed a *translatio imperii* that moved according to secular rather than sacred imperative, we find similar translations of power to a secular realm elsewhere in the narrative. Arthur appoints two archbishops and several bishops at his plenary court with only the consent of his nobles (157-58). In this scene, investiture has become a court-orchestrated ceremony that effectively bypasses the prerogatives of the church. Lay investiture was already a controversial subject at the time Geoffrey was writing as it had caused a rift (documented by Eadmer) between Henry I and Anselm in the early years of the century; the subject would only grow more heated under Henry II.[7]

The *HRB*'s perspective on these matters can in part be explained by Geoffrey's own circumstances: charter evidence suggests that he was a canon of the college of St. George's in Oxford. As a chapel and secular college attached to a royal castle, St. George's was patronized by and received its privileges from the king, a situation that allowed the college a good measure of freedom from local episcopal jurisdiction (this situation lasted at St. George's until its assumption by Osney Abbey in 1149).[8] Secular colleges occupied an unusual position in the medieval church, since the deans of such colleges were appointed by letters patent and installed by lay officers (the deans, in turn, oversaw the appointment of the canons).[9] This arrangement showed 'the possibility of royal supremacy and independence from Rome in an age when the control and discipline of churches were usually matters of episcopal or papal jurisdiction' (Denton ix). A model of rulership that promoted the king's spiritual prerogative would not be unexpected in Geoffrey's work, since it was this model that governed the workings of colleges like St. George's. Geoffrey's generally secularizing view of history can thus be traced to his position as a secular canon.

Valerie Flint rightfully points out that 'all of [Geoffrey's] sees are secular sees. There is no monk-bishop to be found in the whole work' (465). It is, in fact, difficult to find any reference to monastic houses in the *HRB,* and they are certainly never mentioned in the role for which they were best known, as channels for the dissemination of knowledge on the island. As a secular canon, Geoffrey wrote from outside of the monastic tradition which had controlled both historiographical production and the preservation of classical knowledge on the island. Geoffrey's own situation was anomalous in much the same way that the *HRB* was anomalous in terms of the received norms of insular historiography. What the narrative omissions of the *HRB* attest implicitly—that is, the rivalry between secular and regular orders—is witnessed explicitly in the *HRB*'s epigraph, which warned away the monastic historians William of Malmesbury and Henry Huntingdon from discussing the British subject matter Geoffrey had claimed as his own. Geoffrey's denunciation of rhetorical history writing in the preface to his *HRB* can be seen, in part, as a response to his own situation outside of the tradition which produced this kind of history.

Geoffrey's role as a secular canon is also significant because colleges and chapels of royal castles maintained a special relationship with the king's household.[10] The status of St. George's explains why we find Geoffrey as a witness to many royal charters, including the 1153 treaty in which Stephen named Henry his heir. That St. George's was a center of royal patronage may also help explain the wide circulation of the **HRB.** Though Geoffrey probably began writing the **HRB** 'on spec' (as the array of dedications suggests), he found magnanimous, if unfortunately posthumous, patronage in his dedicatee Robert of Gloucester's nephew, Henry II. Lee Patterson and Francis Ingledew have written persuasively about how the **HRB**'s Trojan genealogy was used by Henry II to sanction his shaky succession to the throne from Stephen (as well as how the **HRB**'s resistance to the Anglo-Latin alliance on the island was helpful to the Norman political agenda more generally). But the Arthurian model of secular power was also useful to the new king, and the project of translating Geoffrey became the site of specific political claims for Henry, claims which brought him into conflict with the regular communities. Henry's simultaneous attempts to curb their liberties (while expanding royal privilege) was resented, and monasteries became organized centers of opposition to the demands of Henry's increasingly bureaucratic government. Henry had a series of run-ins with religious houses, most notably the Cistercians with the untimely death of Thomas Becket.

The Becket conflict was in part a conflict over lay investiture. As Beryl Smalley notes, the core of Henry's case against Becket, and in defence of royal prerogative more generally, depended not on readily available political or theological precedents, but on the customs of his forebears (160-4). These 'customs' were finally codified at the Council of Clarendon in 1164 where Henry had summoned Becket along with his other bishops. Henry demanded that all assent to a document codifying such customs as had been observed at the court of his grandfather. The resulting constitutions gave Henry significant powers over investiture (among other privileges), insisting that when an archbishopric or bishopric became vacant, 'the election ought to take place in the lord king's chapel with the assent of the lord king.'[11] In Arthur, Henry had found a model of kingship that mixed spiritual with temporal oversight, a model consistent with Henry's attempts to establish certain inalienable rights of the crown (including royal control over investiture). Henry's appeal to the vague customs and usages of his ancestors made it desirable for him to have a work that documented such customs entering the mainstream of the vernacular; this is one reason we find the project of translating Geoffrey's translation associated with Henry's court. My point in rehearsing these events is to show that the reception of the **HRB** is to some extent the result of the tensions between monastic and secular authorities in the twelfth century. This is to discuss not necessarily what the **HRB** means (or less, what Geoffrey may have intended), bur rather how the work got used in the second half of the century.

We see this dynamic not only in Henry's use of the **HRB** but also in the response of later twelfth-century historians to this work. Modern historians always note that William of Newburgh and Gerald of Wales (both writing in the 1190s) were virtually the only two critics to voice scepticism of Geoffrey throughout the Middle Ages, but no one questions why it was these two writers or why it occured at this particular time. In the preface to his *Historia rerum Anglicarum* (ca. 1196), William begins by reaffirming the norms of rhetorical historiography in the face of a specifically British historiography, such early histories as Gildas's on account of its 'unpolished and rude language' ['sermone . . . impolitus atque insipius'] (1:11). He then compares Geoffrey's history to Bede's, and finds the former lacking. He attacks Geoffrey both as a historian and as a translator:

> Gaufridus hic dictus est, agnomen habens Arturi, pro eo quod fabulas de Arturo, ex priscis Britonum figmentis sumptas et ex proprio auctas, per superductum latini sermonis colorem honesto historiae nomine palliavit
>
> (1:13).

> [This man is called Geoffrey and bears the sobriquet Arthur, because he has taken up the stories about Arthur from the old fictitious accounts of the Britons, has added to them himself, and by embellishing them in the Latin tongue, he has cloaked them with the honorable title of truth
>
> (trans. Walsh).]

William objects to the translation of Merlin's prophecies because 'in translating them into Latin, he has published them as though they were authentic prophecies resting on unshakeable truth' ['dum eas in Latinum transfunderet, tanquam authenticas et immobili veritate subnixas prophetias, vulgavit'] (1:12). He again describes Geoffrey as the one 'who translated the infantile stories of these prophecies from the British tongue' ['qui divinationum illarum nenias ex Britannico transtulit'] (1:12). William objects to Geoffrey's assertion of a new historiographical order which substitutes fables about Arthur for *latinitas,* correctly identifying *translatio* as the agency through which Geoffrey is able to suppress earlier historical narrative. In the *Itinerarium Kambriae* (ca. 1191), Gerald of Wales voices a similar concern over Geoffrey's trustworthiness when he recounts the story of a Welshman called Meilerius who, as a result of his possession by evil spirits, had the ability to point out false passages in books even though he was illiterate. During one such bout of possession, the Gospel of John was placed on his chest, at which point, all the spirits fled, but when the Gospel was replaced with Geoffrey's **HRB,** the spirits returned more thickly than before (I. 5).

We can read the accounts of William and Gerald as 'stigmatizing narratives' whose characterizations of Geoffrey illustrate the increasing anxiety over the proper relation between vernacular and Latin in the realm of rhetorical historiography. In the broadest sense, both of these writers affirm that Bede's view of the relation between the insular languages still holds; they also affirm proper ecclesiastical history in the face of Geoffrey's 'improper' history. In so doing, they have to distinguish between a true and a false Latin textuality. The possibility that Latin did not convey historical truth was obviously a cause of some anxiety for William since he pointedly accuses Geoffrey of using Latin to 'cloak' his vernacular fables. If Latin was supposed to be the transparent language of truth (as we saw in the earlier quotation from Bede), Geoffrey's sin was to make Latin opaque as a historical medium. This anxiety is implicit in Gerald's Meilerius anecdote as well. The illiterate Meilerius has access to Latin texts only through demonic agency, a demonic agency that is, in turn, identified with Geoffrey's *HRB*. The paradox at the center of the Meilerius story—the *illiteratus* who can separate true Latin history from false—speaks to both Gerald and William as writers and readers of such histories. It was a talent that Gerald especially would have loved to possess, since he uses Geoffrey's material in a number of places.[12] Taken together, Gerald's fable and William's indignation point to their own fears about using 'false' Latin sources. Both accounts stigmatize translation as an act which introduces ambiguity into Latin as the language of historical truth, questioning its status as the sole authorized conveyer of that truth.

These concerns over language and the canonicity of historical writing do not sufficiently account for the virulence of their attack on Geoffrey, however. Indeed William's attack on Geoffrey seems singularly unprovoked in light of the fact that his post-Conquest subject matter does not overlap with Geoffrey's narrative, which ends in the seventh century with the reign of Cadwallader, a good four centuries before William's narrative begins. In this context, it is significant that both William of Newburgh and Gerald of Wales were writing their histories at the request of powerful Cistercian patrons. William announces in the preface of the *Historia rerum Anglicarum* that he writes at the behest of Ernald, abbot of the Cistercian house of Rievaulx. In 1188, Gerald had accompanied Baldwin, the Cistercian Archbishop of Canterbury, on a preaching tour of Wales, a trip that resulted in Gerald's *Itinerarium Kambriae*. If these writers were unsympathetic to the translation of Troy that had allowed Geoffrey to unfix the linguistic (and related national) alignments that were currently in place in historical writing in the early twelfth century, they were even less sympathetic to a historian whose work had been adopted by Henry II. Gerald in particular was a fanatical devotee of Becket and took every opportunity in his writings to attack Henry, a treatment he seems more than happy to extend to a writer whose work had become associated with the king's court. If Geoffrey's reception at the end of the century witnesses the primacy of this linguistic realignment to his project, it equally witnesses the significance of the Becket conflict to the writing of insular history at this time.

In the historical writing of the twelfth century, debate over which version of the classical past would be used resonated keenly with contemporary events. Geoffrey's recourse to a primarily Trojan rather than Roman past li-

censed his reapportionment of historical agency on the island. In the preface to the *HRB*, he substitutes the authority of translation from a supposedly authoritative British source for the rhetorical tradition that had licensed the writing of insular history for several centuries, while, in the narrative, he calls on classical rhetoric to define a new model of secular leadership. The model of centralized power embodied by Arthur was eloquent to the unsettled 1130s and 1140s, and it would only become more so as Stephen's reign progressed (or rather, deteriorated). In the *HRB* Henry had found a model of secular authority that represented an idealization of his own dream of acceding to rulership of the entire island, of possessing a power less fettered by the religious orders that would prove so troublesome during his reign. Both William of Newburgh and Gerald of Wales, on the other hand, saw the potential threats posed by Geoffrey's *HRB,* not only to ecclesiastical prerogative, but also to the traditional alignment of Anglo-Saxon and Roman in Latin insular historiography. If Henry emphasized Trojan genealogies and Arthurian 'custom,' these later historians would affirm the priority of Bedean history with its emphasis on the Roman continuity that underwrote monastic privilege. To read the indignation of these later twelfth-century historians against Henry's appropriation of Geoffrey is to see how the *HRB*'s refashioning of the classical past became part of a larger conversation about the rights of the clergy as opposed to those of secular powers.

Notes

1. John O. Ward notes that William appears to be more interested in linking the style of his work to that of Bede than in proving the veracity of his sources (119). For a more general discussion of the aims and effects of medieval rhetorical historiography, see Southern (esp. 177-83).

2. All citations from Geoffrey of Monmouth refer to Neil Wright, ed., *The Historia Regum Britannie of Geoffrey of Monmouth I: Bern, Burgerbibliothek, MS. 568* (Cambridge: D.S. Brewer, 1984), and translations are my own.

3. The concatenation of the terms 'history' and 'translation' appears throughout the work. For example, when Geoffrey dedicates the prophecies of Merlin independently to Alexander, Bishop of Lincoln, he once again stresses its status as a translation ['Coegit me, Alexander Lincolinensis presul, nobilitatis tue dilectio prophetias Merlini de Britannico in Latinum transferre antequam historiam parassem quam de gestis regum Britannicorum inceperam'] (110:1-4). In describing the decline of the British empire at the hands of the Saxons near the end of the *HRB*, Geoffrey mentions the Welsh flight into Brittany and promises to translate another work describing this event more fully ['Set hec alias referam cum librum de exulatione eorum transtulero'] (186:16-17).

4. Although Geoffrey derived the Trojan origins of the British people from Nennius's *Historia Brittonum,*

he was the first to enlarge on these origins. In the *HRB*, the arrival of Brutus and his Trojan band displaces the indigenous population of the island; the establishment of a new Troy occurs at the expense of a place that used to be called Albion and that was inhabited by some unruly giants. This narrative act of displacement covers up the actual historical displacement that occurs, since it is not giants but rather Romans who are being purged.

5. Homi Bhabha describes a paradigm of 'cultural translation' in *The Location of Culture* that complements the idea of 'minor literature' formulated by Deleuze and Guattari. This kind of translation 'desacralizes the transparent assumptions of cultural supremacy, and in that very act, demands a contextual specificity, a historical differentiation within minority positions' (228). In Geoffrey's translation, linguistic difference signifies cultural difference; it demonstrates that the British have a historical existence outside of the position allotted to them in the Saxon narrative of martial and moral domination on the island.

6. For the idea of a 'penitent Rome' and its relation to *translatio imperii,* see Curtius (29-30).

7. For details of this conflict, see Eadmer's preface to his *Historia Novorum in Anglia.* Investiture is but one example of how the *HRB* repeatedly describes a society in which the role of the ecclesiastic hierarchy is diminished in favor of a more centralized, secular administration (another example of this bias is to be found in Geoffrey's transfer of jurisdiction over sanctuary from the church to the state). Henry II's interest in lay investiture is discussed below.

8. Salter documents the relevant charter evidence on Geoffrey's position as a canon ('Geoffrey of Monmouth and Oxford'). Secular canons were collegiate clergy; unlike regular canons, they lived communally but did not follow the Augustinian rule. On the difference between the two in the twelfth century, see Bynum (2). For the particular situation of the college at St. George's, see Denton (118-21). The spiritual freedoms of royal colleges and chapels apparently mirrored those enjoyed by religious houses; thus secular canons and monks occupied similar yet exclusive positions. Denton asserts that the spiritual privileges associated with such secular colleges began to decline in the late twelfth-century (135-36).

9. For an overview of the workings of secular colleges, see Thompson (81-83).

10. According to Denton, 'privileges were granted by the king to St. George's, and the king claimed for the canons of the college that they held their lands in frankalmoign' (120). Evidence of royal intervention on behalf of St. George's is evident in charters dating from about 1127 (Salter, Facsimiles nos. 57 and 58). Additionally, Thompson notes that the deaneries and canonries associated with royal secular colleges were frequently the 'perquisites of king's clerks' (83).

11. Article twelve: the text of these constitutions is translated in Douglas (2:718-22). The constitutions stipulate that, in addition to the conditions laid down therein, 'there are, moreover, many other great customs and privileges pertaining to holy mother-Church and to the lord king and his barons of the realm which are not contained in this document. Let them be safe for holy Church and for our lord the king and his heirs and the barons of the realm. And let them be inviolably observed for ever and ever' (722).

12. It seems that Gerald must share Meilerius's ability to distinguish between true and false passages in historical works. The Meilerius passage can be read as an anxious gloss on Gerald's own literary production in so far as it directly follows his description of Arthur's plenary court at Caerleon, the details of which are taken directly from Geoffrey.

Works Cited

Bede. *Opera Historica.* Ed. and trans. J. E. King. 2 vols. LCL. London: William Heinemann Ltd, 1930.

Bhabha, Homi. *The Location of Culture.* London: Routledge, 1994.

———., ed. *Nation and Narration.* London: Routledge, 1990.

Bynum, Caroline Walker. *Docere Verbo et Exemplo: An Aspect of Twelfth-century Spirituality.* Harvard Theological Studies. Missoula, Montana: Scholar Press, 1979.

Curtius, Ernst. *European Literature and the Latin Middle Ages.* Trans. Willard R. Trask. Princeton: Princeton University Press, 1953.

Deleuze, Gilles and Felix Guattari. *Kafka: pour une littérature mineure.* Paris: Minuit, 1975.

Denton, J. H. *English Royal Free Chapels 1100-1300: A Constitutional Study.* Manchester: Manchester University Press, 1970.

Douglas, David C., ed. and trans. *English Historical Documents.* 12 vols. London: Eyre and Spottiswoode, 1953.

Eadmer. *Historia Novorum in Anglia.* Ed. Martin Rule. Rolls Series 81. London: Longmans, 1884.

Flint, Valerie. 'The *Historia regum Britanniae* of Geoffrey of Monmouth: Parody and its Purpose. A Suggestion.' *Speculum* 54 (1979): 447-68.

Gerald of Wales. *Itinerarium Kambriae et Descriptio Kambriae. In Giraldi Kambrensis Opera.* Vol. 6. Ed. James F. Dimock. Rolls Series 21.6. London: Longmans, 1868.

Ingledew, Francis. 'The Book of Troy and the Genealogical Construction of History: The Case of Geoffrey of Monmouth's *Historia regum Britanniae*.' *Speculum* 69 (1994): 665-704.

Patterson, Lee. *Negotiating the Past: The Historical Understanding of Medieval Literature.* Madison: University of Wisconsin Press, 1987.

Salter H. E., ed. *Facsimiles of Early Charters in Oxford Muniment Rooms.* Oxford: Oxford University Press, 1929.

———. 'Geoffrey of Monmouth and Oxford.' *English Historical Review 34* (1919): 382-5.

Smalley, Beryl. *The Becket Conflict and the Schools.* Oxford: Basil Blackwell, 1973.

Southern, Richard. 'Aspects of the European Tradition of Historical Writing: 1. The Classical Tradition from Einhard to Geoffrey of Monmouth.' *Transactions of the Royal Historical Society,* 5th ser., 20 (1970): 173-96.

Strohm, Paul. *Hochon's Arrow: the Social Imagination of Fourteenth century Texts.* Princeton: Princeton University Press, 1992.

Thompson, A. Hamilton. *The English Clergy and their Organization in the Later Middle Ages.* Oxford: Clarendon Press, 1947.

Ward, John O. 'Some Principles of Rhetorical Historiography in the Twelfth Century,' in *Classical Rhetoric and Medieval Historiography* (ed. Ernst Breisach). *Studies in Medieval Culture* 19. Kalamazoo, MI: Medieval Institute Publications, 1985. 103-165.

William of Malmesbury. *Gesta Regum Anglorum.* Ed. William Stubbs. 2 vols. Rolls Series 90. London: Longmans, 1889.

William of Newburgh. *Historia Rerum Anglicarum. In Chronicles of the Reigns of Stephen, Henry II, and Richard I.* Ed. Richard Howlett. 2 vols. Rolls Series 82. London: Longmans, 1884-85.

———. *The History of English Affairs.* Ed. and trans. P. G. Walsh and M. J. Kennedy. Warminster, Wiltshire: Aris and Phillips, 1988.

Wright, Neil, ed. *The Historia Regum Britannie of Geoffrey of Monmouth I: Bern, Burgerbibliothek, MS. 568.* Cambridge: D.S. Brewer, 1984.

John E. Curran, Jr. (essay date 1999)

SOURCE: "Geoffrey of Monmouth in Renaissance Drama: Imagining Non-History," in *Modern Philology*, Vol. 97, No. 1, 1999, pp. 1-20.

[*In the following essay, Curran argues that playwrights who tried to be faithful in their adaptations of Geoffrey's material met with disappointing results, whereas William Shakespeare's version—which did not treat the* History *literally—is a masterpiece.*]

At the end of *King Lear,* Shakespeare makes a crucial decision that sheds much light on his intentions for the play: contrary to the story he would have read everywhere else, he has Regan and Goneril die without issue. Geoffrey of Monmouth's version, recounted in his twelfth-century *His-toria Regum Britanniae,* required that each daughter have a son so that the family feud could live on into the next generation.[1] Shakespeare avoids any suggestion of this futurity, and the results of his drastic innovation are twofold. First, cutting the story off from its chronicle future precludes a correspondence between the play and any historical reality it might purport to imitate.[2] The play limits itself to its own world. Positioned in no larger, continuing story of British history, Regan and Goneril seem not to be based upon persons conceived as historical. Second, the play's lack of futurity de-emphasizes any political message or lesson that might be extracted from it. Such maxims as "manage the succession well," or "do not divide the kingdom," or "avoid civil strife" seem of little use with all the putatively historical characters dead; apocalypse, not politics, prevails.[3] Leaving the story truncated from its chronicle future is one decision among many by which Shakespeare clearly differentiates *King Lear* from a play like *Antony and Cleopatra*—where his purpose is to imagine what historical figures would have been like and to consider the causes and workings of political actions.

My argument here is that Shakespeare's double escape from history—that is, from having to imagine historical persons and from having to consider exemplarity—makes *King Lear* unique among the extant Galfridian chronicle plays treating the pre-Roman era of British history. The other surviving plays, Thomas Sackville and Thomas Norton's *Gorboduc* and the anonymous plays *Locrine, The True Chronicle History of King Leir,* and *Nobody and Somebody* (chronicling the story of Elidure, the three-times king), fail to make such an escape; these plays are more seriously committed than *Lear* to representing a history, and so the non-historicity of their topic creates a constant disruption for them.[4] These plays, all products of the later sixteenth century, come from a time when belief in the historicity of the Galfridian tradition was unstable and eroding.[5] Thus, those playwrights who drew upon Galfridian personages for history-play material were unsure both whether they were imagining real people and whether they were generating examples from actual history.

As Judith Anderson has explained, a history play—like Renaissance historiography itself—was expected to take liberties with historical events in order to produce imaginative fictions that were true to what events meant; Shakespeare's *Richard III*, like Sir Thomas More's, is designed to represent through an exaggerated caricature a historical person conceived as having been genuinely evil.[6] But what were the parameters in representing historical persons from thousands of years ago, persons about whom so little was known—persons who were probably not historical at all? It is true that treating the ancient British past was widely considered to be the same as treating more recent history. Such writers as William Baldwin, compiler of the first *Mirror for Magistrates,* and later Thomas Heywood, in his *Apology for Actors,* cited all British history "from the landing of Brute" as perfect material to teach people history and the wholesome examples attached to it.[7] But as Arthur B. Ferguson has noted, the problems involved with creating an imaginative interpretation of history—that is, with mixing history and poetry—"naturally increased exponentially" with "inquiry into the prehistoric past."[8] In these four prehistorical Galfridian plays, the authors appear unsure of exactly what they are attempting to write. Are they filling in invented details to embellish a core of fact, or are they simply imagining imaginary characters?

Englishmen of the sixteenth century had every reason to feel that the Galfridian legends were important enough to treat as history. Not only had the legends become a conspicuous part of the Tudor myth, but they also carried substantial weight regarding Britain's own ancient past.[9] They were stories every patriot ought to learn about and learn from. One of the more striking defenses of Geoffrey's historicity, that of Richard Harvey, categorized the Galfridian legends according to the various significances of heroes and events (examples of deceit, examples of intemperance, examples of good government); the implication was that the British History should be deemed true because it looked every bit like a proper history—like a good national story that yielded a wealth of wholesome examples.[10] This attractive utility, however, was undermined by a wave of sixteenth-century criticism of Geoffrey, given voice by Polydore Vergil (1534) and stalwart authority by William Camden (1586).[11] Such skepticism, although often fervently rebutted, affected those who would translate Geoffrey's stories into historical dramas. Even Sackville and Norton, writing near midcentury, would have encountered questions about Geoffrey in chronicles of Robert Fabyan and Richard Grafton;[12] certainly, our three anonymous authors would have found serious doubts articulated in Holinshed's chronicles.[13] These playwrights felt the allure of the stories from their nation's most ancient past but were also exposed to a creeping sense of the adequacy of those skeletal legends and of the inaccessibility of that past.

I am concerned here with identifying aspects of these four plays which reflect the poets' conflicting senses and consequent uncertainty about whether they are actually recreating history. Invariably, the authors' attempts to translate Geoffrey's stories into history plays are undermined by the non-historicity of the material. The resulting dynamic has three principal manifestations: (1) the playwrights move the plays in and out of historical times, (2) they craft history-play plots but only by altering the historical record to the point of fiction, and (3) they imagine the minds of historical persons but with unhistorical-seeming results. Such features mark the differences between Shakespeare's play and *Gorboduc, Locrine, Nobody and Somebody,* and *Leir.* Among the Renaissance Galfridian plays, only *King Lear* is secure in its status as non-history.

I

Chronological situatedness is a prime characteristic of the history play: plays experienced as imitating a historical reality tend to be invested with a sense of where the action is on the time line. Thus Shakespeare's *Richard II* makes many references to the time of Edward III; the characters have a past life. Shakespeare's *King Lear,* on the other

hand, makes no reference at all to a previous era. Of what has happened before, we have no idea, as the playwright cuts off his version of the Leir story from both chronicle past and chronicle future. In the four other plays on Galfridian subjects, however, this is not the case. Like Shakespeare's own *Cymbeline*—which takes place within the bounds of history and not prehistory, being of the Roman era—these four plays make mention of the past and call attention to chronological matters. But while Shakespeare injects chronological details such as the reigns of past kings Cassivellaunus, Tenantius, and Dunwallo into *Cymbeline* with chronological precision, he injects them into a story wholly of his own invention; he is merely using these details to decorate a fiction which has no pretensions of imagining historical persons. The four plays I am interested in do not share this detachment; in each of them, chronological references can be found in a firmly Galfridian plot. But although chronology is suggested in the plays, it is always disrupted. Time is inconstant.

We encounter, for example, an ambiguous historicity in the odd treatment of what would constitute recent history for characters. In *Locrine,* recent history occupies a great portion of the first scene as the dying Brutus, eponymous founder of Britain, recounts to his three sons—Locrine, Camber, and Albanact—his great deeds and their significance; as the great-grandson of Aeneas, he is the rescuer of the Trojan name. The playwright evidently intends that we consider a Brutus who has actually lived through the events he describes. But toward the end of the speech when Brutus recalls his extermination of the giants he says that they "come of Albion's race, / With Gogmagog, son of Samotheus" as their "captain" (1.2.118-20). A historical Brutus would have had no way of knowing about Albion, a legendary figure associated with a time long before the Trojans' arrival in Britain; and "Samotheus" was no giant at all, but the supposed founder of a civilization which predated Albion himself. For the orthodox chronology, the playwright could have gone to Holinshed;[14] but he chose instead to proffer his own muddled version. Whatever his reason for this innovation, its result is clear: we no longer sense that Brutus's speech represents the memories of an actual person. "Samotheus" and "Albion" seem like names drawn haphazardly from the chronicles for mere decoration, and they make the rest of the speech appear more fictional. Does this Brutus exist in time or not?

Nobody and Somebody and *Gorboduc* exhibit similar contradictions when dealing with their characters' recent history. In the first scene of *Nobody and Somebody,* Cornwell, the wise old counselor, notes that he has served four kings (1.54). Although he is an invented figure, Cornwell's memory is sound; since the reigns of the three previous monarchs total some twenty-six years in Holinshed, Cornwell has not violated the time line and actually helps cement it by making a remark suited to the historical context. Later, however, the humble King Elidure pleads with the nobles to let him abdicate and reinstate his deposed brother Archigallo, and he appeals to Cornwell, "As thou didst love our father, let his son / Be righted" (5.998-99).

Such a reference imagines for Elidure and Cornwell a shared past they both understand. But, according to the chronicles, the king before Archigallo was Elidure's eldest brother, Gorbonian, not their father, while their father, king before Gorbonian, was the mercilessly cruel Morindus, whom no one would have recalled with love.[15] Hence the remark undermines the seriousness of the very time frame it suggests: where is Elidure in time and what does he remember about his predecessors? In *Gorboduc*, Philander, the second of King Gorboduc's three counselors on the succession issue, suggests that Britain has been quiet since the civil war in which the ambitious King Morgan (Leir's grandson) was slain by his cousin (1.2.161-65). This remark does much to establish a historical time scheme; a counselor in a historical Gorboduc's court doubtless would comment on the nation's most recent episode of civil strife and characterize it as happening a fairly long time ago, since six reigns intervene between Morgan and Gorboduc.[16] The next mention of the recent past, however, is imprecise. Gorboduc's best counselor, Eubulus, urges him to remember how Brute, Britain's first king, inaugurated the practice of dividing the realm among sons, which resulted in "much British blood" being lost (1.2.269-81). Although recent British history is full of civil strife, none is associated with Brutus's particular bequest; his sons were content in their several kingdoms and cooperated with one another against common enemies. Like Elidure, Eubulus miscites a history he should know very well. In these instances, the authors concentrate on the argument at hand but not consistently on what a person in this particular historical circumstance would be likely to remember or say. In both plays, a time continuum is suggested and then relaxed.

King Leir makes no direct reference to previous reigns or chronicle events, but we are given insubstantial intimations of the previous years of Leir's own reign. Impressed by Leir's attempt to manage the succession by marrying off all three daughters to British kings who could protect Britain from foreign invasion, the good counselor Perillus declares to Leir that for his "care" of the nation he "deserves an everlasting memory / To be enroll'd in chronicles of fame" (1.67, 69-70). There is a hint here that Perillus's praise encompasses more than Leir's latest efforts to care for the kingdom; "care" that deserves everlasting fame suggests that Perillus recalls an entire career, of which the present "care" is only a culmination. But the author can offer no more than a hint of this previous record of care because the chronicles tell him nothing of Leir's long reign except his building of Leicester.[17] Perillus reflects both the playwright's eagerness to praise Leir and his inability to find anything to praise Leir for. The "chronicles of fame," in fact, have not remembered Leir for anything except these incidents of his late reign. The King's dwelling on the absence of his late queen has the same effect. We are told that she was a guiding hand to him, that she educated their daughters virtuously, and that he feels adrift without her (1.1-18). Our playwright feels free to suggest an imagined past family life, yet constricted enough to tell us essentially nothing. We have only a nameless queen

and a vague account of her influence—no mention of anything Leir himself did. The play proposes to add needed color to the chronicle material but also aims to avoid a concocted history. What happened during Leir's reign? The author must offer something, or his people will appear unhistorical, characters with no memory; but he cannot embroider Geoffrey's account very much, or his Leir will appear equally unhistorical. Thus we remain uncertain about *Leir*'s situatedness in historical time. Does Leir have a past?

In these plays, chronology is destabilized not only by a fluctuating sense of the characters' recent past but also by the confused relationship between their world and the realm of myth as it was known in the authors' own day. Since the stories of Locrine (eleventh century B.C.), Leir (ninth century B.C.), Gorboduc (sixth to fifth century B.C.), and Elidure (third century B.C.) all date within the millennium after the Trojan war (twelfth century B.C.), a historic recreation of the worlds in these stories would represent that cataclysmic event as part of the people's cultural currency.[18] They are Trojans; the Trojan war is etched in their national consciousness. In Shakespeare's unhistorical version of the Leir story, the matter of Troy is not much in evidence; Ajax is mentioned once, briefly and proverbially (2.2.125). In *Gorboduc, Locrine,* and *Leir,* by contrast, Troy gets noticeable mention, and some emphasis is placed on the characters' identification with it: this emphasis, however, is in some cases offset by a sense that Troy is merely a proverbial name for ancient misfortune.

The authors of *Gorboduc* are careful to remind us of the Troy connection. Philander, charged now with advising Porrex, expresses his fears that the escalating tension between the prince and his brother Ferrex will wipe out the Trojan line of Brutus: the gods are "since mighty Ilion's fall not yet appeased / With these poor remnants of the Trojan name" (2.2.76-77). Gorboduc himself soon echoes Philander on the wrath of the gods unsatisfied with the fall of Troy, invoking the Simois stained with blood, the Phrygian fields strewn with corpses, and the "slaughter of unhappy Priam's race": "continued rage / pursues our lives and from the farthest seas / Doth chase the issues of destroyed Troy" (3.1.1-10). Gorboduc and Philander see themselves as continuators of the *Iliad* story, the carriers of Troy's legacy, and the guardians of its destiny. Although this reference to Troy is strongly contextualized, the next one appears slightly less so. Gorboduc identifies himself with Hecuba and Priam who were once happy and became miserable (3.1.11-18). Gorboduc might be envisioning his forebears here, but Priam and Hecuba seem more like stock examples, a warning applicable to any complacent "happy wight." The king and queen of Troy appear less as revered ancestors and more as vague myth figures used generally "to make a mirror of," as Gorboduc puts it.

Locrine and *Leir* reveal a greater disparity between the characters' own historical consciousness and a language which figures a Troy myth as universal currency. In *Lo-*

crine, Brutus is considered the last upholder of the name of Troy (1.2.100; 1.2.262), and the invader Humber has heard of the Britons as Trojans (2.2.9; 2.7.4); the Britons' situation as transplanted Trojans is salient in their minds and those of foreign enemies. But when the author uses similes to decorate the story, the matter of Troy can combine with any hackneyed story from the classics. For example, when Locrine compares his grief for Albanact's death with that of Priam, and Gwendoline compares hers with that of Hecuba, Camber then compares his sorrow with that of Niobe (3.2.43-57). That is to say, Niobe, a shadowy, mythical figure, occupies the same category here as do two figures from the speakers' own historical past. In other similes (2.2.89-93; 2.4.32-34; 5.6.7-11), Troy seems indistinguishable from any other mythology as characters resort to conventional hyperbole and do not really consider their relationship to the persons and situations they name. When Leir greets his sons-in-law by telling them they are as welcome "as ever Priam's children were to him" (6.52-53), it seems plausible that he is thinking about his people's past. But then Gonorill greets her husband, Cornwall, by saying he's as welcome as Leander was to Hero, or Aeneas to Dido (6.65-67). As with Niobe in Camber's speech, here the imaginary Leander is given the same status as a Trojan figure, Aeneas, who should not be imaginary for the speaker. The historical merges with the proverbial, the characters' past with the Elizabethan present.

We might expect the most obvious indication of the authors' chronological inconsistencies to be their blatant and frequent anachronism, but this is not the case. The clocks in *Julius Caesar* do not produce doubts about Shakespeare's commitment to historicity because they do not obscure the sense of where the characters think they are within the historical continuum: Caesar understands his own history and situation. That Cheapside and Fleet Street get mentioned in *Nobody and Somebody* or that the ancient Britons of *King Leir* are Christians need not imply the authors' disbelief that they were representing historical persons. More telling are moments such as the mention of Billingsgate in *Leir* (12.78), where a structure which one of Leir's own descendants, Belinus, famously founded is made a feature of Leir's world.[19] Such a reference, like the ones we have examined so far, at once reminds us of Galfridian time and violates it. These authors' dedication to Galfridian time is both serious and sporadic; they seem caught between an imagined time in history and an imaginary, timeless fiction.

II

Since history plays are known for elaborating on truth with fiction, we can expect to find many invented characters and situations. But when a playwright changes the basic Galfridian storyline, he takes a major step. While imagined characters like Falstaff appear in *1 Henry IV*, they serve to further the view of historical truth Shakespeare is trying to convey—the story of the maturation of England's hero-king. By contrast, Shakespeare's reworking of the

end of the Leir story, turning triumph into defeat and continuation into apocalypse, reflects an entirely different approach to the material. Translating the story of Holinshed's Henry V into a dramatic plot was not the same procedure as translating the story of his Leir. Because any given Galfridian story is very sparse in its details, painting its portraits only in brief, broad strokes, any alteration of that story constitutes a drastic revision of history and calls into question the degree to which it can be taken seriously. Shakespeare, disregarding historicity in *King Lear,* felt free enough to take measures comparable to having Henry V lose at Agincourt. Although the four non-Shakespearean plays are more faithful to Geoffrey than *King Lear* is—as we have noted, they all follow Geoffrey's outline with comparable strictness—they do make some striking alterations to their source. The difference between their alterations and Shakespeare's is that the former use unhistorical alterations for historical purposes. To draw a proper history play from Geoffrey's details, these playwrights must invent their own details and adjust Geoffrey's basic storyline. Attempting seriously to treat Geoffrey's stories as history—as true stories which treat people who actually lived and which therefore provide useful lessons of statecraft and patriotism—necessitates violating the historicity of Geoffrey's account. All four plays exhibit tensions between history play and historicity that arise from the difficulties of imagining what actually happened in Galfridian time.

In *King Leir,* the author has determined to render a certain type of Leir conducive to exemplarity, as shown in the representation of Leir handing down the kingdom. Except for his rash misassessment of Cordella, the Leir of this play is totally blameless, and mild, patient, and penitent in his suffering—a man, as he says, "in true peace with all the world" (19.161). He is a Christian saint-king, and the play is a species of hagiography. Giving away his power helps establish this view of him: "here I do freely dispossess my self" (6.84), he says, making the transaction a mark of his contented mind and selflessness. The playwright stresses the ingratitude of the children toward this benevolent and generous monarch-father. The basic Galfridian story is that of a king who loses a throne and gets it back; the playwright adapts this story so that we learn what a good, meek king is like and how good subjects should treat him. In contrast to Shakespeare's turbulent Lear who functions in no such capacity and who is conducive to no neat message, this Leir evokes the feeling that details have been manipulated in order to yield a view of the past which makes sense of it. Leir is christianized and made a saint in order to imagine him as having been, historically, a good king; he is made to relinquish his crown voluntarily in order to prove him the type of king who deserved to reign once more. This attempt to stamp a coherent interpretation, an agreeable example, on Geoffrey's account suggests that the playwright is trying to treat the story as history.

The problem is, however, that the king's voluntary abdication of all the reins of government to his sons-in-law marks a major alteration of the chronicle material. Since this situation is so familiar from *King Lear,* we may overlook its important departure from the chronicles which Shakespeare inherits from the older play. In the Galfridian story, Leir's bequeathing of power to the husbands of Goneril and Regan is to take effect only after his death; this deferral of possession prompts his sons-in-law to rebel against him and snatch it by force.[20] In revising this traditional account of the Leir story, the playwright was probably drawing on Spenser, whose "Briton Moniments" reports that Leir retired after the apportionment, "eased of his crowne"; but although Spenser was a reputable enough source, he himself had almost no precedent for this change and probably made it for brevity's sake.[21] The author of *King Leir* was therefore indeed making an innovative change to the Galfridian account. The standard storyline was evidently unacceptable to the playwright as a narrative of conflict at odds with the saint-king he was striving to imagine; engaging Leir in this armed power struggle with his sons-in-law might make him appear grasping, tenacious, or combative. But, as a consequence, the author's historically imagined Leir conflicts with the "historical" record.

Gorboduc, too, has much to do with dividing the kingdom among children; as in *Leir,* the partition story in *Gorboduc* tries to forge a suitable history play from Geoffrey's bare outline. From Geoffrey's implication that Gorboduc is alive at the outbreak of his sons' civil war, the authors infer an active, causal role for him to play in it: the war ensues from Gorboduc's failure to heed Eubulus's counsel against divesting himself of the throne and allowing his sons, Ferrex and Porrex, equal shares of power. Events have thus emanated from a decision by Gorboduc himself; given agency, he is imagined as having been a king who actually did something with important historical ramifications. This plot affords the opportunity to meditate on what Gorboduc should have done and where he went wrong; it gives the authors the chance to turn history to its proper role of instruction: rule until you die, and make sure you leave an intact kingdom to a clear successor. The authors enhance this message by imagining that Ferrex and Porrex have already been crowned as a result of the partition. While a succession war among princes would signify only evil ambition and disastrous fratricide, a war between reigning kings can demonstrate the impossibility of peaceful coexistence between two kings in one realm— Britain must be unified. That the authors structured their plot to yield these political examples indicates that they were trying to conceive their own drama as a history play, an illumination of truth with fiction.

But in *Gorboduc,* as in *Leir,* a history play has been crafted by making changes only fiction could permit. In fact, the premise that Gorboduc himself was determined to divide his kingdom between his sons seems to be the authors' invention. In Geoffrey's account, we are given no clues about what Gorboduc's role might be in the civil war; we learn only that when he grew old, the princes began to quarrel about who should succeed, and that the younger brother, Porrex, was the more grasping of the two.[22] Giving Gorboduc any agency amounts to inventing a new

story. Fabyan and Grafton give even less cause to ascribe any action to Gorboduc, for they tell us that the king is dead before his sons begin their joint reign.[23] Moreover, while the authors perhaps draw on Fabyan and Grafton for the representation of Ferrex and Porrex as crowned kings instead of warring princes, such a borrowing does not invest the play with chronicle authority; instead, the disagreement among chronicles over the most basic details and the patchwork quality of the play itself become clearer. Sackville and Norton mix Geoffrey with Fabyan and Grafton, adding their own device of Gorboduc's decision to divide the kingdom. This amalgam results in a suitable history-play plot, but at a cost: the authors have manufactured their own peculiar story.

The same tension between history play and "history" is evident in *Nobody and Somebody* and *Locrine*: to pursue one history-play goal of providing negative examples of kingship, the authors must reach beyond the chronicles to refashion kings into tyrants. In scene 10 of *Nobody and Somebody,* Peridure and Vigenius, Elidure's two younger brothers, first join forces to usurp him and then fight a war with each other—a war which the playwright has invented. The usurpers need to usurp each other to underscore the play's warning about ambition and to establish Elidure as a prototypically unambitious, humble monarch; only with a moral attitude such as his can a king survive and end the cycle of civil strife. But this handy message requires a serious departure from the chronicle record, the invention of a major event.[24] Similarly, *Locrine* has its title figure turn from dutiful hero to tyrant as soon as he sees the captured Princess Estrild. Here, to produce a history-play message, the playwright elaborates the traditional idea of the king as falling after committing adultery and fashions a Locrine who undergoes a sudden and total personality change. The author evidently feels compelled to translate Locrine's personal vices into political ones; the history-play lesson of his fall is not complete unless he can be shown wicked in his kingship, his lust rendering him paranoid and tyrannical. To fashion this wicked king, however, the author invents his own Locrine, perhaps even contradicts history's.[25] Again, the pursuit of historical ends necessitates unhistorical means.

Unlike Shakespeare, the authors of the other Galfridian plays demonstrably attempt to treat Geoffrey's plotlines as history—moments from the nation's ancient past that, properly presented, could be instructive for the present. But as we have seen, this proper presentation entailed key distortions in those plotlines beyond the point where the authors' imaginings could cohere with a core of presumptive truth. Inconsistent with chronology, the authors are also inconsistent with their Galfridian storylines; Geoffrey is both historical foundation and malleable fiction.

III

The behavior of the characters in *King Lear* continually defies rational explanations. Why does Lear suddenly become so angry with Cordelia? What do Goneril and Regan have against Cordelia? And is it possible to account for Cordelia's utter goodness? Shakespeare proceeds as if his characters can be driven to extremes without addressing their motivations. And yet, somehow the play sustains its verisimilitude, for people often tend to be inexplicable.[26]

A history play, however, cannot refrain from examining motivation. While it will not completely invent what happened, it must attempt imaginatively to portray how people felt. To draw examples from the past, the history play must make sense of the past, which means the history play must render the causes of events. In the Renaissance, these causes—apart from the first cause, providence—were often identified with the hidden motivations in people's minds.[27] To fulfill its purpose, the history play must make plain the psychology of its characters. Since the rashness of Hotspur's rebellion offered a major lesson, Shakespeare imagines a rash Hotspur; historical actions are put into perspective by virtue of an appropriately imagined personality. Shakespeare is able all at once to reconstruct true history (as he would have understood it), to attend to exemplarity, and to develop a vivid, realistic characterization. In the non-Shakespearean plays on Galfridian materials, this synthesis between historical truth, exemplarity, and realism proves impossible. The mind of Hotspur, a figure from fairly recent history, was not so hard to imagine, and even legendary figures from other traditions, like Jupiter or David, had characters that were relatively well delineated and understood.[28] But the minds of Gorboduc, Locrine, Elidure, and Leir were simply too remote. The imagination had to transcend tremendous gaps in time and in known details, as well as, ultimately, in believability; what is more, these imaginative leaps had to be made without appearing to have created one's own, nonhistorical characters. Thus when the plays on Galfridian materials purport to look into the minds of the characters and produce explanations for the causes of events, their imagined motivations seem both artificial and noncommittal—limited by the impossible project of treating the figures in Geoffrey's meager legends as historical persons. Paradoxically, the more the authors respect their "historical" sources and their history-play agendas—the more they attend to truth and exemplarity—the less realistic and historical-looking their characters can become.

In *Gorboduc,* the authors are especially interested in motivating the scant sequence of events in the chronicles. Geoffrey does not explain why two brothers should begin to fight one another; Ferrex and Porrex, both desiring to reign, have a war, and that is all we know. For the playwrights this fratricide requires explanation. We can hardly expect to derive any political lessons from a merely gratuitous clash, and British princes should not be imagined as attacking one another without reason. Hence the authors of *Gorboduc* render the princes' war more understandable. Because of Gorboduc's ill-advised decision to divide the realm between them, both sons feel slighted. Spurred by this antagonism which their father's poor judgment fostered, and urged on by bad advisors in an atmosphere of mounting tension, the brothers are no mere incarnations of evil ambition. Viewed partly as victims and pawns, they are made more forgivable and the disaster less random. British princes must be imagined as having some good in them, and the disaster as not primarily the brothers' doing but the consequence of the original bad decision to divide the kingdom.

Yet, while the play does develop this perspective on the motivations of Ferrex and Porrex, there is still a sense of how impenetrable their minds are. Ferrex, for one, is given little to say. In act 1, scene 1, next to his ardent mother, Videna, he appears flat, lacking any substantial thoughts. In act 2, scene 1, he has far fewer lines than the counselors around him and he absorbs their counsel like a veritable sponge. He says the minimum of what the plot requires him to say and then disappears. Although Porrex is perhaps more sharply portrayed, he ultimately seems as opaque as Ferrex because we get such contradictory impressions of him. For example, does Porrex's heartfelt plea for forgiveness in act 4, scene 2 merely carry out a plan, mentioned earlier (2.2.64-66), to appease his father? Are we to take his appeal to Gorboduc as premeditated and deceitful? When he cites in his own defense attempts by Ferrex on his life, is Porrex lying? Before either we or Gorboduc can evaluate his speeches, Porrex has been slain and Lady Marcella is praising him as the very image of the chivalric prince (4.2.228-56). What type of men were Ferrex and Porrex? What motivated them?

This and other questions that we might ask about the "historical" figures of the play go unanswered, and the gaps cannot be attributed merely to inept playmaking. Sackville's contributions to the *Mirror* reveal that he, at least, was capable of imagining colorfully the minds of historical figures.[29] But in *Gorboduc* he and Norton are trying to handle non-historical characters with some historical care, and the result is that their creations seem unlike people who might actually have lived. Like his sons, Gorboduc says little and reveals little about himself before being murdered offstage by a mob. The playwrights invent a death for him which fits the history-play message (i.e., the admonition against rebellion), but which also permits them to imagine as little as possible. By killing Gorboduc offstage, they manage to avoid overtly contradicting anything Geoffrey indicates about the man. It is thus not surprising that the most clearly drawn of the play's Galfridian figures is Videna. The playwrights can make her a striking, Medea-like figure because Geoffrey reports something about her mind: she loved her son Ferrex, and she hated Porrex for killing him.[30] But after these emotions have been depicted, Videna, too, is banished from our sight, killed offstage with her husband. Ironically, the play's Galfridian figures seem less like real, historical people because of the authors' effort to assume that they were real, historical people.

Locrine, too, conveys the impression that some liberties have been taken with the characters in order to imagine their minds and satisfy the conditions of a history play; in *Locrine,* likewise, regard for history results in vague characterizations. The best example is Estrild, the princess who came with Humber and who after his defeat became Locrine's concubine. The mind of Estrild was a complete mystery. Taken by Humber as booty, had she become attached to him? Was his fall a calamity for her? Did she go willingly with Locrine or did he force her? Did she feel guilty about being hidden away as his concubine, did she defy such considerations, or did she feel she was his rightful wife? Did his death mean the loss of a man she loved? Was she twice a victim of rape, twice an opportunistic whore, or twice a grieving widow? These unanswerable "historical" questions attracted the interest of at least two other writers, John Higgins in his additions to the *Mirror* and Thomas Lodge in his "Complaint of Estred." Both joined the playwright of *Locrine* in attempting to imagine this woman's mind. But the three depictions of Estrild suffer under the same difficulty of simultaneously embroidering on and remaining faithful to history. All three works fashion an Estrild who had freely accompanied Humber and was grief stricken at his death; they then decide that she loved Locrine as passionately, his loss being a disaster that redoubles Humber's loss.[31] This convenient solution added to Geoffrey's details without contradicting them and served the purpose of exemplarity. An Estrild in love with and mourning both men was able to express lamentations which taught the fickleness of fortune; twice bereft of a glorious lover, she was qualified to lecture against excessive love of worldly pomp, and she does so in all three works. But such a solution made for an inhuman-seeming character. What woman would twice respond so favorably to a captor and to a situation into which she had been forced? Of the three portrayals, only *Locrine* even hints at this problem, lending Estrild a few lines of misgiving about her second lover (4.2.126-44, 5.2.90-93). But these moments are fleeting, absorbed into the Estrild who suddenly loves each king in succession with all her heart. A more complicated Estrild might require adding too much to Geoffrey's account; it would certainly complicate the fine exemplum that the pat solution provides. We are given a history-play woman, but one whose erotic history seems not to correspond to that of anyone who lived such a life.

If it was difficult to recreate the mind of the Estrild who lived through Geoffrey's story, it was equally daunting to imagine the mind of his Elidure. Noted for the improbable feat of being thrice crowned king, this figure, like Estrild, endured the same fate repeated times; as with Estrild, the question of what such a person must have been like appeared intractable. Geoffrey calls him "pius" for his lack of ambition in abdicating in favor of his deposed brother Archigallo, who in Elidure's estimation remained the lawful king.[32] But did this "pius" concern for brotherhood and law reflect a noble heart or an acquiescent one? Did Elidure make a sacrifice to reinstate his brother, or did he relinquish a crown he cared nothing for? In *Nobody and Somebody,* the need to adhere to Geoffrey and to exemplarity results in the most simple Elidure imaginable. Elidure, one of Geoffrey's better kings, was a model of justice, humility, and altruism; hence the play is careful in various places to imagine an Elidure who tallies with this standard impression. But as with Estrild in *Locrine,* with Elidure the simple, history-play solution yields an unreal and inconsistent character. Could a historical person who behaved like Elidure avoid appearing weak and irresponsible, neglectful of his people's wishes? It takes an invented character, the comically ambitious Lady Elidure, to signal Elidure's questionable actions, which she takes to be lapses in duty. In surrendering his throne to his grasping younger brothers, he is permitting his wife to suffer, and she tells him so (10.1438-42). Her frustration might be ours: who is this Elidure? In adapting the Elidure story as a history play, *Nobody and Somebody* proves unable to answer this question.

While *King Leir* appears to imagine the minds of its characters with greater freedom than the other three plays, it too emerges as constrained by history, for this imagining tends not merely to add color but also to account for and rationalize the characters' behavior.[33] Such rationalization leads me to infer that the author aims at a history play—for this is just the strategy he would use if he wanted to produce one. We need understandable motivations to produce explanations of actions and political examples; we also need them to envision what these people must have been like. For example, the playwright chooses to imagine the events preceding Leir's disinheriting of Cordella so that we might understand why he would do such a thing. Here the love contest is not arbitrary, but part of the king's plan to marry off his daughters suitably and ensure the long-term safety of Britain (1.54-89). Cordella's famously truthful answer is thereby given added significance: it is a declaration that she will not marry according to his wishes. His anger at her is made more comprehensible because her reply represents, in his eyes, a refusal to obey his will and to consider her duty to the kingdom (3.86-100). The episode is made to concern statecraft and to resemble the type of decision an actual king might have made. As for the cause of her sisters' hatred of Cordella, the play imagines this explanation: Gonorill and Ragan detest their younger sister because "all the court" holds her above them and because she is likely to gain a better husband than they (2.1-29). They hate Cordella because they have cause to perceive her as a threat to their aspirations; Geoffrey's account of their hatred becomes rationalized. We are given to understand that their hatred is wrapped up in court politics and that their hatred was an emotion which historical people would have been capable of feeling; we get the sense that some such persons could have lived. Thus the imagined motivations in *Leir,* like those in the other plays, are very often controlled by the history-play demands of exemplarity and historical reconstruction.

Yet despite all such attempts to make serviceable history-play figures from Geoffrey's personages, the sense of who they were or of their connectedness to people who actually lived remains fairly weak. While certainly evil, Gonorill and Ragan, for example, are marked in *Leir* by a kind of intermittent conscience, a fitful concern for what others think. Next to their Shakespearean counterparts, the portrayals of Gonorill and Ragan appear inconsistent and wa-tered down, illustrations of just how little access the playwright has to these characters' minds. The best example of all is Cordella. Here, as always, Cordella is without blemish; but to make her more accessible to the audience, the author resorts, as he did with Leir, to using religious commonplaces to establish this goodness. Although happily invested as queen of France (13.1-32), Cordella still pines for her father and hopes to regain his love; these pious feelings find articulation in a long speech replete with references to prayer, church, fasting, pilgrimage, sackcloth, charity, and the "Saviour." Her sister calls her a "puritan" for her brand of piety (29.96). Yet such anachronisms sustain rather than violate the author's sense of historicity. How could this remote figure, known only for her superhuman goodness, be imagined? By letting her display her goodness and by associating it with that of familiar figures like monks and puritans, Geoffrey's woman is made to seem possible. Perhaps we are now meant to grasp why she acted as she did. But the result is a Cordella whose self seems smothered by these conventional tags of "goodness." She becomes "everygoodwoman." What was she like? Who was she? As in the other plays, the attempt to imagine historically the minds of Geoffrey's characters only confirms the difficulty of doing so.

Shakespeare's version, striving neither to recreate history nor to make sense of it, achieves its realism by avoiding rationalization. When Lear marvels at the cruelty of his two elder daughters and asks, "Is there any cause in nature that makes these hard hearts?" (3.6.77-78), we are aware that no answer can be given. And Cordelia, unlike Cordella, has no opportunity to explain the nature of her love for her father. It is simply there. When at last called upon by her father to account for this love, she replies: "No cause, no cause" (4.7.75). Cordelia's love is not made comprehensible to us, nor are we invited to imagine that Cordelia represents a historical person who loved this way. And yet Shakespeare's Cordelia rings humanly true.

. . . . .

I have argued that the disparity between *King Lear* and the other plays on pre-Roman Galfridian material traces not only to differences in dramatic skill but also to differences in attitude toward the source material. In Renaissance drama, the historical often mixes with the fantastical, and in many cases historical elements provide mere decoration. But some plays are clearly more concerned than others with representing historical events and people; and, as I have tried to demonstrate, many of the peculiarities of the four non-Shakespearean plays derive more from their attention to "history" than from their dismissal of it. In attempting to use Geoffrey of Monmouth's prehistorical Britain as history-play material, the dramatist was bound to encounter certain conceptual problems. How should he situate the Galfridian stories in time? Or were they in time? How should he rework the "historical" narrative to provide good examples? Or did the extent of his reworking itself expose a lack of historicity in that narrative? Finally, how should he portray the minds of the persons as

motivating their actions? Or were these minds closed to him by their remoteness or, perhaps, their fictiveness? Shakespeare was able to avoid these questions. In accepting Geoffrey as non-history, he was able to produce a play that took another reality as its subject, one entailing no explanations—no cause.

Notes

1. The standard story was that the sons of Goneril and Regan, Marganus and Cunedagius, joined forces to overthrow Cordelia, and thereafter, unable to share the kingship, fought a civil war won by Marganus. See, for example, the account in Raphael Holinshed's *Historie of England* (in his *Chronicles* [London, 1587], pp. 13-14).

2. On evaluating a history play in terms of the "reality it purports to imitate," see Herbert Lindenberger, *Historical Drama: The Relation of Literature and Reality* (Chicago, 1975), p. 3.

3. For critics who do consider *Lear* a history play because of its political content, see Irving Ribner, *The English History Play in the Age of Shakespeare* (Princeton, N.J., 1957), pp. 247-53; Eric Sterling, *The Movement towards Subversion: The English History Play from Skelton to Shakespeare* (Lanham, Md., 1996), pp. xiii, 43. A great many critics prefer not to treat *Lear* as a history play but to view it instead as a "poetic fable" commenting on Shakespeare's own day. Some examples include Alvin B. Kernan, "*King Lear* and the Shakespearean Pageant of History," in *On King Lear*, ed. Lawrence Danson (Princeton, N.J., 1981), pp. 7-24; Joseph Wittreich, *Image of That Horror: History, Prophecy, and Apocalypse in King Lear* (San Marino, Calif., 1984), pp. 33-38; Jonathan Dollimore, *Radical Tragedy* (Brighton, 1984), pp. 189-203; Richard Dutton, "*King Lear,* 'The Triumphs of Reunited Britannia,' and 'The Matter of Britain,'" *Literature and History* 12 (1986): 137-51; and John Turner, "*King Lear,*" in *Shakespeare: The Play of History,* ed. Graham Holderness, Nick Potter, and John Turner (Iowa City, 1988), pp. 85-118. "Poetic fable" is Kernan's term. For *Lear* as emphasizing tragedy over history, see Richard H. Perkinson, "Shakespeare's Revision of the Lear Story and the Structure of *King Lear,*" *Philological Quarterly* 22 (1943): 315-29; Maynard Mack, *King Lear in Our Time* (Berkeley and Los Angeles, 1965), pp. 51, 84-85. For *Lear* and the obscurity of pre-Roman Britain, see Jodi Mikalachki, *The Legacy of Boadicea: Gender and Nation in Early Modern England* (London, 1998), pp. 68-95.

4. Several other prehistoric Galfridian plays are recorded in Philip Henslowe but do not survive, including plays on Brute, Lud, Dunwallo, and Brute Greenshield. See Geoffrey Bullough, "Pre-Conquest Historical Themes in Elizabethan Drama," in *Medieval Literature and Civilization; Studies in Memory*

of G. N. Garmonsway, ed. D. A. Pearsall and R. A. Waldon (London, 1969), pp. 289-321.

5. *Gorboduc* was written in 1561 and published first in 1565, and then in an authorized version in 1570; see Norman Rabkin's introduction to his edition of the play in *Drama of the English Renaissance I: The Tudor Period,* ed. Russell A. Fraser and Norman Rabkin (New York, 1976), p. 81. (References to this edition are to act, scene, and line.) *Locrine* was published in 1595 and draws upon the first installment of Spenser's *Faerie Queene* (1590), but it seems to have been first written during the 1580s and then reworked; see Jane Lytton Gooch's introduction to her edition of the play, *The Lamentable Tragedy of Locrine* (New York, 1981), pp. 4-10. (References to this edition are to act, scene, and line.) *The True Chronicle History of King Leir* was published in 1605, but a publishing license of 1594 probably refers to this play; see Donald M. Michie's introduction to his edition of the play, *The True Chronicle History of King Leir and his Three Daughters, Gonorill, Ragan, and Cordella* (New York, 1991), pp. 4-5. (References to this edition are to scene and line.) *Nobody and Somebody* was published in 1606, but scholars have argued convincingly for an initial composition date of circa 1592, with subsequent revisions; see David L. Hay's introduction to his edition of the play, *Nobody and Somebody* (New York, 1980), pp. 63-66. (References to this edition are to scene and line.) All references to *King Lear* are from *The Riverside Shakespeare,* ed. G. Blakemore Evans et al. (Boston, 1974).

6. Judith H. Anderson, *Biographical Truth: The Representation of Historical Persons in Tudor-Stuart Writing* (New Haven, Conn., 1984), pp. 110-23.

7. See William Baldwin's second preface, "Baldwin to the Reader," in the 1559 edition of *Mirror for Magistrates,* ed. Lily B. Campbell (New York, 1960), pp. 69-70; and Thomas Heywood, *An Apology for Actors* (London, 1612), fol. 3. The quotation is Heywood's.

8. Arthur B. Ferguson, *Utter Antiquity: Perceptions of Prehistory in Renaissance England* (Durham, N.C., 1993), p. 118.

9. On the Tudor/Stuart uses of Geoffrey of Monmouth, see Edwin Greenlaw, *Studies in Spenser's Historical Allegory* (Baltimore, 1932); Charles Bowie Millican, *Spenser and the Table Round* (Cambridge, Mass., 1932); and Roberta Florence Brinkley, *Arthurian Literature in the Seventeenth Century* (London, 1967).

10. Richard Harvey, *Philadelphus, or a Defense of Brutes, and the Brutans History* (London, 1593), pp. 17-57.

11. For Polydore, Camden, and the discrediting of Geoffrey of Monmouth, see T. D. Kendrick, *British Antiquity* (London, 1950); and Ferguson, pp. 85-105. For an analysis of Shakespeare's subversion of the British Troy myth in response to antiquarian scholarship, see Heather James, *Shakespeare's Troy: Drama, Politics, and the Translation of Empire* (Cambridge, 1997), pp. 20-33, 85-118.

12. *Gorboduc* has been assumed to take either Robert Fabyan's chronicle or Richard Grafton's, or both, as its source. I choose to take Fabyan as the principal source, for Grafton's *Abridgement of the Chronicles of England* did not first appear until 1562, and Grafton tends to follow Fabyan slavishly in any case. Scholars warn us, however, that the authors probably drew upon a number of sources. See James Swart, *Thomas Sackville: A Study in Sixteenth Century Poetry* (Gronigen, 1948), pp. 68-70; and Paul Bacquet, *Thomas Sackville: The Man and His Work* (Geneva, 1966), pp. 218-23. Perusing Fabyan, the authors would have encountered a number of remarks about the oddities in Geoffrey's account. An example would be Fabyan's observation that Geoffrey's mention of France in the Leir story would have been an anachronism (*The Chronicle of Robert Fabyan* [London, 1542], pp. 15-16). Of course, Sackville and Norton could also have been familiar with the criticisms of Geoffrey made by Polydore Vergil.

13. Although each of them draws upon a number of sources, including perhaps Geoffrey of Monmouth himself, all three of these plays are probably heavily influenced by Holinshed; see Felix E. Schelling, *The English Chronicle Play* (New York, 1902), pp. 187-88. Holinshed's strategy of all-inclusiveness led him to incorporate into his chronicles Polydore's criticisms of Geoffrey, and he himself at times questions the British History. When he reaches the story of Caesar's invasion, Holinshed remarks that thenceforth he will have access to more accurate sources; see Holinshed (n. 1 above), pp. 23-24.

14. Holinshed, pp. 1-6.

15. Ibid., pp. 20-21.

16. Fabyan, pp. 16-19.

17. Holinshed, p. 12.

18. I rely on Holinshed for these dates, but Fabyan, who is quite interested in chronology, comes close enough to Holinshed in all four cases.

19. Compare Holinshed, p. 19.

20. Ibid., p. 13. Sterling believes that Leir is made to choose to hand down the kingdom so that blame can be transferred onto him (p. 168). I disagree because Leir's decision to divide the kingdom is not condemned in the play.

21. Edmund Spenser, *The Faerie Queene,* ed. A. C. Hamilton (London, 1977), pp. 258, 263 (2.9.59.6, 2.10.29.6). See Carrie Anna Harper, *The Sources of the British Chronicle History in Spenser's "Faerie Queene"* (Philadelphia, 1910), p. 80. I have found only one possible precedent that Spenser may have been following for Leir's donation of the entire king-

dom within his own lifetime: John Rastell, *The Pastyme of People* (London, 1530), sig. Aiii.

22. Geoffrey of Monmouth, *The Historia Regum Britanniae of Geoffrey of Monmouth,* ed. Acton Griscom (London, 1929), p. 272 (hereafter cited as *Geoffrey*).

23. Fabyan (n. 12 above), p. 19; Grafton (n. 12 above), fol. 4.

24. The standard account has Peridure peacefully coexisting with his brother until the latter's death and then serving as an effective king until his own. Geoffrey indicates that Peridure was more highly esteemed even than Elidure (*Geoffrey*, p. 299); for the debate on whether Peridure was a tyrant, see Holinshed (n. 1 above), p. 21.

25. While Spenser's version could imply a connection between private vice and public negligence (*FQ* 2.10.17), I can find no explicit account of Locrine as a tyrant, and in Caxton's chronicle he is even counted as a good king, "wonder wel beloued" (*Chronicles of England* [1480], chap. 5).

26. See Mack (n. 3 above), pp. 91-98.

27. See, for example, the statements on cause by Thomas Blundeville, *The True Order and Methode of Wryting and Reading Hystories* (1574), ed. Hans Peter Heinrich (Frankfurt, 1986), pp. 9-14, and Sir Walter Raleigh, *History of the World,* in *The Works of Sir Walter Raleigh,* 8 vols. (New York, 1964), 4:612-17. Sir Philip Sidney indicates that the heightened ability to analyze cause by imagining far-off historical persons was a special advantage of poetry over history (*A Defense of Poetry,* ed. J. A. Van Dorsten [Oxford, 1966], p. 36).

28. I am thinking specifically of the portrayal of David in George Peele's *David and Bethsabe* and of Jupiter in Thomas Heywood's *Golden Age* and *Silver Age.* Both characters are rendered with confidence because traditional accounts of them made it easy to grasp their basic personalities. In both plays, the authors almost certainly thought they were embroidering upon fact with fiction or fantasy.

29. See especially Sackville's tragedy on the Duke of Buckingham in Campbell, ed., *Mirror for Magistrates* (n. 7 above), pp. 318-45.

30. *Geoffrey*, p. 273.

31. John Higgins, "Elstride," in *Parts Added to the Mirror for Magistrates,* ed. Lily B. Campbell (Cambridge, 1946), pp. 87-100; and Thomas Lodge, "The Complaint of Estred," in *The Complete Works of Thomas Lodge,* 4 vols. (New York, 1963), 2:59-84.

32. *Geoffrey*, p. 296. For Holinshed he was Elidure the "godlie and vertuous" (p. 21).

33. On this point, see Perkinson (n. 3 above), p. 316.

FURTHER READING

Criticism

Baker, Imogene. "The Arthurian Household in the *Historia Regum Britanniae* and Subsequent Chronicles." In *The King's Household in the Arthurian Court from Geoffrey of Monmouth to Malory,* pp. 22-53. Washington, D.C.: The Catholic University of America, 1937.

> Examines the court's retinue in Geoffrey's work as well as its treatment in writings by Wace, Layamon, and later chroniclers.

East, W. G. "Manuscripts of Geoffrey of Monmouth." *Notes and Queries* 22, No. 10 (November 1975): 483-84.

> Corrects the list by A. Griscom of manuscripts of *The History of the Kings of Britain* held in Oxford libraries.

Howlett, D. R. "The Literary Context of Geoffrey of Monmouth: An Essay on the Fabrication of Sources." *Arthuriana* 5, No. 3 (Fall 1995): 25-69.

> Discusses how writers who followed Geoffrey felt compelled to create secret, unimpeachable sources for their histories.

Jones, Timothy. "Geoffrey of Monmouth, *Fouke le Fitz Waryn,* and National Mythology." *Studies in Philology* XCI, No. 3 (Summer 1994): 233-49.

> Examines the indebtedness of *Fouke le Fitz Waryn,* a late thirteenth-century romance, to *The History of the Kings of Britain.*

Padel, O. J. "Geoffrey of Monmouth and Cornwall." *Cambridge Medieval Celtic Studies* 8 (Winter 1984): 1-28.

> Considers the importance of Cornwall in *The History of the Kings of Britain* and speculates about the reasons for its emphasis.

Pickens, Rupert T. "Arthur's Channel Crossing: Courtesy and the Demonic in Geoffrey of Monmouth and Wace's *Brut.*" *Arthuriana* 7, No. 3 (Fall 1997): 3-19.

> Compares and contrasts the accounts by Geoffrey and Wace of Arthur's channel– crossing episode.

Reiss, Edmund. "The Welsh Versions of Geoffrey of Monmouth's *Historia.*" *Welsh History Review* 4, No. 2 (December 1968): 97-127.

> Surveys the history of scholarly studies of the *Brut y Brenhinedd,* the *Brut Gruffydd ab Arthur,* and other Welsh versions of Geoffrey's chronicle and classifies sixty-five of the known seventy-six manuscripts containing Welsh versions of the *History.*

Roberts, Brynley F. "Historical Writing." In *A Guide to Welsh Literature,* Vol. I, edited by A. O. H. Jarman and Gwilym Rees Hughes, pp. 244-47. Swansea, Wales: Christopher Davies (Publishers) Ltd, 1976.

Summarizes the importance of *The History of the Kings of Britain* for Welsh perceptions of history.

Schlauch, Margaret. "Geoffrey of Monmouth and Early Polish Historiography: A Supplement." *Speculum* 44, No. 2 (April 1969): 258-63.
Reveals Geoffrey's influence on two Polish chroniclers: Mierzwa and Dlugosz.

Tolhurst, Fiona. "The Once and Future Queen: The Development of Guenevere from Geoffrey of Monmouth to Malory." *Bibliographical Bulletin of the International Arthurian Society* L (1988): 272-308.
Examines how and why various authors have recreated the character of Guenevere and explores the significance of her evolution.

Turcotte, Gerry. "Geoffrey of Monmouth and Tennyson: A Paradoxical Parallel." *ANQ* 1, No. 4, new series (October 1988): 140-41.
Discusses an image found in common in Geoffrey, Alfred, Lord Tennyson, and the biblical *Isaiah*.

Grettis Saga

c. 1320-25 (Also known as *Grettir's Saga* and *Saga of Grettir the Strong*) Icelandic prose.

INTRODUCTION

The *Grettis Saga* is the last and highest praised work of the genre of family sagas of old Iceland. It tells the eleventh-century tale of Grettir, a warrior of phenomenal strength and an equally powerful temper. Banished and outlawed, the victim of curses, witchcraft, and magic, Grettir performs heroic deeds, including battles against monsters and ghosts; ironically, these deeds benefit the very society with which he is so often at odds. After his murder, he is avenged by his brother, Thorsteinn. The *Grettis Saga* presents complex characters with rich, wide-ranging personalities. Although much critical interest in the tale derives from its similarities to *Beowulf*, it continues to gain new respect and new readers in its own right. It is also invaluable to historians and folklorists for its vivid, highly detailed descriptions of Viking ways and for help in understanding their perception of the individual and society.

PLOT AND MAJOR CHARACTERS

The story of the *Grettis Saga* is told in chronological order. The prologue, which consists of thirteen chapters, is both a history of the Icelandic region and a genealogical study of Grettir's ancestors. Grettir Asmundarson, the hero of the tale, was a historical person who died in 1031, but probably few, if any, facts about his life remain unembellished by legend and myth. Grettir is introduced at age ten in chapter fourteen, portrayed as lazy, impatient, resentful, disrespectful, and antisocial. He does not hesitate to confront and even assault those who irritate him, including his own father, who has little love for his son. His mother, Asdis, however, loves him dearly no matter how sadistic his actions. The following chapter depicts Grettir at age fourteen, fighting over an unfair play in a ball game, but not losing his sense of reason. Chapter sixteen is the first time that his horrible temper lands him in serious trouble. In an argument over a bag of provisions, Grettir kills a servant, Skeggi, in self-defense. Banished for three years, he heads for Norway. When the ship he is on is hit by a storm, Grettir does the bailing of eight men—perhaps showing that he is not truly lazy, just selective in choosing what tasks warrant his attention. The remaining chapters describe Grettir's heroic deeds: he recovers stolen treasure after defeating the ghost who guarded it, kills a bear, and swims in ice cold water for several miles. Once back in Iceland, Grettir pits himself against one of the undead,

who in life was Glamr, the shepherd. Although Grettir defeats him and thus saves the area's peasants from further attacks, Glamr curses Grettir. The curses are to keep his strength from increasing, to cause his deeds to go awry, and to have the effect of making him afraid to be alone, especially in the dark. Soon, as depicted in chapters 38 and 39, one of Grettir's feats does go astray and he accidentally burns down a hall, killing the twelve men inside, one of whom is the son of a chieftain. He is declared an outlaw and wanders the rest of his life in desolate parts of Iceland, at odds with the curse that makes him afraid to be alone. Chapters 42 through 45 offer accounts of Grettir's brother, Atli, and his death at the hands of Thorbjorn. Grettir eventually kills Thorbjorn and Thorbjorn's son, and is in turn murdered on his own deathbed. The last six chapters of the *Grettis Saga* have been described by Robert J. Glendinning as a novella in both structure and content. They describe the vengeance extracted by Thorsteinn for the murder of Grettir.

MAJOR THEMES

There has been much critical debate over the theme or themes of the *Grettis Saga*. Hermann Pallson interprets it as a warning against an overabundance of pride. Other critics see it as a warning against excessive violence. Kathryn Hume believes the theme has to do with the lack of place for the heroic in a modern society. Still other scholars view it in terms of the outlaw's role in civilization. Such diversity of opinion is part of what makes the *Grettis Saga* appealing to modern critics. With its ambiguous portrayals of Grettir and his motivation, and a wealth of examples to draw from, new interpretations of the main ideas at work in the saga will likely continue to be made.

CRITICAL RECEPTION

Similarities between the *Grettis Saga* and *Beowulf* have been recognized and discussed by scholars for well over a century. Much of the published work concerning the *Grettis Saga* involves comparisons with *Beowulf*; current consensus among critics is that the two works were written independently, but based on the same or similar variants of fairy tales, particularly the story of Bear's Son. Magnús Fjalldal challenges the popularly accepted notion that the works have a lot in common, asserting that similarities are superficial and based on very small portions of the tales, while differences are often ignored altogether. As one of the major Icelandic family stories, the *Grettis Saga* is vital to the study of old northern European literature. Scholars examine the work closely in trying to ascertain developments and progressions in the literary tradition, including the sharing of motifs. Lotte Motz explores how the factual basis of Grettir has been remodeled and transformed until the once-unique man fits in with a common pattern for heroes found in literature. Critics have pointed out that the *Grettis Saga* is flawed in its structure, with folk and romance elements interspersed among history, and with sudden shifts in Grettir's character. Hume argues that the very elements once attacked are now the most studied, and that the author's contrasting depictions of Grettir are a deliberate part of a pattern used to illustrate the theme of the work. Many critics have found fault with the final six chapters, which are believed, as evidenced by their romantic nature, to have been tacked on the tale at a later date. However, the overall merit of the *Grettis Saga* remains unquestioned and it endures as enjoyable reading several centuries after being written.

PRINCIPAL WORKS

Principal English Translations

The Saga of Grettir the Strong (translated by George Ainslie Hight) 1929

Grettir's Saga (translated by Denton Fox and Hermann Palsson) 1974

Story of Grettir the Strong (translated by Eirikr Magnusson and William Morris) 1980

CRITICISM

Robert J. Glendinning (essay date 1970)

SOURCE: "*Grettis Saga* and European Literature in the Late Middle Ages," in *Mosaic: A Journal for the Interdisciplinary Study of Literature,* Vol. 4, No. 2, 1970, pp. 49-61.

[*In the following essay, Glendinning examines elements of the novella genre present in the* Grettis Saga *as well as motifs and devices it shares with the literature of continental Europe.*]

During the second half of the 13th century, when the literature of continental Europe was beginning to move into the new intellectual constellation that was to become the Renaissance, the people of Iceland were still living in that brilliant period which saw the culmination of their mediaeval culture in the classical Icelandic sagas, the so-called Family Sagas. According to the traditional view, the classical Icelandic saga owes little of real substance to the mainstream of continental European literature. It owes nothing

to the courtly vogue which at the end of the 13th century was just past its flowering.[1] In place of the voluptuous ideality of Arthurian romance, we find in the sagas "a hard and positive clearness of understanding, such as is to be found nowhere else in the Middle Ages," according to Ker (p. 59). The Icelanders of the sagas, he adds, "had the faculty of seeing things clearly and judging their values reasonably, without superstition" (p. 61). Even the pre-courtly heroic epic pales beside the saga from the viewpoint of realism, substantiality and the depiction of complex individual characters.

Yet, notwithstanding the polarity underlying the literature of North and South, recent critics have increasingly recognized that Iceland in the Middle Ages was not a world unto itself hermetically sealed off from the European mainstream. Its relationship to the Roman-Christian culture of the continent was one of dialectic tension. Thus, for example, the greatest pagan Germanic cosmological poem that has been preserved, the *Völuspá,* of the *Poetic Edda,* seems to owe the vastness and grandeur of its conception to the inroads of Christian doctrine in the northern world around 1000 A.D.[2] In the case of the sagas, undercurrents both of Christian values and of romantic literary taste become evident in the late works written around 1300. Indeed, if *Laxdæla saga* was written as early as 1250, romantic taste may be said to date from this time. Chivalric literature had in fact made its formal entry into the Scandinavian world as early as 1226, when a monk named Brother Robert rendered Thomas of Brittany's version of *Tristan* into Old Norse prose for the Norwegian king, Hákon Hákonarson. *Njáls saga,* written near the end of the 13th century, and generally considered the greatest of the Icelandic sagas,[3] is a veritable thesaurus of the mediaeval world—but its inner unity nevertheless derives from the tradition inherent in its Icelandic subject matter.[4] Another of the late sagas, the one in fact which vies with *Njáls saga* for the final position in the classical chronological canon, is **Grettis saga Ásmundarsonar.**[5] Written around 1300 or shortly after, it is full of heterogeneous material, with a particularly heavy inlay of motifs from folklore and folktale as well as from the polite literature of the continent.[6] The protagonist of the saga, Grettir Ásmundarson, was the most famous outlaw of mediaeval Iceland. He became a folk-hero by dint of his protean elusiveness and cunning, his strength, endurance and daring, and above all, his Eulenspiegel-like gamesmanship. It is particularly concerning Grettir as a trickster-figure that the saga invites comparison with the themes of European literature popular in the late 13th century.

Although scholars have long recognized that the last six chapters of **Grettis saga** form a "pure novella in the contemporary European taste, made up of familiar motifs from a well-known European literary tradition,"[7] the main body of the saga, that is, the story proper, has not been subjected to the scrutiny that it deserves in this connection. In his characterization of the progress of literature in the 13th century the German literary historian Helmut de Boor says:

Out of the equestrian class, classical literature had succeeded in developing and accrediting the idea of chivalry. It set a high-flown image of man in a real world with which that image had little in common. It paid for this sublimation by the narrowing of the circle in which it was valid, and by a severe limitation of the subjects it could treat in order to reach its high goal.[8]

At the end of the century both the old order and its literature were falling into decay. The emergence of the middle class and the beginning of a new horizontal world-view were preparing the ground for a concept of reality that conflicted with the postulates of mediaeval dualistic thinking. Already the climate was developing for the emergence of a Boccaccio, whose unregenerate world is characterized by Yvonne Rodax as consisting of "the rules of *amour courtois*," "the vanished theological system," and "the precepts of disillusionment."[9] The typical vehicles of literary expression at the end of the 13th century were the miniature forms: *fabliau, Schwank,* and *novella* or *novellino.*

The *fabliau,* or *Schwank,* was not new to the second half of the 13th century. Although we do not encounter it in written form before this time, it was nevertheless well known to earlier generations in an oral form, which was the complementary opposite, according to Erich Auerbach, of the *exemplum.*[10] In his study of the Renaissance novella Auerbach disclaims a contributory role for the *fabliau* in the emergence of this genre. The true novella, he argues, which hardly existed before Boccaccio, is a delicate balance between the ideal and the real, between entertainment and revelation. The *fabliau* is pure sensuality, a form which makes no attempt to master empirical reality, cares nothing for causal relationships or symbolical meanings, and instead indulges itself in sensual gratification. In contrast with Boccaccio's literary world, which is based on "an immanent ethic of sensual love," the *fabliau* is unreflecting and uncritical.[11]

This view is not in agreement with more recent treatments of the subject by Yvonne Rodax and Helmut de Boor, by contrast with which it appears unnecessarily harsh and rigid. Both of the latter consider the novella proper to have begun in the 13th century when all three miniature forms, *fabliau, exemplum* and novella served, at least ostensibly, the purpose of moral didacticism.[12] In contrast with the courtly literature of an earlier generation these forms were rooted in a practical kind of realism.[13] Their didacticism was not confined to their explicit moral precept, the *fabula docet* that was usually appended in a blatantly extraneous way. It was inherent in their commonsense view of the world. In novella and *fabliau* a cure for the world's folly is implicit in the unclouded view with which this folly is recognized and exposed.

> The Schwank-literature above all, which is at this time a recognized form of moral didacticism, revolves around the themes of cleverness and folly and delights itself in the outwitting of the foolish by the clever, for this is the way of the world.
>
> (de Boor, p. 17.)

According to Miss Rodax, the hero of this literary genre, through whom the moral effect in a deeper sense is realized, is a trickster-hero:

> In the fabliau, folk always get exactly what is coming to them. The finest and most lively examples invariably demonstrate this law of compensation which functions like a moral code in that it preserves human existence from falling into chaos. A man or woman can learn how to get along by this rule and, if all the facts are available, can anticipate exact results. He who is poor must depend upon trickery, hypocrisy and deceit; he who is rich can satisfy his desires by force or purchase until he falls victim to one more clever or more powerful than he. . . . In this universe, as in the moral realm, there is a hierarchy of offenses which lead to ignominy, punishment or destruction. The greatest of these is to disobey or disregard the laws of unregenerate human nature.
>
> (Rodax, p. 21)

The office of the new hero was not merely to deflate the pompous, dupe the gullible, and expose the follies of humanity to laughter and derision. It also included an element which was constitutive for a well-known type of *fabliau* and novella: the theme of illicit sexual relations. In the works of this type trickery and the erotic are indeed such complementary themes that it is difficult to imagine one without the other (de Boor, p. 270 ff.). The type has become especially well-known through certain of Boccaccio's novellas.

Returning to the Icelandic saga, it will be useful to enlarge somewhat on W.P. Ker's observations quoted at the beginning of this article, so as to place a brief characterization of this genre beside the better known courtly romance, whose essence has already been indicated here. We shall then be able to trace the converging lines of two literary traditions that were originally antipodal in form and spirit.

Old Icelandic literature realized its highest achievement in the Family Sagas. Although written in the 13th century, their subject matter is made up of the lives and exploits of the original settlers of Iceland and their immediate descendants, that is: the three generations extending roughly from 930-1030 A.D. The great strength of the Icelandic Sagas is their credible and realistic depiction of individual human character. The protagonists themselves reveal their own character by their words and deeds, in a style that is severely economical if not elliptical. Almost every description of the Family Saga begins with a tribute to its realism and objectivity.[14]

> As a rule they treat their matter in an extraordinarily objective and realistic manner, far removed from spiritualism and metaphysical brooding. The ideology which is delineated in the speech and actions of their characters is of pagan origin; traces of Christian ethics are insignificant.
>
> (Hallberg, p. 2)

Scholars have also noted in the sagas an idealizing tendency in their presentation of the past.[15] This apparent contradition is made possible because the idealism of the sagas is of an eminently practical nature. Its goal is human dignity in the everyday world.

> Honor . . . is ethically the key concept in the world of the Icelandic saga. This was not an abstract idea, but a deep and passionate experience, a condition of life as basic as one's daily bread.

(Hallberg, p. 99)

The upholding of this ideal made a man master of his own destiny and victor over life and death. The fulfilment of life in death was thus a temporal fulfilment and was entirely in the hands of the hero himself—therein lies the fundamental distinction between the pagan ethic which informs the action of the Icelandic saga, and the Christian ethic which is assumed in the world of courtly literature. Scholars have recognized, however, that one saga in the classical canon, written in the 1260's or 70's, is unlike all the others. In its treatment of its subject matter, *Bandamanna saga*[16] completely deflates traditional Icelandic values and ideals. It is based on a much cruder story, *Ölkofra þáttr*, which has been preserved. The prototype is closer to the folktale in style and content, and in fact shows a close affinity with the *fabliau* and *Schwank* in its crass indecency and its presentation of a hero of humble origin who triumphs over the mighty of his day by dint of sheer cunning and ingenuity.[17]

The heroes of *Bandamanna saga* are a father and son from the lower stratum of Icelandic society. The son, Oddr, is gifted with business acumen and becomes affluent through his commercial enterprises, an activity disdained by the chieftain class. Father and son become involved in a lawsuit with a group of chieftains who are conspiring to cheat Oddr out of his fortune by manipulating the law. The story of how the father, Ófeigr, not only outdoes the chieftains at their own game, but exposes them to disgrace and derision in the process, moves from raucous farce to razor-edged satire. Gudbrandur Vigfússon has called this saga "an essentially plebian story," W.P. Ker has termed it "the first reasonable and modern comedy in the history of modern Europe," and to Jan de Vries it is a "lustige Novelle."[18]

As we have already observed in passing, *Grettis saga* has the structure and content of the novella in its concluding six chapters. It was written in the same district of Iceland, that of Miðfjördur, as was *Bandamanna saga,* a fact which should not be forgotten when we examine further novella-elements in this saga. The last six chapters of ***Grettis saga*** contain a sequel to the life of the hero, and relate the vengeance exacted for Grettir's slaying by his brother Thorsteinn. After following the slayer to Constantinople and joining, as he had done, the Varangian Guard, Thorsteinn takes his vengeance by slaying him in the presence of the assembled Guard while he is reciting the story of how he had killed Grettir. This carry-over from the northern world—one is tempted to say from the Icelandic saga proper—is, however, only the beginning of Thorsteinn's adventures in Constantinople. A configuration of motifs now emerges which is distinctly atypical of the saga genre, even though at least one of them can be found in an earlier saga. Thorsteinn falls in love with a noble lady of Constantinople named Spes [sic], and she with him. There follows a series of extra-marital intimacies, concealments and ruses that are strongly reminiscent of the novella and *fabliau* literature current in continental Europe at the time the saga was written.

Of special interest is a striking motif correspondence with the romance of Tristan and Isolde which was transmitted in the 12th and 13th centuries in several versions and languages.[19] Spes' honour, like that of Isolde, is eventually put to the test in an ordeal, and both women avoid disgrace by means of an ingeniously ambiguous oath. Although the details vary, the basic idea is the same in both cases: by prearrangement, on the day the oath is to be sworn, the lady's lover appears in the precincts of the church in the disguise of a beggar (pilgrim) and is called upon to carry the lady over a muddy ditch (ashore from a boat). Just as he is about to reach dry land he stumbles and pitches to the ground with his burden; whereupon the lady, jestingly at first, then with increasing earnestness, avers that she is now unable to swear that she has lain with no other man but her husband. This condition is accordingly put into the oath, which, duly sworn, results in a full restoration of the lady's honour and good repute.

Several scholars have drawn attention to the existence of a somewhat similarly ambiguous oath sworn under similar circumstances in a Byzantine Greek novel of the 6th century A.D., *Leucippe and Clitophon,* by Achilleus Tatius. It is conjectured that the motif may have been brought from Byzantium to Iceland in the later Middle Ages by Icelanders returning home after their service in the elite Varangian Guard.[20] According to Odd Nordland, who has more recently devoted a detailed study to the Spes-episode and its sources, there is another correspondence between this part of ***Grettis saga*** and the Tristan material. In both works there is a notch in a sword-blade which was caused by the slaying of a man and later serves to identify the slayer. In *Grettis saga* the sword is carried by the slayer of Grettir, and in *Tristan* it is the hero's own sword with which he slew Morolt. Despite the fact that in the one instance the sword is that of the hero, and in the other, the hero's slayer, Nordland sees no reason for doubting that the motif, like the ambiguous oath, indicates a connection between the Spes-episode and *Tristan,* either in terms of a direct literary borrowing, or dependence on a common source. Indeed, he has demonstrated the probability that the ambiguous oath in ***Grettis saga*** was borrowed from a particular version of the Old Norse translation of Thomas of Brittany's romance. His study of the variants of this oath shows that it is a motif belonging to an international inventory of narrative materials current in Europe in the Middle Ages.[21] Its appearance in the courtly *Tristan* makes for a strange combination of the farcical and the sublime, and in the classical telling of the *Tristan* story by Gottfried von Strassburg, a moderately careful reader will not fail to realize the dilemma confronting the author at this point.[22]

Nordland's reference, to an "europeisk litteraer sameige i mellomalderen" (p. 39) as background and framework for the variants in the motif of the ambiguous oath, makes it possible to account for both a direct relationship between the Spes-episode and *Tristan,* and an indirect relationship between these works and the Byzantine novel by Achilleus Tatius. It is well known that a stream of narrative materials from Greece, the Byzantine world and even India flowed westward and northward from the time of Herodotus up to the close of the Middle Ages, stories which were in the main anecdotal, often lewd and highly ingenious.[23] These stories enriched the indigenous *fabliau* literature of the west and in a number of instances served as prototypes for Italian novellas of the 14th century.[24] The more fabulous kind of Oriental lore was, in fact, a very considerable source of material for a poet of chivalric romance like Wolfram von Eschenbach.[25] But because such stories existed on a plane that was much broader and more productive in terms of the future, they not only outlived the world of chivalry but came into their own in the age that saw the *fabliau* and *Schwank* become popular literary genres. Hence Nordland explains the Spes-episode, which he demonstrates to be fictional and probably a late addition to the older *Grettis saga,* as a love story which addresses itself to a new literary taste, a taste which is evidence of literary impulses reaching Iceland from continental Europe near the end of the 13th century.[26]

One of the concealment devices used by Spes and her lover Thorsteinn occurs, as we have already pointed out, in an earlier Icelandic historical saga, the *Morkinskinna* redaction of *Haralds saga harðráða.* It is generally agreed that the author of the Spes episode in *Grettis saga* borrowed the motif from that source,[27] but he has done more than merely transfer it from one saga to another. He has expanded it by introducing a husband—this figure is lacking in the earlier saga—and by having the lovers use an ingenious trick to avoid discovery not once, but three times. The role of the hood-winked husband and the more or less farcical atmosphere that attaches to it is therefore new. Moreover, it is precisely this aspect of the story that the author intensifies still further by including the motif of the ambiguous oath already mentioned. This combination and expansion of motifs may be seen as a perfect reflection of the shift of the literature in continental Europe from the idealistic courtly forms to the novella and *Schwank* in the later 13th century. The question which must now be considered is whether, in *Grettis saga,* this element is restricted to the Spes episode, or whether it has also influenced the other, more purely Icelandic parts of the work.

One of Grettir's most famous exploits is described in chapters 74 and 75 of *Grettis saga.* He was living with two companions on a barren, unapproachable island off the northern coast of Iceland, called Drangey. One night a crisis occurred when the fire was inadvertently allowed to die. Grettir decided to swim to a farm on the mainland 7½ kilometers away to fetch fire. He not only accomplished his original purpose, but enjoyed an amorous encounter

with one of the farmer's maids into the bargain. This episode has attracted a certain amount of critical attention. Although Grettir himself was most certainly an historical person, the historicity of this particular event is dubious. There is the matter, first of all, of the scaldic verses that Grettir is reported to have extemporized during his visit to the farmhouse. In early sagas, especially the Sagas of the Kings, authentic scaldic verses were a primary historical source for the saga-writers. In later sagas they came to be treated as an artistic device and were invented by the authors for embellishment and as a pseudo-authentication of their material. Critics have agreed that most of the verses in *Grettis saga* were invented either by the last author or by earlier oral narrators. Of the two stanzas spoken by Grettir in this episode, one (No. 65) has been unanimously considered spurious, and the other (No. 64) questionable.[28]

Although Grettir's swim from Drangey to the mainland has been performed in modern times, its authenticity in the saga has been questioned for several reasons. R. C. Boer has noted that this is the second time the motif of swimming to fetch fire occurs in the saga. He considers it a mere variation of the first occasion, with the addition of the encounter with the serving-maid (p. xxii). Arthur Hruby has suggested that the model for the episode is to be found in a number of the myths of the gods found in Eddic poetry, the stealing of the Poet's Mead by Odin, the stealing of Thor's hammer, and the devouring of the sun by the Fenris-wolf at the end of time. One is even reminded, he thinks, of the fire-bearing god Prometheus.[29] While there is other evidence in the saga to suggest that some element of myth occasionally strayed into the author's conception of Grettir, it is difficult to find any convincing parallel between Grettir's swim and Hruby's conjectured mythical sources. The fact that these suggestions are so numerous has the effect of devaluing the theory. Almost as an afterthought Hruby mentions the story of Hero and Leander, but makes no attempt to investigate its possibilities as a possible source for the episode. Since this story was widely known in Northern Europe in the late Middle Ages, the conjecture seems plausible. Friedrich von der Hagen, who edited a mediaeval German *Hero and Leander,* tells us in his introduction that the subject matter originated in India and was bequeathed to the Middle Ages by Roman and Greek authors. Dante refers to the story in the *Purgatorio,* the existence of Old French versions may be assumed, and in Germany and Scandinavia its popularity is attested by a great variety of folksongs and ballads.[30] Yet if this explanation seems to offer a more acceptable source for Grettir's amorous swim than the myths of the Gods, it remains conjecture, and we can only say that if the legend did provide the source, its love ldyll has been badly vulgarized in the saga. An Icelandic farmhouse in the 11th century may not have been an ideal setting for a Hero and Leander. Nevertheless, we may wonder whether the relative crudity of the saga-episode was necessarily inherent in the saga style, or whether this too might not be traceable to a European source, a motif of novella-like character with which the Hero and Leander story could have been contaminated. Such a motif, in fact, exists.

In the *Decameron* (Day 3, Tale 1) Boccaccio tells the story of a certain Masetto who, by pretending to be a deaf mute, obtains employment as a gardener in a convent. His purpose is not to cultivate the convent garden, but to attempt intimacies with the nuns. This he accomplishes, first by pretending to be asleep in the garden when two of the sisters chance to come along, and on another occasion, by really falling asleep with his smock disarrayed in a manner irresistible to the abbess of the convent.[31]

In his study of Boccaccio's sources Marcus Landau notes a corresponding story in another collection of novellas, the *Cento novelle antiche,* and regards oral tales circulating at the time as the common source of the two works (p. 165). According to the evidence cited by Landau the story also appears with rather wide variations in several other works of the 13th and 14th centuries (pp. 175-177). One of these is a Middle High German novella which the Middle Ages mistakenly attributed to Konrad von Würzburg,[32] a poet who flourished around the middle of the 13th century. Although the German poem may post-date Konrad, the literary incidence of the story nevertheless suggests that it was popular in the 13th century as a *fabliau.*

In the various renderings of the story only the basic motifs remain fairly constant. In the pseudo-Konrad novella, for example, Masetto's counterpart is a Ritter Arnold, who pretends to be deaf, dumb and a simpleton. He lingers about his lady's door awaiting his opportunity, and one day is brought into the chamber to serve as a butt for the company's jokes. The lady's concupiscence is aroused by the banter, and the predictable eventually takes place. Here the element of nakedness is absent in the motivation of the event, but the most reliable manuscript appears to include it as a blind motif. We read that Arnold had a habit of lying in front of the lady's door, and that he was observed there one evening by a lady's companion in a certain condition:

> dâ vant si den blâzen
> der dâ ein tôre solte sîn.

(Wolff, ll. 232-233)

The meaning of the "blâz" is uncertain, but one explanation sees it as an Alsatian dialect form of "blôz," "uncovered" (p. xxvii). If this is correct, it is quite clear that the story is based on migratory material comprising three basic motifs that appear in a mixture of persistence and dispensability: a man who is sleeping or pretending to do so, is indecently clad, and is affecting some kind of deficiency.

A closer look at *Grettis saga* is now called for. Here we read:

> He [Grettir] smote the water bravely and reached Reykjanes after sunset. He went into the settlement at Reykir, bathed in the night in a warm spring, and then entered the hall, where it was very hot and a little smoky from the fire which had been burning there all day. He was very tired and slept soundly, lying on right

into the day. When it was a little way on in the morning the servants rose, and the first to enter the room were two women, the maid with the bondi's daughter. Grettir was asleep, and his clothes had all fallen off on to the floor. They saw a man lying there and recognized him. The maid said:

> "As I wish for salvation, sister, here is Grettir the son of Asmund come. He really is large about the upper part of his body, and is lying bare. But he seems to me unusually small below. It is not at all in keeping with the rest of him."

> The bondi's daughter said: "How can you let your tongue run on so? You are more than half a fool! Hold your tongue!"

> "I really cannot be silent, my dear sister," said the maid; "I would not have believed it if any one had told me."

> Then she went up to him to look more closely, and kept running back to the bondi's daughter and laughing. Grettir heard what she said, sprang up and chased her down the room. When he caught her he spoke a verse.

(Hight, p. 195)

Here our fastidious English translator breaks off and leaves us to our own resources. We translate, then, as follows, reducing the intricate scaldic structures, for the most part, to straightforward prose:

> The wanton girl's behaviour is mischievous; few warriors can show the sword in their hair completely to others. I'll wager I have larger testicles than other men, though they may have a larger penis.

> With that he whisked her onto the bench and the bondi's daughter ran out of the room. Then he spoke this stanza:

> The woman has said I have a little sword. The goddess of the scrotum bough has spoken the truth. The horse with the mane down in the forest of the young man's thighs can grow very long. Just wait, girl!

> The serving girl shouted loudly, but when they parted she was well satisfied with Grettir.

(Jónsson, pp. 240-241)

The elements observed in the above passage which are common to it, the Boccaccio novella, and the pseudo-Konrad are: a sleeping male, two or more women who hold a conversation about him,[33] nakedness, a feigned or only apparent incompetence or inadequacy in the male, and the sexual act arising from a combination of the above. The stanzas extemporized by Grettir in the manner of the traditional saga hero during his great moments, are unrivalled in their indecency until the mythical-heroic work *Bósa saga,* written several decades after *Grettis saga.*[34] Although the story told by Boccaccio is mild in this respect, the pseudo-Konrad is more than moderately prurient, and if the episode in *Grettis saga* owes its origin to some such source, that source may well have provided not only the erotic situation, but also its exceedingly lewd treatment.

We cannot, of course, prove that the story of Masetto, that is, the prototype of Boccaccio's story, was one of the forerunners of Grettir's adventure at Reykir. But the plausibility of the theory is much enhanced by the results of a study made by Alexander Krappe, who showed that at least two of a collection of stories written by the Icelandic Bishop of Skálholt, Jón Halldorsson (1322-1339), owe their origin to Italian stories of the 13th century.[35] These stories reached far-off Iceland, Krappe concludes, "through the medium of one of the many Icelanders studying at Italian universities."[36] Jón himself studied at the university of Bologna in the late 13th century, which is the conjectured time of the writing of *Grettis saga*.[37] It is difficult to believe that of these many Icelanders studying at Italian universities, Jón was the only one to bring back Italian novella material to Iceland.

In the light of these conjectures, a glance at Grettir's life and character in other parts of the saga reveals some astonishing affinities. To begin with, he is an almost classic example of the jester and wag prominent, according to Jacob Burckhardt, in Renaissance society.[38]

As a youngster Grettir was a good-for-nothing who refused to earn his keep. While this may be seen as a reminiscence of the Dümmling-motif of fairy-tale, a motif which often occurs in the sagas as well,[39] Grettir combines it with other characteristics that make him both a consummate practical joker and an inveterate lady's man. Chapter 14 of the saga tells of Grettir's boyhood and his father's attempts to set him to work. Three times Grettir is given a task to perform, and three times the result is a rather malicious practical joke. At the same time Grettir composes satirical stanzas whose authenticity is now considered doubtful.[40] At the conclusion of the chapter the saga reports that Grettir played many more childish pranks that are not related, and that he continued composing lampoons. His attitude to work seems to have changed little during his lifetime. We read that in the sixth year of his outlawry (Chapt. 53) he was sent away by an erstwhile benefactor because he refused to work, and again in the same chapter, that he was "a first-rate hand at forging iron, but was not often inclined to work at it."[41] At the age of fifteen Grettir left home and took passage for Norway (Chapt. 17). We are told at the beginning that the mate of the ship had a young and pretty wife. Grettir refused to do any work on the ship and spent his time lampooning the crew instead. As a storm increased in violence, so did Grettir's verses, until the crew became more vexed by this baiting than by their incessant bailing. They reproached Grettir with "patting the belly" of the mate's wife instead of doing his duty and bailing like the others. Finally he agreed to lend a hand, but only to please the mate's wife. At least four of the five stanzas spoken by Grettir in this chapter are spurious according to Jónsson (pp. xxxv, xl).

Grettir's relations with the opposite sex cannot be pursued in detail here, but the above instance, together with the fire-fetching episode, may be considered outstanding examples of his exploits. In the introduction to his edition of the saga, Guðni Jónsson has drawn attention to the sensual vein in the story and provides a list of specific references to the text (p. xii n.) Likewise, a complete list of Grettir's hoaxes and practical jokes would become tedious out of context. The point can, however, be illustrated by citing two examples,

While living on Drangey, Grettir decided one spring to go to the mainland to fetch supplies; he had the secondary motive of joining in the festivities of the spring assembly at Hegranes (Chapt. 72). Arriving in disguise, he persuaded the unsuspecting chieftains to grant him safe-conduct, whereupon he revealed his true identity and stayed on at Hegranes to enjoy the entertainments of the day. The authenticity of the whole episode has been questioned by R. C. Boer, who suggests that it is based on a similar event in another saga.[42]

In the year 1026 or thereabouts, Grettir was living on the Reykir Heath (Chapt. 63) with a companion. One day he suddenly caught sight of his longstanding enemy, Thórir, approaching the spot with a band of armed men. Grettir and his companion, not at a loss to hide their horses in an almost completely open landscape, dragged them, prostrate, into the very low-roofed dairy shed in which they had been living. Thórir passed by unsuspecting. But this was not good enough for Grettir. He donned a disguise and set off after Thórir. "It would be a good jest," he told his companion, "if they didn't recognize me" (Hight, p. 169). He arranged to meet Thórir on the heath, and when the latter asked him if he had seen Grettir Ásmundarson, he replied in the affirmative and sent the company galloping off at top speed into a swamp; they spent the rest of the day extricating themselves. In the meantime, Grettir and his companion rode to Thórir's farm and paid their respects to his daughter with a satirical verse. This verse, like the others, is regarded by Jónsson as spurious (p. xxxviii).

In looking back on Grettir's character traits, it must be conceded that wit, a sharp tongue, and even guile, are characteristics often found in the old saga-heroes. Moreover, as an outlaw, Grettir had particular occasion to develop these qualities. But the striking fact about Grettir is that he used his wits less to elude capture than out of sheer waggery. The theme of the relation of the sexes is not peculiar to *Grettis saga*. It played a prominent role in at least four earlier classical sagas. There, however, it is treated with deep respect in love stories whose outcome is consistently tragic. Grettir's character derives its particular hue from the combination and cumulative effect of his penchant for trickery and his amorousness. This is unique to *Grettis saga*.

Grettir's character and career follow a clearly marked pattern that bears a close affinity to the new kind of literature coming into being in Europe in the latter 13th century, a literature which marked the demise of the great age of chivalry and the birth of a new social and cultural world. If the Icelandic sagas considered here, *Ölkofra þáttr, Ban-*

damanna saga, and above all **Grettis saga,** may be said to form a particular stylistic branch of late saga-writing—and we must remember the connection noted earlier between these works—then it is undoubtedly true to say that in this branch Icelandic literature and the literature of continental Europe in the 13th century moved from what were originally antipodal positions with respect to subject matter, style and spirit, to a point of considerable resemblance in the style of the newly elevated *fabliau* and novella.

All literature is in one way or another a document of the age that has produced it; so also are the sagas of Grettir and the *bandamenn.* In the year 1262 history witnessed the astonishing spectacle of the ancient Republic of Iceland voting in its parliament to eclipse itself and to accept the sovereignty of the crown of Norway, ironically a dynasty that was itself in the twilight of its day. Though the spirit lingered, the world which bore and nourished the Icelandic saga had ceased to exist as a political reality.

Notes

1. Cf. W. P. Ker, *Epic and Romance, Essays on Mediaeval Literature* (1896; reprinted New York, 1957), pp. 57-61, 179-186; Peter Hallberg, *The Icelandic Saga,* trans. Paul Schach (Lincoln: University of Nebraska Press, 1962), p. 2.

2. Cf. G. Turville-Petre, *Origins of Icelandic Literature* (Oxford: Clarendon Press, 1953), pp. 60-61, 64.

3. Cf. *loc. cit.;* W. P. Ker, *op. cit.,* p. 60; Jan de Vries, *Altnordische Literaturgeschichte,* 2 vols. (Berlin, 1942), II, 424-425.

4. Cf. Turville-Petre, *op. cit.,* p. 253.

5. *Grettis saga Ásmundarsonar,* ed. Guðni Jónsson ("Íslenzk fornrit," vol. vii; Reykjavik, 1936); *The Saga of Grettir the Strong,* ed. Peter Foote, trans. G. A. Hight (London, 1965).

6. Cf. Jan de Vries, *op. cit.,* pp. 405-407; *Grettis saga,* ed. Guðni Jónsson, pp. viii, ix, lvii.

7. Odd Nordland, "Norrøne og europeiske litteraere laan i Grettis saga," *Maal og Minne,* xliv (1953), p. 44.

8. *Die deutsche Literatur im späten Mittelalter,* von Helmut de Boor (München, 1962), p. 229.

9. Yvonne Rodax, *The Real and the Ideal in the Novella of Italy, France and England,* (North Carolina, 1968), p. 36.

10. Erich Auerbach, *Zur Technik der Frührenaissancenovelle in Italien und Frankreich* (Heidelberg, 1921), p. 41.

11. *Ibid.,* pp. 6, 21, 30-31.

12. Yvonne Rodax, *op. cit.,* p. 127; Helmut de Boor, *op. cit.,* p. 221f.

13. Yvonne Rodax, *op. cit.,* p. 18-19; Helmut de Boor, *op. cit.,* pp. 16-17, 229-238.

14. Cf. G. Turville-Petre, *op. cit.,* p. 230; Jan de Vries, *op. cit.,* pp. 275-276, 278.

15. Cf. *ibid.,* pp. 98-99; Jan de Vries, *op. cit.,* p. 286; *Bandamanna saga* und *Ölkofra þáttr,* ed. Walter Baetke, Altnordische Textbibliothek, Neue Folge, 4. Band, (Halle, 1960), p. 17.

16. *Bandamanna saga, Odds saga Ófeigssonar* [=*Ölkofra þáttr*], ed. Guðni Jónsson ("Islenzk fornrit," vii, Reykjavik, 1936); Walter Baetke, *op. cit.*

17. Walter Baetke, *op. cit.,* pp. 2-4, 26ff, esp. 28.

18. *Sturlunga saga,* ed. Gudbrandur Vigfússon (2 vols.; Oxford, 1878), I, p. liii; W. P. Ker, *op. cit.,* p. 229; Jan de Vries, *op. cit.,* p. 399.

19. Cf. R. S. Loomis, *Arthurian Literature in the Middle Ages* (Oxford, 1959), pp. 134-159.

20. Cf. H. G. Leach, *Angevin Britain and Scandinavia* (Cambridge, 1921), p. 188; Guðni Jónsson, *op. cit.,* p. lvi.

21. Cf. Odd Nordland, *op. cit.,* p. 34.

22. Cf. *Tristan,* ed. Karl Marold (Berlin, 1969), 1. 15,701 ff, 1. 15,737-15,754.

23. Cf. Eberhard Hermes, *Die drei Ringe. Aus der Frühzeit der Novelle* (Göttingen, 1964), pp. 18, 22-44, (esp.) 27, 42-43. The occurrence of pan-European motifs, of which at least one came from the Orient, has been demonstrated in the cases of several relatively early Icelandic sagas. Jan de Vries has pointed out the presence of one such anecdote in *Ljósvetninga saga;* cf. "Een Indisch Exempel in een Ijslandsche Saga," *Tijdschrift voor Nederlandsche Taal en Letterkunde,* xlvii (1928), pp. 63-80. A better known instance is the Kálfr-episode in *Víga-Glúms saga;* cf. *Víga-Glúms saga,* ed. G. Turville-Petre (2nd ed.; Oxford, 1960), pp. xxxiv-xxxv and Jan de Vries, *op. cit.,* p. 393.

24. Cf. Marcus Landau, *Die Quellen des Dekameron,* 2. Aufl. (Stuttgart, 1884), pp. 1-2, 120-121; *Cassell's Encyclopædia of Literature,* ed. S. H. Steinberg, (London, 1953), p. 216.

25. Cf. Margaret Fitzgerald Richey, *Studies of Wolfram von Eschenbach* (Edinburgh and London, 1957), p. 157.

26. Odd Nordland, *op. cit.,* pp. 38, 43. Nordland conjectures that *Grettis saga* may have been written by the Icelandic historian Sturla Thordarson, a hypothesis which would place its composition in the period between 1270 and 1284 (cf. p. 42). As noted earlier Guðni Jonsson (*op. cit.,* p. xxxi) and Jan de Vries (*op. cit.,* p. 406) argue for a later date, namely around 1300 or shortly thereafter.

27. Cf. *Grettis saga Ásmundarsonar,* ed. R. C. Boer, Altnordische Sagabibliothek, Heft 8; (Halle a.S, 1900), pp. xxvi-xxxi; Odd Nordland, *op. cit.,* p. 39.

28. Cf. Guðni Jónsson, *op. cit.,* pp. xxxii, xli.

29. Arthur Hruby, *Drei Studien zur Technik der isländischen Saga* (Leipzig und Wien, 1936), pp. 11-16.

30. *Gesamtabenteur. Hundert altdeutsche Erzählungen,* ed. Friedrich von der Hagen, 3 vols. (Stuttgart and Tübingen, 1850), I, pp. cxxix-cxxxiii.

31. *The Decameron of Giovanni Boccaccio,* trans. Francis Winwar (New York, 1955), pp. 147-148.

32. *Diu halbe bir, Ein Schwank Konrads von Würzburg,* ed. G. A. Wolff (Dissertation, Erlangen, 1893); H. Laudan, "Die halbe Birne nicht von Konrad von Würzburg," *Zeitschrift für deutsches Altertum und deutsche Literatur,* L (1908), pp. 158-166.

33. Cf. the conversation between the two nuns in Boccaccio, and that between the lady and her mentor in the pseudo-Konrad.

34. Cf. Jan de Vries, *op. cit.,* p. 461.

35. Cf. Alexander H. Krappe, "The Italian Origin of an Icelandic Story," *Scandinavian Studies* xix (1946-1947) pp. 105-109.

36. *Ibid.,* "Parallels and Analogues to the Death of Örvar Odd," *Scandinavian Studies,* xvii (1942-1943), p. 35.

37. Cf. *Ibid.,* xix (1946), 105.

38. Cf. Jacob Burckhardt, *Die Kultur der Renaissance in Italien* (1860; reprinted in "Gesammelte Werke," Bd. III, Basel, 1955), pp. 105-106.

39. Cf. Heinz Dehmer, *Primitives Erzählungsgut in den Islendinga-Sögur* "Von deutscher Poeterey. Forschungen u. Darstellungen aus dem Gesamtgebiet der deutschen Philologie," Bd. 2, (1927), pp. 6 ff.

40. Cf. Guðni Jónsson, *op. cit.,* p. xli, xxxiv-xxxv.

41. G. A. Hight, *op. cit.,* p. 143.

42. Cf. R. C. Boer, *op. cit.,* p. 256 n.

Lotte Motz (essay date 1973)

SOURCE: "Withdrawal and Return: A Ritual Pattern in the *Grettis Saga,*" in *Arkiv för Nordisk Filologi,* Vol. 88, 1973, pp. 91-110.

[*In the following essay, Motz provides instances in which the main character of the* Grettis Saga, *Grettir, conforms to patterns of the hero in myth, tradition, and ritual, with the result that his individuality is sublimated.*]

Grettir Ásmundarson, one of the strongest men of his time, a victim of both ill luck and the tempestuousness of his character, lived almost all of his adult life as an outlaw and was slain according to the saga written about him, as a mortally sick man on the lonely island which had sheltered him and his faithful brother Illugi. He was, his saga asserts in its closing chapter,[1] the most notable of all outlaws for his strength and his many victories over the fiends of darkness, the length of his exile and the effection of his vengeance from abroad. Grettir was a well-born man belonging on his mother's side to the people of Vatnsdal and numbering among his paternal ancestors the famous

Omundr Tréfót. By the time his tale had found its way to the manuscript which underlies our editions of the saga Grettir's figure had grown beyond the boundaries of the area assigned to him by his human parentage.[2]

The oral and written tales which had kept his memory from fading had also altered and extended the factual basis of his life until its historic core lay embedded in a web of imaginary matter. This fate Grettir shares with many a historic personage who has kindled the imagination; these figures are frequently remodeled and redrawn until their life and deeds conform to the same basic patterns which shape the destiny of the heroes of legend and literature. So the great men are remembered less in their transitory and unique appearance in time, less in their own, individual likeness than in that of the more lasting and encompassing type to which they have become assimilated. To illustrate the process Mircea Eliade recounts how in a small Roumanian village the events and characters of an unfortunate incident were reshaped and assimilated into a pattern within the life time of some of the witnesses.[3]

The type of which Grettir appears to be the Icelandic manifestation is that of the gifted fighter, the protagonist of 'heroic literature' who is lifted above ordinary men by his strength and skill in battle, by an excessive sensitivity to any stain on his honor and by a spirit which drives him to both: deeds of glory and an early doom.

There have been attempts to trace the outlines of such a life; Jan de Vries, taking his models from many stages in history and many areas of the world found the following recurrent features (not necessarily present in their entirety in every heroic life): divine or semi-divine parentage, superhuman feats of strength and courage, a voyage to the beyond, the winning of a maiden, defeat of a monstrous being inimical to man, and an early death.[4] It is possible, even on superficial investigation, to ascertain these elements within the tales gathered in Grettir's saga, so that we may be well justified in looking for his spiritual kindred among the traditional heroes, on the battlefield of Maldon, before the ramparts of Troy and in the mountain pass of Roncevaux.[5]

One would, of course, never deny to Grettir his specific place in space and time nor question the saga's rendition of medieval Iceland, her pastures and grazing horses, her mountains and valleys peopled by giants, her drinking feasts and bloody feuds. But one may have to consider that the appeal of the central figure, his hold on our interest and emotion may stem from our response to a configuration which has exercised its spell through the ages.

Ancient as the scenario of the heroic life may be, it is composed of yet more ancient matter: the elements of archaic myth and ritual. The battle with a monster fought and won by the warrior hero may be traced ultimately to the mythical battle in which a warrior god defeated a primordial being, symbolic of chaos, and thus assured the establishment of cosmic order. The heroes' deeds, the exhibition of strength and courage, their solitary passage to non-human regions, may recall the initiation ritual of archaic religion, the ordeals to be endured, the proofs of manhood to be given, the contact with the sacred to be achieved by young men before they are admitted into adulthood or into special classes.[6] Such rites are assumed to have pervaded everywhere, at a certain stage of civilization, the fabric of communal life (therefore also that of the ancient Germanic tribes or their ancestors) and may be observed and studied in modern times among those people who have remained on the appropriate level of cultural achievement.

In a recent study Margarete Arent examines, in the light of the heroic life-pattern, Grettir's repeated struggles against ghosts and monsters in relation to their most famous parallel: Beowulf's encounter with Grendel and his dam, grim night-time visitors from their dank dwellings to the hall of Hrothgar.[7] It is the purpose of this paper to retrace another archaic pattern, less strikingly apparent, but still discernible through the realistic overlay, and to follow the thread of a ritual sequence.

As Grettir's life reaches its culminating moments in the fierce ecstasy of combat with human or non-human foes, its external course follows his pendulum movements between wilderness and settled dwellings, between separation from society and brief integration. The journeys may be understood realistically on the basis of Grettir's inability as dangerous outlaw to receive lasting hospitality and, on the other hand, his need for human companionship. They may also be understood differently.

There is, in fact, in ritual, an analogue to the rhythm of withdrawal and return which actuates Grettir's outlaw existence. Segregation is the indispensable first step in the initiation ceremonies of primitive societies which have earlier been mentioned. A rite of separation, as called by van Gennep, a stay in bush, forest or mountain assures the stripping away of all that is secular and profane, all that belongs to the earlier existence of the individual who, in this ceremony, must die and emerge reborn into a higher mode of living.[8]

Such segregation may extend for several months, as in Ceram,[9] but last up to several years (up to six years in the Congo),[10] especially if the membership desired is that into a secret and selective group. So deeply entwined appears to some Australian tribes the experience of initiation with the stay in the forest that they use one word to designate both (the word '*Jeraeil,*' for example among the Kurnai, or the word '*Kuringal,*' among the Yuin means: 'that which is from the forest,' and 'initiation').[11]

The acts of violence by which Grettir, by necessity, procures the means of sustaining life also find their counterpart in the religious practices. The geographic distance from the normal habitation brings to the novices at times a liberation from the laws which had bound their profane life. In Liberia, for instance, the young men are allowed

and expected to steal and pillage, to obtain in nightly attacks on the villages what they need for their maintenance.[12] The seizing of any food they might like to eat is a license enjoyed by the newly circumcised of Fjuta Djaloon in Australia;[13] in French West Africa, where circumcision also forms part of the ceremonies, the right to steal is granted from the time of cicatrition of the wound to the moment of complete healing.[14] The code of Lykurgus sent the youth of ancient Sparta, for one year, naked into the mountains to live on what could be obtained by dagger, the only implement allowed to the young men.[15]

Thus, truly outside of the community and its norms of life, often subjected to cruel ordeals, such as beatings or the infliction of wounds, the old form of the individual is thought to die; induced, at times, by intoxication, encounter with the sacred is achieved; then the men return, profoundly altered and affected beings, often bearing the marks of their experience on their body (a scarred cheek, a pierced tongue, a circumcised genital). They may also carry less permanent signs of their communion with the godhead, and may appear disguised, masked, their body painted or naked:[16] they may return frenzied and in need of exorcism as do the Kwakiutl of North America.[17]

On their return the men must frequently give proof of the powers which fit their new status: the mastery of magic techniques (in the case of shamans), feats of strength (in the case of the warriors), before they may assume their rightful place in the community or the young men be allowed to marry. There is also periodic and diluted repetition throughout life of the sacred experience.

The ancient rites have left their footprints, easily noticed in the folk customs of nations who have long forgotten the ancient religion. We know, just to cite an example, that in a remote Swiss valley young men in terrifying masks appear yearly among the inhabitants, stealing and looting, spreading fear and horror through the countryside, recalling in this way the lawlessness and sacred frenzy of the newly initiated.[18]

One may also look to literature for the impress of initiatory themes. These are strikingly realized in the tales of the long and weary exile of Odysseus and his eventual return and integration, which we know from the version said to be Homer's. We may remember that in the poem the beings met on the perilous journey are almost always superhuman, that after ordeals on the angry sea Odysseus enters his island kingdom in the disguise of a ragged beggar, unrecognizable even to his nearest kin, that he passes with surpassing skill a test of stringing an ancient bow and shooting an arrow through twelve axes, before he resumes his rightful place as king and husband.[19]

In the northern tale of the Volsungs we may also recognize various stages of the initiation ritual: 1. The young hero Sinfjotli is sent into a forest to stay with the older Sigmund; he passes ordeals, such as baking bread from flour which harbors a living snake; 2. Both heroes transform themselves into wolves by donning wolf-skins (they appear in disguise); 3. Still in this form Sinfjotli slays in a single encounter eleven men without asking Sigmund for help (proof of valor); 4. The two burn their wolf-skins and resume human form (return to society). These events complete the initiation and Sinfjotli is ready to take up his life's work, the act of vengeance for which he was begotten.[20]

We shall now probe five episodes of Grettir's life for the chain of events which parallels the ritual sequence: exile, disguise, proof of valor, revelation of identity, and reintegration into society.

I. HÁRAMARSEY (CHAP. 18-20, PP. 56-73).

The ship which carried Grettir on his first voyage to Norway has foundered on a rock so that the sailors are forced to seek shelter on a small island off the Norwegian coast. Here the farmer Þorfinnr is settled and Grettir stays with this man and his household though he holds himself rather reserved. He is present at the moment when twelve pirates, known for their plundering and ravishing of women, pull their boat unto the shore in a way which indicates that "they do not mean to wait for an invitation."[21] In the absence of the farmer, away at a Yule gathering, Grettir approaches the vikings, welcomes them warmly and bids them enter the hall. Despite the horror and despair shown by the women and servants of the household, Grettir, usually a sullen man, entertains the strangers with merry jests, plies them with food and ale and promises the mistress of the house as a bedcompanion. When the visitors are heavy with drink he leads them into a combination of store- and outhouse and locks them by a ruse into the building. Immediately they are trapped he drops his role, and arming himself, charges against them as they emerge, sobered, through the broken wall. Though they are without weapons and he wields arms it is "a trial of a man's strength to stand up against their superhuman powers,"[22] for they have the ability to turn themselves into 'Berserks.' Ten of them Grettir kills singlehandedly, two escape and find death, exhausted by their wounds, in the snow. The returning hero is treated with the utmost deference and admiration as savior of life and honor, and is later offered by the farmer a place in the household.[23]

Let us note that in this episode the hero arrives on the island after ordeals at sea, shipwrecked, stripped of his belongings, a man completely removed from his former life; on meeting the Berserks he masks his action and reveals his true nature when he commences the battle which is the first to spread his fame. Through this proof of valor he receives definition of his role in society and integration into the small community of the farmstead. The question of old and new personality and the significance of the battle to the revelation of manhood is touched upon in a short dialogue between Grettir and the housewife. "Am I not the same man," he inquires observing her new courtesy towards him, "that I was when you treated me so contemptuously?" "I didn't know that you were such a stout man as you now have proved yourself to be," is her answer.[24]

II. SODULKOLLUVÍSUR (CHAP. 47, PP. 147-153).

Grettir has landed in Iceland only to hear that he has been outlawed for the burning of Þorir's sons (of which he is not guilty). He stays with his ship because "he didn't find a suitable horse," until one night under cover of darkness "for he didn't want the merchants to know," he conceals his giant frame under a black cloak, seizes the best horse of a farmer named Sveinn, as it was grazing on the pasture, and rides off through the countryside. Sveinn laughingly hears the news that a big man in a black cowl has been seen mounted on his swiftest horse, composes a verse and races after the thief. As Grettir gallops through the meadows he encounters a man and entreats him to spread the tale of the theft through the district. The information is dutifully passed on to Sveinn who again chants a verse and moves after Grettir. A woman is next told by Grettir the destination of his journey and again asked to transmit the intelligence. Once more Sveinn answers with a strophe full of threats and the greater speed of his riding. At Gilsbakki, the destination, pursuer and pursued dismount, exchange more merry verse and part in friendship, for Sveinn considers himself amply repaid for the 'borrowing' of his horse. Grettir is warmly received by the owner of Gilsbakki and proceeds after a short stay to his family's home and to his mother in Bjarg.

One would be hard pressed to find a realistic interpretation of the incident; there is little reason for Grettir to leave his ship in the dark, but to seize the horse when dawn has broken and he may be observed, to conceal himself and then to disclose his theft, his destination and his name (the last in verse 34, 3, 4; *lautar áll—ormr*—Grettir). Unfitting also to the character of an Icelandic householder, no matter how 'merry' is the acceptance by Sveinn of insult and theft. We can only think that both Grettir and Sveinn act in accordance with the rules of a certain tradition.

The stanzas themselves might help us to understand this custom; verse 34 contains the word '*gamanvísa*,'—'a playful, joking verse, a jest;' in verse 32 Grettir calls himself one who throws dice, gambles, plays (*drýgja dufl*—to gamble);[25] Grettir also asserts that he would ride so furiously that he might receive hospitality in Gilsbakki.[26]

The poetry thus seems to reveal the vestiges of a gamble or game in which there was furious riding on a stolen horse; the object must have been arrival at a certain place, safe and unimpeded, though information was tossed into the path of the pursuer. It has earlier been stated that theft often belonged to the cultic practices; the right of rapine forms, as stated by Otto Höfler, one of the most characteristic marks of the secret male societies.[27] Mock theft of horses specifically, has been substantiated in the ancient Germanic practices, and may still be observed with the young men of the Alemanic regions on a certain day of the year (*gumpiger Donnerstag*) or with the fur clad *Öja-Busar* of Sweden; the *jolesveinar,* also, figures of Norwegian myth, similarly deplete the stables of horses in their Yuletime frolics.[28]

In a line of strophe 35, spoken by Sveinn, Grettir is abused as 'dogeyed,' (*hundeygr*); this adjective may be expressive of Sveinn's feigned anger, but it could also easily contain a memory of the very widespread custom among Germanic peoples of dog and wolf impersonations, exemplified by the 'Isengrind,' a dog with burning eyes who roams, at the turning of the year, the towns of Switzerland.[29] We may at this point recall the dogheaded warriors, (*Cynocephali*) of the Langobardi.[30]

Black, the verses tell us, are horse and rider (verse 32, 8; *í svortum kufli;* verse 35, 3 *á hrossi svortu*) and ride through a storm (verse 35, 2 *í róstuvedri*), thus painting an image evocative of the black figures on horseback who speed through the stormy night in the furious train which is in legend led by Odin (also related to cultic practices as shown by Otto Höfler).[31] Black is the color favored in numerous folk disguises, as that of the *Schemen* of Bavaria or the Morris dancers of England; it is also the color chosen by the painted warriors of ancient Germanic times who have been described by Tacitus.

With these considerations in mind one may be justified in assuming that the prose and especially the poetry of the episode contain the elements of a folk tradition or game, which in turn had arisen from cultic practices.

When, in the narrative, Grettir has arrived unscathed at his destination, the conditions of the game are apparently fulfilled; he must have removed his concealing clothes, though this is not stated; the warm reception of Grettir by the farmer of Gilsbakki, the friendliness of Sveinn, the owner of the horse, and Grettir's return to his mother's house may be understood to symbolize the return to life in the community.

III. SANDHAUGAR (CHAP. 64-65; PP. 209-214)

The household at Sandhaugar in Bardardal has been sorely troubled by supernatural visitors who carried off in successive Yule seasons its master and later a bondman. Grettir, drawn by the prospect of grappling with troll or giant, turns to the haunted dwelling; naming himself *Gestr* (a stranger), he is received by the young and merry mistress of the household. This young woman, Steinvor, must, in order to attend mass, cross a river so swollen and heavy with floating ice that she despairs of reaching the other bank; but Grettir, placing her daughter on her knee, carries both safely through the turbulent waters, striding firmly through the icy waves, so that the woman, frozen with terror, later reports to her kinsmen that she didn't know whether it was a man or a troll who had served her so bravely.

Back in the hall while the rest of the household is numb with fear Grettir-*Gestr* waits for the ill visit. And indeed, in the dark watches of the night the troll woman enters and seizes the hero. A mighty struggle ensues and continues through the night first in the hall amidst the wreckage of the grim encounter, and later in the open between cliffs

and boulders where Grettir finally cuts off the arm of the troll woman and sees her plunge into the waterfall (or turn to stone according to local tradition).

Steinvor is deeply impressed on her return by the deed and now once more asks for the stranger's name; this time she is told the truth. She extends to him henceforth the utmost of devotion and it is rumored that a child later born to her was fathered by Grettir.

In this episode Grettir does not use physical means of disguise, but hides his name to give it freely after his victory. His respite from the exile's loneliness in the arms of Steinvor, lasting for a winter only, is, as always, shortlived.

IV. HEGRANES THING (CHAP. 72; PP. 229-236)

The spring Thing at Hegranes is well frequented and the men from the proper districts stay long over their business and pleasure, for many in these parts are fond of merriment. Just at this time Grettir decides to lay in new supplies, and concealing himself in shabby clothes, proceeds to the mainland. After he has accomplished his purpose he turns, irresistably drawn, to the place of assembly and arrives when the men have finished their legal affairs and are ready for some sport. As the young begin to wrestle it appears that two brothers, the sons of Þord, emerge as greatly superior to the rest. Looking in their pride of victory for a fiercer challenge they notice Grettir, a huge stranger, sitting quietly in his cloak among the crowd. He gives his name, when asked, as *Gestr*, but does not let himself be drawn into the games until he is solemnly promised safety from attack. After an oath of peace has been pronounced he removes his cloak and all his garments; then a hush falls over the assembled men for they have recognized Grettir in his nakedness. The promise of peace, however, is not broken and the wrestling commences, Grettir holding his own against the brothers who engage him simultaneously, but still cannot defeat him though they are each said to have the strength of two. As the contestants become increasingly bruised and battered and the issue yet remains undecided the onlookers find it an ever more splendid sight to watch such mighty men exert their powers. At the end of the episode Grettir returns unmolested to his island.

In this incident recognition occurs (in contrast to the preceding episodes) before proof of manhood is offered; acceptance by society is indeed shortlived not outlasting Grettir's return to his shelter.

V. REYKIR (CHAP. 74-75; PP. 237-241)

Þorbjorn Glaum who lives with Grettir and Illugi, removed from settled society, on the islet of Drangey has neglected to tend the fire so that it died. The choice is now to wait for a passing boat or to undertake the long swim (one sea mile) to the mainland. Not heeding his brother's counsel who considers the venture beyond human strength Grettir prepares for the swim by having his fingers webbed (animal disguise?); in his usual coarse cloak and breeches he sets out towards evening with the current in his favor and crosses the water. He reaches Reykir at sunset and warms his chilled body in a hot spring. Then he enters a farmer's hall, still filled with the smoke of the day's fire, and soundly falls asleep in the warmth. He lets his garments slide, in his untroubled sleep, to the floor so that he lies naked; this nakedness, as at the Thing, reveals Grettir's identity to the first members of the household who enter the room in the morning: the farmer's daughter and a servant maid, the latter's emotions irresistably aroused by the sight of the sleeping man. Her giggling taunts which awaken Grettir are effectively stopped when he forces her, against her loud protests, onto the bench on which he has slept. Later, the farmer in admiration of the long swim lends the exile a boat for his homeward journey.

To interpret the rape of the bondwoman in the light of the ritual we must remember that initiation often brought the young men admission to the ranks of the sexually mature. A sexual element is, in the words of Jan de Vries, "inseparably linked up with the initiation. This often takes the form of orgiastic promiscuity; the newly-gained virility has first to run its full course . . . so as afterwards to be canalized."[32] Sexual or other aggression against women has been so marked a feature, throughout the ages, of the celebrations of the secret male societies that these are said, by some, to have originated as a force rebelling against the female rulers of a matriarchal society.[33]

Two strophes spoken by Grettir to the maid are suppressed in some editions for the general reader in possibly the same spirit which caused the church to suppress certain relics of the pagan practices: as too gross for a Christian population. These verses emphasize the character of the incident as a challenge extended to prove manly vigor and potency and adequately answered by Grettir. The girl expresses her surprise, for "He is so small below, and that is not in keeping with the rest of him,"[34] and does not stop to wonder at this condition until Grettir assures her in words, before proceeding to deeds, of his adequacy: "The small horse in the forest of my thighs can grow as long as need be, for me a young man."[35] And in truth, the girl complains no longer.

Grettir's long swim may be classed with the cruel ordeals, unnecessary except in the context of the ritual; could not three able-bodied men in possession of tools have built a raft? Bathing in icy rivers is indeed one of the known tests of initiation.[36] The helpfulness of the farmer to a dangerous outlaw, a threat to settled life, who had crept into his hall and done violence to one of his household may represent integration into society after initiation is completed.

It has been seen that in each of the segments of Grettir's life lifted up for our inspection the hero has emerged from some form of unsettled existence to enter into organized society: he came to Haramarsey from a sea voyage and a shipwreck, to Gilsbakki from travel in Norway, to Sandhaugar, Reykir and the Hegranes Thing from his various lonely hiding places. In every case there has been

some form of disguise which was later removed: friendliness towards the Berserks masked his true feelings, a cloak concealed him on his furious ride to Gilsbakki and shabby clothes on his entering the Hegranes Thing; an assumed name hid his identity in Sandhaugar and again at the Thing; no overt mask is mentioned in the Reykir episode; we only hear that he stole as an unknown man into the hall. The mask falls during the combat (the test of manhood) in episode one and his true identity is revealed after the victory; the disguise is lifted in episode two and three after successful completion of the test; recognition of the hero through nakedness precedes proof of valor in episode four and five.

The name *Gestr*, used by Grettir in two of the episodes to hide his identity, describes him as a 'stranger.' A correspondance to this aspect of Grettir may be found with the newly initiated in the Congo who acts upon reentry into the community as if he knew no one and did not understand the language (since he is newly born), who must laboriously relearn customs and speech.[37] Grettir's later naming himself may remind us that the giving of a name often follows or parallels admission into a group (as in Christian baptism). Norse literature offers another analogue: the stranger who visits in the *Norna-Gests þáttr* the court of King Olaf assumes like Grettir the name: *Gestr*. He is indeed a stranger, unbound by the laws of time, who has been living for several hundred years. In both cases the name signifies one who has entered from outside of the boundaries of normal life.

These are the proofs of manhood so easily given by Grettir: victory over twelve Berserks, successful stealing of a horse, defeat of a troll woman, championship in a wrestling match, exhibition of sexual potency. In every case the deed was rewarded by acceptance into a community and the honor and admiration of the group.

The tale of Haramarsey is the only one which could be explained satisfactorily in a purely realistic manner, for here Grettir's disguise was an apt and necessary trick for the defeat of the pirates. Even this episode is lifted from the purely profane by certain features: the action takes place at Yule time, a traditional period for communion with the supernatural, (also a traditional time for the celebrations of male societies); the invaders of the household can turn into Berserks, (supernatural beings) a threat, like the monsters of heroic tales, to settled life; the incident is interlaced with Grettir's preceding adventure, in which he descends a barrow, and which abounds with legendary features.

One might consider the fact that recognition (through nakedness) precedes the test of manhood in episode four and five and follows it in the others a variation of the pattern; there is however a different way of understanding the sequence. Grettir, we hear, takes off *all* his body garments, and his cloak before the assembly at Hegranes. The clothing of a farmer consisted according to Shetelig of a cloak, a woolen shirt, woolen trousers and leg bands;[38] the 'worn, shabby garments' which Grettir had used to conceal himself would not have included the elegance of an undershirt. If he therefore removed, besides his cloak, more than one piece of clothing he was completely naked. Trousers also were not attached to the leg coverings and can not be defined as 'leg clothing;' they would have to be part of the '*bolklædi*', the body coverings removed by Grettir. Wrestling in complete nakedness was not to my knowledge the custom.[39] We may also observe that it seems strange that a man be recognized by his naked body when he has not been recognized by his facial features or general stature.

Weakly motivated also is the disrobing of Grettir in the Reykir episode; he had been dressed for his swim in cloak and breeches; such breeches were in historic times short belted trousers and no longer the short belted skirts from which they had developed;[40] they could not, in this case, have easily slipped off an unwitting sleeper even if the belt was loosened.

We have observed that Grettir was recognized in his nakedness before he had passed a test of valor; such a test shows the novice in the new role he will play in the community, as shaman, warrior, or hunter. It is, in the language of van Gennep, a rite of integration; anything preceding still belongs to the period and practices of sacred isolation. The nakedness in which, in the Congo, the novice emerges from the forest marks him, as would a mask, as still belonging to his spirit.[41] Nakedness as part of the practices is noted elsewhere; it was endured by the young men of Sparta in the *Krypteia,* their year of lonely and wolflike existence in the mountains. Nakedness in a traditional and religious context, similarly, has been found among the Germanic nations; so Tacitus described the sword dances performed by naked youths; partial or complete bareness was required at some of the sacrifices, at the swearing of oaths and some agricultural practices.[42]

The nakedness of Grettir thus seems to have entered the saga through its ritual substructure; we may perceive in it the vestiges of a ritual nakedness; and Grettir was recognized not in his social but in his still numinous aspect, still the carrier and vessel of sacred forces. Such an assumption would be supported by the strong emotions which the sight awakened. The awe of the Thing assembly may recall the shock of the villagers before the masked figures, i.e., the terror before the divine revelation. The fascination of the servant girl may be understood in its original sense: the enchanting of an individual by a supernatural agency. Even the farmer's daughter does not wholly escape the spell and does not run off immediately (as she does later,) a fact noticed by R. C. Boer.[43]

Regarding the structure of the five episodes we find that in each narrative one element encapsules its abstract and numinous content, which we have also tried to extract, or opens a window to the symbolic. The pithy *dialogue* between Grettir and the mistress of Haramarsey shows up Grettir's combat in its purpose: the proof of valor; the *stanzas* exchanged between Grettir and Sveinn and those

spoken by her ravisher to the maid point to the folk custom and the challenge embedded in the tales; the *name Gestr* in episodes three and four (Sandhaugar and Hegranes Thing) reveals Grettir as one who has entered briefly from afar the human community.

It may be significant that Boer considered all these episodes, except for the fight on Haramarsey, as 'interpolations,' as additions which trouble the clear waters of logical sequence.[44] In this latter we may agree for we too have understood the course of action to be stimulated by an agency divorced from rational considerations.

It has been shown in the preceding pages that we may find in the saga not only individual elements of the ritual, such as lawlessness, return from exile, disguise, but also their analogous arrangement. It is this arrangement which allows us to assert more boldly the presence of the pattern of initiation in the narratives. We saw in two and five the elements of folk practices (the wrestling game, the theft and the rape) and in one and three (the Berserks and the troll woman) the incorporation of legendary themes into the sequence.

In the second part of this paper we shall consider the concluding remarks of Miss Arent's comparison who, having ascertained the same archaic pattern in the life of both, Grettir and Beowulf, finds the former wanting in the truly heroic stature reached by the visitor to Hrothgar; for Grettir has become a character in a folk tale, a farmer's son who disports himself with lads of his own class and vanquishes phantoms begotten by local superstition. His deeds, "heaving stones, carrying an ox, flaying a mare, killing goslings emerge from a folk culture . . . the fights with ogres takes place in ordinary farm houses and not in the most illustrious of kingly halls."[45]

We may answer that surely all heroes have been presented in the terms of their own physical environment; within his own country which had not constructed kings' halls Grettir is, as member of one of the leading families, as highly stationed as a prince.

In his coarse cloak and breeches Grettir may, in Miss Arent's view, be an individual who commands our sympathy and compassion, but not, like Beowulf, the admiration reserved for the carrier of heroic virtues who rises like a guiding star before the young.[46]

To counter this interpretation we must investigate how heroic literature uses the inherited themes, and how the heroic character stands in relation to the themes, the physical events, and the conviction of the epics. We cannot help but notice, in this endeavor, how much the emphasis has shifted. The myth of the warrior god slaying the monster of chaos, so often echoed in the poems, surely proclaimed the establishment of civilization, the triumph of order over chaos. The rites of archaic religions surely served to sustain the functioning of the community.

While evidently early religion demanded an occasional retreat from settled life, allowed freedom from the restraints of civilization, it also demanded a return; the novice was

sent into the forest where he recaptured an earlier condition of life in which man and god, or man and beast had
not achieved their separate identities, but he always reen-
tered the human dwellings as a being, and this was the
purpose, more ably fitted to defend them against natural
and unnatural foes, as warrior or magician, more adequately equipped to maintain and propagate life as adult
male.

No such concerns with the safeguarding of life on earth or
establishment of new cultural levels move the warrior heroes of the poems. For they have chosen honor above all
other values, in the words of Heraclitus: ". . . they chose
one thing above all others, immortal glory among mortals."[47] Their striving is not for happiness, their own or that
of their community, though they might slay a dragon; it is
for their bright image among men. So it is not surprising
that a proper hero, holding life lightly, dies young; it is
also not surprising that in works upholding heroic ideals
death and defeat in battle (The Battle of Maldon) or even
the destruction of nations (Iliad and Nibelungenlied) are
not considered the ultimate tragedy, but rather the appropriate background for the awesome and terrifying spectacle of human greatness.

While the monster was slain in myth for the sake of creation, the initiatory ordeal suffered for the sake of rebirth,
heroic literature has often dedicated itself to transmitting
the grandiose and fascinating scene of death and destruction. We must consider such literature to represent a turning away, an emancipation from the original ideals of its
ritual substructure.

In the climate of violence and destruction the hero moves
as in his natural habitat; the dispensing of death is after all
his prime business; and his destructiveness, against his
will, includes often those he loves the most: so Roland destroys Oliver, Achilles Patroklus, and Grettir his loyal
brother Illugi. Heroes cannot, on the whole, foresee and
control the outcome of their action. Their catastrophes are
brought about, in the words of Gertrude Levy ". . . by the
excess of pride arising from their special gift of *mana,* or
manas or *menos:* the heroic energy which is the sign of
their divine ancestry."[48]

With respect to Welsh heroes Marie-Louise Sjöstedt observes "that all the words for 'hero' express the notions of
fury, ardour, tumescence, speed. The hero is the furious
one, possessed of his own tumultuous and blazing energy."[49] To illustrate the violence of the heroic character
she relates how the Welsh hero Kulhwch (probably the
prototype of Parsifal) went to king Arthur's court and
asked for admission into the hall. When courteously told
to return somewhat later because the banquet had already
begun he threatened to emit such shouts that all pregnant
women in the land would abort and those not pregnant be
never able to conceive. And in fact, he gained admission.
Miss Sjöstedt concludes that "it seems to be the rule for a
great hero to enter always by violence even into his own
social group and that before becoming a member of society he must establish himself against it in disregard of its
customs."[50]

Heroes, needless to say, do not listen to the voice of prudence which is often heard in the tales: Odysseus pleading
with Achilles to renounce his private grievance and to return to the Achaian camp, Polydamas warning Hector
against giving battle outside of the city walls (such battle
indeed brings disaster), Þorfinn counselling Grettir against
struggling with Glam whose curse then pursues him
through life, Oliver reasoning with Roland to sound his
horn. Relying on their superior strength and force heroes
fall easy victims to Hybris, the stand against the gods and
the assertion of human achievement, which inevitably
brings ruin, but also, here, deep admiration; for, in this
genre the poets are on the side of men.

One might alternately describe heroes, with reference to
the ritual of initiation, as such in whom is often and easily
induced that state of frenzy and possession which marks
the initiate on his emergence from the sacred wood and
before his integration, as such to whom is rarely granted a
return from their god-haunted wilderness to the sheltering
community. A period of violent destructiveness may occur
in other men's lives as a passing phase, it is the abiding
feature of heroic existence.

Periods of integration, though brief, are nevertheless
present and complete the sequence. To illustrate such an
interlude we may cite the case of Achilles brought back
from his superhuman fury over the slaying of Patroclus by
his compassion for Priam. The old man, come to plead in
the hostile camp for the lifeless body of his son, awakens
in Achilles, through the memory of his own father, an
awareness of his common humanity. Such participation in
general human experience is necessary to the heroic life,
for without it heroes would be wholly gods or monsters.
And heroic literature is above all humanistic, acclaiming
not the divine manifestation, but the man on whom it has
descended.

The literary works admit, of course, an inordinate number
of variations on the basic pattern in varying degrees of resemblance to the abstraction which has here been attempted. But there can be little doubt that to the picture
here drawn Grettir bears a stronger likeness than does Beowulf, a wise and magnanimous ruler who died in the fullness of his years.

Traces of a ruthless striving for glory are, to be sure, de-
tectable in the slayer of Grendel. Did he not lead his faithful band on a voyage from which none thought that he
would return?[51] Yet this trait is dwarfed beside his savior
aspect due undoubtedly to the Christian author of the epic,
eager to present a figure possessing the virtues of his time.

Grettir, on the other hand, little concerned with saving others or himself, cares above else about his honor. Spattered
at one time, in a struggle, with curdled milk, he is more
pained than if he had "received a great wound."[52] In his
exuberant strength he provokes fate wherever he goes, so
in his unnecessary mocking of sailors on his voyage to
Norway for which he nearly pays with his life. Like a true

hero also Grettir does not stop to count the cost of his action; so he strikes down a boy who has taunted him and bars himself from the cleansing ceremony which might have saved him from exile.[53] As his prototype spends large portions of his time in that initiatory frenzy from which ordinary men are swiftly released, so Grettir must stay most of his life in that state of lawlessness which is to those, who practice the ancient rites, a passing interlude. Like the heroic model also Grettir is allowed brief and periodic integration, so in enjoying the acclaim of his prowess, or in finding peace with Steinvor, or in sharing the sorrow of his mother.

In one way Grettir appears to perpetuate a specifically Germanic warrior tradition: in his aloofness from menial work. Tacitus observed: "Whenever they are not fighting, they pass much of their time in the chase, and still more in idleness, giving themselves up to sleep and feasting, the bravest and most warlike doing nothing . . ."[54] True to this pattern, Grettir refuses to participate in the common toil while sailing to Norway, but rises to perform the work of eight men when the safety of the boat is threatened. In his loathing of menial labor, Grettir does not exert himself while staying with Þorsteinn Kuggason, even though he is in desperate need of hospitality, and thereby loses the much needed shelter. Considering that Grettir did not hesitate at the prospect of crossing an icy river, or swimming a sea mile, one must conclude that in the Germanic as well as in Grettir's system of values any effort which did not enhance a man, demeaned him.

We may also ask ourselves whether the time and place of the saga's composition could be favorable soil for the growth of a heroic epic. And we find that conditions were similar to those which had elsewhere fostered such creation. Heroic epics are said to arise at a time of peace which looks back to an earlier age of migration and warfare when men, torn from their familiar surroundings, placed high value on individual courage and loyalty to close comrades. So the Germanic peoples looked back on the battles and conquests of the great migrations which ultimately destroyed Rome, Homer celebrated the deeds of Achaian expeditionary forces of some centuries earlier and Iceland remembered the time of settlement and the Viking raids of her forebears so that with her the old heroic themes received a new habitation, though her sagas were written in prose.[55]

The themes of the ritual retained in the Grettis saga have, in Miss Arent's view, become devoid of their religious meaning while the same patterns appear recharged and revitalized, through contact with Christianity, in the epic of Beowulf, so that it gains close kinship with the religious ideals, the basis of the ritual, which had provided the scenario of the heroic life. While this may well be true it does not make the tale of Beowulf more truly a heroic epic; for these are not religious, intent not on the gods but on the men and their conflicts enacted on a human plane, their loyalties expended on human comrades, their striving directed towards honor in the human community. The poems of warfare and heroism treat of the glory to be gained in combat, the fortitude to be shown in the face of disaster, and the price to be paid for the divine visitation.

Of such stuff is the saga of Grettir, the outlaw who carried to their extremity the violence and rebellion of the traditional heroes and who therefore had to bear the most crushing burden of isolation.

Identical patterns, Miss Arent declares, may be expressive of widely differing values. There is no arguing against such a statement. This paper merely wishes to assert that an utter change of values had already taken place when the poets used the themes inherited from stone age herdsmen and hunters to celebrate the deeds of bronze clad warriors.

Notes

1. *Grettis saga Ásmundarsonar,* Guðni Jónsson, ed. Islenzk Fornrit 7, Reykjavik 1936, ch. 93, p. 289.

2. Recent scholarship assumes that the saga, as we have it, forms an organic whole while earlier scholars (R.C. Boer, Árni Magnússon, Guðbrand Vigfússon) believed in a basic core with later additions. Grettir died between 1030—1040; the first version of the saga is supposed to have been written before 1284 on the basis of oral family tradition by Sturla Þorðarson; a second author expanded this narrative and a third author combined both versions to give us the saga of our editions. It cannot in its present form have been written before 1300 A.D. For more information: Sigurður Nordal, *Sturla Þorðarson og Grettis saga,* Studia Islandica, Reykjavík 1938; also the preface to Guðni Jónsson's edition. No other Icelandic saga contains, according to Guðdni Jónsson, so much folk material.

3. Mircea Eliade, *Le mythe de l'éternel retour,* Paris 1969, pp. 51 ff.

4. Jan de Vries, *Heroic Song and Heroic Legend,* B. J. Timmer, transl. Oxford University Press 1963, pp. 211—217.

5. Grettir numbers Hallbjorn Hálftroll, a supernatural being, among his ancestors; his feats of strength include the carrying of an ox, the killing of a bear, defeat of a superior number of men, victories over supernatural beings who devastate the countryside, such as Glám (chap. 35). He stays for a time in a valley ruled by a giant (þórisdal chap. 61) and in the cave of another giant and his daughter (chap. 57); both places belong to the supernatural landscape. Grettir wins the woman Steinvor after defeating a troll (chap. 64—65); he dies, according to one set of manuscripts at the age of thirty-five, according to another when he is forty-four, in both cases, in the middle of life.

6. De Vries, as in ref. 4, pp. 220—226. Also: Margarete Arent, "The Heroic Pattern: Old Germanic Helmets; Beowulf and Grettis Saga," *Old Norse Literature and Mythology,* Edgar C. Polomé, ed. Univ. of Texas Press 1969, pp. 130—199; p. 144.

7. Arent, as in ref. 6, pp. 186—199.

8. Arnold van Gennep, *The Rites of Passage,* Monika V. Vizedom, Gabrielle L. Caffee trsl., Chicago 1960, p. 82.

9. Heinrich Schurtz, *Altersklassen und Männerbünde,* Berlin 1902, p. 104.

10. van Gennep as in ref. 8, p. 81.

11. Emile Durkheim, *The Elementary Forms of the Religious Life,* Joseph Ward Swain, trnsl., London 1964 (fifth ed.), p. 310.

12. van Gennep, as in ref. 8, p. 115.

13. Schurtz, as in ref. 9, p. 107.

14. van Gennep, as in ref. 8, p. 115.

15. H. Jeanmaire, *Couroi et Courétes; Essai sur l'éducation spartiate et sur les rites d'adolescence dans l'antiquité hellénique,* Lille 1939, pp. 550 ff; the feature was called *Krypteia;* any novice who allowed himself to be seen during this time was punished.

16. van Gennep, as in ref. 8, p. 81.

17. Mircea Eliade, *Birth and Rebirth,* The Religious Meanings of Initiation in Human Culture, Willard R. Trask, transl., New York 1938, pp. 71—72.

18. R. Rütimeyer, *Urethnographie der Schweiz,* Basel 1924, pp. 358 ff.

19. Homer, *The Odyssey,* E. V. Rieu, transl., first published 1946, Penguin books Ltd., XXI, pp. 317 ff.

20. Volsunga Saga, *Fornaldar Sogur Norðdurlanda I,* Gudni Jónsson ed., 1954, pp. 107—218.

21. *Grettis saga,* as in ref. 1, p. 63. . . .

22. *Grettis saga,* as in ref. 1, p. 68. . . .

23. *Grettis saga,* as in ref. 1, p. 72. . . .

24. *Grettis saga,* as in ref. 1, p. 69. . . .

25. *Grettis saga,* as in ref. 1, p. 149, verse 32. . . .

26. *Grettis saga,* as in ref. 1, verse 34. . . .

27. Otto Höfler, *Kultische Geheimbünde der Germanen,* Frankfurt a.M. 1934, p. 259; Ein solches Stehlrecht, an gewisse—zum Teil "heilige"—Zeiten gebunden . . . gehört zu den allercharakteristischsten Kennzeichen kultischer Mannerbünde.

28. Otto Höfler, as in ref. 27, p. 260; the information appears in a footnote.

29. Höfler, as in ref. 27, p. 105.

30. Höfler, as in ref. 27, p. 187.

31. Höfler, as in ref. 27, p. 40—43.

32. de Vries, as in ref. 4, p. 221.

33. Eliade, as in ref. 17, p. 73; the view is advanced by Frobenius.

34. *Grettis saga,* as in ref. 1, chap. 75, p. 239. . . .

35. *Grettis saga,* as in ref. 1, verse 65, p. 241. . . .

36. Höfler, as in ref. 27, p. 30.

37. van Gennep, as in ref. 8, p. 81.

38. Haakon Shetelig and Hjalmar Falk, *Scandinavian Archaeology,* E. V. Gordon, tr. Oxford 1937, p. 338.

39. The word '*bolklæði,*' is glossed on the basis of this occurrence as 'garment (coat, waistcoat) for the body,' in the English-Icelandic Dictionary of Cleasby and Vigfússon, Oxford 1962; R. C. Boer translates the term as: '*Kleidungsstücke für den Oberkörper,*' (*Altn. Sagabibl.* 8, p. 257); Paul Herrmann who translated the saga in *Altnordische Dichtung und Prosa* 5, p. 195, also uses the term: '*Oberkleider.*' In the translation of G. A. Hight for the Everyman's Library, the phrase is: "Then he took off his hood and all of his upper garments", p. 190. Another translation into English (Morris and Magnússon, London 1869, p. 214) has: "all his outer clothes." These translations, based on the picture of the conventionally clad wrestler, are not justified. Could one assume with Cleasby—Vigfússon that "Grettir took of his cloak and all his waist coats?" The word *bolr* from an IE root **bhel,* 'to swell,' means: 'tree, trunk, body;' (acc. to Cleasby—Vigfússon). One of the meanings of *bolr* is identical to *búkr,* m. (acc. to Fritzner, *Ordbog over det gamle norske Sprog*) which means: 'trunk or belly;' the definition of *bolklæði* given by Fritzner as: '*Klædningsstykke som tjener til Kroppens Bedækning*' is therefore more acceptable. Later in the passage Grettir also talks about himself as: *klæðlauss,* 'naked.' It is not surprising that a meaning has to be supplied which is not warranted in the text, if the story is understood on the realistic level alone. M. L. Sjöstedt cites other instances of such dramatic disrobing with strong effect on the audience, also based on a forgotten ritual context; as in ref. 49, p. 66.

40. Shetelig, as in ref. 38, p. 340.

41. van Gennep, as in ref. 8, p. 81.

42. Jan de Vries, *Altgermanische Religionsgeschichte I,* Berlin und Leipzig 1935, p. 257.

43. R. C. Boer, "Zur Grettis Saga," *Zeitschrift für deutsche Philologie* 30, (1898), pp. 1—71; p. 16.

44. *Grettis saga Ásmundarsonar,* R. C. Boer, ed. *Altnord. Sagabibl.* 8, 1900, p. X (Introduction).

45. Arent, as in ref. 6, p. 196.

46. Arent, as in ref. 6, p. 199.

47. As quoted by C. M. Bowra, *Heroic Poetry,* London 1952, p. 2.

48. Gertrude R. Levy, *The Sword from the Rock,* New York 1953, p. 15.

49. Marie-Louise Sjöstedt, *Gods and Heroes of the Celts,* Myles Dillon, transl. London 1949, pp. 58—59.

50. Sjöstedt, as in ref. 49, p. 63.

51. *Beowulf and the Fight at Finnsburg,* F. Klaeber, ed. Boston 1922, lines 691—693.

52. *Grettis saga,* as in ref. 1, chap. 28, p. 96. . . .

53. *Grettis saga,* as in ref. 1, chap. 39, pp. 132—134.

54. *The Complete Works of Tacitus,* Alfred John Church and William Brodribb, trnsltrs, The Modern Library, New York 1942, *Germany and Its Tribes, 15,* p. 716.

55. Levy, as in ref. 48, p. 87.

Joan Turville-Petre (essay date 1977)

SOURCE: "*Beowulf* and *Grettis Saga*: An Excursion," in *Saga-Book,* Vol. XIX, Part 4, 1977, pp. 347-57.

[*In the following essay, Turville-Petre compares and contrasts several specific episodes in the* Grettis Saga *with comparable ones in* Beowulf.]

Beowulf pursues Grendel's mother into her lair, deep below the water.[1] Grettir plunges under a waterfall, to reach the habitat of a troll-woman. Each of them destroys the enemy, after great struggles.

So we have two works, separated by 500 years or more; and in each of them the hero overcomes a visitant from the other-world, in basically similar circumstances.

Direct influence of the poem on the author of the saga is easily ruled out. Even if he could have read the poem, the saga writer could not possibly have constructed his account from this source. Yet there are striking similarities, in general and in detail. We have to ask in what kind of literary tradition this episode was formulated, and how it was transmitted. The affair has been so fully discussed that much that was once taken for granted can bear re-examination. In the literary foreground, how does it fit each of these quite different heroes? And in the background, where did they find it?

One preliminary distinction must be made: Beowulf is a mythical figure, Grettir is not.

There was a real Grettir, who lived in the early eleventh century. His family and contemporaries are independently attested, and some of his own activities can likewise be cross-checked.[2] But essentially the saga is imaginative reconstruction, based on an idea of the kind of person Grettir was, and how he came to live as he did. I take it that the writer of the final recension was not making any significant changes in representing the central figure.[3] Overall there is close attention to character and motive. Although there is a non-human element in Grettir, his humanity is clearly shown in his ready wit: he answers back effectively, and makes shrewd comments.

Beowulf did not live in history; he does not belong to any known dynasty. The poem is organized to show a hero in action. The story is the outline of Beowulf's career, presented in sharply-focused incidents. These are linked by narrative of a more discursive kind: allusions back and forward in time, subsidiary characters and supporting incidents, all held together by comments from the poet or from leading characters (e.g. Beowulf, Hroðgar, Wiglaf). The human society depicted in the poem is generalized and symbolic, a tissue of mutual obligations and benefits.[4] Beowulf is the exemplary figure who illustrates the rules and the virtues of this society.

When I say that Beowulf is a mythical figure, I do not mean that he represents any divine being, nor that his activities have any connexion with ritual practices. I mean "myth" in Northrop Frye's sense:[5] an abstract fictional design, a story (fabula) constructed for a purpose. In this sense, Professor Quinn describes the *Aeneid* as "a poetic myth".[6] The elements of such a story (persons, places and situations) are already familiar to the audience. The central figure also may exist in a previous literary context; but essentially he is the poet's creation. His actions are directly related to the main themes. What the poet particularly has to say is also conveyed in new combinations of stock figures and events (archetypes), used to evoke the main themes.

The poet of *Beowulf* touches on various themes, but there is one central idea, as I see it. This is the ancient religious concept of the deliverer. The hero pits himself against evil powers, the enemy that presses on the borders of the human world. Now Grettir's situation is formally similar to this, though very different in quality. I shall not discuss Grettir as a deliverer; the motive is present, but not dominating. I point only to the entirely different conception of the "outside". Grettir himself has strong connexions with this region and its supernatural inhabitants. *Grettis saga* is the spookiest of the major family sagas, dealing freely with the surrounding world of spirits, which is still a living element of Icelandic culture. This environment is strange rather than terrifying, entirely different from the awesome setting of Beowulf's exploits.

To come now to actual events in the encounter of these two heroes with man-like monsters from the outside. It follows a certain pattern, and the underwater episode is the climax. The essential points are:

(1) the enemy is a male-and-female pair, living underwater;

(2) one of the pair attacks a dwelling at night (Hroðgar's hall, the farm at Sandhaugar), and carries away one or more men to devour in the underwater lair;

(3) the hero waits alone in the house, and when the enemy comes there is a fierce hand-to-hand struggle, indoors;

(4) the enemy breaks out and makes for the water, but is fatally wounded by loss of an arm;

(5) the hero, some time after, plunges into the water, and kills the other member of the pair.

Notice that this pattern does not apply to Grettir's encounter with Glámr (ch. 35). Only point 3 is present here, the indoor wrestling. Glámr is not a member of a pair. He does not live underwater, and he is not a maneater. He is not a nature-monster at all, but the revenant of a heathen Swede: a living corpse, another intruder from outside which is not unusual in Icelandic literature. I think the brilliant description of this episode has led critics of *Beowulf* to overvalue it as an analogue.

Now for section 5 of the pattern. Here, it has often been observed that the account of *Grettis saga* (chs. 64-7) makes sense, whereas in *Beowulf* (1345-1622) neither place nor sequence is clearly visualized. I do not therefore suppose that the prose narrative has preserved some original more faithfully than the poem. It seems rather that certain motifs (archetypal situations) have been used by two artists, each practising the technique appropriate to his work.

The components common to both are logically organised in *Grettis saga.* The hero dives under a waterfall, and his struggles in the eddies are described. He enters a cave, where a good fire is burning. A giant was waiting, and he attacked with a *heptisax;* but Grettir broke the handle with a blow of his *sax* (short-sword). While the giant was reaching back for his own sword, Grettir struck again, sliced out the giant's entrails, and finally killed him. Then he kindled a light and explored the cave.

In *Beowulf*, these same components are not organised into a sequence. There is a special weapon, a *hæftmece,* which like *heptisax* is an isolated compound. But it is identified as the hero's sword, which is found useless at the first encounter. There is a waterfall, but it belongs to Hroðgar's impressionistic description of the environment of the monsters' lair (1357-76). There is no waterfall in the accounts of approach (1400-21) and entry (1492-1517). When Beowulf enters the hall of Grendel's mother, he finds that it is free from water and a fire is burning. A human sword cannot touch her, but in the nick of time he sees a giant-sword. He does not have to kindle a light, for a heavenly light irradiates the place.

Let us leave the *hæftmece* for the moment, and consider the waterfall, the fire, and the miraculous light.

The poet relegates the waterfall to a preliminary general description, where it is an image of the power and peril of the world of nature. In *Grettis saga,* the hero's physical prowess is displayed against a realistic waterfall—although there is no waterfall in Bárðardalr.[7] This is not a normal monster-habitat; in Iceland it occurs otherwise only in reproductions of this episode in later romantic sagas. Trolls live in crags and rocks, but the trolls of Bárðardalr live in a cave accessible only through water.

The fire, in each work, is the focus of domestic life, showing that these underwater creatures use the same means of heating and cooking as human beings.

The sword, which in *Grettis saga* is merely part of the furniture, in *Beowulf* makes the point that no human weapon can penetrate so evil a monster, and Beowulf alone among humans can wield it. As for the light, it is the external sign of God's saving grace, which released Beowulf from the grip of the giantess, and willed the destruction of her evil power. The incident has caused some confusion; first, because of the narrative sequence, and second, because of the inherent symbolism. In the passage 1545-72 the order of narration depends not on logic, but on poetic rhetoric. First, we are told that Beowulf would have perished, if God had not rightly ordained the outcome (1550-6). Next, Beowulf finds the sword, and kills the giantess (1557-69). Third, *se leoma* shines out; it is described as heavenly, i.e. not malignant (1570-2). The reason for the demonstrative *se* is that this light had been a factor at the first stage, but is not identified until the third. Chambers perceived this, and explained the inconsistency with a general reference to Old English poetic technique.[8] On a smaller scale, the device of illogical order was freely used by Virgil.[9] The light is symbolic, in so far as it has no physical origin. At the same time, it is a real light that persists, for it enables Beowulf to explore the whole cave. There is no inconsistency here, for symbolism is not a hard-and-fast scheme, but a momentary allusion to a different level of meaning.[10] When the poet associates sudden emergence of light with the destruction of the monster and God's grace to Beowulf, he strikes out symbolic meanings for the incident. Light projects different images. Two are appropriate here: release, and the cleansing of the infested place.

The *heptisax* or *hæftmece* is the most striking point of agreement. It appears to be a technical term, specifically associated with cave-warfare. Each author interprets this special term in his own way.

The poet equates it outright with a proper sword, but introduces it with some elaboration: "Then, it was by no means the least of strength-supporters [an unusual periphrasis for the sword, but there are paralles[11]] that the spokesman Unferð lent him at his need; that *hæftmece* bore the name Hrunting" (1455-7). He proceeds to describe it as an ancient treasure, a blade of special workmanship.

The author of *Grettis saga* has more trouble, because he is describing realistically. He first states that the giant in the cave seized a *fleinn.* This word means "arrow" or "light spear" in poetry, or in prose derived from verse. But in original prose the word appears as a typical giant's weapon, a pointed iron stake.[12] *Fleinn* does not occur in verse 61 of *Grettis saga,*[13] *heptisax* and *skepti* do (*skepti* only here in poetry). Apparently for this reason, the author adds a *tréskapt* to the *fleinn,* and comments "in those days it was called a *heptisax*". He says also of this *fleinn* that it was suitable for both cut and thrust. This is a typical description of a *sax,*[14] which, unlike the two-edged sword, had a pointed tip. So it seems that the author was describing an impossible composite weapon.

Perhaps it was a mistake to assume that *hepti* had the usual current sense "grip, handhold". This concrete meaning was common for *hepti,* rare for *hæft.* A *hepti* is appropriate to a knife (*sax, knífr*),[15] also to the lower end of an axe-shaft;[16] it is too humble or too unspecific for a sword.[17] *Hæft* usually means "fetter" or "captive".[18] The semantic divergence is best shown in the related verbs: *hepta* "bind, put in bonds; hobble a horse"; *hæftan* "bind, hold captive". This sense is formally distinguished in the OI noun *hapt* "fetter, halter"; pl. "bondage", and *hopt,* like *bond,* is a poetic term for the gods. If *hepti-/hæft-* is a verbal adjective (as in *sendimaðr*), the compound could mean "blade attached / bound in some way". *Hæftmece* would then be comparable to *fetelhilt, Beow.* 1563,[19] derived from a *fetlian* "attach, connect". In historic times, the sword or *sax* could be fitted with a loop to hang on the arm.[20] A weapon attached in this way would be especially useful in an underwater adventure; Grettir "girded himself with his *sax*" before he dived in.

Why was this particular episode brought into the careers of these two very different heroes? In some way it must fit the concept that each author had of his leading character.

The author of the saga shows that Grettir's great strength was his misfortune. In spite of good intentions, he was progressively estranged from society. He was impulsive and uncontrolled, and as a result appropriate outlets for his strength were more and more restricted. Grettir was an outlaw for 19 years. He is depicted as an outsider, a man who naturally consorted with strange beings: such as Hallmundr, who called himself Loptr[21] and lived in a cave, and the half-troll Þórir in his happy valley. Grettir sought out and defeated hostile supernatural beings, partly to meet the challenge, and partly through goodwill. The last of these exploits was the encounter with the trolls of Bárðardalr, and Grettir approached it as an expert: *með því at honum var mjok lagit at koma af reimleikum eða aptrgþongum* (ch. 64) "because he was much by way of getting rid of hauntings and walkings" (or, "had a natural facility for . . .").

Both the first and the last of Grettir's attacks on the supernatural took him into the underworld. The first[22] is set in Norway, where Grettir broke into a grave-mound, overcame the dead man, and returned with all his treasure. He handed it over to the owner, his host Þorfinnr, who later gave Grettir the most precious object of all: a *sax* which Grettir had coveted, and used ever after. So it seems that Grettir, like some other heroes,[23] acquired his special weapon from the land of the dead.

The final underworld adventure is as different in theme as it is in setting. Grettir is now a fugitive, and his enemies are closing in. He is able to deliver the people of Bárðardalr from the attacks of a troll-woman, and through their gratitude he gains a temporary refuge. His feats of strength begin with a happy prelude: Christopher-like, he carries the housewife and her child across the dangerous river to attend church.

In *Beowulf,* the underwater episode is the culmination of the hero's testing-period. Beowulf had become Hroðgar's visiting champion; with this exploit he attains the full status of a hero. At this point, the poet had to project the action beyond the human world. The preliminary account of the setting, given in Hroðgar's speech, contains the same elements as Aeneas' approach to Hades (*Aen.* vi, 237-41), for it has the same purpose of suggesting gloom and horror. There is a great gulf, dark water, shadowing trees, and the place is shunned by wild creatures. Additional elements, frost and fire, are derived from *The Vision of St Paul.* The succeeding factual account of the route taken by Hroðgar and his troop leads steadily away from man's world. Yet a tableau of vigorous human activity is mounted on the very brink. First there is a hunting scene, then the ceremonial arming of the hero. The arming evokes a flashback to court life, when Unferð presents his sword, and Beowulf addresses farewell words to his master. He breaks away from this scene, by jumping into the pool and entering the *ælwihta eard* below.

The symbolism of this setting is in keeping with Beowulf's nature. Beowulf is not a historic person, but an incarnation of the hero-ideal. Like Aeneas, he has a mission, and this is the subject of the epic. Beowulf does not come to found a city; his mission is to deliver mankind, represented by the Danes and the Geats, from attacks by creatures of the otherworld. The historic element, which establishes Beowulf in the human world, is the spread of Northern dynasties, with their political and military involvements.

Grettir did actually belong to his setting of historic contemporaries. Yet the part he plays in public affairs and family rivalries is less important than for other tragic heroes of the sagas. His encounters with the supernatural are the fabric of his life, as this author sees it. For the Grettir shown to us is formed by the story-teller's art, a literary medium which developed rather rapidly in Iceland during the thirteenth century. It seems that this author perceived in Grettir some of the patterns of heroic life which had been set in ancient poetry.[24] Writers of this period could create tragic heroes from people of past ages, because their literary inheritance offered them such patterns. This inheritance had been developed and enriched by the antiquarian interests of their predecessors in the twelfth century.

In *Grettis saga* there is no overt reference to heroic poetry: no straight comparison, as in *Gísla saga,* where some incidents are modelled on events in the Sigurd poems and where there is a direct reference to that story. Yet some association with the heroes of antiquity is implicit when Grettir gets his special *sax* from the land of the dead. Among his great deeds, the two indoor wrestling-matches (the first with Glámr, the second with the troll-woman) had some place in heroic legend, since they are generically related to the cleansing of Heorot. The underwater adventure with its *heptisax* seems more like a direct allusion. If so, the poetic source of this episode has not survived.

The Old English poem stands nearer this source, in literary form as in time. The underwater episode is entirely appropriate to Beowulf himself, indeed it is necessary to his career. In *Grettis saga,* it is one more remarkable adventure.

When we look for the antecedents of this Beowulf in heroic legend, there is something in his name. It pretty certainly means "bee-wolf", circumlocution for "bear". The name was not fanciful; it is recorded for two historic persons. One was a seventh-century Northumbrian monk,[25] the other was Bjólfr the *landnámsmaðr.*[26] The most likely reason for giving this strange name is that it was current in heroic legend. Far back in pagan antiquity, the name would denote a theriomorphic divinity. In historic times, a bear-hero appears in two divergent literary traditions: in heroic legend (*Bjarkamál, Beowulf*) and in the folklore of the Northwest Germanic area. Chambers has shown that a hero of bear-ancestry is well represented here (his chief exploit is to enter the underworld through a hole).[27]

There is not much of the bear left in heroic legend. Bjarki has only his name, and his fierce courage in defence of his lord; according to Saxo, he also slew a bear. In *Beowulf,* the animal attributes implied do survive as poetic imagery. The superhuman grip of the hero reminds us that he is not as other men are. Although his activities are in the human world, he has access to regions beyond it. Beowulf is firmly set in human society, and conforms to its rules. But he can pass beyond these limits, and return unscathed. The excursion increases his human stature; for he begins as a wandering champion, and ends as a king defending his people.

Notes

1. References are to F. Klaeber, *Beowulf and the Fight at Finnsburg* (3rd edition, 1950), by line; and to Guðni Jónsson, *Grettis saga* (Íslenzk Fornrit VII, 1936), by chapter.

2. Saga writers did invent incidents in which historical characters are concerned, and also attributed to them situations borrowed from other sagas; see Kathryn Hume, 'The Thematic Design of *Grettis saga*', *Journal of English and Germanic Philology* LXXIII (1974), 476-82.

3. There are persuasive reasons for thinking that Sturla Þórðarson composed a life of Grettir *c.* 1280, and that this work survives in outline in the present redaction of the early fourteenth century; see Sigurður Nordal, *Sturla Þórðarson og Grettis saga* (Íslenzk fræði 4, 1938).

4. Cf. E. B. Irving, *A Reading of Beowulf* (1968), ch. ii.

5. Northrop Frye, *Anatomy of Criticism* (1957, reprinted 1971), 135; see also 366, "a narrative in which some characters are superhuman . . . a conventionalized or stylized narrative not fully adapted to plausibility or 'realism'".

6. K. Quinn, *Virgil's Aeneid; a Critical Description* (1968), 52-4.

7. This is one sign that conventional elements have been naturalized. Another is the fate of the troll-woman. In the description of the fight itself (ch. 65), Grettir freed himself by cutting off her right arm, whereupon she fell into the gorge. Later in the same chapter, an alternative account is given: "but the people of Bárðardalr say that she was overtaken by daylight as they wrestled, and succumbed when he struck off her arm; and there she still stands on the cliff in the shape of a woman." On the substitution of this popular belief see H. Dehmer, *Primitives Erzählungsgut in den Íslendinga Sögur* (1927), 53 f.

8. R. W. Chambers, *Beowulf, an Introduction* (3rd edition, 1959), 467-8.

9. See T. E. Page, *The Aeneid of Virgil Books I-VI* (1894), 468-9. It consists of two co-ordinate statements, the second of which functions as a clause defining the first in terms of an antecedent event. The *Beowulf* poet achieves a similar effect with a summarising statement explained by a brief *syððan*-clause, in 1554-6 and elsewhere.

10. See Quinn, *op. cit.,* 55 and note.

11. See H. Marquardt, *Die altenglischen Kenningar* (1938), 223.

12. H. Falk, *Altnordische Waffenkunde* (1914), 67.

13. Verses 60 and 61 (ch. 66) concern this adventure. They cannot be dated. The rime *fjón: kvánar* (v. 60) would not have been acceptable in court-poetry of the eleventh century; but this is not court-poetry. On these two verses, see P. A. Jørgensen, 'Grendel, Grettir and Two Skaldic Stanzas', *Scripta Islandica* 24 (1973), 54-61.

14. Falk, *op. cit.,* 9 (quoting *Stjórn* 541).

15. Falk, *op. cit.,* 10.

16. Falk, *op. cit.,* 118.

17. Klaeber's translation "hilted sword" (Glossary, s.v. *hæftmece*) shows the impasse of this interpretation; there is no such thing as a sword without a hilt.

18. *Hæft* is figurative in O.E. poetry and can mean "bondage", "imprisonment" etc., cf. J. Bosworth and T. N. Toller, *An Anglo-Saxon Dictionary* (1898, reprinted 1973), s.v. *hæft.* Cf. also *hæftnyd* "captivity".

19. See J. Hoops, *Kommentar zum Beowulf* (1932), 172, 179.

20. Falk, *op. cit.,* 38.

21. *Grettis saga* ch. 54. Loptr is here an Óðinn-figure; his face is obscured by a drooping hood. In poetic sources, this appellative is applied to Loki only, and its etymology is uncertain.

22. See A. R. Taylor, 'Two Notes on *Beowulf*', *Leeds Studies in English and Kindred Languages* 7-8 (1952), 13-17.

23. Hervor gets Tyrfingr from Angantýr in his gravemound (A. Heusler and W. Ranisch, *Eddica minora* (1903), 15-20). Miðfjarðar-Skeggi robbed the gravemound of Hrólfr kraki and took his sword (Jakob Benediktsson, *Íslendingabók, Landnámabók,* Íslenzk Fornrit I, 1968, 212).

24. As observed by W. P. Ker, *Epic and Romance* (1908), 202; Björn K. Þórólfsson, *Gísla saga* (Íslenzk Fornrit VI, 1943), xxv; J. de Vries, *Heroic Song and Heroic Legend* (1963), 98.

25. H. Sweet, *The Oldest English Texts* (1885), 163. It is interesting that the next name is Arthan, a Welsh diminutive form for "bear", which appears in early genealogies and in a poem of the twelfth-thirteenth century; see references in J. Lloyd-Jones, *Geirfa Barddoniaeth Gynnar Gymraeg* (1931), 43.

26. Jakob Benediktsson, *Íslendingabók, Landnámabók,* 302-3, 306.

27. *Beowulf, an Introduction,* 365-81.

E. J. J. Peters (essay date 1989)

SOURCE: "The Wrestling in *Grettis Saga*," in *Papers on Language and Literature: A Journal for Scholars and Critics,* Vol. 25, No. 3, Spring, 1989, pp. 235-41.

[*In the following essay, Peters discusses the prevalence of* hryggspenna, *a type of combat wrestling, in the* Grettis Saga.]

Two distinct forms of wrestling are employed in *Grettis Saga,* an older Nordic *hryggspenna* style against nonhuman adversaries, and a newer, exclusively Icelandic *glíma* against all human opponents.[1] The *hryggspenna* style is decidedly a combat style whereas *glíma* is practiced as sport. A form of trouser wretling similar to that practiced in southwestern areas of Britain, *glíma* has been practiced in Iceland since at least the twelfth century and is, today, the national sport of Iceland. Glíma appears to have been a summer sport in early Icelandic society, the favored winter sport having been *knattleikr,* a ball or hockey game played on a frozen surface. Yet athletes who were proficient at glíma were asked to participate in knattleikr,[2] since the latter sport allowed for a type of wrestling which is often not distinguished, in the saga accounts, from fighting, but which was probably much like blocking, tackling or boarding in contemporary rugby, North American football, or ice hockey. The objective in glíma is to unbalance the opponent, throw him to the ground, and ultimately pin him with his back to the ground. In *Grettis Saga* Audun does this to the young Grettir, and further humiliates the younger boy by kneeling on his stomach.[3]

Although a precise technique is missing in the bout between Audun and Grettir, there is a clear description of glíma technique in the episode at the end of the saga, where Grettir wrestles Thord during the Thing at Hegranes. Grettir is not moved when Thord charges, but reaches over Thord's back, grasps his trousers, and lifts Thord upwards and over so that the man falls heavily. Because of Grettir's great ability, it is suggested that he wrestle both brothers thereafter. Despite the fact that all three participants in the match are brought to their knees, none of them is able to

effect a pin, and the match is declared a draw. It is clear in this episode that glíma is a style of sport wrestling with rules for determining winners and losers.

Hryggspenna, on the other hand, appears to have been used both for combat and for sport, as inferred from accounts in Nordic sagas as well as from the Old English poem *Beowulf.*[4] Although important details are missing, hryggspenna applied a back grip similar to the hold that is popularly described as a "bear hug." Opponents faced one another, placed hands on the other's waist, and then "snatched" quickly to fasten their hands on the backbone of the opponent at the base of the spine. At this point the opponent was "captured" by being hugged closely to the attacker and was lifted by arm strength alone off the ground.[5] Reports are vague and varied at this point in the procedure. Apparently the captured opponent was driven backwards by the attacker. In the earliest accounts the captured opponent, whose legs become useless when he has been lifted off the ground, appears to have been slammed upright against a wall rather than toppled, the lifting and carrying being a better exhibition of strength than toppling would be. In later accounts the captured opponent was bent over a *fanghella* or wrestling board; and in the most contemporary Norwegian accounts he appears to have been pinned against the ground in the way Audun pins Grettir.[6] In *Grettis Saga* Glámr kills the old cattle steward apparently by smashing his backbone against the cattle stalls. Since the reader is given a report of what has taken place rather than a precise description of the event, reconstruction of the method is difficult. If Glámr has accomplished the back breaking by holding the cow steward upright, he has used a slamming technique; but if he has bent the steward over the top of a stall, his technique is the fanghella. In other *Grettis Saga* reports of Glámr's murderous activities we learn that men and animals have had their bones crushed, and there is sometimes a reference to the rocky ground in the vicinity.[7] This bone crushing is certainly indicative of hryggspenna technique; but the question remains whether it was a slamming, a fanghella, or a crushing technique, like that employed in Beowulf's fight with Dæghrefn.[8]

Sigurðsson's description of hryggspenna reveals that captives were pitted against hryggspenna champions, the ultimate goal of the contest being to snap the backbone across the fanghella. It is possible that this sort of contest was not restricted to captives. Cavill argues that the hryggspenna contest between Dæghrefn and Beowulf was not a battlefield combat, as a literal interpretation of the passage and previous critical consensus suggests, but rather a pre-battle contest to the death between champions.[9] This fight in the *Beowulf* analogue is particularly significant since it clearly depicts a hryggspenna contest and since it is one of the four fights directly paralleling fights in *Grettis Saga.*[10] Despite the fact that Cavill's interpretation removes the combatants from the battlefield, it still supports hryggspenna as a combat form in *Grettis Saga* as opposed to glíma, a sport form. Grettir clearly uses *hryggspenna* in his battles with Glámr and with the troll wife at Sandhaugr. He probably employs the *hryggspenna* style in his battle with Kárr the Old, but the description of the wrestling method in this battle is too sparse for an absolute judgement of style to be made.[11] All of these adversaries are in effect undead or magical figures devoid of the humanity and human characteristics they may have at one time possessed. They are bloated, unreal, and often larger than the living creatures they exploit. In a sense they represent a legend controlling the fate of those who must live with the past.

Grettir apparently intends to use hryggspenna in his fight with the bear, which parallels the dragon fight in *Beowulf.*[12] Grettir is prevented from employing classical *hryggspenna* technique because he must defend himself from the bear's teeth; thus he reaches under the bear's arms, as a hryggspenna wrestler would, but grasps the bear's ears from behind rather than completing the hryggspenna move by clasping the bear's back.[13] It is obvious that Grettir initiates his bear battle with a hryggspenna advance.

In his battle with Glámr, Grettir successfully applies the back grip only to have it broken by Glámr, who smashes downwards on Grettir's arms. As soon as he has broken Grettir's back grip, Glámr applies the hryggspenna hold himself and drags the resisting Grettir to the door, moving backwards in a fashion uncharacteristic of hryggspenna technique but in keeping with his preference for killing outdoors.[14] When they reach the door, Grettir abandons his defensive stance and drives forward against Glámr, in typical hryggspenna style, pushing the monster through the door before him. It is significant that at this point Glámr capitulates since it is unclear that Grettir has the monster in his power. What is absolutely clear is that Grettir has proved himself the better hryggspenna wrestler.

In the initial stage of his battle with the troll at Sandhaugr, Grettir is again prevented from applying the hryggspenna back grip. The troll clasps him fast, pinning his hands to her sides—or to his, the precise hand position being unclear. This counter move by the troll is similar to the arm-smashing counter used by Glámr on Grettir. Grettir and the woman remain in this position for hours; and Grettir is unable to carry out the back-breaking ritual that we find in the various analogues to **Grettis Saga,** for instance the Dæghrefn fight in *Beowulf* or the killing of the cat troll in *Orms þáttr Storolfssonar.* Despite the fact that Grettir's advance has been frustrated, it is indisputable that he has initiated a hryggspenna attack.

On a literal level, the distinctive employment of combat and sport wrestling styles, against nonhuman and human adversaries respectively, owes to the history of the saga. The hryggspenna episodes are borrowed from an older Nordic and older English literary tradition in which these motifs are precisely represented. The glíma episodes, on the other hand, are precisely Icelandic. On a symbolic level, the difference of wrestling forms represents the dichotomous society in which Grettir lives and which he represents. He is the individual in Icelandic society, torn between the old Nordic past and the new Icelandic future.

He is the wrestler who must fight in the old tradition yet manipulate the new, or at least be able to fight differently in contemporary society.

The combat style he uses against legendary enemies enables him to meet the influence from the literary past and to counter this influence. While he does not suffer defeat in any of his battles with legendary nonhuman figures, he carries psychological scars from these battles forward in his life as a new Icelander. Although Grettir defeats Glámr, he is transfixed by the gleam in Glámr's eye, a vision that disturbs him for the rest of his life. What precisely this vision is is difficult to determine, but it appears to be a legacy and burden from the Nordic past. It is significant, perhaps, that Grettir carries off none of the treasure in the underwater lair of the troll and giant at Sandhaugr; rather, he retrieves the bones of slain men. This is a mature Grettir, not the younger one who plundered the treasure, the legacy of the past, hoarded in the dwelling of the defeated Kárr the Old. After his battles at Sandhaugr, Grettir's intent is to bury the bones of the men slain and probably fed upon by creatures of the Nordic past.

Although Grettir is undefeated in his fights with nonhuman adversaries, he loses, wins, and draws in his wrestling bouts against humans. The young and untried Grettir loses his first match to the older and stronger Audun. Yet this match is an unstructured one, a fight between boys which is ungoverned by rules and in which, therefore, Audun is allowed to treat Grettir shamefully. When Grettir wrestles at Hegranes the situation is drastically changed in that a rule of law and society has been imposed. The judgement imposed on him in the past is suspended for the moment, and his conflict with other Icelanders is resolved in a rule-governed contest. Prior to this contest at Hegranes, his applications for a test of strength in which he might prove himself have been denied by the authority that derives from the old order. At Hegranes, on the other hand, Icelandic people decide that he is to be given the opportunity to prove his worth. It is rather ironic that in the interval between his wrestling match with Audun and his matches at Hegranes he has been outlawed and has, by defeating the legendary monsters, proven himself as a champion of the Icelandic people.[15] In his first match at Hegranes he defeats an adversary who might have been an instrument of vengeance under the old order; and he fights to a draw against the two brothers who might be said to represent the collective Icelandic society. Significantly, the glíma style symbolizes a method of arbitration, a system ruled by law and empowered by those assembled at the Hegranes Thing, to resolve Grettir's ongoing conflict. This structured procedure, generated by the people, points to the establishment of a new Icelandic society in which men seek arbitration rather than vengeance.

Unfortunately for Grettir, the wrestler carries the shadow of the past. Although he has had his moment of victory and equanimity at Hegranes, Grettir—and perhaps the fledgling Icelandic democracy to which has contributed—is still subject to influence and vengeance from the past.

When he returns to his sanctuary at Drangey, the magic from the past is used against him. He may have been victorious as hryggspenna champion in battles with legendary magical figures, and he may have been instrumental in building a collective democratic society in Iceland. As an individual, however, he cannot escape the past and falls victim to its magic, dying helpless in his island sanctuary.

Notes

1. In Bjørn Bjarnason, *Nordboernes Legemlige Uddannelse i Oldtiden* (Copenhagen: Hofboghandel, 1905) 105, as well as in other sources we are told that the *glíma* style is unrecorded outside Iceland. Johan Götlind, *Idrott och Lek, Nordisk Kultur,* (Oslo: Forlag, 1933) 24: 17, 39 has reported on *glíma* in Sweden. Pétur Sigurðsson, "Glíma", *Kulturhistorisk Leksikon for Nordisk Middelalder* (Oslo: Gyldendal, 1960) 5:359 refers to a *glíma* match in the year 1119.

2. This is reported in a number of the sagas—for instance, in *Egils Saga Skallagrímssonar,* ed. Vald. Ásmundarson (Reykjavik: Kristjánsson, 1910) 97: "Egill var mjök at glímum."

3. *Grettis Saga Ásmundarsonar, Húnvetninga Sögur* I., *Íslendinga Sögur* 6, ed. Guðni Jónsson (Reykjavík: Íslendingasagnaútgáfan, 1946) 39. . . . All citations are to this volume of this edition, unless otherwise indicated. . . .

4. Cf. Bjarnason 103-05 for the various Nordic sagas. For an explicit *hryggspenna* technique in *Beowulf* see the Dæghrefn fight, lines 2507-08, in Klaeber, *Beowulf and the Fight at Finnsburg,* 3rd ed. (Lexington, MA: Heath, 1950).

5. Among the grips inadequately described are the counter holds like those used against Grettir by Glámr and the troll woman, respectively, in *Grettis Saga* 118, 213. Bjarnason 103.

6. Bjarnason 105; P. Sigurðsson, "Fang," *Kulturhistorisk Leksikon for Nordisk Middelalder* (Oslo: Gyldendal, 1959) 4: 163; Johannes Skar, *Gammalt or Sætesdal* (Oslo: Det Norsk Samlaget, 1961), 2: 222, 223, 262, 299; Reidar Svare, *Frå Gamal Tid: Tru og Tradisjon, Vefsn Bygdebok* (Mosjøen, 1973) 377. . . .

7. The fate of Grettir's horse is pertinent . . . (116). The shepherd Thorgaut suffers a similar fate (112). Thorgaut's body is found on Glámr's rock pile of a grave, and stones are strewn around the area where the human Glámr has been slain (112, 109).

8. Beowulf ll. 2507-08.

9. Sigurðsson 163; Paul Cavill, "A Note on Beowulf, lines 2490-2409," *Neophilologus* 67 (1983): 599-604; R. W. Chambers, *Beowulf: An Introduction to the Study of the Poem with a Discussion of the Stories of Offa and Finn,* 3rd ed. (Cambridge: Cambridge UP, 1967) 12.

10. Grettir fights Kárr the Old, the bear, Glámr and at Sandhaugr. Although only three fights are associated

with Beowulf, he actually fights four in his capacity as champion: against Grendel, Grendel's mother, the dragon, and Dæghrefn. Prior to becoming champion, he fights against sea monsters in the Breca episode.

11. It appears to be a *hryggspenna* match since it begins with a pushing contest (both wrestlers are brought to their knees) yet the contest ends with Kárr crashing backwards. . . . (54).

12. R. McConchie, "Grettir Ásmundarson's Fight with Kárr the Old: A Neglected *Beowulf* Analogue," *English Studies* 63 (1982): 481-86, indicates how the Kárr fight parallels the fights between Beowulf and the Grendels, and suggests a similarity with the dragon fight as well. Yet in the Grettir bear fight there are also locational, companionship, material and thematic parallels with the Beowulf dragon fight. Cf. McConchie on monsters, 483; Chambers 484 appears to allow for the inclusion of animal (bear, wolf) enemies in the same category as undead enemies.

13. . . . Note that Beowulf must also protect himself from the dragon's breath.

14. . . . With the exception of the cattle steward, all Glámr's victims are found outside; the monster takes the trouble to drag Grettir's horse out of the stable before killing it. . . .

15. The unacclaimed champion nevertheless; many of those who had agreed to Gest being granted immunity at Hegranes are afterwards upset when they learn that they have actually granted immunity to Grettir.

Robert Cook (essay date 1989)

SOURCE: "Reading for Character in *Grettis Saga,*" in *Sagas of the Icelanders: A Book of Essays,* edited by John Tucker, Garland Publishing, Inc., 1989, pp. 226-40.

[*In the following essay, Cook demonstrates some ways of discerning and evaluating character in the* Grettis Saga.]

The modern reader, brought up on novels and unused to the Sagas of Icelanders, will at first have a hard time. The sagas present a bewildering array of persons and events, names and details, often without highlighting what is important or pointing to connections or giving the reader any apparent basis for comprehension. The novice deserves some help, and in this essay I will offer some elementary guidelines, with examples from ***Grettis saga.***

I

My starting point will be to contrast the sagas with the Old English poem *Beowulf,* which many who come to the sagas will have read, at least in translation. *Beowulf,* too, is hard reading, but for different reasons. For one thing, it has an irritating way of mentioning only casually things that seem pregnant with importance, such as Unferth's fratricide (lines 585-589, 1167-1168, both times in "although" clauses), Beowulf's "Inglorious Youth" (2183-2188), and the curse on the treasure found in the dragon's hoard (3051-3057)—not to mention the frequent and baffling references to events from Danish and Geatish history and Germanic legend. What are we to make, for example, of this account—the only one in the poem—of Hama? After mentioning a necklace that was given to Beowulf after the slaying of Grendel, the poet says:

> I have heard of no better heroic treasure since Hama carried off to the bright city the necklace of the Brosings, precious gems in a fine setting; he fled from the treacherous enmity of Eormenric, he chose eternal reward.[1]

What bright city? Who is Hama? Did he steal the necklace? What was the cause of his enmity with Eormenric? What does the last clause mean? The poet is not telling, and the modern reader has his hands full tracking allusions, comparing stories, and just guessing.

A second bewildering feature of *Beowulf* is the indefinite way in which characters are presented. The first mention of Grendel comes without preparation after a description of Hrothgar's hall, Heorot: "Then the powerful demon suffered a difficult time of hardship, he who lived in darkness, when every day he heard loud joy in the hall."[2] The introduction of this major character is so faint that modern translators sometimes feel compelled to indicate in a footnote or by some other means that this demon is Grendel;[3] he is not mentioned by name until line 102. The hero Beowulf is also introduced without preparation, after an account of Danish sufferings at the hands of Grendel, merely as "a thane of Hygelac" (line 194)—to be sure, an exceptionally strong and noble one—who heard of Grendel's depredations and decided to do something about them. We do not learn his name until line 343, a hundred and fifty lines after his first mention, and though we learned his father's name in line 263 we don't learn until 374-75 that his father was married to the daughter of the Geatish king Hrethel. It is typical of *Beowulf* that such essential information is not presented concisely but rather in widely spread snippets. The companion of Beowulf who is eaten alive by Grendel in lines 740-745 is not given a name (Hondscio) until line 2076. Grendel's mother carries away a Dane in lines 1294-1295 who is immediately described as someone dear to Hrothgar but is not given a name until line 1323. A more general point following from these observations is that characters are not given physical or other specifying features which would make them three-dimensional. Hrothgar seems to be a wise old man and Hygelac a younger, rash man, Heremod a greedy one and Wulfstan a loyal one, but none of them is more than a pale type. Beowulf himself is an exceptionally strong man of noble blood and purpose, but apart from a possibly inordinate concern for the dragon's treasure (at least to some recent critics) there is nothing interesting about him.

The Sagas of Icelanders contrast with *Beowulf* on both these points. Far from teasing the reader with shadowy stories and allusions to a wide body of traditional lore

which the reader has to piece together on his own, the sagas place everything up front. The anonymous writers of the sagas clearly had a different conception of their task from the author of *Beowulf:* they saw themselves largely as historians and compilers, who gathered as much material as possible on their subject and then shaped it as best they could. The result is a literature that is not *deliberately* obscure. As for characterization, here too the sagas could not be in greater contrast to *Beowulf.* Take for example the initial mention of Skarpheðinn in *Njáls Saga,* Ch. 25:

> Now we shall mention the sons of Njáll. Skarphðinn was the oldest; he was large and strong, a good fighter, could swim like a seal, was very fast on his feet. He was quick at making up his mind and resolute, contradictory and hasty in speech, and yet usually under control. He had brown curly hair and good eyes; he was pale and sharp-featured and had a crooked nose. His row of teeth stood out prominently, and he had an ugly mouth, but he was obviously a very good fighter.[4]

Such vivid portraiture, often at the first mention of a hero, is common in the sagas, and the narrative provides even more individualizing details. The result is, as Paul Schach has written, that "the *Íslendingasögur* (Sagas of Icelanders) contain more memorable portraits of complex men and women than any other medieval literary genre."[5] The writers of the sagas were clearly not as interested in plot or narrative design or abstract ideas as they were in people.[6]

My advice on how to read the sagas arises from the lesson of these contrasts: *read for character,* i.e. try to gain a sense of the uniqueness of the main characters on the pages in front of you. A corollary to this is: *read for genealogy and evidence of other relationships,* i.e. notice the kin and the friends, and also the non-kin and the enemies, of the main character(s). This is important not only for defining the main character(s) but also, in stories which turn so much on feuding, for seeing who is on whose side and why. These elementary guidelines—which no one in his right mind would recommend for *Beowulf*—correspond to the way that native Icelanders have always read their sagas. When an Icelander thinks of *Njáls saga* he thinks of Njáll and Gunnarr, of Bergþóra and Hallgerðr, of Hrútr and Flosi and Hoskuldr and Skarpheðinn and Kári and so on. (I do not mean to imply, of course, that other critical approaches have no validity or that there is no more at stake in the sagas than an interest in character. The authors clearly were interested in concepts of honor, for example, but they always presented concepts concretely through characters and situations.)

As I stated at the outset, however, the sagas are not always easy reading, and discerning character in them is made difficult by at least three factors: (1) the abundance of information apparently unrelated to the central character(s); (2) the flat manner of presentation which often fails to highlight essential information; (3) and the absence of comment or interpretation which would help us to understand character. The sagas may put everything up front, but this does not mean that they put enough up front, and it often seems that they put down too much. The reader has to do for himself much of the work of seeing what is important, of remembering and collecting, and finally of evaluating. In what follows I will use *Grettis saga* as a working example of how to read for character in the face of multifarious yet inconclusive information. I will proceed in two stages, first showing what to look for and remember in order to make sense of the story of Onundr trefótr (Tree-Foot), and then suggesting how to analyse a complex and elusive character such as Grettir.

II

Grettir does not appear until Ch. 14 of the saga, and the first ten chapters contain what must seem to the first-time reader a disorganized mass of names and events. On closer consideration, however, it becomes obvious that everything in these chapters relates one way or another to Onundr Ófeigsson (later dubbed Tree-Foot when he loses a leg in the Battle of Hafrsfjörðr, in Ch. 2). He is a ninth-century Norwegian viking who defeats the Irish King Kjarvalr (Ch. 1), fights on the losing side against King Haraldr of Norway and flees to the Hebrides along with a man named Þrándr Bjarnarson (Ch. 2), who remains his friend until the end of his days. Onundr and Þrándr become engaged to the daughters of two other Norwegian refugees (Ch. 3) and kill two Hebridean vikings in a sea battle (Ch. 4). The two friends then visit Þrándr's half-brother Eyvindr, who at first wants to kill Onundr but then relents (Ch. 5). When Þrándr's father dies in Norway, Onundr returns with him to help him claim his inheritance (Ch. 6) and kills a man named Hárekr who held his own possessions; he also kills a man named Grímr who had killed Ondóttr kráka (Crow) (Ch. 7). Onundr then goes to Iceland (where Þrándr had gone earlier) with one of the sons of Ondóttr kráka; the other son, who had been thought dead in Norway, arrives later (Ch. 8). With help from a wealthy settler named Eiríkr, Onundr builds a farm at Kaldbakr in the North-west of Iceland (Ch. 9). His last deeds are that he prosecutes and has outlawed a man named Þorbjörn who killed Ófeigr Grettir (Onundr's father-in-law) and arranges an important marriage (Ch. 10). In Ch. 11 his death is reported and the author comments: "He was the boldest and most agile one-legged man in Iceland."

All this seems easy and clear when set out in this fashion, but because of the three factors mentioned above, it requires a little effort to see such a clear outline and the meaning of certain details. In Ch. 5, for example, we read that Eyvindr wants to attack Onundr; in response to Þrándr's plea for his friend, "Eyvindr said that [Onundr] had made trouble earlier when he attacked King Kjarvalr and now he had to pay for that." To comprehend this fully the reader must recall three things: (1) Onundr defeated King Kjarvalr of Ireland in Ch. 1; (2) Eyvindr was married to King Kjarvalr's daughter (mentioned in Ch. 3); and (3) Eyvindr has since taken charge of the defence of Ireland (mentioned twice, in Ch. 3 and 4). These things are mentioned separately and, except for the first, without the kind of emphasis which would cause the untrained reader to remember them and draw connections.

Another example of unemphasized but essential matter occurs in Ch. 6 when we read of Ondóttr kráka's concern for the estate of Björn Hrólfsson, the father of Þrándr and Eyvindr. Who is Ondóttr kráka, and what is he to Björn? For this the reader must recall a brief account of Björn in Ch. 3: he was in the past entertained by Ondóttr kráka, for a number of winters in Norway, and when his wife Hlíf died he married Helga, Ondóttr's daughter. Ondóttr kráka is, then, Björn's father-in-law. We also learn in Ch. 3—though unfortunately such genealogical information is snatched from the text and placed in footnotes in the Pálsson-Fox translation—that Hlíf was the mother of Eyvindr and Helga the mother of Þrándr. Ondóttr Kráka is thus Þrándr's maternal grandfather, and this explains Onundr trefótr's actions (in Ch. 7) to avenge the death of Ondóttr, in conjunction with Ondóttr's sons Ásgrimr and Ásmundr (they are Þrándr's uncles). Þrándr had gone to Iceland before the killing of his grandfather (see end of Ch. 6), and Onundr, still in Norway, acts the part of the loyal friend in his absence.

Understanding the career of Onundr trefótr thus requires noticing and retaining a number of discrete pieces of information. When we have put them together we see a full if somewhat flat picture of a ninth-century viking who was a successful marauder and only partly successful opponent of the strong King Haraldr of Norway. A major part of Onundr's story, and one which goes some way toward individualizing him, has to do with his close and enduring friendship with Þrándr, from the time that the wounded Onundr is brought to Þrándr's ship in the battle of Hafrsfjörðr (in Ch. 2) to the simple statement in Ch. 10 that Þrándr invited Onundr to his home in Iceland. The high points of the friendship occur in Ch. 3 when Þrándr, in reaction to Onundr's gloomy verse about life as a one-legged man, encourages him to marry and negotiates his betrothal to Æsa Ófeigsdóttir, and in Ch. 7 when Onundr avenges the slaying of Ondóttr kráka.

Why has the author opened the saga of Grettir with this biography of Onundr? We soon learn that Onundr is Grettir's great-grandfather, and perhaps that was reason enough to tell his story (though we may then wonder why Grettir's grandfather and father get much less attention, in Ch. 11-13). Some critics have suggested a thematic function for the Onundr chapters: that the viking world in which Onundr lived would have suited his great-grandson well, but Grettir had the misfortune of being born instead into a later and more confining society.[7] If there is a thematic justification for the presence of Onundr's story it might in fact work in a slightly different way, by a simple principle of contrast. In the last chapter devoted to him (Ch. 10), Onundr is a thoroughly domesticated viking, functioning as an integrated member of Icelandic society. He arranges a wedding, prosecutes a law-suit peacefully, and is a welcome guest at a number of farms. His great-grandson will never fit into society this well, nor ever have a close friend like Þrándr.

III

If understanding Onundr tréfótr requires noticing and retaining various bits of information which are presented without emphasis, understanding Grettir Ásmundarson is a more complex matter. Here the information is abundant and unavoidable, and the problem is not in retaining it but in reconciling it, harmonizing it into a comprehensible whole. Where Onundr was a faint character, Grettir is a bewildering one, and the modern reader—like Icelanders going back probably to the time before the saga was ever written down—has a hard time coming to terms with him. At times he seems an incorrigible lout, at other times a magnificent hero; on balance, I think, the view is a positive one.

Our first impressions of Grettir come in Ch. 14, in the character sketch and the account of three pranks he plays on his father: when told to mind the geese he kills or mutilates them; when told to massage his father's back he runs a sharp iron comb down it; when told to look after horses he flays his father's favorite mare. These look like the acts of a budding sadist, but on close reading we notice three things which help to excuse Grettir. The first is that, as the sketch puts it, "he did not have much affection from Ásmundr, his father," and this becomes clear in the way Ásmundr speaks to him (e.g. "Now you will have to give up your sloth, you miserable excuse for a man"), and exposes him to the cold in light clothing, a cruel gesture from a man who himself liked to sit by the fire and have his back rubbed. Second, we notice that Grettir has a way of speaking in aphorisms ("He who warns another of evil is a friend." "It is a bad idea to provoke a rash man."), a controlled and prudent form of discourse which contrasts with his father's provocative language. A third consideration is that the pranks must have something to do with the fact that Grettir regards the assigned tasks as demeaning. Like most children, he prefers a challenge to being bored.

If these considerations in fact offset an otherwise unfavorable picture of Grettir, what can we say when he slays the servant Skeggi because of a bag of provisions in Ch. 16? At first glance this seems unforgivable, but here too there are mitigating circumstances. In spite of Grettir's attempt to be companionable—he suggests that he and Skeggi join forces in looking for their lost food-bags—Skeggi goes off on his own when he spots a bag, and he refuses to show it to Grettir. In addition to acting provocatively, he speaks provocatively, as did Grettir's father; and as before, Grettir's language is more temperate than that of his fellow. Finally, it is Skeggi who strikes first. Grettir kills in self-defense when he manages to get Skeggi's axe in his own hands.

These episodes (in Ch. 14-16) thus present a complex picture of Grettir. On the one hand, he is a harsh and violent young man, but on the other hand there are details which suggest that he does not seek violence for its own sake, that he is prone to being badly treated by others, and that when this happens he is likely to react with violence.

For killing Skeggi Grettir is declared an outlaw for three years, which obliges him to go abroad—otherwise he can be killed with impunity in Iceland. On the way to Norway in the ship of a man named Hafliði, Grettir again displays unattractive features: in addition to a scorn for routine tasks (which we already saw in Ch. 14), he reveals a talent for mocking his shipmates in poetry. These traits do not make him popular, and to prevent open violence Hafliði suggests to Grettir that he compose verses about himself (Hafliði) which are insulting on the surface but complimentary on a deeper level. This is a real challenge—something which his father never gave him—and Grettir rises to the occasion. A second challenge in Ch. 17 comes when the ship leaks seriously and needs more than the usual amount of bailing. Now Grettir is ready to work and amazes them all by doing the work of four (or even eight) men. As a result of his responses to these challenges Grettir becomes popular with his shipmates, and presumably with the reader. His scorn for ordinary work seems to be related to his unusual strength—recall that at the end of Ch. 16 he surprised men by lifting a very large boulder— and a sense that this strength should be used for special tasks.

Such a task presents itself in Ch. 18 when as a guest on an island off Norway Grettir hears of a burial mound containing treasure. He digs down into the vault and encounters the powerful revenant Kárr, whom he must fight and behead before he can take away the treasures. This is a truly heroic deed, the first of Grettir's encounters with superhuman creatures, and yet at the beginning of the episode he showed an unattractive side when he spurned the company of his convivial host Þorfinnr. Looking back over the chapter we might excuse this unfriendly behavior by saying that Grettir chose his own way of relating to Þorfinnr: rather than keep company with him (which after all anybody can do), he preferred to do an extraordinary feat and then present Þorfinnr with the treasures from his father's grave mound.

If Grettir "hardly ever spoke" . . . with Þorfinnr in Ch. 18, he suddenly becomes "very chatty" . . . in the following chapter when twelve berserks arrive on the island seeking vengeance against Þorfinnr, who is on the mainland for Christmas. Why does Grettir show such amiable hospitality toward these vicious berserks? By the end of the chapter, of course, the reason is clear: Grettir was only pretending to be friendly in order to trick the berserks into a position where he could kill them. But not all readers will have foreseen this outcome, and for many the pattern of the chapter will be the same as that of Ch. 17 and 18, in which Grettir shows an unattractive side which he later makes up for by means of a stupendous deed (bailing out the ship, subduing Kárr, killing twelve berserks). These three chapters (17-19) thus develop the already complex portrait of Grettir. We are now aware of his extraordinary strength and of the possibility that his unpredictable, even hostile manner might be justified or at least explained by his consciousness that he is in fact superior in strength to other men.

There is not space here to cover all of the saga even in this rapid way, but two further examples will indicate that the process of getting to know Grettir is an ongoing one, in which the reader must be constantly at work assimilating and evaluating an abundance of information. After some chapters (Ch. 21-24) in which Grettir is the victim of malicious types in Norway, and some others (Ch. 25-27) from which he is absent while Icelanders engage in a killing and its legal aftermath which are typical of the sagas (though untypical for Grettir), he returns to Iceland in Ch. 28. Immediately the saga author tells us that "Grettir had then become so arrogant that he thought there was nothing he couldn't do," . . . and a character within the saga calls him "overbearing and stubborn". . . . The reader must not take such statements as the final word, however, for the events themselves provide other and equally important evidence. What happens in Ch. 28 is that Grettir pays a visit to a farmer named Auðunn who had once, when they were young, given Grettir a drubbing (Ch. 15). From his attire and weapons we get the impression that Grettir intends to kill Auðunn, but when he gets to Auðunn's farm and finds Auðunn not at home, he sits down and falls asleep! Later, Auðunn returns and the two have a scuffle which is as comic (Grettir gets covered with curds) as it is serious (Grettir gets the upper hand), until someone comes along and asks them to make up. The next time they meet (in Ch. 34) Grettir gives Auðunn an axe as a token of friendship. This is not the behavior of other saga characters who are labelled "arrogant" or "overbearing"; almost inevitably they resort to killing, whereas Grettir seems content to have demonstrated his superior strength.

In this connection a sentence at the end of Ch. 31, after some additional inconclusive encounters, is significant: "It bothered Grettir very much that he had no occasion to test his strength, and he made inquiries as to whether there was something he could pit himself against." If Grettir is arrogant, he is so in an impersonal and comparatively harmless way, directing his energies not against men who have offended him (unless they are truly vicious and deserve to be killed) but at challenges to his strength, whether in the form of wrestling, or lifting stones, or fighting superhuman and even supernatural beings like Glámr (Ch. 32-35). In such encounters we feel that Grettir is in his element, but unfortunately he must always return to the world of mere men, where bad luck and maliciousness pursue him.

Finally we might glance at the two important chapters set in Norway (Ch. 38 and 39) in which Grettir accidentally burns twelve men to death and then, in Trondheim church, strikes a boy and thus misses his chance to prove his innocence. These events lead to Grettir's being pronounced an outlaw at the Icelandic Althing (in Ch. 46) and condemn him to the long period of lonely exile in the uninhabited parts of Iceland which continues to the end of his life.

In reflecting on these two scenes the reader is again forced to weigh opposing views. From one perspective, both the swim across the channel to fetch fire in freezing weather (Ch. 38) and the striking of the boy who taunted him in the church (Ch. 39) are rash and wild acts. At the same time, however, the author has provided details which are more favorable to Grettir. The swim for fire was, like the killing of Glámr, a beneficial deed which only Grettir could perform; he foresaw danger, however, and was persuaded to do it against his own best judgment; had the sons of Þórir and the others who were burnt not been drinking, they might have been able to distinguish a man whose clothes were frozen from an evil monster; and the boy who taunted Grettir was an unknown who seemed to come from nowhere: "No one seemed to know where the boy had come from or where he went, but it was generally thought that he was an unclean spirit, sent to destroy Grettir." The effect of these details is to portray Grettir as a victim of bad luck and even some malicious force rather than a victim of his own character.

Seen in this way, the saga about Grettir becomes very much like the verse which Grettir composed about Hafliðoi in Ch. 17: on the surface one gets a negative picture, but when one looks more carefully the impression becomes positive. As the saga continues the reader may eventually feel that Grettir is a hero in the mould of Homer's Achilles (though Grettir is more dogged by bad luck than Achilles), a man of extraordinary powers who is doomed to a life of "tragic loneliness in a world he qualitatively transcends but cannot leave."[8]

IV

These remarks have been intended not as an outline of a definitive interpretation of Grettir but as an illustration of how to go about making one's own interpretation. The experience of reading about a character like Grettir or Njáll or Kjartan (in *Laxdæla saga*) is very much like getting to know someone in everyday life. As with a friend or acquaintance, we get a rich variety of perspectives: we see him behave in many different ways and situations; we listen to him talk; we hear what others have to say about him. At times we admire him, at others we feel sorry for him, and occasionally we are disappointed or outraged. Neither in real life nor in the sagas is there someone to pull all of this experience together for us. The job of evaluating, of seeing things whole, is ours. This is not easy, but it is this task of working through the experience of the text to arrive at an understanding of the characters that makes reading the Sagas of Icelanders a very human pleasure.

Notes

1. . . . (ll. 1197-1201) My translation, as thought.

2. . . . (ll. 86-89).

3. E.g. Donaldson, *Beowulf,* p. 3.

4. . . . (IF XII)

5. *Icelandic Sagas,* p. 173. See also Schach's article, "Character Creation and Transformation in the Icelandic Sagas."

6. Although Schach argues in the article just cited that saga characters are "too unique not to have been au-

thor creations" (p. 261), most scholars would agree that the main characters in the sagas must have been shaped to some extent in oral tradition prior to the writing down of the sagas. Possible evidence lies in the references to Sturla Þórðarson in Chs. 69 and 93 of *Grettis saga;* see the remarks by the editor, Guðoni Jónsson, in ÍF VII, p. xlv. The oral tradition has interesting implications for saga composition, which have often been discussed, but also for saga reading, as Robert Kellogg has pointed out to me. A fourteenth-century reader of (or listener to) *Grettis saga* would have come to the saga with a pre-existing notion of what kind of man Grettir was, and I suspect that the response of Icelanders through the centuries has always involved this kind of "intertextuality." An ideal reading of the "saga" of Grettir would attempt to deal with this fact, but for present purposes a close reading of the written text is sufficient. . . .

7. See the Introduction to the Pálsson-Fox translation, pp. viii-ix, and Hume, "The Thematic Design of *Grettis saga,*" pp. 478-79. . . .

8. The phrase is from Schein, *The Mortal Hero: An Introduction to Homer's Iliad,* p. 107.

Magnús Fjalldal (essay date 1998)

SOURCE: "The Making of Heroes and Monsters," in *The Long Arm of Coincidence: The Frustrated Connection between Beowulf and Grettis Saga,* University of Toronto Press, 1998, pp. 17-36.

[*In the following excerpt, Fjalldal refutes critical assertions of relationship between the characters of the* Grettis Saga *with those of* Beowulf, *claiming that many comparatists have shown more evidence of imaginative speculation than of literary research.*]

The purpose of this and of the next three chapters is to examine the basic ingredients of the five genetically related analogues that critics claim to have found in *Grettis saga* against the relevant sections of *Beowulf.* Although a great deal of literature has accumulated around these five texts, comparisons have never been very detailed or thorough, even in the case of the most widely accepted analogues, namely, the Sandhaugar and Glámr episodes. Critical discussion has in most cases revolved around a few fragments of a given analogue, usually to reach the quick conclusion that they presented ample evidence to relate the two works. Differences have, for the most part, been ignored. In this respect, later scholars have too often followed the example of Guðbrandur Vigfússon and F. York Powell, who only touched upon a few examples from the Sandhaugar and Glámr episodes and then pronounced their conviction that in the first text events described in *Beowulf* were repeated 'with little alteration' and that correspondence of incident was 'so perfect' in the second.[1]

BEOWULF AND GRETTIR AS HEROES

The lives of Beowulf and Grettir are to a large extent dictated by the fact that as king and outlaw they inhabit opposite ends of the social spectrum. Before Guðbrandur Vigfússon lumped them together as monster killers no one had seen anything to compare in Beowulf and Grettir,[2] but soon after Vigfússon had published his findings critics began to peel away their differences to find a core of attributes that the two heroes might have in common. Four points seemed obvious: Beowulf and Grettir are sluggish youths; they possess great physical strength; they swim long distances; and, most importantly, they volunteer to overcome evil supernatural beings. But is this sufficient evidence to argue that as a character Grettir is partly fashioned with Beowulf in mind, or that the two share a common ancestor in their heroic exploits? Some critics have not found these apparent similarities enough to outweigh the differences. Guðni Jónsson, for instance, regards Grettir, in his land-cleansing efforts, merely as a new player in an old role,[3] but other critics have insisted that the two heroes are basically cut from the same cloth.[4] Textual comparison is always a treacherous business, and in this case it is more treacherous than usual because of the different techniques that the authors of the poem and the saga employ to present their main characters. *Grettis saga* is cast as the story of Grettir's life in the sense that it relates, in considerable detail, his origin, his career, and his death as an outlaw. *Beowulf,* on the other hand, is not a biographical poem, whether or not a king by that name ever existed. Only certain critical moments in Beowulf's life are ever described. Other information about him as a character is sketchy and incidental.

This lack of concrete information in the Old English poem has often forced critics who wish to claim a special affinity between the two heroes into a position of having to fall back on rather superficial comparisons and speculative arguments as evidence. We have, for example, already come across the observation that both Beowulf and Grettir come from afar to do their deeds and prefer to fight alone.[5] It has also been pointed out that each is a lonely man, who only has one friend in the final struggle, and who ends his life unhappily.[6] These factors do indeed apply to Beowulf and Grettir, albeit in different ways; but they are equally applicable to any number of heroes from Gilgamesh to Tin Tin. Guðbrandur Vigfússon and F. York Powell believed that, like Grettir, Beowulf had been cursed (by Grendel), and suggested that the curse had been 'a trait of the original legend which our poem has not preserved.'[7] They saw the curse as a missing link which explained Beowulf's childlessness and his sad fate as a ruler. But in the poem Grendel is silent on this and other matters, except for one mighty howl, and efforts of this kind have not produced any firm ground for comparing the two heroes beyond the four points mentioned at the beginning of this chapter.

The first of these concerns the question as to whether a background as an inglorious or a sluggish youth can be claimed as a common trait for both Beowulf and Grettir.

The idea was first proposed by Friedrich Panzer, who believed that both Beowulf and Grettir were derived independently from the folktale figure of the Bear's Son, a creature who is often unmanageable or lazy in his youth.[8] The issue, however, is a great deal more complex than Panzer makes it appear. *Grettis saga* devotes a whole chapter (14) to Grettir's youth. We learn that he is not a precocious youngster, and the saga emphasizes this fact by specifically mentioning that Grettir is ten when he begins to show signs of any real growth. When his father asks him to pull his weight on the farm, Grettir promptly explains that he is not suited for such labour. Making the boy do domestic chores only results in a series of memorable, but nasty, pranks. Grettir obviously finds farm work demeaning and has presumably at the age of ten already decided on a career that involves more heroic exploits. In this sense, Grettir's youth may be disappointing or sluggish from a diligent farmer's point of view, but it is not necessarily inglorious for a hero to be. The question as to whether Grettir spent his youth as an ash-lad by the fire is addressed by the narrator of the saga and answered in the negative.[9]

We know that Beowulf is, on his mother's side, related to the royal family of the Geatas, but otherwise the story of his youth and upbringing is very unclear in the poem. The hero's undistinguished boyhood is alluded to only once (lines 2183b-9), where it is stated that he was long despised by the Geatas, who found him slack and lacking in courage and rewarded him accordingly until a change came about. But there are also passages in *Beowulf* that seem to contradict this statement. At the age of seven the boy is at the court of his grandfather, King Hreðel, enjoying treasures and feasts and being treated like one of Hreðel's own sons (lines 2428-31). Furthermore, when Beowulf, presumably still a very young man, arrives at the court of King Hroðgar to fight against Grendel, he does so with impressive credentials. According to the poem he has already performed many illustrious deeds (lines 408b-9a) and is an accomplished destroyer of sea monsters and giants (lines 418-24a and 549-76).[10]

Some scholars, especially those who believe that the poem seeks to depict a model prince, have found it impossible to reconcile these different pieces of information concerning Beowulf's youth and have therefore dismissed the reference to his inglorious early years as incompatible.[11] Others have sought to create a picture of Beowulf's youth that could accommodate his accomplishments as well as a period when something is seriously amiss.[12] There is, in other words, no clear-cut evidence to establish Beowulf as a youngster without promise of becoming a hero, and even if such a case could be made the comparison with Grettir as a boy would still be highly questionable because Grettir rebels against mundane tasks that he considers unworthy of a hero's attention.

Ever since Guðbrandur Vigfússon claimed that *Grettis saga* and *Beowulf* derived from the same legend, the great physical strength of the two monster killers has been considered one of the most obvious traits that they have in common. Ironically, this factor separates them no less than it unites them. The author of *Grettis saga* measures the strength of his hero on various occasions: he bails water like eight seamen (chapter 17); carries an ox single-handedly (chapter 50); and successfully wrestles against two men, each twice as strong as an ordinary person (chapter 72). These and other feats of strength that Grettir performs allow the saga author to conclude that he was indeed the strongest man in Iceland in his time (chapter 93). But strong though Grettir is, his physical prowess is always kept close to the borders of the humanly possible; what he might have become had Glámr's curse not stunted his growth by half we can only guess.

Beowulf, on the other hand, has no constraints of 'realistic' presentation imposed upon his strength. He is the strongest man alive (lines 789-90), with the strength of thirty men in his hand-grip (lines 379b-81a). These references would not necessarily indicate a strength of mythological proportions were they not coupled with descriptions of Beowulf's feats of swimming, which include five days in the sea in full armour (line 545a)[13] and a five hundred mile swim home after Hygelac's disastrous raid on Frisia (lines 2359b-72). Scholars have quibbled over various details in these descriptions, but there is no question that the author of *Beowulf* endows his hero with superhuman qualities of strength and endurance.[14] By comparison, Grettir's achievements in fresh or salt water are understandably paltry, as they are kept within the range of what a strong swimmer can actually do.[15]

The superhuman qualities of Beowulf make it very unlikely that the author of *Grettis saga* merely borrowed the physical attributes of his hero from the poem, but could the two hearken back to a legendary forefather—a strong swimmer who killed monsters? Larry D. Benson has argued along these lines in a well-known article entitled 'The Originality of Beowulf,' in which he maintains that whereas wrestling is a common accomplishment among Germanic heroes, great feats of swimming are more unusual. The idea of combining the two leads him to conclude that 'the fact that both Grettir and Beowulf demonstrate skill at swimming and wrestling raises the possibility that both works are based on some longer work that included the Grendel episode and had other similarities to the central fable in Beowulf.'[16] Benson's observation—i.e., that Germanic heroes who are both strong and can swim are few and far between—is incorrect insofar as it ignores the evidence of the later mythic-heroic *fornaldarsogur,* some of which are known to have influenced *Grettis saga.* *Örvar-Odds saga, Hálfdanar saga Brönufóstra, Egils saga einhenda,* and *Þorsteins saga Víkingssonar* all include swimming heroes, so in this respect Grettir and Beowulf are not as exceptional as Benson would like to think. If, in the original story, it mattered that the hero had to swim to reach a second monster, his journey is not easily reconstructed by comparing the poem and the saga. Beowulf, in full armour, sinks to the bottom of the mere where he is immediately attacked by Grendel's dam and her ilk, whereas Grettir dives beneath a waterfall and uneventfully scales the rock behind it to reach the giant's cave. The real swimming feats of both heroes are reserved for other occasions.

The mythical strength of Beowulf and the human limitations of Grettir do not point to a common ancestor; on the contrary, they indicate different concepts of what comprises heroic prowess. The attitudes of the poem and the saga towards supernatural beings also reveal a wholly different definition of what forces the hero must combat. In *Beowulf,* not only Grendel, his mother, and the dragon, but all mystical creatures, are evil. They are all enemies of man and God alike, and Beowulf fights them and overpowers them by virtue of superior strength (and divine assistance) until his final battle with the dragon. In *Grettis saga,* supernatural beings more or less mirror the world of people in the story: some are hostile, like Kárr, Glámr, and the Sandhaugar trolls, and Grettir destroys them in much the same way as he does his human enemies; others are friendly towards him, like the half-troll Þórir and the mysterious Hallmundr.[17] Furthermore, the saga author always assumes that supernatural creatures are stronger than Grettir. This is abundantly clear in his wrestling bouts with Kárr, Glámr, Hallmundr, and the troll-woman. Grettir's victories against hostile supernatural creatures are won with the aid of good luck or cunning or both; either they trip over something in the course of the struggle and fall flat on their backs, like Kárr and Glámr, or they fail to avoid a wrestling trick, like the troll-woman at Sandhaugar.

GRENDEL AND HIS MOTHER

In their comparisons of Beowulf and Grettir, Guðbrandur Vigfússon and F. York Powell paid little attention to differences in the heroes' supernatural opponents, although the nature of such creatures obviously mattered to the saga author and, even more so, to the *Beowulf* poet. Vigfússon and Powell regarded Grendel and his dam, Glámr, the troll-wife, and the giant at Sandhaugar primarily as hostile otherworldly creatures—'friends' and 'monsters'—not the same thing, perhaps, but easily interchangeable in the two different versions of the legend.[18] This trend has continued, and it is still common practice among critics to lump the supernatural adversaries of Beowulf and Grettir together on the facile assumption that they are all more or less the same, functionally speaking.[19] A structural approach is in itself neither better nor worse than any other, but the problem begins when the same critics start extracting sundry details in the description of the monsters, such as the cannibalism of the Grendels and the Sandhaugar trolls or the evil eyes of Grendel and Glámr, and then proceed to serve them up as evidence to support the idea that the poem and the saga are related.

The shortcuts that have been taken by various comparatists have not stemmed from a lack of critical efforts to determine the origin and nature of Grendel and his mother. The earliest views, however, which favoured rather abstract interpretations of them, did little to support Vigfússon's

theory. The Grendels were most commonly thought to originate in nature myths and Beowulf's victory against them was seen in the context of the prevailing of spring against the forces of winter. Alternatively, they were taken to be symptoms of diseases like malaria or hallucinations by the Danes, brought on by too much drink and lack of proper ventilation. But gradually Grendel and his mother took on more concrete shapes, and scholars began to trace their ancestry to the male-female rulers of the underworld of Persian and Greek mythology.[20] These developments opened the possibility of finding a more immediate forefather of the Grendels, preferably with descendants in *Grettis saga* as well.

In 1912, W.W. Lawrence published an article that offered new and persuasive evidence to link *Beowulf* and *Grettis saga.*[21] Lawrence was convinced that from the bewildering and seemingly contradictory description of the Grendels' abode in different parts of the poem it was possible to glimpse a reference to a waterfall in two places.[22] The waterfall linked the description of the landscape in *Beowulf* to Sandhaugar and led Lawrence to conclude that the original story, a *Märchen* of the Bear's Son type, had been set in Scandinavia and involved waterfall trolls as the hero's adversaries. From such stock the author of *Beowulf* had eventually fashioned Grendel and his mother.[23] Lawrence found further support for his ideas on the habitat of trolls in Icelandic materials such as the *Story of Grímur Helguson* and *Orms þáttr,* and in the presence of water sprites in Norwegian folklore. 'A waterfall among high rocks, in which a supernatural being is believed to dwell, is a common and characteristic feature of Scandinavian mountain scenery,' Lawrence declared.[24] It now seemed as though Vigfússon's hunch about a Scandinavian homeland from which the legend had derived had been correct after all.

Although there are glaring weaknesses in his argument, Lawrence's ideas concerning the origin of Grendel and his mother have had a lasting influence on *Beowulf* studies.[25] To begin with his thesis hinges on the notion that there is indeed a waterfall with a cave behind it to be found in the poem; an assumption that has come under stinging criticism from Kemp Malone, as we shall see in chapter 5. Furthermore, there is nothing in the poem's complex and ambiguous description of Grendel and his dam—other than their enormous size—to support the idea that waterfall trolls were the raw material from which the *Beowulf* poet formed his monsters. But the weakest link in Lawrence's theory is probably the fact that Scandinavian trolls do not as a rule live in waterfalls. They are roaming creatures who traditionally choose to live in mountains or hills.[26]

Grendel and his mother are no ordinary trolls; that much is certain from the poem. They may be huge, misshapen, diabolical, and beastly cannibals, but they are much more 'aristocratic' and have more human attributes than monsters in Scandinavian lore usually do. In *Beowulf* one of the first things we discover about the Grendels is their, criminally speaking, respectable background as descendants of Cain and inheritors of his curse. Like the Danes, they also keep their own court, in the sense that they occupy an underwater hall (*niðsele*) guarded by a band of water-monsters. Furthermore, we learn that for a number of years Grendel literally ruled over the Danes (*rixode*), until Beowulf put an end to his reign. The touch of magic that makes the Grendels immune to normal weapons also sets them apart from ordinary monsters in the poem, and as a tangible sign of family pride, mother and son possess an heirloom, a sword whose hilt records the history of their race. Other human touches are added as Grendel is on several occasions referred to as a man (*rinc, wer, healðegn*), and his misery as an outlaw equated with ordinary human feelings of loss and rejection (*wonsæli, dreamum bedæled*). His mother is similarly presented as a woman (*ides*), and in avenging her son she fulfils her duty as any self-respecting Germanic mother would.

Another factor that separates the Grendels from ordinary trolls in Scandinavian literature is the mystery in which the author of *Beowulf* shrouds them. His audience is never allowed to satisfy their curiosity by having a good look at them, or to discover a simple answer as to what kind of creatures they are. We have to imagine them to be unlike any known monsters, and their strangeness is emphasized by the frequent variation among terms that highlight their threefold nature: human, bestial, and diabolical. In the description of Grendel's mother the *Beowulf* poet goes still further by teasing his audience with contradictory statements about her. She is supposed to be weaker than a male warrior (lines 1282b-7) but, as Beowulf discovers, she is a far more dangerous opponent than Grendel.[27] With the proposed Sandhaugar analogue in mind, however, it is even more important that the poem refers to her with a masculine pronoun on four different occasions (lines 1260a, 1392b, 1394b and 1497b). Is this done to suggest that her sex is unimportant, as Lawrence and Goldsmith have argued,[28] or do we have to think of her separately as a mother and a monster, as Wrenn seems to think?[29] Whatever the answer is, these androgynous qualities make her more analogous to certain modern pop stars than to the troll-woman at Sandhaugar.

Grendel's name is of no help in determining family traits; it only adds to the mystery. Lawrence's theory that the word *grendel* may have been a generic term for a water monster in Old English[30] is pure guesswork, and there is no evidence to suggest that the poem's Anglo-Saxon audience had any more clues as to what the name actually means than modern scholars, who have proposed no less than five different etymologies to account for it:

1 / Old English *grindan* = 'to grind' (Old Norse *grand* = 'evil').

2 / Old English *grindel* = 'bar,' 'bolt.'

3 / Old Norse *grindill* = a poetic term for 'storm.'

4 / Latin *grandis* = 'full-grown,' 'great,' 'large.'

5 / Old English *grund* = bottom, cf. Old Norse *grandi* = sand, bottom ground of a body of water.[31]

Not everything about Grendel is as enigmatic as his name and nature, however. The facts that can be gleaned from different parts of the poem about his physical attributes and behavior as a man-eating monster are briefly as follows:

• Grendel is an (in)famous rover[32] of the fens and the moors that lie outside the borders of human habitation (lines 103-4).

• He is huge. Four men struggle to carry his head back to Heorot after Beowulf's final victory (lines 1637b-9).

• His fingers have nails that seem like steel-tipped spurs (lines 985-7b).

• An ugly, flame-like light emanates from his eyes (lines 726b-7).

• Unlike his mother, he does not care to fight with weapons (lines 433-4), and they do not wound him (lines 794-805b), except for his mother's magic sword (lines 1588b-90), if that is indeed the sword with which Beowulf decapitates him.

• Poisoned or corrosive blood runs through his veins (lines 1615b-17).

• Grendel is a ferocious cannibal who behaves much like an ordinary predator. For twelve years (line 147) he persecutes the Danes with frequent attacks at night (lines 1577b-9) to feast on them.

• Grendel's feeding habits have both predatory and human characteristics. He snatches as many as thirty Danes at a time, eats fifteen on the spot in one go, and carries another fifteen away with him for a later meal (lines 1581b-4a). He tears his victims apart, drinks the blood from their veins, and eats their bodies in huge mouthfuls, leaving nothing behind (740-5a).

• Grendel has a huge pouch or glove made of dragon skins (lines 2085b-8) in which he presumably carries victims that he intends to eat later.

• Grendel has no career as a 'living corpse,' (cf. Glámr and Kárr) either before or after Beowulf cuts his head off.

GLÁMR

Glámr is an uncommon name in Old Norse. Although the origin and meaning of the name are somewhat uncertain, it does not appear to be related etymologically to that of Grendel in any way. Glámr comes from Germanic **glé*, 'to shine with a dim or a faint light' (cf. Modern English 'gloom'), and later derivations of the word are usually associated with light or whiteness of some kind.[33] Scholars are agreed that as a name, or a nickname, Glámr originally denotes someone who stares or looks foolish, but this as-sociation has attracted far less attention than the occur-rence of his name as a poetic term for a giant and for the moon in Snorri's *Edda*. This latter connection has led some critics to believe that it might be indicative of his nature in the saga. Thus R.C. Boer associated Glámr with a moon myth and saw him (or rather his ghost) as the per-sonification of the moonlight in winter.[34] Others, particu-larly Wolf von Unwerth, have stressed the giant-like size and nature of Glámr as a ghost.[35] But Glámr also occurs as an ordinary name in *Sturlunga* (*Íslendinga saga*), so it is by no means certain that the author of **Grettis saga** in-tended his audience to interpret it in a particular way, ex-cept to associate it with *glámsýni* (illusions), as he himself suggests.

It is not clear either what kind of creature Glámr is sup-posed to have been before he became one of the living dead. Boer and von Unwerth regard him as a demon or a magician who only feigns a human form and has evil in-tentions, whether he is living or dead.[36] No one, however, had seen any connection between the pre-ghostly Glámr and Grendel until James Carney found a way to unite them. In *Beowulf* (line 107) we are told of Grendel's de-scent from the exiled Cain, who becomes the progenitor of monsters and giants in medieval lore, and Grendel thus owes his monstrous form to inherited guilt. Carney main-tains that this account in the poem has been transformed in the story of Glámr into his 'personal guilt,' because of his failure as a 'normal human being' to observe Christian rites, for which he is punished by becoming 'not a mere ghost, but a physical monster':

> just as Hrothgar's palace was changed into an Icelandic farmhouse, so too the tale was brought up to date in medieval Iceland by discarding the idea of Cain's guilt for an analogical idea—failure to practice religious ob-servance—that had some relevance in contemporary Iceland . . . Grettir slew the monster Glam who be-came a monster because he, in his own person, had re-fused to attend Mass and had eaten meat on a fast-day.[37]

This is pretty far-fetched stuff, and Carney has to make a few shortcuts through the facts of the matter on his way to his conclusion. In the first place, Glámr hardly qualifies ei-ther as a 'normal human being' or as a 'monster,' the term under which Carney conveniently lumps Glámr and Gren-del together. Secondly, he has no convincing means of ex-plaining why the idea of monsters springing from Cain should have been replaced by a more relevant notion in medieval Iceland. There is indeed a hint of divine retribu-tion in the tale of how Glámr meets his end, but there is no suggestion in **Grettis saga** that his existence as a ghost is a form of punishment or due to anything other than his own evil nature.[38] As opposed to Grendel, Glámr seems to enjoy his supernatural state; the punishment is reserved for Þórhallr's farm and the rest of the community.

Although Glámr as a ghost haunts farms and kills people, he is in most respects entirely different from Grendel. Glámr has no taste for human flesh, he can speak, he is as

vulnerable to weapons as anyone else in the saga, and no mother or a female partner avenges his second and perma-nent death at the hands of Grettir. Icelandic ghosts are as a rule 'more material than the ghosts of English tradition,'[39] as E. V. Gordon so aptly put it, and Glámr is no exception, so a physical presence after death does not *per se* make him a monster on par with Grendel, as some critics like to think. Glámr's ghostly exploits: riding housetops, making a whole region desolate, driving people mad, breaking the bones of and killing animals and people, are all well known ghost story motifs from Icelandic texts, many of which the author of **Grettis saga** has been shown to have been familiar with.[40] It is also possible, as Hermann Páls-son has suggested,[41] that the account of Glámr's nature and powers is sprinkled with ideas that can be traced to medi-eval commentaries on the subject of ghosts and demons. But the main traits that Glámr and Grendel share—haunt-ing places and killing people—are far too common among ghosts and monsters to establish any particular link be-tween the two. Of the contact points between Glámr and Grendel that have been suggested, only three are specific enough to indicate that they might hearken back to a com-mon origin or be directly related in some other manner: their great size, their evil eyes, and the matter of cursing or being cursed.

Grettis saga makes it quite clear that Glámr's size varies. As he enters the farmhouse where Grettir awaits him (chapter 35), he towers up to the ceiling, but a moment later the two wrestle in a manner that would be impossible if Glámr was the giant that he had just appeared to be. Hermann Pálsson has explained this with a reference to the illusionary powers that *Antoníus saga* ascribes to de-mons,[42] and the note which the saga author inserts into his text to relate the word *glámsýni* to the story of Glámr sup-ports Pálsson's reading. Grettir's vision of Glámr as a gi-ant is only a fleeting illusion, whereas Grendel's gigantic size is an integral part of his ancestry from Cain.

It is only as Glámr is about to meet his death that his evil eyes and his stare begin to play a part in the story, whereas the ugly flame-like light from Grendel's eyes presumably scared the Danes all along. The idea that evil persons who possess magic powers can do harm by looking at someone at the moment of their death was, however, already well established in Icelandic literature before **Grettis saga** was composed[43] and has nothing whatsoever to do with Gren-del.

Finally, there is the matter of the curse. James Carney in-cludes Grettir in the second part of his Cain hypothesis and presents the following argument:

> Part of the curse of Cain was that he was to be a '*va-gus et profugus in terra*.' When the monster Glam is dying he curses Grettir and part of his curse is: 'Thou shalt be outlawed and doomed ever to dwell alone, away from men.' This suggests that Cain figured in the author's source material; when Cain was eliminated the terms in which he was cursed were retained; but he is made, in the person of Glam, to utter the curse of which, in the source material, he was the recipient.[44]

Carney's theory is based on his conviction that the author of *Grettis saga* had direct access to a manuscript of *Beowulf,* something which is very unlikely, as we shall see in chapter 6. But the most amazing part of Carney's speculation is that, having just explained how the author of **Grettis saga** felt compelled to substitute Grendel's ancestral guilt for Glámr's personal guilt in order to emphasize the importance of observing Christian customs in Iceland, the same author decided to cast the ghost of that stubborn heathen Glámr in the role of God almighty to banish and curse Grettir, as Cain was banished and cursed.

Whether Glámr's role in the 'old legend' is the same as Grendel's we have yet to examine, but nothing about the origin, nature, or behaviour of Glámr seems to point to any special affinity with Grendel. The differences between them for outweigh any superficial traits that they might seem to share, and statements to the effect that 'after his death [Glámr] distinctly resembles Grendel'[45] are not based on much more than wishful thinking.

THE TROLL-WOMAN AND THE GIANT OF THE SANDHAUGAR EPISODE

Some scholars think that the Old Norse terms *troll* ('trolls') and *jotnar* ('giants') may have indicated a degree of difference between the two at a very early stage, i.e., that giants were considered to be remote, prehistoric figures in comparison to trolls. In late sagas (especially *fornaldarsogur*) and in folktales, trolls and giants have merged and for the most part share the same characteristics.[46] In this literature, trolls and giants are huge, supernatural beings who live in the mountains far to the north and are as a rule hostile towards people. This is, of course, not without exceptions, as we see in **Grettis saga** itself.

Unlike the battle against Glámr, whose curse follows Grettir to the end of his days, the Sandhaugar episode is self-contained and independent; much like a chapter in a picaresque novel. Late in the saga (chapter 64), the reader is informed that at a farm called Sandhaugar in Bárðardalur people are spooked by the presence of trolls. For two years in a row a man has been kidnapped from the farm at Christmas, a season that also inspired Glámr to do evil deeds; however, unlike Glámr, whose persecutions extended throughout the dark months of winter, these creatures only strike once a year. During the first attack, when the farmer was snatched away, there were other people present in the hall of the farmhouse, which clearly shows that these evil beings are only interested in taking a single person. The farmer disappeared without a trace, and no one saw anything, although a great deal of noise was heard by his bed. Then, in one sentence, the saga author makes a year go by and has nothing to say about anyone's reaction to the man's disappearance. It is only after the second attack, when traces of blood are found by the front door of the hall, that people conclude that some evil beings must be responsible for the kidnapping of the two men. Unlike with Grendel and his mother or Glámr, nothing is known about these trolls; they are (and remain) nameless, and no

one knows where they come form. This is how matters stand when Grettir—who after his tangle with Glámr is the last person the reader expects to turn up in a haunted place—appears on the scene.

The above-mentioned account looks like a summary of a story, but in fact it is not; there is no more information in the saga concerning the famous hauntings at Sandhaugar prior to Grettir's fight with the trolls. What little we have is a disappointingly short and incomplete story, especially if we keep in mind that Vigfússon believed his 'old legend' to have been percolating in people's imaginations for hundreds of years. And it is not just that the saga version is short. As it stands, this first part of the Sandhaugar episode, i.e., the counterpart to the national disaster that Grendel brought on the Danes, leaves some awkward questions unanswered. There is no explanation as to why these evil beings only strike at Christmas,[47] why they kidnap people but only take one person at a time, or what they actually do with their victims. The fact that when the troll-woman attacks Grettir she is armed with a long knife and carries a *trog,*[48] and the discovery of the bones of the two missing men in the giant's cave, would seem to indicate that the Sandhaugar trolls are cannibals like Grendel. But if that is indeed the case, it does not say much for their monstrous appetite that they strike only once a year and take one person at a time. Grettir's discovery of the bones in the cave also shows that their eating habits must be a good deal more sophisticated than those of Grendel's. If, on the other hand, we are not meant to think of the Sandhaugar trolls as cannibals, there is no explanation as to why they kidnap people. These uncertainties, which affect the very nucleus of the story, do not give the impression of a legend polished by centuries of oral transmission. The hints which the author drops are inconsistent, as if he has not fully formulated the story that he wants to tell. The blood by the front door would, for example, seem to suggest that someone was attacked and perhaps eaten on the spot, and the troll-woman's long knife and *trog* could create the same impression. But the bones in the cave point in the opposite direction, i.e., towards people being abducted live and in one piece and killed there.

Grettir's involvement does not add a great deal of knowledge about the Sandhaugar trolls, as the reader is never given any information beyond what little Grettir actually sees. They remain without a background, there is no attempt to develop them as characters, and there is nothing about them to suggest that they enter the story with the identifying marks of a long tradition. The troll-woman is big and is armed with a long knife (*skálm*), as troll-women in Icelandic lore commonly are.[49] The *trog* she carries is, however, a more interesting and unusual prop. In his introduction to *Beowulf,* Klaeber states his belief that the *trog* and Grendel's *glof* ('glove,' 'pouch'?) point to a connection between the two stories, as both articles serve the identical purpose of holding food,[50] but this comparison is somewhat misleading. Grendel obviously uses his glove to store and carry his victims, whereas the troll-woman's *trog* might be used as a cutting tray or a container in which to store food, but as a substitute for Grendel's 'rucksack' it will not do. The giant's entry into the story adds very little to what we know (or rather what we do not know); he is huge, black, and ugly, as giants in folklore are expected to be,[51] and like the troll-woman, but unlike Grendel, he uses weapons.

Critics who wish to equate the Sandhaugar pair with Grendel and his mother have usually chosen to ignore the fact that *Grettis saga* suggests no relationship of any kind between the giant and the troll-woman, although in recent years some scholars have seen a ray of hope in one of the kennings that Grettir uses to refer to the giant in a stanza (no. 61) that he composes about the battle against him in the cave. The epithet in question is *mellu vinr,* which literally means 'the troll-woman's friend.' The two main editors of *Grettis saga,* R.C. Boer and Guðni Jónsson, take this kenning to mean 'a giant' and read nothing else into it. It is therefore somewhat surprising to encounter the giant as the 'she-troll's ugly husband' in the translation of this stanza in *Beowulf and Its Analogues.*[52] Unfortunately, the translator does not explain how and when this match has come about. Another attempt to establish a relationship has been undertaken by Peter Jorgensen, who maintains that *mellu vinr* might be taken to mean 'a lover,' but the kennings for lovers that he points to as a basis for his reading are too far removed from *mellu vinr* to prove his point.[53]

The only thing that the Sandhaugar trolls really have in common with Grendel and his dam is the fact that they are male and female, and even that evidence comes with certain caveats. It must be kept in mind that, unlike in *Beowulf,* their sex is of no importance, and that in the saga they appear in the wrong order. Critics who have the imagination to see Grendel and his mother 'in all their monstrosity and superhuman powers' in the giant and the troll-woman of Sandhaugar[54] are only testifying to the might of Glámr's eyes.

KÁRR THE OLD

Nothing but the art of finding the lowest common denominator through a play on words can make Kárr the Old resemble Grendel or his mother. Kárr is a ghost (one of the living dead) who lives in a gravemound on Háramarsey. According to the saga he has managed to increase the wealth and power of his son, Þorfinnr, by scaring other farmers off the island and making Þorfinnr the sole owner of all property there. Only those who enjoy Þorfinnr's favour are unmolested by Kárr's hauntings.[55] R.W. McConchie, who, as we have already seen, maintains that the story of Kárr the Old is a genetically related and neglected *Beowulf* analogue, readily admits that Kárr is quite unlike Grendel, and that the whole episode is relatively unimportant in the context of the saga. Instead he chooses to emphasize the similarity of events and how the two heroes react to them. McConchie suggests that the first of 'several points of similarity between Beowulf's struggle with Grendel's mother and Grettir's fight with Kárr' is the fact that

both 'take place as a result of a series of violent hauntings.'[56] It is, of course, a matter of literary sensibility whether we see fit to equate a national disaster, like Grendel's reign of terror, and Kárr's spooking a few farmers away (he does not kill anyone) under the neat semantic umbrella of 'a series violent hauntings.' However, it is simply not true that Grettir tangles with Kárr as a result of his hauntings, as McConchie maintains. *Grettis saga* makes it quite clear that the hero's motive has nothing to do with cleansing the island of an evil being; Kárr has achieved his goal anyway, and there is nothing to be gained by his destruction except treasure. Like all others who break into gravemounds in the sagas, Grettir does so for precisely this reason.[57]

THE BEAR

A.R. Taylor and A. Margaret Arent, the first scholars to maintain that the bear episode was analogous and genetically related to *Beowulf,* saw nothing in the description of the brown bear that Grettir fights except a brown bear. Their readers were thus spared a detailed comparison of the nature and characteristics of the beast and Grendel. But is there no way of equating the two? Recently, Arthur A. Wachsler has attempted to do so and presents his case as follows:

> According to Norse Lore, a man was said to possess a soul called a *'fylgja'* which could leave the body and reappear in the form of an animal. Indeed, the *fylgja* often shared the personality of its human partner. 'The animal *fylgja* often had some corresponding aspect to that of the character of its owner - bulls and bears attended great chiefs, foxes people of crafty nature.' Along with the bull, then, the bear, according to Norse tradition, was the spirit form of a great leader.
>
> The supernatural and manlike qualities of the bear are attested also in the Norse belief in lycanthropy. Men who had the gift of shape-shifting frequently changed into animals, often appearing as bears as well as wolves . . .
>
> Besides the Scandinavians, other northern races held the bear in special esteem. The Lapps, Finns, Ostiaks and Voguls regarded the bear as the most holy of wild animals and held feasts in its honor. They considered the animal to be more intelligent and stronger than a man. One northern race, the Votiaks, believed that the bear could understand human speech. In addition, these people believed that the bear, if provoked enough, could return from the dead to punish its enemies. The awe in which the Votiaks held the bear was based no doubt on its ghostly nature, on its ability to return from the dead . . .
>
> The evidence in ancient northern lore suggests that the bear, along with more obvious examples, was considered to be a revenant, one of the *draugar* or animated dead. For that reason, the bear can be considered no less formidable and worthy an opponent than Glamr, the female troll at Sandhaugr and Kar the Old to all of whom the animal is related.[58]

Wachsler's method puts the cart squarely before the horse. Even if we accept all his findings at face value, it is still not easy to see how they lead to the desired conclusion. If there is a connection to be made between Scandinavian beliefs in *fylgjur,* or shape-shifting—which, as it happens, only affect living persons—and the Votiaks' belief that the bear could return from the dead, it certainly does not turn the brown bear in **Grettis saga** into a *draugr* on par with Glámr and Kárr, as Wachsler would like us to think. None of this has anything to do with the bear in *Grettis saga,* unless we are meant to think of the animal as someone's *fylgja,* a chief who has taken on the shape of a bear, or the ghost of the beast rather than an ordinary brown bear of flesh and blood.

Various other points that concern the bear episode, in addition to Grettir's fight against the beast and the descriptions of its lair, have been thought to show contact with *Beowulf.* There is, first of all, Taylor's contention that the character and actions of Bjørn, the obnoxious relative of Þorkell, mirror those of Unferð. Taylor based his comparison on their 'discourtesy towards guests and strangers,' which he found so strongly emphasized in the saga writer's portrait of Bjørn that he believed it to have been a 'characteristic of the prototype of the two men.'[59] However this comparison is not as simple as it looks. It is quite true that Unferð challenges Beowulf's credentials in the poem (lines 499-528), but it is by no means certain that he does so out of discourtesy or hostility. As Hroðgar's ryle ('spokesman'?), it may well be that he is merely carrying out his duties.[60] Later in the poem, Unferð appears as Beowulf's friend and lends him Hrunting—the famous *hæftmece*—to use against Grendel's mother. Although Bjørn and Unferð may both be jealous men, there are too many other factors that separate them in the poem and the saga to suggest that they go back to a common ancestor. In the first place, Bjørn has no official position at Þorkell's farm, and he has no skeletons in his closet like Unferð (who is guilty of fratricide). Secondly, Unferð makes no attempt to tangle with Grendel, whereas Bjørn tries to kill the bear. Finally, it must be kept in mind that Bjørn is eventually killed by Grettir. As Geoffrey Hughes has rightly observed, there is no character in Germanic literature with whom Unferð can be readily compared, and Bjørn is no better than previous candidates.[61]

Wachsler, however, thinks that he can detect echoes from 'the original stories' in the way in which Bjørn and his companions arouse the 'primal monster':

> It is not unreasonable to suppose that Bjorn and his company drank to excess and celebrated by playing instruments, singing loudly and generally behaving as drunk men do. They 'lifted their voices' (*reysta*) causing a din (*háreysti*). And there is nothing to suggest the Danes in Heorot were any less boisterous than their Icelandic [*sic*] counterparts. They expressed their joy by celebrating loudly (drēam). During their noisy celebration, both groups, apparently, provoked their neighbors who in great anger retaliated by attacking their inconsiderate tormentors. In keeping with his Christian background, the *Beowulf* poet places Grendel in league with the kin of Cain. In contrast, the author of the saga, with his monstrous bear, remains squarely in the pagan world, and he is probably closer to the original stories.

In each case, however, it is loud noises or the sounds of celebration which arouse a primal monster and cause it to attack those who have disturbed its peace.[62]

This may look convincing, but most of the analogous material that Wachsler claims to find in **Grettis saga** either is not there or is made to appear in a greatly emended form. In the saga Bjørn and his cronies are said to have loitered outside and to have made loud noises (74), but there is no mention of singing or drinking or other forms of celebration; nor are such activities normally practised outdoors in Scandinavia during the winter. It is a also a mere play on words to argue that both Grendel and the bear are 'roused' by noises, which cause them to attack, or to compare them as 'primal monsters.' Grendel is attracted—and presumably tormented—by the happy noises of celebration that he hears coming from Heorot every day; the brown bear is awoken from its hibernation and behaves as a hungry bear might be expected to do: it attacks sheep—anyone's sheep. Þorkell suffers more damage than other farmers simply because he is the wealthiest of the lot, as **Grettis saga** duly explains. To find in the brown bear episode of the saga essentially the same story line as in *Beowulf* can obviously be done, but only if we are prepared to emend both texts in the manner that Procrustes employed to make his visitors fit his infamous bed.

GRETTIR AS A MONSTER

The hypothesis that Grettir has an alter ego as a monster was first suggested by Nora Chadwick in 1959, and has since become increasingly fashionable among *Beowulf* scholars. Chadwick's transformation of Grettir seems to have come about as a result of her failure to fit him into a theory that would make *Beowulf* and **Grettis saga** (along with several other texts in Old Norse) ritualistic repetitions of an ancient story, which supposedly involved 'a hereditary feud between a heroic member of a ruling Scandinavian dynasty and a closely knit group of supernatural foes [a *draugr,* an evil supernatural woman and a dragon], located to the east of the Baltic.'[63] Chadwick finds two of these foes in **Grettis saga,** but no trace of landscapes east of the Baltic or a dragon. As luck would have it, *Bjarnar saga Hítdælakappa* contains these missing elements, and that leads Chadwick to the following extraordinary conclusion:

> It is strongly to be suspected that Grettir's adventures against monsters nowhere else associated with Iceland, but consistently located east of the Baltic in 'Bjarmaland,' have been derived by the author from traditions proper to Björn Hítdælakappi's Russian sojourn with King Cnut.[64]

What Chadwick omits to explain is why, if these traditions are indeed associated with Bjørn, they are not included in his saga? And where does this leave poor Grettir? Given a family tree with half-trolls and warlocks on its distant branches and with no immediate prospects of qualifying as 'a heroic member of a ruling Scandinavian dynasty,' his fate at Chadwick's hands is rather predictable. As she meditates on Grettir's name—which she believes to be unusual and sinister—his metamorphosis from a hero to a monster is a matter of smooth speculation:

> Is it possible that the name itself carries with it a troll connotation? What is its origin? Can it be a Norse form derived from *grandi-*, and is the corresponding Anglo-Saxon form *Grend-il*? Is it possible that in origin Grendel and Grettir are identical, and that in the Norse story the monster has been transformed into the hero—that a story, originally told from the monster's point of view, has left traces on this strange and capricious, pitiful yet very sinister, outlaw?[65]

Nora Chadwick's ideas have been firmly opposed by Anatoly Liberman, who, as we have already seen, also rejects the notion that there could have been an Old English text in which Grendel's story was related from the monster's point of view. But is it possible that the names Grettir and Grendel are related through *grandi-*[66] or *grenja* ('to bellow'), as Margaret Arent has proposed?[67] Grettir's name is normally traced to *grantian* (i.e., related to words meaning 'to snarl' or 'to growl'), but it has also been argued that the name might not be of Norse origin and hence that it is uncertain what it means.[68] Liberman, who has discussed the possible etymologies of the names Grettir and Grendel in detail, sees no possibility of tracing their origin to the same root. His argument may be summarized as follows:

1 / Although the etymology of Grendel is debatable, the root *grend* is probably the umlauted form of **grand*.

2 / Another Germanic root, *gran-*, is related to the root *grant-*, as in **grantjan*, from which we have the verbs *grenja* and *gretta*, and eventually Grettir as a name.

3 / The relevant question is thus whether the roots **grand-* and **grant-* can be related, which they cannot be unless we can find a way of explaining the last consonant in each word: i.e., the *d* in **grand-* and the *t* in **grant-*. This was indeed attempted during the last century by Sophus Bugge, but his hypothesis was demolished by historical linguists a long time ago. In short, the bottom line is that **grand-* and **grant-* have to be taken to be two separate and unrelated etyma and, given that conclusion, there is no possibility of tracing the names of Grettir and Grendel to the same root.[69]

Arent and Chadwick have also used chthonic connotations, which they claim to be present in the names of Grettir and Grendel, as evidence to link them. It goes without saying, however, that in the final analysis the argument stands or falls on etymological evidence, and any speculation about common connotations, chthonic or otherwise, which critics may feel that they share, is simply irrelevant.[70] It may well be that Nora Chadwick's ideas represent 'the most daring questioning to date,' as Richard Harris has stated,[71] but there is not a shred of reasonable evidence to support her hypothesis concerning Grettir's monstrous origin.

As we saw in chapter 1, the fifth analogue that Harris claimed to have found in *Grettis saga* represents an attempt to develop Chadwick's ideas much further than she herself was prepared to do. Harris looks for textual evidence and finds that 'the death of Grettir resembles in at least eleven details the first part of *Beowulf,* particularly the fight at Grendel's Mere.'[72] Harris's evidence inevitably consists of sundry events and details that are extracted from the two texts. Apart from this, his approach to the two texts does not appear to follow any particular method, except to connect them at any cost.[73] Sometimes the order of these elements, as they originally appear in *Grettis saga* and *Beowulf,* seems to matter—and is kept; in other instances it must be re-shuffled to make a comparison.[74] But this is not the only liberty that Harris takes in the presentation of his evidence. There is also a tendency to 'emend' some of it in the process. Take points 2 and 3, for example:

> Grettir has a hut on Drangey;
> nearness to the sea.
> Þorbjörn arrives at Drangey
> toward the end of the day.
>
> Grendel has a waterfall cave,
> possibly near the sea.
> Beowulf takes most of day
> to reach bottom of mere.

Grendel has no waterfall cave like the giant at Sandhaugar; he has an underwater hall, and according to the poem it takes Beowulf *hwil dæges* (line 1495)—'a good part of the day,' not most of it—to reach the bottom of the mere.

In the course of Harris's discussion these seemingly unrelated items are stitched together with literary exegesis of the kind that Isidore of Seville practised to perfection in the seventh century. Take point 4, for example:

> Þorbjörn climbs a ladder
> to reach Grettir's hut.
>
> Beowulf plunges into mere.

For the reader who is slow to see a connection between ÞorBjørn's climbing a ladder to reach Grettir's hut, and Beowulf's plunging into the mere, Harris offers the following explication:

> Þorbjörn climbs a ladder to reach Grettir's hut. Panzer's description of the Bear's Son Tale includes the motif of the hero climbing to a world, the Demon Kingdom, above or below the earth to confront the monster. Presumably an ascent would be involved where the opening in the earth, by which access is gained to the other world, is on a mountain or the top of a hill. The monster is reached only by descent elsewhere in *Beowulf* and *Grettis saga*. The necessity of climbing in the opposite direction doesn't seem to me to rule out the possibility of this being an element parallel to the climbing in the other episodes. The ladder would simply be a modification of the rope used by Grettir in the Háramarsey and Sandhaugar adventures.[75]

In *Grettis saga,* it is perfectly true that Grettir plays many and sometimes contradictory roles,[76] and in conclusion, I want to emphasize that I do not reject Nora K. Chadwick's role reversal theory because I find it shocking that Grettir could be cast as a monster; I reject it because there is no reasonable evidence to support that particular role reversal for Grettir, and Harris's attempt to develop the original theory further changes nothing in that respect. In essence, Harris's fifth analogue shows Grettir to be a sheep-eating outlaw whose death, scene by scene, does not mirror that of Grendel, unless we are prepared to suspend common sense altogether in reviewing the evidence. However, Harris's argument is neither better nor worse than others that we have examined in this chapter from the hands of critics who would like to equate Beowulf and Grettir as heroes or their various adversaries as monsters. Undoubtedly, these arguments are inspired by academic climates that place a great value on critical imagination in literary analysis, but some issues—like the questions we have examined in this chapter—simply cannot be resolved on the basis of what critics would like to imagine. Having considered the ingredients that make up the heroes and the monsters in *Beowulf* and *Grettis saga,* I do not think there is convincing evidence to suggest a relationship between the two. As 'heroes' Grettir and Beowulf have little in common, and as 'monsters' their supernatural adversaries have even less.

Notes

1. Vigfusson and Powell 1879, 404, and 1883, 502.

2. Gering 1880, 87, wonders aloud how earlier scholars like Grímur Thorkelin, N.F.S. Grundtvig, Eiríkur Magnússon, and W. Morris—all of whom knew both *Beowulf* and *Grettis saga*—could have failed to see the connection between them.

3. Jónsson 1936, lv.

4. See, e.g., Powell 1901, 396.

5. See the discussion of the Sandhaugar episode and Grettir's fight with the bear in chap. 1.

6. See, e.g., Stedman 1913, 26 and 17, and Benson 1970, 28.

7. Vigfusson and Powell 1883, 502 and n. 2 on the same page.

8. See Panzer 1910, 32-9 and 44-66, on how this feature is expressed in various tales, and 268-9 and 322-4 on his attempt to apply the idea to Beowulf and Grettir. Panzer's theory is discussed in chap. 7.

9. Jónsson 1936, 42.

10. The first section definitely relates Beowulf's exploits as a boy, but no chronology is given for the second, which may or may not refer to the same event.

11. See, e.g., Chambers 1959, 65 and Klaeber 1950, 207 (note on line 2183).

12. Arguments to this effect are summed up by Wrenn 1953, 218 (note on lines 2183-9), and Kuhn 1984, 245n. 11.

13. Seven days according to Unferð (line 517a).

14. Even Fred C. Robinson's well-known article, 'Elements of the Marvellous in the Characterization of Beowulf,' in which the author finds ways of rationalizing Beowulf's dive into Grendel's mere, his swimming contest with Breca, and his return by water from Frisia, does not alter this fact. I prefer the more traditional reading of the above-mentioned episodes of the poem, not just because it suits my argument, but because I find it futile to try to rationalize the main hero of a poem which is neither consistent nor rational, and which asks us to believe that this same hero fought and defeated a number of supernatural enemies. In short, I prefer the mystery in a mysterious poem like *Beowulf,* and taking it away feels like being told that the parting of the Red Sea took place because of strange and unusual weather conditions.

15. See, e.g., chaps. 38, 58, and 75. Grettir's most famous water adventure, his swim from the island of Drangey to the shore of the mainland of Iceland, has been repeated several times during this century by lesser mortals.

16. Benson 1970, 28.

17. Guðni Jónsson believes Hallmundr to be a half-troll as well; see his introduction to *Grettis saga,* l. The exact nature of Hallmundr is left undefined in the saga.

18. Vigfusson 1878, xlix, and Vigfusson and Powell 1883, 502.

19. See, e.g., Chadwick, 1959, 178-91; Chadwick's use of the term *draugr* for all kinds of supernatural beings is now widely accepted.

20. See Lehmann 1901, 191-2. Early theories on the origin of the Grendels are summed up, e.g., by Kögel 1892, 274-6, and Wardale 1965, 92-3.

21. 'The Haunted Mere in Beowulf.' Lawrence developed his ideas on the subject further in a later study entitled *Beowulf and Epic Tradition.*

22. Lines 1359b and 2128b. Lawrence interpreted the Old English term *fyrgenstream,* 'mountain stream,' to mean a waterfall.

23. Lawrence 1912, 241-5, and 1928, 162.

24. Lawrence 1912, 240.

25. See, e.g., Chambers 1959, 461-4; Liestöl 1930, 371-2; Fontenrose 1959, 527n. 12 and Kennedy 1940, xxi.

26. For a further discussion of this point see, e.g., von Sydow 1923, 31.

27. This has presented a dilemma to critics who look for rational explanations of everything in the poem. Klaeber 1950, 181 (note on lines 1282 ff.), for instance, offers the far-fetched but amusing theory that the reference to her weakness is 'evidently to be explained as an endeavor to discredit the unbiblical notion of a woman's superiority.'

28. See Lawrence 1928, 181-2, and Goldsmith 1970, 104.

29. See Wrenn 1953, 209.

30. See Lawrence 1928, 163-4.

31. For further reference see Klaeber 1950, xxviii-xxix, and Chambers 1959, 309-10. 'Grendel' also surfaces in English place names, often attached to water, but apart from that they throw no light on the meaning of the word according to Chambers. On the place name 'Grendill' in Iceland, see Einarsson, 1956, 79-82. He believes that the name is modern, probably given by a recent surveyor.

32. *Mære mearcstapa.* It has also been suggested, first by Edv. Lehmann 1901, 189, and later by Kiessling 1968, 191, that *mære* (with a long 'æ')—normally taken to be an adjective—might be a noun, *mære* (with a short vowel), meaning an incubus or a night monster (Old Norse *mara*).

33. See Jónsson 1936, 123-4n. 2; Janzén 1947, 51; Magnússon 1989, 252; and Jónsson 1954, 209 and 311.

34. See Boer 1898, 57-8, and 1900, xlii.

35. See von Unwerth 1911, 171-2. Von Unwerth also points to the presence of a giant named Glámr in *Bárðar saga,* chaps. 13-14.

36. See Boer 1900, xlii n. 1, and von Unwerth 1911, 171-2.

37. Carney 1955, 94-5.

38. It has been argued (see, e.g., Hume 1975, 473) that there is a causal relationship between Glámr's becoming a ghost and the fact that his death is caused by some kind of a monstrous creature. There is nothing in the text of *Grettis saga* which confirms (or denies) this view.

39. Gordon 1927, 83. Gordon, it may be added, sees little ingenuity in Glámr's behaviour as a ghost and suspects that his habit of riding the house-top 'may have been suggested originally by the cattle of Iceland getting on the turf roof to nibble the grass.'

40. See von Unwerth 1911, 167-9, and Jónsson 1936, xvii-xxxi.

41. Pálsson 1980, 98-9.

42. Pálsson 1980, 98. . . .

43. It appears both in *Eyrbyggja* and *Laxdæla saga.*

44. Carney 1955, 96.

45. Kiessling 1968, 200.

46. See, e.g., Halvorsen 1974, 656.

47. Christmas is very often the time when such attacks occur, but here there is nothing in the text to indicate that these particular raids are inspired by animosity towards Christianity, like the account of Grendel's ongoing strife against God.

48. There is no single word in English for this vessel. *Trog* is a cross between a tray and a trough.

49. See, e.g., Jónsson 1936, 30n. 1, and Shetelig 1937, 378.

50. See Klaeber 1950, xv n. 2.

51. See, e.g., Motz 1982, 72-3.

52. Garmonsway et al. 1968, 316.

53. Jorgensen 1973, 56. The compounds *ástvinr* and *málvinr,* which occur in the kennings for lovers that Jorgensen found ('*ástvinr meyja*' and '*ekkju málvinr*'), indicate more than just a friendship. It is difficult to see how they can be used as evidence of the semantic range of the uncompounded form *vinr* in Old Norse.

54. See, e.g., Malone 1958, 307.

55. Like the Sandhaugar episode, chap. 18 of the saga is somewhat inconsistent. The story of the high-handed practices of Kárr and his son does not accord well with the description of Þorfinnr's character, and his reaction to Grettir's robbing Kárr's gravemound makes little sense.

56. McConchie 1982, 482-3.

57. It is a fire burning on a promontory on the island that first attracts Grettir's attention, and he immediately interprets what he sees as a sign of a buried treasure. After having broken into the gravemound, Grettir pays no attention to the presence of Kárr; he merely assembles his booty and is about to leave when Kárr attacks him (cf. Jónsson 1936, 57-8). McConchie's statement (p. 484) that 'Grettir's interest in the gravemound is not given a precise motivation' is only true in the sense that the saga author does not spell it out any clearer than this.

58. Wachsler 1985, 382-3.

59. Taylor 1952, 17.

60. It is very uncertain what *þyle* really means and what Unferð's role in Heorot is. See, e.g., Rosier 1962, 1-8, and Eliason 1963, 267-84.

61. For further discussion see Hughes 1977 and Rosenberg 1975.

62. Wachsler 1985, 386.

63. Chadwick 1959, 193.

64. Chadwick 1959, 192.

65. Chadwick 1959, 193.

66. It is not clear what meaning Chadwick wants to assign to this form.

67. Arent 1969, 184-5.

68. Janzén 1947, 155. . . .

69. Liberman 1986, 389-90.

70. For discussion along these lines see, e.g., Arent 1969, 184-5, and Chadwick 1959, 193.

71. Harris 1973, 40.

72. Harris 1973, 36.

73. Anatoly Liberman's objections to Harris's methods were noted in chap. 1.

74. Cf., e.g., item 6 regarding Grettir's death and items 6 and 7 from *Beowulf.*

75. Harris 1973, 43-4.

76. For a thorough investigation of the different roles that Grettir is made to play in the saga itself and in later tradition see Hastrup 1990, 154-83.

Works Cited

Arent, A. Margaret. 1969. 'The Heroic Pattern: Old Germanic Helmets, *Beowulf* and *Grettis saga.*' In Edgar C. Polomé (ed.), *Old Norse Literature and Mythology: A Symposium.* Austin: University of Texas Press. 130-99.

Benson, Larry D. 1970. 'The Originality of *Beowulf.*' In Morton W. Bloomfield (ed.), *The Interpretation of Narrative: Theory and Practice.* Harvard English Studies, 1. Cambridge, Mass.: Harvard University Press. 1-43.

Boer, R.C. 1898. 'Zur Grettissaga.' *Zeitschrift für deutsche Philologie,* 30: 1-71.

———(Ed.). 1900. *Grettis saga Ásmundarsonar.* Altnordische Saga-Bibliothek, Heft 8. Halle: Max Niemeyer.

Carney, James. 1955. *Studies in Irish History and Literature.* Dublin: Dublin Institute for Advanced Studies.

Chadwick, Nora K. 1959. 'The Monsters and Beowulf.' In Peter Clemoes (ed.), *The Anglo-Saxons, Studies in Some Aspects of Their History and Culture Presented to Bruce Dickens.* London: Bowes & Bowes. 171-203.

Chambers, R.W. 1921. *Beowulf: An Introduction to the Study of the Poem with a Discussion of the Stories of Offa and Finn.* Cambridge: Cambridge University Press.

———1929. 'Beowulf's Fight with Grendel, and its Scandinavian Parallels.' *English Studies* 11: 81-100.

———1959. *Beowulf: An Introduction to the Study of the Poem.* 3rd ed. with a supplement by C.L. Wrenn. Cambridge: Cambridge University Press.

Einarsson, Stefán. 1933. *Saga Eiríks Magnússonar.* Reykjavík: Ísafoldarprentsmiðja.

———1938. 'Review of Guðni Jónsson's edition of *Grettis saga.*' *JEGP,* 37: 289-91.

———1956. 'Bjólfur and Grendill in Iceland.' *Modern Language Notes,* 71: 79-82.

———1961. *Íslensk bókmenntasaga 874-1960.* Reykjavík: Snæbjörn Jónsson.

Eliason, Norman E. 1963. 'The Þyle and Scop in *Beowulf.*' *Speculum,* 38: 267-84.

Fontenrose, Joseph. 1959. *Python: A Study of Delphic Myth and Its Origins.* Berkeley: University of California Press.

Garmonsway, G.N, Jacqueline Simpson, and Hilda Ellis Davidson. 1968. *Beowulf and Its Analogues.* London: J.M. Dent & Sons.

Gering, Hugo. 1880. 'Der *Beówulf* und die islaendische *Grettissaga.*' *Anglia,* 3: 74-87.

Gordon, E.V. 1927. *An Introduction to Old Norse.* Oxford: Clarendon Press.

Halvorsen, Eyvind Fjeld. 1974. 'Troll.' In Finn Hødnebø (ed.), *Kulturhistorisk Leksikon for nordisk middelater,* vol. 18. Oslo: Gyldendal Norsk Forlag. 655-7.

Harris, Richard L. 1973. 'The Deaths of Grettir and Grendel: A New Parallel.' *Scripta Islandica,* 24: 25-53.

Hastrup, Kirsten. 1990. *Island of Anthropology: Studies in Past and Present Iceland.* The Viking Collection: Studies in Northern Civilization. Vol. 5. Odense: Odense University Press.

Hughes, Geoffrey. 1977. 'Beowulf, Unferth and Hrunting: An Interpretation.' *English Studies,* 58: 385-95.

Janzén, Assar. 1947. *Nordisk Kultur VII Personnamn.* Stockholm: Albert Bonniers Forlag.

Jónsson, Guðni (ed.). 1936. *Grettis saga Ásmundarsonar. Íslenzk fornrit,* 7. Reykjavík: Hið íslenzka fornritafélag.

———(Ed.). 1953. *Íslendinga sögur.* 12 vols. Reykjavík: Íslendingasagnaútgáfan.

———(Ed.). 1954. *Edda Snorra Sturlusonar, Nafnaþulur og Skáldskapartal.* Reykjavík: Íslendingasagnaútgáfan.

Jorgensen, Peter A. 1973. 'Grendel, Grettir, and Two Skaldic Stanzas.' *Scripta Islandica,* 24: 54-61.

Kennedy, Charles W. (trans.). 1940. *Beowulf: The Oldest English Epic.* New York: Oxford University Press.

Kiessling, Nicolas K. 1968. 'Grendel: A New Aspect.' *Modern Philology,* 65: 191-201.

Klaeber, Fr. (ed.). 1922. *Beowulf and the Fight at Finnsburg.* 1st ed. Boston: D.C. Heath.

———1950. *Beowulf and the Fight at Finnsburg.* 3rd ed. Boston: D.C. Heath.

Kögel, R. 1892. 'Beowulf.' *Zeitschrift für deutsches Altertum,* 37: 268-76.

Lawrence, William Witherle. 1912. 'The Haunted Mere in *Beowulf.*' *PMLA,* 27: 208-45.

———1928. *Beowulf and Epic Tradition.* Cambridge, Mass.: Harvard University Press.

Lehmann, Edv. 1901. 'Fandens oldemor.' *Dania,* 8: 179-94.

Liberman, Anatoly. 1986. 'Beowulf-Grettir.' In Bela Brogyanyi and Thomas Krömmelbein (eds.), *Germanic Dialects: Linguistic and Philological Investigations.* Amsterdam and Philadelphia: John Benjamins Publishing Company. 353-401.

Liestöl, Knut. 1930. 'Beowulf and Epic Tradition.' *The American-Scandinavian Review,* 6: 370-3.

Magnússon, Ásgeir Blöndal. 1989. *Íslensk orðsifjabók.* Reykjavík: Orðabók Háskólans.

Malone, Kemp. 1932. 'Review of *Beowulf: An Introduction to the Study of the Poem with a Discussion of the Stories of Offa and Finn* by R.W. Chambers.' *English Studies,* 14: 190-3.

————1958. 'Grendel and His Abode.' In A.G. Hatcher and K.L. Selig (eds.), *Studia Philologica et Litteraria in Honorem L. Spitzer.* Bern: Francke Verlag. 297-308.

McConchie, R.W. 1982. 'Grettir Ásmundarson's Fight with Kárr the Old: A Neglected *Beowulf* Analogue.' *English Studies,* 63: 481-6.

Motz, Lotte. 1982. 'Giants in Folklore and Mythology: A New Approach.' *Folklore,* 93: 70-84.

Pálsson, Hermann. 1980. 'Glámsýni í Grettlu.' In Jónas Kristjánsson (ed.). *Gripla,* 4. Reykjavík: Stofnun Árna Magnússonar. 95-101.

Panzer, Friedrich. 1910. *Studien zur germanischen Sagengeschichte.* Vol. 1. *Beowulf.* Munich: C.H. Beck'sche Verlagsbuchhandlung.

Powell, F. York. 1900. 'Review of Boer's Edition of *Grettis saga.*' *Folklore,* 11: 406-14.

————1901. 'Béowulf and Watanabe-No-Tsuna.' In *An English Miscellany Presented to Dr. Furnivall in Honour of his Seventy-Fifth Birthday.* Oxford: Clarendon Press. 395-6.

Robinson, Fred C. 1974. 'Elements of the Marvellous in the Characterization of Beowulf.' In Robert B. Burlin and Edward B. Irving (eds.), *Old English Studies in Honour of John C. Pope.* Toronto: University of Toronto Press. 119-37.

Rosenberg, Bruce A. 1975. 'Folktale Morphology and the Structure of *Beowulf:* A Counterproposal.' *Journal of the Folklore Institute* [Indiana University], 11: 199-209.

Rosier, James L. 1962. 'Design for Treachery: The Unferth Intrigue.' *PMLA,* 77: 1-8.

————1963. 'The Uses of Association: Hands and Feasts in *Beowulf.*' *PMLA,* 78: 8-14.

Shetelig, Haakon, and Hjalmar Falk. 1937. *Scandinavian Archaeology.* Trans. E.V. Gordon. Oxford: Clarendon Press.

Stedman, Douglas. 1913. 'Some Points of Resemblance Between *Beowulf* and the *Grettla* (or *Grettis Saga*).' *Saga Book of the Viking Society,* 8 (Part 1): 6-28.

Sydow, Carl W. von. 1923. 'Beowulf och Bjarke.' *Studier i nordisk filologi* 14:3. In *Skrifter utgivna av svenska litteratursällskapet i Finland,* 170. 1-46.

Taylor, A.R. 1952. 'Two Notes on *Beowulf.*' *Leeds Studies in English and Kindred Languages,* 7 and 8: 5-17.

Unwerth, Wolf von. 1911. *Untersuchungen über Totenkult und Ódinnverehrung bei Nordgermanen und Lappen mit Excursen zur altnordischen Literaturgeschichte.* Germanistische Abhandlungen, 37. Heft. Breslau: Verlag von M. & H. Marcus.

Vigfusson, Gudbrand (ed.). 1878. *Sturlunga Saga Including the Islendinga Saga of Lawman Sturla Thordsson and Other Works.* Vol. 1. Oxford: Clarendon Press.

Vigfusson, Gudbrand, and F. York Powell (eds.). 1879. *An Icelandic Prose Reader with Notes, Grammar and Glossary.* Oxford: Clarendon Press.

————1883. *Corpus Poeticum Boreale: The Poetry of the Old Northern Tongue.* Vol. 2. Oxford: Clarendon Press.

Wachsler, Arthur, A. 1985. 'Grettir's Fight with a Bear: Another Neglected Analogue of *Beowulf* in the *Grettis Sage Asmundarsonar.*' *English Studies,* 66: 381-90.

Wardale, E.E. 1965. *Chapters on Old English Literature.* New York: Russell & Russell.

FURTHER READING

Criticism

Arent, A. Margaret. "The Heroic Pattern: Old Germanic Helmets, *Beowulf,* and *Grettis Saga.*" In *Old Norse Literature and Mythology: A Symposium,* edited by Edgar C. Polomé, pp. 130-99. Austin: University of Texas Press, 1969.
    Cautions against drawing quick conclusions from similarities between the *Grettis Saga* and *Beowulf.*

Cook, Robert. "The Reader in *Grettis Saga.*" *Saga-Book* 21, Nos. 3-4 (1984): 133-54.
    Offers modern reader-response interpretations of assorted episodes in the *Grettis Saga.*

Hume, Kathryn. "The Thematic Design of *Grettis Saga.*" *Journal of English and Germanic Philology* 73 (1974): 469-86.
    Proposes that the theme of the *Grettis Saga,* namely that the traditional hero has no place in modern society, came to the author first, and that the plot of the saga followed and conformed to this theme.

Wachsler, Arthur A. "Grettir's Fight with a Bear: Another Neglected Analogue of *Beowulf* in the *Grettis Sage Asmundarsonar.*" *English Studies: A Journal of English Language and Literature* 66, No. 5 (October 1985): 381-90.
    Examines similarities between the bear episodes in the *Grettis Saga* and *Beowulf.*

Heike Monogatari

c. 1218-21. Japanese prose epic.

INTRODUCTION

The *Heike Monogatari (The Tale of the Heike)* is considered one of the greatest masterpieces of Japanese literature. A martial epic deeply influenced by Buddhism, it describes the events that led from the end of a long peaceful period to the revolutionary Genpei War, which was waged between the Taira (or Heike) family and the Minamoto (or Genji) clan from 1177 to 1185. The tale concludes with the annihilation of the Heike clan. Scholars believe that Yukinaga was the author of the original text of the *Heike Monogatari*, called the *Shibu kassenjo*. Yukinaga reportedly taught the blind monk Shobutsu to recite the tale, and Shobutsu helped write the portions dealing with war. This first version, written in a combination of Japanese and Chinese, is now lost. The *Heike Monogatari* was chanted by blind musician-monks who accompanied themselves on Japanese lutes. They wandered the country, singing the tale wherever they found people who were interested. The story enthralled its audience and led to well over one hundred variant editions spanning a period of approximately a century and a half. The text considered standard for the last six hundred years was written by Akashi Kakuichi, a blind singer, who finished dictating his version shortly before his death in 1371. Although the *Heike Monogatari* has been accepted as legitimate history by general readers for centuries, modern scholars realize that the fictional elements of the tale outnumber the factual. For all its romanticism, however, the *Heike Monogatari* vividly describes how the courtier class gave way to the warrior class. It has also inspired countless other Japanese works based on its characters and incidents.

PLOT AND MAJOR CHARACTERS

The period covered in the *Heike Monogatari* is ninety years, from 1131 to 1221. The focus, though, is on eighteen years, from when Taira no Kiyomori assumed leadership in 1167 until the destruction of the Heike forces at Dan-no-ura. The *Heike Monogatari* draws much of its factual material from diaries and temple records. Most of the tale is presented chronologically, although there are generous insertions of myths and legends, often dealing with Buddhist philosophy and practice. Additionally, ninety-seven short poems are included. The first half of the work describes the power and pride of the Taira and includes unsympathetic accounts of Kiyomori's outrageous behavior. Readers have sometimes been disturbed by the central character acting so shamelessly, but the work does not aim to glorify each of its actors. Taira no Shigemori, Kiyomori's son, is much the opposite of his father. He is sound in judgement, practices Confucianism, and is merciful. He represents the traditional rights of the royal family and its courtiers. Some chapters of the *Heike Monogatari* are mostly devoted to individual characters, including Yoshinaka, a great Genji fighter but poor leader, and Yoshitsune, also a victor at war. The second half of the *Heike Monogatari* concerns the battles of the Genpei War, climaxing with the abandonment of the capital by the Taira. Initially, battles are described in general terms, but later the narrative personalizes war by describing the specific acts of heroes. The most famous of all the battles depicted is that which was fought at Mikusa. The Heike are barricaded near the ocean in a fort which Genji forces have found impenetrable. One side of the fort is a steep cliff, and the Heike believed it was unnecessary to protect themselves on that side because no one could possibly climb down such a precipitous cliff and attack from it. The Genji, however, accomplish the impossible and descend on horseback. They vanquish the Heike and order those they spare to swim to their boats in the harbor.

MAJOR THEMES

The *Heike Monogatari* mainly concerns itself with the fall of the Heike courtiers and the concurrent rise of a new warrior class in Japan. Differences between aspects of the old and new moralities constitute one of the main themes of the work, and much attention is focused on the warrior code, so central to Japanese culture. Another thematic focus is Buddhist philosophy, especially as it relates to man's vain nature and the uncertainties and transitory nature of life.

CRITICAL RECEPTION

Critics point out that perhaps no other story has ever captured the imagination of the Japanese public as has the *Heike Monogatari*. It has often been deemed the Japanese equivalent of the *Iliad* and it appeal has been wide; in addition to English, it has been translated into French, Chinese, Russian, and Czech. Scholars frequently focus on the textual development of the tale. Although the exact chronology of the major revisions and the interaction between oral versions and written texts can never be totally resolved, there is much broad agreement. Most scholars believe the *Heike Monogatari* began its life as a written text and then was revised for recitation. There is some disagreement over the matter of whether before the modern twelve-scroll version there existed three-scroll and six-scroll versions; most scholars are skeptical of the existence of the three-scroll version, but more accepting of the possibility of the six-scroll text. Through the process of being told over and over by professional storytellers, the work evolved and improved. Its ultimate form, critics agree, is the nearly perfect rendition of Kakuichi, which unites the best of written and oral styles. Scholars also find the *Heike* a rich source for the study of Japanese history and culture. Kenneth Dean Butler has made a case that the depiction of the Heike as given by the blind singers led to the code of the warrior: "We therefore have the paradox of the Japanese of later ages modeling their actions not on those of the Gempei warriors as they actually were, but rather upon the ideal warrior as conceived by oral singers who formed their heroes by means of formulaic techniques of oral composition." William E. Naff states that although the Heike Monogatari was "created for a society of warriors it is unflinchingly realistic about both the physical and the moral shortcomings of the warrior's trade. It is almost entirely free of the morbid and obsessive preoccupation with the minutiae of slaughter and mutilation which military tales the world around so often offer as a counterfeit of honesty about their subject."

PRINCIPAL WORKS

Principal English Translations

The Heike Monogatari (translated by Arthur Sadler in *Transactions of the Asiatic Society of Japan*) 1918 and 1921

The Tale of the Heike (translated by Hiroshi Kitagawa and Bruce T. Tsuchida) 1975

The Tale of the Heike (translated by Helen Craig McCullough) 1988

CRITICISM

Kenneth Dean Butler (essay date 1966)

SOURCE: "The Textual Evolution of the *Heike Monogatari*" in *Harvard Journal of Asiatic Studies*, Vol. 26, No. 5, 1966, pp. 5-51.

[*In the following excerpt, Butler examines the authorship and dates of creation of the* Shibu *text, arguing for its acceptance as the original* Heike Monogatari.]

. . . THE AUTHORSHIP OF THE *SHIBU* TEXT

The starting point for all investigations of the authorship of the original *Heike monogatari* has been the following section of the *Tsurezuregusa,* a miscellany written by Yoshida Kenkō (1282-1350) about the year 1330.

Section No. 226: During the time of the Retired Emperor Go-Toba,[1] the former Governor of Shinano Yukinaga[2] was renowned for his learning, but because he forgot two of the virtues of the "Dance of Seven Virtues"[3] when he took his turn in discourse on *yüeh-fu,* he was given the sobriquet of "Five Virtues Kanja."[4] Feeling miserable, he forsook scholarship and took Buddhist vows. The Priest of the First Rank Jichin[5] took people even of low rank who had some artistic talent into his service and carefully looked after them, and so he gave this Shinamo Lay Priest a stipend.

This Lay Priest Yukinaga composed the ***Heike monogatari,*** taught it to a blind man named Shōbutsu,[6] and had him recite it. Now he wrote especially well of matters concerning the Enryaku-ji. He was well informed of events concerning Kurō Hōgan,[7] and in writing included them. But evidently not knowing much of events concerning Kaba no Kanja,[8] he failed to record many things. As for matters concerning warriors and the arts of archery and horsemanship, Shōbutsu, being from the Eastland, questioned warriors and had it written down [by Yukinaga]. The natural voice of this Shōbutsu is studied by present-day *biwa hōshi.*[9]

Although Yoshida Kenkō certainly made no particular effort to include in the *Tsurezuregusa* only historically accurate information, research shows that a good part of what he wrote has some basis in historical fact. This is true of the above account. It is not correct in every detail, and contains a certain amount of erroneous interpretation, but some of the information given about the authorship of the ***Heike*** seems to be close to what the actual facts must have been. The three major points made by Kenkō are: (1) the attribution of the authorship of the original ***Heike monogatari*** to the Lay Priest Yukinaga; (2) the statement that Yukinaga was connected with Jichin; and (3) the dating of the ***Heike*** at the time of the retired Emperor Go-Toba (1198-1221). The first two points will be considered here, and the third one taken up in the following section.

The scholarship concerning the above *Tsurezuregusa* section would be tedious to relate in full, but in summary, the accepted interpretation of this entry is that Yukinaga did in fact write the original ***Heike monogatari,*** which was a text written for recitation, but that this text has been lost, and all of the preserved ***Heike monogatari*** manuscripts are revisions deriving from Yukinaga's original recited text. But when the *Tsurezuregusa* information is compared with evidence concerning the textual evolution of the ***Heike*** derived from study and comparison of the early manuscripts, a basic contradiction becomes apparent. Yoshida Kenkō stresses Yukinaga's renown and ability as a scholar of Chinese learning, and other historical records substantiate this. If Yukinaga did write the original ***Heike monogatari,*** it would be reasonable to suppose that he wrote it in *kambun,* the "literary language" of a Chinese scholar.[10] But by the statement, "taught it to . . . Shōbutsu and had him recite it," the *Tsurezuregusa* account implies that Yukinaga's original ***Heike*** was a recited text,[11] and there are no pure *kambun* versions of the ***Heike*** that were written and used as recited texts.

What seems to have happened in the *Tsurezuregusa* account is that while correctly attributing authorship of the original **Heike monogatari** to Yukinaga, Yoshida Kenkō has erred in implying that this was a recited text. In effect, he has confused the later revision of the *kambun Shibu* text for recitation with the original writing of the text, and in so doing has compressed at least thirty years of textual development to make it appear that the **Heike monogatari** was originally written for the purpose of providing a fixed text for recitation. This is a natural mistake for one of Yoshida Kenkō's period to make, since the date of the *Tsurezuregusa* roughly corresponds to the time Kakuichi was producing his refined recited version of the **Heike.** At this time recitation of the **Heike monogatari** was becoming so popular[12] that it obscured the fact that the original **Heike monogatari** prior to revision for recitation was a pseudo-historical chronicle, intended to be read, not recited.

A complete account of Yukinaga's life as it can be reconstructed from the records and diaries of the early Kamakura period is available in Japanese.[13] Here only the highlights need be related. Yukinaga was born about the year 1164,[14] the second son of Nakayama (Hamuro) Yukitaka, a man mentioned in Kujō Kanezane's diary and other records of the period as having been in charge of rebuilding the Great Buddha Pavilion of the Tōdai-ji in Nara.[15] Yukitaka is mentioned many times in the *Gyokuyō,* and it seems clear that he was on intimate terms with Kanezane.[16] Due perhaps to Yukitaka's connections, we find Yukinaga listed in the *Gyokuyō* entry of Bunji 6:4,10 (1190)[17] as one of Kanezane's family retainers, although it is not clear when he assumed this relationship. In the *Gyokuyō* entry of Kenkyū 5:9,17 (1194), Yukinaga is listed as "Yukinaga, Governor of Shimotsuke,"[18] and Japanese scholars have suggested that in the *Tsurezuregusa* account, Shinano is a mistake for Shimotsuke.[19] In an entry in the *Sanchōki* dated Kenkyū 6:8,15 (1195), we find Yukinaga listed as again without court office,[20] and this is generally accepted as indicating that his tenure as provincial governor ended at about this time.[21] The *Sanchōki* entry is of interest also in that Yukinaga's name is listed with that of Fujiwara Teika (1162-1241), of *Shinkokinshū* fame. This is understood to indicate that Yukinaga's position was of a level similar to Teika's.[22] In addition to his court rank and status as a retainer of Kanezane, Yukinaga was quite well known as a Chinese poet and scholar of Chinese learning. He is mentioned in several records as having taken part in various Chinese poetry contests and such, and seems to have been above average in talent.[23] By the year 1212, Yukinaga had become a retainer of Yoshisuke (d. 1218), Kujō Kanezane's son.[24] Yoshisuke is referred to in the *Gukanshō* (p. 323) as being "unparalleled in either past or present in his ability in Chinese learning," and it may have been due to a similarity of interests that Yukinaga became a retainer of Yoshisuke. The fact that Kanezane died in 1207, and his eldest son, Yoshitsune, preceded him in death by one year, is also undoubtedly relevant to Yukinaga's finally entering the service of Yoshisuke.

Now in the *Tsurezuregusa* account, it states that Yukinaga, as a result of humiliation at the time he discoursed on one of Po Chü-i's poems, had taken Buddhist vows and entered the service of the Priest of the First Rank Jichin. Jichin, or Jien, as he is better known to history, was the younger brother of Kanezane, Yukinaga's former master, and uncle of Yoshisuke, Yukinaga's master in the year 1212. This in itself tends to make plausible the *Tsurezuregusa* statement. There is no record giving the date or the fact that Yukinaga took Buddhist vows, but if we follow the *Tsurezuregusa* and consider that it was after formal discourse on the *hsin yüeh-fu* poetry of Po Chü-i during the time of the Retired Emperor Go-Toba (1198-1221), then there are only two possible dates for this event. One is the "Fifth Discourse on *yüeh-fu*" held on Jōgen 4:3,15 (1210),[25] and the other is the "Sixth Discussion of the Works of Po" held on Kempō 6:6,3 (1218).[26] If Yukinaga did in fact retire from the world after one of these two events and then write the **Heike monogatari,** the later date of 1218 would be the more likely, since Yukinaga's name appears in the diary of Fujiwara Teika in the years 1212 and 1213 as still a man of this world.[27] A further fact serving to suggest that Yukinaga may have taken vows in 1218 is that during this year his second master, Yoshisuke, also died. This, coupled with the previous deaths of Kanezane and Yoshisuke's elder brother Yoshitsune, suggests the possibility that with the loss of his secular masters, Yukinaga would renounce the world and enter the service of the Buddhist priest Jien, the remaining adult member of the Kujō Fujiwara family.

From the preceding brief account of Yukinaga's life it can be seen that he possessed the two important qualities necessary for authorship of the *Shibu* text: one, he was a scholar and poet of Chinese literature, hence skilled in *kambun;* and two, he was a retainer of Kujō Kanezane and members of his family, and therefore in a position to have had access to the *Gyokuyō.* When we look at the *Shibu* text itself, in addition to the Kanezane *sesshō* section, several other of its features serve also to point to Yukinaga as its author. First, of all the **Heike monogatari** variant manuscripts, the *Shibu* is most permeated with political and philosophical concepts which are traceable to Jien, the political theoretician of the Kujō family. Jien's political philosophy is presented in his work, the *Gukanshō.*[28] When various sections of the *Shibu* are investigated, it can be seen that the author has incorporated several of Jien's basic ideas. A "Dream Section" of *maki* 5, to be discussed later in connection with dating the *Shibu,* is one of these. Another conspicuous example appears towards the end of *maki* 1, in a section describing an attack on Kyoto by Buddhist monks from a temple connected with the Enryaku-ji on Mt. Hiei. Here there is a long digression, which does not appear in any of the other **Heike** variant manuscripts, concerning the function of the Enryaku-ji, the temple headed by Jien, as spiritual protector of the Japanese Court.[29] This idea was not original with Jien, but it was basic to his over-all scheme of thought and was strongly advocated by him as part of his general plan to seize political control of Japan for the Kujō family in the early part of the thirteenth century.[30] Since this section does not appear in any other *Heike* variant, it seems possible that it was included in the *Shibu* text by Yukinaga due to Jien's influence. Then by a process similar to that observable in the Kanezane *sesshō* appointment section, it was dropped out in the later recited revisions, as being disruptive to the basic narrative of the Heike story.

Another feature connecting Yukinaga with the *Shibu* is the treatment given his father, Yukitaka. Yukitaka was a rather minor official in comparison with the major figures who make up the principal characters of the *Heike monogatari,* but he is mentioned several times in the *Shibu* text in circumstances which suggest the author had a personal reason for including him. The longest account of Yukitaka in the *Shibu* comes towards the end of *maki* 3, and covers four full pages. This account relates that Yukitaka had been dismissed from office and was living in retirement, but that after Kiyomori, the Heike leader, achieved power, he granted Yukitaka many presents and had him reappointed to the office of *ben,* or "Controller." The *Shibu* account reads as follows:

> There was a person called the former Lesser Controller of the Left Yukitaka, eldest son of the deceased Nakayama Middle Counselor Lord Akitoki.[31] During the time of the Retired Emperor Nijō,[32] he was a personal retainer and at the time that he became a Controller, he passed over the Lesser Controller of the Right Nagafusa and attained [the position of] the Left.[33] At the time he was appointed to the Full Fifth Rank also, he passed over eight outstanding men, and [his rise] was phenomenal. But after the death of the Retired Emperor Nijō, he lost his prosperity, and on Nin'an 1:4,18 (1166) he resigned his office. After entering retirement, he for long lost all prospects; he passed fifteen years of spring and fall without changing his summer and winter clothing, and the intervals between the smoke of morning and evening [cooking fires] were many.[34] As he spent his days weeping sad tears, on the sixteenth [of the month (1180)] as evening deepened, there was a messenger from the residence of the Lay Priest Prime Minister[35] who said [for Kiyomori], "Come! There is a matter I must discuss." Yukitaka was greatly excited, wondering what this matter was. "Many people are meeting with misfortune, what should I do? I have not been involved in anything for these [past] fourteen years, but despite this there must have been someone who slandered me and said that I was planning an uprising. He said to come immediately, but I have no oxcart," [he said] worrying. He sent a messenger to his younger brother, the one called the former Major of the Left Military Guards, to tell him of this matter and request that he send an oxcart and court clothing. His wife and sons were sick at heart and wept, wondering what would happen. Finally he went to the Nishihachijō Residence[36] and met the Lay Priest, who said: "In addition to being friends with the deceased Middle Counselor,[37] I especially discussed all matters great and small [with him], and I regret his passing. I do not intend to neglect you. Your retirement has been long and I have regretted this, but since it was the will of the Priestly Retired Emperor [Go-Shirakawa], I have been powerless. [But] now you should be employed. I have

> arranged everything." [Yukitaka] returned to his residence, and when he reported that the Lay Priest had said this, beginning with his wife, [everyone] wept together in happiness. The following morning the Gen Fifth Rank Lieutenant Suesada came bringing a small-eight-leaved cart[38] drawn by the Lay Priest's oxen, with driver and livery, and in addition to presenting [Yukitaka] with one hundred *hiki* and one hundred *koku,*[39] [he said that] [Yukitaka] would immediately be reappointed as Controller. [Yukitaka] was so happy he could not speak and did not know where to wave his arms or stamp his feet. The entire family felt it indeed must all be a dream

> (3.60a1-62a1).

Like the Kanezane *sesshō* appointment section of the *Shibu* discussed previously, this section concerning Yukitaka's reappointment as *ben* has no connection with the narrative preceding or following it. It therefore seems to have been inserted as a result of some direct interest on the part of the *Shibu* author. Considered in terms of Yukinaga's probable authorship of the *Shibu,* the reason for this becomes apparent. By associating his father with the great events and personages related in the *Heike monogatari,* Yukinaga probably hoped to show that his family also had some claim to fame.

In addition to connecting Yukinaga with the *Shibu* text, the Yukitaka section also sheds light on Yukinaga's reason for writing the *Heike monogatari* and on the bias his work displays. First, although the Genji were the final victors in the Genji-Heike confrontation, in the *Shibu* (and subsequently in the *Yashiro* and *Kakuichi* recited variants) the Heike, rather than the Genji, are the focal point of the narrative and are depicted in a sympathetic manner.[40] Secondly, the Cloister Emperor Go-Shirakawa, although nominally the expected rallying point for the court nobles against both the Heike and the Genji warrior groups, is never developed as a character in the *Shibu* to the extent one would expect on the basis of his direct involvement in most of the major events related. When he does appear in the narrative, he is usually depicted from a rather hostile point of view.[41] These two aspects of the *Shibu* would suggest that its author was probably someone with connections with the Heike and also one bearing animosity for Go-Shirakawa. In the early part of the Yukitaka section, Yukinaga's father is pictured as having had a phenomenal career under the patronage of the Emperor Nijō, but being forced to retire completely from court life after Go-Shirakawa emerged as the ruling power in Kyoto. In the latter part of the section the opposition of Go-Shirakawa is made even more explicit by having Kiyomori state that Yukitaka's retirement was due specifically to the will of Go-Shirakawa. In the latter part also, we are shown that it was Kiyomori, the Heike leader, who rescued Yukitaka from retirement and started him once again on his official career. It is perhaps not forcing the interpretation too much to assume that the aid given Yukinaga's family by Kiyomori was responsible at least in part for his motive in writing his account of the Heike, and also for his sympathetic treatment of them. Similarly, by showing that Go-

Shirakawa was responsible for his family's long privations, Yukinaga indicates the basis for his animosity towards Go-Shirakawa, and this is consistent with the treatment given Go-Shirakawa throughout the *Shibu* text.

One further point which tends to fill in the picture of Yukinaga's authorship of the *Shibu* is an entry dated Jōkyū 2:4,22 (1220) in the *Gyokuzui*, the diary of Kujō Michiie (1193-1252), grandson of Kanezane and *sesshō* prior to the Jōkyū War of 1221. Michiie mentions that he sent a certain Nagatame to the residence of Mitsumori, son of Kiyomori's brother Taira Yorimori (1132-1186), to borrow and copy the many "*Heike kiji*" possessed by Mitsumori.[42] There has been some question as to what sense should be given to the term *kiji* in this entry. The most recent interpretation is that it refers to some type of "Heike story" which was written prior to the original ***Heike monogatari***.[43] The normal meaning of the word *kiji* is, however, "records." On the basis of Yukinaga's probable authorship of the *Shibu* text, and his connection with the Kujō family, another possible interpretation of this entry would be that the "*Heike kiji*" were personal family records of the Heike in the possession of the one remaining branch of the Heike, that stemming from Yorimori.[44] As will be shown in the following section, the *Shibu* text was being written during the year 1220, and it is possible that Kanezane's grandson Michiie borrowed and had copied such Heike records for Yukinaga to use as historical source material in writing sections of the ***Heike monogatari***.

THE DATES OF COMPOSITION OF THE *SHIBU* AND *YASHIRO* TEXTS

Internal evidence can be found in the *Shibu* text of the ***Heike monogatari*** which establishes with a fair degree of certainty that it was written during the years 1218-1221. These dates fall within the period when Go-Toba held the title of Retired Emperor (1198-1221), given in the *Tsurezuregusa* as the date for the writing of the original ***Heike monogatari***. The terminal date of 1221 may be derived as follows. At the end of *maki* 12 of the *Shibu* text, following the account of the search for and execution of Heike descendants and retainers, which appears after the Rokudai Gozen story and the Kanezane *sesshō* account, there is the following passage, referring to an incident in 1199:

Mongaku,[45] being by nature a person of immoderate temperament, [felt that] the reigning Emperor [Go-Toba] gave himself over solely to pleasures, and knew nothing of the government of the world. After causing Lord Kujō's[46] retirement, [the reigning Emperor] lived at [the residence of] Kyō no Tsubone,[47] and paid no heed to the afflictions of the people. Since the Second Imperial Prince[48] alone did not neglect learning and put proper principles first, [Mongaku] planned to place him on the throne, and have him carry on the government of the world; but while the Udaishō [Yoritomo] was living it was impossible. But after [the Udaishō] passed away on Shōji 1:1, 13 [1199], when it was reported that [Mongaku] was still planning this matter, Mongaku immediately incurred the censure of the Retired Emperor; *kembiishi*[49] were sent to his residence at Nijō

Inokuma,[50] and he was banished to Tosa province. After that Rokudai Gozen had not been at Takao[51] at all, making pilgrimages . . .

(12.48b3-49a5).

This section presents much that is important in dating the *Shibu* text and connecting it with Yukinaga. First, we again have mention of Lord Kujō (Kanezane). His forced retirement from the office of *sesshō* was an act traceable ultimately to Go-Toba, which paved the way for Go-Toba's own attempt at forming an *insei* government led by himself, and one which incurred for Go-Toba the lasting enmity of Jien and the Kujō family.[52] There is no logical reason for reference to be made to it here, however, unless the author did so in order to express obliquely his dissatisfaction with Go-Toba's dismissal of Kanezane by associating it with criticism of Go-Toba's conduct. Secondly, the Retired Emperor Go-Toba led the attack on the Kamakura *bakufu,* known as the Jōkyū War,[53] in 1221 and was subsequently banished to Oki province. No mention is made of this event in the *Shibu* account, although it does appear in this section in all other ***Heike*** variants. This discrepancy suggests that the *Shibu* account was written prior to Go-Toba's banishment in 1221. Further evidence to this effect is the circumlocution achieved by the term "the Reigning Emperor." Go-Toba was Reigning Emperor from 1184 to 1198. Afterwards he was Retired Emperor until his banishment in 1221; and after other Emperors retired, he was referred to as Senior Retired Emperor. Following his banishment to Oki province in 1221 until his death in 1239, Go-Toba was referred to as "the Retired Emperor at Oki". He did not receive the posthumous title of Go-Toba-in until 1242, three years after his death. The use of proper terminology in the *Shibu* text in referring to Go-Toba prior to 1196 only as *tōkon*, and after this date in 1199 as *in,* and the failure to use the term Oki no In or Go-Toba-in, together with the failure to mention the Jōkyū War and Go-Toba's banishment to Oki, may be adduced as evidence that the *Shibu* text was written prior to 1221. This becomes apparent when the treatment given the same section in the *Yashiro* text, which was definitely written after 1221, is considered. The corresponding *Yashiro* section reads as follows:

At that time the term Reigning Emperor referred to Go-Toba-in. He gave himself over to pleasures, and since all under heaven was following completely the will of Kyō no Nii,[54] the grief and affliction of the world was unending. Mongaku of Takao, viewing this, grieved over the perilous condition of the world, and since the Second Imperial Prince did not neglect learning and put proper principles first, he planned somehow to place him on the throne. However, while Kamakura no Udaishō was living, he did not, after all, mention it, and the Reigning Emperor abdicated in favor of the First Imperial Prince.[55] After Kamakura no Udaishō Yoritomo died on Shōji 1:1 [1199], when Mongaku attempted this affair, it was immediately reported, and he was arrested, and at the age of over eighty-two he was banished to Oki province. Since the Retired Emperor was fond to excess of bat-ball,[56] at the time he was punished by the Punishment Official and the Prisoner Escort,[57] and driven from the capital, [Mongaku] gave vent to many insults. Saying, "Would that in the end I meet that bat-ball scamp in the place where I am banished," he was banished. When he arrived in Oki province he at length died of melancholy. Although he was fearful in manner, he was foolish. However, when in the summer of the third year of Jōkyū [1221], the Senior Retired Emperor attempted to attack Ukyō no Gon no Taifu Yoshitoki,[58] he was defeated in battle; although there were many places, that he should be sent to Oki province was indeed sad. Rokudai Gozen, under the name of Sammi no Zenshi was practicing religious austerities, but after . . .

(12.60b7-61b8).

In this section of the *Yashiro* several revisions and expansions of the *Shibu* narrative have occurred. First, the reference to Go-Toba (*tōkon*, "Reigning Emperor," in the *Shibu* text) is made explicit by the opening statement: "At that time the term Reigning Emperor referred to Go-Toba-in," as though the *Yashiro* revisor were providing a gloss to the *Shibu* text, which he apparently was. The use of the term Go-Toba-in indicates beyond doubt that the *Yashiro* text was written after 1242, the year Go-Toba was given this name.[59] Another important difference between the two accounts is that in the *Yashiro* there is no mention of Kanezane's dismissal from the office of *sesshō*. The *Yashiro* revisor was working at a time more than fifty years after the event, and undoubtedly had no connection with Kujō descendants, whereas Kanezane's dismissal was a very real event to the *Shibu* author, Yukinaga, and probably for this reason given prominence by him in his criticism of Go-Toba.

An even more significant revision in the *Yashiro* text of the *Shibu* account in terms of content, is the mention of the Jōkyū War and the change of Mongaku's place of banishment from Tosa province to Oki province. It is historical fact that after the abortive Jōkyū War Go-Toba was banished to Oki. Knowing of this, the *Yashiro* revisor evidently wanted to provide a more dramatic effect, and therefore changed Mongaku's place of banishment to Oki province also.[60] By the final stage of the *Kakuichi* text of 1371, the end of this passage appears as: "Furthermore, when in the Jōkyū period [the Retired Emperor Go-Toba] raised a rebellion, although there were numerous provinces, that he should be sent to Oki province is indeed unaccountable. It was rumored that Mongaku's ghost was roaming about in that province and frequently talked to him" (*KBT* 33, 421-422).

There are several other elements of the above *Yashiro* section, such as the addition of identifying tags to the titles of personages to make the narrative more suited to oral presentation, and various other expansions, which mark it as a revision of the *Shibu* account. When the *Shibu* section of *maki* 12 is thus considered in terms of this *Yashiro* revision, the evidence seems conclusive that it was written prior to the Jōkyū War in 1221. There are no sections of the twelve *maki* of the *Shibu* which can be shown to have necessarily been written after 1221, so that this may be taken as the approximate terminal date for its writing.[61]

In determining the earliest date the writing of the *Shibu* could have been begun, an account of a dream presented in *maki* 5 is of importance. In brief, it is related that a Genji retainer in Kyoto had a dream which foretold that the Genji would take over rule of Japan from the Heike, and then in turn the Fujiwara would succeed the Genji in power. This section reads as follows:

> A dream had by a person serving Lord Gen Chūnagon Garai[62] was indeed portentous. He dreamed that at a place resembling the Bureau of Worship in the Palace, many people dressed in ceremonial robes and hats were assembled in deliberation. A person seated in the place of lowest rank, [who appeared to be] a partisan of the Lay Priest Prime Minister [Kiyomori], was driven out [of the meeting]. [Then] a person of brave and distinguished appearance, seated at the head [of the gathering], said, "The sword which previously had been entrusted to the Lay Priest Prime Minister should now be entrusted to Yoritomo." [Next] a person seated towards the middle said, "After that it should be entrusted to my descendants." Still dreaming, [Garai's retainer] stood up and approached a person near the door and asked who was [the person] at the head [of the group]. He answered, "The person on the corridor side is Hachiman no Daibosatsu. The one who said 'My descendants,' is Kasuga no Daimyōjin. The one who was driven away is Itsukushima no Daimyōjin." . . . After awaking from his dream [Garai's retainer] thought it was very strange, and because he told about having this dream, people broadcast it about. The Lay Priest heard of this and was very angry. He sent Yukitaka no Ason[63] to question Lord Garai, but nothing came of it. [Lord Garai said,] "After reporting this matter, the one who had the dream, and family, disappeared." That the Itsukushima no Daimyōjin was a partisan [of the Heike] was well known. But Saishō Nyūdō Shunken[64] [said], "Itsukushima is a female god, so I can understand this much. But it is strange that the Kasuga no Daimyōjin said, '[the sword] should be entrusted to my descendants.' Does this mean that in later years there will be a Fujiwara *taishōgun*?"

(5.16a6-18b1).

In this account, the sword is used figuratively to symbolize political and military control of Japan. The Hachiman no Daibosatsu was the protective god worshiped by Yoritomo, the Genji leader, while the Kasuga no Daimyōjin served the same function for the Fujiwara, and the Itsukushima no Daimyōjin was the family god of the Heike. The statement that the sword should ultimately be passed to the descendants of the Kasuga no Daimyōjin, that is, the Fujiwara, and the forecast of a Fujiwara *taishōgun* may be interpreted as referring to the dispatch in 1219 of a great-grandson of Kujō (Fujiwara) Kanezane to Kamakura to be *seii taishōgun* after the extinction of Yoritomo's line.[65] The appointment of Kanezane's great-grandson to the position of Shogun was part of the over-all *bumbu kenkō* (parallel rule by civil and military) scheme of Jien, which envisioned a Kujō family member as *sesshō* and a Kujō descendant as Emperor in Kyoto, at the same time a Kujō family member was Shogun in Kamakura. This, combined with Jien's position as the dominant figure of the Enryakuji, the Buddhist temple which traditionally was the protector of the Kyoto Court, would have given the Kujō family a monopoly on all of the important political and religious offices in Japan, and put them in a position, they felt, to usurp political power gradually from the Hōjō regents of the Genji *bakufu* in Kamakura.[66] This plan seemed to be on the verge of success in 1221, when the son of Kujō Yoshitsune's daughter was enthroned as Emperor, another grandson, the son of Michiie, was in Kamakura as the shogun-designate, and Michiie himself was *sesshō*. But the machinations of the Kujō were brought to an abrupt halt by Go-Toba's ill-advised attack on the Kamakura *bakufu* in the fifth month of 1221. By the time the Jōkyū War had ended, the Hōjō regents were in a position to exert directly their authority throughout Japan, and were in no need of political alliances with Court aristocrats such as the Kujō Fujiwara. Thus all prospects for a Fujiwara return to power were ended.

An awareness of this *bumbu kenkō* plan of Jien provides a key to understanding the *Shibu* dream section reference to power being passed to the Fujiwara. The Kujō had been trying to achieve political power ever since Kanezane first secured appointment as *sesshō* in 1186. But it was only during the later stages of the Kujō conspiracy that efforts were directed toward obtaining appointment of a Kujō as Shogun in Kamakura. Upon the death of Yoritomo's last son, the third Shogun Sanetomo (1192-1219), the Hōjō in Kamakura attempted to have one of Go-Toba's sons appointed as Shogun, apparently hoping by this move to make further inroads into the Imperial prerogatives. Go-Toba, realizing this and also undoubtedly by this time thinking of possibly attacking the *bakufu*, refused to allow it. Next, the infant son of Kujō Michiie was put forward as a candidate for Shogun, and it was at this time (1219) that the possibility of a Kujō Shogun suddenly materialized. Hence, if we take the reference to a Fujiwara Shogun in the dream section as referring to the appointment of Michiie's son, which by all calculations it must, then this indicates that at the time of writing this section, the *Shibu* author knew that his fictional prophecy "Does this mean that in later years there will be a Fujiwara *taishōgun*?" had already been, or was on the point of being, fulfilled. Therefore 1219, the year Michiie's son was sent to Kamakura as Shogun, may be taken as the earliest date possible for this part of *maki* 5. When this is combined with the previously estimated date of 1218 for Yukinaga's vow-taking, after which the *Tsurezuregusa* states he wrote the **Heike monogatari,** the year 1218 may be accepted as the approximate date that the writing of the *Shibu* was begun.

In the dream section of *maki* 5 of the *Yashiro* text, an account similar to the *Shibu* narrative is presented, but with the important difference that all mention of the Kasuga no Daimyōjin and the Fujiwara Shogun is omitted, and the account ends with the forecast of the Genji takeover from the Heike.[67] This is what one would expect from a text produced for public recitation after the year 1242. By this time the Hōjō were firmly entrenched as the legitimate representatives of the Genji *bakufu,* and they would have

undoubtedly objected strongly, just as Kiyomori is said to have done in the dream section, to public prediction of their demise.

In summary, on the basis of the narrative of the Mongaku banishment section of *maki* 12, the dream section of *maki* 5, and the *Tsurezuregusa* account, the composition of the *Shibu* text can be dated during the period 1218-1221. In addition, because the term Go-Toba is used in the *Yashiro* text, it can be dated at sometime after 1242.

THE *SHIBU* TEXT AS THE ORIGINAL *HEIKE MONOGATARI*

All of the foregoing considerations tend to corroborate Yoshida Kenkō's attribution in the *Tsurezuregusa* of the authorship of the original **Heike monogatari** to Yukinaga, and to point to the *Shibu* as being that original text. This poses several contradictions with traditional theories of the genesis of the **Heike.** First, if the *Shibu* chronicle is accepted as the original **Heike monogatari,** the theory that the original **Heike** was written for recitation is no longer credible. Once this idea is rejected, other historical references suggesting that the **Heike monogatari** was first written as a read text and then revised for recitation appear to have more validity than has heretofore been granted them. Two such references are as follows:

The *Heigo gūdan,* a work about **Heike monogatari** recitation written in 1827, states that in a manuscript of the *Nagato* read text of the **Heike,** which the author apparently had seen, there was the following notation: "The twelve *maki* wood-block printed book called the **Heike monogatari** has existed from the middle ages. This is [a work] which the person called Tameie, made on the basis of Yukinaga's original work, for the purpose of *biwa hōshi* singing."[68] It has been recently pointed out that this passage actually appears at the beginning of an early manuscript of the *Nagato* text acquired by Tenri University and that evidently this was the copy of the *Nagato* text viewed by the *Heigo gūdan* author.[69] Thus this notation probably dates from a period earlier than 1827, though just how early is not certain. It has been suggested that the Tameie referred to in this statement was Fujiwara Tameie (1198-1275), the son of Fujiwara Teika, and a Japanese poet of some note.[70] The dates of his life would place him at maturity at about the time the *Shibu* text was beginning to be revised for recitation, but there is no corroborating evidence showing he had a hand in such revision. In this case, like the *Tsurezuregusa* account, the *Nagato* text notation is probably only partially correct. At any rate, it does imply that prior to revision for recitation there was an original read text of the **Heike monogatari** authored by Yukinaga.

In the *kambun* work, *Gaun nikkenroku,* under the date of Bun'an 5:8,19 (1448), an interview with a certain Saiichi *kengyō,* a second generation disciple of Kakuichi, is mentioned. He is quoted as saying: "Of old, Lord Tamenaga wrote this twelve *maki* [**Heike monogatari**] while he was residing in Harima province. Afterwards, Shobutsu set this to music and recited it."[71] Here again, the relationship of both Tamenaga and Shōbutsu to the composition and revision of the *Heike monogatari* is unclear, but the entry does suggest that there was, among people concerned with *Heike* recitation in the fifteenth century, a tradition that the *Heike* was revised for recitation after it was first written as a read work. In addition to these two entries, there are several other records of the history of *Heike* recitation, dating mainly from the Edo period, which, although not accurate in details, contain statements to the effect that the *Heike monogatari* was first a read text and later was adapted for recitation.[72]

A second problem arising from acceptance of the *Shibu* as the original *Heike* results from the theory that the *Heike monogatari* was written first in a short three-*maki* form, and then expanded into six *maki,* and finally, through a process of further revision and expansion, attained the twelve-*maki* form of all the major preserved recited *Heike* variants.[73] According to this concept of the genesis of the *Heike,* the original three-*maki* text and its six-*maki* expansion were somehow lost, and the various early variant manuscripts such as the twelve-*maki Shibu* and *Yashiro,* being later expansions, only preserve the form and content of the original to an imperfect degree.

The idea that originally the *Heike* was in three-*maki* form stems from an account in a work of uncertain date, the *Heike monogatari kammonroku,* which was current during the Edo period, but which was probably written earlier, during the Muromachi period (1336-1573). This work mentions six manuscripts of the *Heike monogatari,* none of which can be identified as any of the preserved manuscripts, ranging in form from thirty-three *maki* down to three *maki,* and assigns an author to each.[74] A good part of the supposedly factual material appearing in the *Kammonroku* is in error, and there is no record of any of the "authors" given for the *Heike* texts having had any connection with the writing of the *Heike.* But due to the fact that the *Hōgen monogatari* and the *Heiji monogatari,* two minor short works of the *gunki monogatari* genre, are in three-*maki* form, succeeding generations of scholars have seized on the statement in the *Kammonroku* that there was a three-*maki Heike* as suggesting that originally the *Heike monogatari* was in this form also.[75] Having accepted this dubious point, they then use it to postulate a three-*maki* recited *Heike monogatari* preceding all of the preserved variants. Since there is no corroborating evidence of a three-*maki Heike monogatari,* the *Kammonroku* account upon which this theory is based should be taken only for what it appears to be—a highly imaginative attempt to manufacture more or less from whole cloth a theory of *Heike* textual development—and undue weight should not be given to the idea that originally the *Heike* was in three-*maki* form.

The theory that there was a six-*maki* text which preceded all of the preserved twelve-*maki Heike* texts has more validity than the three-*maki* theory, and deserves discussion at length. This theory is based on two inserted *kambun* notations in the *Heihanki,* a diary covering the period 1132-1171 by Taira Nobunori (dates unknown). In addition to mentioning the *Heike monogatari,* these notations also mention a year-period change, and on the basis of this it has been established that the two notations date from the year 1240.[76] The first notation states:

> The six-*maki Jishō monogatari,* titled *Heike,* is being copied. Although it is not yet finished, I have requested to see it.

The second notation reads:

> The six-*maki* [*Jishō monogatari*] was expanded into the twelve-*maki* [version] current in the world. The six-*maki* [text] in many places is the same as the current (twelve-*maki* text). Half of the twelve-*maki* [text] has places that are secret.[77]

The very nature of these notations as inserted entries in a work with which they have no connection invites their acceptance as true comments concerning the texts of the *Heike* made by someone who had compared them. Since it has been determined that they were written during the year 1240, they are perhaps the earliest preserved comments about the textual development of the *Heike.* When interpreted in terms of information derived from textual comparison of the major preserved *Heike* variants, these notations shed a good deal of light on how the *Heike* developed as a written text.

First, the record that a text called the *Jishō monogatari* (*The Tale of the Jishō Period,* [1177-1180]), existed prior to the twelve-*maki* version of the *Heike* may be interpreted as referring to the *Shibu* text. The full title of the *Shibu* text as we have it today is *Shibu kassenjō daisamban tōjō,* or "Campaign number three of the four-part battle record." This title is evidently connected with, or derived from, a section in the *Heike monogatari kammonroku* which begins, "This *Heike* is a battle record in four parts . . ."[78] Following this statement is an explanation to the effect that the account of the battle of the Hōgen period [the *Hōgen monogatari*] may be termed the first battle record of Japan, the account of the battle of the Heiji period [the *Heiji monogatari*] may be termed the second battle record of Japan, the account of the battle of the Jishō period [the *Heike monogatari*] may be termed the third battle record of Japan, and finally, the account of the battle of the Jōkyū period [the *Jōkyūki*] may be termed the fourth battle record of Japan. The significant point of all this in terms of the *Shibu* text is that it was written prior to the battle of the Jōkyū period in 1221, hence prior to the *Jōkyūki,* the fourth battle record of Japan. Therefore, at the time it was written it would have been impossible for the author to have given the *Shibu* the title of "Campaign number three of the four-part battle record," since he probably did not know yet of the Jōkyū battle, and certainly did not know of the *Jōkyūki,* which was written later during the Kamakura period.

The fact that the *Shibu* text bears the title of *Shibu kassenjō daisamban tōjō* indicates that as a result of its various copyings over the centuries it has undergone a certain amount of superficial change, and that at sometime after the appearance of the *Jōkyūki*, and possibly after the *Kammonroku* (the work that seems to be the first to have established the four categories of battle records), someone attached the present title to the *Shibu* text. But the *Shibu* must have had some title from the start. The first part of the name "Campaign number three of the four-part battle record" is a circumlocution for what in analogy with the *Hōgen monogatari* and the *Heiji monogatari,* both named after year-periods, would have been termed the *Jishō monogatari*. Since the *Heihanki* notation of 1240 refers specifically to a *Jishō monogatari* being in existence prior to this date, it seems probable that the text presently known as the *Shibu kassenjō daissamban tōjō* is in fact the original *Jishō monogatari* text, which has merely had its title changed to conform to its being the third in a series of four battle records. The only major flaw in such a theory is that the *Heihanki* notation states that the "*Jishō monogatari* titled *Heike*" was a six-*maki* text, rather than a twelve-*maki* text as is the *Shibu*. This apparent contradiction might be explained, however, by the fact that after the appearance of the twelve-*maki Yashiro* and *Kakuichi* recited texts, the twelve-*maki* form came to be accepted as standard for the **Heike monogatari.** Perhaps some copyist of the *Shibu,* influenced by this, revised the six-*maki Shibu* (*Jishō monogatari*) text to make it also conform to this form.[79]

There remains one further problem arising from the *Heihanki* notations. In addition to the reference to the *Jishō monogatari,* it is stated that from the six-*maki* work there developed a twelve-*maki* version of the **Heike.** If it is accepted that the *Shibu* text is the *Jishō monogatari,* then it would seem logical to suppose that the twelve-*maki* text referred to would be the recited *Yashiro* text, since it has been shown that the *Yashiro* is an early revision for recitation stemming from the *Shibu*. But the *Heihanki* notations were written in the year 1240, and it will be recalled that internal evidence shows that the *Yashiro* text was written after 1242. Thus it is hardly likely that the twelve-*maki* text of the *Heihanki* notation is the *Yashiro* text. It is therefore necessary to look elsewhere among the preserved early variants of the **Heike** for a text to fit the *Heihanki* notation's description. . . .

Notes

1. Go-Toba-in (1180-1239) was Retired Emperor from 1198 to 1221.

2. Shinano no Zenji Yukinaga. See pp. 18-19 above for an outline of his life.

3. *Ch'i-te-wu,* a *hsin yüeh-fu* poem by Po Chü-i predominantly in seven-word lines. See Takagi Shōichi, *Haku Kyōi* (Tokyo: Iwanami, 1958) [*Chūgoku shijin senshū,* 12], I, 19-24 for the text and commentary of the poem and a list of the seven virtues.

4. *Kanja,* a title for persons of the Sixth Rank who did not hold office.

5. Jichin *kashō* (1155-1225), more commonly known as Jien. He was a Tendai abbot, author of the *Gukanshō,* and younger brother of Kujō Kanezane.

6. Shōbutsu is generally taken as the first reciter of the *Heike monogatari* (see Atsumi, 34-35), but there is no acceptable corroborating evidence of this fact.

7. Minamoto Yoshitsune (1159-1189), the younger brother of Yoritomo who led the Genji warriors in their defeat of the Heike.

8. Minamoto Noriyori (d. 1193), a younger brother of Yoritomo and a Genji general in various battles with the Heike.

9. *Hōjōki Tsurezuregusa* (Tokyo: Iwanami, 1958) [*KBT* 30], 271-272.

10. The revision of the *kambun Shibu* text for recitation was one of the principal factors in the development of the *wakan konkō* style of writing. Prior to this revision, a mixed *kanji-kana* style such as that of the *Yashiro* and *Kakuichi* texts did not exist. A possible exception to this statement would be the mixed *kanji-katakana* style of the *Konjaku monogatari,* but this style developed from the practice of inserting *katakana* into Buddhist *kambun* texts for *shōdō* lecture purposes; and while this is another factor accounting for the *wakan konkō* style, the *Konjaku* method of writing is inherently different from that of the *Yashiro* and *Kakuichi Heike* texts. *Kambun* was still the standard written language at the time the original *Heike* was written, especially among people like Yukinaga who were concerned with Chinese studies.

11. For what has been the standard Japanese interpretation of the significance of the *Tsurezuregusa* implication that the *Heike* was originally a recited text, see Takagi Ichinosuke, "Heike monogatari no jojishiteki kanren", *Heike monogatari koza* (Tokyo: Sogensha, 1957), I, 5-39, esp. 15-19. This interpretation is followed in Atsumi, 26-27.

12. Yamada Yoshio, "*Heike monogatari kō zokusetsu*", *Kokugakuin zasshi* (April, 1933), 61-62, quotes two sources which mention recitation of the *Heike* by *biwa hōshi* in the years 1315 and 1321.

13. One of the most recent and most accurate and comprehensive accounts of Yukinaga's life appears in Ishida Yoshisada, "Heike monogatari to Shinkokinshū, Yukinaga sakushasetsu no kentō" *Bungaku* 30 (1962). 52-64. Atsumi also has an account and discussion of Yukinaga's life and quotes many of the references to him in historical sources, although her conclusions differ from those presented here (Atsumi, 25-35).

14. Ishida, 56.

15. *Gyokuyō,* Juei 3:1,5 (1184), III, 2.

16. *Gyokuyō,* Juei 3:6,23 (1184), III, 24; Bunji 2:3,17 (1186), III, 173.

17. *Gyokuyō,* III, 605.

18. Shimotsuke no Kami Yukinaga, *Gyokuyō,* III, 891.

19. Atsumi, 29.

20. Quoted in Ishida, 57.

21. *Ibid.*

22. *Ibid.*

23. One such reference is in the *Meigetsuki,* Fujiwara Teika's diary (Tokyo: Kokusho kankōkai, 1911), I, 278 (Kennin 2:8,23 [1202]). In this entry Yukinaga is referred to as Saki no Shimotsuke no Kami ("the former Governor of Shimotsuke"). Yukinaga also took part in the Japanese and Chinese poetry contest held at Go-Toba's residence on Genkyū 2:6,15 (1205). See Ishida, 57.

24. Ishida, 58.

25. *Rakufu mondō goban. Ichidai yōki,* Jōgen 4:3,15 (1210). Quoted in Ishida, 59.

26. *Hakushi monjū rongi rokuban. Hyakurenshō* (Tokyo: Kokushitaikei kankōkai, 1929), 151-152 (Kempō 6:6,3 [1218]).

27. *Meigetsuki,* II, 147 (Kenryaku 2:2,12 [1212]) and II, 286 (Kempō 1:6,11 [1213]).

28. The *Gukanshō* was written during the period 1220-1221. Although it is cast in the form of a record of Japanese history, in the later part of it Jien presents a view of Japanese history slanted to establish the Kujō claim to dominance of the Fujiwara, and advocating the *sesshō* form of government with a Kujō at its head. He also includes a theoretical argument for the validity of his *bumbu kenkō* (parallel rule by civil and military) plan, which envisioned eventual political control of Japan by the Kujō. See especially the concluding *furoku* section, 287-329 (translated by Johannes Rahder, "Miscellany of Personal Views of an Ignorant Fool," *AO* 15(1937).173-230).

29. *Shibu* 1.57a5-60a6. This passage is quoted in Atsumi, 138-139, where it is accepted as representing Jien's thought. The passage is cast in the form of a statement by Chōken, the father of the probable first revisor of the *Shibu,* Shōkaku. See below, pp. 34-35.

30. For a discussion of Jien's concept of the protection of the state by Buddhism, see Taga Munehaya, *Jien* (Tokyo: Yoshikawa Kobunkan, 1959) [*Jimbutsu sōsho,* XV], 135-142.

31. For the genealogy of the Hamuro Nakayama family, see *Heike monogatari,* Takagi Ichinosuke *et al.,* eds. (Tokyo: Sanseidō, 1958) [*Kokugo kokubungaku kenkyūshi taisei* IX], 52. This work quotes all of the early historical references to the *Heike* (47-69) and gives a complete bibliography of *Heike* studies through 1957 (275-304). In the present article some of the more obscure references to the *Heike* are keyed to this source, hereafter abbreviated as Takagi.

32. Nijō no In (1143-1165). He retired in 1165 and died the same year. Here the reference is to the reign of Nijō prior to his retirement, 1158-1165.

33. The Controller of the Left ranked above that of the Right.

34. I.e., he lacked official position and therefore passed his days in poverty.

35. Nyūdō Shōkoku, the title of Kiyomori.

36. Nishihachijō-dono, the residence of Kiyomori on Nishihachijō (street) in Kyoto.

37. Ko-chūnagon, a reference to Akitoki, Yukitaka's father.

38. *Kohachiyō no kuruma,* a cart with small eight-leaved figure decorations on its sides, used by people of the Fourth and Fifth Rank.

39. *Hiki, koku,* measures of silk and rice respectively.

40. The neglect of the Genji in the *Shibu* text is evidenced by the almost immediate composition in Kamakura of the *Gempei tōjōroku,* a revision in the read division of textual development, which added much detail about the Genji and remedied what to them was a serious defect in the *Shibu* account. The transmission of the *Shibu* text from Kyoto to Kamakura may have resulted from the appointment of Kujō Michiie's grandson as Shogun-designate in 1219. For a study of the *Gempei tōjōroku* as a revision of the *Heike* made by eastern warriors associated with the Genji, see Yamashita Hiroaki, "Gempei tōjōroku kanken", *Kokugo to kokubungaku* (August, 1961).24-40.

41. See Yamashita, "Katari to yomi," 39, 44, and Ishimoda Shō, *Heike monogatari* (Tokyo: Iwanami, 1955), 75. Ishimoda acknowledges that Go-Shirakawa is treated unsympathetically and suggests that the cause was in part the original *Heike* author's opposition to the *insei* system and support of the *sesshō* system of rule. Yukinaga would also qualify as author in this respect. See also Yamashita, "Katari to yomi," 35-36 for a brief discussion of the sympathetic treatment of the Heike in the *Shibu* vs. the Genji bias of the *Gempei tōjōroku.*

42. Quoted in Takagi, 51.

43. Atsumi, 59.

44. Yorimori was a brother of Kiyomori who took no direct part in the Gempei battles and therefore survived.

45. See note 28 above.

46. Kanezane. He was dismissed from the office of *sesshō* in 1196.

47. Kyō no Tsubone (1155-1229), daughter of Fujiwara Norikane, and Go-Toba's wet-nurse during his early life. Also known as Kyō no Nii. After Go-Toba became Retired Emperor she was one of his closest advisors and influenced him greatly.

48. Ni no Miya, second son of the Emperor Takakura, who had been passed over at the time Go-Toba was made Emperor.

49. *Kembiishi,* also read *kebiishi,* "police."

50. Nijō Inokuma, the residence of Mongaku at the intersection of Nijō and Inokuma streets in the northern section of Kyoto.

51. Takao, the mountain just north of Kyoto where Mongaku's temple, the Jingo-ji, was located.

52. Kanezane's dismissal is discussed in *Gukanshō, 247-248*. After being appointed *sesshō,* Kanezane had his daughter Taeko made consort of Go-Toba at the time of Go Toba's manhood ceremony at the age of eleven in 1190. He hoped his daughter would bear a future emperor. Then as *sesshō* and maternal grandparent of the Emperor, he would be able to establish a new Fujiwara Regency with his branch of the family at its head. But upon reaching actual manhood, Go-Toba became determined to continue the *insei* or direct rule by Retired Emperor, started by the Retired Emperor Shirakawa in 1086 when he wrested control from the Fujiwara. The removal of Kanezane in 1196 was the first step towards this goal. After Kanezane's dismissal, his daughter was removed from her position as consort, and Jien also resigned his position as Abbot of the Enryakuji. The Kujō family was then forced into total political eclipse. Later Jien was able to persuade Go-Toba to appoint Kanezane's son Yoshitsune as *sesshō* in 1202, again setting the stage for the Kujō family to attempt to seize political power. These details are related in Taga, *Jien,* 46-78.

53. Also read *Shōkyū.* On this war see William H. Mc-Cullough, "*Shōkyūki:* An Account of the Shōkyū War of 1221," *MN* 19 (1964) 1/2.163-215; 3/4.186-221.

54. See note 101.

55. Daiichi no, the Emperor Tsuchimikado, eldest son of Go-Toba. Reigned 1198-1210.

56. *Gitchō,* a game played either on horseback or on foot, using mallets and a wooden ball. See Sakai Kin *Nihon yūgi shi* (Tokyo, 1933), 456-463.

57. *Chakushi; ryōsōshi.*

58. Hōjō Yoshitoki (1163-1224), son of Tokimasa (father-in-law of Yoritomo) and second Regent (*shikken*) of the Kamakura *bakufu* (1205-1224). He was head of the *bakufu* at the time of Go-Toba's attack in 1221.

59. The text of the *Gukanshō* presents another example of a contradiction in referring to Go-Toba by his posthumous name. It has been demonstrated fairly conclusively that the work was written by Jien in 1220-1221, just prior to the Jōkyū War. In the main body of the text (*maki* 3 through *maki* 6, plus the *furoku* appendage), the name Go-Toba is not used, he being referred to as *in* (the Retired Emperor). When, however, at the end of *maki* 2 he is listed as the eighty-second Emperor, he is referred to as Go-Toba. Japanese scholars feel that the latter part of *maki* 2 is a later addition written after 1221. See the introduction to the Iwanami edition, *Gukanshō, 3.*

The posthumous title Go-Toba-in also appears in the *Ujishui monogatari* (story no. 159) and has been used in establishing that this part of the *Ujishui* must have been written after 1242. It is still not clear, however, whether or not this story was inserted after

the original collection had been made. See *Ujishui monogatari* (Tokyo: Iwanami, 1960) [*KBT* 27], 12-15.

60. There is no historical evidence that Mongaku was ever banished to either Tosa or Oki. He was, however, banished several times to Sado, Tsushima, and Izu because of his stubborn efforts to secure contributions for rebuilding the Jingo-ji. The *Shibu* reference to Tosa may be a copyist error for Sado. . . . For a discussion of Mongaku, see Hoshino Kō, "Heike monogatari Gempei jōsuiki wa gobyū ōshi", *SZ* 9 (1898).1-17. This article is quoted in full in Takagi, 80-90. See p. 86 for the reference to places where Mongaku was banished.

61. As possible internal evidence which might aid in dating the *Shibu,* Tomikura Tokujiro mentions an entry appearing in *maki* 11 (11.48a1-2) in his study, *Heike monogatari kenkyū* (Tokyo: Kadokawa, 1964), 245. Here the person Kura no Kami Nobumoto is glossed as being the grandfather of Norisuke and the father of Chikasuke. Norisuke died at the age of forty-three in 1234, during the reign of Emperor Shijō (1232-1242), and Tomikura suggests that the inclusion of his name can be taken as evidence that the *Shibu* was written after the reign of Emperor Shijō. He then combines this fact and the mention of the posthumous title Go-Toba-in in the *kanjō no maki* to date the entire *Shibu* text at sometime after 1242. In the present article I have suggested that the *kanjō no maki* is a later addition to the twelve *maki* of the *Shibu.* My reasons are the complete dissimilarity of writing styles and the use of the posthumous title Go-Toba-in. I therefore prefer to date the *Shibu* only on the basis of internal evidence in its twelve *maki.* As for the appearance of Norisuke's name in *maki* 11, he would have been approximately twenty-eight years old in 1220, and I see no reason to prohibit the use of his name in this way by Yukinaga in 1220.

62. Gen Chūnagon Garai no Kyō, a member of the Murakami branch of the Genji.

63. *Ason,* also read *asomi.* A title of respect attached to the surname of persons of the Third Rank and above, and to the personal name of persons of the Fourth Rank. The usage here would indicate that Yukitaka held the Fourth Rank at this time, and the use of his name is another instance of Yukinaga's attempt to weave his father into the *Shibu* narrative.

64. Saishō Nyūdō Shunken. The details of his life are unknown. In the *Kakuichi* text Shunken appears as Nariyori.

65. Atsumi discusses this dream section in these terms as it appears in the *Kakuichi* text. She mistakenly states, however, that the reference to the Fujiwara Shogun does not appear in the *Shibu* text, an error that throws off her entire consideration of dating the *Heike* on the basis of this section. She also mistakenly gives 1221 as the date of the last Genji Shogun Sanetomo's death (1219) and thus further confuses the is-

sue (Atsumi, 33-35). The vocabulary of this dream section is quite similar to that of references to the appointment of the Fujiwara Shogun in Jien's *Gukanshō*, 305, 317.

66. The theoretical basis of Jien's *bumbu kenkō* plan is related in the *Gukanshō* appended *furoku* section, 287-329. See also Taga, 142ff. Jien's ultimate objective was a unification of civil and military under a *sesshō* form of government (Taga, 149).

67. *Yashiro* 5.11b8-13a6. The *Kakuichi* account, written in 1371, reintroduces in the dream section the part about the sword passing to the Fujiwara, apparently because it makes a better story and because in 1371 there was no longer any fear of reprisal by the Hōjō (*KBT* 32, 342-343).

68. Quoted in Gotō, *Senki monogatari no kenkyū*, 101. See also 526-527.

69. Tomikura Tokujiro, "Heike monogatari no seiritsu ni tsuite," *Kokubungaku* (November, 1956).13.

70. Gotō, 101.

71. Quoted in Takagi, 54.

72. Atsumi, 49, 15, mentions these other works.

73. Tomikura, "Heike monogatari no seiritsu," 9.

74. The relevant passage of this work is quoted in Takagi, 57-62. Atsumi discusses it in *Kisoteki kenkyū*, 47-49.

75. See Yamada Yoshio, *Heike monogatari* (Tokyo: Hōbunkan, 1933), 41-45, for a concise statement of this view, which has been followed by later scholars.

76. Yamada Yoshio, "Heike monogatari kō zokusetsu," 63. I have not translated the line about the year-period change. The title *Heihanki* is also read *Hyōbanki*.

77. These notations are quoted in Takagi, 51, and Atsumi, 41. The Gempei wars began in 1180, the last year of the Jishō period (1177-1180), hence the name *Jishō monogatari*.

78. Quoted in Takagi, 59.

79. There has been a tendency to assume that if the *Jishō monogatari* was in a six-*maki* form, the narrative of the later twelve-*maki* texts must be twice as long as this (Atsumi, 44). That such an assumption is not necessarily valid is easily shown by the existence of a later expanded text in the read division, the *Enkyō* text, which is divided into six divisions, but runs to 1007 pages of fine print as compared with the 733 pages of the standard printed twelve-*maki* version (*Ōei shosha Enkyōbon Heike monogatari* [Tokyo: Hakuteisha, 1961]). Scholars feel that parts of the narrative of the *Enkyō* text are close to that of the original *Heike*. The organization of the *Enkyō* into six divisions (*ichi, ni, san*, etc., the term *maki* is not used) probably also reflects the organization of the original *Heike* text. See the photographically reproduced text of the *Enkyō: Enkyōbon Heike monogatari* (Tokyo: Koten kenkyūkai, 1964). It is interesting to note that the six divisions of the *Enkyō* text are further subdivided into twelve sections as follows: *dai-ichi hon; dai-ichi sue; dai-ni hon; dai-ni chū; dai-ni sue; dai-san hon; dai-san sue; dai-shi; dai-go hon; dai-go sue; dai-roku hon; dai-roku sue*. In copying a text such as this, it would be a simple matter to revise these twelve sections into twelve *maki*, and it was probably through a process similar to this that the *Shibu* original *Heike monogatari* text was changed from six to twelve *maki*. The divisions of the twelve *maki* of the *Shibu* correspond roughly to the twelve divisions of the *Enkyō*. See the comparative charts given in Atsumi, 378-427 and especially p. 406, which shows that the beginning of *maki* 7 of the *Shibu* corresponds exactly with the beginning of *dai-san sue* of the *Enkyō* and *maki* 28 of the *Gempei jōsuiki*, the two texts of the read division which are thought to preserve some elements of the structural division of the original *Heike*.

Hasegawa Tadashi (essay date 1967)

SOURCE: "The Early Stages of the *Heike Monogatari*," in *Monumenta Nipponica*, Vol. XXII, No. 1-2, 1967, pp. 65-81.

[*In the following essay, Tadashi provides an overview of the* Heike Monogatari, *examines the significance of the blind lute players who recited it, and traces the development of its written text.*]

The culture of the Heian period was the product of a small aristocracy which flourished in the metropolis of Heian or Kyoto, capital of a highly centralized political system. It bloomed in the soil of luxury consumption maintained by the produce of lands which the aristocracy held in every province of the country. But the power structure of this society was severely shaken by three disturbances which came in succession after the middle of the twelfth century. These were the Hōgen and Heiji wars of 1156 and 1159, the war between the Taira and Minamoto from 1177 to 1185, and the Shōkyū war of 1221. Centered on the second of these disturbances, the war between the Taira and Minamoto, the ***Heike monogatari*** tells of the eminence of the warrior clan known as Heike or Taira and its ultimate downfall. It is in many ways a description of the age itself.

The warrior class had undergone a considerable period of development before it was ready to play its leading role as a political force in the Hōgen and Heiji wars of the mid twelfth century. The rise of the warrior class and the expansion of its power were intimately related to political and economic changes which took place in the agricultural villages of the provinces. The Hōgen and Heiji wars were waged by military clans matured in the provinces which competed for power in Kyoto by allying themselves with rival houses of the civil aristocracy. But no sooner had the

Taira clan gained the victory than it began an amazingly rapid transformation into a metropolitan aristocracy itself. The reasons for this changing character of the Taira need to be examined here, because it was precisely their transformation into a civil aristocracy which contributed most to their downfall.

In their moment of supremacy, when they controlled half the territory of Japan, the Taira were ruled by their chieftain, Kiyomori, from his palace of Rokuhara in Kyoto, whom the author of the *Heike monogatari* compared with historic Chinese and Japanese rebels in the following words: "Proud in thought and vigorous in deed though all of them certainly were in the histories of our two countries, yet it is the story of this man, who so recently moved in the world and bore the unprecedented titles of Elder of Rokuhara and Former Chancellor of the Empire, His Excellency Lord Kiyomori of the Taira, which does indeed surpass the imagination and defy description." But it was only in the time of Kiyomori's father, Tadamori, that the Taira chief had been granted admittance to the imperial court, and Scroll One of the *Heike monogatari* relates how the exclusive aristocracy tried to ostracize Tadamori when he attended court. The reason for the remarkably swift advance of the Taira into the center of political power lay in the wealth of the clan. Under the leadership of Tadamori and Kiyomori the Taira gained control of the Inland Sea and were acquiring enormous wealth from trade with China. In contrast to the Minamoto clan, which drew its support from the agricultural villages of the eastern provinces, the Taira, established in the more advanced western provinces, conducted trade with China and had a bourgeois side to their character. And so from the outset the Taira were urban warriors, and the Minamoto were rural warriors.

After the Taira emerged victorious from their competition with the Minamoto in the Hōgen Heiji wars, they became participants in the central authority and went on step by step seizing political power at the expense of the Cloistered Emperor. So that now they could rely on the power of the state machinery to secure their rule, whether in the requisition of fighting men in case of civil war or in the levying of taxes for military supplies. However, in order to reach this position, they could not avoid sacrificing vested interests, including the interests of the central aristocracy and prominent religious institutions. Therefore the Taira found themselves in the unfavorable situation of being isolated in the capital from the traditional powers represented by the aristocracy and religious bodies, and being confronted in the provinces by insurrection from the military class. In contrast to the Taira, who appeared as pacifiers of rebellion, as the commanders of the government forces, the Minamoto found themselves playing the rebel. They were obliged to organize insurrection and to that extent had to respect the interests of the provincials, and in particular the interests of the warrior class, which was composed of local proprietors.

Considered in its broad significance, then, the war between the Taira and Minamoto from 1177 to 1185 was not simply a struggle for leadership between these two clans, it was essentially a civil war marking the end of the old order. The author of the *Heike monogatari,* however, sees it as a conflict between these two mightiest of the warrior houses, and tells his story as one depicting the downfall of the Taira.

THE AUTHORSHIP OF THE *HEIKE MONOGATARI*

It is still impossible to establish with certainty either the author of the *Heike monogatari* or the date, place, and circumstances of its composition. However, for the most convincing source relating to these problems we may turn to section two hundred twenty six of the *Tsurezuregusa* (Harvest of Leisure) by the monk Yoshida Kenkō[1] (1281-1350). Kenkō gives his version of the authorship of the *Heike monogatari* in the following words:

> In the reign of the Cloistered Emperor Go-Toba, Yukinaga, a former governor of the province of Shinano, who was reputed to be a scholar of antiquities, was summoned to take part in a discussion of Po Chü-i's poetry before His Majesty.[2] He forgot two of the virtues which figure in the poem "The Dance of the Seven Virtues," and as a result was nicknamed "Young Master Five Virtues." He felt so unhappy over this that he gave up scholarship and abandoned the secular world. But the Abbot Jichin used to take anyone into his service, including persons of low condition, so long as they had at least one accomplishment to their credit; and he took pity on this monk who had once been the governor of Shinano, so that he extended his patronage to him.
>
> The monk Yukinaga wrote the *Heike monogatari* and taught a blind man named Shōbutsu to chant it. The *Heike monogatari* treats the subject of Mt. Hiei with particular gravity. The author was well acquainted with the career of Minamoto no Yoshitsune and wrote it down in detail. The career of Minamoto no Noriyori, however, he has recorded with many omissions, perhaps because he was not well acquainted with his life. As for the doings of the military and the profession of the horse and bow, Shōbutsu, being a native of the eastern provinces, asked the warriors about them and gave the facts to Yukinaga to write down. The minstrels who recite the *Heike monogatari* to the accompaniment of the lute nowadays imitate the natural voice of the first reciter, Shōbutsu.

According to this source, the author of the *Heike monogatari* was Yukinaga, a minor official in the latter days of the old order, who could not get ahead in secular life although he was to some extent a learned man. He composed the *Heike monogatari* after he had taken the tonsure and while he was under the patronage of Abbot Jichin. He had the work chanted by the blind Shōbutsu, who hailed from the eastern provinces, and Shōbutsu helped him to write the parts that deal with the wars by canvassing the military men for the facts. As for Shōbutsu, he seems to have been one of those persons whom Jichin was willing to patronize "so long as they had at least one accomplishment," in this case the accomplishment of minstrelsy.

This account in the *Tsurezuregusa* may be only what Kenkō wrote down as he heard it from others, and it is hardly likely that he did any historical research on it himself before committing it to writing. Nevertheless, it is true that "the ***Heike monogatari*** treats the subject of Mt. Hiei with particular gravity," as Kenkō puts it, for it contains numerous references to the Enryaku monastery, the headquarters of the Tendai sect of Buddhism located on Mt. Hiei near Kyoto. In this connection I might add that the *Shibukassenjō* text of the ***Heike monogatari*** has a deeper religious tone than any of the other versions and is remarkable for its supplements dealing with religious matters. Considering, too, that the chant known as *heikyoku,* characteristic of ***Heike monogatari*** recitation, descends from a type of Buddhist singing called *shōmyō,* which was prevalent in that day, I am inclined to place a high value on the account given in the *Tsurezuregusa.* It is now thought that Jichin, who was the head of the Tendai sect, the monk Yukinaga, and the blind reciter Shōbutsu were all on Mt. Hiei when the ***Heike monogatari*** was written.[3]

The second source concerning the origin of the ***Heike monogatari*** is found in the fifth scroll of that work, in a section entitled *Mokke no sata*—(Rumors of Prodigies). It is an allusion to the installation of a Fujiwara shogun at Kamakura, which took place in 1219, after the extinction of the line of shoguns descended from Minamoto no Yoritomo. On the authority of this passage Kan Sazan, a Japanese Confucianist (1748-1827), wrote in his essay *Fude no susabi* (Playing with a Writing Brush) that the ***Heike monogatari*** was written after the Shōkyū war (1221). However, since the passage does not occur in the *Yasaka* text, Yamada Yoshio thought the original ***Heike monogatari*** was written before the Shōkyū war, that is, in the era of the Minamoto shoguns. But now we know that the old manuscripts which do not have the passage include not only the *Yasaka* text but also the *Yashiro* text and the *Shibukassenjō* text. In my opinion the passage was probably added to later texts, because the older manuscripts which stand near the original do not have it. Therefore this passage alone is not sufficient to ascertain the earliest date of the original ***Heike monogatari.***[4]

The third source is an entry in the diary *Gyokuzui* (The Jade Stamen) written by Fujiwara no Michiie, an aristocrat and chief adviser to the Emperor Chūkyō. Dated the 20th day of the 4th month of 1220, it states that Michiie borrowed from Taira no Mitsumori "the many Heike which he owned." If we suppose that the *Heike* mentioned in the *Gyokuzui* were copies of the ***Heike monogatari,***[5] it means that the ***Heike monogatari*** was written before 1220.

The assertion in the *Tsurezuregusa* that the ***Heike monogatari*** was written in the reign of the Cloistered Emperor Go-Toba, which covers the period from 1198 to 1221, will thus be reinforced. It is now generally accepted that the entry in the *Gyokuzui* does indeed refer to the ***Heike monogatari.***

On the basis of the above three sources it is now provisionally recognized that the original ***Heike monogatari*** was composed not later than 1221.

THE *HEIKE MONOGATARI* AND THE *BIWA HŌSHI*

The wars which in their aggregate effect put an end to the old order were, it will be remembered, the Hōgen and Heiji wars of 1156 and 1159, the civil war involving the Taira and Minamoto from 1177 to 1185, and the Shōkyū war of 1221. Each of these upheavals has its story enshrined in a *monogatari* (tale), the four of them being referred to collectively as "the four battle stories." There are records showing that the Hōgen, Heiji, and Heike tales were recited by minstrels known as *biwa hōshi,* blind men who entertained audiences by intoning a text to the accompaniment of the *biwa* (lute). As for the *Shōkyū ikusa monogatari* (Tale of the Shōkyū War), however, this work does not have much literary value, and so it seems that no one took the trouble to make a note of it; in any case there is no record of its recitation by *biwa hōshi.* Nevertheless it was probably part of the minstrels' repertoire together with the other battle stories.

The existence of *biwa hōshi* is attested by documentary evidence going back early into the Heian period. They figure in the *Genji monogatari,* which dates from the beginning of the eleventh century, and there are numerous references to them in aristocratic diaries and other documents, the earliest being an entry in the diary *Ouki* dated 985, which says: "Summoned *biwa hōshi* and had them display their talent and skill. Granted them a small gratuity."[6]

The greatest patrons of the *biwa hōshi* were the larger Buddhist monasteries, probably because the monasteries required performers and artists for religious services. Some scholars claim that the origin of the *biwa hōshi* is connected with a type of dance performance known as *gigaku,* which flourished in the eighth century.[7] Although the music and dances accompanying public functions in the aristocratic society of the eight century were refined arts imported from China, the *gigaku* dances were something like pantomime with a touch of the comic in their mood, and they apparently served to relieve the solemnity of the other performances. It is said that *gigaku* probably originated on the continent too.

Whatever their origin, the *biwa hōshi* were wandering singers of low social status, and they evidently used texts of one kind or another in their performances.[8] Nevertheless these purveyors of a minor plebeian art, who were treated as on a par with puppeteers, acrobats, and magicians, are not thought to have possessed texts of a quality which might have entitled them to the same high place in the literature of antiquity as the *biwa hōshi* texts were later to attain in the literature of the middle ages.

When exactly did the *biwa hōshi* take custody of the battle stories and especially the ***Heike monogatari?*** This question, which is of prime importance for the history of Japanese medieval literature, is still far from being elucidated despite the existence of numerous scholarly studies; and what we know about it so far is accurately summed up in the following words: "The very fact that is is obscured in a fog of legend is highly suggestive of the position of *Heike* recitation at the time of its origin; it indicates that for some time after the appearance of minstrels reciting the *Heike monogatari,* the people who had a literature, in other words the aristocrats of the capital, were not yet aware of this art as something worthy of notice."[9] The earliest source we know of which mentions a *Heike* recital before an audience is a collection of Buddhist stories entitled *Futsū shōdō shū* (Popular Sermons) with a preface dated 1297. Another important reference to *Heike* recitals is an entry dated 1321 in the diary of the Cloistered Emperor Hanazono (*Hanazono shinki*):

> I made an unexpected visit to the Nakazono Palace this evening. We went on foot. We summoned the blind man Yuishin to play the *biwa.* He took the *biwa* and strummed it like a zithern *(koto).* The excellence of his performance was truly indescribable. He sang of the Heiji and Heike wars and other events of those days. There were many ladies of the Court in the audience. We left at dawn.

This is the first record that an emperor listened to a recitation of the *Heiji* and *Heike* tales. It reveals that recitals of the war tales such as the *Heiji* and *Heike* were now much in vogue in aristocratic society.

The *Heike monogatari* gained a decisive popularity because it was recited by the blind lute players called *biwa hōshi,* because, in short, the *biwa hōshi* took charge of the recited versions—the *heikyoku,* as they came to be known, which were intoned to the accompaniment of the *biwa* in a melody reminiscent of the *shōmyō* chant of Buddhism. This fact marks a new development in the history of Japanese literature. As is evident in the case of the *Genji monogatari,* in the literary world of the Heian period authors and readers could hardly be distinguished as separate groups, confined as they were to the narrow social circles of aristocratic gentlemen and ladies, where each member was expected to be an artist as well as a connoisseur. The amateurism of Heian literature is further revealed in the circumstances surrounding the authorship of the *Ōsaka koenu gonchūnagon* (The Counsellor Who Failed in Love), which is found in an eleventh-century collection of short stories. It was written by a court lady named Koshikibu, who entered it in a prose writing contest held at the residence of Princess Baishi in 1055. Here it is evident that the ladies of Princess Baishi's circle wrote for each other's enjoyment. But the world of the *Heike monogatari* was a professional one, in which there existed both a clear-cut division of functions and a unity of purpose between author, reciter, and audience.

Nevertheless, whether or not the *Heike monogatari* was from the first recited to musical accompaniment, in short, whether or not it was composed originally to serve as a minstrel's script, is a point on which opinions are still divided. Both sides of this controversy originate from two different interpretations of the passage in the *Tsurezuregusa* which I quoted earlier. Dr. Atsumi Kaoru believes that the original *Heike monogatari* was written as a recit-

er's text and that *Heike* recitation is coeval with the authorship of the work.[10] In support of this opinion she cites the fact that Jichin, the head of the Tendai sect, who patronized Yukinaga, was an ardent promoter of popular education; and she supposes that Yukinaga, with his knowledge of Chinese poetry, had a part to play in the furtherance of popular education under Jichin's auspices, so that he observed how stories about the Taira were being used to illustrate Buddhist teachings in the monasteries and were being sung before audiences by blind monks playing the *biwa,* and from this practice he got the idea to compose the *Heike monogatari* for *biwa* recitation.[11]

On the other hand, Dr. Sasaki Hachirō maintains that the *Tsurezuregusa* does not give enough information to support a conclusion that Yukinaga intended from the outset to have the *Heike monogatari* recited by *biwa hōshi* and so composed it in a form suitable to recitation. No one can give a conclusive answer to this question, now that there is no chance of discovering the original *Heike monogatari* that is supposed to have been written by Yukinaga. Nevertheless Dr. Sasaki goes on to say, "I assume that the *Heike monogatari* supposed to have been written by Yukinaga was essentially in a form designed for reading."[12] But in considering Dr. Sasaki's assumption we must take into account that even in the oldest manuscript of the group classed as 'reading texts'—the *Gempei tōjō roku* (Record of the Conflict Between the Minamoto and the Taira)—there are unmistakable traces of the reciter;[13] therefore one cannot dismiss the possibility that the original *Heike monogatari* was used for recitation, even though one may not accept the *Tsurezuregusa*'s version of its composition.

Still, it is self-evident that the *Heike monogatari* can not have been created by simply fitting together around a central plot stories about the Taira which the *biwa hōshi* may have been circulating at the time. Therefore Dr. Sasaki is correct when he emphasizes the form characteristic of chronicles which is present in the extant versions of the *Heike monogatari* and makes use of this fact to support his assertion that the original *Heike monogatari* must have been quite different from any of the earlier minstrel texts.

Nevertheless, inasmuch as there is not a single source existing today which refutes the *Tsurezuregusa*'s version of how the *Heike monogatari* was written, I am inclined to give the *Tsurezuregusa* the benefit of the doubt.

It is not hard to imagine that various stories about the Taira should have sprung up immediately after their destruction at the Battle of Dannoura in 1185. The original *Heike monogatari* did not appear on the scene until some thirty years after the collapse of the Taira, and the nature of this type of literature—the battle stories—resists the notion that nothing about this collapse was made into story form during those thirty years. There must have been many stories current at the time that the *Heike monogatari* was written, and so it is with good reason that later historical sources name a variety of persons as putative authors of the *Heike monogatari.* The *Tsurezuregusa,* as we have seen, offers us a former governor of Shinano Province, named Yukinaga, but there is no other evidence that such a person existed. On the other hand, we do have historical evidence that Fujiwara no Yukinaga, formerly a governor of Shimotsuke Province, lived during the period when the *Heike monogatari* was written, and he had also been the steward of Abbot Jichin's brother, Fujiwara no Kujō Kanezane who was the chief adviser to the Emperor. This historical Yukinaga may well have been the author of the *Heike monogatari.*[14] But no matter whether Yukinaga wrote the *Heike monogatari* or not, the extant versions leave little doubt that the author was a ruined aristocrat with education and a monk closely associated with the Enryaku monastery.

The monastery in this period was not only the last citadel of representatives of the old aristocratic culture, it was also an epitome of the chaotic social conditions which prevailed in Japan. For it housed a medley of all classes of people, who were forced to leave secular life from the most backward areas of the country as well as from the most advanced. The blind Shōbutsu mentioned in the *Tsurezuregusa* was one of these. If we suppose that in this gigantic retreat on Mt. Hiei with its complex population Yukinaga, or anyone else in the same circumstances, were to describe those amazing times from his personal experience, we would expect him to identify his own fate with the fall of the Taira and respond sympathetically to the tragedy which overtook that once prosperous clan.

The *Heike monogatari* itself relates how Prince Shukaku, abbot of the Ninna monastery, secretly invited Minamoto no Yoshitsune to come and tell him about the battles, and then made a record of what he heard. The prince was deeply affected by "the rule that man should prosper only to decline and rise only to fall, and the pathos of earthly vicissitude and heartlessness";[15] and even as he remembered sadly those among the sinking Taira who had accepted aristocratic culture, he could not help but be attracted to the valiant warriors like Yoshitsune who were sinking them. But it was not only Prince Shukaku who experienced this ambivalence to the wars; contemporary records show that aristocrats like Jichin and Fujiwara no Kanezane vied with each other to hear stories about the warriors great and small, and particularly about the heroic Yoshitsune. These accounts reveal how interested people were to find out what happened in the civil war. And for someone like Yukinaga, living under the patronage of Jichin, would not the best way of satisfying the curiosity of the aristocrats and others in the capital have been to compile a *Heike monogatari* from the records and narratives concerning the Taira? Would not his most effective procedure have been to narrate the fall of the Taira in the melodic measures used for the intonation of stories about paradise and hell prevalent at that time in the Buddhist monasteries? In this he would have had ample precedent, for the practice of reciting battle stories of *biwa* accompaniment is documented from times prior to the age of the Taira.

Though its origin is obscure, we can at least say that the *Heike monogatari* which we have today is the product of extensive revision undergone during the centuries when it was recited by the *biwa hōshi.* The text was altered to enhance its effect as a piece of musical recitation and to adjust the melodic quality of its phrases, it was rearranged to sharpen the dramatic impact of the narrative, and it was supplemented with romantic episodes and half-legendary tales recast in a form suitable to intonation.[16]

THE PROTOTYPES AND DEVELOPMENT OF THE *HEIKE MONOGATARI*

The original *Heike monogatari,* written at the beginning of the thirteenth century, did not consist of twelve scrolls as its successors do today. According to one account from the fifteenth century (*Heike kammon roku*), there were six different versions of the *Heike monogatari,* in addition to the reciter's text, one of them had grown from three scrolls to six scrolls, and the *Heike monogatari* which Shōbutsu recited was composed of six scrolls. However, such statements should not be accepted at face value, since they appear in documents of a later time and seem merely to reflect oral traditions.

A document which helps to clarify this problem was discovered by Dr. Yamada Yoshio in the Higashiyama Library of the old imperial palace in Kyoto. It bears the date 1240 and states that the *Heike monogatari* used to be called *Jishō monogatari* (The Tale of the Jishō Era) (1177-81) and consisted of six scrolls; that while the six-scroll version circulated widely, there also existed a version in twelve scrolls. The discovery of this document suggests that the text of the *Jishō monogatari* underwent a gradual revision. The original six scrolls must have remained substantially unchanged, having reached the stage of an established recitation text; so that the twelve-scroll version was doubtless formed by the addition of a further six scrolls consisting mainly of stories about the battles which took place after Kiyomori's death in 1181.

Before the discovery of the above document, Dr. Yamada proposed a theory that the original *Heike monogatari* consisted of three scrolls.[17] He adduced in support of his theory the fact that the opening lines of scrolls one, six, and nine agree in all versions of the work, and the fact that the other three battle stories—the *Heiji, Hōgen,* and *Shōkyū* tales—are each composed of three scrolls. But this theory has not gained general acceptance because no reliable source has yet been uncovered to corroborate it. In any case, we still have no definite clue to tell us what the form of the six-scroll version might have been, not to mention Dr. Yamada's hypothetical three-scroll version. And of course it is not clear either whether the six-scroll text we are dealing with here is really the *Heike monogatari* presumed to have been written by Yukinaga.

Professor Ishimoda Tadashi attaches importance to the fact that the opening lines of scrolls one, six, and nine not only agree in all texts of the twelve-scroll *Heike monogatari,* but are also in a style characteristic of chronicles. "This fact," he writes, "raises the question that if we could trace back the successive stages in the development of the present texts, we might well find that they took on more and more distinctly the form of a chronicle the farther back in time we went. Or else it permits the hypothesis that the *Heike monogatari* was originally in chronicle form, and even though it passed from a three-scroll stage to a six-scroll stage and was finally divided into twelve scrolls, there was still an attempt to preserve its original form at least at the beginning of each scroll."[18] The originality of Professor Ishimoda's view is well appreciated in his conjecture that there may be a relationship between the chronicle form of scrolls one, six, and nine and the original form of the *Heike monogatari.*

All extant versions of the *Heike monogatari* combine two modes of presentation. One is the chronological mode, and the other is the biographical mode, which is a method of narrating events by centering them around the personalities concerned, without necessarily following a chronological order. Both modes of presentation belong properly to the writing of history; but the *Heike monogatari,* while following the example of such antecedent historical narratives as the *Ōkagami* (Great Mirror), has achieved a brilliant success in the use of these modes for a literary purpose. That is, the parts consisting of story and legend organized by the biographical method have been squeezed into the middle of the chronological organization, yet every effort has been made to maintain an over-all harmony.

The following passage illustrates the chronological method employed in the *Heike monogatari:*

> Twenty-second day of the second month of the second year of Juei:
>
> His Majesty pays a visit to the imperial parents at the Hōjūji palace. His Majesty's visit to his parents in the sixth year of the Cloistered Toba has been taken as the precedent for this.
>
> Twenty-third day: Munemori receives the Junior First Rank.
>
> Twenty-seventh day: He resigns his ministership.

This passage introduces the seventh scroll of the *Tashiro* text, which is the oldest reciter's text we have. But in the other texts of this category, which are further advanced in their development as minstrels' scripts, the seventh scroll begins as follows:

> The New Year's banquet and other court functions from the first day of the first month of the second year of Juei take place as usual. The duties of the Master of Ceremonies are performed by the Minister, Munemori of the Taira.

The passage is further adjusted by shifting the events of the second month in the earlier text backward to the sixth day of the first month. This comparison shows that by the end of the thirteenth century reciters had begun to concern themselves that there should be a mention of the New Year to start off each scroll.

The above examples have been adduced to illustrate the fact that the chronological mode of presentation, by which events are recorded day by day, is fundamentally consistent throughout all versions of the *Heike monogatari* from those texts which were clearly organized for *biwa* recitation to others like the *Gempei seisui ki* (Record of the Fortunes of the Minamoto and the Taira), whose Chinese vocabulary has rendered them unintelligible except to the eye. Furthermore, the judgment applies generally to the category of reciters' texts that the earlier ones like the *Tashiro* text appear simple in form, even documentary, in comparison with the later ones like the *Kakuichi* text, which are more fully developed to suit the needs of the reciter's art.

Little though we know of the origin of the *Heike monogatari,* it is clear that it depends for its material to a large extent on aristocratic diaries and temple records of the period. Passages introduced by a date, such as the foregoing examples, are found everywhere in all the extant versions. They are almost like entries in a record and demonstrate conclusively that the style of aristocratic diaries was taken over directly as a mode of presentation in the *Heike monogatari.* This fact suggests something of the nature of the *Heike monogatari* as a literary work in the time of its formation, when it went by the name of *Jishō monogatari* (The Tale of the Jishō Era).

The next question I wish to consider is how the two modes of presentation, the chronological and the biographical, are intertwined in the *Heike monogatari.* For an example I shall use scroll six in the centre of which the death of Kiyomori is related. In the standard edition this scroll is divided into thirteen chapters, which fall into four groups.

The first group (chapters one to four) concerns the Cloistered Emperor Takakura, who died at the early age of twenty-one. Chapter one "The Death of the Cloistered Emperor" is a chronological record of events having to do with the Emperor Takakura. Chapters two to four are not organized chronologically. Chapter two, "Autumn Leaves" and three, "Lady Aoi" contain traditional stories illustrating the cloistered emperor's gentleness; and chapter four, "Kogō" is an independent romance which was developed from a simpler tradition concerning the emperor.

The second group (chapters five and six) tells of the national insurrection against the Taira. Chapter five, "The Summons to Arms" contains traditional stories about the birth of Kiso Yoshinaka, a member of the Minamoto clan who raised troops in the south of Shinano close to the capital, and it tells the motives of his uprising. Chapter six, "The Coming of the Couriers" is entirely a record organized like a chronicle, which reports on the progress of the insurrection in the home provinces, Kyushu and Shikoku.

The third group (chapters seven to ten) deals with Taira no Kiyomori. Chapter seven, "The Monk's Demise" records the death of Kiyomori, and while organized chronologically, has a few legendary stories mingled in the chronicle. The remaining three chapters in this group—"The Artificial Island," "The Monk Jishin," and "The Lady of Gion"—follow the biographical mode of presentation and consist of stories handed down about the deceased Kiyomori.

Group four comprises chapters eleven, twelve, and thirteen, entitled respectively: "The Battle of Sumata," "The Hoarse Cry," and "The Battle of Yokotagawara," which resume the progress of the fighting from the point to which it was carried in chapter six, "The Coming of the Couriers." Although organized like a chronicle, these chapters include descriptions of fighting and amount to something more than a plain record.

Thus the sixth scroll is composed of a variety of ingredients consisting of chronicles, traditional stories, a romance, and battle descriptions. This sort of motleyness is not found in the *Hōgen* and *Heiji* tales, let alone the prose literature of the Heian court, epitomized in the *Genji monogatari*. For it is in the nature of the court novels and stories that they should be devoid of chronological records and descriptions of battles, while on the other hand it is most difficult to find in the *Hōgen* and *Heiji* tales any sort of subjective treatment of events or delineation of character and feelings. The *Heike monogatari*, while belonging to the succession of battle tales which began with the *Shōmonki*, an account of the rebellion of Taira no Masakado in the tenth century, has been heavily influenced by traditional, half-legendary stories such as are found in the eleventh-century collection entitled *Konjaku monogatari* (Once-Upon-A-Time Tales), and has imitated extensively chronological records like the *Ōkagami* (Great Mirror), which is a history of the imperial court in the ninth and tenth centuries. At the same time it differs markedly from its immediate predecessors in the line of battle stories, the *Hōgen* and *Heiji* tales, in that it betrays considerable influence from such products of the court literature as the *Genji monogatari*. Its tendency to portray emotion is realized in its successful depiction of the life and sentiments of the declining aristocracy by adopting on a large scale the classical diction and style developed in the literature of the imperial court. For example, in contrast to the *Hōgen monogatari*, which shows little sympathy with the Cloistered Emperor Sutoku, the central character of the Hōgen war, by cutting short his lament on defeat after only two lyric poems and two lines of prose, the *Heike monogatari* devotes two long chapters to the Cloistered Emperor Go-Shirakawa when he is reduced to a similar plight and describes his grief with a minuteness born of sympathetic understanding.

However, this concern with personal feelings, which is so evident in the reciters' versions and the standard text, both alike derived from the *Kakuichi* manuscript, is not characteristic of all the texts. Which means that not all of the

sentimental passages in the reciters' texts date from the origin of the *Heike monogatari*. To illustrate this point we may take the famous chapter in scroll five entitled "Moon Viewing," which has a direct bearing on the *Genji monogatari*.

With the Minamoto pressing upon them, the Taira have abandoned the capital and moved the court to Fukuhara. One autumn night the aristocrats hold moon viewing parties at Fukuhara, but Tokudaiji Jittei returns to the capital to enjoy the moon in the deserted haunts of better days. He stops at his sister's house and is received by her as she sits playing the *biwa*. The sight reminds him of another lady, described in the *Genji monogatari*, who long ago spent an autumn night in contemplation as she strummed the *biwa*, and on perceiving the pale moon still riding the sky at daybreak, beckoned to it with her plectrum. One of his sister's maids is called Matsuyoi (Waiting at Nightfall), because she was once asked what was more pathetic, waiting for one's lover at nightfall or watching him depart in the morning, and she replied with the poem:

> How cheap is the early song of the birds
> When they greet his departure at sunrise
> Compared with the boom of the temple bell
> As it tolls the hours of waiting at nightfall.

These passages evoke the heyday of a dying culture—the days when it could produce a masterpiece like the *Genji monogatari*, when a courtier might spend his youth in nothing more serious than nighttime love affairs, and when impromptu poems were essential components of courtly converse—and by this evocation could touch the heart of a listener whose sympathies lay with the past. They are, however, not to be found in the *Shibukassenjō* manuscript, which is a reading text, nor in the early reciter's text, the *Yashiro* manuscript. It is evident, then, that the original form of the *Heike monogatari* is best inferred from the plain narration characteristic of the *Shibukassenjō* and *Yashiro* versions, and that the sentimental passages, which differentiate the *Heike monogatari* from its predecessors in the genre, were added gradually at a later date.

Returning now to scroll six, we may remember that chapters two, three, and four—"Autumn Leaves," "Lady Aoi," and "Kogō"—present stories illustrating the gentleness of the Cloistered Emperor Takakura. "Autumn Leaves" contains two stories, which are summarized as follows:

I

When the emperor was ten years old, he kept maple trees in his garden because he loved the autumn colours. The leaves were scattered one night by the wind and a gardener raked them up for a fire to heat his *sake*. Instead of punishing the culprit as his courtiers expected, however, the emperor accepted the situation philosophically and did nothing.

II

The emperor, on the way to one of his residences, encountered a poor girl who had just been robbed of her master's garment. He presented her with a new set of clothing and sent her home under the protection of one of his guards.

Originally these two episodes were separated by the independent story entitled "Lady Aoi," and subsequently they were put together to form a single chapter because they complement each other as examples of the emperor's gentle nature.

The very moving chapter entitled "Kogō," which follows "Lady Aoi" in most texts, does not occur in the *Shibukas-senjō* manuscript. It is summarized below according to the version found in the *Kakuichi* and the standard texts.

When the emperor lost his mistress, Lady Aoi, he was so grief-stricken that his consort hoped to console him by presenting him with a lovely girl named Kogō. But Kiyomori took offense because Kogō was the mistress of his son-in-law, Reizei Takafusa, and his anger vented itself on the girl. Therefore, Kogō, heedless of the emperor's pleas, went into hiding. One autumn evening the emperor was informed that Kogō had gone to Saga, and he sent his attendant Nakakuni there to find out where she was hidden. Nakakuni made his way to Kogō's house, guided by the music of her zithern. He returned her to the palace, where eventually she bore the emperor a daughter. But Kogō's presence in the palace came to the attention of Kiyomori, and at length she was compelled to go into a convent. This incident was one of several which contributed to the emperor's early death.

The "Kogō" chapter, which is not found in the *Shibukas-senjō* text, was introduced into the **Heike monogatari** through the *Nagato* text. In its tone it resembles closely many of the "once-upon-a-time" tales in the *Konjaku monogatari,* and it depicts Kiyomori as both a rough and a licentious character. However, in the *Enkyō* manuscript, which follows the *Nagato* manuscript in the lineage of reading texts, the realistic description of the give and take between Kiyomori and Kogō disappears; the Kogō who in the *Nagato* text boldly stood up to Kiyomori has now become a pliant female; and the scene where she bears the emperor a daughter appears for the first time. Moreover Kiyomori has been transfigured from a strong personality into a stereotyped authoritarian, the father of the emperor's consort. This change is carried further in the *Kakuichi* manuscript, a reciter's text, where the centre of attention recedes from the character of Kiyomori and shifts over to the first half of the story, that is, the love between the emperor and Kogō. Thus the "Kogō" chapter, as one of the legends concerning the Emperor Takakura, has attained its completed form, and the process illustrates the fact that the **Heike monogatari** developed a deepening sensitivity to the portrayal of sentiment during the period when it was in the hands of the *biwa hōshi.*

The basic rhythm of the **Heike monogatari** resolves itself into alternating lines of seven and five syllables, which is the characteristic metre of Japanese poetry. The smooth-

ness of this rhythm may be appreciated in the opening lines of the scene where Lady Hotoke pays a visit to the retreat of Giō, Kiyomori's cast-off mistress, who now, with her mother and sister, devotes herself to religion.

Kakute haru sugi
natsu takenu.
Aki no hatsukaze
fukinureba
hoshiai no sora o
nagametsutsu
amanoto wataru
kaji no ha ni
omou koto kaku
koro nare ya.

And so the spring is gone
and summer has passed the zenith.
With the first breath
of autumn in the wind,
now is the season when youngsters look up
to the star lovers united in the sky,
the Weaving Maid and Herdboy,
who come together but once a year,
and between their upward glances
write words of love
on leaves of the paper mulberry,
leaf-boats to bear their thoughts
as the Herdboy is borne across
the river of the milky way.

. . . . .

Tasokaredoki mo
suginureba
take no amido o
tojifusagi
tomoshibi kasuka ni
kakitatete
oyako sannin
nembutsu shite
itaru tokoro ni
take no amido o
hotohoto to
uchitataku mono
idekitari.

The hour of dusk is past:
with the bamboo door secured
and the lamplight burning low
a mother and her daughters
are telling their beads
when suddenly on the door without
beats a sharp rap rap
of one who has come.

The "Giō" chapter does not occur in the *Gempei tōjō roku,* the *Shibukassenjō* text, and the *Nagato* text, all of which are meant to be read and not sung. This story of the rival dancers, Giō and Lady Hotoke, had originally been an independent piece, but was incorporated into the **Heiki monogatari** as another demonstration of Kiyomori's "extraordinary" behaviour. In the *Enkyō* text the same scene is rendered concisely thus:

It is now about the third day of the month, when about midnight there comes a rapping on the door of their retreat.

In this objective description of what happened, devoid of lyricism, we get an idea of the form in which this story was cast in the early period of the *Heike monogatari*'s development.

Let us go back again to scroll six. On the basis of this scroll as it appears in the *Kakuichi* text I shall discuss the relationship between chronological form and literary quality, for nearly half of the scroll is organized chronologically. The opening paragraph of chapter six, "The Coming of the Couriers," describes, as a sort of prologue to the national insurrection, the reaction of Kiyomori and the Taira clan to the report of Kiso Yoshinaka's rebellion. This part is not in chronicle form, and it stands in relation to the rest of the chapter as a kind of preface. The remainder of the chapter is taken up by chronological entries each preceded by a date: the first day of the second month, the seventh day of the same month, the ninth day of the same month, and so forth. These entries are written in a Japanese burdened with Chinese vocabulary, a style called *wakan konkōbun* which is characteristic of aristocratic diaries and historical records like the *Azuma kagami* (Mirror of the East). The entries from the first to the sixteenth day of the second month are selected to focus attention on the repercussions and countermeasures evoked in the capital by the anti-Taira movement which was gathering force throughout the country. Accordingly, any passage in this section from an earlier text was deleted from the *Heike monogatari* as represented by the *Kakuichi* text if it did not conform to the principle of selection adopted in the *Kakuichi* text to unify this part of the chapter.

When we consider the *Heike monogatari* as represented in the reciters' texts, there is nothing in particular to hold our interest in the choice of vocabulary; for, to state the matter in an extreme form, the reciters did not care whether their audiences could understand every word of the Chinese vocabulary they frequently employed. The essence of *Heike* artistry lies rather in the beauty resulting from the union of written style with the style of recitation, therefore what is required is a mode of recitation suitable to the passage at hand. Nevertheless, even when we consider the *Heike monogatari* simply as a piece of written literature, ignoring the tonal beauties that go into its recitation, its literary qualities are quite obvious. For example, the chronological and non-chronological parts of the "Coming of the Couriers" are not merely juxtaposed but have an organic relation. Kiyomori's contempt when he received the report of Kiso Yoshinaka's rising was shared by the men of the Taira. But others, who knew that the Taira had been losing the regard of the nation, thought differently. This is the situation set forth in plain narrative at the beginning of the chapter. Now begins the chronicle, which proceeds step by step to verify the misgivings of those in the capital who had not shared the Taira's disregard of the first report. Here it is necessary to note that the method in the reciters' texts of ending these reports of rebellion with the formula "so it is reported" serves the purpose of presenting the facts as objectively as possible. The recitation progresses, piling one fact upon the other without the slightest qualification. The Taira, who have discounted the report of Yoshinaka's rebellion, are shocked to hear the news from Kyushu, when hard upon it comes the news from Shikoku to complete their dismay. In this way the uneasy murmuring of observers at the beginning of the chapter culminates by chronological stages into a despairing cry at the end that "the world is on the brink of disaster"; and we find before us a graphic description of an age trembling at the portents of an unprecedented civil war. In such a manner, then, the literary quality of the *Heike monogatari* transforms its value in the process of shifting, or being absorbed into the reciting texts from the reading texts, losing the chronological character of the reading texts, and at the same time its function as a piece of recitation is realized in the literary value of the minstrels' texts.

Notes

1. "Monk" translates *nyūdō* "one who has entered the way." A *nyūdō* had his head shaved and wore the habit of a monk, but he did not live in a monastery and was not necessarily aloof from worldly affairs.

2. This was a discussion of *shingafu* (hsin-yüeh-fu) in the *Hakushi monjū* (Po-shih-wen-chi), which is thought to have been held on the 15th of March, 1210 (fourth year of Shōgen) at the *Kōyōinden* palace where the Cloistered Emperor Goshirakawa resided.

3. *Heike monogatari* in *Nihon koten bungaku taikei* XXXII, Iwanami shoten, Tokyo, 1952, p. 12.

4. Matsui Takeshi, "Heike monogatari to Shōkyūki to no kankei," *Bungaku*, July 1934, II, No. 7, pp. 64-65.

5. But Takahashi Sadaichi thinks the reference might be to the records of the Heike family rather than the *Heike monogatari* (*Heike monogatari shohon no kenkyū*, Fuzambō, Tokyo, 1943, p. 449); and Atsumi Kaoru believes that it concerns some tales about the Heike which existed in written form before the *Heike monogatari* itself (*Heike monogatari no kisoteki kenkyū*, Sanseidō, Tokyo, 1962, p. 49).

6. This is the diary of Fujiwara no Sanesuke, the Minister of the Right.

7. Ishimoda Tadashi, *Heike monogatari*, Iwanami shoten, Tokyo, 1957, p. 183.

8. Fujiwara no Akihira, "Shin sarugakuki" (1058 AD) in *Gunshorui jū*, VI, 1046.

9. Kazamaki Keijirō, *Nihon bungakushi no shūhen*, Hanawa shobō, Tokyo, 1954, p. 169.

10. *Heike monogatari* in *Nihon koten bungaku taikei*, XXXII, 44.

11. *Heike monogatari no kisoteki kenkyū*, pp. 14-15.

12. *Heike monogatari hyōkō*, Meiji shoin, Tokyo, 1963, 1, 17.

13. Yamashita Hiroaki, "*Gempei tōjō roku* to kenkyū" in *Mikan kokubun shiryō*, Toyohashi, 1963, p. 221; "*Heike monogatari* no katari to yomi ni kansuru shi-

ron" in *Kinjōgakuin daigaku ronshū,* No. 25, July, 1964, pp. 46-49.

14. On the other hand, the *Daigo zasshō* "Records of the Daigo Monastery," which was written by the monk Ryūgen (1343-1426), says that the *Heike monogatari* was written by Fujiwara no Tokinaga, a cousin of the historical Yukinaga, at the suggestion of the blind *biwa hōshi* Jōichi. Jōichi was an eminent reciter, and his name appears in a record of 1328.

15. Prince Shukaku's diary *Saki, Gunshoruijū* XVI, 764. Cf. Nagazumi Yasuaki, *Chūsei bungaku no tembō,* Tōkyō daigaku shuppankai, 1956, p. 111.

16. The manuscripts of the *Heike monogatari* fall into two lines of descent: the *katari-kei* "recitation texts" and the *zōho-kei* "supplemented texts" or *yomihon* "reading texts." In 1371 Kakuichi, a gifted reciter, stabilized the recitation text of his school to forestall disputes among his followers after his death. The *Kakuichi bon,* as this version is called, is one of the best known recitation texts.

17. *Heike monogatari,* Hōbunkan, Tokyo, 1933, pp. 42-45.

18. *Heike monogatari,* pp. 140-141.

Kenneth Dean Butler (essay date 1969)

SOURCE: "The *Heike Monogatari* and the Japanese Warrior Ethic," in *Harvard Journal of Asiatic Studies,* Vol. 29, 1969, pp. 93-108.

[*In the following essay, Butler argues that the code of the Japanese warrior as presented in the* Heike Monogatari *is more a creation of the tellers of the tales than historic fact.*]

The *Heike monogatari* has exerted a strong influence on many aspects of the later development of Japanese society. In the political sphere, it is well-known that the accounts of warrior battles contained in the *Heike* provided a model for the attitudes and standards of conduct of the warrior class until the nineteenth, and even into the twentieth, centuries.[1] The degree of historical validity of these accounts, and their relationship to the actual battles themselves, is less well-known. The present article is an attempt to outline briefly the process by which the narrative passages, which taken as a whole define the warrior code at the time of the Gempei battles of 1180-1185, came to be a part of the *Heike monogatari* text. The manner in which these passages came to be accepted as historical fact, and how they came to be regarded as superior examples of the code of the Japanese warrior, is also considered.

It is possible to isolate in the standard *Heike monogatari* text all of the important qualities which later came to be accepted as the ideal and necessary attributes of a warrior. The concepts of personal loyalty, a willingness to sacrifice one's life for one's lord, and the determination to fight on

to an honorable death rather than give in to a superior foe, to name but a few, all find frequent and varied expression throughout the sections of the *Heike monogatari* devoted to the Gempei battles.

It would seem to be a rather simple task to assemble a sufficient number of examples illustrating these concepts, arrange and classify them, and then come up with a model of the feudal warrior ethic as it existed in the late twelfth century. But before one becomes too involved in constructing such a model, it is well to give some attention to the circumstances of the textual development of the *Heike monogatari.* There exists an extremely large number of variant manuscripts of the *Heike,* more than a hundred, by recent estimates.[2] But a clear picture of the exact sequence in which the major variant manuscripts appeared, and the process of interaction between oral and written literature which produced the perfected narrative of the standard *Heike* text, has only recently begun to emerge.

For about the last six hundred years the text which has been taken as standard has been one dictated in 1371 by the famous *biwa hōshi Heike* singer, Akashi Kakuichi (d. sixth month, 1371). It has been realized by most people that there had been earlier written versions of the *Heike monogatari.* In fact, the original *Heike monogatari* has traditionally been thought to have been written during the time of the Retired Emperor Go-Toba (1198-1221), not long before the Jōkyū War of 1221.[3] But little information has been available concerning the textual development of the *Heike monogatari* during the 150-year period from 1221 to 1371, and consequently the popular audiences after 1371 who heard or read Kakuichi's *Heike monogatari* text (and its later minor revisions) accepted it as a contemporary account of the events it relates. Even scholars, who knew of the late date of the Kakuichi text, tended to assume that in its essential parts the Kakuichi narrative was identical with the original version. Until quite recently, most scholars have only mentioned in passing that the *Heike* text has suffered some degree of modification as a result of its textual development, and they then go on to base whatever aspect of the period 1180 to 1185 they may be dealing with on the *Heike monogarati* narrative as it appears in the Kakuichi text of 1371.[4]

One of the factors which has been conducive to the adoption of such an approach is that it is possible to find in certain of the historical records of the Gempei period many entries which seem to corroborate the Kakuichi *Heike* narrative. In the past, the historical chronicle of the Kamakura feudal government, the *Azuma kagami,* has often been cited in asserting the historical accuracy of the *Heike monogatari.* We know that the *Azuma kagami* was not compiled before about the year 1270, or almost one hundred years after the Gempei battles. But the general consensus has been that the *Azuma kagami* entries are based on earlier records kept by the Kamakura warriors and that therefore they should be reasonably accurate. In the early portion of the *Azuma kagami* there are many entries concerning the major Gempei battles which accord quite closely with similar passages in the *Heike.* This correspondence tends to reinforce the impression that the major part of the *Heike* narrative should be accepted as presenting a valid picture of the battles.[5] But on the basis of a preliminary comparison of the *Azuma kagami* with the earliest of the preserved *Heike monogatari* variants, which date from before 1270, the indications are that much of the early part of the *Azuma kagami,* particularly such sections as the ones describing Mochihito's flight from Kyoto, the Fuji River battle, Ichinotani, and Yashima, is in fact based directly on the accounts as they appear in the early *Heike* variants rather than on separate historical records. It is therefore rather risky to cite the *Azuma kagami* to substantiate the validity of the *Heike monogatari* narrative.

If we put aside the *Azuma kagami,* the one other major source most often cited to support the *Heike* narrative is the *Gyokuyō,* the *kambun* diary which was kept as a day-to-day record of the events of the period as observed in Kyoto by the Fujiwara nobleman Kujō Kanezane (1149-1207). There was a definite and legitimate influence from the *Gyokuyō* at the time the original *Heike monogatari* was written, but comparison of the *Gyokuyō* and the early extant *Heike* manuscripts reveals that the type of narrative element which finds substantiation in the *Gyokuyō* is not such passages as those that treat of the actions and mentality of the Heike and Genji warriors in battle. Instead, the sections which can be shown to be based on the historical *Gyokuyō* account are for the most part merely those which relate specific dates, or deal with such matters as who was where at what time, what kind of court ceremonies were held when and where, who was promoted to what office in the civil government, and the like.[6] Kujō Kanezane was a civil official who did not leave Kyoto. With the exception of a few scathing attacks on warriors such as Kiso Yoshinaka, or accounts describing his own negotiations with the Genji leader Yoritomo concerning his later appointment as *sesshō* or "Regent," Kanezane did not deign to mention much concerning matters pertaining to warriors.

So, if we get no help from the *Azuma kagami* or from the *Gyokuyō* in determining the validity of the warrior ethic as it appears in the *Heike monogatari,* we are left with little choice other than to do it on the basis of the variant *Heike* manuscripts themselves. Fortunately our understanding of the textual development of the *Heike monogatari* has improved greatly during the last decade, and it is now possible not only to appreciate much better the *Heike* as a work of epic literature but also, by comparative study of the early manuscripts, to gain a much more accurate insight into the events of the Gempei wars as related in this work.

In a recent study I have cited several major variants of the *Heike monogatari* which are crucial to any consideration of the *Heike.*[7] Of these, four are of particular importance to an understanding of the development of the warrior ethic within the *Heike* text. The earliest of these manuscripts is known by the title *Shibu kassenjō daisamban tōjō Heike monogatari,* or "*Heike monogatari,* the third

battle of a battle-record in four parts." This is a version of the *Heike monogatari* written in a *kambun* style which verges on pure Chinese. On the basis of internal evidence I have shown that this text was written between the years 1218 and 1221. With the aid of these dates and also as a result of detailed textual comparison with the other early *Heike* variants, I have suggested that the *Shibu kassenjō* text is in fact the original written form of the *Heike monogatari.* The style of the *Shibu kassenjō* text is much closer to that of a straight historical chronicle than is the style of any of the other *Heike* variants, and by comparison with the *Gyokuyō,* it can be shown that the greater part of the factual information in the *Shibu kassenjō* is based directly on the *kambun* entries of the *Gyokuyō.*[8] The second major variant is the Yashiro *Heike monogatari* text. The Yashiro text was written sometime after 1242, but probably before 1300. It represents the earliest attempt to revise the *kambun* narrative of the *Shibu kassenjō* original *Heike monogatari* for use as a fixed text for memorization and recitation by rhapsode-type *biwa hōshi* reciters. The Yashiro text is written in Japanese, rather than *kambun,* and uses the *katakana* phonetic script with Chinese characters. The third major variant is the Kamakura *Heike* text. The Kamakura text was made at some time during the period from about 1300 to 1340, and it represents an expanded and more sophisticated revision for recitation of the original *Heike* narrative. The Kamakura text is also in Japanese and uses the *katakana* script. The final major variant necessary for an understanding of the *Heike monogatari* is the Kakuichi text of 1371. In essence, the Kakuichi text is a combination of the best elements of both the Yashiro and the Kamakura divisions of textual development. Because of the perfection of its narrative, which uses the *hiragana* script rather than *katakana,* from about 1400 the Kakuichi text became accepted as the standard version of the *Heike monogatari.* Copies of the earlier variants such as the *Shibu kassenjō,* the Yashiro, and the Kamakura texts, dropped from sight. These texts were relegated to the archives of Buddhist temples and private collections, where they remained until discovered by manuscript collectors of modern times.

How does a knowledge of the textual development of the variant *Heike monogatari* texts aid in understanding the basis of the development of the warrior ethic in Japan? The best way in which this question may be answered is by reference to a particular passage as it appears in the four major *Heike monogatari* variants themselves.

In Book 7 of the standard Kakuichi text of 1371 a detailed account is given of the battles in 1183 north of Kyoto between the attacking Genji force of Kiso Yoshinaka, and the defending forces of the Heike.[9] This section opens with the statement that Yoshinaka was poised in the north with 50,000 warriors, ready to attack the Heike in Kyoto. We are told that the Heike, led by Kiyomori's grandson Koremori, raised a force of 100,000 and advanced to meet Yoshinaka. The validity of these figures need not concern us, since they are probably inflated, but at any rate, in the present account, after a passage describing how the two opposing warrior groups are divided, we find Yoshinaka, with a force of 40,000, confronting the main Heike force of 70,000 in the Tonami mountains. Yoshinaka decides that since his force is so much smaller, he must rely on superior strategy to defeat the Heike. Accordingly he devises a plan of boxing up the Heike warriors in Kurikara Canyon, at the foot of the mountains. After the initial encounter, the Heike force is deceived into thinking that Yoshinaka's force is much stronger than their own, and at the time of the major charge by Yoshinaka, the entire Heike force turns and flees in confused retreat without joining battle. The Heike force flees into Kurikara Canyon, and Yoshinaka, as planned, boxes them in. Of the 70,000 Heike only 2,000 manage to escape with their lives. After this encounter, Yoshinaka takes his troops to help defeat the smaller Heike force of 30,000 at Mt. Shiho, and this Heike force also flees. With this defeat, the section describing the major encounter between the Genji and the Heike ends.

In the narrative up to this point the battle has been presented only in general terms, and there is no mention of fighting between individual warriors, or of any details which would provide a direct insight into the actual code of the warrior as it was expressed in action. On the contrary, by placing the emphasis in the narrative on the fact that the entire Heike force of 100,000 retreats without fighting at the first sign of the Genji battle flags, the *Heike monogatari* at this point seems to be advocating cowardice as the better part of valor, and this of course is the exact opposite of the warrior code as it is known in later ages.

But the narrative of the Kakuichi *Heike* text of 1371 does not stop here. After the description of the major battles at Kurikara Canyon and Mt. Shiho, there is a series of accounts of battles between individual warriors. It is in these later sections that the narrative elements commonly accepted as reflecting the warrior code of the Gempei wars emerge.[10] First there is a section which bridges the gap between the general battle and the individual acts of heroic sacrifice which are to come. In this section we are told that before the Heike warriors set out from the capital, a certain Saitō Bettō Sanemori had tested twenty of the leading Heike warriors, who had their origins in the East, by suggesting that since the Genji were obviously going to win, they should desert the Heike and align themselves with the Genji forces of Kiso Yoshinaka. The men are about to decide to do this, when one among them remonstrates with Sanemori saying that it is most disgraceful for a warrior to change from one side to the other according to the will of fortune, and he urges them all to die in fighting for the Heike. Saitō Bettō Sanemori replies that he had only been testing the loyalty of the warriors, and that they should all make a vow to die for the Heike. In an aside, the *Heike* text tells us that tragic as it may be, all twenty of the men kept their vow and died at the time of the battles in the north with Yoshinaka.

Here we have a classic expression of a concept which later became central to the code of the warrior in Japan. A warrior should not serve two lords, and should choose death

in battle rather than go over to the enemy. Following this section in the Kakuichi text it is related that after fleeing from Kurikara Canyon and Mt. Shiho, the remnants of the Heike force stopped to rest at Shinohara in Kaga. Yoshinaka pursues them, and it is at this point, coming after the previous brief section stressing the loyalty of a warrior, that we get three actual examples of the warrior code at its best.

After describing the preliminary encounter at Shinohara, an account of the fortunes of one Takahashi no Hōgan Nagatsuna is given. He joins battle with 300 of the Genji with a mixed force of 500 warriors from various provinces who have straggled into the Heike camp. Although Takahashi fights valiantly, his men are a motley lot and most of them flee. Takahashi himself is finally forced to retreat, but his intention is to try to find some of his own loyal personal retainers and once again to join battle with the Genji. As he is searching for his men, he encounters a young Genji warrior named Yukishige. Takahashi starts to kill him, but then remembers that his own son who had been killed in battle the previous year was about the same age as Yukishige, and he decides to spare the young Genji warrior. But Yukishige, for his part, is filled with warrior spirit. Even though Takahashi has just spared his life, Yukishige waits for a chance to take Takahashi by surprise and kill him. This he does, with the aid of three of his retainers who happen along, and thus ends the great warrior Takahashi.

The second example of a warrior in action concerns a certain Arikuni, who penetrated far into the Genji ranks with a force of 300. The *Heike monogatari* narrative is particularly vivid at this point, and is worth quoting in part.

> Arikuni, having penetrated deep within the enemy ranks, exhausted all his arrows and had his horse shot from under him. Then afoot, he drew out his sword and fought on, killing many warriors. Finally, pierced by seven or eight shafts, he met his death, still on his feet. Their great general thus fallen, his forces all fled in retreat.[11]

The final example appearing in this section of the Kakuichi text is one involving Saitō Bettō Sanemori, the warrior who appeared earlier as the one who admonished his twenty men to die fighting. This passage is rather long, and there is no need to trace it out in detail. The importance of it as it bears on the warrior ethic is that after the Heike forces have been completely routed and are retreating as fast as their horses will carry them, Sanemori alone among the Heike warriors refuses to retreat, and despite his advanced age, constantly turns back to engage the enemy and protect the rear of the retreating Heike. He is finally killed, but not before he has displayed by personal example the manner in which a true warrior should act in battle. The Sanemori section ends the portion of the Kakuichi *Heike monogatari* text dealing with the battles in the north against Yoshinaka. Not long after this time, Yoshinaka and his forces enter the capital, and the scene soon shifts to an account of the battles in the west—Ichinotani, Yashima, and finally Dannoura, where the Heike meet their end.

On the basis of the four sections coming after the general account of the Kurikara Canyon battle in the Kakuichi text of 1371, we can discern several of the qualities previously mentioned which later ages held up as shining examples of the Japanese warrior code. In the earlier Sanemori section we saw that loyalty to one's lord, even if the cause is hopeless, was defined as one of the cardinal virtues. In the Takahashi passage, we get the young warrior Yukishige appearing as the cold-hearted warrior who thinks only of killing the enemy, even if the enemy, as in this particular case, has shown him mercy. The actions and feelings of Takahashi in this passage are almost identical to those of Kumagai Naozane in the famous Atsumori section of the battle of Ichinotani, related in Book 9. Naozane, however, while regretting his action, does in the end kill Atsumori.[12] In the Takahashi section, Takahashi's actions should probably be interpreted as an example of the fact that if one's enemy is weak, the true warrior should take advantage of this and accomplish his objectives with no thought of human feelings. The Arikuni section, while short, presents an example of the warrior fighting on to the bitter end, and in the final Sanemori section once again we get the picture of the true warrior refusing to retreat before superior odds and sacrificing his own life so that his lord might live.

All of these actions are examples of the qualities that have been emulated by Japanese warriors of later ages, and are also the ones which together with a liberal dosage of Confucian teachings were developed into the code of Bushidō by such theorists as Yamaga Sokō (1622-1685) during the Tokugawa period. If these events as related in the Kakuichi text of the *Heike monogatari* were only true or at least bore some demonstrable resemblance to the actual situation, there would be no problem, and a survey of the warrior ethic in the *Heike monogatari* would end at this point. But when we look at the *Shibu kassenjō* text of 1221, and also the other early *Heike* variants, the picture is quite different.

In the *Shibu kassenjō* text there is a general description of the battles at Kurikara Canyon and at Mt. Shiho which is more or less identical to that of the Kakuichi text. The numbers of warriors involved are stated as being slightly less, but for the most part the account is the same. But following this general account of the major battles, in which the Heike are described as fleeing without attempting to fight, we get a very different sort of narrative. First, the sections of the Kakuichi text devoted to Sanemori and his twenty warriors, the adventures of Takahashi and Yukishige, and the death in battle of Arikuni are completely missing. We do get the final section describing the death of Sanemori in battle, but even here the emphasis is entirely different. In the *Shibu kassenjō* version Sanemori is not presented as having remained behind to protect the rear. Instead, he is fleeing like all the rest, and it is only because he is old that he is overtaken by a younger Genji, who dispatches him with ease and takes his head to Yoshinaka. In short, at no point in the *Shibu kassenjō* account, which is the version of the *Heike mongatari* written at a time closest to the events it relates, is there any developed

presentation of individual warriors acting in a way we have come to believe they did on the basis of the narrative of the standard Kakuichi text of 1371.[13]

When we consider the Yashiro text, we can see some expansion of the narrative, but it also is still far from presenting any sort of concrete picture of a developed warrior ethic. The story about Arikuni has been added, in a rather terse form, but both he and Sanemori are still presented as having become separated from the main group of fleeing Heike, and fighting for their lives out of necessity, rather than choice.[14]

It is only when we get to the Kamakura text, which was not written until about 1300, more than one hundred years after the Gempei battles, that we find the narrative developed to a point approaching that of the Kakuichi version of 1371. In the Kamakura text, in addition to the story of Sanemori, there are also the stories of both Arikuni and Takahashi. The only major difference with the Kakuichi text is that the final brief general battle at Shinohara is not described at length.[15] But even more importantly, in the Kamakura text we find a major shift in emphasis. No longer is Sanemori presented as an old warrior who has fallen behind. Instead we find him possessing all the attributes of a great hero in the best tradition of the warrior ethic. Sanemori stays behind by choice, to defend his lord who must live to fight another day. The other warriors, Takahashi and Arikuni, have also taken on heroic attributes. In the earlier Yashiro text Arikuni is presented not as having charged into the enemy ranks, but rather as having fallen behind along with Sanemori in attempting to flee and as having been finally overtaken by the enemy who shoot his horse from under him and then kill him. In the Kamakura text Arikuni appears as a stout-hearted warrior, one of the leading generals in the battle, who charges into the enemy ranks in much the same manner as he does in the account quoted from the Kakuichi text.

There is much more that can be said about the evolution of the *Heike monogatari* narrative throughout the variant texts, but it should be clear from the brief outline given that the elements of the *Heike* narrative which in the past have commonly been accepted as representative of the warrior spirit at the time of the Gempei wars of 1180 to 1185 did not enter the *Heike* text until about 1300 at the earliest—or more than a century after the actual events. If we examine all the other battle sections of the *Heike monogatari* as they appear in the four major variants, the situation is the same. All of the battles begin with a general description of the large battle itself. Then the general account is followed by a section in which the actions of the individual warriors are described. The *Shibu kassenjō* text, however, contains the general account of the battle, but lacks the appended sections of the actions of the individual warriors. Similarly, it is only at the stage of the Kamakura text of about 1300 that we find the accounts of the individual warriors appearing in a fashion similar to that of the Kakuichi text.

There should be little doubt that the details of the heroic actions of the warriors as they are presented in the Kamakura and Kakuichi texts are entirely fictional. There are no acceptable historical records which corroborate any of the Kakuichi text narration of the specific incidents of the Gempei battles. Since little or none of this detail appears in the original *Shibu kassenjō Heike* text and very little of it in the Yashiro, it is difficult to imagine that suddenly about the year 1300 someone would discover complete historical accounts of these battles and insert them into their appropriate places in the *Heike* narrative. But the fact remains that these accounts in the standard *Heike* text have, with only minor reservations, been accepted over the centuries as being more or less historically accurate. There is an inherent, built-in feature of the standard Kakuichi *Heike monogatari* narrative which to a large extent explains this rather unusual phenomenon. The remainder of the present article is devoted to outlining how this came about.

Anyone who has read the battle sections of the Kakuichi text cannot help but have been impressed by the detailed and vivid nature of the description of the warrior and his actions. These passages seem to have a certain living force of their own, which tends to pull the audience into the narrative and causes one to feel that he himself has been a part of what has taken place. Space limitations prohibit a detailed discussion of how the narrative of the entire twelve books of the *Heike monogatari* reached its perfected written form, but it is possible to state that much of the striking effect of the battle tale narrative in the Kakuichi text is accomplished by the use of narrative techniques which had their origins in orally composed battle tales sung by a class of singers who originally accompanied the warriors to battle.[16]

The details of orally composed tales, no matter what the country or what the subject matter, are by definition largely fictional. Oral tale singers utilize a very definite method of composition based on the use of formulas and a formulaic method of elaborating themes. The fundamental features of such a method of oral composition have been defined by Professor Albert Lord of Harvard in his book *The Singer of Tales*.[17] The oral singer traditionally takes his subject matter from historical events and personages, but the specific content of his story is entirely fictional. He does not recite his tale from memory, as was the case of the recitation of the written *Heike monogatari* after 1371. Rather, each time a true oral tale singer tells his tale he recreates it anew by means of oral formulaic techniques of composition. The oral singer is able to establish a special rapport with his audience by means of this method of composition, and even though the audience might know in one part of their minds that the details of the tale sung by the singer cannot possibly be true, by the very nature of the art the audience is drawn into the story, and by the end is left with the distinct feeling that what they have heard is an accurate version of the historical event as it actually happened.

We can see the hand, or rather the mind and voice, of the oral tale singer at work in all of the battle tale sections of the Kamakura and Kakuichi *Heike monogatari* texts. The largest themes contained in these two texts are the overall battles themselves. But it is in the latter sections of the battles, the ones describing individual warriors, that we find descriptions which betray a stereotyped pattern which establishes them as having been developed originally by means of the process of formulaic composition and thematic elaboration which is the hallmark of the oral tale singer. This kind of oral composition can be classified on the basis of the themes related. By way of illustration a short section from the Kakuichi text is quoted below, which in addition to displaying formulaic language, contains classic examples of two of the shorter oral tale themes, those of "dressing the hero," and "naming one's name," which appear frequently throughout the *Heike monogatari.*

The setting is the Battle at the Bridge at the time Prince Mochihito and his Genji supporters are fleeing from Kyoto in 1180. A monk-warrior from among the temple troops supporting Mochihito steps out to fight, and is described as follows:

> From among the monk-warrior group Tsutsui no Jōmyō Meishū wearing black leather-threaded armor over a dark blue "victory" robe, and a five-plated helmet, and with a black-lacquered sword at his side, and a quiver of twenty-four black-feathered arrows hung at his back, together with a lacquered bow and his favorite white-handled halberd in his hands, advanced onto the bridge. In a mighty voice he named his name, saying: "You have long heard of me, now take a good look. I am Tsutsui no Jōmyō Meishū, known to all of Mii Temple as a warrior worth a thousand men. Let those who will advance, and we shall see the outcome," and he then mercilessly let fly his twenty-four arrows. Immediately twelve warriors fell dead and eleven were wounded, and still one arrow remained in his quiver. He threw down his bow and stripped off his quiver. Then, kicking off his foot-gear, he sprang barefoot onto the beams of the bridge, and charged across. None would advance to meet him, and Jōmyō proceeded on, as though strolling the wide streets of the capital.[18]

The theme of "dressing the hero" as it is applied to the monk-warrior Meishū in this passage is almost identical with a similar theme used repeatedly in the *Iliad* and the *Odyssey,* and it also resembles one used in the Yugoslav oral tale tradition as described by Albert Lord.[19] Both the themes of "dressing the hero" and "naming one's name" are repeated over and over in the *Heike monogatari,* and it is on the basis of such minor themes as these and others that the larger themes of entire battles are put together. Furthermore, it is the kind of specific detail that a singer of oral tales is able to include as a result of the process of formulaic oral composition which builds a theme, that contributes the realistic element to the narrative. In addition to exact descriptions of his armor, in the passage quoted we are told that Meishū was carrying not just a halberd, but rather a "white-handled" halberd. And not only this, but it was his "favorite" white-handled halberd. Although such detail-producing formulas are repeated over and over throughout the *Heike monogatari,* this fact should not lead one to assume that their use is in any way stereotyped or hackneyed to an extent which would limit the range of personalized description in any given case. Concerning the monk-warrior Meishū, the "dark" and "black" images in the early formulas describing his robe, sword, and arrows, when viewed in comparison with dozens of other such passages in the *Heike,* particularize Meishū as an especially "ferocious" warrior, one indeed who is "worth a thousand men" (another recurring formula) in his own distinctive way. The point to make is that while oral formulaic repetition distinguishes the *Heike monogatari* as being at once different from a normal written work of literature, the technique itself admits of a particularized use which transcends a mere mechanical repetition of set, stereotyped phrases, and this in turn works favorably towards creating the special aura of authenticity which surrounds all such epics emanating from an oral tradition.

It is by the method of stringing the smaller themes (or motifs, as they are sometimes called), which themselves are based on formulaic composition, together into larger themes that the type of battle narrative we find in the perfected *Heike monogatari* is produced. There is an overall governing principle to this method in the orally composed literature of any country. In the case of the *Heike monogatari,* this governing principle demanded that after a general description of a large battle, there should be a series of accounts describing the actions of individual warriors. But the actions as they are described are not factual. Rather they are defined and limited by the range and extent of the oral formulas and themes available to the singer in his tradition. As an example of how this works out, it will be recalled that the actions of Takahashi in sparing the life of Yukishige are essentially the same as those of Kumagai Naozane in his encounter with Atsumori. In terms of oral composition both Takahashi and Kumagai Naozane are in fact the same person. Their actions might be described in oral terms as the theme of "the older warrior sparing the life of a younger warrior because of resemblance to his own young son." There is no way of knowing whether Takahashi or Kumagai Naozane actually performed actions similar to those attributed to them in the Kakuichi text of 1371. It is certain, however, that no matter what their actions, the details were not like what is described.

The descriptions of the actions of warriors in the other battles recounted in the *Heike monogatari* can also be reduced to general stereotyped themes of a similar type, which can be shown to be the kind of themes that the oral singer has at his disposal. As for why these oral themes appear in the late Kamakura text but not in the earlier *Shibu kassenjō* and Yashiro texts, this has to do with the manner in which the different texts were composed. First, it can be shown that it takes considerable time for a tradition of oral tales such as these to develop to perfection. The available evidence points to the interpretation that these oral battle tales were not current in Kyoto at the time both the original *Shibu kassenjō* text and the Yashiro

revision were made. But it also appears that the Kamakura text was made at the Buddhist center of Shoshazan in Harima province. The indications are that after the last of the Gempei battles, a group of oral battle tale singers settled at Shoshazan and that it was on the basis of the tales they sang that the existing *Heike monogatari* narrative was revised to include these elements.[20] This process produced the text we now know as the Kamakura text of the *Heike monogatari.* The Kamakura text was subsequently revised further by Kakuichi, using techniques of oral composition, and this resulted in the final perfected Kakuichi version of 1371.

In conclusion, two final comments may be made concerning how a knowledge of the oral basis of the battle sections applies to understanding the Japanese warrior ethic as it developed in conjunction with the textual evolution of the *Heike monogatari.* First, it is because of the techniques of oral composition that we get our warriors, who in the *Shibu kassenjō* text are presented in very human terms, changed into stereotyped heroes exhibiting all of the qualities later accepted as proper for a warrior. In this respect, the warrior ethic as contained in the *Heike monogatari* is not the result of an attempt at a factual description of the actions of actual warriors in the Gempei battles. Rather it should properly be attributed to the skill of the oral tale singers as they developed their tales in later years. We therefore have the paradox of the Japanese of later ages modeling their actions not on those of the Gempei warriors as they actually were, but rather upon the ideal warrior as conceived by oral singers who formed their heroes by means of formulaic techniques of oral composition. Secondly, it is as a result of the combination of oral tale narrative of this type, which itself has elements conducive to its acceptance as historical fact, with the completely factual elements derived from the *Gyokuyō* and other court records, that there was produced the perfected Kakuichi version of 1371 of the *Heike monogatari,* which has an imprint of reality sufficient to make it acceptable to later Japanese as an historically accurate and valid account.

Notes

1. See Edwin O. Reischauer and John K. Fairbank, *East Asia: The Great Tradition* (Boston, 1960), 534-544.

2. An early attempt at classification of the variant manuscripts appears in Takahashi Teiichi, *Heike monogatari shohon no kenkyū* (Fuzanbō, 1943), 569 pp.

3. See my article, "The Textual Evolution of the *Heike Monogatari,*" HJAS 26(1966).16-17.

4. Two of the best such studies are Ishimoda Shō, *Heike monogatari* (Iwanami, 1955); and Sasaki Hachirō, *Heike monogatari no kenkyū* (Waseda, 1948), 3 vols.

5. For a short general discussion of the relationship between the *Azuma kagami* and the *Heike,* see Minoru Shinoda, *The Founding of the Kamakura Shogunate, 1180-1185* (New York, 1960), 9-12.

6. In his monumental study, *Heike monogatari ryakuge* (Hōbunkan, 1929), Mihashi Tokugen has pointed out many of the passages in the standard *Heike* text which have a basis in the *Gyokuyō* and other court records of the period.

7. "The Textual Evolution of the *Heike Monogatari*," 8 ff.

8. The most recent study of the *Shibu kassenjō* and *Gyokuyō* connection is Shida Itaru, "Rekishi sono mama tor ekishibanare—Shibu kassenjōbon Heike monogatari o megutte", *Bungaku* (Nov. 1966).11-21.

9. *Heike monogatari* (Iwanami, 1959, 1960), 2 vols., II, 61-82.

10. *Heike monogatari*, II, 75-82.

11. *Heike monogatari*, II, 78.

12. *Heike monogatari*, II, 219-222. Translated in *Anthology of Japanese Literature, Earliest Era to Mid-Nineteenth Century*, ed. Donald Keene (New York, 1955), 179-181.

13. *Shibu kassenjōbon* (Shōwa Women's University MS.), 7.7a-27b. Atsumi Kaoru, in *Heike monogatari no kisoteki kenkyū* (Sanseidō, 1962), 353-356, was the first to point out the evolution of these passages through the four variant texts. Her discussion and the charts appearing on pp. 407-408 were of great help in the early stages of preparing the present article.

14. *Yashiro Heike monogatari* (Kadokawa, 1966), 511-516.

15. Kamakurabon *Heike monogatari* (MS.), 7.15a-18b.

16. For a general account of the oral basis of the *Heike monogatari*, see my article, "The *Heike Monogatari* and Theories of Oral Epic Literature," *Bulletin of the Faculty of Letters, Seikei University* 2(Tokyo, 1966).37-54.

17. *The Singer of Tales* (Cambridge, 1960).

18. *Heike monogatari*, I, 310. The equivalent passage in the *Shibu kassenjō* text appears in Nomura Seiichi, "Shibu kassenjobon Heike monogatari kan-shi", *Bungaku*, (Nov. 1966).96. This *Shibu kassenjō* passage, which does not display the oral thematic technique in developed form, is discussed in Yamashita Hiroaki, "Heike monogatari no katari", *Bungaku*, (Nov. 1966).7-10.

19. James I. Armstrong, "The Arming Motif in the *Iliad,*" *American Journal of Philology*, 79.344; *The Singer of Tales*, 92.

20. "The Textual Evolution of the *Heike Monogatari*," 37. See also note 144.

William E. Naff (essay date 1976)

SOURCE: "A Tale of the Heike," in *Monumenta Nipponica*, Vol. 31, No. 1, Spring, 1976, pp. 87-95.

[In the following essay, Naff discusses the difficulties in translating the Heike Monogatari *and specifically criticizes the efforts of Kitagawa and Tsuchida.]*

The ***Heike Monogatari*** occupies a seminal position in the Japanese literary tradition. For the greater part of a millenium it has been the model in Japan for treatments of the human and religious implications of war. Among epics and military tales, the ***Heike Monogatari*** is notable for its posture toward war, the occasions of war and the roles of the contending sides in war. It was developed by chanters whose most important audiences were the victors of the wars of the twelfth century and the heirs of those victors, yet it is the vanquished who are most frequently sympathetic. Although created for a society of warriors it is unflinchingly realistic about both the physical and the moral shortcomings of the warrior's trade. It is almost entirely free of the morbid and obsessive preoccupation with the minutiae of slaughter and mutilation which military tales the world around so often offer as a counterfeit of honesty about their subject. Although it tells of what was becoming a man's world, many of its most important and most fully-realized characters are women.

The twelfth century in Japan constituted a brutal and horrifying coda to the long centuries of peace and elegance that had been enjoyed by the artistically productive core of the Japanese aristocracy. The Heian period had been one of the world's great ages for humanistically oriented exploration of the human condition. Now that age of cultivation and courtly love had suddenly been replaced by a world of betrayal and terror and death and the ghosts seemed to outnumber the living, but much of the Heian sophistication and sensibility remained at the disposal of those who would try to comprehend this terrible new time.

> Nor certitude, nor peace, nor help for pain;
> And we are here as on a darkling plain
> Swept with confused alarms of struggle and flight
> Where ignorant armies clash by night.

Matthew Arnold's lines from 'Dover Beach' might almost have been written as an epigraph for the ***Heike Monogatari***. It is this vision, informed by a world view in which Buddhism predominated, that calls forth the special ambience of the ***Heike***. In its magnificent sweep from the tolling of the bells of the temple of Jetavana in India in the opening lines to the tolling of the bell of the small, poor temple of Jakkō-in deep in the mountains north of the capital on the death of the Empress Kenreimon-in, the ***Heike Monogatari*** tells one of mankind's greatest and most illuminating stories.

Medieval entertainers chanting the ***Heike*** to lute accompaniment played a key role in linking the entire nation together with a common heritage. The ***Heike*** has provided the source material for a large part of the repertoire of the Noh and Kabuki theatres. Down to the present day it continues to raise echoes, both direct and indirect, in fiction, theatre, and film. A work that has played such a role in a literary tradition as vast and rich as that of Japan must surely have an important role to play in world literature if its excellences can be made accessible to readers of other languages. The responsibilities that must be borne by the translators of such a work are of the heaviest and the expectations with which such translations will be met are unavoidably of the highest. A level of the translator's art which could lead to brilliant success with a lesser work might prove to be altogether inadequate for a work of such richness, range, and power as the **Heike Monogatari.** Such is the context in which the new translation of the **Heike Monogatari** must be read. To the extent that one agrees that the **Heike Monogatari** is worthy of a place alongside the *Iliad* or the *Odyssey,* one must hold the same standards in judging a new English translation of the **Heike** as in judging a new English translation of Homer.

The present translation makes a splendid physical impression in spite of a bulk that may make readers wish that it could have been bound in two volumes. Exactly the right tone of somber elegance has been struck in the slipcover, the dust jacket, and the interior layout. The reproductions from the *Heike Nōkyō* which they bear are appropriate in their restrained richness and sophistication for those who might wish to orient themselves through a brief reflection on the twelfth century in Europe and Japan. The calligraphic frontispieces for each of the twelve books of the **Heike** are a splendid inspiration beautifully realized.

Edward Seidensticker's foreword is graceful and informative for the general reader as it locates the **Heike** in the Japanese literary tradition. The translator's preface is also helpful, although it could have profited from both greater length and tigther focus. Appendices include an extremely useful chronological table, illustrations of the more important articles of clothing and their wearing, and maps of major sites and battles. Most readers would probably be grateful for some additions to these latter, particularly for such crucial and complicated actions as Yashima and Ichino-Tani. The volume is brought to an end with a bibliography and an index. Proofreading was excellent. Only one obvious typographical error was found: 'the might roar' on page 409, line 3, should be 'the mighty roar'. In its physical layout and in the aids to the reader that have been provided in the introduction, the appendices, and the notes at the end of each chapter, the presentation is highly reassuring to the reader, but it is the text itself which must be judged.

In order to translate successfully a great work of literature, it is necessary to find a voice or a set of voices for the work in the new language; to establish a style and stance which will give the readers of the translation a sufficiently clear perception of both the manner and the matter of the original so that claims of literary excellence made for the original will be credible. There are many ways in which this requirement may be met, but if a translation into English does not on some level come to life as English literature it cannot be counted a success, whatever may be said about the literal accuracy of the translation. It is never easy to bring a translated masterpiece to life and it is especially difficult for the **Heike.** Surely every foreign reader who has ever experienced the thundering majesty of the prologue has dreamed at least fleetingly of publishing his own version in his native language. That in a century of translations from Japanese literature this is only the second complete English version is testimony to the extreme difficulty of realizing such dreams. The present translators have had the courage to undertake a task of heroic proportions and the tenacity to see it through.

A. L. Sadler's pioneering English version,[1] a creditable first effort, is well over a half a century old and even his revised selections date from 1928. It has passages of great force and effectiveness even though the archaic English style that Sadler chose to affect was not always under firm control. His **Heike** did not find a place in world literature in any way comparable to that earned by Waley's *Genji.* But if it failed to provide a definitive English version of the **Heike** for our time, it nevertheless set a very respectable standard for those coming after. The first question that must be addressed to any new English **Heike** is whether or not it represents the kind of advance that it should after a half-century that has seen perhaps ninety percent of all Japanese-English translation. Unfortunately the answer here is by no means the clear-cut and simple one that we might wish for. The present **Heike** is an earnest version, obviously a labor of love and equally obviously the product of many thousands of hours of effort over many years. In spite of these sympathetic qualities, however, a careful reading of this translation raises many serious questions about its stance vis-à-vis the reader and its relationship to both the English language and the original Japanese.

Donald Keene is one of many distinguished and successful translators who have pointed out that successful literary translation into English depends first of all on 'a love for the English language and a sensitivity to its possibilities and limitations'.[2] He goes on to agree that a thorough grasp of the original is also absolutely essential; that errors traceable to carelessness or ignorance before the original text are inexcusable, but that their absence in no way guarantees a successful translation. These considerations make clear that there are almost impossible demands on the translator from Japanese to English and these demands would seem to be best met by collaboration between a Japanese specialist and a writer whose native language is English. There have been some brilliant successes for this approach in the translation of Japanese poetry, but even in poetry the rate of success of collaborative efforts has not been impressive. The collaborative approach has usually been unsuccessful in the translation of prose. All too often the end product combines the felicity in English idiom of the Japanese collaborator with the English-speaking collaborator's grasp of the text. Something of the sort seems to have happened with the present **Heike.** I have no direct knowledge of the quality of Professor Kitagawa's English or of Mr Tsuchida's Japanese, but there are problems with both languages in the translations as it stands.

The first disappointment comes at the very beginning. The deep sonorities of bronze bells and the sharp clash of steel that lies behind the original has been replaced by the drone of the lectern. The reader is told with a fair degree of precision *what* the original said but he is given no idea of *how* it was said. The words of the original strike like great hammers; the words of the translation like great feather pillows. Their variance from the literal meaning of the original tends consistently in the direction of diminished specificity. In an inconsistency with Japanese terms and words of ultimate Sanskrit derivation, about which more will be said later, the failure to go back to the original Jetavana, staying instead with the Japanese Gion, will leave the non-specialist reader in Japan instead of in India unless he stops after the sixth word of the text to consult a footnote at the end of the chapter. The absolute concreteness of the original in its allusion to the *Gion Zukyō* is lost as is the great sweep from India to China, from China to an earlier Japan and finally to twelfth-century Japan and Taira no Kiyomori. We have a rather close paraphrase of the surface meanings of the text but the force of allusion, the sense of movement in time and space and the exquisitely controlled rhythms that give the original its magnificence are gone. The tiger has been reduced not to a housecat but to a jellyfish.

The rendering of the title of Book Five, Chapter XII, *Gosechi no Sata*, as 'The Five Dancers Bountiful Radiant Harvest Banquet', is symptomatic of much that makes the reader uneasy about this translation. It is as casual toward the literal meaning of the original (five dancers indeed!) as it is toward the limits of idiomatic English. Such grammar as the English title possesses is Japanese, not English. Comparable difficulties appear on almost every page although few are as extreme as this. If they had been, the translation would of course never have found a publisher. At this point a few more typical examples need to be considered.

On page 182, lines five through eight, is this description of an abandoned villa: 'As the villa had not been occupied for many years, the walls were without a roof, and the gateway without doors.' Then, five lines later we read, 'The building still stood, though everything around it was in ruins.' Since the first passage quoted seems from its context to be describing a ruined building, one is forced to turn to the original to account for its sudden restoration. The original of the passage is, '. . . *tsuiji wa aredomo, ōi mo naku, mon wa aredomo, tobira mo nashi,*'[3] that is to say, '. . . although the earthen walls of the garden still stood, they had lost their protective roofs; although the main gate structure still stood, its doors were gone.' The first passage was not about the house at all but about the garden walls. This is self-evident in the original but not at all so in the translation, even on rereading.

Again, on page 213, two men are trying to flee from the wrath of the Heike, who were still at the height of their power and arrogance. As the fugitives discuss their limited possibilities, they say, 'Is there any manor in Japan that is not controlled by the Heike?' The reader is puzzled and impatient. If these men are really so hard-pressed, why do they insist on going to a manor? Why do they not flee into the wilderness that still had not vanished in twelfth-century

Japan? But the original says, '*Nippon-koku ni, Heike no shōen naranu tokoro ya aru*'[4] or, 'Is there any place in Japan that is not a Heike manor?' The difference is small but crucial. In the original we can share the despair of the fugitives because we understand that they are trying to hide in a country where even the backwoods seem to have become Heike manors. The imprecision of the translation has betrayed the sentence. This sentence is the key sentence of the opening paragraph of Book Three, Chapter XVII. The entire thrust of the chapter becomes vague because of its failure.

There is a similar example at the beginning of the fifth paragraph of page 24. Where the original text says, '*Giō motoyori omoi-mōketaru michi naredomo, sasuga ni kinō kyō to wa omoiyorazu*',[5] the translation says, 'Lady Giō had long brooded over the possibility of such a turn of events, but she had not expected her lot to change so precipitously, favor yesterday and banishment today.' Here the English line is considerably longer than the Japanese line, but it says less than the original and says it less clearly. The allusion to Narihira's poem is probably unsalvageable in translation, but the grace of the original is replaced by a heavy, unnatural, and slightly pedantic tone. The translation also makes two misleading additions. There is no reason why a female entertainer from a tradition that was a distant forerunner of the geisha should be gratuitously given the title 'Lady' with its specifically aristocratic implications and every reason why she should not. Nor is there anything in the original that in any way hints that she had 'long brooded over the possibility'. The original simply says that she had been aware all along that such a thing might happen. 'Brooding' ascribes a weakness which is nowhere hinted at in the **Heike**'s treatment of Giō, whose failing, if any, seems rather to lie on the side of impulsiveness.

The translation of the **Heike** involves the translation of a great deal of poetry, mostly *waka*. In some ways this is the greatest challenge of all. The *waka* is notoriously resistant to translation. Yet it is necessary to say that the translations of the *waka* and *imayō* made by Kitagawa and Tsuchida are for the most part disappointing. It is often difficult to tell just what the English versions are supposed to be about. There is seldom anything particularly poetic about them either in phrasing or imagery, which is not surprising since in many cases (e.g., pages 35 & 69) they are not translations of the poems in question at all but of the prose paraphrases given in the headnotes of the *Nihon Koten Bungaku Taikei* edition.

These examples would not make a significant case if they constituted anything remotely approaching an exhaustive list. They are, however, unfortunately typical rather than exceptional. An exhaustive citation of similar blurrings or distortions of the original would in itself run to several hundred pages. Even more unfortunate is the fact that translations with such shortcomings are likely to have other kinds of shortcomings as well.

There are usually a few howlers in the most careful translation. There are very few in this translation. On the next-to-last sentence of page 372, *issaikyō* becomes 'the sutra of Issai'. A far more frequent and serious problem is the rendering of proper nouns as common nouns and *vice versa*. In the first line of the second paragraph of page 620 is the phrase 'the Shōjō-den of Hongū'. To render this as 'the Shōjō-den of the main shrine [of Kumano]' is not simply more helpful to the reader who has no Japanese; it is also more accurate. This is only one of many such cases, all of which in turn are part of a strange reluctance to come all the way into English with the translation.

If the reader's intelligence seems sometimes to be underrated by the translation, his probable knowledge of Japanese is highly overrated. The linear measurements *shaku* and *ken* are consistently left untranslated and unexplained, making the passages in which they occur unnecessarily mystifying to the general reader. The term *on-pei-shi* is defined in a note at the end of the chapter in which it first appears, but since the word appears at other places in the work the general reader would probably be better served by an English term whose inevitable shortcomings could then be explained in a note. On p. 178, *shakujō* (a priest's staff) appears without explanation. On p. 60, *marōto* (guest) is given as *marouto,* which lies somewhere between a phonetic representation and the *kana* spelling and is no guide to pronunciation for the unprepared reader. The term *nyūdō* is left untranslated in the text although its first appearance in the text is footnoted (page 6, note 12). Unfortunately the note is partially inaccurate and wholly misleading: *nyū* does mean 'entering', but *dō* of course means 'way', not 'priesthood'. The general reader will know a little bit less after reading this note than he did before. Why not use the term 'lay priest' as both Waley and Sadler have? It eliminates the need for a note and helps the reader instead of confusing him.

Buddhist terms are treated with a casual inconsistency, sometimes presented in Sanskrit or Pali, sometimes in Chinese, and sometimes left in Japanese, a Japanese which is often incomplete, making it impossible in many cases for the reader who cannot consult the original to follow the references and allusions. There is nothing to suggest that the translators ever really came to grips with this problem, in spite of the central role that Buddhism and Buddhist ideas, texts, traditions, and historical figures play directly or indirectly in setting the tone and establishing the themes of the *Heike.* Here again, the English reader, although often not credited for knowing things that he can hardly help knowing or deducing, is left to his own devices in areas where he can scarcely be expected to know anything at all unless he happens to be a specialist.

The mixed Japanese-Chinese language of the *Heike* is a difficult style in the original, making great demands on its readers or listeners, but bestowing great rewards in turn. In its careful control of the mixture of soft, flowing *yamato-kotoba* and terse, pithy Chinese loan words to suit the mood and set the tempo of each passage, the *Heike* makes the first full use of what was to prove to be one of the greatest resources of one of the world's great literary

languages. An English version which consistently risks boring its readers and sometimes comes close to insulting their intelligence through its blurring of the impact and evasion of the difficulties of the original is not going to be able to make credible or even perceptible the central concerns of the *Heike.* Careful comparison of this English version with the original immediately demonstrates that the problem is not solely one of English.

On page 268, in note 2, is found this remarkable sentence: 'To honor the prominence of the *Heike* among war tales, the translator rendered this passage faithfully in the style of the original Japanese.' Even if we sidestep the host of philosophical problems that this statement raises, it remains an extraordinary remark for a translator to make. It raises the question of just what the translator was doing elsewhere. The passage in question, which begins on the bottom of page 264, is much closer to the original text than is the general rule for this translation. It is also an exceptionally effective passage. It shows that the translators were entirely capable of standing in a more rigorous relation to the original text than they generally did. It further shows that the effectiveness and accuracy of the translation would have been greatly improved had they done so consistently as a matter of policy. Why did they choose to do otherwise? Why did the translators not place more trust in a text which they so obviously and so rightly revere?

Here, then, is the central failing of this translation. Almost every sentence is longer than its original and almost every sentence says less than its original. Far too many of the sentences say something significantly different from their original. The defense that the demands of literary English necessitated such departures might be brought forward if the English of the translation were of the quality that was needed, but the English of the translation not only fails to be adequate for the recreation of a literary masterpiece but sometimes seems to be actively hostile to the very idea of literary English. The taut, austere, demanding, but ultimately magnificent language of the original has become a slack, prolix, unfocused, patronizing, and ultimately alienating retelling in English.

Very few people develop an adequate literary style in any language and particularly in one that is not their own. At the same time the process of translation between languages as divergent as Japanese and English tends to distort even the soundest style unless constant vigilance is maintained. Theory would therefore suggest that successful literary translation is inescapably the nearly exclusive province of native speakers of the language of the translation. Experience so strongly supports theory that it would seem to be scarcely necessary to make the point one more time here. Just how seriously would (or should) a publisher take the most conscientious effort by an American professor to render Geoffrey Chaucer or Sir Thomas Malory into Japanese, even if he had had copious assistance from Japanese friends?

This translation attempted much and much was expected of it. The fact that it constitutes an astonishing accomplishment given the conditions under which it was done cannot, unhappily, make it the translation of the **Heike** for which we have been waiting.

The question of whether or not the present translation represents an advance over that of Sadler has to be answered in the affirmative but not a strong affirmative. If a reader of English wants to know what the **Heike Monogatari** was about in general terms, this translation will tell him in great detail. If he wishes to understand why the **Heike** has played such an important part in Japanese literary history, this translation will stand in his way more often than it helps him. The state of the art of translation demonstrated here is much closer to that of 1920 (always excepting the work of Arthur Waley, who made his own epochs) than to that of 1975. The introduction of the **Heike Monogatari** to its proper place in world literature, an introduction that can only be made by a brilliantly successful translation into a language more widely read than Japanese, still remains to be done.

Notes

1. A. L. Sadler, trans., 'The Heike Monogatari', in TASJ, XLVI, 1918, & II, 1921; reprinted in *The Heike Monogatari,* 2 vols., Kimiwata Shoten, Tokyo, 1941.

2. Donald Keene, *Landscapes and Portraits,* Kodansha International, Tokyo & Palo Alto, 1971, pp. 322-3.

3. Takagi Ichinosuke *et al.,* ed., *Heike Monogatari,* I (*Nihon Koten Bungaku Taikei,* 32), Iwanami Shoten, 1959, p. 229.

4. Ibid., p. 259.

5. Ibid., p. 98.

Helen Craig McCullough (essay date 1988)

SOURCE: An introduction to *The Tale of the Heike,* translated by Helen Craig McCullough, Stanford University Press, 1988, pp. 1-11.

[In the following essay, McCullough considers the political and social changes taking place in twelfth-century Japan which inspired the creation of the Heike Monogatari.*]*

As the twelfth century waned, no thoughtful Japanese could have failed to recognize that the long Heian interlude of peace, economic security, and cultural florescence was nearing its end, and that a new political force was threatening the imperial court's hegemony. The signs were unmistakable.

In the countryside, there had been a steady evolution away from the institutions established by the seventh-century Taika Reform, which had brought all rice lands under state control and had created organs of local government to collect taxes and maintain order. At the time of the Reform, some powerful families had stayed on the land, where they had typically occupied subordinate government offices;

others had moved to the capital and, as members of a new aristocracy, had helped create the brilliant civilization depicted in the eleventh-century *Tale of Genji.*[1] Over the years, the court's preoccupation with the immediate concerns of aristocratic life had led to the discontinuance of the periodic land allotments on which the Taika economic system was based; to the widespread growth of private landholdings, known as *shōen;* and to the rise of a provincial armed élite, brought into existence by the government's military impotence.

Many among the new warrior class traced their roots to pre-Taika forebears who had remained in the provinces; others were aristocrats who had come from the capital as *shōen* managers and provincial officials, or were the descendants of such men. The court had become accustomed to calling on them in case of need, and during the tenth century, in particular, had used some of their prominent leaders to quell two protracted civil disturbances in eastern and western Japan, the rebellions of Taira no Masakado and Fujiwara no Sumitomo, respectively. The result had been a great increase in the power and prestige of two warrior clans of aristocratic lineage, the Taira, or Heike ("House of Taira"), and the Minamoto, or Genji ("Minamoto Clan"), whose chieftains had become actual or potential overlords for large numbers of local warriors and warrior bands. The main Minamoto strength was in the east; the Taira had established themselves both in the east and in the west, where they had enriched themselves through the China trade.

In the capital, little heed had been taken of the potential threat such power bases represented. The court aristocrats had continued throughout to view the rural warriors as bumpkins, useful for punishing rebels, furnishing guards to make city life safer, and repulsing incursions of soldier-monks from the Enryakuji, Kōfukuji, and Tōdaiji temples (which had developed a tendency to press their grievances by marching on the imperial palace), but otherwise unworthy of serious notice, except insofar as the economic resources of the wealthier ones might be tapped. Their attention remained fixed on the annual round of public and private ceremonies, amusements, and religious observances in the capital, and on the ceaseless quest for influence and preferment in the Chinese-style central bureaucracy, which was another Taika legacy.

In theory, the Taika Reform had made the Emperor the supreme court figure, the source of all social status and bureaucratic position. As early as the ninth century, however, one clan, the Fujiwara, had succeeded in controlling the sovereigns—many of them children who either died young or abdicated after a few years—by providing them with Fujiwara mothers, uncles, grandfathers, and Regents; and had consequently monopolized the desirable offices, acquired large numbers of shōen, and otherwise prospered. Their ascendancy had endured until late in the eleventh century, when Emperor Go-Sanjō, the able, mature offspring of an imperial princess, had abdicated and established what was thenceforth to function as a second center of prestige and power, the Retired Emperor's Office (Innochō), with edict-issuing authority comparable to that of the Emperor.

The principal figures in an Innochō were a small group of from five to twenty *kinshin* ("close attendants"), who typically included rich provincial Governors, relatives of the former sovereign's nurses, talented figures with no future in the bureaucracy, and men who enjoyed the Retired Emperor's personal favor. Rivalries and shifting alliances involving the kinshin, the members of the regular bureaucracy, the Fujiwara Regent, and the reigning and retired sovereigns had exacerbated the already fierce competition for rank and office, affected the distribution of economic plums, and, in the absence of a rule of primogeniture, vastly complicated the selection of new Emperors.

It was under such circumstances that the imperial succession fell vacant in 1155. Complex, deep-seated animosities flared after the Retired Emperor of the day, Toba, chose the future Emperor Go-Shirakawa, and Toba's death in 1156 set off the brief armed clash known as the Hōgen Disturbance. (See Appendix A.) With the aid of the Minamoto and Taira clan chieftains, Yoshitomo and Kiyomori, Go-Shirakawa's supporters triumphed over their opponents, who had relied on Yoshitomo's father, Tameyoshi (the former Minamoto chieftain), and a minor Taira named Tadamasa. But in a larger sense both sides lost, because the affair brought the warrior class forward as an independent force, capable of determining events at the highest political level.

Less than four years later, Go-Shirakawa, by then the Retired Emperor, encountered a second challenge from a faction resentful of the privileges granted to his kinshin, and Kiyomori again defeated the insurgents, whose chief military support had come from Yoshitomo, Kiyomori's erstwhile ally. In that clash, known as the Heiji Disturbance, the Minamoto were rendered leaderless, bereft of Tameyoshi, Yoshitomo, and Yoshitomo's heir, Yoshihira. It was only thanks to the plea of a compassionate Taira woman, Lady Ike, that the next in line for the chieftainship, Yoshitomo's fourteen-year-old son Yoritomo, was spared and allowed to live in exile in eastern Japan. Kiyomori and his relatives, on the other hand, entered a period of prosperity such as no military clan had dreamed of.

The groundwork for the Taira ascendancy had been laid by two members of the clan's western branch, Kiyomori's father and grandfather, Tadamori and Masamori, who had managed to break into court society as kinshin of Go-Shirakawa's great-grandfather and father, Retired Emperors Shirakawa and Toba. As a result of their military services, and of their lavish expenditures on projects dear to the imperial hearts, Kiyomori himself had received significant preferment in office and rank from his twelfth year on. His exploits in the Hōgen and Heiji disturbances were rewarded with substantial appointments: by 1160 he had already joined the exalted ranks of the senior nobles (*kugyō*), and in 1167 he advanced from the lowest ministe-

rial office, Palace Minister, to the pinnacle of the bureaucracy, the chancellorship, without passing through the intermediate positions of Minister of the Right and Minister of the Left. Following the usual practice of ambitious courtiers, he also established kinship ties in high places. His principal wife was sister to Go-Shirakawa's favorite, Kenshunmon'in, and thus aunt to Kenshunmon'in's son, Emperor Takakura; one of his daughters, the future Kenreimon'in, became a consort of Emperor Takakura; and other daughters married important Fujiwara noblemen.

Retired Emperor Go-Shirakawa, under whose auspices Kiyomori's spectacular rise occurred, seems to have been willing enough to bring the Taira leader and his relatives forward. The clan's military support was vital to the former sovereign's position, and his interests and Kiyomori's coincided during the period when both were maneuvering to place Kenshunmon'in's son on the throne. Moreover, Kiyomori carried out his activities with considerable prudence—not only during the tense early 1160's, when Go-Shirakawa and the reigning Emperor, Nijō, were at loggerheads, but throughout his public career, which ended in 1168, within months of Emperor Takakura's accession, when he took Buddhist vows in consequence of an illness.

But Kiyomori's circumspection disguised the fact that his clan had become a potentially dangerous power center. By the mid-1170's, dozens of its members had acquired coveted offices, profitable provincial governorships, and extensive shōen; the Retired Emperor found himself competing with Emperor Takakura's Taira kinsmen for his son's ear; and Kiyomori's daughter was an imperial consort, the potential mother of a future sovereign. Members of the clan had begun to display an arrogance that was profoundly offensive to the established aristocracy, many of whom remained unreconciled to the presence of military upstarts in their midst. Kenshunmon'in's brother, Taira no Tokitada, had been heard to remark, "All who do not belong to this clan must rank as less than men," and one of Kiyomori's young grandsons, Sukemori, had created a scandal in 1170 by insulting the Regent—an incident particularly galling because the boy's conduct had been defended by his father, Shigemori, Kiyomori's successor as clan chieftain.

In 1177, Retired Emperor Go-Shirakawa attempted to neutralize the Taira threat. With his encouragement, a group of kinshin planned a military action against the clan, relying on the assistance of Yukitsuna, a minor Genji from nearby Settsu Province. The plot collapsed when Yukitsuna betrayed his associates, and the kinshin were arrested and punished as Kiyomori saw fit.

No issue was made of Go-Shirakawa's involvement, but the affair left an irreparable breach between the Retired Emperor and Kiyomori. There was a period of uneasy truce, during which the two came together in a show of amity for the birth of their mutual grandson, the future Emperor Antoku, in 1178. Then, in 1179, the Taira suffered a devastating blow: Shigemori, their forceful, talented leader, died at the age of forty-three and was succeeded as chieftain by his brother Munemori, whose cowardice and poor judgment were to be among the causes of the clan's ruin. Go-Shirakawa seized the opportunity to deprive the clan of tax rights and properties to which Kiyomori felt entitled, and to decide against Kiyomori's candidate for an important court office. Kiyomori promptly took an army to the capital from his villa at Fukuhara (modern Kōbe), terminated the official appointments of more than three dozen of the Retired Emperor's kinshin and other supporters, and confined the former sovereign to the Toba Mansion, an imperial villa outside the city.

Kiyomori made his démarche toward the end of 1179. A few months later, he completed the sweep of actual and potential rivals by installing his one-year-old grandson on the throne, which Emperor Takakura was forced to vacate. But the Taira clan had become a vulnerable target for anyone who chose to put himself forward as a defender of the imperial house and the traditional order. At the instigation of Minamoto no Yorimasa, a respected elderly Buddhist Novice who lived in the capital area, one of Retired Emperor Go-Shirakawa's sons, Prince Mochihito, summoned the provincial Genji (Minamoto) to arms within two months of the infant Emperor Antoku's accession.

Before the year was out, two ambitious Genji, the now grown Yoritomo and his cousin, Kiso no Yoshinaka, were fighting Heike armies in the provinces. Yoritomo won an important psychological victory at the Fuji River in late 1180. He then retired to his headquarters in eastern Japan, where, as the "Kamakura Lord," he concentrated on establishing feudal relationships with local warriors to whom he guaranteed land rights in exchange for allegiance (a tactic the Taira sought in vain to counter by recruiting men through bureaucratic channels).

In early 1181, the Taira, already at a disadvantage, were further staggered by the death of Kiyomori, which left the hapless Munemori in control of the clan's destinies. Widespread famine and pestilence produced a lull in the fighting, but by mid-1183 Yoshinaka was threatening the capital. Munemori fled westward at the head of his kinsmen, overriding the objections of his brother Tomomori and others who wanted to mount a last-ditch stand, and taking along Emperor Antoku in an attempt to legitimate the clan's status. The Retired Emperor promptly enthroned another of his young grandsons, the sovereign known to history as Emperor Go-Toba.

Meanwhile, three days after the flight of the Taira, Yoshinaka made a triumphant entry into the city, accompanied by his uncle Yukiie. Hailed as a savior at first, he soon wore out his welcome. His men foraged for provisions in the famine-stricken countryside, the volatile Yukiie slandered him to Retired Emperor Go-Shirakawa, his rustic ways alienated the snobbish aristocrats, and his efforts to launch an effective campaign against the Taira in the west failed miserably. Four months after his grand entry, the Retired Emperor mustered a ragtag collection of soldier-monks and local warriors and ordered the "savior" to withdraw from the capital. Yoshinaka crushed the imperial forces, carried out wholesale demotions of high court officials, made a futile attempt to persuade the Heike to ally themselves with him against his cousin Yoritomo, with whom the Retired Emperor was in active communication, and finally died at the hands of Yoritomo's eastern forces, which were commanded by two of the Kamakura Lord's half-brothers, Noriyori and Yoshitsune.

Less than a month later, the eastern forces attacked Ikuta-no-mori and Ichi-no-tani, the eastern and western entrances to a stronghold the Taira had established between the mountains and the sea, in what is now the Kōbe area. Thanks to a surprise assault from the mountains behind Ichi-no-tani, executed by Yoshitsune and a few of his men, the stronghold fell, and the Taira fled over the water to Yashima in Shikoku, crippled by the loss of many of their leading kinsmen and retainers.

Noriyori returned to Kamakura after the Ichi-no-tani victory, but in mid-1184, Yoritomo sent him westward again, with instructions to seek out and attack the Taira. Meanwhile, Yoshitsune had been guarding the capital. Yoritomo had indicated to Retired Emperor Go-Shirakawa that he would also send Yoshitsune against the Taira, but now he changed his mind, angered because the Retired Emperor had granted his brother two desirable court offices without consulting him. Noriyori therefore advanced alone to Suō and Nagato provinces, where he presently found himself bottled up by two Taira forces—one, under the able Tomomori, threatening the Kyūshū sea lanes from Hikoshima, and the other, imperiling his rear, dispatched to Kojima in Bizen Province from Yashima, where Munemori remained with Emperor Antoku. Further hampered by supply problems and a lack of boats, Noriyori idled away half a year in the vicinity.

Finally, in early 1185, Yoritomo ordered Yoshitsune into action. Yoshitsune crossed to Shikoku during a storm, took the Taira by surprise, and drove them from Yashima. Munemori joined forces with his brother Tomomori, and the opposing sides met in a last major engagement, the naval battle of Dan-no-ura, which ended with the defeat of the Taira and the deaths of Emperor Antoku, Kiyomori's widow, and most of the male clansmen. Thereafter, Yoritomo and Go-Shirakawa reached a tacit understanding, with ultimate authority exercised by the court in form and by the new Kamakura military government in fact. The Genji ruled Japan, and Kiyomori's descendants disappeared from the pages of history.

Like other dramatic events of far-reaching import, the rise and fall of the house of Taira, and particularly the protracted five-year struggle known to scholars as the Genpei War, constituted a rich source of materials for the storyteller. Even before the final Heike defeat in 1185, tales must have been circulating about isolated events in the conflict. And at some point, probably early in the thirteenth century, the ancestor of the present *Heike monogatari* made its appearance.

The Tale of the Heike is known today in numerous versions, probably dating from the thirteenth century to the Edo period (1600-1868): some are relatively short, some very long; some have variant titles; some are written in Chinese; some were seemingly designed to be read; and some contain internal evidence suggestive of use by Buddhist preachers (*sekkyōji*). By far the most characteristic, however, are texts of intermediate length, known to have been narrated by a class of blind men called *biwa hōshi*. Biwa is the Japanese name for the *pipa*, a Chinese musical instrument resembling a lute that had entered Japan with the introduction of Buddhism many centuries earlier; hōshi ("master of the doctrines") designates a monk or, as in this case, a layman in monk's garb.

The *biwa hōshi* had appeared in the countryside several centuries earlier. Many of them frequented Buddhist temples, institutions traditionally hospitable to the unfortunate, where they probably learned to play the biwa, and where they may have acquired the habit of wearing clerical robes. Thanks to their attire, to their acute nonvisual senses, and to their mastery of the biwa—which, like other stringed instruments, was considered an efficacious means of establishing contact with unseen powers—they seem to have impressed country folk as capable of communicating with the otherworld, and they were thus called upon to drive away disease gods and pacify angry spirits. They also functioned as wayside entertainers, telling stories (often of a sermonizing nature), reciting poems, and singing songs.

By the thirteenth century, large numbers of such men had congregated in the capital, where they must have encountered a demand for stories about the Genpei War—in particular, tales of tragic or violent death, which, when related with sympathy, would serve to quiet the restless spirits of the deceased. Some of them are known to have frequented the Enryakuji on Mount Hiei, the home base of a school of preachers famed for their eloquence and erudition; some almost certainly used their art to become acquainted with mid-level court nobles, the kind of men who collected oral stories as a hobby. Although the details are elusive, the ancestral **Heike monogatari** almost certainly emerged from such circumstances—from a pooling of the talents and practices of religiously oriented professional entertainers with the literary skills of educated men.

Medieval writings proffer several explanations of our work's origins. The best known appears in *Tsurezuregusa* (Essays in Idleness), a collection of jottings set down around 1330 by Yoshida Kenkō, a monk and former courtier with a reputation as a scholar and an antiquarian:

> In Retired Emperor Go-Toba's time, the Former Shinano Official Yukinaga won praise for his learning. But when commanded to participate in a discussion of *yuefu* poetry, he forgot two of the virtues in the "Dance of the Seven Virtues," and consequently acquired the nickname "Young Gentleman of the Five Virtues." Sick at heart, he abandoned scholarship and took the tonsure.
>
> Archbishop Jien [the Enryakuji Abbot] made a point of summoning and looking after anyone, even a servant, who could boast of an accomplishment; thus, he granted

this Shinano Novice an allowance. Yukinaga composed **The Tale of the Heike** and taught it to a blind man, Shōbutsu, so that the man might narrate it. His descriptions of things having to do with the Enryakuji were especially good. He wrote with a detailed knowledge of Kurō Hōgan Yoshitsune's activities, but did not say much about Gama no Kanja Noriyori, possibly for lack of information. When it came to warriors and the martial arts, Shōbutsu, who was an easterner, put questions to warriors and had Yukinaga write what he learned. People say that our present-day *biwa hōshi* imitate Shōbutsu's natural voice.

(*Tsurezuregusa,* Sec. 226)

If we assume Emperor Go-Toba's "time" to mean both his reign (1183-98) and his period of authority as Retired Emperor (1198-1221), and if scholars are correct in ascribing the original **Heike monogatari** to the early thirteenth century, then Kenkō's dating is approximately accurate. Moreover, Yukinaga is a historically identifiable figure of the right period. In the absence of independent evidence, we cannot go further, but Kenkō's statements probably reflect the kind of thing that actually happened, even though they may be wholly or partially inaccurate in their particulars. The same may be said of the attributions to other authors put forward in other sources, along with purported information about textual evolution. Although none of those attributions can be substantiated, they seem to support the assumption that a number of different people had a hand in the work's creation, and that some versions, at least, were the product of collaboration between *biwa hōshi* and mid-level courtiers or Buddhist monks (or both).

The available evidence also suggests that a number of **Heike** texts were in existence by the end of the thirteenth century. It is impossible to know how much the earliest versions may have resembled one another in content and style, or whether they all sprang from a single original, but we can say that any versions entirely unrelated to our present texts have disappeared without a trace. Although there are many points of difference between extant texts, they have all descended from a common parent, even the huge forty-eight-chapter *Tale of the Rise and the Fall of the Minamoto and the Taira* (Genpei jōsuiki), which bears a unique title and was once considered an independent work.

This Introduction is not the place for a discussion of the immensely complicated, ill-understood connections between surviving **Heike** texts. We shall be concerned only with the version perfected over a thirty-year period and recorded in 1371 by a man named Kakuichi, a *biwa hōshi* who took traditional materials, reshaped them into a work of great literary distinction, and established a standard text, memorized and narrated by many successive generations of blind performers.

By the first half of the fourteenth century, the *biwa hōshi* in the capital had become sufficiently specialized in what came to be called *heikyoku*, or "**Heike monogatari** narration," to form a guild, the Tōdōza, with a noble house as patron. A court noble's diary tells us that Kakuichi was active in the guild by 1340, when he is conjectured to have been about forty years old. There is no reliable information concerning his earlier life—merely a legend preserved in a seventeenth-century collection of Tōdōza traditions and precepts, *Saikai yotekishū*, that identifies him as having been a Shoshazan monk.[2] According to that work, he became a *biwa hōshi* after the sudden loss of his vision, went to the capital, joined the Tōdōza, and rose to the guild's top ranks. Whatever his origins, by 1340 he was presenting heikyoku performances that the same noble diarist described as "different" (*ikei*), a comment probably inspired not only by his textual revisions but also by his performance style, which seems to have been more complex, colorful, and melodic than anything previously attempted by the guild members.

Some scholars have theorized that Kakuichi drew on the Buddhist chants (*shōmyō*) used at Shoshazan. We know that Shoshazan was a recognized center of Buddhist music by the fifteenth century, but it is not certain whether this was the case in Kakuichi's day—or, indeed, whether there is any truth in the legend associating him with the temple. Nevertheless, he undoubtedly revolutionized heikyoku performance. During his lifetime and probably soon after the appearance of the original Kakuichi text, the Tōdōza split into two schools, the Ichikata-ryū and the Yasaka-ryū. Personalities and other issues may have been involved, but the main reason for the disagreement seems to have been that a conservative faction, the future Yasaka-ryū, refused to accept the innovations introduced by Kakuichi and adopted by the rest of the community, who became the Ichikata-ryū.

Thanks largely to Kakuichi, heikyoku won upper-class acceptance and became recognized as the leading contemporary performing art. Both the Ichikata-ryū and the Yasaka-ryū continued to flourish in the so-called golden age of heikyoku narration, the century from Kakuichi's death in 1371 to the Ōnin War, which was fought in the capital between 1467 and 1477. Five or six hundred *biwa hōshi* are reported to have been active in the city in 1462, and the best of them enjoyed the patronage of aristocrats or leading warriors, for whom they sang on demand. But the Ōnin War marked a turning point in heikyoku history. Thereafter, other types of entertainment became more popular—for example, the noh drama, the comic kyōgen play, and the recitation by "narrator monks" (*katarisō*) of the military tale *Taiheiki* (Chronicle of Great Peace).

This does not mean that *Heike monogatari* fell into obscurity. Stories about the Genpei epoch were never to lose their appeal, and *The Tale of the Heike,* the principal repository of such materials, continued to attract readers. *Heike monogatari* also served as a model for medieval chronicles of later military campaigns, and as a point of departure for countless dramas and prose stories. Of the sixteen warrior pieces (*shuramono*) in the modern noh repertoire, a majority are based on *Heike monogatari,* and many follow its text closely, a practice specifically advo-

cated by Zeami, the leading noh dramatist. Other types of noh plays retell *Heike* anecdotes about music and poetry, or center on some of the work's most pathetic figures. *Heike* heroes appear as protagonists in thirty-three of fifty extant ballad dramas (*kōwakamai,* a form prominent in the sixteenth century). They figure in innumerable kabuki and puppet plays (*jōruri*) as well, many of which continue to enjoy great popularity, as do modern films and television dramas dealing with the Genpei period. *Heike* characters also play important roles in all of the half-dozen or so popular prose-fiction genres of the Edo period. As a measure of the work's enduring appeal, we may note that a potboiler called *Shin heike monogatari* (New Tale of the Heike) was a national best-seller as recently as the 1950's. There are medieval and later *Heike* picture books, songs, comic verses, and parodies.

It would be wrong to claim direct influence from *Heike monogatari* for all of the hundreds of literary and artistic productions inspired by the Genpei campaigns. Some authors retold old anecdotes missing from *Heike monogatari;* others launched Genpei figures on adventures of their own devising. But we can probably say that no single Japanese literary work has influenced so many writers in so many genres for so long a time as the *Heike,* and that no era in the Japanese past can today match the romantic appeal of the late twelfth century. It is not surprising, then, that one of the two heikyoku performing schools managed to survive the medieval period despite the competition of newer forms of entertainment. The Yasaka-ryū dropped out of sight around 1600, but the Ichikata-ryū obtained shogunal protection, lingered into the twentieth century, and still claims a handful of performers.

In seeking an explanation for the Ichikata-ryū's greater longevity, we may note its tighter organizational structure, an advantage traditionally ascribed to Kakuichi, who is said to have created its four grades and sixteen subgrades of performers. The school also possessed a superior text, as is evident from a comparison with extant Yasaka-ryū texts. And, finally, it seems to have offered a more appealing performance style.

There are comments on performance in various Tōdōza documents, including extensive discussion in the seventeenth-century collection *Saikai yotekishū,*[3] and there are also Edo-period scores, compiled when sighted amateurs took up heikyoku as a hobby. In view of the prestige enjoyed by Kakuichi and his text, and of the generally conservative nature of the Japanese arts during and after the medieval period, we can probably assume that such sources, and the modern performers who use them, reflect Kakuichi's own practice to a considerable extent.

Drawing on these sources, then, we can say that the performer was silent while the biwa was played; that the biwa music was relatively uncomplicated, as compared with, say, the samisen music in the jōruri puppet play; and that the biwa passages were short. The instrument sounded the opening pitch for a vocal passage, gave the pitch for the succeeding passage, or heightened the mood conveyed by the text. The vocal part of the performance was a combination of declamation and singing. For each section (*ku*)—that is, each titled subdivision of a chapter (*maki*)—there was a prescribed *katari,* or narrative, pattern, designed both to suit the context and to provide the variety and drama necessary to capture and hold an audience's attention. There are said to have been as many as thirty-three types of melodies in use at one time or another, of which some eight or nine were especially important.[4] A brief look at four of them will give a general idea of their nature.

The most musical was the *sanjū* ("threefold"), used for passages that dealt with the imperial court, the supernatural, the arts, or the classical past, or wherever an effect of gentle, elegant beauty was desired. High-pitched and leisurely, it was compared in *Saikai yotekishū* to the flight of a large crane rising from the reed plains: the voice soared like the bird, wavered gracefully as though flapping its wings, and settled slowly to earth again.

A quavering, slow melody called *origoe* ("broken voice") was employed in pathetic or tragic passages, such as the description of little Emperor Antoku's death, or to express heroic resolve on the part of a character, or to convey an address to the throne, or for letters, some kinds of dialogues, and soliloquies.

A livelier melody, *hiroi* ("picking up"), was associated especially with fighting and deeds of valor, but might also be prescribed for descriptions of disasters, scenes of confusion, or any other sort of dramatic action.

For straightforward narration, the performer might employ *kudoki* ("recitation"), a relatively fast, simple melody close to ordinary speech. (Narration was also rendered in *shiragoe,* "plain voice," a brisk declamatory style making no use of melody.)

Kakuichi's art as a performer manifested itself not only in the development of a superior repertoire of melodies, but also, and more significantly, in the painstaking combination of individual melodic elements into patterns that were dramatically effective and appropriate to the content. Armed with the model he provided, which regulated every nuance of every section, the Ichikata-ryū rank and file enjoyed an invaluable advantage over their competitors. We cannot fully appreciate that advantage, nor can we recapture the medieval audience's experience, even if we are fortunate enough to witness a brief performance by a modern narrator. Limited for all practical purposes to the printed page, we find ourselves in the position of those who must read a script instead of seeing the play performed. But just as the best dramatists surmount such obstacles, so Kakuichi and his fellow authors have created an independent literary work of remarkable status. Appendix C, which can best be approached after an initial reading of the text, attempts to sketch some of the dimensions of their accomplishment. Here it is enough to say that it is the translator's fault, not theirs, if this English version fails to convey at least some of the heroic spirit, humor, pathos, and lyric beauty of the original.

Notes

1. After frequent early moves, the court had settled first at Nara (8th c.) and then at Heian[kyō] (794on; modern Kyōto).

2. Shoshazan was another name for the Enkyōji, a Tendai temple on Mount Shosha in Harima Province (now in Himeji City, Hyōgo-ken). Monk Jigu, *Saikai yotekishū,* ed. Tomikura Tokujirō (Tōkyō, 1956), p. 94.

3. Summarized in Makoto Ueda, *Literary and Art Theories in Japan* (Cleveland, Ohio, 1967), pp. 114-27.

4. *Saikai yotekishū,* pp. 48-55.

Paul Varley (essay date 1997)

SOURCE: "Warriors as Courtiers: The Taira in *Heike Monogatari,*" in *Currents in Japanese Culture: Translations and Transformations,* edited by Amy Vladeck Heinrich, Columbia University Press, 1997, pp. 53-70.

[*In the following essay, Varley examines how later interpretations of the* Heike Monogatari *served to lend an aristocratic character to various warriors.*]

Japan's entry into the medieval age (1185-1573) in the late twelfth century was accompanied by an epochal transition in leadership of the country, when the emperor and the ministers who served him at his court in Kyoto relinquished national rule to provincial warrior chieftains. But this transition did not occur immediately, nor was it ever carried to completion in medieval times. Through much of the Kamakura period (1185-1333), for example, government continued to be divided between the court and the new warrior regime (bakufu) that was founded by Minamoto no Yoritomo in Kamakura. And even during the Muromachi period (1336-1573), when the court's political fortunes sank to their nadir, the emperor and his ministers still held high authority and the potential to exercise at least some political power.

In addition to thus retaining a measure of rulership, however slight, throughout the medieval age, the court (comprising imperial and courtier families) influenced and in various ways shaped and even culturally transformed the character of the warrior elite that increasingly dominated the age. Court influence was especially intense during the times when warrior rulers resided in Kyoto. These rulers included the Rokuhara magistrates (*tandai*), who were in Kyoto from 1221 until the overthrow of the Kamakura bakufu in 1333; the Ashikaga shoguns of the Muromachi period; and the daimyos or regional barons who served the Ashikaga and, from at least the late fourteenth century, also lived more or less permanently in Kyoto and visited their domains only infrequently.[1]

THE ISE TAIRA

The forerunners of the medieval warrior rulers who resided in Kyoto were the Ise branch of the Taira (or Heike) family. Victors in the Heiji Conflict in 1159-1160, the

Taira under their leader Kiyomori rose to power in Kyoto during the two decades or so from the Heiji Conflict until the Genpei (Minamoto-Taira) War of 1180-1185. Unlike their medieval successors, the Taira did not establish new institutions of warrior rule; rather, they entered court government and in large part emulated the political practices of the Fujiwara regents, even marrying into the imperial family and becoming maternal relatives of the emperor.

The great war tale *Heike monogatari* (*The Tale of the Heike*) tells us that the Ise Taira were—to coin a word—"aristocratized"[2] during their decades of prominence in Kyoto. Not only did they engage in court government; they actively participated in court society and embraced courtier culture and ways. The *Heike,* although based on history, is—as is well known—a highly embellished work of literature, having been molded and developed over a period of at least two centuries, especially by tale singers who chanted its stories while accompanying themselves with lutes (*biwa*).[3] Hence the *Heike*'s account of how the Ise Taira were aristocratized during their years in Kyoto cannot be accepted uncritically as history. But it is history of a kind, since Japanese through the centuries—even until very recent times—have believed it to be a generally accurate record of the past.[4] The image of the Ise Taira as "courtiers" or courtly warriors was particularly powerful during the medieval age, making their story, primarily as it is given in the *Heike,* the starting point for any study of how the court, court life, and court culture recurrently affected the warrior elite as it evolved during medieval times.

The Taira, along with that other famous warrior family, the Minamoto (or Genji), were descended from the imperial family. Historians have traditionally recounted how surplus princes, excluded from the imperial family in a process of "dynastic shedding" and given the surnames of Taira or Minamoto, went out from the capital during the early Heian period (794-1185) to occupy offices in the provincial governments and, after completing their terms of office, settled down to become leaders in the emerging warrior society of the provinces. In fact, many of these men also continued to maintain residences in Kyoto and, in some cases, to spend more time there than in the provinces. An example is the Minamoto chieftain Yoshiie, victorious commander in the Later Three Years War (1083-1087) in northern Honshu in the late eleventh century, who spent most of his life after the war (he died in 1106) living in Kyoto.

Many provincial warrior chieftains also established patron-client (*shujū*) relations with leading courtiers or members of the imperial family that were very much like the lord-vassal ties of warriors and their followers. The Ise Taira from the time of Kiyomori's grandfather, Masamori, in the late eleventh century, for example, became clients of the senior retired emperors (*in*) who, from about the same time, increasingly surpassed the Fujiwara regents as wielders of power at court.

Not only did provincial warrior chieftains establish private patron-client relationships with courtiers and members of the imperial family, they also avidly sought court titles and posts in both the central and provincial governments. Thus, by the time the Ise Taira rose to national prominence in the second half of the twelfth century, the provincial warrior chieftains as a class had become, both privately and publicly, deeply involved in court life and court affairs; they had, in short, become substantially aristocratized. This does not mean that they were accepted as equals by court society. On the contrary, as the case of the Ise Taira in *Heike monogatari* clearly illustrates, warrior chieftains in Kyoto continued to be despised by courtiers as essentially barbarians, even though—as in the cases of the Taira and Minamoto—they may have been descended from royalty.

Taira no Tadamori

In its famous introduction, *Heike monogatari* announces the theme of and sets the tone for the story that is to be told. It will be a somber story, heavily colored by pessimistic Buddhist views of the impermanence of all things and, especially, the decline of the world during what was believed to be the age of *mappō,* or the "end of the Buddhist Law." The Ise Taira family, under the leadership of Kiyomori, has risen to a dizzying height of grandeur and is headed for a fall, a fall that will be particularly great, and perhaps also very swift, both because of the height to which they have risen and the wickedness of Kiyomori as a ruler.

But before embarking on the story of the Ise Taira under Kiyomori, the *Heike* relates an incident in the life and career of Tadamori, Kiyomori's father, who greatly advanced the family fortunes while in the service of the senior retired emperor Toba during the middle decades of the twelfth century. Toba, we are told, wishes to bestow special reward on Tadamori for building a Buddhist temple that he, Toba, has personally promised to have erected. The reward is appointment to a provincial governorship and permission to "attend," that is, to participate in courtier affairs, at the imperial palace (Seiryōden).[5] This permission is extraordinary, if not unprecedented, both because it is granted to a warrior and because Tadamori holds only the senior fourth rank, lower grade, and attendance has by tradition been restricted to courtiers of the third rank and higher.

It is difficult, if not impossible, for us living in the present age to appreciate fully the pervasive importance of social status to a class such as the courtiers of ancient Japan. This status, believed to be granted by the gods and based almost exclusively on birth, was figuratively the air that the courtiers breathed. Violations of status were regarded as ethical transgressions of the most serious kind. We can imagine that the courtiers responded in a spirit of truly righteous indignation when Tadamori, in 1132, was granted the right of attendance at the palace. In the *Heike* account, the courtiers' indignation gives rise to a plot to assassinate Tadamori when he first appears at the palace, which is on the occasion of a banquet in the twelfth month.

Although brief, the account of this assassination plot and how Tadamori foiled it (told in "The Night Attack at the Palace") is critical to an understanding of the *Heike* as a whole. We usually think of the *Heike* as the story of the rise and fall of the Ise Taira, but in a larger sense it is a record, admittedly much romanticized, of how and why warriors supplanted courtiers as the ruling elite of Japan in the late twelfth century. Seen in this light, the confrontation between Tadamori and the courtiers in "The Night Attack" becomes a parable for this momentous historical transition in ruling elites.

Informed in advance of the plot, Tadamori, upon his arrival at the palace, ostentatiously displays a large dagger he has brought with him in what is evidently a breach of proper court conduct. Startled by the display of this weapon, the courtiers are truly alarmed when they observe that one of Tadamori's retainers, armed with a sword, is seated in a garden outside the hall where the banquet is being held. When questioned, the retainer states that he has come because he has heard that there is to be an attempt to kill his lord that night.[6]

Obliged to abandon their plot, the courtiers seek some satisfaction by singing, while Tadamori dances as part of the evening's entertainment, a satirical verse that contains a phrase with several plays on words that can be taken to mean either "the Ise Heishi (or Heike; Tadamori) is squint-eyed" or "the bottle from Ise is a roughly made article" (or "is a vinegar bottle"). One meaning mocks Tadamori as physically flawed, and the other characterizes him as a countrified boor from the wilds of Ise.[7]

After the banquet, the courtiers submit their complaints about Tadamori to retired emperor Toba, claiming that he has violated court regulations, which stipulate that one may not, without special imperial authorization, enter the palace with a weapon or in the company of an escort. But Tadamori proves he has not broken the regulations because his dagger is a sham weapon, made of wood, and the retainer came not as an escort but of his own accord. Far from punishing Tadamori, Toba praises him for his resourcefulness in dealing with a difficult situation.[8]

This story of Tadamori and the courtiers is like a parable because it can be taken to signify, although in exaggerated form, the qualities that distinguished courtiers from warriors (represented by Tadamori) in this age and made inevitable the victory of the latter as the future rulers. Whereas Tadamori is determined, realistic, and resourceful, the courtiers are arrogant and aloof, unbending in their commitment to status and class privileges and to the rules that for centuries have tightly governed conduct at court. As Nagazumi Yasuaki points out, the *Heike* subtly enforces the courtiers' rigid commitment to privileges and rules by having them employ elaborate, Chinese-style language when they lodge their complaints about Tadamori with Toba.[9]

Although it may be interpreting too much from a few words voiced in anger, we can regard the courtiers' description of Tadamori as a "vinegar jar from Ise" as an indication of their unwillingness to recognize him as any-

thing other than a barbarian. Yet we have observed that provincial warrior chieftains of this age frequently visited and resided in Kyoto, served at court, and participated in court life and culture. As heir to his father's (Masamori's) preferment in the service of the senior retired emperor, Tadamori had probably spent most of his life in Kyoto. Even the *Heike* alludes to Tadamori's courtliness when, in mentioning an affair he had with a court lady "of refinement," it describes him as a man of "elegance."[10]

TAIRA NO KIYOMORI

As he is portrayed in the *Heike,* Kiyomori is an archvillain who rivals all those heinous characters of Chinese and Japanese history who "did not obey the rule of their lords or former sovereigns, led dissolute lives, ignored admonitions, were not aware of the world's disorders, and were blind to the suffering of the people."[11] Through the first half of the *Heike,* until his death in book 6, Kiyomori as archvillain looms over the story, representing a primary (although not the sole) reason that the Ise Taira are headed for decline and destruction.

The organization of book 1 of the *Heike* conveys the sense that the rise of the Ise Taira under Kiyomori occurred very rapidly. If Tadamori faced formidable social and status barriers at court, his son Kiyomori, in the *Heike* account at least, seems scarcely troubled by them. With little commentary, the *Heike* relates Kiyomori's almost meteorlike ascent of the twin ladders of court rank and office to become chancellor (*daijō daijin*) with junior first rank. As he thus rises to the summits of court society and status, Kiyomori carries his entire family in his train, as we quickly learn from a listing of the preferments in office and rank given to other Ise Taira men and from the marriages arranged between Ise Taira women and members of the highest courtier families, including the Fujiwara regent family and even the imperial family (Kiyomori later becomes the grandfather of an emperor, Antoku).[12] So grand do the Ise Taira become that in the words of one of them, "all who do not belong to this family cannot be considered human beings."[13]

Although Kiyomori is now, in regard to office and rank, the preeminent courtier of the land, the *Heike* tells us almost nothing else about how aristocratized or courtly he may have become. Aristocratization does not mean simply the attainment of office and rank at court but also the acquisition of those special qualities of attitude, bearing, and taste that distinguish courtiers from others. As portrayed in the *Heike,* Kiyomori is essentially a political leader, and not a very courtly one at that. Despite his occupancy of the office of chancellor, in times of crisis, for example, he usually responds not as we would expect a courtier of such exalted position to respond but rather like a warrior chief, by resorting to arms. In this, he differs most markedly from his oldest son and heir apparent, Shigemori.

TAIRA NO SHIGEMORI

In earlier war tales—*Hōgen monogatari* (The Tale of Hōgen) and *Heiji monogatari* (The Tale of Heiji)— Shigemori is the leading battlefield commander of the Ise

Taira. In the *Heike,* however, he is almost entirely divested of his military attributes, becoming not only a "courtier" but one who exemplifies the highest ideals of the courtier as minister. We must here distinguish between two personae of the courtier: the courtier as minister and the courtier as romantic or lover. Shigemori's courtliness is completely in the ministerial realm; the *Heike* says nothing about his possessing a romantic side. He is married to a court woman, but we are told almost nothing about her or their marriage. Yet others among the Ise Taira, as we will see, display their courtliness primarily as romantics, reciting *waka* poems, playing musical instruments, having affairs with elegant court ladies.

As many commentators have observed, Shigemori the courtly minister functions in the *Heike* as a medium to defend the traditional rights of the imperial family and the courtier class in the face of the relentless assault on them by Shigemori's own family, led by his father Kiyomori.[14] Shigemori defends these rights primarily in two sustained admonitions he delivers to his father in 1177, at the time of discovery of the Shishigatani plot to overthrow the Ise Taira. Kiyomori reacts to the revelation of the plot by summarily executing some of the conspirators and preparing to take military action against others, including the senior retired emperor Goshirakawa.

Shigemori delivers his second, longer admonition after rushing to Kiyomori's residence to forestall a plan to march on and seize Goshirakawa. In contrast to Kiyomori and the other Taira and family retainers assembled at the residence, who have donned their armor, Shigemori is attired—as he is always attired in the *Heike*—in courtly robes.[15] Kiyomori, invariably flustered when confronted by this son who is universally admired for his unswerving adherence to the highest Confucian and Buddhist precepts, tries to hide his armor by hastily pulling a monk's robe over it. He then sits in silence as Shigemori speaks.

In the admonition, Shigemori talks of fate and karmic retribution, touching on themes that permeate the *Heike.* But the central point of his argument is the theory of imperial absolutism.[16] After chiding his father for violating the law that a chancellor must never wear helmet and armor, he calls on Kiyomori to adhere to the supreme obligation of men to obey their sovereign.[17] Although in fact the sovereign is the emperor, Shigemori here refers to senior retired emperor Goshirakawa who, as Uwayokote Masataka notes, is a political schemer capable of straining the faith and commitment of any subject.[18] Shigemori acknowledges that Goshirakawa's thinking can be "unpredictable" but nevertheless asserts that it is the subject's duty to serve him and the court with unstinting loyalty.

Shigemori's courtliness is unique among Ise Taira in the *Heike.* No other member of the family assumes, in any significant way, the qualities of the courtier as minister. Rather, the aristocratization of other Ise Taira, apart from the receipt of court ranks and offices, lies largely in their acquisition of what I have called the romantic attributes of

the courtier. But little is said about the Ise Taira as courtly romantics until the *Heike*'s second half, when the Genpei War has begun and the family is launched on the road to what we know will be defeat and doom.

COURTLY WARRIORS IN THE GENPEI WAR

The Genpei War began in 1180 when an imperial prince, Mochihito, disgruntled because he had been bypassed through Kiyomori's interference in the succession to the emperorship, dispatched an edict to Minamoto chieftains in the provinces calling on them to rise up and overthrow the Ise Taira. Among the first to accept this call to arms against the Ise Taira were Minamoto no Yoritomo in the Kantō and his cousin Yoshinaka in Shinano Province.

In the Genpei War, as it is narrated in the second half of the *Heike,* there is little doubt about the eventual outcome of the warfare between the Minamoto and the Ise Taira. The Minamoto, especially those from the eastern provinces of the Kantō, are famous as fierce fighting men—they are the cream of the horse-riding warrior class that had evolved in the provinces since early times. The Ise Taira, on the other hand, represent what the *Heike* categorizes as "western" warriors, who lack both the martial prowess and physical and mental toughness to stand up to their eastern adversaries.[19] Although some Taira chieftains, such as Noritsune and Tadanori, are in fact impressive fighters, most are no match for their Minamoto counterparts.

The Taira problems in the *Heike*'s version of the Genpei War begin with weak leadership. In 1179 Shigemori dies, convinced that the fortunes of the Ise Taira are nearing their end, and then in 1181 Kiyomori dies, angry and unrepentant to the last, less than a half year after the war's start. Although dictatorial and erratic, Kiyomori was at least a decisive leader. His successor as the head of the Ise Taira, his second son Munemori, is not only indecisive; he is quite devoid of martial spirit. When, for example, Minamoto no Yoshinaka leads his army to the gates of Kyoto in 1183, Munemori decides to take the child emperor Antoku (his nephew and Kiyomori's grandson) and flee the capital, rejecting the advice of other Taira chieftains who wish to remain and defend against Yoshinaka. Munemori gives as his reason for abandoning the capital his unwillingness to expose members of the imperial family, including the emperor and his mother, Kenreimon'in (Munemori's sister), to the distress of battling with Yoshinaka.[20]

Munemori's fainthearted—one is tempted to say courtier-like—behavior in the face of the Yoshinaka threat sets the tone of the chapters in book 7 of the *Heike* that describe the sad departure of the Ise Taira from Kyoto and, indeed, of the work's entire second half. Until this point, the reader has generally despised the Ise Taira because of the evilness of Kiyomori and the hubris of the family as a whole; from here on, however, the reader is increasingly led to sympathize with them.

One reason for this newly felt sympathy is the disparity in fighting ability between the Ise Taira and their Minamoto adversaries: the reader pities the Taira as manifest underdogs. But another and, I believe, stronger reason for the elicitation of the reader's sympathy is the series of revelations about the romantic courtliness of Taira leaders. It can even be suggested that the Ise Taira become surrogates for the courtier class and that their destruction in the Genpei War symbolizes the historical displacement of this class as a ruling elite by rough warriors from the provinces.

The Ise Taira flight from Kyoto in 1183, at least as described in the *Heike,* is less tragic than pathetic. Some of the Taira are tough and are ready to fight. But the family in general is bewildered and in disarray. Munemori sets the tone by weeping when he informs his sister Kenreimon'in that they must leave the capital.[21] The Minamoto also cry in the *Heike,* for example, Yoshitsune when his intimate follower, Satō no Tsuginobu, is killed defending him at the battle of Yashima early in 1185.[22] But the Minamoto shed only "manly" tears—tears for fallen comrades or for the anguish of war itself. Munemori, on the other hand, cries like a courtier—drenching the sleeve of his robe—from a sense of frustration and impotence. Other Taira weep in similar courtly fashion, for example, Shigehira when parting from a mistress he is allowed to see briefly after he is captured by the Minamoto following the battle of Ichinotani.[23]

In preparing for flight, the Taira decide to take their women with them (they also take Emperor Antoku, but that is for an important political reason: to give legitimacy to their cause). With the women in tow, the Taira are far from a typical army. Women seldom accompany armies in the war tales, and the presence of the Taira women during the flight from the capital contributes as much as anything to the sense of courtly poignancy surrounding what we know will be the family's inevitable fate in the Genpei War.

Although they occasionally rally and win battles, after Kyoto the Taira are essentially pathetic fugitives, afflicted at every turn by homesickness and depression resulting from grief over their plight and ceaseless longing for the capital and the life of luxury and glory they once knew. The Taira men would surely have been homesick and depressed without their women, but the presence of the women intensifies these feelings and, I believe, enhances the impression that the *Heike* conveys of the Ise Taira as surrogate victims for the courtiers who are losing out as a ruling elite in the transition to the medieval age.

After leaving Kyoto, the Taira visit Fukuhara, their former base on the Inland Sea to which Kiyomori had once moved the imperial capital.[24] Assailed by memories of Fukuhara's transient grandeur and made wretched by its present desolate and deteriorated state, the Taira spend only one night there, "their tears mixing with dew on the grassy pillows of their travellers' beds."[25] The description of the Taira departure from Fukuhara the following day is one of the saddest and most courtierlike passages in the *Heike:*

> As dawn broke, the Taira set fire to the Fukuhara palace and, with the emperor, they all boarded the boats. Departing the capital had been more painful, but still

their feelings of regret were great indeed. Smoke at eveningtime from seaweed burned by fisherfolk, the cries of deer on mountain peaks at dawn, waves lapping the shore, moonbeams bathing their tear-drenched sleeves, crickets chirping in the grasses—no sight met their eyes nor sounds reached their ears that failed to evoke sadness or pierce their hearts. Yesterday they were tens of thousands of horsemen with their bits aligned at Ōsaka Barrier; today, as they loosened their mooring lines on waves in the western sea, they numbered a mere seven thousand. The sky was cloudy and the sea calm as dusk approached. Lonely islands were shrouded in evening mists; the moon floated on the sea. Cleaving the waves to the distant horizon and drawn ever onward by the tides, the boats seemed to row up through the clouds in the sky. Days had passed, and they were already separated far from the mountains and rivers of the capital, which lay behind the clouds. They seemed to have gone as far as they could go. All had come to an end, except their endless tears.[26]

As Ishimoda Shō has observed, the *Heike* differs from the earlier war tales in containing passages such as this one, written in a tone of classical lyricism and presenting visual images like scenes from *Yamato-e* (Japanese-style pictures).[27] Drawing on the *aware* aesthetic of courtly taste, the scenes in this passage are suffused with a sadness deriving from the haunting sights and sounds depicted and the uncontrollable grief of the Taira and also from the many metaphors related to water—sea, waves, tears, floating, tides, mists. These images heighten our awareness that the once supremely proud family of Kiyomori, now greatly reduced in strength, has literally lost its political and social moorings ("with the loosening of their mooring lines") and is drifting toward an unknown, but inevitably dark, fate.

There is irony in the water metaphors inasmuch as the Ise Taira first gained fame as a sea power in the Inland Sea. The once great "kings of the water" are now its victims, carried along by its changing tides and shifting currents. There is irony also in the fact that the Taira are fleeing to the west, for they were not just a sea power but a "western" sea power as well. In the *Heike,* the war between the Ise Taira and the Minamoto is presented geographically as a conflict between the Minamoto of the east (land power) and the Taira of the west (sea power). The ultimate irony of this pairing is revealed, of course, in the final defeat of the Taira by the Minamoto in the sea battle of Dannoura in the west in the third month of 1185. But another irony deriving from the association of the Taira with the sea and the west appears in the *Heike* in the description of the family's flight from Kyoto and Fukuhara. Although by heading westward to Kyushu, the Taira hope to gather support from former adherents in that region, the *Heike,* as in the passage just quoted, portrays the west as remote and lonely, distant from the high civilization of the capital. The Taira, who have become aristocratized, now see their western heritage differently: compared with the "civilized" capital, the west is "uncivilized." Sharing the sentiments of courtiers through the ages, they are agonized by their forced departure from the capital and can conceive of happiness only in terms of returning to Kyoto.

TADANORI AND TSUNEMASA

The *Heike*'s description of the Taira flight from Kyoto emphasizes their courtliness also by highlighting the departure of two members of the family who exemplify acquisition of the courtly arts: Tadanori the poet and Tsunemasa the musician.

Tadanori was a younger brother of Kiyomori and one of the leading field commanders of the Ise Taira. More than any other member of his family as they are portrayed in the *Heike,* he combines the qualities of warrior and romantic courtier. In one of his early appearances in the *Heike,* Tadanori serves as the second in command of an ill-fated expeditionary force sent by Kiyomori to the Kantō against Minamoto no Yoritomo, shortly after Yoritomo rises in rebellion in 1180. We are told that for many years, Tadanori had been conducting an affair with the daughter of a princess and that the daughter, distressed that he must now leave on a military expedition, sends him a poem along with the gift of a robe. In responding to the daughter, Tadanori composes a poem that is described as containing lines of "great refinement":

> *Wakareji o*
> *nani ka nagekan*
> *koete yuki*
> *seki mo mukashi no*
> *ato to omoeba*

> Why lament
> Our parting,
> When the barrier I cross
> Leads to the sites
> Of bygone days?[28]

Among the warriors in the *Heike,* only the Taira recite poetry. Even in the affairs they occasionally have with courtly women, the Minamoto are poetically silent.[29] The inclusion in the *Heike* of thirty or so poems by Taira—most of them in the work's second half, which describes the Genpei War—is one of the more important indices of how courtly the Taira have become during their years of ascendancy in Kyoto.

We know that Tadanori was, in historical fact, a poet of some distinction.[30] The *Heike* develops Tadanori's courtier poet side to make his flight from Kyoto with his Taira kinsmen and his subsequent death at the battle of Ichinotani one of the more poignant of the many tales of how the Taira perish, one after another, in the various battles of the Genpei War. As the Taira prepare to leave Kyoto, Tadanori visits Fujiwara no Shunzei, one of the leading court poets of the day, with whom he has studied poetry for many years. He implores Shunzei to read a scroll of poems he has written, in the hope that one or more may be included in a future anthology of imperially authorized poetry.[31]

Tadanori is killed attempting to escape when the Minamoto, in the second month of 1184, rout the Taira from the fortress they have established at Ichinotani on the shore of the Inland Sea. The enemy knows Tadanori to be a high-ranking Taira commander because his teeth are blackened in the courtly fashion. He is able to make a precise identification when he finds a poem, written and signed by Tadanori, by Tadanori, in Tadanori's armor. There are none among friend or foe, we are told, who do not shed tears upon hearing of Tadanori's death: "How sad! [everyone said]. He was a person who excelled in both the martial arts and the way of poetry. He is a general who will be sorely missed."[32]

When Shunzei compiles the anthology *Senzaishū* in 1187, he in fact includes one of Tadanori's poems. But because the Ise Taira, having by then been defeated and destroyed in the Genpei War, are regarded as enemies of the court, Shunzei is obliged to label the poem "anonymous":

> *Sazanami ya*
> *Shiga no miyako wa*
> *are ni shi o*
> *mukashinagara no*
> *yamazakura kana*

> Though the old Shiga capital
> Lies in ruins,
> The mountain cherries
> Ripple like waves
> As of yore.[33]

Tsunemasa was a nephew of Kiyomori, who as a youth had served at Ninnaji (temple) in Kyoto and who, because of his extraordinary musical talent, had been entrusted by the temple's abbot with the famous lute Seizan, which centuries earlier had been brought to the Japanese court from China. The bestowal of Seizan, an instrument once prized by emperors, upon a young Taira was an extraordinary tribute to the skill of a warrior in one of the courtly arts. Although it is possible that Tsunemasa was given Seizan to curry favor with the powerful Taira family, the *Heike* avers that he fully deserved it—presumably above potential courtier recipients—on grounds of his musicality alone.[34]

As the Taira prepare to abandon Kyoto, Tsunemasa hurries to Ninnaji to return Seizan to the abbot. Weeping, Tsunemasa says that he cannot bring himself to take such a treasured instrument into "the dust of the hinterland."[35] What he means, metaphorically, is that he must leave behind "civilization" (or culture, represented by Seizan) because he is heading into the "uncivilized" (and hence uncultured) western provinces. He expresses the hope that if the fortune of the Taira should through some miracle change and he is able to return to the capital/civilization, he might be given Seizan to play once again. After exchanging poems of parting with the abbot, he leaves Ninnaji. Tsunemasa's performance in this touching scene—his relinquishment of the lute, his weeping, his dread of venturing into the "hinterland," his exchange of poems with the abbot—is thoroughly courtly.

The theme of the Taira warrior as musician reappears in the famous story of Tsunemasa's younger brother Atsumori. The setting is again the Minamoto rout of the

Taira at Ichinotani. Atsumori, who is only sixteen or seventeen, is attempting to escape to the Taira ships moored offshore and fights with the fearsome Minamoto adherent Kumagai no Naozane. Wrestling Atsumori to the ground and tearing off his helmet to behead him, Naozane is amazed to see the face—with blackened teeth—of a beautiful youth. To Naozane, Atsumori is like a courtier. He also reminds Naozane, who wishes to spare him, of his own son. But Naozane is forced to kill Atsumori when he sees a band of Minamoto approaching and knows they will show the youthful Taira no mercy. Later, Naozane discovers a flute in a pouch at Atsumori's waist and realizes that it had been Atsumori playing the flute in the Taira fortress that morning. Observing that none among the Minamoto would think of bringing a flute to a battle, Naozane proclaims: "These lofty people [the Taira] are truly men of refinement!"[36]

THE END OF THE ISE TAIRA

The Taira journey to Kyushu in the distant west avails them little, for they are driven also from that region, which had once been an important family base, by a renegade former vassal. Adrift again, they make their way to Yashima off Shikoku Island, where Munemori and the other Taira, all of whom hold high court ranks, must "spend their days in the rush-thatched huts of fishermen and their nights in mean hovels."[37] The Taira are, however, able to win some battles against forces sent from Kyoto by Yoshinaka, who is under increasing threat from his cousin and rival for Minamoto leadership, Yoritomo of Kamakura.

In the first month of 1184, Yoshinaka is destroyed by an army under the half brothers Minamoto no Yoshitsune and Noriyori, dispatched from Kamakura by Yoritomo (another half brother). With Kyoto secured, the quick-acting Yoshitsune attacks the fortress that the Taira have meanwhile established at Ichinotani on the Honshu littoral of the Inland Sea, near Fukuhara. The Taira loss at Ichinotani is devastating; the *Heike* lists among the family dead ten of its most prominent members, including all three of those discussed in the last section—Tadanori, Tsunemasa, and Atsumori.[38]

Only one Taira commander, Kiyomori's son Shigehira, is captured at Ichinotani. Shigehira, as we find him in the *Heike,* rivals his uncle Tadanori as a possessor of outstanding qualities as both warrior and romantic courtier. Much of the *Heike*'s book 10 is devoted to Shigehira in captivity (he is held for about a year and a half before being executed after the Genpei War), during which time he is taken to see Yoritomo in Kamakura. In an earlier meeting with a mistress (mentioned earlier) and while on the trip to Kamakura, Shigehira shows himself to be a person of great courtly sensitivity, composing waka poetry, engaging in a brief affair with a girl at an inn, and charming people with his lute playing and chanting at Kamakura. Yoritomo pronounces him to be "the most cultivated of men."[39]

There is no need, for the purpose of this chapter, to describe the final year of the Genpei War; it is enough to note that the Ise Taira are badly defeated again at the battle of Yashima in the second month of 1185 and are driven westward once more in their boats. A month later they are decimated in the naval battle at Dannoura. Most of the remaining Taira leaders are killed or drown themselves, along with the child emperor Antoku, at Dannoura. The few Taira who are captured, including Munemori, are subsequently executed, and other Taira who did not participate in the Dannoura fighting, including children, are hunted down and killed. The *Heike* is brought to a conclusion with the final pronouncement, after the execution of Shigemori's grandson (and Kiyomori's great-grandson) Rokudai, that "thus the progeny of the Heike [Taira] came finally to an end."[40]

CONCLUSION

As I noted at the beginning of this chapter, the Kakuichi version of the *Heike monogatari* that I used was completed in 1371 and was the product of nearly two centuries of textual development and embellishment, especially by itinerant tale singers. The picture of the Ise Taira as aristocratized or courtly warriors in the Kakuichi *Heike* is therefore historically inaccurate (although the Taira certainly became aristocratized to some extent during their years of ascendancy in Kyoto), and it does not even necessarily represent the tastes and attitudes of the late twelfth century, the time of the *Heike*'s story. Rather, at least some, if not a great deal, of what we find in the Kakuichi *Heike* reflects the tastes and attitudes of the early Muromachi period. We know, for example, that in the early Muromachi period, the Ashikaga and other members of the warrior elite, most of them maintaining their principal residences in Kyoto, were commencing a historical process in which they themselves became aristocratized and that they enjoyed being informed about courtier-warriors of the past, especially the Ise Taira of the Genpei age. Zeami, one of the creators of the nō theater, who began his career in the theater about the time of the completion of the Kakuichi *Heike,* catered to this desire of the Muromachi warrior elite to learn about the Ise Taira as courtier-warriors by creating the warrior category of nō plays and by basing all his warrior plays on the Kakuichi *Heike.*[41]

The transformation of the Ise Taira into courtly warriors in the Kakuichi *Heike* is achieved by various means. Among these are the constant use, and thus highlighting, of Taira-held court ranks and titles (the Minamoto in the *Heike,* with few exceptions, have no such ranks and titles); the recording of poems composed by Taira; the description of Taira, especially from the time of their forced departure from Kyoto in 1183, weeping when moved by such unmanly or un-warrior-like feelings as longing for a loved one, homesickness (for Kyoto), and the bewilderment and frustration caused by the disruptions of the Genpei War; and the narration of the love affairs the Taira have with court ladies. Among the most prominent Taira lovers, as they are identified in the *Heike,* are Tadamori, Tadanori, Michimori, and Shigehira.[42] Although the Minamoto also occasionally engage in affairs with court ladies in the *Heike* (for example, Yoshinaka and Yoshitsune), we are told nothing about their styles of courtship.

When speaking of the intrusion of Muromachi tastes into the war tales that recount the Taira-Minamoto stories of the Genpei age, Helen McCullough has commented on "the idealization of the fleeing Taira as elegant and bewildered aristocrats."[43] This comment appears, in fact, in a discussion of how Minamoto no Yoshitsune, who remains manly and warriorlike throughout the **Heike,** is aristocratized in *Gikeiki* (Chronicle of Yoshitsune), a Muromachi-period work whose primary focus is on the flight of Yoshitsune and a small band of supporters to the northern provinces after the Genpei War to avoid the wrath of Yoritomo, who is determined to destroy—and finally succeeds in destroying—Yoshitsune. One should be cautious about drawing analogies between **Heike monogatari** and *Gikeiki,* since they are very different kinds of works. Nevertheless, in both we see the "flight" used prominently as a narrative device for the purpose of transforming warriors into courtly warriors.

Still another important means by which the **Heike** transforms the Taira into courtly warriors is through the use of classical court language, such as the language in the description quoted earlier of the Taira flight from Fukuhara and in the stories of their affairs with court ladies. The classical language we find in this and other sections of the **Heike** is one of the reasons it, alone among the war tales, is admired as a literary masterpiece.

Many other examples of Ise Taira aristocratization or courtliness in the **Heike** could be cited. But I hope what I have presented conveys a general sense of the extraordinarily rich tradition, in both history (insofar as people regard the **Heike** as history) and literature, of this family as courtly warriors, especially romantic courtly warriors, as they are portrayed in the **Heike**'s second half when they flee from Kyoto, are hunted down, and are annihilated in the Genpei War and its aftermath.

Notes

1. Records of the fourteenth century, especially the war tale *Taiheiki,* suggest that many daimyos had already voluntarily taken up residence in Kyoto before they were required to do so by the third Ashikaga shogun Yoshimitsu. The first third of *Taiheiki* can be found in English translation in Helen Craig McCullough, trans., *Taiheiki: A Chronicle of Medieval Japan* (New York: Columbia University Press, 1959).

2. The Japanese term for aristocratization is *kizoku-ka.* See the reference to this in Yasuda Motohisa, *Heike no gunzō* (Tokyo: Hanawa shobō, 1967), p. 18.

3. See Kenneth Dean Butler, "The Textual Evolution of the *Heike Monogatari,*" *Harvard Journal of Asiatic Studies* 26 (1965-66): 5-51. See also the summary of the *Heike*'s textual evolution in Paul Varley, *Warriors of Japan, as Portrayed in the War Tales* (Honolulu: University of Hawaii Press, 1994), pp. 82-85.

4. Yasuda, *Heike no gunzō,* pp. 14, 77. Yasuda cites two important Tokugawa-period histories, the Mito

school's *Dai Nihon shi* and Rai San'yō's *Nihon gaishi,* that use the *Heike* as a primary source.

5. Takagi Ichinosuke et al., eds., *Heike monogatari,* vol. 1, in *Nihon koten bungaku taikei,* vols. 32-33 (Tokyo: Iwanami shoten, 1959), p. 84. This is the 1371 Kakuichi text of the *Heike,* which is the work's *rufubon,* or the most widely disseminated of the hundred or more surviving versions of the *Heike.* My chapter is based solely on the Kakuichi *Heike,* and the translations are mine. For a full English translation, see Helen Craig McCullough, *The Tale of the Heike* (Stanford, CA: Stanford University Press, 1988). The reference to Tadamori's receipt of a provincial governorship and permission to attend at the imperial palace appears on p. 24 of the McCullough translation.

6. Takagi et al., *Heike monogatari,* vol. 1, p. 85; McCullough, *Tale of the Heike,* p. 24.

7. Ibid.

8. Takagi et al., *Heike monogatari,* vol. 1, pp. 87-88; McCullough, *Tale of the Heike,* pp. 25-26.

9. Nagazumi Yasuaki, *Heike monogatari o yomu* (Tokyo: Iwanami shoten, 1980), pp. 19-20.

10. Takagi et al., *Heike monogatari,* vol. 1, p. 89; McCullough, *Tale of the Heike,* p. 27.

11. Takagi et al., *Heike monogatari,* vol. 1, p. 83; McCullough, *Tale of the Heike,* p. 23.

12. Takagi et al., *Heike monogatari,* vol. 1, pp. 92-94; McCullough, *Tale of the Heike,* pp. 27-30.

13. Takagi et al., *Heike monogatari,* vol. 1, pp. 90-91; McCullough, *Tale of the Heike,* p. 28.

14. For example, Tomikura Tokujirō, *Heike monogatari* (Tokyo: NHK, 1972), p. 56.

15. Takagi et al., *Heike monogatari,* vol. 1, p. 171; McCullough, *Tale of the Heike,* p. 74. There is one occasion in the *Heike* when Shigemori presumably wears armor: in book 1, where he is said to assume responsibility for defending several gates of the imperial palace against warrior monks. Takagi et al., *Heike monogatari,* vol. 1, p. 135; McCullough, *Tale of the Heike,* p. 53.

16. See the discussion of this in Uwayokote Masataka, *Heike monogatari no kyokō to shinjitsu* (Tokyo: Hanawa shobō, 1985), vol. 1, pp. 81-88.

17. Takagi et al., *Heike monogatari,* vol. 1, p. 172; McCullough, *Tale of the Heike,* p. 75.

18. Uwayokote suggests that the *Heike*'s author(s) used Shigemori to criticize Kiyomori because Goshirakawa was too embroiled himself in court politics to be a credible critic. *Heike monogatari no kyokō to shinjitsu,* vol. 1, pp. 85-86.

19. See the analysis of the differences between "eastern" and "western" warriors by Saitō no Sanemori, an eastern warrior allied with the Taira. Takagi et al.,

Heike monogatari, vol. 1, pp. 372-73; McCullough, *Tale of the Heike,* pp. 188-90. See also the discussion of this subject in Varley, *Warriors of Japan,* pp. 91-92.

20. Takagi et al., *Heike monogatari,* vol. 2, p. 94; McCullough, *Tale of the Heike,* p. 242.

21. Ibid.

22. Takagi et al., *Heike monogatari,* vol. 2, pp. 314-16; McCullough, *Tale of the Heike,* pp. 365-66.

23. Takagi et al., *Heike monogatari,* vol. 2, p. 247; McCullough, *Tale of the Heike,* p. 330.

24. Kiyomori moved the capital to Fukuhara in the sixth month of 1180 and returned it to Kyoto five months later.

25. Takagi et al., *Heike monogatari,* vol. 2, p. 115; McCullough, *Tale of the Heike,* p. 254.

26. Takagi et al., *Heike monogatari,* vol. 2, p. 116; McCullough, *Tale of the Heike,* pp. 254-55. Tomikura Tokujirō notes that this passage of the Taira flight from Fukuhara has, because of its lyricism, been one of the favorites of the *Heike* tale singers. See his *Heike monogatari* (Tokyo: Kadokawa shoten, 1975), p. 235.

27. Ishimoda Shō, *Heike monogatari* (Tokyo: Iwanami shoten, 1957), pp. 167-68.

28. Takagi et al., *Heike monogatari,* vol. 1, pp. 367-68; McCullough, *Tale of the Heike,* pp. 185-86. The *Heike* goes on to say that the "sites" Tadanori refers to must be the places where Taira no Sadamori was victorious when he led an expedition eastward in the ninth century to subdue the rebel Masakado.

29. There are two exceptions to this statement. Kajiwara no Kagetaka recites a poem before charging into battle at Ichinotani in book 9, and Minamoto no Yorimasa, identified in the *Heike* as an ardent poet, is the author of several poems in book 4. But the case of Yorimasa is unusual, since he was the only prominent Minamoto to side with the Taira in the Heiji Conflict of 1159-60 and, as a result, the only one to remain in the capital thereafter. Despite his Minamoto surname, Yorimasa is really like a Taira in the *Heike,* that is, one who was aristocratized in the years leading to the Genpei War.

30. Sixteen of Tadanori's poems are in imperially sponsored anthologies. Kajiwara Masaaki, *Heike monogatari* (Tokyo: Shōgakkan, 1982), p. 230.

31. Takagi et al., *Heike monogatari,* vol. 2, pp. 102-4; McCullough, *Tale of the Heike,* pp. 246-47.

32. Takagi et al., *Heike monogatari,* vol. 2, pp. 215-17; McCullough, *Tale of the Heike,* pp. 313-14.

33. Takagi et al., *Heike monogatari,* vol. 2, p. 104; McCullough, *Tale of the Heike,* p. 247. Shiga, in Ōmi Province, had once in ancient times been the imperial capital.

34. Takagi et al., *Heike monogatari,* vol. 2, pp. 107-8; McCullough, *Tale of the Heike,* pp. 249-50.

35. Takagi et al., *Heike monogatari,* vol. 2, p. 106; McCullough, *Tale of the Heike,* p. 248. I have taken the word *hinterland* from the McCullough translation.

36. Takagi et al., *Heike monogatari,* vol. 2, pp. 219-22; McCullough, *Tale of the Heike,* pp. 315-17.

37. Takagi et al., *Heike monogatari,* vol. 2, p. 135; McCullough, *Tale of the Heike,* p. 266.

38. Takagi et al., *Heike monogatari,* vol. 2, p. 226; McCullough, *Tale of the Heike,* p. 320.

39. Takagi et al., *Heike monogatari,* vol. 2, p. 226; McCullough, *Tale of the Heike,* pp. 340-41.

40. Takagi et al., *Heike monogatari,* vol. 2, p. 422; McCullough, *Tale of the Heike,* p. 425. Helen McCullough provides a freer, more dramatic translation of this passage: "Thus did the sons of the Heike vanish forever from the face of the earth."

41. See the discussion of this in Thomas Blenman Hare, *Zeami's Style* (Stanford, CA: Stanford University Press, 1986), p. 185.

42. Michimori's courtship of and marriage to the court lady Kozaishō and her suicide by drowning when she learns of his death in the battle of Ichinotani are recounted in "Kozaishō's Suicide," the last chapter of book 9. Tadamori, Tadanori, and Shigehira as lovers have been discussed.

43. Helen McCullough, trans., *Yoshitsune* (Stanford, CA: Stanford University Press, 1966), p. 54.

Herbert Plutschow (essay date 1997)

SOURCE: "The Placatory Nature of *The Tale of the Heike*: Additional Documents and Thoughts," in *Currents in Japanese Culture: Translations and Transformations,* edited by Amy Vladeck Heinrich, Columbia University Press, 1997, pp. 71-80.

[In the following essay, Plutschow contends that a major purpose for the Heike Monogatari *was to appease angry gods and guilty consciences.]*

In my book *Chaos and Cosmos: Ritual in Classical Japanese Literature,* I discuss a number of texts suggesting that the ***Heike monogatari (The Tale of the Heike)*** was recited in part to placate the spirits of its heroes. These texts range from legends such as "Earless Hōichi" and "Earless Danichi" to war tales (*gunki-mono*), historical works, and diaries. I introduce the pioneering research of Tsukudo Reikan and others who interpret ***The Tale of the Heike*** as placatory literature. Furthermore, I support my hypothesis with a discussion of the fear of vengeful spirits in Japanese religion and refer to the traditional role of blind performers in placating them.[1]

Based on a combination of these factors, I conclude that the account in *Tsurezuregusa* (Essays in Idleness) of the role of Priest Jien (1155-1225) in producing **The Tale of the Heike** needs serious reconsideration:

> During the reign of the Emperor Go-toba, a former official from Shinano named Yukinaga enjoyed a reputation for learning. . . . The priest Jichin [Jien], who made a practice of hiring men with artistic talent even as menials and treating them kindly employed this lay priest of Shinano.
>
> Yukinaga wrote the **Heike monogatari** and taught a blind man named Shōbutsu to recite it. . . . *Biwa* entertainers today imitate what was Shōbutsu's natural voice.[2]

Although Jien fails to mention **The Tale of the Heike** in his own writings, he is well-known through his *Gukanshō* (a moral history of Japan based on imperial and Buddhist law written around 1219) as the most vehement proponent of the need to protect the nation by placating evil spirits. Moreover, as a prominent member of the most powerful (*sekkanke*) branch of the Fujiwara aristocracy and high priest of the Enryakuji (since 1192), a temple that owes its existence to warding off evil, Jien is likely to have played a role in the inception of the **Heike**.

Additional texts further support this theory. The following are excerpts from Jien's *Hatsugan-bun* (Petition) to build the temple Daisenpōin:

> Thus from the Hōgen era [1156-1159] until now when the nation is in turmoil, vengeful spirits fill the heavens. The spirits of fallen warriors are all over. However, no amnesty has yet been proclaimed to save the nation from their evil. Furthermore, no deliberations have yet taken place about national renewal. . . . Appeasing these evil spirits helps the state. In so doing, we must rely solely on the power of the Buddhist dharma. . . . Among these evil spirits stand out the sacred soul of ex-Emperor Sutoku [1119-1164] and the vengeful ghost of Chisokuin [Kujō Yoshitsune, 1169-1208]. . . . Therefore vengeful spirits and the spirits of fallen warriors fill the nation. By performing *ekō*, we must have them abandon their evil ways, return to normal and help them overcome their pains by providing them with *raku*. By practicing the Buddhist dharma and the laws of good government and by the Buddhas and deities invisible to them, we must turn misfortune into fortune and bring about happiness and peace. This is not only my own wish, but is has always been the desire of the Buddhas and deities to benefit mankind.[3]

Jien expresses the same thoughts in his *Gogan-bun* (Petition for Special Services at Daisenpōin):

> Since the disturbances started in the Hōgen [1156-1159] and Genryaku [1184-1185] eras, warriors were constantly on the move, causing anxiety among the people. . . . Evil ministers and rebellious warriors disturbed the nation and caused war, and many died away from home and turned into evil demons. It is like the southern barbarians aspiring to high office and eastern barbarians who lost their way on the path toward prosperity. We must protect the country by escaping from the pains of these evil times and turning these evils around.[4]

Through these petitions, Jien reiterates the need to placate by means of *ekō* and *raku* the many malevolent spirits of those who died away from home. *Raku* means to guide someone back to a normal, desirable mental and physical state. *Ekō* means that someone uses power or merit accumulated through discipline to benefit someone else and to guide that someone toward enlightenment. Both terms can be applied to the recitation of the **Heike**. Jien fails to mention the Heike by name in these petitions and concentrates instead on the spirits of ex-Emperor Sutoku and Chisokuin. He does, however, mention the Heike (also Taira) in his *Gukanshō*: "The Heishi all disappeared without leaving a trace . . . there are numerous vengeful spirits of the Heike who, from the invisible world, act out [their vengeance] according to the laws of cause and effect."[5]

Unfortunately, little is known about the early stages in the development of the **Heike**. According to the *Tōdōyōshū*, the first **Heike** text was written under Jōichi, who lived about half a century after Jien.[6] We must therefore resort to other evidence to support the view that the **Tale** was recited to placate the Heike.

One such piece of evidence comes from a close examination of the passages about the drowning of the child emperor Antoku at the battle of Dannoura in 1185. Before throwing herself into the ocean with the emperor in her arms, the wet nurse Nii-dono (Lady Second Rank) consoles him, saying: "There is also a capital at the bottom of the sea," implying the existence of a paradise at the bottom of the ocean. In addition, according to the Enkei text version of the **Heike**, Nii-dono composed a death poem expressing the same sentiments:

> *Ima soshiru*
> *Mimosusogawa no*
> *Nagare ni wa*
> *Nami no shita ne mo*
> *Miyako ari to wa*[7]
>
> Now you will know
> There is also a capital
> At the bottom
> Of Mimosuso River.

The Mimosuso River stands for the Ise shrine (Naikū), where the ancestral deity of the imperial family is enshrined. By mentioning this, Nii-dono suggests that Antoku will control the gentle flow of the river and live in peace at the home of his ancestors. According to the Kakuichi text, in the "Rokudō no Sata" section, Kenreimon'in, Antoku's mother and the daughter of the Taira chieftain Kiyomori, dreams that Nii-dono told Antoku: "There will be for you a palace by far more splendid than the one in Kyoto, where the late emperor and all the nobles of the Heike will offer you a banquet." Having never heard about such a palace, Antoku asked: "Where is this?" Nii-dono replied: "The dragon's place."[8] The Enkei copy reports similarly: "Thus all those who sank into the sea will no doubt become one with the dragon."[9] The Kakuichi version even suggests that Antoku was the dragon who "came down from heaven and turned into a fish at the bottom of the sea."[10]

When Emperor Antoku drowned at Dannoura, the imperial sword, one of the three symbols of imperial power, sank with him to the bottom of the sea. According to the *Gukanshō*, only the sword's empty box was picked up by a warrior.[11] This sword, according to the Enkei text, was never found, despite special prayers ordered to be held at temples and shrines, because it "was taken by the dragon and placed in his place."[12] The Enkei text in fact suggests that the sword was taken back by its original owner, the dragon killed by the deity Susanoo. The *Genpei seisui ki* recounts the story of two divers who, when searching for the lost sword, met the dragon and saw the sword at his place.[13]

All *Heike* texts attribute the great earthquake of 1185 to the vengeful spirits of the Heike, but by implication it also is ascribed to the dragon, which is seen as the main cause of earthquakes, floods, landslides, and other natural calamities. Jien's *Gukanshō* confirms this: "This is an extraordinary event that was caused by the earth-shaking dragon deity and people claimed that the dragon had become Taira Shokoku [Kiyomori] and that it was he who shook the earth."[14] In his chapter entitled "Why Emperor Antoku Was Drowned," Jien elaborates:

> This emperor [Antoku] became emperor because Kiyomori offered prayers at Itsukushima shrine. It was the blessing of this deity of Itsukushima in Aki Province. This Itsukushima deity is the dragon's daughter, they say. A person knowledgeable in these matters said that the deity responded to the deep respects Kiyomori had paid and turned into this emperor who, in the end, returned to the sea. I think this is true.[15]

Perhaps Kiyomori selected the Itsukushima shrine on Miyajima (island) as his ancestral shrine because the shrine was believed to be the abode of the dragon's third daughter. The Enkei text agrees with Jien's *Gukanshō* interpretation that the dragon sought revenge for having been killed by Susanoo by introducing the Taira into the imperial line.[16] Before that, only Fujiwara—and not Taira—women were eligible to produce emperors. The *Heike*'s section on the loss of the imperial sword also agrees with Jien's interpretation:

> An expert made a divination and revealed: "The great snake that Susanoo-no-mikoto slew at the upper course of Hino River in Izumo Province has deeply resented the loss of the sacred sword and, according to its eight heads and eight tails, retook it after the eightieth human reign from an eight-year old emperor and returned to the bottom of the sea."[17]

In his *Gukanshō*, Jien affirms that thanks to Kiyomori's fervent prayers, the dragon became Antoku. That is, Antoku and the dragon are one and the same. The *Heike* also makes this association quite clear. It describes Antoku just before his death as an exceedingly handsome boy wearing a *binzura* hairstyle.[18] Indeed, Ubukata Takashige and others believe that Antoku's hairstyle, usually worn by deities and buddhas, suggests an unearthly being.[19]

The dragon not only appears in texts such as ***The Tale of the Heike*** but also was related in many ways to their blind reciters. According to the *Mōsō yurai*, blind reciters were summoned by Empress Genmei (661-721), when the court was disturbed by unusual events.[20] In order to ward off the evil, the blind recited the *Chijin-kyō* (literally, Earth deity's sutra) accompanied on the biwa.[21] It reports that during the rites, a snake appeared and fell on the white sand of the Shishinden palace but was chased off. The *Chijin mōsō engi*, which deals with the *Chijin-kyō* in particular, mentions a large snake seeking "revenge against the court."[22] The text explains the origin of the snake not in terms of the dragon but as the snake that prevented Priest Saichō (767-822) from building the Enryakuji (temple). Such stories may be mythical rather than historical in nature, but they well represent the ideology of the blind reciters and of the court that regarded the placation of opposed forces as one of its most important functions.

By reciting the *Chijin-kyō*, the blind priests were engaging in a placatory effort of national proportions. Yanagita Kunio points out that blind priests were often summoned to perform rites in villages suffering from droughts or floods.[23] The popular legends that resulted reveal the belief that all blind people were related to the dragon, that they controlled the dragon and therefore had the power to appease it when it caused calamities. The *Chijin-kyō* refers to the dragon king and the deities who served the dragon, such as the snake and water deities. According to this text, the five directions (east, west, north, south, and center) are controlled by the dragons. One of them has controlled the wind and waves of Japan ever since it was pacified. The Heike thus must be placated because they were related to this dragon.

Finally, we can gain insight into the purpose of reciting ***The Tale of the Heike*** by considering where and when it was recited. The Tōdō group gathered every year on March 24, the anniversary of Emperor Antoku's death, on the bank of the Kamo River at about the level of the Shijō Street to recite the ***Tale***.[24] Before beginning their recitation, the group built a pagoda with pebbles and stones, a custom still observed today in the construction of stone pagodas (five-storied pagodas, *sotoba* and other forms of stupas, *jizō* [guardian deities], and simple earth mounds) in dry riverbeds, crossroads, slopes, and passes. The erection of such pagodas probably goes back to the *nenbutsu* priests who placated evil spirits at such places. The locations of these pagodas are unmistakably liminal, to use the term that Victor Turner labeled much ritual activity. These places were believed to separate the world of the living from the world of the dead.

Pagodas built at such places served as *yorishiro*, that is, places in which priests invoked the spirits to descend so that the ritual could be performed in their presence. As such, stone pagodas are mentioned in many documents, including the *Honchō seiki* (a history covering the years 935 to 1153) and the *Meikō orai* (text of the late Heian period describing the daily ceremonies of nobles and commoners).[25] According to the *Nihongiryaku* (a history from the first emperor until 1036, of unknown authorship and date), stone pagodas were ordered to be built at all crossroads in the vicinity of Kyoto during the epidemic of 994.[26] From such sources, we learn that pagodas were built at crossroads, gates, and other important locations in order to prevent the evil spirits that cause natural calamities from entering the capital and disrupting the conduct of state affairs.

A good example of such a liminal place is Shinomiya-gawara (dry bed of the Shinomiya River) in Yamashina in northeast Kyoto. Believed to be inhabited by the Shuku or Shiku deities (potentially evil water deities), this was a place where one could link the world of the living with the world of the dead in order to placate evil spirits who seek revenge on the capital from the northeastern *kimon,* or the gate of hell. It was not far from the Seki myōjin (shrine) on Mount Ausaka (or Osaka, between Kyoto and Ōtsu), dedicated to the blind Semimaru, who was worshiped as a tutelary deity of biwa players and also as a deity that protected the access to Kyoto at the Ausaka pass. Semimaru was the fourth prince of Emperor Daigo (885-930) and is thought to have lived near the site of today's shrine.[27] Since he was the fourth prince, the area was also known as Shinomiya (Fourth Prince) and was the place where the Tōdō group performed their rites. Saneyasu, who is worshiped by the Tōdō reciters as their artistic and tutelary deity, also happened to be a fourth prince (of Emperor Ninmyō, 810-850).[28] The two fourth princes were therefore amalgamated in the tradition of the *Heike*'s reciters.

Through folk etymology, which played an important role in Japanese religion, these two fourth princes also were associated with the Ten Deities, called Shiku, of Mount Hiei's Sannō deity. In its Japanese reading, Shiku can also be read Shinomiya, hence the association. In the Shinomiya area, we also find a jizō and the temple *Jūzenji gongen.* Jūzenji refers to ten priests (*naigubu*) selected by Emperor Kōnin in 772 to hold prayers at the imperial palace and included Saichō (797) and Ennin (848). They were believed to be reincarnations of the jizō. The jizō were worshiped as deities that saved souls who erred in the unenlightened Rokudō realm, of which Shinomiya was believed to be one of the crossroads.[29]

There the blind *Heike* reciters built a stone pagoda on a biwa-shaped rock. The pagoda served as a symbol of the prince who was called on to assist the reciters in their art. At the same time, it served as *yorishiro* for the evil ghosts of the Heike that had to be appeased there to prevent their intruding into the capital and wreaking havoc. These spirits are the *mono* that the *monogatari* addressed.

There is still another dimension to the *Heike* recited at such places as Shinomiya-gawara and Shijō-kawara. These were liminal places where the blind reciters were able to identify with their heroes, where they could lend their bodies to these vengeful spirits. As is amply demonstrated in the nō theater, spirits are more effectively placated when the identities of the ghost and his storyteller blur and the reciter speaks as if it were the ghost himself telling his own story. For example, in the nō play *Sotoba Komachi,* nenbutsu prayers are offered at a stone pagoda in an effort to appease the spirits of Ono no Komachi and her unfortunate lover Shii no Shōshō. Not only do they end up exchanging their identities, and therefore their sins and pains, but they also assume the role of the nenbutsu performers as well. These are the ending lines of the play, sung by all:

> By building a pagoda out of sand
> We make a Buddha and offer flowers;
> We are entering the way of enlightenment,
> We are entering the way of enlightenment.[30]

Such shifts and mergers of various identities frequently encountered in the nō theater were no doubt placatory devices available to exorcists and placators, including the blind reciters of **The Tale of the Heike.**

From the Edo period on, Tōdō group reciters also performed their rites at Shijō-kawara, as we have seen. Shijō-kawara was also a liminal place, used for the execution of criminals, for worship of the dead such as *segaki-e* (Buddhist offerings of food to the hungry ghosts feared to cause calamities), and also as a place of purification and divination.

Socially, Shijō-kawara was a place frequented by itinerant nenbutsu priests, outcasts, artists, and low-class performers. The performance of so many different rites at the same place points to the ambivalence we observe in much Japanese art and religion. Placation also means purification, a place polluted with evil spirits that is also a place of renewal. As is clear in the myths of Izanagi's pollution resulting from his visit to the world of the dead and his subsequent purification in a nearby river, purification and world-renewing rituals are often held at the most polluted sites. This fact is consonant with Japanese religion, which places its emphasis not so much on the simple expulsion of evil but, rather, on its conversion to good. The example of Sugawara no Michizane (845-903) is a case in point. Worshiped as Tenjin, a deity of learning and agricultural fertility, Tenjin is a converted devil who, in revenge for having been unjustly exiled, inflicted calamities on the emperor and his rivals.

At Shijō-kawara, the blind reciters performed a ritual called *kyō-nagashi* or *nagare gonchō,* consisting of floating downriver portions of the Lotus sutra that they had copied themselves.[31] On March 24, they did so expressly for the appeasement of Emperor Antoku's soul. Yet there is also another dimension to this rite. Shijō-kawara is in the vicinity of the Yasaka shrine dedicated to Gozu Tennō, who was a deity of epidemics, that is, a deity who could both cause epidemics and prevent them. Gozu was believed to be a manifestation of none other than the deity Susanoo whom we have already encountered. Maybe Gozu was associated with Susanoo—a bull-headed demon of hell—because Susanoo was exiled by the heavenly deities to Izumo, an area associated with the netherworld in ancient Japanese cosmology. At Shijō-kawara, therefore, **Heike** reciters worshiped the spirits of Emperor Antoku and the Heike and also that of Susanoo, in an effort to combine the worship of these original antagonists into one ritual.[32]

Given such multidimensional values and different, that is, malevolent and benevolent, identities, Susanoo was perhaps a kind of scapegoat on whom one could heap all the evil ravaging of a community. But he was also a deity who could purify and appease evil spirits. Susanoo therefore fulfilled many of the same functions as the jizō and other such scapegoat deities one finds all over Japan. As a prominent heroine of **The Tale of the Heike,** Empress Kenreimon'in was also a kind of scapegoat who, according to the "Rokudō no Sata" section of the **Heike,** assumed all the sins committed by the Heike. The **Heike**'s reciters, too, are scapegoats as they heap on themselves the sins of the very heroes whose stories they recite. Their highly dramatic and lyrical recitations help erase the separation between reciters and their heroes.

In conclusion, a thorough study of where, when, and by whom **The Tale of the Heike** was recited is likely to reveal dimensions that hitherto have remained hidden from us. The result of such study would help us show that the heroes and the reciters of the **Heike** were related to one another and to the heterogeneous religious rituals and deities in a multidimensional, grandiose scheme through which the nation sought to rid itself of its past violence and the bad conscience it was causing. By trying to associate Antoku's death with mythical traditions concerning the creation of Japan, the **Heike**'s reciters seem to have abided by a historical determinism from which Japan seeks delivery. In the light of these facts, it is evident that the **Tale** was recited for placatory, and not exclusively artistic, purposes.

Notes

1. Herbert Plutschow, *Chaos and Cosmos: Ritual in Early and Medieval Japanese Literature* (Leiden: Brill, 1990), pp. 220-28.

2. Donald Keene, trans., *Essays in Idleness: The Tsurezuregusa of Kenkō* (New York: Columbia University Press, 1967), p. 186 and n. 1, 3, 4, and 7. Jien was the son of the *kanpaku* (chief adviser) Fujiwara no Tadamichi. At the age of eleven, Jien entered the Enryakuji (temple) and was ordained two years later. In 1192 he became the head priest of Enryakuji. He is known as the author of the *Gukanshō* and as one of Japan's most prolific poets.

3. Added to the end of the *Daisenpōin jōjō keisei no koto,* reprinted in *Dainihon shiryō,* vol. 5, part 1 (Tokyo: Tōkyō daigaku shuppan-kai, 1981), p. 529. See also *Jien, jinbutsu sōsho,* vol. 15 (Tokyo: Yoshikawa kōbunkan, 1963), pp. 126-27. Kujō

(Fujiwara) Yoshitsune was assassinated the night before he expected the emperor's visit.

4. *Dainihon shiryō,* vol. 4, part 10 (1910), pp. 259 ff. See also Fukuda Akira, "Kataribon no seiritsu," *Nihon bungaku,* June 1990, p. 58.

5. *Nihon koten bungaku taikei,* vol. 86 (Tokyo: Iwanami shoten, 1967), pp. 304-5 (hereafter abbreviated *NKBT*). See also Delmer Brown and Ichirō Ishida, trans., *The Future and the Past: A Translation and Study of the* Gukanshō, *an Interpretive History of Japan Written in 1219* (Berkeley and Los Angeles: University of California Press, 1979), p. 182.

6. The *Tōdōyōshū* is a collection of documents pertaining to the Tōdō-za group of blind *Heike* reciters, of unknown date and authorship, and containing information about the origin of the Tōdō group; legends about the founder, Prince Saneyasu; the ritual calendar; protective deities and buddhas; the origin of the various *Heike* texts; and the establishment by Kakuichi of a bureau of blind priestly reciters. It also includes instructions (and punishments) for the reciters. The *Tōdōyōshū* tried to establish the art of reciting the *Heike* as a sacred art related to emperors and the Tendai school of Buddhism. The earliest extant copy is dated 1741, copied from a 1684-1688 manuscript. It is printed in *Nihon shomin shiryō shūsei,* vol. 17 (Tokyo: Sanichi shobō, 1972), p. 231.

7. Yoshizawa Yoshinori, ed., *(Ōei shosha Enkei-bon-) Heike monogatari* (Tokyo: Hakuteisha, 1971), p. 881. The Enkei text is a 1310 version of the Kakuichi manuscript of the *Heike monogatari* related to the Kajūji family in Kyoto.

8. *Heike monogatari,* part 3, *NKBT,* vol. 33 (Tokyo: Iwanami shoten, 1960), p. 439. Kakuichi (d. 1371) established the Kakuichi *Heike* text and helped form the Tōdō-za group. He is said to have recited the *Heike* as a prayer for Kō no Moronau's health. The Kakuichi text, issuing from an earlier Yashiro text version, was the main recitative text of the Tōdō-za.

9. "Hōō Ōhara e gokō naru koto," in Yoshizawa, *Heike monogatari,* pp. 989-90.

10. *NKBT,* vol. 33, p. 337.

11. *NKBT,* vol. 86, p. 246.

12. Yoshizawa, *Heike monogatari,* pp. 889-93.

13. *(Kōtei-) Genpei seisuiki* (Tokyo: Hakubunkan, 1911), pp. 1158-61.

14. *NKBT,* vol. 86, p. 268.

15. Ibid., p. 265.

16. Yoshizawa, *Heike monogatari,* p. 893.

17. *NKBT,* vol. 33, pp. 348-49.

18. Ibid., pp. 336-37.

19. *Heike monogatari no kisō to kōzō—Mizu no kami to monogatari* (Tokyo: Kindai bungeisha, 1984), pp. 22-23.

20. Printed in *Nihon shomin seikatsu shiryō shūsei,* vol. 17, p. 247. The *Mōsō yurai* explains the origins of the blind priestly reciters, their cults and exploits. According to this text, the ancestor of the reciters is not Prince Saneyasu but a person recorded as Yukyō-reishi. The oldest text, in the possession of Iwata Koyata, is dated 1301.

21. The *Chijin-kyō* is printed with its various versions in *Nihon shomin seikatsu shiryō shūsei,* vol. 17, pp. 119-29.

22. *Nihon shomin seikatsu shiryō shūsei,* vol. 17, pp. 225-27. The *Chijin Mōsō engi* is a religious text related to the Myōonji in Chikuzen Province and used by the Chikuzen and Hizen groups of reciters.

23. *(Teihon-) Yanagita Kunio shū,* vol. 8 (Tokyo: Chikuma shobō, 1962), pp. 309-11.

24. *Nihon shomin seikatsu shiryō shūsei,* vol. 17, p. 230.

25. See in particular *Honchō seiki, (shintei zōho-) kokushi taikei,* vol. 9 (Tokyo: Yoshikawa kōbunkan, 1933), p. 12.

26. *(Shintei zōho-) kokushi taikei,* vol. 11, pp. 177-79.

27. See Susan Matisoff, *Legend of Semimaru: Blind Musician of Japan* (New York: Columbia University Press, 1978), pp. 38 ff.

28. *Tōdō yōshū,* in *Nihon shomin seikatsu shiryō shūsei,* vol. 17, p. 229. Prince Saneyasu (831-872) entered the priesthood in 859. He was the younger brother of Emperor Kōkō.

29. For further discussion, see Hyōdō Hiromi, *Katarimono josetsu: Heike-gatari no hassei to hyō gen* (Tokyo: Yūseido, 1985), pp. 119 ff.

30. *Yōkyoku taikan,* vol. 3 (Tokyo: Meiji shoin, 1931), p. 1730. The pagoda (*sotoba*) is referred to earlier in the play as a prayer allowing one to leave the Three Evil Paths.

31. Hiromi, *Katarimono josetsu,* pp. 122 ff.

32. For more discussion, see Fukuda Akira, "Shukujin-gatari no keifu," *Ritsumeikan bungaku,* nos. 472, 473, and 474 (October, November, and December 1984): 22 ff; and Neil McMullin, "On Placating the Gods and Pacifying the Populace: The Case of the Gion *Goryō* Cult," *History of Religions* 27 (February 1988): 270-93.

FURTHER READING

Criticism

Arnn, Barbara Louise. "Medieval Fiction and History in the *Heike Monogatari* Story Tradition." *Dissertation Abstracts International* 45, No. 5 (November 1984): 1402-A.
    Outlines study of the role played by the *Heike Monogatari* in passing on Japanese cultural traditions.

Bialock, David Theodore. "Peripheries of Power: Voice, History, and the Construction of Imperial and Sacred Space in *The Tale of the Heike* and Other Medieval and Heian Historical Texts." *Dissertation Abstracts International* 58, No. 2 (August 1997): 459-A.
    Outlines study which emphasizes the historiographical tradition of the *Heike Monogatari* and the *Kakuichi* variant, which is the product of a marginalized group.

Keene, Donald. "Tales of Warfare." In *Seeds in the Heart,* pp. 613–42. New York: Henry Holt and Co., 1993.
    Explains why the *Heike Monogatari,* defined by its dramatic contrasts and brutal portrayals of warriors, deserves its reputation as the foremost example of the Japanese martial tale.

Kitagawa, Hiroshi. "Translator's Preface." In *The Tale of the Heike: Heike Monogatari,* Vol. 1, Books 1–6, translated by Hiroshi Kitagawa and Bruce T. Tsuchida, pp. xxi-xl. Tokyo: University of Tokyo Press, 1975.
    Offers background information on a wide variety of subjects relevant to the time of the *Heike Monogatari,* including Buddhist influence; ethics; superstitions; ranks and titles; clothes; weapons; and food.

Konishi, Jin'ichi. "The Advance of Prose in the Mixed Style." In *A History of Japanese Literature, Volume Three: The High Middle Ages,* translated by Aileen Gatten and Mark Harbison, edited by Earl Miner, pp. 297-349. Princeton: Princeton University Press, 1991.
    Explores the strong influence of Buddhism on the *Heike Monogatari.*

Yamagata, Naoko. "Young and Old in Homer and in *Heike Monogatari.*" *Greece & Rome* XL, No. 1 (April 1993): 1-10.
    Comparative study of the *Iliad* and the *Heike Monogatari* that focuses on the generation gap.

Roman de Renart

c. 1171-1250 (Also known as *Roman de Renard*) French fables.

INTRODUCTION

The *Roman de Renart* is a 40,000-line collection of comic, sometimes bawdy, verse narratives from twelfth- and thirteenth-century France in which the characters are animals that behave like humans. While usually described as fables, the stories have also been termed epic romantic tales. Composed and collected circa 1171-1250, the *Roman de Renart* is the work of many different unknown authors and poets, whom many scholars contend were clerics. The central character and hero is Reynard the Fox, a devilish trickster. Many tales featuring Reynard were produced up to the fifteenth-century, including those of William Caxton, who translated and printed his version, *The History of Reynard the Fox*, in 1481. Reynard and his fellow animals who satirize the acts of man are also known today in the form of *Reinaerts Historie*, an adaptation that dates from circa 1380.

PLOT AND MAJOR CHARACTERS

The *Roman de Renart* comprises twenty-eight separate tales, or branches, as they are often called. Usually the stories feature the perpetually hungry fox involved in one antisocial activity or another. Typically he is captured for his misdeeds but escapes punishment through his cleverness. Reynard is essentially undefeatable, as demonstrated in branch XVII, which tells of his death and funeral services; while the ceremony is proceeding, Reynard jumps out of his coffin and thereby escapes even death. Reynard's animal associates include King Noble the Lion, who is king of the beasts; Isengrim the greedy wolf, Reynard's chief rival; Chantecler the rooster; Tiecelin the crow; Tibert the cat; and Brun the bear. The plots of the various tales are simple but enduring, as these two examples illustrate: Reynard flatters Chantecler on his fine voice until the vain rooster concentrates so much on demonstrating his skill that he forgets to be on guard against the fox, who seizes him by the neck. Another time Reynard and Isengrim chance upon a flock of sheep grazing on a hill. Anticipating the taste of lamb, Reynard devises a plan: Isengrim will put on shepherd's clothes—the smell of which will fool the guard dogs—and capture the newborn lambs when they answer to his calls. But Reynard knows that when Isengrim calls, the sheep will panic at the wolf's howls and the dogs will give chase, allowing Reynard in the confusion to snatch his pick of the sheep for dinner. Many of the other fables lampoon the courts as various animals testify against Reynard.

MAJOR THEMES

The tone and intention of the *Roman de Renart* varies considerably through its many branches. For the most part, however, the satire of man and the follies of feudal society are in the forefront. The hypocrisy of the nobility and of churchmen is a favorite target, but no part of society is left untouched. H. J. Blackham describes Reynard as the "comic hero of beguiling guile," and this charm of the fox while he is busy deceiving has made him a most popular and influential character for centuries, for he shows how, through cunning, one can defeat superior brute strength.

CRITICAL RECEPTION

The *Roman de Renart* met with instant success, demonstrated by many manuscript variants, translations into other vernaculars, and abundant representations in iconic art. Kenneth Varty has written of hundreds of depictions of the fox in medieval art. Much scholarly activity centers around attempts to determine the order of creation of the various branches. Critics have also debated the ultimate sources of the *Roman de Renart*: some concentrate on features apparently borrowed from traditional oral narratives, while others assert that the tales evidence a learned mentality at work. Studies have also been made of the collection's indebtedness to fables derived from Greece and Rome, as well as of its long and complicated printing history. Several critics have emphasized social concerns in *Renart*: Kathryn Gravdal, for example, writes of branches of the *Renart* that have to do with the application of the rape law. She contends that "the principal relation of the *Renart* trial scenes to medieval legal philosophy and procedure is one of subversion. The *Renart* stories undermine the feudal principle of immanent justice, which grounds centuries of legal thought, institutions, and practices." Her explication of the text shows authorial deliberateness in emphasizing the fallibility, superstition, dishonesty, and impotence of feudal law enforcement. Kenneth Varty writes on a similar subject, examining the fables for what they tell the modern reader about medieval notions on the giving and withholding of consent, and how these ideas interacted with notions of social status and of what constituted a legal marriage. Historians find the *Roman de Renart* an invaluable guide to the customs of the medieval world.

PRINCIPAL WORKS

Principal English Editions

The History of Reynard the Fox (adapted by William Caxton; edited by N. F. Blake) 1970

Renard the Fox (translated by Patricia A. Terry) 1992
The Romance of Reynard the Fox (translated by D. D. R. Owen) 1994

CRITICISM

N. F. Blake (essay date 1965)

SOURCE: "English Versions of Reynard the Fox in the Fifteenth and Sixteenth Centuries," in *Studies in Philology,* Vol. 62, 1965, pp. 63-77.

[*In the following essay, Blake surveys several editions of* Reynard the Fox, *noting a trend toward standardizing the English language.*]

All writers on the history of the English language agree that the introduction of the printing press was an important landmark in the development of the language. McKnight, for example, writes: "The printing press introduced by Caxton was one of the most important factors in fixing the English language in permanent form."[1] But although Caxton's language has been investigated,[2] few scholars have made any study of the language of the other printers of the late fifteenth and early sixteenth centuries to determine how this trend to conformity developed or how quickly the establishment of English in permanent form was achieved. Yet several books were constantly reprinted in the fifteenth and sixteenth centuries and by investigating the changes in orthography made in the printed versions of one of these minor best-sellers, it should be possible to make a contribution to the study of "the process and progress of the move towards conformity."[3] A study of this sort might help to show how the individual master-printers approached the language in which they were printing, the sort of changes they made and whether they attempted to standardize it.

One of the popular books of this period was William Caxton's **Reynard the Fox,** which he himself translated and then printed in 1481 (WC). This book was evidently so successful that Caxton reprinted it in 1489 (PL). This version is extant only in one copy now in the Pepys Library, Magdalene College, Cambridge; it lacks a couple of leaves at the end. Another reprint was issued about 1500 by Richard Pynson (RP). This version also survives only in one copy, which forms part of the Douce bequest to the Bodleian Library, Oxford. It likewise lacks several leaves at the end. A further edition, this one by Wynkyn de Worde, appeared about 1515 (WW). Only two leaves of this edition are known to exist and they are now in the University Library, Cambridge. The last edition I shall deal with was printed by Thomas Gaultier in 1550 (TG). This edition survives in several complete copies, one of which is in the Bodleian Library and another in the British Museum.[4] I shall confine my attention to the editions so far listed, for

all subsequent editions, and there were many of them,[5] contain such extensive alterations that it is hardly possible to compare the language of these later versions with that of the earlier ones satisfactorily. Nevertheless between the first and the fifth edition there is a span of eighty years which should be sufficient to show whether there was any trend to conformity. Unfortunately only a small part of WW is extant so I have not always been able to use it in tracing the development of certain written forms because WW does not contain sufficient examples.

Before any discussion of the language can be attempted, it is necessary to elucidate the relationship of the various reprints. It is normally assumed that a reprint would be reprinted from the latest printed version.[6] This is not the case with **Reynard the Fox,** for although all the texts are closely related to one another, there is not a straightforward chronological progression in their printing history. PL is naturally a reprint of WC, for WC was the only English version available when PL was printed. RP is not, however, a reprint of PL, but it also is a reprint of WC. WW is likewise not a reprint of RP, but a reprint of PL. TG, on the other hand, is a reprint of WW. Thus RP might be said to stand outside the main line of descent of **Reynard the Fox.** This fact may be readily proved because the changes which are made in PL do not appear in RP, though they are found in the two later reprints. Consider, for example, the following passages:

> WC he that shoef your crowne
> PL he that shoere your crowne
> RP he that shoef your crowne
> TG he that shore your crowne
> WC but now he sorowed that
> PL but now he trowed that
> RP but nowe he sorowd that
> TG he trowed his iourney

Examples like these could be multiplied. Unfortunately the corresponding passages from WW are not extant for comparison, for the leaves of WW which survive correspond to a part of RP which is missing. Yet it is possible to show from the surviving leaves of WW that it reproduces a mistake made in PL and that therefore it must be a reprint of PL:

> WC I wyl al otherwyse on yow yet / abyde I shal brynge
> PL I wyl al otherwyse oon you yet byte I shal brynge
> WW I wyll yet al otherwyse byte you I shal brynge
> TG I wyll yet all otherwyse by you I shall brynge

From the above examples it can be accepted that there is a straight-forward sequence of printing for four of the versions, *viz.* WC—PL—WW—TG, and that RP stands outside this sequence and is a reprint of WC.[7]

Throughout the eighty years covered by the survey there is no noticeable change in the haphazard use of *i* and *y.* PL differs considerably from WC in its use of these graphemes, but the changes made are purely random. Thus when the compositor was setting from WC a4ʳ, which includes all chapter 1 and some of chapter 2, he changed *i* to *y* eight times and *y* to *i* four times. In addition *e* is once changed to *y* and *i* once to *e*.[8] If anything *y* is used somewhat more frequently than *i* in PL, especially in such words as *wyth* etc., but both letters are used indiscriminately. There is certainly no attempt at standardization. The same state of affairs is to be found in all the later versions. Individual words are not necessarily spelt in the same way as in the copy-text, but no version shows a particular preference for one letter or the other. In the endings of the preterite of weak verbs and the plurals of nouns, however, *e* did become the standard spelling by the end of the period. In WC, PL and RP *-yd/-id/-ed* and *-ys/-is/-es* interchange freely, though spellings with *e* are not common. In WW *e* spellings are introduced a little more frequently; and in TG they become regular. The *-yd/-id* and *-ys/-is* forms do not survive in TG. Similarly in TG in the preterite of weak verbs the ending *-ed* is extended to words which in the earlier versions formed their preterites by adding *-d* or *-de: sauourd* and *prayde* appear as *sauoured* and *prayed*.[9] The spellings with *-ed* are not found with any regularity before TG. Although conformity was established in this case, WC's standardized spellings were not always respected in later editions. In WC *-y* is always used at the end of a word. There is only one exception to this in the whole text: *herbi*. In PL, however, this final *y* is often changed to *i*, so that words can be spelt ending in *i* or *y*. The latest three versions also use either spelling. The development of spelling in this period was not always towards conformity.

It is well known that a final *e* was added or omitted indiscriminately in early printed books. The five versions of **Reynard the Fox** are no exception. From WC through TG there is no discernible reason for the omission or addition of the *e* in most instances, and, as in the case of *i* and *y*, no version agrees with its copy-text as to when final *e* is found or not. On the other hand, WC rarely includes a medial *e* before the adverbial ending *-ly*. PL often adds *e* in this position, especially after dentals and stops, so that WC's *sharply, frendly* and *goostly* appear as *sharpeli, frendely* and *goostely*. RP likewise frequently adds an *e*, and WW and TG reflect the orthography of PL.

In WC *a* and *o* when followed by a nasal interchange freely. This confusion is retained in PL where even the preposition *on* and the article *an* are spelt indifferently with *a* or *o*. PL often changes the spellings found in WC: *songe (sange), domage (damage),* and *stande (stonde)*,[10] but not systematically. In RP there is a marked preference for the *o* spellings: *vnderstonde, londe, stondyng*, except in the preposition and the article where *a* is common. There are insufficient examples in WW upon which to base any conclusions, but in TG an *a* is generally found where the copy-text has an *o: stande, lande, any, husbande*. Regularity is not achieved in TG, though the *a* spellings are dominant. The preposition, however, is spelt *on*. In all texts whether they use *a* or *o*, a *u* is frequently inserted between the *a/o* and the nasal when it is followed by another con-

sonant. This change is found particularly in words of Romance origin: *penaunce, commaunde, condicious*. In PL and RP reverse spellings when the *aun/oun* is simplified to *an/on* do occur, thus PL has *danger* for WC's *daunger*. But these examples are few in comparison with those which show the change *an/on* to *aun/oun*. In TG there are examples only of a *u* being added; there are no words which drop a *u* which was found in the copy-text. The spelling *aun/oun* is not regular yet in TG in words of Romance origin, but this development is one of the few regular trends towards conformity which is found consistently in all the texts.

In WC words like *do* and *see* can be spelt with a final single or double vowel. PL does not differ much from WC, though some changes which are made in PL tend towards simplification of the final double vowel: *doo* and *see* appear as *do* and *se;* but *go* becomes *goo*. In RP, however, there is a very strong tendency to double all final single vowels: thus WC's *be, se, go, to, do, so, nothyng* appear as *bee, see, goo, too, doo, soo* and *noo thyng* respectively. The limited evidence from WW suggests that in that text whereas final *oo* was simplified, final *ee* was retained; this is the trend found also in TG. In neither WW nor TG are these spellings carried through consistently.

There is no uniformity in the use of *ou* or *ow* and *au* or *aw* in WC. In PL one can glimpse the beginnings of a tendency to use *au* and *ou* internally, as in *hauthorn* (*hawthorn*) and *coude*, and *aw* and *ow* finally, as in *yow* and *now*. Nevertheless there are many exceptions. RP still uses the spellings indiscriminately. WW develops the trend found in PL: it uses *ou* and *au* internally, except in the word *downe*, which is almost invariably spelt *doun(e)* in PL, and *ow* and *aw* finally, except in *you* where the *ou* spelling is regular. TG follows WW, though regularity is not achieved. But whereas in PL there are times when an internal *ou* or *au* in WC is changed to *ow* or *aw* respectively, there are no occurrences of this reverse spelling in TG so that one may perhaps suggest that a preference had evolved. The spellings *ei, ey, ai, ay* vary freely among themselves in all texts, except that in TG a slight preference for *ay* may be noted. The variation between *er* and *ar* in such words as *merchant* and *Reynard* is decided finally in favour of *ar*. In WC and PL either spelling is used; in RP *ar* is found more commonly in common nouns: *marchauntes*, but *er* is used regularly in the names of the animals: *Grimberd, Reynerd*; and in WW and TG *ar* is the regular form in all words which had previously exhibited variation. One of the most remarkable features of this study of the five versions of **Reynard the Fox** is how the grapheme *ea* appears suddenly and becomes accepted as the standard spelling in some words in such a short time. It is rarely found in the three earliest versions which use *e* or *ee* instead: *grete, heed* etc. In WW *ea* makes its first regular appearance in the word *great*, though it is also found sporadically in other words in WW. Otherwise WW prefers to represent this long vowel sound by an internal *a* and a final *e:* it changes PL's *breed, leep* and *feet* to *brede, lepe* and *fete*. In TG the spelling *ea* has become almost regular in such words as *teache, head, heade* ("heed"), *great* and *beast*.

As for the spelling of consonants and consonant groups a tendency to conformity can be noticed in the spelling of such words as *enough* and *through*. In WC *enough*, for example, is spelt as *inowh* and *inough*. The beginnings of the spread of spellings in *-ough* is found in PL, where, although many *-wh* spellings are retained and isolated examples are changed to *-uh: ineuh (inewh)*, there are frequent occasions when the *-wh* is altered to *-ugh: thaugh, inough* etc. It is noteworthy that there are no examples of the reverse spelling *-ugh* to *-wh* in PL. RP, however, shows no particular advance over WC. But in the short passage from WW extant there are several examples where PL's *-wh* has been changed to *-ugh,* and in TG *-ugh* has become regular. A similar trend to standardization is apparent in the use of the graphemes *-tch* and *-dg-*. These spellings are already found in WC, but they are not as common as *ch* and *g(g): cache, juge* etc. Already in PL many of the *ch* and *g(g)* forms give way to *-tch* and *-dg-* respectively: *fetche (feche), pledge (plegge)* etc., though reverse spellings also occur so that one cannot assume that *-tch* and *-dg-* were yet the dominant forms. RP tampers little with WC's spellings of these consonant groups, but in WW and TG *-tch* and *-dg-* become the most frequent forms, although they have not yet become the only ones.

It is not possible to trace such a consistent trend to standardization in the other consonant spellings. For example, both *k* and *ck* are used in WC. But many of the examples which have *k* in WC appear with *ck* in PL: *spack (spak), dranck (drank)* and *stomack (stomak)*, whereas in RP many of WC's *ck* spellings are simplified to *k: spak (spack)* and *cok (cock)*. In WW there is no sign of consistency: sometimes a *ck* is changed to *k* and sometimes a *k* to a *ck: spake (spack)* and *ducke (doke)*. This variety is also characteristic of TG so that at the end of the period there is as much freedom in the use of *ck* and *k* as there had been at the beginning. Standardization did, however, begin to make itself felt in the question of whether a consonant should be doubled or not, either internally or finally. PL differs considerably from WC in its use of single and double consonants, but it does not reveal a decisive preference one way or the other. Sometimes a double consonant is simplified: *vylonye (vyllonye)* and *april (appryl)*; and sometimes a single consonant is doubled: *ballock (balock)* and *fell (fel)*. When a word ends in a double consonant followed by an *e* in WC, there is a tendency to reduce this group to the single consonant in PL: *at (atte), al (alle)* and *had (hadde)*; though there are exceptions: *ranne (ran)*. RP, on the other hand, exhibits the opposite tendency. Although internally consonants are not regularly doubled, a single final consonant is, particularly if the word is a monosyllable ending in *f, off, yff, wyff, selff, att, shall* etc. In certain words the final consonant is doubled and an *e* is added: *hadde (had), ferre (fer)* and *uppe (up)*. WW has a different spelling system. In this text final *l* is usually doubled: *shall, lytell, all, tyll* and *well*. Other single final consonants are either retained or else they are doubled and an *e* is added, so that

both *bad* and *badde* are found. Internally a few double consonants are simplified, but there is otherwise little change. TG follows the pattern of WW: its only consistent trend is to double final *l*, though there are examples where this has not been carried out. Otherwise single and double consonants occur side by side.

In WC the personal names often retain a Dutch form, many of them ending in *-aert*, e.g. *Reynaert*. In PL these Dutch forms are eliminated by the omission of the *a* or the *e* of *-aert*. Similarly the names which had been spelt with a final *-ard/-erd* in WC are changed to *-art/-ert* in PL: *Grimbart (Grimbard)*. This preference for a final *t* is not found in the later versions which generally change it to a *d*. In RP this change of *t* and *d* when final is particularly marked and it may have influenced the forms of such words as WC's *market* which appears in RP as *marked*. The change of final *t* to *d* in the beast names is also found in WW and TG, in which such spellings as *Raynard* had become the standard ones. In WC and PL initial *w* and *wh* are interchangeable: *what/wat, where/were*. This confusion does not appear in RP or TG which both use initial *w* and *wh* in conformity with modern orthographic practice. The position in WW cannot be reliably checked, but it appears to approximate to the earlier confusion rather than the later regularity.

A few final minor points may also be recorded. WC and PL use *c* and *s(s)* interchangeably for the voiceless dental spirant *s* in the neighbourhood of front vowels, though the latter spelling is commoner. In RP there is an increase of the *c* spellings: *counceillys (counseyllys), Iustice (Iustyse)* and *seruyce (seruyse)*. This preference also occurs in WW and TG, although in neither text does the *c* spelling predominate. Final *-re* in WC is changed occasionally to *-er* in PL: *Flaunders, togyder* and *lengher*. The trend to *-er* spellings does not manifest itself at all in RP, but it reappears again in WW and TG. A conflict in the expression of the initial palatal *g* is evident between some of the versions. In WC and PL it is represented by a *y* or a *g;* in RP many of the forms with *g* in WC are changed to *y: yates (gates), foryeue (forgyue)* and *foryeuenes (forgyuenes)*; and in TG the *y* of its copy-text is changed to *g: gate (yate)* and *giue (yeue)*. Finally mention should be made of the variation between *d* and *th*. Internally in words the variation appears first in RP which changes WC's *fader* and *vnther* to *father* and *vnder*. In TG this change is common: *murtherer (murderar), thyther (thyder)* and *wether (weder)*. The variation between *d* and *th* occurs also in a final position. This variation appears not to have been remarked upon before, for it would often be impossible to detect were it not that each version can be checked against its copy-text. *Had* often makes as good sense as *hath* in individual contexts. The confusion occurs sporadically in all texts, but it is most frequent in RP where such examples as *hath byldeth* for WC's *hath bylded* occur. But even in PL we find that WC's *complayneth, sklaundryth* and *thanked* appear as *complayned, sklaundryed* and *thanketh* respectively.

In PL and RP there is little change from WC in the relative frequency of such pairs as *here/there, hem/them, fro/ from* and *tho/then(ne)*. Changes are made occasionally, but they appear to be fortuitous. It is first in WW that one can notice a marked change in the spellings of these words. Although the extant passage of WW is little more than a thousand words long, *hem* is changed twice to *them,* and *tho* to *than* seven times. *Fro* is altered to *from* twice and remains only once. These changes do not eliminate all the *hem, tho* and *fro* forms, but they do indicate a marked preference for the more modern forms. In the passage in TG which corresponds to the extant part of WW all the older forms which had survived in WW are changed. *There, them, from* and *than* were standard in TG.

It has naturally not been possible to record all the variations in orthography in the individual versions: only the more significant forms have been dealt with. In each individual spelling treated one of three possible developments may be noted. (i) There is no appreciable difference in spelling habits: the letters *i* and *y* are used interchangeably throughout the period. (ii) There are definite and marked changes in orthography, but these do not show any consistent pattern: PL favours the spelling *ck,* RP favours *k* and the two later versions use either. Individual compositors had their own spelling habits, which were not always uniform among all compositors. (iii) There is a definite trend to consistency. Although in WC *-wh* and *-ugh* are found finally in such words as *though* and *enough,* by the time of TG only *-ugh* is found and most versions show a gradual spread of *-ugh* forms over *-wh* ones. Naturally all trends do not emerge at the same time. The preference for the spellings *aun/oun* in Romance words can be traced back to PL, whereas that for *ea* as against *e/ee* in such words as *great* is not manifest until WW. Consequently it will be appreciated that such general statements as that by McKnight with which I opened this paper demand so much qualification as to be virtually valueless. The printing press *can* be an important agency for the spread of uniformity, but it does not follow that it *was* at the end of the fifteenth and the beginning of the sixteenth century. Uniformity did not materialize overnight and the history of each separate grapheme has to be investigated, for consistency was achieved in some fields long before any trend to consistency can be noted in others. Before we can even begin to appreciate how uniformity developed, full studies of individual graphemes are essential. How else will we be able to tell why the grapheme *ea* makes such a forceful appearance in **Reynard the Fox** at the beginning of the sixteenth century and quickly becomes the standard spelling in some words. Ultimately the printing press will help the spread of conformity, but only when the printers themselves achieved a standardized orthography. This was not accomplished quickly and it may even be suggested that the initial result of the introduction of the printing press was to provoke variety in spelling rather than to promote uniformity. There were after all many printers and an enormous number of books was issued, the majority of which may have differed in orthography among themselves as much as the five texts examined here do. Even if there were

trends to conformity which we can spot today, they might not have been apparent to contemporary readers, because in 1500 people were still buying and reading books printed years earlier. Furthermore although the scribes in the fifteenth century were generally fairly educated and probably went through some training,[11] the compositor was perhaps little more than a workman and even the master-printers were not necessarily very educated. For them a standard orthography may not have appeared so important as it did to the scribes.

The changes in the versions of **Reynard the Fox** are not confined to orthography. There are also many variations in vocabulary and syntax. As these offer some interesting sidelights on the attitude of the printer to his copy-text and to the language, a short account of these other changes will be given. In WC Caxton had introduced a great many Dutch words from his original some of which are replaced by English words in PL: thus *dasse* becomes *brocke* or occasionally *gray, hammes* becomes *buttockes,* and *rore* becomes *styre.* Even English words are occasionally altered in PL: *cryde* is replaced by *sayde, lerynge* by *lernynge,* and *that leep becam yl to the preest* by *that leep becam euyl to the preest.*[12] PL frequently changes phrases with a *many a* plus a substantive by omitting the *a* and putting the substantive in the plural: *many shrewd strokes* (*many a shrewd stroke*), and *many yeopardys* (*many a iepardy*). In RP, however, changes in vocabulary are kept to a minimum. It differs from the other versions in making virtually no changes in WC's many Dutch loanwords: *dasse* remains unaltered. RP does contain a type of addition not found in the other texts: a word is added to form a doublet for a word already in the text. Thus *shame* (WC) becomes *shame and rebuke,* and *synnes* (WC) becomes *synnes and trespaces.* The changes made in the vocabulary of WW are extensive. Here is a selection: (a) Dutch loanwords replaced: *voyded* (*romed*), *scrapynge* (*skrabbyng*); (b) older English words replaced: *thought* (*wende*), *vauntage* (*fordele*); (c) older phrases replaced by more up-to-date idiomatic expressions: *on fote* (*to fote*), *she bad hym take hede* (*she said se wel to*), *it flewe in the wolues eyen* (*it flewe the wulfis eyen ful*).[13] In TG changes in vocabulary are also common, but since most of WW is missing it is not always possible to tell whether the changes were introduced in TG or in WW. TG's changes are similar to those in WW, except that in TG a latinizing tendency appears for the first time: *set* is replaced by *appointed, full* by *sacyate,* and *see* twice by *perceiue.* Such words as *auyse* and *auenture* are given a Latinate spelling: *aduise* and *aduenture.*

Changes in word order are found in all the texts. PL contains many instances of such changes, some of which were certainly caused by the compositor's carelessness for the sense of the resulting passage is clumsier than that of the original. Thus WC's *beware that reynart goo not away* becomes *beware that reynart not goo away.* On other occasions it would not always be obvious that a change had been made, were it not that we can compare PL with WC: thus WC's *I muste kepe it in secrete* appears as *I muste it kepe in secrete* in PL. This type of change is found in all versions, but they are especially common in RP. It is not always clear whether individual changes were made to modernize the language or whether they were dictated by some typographical reason. Some changes appear to be attempts at correction by the compositor. Not infrequently in RP, and occasionally in the other texts, the phrase *Noble the king* is changed to *the noble king*. It may be assumed that to a compositor with only a page of text in front of him the phrase *Noble the king* appeared to be a mistake, for he did not realise that Noble was the king's name. This is presumably why it is changed sporadically in all texts. There are a few changes in WW all of which modernize the language. For example the group *to . . . ward* is replaced by *toward.* In TG changes do occur, but they are not frequent.

All the changes that are made between a text and its copy can be classified in three groups which I shall call (1) editorial, (2) compositorial and (3) typographical. By a typographical change I mean a mistake which occurs because one piece of type has been incorrectly inserted into the composing stick in place of another. This mistake can arise through the compositor actually picking up the wrong piece of type and inserting it or through the compositor misreading a certain letter because its shape resembles that of another. I have not discussed this group of changes in the paper, because they have no relevance to the history of the language: they are mechanical errors. In these texts pairs of letters interchange: *f* and *s* (*fighte* WC: *sight* PL), *th* and *w* (*that* WC: *wat* PL), and *th* and *t* (*Thise, tho* WC: *Tise, to* PL). It is only necessary to recognize that this group occurs in early printed books and that all changes in it are mistakes which ought to be corrected in modern editions. This has not always been done.[14] Similarly by tabulating these confusions it is possible for an editor of a first edition of a Caxton translation, who is naturally unable to make a comparison with an English copy-text, to recognize what are typographical mistakes in the text.[15] A compositorial change (group 2), on the other hand, is a change made in the spelling or word order of the text by which one variant spelling or syntactical usage is replaced by another. These changes are not mistakes and should therefore never be emended in a modern edition. Until a standard spelling emerges it is just as "correct" to spell *with* as *with* or *wyth.* The changes may be considered compositorial, for they are haphazard in their occurrence: sometimes the copy's *with* will appear as *wyth,* and sometimes the copy's *wyth* will be changed to *with.* It is hardly credible to think that Caxton or any other master-printer went through a text changing some spellings one way and other spellings the opposite way.[16] Most changes between one fifteenth-century text and the next probably fall into this group. Even changes in word order were no doubt generally made by the compositor, probably to justify his line. It has already been noted that RP contains a considerable number of these changes. RP differs from the other texts in that it was set up in two columns per page and therefore the problem of justifying the line was more acute. This is probably why the compositor had to tamper with the word

order more frequently. Changes in group (1) I have entitled "editorial"because they are made consistently throughout a text. They reveal an attempt to eliminate a certain spelling, word or syntactical usage from a text. The changes are therefore different from those in group (2). It is not always easy to decide whether editorial changes were made by an editor such as Caxton or by the compositor or even in individual cases by both of them. It may be that in the earlier texts the editorial changes, which are few, were made by the editors and that in the later texts both compositor and printer had a hand in them. It is perhaps more important to recognize that the only changes that a master-printer would have made are those in group (1), and consequently it is from an examination of them that we may gain some idea of his attitude to the text. PL shows that Caxton, for example, made very few changes in his second edition: only a few Dutch loanwords are altered. There is no attempt to improve the style or language of **Reynard the Fox** and those scholars who think of Caxton as a man of letters would have to explain why he failed to improve his work.[17] The explanation may well be that Caxton was more of a businessman than a scholar and that he was more interested in producing a great number of printed works than in their merit as works of art. Certainly everything he translated seems to have been completed at great speed.[18] The changes made by Pynson in group (1) are likewise minimal. On the other hand, the changes from this group in WW are extensive. This is surprising for the attitude of modern scholars to de Worde is that he was an unimaginative printer who had not the same scholarly ability and interest as his former master Caxton.[19] Yet the changes indicate that there was an attempt to modernize the language in WW. It must be admitted that it cannot be proved that de Worde was responsible for the changes, for his compositor might have made most of them. It is, however, a matter that deserves further investigation, for it may be that we have been unjust in our estimation of de Worde in the past.

Some scholars, especially those working in the Renaissance field, may think that I have laboured the difference between the various groups of changes in early printed books which has revealed how large a part a compositor played in the final make-up of the language of a text. I have done so because scholars who have worked on Caxton and other fifteenth-century printers have often been specialists in the medieval field who appear not to have appreciated many of the difficulties connected with early printed texts. Wiencke made a thorough study of Caxton's language based on a survey of four of his printed books.[20] Yet nowhere in his study does he even mention the problem of how accurately the printed books represent the copy-texts that were being set up. Nevertheless general conclusions are drawn about the language of London in Caxton's own day. Individual forms interpreted as having philological significance might have arisen as typographical changes;[21] and a book which shows marked variations in its forms might have been set up by two compositors.[22] Similarly it has been pointed out that in all the versions of **Reynard the Fox** investigated there are many examples of changes in the word order. Though some of these changes might have been made to modernize the word order, many of them were made by the compositor either to justify the lines or through sheer carelessness. In Šimko's recent investigation of word order in Caxton's printed version of Malory's *Le Morte Darthur* it is assumed that the printed text represents Caxton's own word order accurately.[23] If this investigation into **Reynard the Fox** is any guide, this assumption is at the best only very doubtful. The number of examples that Šimko produces for some of his changes in the word order is so small that one is tempted to think that they might be compositorial rather than editorial changes. In any investigation of this sort the nature of the compositorial changes in the text must be examined before an evaluation of the editorial changes can be attempted.

The study of the development of a standard orthography and of the attitude of the early master-printers to language is fraught with difficulties which have not always been taken into consideration. An enormous amount of work remains to be done in this field, but I hope that this brief survey of a minute part of the material available has shown what directions future investigations into the relationship of early printing to the English language could take and what difficulties will have to be overcome.

Notes

1. G. H. McKnight, *Modern English in the Making* (New York, 1928), p. 68.

2. H. Wiencke, *Die Sprache Caxtons,* Kölner Anglistiche Arbeiten No. 11 (Leipzig, 1930).

3. The phrase is that of Professor N. Davis in his "Scribal Variation in Late Fifteenth-Century English-,"*Mélanges de linguistique et de philologie: Fernand Mossé in memoriam* (Paris, 1959), p. 95. Professor Davis stresses the need for investigations of this process.

4. *A Short-Title Catalogue 1425-1640* (London, 1946), No. 20919-20925a and E. G. Duff, *Fifteenth-Century English Books* (London, 1917), pp. 99-100.

5. C. C. Mish, *"Reynard the Fox* in the Seventeenth Century,"*The Huntington Library Quarterly,* XVII (1953-1954), 327-344.

6. See R. B. McKerrow's postscript to C. Bühler's article on *The Dictes or Sayengis of the Philosophres* in *The Library,* 4th series, XV (1934), 326-9.

7. It is difficult to think of any satisfactory reason why RP is an isolated text, but it might be a fruitful matter for further investigation.

8. The examples are as follows, the forms being given from WC: (i) *i* is changed to *y:* with, beestis (3), assemblid, his (2), first; (ii) *y* is changed to *i:* leuys, thys, thyder, wylle; (iii) *i* is changed to *e:* flowris; (iv) *e* is changed to *y:* wete.

9. But this change does not refer to *saide/sayde.*

10. When examples are given with a similar form immediately following in parentheses, it is to be under-

stood that the first form is from the text under discussion (in this case PL) and the form in parentheses is from its copy-text (in this case WC).

11. See particularly C. F. Bühler, *The Fifteenth-Century Book: the Scribes, the Printers, the Decorators* (Philadelphia, 1960).

12. Some apparent changes in vocabulary, such as *truantyse (truantrye),* may be purely typographic, for *truantyse* is not recorded in *OED.*

13. As so little of WW survives it is not possible to tell whether these changes were carried out consistently.

14. Despite the typographical variation between initial *t* and *th,* E. Arber, *The History of Reynard the Fox* (London, 1878) does not emend *thybert* (p. 31), *thibert* (p. 32), *thoucheth* (p. 68) and *thybert* (p. 116), although forms with *t* are otherwise regular and in the Dutch text *Tibert* is never spelt with a *th-.*

15. In the discussion on orthography above I did mention that final *d* and final *th* interchange in all texts. But it seems probable that this variation is a typographical change, because such spellings as *byldeth* (for *bylded*) do not occur in manuscripts of this period. Mrs. Offord, who is at present editing Caxton's *The Knight of the Tower,* has kindly pointed out to me several examples of this mistake in that work: e.g. "And yf god gyue yow youre husbondes / soo that soone after ye be wydowes / *wedded* yow not ageyne for playsaunce ne for loue /"(ch. 113). (I am greatly indebted to Mrs. Offord for this quotation and for other help with this article.) G. Legman, "A Word on Caxton's *Dictes,"The Library,* 5th series, III (1948), 172, suggests that *departeth* in the first edition has been corrected to *departed* in the second edition of the *Dictes* and that this helps to prove that the editions were issued in this order. But this evidence is inconclusive in itself, because the interchange of final *d* and final *th* is a frequent typographical change. It is conceivable that a first edition had *departed* which was incorrectly set up as *departeth* in the next one, just as RP has *byldeth* incorrectly for WC's *bylded.*

16. It is, of course, theoretically possible that the master-printer had the text embodying his changes copied out by a scribe before it was passed on to the compositor and that changes in orthography could have been introduced by the scribe. But this is somewhat improbable.

17. H. R. Plomer, *William Caxton (1424-1491)* (London, 1925), *passim.*

18. Most editors of Caxton editions comment upon the hastiness of his translation, see for example M. N. Colvin, *Godeffroy of Boloyne,* EETS extra series 64 (London, 1893), p. viii.

19. "He was in no sense a scholar, and knew little about the literary value of books . . . no reason to believe he had any literary talent. . . . He had no high ideals, and his printing was solely a commercial under-

taking for profit."H. R. Plomer, *Wynkyn de Worde and his Contemporaries* (London, 1925), p. 44 *et passim.*

20. H. Wiencke, *Die Sprache Caxtons* (Leipzig, 1930). The four texts were *The Histories of Troy, Jason, æsop's Fables* and *Eneydos.*

21. Wiencke, *op. cit.,* p. 74, suggests that the only occurrence of *hondreth* in *Eneydos* for otherwise regular *honderd/hundred* exhibits Scandinavian influence. Although this is possible, it could be that this is another example of the confusion by a compositor of final *d* and final *th.*

22. Wiencke points out that the orthography in the first 160 pages of *The Histories of Troy* differs from that in the rest of the text. For example in the first 160 pages the proportion of *from* to *fro* forms is 94: 41. In the text as a whole, however, the number of *from* forms amounts to only 29

    of all occurrences of both *from* and *fro* forms, because *from* occurs so rarely in the latter part (p. 67).

23. J. Šimko, *Word-Order in the Winchester Manuscript and William Caxton's edition of Thomas Malory's Morte Darthur (1485)—A Comparison* (Halle, 1957).

Kenneth Varty (essay date 1967)

SOURCE: "The Fabulists' Fox," in *Reynard the Fox: A Study of the Fox in Medieval English Art,* Leicester University Press, 1967, pp. 95-101.

[In the following excerpt, Varty describes the spread of fox fables and summarizes some of the tales most often depicted in art.]

In the preceding chapter we have seen how the Bestiary fox was drawn into the **Roman de Renard** and how Reynard came to be identified with him. Pierre de Saint Cloud, his continuators and imitators similarly drew on the fabulists' fox for inspiration and, as Reynard's reputation grew, he moved into many of their fables, both in France and England.

Most fables told in the Middle Ages go back to Phaedrus, a slave born in Macedonia who spent the greater part of his life at Rome and became a freedman of the Emperor Augustus. Another important source of the medieval fable is the Roman Avianus who wrote about A.D. 400. Paraphrases of the fables of Phaedrus and Avianus began to be made from the fifth century onwards, and it was chiefly through the medium of these paraphrases that later centuries obtained their knowledge of fables. A collection of French versions appeared as early as the tenth century and many others followed throughout the Middle Ages. Medieval English collections were largely based on the French which were called *Isopets* (from the name of Aesop, thought to be the inventor of this literary form).[1]

After the creation of the **Roman de Renard** we find the proper names of some of the protagonists of the animal epic appearing in the fables, but the process was a slow one.[2] For example, in the thirteenth-century collection of fables called the *Isopet de Chartres* there is a fable about the fox and the eagle in which the fox is always described by his generic name, *goupil.*[3] This same fable reoccurs in the fourteenth-century *Isopet II,* (derived from exactly the same Latin source as the *Isopet de Chartres,* that is, from the *Novus Aesopus* by Alexander Neckam) and in it the fox is described by his generic name, *goupil,* both in the title and the first two textual references. In the third textual reference, however, we find *Renart li goupil,* Reynard the Fox.[4] The *Isopet II* also contains the well-known fable of the fox and the crow in which all three textual references to the fox are to *Renart.*[5]

If we turn to two other Isopets, the thirteenth-century *Isopet de Lyon* and the fourteenth-century *Isopet I,* both derived from a different, but common source (namely, the verse *Romulus* attributed to Walter the Englishman), we find an altogether more marked influence of the **Roman de Renard** and a similar increase of this influence on the later collection. In the earlier collection, the *Isopet de Lyon,* there are four fables about the fox: the fox and the eagle,[6] the fox and the crow,[7] the fox and the stork[8] and the fox and the monkey.[9] In every case the name *vulpil* (= *goupil*) is used in the title, but in every case *Renart* is used in the text. In the later *Isopet I* there are six fables about the fox and in all six, both in the title and the text, he is called *Renart.*[10] What is more, we also meet here a wolf called Ysangrin,[11] a dog called Rouneaus (= Roonel),[12] a crow called Tiecelin[13] and a stag called Brichemer,[14] all proper names made famous by the **Roman de Renard.**

The presence of Reynard, Isengrin and Tibert, etc., in the works of some English fabulists writing in the thirteenth and fourteenth centuries suggests that the animal epic was also known in England and that the reynardization of fables was also taking place here.[15] The English fabulists to whom I refer did not, however, write in English. One, Odo of Cheriton,[16] wrote in Latin and the other, Nicole Bozon,[17] wrote in Anglo-Norman. Latin and French were, of course, the languages of a large section of the intellectual and aristocratic elite of the earlier Middle Ages in England. It is perhaps significant that the first of these fabulists, Odo of Cheriton, had strong links with France, and G. R. Owst, in his *Literature and Pulpit in Mediaeval England,*[18] argues that 'the animal fable proper, so far as England is concerned, seems to have been an importation from France along with the other Norman influences upon our language and literature, following the Conquest. . . . Whether or not the appetite for such fables was strong and indigenous, at all events the comparative rarity of this animal fiction in English sermons suggests that it remained, with few exceptions, as it had begun, the particular entertainment of the Anglo-Norman aristocracy. Nevertheless, England produced at least one leading fabulist of the Middle Ages in the person of Odo of Cheriton, and two

Page from a 13th century manuscript of Roman de Renart.

subsequent preachers who made rich use of this same material (Bozon and Bromyard). Like many of his English fellow-clergy of the early thirteenth century, Odo the Cistercian, it seems, had certainly studied in Paris; and there he had collected, no doubt, the Aesopic and romantic fables which later graced his own sermons and collections of *exempla*. Many of these fables, simple enough in their construction, present us with the natural humour and vivid imagination of those who watch the animal and insect world with the eyes of lively, mischievous children. These animals themselves are regarded as little people, precisely as they appear in frequent representations upon the margins of illuminated manuscripts,[19] engrossed in earnest conversation, fighting in miniature tourneys, playing on musical instruments, indulging in the various pastimes and mischiefs of men and women of the day. . . . Like impish children, or merry rustics, the beasts play tricks upon each other, wild practical jokes that not infrequently lead to disaster. Thus the fox pretends to be dead in order that he may catch the unwitting raven, or is admitted into the hen-roost on the plea of sickness, whereupon he straightway devours the hens. . . . Teburg the cat (obviously Tibert of

the *Roman de Renard*) from his point of vantage in the tree mocks Reynard, who, for all his bag of tricks and his boasting, cannot escape so easily from his pursuers. . . .'[20]

Odo of Cheriton was born between 1180 and 1190, only a decade or so after the beginning of the *Roman de Renard*. He belonged to the aristocracy and lived in Folkestone. He studied at Paris and travelled through France and Spain. He inherited a very sizeable domain in 1232-33 and died in 1246-47. He published sermons, theological works and fables. These fables seem to have been composed after 1225, and they must have been immensely popular to judge by the many medieval manuscripts which survive from all over Europe. They were used again and again by priests in their sermons as *exempla*. Although they are in Latin there can be no doubt that they were retold in English because, from time to time, English expressions or proverbs interrupt the Latin text. In three of his fables[21] he writes of a fox called Reinardus or Renaldus who encounters a cock called Chantecler, a cat called Tebergus and a wolf called Ysingrinus. These proper names, especially that of the cock, point to a knowledge of Pierre de Saint Cloud's poem. In fact, eight of Odo's fables which feature animals with proper names similar to, or identical with those used in the *Roman de Renard* also correspond to branches in the *Roman de Renard*.

Nicole Bozon, a Franciscan, lived in the first half of the fourteenth century, probably near Nottingham. Owst says that he 'is the English preacher on whom the mantle of Odo of Cheriton seems to have fallen in the early years of the fourteenth century.'[22] He wrote in Anglo-Norman and retells, much modified, many of the fables formerly told by Odo. For example, whereas Odo told how Renaldus enticed Ysingrinus into a larder with a narrow opening, Nicole tells how, in similar circumstances, a cat seduced a fox with talk of meat, cheese and milk.[23]

If Odo of Cheriton and Nicole Bozon used some of the proper names made familiar by the *Roman de Renard* we may surely presume that not only they but their readers and audiences were acquainted with the French epic and its derivations, and that they liked to identify the fox of these fables with Reynard. Many of the fox fables were, however, drawn into the mainstream of the *Roman de Renard* right from the beginning and in this way lived a double life. One of the best examples of this is the fable of the fox and the crow.

THE FOX AND THE CROW

The story of Reynard's encounter with Tiecelin the Crow forms the fourth episode of Pierre de Saint Cloud's poem. After his brushes with the cock, titmouse and cat, Reynard next skirmishes with the crow. Nearly two hundred lines of octosyllabic verse are needed to relate the episode. First, the poet tells how Tiecelin acquired the cheese. He saw it put out to dry in the sun by a dairymaid whom he taunted as he stole it. Then he flew off to a tree below which, unknown to him, Reynard was resting from his last adventure. As Tiecelin began to eat his cheese a piece fell down right in front of Reynard's nose. The fox looked up, saw the crow and the cheese and immediately began a campaign to win both. He got the cheese by flattering Tiecelin about the quality of his voice. He nearly got the crow by pretending to be so badly injured as to be unable to move and the gullible bird was lucky to escape with the loss of only four feathers.

This fable obviously goes back to the well-known account attributed to Aesop,[24] though Pierre de Saint Cloud's immediate source seems to have been the fable by Marie de France.[25] It must have been very popular in its epic form, at least in France, for it was soon thoroughly reynardized. In the *Isopet de Chartres* this fable shows no obvious influence of the **Roman de Renard**,[26] but in the *Isopet II* the fox is Renart, though the crow is referred to only by the generic term, *corbel*.[27] In the *Isopet de Lyon* the fox is even Don Reynard (*Dam Renar*) but the crow remains the impersonal *corbel*.[28] In the *Isopet I* both animals have their proper names; the crow is even Sire Tiercelin.[29]

Curiously enough, in spite of the great popularity of the fable, carvings and drawings of it are relatively rare. Perhaps its most famous representation is the one in the Bayeux Tapestry, predating the **Roman de Renard**.[30] Even in the few representations which postdate the **Roman de Renard** there is no conclusive evidence of the epic's influence. This is not really surprising. One has only to look at a French manuscript-painting which does illustrate this episode in the epic to see that there is nothing specially distinctive about it <158>.[31] The one carving which does seem to illustrate the epic is in fact a nineteenth-century product.[32] This is on a misericord in Chester Cathedral where we see two foxes below a tree in which is perched a crow holding a piece of cheese in its beak <159>. If this were medieval, I would have said that it was one more of those carvings which depict two consecutive events in one. I would have said that the fox resting below the tree is Reynard in the earlier stage of Pierre de Saint Cloud's poem, and that the fox sitting up and looking at the crow is Reynard a few moments after Tiecelin has roused him by accidentally dropping a piece of cheese right in front of his nose. It is, of course, possible that the nineteenth-century carver used a medieval model. We know that he replaced an indecent medieval carving with this fox-scene, and that he did the same with at least two other fox-scenes <160 and 167>,[33] thereby showing a marked predelection for the fox. Perhaps he was using an early, illustrated edition of fables in which the illustration of the fox and the crow fable was influenced by Pierre de Saint Cloud's poem.

THE FOX AND THE GRAPES

The Aesopian fable of the fox and the grapes also finds its way into the **Roman de Renard;** to be precise, into Branch XI, composed about 1200.[34] This is one of the briefest of the Classical fables: A hungry fox tried to reach some clusters of grapes which he saw hanging from a vine trained on a tree, but they were too high. So he went off and comforted himself by saying, 'They weren't ripe, anyhow.'[35] This is expanded into some seventy lines of octosyllabic verse in the French epic, and the grapes are turned into blackberries: Reynard is out walking in the country when he suddenly comes upon a deep and wide ditch. He inspects the powerful network of brambles which bar his way. Bunches of blackberries hide the leaves, so numerous are they. 'Goodness me,'says Reynard, 'anybody who likes blackberries should build his house here.'Then he tries to reach the berries, but he can find no access to them, the brambles are so dense. He growls with displeasure. His tongue hangs out with desire. Excitement spurs him on and he jumps up the prickly branches, then tries to hold on. He fails and falls to the bottom of the ditch, badly scratched. How to get out? At last, after many a sigh, scratch and bruise he scrambles out. 'Do you, Lord God, deny me these blackberries? Surely not? Even if I stay here till night falls, I shall have some of them, in spite of everything.' He gathers lots of stones and piles them up. At last he can reach the berries. He knocks about thirty of them down, but, alas! they fall into the ditch. He curses, in a low voice. At last he gives up. 'How stupid of me,' he says to himself, 'Blackberries? Why, I never eat them. I once used to like them, but I vowed I would never eat them again. I must keep my vow.' And off he went. . . .[36]

The nineteenth-century guardian of decency in Chester Cathedral has left us a delightful scene of the fox first contemplating and then struggling to reach a luscious bunch of berries <160>. Once more he employs the medieval technique of two consecutive scenes in one. Or are these the little foxes of the Bible who spoil the tender vines?[37]

This may well be the case of the nineteenth-century stone sculpture in the Chapter House of Salisbury Cathedral which shows two foxes contemplating a colossal bunch of grapes. There is good reason to believe that this modern sculpture replaces a similar one of medieval origin.[38] The only genuine medieval carving I have found of this episode (if 1533 can be called medieval) is on a misericord in the parish church at Faversham, Kent.

THE FOX AND THE STORK

The fable of the fox and the stork is depicted relatively often in medieval art. The Aesopian version tells us that a stork which had arrived from foreign parts received an invitation to dinner from a fox, who served her with clear soup on a smooth slab of marble, so that the hungry bird could not taste a drop of it. Returning the invitation, the stork produced a flagon filled with pap, into which she stuck her bill and had a good meal, while her guest was tormented with hunger. 'You set the example,'she said, 'and you must not complain at my following it.'[39] One can well understand that this fable, which vividly illustrates Christ's teaching 'whatsoever ye would that men should do to you, do ye even so to them'[40] should have been depicted in churches and religious books.

This fabulist's fox was never drawn into the **Roman de Renard,** but he did become identified with Reynard as this translation of a fourteenth-century French version proves: Reynard, who never did any good, invited his good friend the stork to dine with him. She did not refuse. She thought she would be well received, fed and feasted. She did not expect any trickery. Reynard poured a pot of honey over the table, and offered this to his guest. . . . She wondered in what way she could pay Reynard back. She invited Reynard, and prepared a pot full of the very best meat. This pot had a very long and narrow neck so that Reynard was unable to taste the meat. But the stork took her fill of it. . . .[41]

There is no similar proof of this fable's reynardization in English literature, nor, for that matter is there much to say about its iconographical forms. There is, however, one example whose context is such as to suggest that the sculptor may have been thinking of Reynard. This is a very worn, twelfth-century carving in St Michael's, Melbourne, Derbyshire <161>. Only the stork, to the extreme left, is fairly clear, and the tall vessel from which it feeds. To the right of this vessel are the vague outlines of a fox standing on its hind legs. On the capital next to it, further to the right (south), it is just possible to make out a fox pursuing a bird through some stylized leaves and branches. Only the bird is reasonably easily recognized. The pointed ears and snout are all that can be distinguished of the fox. On another capital to the left (east) of the fox and stork scene is a clearly visible fox scene <162>. A long-nosed, thick-lipped, big-eyed peasant leans backward with the effort he makes as he tugs at a fleeing fox's brush. The fox has something in his open jaws, possibly the head of a bird. On a capital on the opposite side of the Chancel, facing this peasant and fox, is a lion-like creature <163>. If he wore a crown like the lion at Tilton <55> I would have guessed him to be Noble before whom Reynard will soon have to account for this attack on one of his feathered subjects. As it is, he may be the Lion of Judah, rather like the one at West Keal <59>. This is perhaps confirmed by the serpentine creature before him.[42]

An early and much-worn carving of the fox and stork fable is to be found on a doorway of St Martin's, Holt, Worcestershire <164>. The fox is shown, as always, with the tables turned on him. There is no contextual evidence here to suggest any Reynardian overtones.

Another early, much-worn carving is to be found on a coffin lid in the Priory church of Bridlington, Yorkshire <165>.[43] Here, as at Holt, the fox is trying to get his snout into the mouth of the vessel at the same time as the stork. Curiously enough, immediately below the fox and stork is a lion-like figure. (None of the creatures depicted on this stone slab is particularly realistic.) This lion (?) is carved upside down in relation to the fox and stork so that he witnesses the fox's discomfiture. This recalls the scene and situation at Melbourne, but there is no serpent here.

A beautiful, sixteenth-century representation of this fable is to be found in the choir of the parish church, Swavesey, Cambridge. Here the fox licks at the liquid as it overflows

from the long-necked vessel into which the stork dips its bill <167>. This carving is one of the poppyheads of the priest's prayer desk. The other poppyhead shows a lion-like creature. The carver may have intended to depict a griffin which should have the head, neck, wings and talons of an eagle and the hind quarters of a lion.[44] What he has produced is a winged lion. It is indeed curious how frequently, in the few extant carvings of this fox and stork fable, the lion or a lion-like creature is to be found close by.

A particularly fine, nineteenth-century misericord carving of this fable may be seen in Chester Cathedral <166>.[45]

THE FOX AND THE EAGLE

One other fox fable, not drawn into the **Roman de Renard,** is represented by carvings in St Olaf's, Poughill, Cornwall and in Gloucester Cathedral. This is the fable of the fox and the eagle. The Classical version goes like this: An eagle and a vixen became friends and decided to live near each other in the hope that closer acquaintance would cement their friendship. The eagle flew to the top of a very tall tree and laid her eggs there, while the vixen gave birth to her cubs in a thicket underneath. One day she went off in search of food. The eagle, feeling hungry, swooped into the bushes, snatched up the cubs, and made a meal of them with her brood. The vixen came back and saw what had happened. She was less distressed by the loss of her young than by the difficulty of punishing the eagle. How could she, tied down to earth as she was, pursue a bird? All she could do was to stand far off and curse her enemy, like any weak and feeble creature. But it chanced before long that the eagle was punished for violating the sanctity of friendship. Some men were sacrificing a goat in a field, and the eagle darted down on to the altar and carried off a burning piece of offal to her nest. Just then a strong wind sprang up and fanned into a blaze the bits of dry stalk of which the nest was made. The result was that the nestlings, which were not yet fully fledged, were burnt and fell to the ground. The vixen ran to the spot and gobbled up every one of them right under the eagle's eyes.[46]

This fable appears in most medieval collections, slightly modified. In the French *Isopet I* the vixen becomes Reynard (*Renart*) and he manages to rescue his cub before the eagle feeds it to his young. He does so by piling up lots of green twigs against the tree in which the eagle has nested. Then he sets fire to the twigs and smokes the eagle into submission.[47]

At Poughill, a bench end depicts the first part of this fable when the eagle makes off with the fox cub <168>. I think the carver meant to depict this incident, but departed slightly from it by portraying a creature rather more like a rabbit than a fox cub in the eagle's talons. The fox looks on, helplessly, from the left. In Gloucester Cathedral a misericord shows only the eagle pouncing on a cringing fox cub <169>.

It is a curious fact that, in all these representations of the fabulists' fox, he is never shown getting the better of his opponent, even when, in the fable, he does so at one stage or another.

Notes

1. The history of the fable is very complex. My résumé glosses over many thorny problems. A slightly expanded history of the fable may be read in the introduction to S. A. Handford's translation of the *Fables of Aesop*. For the French *Isopets, see* the editions by J. Bastin, *Recueil Général des Isopets*, 2 vol. (1929-30).

2. For a general study of this phenomenon, *see* J. Flinn, *op. cit.*, pp. 125-131.

3. J. Bastin, *op. cit.*, vol. 1, pp. 140-141.

4. *Ibid.*, pp. 75-74.

5. *Ibid.*, pp. 83-84.

6. *Ibid.*, vol. 2, p. 108.

7. *Ibid.*, pp. 110-111.

8. *Ibid.*, pp. 136-138.

9. *Ibid.*, pp. 181-182.

10. *Ibid.*, pp. 222-227, 256-257, 265-267, 280-283 and 303-304.

11. *Ibid.*, p. 280.

12. *Ibid.*, p. 297.

13. *Ibid.*, p. 258.

14. *Ibid.*, p. 253.

15. A study has been made of this subject by F. Mossé, 'Le Roman de Renart en Angleterre,'in *Les Langues Modernes*, fasc. A, mars-avril, 1951, pp. 70-84.

16. *See* L. Hervieux, *Les Fabulistes latins depuis le siècle d'Auguste . . . IV, Eudes de Cheriton et ses dérivés* (1884 and 1893-99).

17. *See* L. Toulmin-Smith and P. Meyer (eds.), *Les Contes moralisés de Nicole Bozon* (1889).

18. G. R. Owst, *Literature and Pulpit in Medieval England* (1933).

19. *See*, for example, L. M. C. Randall's 'Exampla as a source of Gothic marginal illumination,'in *The Art Bulletin*, June 1957, Vol. XXXIX, No. 2, pp. 97-107.

20. G. R. Owst, *op. cit.* (note 18) pp. 204-205.

21. These fables are quoted in French by F. Mossé, *op. cit.*, pp. 30-31.

22. *Op. cit.* (note 18), p. 206.

23. *Op. cit.* (note 17), p. 184.

24. *See* p. 12 of S. A. Handford's translation (note 1).

25. *See* L. Foulet, *op. cit.* (note 5 to the Introduction), p. 158.

26. *See* J. Bastin, *op. cit.* (note 1), vol. 1, pp. 146-148.

27. *Ibid.*, pp. 83-84.

28. *Ibid.*, vol. 2, pp. 110-111.

29. *Ibid.*, pp. 225-227.

30. See *The Bayeux Tapestry* (1965), plates 5 and 6; also E. Maclagan's *The Bayeux Tapestry* (1953), plate 80a.

31. MS Douce 360, f. 29 v., kept at the Bodleian, Oxford. 14th C.

32. A Mr G. E. Armitage, whose initials are clearly visible on the misericords he carved. *See* T. Cann Hughes, 'Misericords of Chester Cathedral,'in the *Chester Archaeological Journal*, vol. V, no. 1.

33. *See* T. Cann Hughes, *op. cit.*

34. This branch is usually called *Renart l'Empereur. See* R. Bossuat, *op. cit.* (note 5 to the Introduction), pp. 54-55.

35. *See* Handford's translation (note 1), p. 5.

36. *See* Méon's edition, vol. 3, pp. 176-179.

37. The Song of Solomon, Chapter 2, verse 15.

38. *See* above, Chapter 6, p. 71.

39. *See* Handford's translation (note 1), p. 81.

40. St Matthew, Chapter 7, verse 12.

41. Translated and abridged from J. Bastin, *op. cit.* (note 1), vol. 2, pp. 256-257.

42. *See* above, Chapter 3, p. 49.

43. This slab could be a foreign importation.

44. *See* F. Bond, *Misericords*, pp. 60-62.

45. *See* note 32.

46. *See* Handford's translation (note 1), p. 71.

47. 46 *See* J. Bastin, *op. cit.* (note 1), vol. 2, pp. 222-224.

Donald B. Sands (essay date 1974)

SOURCE: "Reynard the Fox and the Manipulation of the Popular Proverb," in *The Learned and the Lewed: Studies in Chaucer and Medieval Literature*, edited by Larry D. Benson, Harvard University Press, 1974, pp. 265-78.

[*In the following essay, Sands analyzes the proverbs found in great abundance in* Reinaerts Historie *and explains their purpose in terms of truth and irony.*]

The anonymous Middle Dutch poem *Reinaerts Historie* (usually referred to as *R II*) was written sometime around 1375.[1] Its first half (3,480 lines) amounts to a close retelling of a poem written perhaps one hundred years before called *Van den vos Reinaerde*.[2] Its second half (4,314 lines) is a continuation and conclusion of the earlier poem. *Van den vos Reinaerde* (usually referred to as *R I*) is a surprisingly unified piece of narration, but it can also be said that a sense of unity—this, however, arising chiefly from tone and style—informs *R II*. A modern reader feels he has before him in the later poem the product of one man's creative skill; and *R II*, although it is little read outside Dutch- and Flemish-speaking areas, is the seminal work of much English and German Reynard material. Via Caxton's translation of a prose version, it sired numerous English adaptations. Via its eventual translation into Low German verse, and Gottsched's translation of this into prose, it is the source of Goethe's *Reineke Fuchs*.

There are 73 proverbs in *R II*. For a medieval work of just under 8,000 lines, the number is neither large nor small. It means that there is 1 proverb, on the average, for every 100 lines. The statistic, however, does not give a true picture. *R I* contains in its 3,500-odd lines only 13 proverbs—hence, approximately, 1 proverb for every 260 lines—and the *R II* poet neither adds to nor subtracts from that number in his adaptation of it; but in the 4,300-odd lines he adds to *R I*, there are 60 proverbs—hence, about 1 proverb for every 70 lines. This, indeed, is a high number, even for a medieval work; and it leads to speculation as to whether the *R II* poet used proverbs with an intention the *R I* poet either did not need to utilize or, more probably, was really unaware of. Predominant in *R I* is a succession of narrative motifs; in *R II*, these give way to numerous, chiefly hypocritical, confessional speeches. The *R II* poet, being, in all probability, a learned cleric, could have padded out his speeches with learned "sentense,"as Chaucer padded out Pertelote's presentation of her "doctrine," and he could have drawn heavily on the *topoi* of late medieval Latinity. In fact, one is forced to conclude that the *R II* poet, however well he duplicates the idiom of the earlier poem, is a very different fellow from the man who put *R I* in final form. Not only is his narrative technique different from the *R I* poet's, his Reynard is an altogether different fox from the Reynard of *R I*, where he is primarily a prankish folk figure; the *R II* Reynard is psychologically top-heavy, an angry brooder over the discrepancies between social appearance and inner intention.[3]

Criteria for proverb selection vary, but in culling the 73 proverbs from *R II* I followed those laid down by J. Allen Pfeffer in his *The Proverb in Goethe*.[4] A proverb, he says, is "human experience and reflection distilled in the form of a lucidly phrased, variable saying"of "known or unknown origin and of limited or wide prevalence"whose "currency must be attestable."Hence, I exclude, as some paroemiologists do not, metaphorical turns of phrase, any expression of incomplete predication, and numerous non-attestable proverb-like utterances.

What gives a proverb its aura of truth is not truth itself but the sheer currency of the proverb. The fact that a multitude of unreflecting minds accept a proverb as true makes it appear true. An illustration is that almost any proverb when negated contains just about as much "truth"as does the original. "Clothes do not make the man"is just as true, given proper context, as its more usual positive expression.

But the medieval *Spielmann*—why did he often interlard his fictions so heavily with proverbial lore? The answer, it seems to me, lies in the fact that as a purveyor of fictions, he, like the *pícaro*, views the world aesthetically, not morally. He uses the proverb, over and above the stylistic heightening it lends his tale, not for its "truth,"but for the impact of credence it carries with it. If the *Spielmann*'s game is primarily deception—making his audience believe for a period what is manifestly untrue—what better device than the proverb could he use to promote an audience's belief in his fictions?

But does the Middle Dutch *Reinaerts Historie* itself differ from the usual medieval narrative—whether romance, *Märchen*, lay, or fabliau? Its date of composition places it in the later stages of the medieval period, although by no means at its very shag end. Literary histories label it a "comic beast epic,"and one can wonder how accurate the label is. If it is "comic," it is so in a "black humor"sense quite foreign to the slapstick of the fabliau and the *Fastnachtspiel*, the late medieval German Shrovetide play. If it is a "beast epic," it is also one of the few medieval narratives that produces characters, albeit in the personas of animals, that duplicate the treacherous contradictions in human makeup. And if it is indeed an "epic,"it is so, I feel, because it is, unlike many long medieval narratives, whether by design or by accident, well plotted and well constructed. Nor do I feel, as is sometimes assumed, that it is someone's satire of something socially out of phase. It pillories humanity rather than human institutions—it is only incidentally anticlerical and antiestablishment. Finally, I question the occasional allegation that it is allegory or allegorical. Its orientation is foreign to the system of concepts on which medieval writers based their allegories—the moral philosophy, the theocratically sanctioned hierarchies, the mandarin conventions of an aristocratic society. It transcends the intermediary of allegory—it is more a direct appraisal of *zoon politikon* himself.

There is, furthermore, in the latter half of *R II*, an implied social ethic. Society splits into those covetous of power and those attempting to evade its machinations. The former, once in power, suffer from the myopic stupidity power engenders. The latter are constrained by the sheer effort of evading those in power to acknowledge the virtue of mutual loyalty. They develop Socratic adroitness. They become intuitive manipulators to whom proverbial "truth"is useful as a psychological ploy. They find the chink in the armor of moral pretense to be the public's unreasonable veneration of its own version of "truth"—and it may be that the implied social ethic of *R II* prompted Goethe to refer to it as an unholy universal Bible.

But turning to the proverbs themselves: How do they operate? They can be arranged according to the degree the import of "truth"disappears from their contextual use and the impact of ironic virulence takes its place. On one level, they are to be taken "straight."The narrator, for example, reassures his audience with comfortable words in proverb form. Grimbart the badger, within context, supplies a sort of choric wisdom—voices proverbially the reactions and conclusions any honest burgher might have. Reynard himself, in confession to his friend Grimbart, voices bitter wisdom in proverb form that could only come from a member of society with the tragic perspective of an outcast. In all three instances, the proverbs establish audience-narrator rapport, even though those of the narrator are platitudinous, those of Grimbart conventional, and those of Reynard in confession to Grimbart anguished and bitter. A few examples will help highlight the "ironic proverbs" to be noted later.

The narrator of *R II* does obtrude on occasion, as most medieval narrators do. He says of Reynard, who fails to appear at court, "Wie quaet doet, die scuwet dat licht"—"Whoever does evil shuns the light"(63). He remarks, as Reynard leads the credulous Bruin to a meal of honey in Lantfreit's farmyard (and to a physical disaster), "Mer het is dicke also ghesciet / dat hem die menich verblijt om niet"—"But it often happens thus / that many look forward to something in vain" (697-698). He observes, as the various animals gather to make accusations against an all-but-forsaken Reynard, "Die crancste heeft die minste crode"—"The weakest have the least retinue"(1911). At the very end of the poem, where Reynard emerges victorious from his trial by combat with Isegrim the wolf and wins thereby the support of king and queen, he directs a proverbial observation toward the audience which embodies a truism applicable to the whole narrative: "Diet wel gaet, gheeft man eer ende lof: / mer diet misgaet, daer vliet men of"—"To those with whom things go well people give honor and praise: / but those who fail, people flee from them"(7393-94). As if to drive home the point, he repeats it a few lines later in terser form: "Diet wel gaet, die crijcht veel maghen"—"Those who succeed get many relatives"(7409).

Grimbart, as noted earlier, is a choric figure. He reacts laconically and usually in proverb form. One can imagine that the narrator lets the audience via Grimbart into context and lets it speak the wisdom an honest audience might. In defending Reynard against the deluge of accusations leveled at him during his absence from court, Grimbart says, "Dat viants mont sprect selden wel"—"An enemy's mouth speaks seldom well" (189). When Courtois the hound accuses Reynard of stealing a pudding he himself had stolen, the badger excuses the act with "Met recht so wart mens qualic quijt / dat men qualic heeft ghewonnen"—"With justice is one dishonestly freed / of that which he has unjustly acquired"(269-270). At the end of Reynard's second private confession of his sins, when the badger is less aghast at Reynard's transgressions than overwhelmed by his wisdom, he exclaims, "Die beste clerke . . . dicke die wijste liede niet ensijn: / die leken vervroedense bi wilen"—"The best scholars . . . aren't often the wisest people: / the laity outwit them on occasion"(4102-03). He says, by way of giving Reynard absolution, "Die doet is, moet bliven doot"—"What's dead ought to remain dead"(4116). As the pair make their way into a crowd of hostile courtiers, he reassures his uncle,

the fox, with three proverbs on the wisdom of being bold in the face of danger:

> Die blode endooch tot gheenre ure:
> Den coenen helpt die aventure.
> Een dach is beter dan sulc een jaer.

> The cowardly aren't worthy of any honor.
> The courageous are helped by hazard.
> One day for many is better than for others a year.
>
> (4285-87)

Reynard himself delivers four long confessions in *R II*. Two are given before the court of Noble the lion, and these presumably are comic because the narrator's audience knows, though the court is not quite sure, they are bare-faced fabrications. The two other confessions are private. They are given on the way to face various charges before a royal tribunal and are made to Grimbart, Reynard's brother's son. The first consists chiefly of Reynard's enumeration of his misdeeds against Bruin the bear, Tibert the cat, and Isegrim the wolf. There are two encapsulated *Schwänke*—Isegrim, as monk, caught and beaten when he becomes entangled in the bell-ropes of a monastery and Isegrim duped into falling into a peasant's henhouse. There is only one proverb and this an item of deceiving rhetoric. As Isegrim inches his way into the blackness along the hen-roost in the peasant's barn, Reynard urges him on with the words "Men moet wel pinen om ghewin"—"One must take pain for profit"(1642). In contrast, the second confession to Grimbart, even though it does, like the first, contain encapsulated *Schwänke*, evolves into a lengthy and angry denunciation of greed. One imagines the poet in the persona of Reynard assessing the moral composition of the audience itself, and the lines might well create a narrator-audience nexus which in its potential impact might far surpass that produced by the few proverbial asides that the narrator as narrator addresses to his audience. Reynard admits transgressions, but observes, "Wie honich handelt, vingher lect"—"Whoever touches honey licks his fingers"(4129). Deception is a fault, he concedes, but a necessary art of survival: "Dus moet men hier ende daer / nu liegen ende dan segghen waer"—"Thus must one here and there / first lie and then tell the truth"(4189-90). Telling the truth consistently is fatal: "Want die altoos die waerheit sprake, / enconde die strate nerghent bouwen"—"For those who ever spoke the truth / couldn't travel anywhere"(4252-53). At the point when fox and badger draw near the court, Reynard, prepared to lie his way out of the charge of murdering Cuwart the hare, speaks three proverbs in a row:

> Man moet wel lieghen alst doet noot,
> Ende daer na beteren bi rade.
> Tot allen misdoen staet ghenade:
> Ten is niemen, hi endwaelt bi tiden.

> One has to lie as necessity dictates
> and afterward make amends according to experience.
> For all transgressions there's pardon.
> There's no one who doesn't at times transgress.
>
> (4260-63)

When the confession ends, there is little for the loyal Grimbart to say except concede the wisdom of his uncle's words and admit, "Ghi sout selve sijn die paep"—"You ought yourself to be the priest"(4269).

Elsewhere the narrator may also express his views, but more indirectly and precariously—namely, in those speeches given Martin the ape, speeches punctuated by proverbial summations of things as they are. Here the proverbs are probably to be taken "straight,"just as "straight" as those the narrator addresses to his audience directly or as those spoken by Grimbart or as those spoken by Reynard privately during the second confession. But Martin's proverbs possess an insulting quality. They express unpopular "truths," ones that might be expected from a *déclassé* opportunist like Martin himself, but ones that also unmask the righteous and godly pretentions which camouflage human motivation. An audience, on hearing these particular "truths,"probably undergoes several reactions—first, a shock on hearing utterances they suspect are true, but are forbidden by convention to voice; second, a suspicion that repugnant imputations are ricocheting in their direction; third, an apprehension that one "truth"may exist for those respectably ensconced behind legality and another for those entangled in it. Such proverbial wisdom could probably produce a subtle and unsettling *Verfremdungseffekt*.

Martin the ape is a repellent character. The poet seems to intend in him a caricature of a papal emissary whose one faith lies in the power of money. His long sermon on the ways of venality is addressed to Reynard and Grimbart just before the opening of the second trial. Justice, he begins, is a delicate matter: "Trecht is elken swaer ghenoech"—"Justice is for everyone hard enough"(4609). Faced with the possibility of becoming involved in it, one needs, above all, an extralegal prop: "Een trou vrient is een hulpe groot"—"A true friend is an enormous help"(4422). But one needs a particular kind of friend, one to whom personal loyalty transcends all else: "Een trouwe vrient sel lijf ende goet / voor sinen vrient setten, alst noot doet"—"A faithful friend ought to hazard life and property / for his own friend as necessity dictates"(4555-56). He adds that justice must be cajoled: "Want trecht heeft dicwijl hulpe noot"—"For justice often has need of help"(4576)— such "help"coming via petitions cushioned with money: "Die bede is mitter ghiften coen"—"A petition becomes bold with gifts"(4552). Hence, learning the value of the one means that can influence justice is the root of all wisdom: "Men sel den pennic houden leren / ter noot dat onrecht mede to keren"—"One must learn to cherish money / in order to avert injustice with it"(4553-54). And whoever does not use friend and money to buy himself off as occasion demands is lost: "Wel is die vrient ende tghelt verdoemt / daer niemen troost of baet of coomt"—"Indeed money and friend are damned / where no one derives comfort and advantage from them"(4557-58). When Martin hastens away, Reynard and the little badger look after him in wonder, and one senses that the poet has let him echo the judicial *Realpolitik* of his time.

With the figure of Martin's consort, Rukenaw the she-ape, the *R II* poet reduces proverbial wisdom to sophistical blather. Her great moment comes when she champions Reynard at the beginning of his second trial. She immediately thrusts at her royal audience with a weapon of highest potency—proverbial lore of Biblical origin. She quotes Luke 3:36, initially the Latin "Estote misericordes"(4776) and then the vernacular "Weest ontfermich"—"Be merciful" (4777). This she reinforces with Matthew 7:1, initially again the Latin "Nolite judicare, / et non judicabimini"(4778-79) and then the vernacular "Oordeelt niemen, so enseldi / selve oordeel liden gheen"—"Judge no one, thus you shall / yourself suffer no judgment"(4780-81). After relating the parable of the woman taken in adultery, she adduces her third Biblical proverb (Matthew 7:3): "Sulc siet in eens anders oghe een stro, / die selve in sijn oghe een balc heeft"—"Many a one sees a straw in another's eye / who himself has a beam in his own"(4792-93), which, just to be sure king and queen fathom its import, she paraphrases in plain words: "Tis menich, die over een ander gheeft / een oordeel, ende hi is selve die quaetste"— "There's many a one who makes judgment on others who himself is most evil"(4794-95). Biblical allusion persists. She notes that the lowly shall be exalted and that God shall receive those who desire him (4796-97 and 4798). She caps her exordium, her portentous call to justice, with a third and freer paraphrase of Matthew 7:3:

> Niemen ense den anderen condempneren,
> Al wist hi wat von sinen ghebreke,
> Hi endede eerst of sijns selfs bleke.
>
> No one ought to condemn another
> even though he knows something of his transgression
> unless he first be rid of his own blemish.
>
> (4800-02)

Noble at first rejects her plea that Reynard be heard by remarking curtly, "Hi strijct altoos sinen steert"—"He's always stroking his tail"(that is, always deceiving)—and her rejoinder is a concatenation of six proverbs, all of which are, like the proverbs of Sancho Panza, overwhelming in their aura of wisdom and none of which are particularly pertinent:

> Dat swaerste moet noch meeste weghen.
> Een sel sijn lief minnen to maten
> Ende sijn leet to seer niet haten.
> Ghestadicheit voecht wel den heren.
> Tis misselic, hoe die saken verkeren.
> Men sel den dach te seer niet
> Loven noch laken, eer men siet
> Dat hi ten avont is ghecomen.
> Goet raet can dic den ghenen vromen
> Die hem met vlijt daer keret an.
>
> The heaviest must indeed weigh the most.
> One ought to love his pleasure in moderation
> and not hate his anguish too much.
> Constancy well beseems a lord.
> It is unforeseeable how things will turn out.
> One ought not to praise too much

or blame the day before one sees
that it has reached evening.
Good counsel can often help
those who diligently apply themselves to it.

(4848-58)

The inundation of wisdom silences the royal couple. The she-ape keeps the floor and eventually affords Reynard opportunity to contrive his own defense. Here the sweet reason of the proverb prevails: it subverts justice, and the rational king and queen succumb to it where, by rights, they should have executed the fox on the spot.

It is a curious fact that the *R II* poet gives no proverbs to the three power figures—Bruin the bear, Isegrim the wolf, and Tibert the cat—although there is one exception. Once and only once the poet allows Bruin to proverbialize, and his wisdom encourages his own downfall. As he is obviously on the verge of being trapped within the tree-trunk in which Reynard has convinced him there is a cache of honey, he smugly reassures the fox of his continent habits: "Waendi dat ic bem onvroet? / Maet es tot alle spele goet"—"Do you think I'm foolish? / Measure is good in everything"(723-24).

One assumes that the poet implies by not larding the speeches of his power figures with proverbial truisms that they are so obsessed with greed that they have lost all mental agility. But king and queen, though power figures also, are of a different sort. Their position is secure, and hence they have opportunity to lapse into attempts at wisdom. When Noble tries to persuade Tibert to bring Reynard to court, the cat is apprehensive. Bruin has been mauled, and Tibert feels he might fare no better. The king urges him on with "Het is menich die mit listen can / meer dan sulc mit crachten doet"—"There's many a one who can do more with cunning / than others can do with force" (1062-63). When Noble wishes to execute Reynard without legal formality, the queen, both Francophile and stickler for protocol, rebukes her spouse with "Sir, pour dieu, ne croies mie / toutes chose que on vous die (3665-66) and caps her demand with "Alteram partem audite! / Sulc claect, die selve meest misdoet"—"Hear the other side! / Many accuse who themselves misdo most"(3678-79). When Reynard seems hopelessly within the clutches of Isegrim and his henchmen, the king evokes Aesopic wisdom: "So langhe gaet te water die cruuc, / Dat si breect ende valt aen sticken"—"The pot goes only so long to water / before it breaks and falls to pieces" (4356-57). When Reynard, victorious in combat with Isegrim, desires to address those loyal to him, both king and queen consent, saying:

Tis reden, dat men den vrienden seit
Grote saken, daer macht aen leit,
Ende men des volghet haren rade.

There's reason that one tell friends
important matters that concern power
and that he follow their counsel.

(7381-83)

Here, with the royal pair, the proverb is the cipher of unwisdom. As in the speeches of Polonius, its function is to underscore vacuousness of character.

The proverbs, allotted Reynard are, with the exception of those addressed to Grimbart during the fox's second confession of his sins, ironic sallies that are both hypocritical and candid at once, that have both a surface pertinence and a subterranean barb. They are the *R II* poet's masterpieces of ambiguous truisms. Only a few may be cited here. One exhorts to religious renewal. Reynard quotes Matthew 24:44—"et vos estote parati"(4458)—as he, in the guise of an eremite, is about to take the life of Lampreel the cony. Another enjoins legal impartiality. He cries, "Dat recht endoet niemen onghelijc"—"Justice treats no one unequally"(4627)—as he is about to demand special dispensations from the royal tribunal. Another warns against incompetents in authority. He says to king and queen that Isegrim, Bruin, and Tibert have dangerous ambitions and points up his argument with "Waer esels crighen heerscappien / daer siet ment selden wel ghedien"—"Where jackasses get power / one seldom sees things turn out well"(5749-50)—and here the listeners, both the animal courtiers of the poem and the human audience of the narrator, are fully aware that the dig is as appropriate to the royal pair as to the trio of political scoundrels. Several—hypocritically—warn against the prevalence of hypocrisy:

Want daer veel op eerden leeft,
Die van buten draghen schijn
Anders, dan si van binnen sijn.

For many live on earth
who outwardly show appearances
different from what they are within.

(4310-12)

On occasion, Reynard's proverbs are instruments of cruel sarcasm, of the *Schadenfreude* which characterizes much of the humor in the late medieval *Schwankbücher*. When Bruin is firmly caught in Lantfreit's tree-trunk and is about to suffer a horrible beating at the hands of the local farmers, Reynard announces their approach and tells Bruin they will give him something to drink since he has enjoyed Lantfreit's honey so thoroughly (which he certainly has not), adding as justification, "Het is goet dat men die spise wel net"—"It is proper that one moisten food (with drink)" (764). The cruelty of the remark is rounded off a few lines later when Reynard finds Bruin on a river bank where he has collapsed from exhaustion and, presumably, loss of blood. Seeing that the scalp has been torn from his head, the fox addresses him as "Sir priester, dieux vous saut"(957) and then asks, "In wat oorden wildi u doen / dat ghi draecht dat rode caproen"—"What order do you wish to enter / by wearing that red cowl?"(969-70).

The ultimate purpose of any paper such as this is to enhance the aesthetic potential of its subject. Too much esteem, I feel, is allotted the progeny of the Middle Dutch poem and too little the progenitor. Few medievalists I know have ever bothered to read *R II.* Elsewhere, in an earlier paper, I attempted to give paternity its due.[5] I pointed out that if Lazarillo de Tormes and Guzmán de Alfarache are *pícaros,* then Reynard is also, just as much as Simplicius and Felix Krull are *pícaros,* even though they are outside the seminal picaresque tradition of the Spanish sixteenth and seventeenth centuries. I urged that *R II* be accorded the dignity of being read as picaresque fiction, despite the fact that it is written in iambic tetrameter couplets; despite the fact that its narrative technique is not linear, but complex and heavy with encapsulated flashbacks; despite the fact that its picaresque earthiness and vulgarity are informed by an ever ironic and worldly eloquence. Here I must concede that much of the humor in *Reinaerts Historie* is gross and heavy-handed. The two major crises of the poem utilize the motif of the "lying confession": in both we see Reynard condemned to death and allowed, grudgingly, to make public confession of his sins. We, the external audience, know he is lying and know also the internal audience, the assemblage of beasts at King Noble's court, eventually feel he is telling the truth. This sort of thing is pretty obvious, and its humor may strike us today as stale. I concede also that the numerous fabliau-like *Streiche* in *Reinaert*—like the two in the first half where Reynard does in both Bruin and Tibert—belong in *Schwankbücher:* their level of humor is that of the pratfall and custard pie. But the ironic humor that plays on conventional conceptions of "truth" is pervasive and subtle. It does not merely reverse the positions of apparent truth and apparent falsehood, but indirectly casts doubt on whether there is any basis for conventionally received "truth" outside of that produced by public consensus abetted by repressive power. The signal for this sort of epistemological irony is the persistent use of the popular proverb in ever-varied contextual situations. Indeed, the proverbs are, in a large sense, heuristic: they tend to disestablish any unreflected acceptance of "truth" and to keep Pilate's question open.

Notes

1. Still the handiest annotated text of *R II* is Ernst Martin, ed., *Reinaert/Willems Gedicht Van den Vos Reinaerde und die Umarbeitung und Fortsetzung Reinaerts Historie* (Paderborn: Ferdinand Schöningh, 1874). Line references to *R II* in the present context are to the Martin edition, and quotations from *R II* are also from the Martin edition.

2. The most heavily annotated edition of the older poem is J. W. Muller, ed., *Van den vos Reinaerde,* 2 vols., Leidsche Drukken en Herdrukken (Leiden: E. J. Brill, 1939 and 1942). Diplomatic printings of both the early poem and its continuation are in W. Gs. Hellinga, ed., *Von den vos Reynaerde/I Teksten* (Zwolle: W. E. J. Tjeenk Willink, 1952), where line numeration differs slightly from Martin's edition (see n.1 above).

3. Coverage of the literary history of Reynard the Fox in the Low German areas is in my edition, *The His-*

tory of Reynard the Fox Translated and Printed by William Caxton in 1481 (Cambridge, Mass.: Harvard University Press, 1960), pp. 14-30, and in N. F. Blake, ed., *The History of Reynard the Fox Translated from the Dutch Original by William Caxton,* Early English Text Society, 263 (London, 1970), xi-xxi.

4. New York: King's Crown Press, 1948, pp. 1-2. On the skepticism that must inevitably arise concerning anyone's clear-cut definition of the proverb, see B. J. Whiting, *Proverbs, Sentences, and Proverbial Phrases from English Writings Mainly before 1500* (Cambridge, Mass.: Harvard University Press, 1968), pp. x-xvii.

5. "Reynard the Fox as *Pícaro* and *Reinaerts Historie* as Picaresque Fiction," *The Journal of Narrative Technique,* 1 (1971), 137-145.

N. F. Blake (essay date 1975)

SOURCE: "Reynard the Fox in England," in *Aspects of the Medieval Animal Epic,* edited by E. Rombauts and A. Welkenhuysen, Leuven University Press, 1975, pp. 53-65.

[In the following essay, Blake examines several Middle English fox tales and concludes that there is not enough evidence to show a direct connection between them and the Roman de Renart.*]*

The **Roman de Renart** is such an important text in medieval French literature and exerted such an influence on several other medieval vernacular literatures that it has usually been assumed it was also known in medieval England and influenced Middle English writers. Two attempts have been made to document this influence: one by F. Mossé and the other by J. Flinn[1]. Since both scholars were intent on tracing the influence of the **Roman de Renart,** their surveys excluded some Middle English works containing stories of foxes in which the fox is not called Reynard. The omission of these works distorts the general picture of fox literature in England for it suggests that only those stories which have some connexion with the **Roman de Renart** were found. It is therefore worthwhile reopening the question of whether the **Roman de Renart** was known in England, partly to investigate the occurrences of the fox in a wider context, and partly to consider to what ends the English poets used their material since this may provide us with a clue as to the possible sources they used. My investigation will be concerned principally with works written in Middle English, though it should not be forgotten that the fox is frequently portrayed in the art of the later Middle English period and that stories about the fox were composed also in Latin and French in England.

It is natural to start with a consideration of *The Fox and the Wolf,* a poem which survives only in one manuscript and which was probably composed about 1250[2]. A relatively short poem of only 295 lines, it corresponds in general with Martin's branch IV of the **Roman de Renart**[3], which is taken to be its source. Apart from an article by Bercovitch, which was in any case confined to the satirical intention of the author, no attempt has been made to explain the overall structure and purpose of the poem[4]. It is indeed usually dismissed as a work of little literary merit, with the implication that the English poet simply bungled his task of adapting his French source[5]. There are, however, important differences between the English poem and branch IV of the **Roman**. The animals in the former are introduced as 'a fox' and 'a wolf'; and the names *Reneward* and *Sigrim*[6], which preserve distinctively English forms, are referred to only incidentally. Furthermore the one monk who is named is called Aylmer, a purely English name. There are also important differences in the details of the two versions, particularly in the ending, and the author of *The Fox and the Wolf* has introduced two episodes not found in branch IV. In the **Roman** when Reynard enters the barn he eats his fill of the hens. In the English poem Reneward does not explicitly eat any of the hens, and his attempts to make Chanteclere, who is so named, come down off his perch so that he can eat him are unsuccessful. The fox leaves the barn in disappointment. This episode is not identical with any branch in the **Roman** though it has general similarities with some. The second insertion occurs in the wolf's confession to the fox. Here the wolf says that he once saw Reneward in bed with his wife. This may be based on branch Va of the **Roman,** in which Reynard raped the wolf's wife, but as in *The Fox and the Wolf* the wolf found the two in bed it need be little more than seduction which was implied.

Despite these differences most commentators have felt that the author of *The Fox and the Wolf* was familiar with the **Roman** and used it as the basis for his own poem, because the inclusion of these two extra episodes implies a knowledge of the Reynard cycle in which stories about Reynard are linked in a united whole. One may well question, though, whether the inclusion of these episodes does point to a knowledge of the **Roman** by the English poet since neither episode has an exact parallel there. Furthermore, this theory fails to provide a reason for the inclusion of these episodes in *The Fox and the Wolf* and it presupposes that the **Roman** was so well known that the English author felt obliged to include stories found in it even though such inclusions had no particular relevance to his own story and may indeed have impeded its logical development[7]. It also raises the problem of why a poet who knew the cyclic **Roman** was content to adapt only one small part of it and to refer so briefly to two other parts. If he knew the **Roman,** his method of procedure was completely different from that of the German and Flemish adaptors.

A clue to the poet's source may be provided by the purpose of his poem. Its relative brevity, the introduction of the animals without names and the incidental references to their names are features characteristic of fables. A fable is essentially a short story with a moral, whereas the **Roman** is a *conte à rire*. It may be that the poet of *The Fox and the Wolf* was composing a fable. In structure the poem is divided into two unequal halves: the fox's relations with Chanteclere and his relations with Sigrim. The outcome of the two halves is strikingly different: Reneward is unable to deceive Chanteclere, but he is able to hoodwink Sigrim. *The Fox and the Wolf* may best be explained as a fable illustrating deceit and how one should guard against it, with the fox playing the role of a devil or arch-tempter—one frequently given to him in fable literature[8]. It is important to remember that Reneward had deceived both animals previously. Because the fox had eaten many of his chickens on previous occasions, Chanteclere knew Reneward's treachery and is not taken in by the story of blood-letting. But Sigrim, even though he had seen Reneward in bed with his wife (which ought to have been sufficient warning), is prepared to disbelieve the evidence of his own eyes and to accept Reneward's present story at its face value. He is justly punished and thus the moral is underlined. The disproportion between the two halves is explained by the moral: the poet is principally concerned with those who succumb to temptation and how they will suffer. The added episodes are an essential part of the poem's meaning and should not be dismissed as a mere reference to the cyclic story of Reynard the Fox.

Yet the poet's ability to use these interpolations meaningfully need not preclude the possibility that he took them from the **Roman de Renart**. In this connexion two points should be borne in mind. The first is that most stories about animals are arranged in groups, if not exactly in cycles. *æsop's Fables* is a collection of stories in which many animals reappear and the whole has more than a mere formal unity. In England, Odo of Cheriton produced a collection of Latin fables in which some of the animals are occasionally named. It would have been as practical for the poet of *The Fox and the Wolf* to have taken his episodes from three fables in one collection as from three branches in the **Roman,** for the three episodes in the **Roman** have no more particular connexion than would three fables in a collection. References to other stories are not in themselves sufficient to prove a knowledge of the **Roman**. The second is that one must evaluate whether the English poet is more likely to have had access to and modelled his stories upon fables than the **Roman**. If it is argued that the **Roman** was so well known that the poet of *The Fox and the Wolf* would not fail to refer to it, it might be suggested that he is hardly likely to have altered the episodes so much that the resemblance of his poem to the **Roman** is problematical. But evidence for knowledge of the **Roman** in England during the thirteenth century comes only from this poem. No manuscripts of it were either written or found in England by 1250. On the other hand, collections of fables and other animal stories were common. An English version of the *Bestiary* was made about 1200[9]. Marie de France based her French collection of fables on English models during the latter part of the twelfth century. Odo of Cheriton's fables survive in many manuscripts both in England and abroad. His fables were in Latin, but from one or two English verses found in some manuscripts it seems probable that English versions existed. As Odo's fables were composed soon after 1225, they may even have provided the spur to our poet for the composition of his own poem. The reasons adduced in favour of our poet's use of the **Roman** as his source are not convincing. Because *The Fox and the Wolf* is a fable-type story with moral and because fables about animals, with or without names, were quite well-known in the first half of the thirteenth century in England, it seems more reasonable to assume that our poet both used as his source and modelled his poem upon fables then current in England.

The poem *A Song on the Times* of about 200 lines from British Museum Harl. 913, dated to the early fourteenth century, has never been considered in surveys of literature about the fox in Middle English[10]. Yet it could be an important text coming as it does midway between *The Fox and the Wolf* and the *Nun's Priest's Tale*. It is a complaint about the perversion of justice through bribery and influence which is illustrated by a *vorbisen* or exemplum. This example includes four animals: the lion who is king of the beasts, the fox and the wolf who are the king's companions and hence represent his aristocratic subjects, and the simple ass who represents the lower classes. The fox, wolf and ass are accused in the king's court of various misdeeds, the chief of which is the slaughter of sheep and poultry. The fox and wolf bribe the king and are consequently released; the ass who does not is found guilty even though he assumed that as he eats only grass he would be found innocent. The animals are not named, but there are some general similarities between this poem and the **Roman:** the lion is the king of the beasts; the fox and wolf are his barons; and the lion holds court where his subjects may bring suits against others. However, the story can hardly have been taken from the **Roman,** and it is probably based on a fable though no exact parallel is known. The exemplum is significant since it shows that fables were used as illustrative material in vernacular poetry at this time and since it underlines the popularity of this type of moral story. It reinforces the impression gained from *The Fox and the Wolf* that the **Roman** itself was not known in England and was not used as a direct source by poets writing in English.

The second major work about the fox in Middle English literature is Chaucer's *Nun's Priest's Tale*. Its authorship has assured it far more scholarly enquiry than has been accorded to *The Fox and the Wolf,* though it is neither possible nor necessary to review that literature here[11]. It was recognised at an early date that the tale bore a general similarity to Martin's branch II of the *Roman* as well as to the German poem *Reinhart Fuchs*. At a time when it was fashionable to look for earlier lost versions of Middle English texts, this similarity led K. Petersen to assume that Chaucer had used an earlier lost version of the **Roman,** a version which stood halfway between it and *Reinhart Fuchs*[12]. But Foulet's study of the sources of the **Roman** questioned whether there were any lost versions, since in his opinion Pierre de St. Cloud's poem is based directly on certain Latin texts[13]. Lecompte accepted this theory and was therefore forced to conclude that Chaucer had access to the **Roman** itself and that any differences from it are the

result of his own creative inspiration[14]. A theory of this sort, which relies on the poet's creativity, can never be entirely disproved, but it is seriously undermined by the parallels found elsewhere for the many places in which the *Nun's Priest's Tale* differs from the **Roman.** Therefore Sisam in his edition assumed that the complete **Roman** may never have been known in England or to Chaucer and that it may have been disseminated here in the form of independent tales[15]. Each tale was told without reference to the others. This theory would mean that the **Roman** was constructed from certain independent Latin texts to form a cyclic whole and then broken down again into independent sections. Though perhaps unlikely, this view is not impossible; unfortunately there is no evidence that the **Roman** was preserved in this way in England. Even in France, though the manuscripts may contain a varied number of branches, they never contain only a single branch.

Because scholars have taken the **Roman** as their point of departure, they have been forced to offer the only three possible theories: that Chaucer used a pre-**Roman** version, that he used the **Roman** itself, or that he used some **Roman** derivative. As we have seen there are serious objections to each hypothesis, though in view of the time-gap between the **Roman** and the *Nun's Priest's Tale* Sisam's theory that Chaucer used a **Roman** derivative would be the least unlikely, were it not for the lack of any evidence of such derivatives. I suggest it is possible to adapt Sisam's theory; perhaps Chaucer used not an independent branch of the **Roman,** but a fable which was at some earlier stage influenced by it. In other words, his source was of the same type as those used by the authors of *The Fox and the Wolf* and *A Song on the Times*. As the fox is only a minor character in the *Nun's Priest's Tale,* it seems unlikely that Chaucer borrowed directly from the **Roman.** In the fables, however, the roles and importance of the various animals constantly changed, and it is not unusual to find the fox as a minor character. Furthermore, the *Nun's Priest's Tale* shares certain characteristics with *The Fox and the Wolf*. Chanteclere is so named in both texts, but the fox is introduced simply as 'a fox'; in the *Nun's Priest's Tale* indeed he is 'a col-fox'. Can this mean that Chanteclere was a more familiar figure in English fable than Reynard? Otherwise, the animal names in the *Nun's Priest's Tale* do not reflect those in the **Roman.** In Chaucer's tale the fox is Daun Russell and Chanteclere's wife is Pertelote and not Pinte. Both these names are of French origin, but it is unlikely that Chaucer got them from the **Roman**[16]. These names may be an indication of the fluidity of nomenclature in the fables. Just as the poet of *The Fox and the Wolf* introduces new names such as that of the monk Aylmer, Chaucer also adds other names. These include Malle, Talbot, Gerland, Malkyn and Colle. Finally, the *Nun's Priest's Tale* is like *The Fox and the Wolf* in that it is a tale with a moral.

This latter point deserves further consideration. In Chaucer's tale the story of Chanteclere and the fox forms only a small part of the whole, for the tale contains much rhetoric, decoration and moralising. What then is the tale about and what was Chaucer's purpose in writing it? These questions cannot be answered fully here, but most modern interpretations start from those lines at the end of the tale which lead the reader to look for a moral[17].

> But ye that holden this tale a folye,
> As of a fox, or of a cok and hen,
> Taketh the moralite, goode men.
> For seint Paul seith that al that writen is,
> To oure doctrine it is ywrite, ywis;
> Taketh the fruyt and lat the chaf be stille.
>
> (VII 3438-43).

Modern scholars have understood this passage either at its face value or else ironically. Those who take it literally see in the tale a sermon against a particular sin, usually flattery, with an indication as to how man may learn from his mistakes. The moral is identical with that in *The Fox and the Wolf:* one should learn to recognise evils such as flattery and deceit and so be armed against them. In this connexion it is interesting to note that in Chaucer's version the fox tries to deceive the cock twice[18]. This addition, which has been criticised by some critics on literary grounds, reinforces the moral and thus serves the same purpose as the additions in *The Fox and the Wolf.* Those who understand the tale ironically work from the assumption that Chaucer was satirising sermons based on animal exempla and symbolism. Whichever view one takes, the basis of the tale is the fable or sermon with animal examples, and parallels from sermon literature have been adduced[19]. Chaucer and his audience were using the fable as their point of reference. The modern interpretations make it less likely that Chaucer used the *Roman* or a derivative as his source, for it is reasonable to accept that he took both story and model from some fable. Yet, the attraction of the *Roman* has been so great that even those who have pointed out the fable-like character of the *Nun's Priest's Tale* have refused to consider the possibility that Chaucer used a fable as his source[20], though surely we should allow the meaning of a text to guide us in our search for its sources.

Once more, it is necessary to consider the availability of texts. Here we must recognise that as elsewhere Chaucer used French texts not generally available in England, he may have become acquainted with the *Roman* in France. Otherwise, evidence that it was known in England in the fourteenth century is as difficult to come by as it was for the thirteenth. On the other hand, fables about animals were common then. John of Sheppey, who studied at Oxford and Paris and who died in 1360, wrote a collection of fables in Latin. Many were copied from Odo's work, but some were evidently his own. These latter may have been influenced by the *Roman* either directly or indirectly, for John had been to Paris. About the middle of the fourteenth century Nicholas Bozon, an English Franciscan, wrote some fables in Anglo-Norman. In his collection Reynard is himself sometimes duped and is not always the principal character. Some of these fables are based on Odo, others have a general similarity with the *Roman,* and several have no parallel with either. Yet, the name Reynard is used

in fables whose stories have no relation to the *Roman.* Nicholas may have had access to fables in English since he uses a wide variety of English names, for if he had invented the names one might have expected him to use French ones as he was writing in Anglo-Norman. Finally, at the end of the fourteenth century, John Bromyard the Dominican reproduced several fables from Odo's collection in his *Summa predicantium;* he also uses the names Reynard and Tibert. All these collections were designed as teaching aids and they underline the essentially clerical nature of such stories in England. It is not without significance that Chaucer gave his story of Chanteclere and the fox to the nun's priest. There was no attempt, as some have supposed, on the part of the Church to prevent the dissemination of these stories; on the contrary the Church was responsible for propagating them. In England animal stories were religious and not secular.

Since these fable-collections contain many stories about animals not found in the *Roman,* it is unlikely that the *Roman* exercised more than a general influence upon them because it cannot have been the primary impetus for their creation. As a genre they existed before the *Roman* and probably they absorbed material from many different sources, both written and oral. The *Roman* may have been one of those sources, for many of the English fable-writers had been to France, but one should not overemphasize its importance. The continuous development of these fable collections is an important factor to be taken into account in a consideration of the wide range of carvings and manuscript illumination of foxes in England[21]. The latter should perhaps be omitted from the discussion here since we do not usually know where they were made, who made them and what models the artists were following. Isolated pictures of the Reynard story may have been copied from Continental models. The carvings are more important. They are so plentiful we may accept that Englishmen were largely responsible for them. Yet, certain points need to be taken into consideration about them. Although there are isolated carvings from the twelfth and thirteenth centuries, most English representations date from the fourteenth and fifteenth centuries or even later. In other words, the direct impetus for them is hardly likely to have been the *Roman* since the disparity of dates precludes that. It must also be recognised that interpretation of the scenes depicted is not simple, and often a viewer sees there what he expects to find. The only unambiguous representations of Reynard stories from the *Roman* are in my opinion those on some misericords of Bristol Cathedral, dating from 1528[22], and it is surely significant that the only clear examples of the Reynard story as found in the *Roman* date from after 1481. In many cases, the scenes portrayed remind one of English rather than of French literary works. Almost all portrayals of the chase of the fox with a fowl in his mouth show a woman in front of the house, as in the *Nun's Priest's Tale,* and not a man, as in the *Roman.* This, it may be suggested, simply proves the popularity of the *Canterbury Tales;* but as some of these scenes probably antedate Chaucer's poem it is more reasonable to assume that both drew on the same story current in England. Similarly, the fowls usually carved with the fox are geese, not chickens, and this echoes such English poems as *The Fox and the Goose.* Finally, it may be significant that carvings of foxes rarely occur in isolation. They may occupy only one or two misericords in a choir given over to animal symbolism. It is necessary to account for the iconography of the whole series—and it seems likely that most such series were based on bestiaries or fable collections. It is simplest to accept that the fox scenes were part of this general iconography rather than that they were taken from a special source. Many of these points which have been raised in relationship to the carvings could equally well apply to the short poems in which the fox is mentioned[23]. They are late and have points of contact with the longer English works. Although their meaning is often obscure, they rarely reflect the stories found in the *Roman.* Whether they are to be regarded as popular or not is problematical, but it is quite likely that they were written by clerics. Like the carvings, they point to the popularity of animal stories in England which have little or no connexion with the *Roman.*

Just as surveys of fox literature in Middle English omit *A Song on the Times,* so they also overlook Henryson's *Morall Fabillis* written at the close of the Middle English period[24]. This is unfortunate since like *A Song on the Times* it can be regarded as a significant text. It is a collection of versified fables, each of which concludes with a moral. The collection includes versions of such well-known fables as the fox in the well, the prosecution of the fox, and the fox and the herrings. Yet not only do these versions differ considerably from those found in the *Roman,* but also the *Morall Fabillis* includes fables about animals not mentioned there. This is not surprising since Henryson almost certainly used a version of the French *Isopet* as his principal source, though he may in some fables have been influenced by Chaucer[25]. The names given to the animals in the *Morall Fabillis* are of interest. Some preserve English or Scots usage: the fox is always called Lowrence, a name found in Scotland, and the wolf is called Waitskaith, a name found elsewhere only in Caxton's *Reynard the Fox.* These names suggest that Henryson was able to draw on English and Scots stories in which they occurred. The importance of Henryson is that right at the end of the Middle Ages a writer, who is a follower of Chaucer, thought it worthwhile to compose versified fables and to use a French fable collection and not the *Roman* as his source. Like Chaucer, he may have been ignorant of the *Roman*'s existence. But fables were available right through the Middle Ages, and it is time we reconsidered their position as potential sources for writers and artists.

The final text I shall consider is Caxton's *Reynard the Fox* published in 1481 since with this work we can trace the influence of the *Roman* in English literature as Caxton's version is a translation of the Dutch prose *Van den Vos Reynaerde* published at Gouda in 1479[26]. It is indeed the only translation he made from Dutch, and a question that inevitably arises is why he should have used a Dutch rather than a French version. Unfortunately, his epilogue in *Reynard the Fox* contains no answer to this question. But from Caxton's prologues and epilogues to his other texts we get a good idea of his prejudices and attitudes[27]. We know that he thought French literature and culture were far superior to either English or Dutch, and his translations from French keep as close to the original as possible for in this way he hoped English would take on some of the elegance of French. It is a reasonable inference that Caxton would have translated a French text of the *Roman* if he had known the French version existed. This means that he was unfamiliar with the *Roman* during his stay in Bruges, which is hardly surprising since it was less well-known in the fifteenth century and no reference to it occurs in the inventories of the libraries of the Dukes of Burgundy. It also implies that the French version was unknown in England during Caxton's lifetime. For Caxton was not only a publisher, he was also a bookseller. Many manuscripts passed through his hands and he occasionally made special efforts to acquire a manuscript to print when he knew of its existence. Since he was content to use the Dutch text of *Van den Vos Reynaerde,* it seems certain he was unfamiliar with the *Roman.* Why then, we may ask, did he choose to translate and print the Reynard story at all? He generally picked texts to translate which contained stories known of in England, but which were not familiar in the form he printed them in. Thus stories about Charlemagne were not uncommon in England, but the particular version Caxton printed was unknown before he translated it. He knew that animal stories were popular in England for he was familiar with the *Nun's Priest's Tale.* Some of the names in his own *Reynard the Fox* were altered to make them agree with those in Chaucer's version. The *Nun's Priest's Tale* assured him that animal tales were fashionable, so it required no great imagination on his part to provide England with the complete cyclic version of Reynard the fox. Its immediate popularity proved the wisdom of his choice. The text was frequently reprinted, and this fact may also indicate that the whole story was previously unknown in England, since in so many other countries Reynard had fallen or was soon to fall into oblivion.

From this discussion of Reynard the fox in England it may be concluded that there is insufficient evidence to show that the *Roman* was known in England. The complete Reynard cycle was introduced here only in 1481. Whatever influence the *Roman* may have exerted was at second hand through the fables. Fables were common throughout the medieval period and were the primary source for animal stories in England. Some fable-writers may have been familiar with the *Roman,* but as several of them are known to have visited France they may have become acquainted with it there. What is needed now is a survey of fable literature and how fables influenced works in the vernacular. The *Roman* is considered such an important text that it has tended to draw attention away from the fables; as far as Middle English Literature is concerned I would suggest that this has led to a distorted picture. But even in other medieval literatures the role of the fable deserves fuller investigation. A proper assessment of the development of animal literature in England can come only from an examination of all works dealing with the fox and an understanding of why they may have been written. It may be that English as a medieval literature is different from the other vernacular literatures of Western Europe in its ignorance of the cyclic Reynard story. If so, it could provide an important basis of comparison with those literatures for an evaluation of the influence of the **Roman de Renart**[28].

Notes

1. F. Mossé, *Le Roman de Renart dans l'Angleterre du Moyen Age,* in: *Les Langues Modernes,* XLV (1951), pp. 70-84; and J. Flinn, *Le Roman de Renart dans la littérature française et dans les littératures étrangères au Moyen Age.* Toronto, 1963.

2. Edited in B. Dickins and R. M. Wilson, *Early Middle English Texts.* London, 1951, pp. 62-70; and J. A. W. Bennett and G. V. Smithers, *Early Middle English Verse and Prose,* 2nd edition. Oxford, 1968, pp. 65-76.

3. E. Martin, *Le Roman de Renart.* Strassburg, 1882-7; a different numeration is used in M. Roques, *Le Roman de Renart.* Paris, 1948-63.

4. S. Bercovitch, *Clerical Satire in 'þe Vox and þe Wolf',* in: *Journal of English and Germanic Philology,* LXV (1966), pp. 287-94.

5. As in Dickins and Wilson, *o.c.,* p. 62, and in G. H. McKnight, *The Middle English 'Vox and Wolf',* in: *Publications of the Modern Language Association of America,* XXIII (1908), pp. 497-509.

6. It has often been pointed out that the form *Sigrim* is also found in Lydgate.

7. Cf. Bennett and Smithers, *o.c.,* p. 300; and Flinn, *o.c.,* p. 676.

8. Cf. Henryson's *Morall Fabillis,* ll. 1132-6:

   This Tod I likkin to Temptationis,
   Beirand to mynd mony thochtis vane,
   Assaultand men with sweit perswasionis,
   Ay reddy for to trap thame in ane trayne.

9. Edited in J. Hall, *Selections from Early Middle English 1130-1250.* Oxford, 1920, I.176-96 and II.579-626. In this article I have not added bibliographical references for the Latin and French works mentioned, since Mossé and Flinn give full details.

10. Edited in T. Wright, *The Political Songs of England from the Reign of John to that of Edward II.* London, 1839, pp. 195-205.

11. See A. C. Baugh, *Chaucer.* New York, 1968, and W. R. Crawford, *Bibliography of Chaucer, 1954-1963.* Seattle and London, 1967, for bibliographies.

    See now *The New Cambridge Bibliography of English Literature,* vol. 1 (ed. G. Watson 1974), p. 581.

12. K. O. Petersen, *On the Sources of the Nonne Prestes Tale.* Cambridge, Mass., 1898.

13. L. Foulet, *Le Roman de Renart.* Paris, 1914.

14. I. C. Lecompte, *Chaucer's Nun's Priest's Tale and the Roman de Renart,* in: *Modern Philology,* XIV (1916-17), pp. 737-49.

15. K. Sisam, *The Nonnes Prestes Tale.* Oxford, 1927, pp. xiii ff.

16. Cf. C. Dahlberg, *Chaucer's Cock and Fox,* in: *JEGP,* LIII (1954), pp. 277-90.

17. As, for example, M.J. Donovan, *The Moralite of the Nun's Priest's Sermon,* in: *JEGP,* LII (1953), pp. 498-538; S. Manning, *The Nun's Priest's Morality and the Medieval Attitude towards Fables,* in: *JEGP,* LIX (1960), pp. 403-16; and C. B. Hieatt, *The Moral of The Nun's Priest's Tale,* in: *Studia Neophilologica,* XLII (1970), pp. 3-8.

18. As pointed out in J. B. Severs, *Chaucer's Originality in the Nun's Priest's Tale,* in: *Studies in Philology,* XLIII (1946), pp. 38-9.

19. Particularly in J. B. Steadman, *Flattery and the Moralitas of The Nonnes Prestes Tale,* in: *Medium ævum,* XXVIII (1959), pp. 172-9.

20. R. T. Lenaghan, *The Nun's Priest's Fable,* in: *PMLA,* LXXVIII (1963), p. 301.

21. See K. Varty, *Reynard the Fox.* Leicester, 1967.

22. Illustrated in Varty, *o.c.,* plates 48-52, and discussed by him on pp. 45-8. See also figures 10, 12 and 15 in the present *Proceedings.*

23. See R. H. Robbins, *Secular Lyrics of the XIVth and XVth Centuries,* 2nd edn. Oxford, 1955, pp. 43-5.

24. Edited in H. Harvey Wood, *The Poems and Fables of Robert Henryson,* 2nd edn. London and Edinburgh, 1958, pp. 1-102.

25. See J. MacQueen, *Robert Henryson: A Study of the Major Narrative Poems.* Oxford, 1967, pp. 200 ff.; and cf. D. Fox, *Henryson and Caxton,* in: *JEGP,* LXVII (1968), pp. 586-93.

26. Edited in N. F. Blake, *The History of Reynard the Fox,* in: *Early English Text Society,* o.s. 263. London, 1970.

27. See N. F. Blake, *Caxton and his World.* London, 1969, pp. 64-78.

28. See now also R. A. Pratt, *Three Old French Sources of the Nonnes Prestes Tale,* in: *Speculum,* XLVII (1972), pp. 422-44, 646-68.

Nancy Freeman Regalado (essay date 1976)

SOURCE: "Tristan and Renart: Two Tricksters," in *L'Esprit Créateur,* Vol. XVI, No. 1, Spring, 1976, pp. 30-38.

[*In the following essay, Regalado compares the Renart stories with the tale of Tristan and Iseut, contending that both stemmed from similar narratives of ambiguous tricksters.*]

Seignor, oï avez maint conte
que maint conteor vos raconte,
coment Paris ravi Elainne,
les max qu'el en ot et la paine:
de Tristant, dont La Chievre fist . . .

(**Roman de Renart**, Br. III, vv. 1-5[1])

With these words, Pierre de Saint-Cloud, author of the earliest French branch of the **Roman de Renart,** set his story of the war between Renart and Ysengrin the wolf in the line of stories about celebrated adulterers: Paris and Helen, Tristan and Iseut. The contemporary stories of Renart and Tristan are indeed alike in many ways[2]; both revolve around a primordial sexual transgression involving Renart or Tristan and the wife of a noble personage often, but not always, called an uncle in both the Renart and Tristan stories. The sexual offense is eventually followed by a flight or chase into the woods where the offense is repeated, and, moreover, where the offended husband plainly views the lovers, as Mark sees Tristan and Iseut in the leafy bower (Béroul, vv. 1981-2051),[3] as Ysengrin sees his wife Hersent caught headfirst in Renart's den while Renart "helps"her out from behind (Br. VIIa, vv. 5911-6038). In both the Renart and Tristan stories we find trials by ordeal and a public justification by the accused wife. Béroul even says that Tristan knows much of foxy ways, "Tristan set mot de Malpertuis"(v. 4286).

We have not chosen to study the influence of one group of texts upon the other, nor to determine if the Renart cycle is a parody of the Tristan stories. We suggest, rather, that the twelfth-century French Tristan stories and Renart branches are serious and comic versions of fundamentally similar narrative material, material we can identify as trickster stories. If we borrow the ethnological term *trickster*[4] for our stories, for the protagonists of both comic and serious versions, if we call both Renart and Tristan tricksters, we find we are able to describe and explain the similarity of their stories, and perceive narrative patterns as typical and as predictable as those of stories about heroes.[5]

How can we call Tristan a trickster? It is easy to call Renart a trickster, since it is his nature to trick, to practice his *renardie.* We do not hesitate to speak of Renart's cunning and guile, while we would hardly say that Tristan "foxes"King Mark. Yet we must not be fooled by our own words. Tricks, and our words for talking about them, are quite ambiguous. We speak of craftsman and crafty, beguile and hoodwink, mischief and fraud with very different feelings. We are happy to be called artful, shrewd, clever, even wily, but not sly. We like to play tricks, but not to be taken for swindlers and cheats. We can take Odysseus or Prometheus seriously, Don Juan perhaps, but not Till Eulenspiegel, Panurge or Brer Rabbit.

Our medieval authors have made good use of the ambiguous nature of tricks to characterize their texts.[6] We find that when sly deception is emphasized, when the tricks are described in grossly physical terms, and when the author and other characters call the protagonist a trickster, we have a comic trickster's story like the **Roman de Renart.** Although there are dozens of negative words for calling Renart a deceitful cheat, seventeen in the first hundred verses of Branch I alone:

> . . . cil qui tot le mont conchie,
> Renart, icil mavés lechierres,
> cil rous puanz, cil orz trichierres,

> (Br. I, vv. 90-92)

Renart himself never admits to being a trickster nor regrets a trick, and the moral point of view in the Renart branches remains unresolved. The branches end abruptly, break off with a formula like "De ceste branche n'i a plus"(Br. VI, v. 5550), omitting the usual moralizing or proverbial reflection that commonly concludes most comic tales like the *fabliaux.*[7]

When the words for tricks are underplayed in a text, or when, as in the Tristan stories, what might be termed greedy lust is called love and is represented as an elevated emotion, an author can write a serious, even tragic trickster's story. He can lead us to admire without reservation the cleverness of his hero without ever calling him a trickster. The authors of the Tristan stories keep our admiration in several ways. They always emphasize that Tristan's disguises cover his real self, and his true, beautiful and admirable body is usually easily perceived through his costumes.[8] The Tristan authors, moreover, confine themselves to a small number of ambiguous or positively valued terms to describe Tristan's tricks. The author of the Oxford *Folie Tristan* calls Tristan's trick, his disguise as a fool, a *veisdie* (v. 180), a word related to our "wisdom,"*engin* (v. 158), a neutral word meaning artifice or means, *cuintise* (v. 181), meaning "worldly prudence," and *art* (v. 734) meaning wit in the context. Although the tricks themselves are fully narrated, the vocabulary in the Tristan stories remains consistently elevated. Where the Renart author may crudely say "Hersant a la cuisse haucie"(Br. VIIa, v. 5792), lovers' politer pleasures in the Oxford *Folie* are "parler, envaiser e jüer"(v. 736). Finally, the Tristan authors never call Tristan himself a trickster. In Thomas' *Mariage* fragment, Tristan may torture himself with the words *trichier* et *enginner,* seeing he must prove a deceitful lover or a faithless husband. But only the lovers' helper Brangien can be directly called a trickster (Béroul, v. 519; Thomas, vv. 323-24), and only the lovers' enemies, the evil barons and Frocin the dwarf, are morally characterized as well as condemned for their deceitful trickery or *traïson.* As in the **Roman de Renart,** the reader is not invited to sit in judgment upon the protagonist and no moral conclusions are drawn from his actions.[9]

Although our admiration for Tristan is carefully maintained, Tristan certainly behaves quite differently before and after drinking the love potion. Before the potion, Tristan counts on his physical skills, and what he does—killing the Morholt and the dragon, winning Iseut—is seen as beneficial to everyone. After drinking the potion, however, Tristan is transformed: he becomes a trickster, an a-social, a-moral being who acts only through tricks. After the potion, Tristan never again openly and straightforwardly confronts his enemies in Mark's court, using only the simple physical skill which was one of his original attributes. He is no longer able to act as a model hero both for the good of society and according to society's code of good and evil. He becomes a wanderer, an outcast, "fors de gent"(Béroul, v. 3759); like Renart, he is repeatedly banned and exiled. Tristan's former prowess is now worthless, the author of the Oxford *Folie* tells us, since only *veidise, engin, art* and *cuintise* can bring the lovers together (vv. 159, 733-34). Tristan cannot clear his name through a trial by combat; he cannot appear at tournaments except in disguise; he cannot kill the King. Because he cannot make full use of his strength, he must, like Renart, use his wits: "engingneus est, mes n'est pas fort" (Br. VIII, v. 8109).

Tristan, as a trickster, can act only through tricks because his desire, like Renart's hunger and lust, is insatiable *and* because what he wants does not and cannot belong to him. There can be no tricks without both desire and prohibition. Tristan would not be a trickster if he could marry Iseut or forget her. A trick is, narratively speaking, what we may call the getting of a desired but forbidden object. In an exploit, a heroic deed, on the other hand, the hero desires an object which it is legitimate for him to win. No matter how hard the task, the object is his for the taking.

Tricks are, moreover, as morally ambiguous and unresolved as the words for talking about them. We see that Tristan and Renart get away with everything. The normal social, legal or moral consequences of their tricks against others simply fail to operate: there are "miracles,"like Tristan's leap, narrow escapes and tight squeaks, but the tricksters are never "gotten" for good.[10]

Although Tristan and Renart get away with everything, they have nowhere to go. After Tristan drinks the love potion, his acts, his tricks, lead to nothing more than repeated meetings with Iseut, just as Renart's tricks lead only to repeated meals, repeated escapes. Renart's desire for, say, an *andoille* (Br. IIIb) does not imply any long-term objective. Tristan's meetings with Iseut, although joyous, cannot lead to a permanent union nor to eternal satisfaction. Their meetings, like Renart's pranks, are not steps towards any recognizable further goal. Neither Tristan nor Renart could ever be engaged in a quest.

As events in a narrative, then, tricks do not seem to lead to the end of a story, to a denouement, but only to the end of each trick. Tricks are thus quite unlike the disguises and subterfuges of other heroes, ruses which clearly advance some other ultimate goal, as Guillaume d'Orange's strategic use of the salt wagons wins new lands for King Louis in the *Charroi de Nimes,* as Alexandre's disguise saves the day for King Arthur in *Cligès,* indeed, as Tristan's disguises as Tantris the Harper and as a merchant win Iseut for King Mark. Occasional claims may be made for a necessity putting the protagonists beyond ordinary human law. King Noble's excuse to the cuckolded Isengrin, "Ce, fait il, que Renart l'amot / l'escuse auques de son pechié, / c'il par amors vos a trichié" (Br. VIIb, vv. 6248-50), rings much like the kindly sympathy of Ogrin the Hermit for Tristan and Iseut: "Gent dechacie, a con grant paine / Amors par force vos demeine!"(Béroul, vv. 2295-96). But such necessity is nothing like the ultimate goal that transcends each adventure of the hero. It is rather a thematic articulation of the insatiable desire characterizing all tricksters, whatever their object.

Lack of finality in the tricksters' stories does not only appear in the absence of narrative linearity and sequence, so strongly related to a sense of moral causality and finality. It may appear thematically as "funning" or playfulness arising unexpectedly at critical moments in a story, through deliberately insulting, teasing, taunting words and gestures accompanying tricks. Renart, after enjoying Hersent, quite gratuitously beats, bepisses and insults the wolf-cubs, reveling in the trick he has played (Br. VIIa, vv. 5794-5811). The winks exchanged by Tristan, Iseut and Dinas, the by-play and equivocal language underscoring the erotic aspect of Iseut's "ride" at the Mal Pas ford emphasize the fun of the trick, confirming that these tricks have no moral function, are indeed played for fun.[11]

The a-morality of the trickster and the lack of transcendant finality in a trick mean that all stories about tricksters and tricks tend to break apart into separate episodes, since a trick, as an event in a story, does not lead functionally to the end of a narrative, but only to its own conclusion. In contrast with the dramatically organized *roman* like the *Chevalier au lion* or *Erec et Enide,* where each episode is linked to a past moral crisis and a future goal, where the narrative and moral structures impose their *conjointure* upon the story's events, the Tristan and Renart stories are so strongly episodic that they are constantly on the verge of breaking up into separate fragments like many of the short branches of the **Roman de Renart** or like the two *Folies Tristan* and Marie de France's *Lai du Chèvrefeuille* which tell only one trick, one meeting. In Branch I of the **Roman de Renart** Isengrin's case against Renart is dismissed after the first three hundred verses, and the story would stop there were it not for the timely arrival of Chantecler and Pinte, bearing the funeral litter of the martyred hen Coupee. While events in Tristan's story up to the love potion follow a logical and essentially irreversible order, the events following the potion are, like those in the **Roman de Renart,** fragmented, reduplicated, and seem to lead nowhere.[12]

Identifying a story as a trickster's tale will, then, tell us much about the type of event which may occur; the protagonist will (repeatedly) try to satisfy an insatiable desire for a forbidden object. Knowing we are dealing with a trickster story will, however, give us virtually no information about the order of events and no means of anticipating the length or the end of a story. The structure of the trickster's story, then, appears to be quite different from that of the hero, which includes a variety of predictable events such as the testing of the hero, recognition of the hero, marriage and coronation of the hero, that appear in a relatively fixed sequence of causal links.[13] The variety of narrative events in a trickster's story is also quite limited, in contrast to the hero's story. Those key events which consecrate the hero's achievement of power within his society are missing in the trickster's story, while those Propp calls "liquidation of lack"[14] are emphasized and reduplicated, but do not constitute irreversible links in a sequence of events leading to the end of a story. Where the hero's story is strongly sequential, then, the trickster's story is strongly episodic.

Yet twelfth-century authors like Béroul and Thomas were particularly interested in creating orderly forms, in overcoming episodic fragmentation. As Thomas says, "Seignurs, cest cunte est mult divers, / E pur ço l'uni par mes vers"(vv. 835-36). Béroul's disparagement of "li conteor"(v. 1265) implies at least a taste for choice, and, like Thomas, for making a work out of a number of episodes. The Tristan authors usually try to provide a satisfactory rounding out of their story and to impose a denouement, if not moral causality and finality, through revenge in Béroul, death in Thomas, the lovers' joy in the two *Folies Tristan* and the *Chèvrefeuille,* this last further rounded out by a preview of the lovers' death and a song commemorating their meeting. There are also some efforts in the longer stories to interlace episodes, often with messengers and spies.

In both the **Roman de Renart** and the Tristan stories, however, it is in the renarration of the episodes themselves that the authors find their principal means of overcoming episodic fragmentation. The most striking narrative technique common to the Renart and Tristan stories is their frequent retelling of past episodes within a single episode or single branch to create a sense of unity, a sense of a larger context, if not of a whole story. Retelling keeps the story going and helps to give a feeling of order to the sometimes random sequence of episodes. Iseut saves Tristan's life by reminding Mark of Tristan's exploits (Béroul, vv. 26-31, 50-53, 136-44); Tristan's message in the *Chèvrefeuille* recalls other ruses. Hersent gives herself to Renart because she recalls Isengrin telling stories of her infidelity; Renart finds he must keep Isengrin's word: "Mais por ce qu'il s'en est clamez / voil ge certes que vos m'amez" (Br. VIIa, vv. 5783-84). In branches like the first of the **Roman de Renart** each episode, retold, seems to engender a new episode: the often recalled ravishing of the wolf's wife is reduplicated by the rape of the lion's Queen Fiere; this rape is recounted by Isengrin to the fake Breton jongleur Renart-Galopin, who pretends to be a story-teller, etc. Renarration of past episodes is often used, in itself, as a trick by Renart or Tristan. They turn stories into tricks by retelling them trickily—cleverly, artfully, deceitfully—as Renart tricks his cousin Grinbert in Branch I by his hypocritical confession of tricks, and as Tristan fools Mark in the Oxford *Folie* by telling him true stories about his love for Iseut.

Repetition of episodes is often very stylized and artfully cultivated within a number of Renart and Tristan texts. The author of Br. VIII, "Le Duel judiciaire,"clearly enjoys the shift in point of view and tone when the ravishing of Hersent is retold successively by the furious cuckold Isengrin, the willing victim herself, the complaisant King Noble and, above all, the fox who relishes the story. Recollection of past episodes is lyrically expanded in the Oxford *Folie Tristan* where the stylized past tenses, the refrain-like repetition of *membre vos,* "do you remember," the stanzaic shape of each episode retold form a beautiful contrast with the continuous thread of present tenses and make the relation of Tristan to the stories he tells especially touching and pathetic.

Episodic renarration also enables the authors of Renart and Tristan stories to retell within one episode a whole nucleus of episodes traditionally told about Renart or Tristan. Renart is often called upon to confess his sins, which gives him a chance to recall his favorite tricks as he does in Branch I where, confessing to Grinbert, he recalls his rape of Hersent and eight other tricks played on Isengrin, including celebrated stories like that of the wolf's tail frozen in the ice. 21 different tricks are told in Branch I in the course of Renart's confession, in the accusation brought against him, and in Renart's jeering speech to Noble's army. In Branch VI there are 23 renarrations of some 14 tricks told by Noble as the judge, and by Isengrin and Renart as plaintiff and defendant. The list of tricks and density of renarration vary from branch to branch, but invariably includes the ravishing of Hersent, the original sin. In the Oxford *Folie Tristan* there are 16 separate renarrations, including two retellings of the drinking of the love potion. Retelling might thus be called the artful authors' best trick, enabling them to show off their repertoire and to tell the "whole"story of Renart or of Tristan within a single episode.

We may finally ask why these two groups of trickster stories were so particularly enjoyed in the twelfth century, and why they seem to us as typical of their time as do stories like *Erec et Enide,* where heroic effort and virtue are amply rewarded. Perhaps it is because the twelfth century reserves a special admiration for stories not about the everyday social world, not even about the hero's world, but stories that suggest a refusal of our imperfect and mortal world, whether they be stories of a-social tricksters like the outlaw fox, of lovers who count the world well lost for love, or of the higher orders of monks and saints who lived, as the Rule of Saint Francis says, as pilgrims and strangers in this world.

Notes

1. Ed. Mario Roques, Coll. Classiques français du moyen âge, Vols. 78, 79, 81, 85 and 88 (Paris). Subsequent references to the *Roman de Renart* will be taken from this edition.

2. A brief article by W. A. Tregenza, "The Relation of the Oldest Branch of the 'Roman de Renart'to the Tristan Poems,"*MLR,* XIX (1924), 301-05, confirms similarities noted by many critics.

3. Ed. Ernest Muret, 4th rev. ed. L. M. Defourques [Mario Roques and Lucien Foulet], Coll. Classiques fr. du moyen âge, Vol. 12. Subsequent references to Béroul will be taken from this edition, while those to Thomas will be from the edition by Bartina H. Wind, Coll. Textes litt. fr., Vol. 92 (Geneva-Paris, 1960), and those to the *Folies Tristan* from the edition by J. C. Payen, *Les Tristan en vers* (Paris, 1974).

4. Key ethnological and psychological studies of the trickster are to be found in Paul Radin, *The Trickster: A Study in American Indian Mythology* (New York: 1972), which also reprints Carl Jung's article, "On the Psychology of the Trickster Figure"(pp. 195-

211), and Karl Kerényi's "The Trickster in Relation to Greek Mythology" (pp. 173-91). See also Claude Lévi-Strauss, *Anthropologie structurale* (Paris, 1958), pp. 248-51, Norman O. Brown, *Hermes the Thief, The Evolution of a Myth* (Madison, 1947), and E. E. Evans-Pritchard, *The Zande Trickster* (Oxford, 1967).

5. The term hero, originally "demi-god,"having passed from mythologists in the early Renaissance to historians like Vico and Michelet, appears in literary criticism in the 19th century. The concept of the hero has been studied particularly by psychologists and mythologists like Joseph Campbell, *The Hero with a Thousand Faces* (Cleveland, 1962), Eric Neuman, *The Origins and History of Consciousness,* tr. R. F. C. Hull, Bollingen Series, Vol. 42 (New York, 1954), and by structuralists like Lévi-Strauss, V. Propp, in his *Morphology of the Folktale,* tr. Laurence Scott, 2nd rev. ed. by Louis A. Wagner (Austin, 1968), Lord Raglan, *The Hero, A Study in Tradition, Myth, and Drama* (New York, 1937). See the anthology *The Hero in Literature,* ed. Victor Brombert (New York, 1969) and the convenient summary of structuralist writings on narrative in Robert Scholes's *Structuralism in Literature* (New Haven, 1974), pp. 59 ff.

6. Johannes Dietrich Schleyer's valuable study, *Der Wortschatz von List und Betrug im Altfranzösischen und Altprovenzalischen,* Romanistische Versuche und Vorarbeiten, 10 (Bonn, 1961), convincingly documents the ambiguity of virtually every one of the more than 300 medieval French and Provencal words for trickery. Indeed, Schleyer's text is organized around his distinction between the positive and negative meanings of each word family, and his examples are drawn from both serious and light works. See also St. Thomas Aquinas, "De vitiis oppositis prudentiae quae habet similitudinem cum ipsa,"Quaes. 55, "De prudentia,"ed. Fr. Francisco Barbado Viejo in *Suma Teológica,* Coll: Biblioteca de Autores Cristianos (Madrid, 1956), VIII, 133-49, where the cardinal virtue *prudentia* is distinguished from worldly prudence (*prudentia mundi*) and also from *astucia, fraus* and *dolus.*

7. See Marie-Noëlle Lefay-Toury, "Ambiguité de l'idéologie et gratuité de l'écriture dans la branche I du *Roman de Renart,"Le Moyen Age,* LXXX (4e série, 29), No. 1 (1974), 89-100.

8. As in Béroul, vv. 3622-24, 3855. Recognition in the Oxford *Folie* is rendered difficult because it is tied to a series of testing motifs.

9. See Stephen G. Nichols, Jr., "Ethical Criticism and Medieval Literature: *Le Roman de Tristan,"in Medieval Secular Literature: Four Essays,* ed. Wm. Matthews (Berkeley and Los Angeles, 1965), 68-89.

10. The strongly eroticized death at the conclusion of Thomas' version suggests a supreme and final trick enabling the lovers to rejoin.

11. Especially Béroul, vv. 3853-58, 3913-80. See Johan Huizinga, *Homo Ludens, A Study of the Play Element in Culture* (Boston, 1960), p. 6.

12. Jean Frappier, in his "Structure et sens du *Tristan,* version commune, version courtoise"(*Cahiers de civilisation médiévale,* VI, Nos. 3-4 [1963], 255-80, 441-54), underlines what he calls the substantive value of narrative structure in Béroul following the meeting under the pine, to the flour, Tristan's leap, the lepers, life in the Morrois, the weakening of the potion, Ogrin, the return of Iseut and the ordeal. Frappier does not agree with LeGentil's view of Béroul's "art fragmentaire" ("La légende de Tristan vue par Béroul et Thomas,"*Romance Philology,* VII [1953], 111). But substantive value is not the equivalent of necessary sequence, since we see these same episodes presented in quite a different order by Gottfried von Strassburg who places the ordeal after the flour episode. In Gottfried, only after Tristan has returned from his victory over the hairy giant Urgan do the lovers set off for their love grotto, more in cool regret than in hot haste.

13. *Morphology of the Folktale,* pp. 53-55. See Scholes, *Structuralism* pp. 63-67.

14. See Peter Haidu's comments on the combination of linear narrative with "vertical non-narrative formal traits"in "Text, Pretextuality and Myth in the *Folie Tristan d'Oxford,"MLN,* LXXXVIII (1973), 712-17.

Paul Wackers (essay date 1981)

SOURCE: "The Use of Fables in *Reinaerts Historie,*" in *Third International Beast Epic, Fable, and Fabliau Colloquium,* edited by Jan Goossens and Timothy Sodmann, Böhlau Verlag, 1981, pp. 461-83.

[*In the following essay, Wacker defends the use of the fables found in* Reinaerts historie, *explaining how and why they effectively illustrate the author's message.*]

Reinaerts historie is one of the most influential Middle Dutch stories. In the Netherlands it was printed and reprinted until the second half of the nineteenth century. And indirectly it has been the source of William Caxton's **The History of Reynard the Fox** (1481) and of the Lübeck edition of *Reinke de vos* (1498). And thus, for more than four centuries, the principal version of the Reinaert story as it circulated in Northern Europe has been a more or less adapted version of *Reinaerts historie.* But in the histories of Dutch literature, *Reinaerts historie* has traditionally been described as worse than its forerunner and model *Van den vos reynaerde*[1]. This much is clear from the characterizations which have been applied to it: it has variously been accused of lacking the fresh note of epic poetry, of being pedantic ostentation and a feeble imitation, of displaying an irritating degree of anthropomorphism, and of being offensive, excessively bourgeois, schoolmasterish, wholly improbable, and without any artistic purpose[2].

Now it is not my intention to dispute the view that *Van den vos reynaerde* is the better story. What I would like to do is examine the question of whether the implicit conviction which emerges from the literary histories and textbooks—that is, that the author of *Reinaerts historie* couldn't write poetry—is justified. I shall try to do so by reference to some detailed research into the fables in the story. Five times the curious situation arises in which the principal figure, Reinaert, tells the court a fable. On four of these occasions the fable is complete with moral.

One of these fables is the famous fable of the frogs, which the author of *Reinaerts historie* has taken over more or less accurately from *Van den vos reynaerde*. The other four appear in the second part of *Reinaerts historie,* which is all the author's own work. Here we find Reinaert describing three articles of jewellery which he claims he sent to the king instead of the newly arrived head of Cuwaert. One of these jewels is a looking-glass whose frame is decorated with pictorial representations of fables, and it is these fables which Reinaert relates.

When people began to take a closer interest in *Reinaerts historie* in the last century, these inserted fables did not come in for a great deal of approbation. Muller, writing in his thesis, says for example[3]:

> Now as regards the interpolated stories and fables, it is remarkable that, as I have already observed above, only a few of them have anything to do with the main content, so that they fractionate and distract attention and break the unity in an exasperating manner. One has only to compare again part I, where nothing is inserted unless it is in direct connection with the main theme (even the fable of the frogs, which many regard as an insertion, is cleverly put to good use). By contrast, here the writer's intention, i.e. to deliver himself of these fables whatever the cost may be, is so apparent, and the thread which connects them to each other so thin, and the connection between the content and the rest so slight, that it all reveals to us an unskilled poet far inferior to that of part I.

This estimation ties up with the more general pronouncements to be found in the text-books. At the same time it is a pointer to the question to be discussed here: are the inserted fables really pure interpolations and do they have nothing to do with the main thread of the story, or do they illustrate that main thread by presenting the reader with important themes from the story in a different form? To find the answer to this question I shall compare the inserted fables, and in particular their morals, with the *Esopet*[4], a thirteenth-century Middle Dutch translation of a Romulus version of the fables of Aesop which served as a direct source for the wording of three of the five fables. In the one of the other two fables there are some correspondences between *Reinaerts historie* and the *Esopet* at the word level. The fifth fable does not appear in the *Esopet*[5].

So as to have material for comparison for all five fables, I have also drawn on the version of them which appears in the incunabulum *Dye hystorien ende fabulen van Esopus,* printed by Geraert Leeu in 1485[6].

The first fable in the story is that of the frogs who want a king, and are given one in the form of a stork which then proceeds to devour them. Here the author of *Reinaerts historie* follows his model in *Van den vos reynaerde* fairly closely[7].

Reinaert tells this fable to clarify his reasons for trying to break up the conspiracy against Nobel. Thus the fable serves as an *exemplum*. Now at first sight it seems as if the situation in the fable does not correspond to that at court. After all, unlike the frogs, the animals already have a king. They are not asking for one. In fact, however, Reinaert is passing veiled comment on the situation at court. The fable's phrasing is probably[8] borrowed from fable 25 in the *Esopet*[9], but in the use of words a number of new themes are introduced. The most important of these is the distinction between free and unfree. This is indicated by words like free, without domination, king, oppressed, violence, cruelty, free, unfree, fear, and king[10]. In the fable, this use of words is used to present King Stork unambiguously as a cruel tyrant.

A second theme is that very cruelty. In the *Esopet* all that is said about the king's behaviour is that he subdued them and bit them all to death[11]. In *Van den vos reynaerde* this becomes: 'who bit them to death and devoured them in every place where he found them, both in the water and in the field; wherever he found them in his power, he was always cruel towards them'[12]. Finally, the silly way the frogs asked for a king is emphasized[13].

These themes also describe the situation at court. Nobel is a tyrant who oppresses his subjects and, so to speak, 'devours' them. The story makes this clear in no uncertain manner. And just as the stupid frogs ask for a king, so the stupid animals at court swallow Nobel's behaviour with approval.

In *Reinaerts historie* the fable is related in a comparable manner. Here, however, the theme of unfreedom is given even greater emphasis, and to achieve this effect new sub-themes are added, in particular the king's high-handedness and the necessity for a people to be oppressed[14].

Reinaerts historie and *Van den vos reynaerde* correspond closely in their portrayal of the behaviour of Nobel (as King Stork), but in *Van den vos reynaerde* it can be attributed to chance or to Nobel's own personality, whereas in *Reinaerts historie* it is seen as a sort of 'law of nature'. All rulers act like this because they cannot do otherwise, so Nobel does too.

The meaning of the fable in the two versions of the Reinaert story is quite different from its meaning in the fable collections. In the *Esopet* the moral is, that he who rejects good deserves to end up in misery. In the incunabulum the subject of the moral is again the contrast between free and unfree, but there it is approached from the other side: freedom is more precious than gold or silver[15].

The first fable on the frame of the mirror describes the hatred felt by a horse towards a stag. In order to kill the stag, the horse enters into a compact with a man: together they will hunt the stag, the horse serving as the huntsman's mount. The stag manages to escape, but the horse has to remain a riding-animal against his will.

In this instance the correspondence between the phrasing in *Reinaerts historie* and that in the *Esopet* is extremely close[16]. However, there are two relevant differences. In *Reinaerts historie,* where the horse's hatred for the stag is being described we read: 'The horse thought he would bring the stag down, even if it brought woe upon himself'[17]. These lines, which do not appear in the *Esopet,* are a clear pointer to the end of the fable, where that is precisely what happens. The moral, which stresses the notion of this self-inflicted pain, is thereby given greater force.

The second difference lies in the way in which the horse tries to entice the man into joining in in the hunt. In *Reinaerts historie* the horse uses the word 'profit'—*baet*. This concept, which does not appear in the *Esopet,* is quite common in *Reinaerts historie,* since one of the story's themes is greed for material gains. I shall give clearer examples of this in a moment. I only draw attention to it here because it is an indication that the author of *Reinaerts historie* chooses his words carefully. Certain concepts recur repeatedly.

The moral in the *Esopet* is twofold: he who ends up in the trap which he sets for another deserves what he gets, and: a fool is he who starts something without knowing that he can complete it[18].

In *Reinaerts historie* the moral stresses twice over that no one can be more easily injured than he who had wanted to injure another[19]. Thus in its moral *Reinaerts historie* places the emphasis exclusively on the justly negative fate of the malevolent.

In the incunable the moral is that one should not surrender one's liberty in order to take revenge on another. Later one is bound to regret is, for liberty is a great good. This moral, then, links up with that of the frog fable in the incunable[20].

The second fable on the frame of the looking-glass concerns an ass and a dog. The ass is jealous of the attention which their master lavishes on the dog, while he, the ass, just has to work all day. He wants to be treated like the dog, so he starts behaving like the dog—jumping up against his master and licking him. The master calls for help and the ass is given a beating.

Here too the *Esopet* version was clearly the source for the version in *Reinaerts historie*[21]. Many verses are copied word for word or almost word for word, but the version in *Reinaerts historie* is somewhat more elaborate and the moral is quite different.

In *Reinaerts historie* the ass's jealousy, in particular, receives more detailed attention. Here, material aspects play an important part. In the *Esopet* version all the ass has to say is: 'I am better than the dog, I am master of many a trade. I work harder than they two, I carry, I fetch, I suffer'[22]. In *Reinaerts historie* this is expanded to this: 'But I am forced to work, to carry sacks, to run and pull. Five of him wouldn't be able to do in a year what I do in a week. Yet he sits by my master at table and gets all he desires of bones to gnaw, of greasy plates, and I get nothing but thistles, nettles and prickly teasels, and at night I have to lie on the ground without straw and without a place to rest'[23].

One particularly striking thing about the *Reinaerts historie* version is that the ass is so extravagant in his account of the work he does, whereas at the same time he says that he is forced to work, which puts him in a more negative light. The ass in the *Esopet* expresses himself in much more positive terms: he is capable of all sorts of things. One is also struck by the emphasis on food and comfort. This is all the more striking because this theme returns in the rounding-off of the story: after receiving a beating the ass goes back to his stall and again eats thistles, nettles and grass, for he is still an ass[24].

In both versions the story ends in more or less the same way. The moral which then follows is, in the *Esopet,* that there are many who strive after the position of another, usually because they think it is better. They do this out of jealousy[25]. In *Reinaerts historie* the moral is more verbosely worded. The ass remains an ass, begrudging another his good fortune even though he himself would be unable to make use of it if he had it. Even if he were to hold the position of the object of his jealousy, it would not become him. That is why it is best to leave the ass an ass—that is, to let him eat thistles and make him carry loads. There is nothing else he can do. Even if one were to pay him homage, he would continue in his old ways. Where asses come to power things seldom go well, for they take account of no one and seek only their own welfare. And yet at the moment, says Reinaert, they are acquiring more and more power. And that is what he deplores most of all[26].

In this way the moral is made much more specific and is applied to the power situation. Asses in power are greedy tyrants. Yet despite this they increasingly often rise to positions of leadership, even if, because of their greed, they cannot fill those positions properly. This moral links up with the fable of the frogs. Rulers are tyrants. The emphasis here is on the egotism of rulers. The idea that rulers are often upstart rogues is new.

In the telling of the story the incunabulum broadly follows the *Esopet* version, but the moral changes: you mustn't do things you aren't capable of or which are not appropriate to you, because that arouses anger towards you[27].

The third fable on the looking-glass is about a fox and a cat. They are seen together by a group of dogs. When the dogs attack them, the cat climbs a tree and the fox has to flee for his life.

This fable does not occur in the *Esopet*[28], but it is in the incunabulum. There are wide differences between the versions in the incunabulum and *Reinaerts historie*[29]. In the incunabulum the fox is the negative figure. He shows off his knowledge, says that he has a sack full of tricks, and is full of contempt for the cat, who says he has only one skill, and that is climbing trees. When the cat catches sight of the dogs, the fox firstly says that there is no reason to be afraid, but if the dogs go for them he intends to run. Then the cat climbs a tree and—not without some justification—mocks the fox, saying: 'Now let's see you open that bag of tricks—you're going to need them'. But the fox is caught and killed by the dogs. The moral is that wise men must not despise the simple, for sometimes people think they are wise when in fact they are very stupid[30].

The author of *Reinaerts historie*, of course, could not let Reinaert tell a fable like that, because then Reinaert himself, or at least his own species, would be the butt of the story, and that would be wholly contradictory to the rest of the narrative. So in *Reinaerts historie* it is the cat that is the villain. A curious feature is that Reinaert tells the tale as if it were a real event. The cat is Tybeert, and the fox is Reinaert's father. However, apart from this identification of the main characters, the tale is clearly of a fabulous nature.

In *Reinaerts historie* Reinaerts's father and Tybeert swear eternal allegiance to each other. Whatever they acquire they will always share and they will always come to one another's help. When the hunters and the hounds appear on the scene, Tybeert asks what they should do. By way of encouragement Reinaert's father then reminds him of the bag of good advice; together they are sure to pull through. But Tybeert leaves Reinaert's father in the lurch and climbs a tree, from the safety of which, moreover, he mocks him. Reinaert's father can only listen to the traitor and can't retaliate, for he has to take to his heels. There is a long and detailed description of the perils of the flight, and Reinaert's father only just manages to escape down a hole in the ground[31]. The moral is that there are many who break their promises if they can thereby realize their own desires[32].

Reinaert then adds a reflection on his own attitude towards Tybeert. It would be perfectly normal for him to hate Tybeert for such a piece of treachery, but he doesn't. He will forgive him, he says, for God's sake. But he hasn't forgotten it; Tybeert's suffering would not affect him, and he still feels angry, but that is the flesh, which contradicts reason and presents his unjust desires as just[33]. Here, then, Reinaert paints a black picture of Tybeert and at the same time makes himself out to be a religiously almost flawless being. In the moral of the fable he again expresses a pessimistic view of things: many people are egotists and are only out to realize their own desires. If this means that promises have to be broken, that is no problem.

The last fable relates the story of a wolf who gets a bone stuck in his throat. Tempted by the promise of a reward, a crane pulls it out. When he asks for his reward, the wolf tells him he has already had it: he has been allowed to put his head in the wolf's mouth and take it out again unharmed.

The versions of this fable in *Reinaerts historie* and the *Esopet* correspond in some lines, but the differences are much greater, and the version in *Reinaerts historie* is also longer[34].

The most striking differences occur at the beginning. The *Esopet* introduces the wolf gnawing at a bone. In *Reinaerts historie* he is described at length. He is someone who never did anything good of his own free will[35]. On a wild heath—that is, in an evil place—he finds the fleshless carcass of a horse. Because he is so hungry he eats the bones, but due to his voracity one bone sticks in his throat[36]. The wolf, in other words, is portrayed as an unpleasant and, specifically, greedy individual.

By contrast to the *Esopet*, he does not meet the crane immediately, but first calls on all sorts of learned people, none of whom, however, is able to help. It is possible that this is implicit criticism of scholarly learning, a theme which comes very clearly to the fore in several places in *Reinaerts historie*[37].

The rejection of the claim for a reward by the crane is reasonably similar in the two versions. In *Reinaerts historie* the wolf is again presented in a worse light: in the *Esopet* he calls the crane 'sir', in *Reinaerts historie* he calls him 'fool'. Peculiar to *Reinaerts historie*, too, is the fact that the wolf refers to the pain inflicted on him by the crane, which is all the more reason why he deserves a reward more than the crane. The reward is again referred to by the word *baet*, profit. The author of *Reinaerts historie* is consistent in his terminology.

The chief feature of the version in *Reinaerts historie*, then, is the negative picture painted of the wolf and the greater emphasis on material things.

At one point the crane calls the wolf Isegrim, so that here again the fable is put into some relationship with narrative reality, though to a much lesser extent than in the previous fable. Here Isegrim is denigrated, but in fact this would also have happened even if his name (which functions here more as a generic name than as a personal one) had not been used.

The moral is that this is how villains and rogues reward those who do them a service. Therefore, where they are allowed to wield power, right and honour perish[38]. So this moral again ties up with the moral of the fable of the ass and the dog. Those who are morally base ought not to be given power because their greed makes them look only after themselves and exploit other people. Despite this, they increasingly often reach high office.

There then follows a further moral which is much more general in nature and may equally well be seen as an observation referring to all the fables: many people who wish to harm others by exploiting their shortcomings would find those same shortcomings in themselves, only to a greater degree, if they examined themselves properly. Therefore it is justly said: he who wishes to criticize must himself be free of blame[39]. This pronouncement supports Reinaert's cause in the sense that he is advancing a moral argument against his opponents in order to make them withdraw their complaints. However, it also functions on a more general plane. So many people's lack of self-knowledge is the reason for their trying to harm others by taking advantage of their faults, while all the time they have the same faults to a far worse degree. One might regard this statement as an indication of the cause of the human badness illustrated in the four fables.

The morals in the *Esopet* and the incunable are identical in their content: it is not worth doing favours to ingrates and blackguards[40]. Here, in other words, the subject is approached from another angle. As a good man you mustn't help the wicked. This is a more optimistic moral than that of *Reinaerts historie,* where the argument starts from the wicked end. The implicit conviction there seems to be that you cannot avoid them.

To summarize briefly: the various different morals in the fables in *Reinaerts historie* amount to this: the implicit moral of the frog fable is that rulers are always tyrants and that their peoples are therefore oppressed and exploited. The moral of the fable of the stag and the horse is that jealousy is bad and that the jealous are rightly punished. The moral of the fable of the ass and the dog is that rogues and scoundrels frequently attain positions of power. They do not, however, deserve their elevated positions because they are exploiters and tyrants. Other people suffer under their high-handedness and their greed. The moral of the fable of the fox and the cat is that promises are not kept if breaking them is to the advantage of the promiser. The moral of the fable of the wolf and the crane is that scoundrels reward good with evil and therefore destroy things like right and honour when they come to power. Reinaert's closing remarks imply that many people have themselves the faults of others—which they criticize—to an even greater degree. Because they do not realize this they continue to try to exploit the others.

In the manner in which the fables are worded it is striking how much importance is attached to the acquisition of profit. This profit is principally of a material nature. Furthermore, the author has a tendency to exaggerate in his portrayal of badness. This is especially noticeable in the way he describes the ass and the wolf.

If we place the fables from *Reinaerts historie* alongside those from the *Esopet* and the incunabulum we find that in the last two—that is, in the Esopet and the incunabulum—the morals are far more general and far more varied: a larger number of different human failings are dealt with, but they are described in less detail. Moreover, the moral is not always negative: sometimes it contains instructions or advice on how one ought to behave. This last kind of moral does not appear in *Reinaerts historie.* Conversely, the strongly material orientation which is a feature of the fables in *Reinaerts historie* is absent from the two other works.

What this comparison has shown is that the author of *Reinaerts historie* took his source—whatever it may have been—and adapted it creatively. When he wrote his fables he had a clear aim before him. He paints an exceedingly pessimistic picture of the world. Human behaviour is determined by egotism, greed and materialism. Attention to spiritual values is absent. This also applies to the leaders of men, even if they are often described as parvenus or usurpers. That is precisely why the situation of the people is so bad: their rulers are the greatest egotists of them all.

Only the fable of the stag and the horse fails to conform wholly to this pattern. There a bad person is punished. On the other hand, things go wrong for the horse partly because in his jealousy he throws all caution to the winds. Now to Reinaert, stupidity is a despicable characteristic. Elsewhere in the story he makes clear that only the wise man, capable of bending circumstances to suit himself because he can oversee the situation, can make headway in this world[41]. The horse fails to appreciate the consequences of its actions and thus brings about its own downfall. The same is true, in fact, of the ass in the fable of the ass and the dog, though no attention is paid to this fact in the moral. Thus we find another theme of the story coming to the fore in the fables: only the wise can acquire an advantage. Reinaert himself is the living proof of the rightness of this idea.

In their content, then, we find that there is a clear link between the fables. However, to say that is not to dispose of Muller's contention that they were simply inserted into the story for no particular reason. So we are left with the question of how the author goes about interpolating them into the main narrative.

As regards the fable of the frogs, the answer will by now have become clear. It is an *exemplum,* which abstracts itself from concrete instances in order to provide greater insight through the medium of a more general plane. The use of *exempla* is a recognised technique in oratory. Moreover, as we have already seen, the fable of the frogs contains veiled criticism of the court, and of Nobel in particular.

The four other fables draw their unity from the fact that they are illustrations on the edge of a looking-glass. Now the mirror is a literary motif which recurs throughout the Middle Ages and can be traced back to the ideas of St. Augustine. In the tradition founded on his thinking, parts of reality are seen as a mirror. This image is often used for books (in particular, of course, for the Holy Scripture). One has to make use of these symbolic mirrors in order to gain insight into one's own situation: into what one is and what one ought to be. Thus the looking-glass points the way to the ideal and to God. To use a mirror to see the faults of others is to use it wrongly[42]. By the same token, the shape of the mirror is of no significance: what is important is the clarity of the glass, not its decoration. The author of *Die spiegel der sonden* puts it like this: 'The strength [of the mirror] lies in the glass, not in how it is worked. Even if a mirror were gilded at the edges, if the glass were dark and dull it would be wrongly praised'[43].

If we analyse the situation in the story from the angle of these ideas, we can draw some surprising conclusions. The young foxes and Reinaert himself have looked in the mirror. The fox cubs have looked at themselves (ll. 5893-8) and through the clarity of the glass Reinaert has been able to see everything happening up to a mile away, both among the animals and among men (ll. 5568-9). In other words, this is a very good mirror: you can see a lot in it. Its glass is so good, indeed, that anyone looking into it is cured of any eye disorder and thus acquires clear and unhindered vision (ll. 5771-6). This mirror thereby approaches closely the ideal mirror. Anyone looking into it acquires insight. It is easy to see the suggestion that he thereby comes closer to God, from whom the clarity of all mirrors flows[44].

But . . . at court Reinaert behaves in such a way that all attention is focused on the frame of the mirror. There, for the court, lies the mirror's strength: at least, that is what Reinaert says. The chance that the court will gain insight into what it is and what it ought to be, that it will find God, is thereby reduced virtually to nil. The court is blind and stays blind.

But the real point of the situation, of course, is that there *is* no looking-glass. Reinaert, after all, is lying about the jewellery. The real mirror is in Reinaert's words. They paint the disconcerting reality of a word ruled by egotism and greed, the reality of the court. In effect Reinaert is telling the court: you haven't the faintest idea of your own situation. That is why you won't change. You cannot see the reality which I describe to you. It will therefore continue to exist. And, as usual, Reinaert is right. At the end of the story, with the help of the qualities he demonstrates in the fables he has acquired the real power at the court. And in the epilogue the author expresses his conviction that things will inevitably always work out that way. At any court it is a matter of eating or being eaten, and that is why only one who combines ruthlessness with a superior insight into the situation, Reinaert that is, will always achieve power in the end.

I believe I have now demonstrated that the author of *Reinaerts historie* not only succeeds in attuning his fables to each other by their substance, and also to his intentions in writing the work as a whole, but also, by his use of the symbolism of the looking-glass, succeeds in presenting his fables structured within a clear framework.

Muller's view, that the fables were dragged in from just anywhere and were put in without there being any inner relation between them individually and between them and the story, does not, therefore, stand up to scrutiny. The au-thor of *Reinaerts historie* knew very well what he was doing when he added these fables. And we now know, better than Muller could have, that for a fourteenth-century writer it is no disgrace to borrow material from elsewhere. It was part of the job, just as long as it was done in the right way: that is, as long as the inserted material contributed to conveying the message the author had in mind. I hope I have shown that the author of *Reinaerts historie* meets this criterion.

In the light of this it also seems to me that the historians of Netherlandish literature have unjustly neglected the author of *Reinaerts historie*. A man who is capable of taking material as heterogeneous as these fables and shaping it in such a way that it fits into his story as if it had grown there, and, moreover, so that it is a continuing illustration of the chief themes of that story, such a man deserves attention. In other words, I would endorse Heeroma's plea, made some years ago now, for a reassessment of *Reinaerts historie*[45].

But Heeroma sees *Reinaerts historie*, like Goethe[46], as a humorous reflection on princes and regents, written by 'an ironic wise man who can put everything into perspective, including his own poem'[47]. But in the fables I have analy-sed here there is no question of irony or relativization, rather the contrary. And the spirit of the entire story, it seems to me, is in tune with that of the fables. To my mind *Reinaerts historie* illustrates better than any other Middle Dutch narrative the emptiness which medieval man must have felt between the fading of Gothic and the flowering of humanism. Nowhere else do we find so cynical and so hopeless a picture of the misdoings of those who wield power. It is my hope that this talk may to some extent have demonstrated the reliability of my view of things.

APPENDIX

The moral of the fable of the frogs Esopet, fables 25, ll. 13-14:

> Hets recht, die wederseget tgoede,
> Dat hi hebbe armoede.

It is just that he who rejects good should live in misery. *Incunabulum,* book 2, fable 1 (f. 38[R] - f. 38[V]):

> Die eerste fabule is vande*n* vorsschen en*de* van iupiter den afgod die / ons bewijst en*de* leert dat Gheen dinck en is beter. dan te leu*en* recht- / uaerdelijcken en*de* niet eyghen te wesen. want vriheyt is beter dan eenich si-luer ofte gout . . . want als men heuet datmen met re-den hebben sal soe salmen te vreden ende / blijde we-sen Ende die niet eyghen en is. die sal zyne vryheyt wel beware*n* Wa*nt* / gheen dinck en is beter dan vry te wesen ende niet eyghen te sijn Want voer al / le die werelt vol van goude. men vryheyt te recht niet coopen en soude.

The first fable is about the frogs and Jupiter, the idol, and it proves to us and teaches us that nothing is better than to live righteously and not to be unfree, for liberty is better than any silver or gold . . . for if one has what it becomes one to have, then one must be satisfied and happy. And he that is not unfree, he had better protect his liberty well, for nothing is better than to be free and not subject, for one might justly not purchase liberty for all the gold in the world.

The moral of the fable of the stag and the horse

Reinaerts historie, ll. 5679-83:

> Hoe mach een sijn gevangen bet
> Dan die om synen fellen nijt
> Hem selven so vaet dat men hem rijt?
> Sulc pijnt seer om eens anders scade
> Ende het loont hem selver almyt quade.

Who can be more easily trapped than he who on account of his fierce jealousy traps himself so that people ride on him? Such a one makes great efforts to harm another, and it rewards him with misery himself.

Esopet, fable 20, ll. 29-34:

> Die valt in sijns selfs net,
> Dat hi spredet ende set,
> Hine mochte geenszins varen bet
> Te sinen rechte, te siere wet.
> Hi es sot die daer begint vechten
> Daer hi hem niet en can verrechten.

He who falls into his own net which he spreads and sets, deserves in no way to fare any better. He is a fool that takes on something he cannot bring to a good conclusion.

Incunabulum, book 4, fable 9 (f. 63^R):

> Die neghende fabule is vanden paerde vanden iagher ende van dat hert. / die ons leert. Dat nyemant hem se-luen sal setten onder bedwanck te willen / sijn oft eyghen te wesen ouermits dat hij wrake van eenen an-deren hebben en*de* / vercrijghen mach. want het is veel beter dat hem een mensche niet eyghen en / maect dan dat als hij hem selven yemande eyghen heeft ghemaect namaels / berou daer af heeft alst te late is . . . Hier om en eest niet / goet dat hem yemant onder enen an-deren in eyghenscap stelt om hem alsoe te / wreeken ouer den ghenen daer hy haet ende nijt teghens heeft. want wie hem / seluen on*der* die heerscappie va*n* ee-nen anderen settet die verbint h*em* seluen onder / des ghenen ghebots. daer hi h*em* onder gheset en*de* ghes-tellet heeft

The ninth fable is about the horse, the hunter and the stag, and it teaches us that no one must go so far as to place himself in someone's power or subject himself to him be-cause he wishes to take revenge on someone else, for it is far better that a man should not make himself unfree than that, when he has subjected himself someone, he should afterwards regret it, when it is too late . . .

Therefore it is not good that someone should subject him-self to someone else in order thus to avenge himself against the one to whom he nurtures hatred and envy. For anyone who places himself in the power of another places himself at the behest of the one to whom he has subjected himself.

The moral of the fable of the ass and the dog

Reinaerts historie, ll. 5734-52:

> Ende bleeff een ezel als hi was,
> Die een anderen sijn welvaren vergan,
> Dat hem niet en cost nochtan.
> Ende al wair hi inden staet
> Des geens geluc dien hi haet,
> Het soude hem recht so wael vuegen
> Als myt lepelen teten der suegen.
> Dair om is die beste raet
> Datmen den ezel den ezel laet,
> Dijstel eten ende dragen den sack.
> Hy en can hem vuegen in geen gemac.
> Al deed men hem oec duechd en eer,
> Hy pleecht altijt sijn oude leer.
> Wair ezels crigen heerscappien,
> Dair siet ment selden wel dyen,
> Want si op nyement sien off roeken
> Dan hairs selfs bate zoeken.
> Nochtan rysen sy alle dage
> In machten, dits dat ic meest clage.

. . . and remained as ass, as he was, who begrudged an-other his good fortune, which was not yet to be his. For even though he were in the same fortunate position as he whom he hated, it would become him just as well as it be-comes sows to eat with spoons. Therefore the best advice is to leave the ass an ass, to let him eat thistles and carry sacks. He cannot adapt to a pleasant situation. Even if one were to be good to him and pay tribute to him, he will al-ways carry on as he was. Where asses get power things seldom go well, for they pay attention to none, but only seek their own profit. Yet every day they acquire more power. This is what I complain of the most.

Esopet, fable 17, ll. 31-34:

> Aldus sijn vele liede, die prien
> Om eens anders heerscepien;
> Si hebben nijt, si hebbens sprake
> Dat iemen es met ghemake.

Thus there are many people who strive for the position of another. They are jealous, they object to someone doing well.

Incunabulum, book 1, fable 17 (f. 34^V - f. 35^V):

> Die seuenthyende fabule is vanden Ezel / ende va*n* een cleyn hondekijn. die ons leert / dat niemant en sal hem on*der*winden te doe*n* / dinghen die hie n*iet* doen en can oft he*m* n*iet* en voeghen . . . Ende daerom sal hem nyema*nt* on*der*winden te doe*n* din- / ghen die hi niet doen en can. want die onwijse die mishaghet altijt daer hi wa*e*nt / te behaghen en*de* te sijn verblijt

The seventeenth fable is about the ass and a little dog, and it teaches us that no one must try to do things that he can-not do or which do not become him . . .

And therefore no one must try to do things that he cannot do, for the fool always arouses antipathy when he fancies that he pleases and is being treated kindly.

The moral of the fable of the cat and the fox

Reinaerts historie, ll. 5812-14:

> Och hoe veel vijntmender noch
> Die luttel achten wat zij loven
> Op dat sy haers willen comen boven.

Oh, how many of them does one still find, that belittle what they promise if thereby they can bring their will to pass.

Incunabulum, 'appendix', fable 5 (f. 70^R - f. 70^V):

> Die vijfste fabule is vanden vos reynaerdt ende vander Catten. Men vint ve / le menschen die hem seluen zeer wijs ende subtijl vermeten te wesen die nochtans gro / te sotten ende dasaerts zijn . . . Ende daer om soe selen die wijse die simpe- / le niet mysprijsen. want die sommighe bywijlen hem vermeet te wesen zeer wijs / ende vroet. die nochtans zeer sot is ende gheen wijsheit en doet.

The fifth fable is about Reynaerdt the fox and the cat. One finds many people who regard themselves as very wise and clever, but who are nevertheless great sots and fools . . . And therefore the wise must not misprize the simple, for many a man sometimes thinks he is very wise and sensible, and all the while is very silly and acts unwisely.

The moral of the fable of the wolf and the crane Reinaerts historie, ll. 5872-75:

> Eens lonen scalcken ende knecht
> Den genen die hem ducht bewisen.
> Wair men den scalc laet risen
> So gaet te niet recht ende eer.

Thus do rogues and knaves reward those who do them favours. Where rogues are allowed to come to power, there right and honour do dissapear.

Esopet, fable 8, ll. 19-20:

> Dus mach hi winnen, die doet
> Den quaden ere ende goet.

Thus may he be rewarded who pays tribute and does favours to the wicked.

Incunabulum, book 1, fable 8 (f. 30^R - f. 30^V):

> Die achste fabule is vanden wolf ende vander craene Soe wie den / quaden ende onwetende doet eeneghe duecht. verliest sijn pijne ende sondighet oft misdoet seer . . . Ende aldus blijcket bij dese fabule dattet niet en profiteert / den bosen ende den ondancbaeren duecht oft goet te doene Mer het is een dinc / dat alder meest verloren is

The eighth fable is about the wolf and the crane. He who does the wicked any favour, even if unwittingly, wastes his pains and sins or acts very wrongly . . . And so it is clear from this fable that is does not profit one to do the wicked and ungrateful any favour or good. On the contrary, it is something that is always quite wasted.

Closing moral in Reinaerts historie, ll. 5876-81:

> Het is mennich die enen anderen zeer
> Wil doen ende sijn gebrec verswaren,
> Mer soude hi hem selven claren
> Te grond, hi souds meer aen hem vijnden.
> Dair om seit men, en tis waer:
> Wie scelden wil sel wesen claer.

There is many a man who will do another harm and make his failings worse, but if he were to look into the depth of his heart he would find them even more in himself. Therefore it is said, and it is true: he who will scold must himself be free of blame.

Notes

1. A diplomatic edition of the texts is: W. Gs. Hellinga, *Van den vos reynaerde. I Teksten, diplomatisch uitgegeven naar de bronnen voor het jaar 1500* (Zwolle 1952). I quote *Van den vos reynaerde* from the critical edition: D. C. Tinbergen and L. M. Van Dis, *Van den vos reynaerde* 20e druk (Groningen 1972). Quotations from *Reinaerts historie* are from the working text of a new critical edition at present in preparation (by myself). In both critical editions the verse numbering is identical to that of the Hellinga edition.

2. Cf. K. Heeroma, *De andere Reinaert* (Den Haag 1970), p. 119.

3. Jacob Wijbrand Muller, *De oude en de jonge bewerking van den Reinaert* (thesis, Leiden: Amsterdam 1884), p. 166.

4. The edition I have used is: Garmt Stuiveling (ed.), *Esopet*. Facsimileuitgave naar het enig bewaard gebleven handschrift. 2 vols. (Amsterdam 1965).

5. The correspondences and differences in the different versions of the fables can, according to Muller (pp. 153-5; see n. 3 above), be explained in two ways: by assuming that the author of *Reinaerts historie* used both the *Esopet* in the version which we know today, and a Latin Romulus text, or by assuming that he had another Middle Dutch *Esopet,* not known to us today, which contained all the fables used by him. Muller considers the second explanation the more likely.

6. See: *Gesamtkatalog der Wiegendrucke*. Hrsg. von der Kommission für den Gesamtkatalog der Wiegendrucke (Leipzig 1925-40), Band I, col. 169. no. 374.

I am grateful to the Museum Meermanno-Westreenianum for their kindness in making available to me a microfilm of their copy of the incunabulum.

Geraert Leeu also printed *Reinaerts historie* twice: in 1479 at Gouda, in prose, and in 1487 at Antwerp, in verse.

7. Tinbergen, pp. 172-3, ll. 2299-2322; *Reinaerts histo-rie,* ll. 2327-49.

Studies of the function of the fable in *Van den vos reynaerde* are therefore also useful. I have drawn on: G.-H. Arendt, *Die satirische Struktur des mittelnied-erländischen Tierepos 'Van den vos reynaerde'* (Köln 1965; thesis), pp. 274-8; and on K. Heeroma, *Rein-aert en Esopet,* in: Tijdschrift voor Nederlandse Taal-en Letterkunde 88 (1972), pp. 236-51.

8. Arendt (see n. 7 above), p. 276, considers direct bor-rowing unlikely, but Heeroma (see n. 7 above) has made a case for it.

9. Stuiveling vol. II, p. 31.

10. *vri* (l. 2299), *sonder bedwanc* (l. 2301), *coninc, dwonghe* (l. 2305), *ghewelt* (l. 2314), *onghenade* (l. 2315), *vri* (l. 2318), *eighin* (l. 2320), *vare* (l. 2321), *coninc* (l. 2322).

11. Stuiveling vol II, p. 31, l. 9: *Diese dwanc ende al verbeet.*

12. Tinbergen, p. 173, ll. 2311-15: *Diese verbeet ende verslant / In allen landen daer hise vant, / Beede in water ende in velt, / Daer hise vant in sine ghewelt, / Hi dede hem emmer onghenade.*

13. Tinbergen, p. 172-73, l. 2303 *groot ghecrai,* 1.2307 *Met groten ghecraie, met groten ghelude.*

14. See esp. ll. 2332-34: *enen heer / Diese bedwonge na sijnre geer. / Want ten dooch geen meent sonder dwanck.*

15. Stuiveling vol. II, p. 31, ll. 13-14; incunabulum: 2nd book, 1st fable. The text is given in the appendix.

16. See Stuiveling vol. II, pp. 25-26; *Reinaerts historie,* ll. 5643-83.

17. ll. 5651-52: *Hem dochte het soude hem neder vellen / Al sout hem dair om raden we.*

18. Stuiveling vol. II, p. 26, ll. 31-34. The text is given in the appendix.

19. *Reinaerts historie,* ll. 5679-83. The text is given in the appendix.

20. Incunabulum: 4th book, 9th fable. The text is given in the appendix.

21. Stuiveling vol. II, p. 21; *Reinaerts historie* ll. 5684-5752.

22. Stuiveling vol. II, p. 21, ll. 11-14: *Ic ben beter dan die hont, / Menech ambacht es mi cont, / Ic doe meer pinen dan si twee, / Ic draghe, ic hale, ic hebbe wee.*

23. *Reinaerts historie,* ll. 5698-5709: *Mer my die men ten orber dwinct, / Die sacken te dragen, te lopen, te driven. / Hy en soude niet myt hem vyven / Den ar-beit doen in enen jaer, / Die ic in eenre weeck vol-vaer. / Nochtan sit hi by mynen heer / Ter tafel ende crijcht al sijn begeer / Van been te cluven, van vetten telyuren. / Ende my mach anders niet gebueren / Dan dijstel. netel ende scerpe kaerden / Ende des nachs te leggen op die aerde / Sonder stro ende sonder letier.*

24. *Reinaerts historie,* ll. 5731-34: *Doe liep hi weder op synen stal / Ende at dijstel end had ongeval, / Netel, kaerden ende gras / Ende bleef een ezel als hi was.* See also l. 5743: *Dijstel eten ende dragen den sack.*

25. Stuiveling vol. II, p. 22, ll. 31-34. The text is given in the appendix.

26. *Reinaerts historie,* ll. 5734-52. The text is given in the appendix.

27. Incunabulum: first book, 17th fable. The text is given in the appendix.

28. It does however appear in three Latin Romulus ver-sions. See L. Hervieux, *Les fabulistes latins,* tome II (Paris 1894), pp. 277-8, 551, 644-5.

29. *Reinaerts historie,* ll. 5753-5830; incunabulum: 'appendix'after the 4th book, 5th fable.

30. The text is given in the appendix.

31. *Reinaerts historie,* ll. 5798-5809.

32. *Reinaerts historie,* ll. 5812-14. The text is given in the appendix.

33. *Reinaerts historie,* ll. 5828-30: *Doch dat is dat vley-sch / Dat dicke op reden vecht / En doer wil gaen voer recht*

34. Stuiveling vol. II, p. 11; *Reinaerts historie,* ll. 5831-81.

35. l. 5832: *Die sijns dancks nye goet en dede.*

36. *Reinaerts historie,* ll. 5836-41: *Doe ghinc hi biten grote beten / Aen die beenre, die hi in swalch / Drie, vier tevens in sijn balch, / Want hi had den honger groot. / So gierich was hi dat hem scoot / Een been dwars in sijn keel.*

37. See for instance *Reinaerts historie,* ll. 3990-4096.

38. *Reinaerts historie,* ll. 5872-75. The text is given in the appendix.

39. *Reinaerts historie,* ll. 5876-81. The text is given in the appendix.

40. Stuiveling vol. II, p. 11, ll. 19-20; incunabulum, first book, 8th fable. The text is given in the appendix.

41. *Reinaerts historie,* ll. 4168-4265.

42. See: Ritamary Bradley, *Backgrounds of the title speculum in medieval literature,* in: Speculum 29 (1954), pp. 100-15.

The use of mirror-symbolism was suggested to me by prof. dr. H. W. J. Vekeman.

43. *Die spiegel der sonden* vanwege de maatschappij der Nederlandsche letterkunde uitgegeven door J. Ver-dam. Eerste deel, de berijmde tekst naar het Mun-stersche handschrift (Leiden, 1900), ll. 16896-900: *Want int glas leghet die cracht, / Niet an dat daer is ghewracht. / Al ware een spieghel vergult omtrent, / Ware dat glas doncker ende blent, / Tonrechte soude hi geprijst wesen.*

44. *Die spiegel der sonden,* l. 16911: *daer aller spiegels claerheit uut spruut.*

45. Heeroma (see n. 2 above), pp. 115-51.

46. Goethe's *Reineke Fuchs* is a re-versification of an adaptation of an adaptation of *Reinaerts historie*.

47. Heeroma (see n. 2 above), p. 122.

H. J. Blackham (essay date 1985)

SOURCE: "*Renart* to *Volpone*"in *The Fable as Literature*, The Athlone Press, 1985, pp. 33-84.

[*In the following excerpt, Blackham provides an overview of the* Roman de Renart, *including its origins, themes, and influences.*]

(I)

Although a masterpiece of medieval French literature with an influence throughout Europe for more than four centuries, *Le Roman de Renart* is not a single work by one author. As J.J. Jusserand described it at the end of the last century, 'It was built up, part after part, during several centuries . . . like a cathedral, each author adding a wing, a tower, a belfry, a steeple . . .'I risked likening the great Indian fables to opera in some aspects, and with the same looseness might liken *Renart* in some respects to jazz; not mainly in its popular appeal, but structurally in its improvisations, its continuations and repeats, its co-operation and virtuosities, even its differences of mood. Before the French performances broke off, the play was taken up by other hands in other lands, returning to the classical structure of a single work with a beginning, middle, and end.

Inspired by the Aesopic fables, and using these fables freely in its making, *Le Roman de Renart* is obviously not itself an Aesopic fable. Described as a 'beast-epic', whether it is itself a kind of fable, or is a parody of heroic poetry, or an allegory, or something else is hardly a profitable question, since in the long run it is all these and not consistently anything. It originated in fable, and it contributed through its popularity and versatility to the literary value and resources of fable. What distinguishes the work is not characteristic of fable—the creation of Renart as a literary figure, a 'character' as familiar as Mr Pickwick in his day, who walked out of the pages that brought him to life into the sun. Emerging as an amusing rogue, entertaining the world with ingenious tricks played upon Isengrim, his compère, and others, and by even more ingenious escapes from the consequences of his audacities, Aesop's fox becomes Renart, the comic hero of beguiling guile, who in later sequels, when his outrages trail death and desolation, achieves an apotheosis as the devil of the Bestiaries, symbol in particular of that aspect of evil with which the Middle Ages were most preoccupied, the hypocrisy which infected the Church, like the double-think feared as a modern manifestation of a righteous order imposed upon the world. The literary acclaim of this creation of French genius is perpetuated in the word 'renard'in

French dictionaries, a proper name that has superseded 'goupil', which was the word for the anonymous animal imported from the fields and woods.

The twenty-eight 'Branches'of **Renart** cannot be integrated into one poem. (There really is no 'cathedral'.) Study of the work has to follow an attempt to piece it together chronologically in order to see how it developed, what individual contributions were made by the score of poets who took it up, and the changes in tone and intention that occurred.

How it all began has been a matter of controversy, in the main between those who wanted to find the roots in folklore and oral tradition, whether immemorial or contemporary, and those who found it evident that the source is bookish and clerkly, in the Latin collections of fables derived from Greece and Rome that were in the schools and in clerical hands. In particular there was a long satirical Latin poem, *Ysengrimus,* composed about 1149 by a Flemish cleric, Nivard de Gand, in which the dominant theme of **Renart** was already broached—an implacable conflict between Renart and Isengrim, the Fox and the Wolf, who enter on their literary careers with these proper names. Some close parallels between parts of **Renart** and *Ysengrimus* indicate the earlier poem as chief source and inspiration. Contemporary poets (Chrétien de Troyes, Marie de France) and the Arthurian cycle of romances were encouragement not only as objects of parody but also as models of narrative scale and tempo. King Arthur and his knights, Louis VII and his feudal nobility, Noble the Lion and the animal seigneurs of his court, Aesop's lion and the beasts he rules and injures, are variations of one pattern. The court of Noble makes the *mise en scène* of **Renart,** where the action starts or to which it returns; and behind it is the feudal order of Christendom, which provides whatever organizing principle there is in the ramifications of the stories. This is the framework of parody and satire, containing a family of familiar personages of whom first and last is Renart, with Isengrim his foil, his compère and his enemy, and with Noble, his suzerain and his dupe. Although satirical, even outrageous in the burlesque of liturgical rites, the twenty-eight Branches contain nothing subversive, no attack upon the institutions. The *trouvères* belong to the establishment and share the contempt of their class for the people, including the parish clery who come from and belong to the people. There is nothing bourgeois, still less populist, about **Renart,** however popular, until the appearance later of independent polemical works based upon it. The stories show the class prejudices and assumptions that still show in Froissart, although perhaps some boredom with the ethos and the literature of chivalry. When Renart describes to Noble with relish his degrading treatment of a *vilein* asleep under an elm, he provokes the remark from Noble:

> Je n'ai mis vilain tant chier,
> Autant ameroie a touchier
> A un ort vessel de ma main
> Comme je feroie a vilain.

(XVI, 1183-6)

(I don't count a villein of much worth, I would as soon touch a dirty pot with my hand as I would a villein.)

Although it is very clear that the framework and temper of *Renart* are bookish and feudal and that the source is Aesopic, the content of some of the stories is drawn from folk-tales. Thus Branch III has the story of the fox who lies in the road shamming dead, to be picked up by a carter and thrown on a wagonload of fish. The fox then throws out the fishes, and jumps off. Later, he tricks the wolf into fishing by dropping his tail in the water and holding it there, until it freezes into the pond. The story, with some of the same elaborations, is to be found among Ukrainian folk-tales (*Ukrainian Folk Tales,* selected and translated by Anatole Bilenko; Kiev, 1974).

The twenty-eight Branches of *Renart* were composed between 1174 and about 1250. They were followed by continuations markedly different in tenor and intention, until the end of the fourteenth century. As a pendant some hundred years later, Guillaume Tardif, professor at the Collège de Navarre, translated for Charles VIII the Latin fables of Laurent Valla in what were in effect new versions that recovered the authentic *Renart.* After that, there is scarcely a reference to *Renart* in French literature.

(II)

The original tales composed in the last quarter of the twelfth century created the dramatis personae and some of the action out of Aesopic material. The lion's court was there (Perry, 285; 585). The lion was acknowledged king of the beasts (*Babrius,* 102, 103, 106; *Phaedrus* IV, 14). The fox was linked with the lion, in out-smarting him or in some kind of partnership (Perry, 394, 258, 416, 585; *Babrius,* 103). The fox was notorious for his ruses, and already there was the rivalry and enmity between fox and wolf, or identity in different versions of a few fables. In short, there was linked material in Aesop's fables, and actual episodes, for adoption and adaptation and further invention, whether in *Ysengrimus* or the *Renart* sequence. With this material, in a setting that reflected the feudal scene—with a courtly literature to be parodied structurally by the device of setting this material in this scene—there were the ingredients to hand for the first comic mix. Aesop's fox, like Napoleon, already knew how to make tools of others, including the royal beast, by manipulating their greed, vanity, fears, as well as by his own rhetorical art of making the worse seem the better case. Some of the fables are woven into the narrative incidentally for their episodic and cumulative effect, adding to the tale of Renart's villainous mischiefs, triumphant or baffled, multiplying Isengrim's misfortunes and grievances. The old apologues which thus reappear in this context disappear like candles in daylight, having no application, general or particular. In this they are unlike the constantly occurring fables in an Indian context, where the fable, however forced, is always a literary ritual introduced to further some matter in the course of the main narrative. Here in *Renart* fables are remade with their sequels to make the fabric of the tale, and

unless the tale is itself a fable, there is no fable any more. What does emerge, apart from parody, is at first a playful satire on the behaviour of men and women in the institutions of their time and in domestic scenes: their cupidities, lusts, deceits, revenges, whims, predicaments, frights; their relationships and solidarities, temporary or enduring; above all, their hypocrisies. Thus in the early Branches of *Renart* are developed the public features of a resourceful and subtle fiction, which is too deadly not to be seized and used in personal and partisan causes, in several serious and powerful fables that transcend the original Aesopic material and turn to profit the success achieved in the first phase of *Renart.* If the Aesopic fable disappears as a fable when it appears in the context of *Renart,* in turn when it reappears later as an apologue again the narrative is longer and richer—as most notably in Chaucer's version of the Cock and Fox. Conversely, when *Renart* offers a later fabulist material for his purpose, it is stripped for that purpose of its narrative complications and circumstantial detail—as Odo of Cheriton simplifies the *Renart* story of Renart and Isengrim in the well (IV).

(III)

The burlesque note is struck at the outset, at the beginning of Branche 2, which is chronologically first:

> Seigneurs, oi avez maint conte
> Que maint conterre vous raconte,
> Comment Paris ravi Elaine,
> Le mal qu'il en ot et la paine;
> De Tristan qui la Chievre fist,
> Qui assez bellement en dist
> Et fabliaus et chancon de geste.
> Romanz de lui et de sa geste
> Maint autre conte par la terre.
> Mais onques n'oistes la guerre,
> Qui tant fu dure de grant fin,
> Entre Renart et Ysengrin,
> Qui moult dura et moult fu dure.

(Lords, you have heard many tales which many story-tellers have told you, How Paris carried off Helen, the ill which he had of it and the punishment; of Tristan who caused *Chevrefeuille* [Marie de France], and who fares so nobly in common report and in *fabliaux* and *chansons de geste.* Of him and of his exploits stories abound. But never have you heard of the war which was so hard and great a conflict, between Renart and Ysengrin, which lasted long and was very bitter.)

There follow the familiar episodes of Renart with Chantecler, with Tibert the cat, and with Tiecelin the crow. He is then close upon his most notorious exploit, the violation of Hersens in the full view of Ysengrim her husband, described circumstantially as a piece of animal behaviour; thematically, a piece of malice that sticks, a wound that becomes a running sore—and a parody of the infidelities of romance.

The matter of the Branches is varied, from Renart's fast ones in the manner of a trickster in a folk tale (III), to parody of a jongleur's indecent *fabliau* (Ib), or to planned episodes of break and enter, with no honour among thieves (XIV, XVI), or to set pieces at Noble's court. The same characters pass from animals in a folk-tale to propertied seigneurs and ecclesiastics, of set and deft purpose. Of the regular appearances (and non-appearances) of Renart at court to answer charges occasioned by his outrages, the one that issues in his single combat with Isengrim is the most dramatic, and is a detailed burlesque of feudal protocol.

After everyone with a grievance has laid his complaint against Renart, Isengrim sums up his own:

> En un des plus lons jors d'este
> N'auroie je pas reconte
> Les mals, les anuis que m'as fes.
>
> (VI, 769)

(During one of the longest days of summer I should not be able to recount the wrongs and hurts you have done me.)

But it is vengeance rather than justice for which he thirsts, and he challenges Renart to the test of arms. Noble allows the challenge, hostages are taken from both sides and a day is appointed for the meeting. When the court reassembles for this public event, the contestants refuse appeals for reconciliation and neither will modify his position. An oath is administered to each: Renart denies the acts with which he is charged and reaffirms complete innocence; Isengrim maintains that Renart is perjured and he himself is in good faith. In detail, all the procedures are duly completed, the behaviour of the supporters of both parties is described and the fight, with shields and weapons, begins. The combat is long and grievous, accompanied by verbal exchanges between the combatants. At one point Renart taunts his adversary, galling him with the thought that many of the spectators will be amused to see them made to work like this to mollify him for his wife's amour. Isengrim breaks out in a bitter cry, eight lines summed up in:

> Par famme est plus guerre que pais,
> Par famme sont honis maint homme,
> De touz les maus est fame somme.
>
> (VI, 1284-6)

(Women bring more war than peace,
Women bring shame to many men,
Women are the sum of all evils.)

Isengrim is partially disabled as the fight goes on, but his superior strength is too much for Renart, whose ruses do not prevail. The end comes with a collapse of Renart's morale when in his extremity, aware of his perjury, conscience takes sides against him. He is beaten to the ground, and left for dead. Isengrim and his party celebrate their triumph. But Renart is not dead, and the outcome of the trial by combat condemns him: he must be hanged. He repents, to save his skin, and by the intervention of his friends and the partiality of Noble he is allowed to seek absolution and to become a monk. Of course this does not last long,

and all is as before. In all these earlier Branches Renart is often defeated, humiliated, punished, and here frightened to death, always resilient. This is in contrast with the later Renart in whom resilience has hardened into a tough mastery of this world worthy of the devil.

The issue of the combat is different in the later Dutch version of **Renart,** translated by Caxton. Renart's ruse does prevail, and by victory he wins friends and influences the great. He is taken by Noble as his chief counsellor, despite his treachery of which Noble has had bitter experience. This shows the indispensability of 'renardie' for worldly success, the keynote of the later versions and adaptations. The other main variant in the Dutch version is the careful preparation—mental, moral, and physical—of Renart for the fight by the she-ape his aunt. They are to fight with teeth and claws, and he is shaved and oiled, to be made as slippery to the touch as he has been elusive to his victims and enemies. The difference in the versions illustrates the evolution in the story from Renart as folk-hero in burlesque of the knights of chivalry to Renart as cynical Lord of Misrule outside the licensed revel, infiltrating Christendom with 'renardie'—as it were, from a university rag to the urban gangster.

Branche XVII narrates the death and funeral of Renart. He is taken ill, his relatives are summoned, he dies. There is a state funeral, with an elaborate burlesque of the office. Bernart, the archpriest, delivers a funeral oration in which the deceased is lauded with the usual bland falsehoods, carried to absurdity: he has lived the life of an apostle and martyr:

> Que de lui ne sui en dotance
> Qu'il ne soit en bonne fin pris.
> Onques ne fut Renart repris
> Nul jour a nule vilanie.
> Il a este sanz felonnie
> Et sanz malice et sanz orgueil.
> Onques jour ne virent my oeil
> Prince qui fust de sa vertu.

(I am in no doubt that he has ended a good life.
Never at any time was Renart found in any villainy.
He has been without crime and without malice and without pride.
At no time would be seen a prince of his virtue.)

A prayer for the deceased follows, in which to the absurdity of his superhuman virtues is added the incongruity of reference to his life and work as a fox:

> En maint peril vous estes mis
> En bois, en forest et en plain
> Pur avoir vostre vantre plain,
> Et pour porter a Hermeline
> Vostre fame coc ou geline,
> Chapon ou oe ou cras oison.

(You were put in many perils, in wood, in forest, and in open field, in order to fill your belly, and to bring home to your wife Hermeline a cock or fowl, a capon or goose or plump bird.)

After this bathos comes the interment by Brun. At the conclusion of the archpriest's benediction, Renart pushes up the lid of the coffin and escapes. Noble is furious. The barons, Chantecler in the van, give chase. Renart is caught between a dog which a vilein has loosed on him and the pursuing court. Chantecler is near, and Renart appeals for help. The upshot is that Chantecler is mounted on Renart's back, and tears him with beak and claws. He is left for dead in a ditch, deserted by everyone. His family carry him home, and his friends demonstrate his death to Noble by annexing a fresh open grave.

Although Renart lives to fight another day as usual, this is the end in 1205 of the **Renart** created by Pierre de Saint-Cloud and his successors. The nine numbered Branches that remain differ in spirit and in manner and in themes, and Isengrim is the central figure in several. 'Les semailles, ou le labourage en commun' (XXII) stands apart as an independent fable. The composition of these last Branches goes on till the mid-thirteenth century.

(IV)

In the second half of the century there were three independent satires based on **Renart**: *Renart le Bestourné* (1261), *Le Couronnement de Renart* (1263-70), *Renart le Nouvel* (1289). The first is a savage attack on the mendicant orders and their influence over Louis IX by the *trouvère* Rutebeuf, who was biased against the orders for personal reasons. The second, by an unknown author, is a political pamphlet in the allegorical form of a fable against the rising bourgeoisie. Renart conspires with Jacobins and Franciscans to overthrow and replace Noble. Money has taken over with the new rich, and can do or undo anything, save raise the dead. The reign of Renart—displacing the old virtues and values represented by Noble—is the rule of money, with the greed, pride, and double-dealing that go with that. The satire reflects the industrial revolution in the Netherlands which left the cities entirely in the hands of patricians enriched by trade.

In *Renart le Nouvel* by Jacquemart Gelée, the allegorical method is used for an attack on the corruption of the Church by the clergy, who have totally submitted to the rule and the arts of Renart. The chaotic poem ends with a tableau in which Renart, crowned, sits on top of Fortune's wheel, flanked by Pride and Guile, with his sons at the foot. He has been assured that the wheel will no longer turn, since he has destroyed Faith, Loyalty, Right, and Humility, and given all power to Pride and Duplicity. This is far removed from the world of **Le Roman de Renart.** At the same time, the allegorizing and moralizing are relieved by superbly comic episodes, involving the degradation of Noble and some of the most outrageous tricks of Renart, which recall the best of the earlier branches and of the *fabliaux.* This was the first of all the Renart tales to be printed in France.

The last and most curious independent work based on **Renart** was *Renart le Contrefait* by the Clerc de Troyes (1319-42). The author states what he and Renart have learned from experience: 'C'est l'art de Renart qui confère la Fortune et la réussite dans le monde; sans lui, tout savoir, toute connaissance des autres arts ne servent à rien. C'est l'art que doivent apprendre rois et comtes, empereurs et papes.'(It is Renart's art which brings Fortune and success in the world; without that, all wisdom, all knowledge of other arts are worth nothing. It is the art which kings and counts, emperors and popes ought to learn) Here, explicitly if ironically, is justification of the drift of so many of the Renart poems, in which, in spite of inexpiable crimes and unforgivable outrages, Renart is perforce restored to royal favour, and is made steward or chief counsellor. This seems to say that he is necessary to worldly wisdom and successful statecraft. Machiavelli said the same, in a treatise, but using the similitude offered by the fables. Of the way in which princes must keep faith, he wrote:

> A prince being thus obliged to know well how to act as a beast must imitate the fox and the lion, for the lion cannot protect himself from snares, and the fox cannot defend himself from wolves. One must therefore be a fox to recognize snares, and a lion to frighten wolves. Those who wish to be only lions do not understand this.
>
> *(The Prince,* ch. xviii)

To digest such 'reasons of State' has always been painful for moralists, and although in the **Renart** tales it is seen as corruption rather than statecraft, there is in the end recognition that there is no hope of success in managing the affairs of this world without 'renardie'. The solution has to be in transcendental terms, and the author of *Renart le Contrefait* engages in metaphysical discussion to try to resolve the problem of evil. But it is Noble advised by Renart who is the principal target, the absolute and arbitrary power of monarchy. This is the voice of the new bourgeoisie, in revolt against tyranny, and in defence of the oppressed and dispossessed poor. The author is no longer of the establishment, and this *Renart* is 'contrefait'.

(V)

Attempts to integrate the original **Roman de Renart** into a single self-contained and self-explanatory poem were made outside France, first in Alsace by Heinrich der Glichezaere at the end of the twelfth century with *Reinhart Fuchs,* and then in Flanders in the first half of the thirteenth century with *Reinaert de Vos,* by an author unknown. This version was in the next century remodelled with additions drawn from **Renart;** and it is this second version, *Reinaerts Historie,* which has been endlessly reproduced and translated and is the source of the survival of the Renart story today.

Reinaert de Vos was sharply satirical (it classed itself with hagiography, lives of the saints and martyrs), realistic in description, and subtle in portraiture. Noble is no longer the rather stupid, impulsive, and good-humoured feudal lord, with an obvious weakness for Renart the rascal; he is calculating, not easily deceived, and with the utmost distrust of Renart, whom he is anxious to get rid of. Renart is therefore driven to outwit an astute and watchful adversary, which he does by preying on the king's cupidity, at the same time dealing him a last insulting piece of malignancy before making his exit from the story, totally triumphant, leaving Noble and his peers to escape their guilt and slake their fury by seizing an innocent scapegoat. A Latin translation of the poem was one of the first books printed in Utrecht, about 1474.

Some hundred years later appeared the new version, *Reinaerts Historie,* in which the language is modernized and a sequel added. Renart does not quit the scene, but comes back to trial and once more outwits the king and his enemies, ending as the king's chosen counsellor, after his victory in single combat over Isengrim. It is the triumph of his influence: 'In any court where kings or lords assemble, when counsel is wanted, it is Renart who provides it'(verse 1425). That his gospel has thus been received has been made possible by submission of the clergy to his example.

Impressions of **Le Roman de Renart** gained by acquaintance with any of these vernacular versions of a complete poem will not be a fair impression of Branches I-XVII of the original, but the vitality of Renart forces its way through in all the productions inspired by the original. Even the later independent French poems mentioned above, so different in mood, method, and purpose, having hitched their wagons to **Renart** for its drawing power, had to keep the engine in good repair to make that use of it. Utility as much as literary respect served and saved the original; and in some cases contributed new wealth to the inheritance.

In review of these diverse **Renart** productions in verse and prose during some three centuries, there are two main things to be said. The original **Roman** composed of Aesopic materials was too loose and episodic to be itself a fable—as, conversely, other material may be used to make a fable. The original showed, however, that this was serio-comic fiction that could be used for a concentrated purpose; and it was adapted in the later independent French poems, in an allegorical form, for particular polemical attacks. In the final Dutch form the original is restructured to make what is a telling fable, profiting by the cumulative transformation of Renart to use the action as an image of 'renardie', general and permanent, the mark of a fable.

Works Cited

Bacon, Francis, *Works,* ed. R. Ellis and James Spedding, 7 vols, (1857-9)

Bilenko, Anatole, *Ukrainian Folk Tales* (Kiev, 1974)

Burns, C. Delisle, *The First Europe: a study of the establishment of medieval Christendom, AD 400-800* (1947)

Caxton, William, *The History of Reynard the Fox,* tr. from Dutch, ed. N.F. Blake (1970)

Fabliaux Anthologies: Reid, T.B.W. (1958); Johnston, R.C. and Owen, D.D.R. (1957); Bédier, Joseph, *Les Fabliaux:*

Études de littérature populaire et d'histoire littéraire du Moyen Age (Paris 1893; 5th edn, 1925)

Fletcher, Angus, *The Prophetic Moment: An essay on Spenser* (1971)

Fowler, Alastair, *Spenser and the Numbers of Time* (1964)

Flinn, John, *Le Roman de Renart dans la littérature française et dans les littératures étrangères au Moyen Age* (Paris, 1963)

Huizinga, J., *The Waning of the Middle Ages,* tr. F. Hopman (1924)

Isidore, Saint, *Etymologiae,* rec. W.M. Lindsay, 2 vols, (1910)

James, M.R., 'The Bestiary', *History,* xvi (April 1931) 61.

Jusserand, J.J., *A Literary History of the English People to the Renaissance* (1895)

Kean, P.M., *Chaucer and the Making of English Poetry,* vol. 2, *The Art of Narrative* (1972)

Ker, W.P., *English Literature: Medieval,* Home University Library (London, n.d.)

Kermode, Frank, (ed.) *The Tempest,* Arden edn (1954)

Keidel, G.C., *A Manual of Aesopic Fable Literature* (Baltimore, 1896)

Kieckhefer, Richard, *European Witch Trials* (1976)

Knowles, David, *The Evolution of Medieval Thought* (1962)

Kott, Jan, 'Prospero's Staff', *Shakespeare our Contemporary,* tr. Boleslaw Taborski (1965)

Lenaghan, R.T., *Caxton's Aesop,* ed. with Introduction and Notes (1967)

Lenmi, Charles W., *The Classical Deities in Bacon* (1933)

Lever, J.W., 'Shakespeare's Narrative Poems', *New Companion to Shakespeare Studies,* ed. K. Muir and S. Schoenbaum (1971)

Lydgate, John, *Minor Poems,* ed. H.N. MacCracken, 2 vols, Early English Text Society, Original series, 192; Extra series, 107.

Marie de France, *Fables,* sel. and ed. A. Ewert and R.C. Johnston (1942)

Migne, J.-P. (ed.) *Patrologiae cursus completus accurante,* series Latina No 117 (Paris, 1844-1904). Ignatius the Deacon's rendering in twelve-syllable tetrastichs of Aesop's fables (early 9th century)

Morris, R. (ed.), *An Old English Miscellany,* 49, Early English Text Society (1872)

Owst, G.R., *Literature and Pulpit in Medieval England* (1933)

Phillips, Margaret Mann, *The 'Adages' of Erasmus: A study with translations* (1964)

Reynolds, L.D. and Wilson, N.G., *Scribes and Scholars: A guide to the transmission of Greek and Latin literature* (1968)

Righter, Anne, Introduction to New Penguin edition of *The Tempest* (1968)

Rolle, Richard, 'The Nature of the Bee', *Fourteenth-Century Verse and Prose,* ed. K. Sisam (1921)

Ross, W.O., *Middle English Sermons,* Early English Text Society (1940)

Sidney, Sir Philip, *Apologie for Poetrie* (1595); ed. E. Arber (1905)

Waddell, Helen, (tr.), *Beasts and Saints* (1934)

Welter, M.J. Th., *L'exemplum dans la littérature religieuse et didactique du Moyen Age* (Paris, 1927)

White, T.H., *The Book of Beasts,* translated from a twelfth-century Latin Bestiary (1954)

Yates, Frances, *Astraea: The imperial theme in the sixteenth century* (1975)

Roger Bellon (essay date 1986)

SOURCE: "Trickery as an Element of the Character of Renart," in *Forum for Modern Language Studies*, Vol. 22, No. 1, 1986, pp. 34-52.

[*In the following essay, Bellon examines Renart's ability to innovate, his tactics, and the nature of his defense arguments.*]

If trickery is defined as a "means of obtaining from others that which cannot be obtained by force, work or right", it clearly emerges from the full text of the *Roman de Renart*[1] that trickery is vitally important to Renart, both as animal and man, for several reasons:

—to obtain food. Without trickery, a predator of Renart's size and strength would almost certainly die of hunger.

—to avenge himself.[2] His hereditary enemies all have a decisive advantage over him: Isengrin for example possesses the physical strength which Renart lacks, while Tibert can climb trees.

—to defend himself. At the Court, where he has been taken because of his earlier tricks, Renart can only escape a death sentence and execution by another trick.[3]

It should be noted that the Old French term *enging* has two senses: it is both a trick, wile or dodge, and in a more abstract sense an attitude of mind, a rule of conduct, and an approach to life. A detailed moral and intellectual portrait of Renart can therefore be drawn; in P. Jonin's study[4] Renart is described as cruel, knavish and perverse[5] from a moral viewpoint, but his intellectual qualities can be summed up in one word: Renart is a trickster. The distinction between moral and intellectual characteristics surely fades into insignificance when set against one essential truth: like other heroes of mediaeval literature, Renart possesses a *teche* (*l'enging*), and all Renart's other characteristics are subordinated to his innate and unfailing trickery. All the authors of the **RdR** agree on this matter, and all repeatedly emphasise this unchanging characteristic by means of a standard line with the same syntactical structure, in three variants:

> Renart, who is cunning,
> Renart, who is a master of tricks,
> Renart, who deceives everyone.[7]

However, the character of Renart is far from monolithic, restricted to a single trait of character[8] or caricatural. On the contrary, the character is fully rounded, with a psychological richness which is the product of his trickery. Trickery itself is not an attitude, but is rather the art of manipulating attitudes. Renart reveals himself as a lively, protean character by virtue of the inexhaustible resources of his trickery, which make him a multi-faceted character: Renart is not merely the instinctively motivated fox, but also (and often simultaneously) a thinking and talking human being. Indeed, is not the originality of the character of Renart precisely the consequence of this subtle and fundamentally important interplay between instinct and reflection? I will attempt to answer this question by examining in turn the three essential aspects of the character: Renart as the strategist who stages the trick, the actor who plays a part to deceive others, and the advocate who defends himself with all the resources of consummate rhetoric.

I. RENART THE STRATEGIST

When confronted by a crisis,[9] Renart's only weapon is his trickery. Many types of crisis can arise: situations resulting from an external event (an obstacle on the path leading to the satisfaction of hunger, or the presence of a physically superior opponent) or the consequences of tricks Renart has played on his opponents (Renart must accept responsibility for his tricks at the hour of reckoning). Whatever the nature of the crisis, Renart's only reaction is the use of *l'enging:* only *l'enging* can bring salvation, and he invariably tries to *s'estordre par enging* from the crisis he faces.[10] This is not to say that Renart, as fox and man, is enslaved to a single attitude: Renart can act on reflex, or can on the other hand reflect on the problem, before acting or adopting a waiting strategy. All this demonstrates that the essential feature of Renart's nature as a strategist is his remarkable ability to innovate, which again is the result of the combination of animal instinct and human intelligence.

At first, the fox's instinct[11] often takes over, causing Renart to take immediate action, so as not to compromise fatally the success of his manœuvre. In such cases, Renart simultaneously assesses the situation, devises the *enging* and puts it into practice. When he sees a potential prey, Renart's instinctive reaction is to hide, so as not to alarm the chosen victim:

3a, 4115 Renart i vint, outre s'en passe,
cheoir se laisse en une masse
por ce que les genz ne le voient.
18, 15632 Tapiz s'est desouz une espine
que il ne viaut estre veüz,
ne s'est crolez, ne s'est meüz
einz se tient coiz et si escoute.
XXVI, 35 Renars le vit, la teste abaisse,
a la terre cheoir se laisse.

But instinct can also cause Renart to adopt a more sophisticated approach: instead of hiding, Renart conceals the fact that he is still alive. This trick is familiar to fox hunters, and had already been recorded by the authors of the *Bestiaires:*

Quant preie volt cunquerre
met sei en ruge tere,
tuz s'i enpuldérat,
cume mort se girat.[12]

The author of branch 17 uses a familiar phrase to emphasise the speed of Renart's reaction:

17, 15136 Si tost conme Renart la voit,
ez le vos a terre estandu.[13]

On the other hand, when in branch III Renart acts instinctively to feign death, the aim is not to deceive another animal, but to dupe the men who are carrying food coveted by our starving hero:

III, 36 Quant vit la carete cargie
des anguiles et des lanproies
muçant fuiant parmi ces voies,
court au devant por aus deçoivre,
qu'il ne s'en puisent apercoivre
Lors s'est cochés enmi la voie.[14]

On other occasions animal instinct comes to the rescue not of the hungry fox but of Renart the baron, just as in common parlance we often say that a man acts instinctively. Two examples may be cited to show how in the case of Renart—a member both of the animal kingdom and of mankind—animal instinct can come to the assistance of man. At the end of the primitive trunk,[15] Renart realises that a trap has been set for him, and he is saved only by an instinctive action:

Va, 1141 Arier se tret . . .

At the end of branch 1a, Renart finds himself in another critical situation, and this time he begins by taking precautionary measures in the face of a worsening crisis:

1a, 2130 Sa feme en envoia arere
et sa mesnie et ses enfans.

As the nature of the danger becomes clearer, Renart the baron adopts the instinctive attitude of the fox, and takes flight:

2145 Et li rois si volt Renart prendre,
mes il ne le volt pas atendre,
ains s'en foï.[16]

Whether hiding, pretending to be dead, or running away, Renart's action is in each case guided by instinct.

As I have already emphasised, the originality and the indisputable psychological depth of the character of Renart are the result of the subtle and fundamentally important interplay of animal instinct and human intelligence, or *porpens.* I do not propose to analyse all the passages in which Renart *se porpanse,* but it is significant that the author of the first narrative in our corpus clearly shows how Renart combines instinct and intelligence. When confronted by an obstacle in the form of the fence of the *cortil,* Renart instinctively tries to remain unseen as he thoroughly inspects the surroundings with instinctive animal cautiousness, while at the same time reflecting on the situation. The dual nature of the character clearly emerges: the fox *mout coloie* (1.4100), whereas the man *porpanse soi* (1.4101). Reflection sometimes however contradicts instinctive impulses, and in such cases Renart must make a choice between instinctive action and considered conduct. In branch 7, the starving Renart[17] sees the object of his desire finally fall just in front of him:

7, 5646 Et li lechierres frit et art
et tout se frist de lecherie;

but Renart overcomes his instinctive impulse, for he has developed another strategy in the midst of the action. The author tells us only of the result of the fox's reflection:[18]

7, 5648 Mais n'en touche une seule mie,
car encor, s'il puet avenir,
vodra il Tiecelin tenir.

The interplay between instinct and reflection is even subtler at the start of branch 2. At first, Renart is torn between two fundamental instinctive tendencies: desire for food causes him to enter the barn of the *abaïe de blans moines,* but cautiousness then makes him turn back. At each stage, he reflects on the situation. Once inside, Renart assesses the risks involved in a "pseudomonologue au style indirect":[19]

2, 3357 . . . S'il püent aparcevoir
que il les voille decevoir
li moine retendront son gage
ou li meïmes en ostage.

Then, as he retreats, Renart is stopped by *porpens:*

2, 3370 Ist de la cort, entre en la voie
et se conmence a porpanser

and finally hunger outweighs instinctive cautiousness, even though the latter is reinforced by an accurate appraisal of the situation:

2, 3366 C'est veritez que mout se doute
qui bien set qu'il fait musardie.

However, there are other cases in which Renart is not torn between contradictory impulses, and in which on the contrary instinct and intelligence are harmoniously combined.

The most striking example of this complementarity is perhaps the one given at the start of branch 18. Renart's quest for food makes him head instinctively towards a *vile:*

> 18, 15540 Bien cuide qu'il i trovera
> chose qui li avra mestier.

After an initial inspection of the terrain, and after the identification of a more specific objective, certainty (the verb *panser*) replaces hypothesis (the verb *cuidier*):

> 18, 15599 Renart vint cele part le cors,
> qui bien pansoit, n'en dotez mie,
> que la maison iert bien garnie
> de ce dont il avoit mestier.

But Renart soon realises that the task is impossible:

> 18, 15614 Bien voit par anging ne par art
> n'i enterra.

Guided as much by instinct as by intelligence, Renart does not however concede defeat, and his perseverance is rewarded. He reverts to the most elementary form of vulpine cautiousness:

> 18, 15627 Par la s'en est entrez dedanz
> tot soef, . . .
> 18, 15632 Tapiz s'est desouz une espine.

Similarly, a little later in the same branch, the author again emphasises that Renart behaves like a fox while thinking like a human being, in order to overcome the herdsman:

> 18, 16418 Maintenant cele part s'en torne
> tout pas por pas, le col baissant;
> durement se va porpansant
> dedanz son cuer que il fera.

It is interesting to note in this respect that some of the authors seem to encourage readers to admire their hero's propensity for reflection and logical reasoning, as when the train of Renart's *porpens* is related in a long monologue, during which various possible responses to the crisis are explored. Passages of this type can be found in branch 1b (ll.2382-2390) and branch XVII (ll.1172-90).

In some crises, Renart decides to wait, after making a more or less rapid analysis of the situation. Waiting is not here the result of atony of instinct or mental paralysis in a hero rendered incapable of reaction, but is in fact a form of opportunism: he is awaiting a favourable opportunity to gain an advantage. Indeed, Renart the strategist is often worthy of the nickname *cunctator,* given by the Romans to one of their generals. The waiting strategy is based on a proverb quoted by Renart:

> 10, 11172 Mais bien atant qui par atant.[20]

Renart reserves his most subtle approach for dealing with Isengrin: he waits not in the hope of finding an opportune moment, but in order to wear down his adversary in a war of nerves. The strategy in this case is the psychological conditioning of the victim:

> 2, 3485 Que qu'Isengrin se dementoit,
> et Renart trestoz coiz estoit
> et le laissa assez huler.
> 12, 13152 Renart l'oï, bien le conut,
> mais de tot ce ne li fu rien,
> ainçois li a fait sorde oroille.

In both cases, when Renart finally speaks, he pretends not to recognise Isengrin, an attitude which is the logical culmination of the fox's waiting strategy.

Whether calling on animal instinct or human intelligence, and whether acting on reflex or after reflection (sometimes followed by a waiting strategy), Renart's character is never caricatural or stilted. On the contrary, Renart's trickery, the product of instinct and intelligence, is characterised by a remarkable flexibility of reaction to external stimuli, and an unfailing ability to adapt to environmental characteristics in the widest sense. After all, trickery is surely the art of always using available resources as effectively as possible in pursuit of a particular objective. A parallel may also be drawn with the fox's instinctive ability to blend into its surroundings, known to naturalists as homochromatism. On one occasion in the *RdR,* the author makes use of this characteristic in an almost absurd context: in branch XIII, Renart, pursued by hunters, escapes by concealing himself amongst the fox furs hanging in the hall of the chateau.

Renart also shows himself to be a master in the art of graduated response, calculated to allow for the strengths and weaknesses of his opponent. When dealing with Liétart, Renart shuns the frontal attack and prefers to blackmail him with the threat of denunciation (br.10, ll.11186-11187). Isengrin and Tibert are handled with similar skill: Renart makes no declaration of war, but instead speaks soothingly and deceitfully[21]

It is useful at this point to analyse more closely Renart's ability to improvise in a specific situation, when he receives the messengers sent to summon him to the Court. The situation remains identical in each case, but the messenger is different. As a result, the authors have an excellent opportunity to show Renart adopting a strategy which is appropriate to the personality of each messenger.

Twice in branch 1, Renart speaks to the messengers in the language of the senses. Renart begins by pitying Brun, who has been entrusted with an exhausting but unnecessary task (as Renart was in any case about to leave for the Court)[22] and then lectures him with a lengthy condemnation of the rich and the *parvenus.* Renart is trying to lull Brun into a false sense of security. Finally, Renart slips into the conversation the words he hopes will catch out the gluttonous bear, who immediately abandons his ambassador persona. The mission is forgotten as Brun poses a far from disinterested question:

> 1, 559 Renart, ce miel dont vos abonde?

The king's messenger soon becomes a mere beggar:

> 1, 562 Car m'en donez ore, biau sire,
> par le cuer bien, la moie coupe!

Brun's fate is now sealed. Renart's strategy has succeeded, and the rest is merely a matter of tactics, as Renart acts out his role. Tibert cautiously tries to tone down the terms of the message,[23] but inadvertently falls into the trap Renart has prepared for him. Exhausted by his mission, he asks spontaneously for something to eat:

> 1, 818 Avez vos ne coc ne geline
> ne chose c'on peüst mengier?

Renart's proposal is enough to make him naïve and careless, and he totally forgets the purpose of his mission:

> 1, 830 Et Tibert le sieut par derriere,
> qui n'i entent barat ne gile.

The combination of hunger and Renart's proposal have completely lowered Tibert's defences of cautiousness and vigilance.[24]

The author of branch 19 again adopts the convenient device of the triple embassy, but cannot of course merely duplicate the events of branch 1. The author and his hero must therefore use another approach when faced with the three messengers.[25] Roonel is a zealous and loyal messenger, and Renart realises immediately that his task will not be an easy one:

> 19, 17343 S'a veü venir Roonel;
> sachiez, ne li fu mie bel,
> que vers lui n'a mestier treslue.

Renart has sized up his opponent, and answers him in a most accommodating manner. Above all, he gives the reply which is expected of him. Renart answers the baron of unimpeachable fidelity with the credo of the loyal vassal:

> 19, 17386 Tot qant il commendera
> ferai sanz contredist de rien.

Renart decides to await developments: he leaves for the Court, but is determined to get rid of the messenger before they arrive. When he sees a trap, his instinct and intelligence combine to devise a suitable strategy:

> 19, 17427 Et vit le morsel en la corde,
> mais n'a talant que il i morde,
> einz jure qu'il i fera prandre
> son conpaignon, . . .

There is to be no escape for Roonel.[26] In branch XIII, Renart again speaks the language of the senses, but this time in a slightly different context. It is not Renart who must be summoned, but Chuflet, accused of crimes of a very precise nature. Tibert does not recognise Renart behind his black mask, and the fox can therefore revert to the stragegy used so successfully in branch 1. Renart responds to Tibert's blunt request[27] with feigned naïvety and then refined politeness:

> XIII, 1688 Se il ne vos torne a ennui,
> je vos voudroie ore proier,
> avoe moi venissies mangier
> en ma meson qu'est pres de ci.

So much politeness causes Tibert to lower his guard of cautiousness and forget himself. When he accepts, his fate too is sealed. The same strategy proves successful against Belin, the second messenger. Renart has only to offer Belin food (*il a jusqu'a la cort grant voie,* Renart adds innocently) and Belin—like Brun in branch 1—forgets his role as a messenger, and makes the fatal request which marks the failure of his mission.[28] In the last ambassadorial visit of the cycle,[29] Renart for the last time proves his talent as a strategist. With Grimbert's connivance, he devises the tomb substitution stratagem, and the cycle thus ends with the feigned death of the hero.

Throughout the cycle, from his first appearance until his "death", Renart proves his considerable strategic abilities. But once the stratagem has been devised, it must be put into practice. How can Brun, ensnared by his own gluttony, be led to the imaginary honey of Lenfroi? How can Roonel be imprisoned inside the supposed tomb of the saint? Here we discover another aspect of Renart's trickery, which is in fact an extension of the first.

II. RENART THE ACTOR

Renart's tactics[30] are almost always based on pretence or dissimulation by means of action or words. It is impossible to dissociate the verbal and gestural fields; words and actions are intimately linked (as in acting) both to create that which does not exist, and to conceal that which does exist. Lying, it must be emphasised, plays a vital part in Renart's trickery. It is used to create a sense of trust and security in the victim, and to overcome his instinctive cautiousness and vigilance.[31] The victim thus becomes unable to detect what Renart is concealing, or to understand the duplicity of Renart's words.

Lying is the main weapon used by Renart the actor, but in most cases the lie is an elaborate tissue of falsehood, whose full implications Renart is quick to exploit. Renart's first five adventures in the primitive trunk (Chantecler, the tit, Tibert, Tiercelin and Hersent) centre on an initial lie, which in each case is chosen to serve Renart's purpose. When faced with a prospective prey, Renart can adopt any of a number of tactics, all of which are ultimately based on a lie, to bring the prey within his reach. To trick the tit, Renart begins by immediately making the fatal proposal:

> 3a, 4465 Car descendez, si me baisiez.

Only afterwards does he give the reason for his request: universal peace has been declared. He is lying, and indeed even if it were true, Renart would surely not respect the truce. Similarly, when dealing with Chantecler and Tiercelin, Renart speaks a language which is well calculated to exploit their respective weaknesses. To flatter them, he speaks of an imaginary family connection with Chantecler, and also lies about the supposed renown of Tiercelin's father.[32] The two untruths are chosen with a particular purpose in mind: to make Chantecler sing with his eyes closed, and to make Tiercelin open wide his beak. Tibert is however not tricked so easily, and Renart has to devise a more complex stratagem. When intimidation fails, he says that he is waging war against Isengrin, and asks Tibert to become his mercenary. Renart's lie does in fact become a reality later, but it is used here for one reason only: to overcome Tibert's suspiciousness while Renart is awaiting a favourable opportunity to achieve his ends. Renart's ability to tailor his untruths to suit the situation emerges most clearly when Renart finds himself caught in a position of inferiority with Hersent.[33] His lies are carefully calculated to exploit Hersent's vanity:

> 7a, 5757 Si m'espie dant Ysangrins
> et en voies et en chemins.
> 7a, 5765 Je vos aim, ce dist par amors.

Remarkably enough, the lie again only anticipates the actual course of events. Hersent later wishes to commit adultery with Renart, provides the opportunity and then performs the act, and Isengrin does in fact set an ambush for Renart.

However, it is in branches 2 and 12 that Renart's almost innate ability for duplicity most clearly emerges. When confronted by Isengrin, he opens hostilities (34) by lying, and then develops the lie by recreating the world around him to match his affirmations. The initial lie in branch 2 in fact contains two elements: Renart says he is dead but *en paradis celestre* (1.3524), and expands on his theme, speaking the language of the senses to the hungry Isengrin:

> 2, 3527 Ceenz a riche pecunaille,
> ceenz puez veoir mainte aumaille.

Pursuing the logic of his lie, Renart gives free play to his imagination, while anchoring his tale convincingly in reality. The well bucket has become the balance of Good and Evil:

> 2, 3555 Renart set bien son sen despandre,
> que por voir li a fait entendre
> poises sont de bien et de mal.

At the last moment, he admits to the still unsuspecting Isengrin (35) that he was lying, but still does not reveal the whole truth. Remaining in the universe he created by his first lie, Renart tells Isengrin that the bottom of the well is in fact Hell. A parallel may clearly be drawn between branch 2 and branch 12: in the former Renart invents Paradise, and in the latter he creates an imaginary monastery. In both cases, Renart exploits Isengrin's gluttony and credulity to ensure the success of his lie.[36] After a moment's hesitation, Isengrin enters wholeheartedly into Renart's imaginary world: enslaved and blinded by his hunger, he is in a state of total dependence on Renart, and behaves with exemplary docility:

> 12, 13293 . . . mout bonement
> ferai ge ce qu'a l'ordre apent;
> ja mar en serez en doutence.

When he has succeeded in trapping his victim in the ice-covered pond by expanding on his initial lie, Renart refers to a proverb,[37] and he reconstructs events to show that Isengrin is solely responsible for his own misfortune.

Renart does not, however, trick all his victims with words;[38] in many cases, words would be useless, or at least insufficiently convincing if not backed up by appropriate gestures. Renart must play a part, and his ability to adapt to his environment enables him to do so with considerable verve. To achieve his ends, Renart is capable of simulating a wound. Renart pretends to be seriously injured twice in the corpus, and a comparison of the two passages shows the full range of Renart's acting abilities. In the first incident, the peasant carrying a *bacon* sees Renart as a fox with a valuable fur. Renart's stratagem is simply to make the peasant chase him, and so have to set down his burden. To this end, Renart pretends to be seriously injured:

> 17, 15267 Renart sot mout dou fandement,
> senblant fait ne l'en soit neant,
> et que ne puist plus tost aler.

and once he has succeeded, he takes flight, leaving the peasant *toz esmariz*. When dealing with Tiercelin, however, Renart has the power of speech, and his act is more complicated to stage, as it consists of superimposing an imaginary serious injury on to a real minor wound:[39]

> 7, 5652 Il leva sus en sozlevent,
> le pié tant avant dont il cloche
> et la pel qui entor li loche:
> bien veut que Tiercelin le voie.

As Renart's aim is to make Tiercelin come down from the tree, the fox must make him feel pity. After mimicking injury, Renart cries and speaks. By coherent argument, he provides a rational explanation for his deadly proposal (1.5663, *car descendez*), and succeeds in reassuring Tiercelin, despite the reluctance of the latter to perform the irreversible action:

> 7, 5678 Quel mal vos puet faire uns plaiez?

But finally the skilful act fails, and Renart the advocate takes over from Renart the actor:

> 7, 5686 Renart s'en ofre a escondire
> mais n'est mie jornez de plait
> a Tiercelin.

However, Renart's acting range is not limited to a momentary attitude; he is capable of entering into a character and of usurping his function so perfectly that everyone is fooled, as when Renart plays the doctor, the *jongleur* or the monk. Once he has gained the patient's trust and complete submission to the powers of medicine,[40] Renart truly enters into the spirit of his character and "becomes" a doctor. He speaks with the assurance of a learned medical man[41] and performs the whole gamut of ritual actions, including the examination of the *orinal* and taking the patient's pulse. Renart alternately worries and reassures his patient,[42] but all his mimickry is bent to a single purpose, as the vengeance-seeking baron peeps through the doctor persona. It is Renart the executioner rather than the doctor who says:

> 19, 18652 Et si me faites aporter
> tot quant que vos demanderai.

The hour of reckoning has come for Renart's enemies. For most of branch 1b, Renart pretends to be a *jongleur.* Dyed yellow, he speaks a mysterious language which makes him unrecognisable, but invents a credible story which holds Isengrin's attention. Renart takes his hypocrisy (or, to put it another way, his professional conscientiousness) so far that he feigns cowardice to bear out the proverb quoted by Isengrin.[43] Similarly, at the end of branch 8, Renart pretends to be a monk,[44] while awaiting the coming of happier days:

> 8, 8699 Et il fait mout le papelart,
> tant que s'en puisse issir par art.

The author is careful to note the sophistication of Renart's acting skills:

> 8, 8693 Bien retint ce c'on li ensaigne,
> ne fait sanblant que il s'en faingne,
> le singne fait dou moniage.

Similarly, at the end of branch 1, Renart briefly plays the part of a pilgrim, in order to escape death and keep himself well clear of his enemies.

As was mentioned earlier, playing dead is a vital reflex action for the fox, as in this way he can obtain food or avoid being seen by an enemy. But in the *RdR,* in which the hero is both fox and man, Renart the baron does not forget this animal stratagem. Indeed the simulation of death becomes a literary motif, which appears both in the narratives in which the fox—a small predator—tries to find food (branches 17, XIII and 12, as shown above) and in the branches in which the baron Renart must face the Court and the king's justice. If special importance attaches to the simulation of death, which is after all merely another wile used by Renart the actor and which confirms Renart's constant propensity for dissimulation and pretence, this is because the combination of animal instinct and human intelligence constitutes the originality of our hero. On three occasions in the *RdR,* the hero simulates death as a stratagem to end a trial by combat in which he has been defeated:

> 8, 8579 Samblant fait d'ome qui soit morz
> XIII, 2266 Comme mors s'est aparelliez
> XVII, 1380 Et Renart fet semblant de mort.[45]

But in the last mentioned branch, when the baron feigns death to avoid admitting defeat, he does not forget the fox's instinct: Renart adopts the instinctive behaviour of the predator, although he is only partially successful. However, his reflex action in devouring the leg of a raven

causes the victim to submit a *clamor* to Noble's Court. The ensuing judiciary procedure ends when Renart again simulates death, this time in a highly original manner: he "borrows"someone else's tomb (the tomb *d'un vilain qui Renart ot non* (1.1621)). Renart thus leaves the centre of the stage with a new mask, and for the last time he *engigne* everyone, with the exception of Grimbert.

Lies, broken promises, mendacious explanations and deliberately misleading actions: in both action and word, Renart is a master of pretence and dissimulation.[46] One further remark should be made to conclude our analysis of the resources of Renart the actor. The same devices are sometimes used by others against Renart, particularly as a riposte to an initial trick played by Renart. In this way, the character concept (Renart the master trickster) can be linked to that of the narrative (the trickster tricked) and ultimately to that of the literary genre.

III. RENART THE ADVOCATE

Jean Batany calls Renart "le d'etenteur d'un logos utilisé de façon égocentrique".[47] We have already seen Renart's virtuosity in falsehood and hypocritical speech, but we have not yet considered how Renart uses a perverting *logos* to defend himself when he must answer for his earlier ruses, and face the consequences of his tricks. Renart praises his own all-powerful rhetoric to Liétart:

> 10, 9727 Je sui bons maistres de plaidier,
> a la Cort Noble le lïon
> ai ge meü maint aspre plait
> et ai sovent de droit tort faiz
> et mainte foiz du tort le droit.

These are no empty boasts, and it should also be noted that Renart has total faith in the power of his own words.[48] Indeed, Renart's opponent twice refuses to answer him, as he knows that Renart cannot be beaten in a discussion.[49]

Renart's defence when he is surprised by Isengrin in the very act of rape deserves more detailed examination. In this case, the advocate is not pleading before the Court. Renart continues to commit the offence of which he is accused, while at the same time denying the reality of the facts, and even accusing the eye witness of fabrication. Renart's defence is spontaneous, and totally improvised in the very thick of the action! This is a diabolical system of defence in the true sense of the word. Renart bases his argument on two actual facts—the layout of his earth (1.6020) and his recent injury (1.6024)—and denies *l'aventure aperte:*[50] he is not forcing Hersent, he says, but only helping her out of a ditch where she had been stuck. He even accuses Isengrin of ingratitude[51] and invention, and says he is telling the truth and Isengrin is lying:

> 7a, 6024 Or en avez oï la voire.
> Si m'en devez bien a tant croire,
> se vos controver ne volez
> achoison, si com vos solez.[52]

From a strictly legal viewpoint, this is supremely clever. Renart denies the rape and makes no admission of guilt. As there is no acceptable witness, justice must be satisfied with the sworn statement Renart is already giving to Isen-grin, although it is in fact perjurous. Renart ends his con-struction of the facts with a final flash of bitter irony, im-plying to Isengrin that Hersent is in any case a willing victim:[53]

> 7a, 6030 Je ne cuit clamors en soit faite,
> ne ja, s'ele ne viaut mantir,
> ne l'en oroiz un mot tantir.

However, the full measure of Renart's talent as an advo-cate is to be found in the *plait* branches. The situation en-ables Renart to give full expression to his rhetoric, which is moreover stimulated by the high stakes involved:

Renart is defending his own life, and can rely solely on the power of his words. In two branches,[54] Renart's de-fence is brief, as he stands accused only of minor offences. In branch XIII, Renart-Chuflet, after offering obsequious greetings,[55] feigns naïvety. When threatened with hanging, however, he devises a simple method of defence: in re-spect of four of the offences with which he is charged, he argues that his accusers are responsible for their own mis-fortunes, and the victims not of a trick but of their own vices; he does not know the fifth plaintiff, and therefore pleads not guilty, ending with a bluff intended to silence his opponents:

> XIII,2033 Et s'il en vout son escu prendre,
> je sui tos prest de moi deffendre,
> contre lequeil que voudrez d'eus.[56]

At the end of branch XVII, Renart stands accused of a single crime: the attempted devouring of Chantecler. When the king begins to talk prematurely of punishment, Renart reminds him of his obligation to observe the due course of law.[57] He demands a judgment, and without even hearing the plaintiff's *clamor,* he makes his defence, accusing Chantecler of *traïson* and then of falsehood, but the narra-tor hurries on to describe the trial by combat.

Other authors seem to delight in allowing Renart to de-velop his defence, although this does not necessarily mean extending Renart's argument interminably. Renart's ad-dress in branch 1 is relatively short (73 lines), but is a model of the genre. Renart begins by recalling the services he has rendered, develops the theme of royal ingratitude,[58] and then attacks the flatterers responsible for his fall from favour, the *losengiers* and the *parvenus.* With regard to his own case, Renart denies any responsibility for the misfor-tunes of Brun and Tibert, and ends by accusing them of cowardice. Carefully omitting to mention the murder of the Dame Coupée, Renart denies raping Hersent, but ad-mits having committed adultery, and offers a courtly ex-cuse:

> 1, 1289 S'ele m'a chier et ele m'ame,
> cil fous jalous de coi se claime?

Renart ends his address with a misleading question, which in fact strongly states his case for the defence:

> 1, 1291 Est-il por ce droit c'on me pande?

In his summing-up he alternates between submission and threats, and once more demands a true judgment.[59]

The high point of Renart's rhetorical artistry comes in branch 8,[60] when Renart proves that he was not lying when he described himself to Liétard as *bons maistres de plai-dier* (br.10, 1.9727). Renart responds to the king's detailed threats by repeating arguments with which the reader of the cycle will be familiar: Renart protests that he is a good and loyal vassal, attacks his lying detractors, and recalls the services he has rendered:

> 8, 7414 Mais onques puis home n'eüstes
> por vos ait tante paine eüe.

As soon as the interminable list of accusations has been read (ll.7425-7695), Renart begins his defence. He admits two minor offences, only to reject the other accusations. His entire defence centres on the theme of innocence ca-lumniated:

> 8, 7736 Que tel ne peiche qui encort.

From this moment onwards, the trial is a confrontation be-tween Renart and his main accuser Isengrin, who enters the arena with good intentions:

> 8, 7819 De traïson t'en proverai
> si que garant en troverai,
> et mosterrai tot par raison
> et felonie et traïson.[61]

To the first accusation (the rape of Hersent) Renart replies with the arguments he used at the time of the events. To answer all Isengrin's other accusations, Renart consistently uses the same defence: Isengrin is the victim of his own weaknesses and vices. Renart backs up his argument with a proverb, of which he says Isengrin's misfortune provides an illustration:

> 8, 7961 . . . qui tot covoite tot pert
> 8, 8006 Qui mal chace, mal li avient
> 8, 8063 Et cil qui trop ment s'ame pert.

Faced with such a flow of rhetoric, Isengrin is helpless. He returns to his favourite field of conflict, physical strength, and confident of his physical superiority requests and is granted a trial by combat. Nonetheless, Renart's "logos pervertissant et utilisé de façon égocentrique"[62] remains undefeated.

In conclusion, it may fairly be said that trickery is the dis-tinguishing feature of Renart's character. Renart exudes trickery through every pore of his skin, but this omnipres-ent trickery does not make Renart a caricatural figure.[63] Renart's character is not solely defined by the deceiving action he accomplishes ("action" is used here in its widest sense, as the stratagem Renart devises, the mask he wears, or the misleading speech he makes to dupe his victim). Renart is also capable of feeling sentiment. The authors pay more attention to some types of sentiment than others, but all invariably revolve around trickery. Renart is joyful or unhappy depending on whether his trick triumphs or fails; Renart's joy can be that of the satisfied predator, or the sadistic joy of wreaking vengeance. The author of branch 3a clearly shows how in Renart the expression of sentiment is linked to the success of his trick. At first, Renart's *enging* achieves its purpose:

> 3a, 4397 Fuient s'en va et fait grant *joie*
> de ce qu'il a encontré proie.

but then Chantecler counters Renart's trick with one of his own:

> 3a, 4455 Fuient s'en va toute une sente;
> mout fu *dolanz,* mout se demente
> dou coc qui li est eschapez.

On other occasions, Renart is motivated by fear, which in its first stage is only an exacerbated form of instinctive animal suspiciousness:

> 2, 3362 Or va Renart par le porpris
> (grant poor a d'estre sorpris),
> vint as gelines, si escoute:
> c'est veritez que mout se doute.[64]

Renart's fear can also be that of the baron who fears for his life, as he is brought before the Court for judgment:

> 19, 18130 Et Renart mout durement tranble
> car grant paor a dou lïon.[65]
> XXIII, 1272 De la poor Renart tressue.

Renart's sentiments are invariably directly related to trickery. What is more, Renart is totally incapable of living without trickery and thus going against his nature, even when he makes a firm resolution to change his ways (not by rejecting sin, but by rejecting trickery). After his confession, Renart swears that he will no longer *rancheïr* (b.1,l.1119), but he cannot stop himself from instinctively heading for a farm, attracted by the *gelines.*[66] The end of branch 8 confirms the proverb: *miaus vaut nature que norreture,* which is not quoted by the authors[67] but which perfectly illustrates Renart's situation. The fox in the monastery cannot go for long without *mangier char* (l.8725) and very rapidly:

> 8, 8746 Mout se retrait a sa nature.[68]

Renart is and will always remain the trickster *par excellence,* and the trickster motif is the nerve centre of the whole **RdR.** Renart is a trickster in whom instinct and intelligence are combined for purposes of mystification. Just as critics have pointed to the presence of a war theme in the *chanson de geste,* the **RdR** has a thematic structure based on trickery. The theme is manipulated by the interplay of anthropomorphism, a central aspect of the **RdR.** As the hero belongs both to the animal kingdom and to mankind, Renart's nature encompasses both the instinctive behaviour of the fox and the cynical and Machiavellian conduct of the baron. But as fox or baron, and as fox and baron, Renart is, in the words of the author of branch XXV, the hero *qui de tous baras est mestre* (l.29).[69]

Notes

1. The title is hereafter abbreviated to *RdR*. By *RdR* I mean the 29 branches included by Martin, that is branches I to XXVI, together with Ia, Ib and Va. The text referred to is that edited by M. Roques (Champion, C.F.M.A., nos. 78, 79, 81, 85, 88 and 90, Paris, 1951-1973); for branches not included in this edition, references are to the E. Martin edition (3 volumes, Strasbourg and Paris, 1882-1887). At the time of writing, the edition based on the C and M manuscripts, edited by N. Fukumoto and N. Harano, has not yet been completed; the first volume of this complete edition was published in 1983 (Editions France-Tosho, Tokyo), and the second is due to be published in 1985. For the sake of clarity, the numbers of branches in the Martin edition are in Roman numerals, and those in the Roques edition in Arabic numerals.

2. In his paper entitled *Les structures narratives dans le RdR* (Helsinki, 1981), E. Suomela-Harma divides the branches into two categories: those based on a quest for *food,* and those based on a quest for *justice* (p.94). A further distinction could I believe be drawn in the latter category between the quest for private justice and for public justice. In the latter case, the instigator is an enemy of Renart.

3. By convention, the hero of a cyclic work cannot die.

4. P. Jonin, *Les animaux et leur vie psychologique dans le RdR (branche I), Annales de la Faculté des lettres d'Aix,* vol.XXV, 1951, pp.63-82.

5. In a paper given in 1977 at the Amsterdam Congress (*The Behaviour of the Fox in Nature,* unpublished) the biologist D. Macdonald explains why mediaeval authors describe the fox, known mainly for its attacks on hen houses—as wicked and cruel: when faced with an abundance of prey, the fox kills more than he can eat, to provide for his needs on the next day. This is exactly what Renart does at the start of branch 2: when he notices three hens on a beam, he devours two immediately (ll.3389-3394). No further mention is made of the third victim. The author subtly underlines Renart's dual nature: the fox devours his victims raw, whereas Renart the man cooks them.

6. In this we are in agreement with R. L. Wagner in his preface to the N. Fukumoto edition (*Le RdR, branches I et Ia, éditées d'après les mss C et M,* Librairie France—Tosho, Tokyo, 1974): trickery is for Renart a distinguishing mark, "une qualité typifiante qui règle sa conduite".

7. It would be impossible to list all the examples of the standard line in the *RdR;* one example of each variant is given in the first narrative, in br.3a, lines 4066, 4067 and 4320.

8. Renart is the incarnation of trickery, but on many occasions he fails to devise a trick, or his ruse is un-

successful. It should be borne in mind that if his stratagems always worked perfectly, the character of Renart would be psychologically unrealistic (and from a dramatic viewpoint, the theme of "the trickster tricked" could not be used).

9. The most common narrative scheme in the *RdR* is the following: the hero is driven by an initial motive (hunger, desire for vengeance, or self-preservation). Renart takes action, but an obstacle of some description must be overcome.

10. Cf. br.9, ll.9177-78, br.10, ll.10977-78, and br.XXVI, ll.101-102.

11. Experts on animal behaviour have pointed out that the motivation of all animal conduct can be explained by two fundamental aspects of instinct: desire (for food or sexual pleasure), and suspiciousness (neophobia or suspiciousness of a stronger animal).

12. *Le Bestiaire* by Philippe de Thaün (1779-1782). The authors of the *RdR* make no mention of red earth, but it is interesting to note that the text of *Le Bestiaire* seems to have provided a scenario for the authors of branches 17 and XIII, when Renart pretends to be dead in order to devour a crow. The original story is expanded in the *RdR* narrative.

13. The same scene and the same instinctive behaviour are to be found in br.XIII, ll.865-868.

14. This is taken from the Martin edition, as it is clearer than the corresponding passage in the Roques edition (br.12, ll.12970-12975).

15. By primitive trunk, I am referring to branches II and Va, which constitute the first narrative of the *RdR,* as shown by L. Foulet (*Le Roman du Renart,* Champion, Paris, 1968, pp.190-216).

16. *Fuiant s'en va* is a refrain hemistich frequently used in the primitive trunk, as Renart the fox flees from dogs and men: br.3a, ll.4397, 4455, 4637, 4774 and 4787, br.7, l.5705. The same phrase is used at the end of br.1, when Renart the pilgrim leaves the Court (l.1522).

17. If we accept Foulet's thesis concerning the unity of time in the primitive trunk, this means that in a single day Renart has failed to trick both Chantecler and the tit, and has been injured by a trap. The starving fox understandably flings himself onto the first prey he finds within his reach.

18. This may be the result of the constraints of brevity. However, in branch XXV the author describes the meanderings of Renart's thoughts in a twenty-one line monologue.

19. In the words of J. Rychner, from his article on the first eighty lines of br.2, *Renart et ses conteurs, ou le style de la sympathie, Travaux de linguistique et de littérature,* Strasbourg, IX, fasc.l, 1971, pp.309-322.

20. The whole of branch 10 is based on a delaying strategy; in order not to have to fulfil the promise made to Brun, Liétart pleads for more time, but Brun, the intended victim, replies with another proverb:

10, 9504 Qui aise atant, aise li fuit.

21. Cf. br.V, ll.14-17 and br.XIV, ll.13-15.

22. This is a blatant lie, as the author has already told us (ll.500-507).

23. The message says that Renart should bring only *la hart a sa geule pandre* (l.752).

24. When confronted by Grimbert, the third messenger, Renart has to change his strategy, Grimbert has taken the precaution of bringing a letter stamped with the royal seal; moreover he knows Renart too well to commit the foolish mistakes which proved fatal to his predecessors, and has eaten before delivering his message. In the face of such resolution, Renart is forced to concede defeat. The third messenger must in any case succeed, in order to comply with the legal procedure of the time and so as not to lose the interest of the audience.

25. This is a fine example of the combination of psychological and dramatic interest. Psychologically, Renart is not restricted to a single attitude, for his trickery is shown to be a capacity for continuous innovation. From a dramatic viewpoint, there is a need for the author of each branch to produce something original using a well-defined and familiar hero.

26. Renart has no difficulty in getting rid of the second messenger, Brichemer, a pale stand-in for Roonel. The account of his mission is dull and uninteresting.

27. He asks Renart to come to the Court *entor vostre col une hart* (1674). As mentioned earlier, Tibert in branch 1 has the foresight to palliate the terms of the message.

28. The situation is different in the case of the third embassy of three barons, sent by the king to bring back the culprit. Renart feigns incomprehension when Bernart makes his firm request, but his efforts are in vain. The other two barons appear, after cautiously keeping their distance, and Renart is defeated. The commando approach leaves Renart no time to devise a strategy, he is captured *manu militari,* and taken back to the Court as a prisoner.

29. That of branch XVII, in which the author, instead of sending three successive messengers, sends a single embassy with three members.

30. This term is used in the sense given by Littré: "La tactique exécute les mouvements qui sont commandés par la stratégie."

31. In br.XXIII, when Renart invents a character called Yvoris, said to be the king's daughter (lying tactics) in order to win time (delaying strategy), the author provides a revealing analysis of the lying mechanism:

XXIII, 1061 Tel chose li faisoit acroire qui ne pooit pas estre voire.

Mes si le voloit enivrer
que il se peüst délivrer.

32. Br.3a, 1.4352 and br.7, 1.5620.

33. Renart has entered his enemy's lair by chance (br.7a, ll.5719-5721) and he fears Isengrin's return (l.5796).

34. In br.2, Renart tries to make Isengrin take his place in the bucket at the bottom of the well; in br.12, the problem is how to keep the starving Isengrin away from the fish Renart has stolen and taken home to his family.

35. Isengrin, at first obsessed by the vision of the adultery, is then completely blinded by hunger. As Renart's trap closes on him, he asks a final question which reflects his total credulity:

    2, 3603 Renart, biau frere, ou va tu?

    In br.12, Isengrin's gullibility emerges again:

    12, 13363 Renart, fait il, trop en i a,
    tant en ai pris, n'en sai que dire.

36. Here again, Renart's skill in speaking the language of the senses should be noted. Isengrin's natural gluttony, exacerbated by hunger (cf. 13115 *de jeüner estoit estens*), undermines the animal's instinctive suspiciousness.

37. Cf.

    br.12, 1.13366 Qui tot covoite tout pert.

    The same proverb is used by Renart in br.8, when defending himself against Isengrin's accusations.

38. In br.12, the author notes the part words play in duping the victim:

    12, 12999 Or tant a fait et tant roté
    Renart que bien l'a asoté.

39. As Renart explains later to Tiercelin (l.5666), this is the foot which was bruised by the *broion* into which he fell, after vainly trying to make Tibert do so. Once more, Renart turns everything to his advantage, including his failures.

40. Cf.

    br.19, 1.18594 Je me met dou tot en voz mains.

    This submissively is only obtained when Renart lies about journeys he has undertaken in search of a remedy; Renart's statement is endorsed by Tibert, who tells a further lie at Roonel's expense. Once again, Renart skilfully uses argument to take advantage of a character's weaknesses (the king is blinded by his desire to be healed).

41. Cf. 1.18613.

42. Cf. 1.18639.

43. Cf.

    br.1, 1.2569 Einz ne vie hardi juglaor
    ne saige clerc ni saige fame.

44. With regard to the motif of the wolf or fox disguised as a monk, see Jean Batany's study: *Approches du Roman de la Rose,* Bordas, Collection Études, Paris, 1973, p.104.

45. Despite the consistency of Renart's behaviour in defeat, the authors create diversity in the fate reserved for the vanquished fox: in br.8, Renart "ressuscite", and is going to be hanged when an *aventure* occurs, in br.XIII it is decided to throw the body into the river, and in br.XVII, Chantecler pushes it into a ditch.

46. The analyses of W. R. Connor, in his book *The New Politicians of 5th Century Athens* (Princeton University Press, 1971) and M. I. Finley, in his article on *Les démagogues athéniens,* in *Past and Present* (vol.XXI, 1962, pp.3-24), suggest that Renart is a prototype of the demagogue. The weapons of the demagogue are, it is argued, lying, false promises, flattery, bribery and calumny. The use of the last four of these resources cannot be discussed in the space of this short study.

47. *Le lion et sa cour: autour du Pantchatantra et du jugement de Renart,* in *Marche Romane, Medievalia 1978,* vol.XXVIII, 3-4, p.22.

48. Renart's talent is acknowledge both by the author:

    19, 17477 Bien sot Renart gent amuser
    et soi par parole escuser.

    and by Renart's main accuser:

    8, 7977 Renart, bien de ses escuser
    et gent par paroles muser.

49. Br.7, ll.5686-5688 and br.XIV, ll.136-138. It should, however, be noted that in neither case is this a courtroom scene between the accused and the accuser.

50. It is Isengrin who naïvely asserts:

    7a, 6001 N'i covient nule coverture:
    tote est aperte l'avanture.

51. This accusation is repeated in br.8:

    8, 7879 Mais je nel fis se por bien non:
    or m'en rendez mal guerredon.

    This argument may usefully be compared with the scenes in which Renart the murderer pretends to be a Good Samaritan to his victim. It also announces the theme (used by Renart on several occasions in his defence before the Court) of royal ingratitude to faithful vassals.

52. Isengrin is incidentally calumniated as a habitual liar.

53. Hersent vigorously defends herself on her release:

    7a, 6080 Sire, il est voirs qu'il m'a fait honte,
    mais n'i ai mie tant mesfait,
    endroit ce que force m'a fait.

54. We will not linger on the remarkably weak defence Renart makes at the end of br.XI. Caught *in flagrante delicto* of the attempted murder of the king, he asks to be spared for services rendered in br.19, and the king immediately agrees.

55. Cf.

    XIII, 1985 Bons rois, cis sires qui ne ment,
    il gart vostre cors de torment.

56. Renart's surprise when Roonel takes up the challenge shows that it was a pure bluff:

> XIII, 2046 Bien sout qu'il covint defendre:
> Durement en est esbaïs.

57. This request is made repeatedly by Renart, and in his absence by Grimbert. In branch 1 and in the presence of Renart, Grimbert reminds the king—who is already speaking of punishment—of the need to observe the due course of law.

58. On the question of the *topos* of royal ingratitude, used earlier in the *Chansons de Geste,* see Jean Frappier's study in *Les chansons de Geste du Cycle de Guillaume d'Orange,* SEDES, Paris, 1967, vol.2, p.192.

59. Renart's argument concerning *la gorje chanue* (l.1296) is analysed by Jean Dufournet in *Petite introduction aux branches I, Ia et Ib du RdR,* CDU, Paris, 1970, p.107.

60. I do not propose to analyse in detail Renart's original system of defence in br.XXIII. Renart confronts his accusers one after the other, and reduces them to silence. The only crime of which he is found guilty is the murder of the Dame Coupée, and for this he is sentenced to death.

61. Cf.

> 8, 7379 Tel guerredon t'en ferai randre
> que as forches te ferai pandre.

62. To repeat the quotation given above.

63. As suggested in the first part of this paper, trickery does not restrict Renart to a particular attitude, but is in fact the art of manipulating attitudes. Similarly, the language used by Renart the trickster is not stereotyped, as trickery is precisely the art of speaking all langauges.

64. Similarly in br.7a, when Renart's suspiciousness fails him, he is paralysed by fear:

> 7a, 5750 Cil a tel paor et tel hide
> ne puet müer qu'il ne responde.

In br.3a, the author on three occasions notes Renart's fear when threatened with death (ll.4567, 4607 and 4792).

65. Renart's reaction is the same in branch XXIII:

> XXIII, 934 Or trenble Renart plus que fueille
> quant de sa mort oï plaidier.

66. Renart follows the path of duty, and civil and religious law, but the law of nature turns his head: *sovent coulie / vers les gelines cele part* (ll.1204-1205).

67. As the author of br.11 emphasises in the epilogue, no one can *guerpir sa nature* (l.12929). He is in fact referring to himself and his Norman provincial expressions, rather than to the hero.

68. In br.9, Renart again tries in vain to change his life and deny his past existence.

69. This article is a shortened version of one chapter of a doctorate thesis entitled *La ruse dans le RdR,* presented in 1982 at the University of Lyons II.

Kenneth Varty (essay date 1986)

SOURCE: "The Giving and Withholding of Consent in Late Twelfth-Century French Literature," in *Reading Medieval Studies,* Vol. 12, 1986, pp. 27-49.

[*In the following essay, Varty analyzes aspects of the* Roman de Renart *to illustrate and explain medieval views on rape and adultery.*]

My investigations into the depiction and punishment of rape in late twelfth-century literature in northern France stem from a particular interest in some of the earlier branches of the **Roman de Renart.** One of these early tales recounts how Renart first committed adultery with the wolf's wife, Hersent, and then how, soon afterwards, he raped her, and was seen to rape her by her husband, Ysengrin.[1] There is also a closely related story, a sequel, in which Ysengrin and Hersent complain to Noble, the lion and King of the Animals, their feudal overlord, about this crime, and seek justice at his hand.[2] In my efforts to see how far these stories reflect or distort relevant legal practice and to assess some aspects of their authors' art, I have been examining the depiction of rape and the giving and withholding of consent in other tales, and exploring medieval law on serious sexual offences. What follows is in the nature of an interim report on the progress I have made in these areas.

The prologue to the Reynardian tale of adultery and rape contains a strong hint that it will be about men who fight over a woman and get involved in conflicts which are the result of their committing serious sexual offences:

> Seigneurs, oï avez maint conte
> Que maint conterre vous raconte,
> Conment Paris ravi Elaine,
> Le mal qu'il en ot et la paine:
> De Tristan . . .
>
> Mais onques n'oïstes la guerre,
> Qui tant fu dure de grant fin,
> Entre Renart et Ysengrin . . .[3]

The story which unfolds divides into two parts: in the first there is a scene of seduction and adultery, and in the second of rape. In the first part a prowling fox accidentally stumbles on the entrance to a wolf's den and falls into it. The animal setting suddenly changes and we are in a castle, in the chatelaine's room where the chatelaine, Hersent, is nursing her young children. Renart, now a noble baron, is at first afraid; but Hersent is very welcoming and, within a short time, offers herself to him. He is delighted and, in an outburst of frenzied triumph after they have made love, throws the children—sons of the King's constable—out of their bed, urinates and defecates all over them, calls them bastards, and vandalizes the room. Hersent is left with a lot of explaining to do when Ysengrin returns home from the hunt. There is a terrible scene, but Hersent manages to explain everything away by describing Renart as an unprovoked aggressor. Ysengrin gets her agree that they must declare war on Renart and attack him at the first opportunity. A week passes by. Out hunting together, Hersent and Ysengrin come across Renart. They promptly give pursuit, and Renart returns at high speed to his castle-den. Hersent outpaces her husband and, right on Renart's tail, pursues him into his den, but the entrance is too small for her. She gets stuck, half in, half out. Renart emerges from another passage and takes advantage of the situation. Hersent defends herself as best she can, with her tail:

> Il n'est ileuc qui la resqueue
> Fors que seulement de sa queue,
> Qu'ele estraint si vers les rains
> Que des deus pertuis deerains
> Ne pert un dehors ne dedens . . .[4]

But to no avail:

> Et Renars prist la queue aus dens
> Et li reverse sor la croupe
> Et les deus pertuis li destoupe:
> Pui li saut sus liez et joianz.[5]

And while Renart enjoys himself, she cries out:

> Renart, c'est force et force soit![6]

A recent French translation of this line reads:

> Renart, c'est un viol. Eh bien, vas-y.[7]

(Renart, this is rape. Ah well, carry on). My own translation of this line would be:

> Renart, this is rape; let it be understood that it is rape.

The difference in sense and emphasis is all-important for, as I hope to show shortly, Hersent—and her creator—had the laws concerning rape in mind here.

Renart's assault on Hersent causes the whole den to echo; and when he has finished the first time, he begins again. Eventually Ysengrin catches them up and witnesses the coupling. He cries out:

> Haï, Renart, or bellement!
> Par les sainz dieu mar m'i honnistes.[8]

One notes that he considers himself to be the injured party, the one who is dishonoured. Renart quickly withdraws, insisting that he was really trying to do Hersent a service by extracting her from the narrow passage:

> Veez con Hersent est ci prise! . . .
>
> Pour dieu, biau sire, ne creez
> Que nulle rien i aie faite,
> Ne draps levez ne braie traite.[9]

And he goes on to argue both his and Hersent's innocence, and says he is prepared to swear on oath, before Ysengrin's best friends, that this is so:

> Onc par cest corps ne par ceste ame
> Ne mesfis rien a vostre fame.
> Et pour moi et pour lui desfendre
> Partot la ou le voudrez prendre
> Un serement vous aramis
> Au los de vos meillors amis.[10]

Readers familiar with the Tristan story may well think there is some parodying going on here, and this may be so. Contemporary audiences would also, however, recognise an allusion to a controversial legal procedure. Ysengrin brushes aside both protestation and offer:

> Serement? traîtres prouvez,
> Voir pour noient i conterez . . .
>
> Cudez vous que ne voie goute?
> En quel terre empaint on et boute
> Chose que on doit a soi traire,
> Con je vous vi a Hersent faire?[11]

Renart continues to use, ironically, arguments which relate to the nature of eye-witness evidence—he had to push Hersent, and repeatedly, to get her out, for the entrance to his den got wider as you went further in. In any case, a few days ago he broke a leg so he could only push, not pull. Thereupon Renart disappears down a hole out of Ysengrin's reach, leaving him to extricate his wife from her predicament. When he has freed her he rains blows and abuse upon her until she manages to calm him by clever argument, stressing that she was raped, not consenting, and that by laying charges at Noble the Lion's court they could get their revenge:

> Sire, voirs est, il m'a fet honte.
> Mes n'i ai mie tant mesfet
> Endroit ce que force m'a fet . . .
>
> Ja cist meffez n'iert amendez
> Por cose que nos en dïon.
> En la cort Noble le lion
> Tient on les plez et les oiances
> Des mortex gueres et des tences:
> La nos alons de lui clamer.
> Bien le porra tost amender,
> Se ce puet estre champete.[12]

In the sequel (Martin's Branch Va) which tells what the wolves' charges were, and how they were presented and received, much is made of the nature of the evidence and the standing of the chief witness. In both baronial and royal feudal courts in late twelfth-century northern France, the judge (i.e. the presiding baron or king, or their chosen representative) hoped first and foremost for an admission of guilt. This was regarded as the best kind of proof. (Renart consistently denies the charges anticipated in Branch II and made at the royal court in Va.) Failing an admission, the judge preferred the oral evidence of reliable witnesses to the alleged crime. This means he preferred the evidence of noblemen of good standing, especially when supported by other noblemen of good standing (often kinsmen or close friends of the witness) sometimes called 'oath helpers'. (In Va much is made of Ysengrin's standing, for he is the king's constable and the only witness to the alleged crime.) Most relevant *Coutumiers* listed unacceptable, unreliable kinds of witnesses. These include convicted criminals, lepers, Jews accusing Christians, the excommunicated, non-believers, perjurers, anybody defeated in a judicial duel, women, children and serfs. Failing oral testimony by reliable witnesses, the judge looked for written evidence by acceptable witnesses; i.e. by noblemen or by letters bearing a seal of authority. But this was considered inferior evidence. (There is in fact no attempt in the **Roman de Renart** to introduce written evidence.) Failing an admission of guilt, or oral or written evidence by acceptable and reliable witnesses, the judge would accept—but only in Normandy and Picardy during the period under consideration—a *serment purgatoire* with oath-helpers. Elsewhere this practice had fallen into disfavour, and was soon to do so in Normandy and Picardy. In Normandy this was known as the process of *deresne* (*diraisna*), while in other areas, and especially in Reims, it was known as *escondit* and the oath-helpers as *escondisseurs*. (Renart, it will be recalled, offers to make this kind of oath in Branch II, and in Va it is finally decided that he shall make such oath, with oath-helpers, and that Roonel the Dog shall be president of the court in place of Noble the Lion.) Lastly, failing all these other kinds of 'evidence', the judge might accept that of a judicial duel.[13] (This is not even considered in Branch Va, but it does seem as if Hersent thought—perhaps even hoped—the judicial duel would be acceptable to Noble since, at the end of Branch II, she refers to a form of justice she describes as *champete,* presumably justice determined in the *champ clos* of the judicial duel. Such a duel takes place only in Branch VI.)

From these more general considerations, let us turn to the specific crime of rape. Here it is particularly important to grasp the medieval concept of rape. Rape occurred when an unmarried woman was forced to have sexual intercourse against her wish, or when a legally married woman was forced by somebody other than her husband. She could not refuse her legally wedded husband. Apart from the fact that in some countries a woman can now bring, in certain circumstances, a charge of rape against her husband, this definition of rape may at first seem modern rather than medieval. The real difference lies in what is understood to be a legal marriage, and the social status of the man and the woman concerned.[14]

In general the legal position on almost any matter is difficult to ascertain for any one place or period. Did Germanic customary law, or did written Roman law prevail? If it was Germanic law, was it the customary law, of say, the Duchy of Normandy or the County of Flanders? Furthermore, is this a period and area where an *ordonnance seigneuriale*, a law promulgated by a feudal overlord, might be relevant and applicable? These began to appear in the eleventh century, and were quite numerous and re-

ally effective in the twelfth century. As Beaumanoir wrote in his version of the *Coutumes de Beauvaisis:* 'Chascuns barons est souverain en sa baronie'and in the *Etablissements de Saint Louis* we read 'li rois ne puet metre ban en la terre au baron sans son asantement.'[15] Some barons and indeed some kings prmulgated laws affecting marriage, and in the **Roman de Renart,** Branch Va, we hear the echo of one of these laws when Ysengrin complains to Noble:

> Vos feïstes le ban roial
> Que ja mariage par mal
> N'osast en freindre ne brisier:
> Renars ne vos velt tant prisier
> N'onques ne tint por contredit
> Ne vostre ban ne vostre dit.[16]

I must admit that I have not yet traced a twelfth-century royal proclamation of the kind apparently referred to here. Fortunately where marriage is concerned it seems that we do not have to take into account the laws which applied to particular towns or communes since, as far as I can discover, none of these affected the marriage laws embedded in either Germanic customary law or in written Roman law, or the laws issued by great feudal overlords. In this list of the different kinds of law which we have to take into consideration, I have left till last canonical law, at the height of its influence and power in the first feudal period (tenth to thirteenth centuries). Canonical law was immensely powerful by the end of the twelfth century in northern France (as elsewhere) where marriage is concerned. This fact considerably simplifies the otherwise complicated and complex, ever-evolving legal situation in the areas we think of as northern and central France.[17]

In *Le Chevalier, la Femme et le Prêtre,* Duby is at pains to show how, over two centuries (from the tenth to the twelfth) the Church concerned itself with marriage; and how, by the end of the twelfth century, its authority was, in this area, by and large, accepted.[18] And Chénon shows that the Church aimed above all, in the marriage contract, to establish the *consent* of both parties; and then having got its way in this, to impose its views on divorce, incest, polygamy and rape. Chénon also shows that customary Germanic marriage law slowly gave way in northern and central France to Roman law which had, by this time, also become *customary;* and this was done under the growing, powerful influence of canonical law.[19]

In early customary Germanic law, a woman became a wife when she was in effect bought by her future husband from her father. In short, she became a married woman *when her father consented to her wedding* with a particular man. Agreement had to be reached only between these men, and what they had to agree on was the size of the sum involved. In later customary Germanic law the price of the woman became less important. Nevertheless, as Cecily Clark has recently shown, in the Anglo-Norman kingdom of 1180, lists of noble orphans and widows were kept at the royal court with the express purpose of ensuring that a large sum of money was obtained by the king (who was legal guardian of these orphans and widows) in exchange for their hand in marriage.[20] The important legal point in Germanic customary law was that, on payment of the agreed sum and the performance of a simple ceremony, the woman passed from her father's to her husband's jurisdiction. And here Germanic and Roman law coincided. In Roman law, however, not only did the woman's father have to agree to hand her over to a particular man, but the couple also had to agree to take each other, and to do so publicly.[21] (Up to the twelfth century the woman said nothing at the wedding ceremony; but by letting her father place her right hand in her husband's right hand, she in effect gave her consent. Only after the twelfth century was the woman allowed to signify her consent by saying a word or two in the vulgar tongue.)[22] In short, in Roman law, not only was consent required between father and future son-in-law, but also between bride and groom, and this had to be done before witnesses, and demonstrated to them if only by gesture. The marriage contract was complete when their public acceptance of each other was followed by the *deductio uxoris in domum mariti*.[23] Then, as in Germanic law, the woman passed from her father's to her husband's jurisdiction. In practice, however, the father's consent was *far* more important than the daughter's. If she did not accept the agreement her father made, he could make her life very difficult; and might even disown her.[24] Also as important as the daughter's consent, and possibly more important, was open and public acceptance of the marriage—Society's consent.[25] Clearly elopements were illegal. A man who eloped with a woman would be seen as an abductor, and her father would probably see him as a rapist.[26] One recalls the verb used by the author of the prologue to that branch of the **Roman de Renart** which is in part about rape when he recalls the story of Paris and Helen: 'Paris (qui) *ravi* Elaine'.[27]

Let us now consider the punishments which might be meted out to a proven rapist. In defining the medieval concept of rape I asserted earlier that the real difference between it and the modern concept depended primarily on what was understood by a legal marriage, and by the social status of the man and woman involved. Where the punishment of a proven rapist is concerned, social status was all-important. In principle rape was a major crime subject to capital punishment. In this respect it ranked with pre-meditated murder, certain kinds of robbery, and arson.[28] But rape was a capital offence only if the victim was of noble birth, or the wife of a nobleman. It may be recalled that in Andreas Capellanus's *De Amore*, a treatise pre-occupied by class distinction, a nobleman is encouraged to rape a peasant woman if he lusts after her. Peasants, Andreas tells us, are naturally led to accomplish Venus's work as a horse and a mule accomplish it. If however a man who may serve in Love's court (i.e. a nobleman) is attracted by a peasant woman, he should, if a suitable occasion presents itself, take her by force ('. . . si locum inveneris opportunum, non differas assumere quod petebas et violento potiri amplexu').[29] In passing, I draw attention to the fact that the only genre other than the courtly romance and the **Roman de Renart** in which rape is occasionally depicted in the period and place under consider-

ation is the *pastourelle*, the lyric poem in which a wandering knight accidentally comes upon a lonely shepherdess: he beseeches her to love him, and she either refuses or consents; if she refuses, she is either rescued by nearby peasants who hear her shouts, or she is taken by force . . . A man of standing, a nobleman, might with impunity rape a peasant woman, a woman of no standing—or so literary texts such as the *De Amore* and the *pastourelles* tell us. Conversely, in literary texts, one of the worst punishments or fates that men can think up for a woman of standing is to give her to men of no standing, to *vilains*, etc. for them to rape. For example, in Chrestien de Troyes' *Chevalier au Lion*, Yvain rescues a baron's daughter from the giant Harpin who threatens to give her to be the sport of the vilest and lewdest fellows in his house, for he would scorn to take her for himself. As the baron reports this to Yvain:

> . . . et quant il l'avra
> as plus vix garçons qu'il savra
> en sa meison, et as plus orz,
> la livrera por lor deporz,
> qu'il ne la deigneroit mes prandre.[30]

Later, hurling insults at the baron whose sons he already has in his possession, Harpin is reported to say:

> . . . il desfie
> ses filz de mort, s'il ne li baille
> sa fille; et a sa garçonaille
> la liverra a jaelise,
> car il ne l'ainme tant ne prise
> qu'an li se daingnast avillier;
> de garçons avra un millier
> avoec lui sovant et menu,
> qui seront poeilleus et nu
> si con ribaut et torchepot,
> qui tuit i metront lor escot.[31]

This incident may remind one that the vicious raping of a noblewoman by a giant, and the punishing of the rapist, has an ancient and honorable pedigree in Arthurian romance. It first appears in Geoffrey of Monmouth's *Historia Regum Britanniae* and in Wace's *Brut* when King Arthur himself fights a giant called Dinabruc because he had taken prisoner a young beauty called Elaine, and raped her, causing her death. Arthur challenged the giant because of this misdeed and killed him in single combat. In so doing Arthur adds to his personal glory as does Yvain in Chrestien's story. I have not found any documentary evidence to prove that a noblewoman might be punished for certain crimes by being given to commoners as a kind of whore, nor have I uncovered any documentary evidence which proves that a peasant woman might not bring a nobleman to trial for rape. However, one may guess that Andreas's advice was within the law.

When one turns to the punishments which might be imposed on a man convicted of raping a noblewoman, one discovers that much depended on her marital status—virgin, widow or wife. If the size of fines which might be imposed is any guide, the least severe punishments were reserved for virgin victims; punishments considered to be of medium severity were imposed when the victim was a widow; severest punishments were imposed when she was married.[32] Much also depended on her character. If she was of good character, then the severest punishments reserved for each category (virgin, widow, wife) were likely to be imposed. If she were of bad character, her assailant might get off scot-free. In this connection, Heath Dillard has recently pointed out that in eleventh-century Castile 'women who ignore expected norms of behaviour lose the protections the law provides for women who adhere to standards set by the society. Thus, it is lawful to strike the shameless woman . . . who insults verbally any person of repute, and it is permitted to kill her without penalty if it is discovered that she has slept with two or three men. Public prostitutes are totally without honour, and may be defamed or raped with impunity, but many fines result when an honorable woman is physically or verbally abused.'[33]

In the period which concerns us the convicted rapist of a noblewoman of good character would almost certainly be put to death, and he risked being physically maltreated, possibly tortured first.[34] The form of execution varied from place to place. He might be burned at the stake, drowned, hanged, broken on the wheel, decapitated or garrotted. The most vicious punishment I have discovered was imposed in thirteenth-century Germany where, if the victim, whether virgin, widow or wife, was forced into her violator's house and raped there, and if she shouted out for help and was heard by three people, not only was the rapist condemned to death, but every animal and every person in the house at the time of the crime. The law specifies what or who they might be in this order: oxen, horses, cats, dogs, hens, geese, ducks, pigs, and all other inhabitants of the house, male or female, young or old. The house was then to be razed to the ground.[35]

The punishment of rapists in literature generally and in Arthurian literature in particular seems rather swifter and more dignified than it was at law; that is to say they are usually killed in single combat by the victim's knight rescuer-avenger. Occasionally however, literary artists allowed their imagination to inflict punishments which I have yet to discover ever existed in the minds of their judge-contemporaries, as when, in Chrestien's *Conte del Graal*, Gauvain punishes the rapist Greoreas by making him eat with the dogs for a month, his hands tied behind his back.[36]

The reader will recall that, at the moment of Renart's sexual assault on Hersent, she cries out:

Renart c'est force; force soit!

It seems to have been very important for the woman to cry out as she was attacked, and if possible to name her assailant.[37] It is not only mentioned in customary laws (such as the one referred to above which prescribes the killing of everything and everybody in the violator's house) but also

in sermons. Speaking of the example of the woman who did not defend herself and did not cry out at the time of the attack, one preacher imagines himself asking her, on this last point, 'how loud did you shout?' and when she answers that she did not shout out at all, he says she was at fault not to do so.[38] Then he imagines the case of a woman raped by a man of great strength who held his hand over her mouth, and raped her in the open country out of earshot and sight: provided she defended herself and shouted out as loud as she could, naming her attacker, she had not committed any kind of sin. On the contrary, she had been the victim of awful torture.[39] The preacher concludes with advice to his imaginary victim: 'she should bite, scratch and struggle with all her might'.[40] I therefore conclude that Hersent's 'Renart c'est force; force soit' is because she knew she was required to name him and to shout out in the hope that witnesses would hear her. And her physical resistance (tail between her legs) was not just a natural reaction but an attempt to conform to the law's requirements and, perhaps, to the Church's teaching on this. Indeed, if the medieval Church took to heart the only teaching there is in Holy Scripture on rape, its preachers will have called to mind those words in *Deuteronomy* which say: 'If a girl who is engaged is seduced within the walls of a city, both she and the man who seduced her shall be taken outside the gates and stoned to death—the girl because she did not scream for help, and the man because he has violated the virginity of another man's fiancée . . . But if the deed takes place out in the country, only the man shall die. The girl is as innocent as a murder victim; for it must be assumed that she screamed, but there was no one to rescue her out in the field.'[41]

Before I bring this essay to an end with some further comments on rape in the **Roman de Renart,** I would like to draw attention to a few other examples of rape, or near rape, in the romances of Chrestien, and to some aspects of the way he treats the question of consent and nonconsent.

At the beginning of the partnerships between Chrestien's heroes and heroines, reference is nearly always made to the giving of consent in the narrower legal sense—consent of the woman's legal guardian, and consent which is publicly made and accepted by Society. In *Erec et Enide*, Erec asks Enide's father for her hand without any prior reference to Enide; and Enide's father gives her to Erec without any prior consultation with her:

> tot a vostre comandemant
> ma bele fille vos comant.'
> Lors l'a prise par mi le poing:
> 'Tenez, fet il, je la vos doing.'[42]

Enide clearly consents by allowing the language of gesture to speak for her. And the story makes it plain that the vavassour loves his daughter dearly, and she him. Though neither father nor suitor discusses the price to be paid for Enide, Erec does tell the vavassour immediately after asking for her that he is the son of a king and that Enide will eventually become the queen of three cities. Furthermore, it is not long before her parents are sent the most generous gifts, apparently promised to them.[43] As for general acceptance of the union: first we learn that *both* Enide's parents are happy about it,[44] and then that so is Arthur's court to which Erec takes her, where royal approval is readily given, and where numerous representatives of aristocratic society assemble to witness the ceremony.[45] In the first two and a half thousand lines of *Cligés* where the story of Alexandre and Soredamors is told, emphasis is put on Soredamors' consent, coupled with that of her immediate feudal superior, Queen Guenievre:

> . . . a lui s'otroie an tranblant,
> Si que ja n'an metra defors
> Ne volanté, ne cuer, ne cors,
> Que tote ne soit anterine
> A la volanté la reïne . . .[46]

Guenievre then gives Soredamors to Alexandre:

> La reïne andeus les anbrace
> Et fet de l'un a l'autre don.
> Ansimant dit: 'Je t'abandon,
> Alixandre, le cors t'amie;
> Bien sai qu'au cuer ne fauz tu mie.
> Qui qu'an face chiere ne groing,
> L'un de vos deus a l'autre doing.
> Tien tu le tuen, et tu la toe.'[47]

And immediately afterwards we learn that Gauvin, Soredamors's brother, approves of the union, as does King Arthur.[48] Private, then family, then public consent to the marriage are thus given, but Chrestien passes rapidly over family and public consent. In this part of his romance, Chrestien seems to be taking greater pains than he did in *Erec* to show how much the couple were attracted to each other before the heroine was given to the hero. And he is no doubt preparing for a vivid contrast with the fate of the heroine in the second part of this romance. In the *Chevalier au Lion*, Laudine, a sovereign lady and widow without father, other legal guardian or overlord, is first urged by her barons to take a husband, then gives her hand privately to Yvain, then publicly, with her barons' consent.[49]

It is in *Cligés* that Chrestien focusses most powerfully on the problem a woman faced when she was married to a man with whom she had no desire to have sexual relations: in short, with threatened rape by husband. In a recently-published study, David Shirt has tried to show that the marriage between Alis and Fenice was not really legal. He may well be right.[50] But it is a fact that Fenice is first promised to Alis by her father, and this is done publicly.[51] Fenice then goes through a marriage ceremony with Alis even though she has fallen in love with Cligés since being promised to Alis. Like most women she evidently felt she could not refuse to comply with the agreement made between her father and her suitor:

> Comant puisse le cors avoir
> Cil a cui mes cuers s'abandone,
> Quant mes peres autrui me done,
> Ne je ne li os contredire.[52]

One notes that Chrestien does not describe the marriage ceremony between Alis and Fenice, thereby avoiding mention of Fenice's formal acceptance, in public, of Alis—if only by letting the customary language of gesture speak for her. However, Fenice's statement (just quoted) highlights the supreme importance of the father's (or other legal guardian's) consent to the marriage, and shows how empty, really, was any question of public consent given by the daughter at a marriage ceremony—a situation which was bound to last as long as, in law, a family's property and wealth were at stake and a woman remained permanently under her father's jurisdiction until she was legally given to the man who became her husband and under whose jurisdiction she remained for as long as the marriage lasted.

Chrestien's romances abound in episodes which are centred on the giving or withholding of consent, each of them illustrating, sooner or later, the awful consequences of relationships which are not fully consenting ones. The large majority of these episodes concentrate on the non-consenting woman's viewpoint and on her suffering, although the man who forces himself upon her is always shown to suffer too, eventually, as a direct consequence of his lusting. In *Erec et Enide,* for example, both Count Galoan and the Count of Limors attempt to wed Enide against her wishes.[53] Erec severely wounds the former, kills the latter. In the *Joie-de-la-Cort* part of this romance we are presented with the relationship between Mabonagrain and Enide's cousin, clearly meant to be contrasted with the relationship between Erec and Enide herself. Here I would draw attention to the cousin's description of how she and Mabonagrain came together: when she was very young indeed ("ancor estoie anfes asez")[54] she fell in love with him; they pledged themselves to each other; eventually they eloped:

> si nos an venimes andui
> que nus ne le sot mes que nos . . .[55]

Their union was not legal. They lacked parental consent (her father could have charged Mabonagrain with abduction) and they lacked Society's consent. In stark contrast to this are Enide's first words to her cousin after being told these things:

> Bele cosine, il (i.e., Erec) m'espousa,
> si que mes peres bien le sot
> et ma mere qui joie en ot.
> Tuit le sorent et lié en furent
> nostre parant, si com il durent . . .[56]

The non-consenting male victim is also found in Chrestien's romances. Perhaps the most striking and interesting example is to be found in the *Chevalier de la Charrete* where Lancelot is greatly distressed. This is when, after a particularly trying day as he searches for the missing Guenievre, he meets a beautiful maiden who offers him hospitality provided he promises to share her bed. After dinner, the lady disappears from Lancelot's view, but is soon heard by him screaming for help. He rushes to her only to find her unclothed, thrown across a bed by a man clearly intent on raping her. He jumps in to the rescue and is wounded in the ensuing fight. It turns out, however, that this was a 'put-up'job; that the lady was, in some way that is not entirely clear, trying Lancelot out. Anyway, she dismisses the assailant who dutifully goes away and then insists on Lancelot getting into bed with her. This he does, but most reluctantly. The way Chrestien describes this moment, and the vocabulary he uses, shows that he thought of it as an attempted rape by a woman of a man:

> Et cil a molt grant poinne mise
> au deschaucier et desnüer:
> d'angoisse le covint süer;
> totevoies par mi l'angoisse
> covanz le vaint et si le froisse.
> Donc est ce force? Autant le vaut;
> par force covient que il s'aut
> couchier avoec la dameisele . . .[57]

Chrestien no doubt meant these incidents to show Lancelot's bravery (going to the damsel's rescue against great odds) and his loyalty (not wanting to be unfaithful to Guenievre), as well as contributing to his narrative-poetic commentary on consent; the main point of which, it seems to me, is to stress the need for consent and the importance of the love that makes consent natural, and all this within the bonds of marriage.

While the giving or withholding of consent may, to some extent, inform Chrestien's first two romances and provide a centre of interest for many an isolated incident in them and in his three later romances, only Branch Va of the *Roman de Renart* provides a full-length narrative of the trial of a rapist in the period which concerns us.

At the end of the tale about seduction, adultery and rape told in the last part of Branch II, it is Hersent who suggests to Ysengrin that they should lay formal charges against Renart at King Noble the Lion's court. It seems that it was indeed for the woman to instigate proceedings for rape, and to have charges laid on her behalf.[58] This practice seems to have been widespread in western and central Europe. For example, we learn from the *Dresdener Bilderhandschrift des Sachsenspiegels* that, in the twelfth century a woman alleging rape, after having cried out in distress at the time in the hope that witnesses would see the assailant, had to display torn garments and dishevelled hair; but if there were no witnesses, she had to tell the first person she met what had happened, and go straight to a tribunal to lay a complaint before it.[59] This is in effect what Hersent does in Branch II. However, the first person she meets is her husband!

As I have suggested, Hersent probably hoped that the King would agree to their complaint being decided by a judicial duel between Ysengrin and Renart; if that were so she could be fairly sure they would win their case since Ysengrin was much bigger and more powerful than Renart. In spite of frequent criticisms and even condemnations by kings (e.g. St Louis, c. 1258) and other powerful authorities, the judicial duel was common among nobles well into the fourteenth century, and did not die out until

the first half of the sixteenth century.[60] The fact is, when the wolves get to court, Noble never even contemplates the possibility of the duel, reflecting perhaps the author's contempt for this form of the dispensation of justice.

At the beginning of Branch Va, Ysengrin emphasises that the complaint is indeed about rape and not about the adultery alleged by his children and denied by his wife. He lists first the crimes against his children, his home and his honour, and deliberately excludes the possiblity that his wife had committed adultery:

> Por ce m'en cleim au conmenchier
> Que dant Renars ala tencher
> A mes loveax en la tesniere,
> Et si pissa sor ma loviere,
> Si les bati et chevela,
> Et avoutres les apela,
> Et dist que cox estoit lor pere,
> Qu'il avoit foutue lor mere.
> Tot ce dist il, mes il menti.[61]

He insists on rape, reminding the court of the circumstances in which it happened as already described by Hersent, and confirmed by himself as an eye-witness:

> L'autrer estoie alez chacer,
> Hersens estoit o moi venue.
> La fu ceste descovenue
> Que je vos ai ci acontee.
> Je les sorpris a la montee . . .[62]

It is interesting to compare what Ysengrin says about the crime against his honour with what medieval law said on this subject. It will be recalled that Ysengrin's first words on witnessing the rape were:

> Haï, Renart, or bellement!
> Par les sainz dieu, *mar m'i honnistes!*[63]

Bringing shame on the husband and dishonouring him in this way was an offence at law,[64] and it was in eleventh-century Castile that it was dealt with particularly severely. As Heath Dillard writes: 'a husband or male relative of the victim is allowed to select a kinswoman of the offender and dishonor her with the same offence committed against his kinswoman.'[65] But in Flanders and areas where Germanic customary law prevailed, it was the woman's honour with which the laws were most concerned, and which they intended above all to protect. Nevertheless, even here, the victim's menfolk had much liberty in avenging her (and their own) shame. As Jacoby has pointed out, ever since the *Lex Salica,* the defamation of a free and honourable woman was a particularly grave crime (even without rape) and from the time of Charlemagne the inviolability of a royal vassal (and Hersent, through Ysengrin, is a royal vassal) was guaranteed, on pain of death, by royal power.[66]

Soon Noble has begun to examine the married couple about the alleged crime. By the questions he asks, the author of this tale seems to show how important he felt it was to eliminate the slightest suspicion of encouragement by the woman who makes the charge, and of possible connivance by her husband:

'Hersent'dist li rois, 'respondez
Qui vos estes ici clamee
Que dant Renars vos a amee:
Et vos, amastes le vos onques?'
'Je non, sire.'—'O me dites donques
Por qei estiez vos si fole
Qu'en sa meson aleez sole . . . ?'[67]

and later, Hersent to Noble:

'Selonc le cleim que vos oez
Que je vos di, li connestables
Mes sires qui bien est estables,
Que il ensemble o moi la vint
Ou ceste vergoigne m'avint.'
'Ere il o vos?'—'Oïl sanz faille.'
'Qui cuidast ce, que diex i vaille,
Que il esforcier vos doüst
La ou vostre mari soüst?'[68]

Eventually the King decides to seek advice, and he first calls on the Camel, Musart, a visiting papal legate from Lombardy. He babbles away at great length in almost incomprehensible Italianate French, obviously comic to his audience even in its linguistic apparel alone. He concludes that Renart is either guilty or not guilty, so he must either be severely punished or exonerated.[69] It is possible that through this speech by which the author gave the Church the first chance to help solve the problem, he shows that neither the Church nor Holy Scripture had a solution to it. Adultery, yes; rape, no.[70]

Noble then turns to the State, to the secular arm, represented by the barons who surround him. They arrive at a solution chiefly through the persuasive powers of Brichemer the Stag. Perhaps it should be remembered here that the stag was an ancient symbol, especially in celtic civilisations, of justice. Rouen's fifteenth-century *palais de justice* is liberally decorated with stags. And the main hall of Paris's *palais de justice* which was burned down in the seventeenth century was dominated by a giant statue of a gilded stag and called the *gallerie du cerf*.[71] Brichemer's decision is that there must be an independent witness to a serious crime; clearly neither a husband nor a wife could provide independent testimony.

In the end, the barons accept that proof of the alleged crime by admissable evidence is not possible, but not without much argument about accepting or rejecting Ysengrin's allegations on the grounds that he is a nobleman of high standing. This argument revolves round the fact, already referred to, that medieval law normally accepted the evidence of a nobleman of good repute provided he could produce witnesses to his good character, witnesses known as 'oath helpers'. In this connection I return to Heath Dillard's comments on the way a raped woman should proceed if she wanted to bring her rapist to justice: 'Like murder, theft, and arson, rape is one of the most serious offenses in Castilian customary law. If a woman of Sepúlveda is raped, she must walk around the walls of the town and call out her complaints and the name of the rapist as she makes her way up to the gate of the castle, there summoning forth the town's elected officials to hear her grievances. The following Sunday she issues a complaint against the man with two kinsmen and two other citizens; the man can prove his innocence with twelve witnesses: five kinsmen, six citizens, and the tithe collector. If he is unable to do so, he pays fifty *moravedis* and becomes the personal enemy of the woman's kinsmen, pending appeal to the king if he chooses. At Cuenca a woman has three days to make her complaint and show her injuries to the town officials, a somewhat less public and spectacular, but equally degrading, accusatory process. Here, too, the man can absolve himself with twelve witnesses (citizens, not kinsmen); if he cannot, he is fined three hundred *solidos* and exiled, any accomplices being fined and exiled for a year. In both *fueros* rape is treated with the same gravity as regards penalties and follows similar procedure. The important difference is the presence in F. Sepúlveda of the kinsmen, both as witnesses supporting the woman and oath helpers supporting the man; these are not found in F. Cuenca.'[72] The presence of oath helpers is clearly meant to guarantee the high standing of the accused, and of their trust in him because if things go wrong, they can be found guilty of the same crime as the defendant, as accessories.

One recalls the fate of Guanelon's oath helpers in the *Chanson de Roland*. So, when it is decided that the way out of the problem in Branch Va is to have Renart swear a solemn oath that he did not rape Hersent and was not guilty of the other crimes of which he is accused by Ysengrin, and when we are shown how first Ysengrin, then Renart marshal their kinsfolk to be with them at the oath-taking ceremony, they do, at least in part, what was normal at law. In fact, it looks as if what Heath Dillard says of eleventh-century Castile was by and large true of large areas of western and central Europe where customary law held sway. Of Flemish, Frankish and Germanic practices in the twelfth and thirteenth centuries, Jacoby observes that 'under old-fashioned formal procedures the man of unblemished reputation appeared without coercion to stand trial. He obeyed the summons. He was judged by his peers . . . he proved his innocence by his oath in which he was supported by the oaths of his friends and relatives, and his oath helpers . . . If he found himself in physical danger, he could flee to a place of asylum where his personal safety was guaranteed normally for a long period of time . . .'[73] This is especially relevant to Branch Va where Hersent and Ysengrin pose as high-ranking people of unblemished reputation, as does Renart, who claims to have been wrongly accused and who, in the end, feels compelled to flee to the safety of his own castle when he perceives himself to be in serious physical danger. The only reason Brun the Bear advances for insisting that they would be justified in dealing summarily with Renart is the fact that Ysengrin is the king's constable and ought to be treated as a man of very high standing indeed, while Renart is not of anything like the same standing.[74] Ysengrin should therefore be taken at his word.

Renart sees the trap which Ysengrin and Roonel, the presiding judge, have laid for him, and at the last minute decamps. He escapes, but only after quite a battle involving plaintiff, defendant, oath helpers, president of the court and onlookers. Could it be that the author of this branch also had reservations about the solemn oath as a means of resolving a rape charge? or any other charge for that matter?

The rape is not proved, but a kind of poetic justice *is* dispensed because we, the spectators of all these events, know that Hersent is a liar and an adulteress, and that Ysengrin has conspired to undermine the proceedings of a court of justice; and that, for Renart, there are extenuating circumstances. He was constantly set upon and plotted against by Ysengrin; and Hersent seduced him. The king, the premier judge in the land, was therefore right to ask the question of his assembled barons:

Se cil qui est sorpris d'amor
Doit estre de ce encopez
Dont ses conpainz est escopez?[75]

can one find one member of a couple overwhelmed by love uniquely guilty and the other totally innocent?

Judges, it seems, found it as difficult in twelfth-century France as they do now to find an accusation of rape proved, especially when it was committed, as it so often is, without witnesses, or with family, even husband, as only witness.

It looks as if only *courtly* French literature is concerned with the depiction and punishment of rape. This is not surprising for rape was only of major concern to noblemen, one of whose compelling preoccupations was the continuation of the family line and the passing on of family property and wealth through legitimate male offspring. Hence also the obvious abhorrence of adultery too in aristocratic circles. It is significant that rape is rarely depicted in the *fabliaux*, though adultery abounds in them. Rape is never entirely funny, but the depiction of adultery can be, especially when it happens in a social stratum where the family line may zigzag as much as it likes and there is no family property or wealth to hand on.

Notes

1. *Roman de Renart*, ed. E. Martin, Branch II, 1027-1314, and Va, 257-88.

2. Martin, Br. Va, 289-1272.

3. Br. II, 1-22.

4. 1269-73.

5. 1273-77.

6. 1282.

7. *Le Roman de Renart*, éd. bilingue, trad. de Micheline De Combarieu du Grès et Jean Subrenat, Paris 1981, I, p. 225.

8. 1302-03.

9. 1308-14.

10. 1315-20.

11. 1321-34.

12. 268-81.

13. This summary of the different kinds of admissible evidence and procedures preferred by medieval courts in northern and central France is very simplified and drawn from E. Chénon, *Histoire Générale du droit français des origines à 1815*, Paris 1926, I, 669-74.

14. The definition which I have given is, of course, my own. Medieval definitions do not refer to the woman's status (virgin, married, widow) and rarely to her rank or character. Typical is this definition from Ph. de Beaumanoir: 'Fame esforcier si est quant aucuns prent a force charnel compaignie a fame contre la volenté de la fame et sour ce qu'ele fet son pouoir du defendre,' vol. I, p. 430, para. 829. But see also n. 37, below.

15. Both quotations are to be found in Chénon, p. 518, together with precise references to their sources.

16. 319-24.

17. This summary of the different kinds of law which were to be found, sometimes overlapping and simultaneous, in northern and central France, is based on Chénon, pp. 489-538.

18. G. Duby, Paris 1981.

19. Chénon, pp. 381-84.

20. C. Clark, 'La réalité du mariage aristocratique au XII siècle'in *Amour, Mariage et Transgressions au Moyen Age,* ed. D. Buschinger and A. Crepin, Göppingen 1984, pp. 17-24.

21. Chénon, p. 384; M. Closson, 'Cour d'amour et célebration du mariage'in Buschinger pp. 515-34.

22. Closson, p. 521.

23. Chénon, pp. 62-3 and 381; see also illustration in Closson, p. 533.

24. Clark, p. 20.

25. Chénon, p. 384: 'cette nécessité de la *traditio* tomba en désuétude, et l'on finit par se contenter de l'échange *public* des consentements entre les époux. Il y a lá une influence évidente du droit canonique . . .'and 'les mariages se faisaient par le consentement des deux époux et *le consentement de ceux sous la puissance desquels ils se trouvaient*". The concluding part of the ceremony, the *deductio uxoris in domum mariti* (Chénon, p. 381) was clearly meant, in part at least, to notify the general public that the wedding had taken place, and the woman had passed

from her father's jurisdiction to her husband's, and thereby received society's (tacit) consent. See also Closson, p. 519, under *Echange des anneaux* (2nd. para.); and p. 520: 'au second concile de Latran, en 1215, on impose la publication des bans . . .'

26. J. Graven, *Le Procès criminel du Roman de Renart*, Geneva 1950, p. 40: '. . . le ravissement ou l'enlèvement, souvent confondu avec le viol parce qu'il en est "le prélude"sont menacés de sanctions graves.' See also Heath Dillard, 'Women in reconquest Castile'in *Women in Medieval Society*, ed. S.M. Stuard, Philadelphia 1976, p. 80 and p. 92 note 41. F.R. Jacoby, *Van den Vos Reinaerde*, Munich 1970, also points out (p. 30) that 'for the written laws . . . the definitions of the crimes of rape with violence, forcible abduction of a woman, and extra-marital immoral conduct do not show codified terminology. Several terms—some with overlapping meanings—were in use.'

27. 1.3

28. This is often stated in the authorities. It is perhaps most clearly set out by Graven, pp. 35-44. See especially pp. 39-40. Ph. de Beaumanoir, after describing the major crimes, sums up thus: 'Quiconques est pris en cas de crime et atains du cas, si comme de murtre, ou de traïson, ou d'homicide, ou de fame esforcier, il doit estre trainés et pendus et si mesfet quanqu'il a vaillant, et vient la forfeture au seigneur dessous qui li siens est trouvés et en a chascuns sires ce qui en est trouvé en sa seigneurie,'vol. I, p. 429, para. 824.

29. *Andreas Capellanus: De Amore*, ed. E. Trojel, Munich 1972^2, Bk. I, ch. 11.

30. ed. M. Roques, Paris 1960, 3865-69.

31. 4108-18.

32. Graven, p. 40; and note 71, p. 131. Also, and particularly important, Dillard, p. 85.

33. Dillard, p. 86.

34. Graven, p. 40.

35. *Schwahenspiegel*, 1961 reprint of 1840, Aalen ed., para. 254, p. 115.

36. ed. W. Roach, Geneva 1959, 11. 7109-15.

37. See, for example, the *Coutume de Bretagne*, art. 155, quoted by Graven, p. 131, note 71: 'Et si aucun forceit famme, pour ce que elle ne fust putain, et il eust sa compaignie par force et oultre sa volonté comme il apparust *par le cri* . . .'

38. Quoted from *Berthold von Regensburg, Sermons*, ed. Fr. Pfeiffer, Berlin 1965, 347, 16 and 18: '"wie lûte riefe aber dû" . . . "Jâ sô habe dir die sünde mit den êren."

39. *Berhold . . .* , 347, 30-31: 'sô ist ez ir deheine slahte sünde weder klein noch grôz, wen sô ist ez ir ein rehtiu martel.'

40. *ibid.*, 347, 24, 26: 'dû sol sie bîzen unde kratzen unde sol sich wern mit allen ir sinnen sô sie aller, meiste mac, unde sol schrîen sô sie aller lûtest mac.'

41. Quoted from *Living Bible Paraphrased*, London 1971; *Deuteronomy*, 22, starting at verse 23.

42. ed. M. Roques, Paris 1970, 11. 675-78.

43. 1845-1914.

44. 680-83.

45. 1915-2074.

46. ed. A. Micha, Paris 1975, 11. 2296-300.

47. 2302-09.

48. 2312-15.

49. ed. Roques, pp. 62-65; in particular, 2038-42 and 2115-36.

50. D. Shirt, 'Cligés: a 12thc. matrimonial case-book?', *Forum for Modern Language Studies*, 18, 1982, 75-89.

51. ed. Micha, 11. 2626-33.

52. *ibid.*, 11. 3126-29.

53. ed. Roques; for the Galoan episode, see 3086; for the Limors episode, see 4580 ff.

54. 6222.

55. 6234-35.

56. 6242-46.

57. ed. Roques, 1204-11.

58. Jacoby, p. 30 and notes 75 and 76.

59. J. Grimm, *Deutsche Rechtsaltertümer*, vol. 2, Berlin, 1956 reprint, pp. 190-191.

60. Chénon, pp. 673-74.

61. 363-71.

62. 374-78.

63. 1302-03.

64. Graven, pp. 40-2; also, Dillard Heath, p. 85: 'The married woman's honor and sexual shame reflect not only on herself but on her husband.'

65. Dillard Heath, pp. 86-87.

66. Jacoby, pp. 30-32.

67. 394-400.

68. 404-12.

69. pp. 172-74, 11. 444-97.

70. Exception made, of course, for *Deuteronomy* ch. 22 see note 41, above).

71. On stag symbolism, and on these facts, see Adrian Blanchet, 'Cernnunos et le Cerf de Justice'in *Bulletin de l'Académie Royale de Belgique*, lettres XXXV (1949), 316-28.

72. Dillard Heath, pp. 80-81.

73. Jacoby, pp. 43-44.

74. 539-51.

75. 502-04.

Kathryn Gravdal (essay date 1991)

SOURCE: "Replaying Rape: Feudal Law on Trial in *Le Roman de Renart*," in *Ravishing Maidens: Writing Rape in Medieval French Literature and Law*, University of Pennsylvania Press, 1991, pp. 72-103.

[*In the following excerpt, Gravdal argues that by allowing legal procedures to dominate the rape trial episodes of the* Roman de Renart, *its authors challenged societal respect for feudal court practices.*]

The archeology of feudal rape law discloses itself in a group of twelfth- and thirteenth-century Old French texts entitled **Le Roman de Renart,** a cycle of narratives in which the characters are humanized animals.[1] The genre draws its sources from universal folklore. In the French medieval avatar, the hero is the trickster fox Renart. Composed between approximately 1171 and 1250, the collection is made up of elements, of varying length and homogeneity, called "branches."A great number of poets participated in the cycle, but we know nothing of them and most of the branches are anonymous. It is assumed the different authors were literate clerics. The genre enjoyed immediate success, a fact attested to by the considerable number of manuscripts, translations into other medieval vernaculars, and also the abundance of iconographic references to Renart in medieval art. The material was initially addressed to a chivalric audience, but was soon aimed at and heard by a broader, general public. Some branches are epic, staged in feudal courts, some parody romance and other popular literary genres, some are situated in the animal world. All are marked by the one permanent feature of the genre—its constant irony.

One group of the **Renart** texts is about the formulation, the authority, and the application of rape law in society. The authors of Branches VIIa, VIIb, I, and VIII display a detailed knowledge of French feudal law, apparent in their construction of legal discourse, their elaborate representation of the feudal judiciary in trial scenes, and their insistence upon posing sexual conflicts in judicial terms. Far from condensing their legal erudition to spare their audience, these poets foreground and highlight the legal procedure of the day, confident that their listeners take great interest in feudal law and are perfectly capable of assimilating its technical points. Indeed, law and legal learning held an important place in the value system of the noble elite in feudal society.[2]

Practitioners of the comparative study of law and literature today have discussed various ways in which the literary text relates itself to law, none of which can begin to account for the complex interweaving of literary and legal models in **Le Roman de Renart.** Legal discourse in the **Renart** is not a metaphor of something else, of another preoccupation or theme.[3] Nor can these *récits* be scrutinized for impassioned human voices, protesting the harsh impartial reason of medieval law.[4] These branches of **Le Roman de Renart** can be read as a set of social texts, to be juxtaposed to another, closely related set of social texts, the legal documents of the same period.[5] The **Renart**'s depiction of trial procedures, oaths, ordeals, trial by combat, and royal pardon, reveals that the preoccupations of the legal and social communities overlap.

A dialectical reading of literature, history, and law is certainly not without precedent among medievalists. There is a methodological tautology inherent in medieval studies, whether we read poetic works in light of secondary sources or study feudal history in light of contemporaneous literary texts. Textual interpretations have for centuries been conceived dialectically, based on historical accounts themselves based on the objects of inquiry. The hermeneutic power of this paradox is double. It plunges us into the medieval way of conceptualizing, which established no epistemological distinction between factual and fictional texts. Second, it teaches us there is no "source,"there is no original object or fact that can be retrieved and that is the Middle Ages. There is only the study of the ways in which discourse is constituted and comes to construct relations of power in society. We cannot produce records of historical fact, but only analyze texts, whether legal, literary, religious, or scientific, as they work to produce representations of "reality."

R. Howard Bloch's *Medieval French Literature and Law* illuminates the singular exchange between literary and legal texts in the French Middle Ages:[6] "Based upon formula, gesture, and ritual, the procedures of the feudal court resembled more than superficially the literary performance. Both fulfilled in different ways a common purpose—the affirmation of an acknowledged set of shared beliefs and aspirations through the articulation of a collective history.'"[7] As Bloch demonstrates, the languages of poems and of legal documentary material are strikingly similar. Their narrative structures draw on shared paradigms. Legal documents are written with conventional literary forms; and literary texts like the **Renart** that focus on legal issues are as documentary in nature as the vernacular *coutumiers,* or collections of customary law.[8] An earlier example of such a reading practice in legal history is Yvonne Bongert's rich tome, *Recherches sur les cours laïques du Xe au XIIIe siècle,* a legal examination that draws with great profit on texts of medieval literature and underscores their detailed representation of legal procedure as prescribed in customaries, charters, statutes, and other records.[9]

The goal of this chapter is to examine the ways in which legal and literary languages subvert cultural models in **Le Roman de Renart.** I hasten to add that their relationship to medieval society is not always subversive, however, as Bongert and other scholars have documented correctly. The images of the feudal court and the courtroom speeches offer an accurate mimesis of twelfth-century royal justice and litigation procedure. Branches VIIa, VIIb, I, and VIII often reproduce exactly legal practices such as summons, ordeals, juries, rules of evidence and procedure. They make clear reference to actual twelfth-century controver-

sies over rape law, sexual crime, and the influence of canon law on royal jurisprudence. But the principal relation of the **Renart** trial scenes to medieval legal philosophy and procedure is one of subversion. The **Renart** stories undermine the feudal principle of immanent justice, which grounds centuries of legal thought, institutions, and practices. Immanent justice is the ideological basis of trials, oaths, and ordeals in the secular medieval court. In the feudal legal system, innocence or guilt is deduced from visible evidence. The innocent party will win the combat or remain unscathed in trial by fire. God makes the truth seen and tangible.[10]

The authors of the **Renart** trial scenes demonstrate, with comic accuracy, the fallibility of oaths, the superstitious nature of ordeals, the dishonesty of the secular judiciary, and the impotence of feudal law enforcement. The characters who take the role of judges are so filled with personal prejudices that their partisan willfulness makes a mockery of divine justice. The jurors on the council of peers are motivated by spite, fear, family ties, and greed. Visibly, they do not seek to follow God's leading. Oaths are so easily manipulated that they prove nothing if not the cleverness of liars. Trial by combat is shown to be an arbitrary matter of physical strength and simple luck. Furthermore, the "divine" outcome of such combats can be quickly overruled by royal whim. Finally, the central character of the trickster hero reveals, with hilarious regularity, the impotence of the royal court to enforce its rulings or make itself respected.

The legal notion of immanent justice and the judicial practices that support that principle are not the simple or sole objects of subversion in the **Renart** rape trials. They seek also to undermine a powerful cultural discourse, that of *fin 'amors,* and one of the literary models that disseminates that discourse, courtly romance. The character of Hersent and the story of her rape by the hero open a space for a cynical parody that strips courtly discourse of its idealizing pretensions and scathingly mocks the feminizing ethos of romance. The teeth of medieval misogyny are bared in and through the discussion of Hersent's rape and the successive trials of Renart the rapist. The depiction of outrageous and joyous indifference to women challenges any literal-minded acceptance of the courtly "celebration" of the feminine. The transformation of Hersent's love affair with the hero into a story of rape demystifies the reigning literary ethos of courtly romances.

The **Renart** poets take advantage of literary parody to reveal the absurdities of feudal law and exploit legal language as an opportunity to parody the reigning models of the feudal literary hegemony. The effect of the ceaseless irony in these animal stories is to lay bare the repressive potential, aesthetic as well as moral, of literary and legal norms. **Le Roman de Renart** offers a subversive thesis which may seem strangely modern to the twentieth-century reader: legal discourse is an exercise in power, changing the way people live; literary discourse constructs ideology and shapes the way people view one another and institu-

tions, a subtler exercise in power. Furthermore, the **Renart** reveals the two discourses are not dichotomous: legal concepts also frame views of relationships, purvey ideology, and shape moral aspirations.[11] The organic interweaving of the two offers a medieval version of the unity of discourse. The authors' repeated choice of a subject as controversial as rape law reveals the deliberate nature of this subversion.

To foreground the specificity of legalism in **Le Roman de Renart,** let us first examine its most immediate textual model. Branches VIIa, VIIb, I, and VIII (Roques's edition) relate Renart's rape of a married woman, his summons, trial, escape, retrial, sentencing, and eventual pardon. The initial plot, the sexual assault, is directly inspired by an almost identical story in a slightly older twelfth-century Latin text, the satirical *Ysengrimus,* signed by one Magister Nivardus.[12]

The *Ysengrimus* is monastic satire built on a series of beast fables drawn from medieval folklore and the Latin stories of Aesop.[13] It relates the conflicts between its hero, Ysengrimus the wolf; the villain, a fox named Renardus; and various members of the animal kingdom. It is composed of seven books, which total 6,576 lines, and is dated in the 1150s. It was probably composed in northern France or Flemish Belgium for performance by monks within conventual walls.

Liber V contains three narrative sequences: the tonsure of Ysengrimus by Renardus; the rape of Ysengrimus's wife by Renardus; the wolf's conversion to monastic life. The rape story (lines 705-820) is relatively brief, as the following summary shows:

> Renardus arrives in the wolf lair where he finds Ysengrimus' little cubs gathered around their mother, who is confined to bed. Renardus defecates on the little ones and runs away. Enraged, the ailing mother tries to persuade the fox to come back. She intends to take revenge. With saccharine blandishments she coaxes him back, then hides behind the door in order to punish him. But when Renardus throws mud and sticks at her, the wife loses all patience and makes the mistake of chasing after the fox. Delighted, he leads her to his den. The small fox enters easily, but the she-wolf is too large and becomes wedged in the entry, unable to move in or out. Renardus exits by another hole, circles back to his enemy's wife, and gleefully violates his captive from behind, joking:

> "Alter," ait, "faceret, si non ego; rectius ergo
> Hoc ego, quam furtim quis peregrinus, agam."

> "Someone else," he said, "would do this, if I didn't; it's better therefore that I should do it than some passer-by on the sly."[14]

The Latin version is doubtless archaic because it remains isolated in the poem and does not affect later episodes or events, as Léopold Sudre demonstrated in his nineteenth-century study of the **Renart**'s sources in folklore.[15] The female wolf character bears no name and does not play a

large role. Her characterization is simple: she wants to protect her children. Only in the later, interpolated verses, 818.1 to 818.18, do we find the suggestion that the she-wolf "warmed to the game." If it is correct, as many have assumed, that *Ysengrimus* was composed for entertainment within the monastery, a performance in which the monks played the roles of the animals, this sexual assault from behind may have functioned as an in-house satire of homosexual practices.

The authors of the French ***Roman de Renart*** use that brief episode to quite different ends. It is greatly expanded and generates three more narratives devoted to a detailed representation of legal practices in secular courts. More interesting still, the expansion incorporates an exposition of various attitudes toward male sexual violence against women.

Branches VIIa and VIIb, the oldest of the French branches, are dated between 1170 and 1177 and are signed by Pierre de Saint-Cloud, of whom we know nothing other than his name.[16] Branch VIIa is cast in the world of the beast fable, not the feudal world of epic. Gustave Cohen opined that "La plus belle branche et la plus caractéristique est la deuxième qui tourne autour du viol de la louve par Renart en présence de ses louveteaux."[17] Whatever the critic may mean by "beautiful," the narrative function of rape in Branch VIIa remains similar to its function in the Latin text; it is neither a testimony to the power of female beauty nor a vehicle to prove male prowess, but an act of violent humiliation.

Maintaining the fundamental element of humiliation, the French poet deviates from the path traced by Master Nivard in essential ways. For one thing, Pierre de Saint-Cloud develops the characterization of the female victim by interpolating a prior act of adultery, making Hersent complicitous with Renart. For another, Pierre transforms the question of sexual violence into a legal issue.

The French author begins his version by doubling the *Ysengrimus* story of the fox's visit to the she-wolf, adding a previous encounter between Renart and his enemy's wife. By introducing this new scene, Pierre will reorient this and several other branches. The female character, now endowed with a name and personality, is no longer a cipher of the maternal: she becomes a bold woman of sexual appetite who is not only a willing partner in her sexual relations with the fox but actually initiates them.

> Hersant saut sus, lieve son chiez,
> si le rapele de rechief
> et açaine a son graille doit
>
> (Roques, VIIa, 5743-45)

Hersent lifts her head and leaps up. She calls Renart to her side and beckons him with her skinny finger.

Pierre portrays Renart as the reluctant lover who finally relents to Hersent's sexual appetite:

> Hersant a la cuisse haucie,
> a qui plaissoit mout son ator.
>
> (Roques, VIIa, 5792-93)

Hersent, thoroughly pleased with the situation, has her thigh lifted in readiness.

The two characters commit adultery with mutual satisfaction and zest.

At this point in the branch, Pierre de Saint-Cloud conflates his rewriting of the *Ysengrimus* with that of another literary model. Pierre here begins his cynical parody of Béroul's romance of Tristan and Iseut, composed c. 1160,[18] by adding this episode, which is without precedent in Nivard's *Ysengrimus*. This cynical scene of adultery between Hersent and Renart invites a comparison with courtly romance. Both the "Romance of Tristan" and the "Romance of Renart" make a mockery of immanent justice and show the fallibility of the feudal legal system.[19] In Béroul's *Roman de Tristan,* Iseut, the married woman, is guilty of adultery, but her husband—who is the king—believes her to be innocent. She will be exonerated. The very different result of the "courtly love" affair between Renart and Hersent will be seen in the subsequent episode, when Hersent's courtly lover rapes her. Hersent will be an innocent victim, but her husband—and the king—believe her to be guilty. Iseut's word is sufficient: she need only take an oath, which the audience knows to be cunning and false, to be cleared. Hersent's word is not sufficient in the eyes of the court: she must offer to undergo the ordeal of cold water to clear herself, even though the audience knows she is innocent. The romance, as cynical as it is, maintains the myth of courtly love while Pierre de Saint-Cloud undermines it by presenting Renart's "uncontrollable love" as rape.

Many critics have stated that Pierre echoes the Tristan and Iseut story, but none has noticed the brilliant economy of this move. By turning to Béroul's text, Pierre accomplishes three important goals. First, he embarks on his parody of courtly romance. Next, the interpolation of the romance allows him to introduce the theme of adultery. Finally, the parody of adulterous courtly love shapes (and perhaps explains) the rewriting of *Ysengrimus* as a legal drama. The construction of Hersent's carnal delight authorizes a substantial *glissement* in the story: what was, in the Latin satire, the question of an innocent victim's rape will be shifted to a debate on the role of the female in the crime of adultery.[20] Pierre de Saint-Cloud can now frame sexual behavior as a *legal* matter.

When Isengrin returns home, his indignant cubs inform him that he has been cuckolded. Hersent immediately defends herself, offering to swear a legal and binding oath that she did not commit adultery:

> que, s'om me laissoit escondire
> par sairement et par joïse,
> jel feroie par tel devise
> c'om me feïst ardoir ou pandre.
>
> (Roques, VIIb, 5872-75)

If I were allowed to defend myself by oath or by ordeal, I would do it even if I were to be burned or
hanged.

Georges Duby has documented the faithfulness with which
Old French texts such as the *Roman de Tristan* and the
Renart obey actual legal procedures. The details of the lit-
erary text

> show to what extent such infractions of the marriage
> laws were viewed as matters of secular justice and did
> not fall within the jurisdiction of the Church. . . . It
> was for the members of the household involved to ob-
> serve the effect of the red-hot iron and to hear the wife
> swear her innocence, taking God as her witness and
> laying her hand on the Gospels or some holy relic. Cer-
> tainly it was not a matter for the husband to decide on
> his own. He had to heed counsel.[21]

As Duby's remarks suggest, Pierre's text may subvert the
literary discourse of courtly romance but is not yet subversive with respect to feudal law, which it faithfully portrays.

At this point Pierre de Saint-Cloud returns to the Latin
model. In the next scene, the couple comes upon the fox
in the woods and gives chase. Pursued by Hersent, the
small fox easily enters his *chastiaus,* or lair; Hersent tries
to follow, but she is still so round from her recent pregnancy that she gets stuck. Delighted, Renart sees his opportunity to "faire de lui son plaissir"(5940). Unlike Chrétien de Troyes, Pierre de Saint-Cloud does not veil or
romanticize the assault but makes it unambiguous that this
assault is wholly unlike the lovers' previous tryst:

> Il n'est ileuc qui la resqeue,
> mais que seulement de sa queue,
> que ele estraint si vers les rains,
> que des.II. pertuis daerains
> n'en pert.I. defors ne dedanz.
>
> (VIIa, 5945-49)

There is nothing that can rescue her, except for her tail,
which she squeezes so tightly between her legs that it
hides the two holes in her behind.

The poet makes it clear that Hersent does not want to be
violated and struggles to protect herself as best she can.

> Et Renart prist la qeue as danz
> et li reverse sor la crope
> et les.II. pertuis li destoupe,
> puis si saut sus, liez et joianz,
> si li fait tot, ses iauz veanz,
> ou bien li poist, ou il li plaise.
>
> (5950-55)

But Renart grabs her tail with his teeth to pull it up
over her and uncover the two holes. Then he jumps on
her, gay and happy, and does it to her whether she likes
it or not.

Hersent is in no doubt as to the nature of Renart's action:
"Renart, c'est force et force soit"(Renart, if this is rape

then you'll have to rape me [5958]). As if to make certain
the audience has understood that there is no complicity on
the part of Hersent, the poet has Renart redouble his efforts:

> Sire Renart tel li redone
> que toute la fouse en estone.
>
> (5959-60)

Sir Renart gives it to her again, so hard that the whole
earth resounds with the noise.

The humiliation of the female character was already itali-
cized in the Latin text by the wife's degrading position:
she is trapped in a hole and subjected to a sodomistic entry from behind. The French poet underscores still more
heavily the humiliation of rape. Insult is added to injury
when Isengrin appears to witness his wife's shame. As if
such a multiplication of degradations were not sufficient,
Pierre invents a new, scatological insult. While Isengrin
strives mightily to free his wife from the hole, she loses
control of her bodily functions: "Isangrin voit qu'ele se
voide" (Isengrin sees her soil herself [6047]).[22] The wolf
frees his wife and then turns his rage on her:

> "Hä! fai il, pute orde vivre,
> pute serpant, pute coleuvre,
> bien ai veüe toute l'euvre;
> bien me sot Renart acupir:
> je le vi sor voz rains croupir,
> ne vos en poez escondire."
>
> (VIIa, 6069-75)

"Ha!"says he, "whoring piece of living filth, whoring
snake, whoring serpent, I saw the whole job; Renart really knew how to cuckold me! I saw him humped over
your back. You can do nothing to excuse yourself."

The irony of this colorful diatribe lies in the audience's
knowledge that Hersent is falsely accused.

Definitively altering the character of the Latin *Ysengrimus,*
Pierre opens a generous opportunity for the scrutiny of
feudal law and the examination of rape as a legal question.
Although Hersent does tell the truth about her innocence,
her earlier willingness to perjure herself when guilty colors this declaration:

> "A la cort Noble le lïon
> tient l'en les plaiz et les oiences
> de mortés guerres et de tences;
> la nos alons de lui clamer:
> bien tost le porroit amander,"
>
> (VIIb, 6088-92)

"At the court of Noble the lion trials and assizes are
held in cases of wars and disputes. That is where we
should go to bring a complaint. He could rectify the
situation very quickly."

Even the truth, coming from the wolf's wife, no longer
sounds like the truth. Branch VIIa ends as the married
couple decide to take their case to court.

As in Arthurian romance, so too in the **Renart:** rape affords the characters their *lettres de noblesse.* In a cynical twist, Pierre shows that rape may humiliate females but it makes male animals into noblemen. Branch VIIb (Martin Va), by the same author and dated c. 1174-77, is known as "La Cour de Noble."It is the first of the French branches in which the animals leave the rural space of the beast fable and enter the feudal kingdom of mock-epic. In other words, as a result of the rape episode, these animals metamorphose into knights, proudly strutting about the royal court.

In its initial passages, Branch VIIb matches the historical information we possess of a feudal king's assembly.[23] As king, Noble is judge at his court. Isengrin comes forward to make his accusation, which he frames astutely:

> Renart est cil qui toz max same,
> car il m'a honi de ma fame;
> Renart ne doute marïage,
> ne loiautez ne conparage.
>
> (VIIb, 6137-40)

Renart is he who sows all evil, for he shamed me by dishonoring my wife. Renart does not respect marriage or loyalty or family relations.

Isengrin's argument is that the rape was a crime against the king's peace, the husband, and patriarchy.

Pierre de Saint-Cloud further problematizes his portrait of the wife, complicating the nameless and marginal motherwolf in the Latin version. Hersent is not romanticized as a helpless victim, nor is she painted cynically as a vindictive liar. Acting as her husband's witness, she prudently begins her testimony with the history of her past relations with Renart. Knowing that in a rape trial the sexual history of the victim is always in question, Hersent's intelligent strategy is to prevent any insinuation of her complicity in the attack:

> —Voire voir, sire, ce dist ele:
> des le jor que je fui pucele,
> m'ama Renart et porsüi;
> mais je li ai toujorz fouï,
> n'ainz ne voil mon cuer aploier
> a riens qu'il me seüst proier.
>
> (VIIb, 6147-52)

"True, true, sir,"she said. "Since the day I became a maiden, Renart loved and pursued me. But I always ran from him. I did not allow my heart to be swayed by anything he promised me."

The audience has a conflicted reaction to Hersent's testimony: having witnessed her lusty seduction of the fox during his initial visit, we know she is capable of lying. But we also know she tells the truth about the rape:

> serree me vit ou pertuis,
> si sailli fors par un autre uis,
> par derriers vint, si me honi
> tant con li jeus li abeli.
>
> (VIIb, 6159-62)

He saw me squeezed in the narrow space and jumped out of his den by another hole. He came up behind me and dishonored me, enjoying the fun as long as he liked.

Pierre portrays a rape victim who believes that the only way she will receive justice in a court of law is by telling half-truths. In a moment of legal philosophizing unusual for the twelfth-century, Hersent adds that her husband's grief and rage are great indeed, but "Je sui cele qui en ai honte"(It is I who bear the shame of this [6165]).

Turning to the character of the king, rightful judge, Pierre begins to undermine his mimesis of actual feudal practice. The lion's first action as judge is to interrogate the victim: "si conmance un poi a sourire"(then he begins to smile a little [6201]). His questions show undisguised cynicism and suspicion: Are you certain you never loved Renart (6209)? Why were you so foolish as to let him enter your house alone, if you were not his lover (6212-13)? How can you expect us to believe that he actually raped you in front of your husband (6222-24)?

Isengrin, official constable of Noble's court, is a character who knows his feudal law well: the role of the judge in a secular court is that of mediator, not decision-maker. It is the council of peers that will take charge of the actual sentencing.[24]

> "Sire, fait il, vos ne devez,
> se vos lest, moi ne lui desfandre.
> Ainz devez plainement entendre
> a sa clamor, que que nus die,
> tant c'on l'ament ou l'esconduie;"
>
> (VIIb, 6226-30)

"Sire,"says he, "you should not, if it please you, take sides with me or with him. You should just listen to Hersent's complaint, regardless of what anyone says, and decide whether to retain or dismiss the case."

Noble hopes to solve the problem between his vassals quickly by projecting blame onto the female character, scapegoating the woman for feudal conflicts and the inadequacies of the legal apparatus.[25] As the scene progresses, the king shows increasing reluctance to pronounce any judgment at all. Pierre shakes the audience's faith in divine justice by portraying a judge eager not to mediate but rather to avoid taking any action in a conflict between two powerful barons, Renart and Isengrin.

Next, Pierre takes on the hypocrisy of courtly love discourse. In verses 6201-24, the king gave the lie to the courtly idealization of women by being openly contemptuous of the alleged rape victim. A few verses later, like a good romance reader, the king interprets forced sex as an expression of passion; he does not want to see anyone mistreated in his court simply because they are accused of love (6237-40):

> "Ce, fac[il], que Renart l'amot
> l'escuse auques de son pechié,
> c'il par amors vos a trichié."
>
> (VIIb, 6248-50)

"The fact,"said he, "that Renart loved her excuses him somewhat from his sin, because he cheated you out of love."

Duby redefines this use of "love"in his analysis of *Le Roman de Renart:*

> The people who laughed at these tales were on the side of the rapists, who embodied the power of aggressive virility. For there is no doubt about it: what these works called "love,"whether in Latin or in various dialects of the vernacular, was quite simply desire, the desire of men, and men's sexual exploits. This is true even of the tales of courtly love. Their theme was violent, sudden "love,"which, like a flame, once kindled was irresistible.[26]

In the case of Pierre de Saint-Cloud, his juxtaposition of rape and "love" is a deliberate part of his literary parody as well as his undermining of feudal justice.

Feudal law, oral, unfixed, traditional, finds itself in a state of crisis as the nature of feudalism itself begins to change dramatically in the twelfth century. Secular courts are turning to the example of canon law, which has retained a written tradition for centuries, and which has a strict and highly codified procedure.[27] The role played during the trial by the Italian camel reveals Pierre's grasp not only of international law but also of the legal situation in the mid-twelfth century. As was the practice in real medieval court sessions, the king turns to an eminent guest, the papal legate and "jurist of great authority"(6263), Chameau. Like a true canon lawyer, Chameau claims to hold the institution of marriage in high regard. But Pierre's comic use of legal language in his portrait of the camel undercuts the legal position of the ecclesiastic dignity:

> "Qare, mesire, me audite.
> Nos trobat en decret escrite
> legem expresse plublicate
> de matrimoine vïolate."
>
> (VIIb, 6269-72)

> "Hear ye, signore, leesten to me. We finded written in zee Decretum these law, she plublicly expresses against violating of matrimonkey."

The esteemed canon lawyer goes on at great length about the seriousness of Renart's crime, but he does so in unintelligible foreign jargon that hints pointedly at his stupidity.

The twelfth century saw an important revival of the study of Roman law in northern Italy and France. Roman law traditionally punished rape by death and confiscation of property. Pierre, perhaps mockingly, assigns the camel the wrong position: this churchman's proposed sentence conforms to Roman, not canon, law.

> Primes le doiz examinar,
> et s'il ne se posse espurgarrr,
> grever le puez si con te plasche,
> que mout a grant chose mesfache.

> Hec est en la moie sentanche;
> s'estar no vel en amendanche,
> de si que parmaine comune
> universe soue pecune,
> de lapidir la corpe ou arde
> de l'aversier de la renarde.
>
> (VIIb, 6273-82)

First you must question zee accused and if he cannot defend for himself you must sentence him as you will, for he has committed a very gravious crime. Ecco my sentence: if he does not will to pay damages, let his fortune be confiscated and let him to be stoned or to burn, this she-devil Renarte.

The **Renart** poet deliberately uses the animal frame to set up a public forum on rape; he devises the courtroom setting and invokes the controversially severe Roman law to survey existing attitudes toward sexual violence. The length of the ensuing debate and its central position in this branch indicate that both Pierre and his medieval audience were interested in the question of rape law and were aware of the controversy surrounding rape's punishment. Unlike Chrétien de Troyes, the author of Branch VIIb presents assault not as a romantic compliment but as a disruptive offense, tearing at the fabric of the social community.

The trial scene undermines the idea of immanent justice by showing the effect that the judge's subjectivity has on the court. Noble tries once again to pose the question of sexual violence as a personal matter of passion, to be seen from the viewpoint of the rapist:

> si jugiez de ceste clamor,
> se cil qui est sorpris d'amor
> doit estre de ce ancorpez,
> se ses conpoinz est acoupez.
>
> (VIIb, 6313-16)

> Go judge this accusation and decide whether he who is under the influence of love must be punished if the other partner is implicated.

Pierre—who never misses an opportunity to ironize—does not entirely suppress the romance version of rape. King Noble is there to represent that school of thought.

Brichemer, the seneschal, begins the instruction. He invokes correct legal procedure, inflecting it to obey the king's wishes: the plaintiff must provide a witness. Furthermore, a wife cannot be trusted as a witness; Hersent's testimony must be dismissed because she will gladly lie on behalf of her husband (6332-50). Pierre here illustrates one of the differences James Brundage identifies between secular and canon law in the twelfth century:

> Gratian had little to say about specific procedures in sex cases. He opposed the use of ordeals in ecclesiastical courts and . . . preferred that Church courts rely upon proof through the testimony of witnesses and he included in his work several canons relating to the evaluation of their evidence. . . . Although he believed

that women were inherently incapable of exercising jurisdiction, Gratian was willing to allow them to testify, particularly in adultery cases.[28]

Soon the jurors abandon their quibbling over the trustworthiness of Hersent's testimony to express their outrage on a more pressing legal point. Plateau provokes a significant change in the deliberation when he informs the council that Renart also stands accused of theft: Renart stole from Isengrin's provisions (6387-6400). Reminded of this, the jurors suddenly take the affair more seriously. The animals are indignant: Renart has bilked almost all of them of food. Indeed, as later chapters will show, theft is an extremely grave crime in feudal law and court records agree that it is punished more severely than sexual assault.[29]

During the rape trials, the character of Brun, the bear, moves to center stage and functions, like Noble, as a focalizer in the legal debate. With the exception of Chameau, the papal legate, Brun is the only member of the court to regard rape as a serious offense. Like the canon lawyer, Brun is in favor of a stricter provision for sentencing:

> Por ice seroit avenant
> que Renart fust pris maintenant,
> si li lïast on mains et piez,
> puis fuist gitez trestoz lïes
> en la chartre ou en la joole,
> puis n'i eüst autre parole
> que de fuster ou d'escoillier,
> des qu'il esforce autrui moillier.
>
> (VIIb, 6633-40)

For this reason it would be appropriate to arrest Renart now, to tie his hands and feet, to have him thrown in jail or prison, and without further ado to whip or castrate him, because he raped another's wife.

Literary critics have frowned upon this passage as an example of Brun's personal vindictiveness. But Brun's speech accurately reflects twelfth-century legal principles. Feudal law, from the time of the Carolingians, subscribed to the *lex talionis;* that is, in any crime the offending member should be severed.[30] The call for castration is legally correct.

Brun stands out not only as the best informed peer but also as the advocate of a legally innovative position. In Pierre's survey of opinions on sexual violence, Brun's position is striking to the modern reader because he examines rape from the viewpoint of the victim, rather than the rapist:

> d'esforcier fame n'i a el,
> ne se c'estoit fame jael;
> on en doit fort justise pandre,
> que autre foiz n'i ost atandre;
> et qu'est donc d'une fame espouse
> qui dolantre en est et hontouse
> de ce que ses mariz le sot?
>
> (VIIb, 6641-47)

There is no other way to punish the rape of a woman, even if it is a woman of ill repute. We must enforce a severe judgment, so that Renart does not dare attempt it again. And why would we be more indulgent when it is a married woman, who suffers and feels shame because her husband knows what happened?

Brun's notion that the punishment should not be less for raping a dishonest woman or a nonvirgin is a legal idea not yet current in the twelfth century but one that will become law later in the Middle Ages.[31] Pierre de Saint-Cloud is not always playing around in his legal debates: his mockery of the current legal system is inspired by or at least open to serious thoughts of reform.

The seriousness never lasts, however, and that is one of the permanent features of trickster literature. When Pierre describes the most recent developments in canonistic thought on rape prosecution, he places those ideas in the crooked and grimacing mouth of the caustic ape. Cointereau, the court cynic, counters Brun's impassioned plea by spouting the position of Gratian, the influential canonist who revised rape law in the first part of the twelfth century:[32]

> Por Dieu, se Renart a mesfait,
> de pecheor misericorde.
>
> (VIIb, 6658-59)

For the love of God, if Renart has done wrong, let us have mercy on the sinner.

Pierre makes a mockery of Gratian's call for brotherly love by assigning it to the jeering ape.

Anxious to placate the king, Brichemer, "conme bons rectorïens," dutifully summarizes the proceedings for Noble:

> "Sire, fait il, nos estïens
> alez le jugement enquerre,
> selonc la guise de la terre."
>
> (VIIb, 6704-6)

"Sire,"said he, "we have acted in accordance with the customs of the land in this matter."

Brichemer reassures Noble that Isengrin must find another witness because Hersent's testimony has been dismissed. Renart is to appear the next day to swear an oath. Roonel, a dog, will preside. Whatever Roonel decides will bind both parties (6713-40). Again, Pierre describes actual feudal procedure: the role of the judge is essentially conciliatory; as mediator, he tries to find a solution to which both parties will freely agree in order to avoid further conflict.[33] But in respecting this procedure, Brichemer uses the technicalities of feudal law to carry out the king's obvious wish that the court take no action against Renart. Furthermore there is heavy irony as the role of judge is handed from a lion to a dog.

The poet portrays the feudal court as a place in which it is easy to put the question of rape aside. No audience could mistake Noble's delight upon being relieved of his responsibility as judge:

Li lïons respont en rïent:
"Ja, par les sainz de Belleant,
ne fuse si liez por.C. livres
con de ce que j'en sui delivres."

(VIIb, 6741-44)

The lion answered joyfully: "By all the saints in Beth-
lehem, if someone gave me one hundred pounds I
would never have been as happy as I am to be rid of
this case."

This is one of the passages that led John Flinn, an important *Renart* scholar, to conclude that Noble is a specific
satire of Louis VII.[34] But the lion's reluctance to take on
the role of judge accurately represents a commonplace historical reality, as we have seen: it was very difficult, in
early medieval France, to persuade any powerful person to
judge disputes, so unpopular was the responsibility.[35] By
painting the king's uncontained and undignified glee,
Pierre de Saint-Cloud suggests that the feudal judiciary
system, far from being an instrument of immanent justice,
is a farce. Noble tries from the outset to sabotage the procedure, first by placing the blame on the victim, then by
foisting responsibility on others. Were it not for the stubborn persistence of one peer, Brun, the rape case could
have been summarily dismissed.

Pierre de Saint-Cloud has reproduced the legal language
and the trial procedures of a feudal court with such attention to legal detail that Flinn refers repeatedly to Pierre's
profound respect for the legal system of his day.[36] Such an
interpretation can scarcely account for the implications of
the subsequent passage in Branch VIIb, which reveals neither admiration nor respect for feudal law. The irreverent
poet undermines his mimesis of the legal system when he
abruptly shifts back to the beast-fable world, ridiculing the
medieval practice, still current in twelfth-century France,
of taking oaths on saints' relics. On the day Renart comes
to court, the council scene dissolves in comic bathos.
Roonel, the canine judge, is easily bribed by Isengrin and
invents a harebrained scheme: the dog will roll over and
play dead; the other animals will force Renart to swear by
the dead dog's tooth; then Roonel will leap to life and
catch the traitor. The branch ends predictably enough as
the fox escapes in his inimitable fashion and returns to his
castle, mocking exultantly.

The seriousness of the rape trial is converted into laughter.
The final irony in trickster literature is that its subversiveness never fully articulates any reform. Ultimately the
trickster overturns anything that may initially appear to resemble a moral program. It is the law of the genre, the
ideology of the form, that the trickster text will always remain finally amoral. Pierre's cynical closure is appropriate
both to the ideology of trickster literature and to the episodic nature of the *Renart* stories.[37] Nonetheless, the modern reader cannot fail to notice the number of important
ideas that Pierre managed to raise along the way.

Pierre de Saint-Cloud altered Nivard's tale of rape in important ways. The French poet problematized his model by
turning the wife into an adulterous liar: he doubled the

Latin scene of sexual transgression by interpolating an
adultery trial scene from the "courtly"Tristan and Iseut
story. But in Pierre's text that sexual transgression is not
mystified as an expression of desire. It serves to develop
the character of the she-wolf from that of an anonymous
mother into a more complex, conflicted, intelligent, and
imperfect wife, falsely accused of lying. Equally important, the French author presented rape as a political, social,
and *legal* matter. He undertook a discursive investigation
of the varying attitudes toward sexual violence in the legal
community: an expression of overwhelming love; an inevitable and predictable fact of life; an error to be forgiven
in the spirit of Christian love; a serious harm to social institutions; a criminal offense that damages all women.
Most important, Pierre subverted the notion of immanent
justice by showing the many foibles of the feudal legal
system, its jurors, judges, and rules of evidence, weaknesses that could only impede a display of God's will.

For all the antifeminism in the images of Hersent's concupiscence and subsequent humiliation, in the cynicism of
Renart's joyful immorality, and in the contemptuous impatience of the king, this openly misogynist examination of
sexual violence is in many ways less repressive than Chrétien de Troyes's aestheticized ravishments. First of all, literary and legal languages play off one another not in order
to moralize rape as a male test or romanticize it as a compliment to female beauty, but to show that the inadequacies of feudal law open a generous space for the legal protection of the rapist and the silencing of the most
appropriate witness: the victim. Secondly, as Roberta Krueger has argued in the context of romance, the egregious
nature of this literary misogyny cannot have escaped the
notice of medieval listeners. Its controversial cynicism
must have invited the audience to consider women's place
in courtly love, as well as in feudal courts.[38] Pierre's depiction of a failed rape trial sows the seeds for the audience's reflection on sexual violence.

Pierre de Saint-Cloud did not miss the mark when he
banked on his audience's taste for legal controversy. In
1179, approximately four years after Pierre ends Renart's
trial in comic chaos, an anonymous poet composed what
would become perhaps the most popular *Renart* branch in
the French Middle Ages, Branch I, "Le jugement de Renart."[39] It is the account of Renart's second trial for rape,
and as such it raises many questions. Why does this later
writer continue Pierre's story, rather than choose fresh material? Why stage yet another rape trial, foregrounding
once more the question of medieval law? And why does
this second trial narrative become so popular, despite its
repetitive character?

The author of Branch I, fully aware of Pierre's success, is
eager to avail himself of the strategy: he, too, poses rape
as a legal matter and uses Noble's court as a dramatic forum on the topic of sexual violence. The continuator begins by explicitly invoking the authority of Pierre de Saint-
Cloud, in an ironic *auctoritas*. He criticizes Pierre for
abandoning the best part of the story:

Perroz . . .
laissa le mieuz de sa matiere
quant il entroblia les plaiz
et le jugement qui fu faiz,
en la cort Noble le lion,
de la grant fornicacion
que Renart fist, qui toz max cove,
envers dame Hersent la love.

(I, 1:3-10)

Pierrot . . . abandoned the best of his material when he neglected to continue the trial and the judgment that took place in the court of Noble the lion, for the great fornication committed by Renart—in whom all evil smoulders—against Hersent the she-wolf.

At the same time, this author begins his version with a notable shift in emphasis. The opening lines refer to the rape as *fornicacion,* which in the medieval taxonomy of sexual sins falls under the heading of adultery, not *raptus.* It is no coincidence that in medieval penitentials there is no category for rape per se, but it is classified as a form of adultery.[40] The *glissement* in Branch I is subtle but definite: the issue of sexual assault is recolored and squarely presented as a question of adultery.[41]

As in Branch VIIb, Isengrin steps forward at Noble's court and cries for justice. But even in the husband's language a change manifests itself:

et dist au roi: "Biax tres douz sire,
faites me droit de l'*avoutire*
que Renart fist a m'espousee,
dame Hersant, qu'ot enserree
a Maupertuis, son fort repere,
qant il a force li vost faire.
A force li fist il li rous!"

(I, 29-35 [emphasis added])

Isengrin said to the king: "Esteemed and noble sire, let me have justice in the *adultery* that Renart committed with my wife, lady Hersent, who was stuck in Maupertuis, his fortress, when he wanted to rape her. He raped her, that redhead!"

This poet employs a new term, *avoutire,* the Old French word for adultery. In fact, in verse 40, Renart is accused of *avoutire* a second time.

Following Pierre's lead, the anonymous poet "holds court" to survey the opinions of the legal and social community. The king is assigned the same role: eager to minimize the seriousness of rape, Noble advises Isengrin not to embarrass himself by exposing the matter in front of everyone: it is a very small thing and does not deserve such grief and rage (I, 45-52). Brun, still positioned at the head of the legal avant-garde, exhorts Noble to carry out his responsibility and to ensure justice and protection to all his people (53-78). Bruyant scoffs at Brun's seriousness; since everyone knows that Renart is incorrigible, Isengrin should simply take matters into his own hands, rather than make such a nuisance at court (79-102). Grimbert, ever the yes-man,

sides with the king: if Renart did it for *love,* what is the harm? Insengrin takes this much too seriously. The fault is all with Hersent; she is not an honorable woman (103-31).

Like the earlier texts, Branch I represents Hersent as a complex and somewhat contradictory character. Hersent finds herself, as in Branch VIIb, on trial and accused. She blushes and feels ashamed; her pulse races; she is overly dramatic:

"Sire Grinbert, je n'en puis mais:

. . . . .

j'en feroie bien un jouïse
en eve chaude ou en feu chat,
mais esconduire riens ne vaut,
lasse, chaistive, mal ostrue!
que je n'en serai ja creüe."

(I, 135, 140-44)

"Sir Grimbert, I can not bear this any more: . . . I would be more than willing to undergo the ordeal by hot water or trial by hot iron, but my denial would be worthless, unhappy me! pitiful woman! unfortunate one! because I would never be believed."

In medieval jurisprudence, both plaintiff and defendant can be asked to undergo ordeals: the burden of proof is shared. All the ordeals mentioned in this branch were in use in the mid-twelfth century. The trial by cold water consisted of plunging the accused, usually a woman, into a vat of freezing water: "And in the ordeal of cold water whoever, after the invocation of God, who is the Truth, seeks to hide the truth by a lie, cannot be submerged in the waters above which the voice of the Lord God has thundered."[42] In other words, if she sank, she was innocent; if she floated to the surface, she was guilty.

The ordeal of the glowing iron consisted in heating an iron until it was red hot; the plaintiff or the accused then took the iron in hand and attempted to tell the sworn truth: "Afterwards let (the iron) be placed on a frame, and let no one speak except to pray diligently to God, the Father Omnipotent, to deign to manifest His truth in the matter."[43] An unscathed hand was the proof of innocence.

It was not uncommon, according to medieval records, for plaintiffs and defendants to propose to take oaths, only to rethink their bravery at the last moment and retract the offer.[44] Hersent has already volunteered more than once to undergo a *judicium.* Here she appears to lose heart and claims that such an ordeal would be pointless because no one would believe her. Pierre's cynicism betrays reservations about the supposedly sacred character of ordeals and their inherent justice. Indeed, most forms of ordeal gradually fell out of practice after the twelfth century, even though the feudal courts preferred them to duels.[45]

Following Pierre's lead, the author of Branch I extends the parody of Béroul's *Roman de Tristan.* When Iseut is accused of adultery, she is not required to undergo an ordeal, but composes an oath of her own in which she declares that no man has been between her thighs except the king and the leper (Tristan disguised as a leper) who carried her across the ford. As E. Jane Burns demonstrates in her study of Béroul's text:

> This recasting of the standard legal oath is in blatant violation of the judicial code which requires that trial by ordeal and oath be conducted according to precise verbal formulas. In feudal jurisprudence, the slightest alteration of the verbal text could automatically render the proceedings invalid. But within the structural composition of Béroul's romance, the twisted truth is *de rigueur*, a necessary tool in protecting the lovers from unjust punishment.[46]

Like Iseut, the character she parodies, Hersent renders her plea of innocence with an oath she herself invents and which bears a double sexual meaning:

> Mes, par les sainz que l'en aeure
> ne se Damedieu me sequeure,
> onques Renart de moi ne fist
> que de sa mere ne feïst.
>
> (I, 145-48)

> By the saints we all worship, may God save me if I lie, never did Renart do to me anything he did not do to his mother.

At the same time as she attempts to vindicate her reputation, Hersent succeeds in insulting Renart with a slur that retains its power to offend even in the twentieth century. Such an obscene travesty of an actual legal procedure functions both to make a mockery of feudal law and to unveil the lie at the heart of courtly love. The deceitfulness that was cast in a romantic light in Béroul's romance is demystified as Hersent's obscene cunning.

Branch I continues to replicate the format of Branch VIIb. The poet circles the council of peers to present a variety of opinions. The members are of a mind to arrest Renart by force (233-43). Noble, however, ever fearful of alienating a formidable baron and eager to shift blame on a powerless individual, objects strenuously. The king wants Hersent, the plaintiff, to undergo the ordeal (244-55). When her husband demurs, Noble angrily informs Isengrin that there will be no more discussion of this conflict with Renart and that anyone who breaks the king's peace will be dealt with harshly (270-82). Isengrin has lost "his" case. Renart will go untried and unpunished, in the name of peace.

During the twelfth century the medieval judiciary strives to suppress private wars between vassals and encourages them to have recourse to the court system. Hersent and Isengrin are the literary construct of one attempt to adhere to the new feudal law, to desist from private warfare and individual revenge, and to bring political conflict into a court, to be solved in a way that will satisfy both parties. It is the king who is represented as inadequate to the new legal philosophy. He fails to honor Hersent and Isengrin's adherence to legal reform, fails to promote legal reform, and seems to yearn for earlier days, when vassals took the law into their own hands.

All would be lost for Isengrin and Hersent, heroes of the new law, were it not for the arrival of a dead chicken. The author of Branch I, eager to exploit his narrative framework, spins the trial into motion again with new impetus. Lady Coupée, Renart's latest victim, is at that moment wheeled before the court on a funeral bier, accompanied by the dirges of her fowl friends (295-351). This new crime functions just as did Plateau's mention of theft in Branch VIIa: rape was not serious enough to warrant the king's justice, but murder is. It is the sorrow of Chantecler the cock, whose manhood is injured, that moves the patriarch to feeling:

> Je ferai ja Renart mander
> qant cist cors sera anterrez,
> si que vos a voz iaux verrez
> com grant vangance en sera prisse.
>
> (I, 388-91)

> When this corpse has been buried, I will command Renart to come, so that you can see with your own eyes what great vengeance will be exacted for this.

In faithful accordance with actual practice, Renart is entitled to receive three summons to court.[47] First, Noble sends Brun to arrest the fox, invoking once again "l'*avotire* et de l'orgoil, de la traïson qu'il a faite" (the *adultery*, the overweening pride, the treason that Renart committed [410-11; emphasis added]). Renart tricks the bear with honey (492-720). Badly wounded, Brun returns to Noble's court where he faints. The king's sympathy for Chantecler now turns to rage at the prospect of losing a vassal:

> "Bruns, dist li rois, Renart t'a mort,
> ne cuit qu'autre merci en aies;
> mes par la mort et par les plaies
> je en ferai si grant vangence
> q'on en parlera jusqu'an France.
>
> . . . . .
>
> dites moi au rous de pute aire
> que il viengne a cort por droit faire
> en ma sale devant la gent;
> si n'i aport or ne argent
> ne parole por lui desfandre,
> fors la hart a sa geule pandre."
>
> (I, 740-44, 747-52)

> "Brun," said the king, "Renart has done you in. Do not believe that I will have mercy on him again. In the wounds and death he will suffer, I will take such great vengeance that even as far as France people will talk of it. . . . Tell the redhead of ignoble birth that I say he must come to court so that justice be done in my hall before the people. Let him bring neither gold nor money nor words to defend himself, nothing but a noose to hang about his neck."

The second messenger is Tibert, the frightened cat, whom Renart also tricks with a promise of food (752-934). Then Noble sends a written letter, his seal affixed, with the third messenger, Grimbert. The written summons appears to convey greater force. When Renart opens the letter and reads that he is sentenced to hang, his fear is great and he confesses a litany of sins to Grimbert:

Sire, gié esté entechiez
de Hersent, la fame Isangrin;
mais ore vos di en la fin
que ele est a droit mescreüe,
que voirement l'ai ge foutue.

(I, 1048-52)

Sire, I was infatuated with Hersent, the wife of Isengrin. But I will tell you the whole story: she is rightly
suspected, because I really did fuck her.

When Renart finally confesses, it is to adultery, not rape.
He vigorously adds that Hersent is guilty, too. And when
the fox appears in court the next day, he shrewdly changes
foutue to *amee*, whitewashing his crime in a romantic turn
that is sure to appeal to the king. It is no longer adultery,
but the crime of love:

D'Isangrin ne sai ge qui dire:
ce ne puis ge pas escondure
que je n'aie sa fame amee,
mes puis que ne s'en est clamee
et puis qu'i n'i ot braies traites
ne huis brisiez, ne portes fraites,
s'ele m'a chier et ele m'ame,
cil fous jalous de coi se claime?

(I, 1283-90)

As for Isengrin, I do not know what to say. I cannot
deny that I loved his wife, but since she never com-
plained, and since I did not pull off her knickers or
break into her house or push down her door, if I was
dear to her and she loved me, what is this jealous fool
complaining about?

The council of peers assembles. Renart is blindfolded and
led to the gallows, but his desperate pleas for mercy finally move the king, who agrees to let Renart make a pilgrimage. No sooner is the fox released then—cursing and
insulting Noble—he wipes his arse with his pilgrim cloak
and throws it at the council members. As in Branch VIIb,
the text ends when Renart escapes to his castle.

The trial scenes in Branches VIIb and I of *Le Roman de
Renart* scrutinize the medieval hesitation in cases involving the sexual violation of a married woman: is it rape or
adultery? It was assumed that a wife, knowledgeable about
sex and men, could only be complicitous in her own rape.
The authors undermine this ideological assumption by depicting a wife who, despite her zestful taste for sexual activities, resisted Renart as best she could and was not at all
complicitous in his assault.

At the same time as they scrutinize secular medieval law,
highlight its inherent contradictions, and illustrate its failings, the authors of Branches VIIb and I parody medieval
romance. Both poets subvert Béroul's version of the
Tristan and Iseut story by highlighting the ambiguity of
those characters, and the discourse of courtly love.

Despite the moments of broad obscenity, scathing misogyny, and grotesque bathos, neither Pierre de Saint-
Cloud nor his continuator falls into a simplistic stance.

These branches of *Le Roman de Renart* examine a range
of medieval attitudes toward sexual violence and actually
point out the ways in which the feudal legal system supports cultural indifference to male violence against women.

In 1190, approximately fifteen years after Pierre de Saint-
Cloud wrote the first trial and ten years after the composition of the second *jugement,* another continuator takes up
the case of Hersent's rape one last time. Branch VIII, "Le
Duel judiciaire," returns to Noble's court where we hear
the king renarrate Renart's countless sins. The events are
by now highly familiar; the medieval audience has heard
them repeated but apparently without diminished pleasure.

The author of Branch VIII continues to exploit the trial
format. Renart offers to undergo an ordeal or combat to
prove that all the charges are lies. Jealous of his wife's
honor, Isengrin is still intent on proving that the fox raped
Hersent:

Dist Isengrin: "Certes, Renart,
jel moterroi de moie part
que vos a force l'asaillites,
en con trover pas ne faillites;
voienz mes iauz, vousist ou non,
li batites vos le crepon.

. . . . .

ce ne porrïez vos desfandre
ne vos en veïsse descendre
et voz braies sus remonter;
ne m'est honte del raconter."

(VIII, 7842-48, 7853-56)

Isengrin said: "Renart, in truth, I will for my part show
that you attacked and raped her, and did not fail to find
her cunt; before my very eyes, against my will, you
rode her rump. . . . You can not defend yourself against
the fact that I saw you get off her and pull up your
breeches. It is no shame for me to tell."

Renart exhorts Isengrin to stop embarrassing himself by
saying such indecent things about Hersent in public, but
the impassioned husband will not be still (7859-8068).

In faithful mimesis of medieval practice, a trial by combat,
the *Judicium Dei* or *jugement de Dieu,* is arranged.[48] Each
combatant lays down his security and names four guaran-
tors. The duel deserves our full and final attention because
it culminates the intertextual saga of Hersent's rape and
shows how the anonymous author of the 1190 branch re-
writes the work of his predecessors. On the day of the
duel, Hersent prays for her husband, and this is what she
asks of God:

Hersant prie por son saingnor
que Diex li face tele honor
*que ja de la bataille n'isse
et que Renart vaintre le puisse,
qui mout souëf li fist la chose
en la tesniere ou iert enclose.*

(VIII, 8191-96 [emphasis added])

Hersent prays for her lord, that God might so honor
him *that he not come out of the combat alive and that
Renart defeat him, Renart who did it to her so sweetly
when she was wedged in the burrow.*

After thousands of verses debating the question of Hersent's violation, the second continuator undoes the complexities of Branches VIIa, VIIb, and I in order to reveal the "truth": Hersent enjoyed being raped.

In the thick of the fighting, the faithful Isengrin finally yields to public opinion:

> [Isengrin] dist: "Foux est qui met s'entente
> en fame n'en riens qu'ele die:
> poi est de fames qui voir die,
> par fame est plus noise que pais,
> ja la moie ne querrai mais.
> Fame fait haïr pere et mere,
> fame fait tuer son conpere,
> par fame sont ocis.M. home,
> fame est de toz max la some,
> fox est qui trop i met s'entente."
>
> (VIII, 8522-31)

[Isengrin] said: "He who places his thoughts in a woman or in anything she says is mad: few are the women who tell the truth. Women are responsible for more discord than peace. Never again will I seek out mine. Women make you hate father and mother; women make you kill your friend; because of women a thousand men are slain; women are the sum of all evil. Whoever fixes his thoughts on them is mad."

In this misogynist diatribe against women, the language usually reserved for Renart is now shifted to womankind: "de toz max la some." The discourse is unlike the studied ambiguities in the representation of the feminine in earlier branches. If we look at this shift in chronological terms, we notice that its date, 1190, corresponds to the approximate date of Chrétien de Troyes's *Conte du Graal,* the one romance in which Chrétien inserts diatribes that are overtly degrading to women. It is possible that Chrétien and the author of Branch VIII are both responding to a historical shift in attitudes toward women, an early example of the backlash against the courtly positioning of the feminine that will break out more virulently in the thirteenth and fourteenth centuries.[49]

Thus the controversy closes. Isengrin will eventually win the duel, but Noble will grant Renart a royal pardon regardless. It would appear that the anonymous poet of Branch VIII could not endorse or sustain the multiple ambiguities of the earlier trials, in which the difficult questions of Hersent's motivations, Renart's violence, the king's indifference, and the court's inadequacies were tossed into the air. Like skilled jugglers, the authors of Branches VIIa, VIIb, and I kept the many pins in constant play. It is as if this movement, this open-ended uncertainty, were too much for the author of Branch VIII, who allowed the juggling pins to drop, and brought in a final verdict against the victim. The miracle of the earlier branches is their brash willingness to portray outrageous contempt for women, to entertain the complexity of social attitudes toward sexual violence, and to scrutinize the existing legal apparatus for judging rape.

We have stressed the ways in which *Le Roman de Renart* undermines the literary discourse of courtly romance and

the legal principle of immanent justice. The *Renart* is not always subversive, however. Its relationship to the legal system of the day is in many passages mimetic; it faithfully reproduces actual medieval practices. While these images are not subversive, they are profoundly cynical and pessimistic. The *Renart* appears to trace the disintegration of the feudal court system. In the earliest trial, Branch VIIb depicts an attempt at legal adjudication. But the judge himself thwarts correct procedure, and the court falls back on the practice of swearing on saints' relics. In the second trial, Branch I reveals the failure of adjudication. The court has recourse to oaths and even threatens the old-fashioned ordeal. In the third trial, the courtroom itself has vanished: the king resorts to the violence of a duel on the field of combat. Concomitantly, Branch VIII ends with the scapegoating of the female plaintiff, implying that her dishonesty is the cause of this conflict. The audience watches images of the feudal law system degenerate from branch to branch. *Le Roman de Renart* documents the slow disintegration of feudal practices, as an oral tradition collapses under the increasing predominance of the written. This literary text uses the legal question of rape as a vehicle to convey the conflicts tearing at the tenuous judicial and political order in feudal society.

In conclusion, lest the modern reader imagine that *Le Roman de Renart* can be made to disclose a well-hidden medieval strain of protofeminism, I want to bring to the center the question that lingers in the margins of this chapter. The female reader cannot fail to notice that Hersent's raped body is the text on which this legal debate, however subversive or thought-provoking, is inscribed. The violated female body stands patiently before the court, in branch after branch, as the vehicle for a male study of feudal jurisprudence. As in Chrétien's romances, sexual violence is construed as a problem for men. Rape is only part of a larger dilemma: that of maintaining order and strength in the chaotic feudal world.

Notes

1. References are to Mario Roques's edition (Paris: Champion, 1950-63). Later branches were edited by Ernst Martin, *Le Roman de Renart* (Strasbourg: K. J. Trubner, 1882). A new bilingual edition of certain branches has been translated by Micheline de Combarieu du Grès and Jean Subrenat (Paris: 10/18, 1981). The first twelve branches are dated between 1175 and 1205; the terminus ad quem for the others is fixed as 1250. The later branches contain several allusions to "les amours de Renart et de Hersent": Martin, XI, 1396-1400; Martin, XIII, 1056-9; Martin, XVII, 976-81. All English translations of *Le Roman de Renart* are mine.

2. Philippe de Navarre, for example, remarks on the importance of legal training for members of the feudal elite in *Le Livre de Phillippe de Navarre,* in *Recueil des historiens des croisades* (Paris: Académie des Inscriptions et Belles-Lettres, 1841-1906), Loi 1, 17:569. See also J.S.C. Riley-Smith, *The Feudal Nobility and the Kingdom of Jerusalem, 1174-1277*

(London: Macmillan, 1973), 133. I am grateful to James Brundage for familiarizing me with these texts.

3. Richard Posner, *Law and Literature: A Misunderstood Relationship* (Cambridge: Harvard University Press, 1988), argues that in most texts on the subject of law, the legal matter is peripheral to the meaning of the text because "great literature deals with the permanent and general aspects of human nature and institutions" (15). Posner implies that a faithful and detailed representation of law would render a "great book"tedious and local. He concludes that "law as depicted in literature is often just a metaphor for something else that is the primary concern of author and reader" (15).

4. James Boyd White, *Heracles' Bow: Essays on the Rhetoric and Poetics of the Law* (Madison: University of Wisconsin Press, 1985), offers Arnoldian readings of great works of literature that take law as their subject and proposes that they be placed in law school curricula in order to make better lawyers.

5. Robert Weisberg, "The Law-Literature Enterprise,"*Yale Journal of Law and the Humanities* 1 (December 1988):3. I am grateful to Daniel Alter for this reference.

6. R. Howard Bloch, *Medieval French Literature and Law* (Berkeley and Los Angeles: University of California Press, 1977). This chapter owes an important debt to the thesis Bloch presents in his Introduction.

7. Bloch, 3.

8. The earliest sources of information on feudal law date from the thirteenth century: *Le Très ancien Coutumier de Normandie*, ed. Adolphe F. L. Tardif (Rouen: Lestrignant, 1896), part written c. 1199-1200 and another part c. 1220; *Le Grand Coutumier de Normandie*, ed. A.F.L. Tardif (Rouen: Lestrignant, 1896), c. 1230-40; *La Très ancienne Coutume de Bretagne*, ed. Marcel Planiol (Rennes: Plihon & Hervé, 1896), probably written between 1312 and 1325; *Le Livre de Jostice et de Pletz*, ed. P. N. Rapetti (Paris: Firmin Didot, 1850), the customary of Orléans, dated 1254-60. Philippe de Beaumanoir, *Les Coutumes de Beauvaisis*, ed. A. Salmon (Paris: Picard, 1899), perhaps the richest source of information on secular law, was drafted c. 1283. *Les Establissements de Saint Louis*, ed. P. Viollet (Paris: Renouard, 1881), is a private customary relating practices in Orléans, Touraine, and Anjou, dated November 1272-June 1273. For an overview of secular law at this time, see A. Esmein, *Histoire de la procédure criminelle en France* (Paris: Larose et Forcel, 1882) and also his *Cours d'histoire du droit français* (Paris: Sirey, 1907). For the peculiarities of Normandy, see J. Le Foyer, *Exposé de droit pénal normand au treizième siècle* (Paris: Sirey, 1931).

9. Yvonne Bongert, *Recherches sur les cours laïques du Xe au XIIIe siècle* (Paris: A & J Picard, 1949). A similar study, specifically comparing feudal law to

Le Roman de Renart, is Jean Graven's *Le Procès criminel du Roman de Renart: etude du droit criminel féodal au XIIe siècle* (Geneva: Librairie de l'Université, 1950). See also Guido Van Dievoet, "Le *Roman de Renart* et *Van Den Vos Reynaerde*, témoins fidèles de la procédure penale aux XIIe et XIIIe siècles?" in *Aspects of the Medieval Animal Epic*, ed. E. Rombauts and A. Welkenhuysen (The Hague: Martinus Nijhoff, 1975), 43-52.

10. On procedure and proof in feudal law see also John W. Baldwin, "The Intellectual Preparation for the Canon of 1215 against Ordeals,"*Speculum* 36 (1961): 613-36; Paul Hyams, "Trial by Ordeal: The Key to Proof in Early Common Law," in *On the Laws and Customs of England*, ed. Morris Arnold et al. (Chapel Hill: University of North Carolina Press, 1981), 90-126; Richard M. Frather, "Preventing Crime in the High Middle Ages: The Medieval Lawyers' Search for Deterrence," in *Popes, Teachers, and Canon Law in the Middle Ages*, ed. James Sweeney and Stanley Chodorow (Ithaca: Cornell University Press, 1988), 212-33.

11. I am grateful to James Brundage for making this point clear to me. For a more detailed discussion, see H.L.A. Hart, *The Concept of Law* (Oxford: Clarendon Press, 1961), 181-207.

12. Nivardus, *Ysengrimus*, ed. Ernst Voigt (Halle, 1884).

13. Lenard Willems's *Etude sur l'Ysengrinus* (Ghent: E. Van Goethem, 1895) remains one of the few studies of this work with a great deal of useful information on the text's sources.

14. Jill Mann, *Ysengrimus: Text with Translation, Commentary and Introduction* (Leiden: E. J. Brill, 1987), 460-61. Mann's volume is a welcome and invaluable contribution to impoverished *Ysengrimus* studies. I am also grateful to Kathy Hardison for her comments and for sharing her translation of Nivardus with me.

15. Léopold Sudre, *Les Sources du Roman de Renart* (Paris: Bouillon, 1893), 21. There is in fact one passing reference to the rape (missed by Sudre) in *Liber* 1:51-52. Sudre's excellent and still useful chapter on the rape episode ("Renart Adultère," 141-58) demonstrates the way in which the French authors of the *Renart* drastically transform a folk tale by investing it with their own cultural preoccupations. Sudre notes that we recognize a version even more archaic than Nivard's in the *Romulus* or *Fables* of Marie de France. See Marie de France, *Fables*, ed. Harriet Spiegel (Toronto: University of Toronto Press, 1987), 184-85.

16. It is commonly supposed that Pierre de Saint-Cloud was a priest or church official. Doubtless he was a cleric, educated within the Church. See Robert Bossuat, *Le Roman de Renard* (Paris: Hatier, 1967).

17. Gustave Cohen, *La Vie littéraire en France au moyenâge* (Paris: Tallandier, 1949), 131.

18. Béroul, *Le Roman de Tristan,* ed. Ernest Muret (Paris: Champion, 1974).

19. I have drawn throughout on E. Jane Burns's informative discussion of law and literature in Béroul's *Roman de Tristan,* "How Lovers Lie Together," *Tristania* 8 (Spring 1983):17, 36. On the important and perhaps unexpected parallels between Renart and the character of Tristan, see Nancy F. Regalado, "Tristan and Renart: Two Tricksters," *Esprit Créateur* 16 (1976):30-38.

20. Two critics who have studied the sexual violence in *Renart* are Dietmar Rieger, "Le Motif du viol dans la littérature de la France médiévale: entre norme courtoise et réalité courtoise," *Cahiers de Civilisation médiévale* 31 (July-September 1988):263-65, and Kenneth Varty, "Le Viol dans l'*Ysengrimus,* les branches II-Va, et la branche I du *Roman de Renart,*" in *Amour, mariage et transgressions au moyen âge,* ed. Danielle Buschinger and André Crépin (Göppingen: Kümmerle Verlag, 1984), 411-18. Rieger, 263, and Varty, 413, underline the discursive *déplacement* from rape to adultery and its misogynist connotations.

21. Georges Duby, *The Knight, the Lady, and the Priest: The Making of Modern Marriage in Medieval France,* trans. Barbara Bray (New York: Pantheon Books, 1983), 220.

22. Unknowingly reiterating Hersent's strategy following the adultery, Renart himself reintroduces the legal context by mockingly offering to swear that he did nothing dishonest to Hersent: "et por moi et por lui desfandre, / tot par la ou le vodrez prandre, / un sairement vos aramis / au los de voz meillors amis" (VIIa, 5993-96) (To defend my honor and hers, I will take an oath, anywhere you choose, before your closest friends).

23. On the *curia regis* see Bongert, 62-67, 137-48, and Bloch, 129, 136, 138, 231. Rape or *raptus* is classed among the most serious crimes against peace and is judged in royal or high courts (Bongert, 124-26).

24. The council of peers is described in Bongert, 66, 270; and Graven, 21.

25. For a discussion of similar strategies in modern literature, see Weisberg, 35; and Barbara Johnson, "Melville's Fist: The Execution of *Billy Budd,*" in *The Critical Difference* (Baltimore: Johns Hopkins University Press, 1981), 79-109.

26. Duby, 221. Studying medieval England, John Marshall Carter shows that royal justice discriminated against rape victims: "However, this same royal justice which helped to maintain order in times of crisis was a great factor in the lessening of women's status in the thirteenth century. Royal justices from distant counties or towns were less concerned about the feelings of an individual female in a county they might not visit again, than they were about law and order, generally, and revenue, specifically. It was much easier to fine a woman for not appearing at an eyre court than it was to pursue the case further" (*Rape in Medieval England: An Historical and Sociological Study* [Lanham, Md.: University Press of America, 1985], 128-29). Of course, in the fiction of the *Renart,* Hersent is well known to the king since she is the wife of his constable.

27. For examples of the influence of canon on feudal law, see Bloch, 9, 231; and Bongert, 37-38, 181, 201. Readers who seek a thorough survey of these exchanges should consult Harold J. Berman, *Law and Revolution: The Formation of the Western Legal Tradition* (Cambridge: Harvard University Press, 1983), and James A. Brundage, *Law, Sex, and Christian Society in Medieval Europe* (Chicago: University of Chicago Press, 1987).

28. Brundage 1987, 253.

29. On the heaviness of penalties for theft, *La Très ancienne Coutume de Bretagne,* for example, stipulates "que il ait emblé plus de cinq soulz, ou la value, il doit estre jugié a mort par coustume" (Article 117). For further examples, see Chapter 5 and also Graven, 43-44.

30. On the status of the *lex talionis* in the Middle Ages, see Graven, 35-42, and Bloch, 68.

31. James A. Brundage, "Rape and Marriage in the Medieval Canon Law," *Revue de droit canonique* 28 (June-December 1978):62-75. *La Très ancienne Coutume de Bretagne,* c. 1312-1325, states: "Et si aucun forceit famme, pour ce que elle ne fust putain, et il eust sa compaignie par force et oultre sa volonté comme il apparust, ou il la raveist par force, celui qui ce feroit en devroit estre puni comme d'autres crimes. . . . Et auxi ne le devroit justice soustenir contre nulle famme mariée que il ne desut estre puni sans remede" (Article 155).

32. For more general bibliography on Gratian, see Brundage 1978 and 1987, and also my Introduction.

33. Bongert, 103-7; Graven, 53-58; and Bloch, 50, 134-37, describe this aspect of the judge's function. *La Très ancienne Coutume de Bretagne* waxes poetic on the judge's duty to be extremely prudent in sentencing: "Ainczois doit être toute justice plus esmue d'absoudre que de condamner, car homme et femme sont trop forz a nourrir, et ils sont tantôt détruit; et homme vaut plus, pour tant ce qu'il soit bon, de cent et de mille livres. . . . [La cause] doit être plus claire que nulle autre et plus claire qu'étoile au ciel, dont homme est condamné a mort."

34. John Flinn, *Le Roman de Renart* (Paris: Presses Universitaires Françaises, 1963), 35-157. For an argument against reading the *Renart* as satire, see my "1175: Fables and Parodies," in *A New History of French Literature,* ed. Denis Hollier (Cambridge: Harvard University Press, 1989), 46-50. Hans Robert Jauss described the *Roman de Renart* as parody in his *Untersuchungen zur Mittelalterlichen Tierdich-*

tung (Tübingen: Max Niemeyer, 1959). See also Danielle Buschinger and André Crépin, *Comique, satire et parodie dans la tradition renardienne et les fabliaux* (Göppinger Arbeiten zur Germanistik, no. 391; Actes du Colloque des 15 et 16 Janvier, 1983 [Göppingen: Kümmerle Verlag, 1983]).

35. The difficulty of finding lords willing to act as judges is documented in Bongert, 57-61, and Bloch, 65. See also Georges Duby, *La Société aux XIe et XIIe siècles dans la région mâconnaise* (Paris: Armand-Colin, 1953), 202.

36. "La scène de discussion est traitée avec un réalisme et une attention aux détails qui trahissent une grande connaissance en même temps qu'*un profond respect* de la part de Pierre de Saint-Cloud pour la procédure de son temps, et sa satire des jugements de Dieu se révèle par conséquent comme *un sincère désir de perfectionner un système auquel il est très attaché.* Les preuves *de son admiration et de son respect* pour les principes fondamentaux et pour les formes de la justice abondent dans la branche II-Va" (Flinn, 39-40 [emphasis added]). Flinn consistently declares that Pierre's descriptions of feudal justice are respectful while his descriptions of the nobility are severely critical. Without justification, however, this seems an arbitrary reading of similar comic techniques. The representation of the king's court can be interpreted as subversive and as disrespectful as the representation of feudal aristocracy.

37. Regalado 1976. See also my *Vilain and Courtois: Transgressive Parody in French Literature of the 12th and 13th Centuries* (Lincoln: University of Nebraska Press, 1989), 81-112.

38. For her persuasive argument on the value of overt misogyny for the female audience of medieval literature, see Roberta L. Krueger, "Misogyny, Manipulation, and the Female Reader in Hue de Rotelande's *Ipomédon,*" in *Courtly Literature: Culture and Context,* ed. Keith Busby and Erik Kooper (Amsterdam: Benjamins, 1990).

39. For a general introduction to this branch, see Flinn, 57-58, and also Lucien Foulet, *Le Roman de Renard* (Paris: Champion, 1914), 323-54.

40. Pierre J. Payer, *Sex and the Penitentials* (Toronto: University of Toronto Press, 1984), 117.

41. Varty (1984) and Rieger (1988) were, to my knowledge, the first to point this out.

42. Hincmar de Reims, *De divortio Lotharii regis et Tetbergae reginae,* C. 6, in *Patrologia Latinae,* ed. J. P. Migne (Paris: Garnier, 1844-64), 125:619-77; trans. cited in Burns, 27 n. 2. See also Robert Bartlett, *Trial by Fire and Water: The Medieval Judicial Ordeal* (Oxford: Oxford University Press, 1986), *passim;* F. Carl Riedel, *Crime and Punishment in the Old French Romances* (New York: AMS Press, 1966), 36, 77; and especially Bongert, 216, 223-25, and Graven, 28-29.

43. Cited in Burns, 27 n. 2. For further commentary and descriptions of the trial by glowing iron, see Brundage 1987, 224; Bongert, 216, 221-25; Graven, 28-29; and Riedel, 36.

44. Bongert describes such changes of heart (218).

45. As early as the eleventh century, Ivo of Chartres expressed grave reservations about this type of proof. See Brundage 1987, 224; and Bongert, 218, as well as Baldwin 1961 and Hyams 1981. In 1215, the Latern Council officially prohibited ordeals.

46. Burns, 19-20. Iseut's oath is found in Béroul, ll. 4197-4216. On the rules of the *serment purgatoire,* see Bongert, 205-10; and Graven, 28.

47. Bongert, 188-90, and Graven, 25-27, document the practice of summoning the accused three times. The same rule continued to be observed in the thirteenth and fourteenth centuries, as the legal records studied in Chapter 5 will show.

48. On the nature and history of the *judicium dei,* see Bloch, 18-19, 21-22, 48-49, 63-64; Bongert, 211, 228-52; and Graven, 29-30.

49. It is also possible to speculate that changing attitudes toward women parallel the degeneration of the feudal law system.

Thomas W. Best (essay date 1993)

SOURCE: "Early *Branches* of the *Roman de Renart,*" in *Reynard the Fox,* Twayne Publishers, 1983, pp. 33-69.

[*In the following excerpt, Best describes and summarizes the various French tales collected under the name of the* Roman de Renart.]

About the year 1176 a trouvère named Pierre de Saint-Cloud wrote what seems to be the first medieval beast epic in a popular language.[1] It consists of some 2,410 eight-syllable verses in rhymed couplets, and its plot is devoted principally to another feud between the fox, named Renart, and Ysengrin the wolf, both of whom are barons in Noble the lion's kingdom. It was so well received that imitations soon appeared. By circa 1250 some twenty-six Gallic tales about Reynard (the exact number depending on how one counts) were circulating as so-called *branches,* in the same verse form as Pierre de Saint-Cloud's poem, and were being collected as the ***Roman de Renart.*** Initially the public may have referred to Pierre's novelty as the "Romance of Reynard," and the poets who first followed his example possibly thought of their creations as offshoots from that trunk. If so, the title nevertheless soon became generic, while *branche* was kept as the technical term for a Reynard epic in French.

Extant manuscripts of the ***Roman de Renart*** do not preserve its *branches* in any meaningful order. They deny Pierre's pioneering venture due prominence, for example, and even break it up most ignominiously. Standard numbering of the *Roman*'s *branches* today still reflects that confusion, despite the chronology established by Foulet.[2] Those poems are usually identified according to their order in Ernst Martin's edition of 1882-87,[3] which does not improve on the manuscripts. Pierre's original is known as *Branches* II and Va combined, and what is termed *Branche* I was not produced until after II-Va, III, IV, and XIV were already in existence (circa 1179).

Branches XV and V (which share the curious fate of having been joined to parts of II-Va)[4] probably also antedate I, though we cannot be sure that they do. There are allusions in I to II-Va, III, IV, and XIV but not so definitely to XV and V, while XV failed to influence the Middle-High-German epic *Reinhart Fuchs,* which was written during the 1190s and combines material from *Branches* I, II-Va, III, IV, V, VI, X, and maybe VIII. *Branche* V seems to anticipate XIV, however, and to be indebted to XV in turn. Because XV refers only to II-Va and III for certain, we will place it chronologically right after III, with V immediately following IV. The *branches* concerning us in this chapter are therefore II-Va, III, XV, IV, V, XIV, and I, in that presumptive order of composition. Among all the ***Roman de Renart***'s *branches* only II-Va and I are major works, but tracing the likely development of the beast epic from II-Va to I is an interesting part of our whole endeavor.

We will utilize Martin's edition rather than more recent ones, since it seems closest to the original version of each *branche* which we want to study.[5]

BRANCHE II-VA

Whereas Nivardus composed *Ysengrimus,* with its difficult Latin, inverted structure, and comments on ecclesiastical personages, to be read by educated clerics, Pierre de Saint-Cloud wrote for recitation to lay nobility, addressed at the very beginning of his poem as *seigneurs.*

In a twenty-two-line prologue he asserts that he is breaking new ground, and he indicates that *Ysengrimus* was unknown to the general public. To familiar stories like those about Paris and Helen or Tristan, he declares, he will add an account of Renart's vendetta with Ysengrin, about which his audience has never heard. Because he ends his prologue by telling us to listen to what brought about the two barons' feud, we expect his work to open with the casus belli or at least with some background history, but we find that the first 1,000 lines contain only a series of episodes involving Renart's attempt to prey upon the rooster Chantecler, upon an unnamed titmouse, and upon Tiecelin the crow, as well as to injure the wildcat Tibert. Those verses do not at all deal with reasons for a war against the wolf.

As Foulet has pointed out,[6] Pierre was evidently influenced by Bruno the bear's poem in *Ysengrimus,* which relates how Reinardus endangered Sprotinus the cock and

then befouled the wolf cubs. Pierre composed his narrative by building onto each of those disparate incidents, for he wanted to portray more than just a feud, despite not saying so in his prologue. We will see that what he created is in fact a satire on the seamy side of knighthood, so that the two major parts of his work are thematically related.

Whereas Nivardus identifies Reinardus right away as a fox, Pierre does not explain who Renart is, implying that in the folklore of northern France the fox had become better known during the generation since *Ysengrimus* appeared. The gentlemen for whom Pierre wrote seem to have been acquainted in advance with both Ysengrin and Renart, though not with a conflict between them. In contrast to that pair, all other named animals are carefully introduced. Because they are, Pierre should probably be credited with having christened most of them himself, following Nivardus's example. Only in regard to the fox, the wolf, and Brun the bear was he clearly not original.

Branche II, Verses 23-1026. Altering Sprotinus's seduction and escape, Pierre handled in his own way the first episode which he borrowed from Nivardus. The French version appears to begin on a morning in July.[7] Renart, characterized as a master of devilish deceit, dives through the palisade around Constant des Noes's garden, landing among cabbage plants that conceal him. Constant's hens, who see something sail through the air, run for their roost, but Chantecler is sure that all of them are safe. So convinced is he that he acts like a fool, says Pierre (line 121), for he goes to sleep on a manure pile. He even dismisses a dream which his favorite wife Pinte interprets as a warning that before noon a fox will seize him by the throat.

During the second nap Renart lunges at him but misses out of impetuosity. To prevent him from flying away, the fox pretends that no harm is meant because the two are cousins. A resultant cry of relief inspires Renart to claim that the song of Chantecler's father, who crowed with his eyes shut, could be heard for a league, and the fox declares that losing a foot would be better than hurting a relative. What Renart does not intend to be a two-step process becomes one, as in *Ysengrimus,* for the cock initially preserves sufficient caution merely to wink. When he is persuaded to close both eyes, his beguiler grips him by the neck and prances off.

In order for Chantecler's plight to be discovered, Pierre has the time suddenly become evening (line 371), even though Pinte's prediction of an attack before noon (line 252) indicated that only slightly earlier it was still morning. The sun has lurched, as in Nivardus's fishing episode. Because of the late hour, at any rate, a woman comes to put the chickens in their coop and espies the rooster slung across his abductor's back. She cries for help, sending all the farm hands in pursuit, and Constant sics dogs on Renart, who has managed to carry his booty back through the palisade.

Chantecler grows clever in adversity, appealing to the fox's pride just as the fox has appealed to his. Without telling Renart to lay him down first, he maintains that

Constant should be taunted. Cooperatively the fox then barks, "In spite of you I'm taking what is mine," permitting what he thought was his to fly into an apple tree. He squats below on a dungheap by way of showing that he has assumed the rooster's role as dupe. Like his counterpart in several of the fables reviewed in connection with the Sprotinus incident, he curses the mouth which opens when it should be shut, while a wiser Chantecler curses the eye which shuts when it should be open. Despite the latter's sneer that Renart must move along to keep his fur intact, his pursuers have vanished, as not only in *Ysengrimus* but also in *Gallus et Vulpes* and Marie de France's *Esope*.

Rather than keep Chantecler in his remark of the Sprotinus episode's second stage, Pierre substituted another bird, the titmouse. With a different prey the peace ploy stands a better chance of succeeding. Pierre must have known either Marie's *Esope*, in which her fable about the fox and the dove immediately follows the one about the fox and the cock, or an earlier version of it, but perhaps he considered the dove a less worthy match for Renart than the tit, whom Marie presents elsewhere as "very wise, perceptive, and sly."[8]

Still reproaching himself for his stupidity, Renart spots that bird near her nest in a hollow oak. He asks her to come down and greet him with a kiss, but instead of complying she scolds him for his deviousness. To put her off guard, he says very nearly what he told Chantecler, lying that he never dreamed of displeasing her and reminding her that he is her son's godfather. He justifies his demand for a peck by claiming that King Noble has suspended all hostilities, to everyone's relief, though rather than wave a piece of birch bark in specious confirmation, like Reinardus, he encourages the tit to kiss him by promising to close his eyes.

She purports to acquiesce, but only in order to tease him. While he squints, she brushes his whiskers with leaves and moss. Of course he snaps, and she chides him for nearly breaking the putative law he has just cited. Excusing himself with the assertion that he was only joking, he urges her to kiss him again, just as he twice coaxed Chantecler to crow with eyes closed. The tit darts past his jaws, but too quickly to be caught. When Renart tries to elicit a third kiss, "in the name of holy charity," he gets no response at all. The stalemate that has developed is ended—not, as in *Ysengrimus* or *Esope*, by the bird professing to see hunters approach—but by a group of riders who really do intervene with their dogs, forcing Renart to search elsewhere for dinner, while the titmouse jeers.

So far in this escapade Pierre has combined three motifs, adding to the truce idea the complementary concepts of osculation and nictitation. The kiss's likeliest source is the Salaura episode of *Ysengrimus*, where bussing is also sought in the name of peace and where it is only a euphemism for biting. Foulet argues reasonably that closing the eyes is a carry-over from the Chantecler adventure.[9] Be-

sides mingling several borrowed motifs in this episode, Pierre also extended it by annexing a subordinate affair apparently of his own invention.

Running down a path, Renart meets a lay brother with two bloodhounds on a leash. Such a pious gentleman should be fair and not interfere with the race in progress, the fox requests, for its stakes are high. Moved by Renart's eloquence, the lay brother turns away, commending to God and Saint Julian what would have made a splendid trophy. By galloping as if on horseback the fox outdistances his pursuers, who were stopped mysteriously while he conversed, reminding us of the peasants in Nivardus's fishing fiasco.

Tibert the cat approaches, twirling along as he chases his tail. Renart pretends to be at war with Ysengrin already and asks the bearer of sharp claws to join his mercenary army. Tibert consents, having a bone to pick with the wolf hic[elf, and pledges his loyalty. Soon the perfidious fox attempts to lure him into a trap beside their trail by facetiously asking for a sample of his "equitation." Though neither of them is actually mounted, Renart requires the cat to demonstrate a make-believe charger. Tibert humors the fox by acting as if he were riding, but he discovers the trap in time to dodge it.

While the cat is dashing back and forth, on orders from his commander, two mastiffs burst into sight, just as other dogs terminated Renart's mischief with the tit. The fox's retreat on this occasion is less felicitous, however, because Tibert pushes him so that he steps into the trap himself, as he flees past it with the cat, and in place of an obliging lay brother he is confronted by the owner of the two mastiffs—a peasant with an ax. Tibert bounds away, scoffing like the cock and the tit. The peasant swings the ax but misses, smashing the trap and releasing Renart, who outruns the dogs despite having been injured. Though his foot was not cut off, we are still reminded of Nivardus's wolf on the frozen pond.

The affair with Tibert differs in a couple of ways from the adventures with Chantecler and the titmouse, as well as from the contest with Tiecelin, which follows. All three of those episodes have known antecedents, while the Tibert incident does not. It was probably invented by Pierre, like the brush with the lay brother. The other three encounters are also attempts at fowling for the sake of food, whereas with the cat Renart is only proving how gratuitously malicious he can be.

The dialog with Tiecelin the crow is carefully placed in a *locus amoenus*, which augurs a happy end. While the fox reclines on grass beneath a beech tree, near a river between two mountains, Sir Tiecelin lights on a limb above him, successfully completing what Pierre portrays as a knightly adventure. The crow has stolen a cheese. Instead of holding it in his beak, like his counterpart in such fables as Marie de France's thirteenth,[10] he presses it between his feet and pecks at it. This procedure is more practical and also permits a dramatic crescendo, since Tiecelin can talk without at once dropping his prize. Alerted by a falling crumb, Renard eulogizes the crow's late father Rohart, "who knew how to warble so well." To prove that he too can sing, Tiecelin curdles the air with his sour croak, which the fox sweetly praises. This routine is twice repeated, the raucous caw growing louder and shriller each time, until with the strain the cheese is released. Thus Pierre has Renart reuse the technique which proved effective with Chantecler[11] rather than compliment Tiecelin on his beauty and wish that his song were comparable.

Fox-crow fables regularly conclude when such cajolery pays off, but Pierre decided to append a second act to his version of the little farce, in order to impress on us Renart's (and many a cavalier's) wicked cunning. Just as he sought to murder Chantecler and the tit and at least to hurt the cat, so Renart now has designs on the life of Tiecelin. Rather than gobble up the redolent cheese, he spurns it as if it were nauseous. Exposing his damaged foot, much as foxes in bestiaries trick crows by playing dead, he whines that strong odors are bad for cripples. Tiecelin believes him and hops down, having not yet eaten enough. As with the rooster, Renart's inevitable pounce goes awry, leaving him with only a mouthful of feathers. He wants to soothe the crow as he soothed the cock, but Tiecelin flutters away. The episode, and thus the whole series of episodes, concludes with Renart being forced to dine less harmfully than intended.

Although the four little dramas are not a part of the feud which Pierre heralds in his prologue and they even lack unity among themselves, on account of the lay brother and Tibert, Pierre must have included them not just to introduce the fox, as Foulet surmises,[12] but to caricature various types of unworthy knights—complacent ones, like Chantecler; thieving ones, like the crow; and deceitful, vicious ones, like Renart, who did not even scruple to scheme against allies and ladies. Surely the fox's failure in each of these early capers reflects his author's disapproval of him. His acquisition of the cheese is not so much his reward as Tiecelin's punishment, and it is more than offset by his wounded foot. (Lameness serves him right especially on account of his assertion that he would rather be a cripple than harm Chantecler.) Pierre was most concerned about the causes and conduct of feuds, however. Not only does his prologue indicate that he was; he also devoted the greater part of his poem to Ysengrin's struggle with Renart. In doing so he no longer strung episodes together like Nivardus but rather told a single, continuous story. Though it has different stages, the one underlying conflict throughout is between the fox and the wolf.

Branche II, Verses 1027-1392, and *Branche* Va, Verses 257-1272. After nourishing himself with the cheese, Renart roams about and chances upon a cave. In a parenthetical comment the author informs us that the long-awaited fray with "Constable Ysengrin" is about to begin. Nivardus's unfrocked monk has been promoted to high officialdom, like the earlier wolf in *Ecbasis Captivi* or as in Marie de France's sixty-eighth fable. (See the sick-lion episode in Chapter One.)[13] Pierre had no use for a mindless embodiment of clerical rapacity, and he wanted the fox's foe to be politically powerful, for a reason that will become apparent near the end of the epic.

Not until Renart enters the cave does he realize that it is Ysengrin's abode. The master is out on the prowl, but the mistress Hersent is nursing four cubs. She jumps up, reproaching her guest for his unsociableness in not having visited her sooner. Renart apologizes by explaining that her husband hates him in the belief that he loves her. Thus the fox and the wolf are at odds here not, as in *Ysengrimus,* on account of the universal threat posed by lupine gluttony but rather because Ysengrin fears being cuckolded. Treated as a rival, Renart reacts as one, especially now that Hersent encourages him. She makes her spouse's jealousy the grounds for a real affair, since unlike her equivalent in Nivardus's epic she is too lascivious to be faithful. She is what Ysengrimus's loyal wife became in the interpolation at the end of Nivardus's wolf-den episode, giving Ysengrin good reason to be suspicious. In a parody of courtly love à la *Tristan* she asks the red knight to kiss her, and the couple embrace.

Before departing, Renart also takes advantage of the chance to gorge himself at his adversary's expense and to mistreat the latter's offspring. In effect he declares war by sprinkling the whelps with his urine, throwing them from their bed, and calling them bastards. As though she despised them too, Hersent does not interfere. Insead of chasing the fox, she even pleads with her young not to inform their father. They tell him everything when he returns, however, and he furiously berates his wife. She placates him by offering to vindicate herself with a test of her innocence, by pledging him total obedience, and by vowing to kill Renart if she ever can. At this point the sun, which was already sinking low more than 800 lines earlier, is finally allowed to set.

Several days later the two wolves chance upon the fox and run after him as he figuratively "spurs" for home. Ysengrin falls behind, leaving Hersent to pursue vengeance alone. When she reaches Renart's den, called Valcrues,[14] she tries to ram herself through its narrow entrance, like her counterpart at Reinardus's burrow in *Ysengrimus,* and becomes stuck. She is also raped, although the fox knows that her mate is looking for him. He may be motivated less by lust than by malice, and he does not stop belaboring Hersent until he is discovered at work. In typically two-faced fashion he denies the obvious, however, insisting to Ysengrin, who is still at a distance, that he has only been trying to dislodge the impetuous lady. He offers to swear formally that he is above reproach, for he fears God no more than the wolf. After he has withdrawn, Ysengrin concludes *Branche* II by digging Hersent loose.

Her efforts to please her husband have backfired. He is as angry at her as he was in their cave, when the story is resumed in *Branche* Va. She calms him down this time by pointing out that she has obviously been abused, and he welcomes her proposal that they complain of the assault at Noble's court, to which they make their way at once. Since Renart has committed a crime, the shortest route to revenge could be the one to the royal throne. The wolves' decision seems reasonable, and it is indeed logic more than *Ysengrimus*'s influence that determines how the plot unfolds from this point on.

Because of his position, his smartness, and his learning (he knows several languages) Ysengrin is likely to win out over Renart provided he can bring the latter to trial, Pierre remarks (lines 292-98). Even though we may be surprised to see intelligence attributed to the wolf, the author is not ironic here, since Ysengrin definitely does have rank. The comment helps reveal, instead, to what extent Nivardus's dolt has been altered.

When the wolf couple enter Noble's palace (or tent, according to line 506), they find all manner of subjects there, with the sovereign's suite in a circle around him. Everyone is silent. Ysengrin steps forward and charges Renart with having broken an imperial law safeguarding marriage, as Hersent can confirm. She testifies that since she was a girl Renart has hounded her, finally possessing her against her will. Ysengrin, who reports having observed the outrage, adds an account of what its perpetrator also did to his children and concludes with a reference to the oath which Renart volunteered to swear.

Averse to chastising a gentleman for an amour, despite the law against adultery, Noble impugns the she-wolf's credibility until her mate objects, whereupon he seeks advice from one Musart, a Lombard camel. This droll creature is a papal legate visiting the lion's court (and the caricature of an actual legate, Pietro di Pavia, in France from 1174 to 1178).[15] Surely with tongue in cheek now, since *musart* means "foolish," Pierre terms the camel "very wise and a good jurist." In pidgin French flavored with Italian and Latin Musart proclaims that the fox must be severely punished if not exonerated; but Noble hints, when calling for a verdict from his barons, that Renart should be pardoned for gallantry.

Pierre informs us that "more than a thousand" courtiers huddled to argue the fox's case. We hear from only Brichemer the stag (Noble's seneschal), Brun the bear, Baucent the boar, Plateax the fallow deer, and the monkey Cointereax, however. While sympathizing with Ysengrin, Brichemer goes objectively and at once to the heart of the matter—the absence of a reliable witness, since a spouse's testimony is suspect—only to be contradicted by Brun, who contends that the constable is too eminent to be doubted. Baucent sides with the stag, while Plateax seconds the bear.

In an effort to support the wolves, Brun relates in a 141-line digression how he himself was victimized not long ago, Renart having duped him into believing that he would find honey at Constant des Noes's farm when in reality he only served to decoy both men and dogs, who nearly killed him, while the fox abducted a chicken unscathed. Brun also reports that Tiecelin, Tibert, and the tit have recently lodged complaints against Renart. Returning to the present situation, Baucent, endorsed by Cointereax, maintains that standard procedure demands an examination of the defendant. Again Brun prolongs the debate, insisting that justice be short-circuited and the accused, against whom he is biased, be summarily treated as a convicted adulterer. Pierre's attention to the bear's lynch mentality implies that it was of topical importance, but a modern reader is likely to sigh with relief over Brichemer's resolution of the 360-line controversy. What the stag proposes, winning the court's approval (though surely not the wolves'), is that Renart should swear his oath of innocence. Since Noble is about to leave the country, the universally respected mastiff Roonel should officiate at the ceremony, to be held the following Sunday.

His Majesty happily sanctions this compromise and dispatches Grimbert the badger to apprise Renart, the two being kinsmen.[16] With court adjourned, Grimbert travels straightway to the fox's residence, which is now called either Malpertuis, Valpertuis, or Malcrues, depending on the manuscript.[17] Renart concurs, intending to perjure himself, but Ysengrin takes steps to overtrump him.

The constable visits Roonel, requesting that this court-appointed judge side with him. Despite having been portrayed by Brichemer as a paragon of virtue, Roonel suggests a particularly impious way of tricking Renart. Since the latter is to swear on a holy relic, the mastiff will pretend to have died; Renart can be asked to sanctify his oath by touching the open jaws of this "saintly" personage. Of course they will snap shut, like the trap in the perjury episode of *Ysengrimus*. Ironically, Roonel will be borrowing the vulpine ruse which Renart varied with Tiecelin and subjecting the fox to what Reinardus brought upon the wolf in Nivardus's poem. Should Renart balk, a small army of other dogs will be lurking in ambush. Not yet content, however, Ysengrin recruits more supporters, including Brichemer, Baucent, and Cointereax, who thus abandon their prior impartiality. In the France of his day, Pierre wanted to say, equity was undermined by politics. The wolf has become a dignitary in order to possess enough influence for that point to be made. He cannot obtain an improper verdict, but he can subvert the verdict which he does obtain. Musart sides with him, and Noble sends him a personal deputy, the leopard, while Tibert, once an opponent of the wolf, understandably joins Ysengrin's party now. Renart is not without allies, too, his principal backer being Grimbert.

At the appointed time both factions come to where the mastiff is playing possum, sprawled on his back with fangs bared. Hidden in a nearby orchard are more than a hundred canine cronies, thirsting for fox blood. Brichemer instructs Renart to acquit himself by proclaiming, with his right hand on Roonel's teeth, that he has been falsely accused. At this climactic moment the fox detects the "corpse's" breathing and steps back. Grimbert, who has also noticed Roonel's ruse, asserts that the crowd is pressing too close. When Brichemer has everyone make room, Renart decamps.

The dogs from the orchard race after him, parodying knightly chases and terminating the conflict with Ysengrin in much the same fashion as the designs on Chantecler, the titmouse, and Tibert were concluded. Pierre spends the last eighty-eight lines of his poem identifying seventy-eight of the pursuers and describing how they nipped the fox's fur before he reached home (Malpertuis). As if everyone were mounted, the leader of the pack, Roonel, is said to carry a lance. Bleeding in more than thirteen places, the scoundrel Renart escapes death but not vengeance, so that a moral of "crime does not pay" can be inferred. Both in the first 1,000 lines of the story and in the last 1,400 he neither fails nor succeeds completely. More sinned against than sinning as regards the fox, Ysengrin ultimately seeks justice in an unjust way, making it appropriate that he settle for less than he likes.

Pierre burlesques deceit, violence, and corruption on the part of supposedly noble knights. All too often, he hints, they behaved like animals, especially when feuding. Some of them were not above rape and the abuse of children in their belligerence, which was frequently occasioned by a woman (like the Trojan War, referred to in the prologue).[18] Even society's pillars might lean toward one of their number when he himself ethically sagged. Albeit inspired by *Ysengrimus,* Pierre was not preoccupied with greed, and he was in no way critical of the clergy. He lampooned Pietro di Pavia because he objected to that dignitary as a person and a lawyer[19] rather than as an ecclesiastic. Musart's religiousness is never impugned. It was the secular elite—the kind of men who must have listened to his poem—that Pierre took obliquely and facetiously to task.

Another facet of *Ysengrimus* which he forsook, perhaps because his plot compelled him to drop it, is Reinardus's role as the wolf's invidious adviser. Brun's account of how Renart misled him once is the only instance in II-Va of malign counsel by the fox. Renart does not really give advice even to Tibert, while he has no occasion to urge a course of action on Ysengrin. The relationship between fox and wolf established by Nivardus was implicitly restored in *Branches* III, IV, XIV, and I (Renart's confession), and it was made explicit again in *Branche* V, as we will see.

That Pierre bestowed more attention on Renart than on Ysengrin overall did not result from a preference for the former but, on the contrary, from aversion to the combination of duplicity and viciousness which characterizes a fox better than a wolf. Renart may not have been more popular than Ysengrin before 1176, though most of Pierre's imitators certainly did favor the fox, probably on account of his prominence in the first 1,000 lines of *Branche* II-Va and also because a wolf is not supposed to be so capable and clever.

BRANCHE III

In what must have been a very short time after Pierre's epic became known, an anonymous minstrel composed 510-line *Branche* III. The fact that III resembles II-Va in containing no allusions to any other *branche* suggests that it was produced quite early, yet Pierre's prologue indicates that his work still takes precedence chronologically. In III the fox also starts a feud with the wolf, moreover, so that Pierre could not have made his claim to "originality" if III antedated II-Va.

Like him, the author of III begins by addressing an audience as *seigneurs,* but in contrast to Pierre he wanted to entertain rather than to satirize. Another difference is that no prologue follows in III, just as there is none in *Ysengrimus.* We are plunged immediately into the narrative by being informed that the season is winter. More precisely, we are later told, it is shortly before Christmas. As hungry as at the outset of II-Va, Renart leaves his now nameless burrow and hunts for food. In the first two of the *branche*'s three episodes (though only for the sake of the second) the den is said to be a castle with windows and a door that opens and closes.[20]

As he lurks beside a road, the fox sees a couple of fish merchants driving their wagon toward him. He plays dead, better than Roonel in II-Va, and for the sake of his pelt the two men toss him atop their load. While they travel on, he gobbles over thirty herring and wreathes himself with eels. His astonished benefactors chase him when he bids them adieu, but he has too fast a horse, as the author jokes in line 141.

One of that poet's major innovations is to have blessed the fox with a family. Although Reinardus indicates that he has cubs in the wolf-den episode of *Ysengrimus,*[21] we never see them or hear of them again, and his wife is not even mentioned. Pierre de Saint-Cloud drops no hint that Renart has either a mate or offspring in II-Va, but in III we find him married to gentle Hermeline, who has borne him two sons, Percehaie and Malebranche. The three of them welcome him heartily, and not just because of his viands, though they quickly prepare the eels for roasting.

Their supper's aroma reaches the nostrils of half-starved Ysengrin, who in his stupid voraciousness is much more Nivardus's wolf than Pierre's. He squats outside a window to the fox's residence and howls for its door to be opened, but Renart, who pretends that the building is a cloister belonging to the order of Tiron (which actually existed), refuses to admit a layman. "*Nomini dame!*" Ysengrin exclaims, introducing into vernacular Reynard epics the use of comically corrupt Latin, reminiscent of *cominus ovis cum* in the monastery episode of *Ysengrimus.* When the wolf asks what the brothers are eating, Renart alleges that they always dine on seafood (and the Tiron monks did).[22] He extends a sample, expressing the hope that Ysengrin will join their congregation. Just for being tonsured the wolf can consume any amount of fish, Renart affirms. Naturally Ysengrin consents, so the fox has him stick his head inside and pours boiling water over it.

In addition Renart stipulates that the "novice" must be tested for a night, by catching fish for the "abbey." He leads Ysengrin to a frozen pond, where there is still a hole in the ice cut by farmers for their cattle. The wolf sits there till dawn, with a bucket tied to his tail. Renart does not have to lure a mob to the scene, because a vavasor named Constant des Granches (after Pierre's peasant Constant des Noes) comes hunting with his men. Drawing a sword, the chasseur tries to accomplish what Aldrada sought in *Ysengrimus,* yet he also misses twice, whacking the fisher's tail in two on his second attempt. After fighting off the hunters' dogs and escaping, Ysengrin ends *Branche* III by vowing enmity against Renart, who has meanwhile returned to his home, now called a den (line 445).

Ysengrimus probably inspired both the second and third episodes of this poem, as Foulet has argued,[23] but whereas Nivardus included a sham ordainment primarily so that monks in general might be satirized by means of his wolf, the author of *Branche* III saw Ysengrin's induction into a putative cloister as merely an excuse for twofold torture (through both tonsuring and testing). While Renart, like Reinardus, entices the wolf into monasticism for the sake of food, moreover, the author of *Branche* III changed the kind of food initially proffered. Instead of cakes he has his fox bait Ysengrin with eels, in anticipation of the fishing affair and in accordance with medieval folklore, which often combined the first caper with the trick on the frozen pond.[24] Although *Branche* III is episodic, it is unified both by the importance of fish throughout and also by the fact that the third adventure develops from the second and the second from the first. The Tiron order's ban on meat, making the order apropos, is probably why Renart identifies with it.

BRANCHE XV

Consisting of two episodes rather than three, 522-line *Branche* XV is also well integrated. Its pair of tales resemble each other to some extent, sharing the same moral. They also share one of the same characters, but he is Tibert rather than Renart. Even though Ysengrin is totally absent, the unknown author ridicules greed, like Nivardus, particularly on the part of clergymen. His first anecdote, involving Tibert, Renart, and a sausage, is varied in the second, where two priests replace the fox and the cat. Tibert then partly functions like the sausage, which has been appropriately eliminated because the cat himself has eaten it. The avarice of both Renart and Rufrangier, the fox's substitute in the later episode, is punished by Tibert, with the priest being chastised worse, since his is the greater sin. Probably no accident in this thoughtfully constructed piece is the alliteration linking Renart to his equivalent, while Torgis is the name of the cat's counterpart.

Without any prologue we are informed that the treacherous fox sets out to appease his hunger. Though Pierre de Saint-Cloud does not indicate that Renart would eat Tibert in *Branche* II-Va, the author of XV states that the fox is eager to devour the cat, so famished is he, when he meets Tibert again. He also wants revenge for what happened in II-Va. To put his quarry off guard, he acts friendly, telling the cat not to run away but to honor the pledge of assistance made in Pierre's poem. Tibert remains, monitorially sharpening his claws, and for thirty-nine lines he is lectured on selfishness. Like Ysengrin, who recently became a monk, says Renart in an illusion to *Branche* III, everyone seeks his own advantage at others' expense, but malice will backfire. For that reason he does not want to be false, the fox alleges falsely. It was egotistic of Tibert to abandon him before, Renart continues, referring once more to their encounter in II-Va, but he pretends that the cat must still have been distressed over his peril. He concludes his sermon by relating that the peasant missed him. With a show of good will on both sides, the fox and Tibert restore their previous relationship, vowing mutual loyalty, but the author warns that it will not be of much duration.

Indeed, the pair soon find a long sausage, which Renart is unwilling to share, despite his championship of altruism. As he carries it in his mouth, dragging each end on the ground, the cat protests that he is spoiling it. Tibert offers to demonstrate a proper manner of conveyance, and the fox acquiesces, thinking that he can overpower his partner when the latter is encumbered. Seizing one tip of the sausage and tossing the rest across his back (the way Renart shoulders Chantecler in II-Va), the cat declares that they will be safe on a nearby hill, where a tall cross stands. There they can see whoever approaches. The fox, who wanted to seduce Tibert, is hoist by his own petard in accordance with his speech on perfidy, for the cat dashes ahead and scampers up the cross, on an arm of which he eats the meat. All in all, therefore, Tibert essentially repeats his role at the trap in II-Va, though the fox has a different part to play on this occasion. He essentially repeats his role at the foot of the oak tree in Pierre's titmouse episode, since he is teased at length. Ultimately he is even forced away by a hunter with dogs. A feud, observes the author, has now commenced between Renart and Tibert.

After the fox has been removed, Rufrangier and Torgis ride toward the cross on their way to a synod. Discovering Tibert still perched on high, they long for his pelt, much as the two fish mongers crave Renart's in *Branche* III. Rufrangier, who dreams of a cat-skin hat, consents to pay Torgis one-half of Tibert's appraised value. Ignoring the cross's symbolism in his avarice, he stands on his horse in order to reach the cat, who slaps him to the ground with those claws which threatened Renart. Tibert then leaps onto the empty saddle and is whisked to Rufrangier's house. When he arrives, his galloping palfrey bowls over the priest's concubine, so that she is punished in roughly the same fashion as her lover. He suffers more, however, for he is scratched as well as felled, and he hits his head when he lands, nearly braining himself. Instead of proceeding to his conference, he goes back home, convinced that a devil has hexed him.

BRANCHE IV

This little work in 478 verses has a thirty-two-line prologue in which a nameless minstrel tells his listeners that he is going to amuse them with a *branche* (and he uses that word) comprising a single anecdote about the fox. To arouse our curiosity and maybe also to incline us toward accepting what will happen to Renart, the author concludes his introduction with a proverb cited by both Nivardus and Pierre de Saint-Cloud when their roosters trick their foxes: "No one on earth is so wise as not to be sometimes a fool."

If the anecdote is single, it still has two main parts (like *Branches* II-Va and XV), and they can be further divided. The first principal section, inspired by Pierre's Chantecler episode, sets up the second, in which Renart blunders by riding a bucket to the bottom of a well like Brer Rabbit in *Uncle Remus*. As we will see, however, he does not do so for the same reason as Brer Rabbit, who seeks a cool respite from hot summer work. His motive is also different from his counterpart's in the fable which must have served as the source for the second half of *Branche* IV.[25] Chapter 23 of Petrus Alphonsi's early twelfth-century storybook *Disciplina Clericalis* is about a fox taking a wolf at night to a well in which the full moon is mirrored. Believing this reflection to be a cheese the fox has promised him, the wolf orders the fox to bring it up, though he offers to help if needed. The fox descends in a bucket and claims that the cheese is too big for him, so the wolf climbs into the other bucket, not realizing that when the second goes down the first will go up. Being lighter, the fox ascends, hops out, and leaves the wolf to thrash about in the water.

The plot of *Branche* IV begins one evening as Renart, again half starved, comes upon a Cistercian abbey, the barn of which houses delectable chickens. After leaping through the surrounding wall, he has second thoughts about risking his life any further, but hunger drives him on. He sneaks into the barn and kills three chickens, at once devouring two of them. The third he plans to take home and cook, though whether he ultimately does so the author neglects to state.[26] A comic touch is applied by portraying the chicken thief parodically as a knight attacking a castle, rather like the way Pierre handles Tiecelin's theft of the cheese. Renart is said to want to "joust," for example, and to be in danger because the monks might hold him for ransom. Thus, and not because he is actually on a horse, we are also told that he does not "rein in" until he reaches the chickens.

The whole point of the preliminary incident is to bring the fox into the monastery and make him thirsty enough to inspect its well before leaving. Aware that he cannot safely reach the water, he gazes at it sadly and discovers his reflection, even though no moon is mentioned, in contrast to the *Disciplina-Clericalis* story. Mistaking his image for his wife Hermeline, he asks what she is doing down there, and the echo strengthens his illusion. In order to check on the woman he loves, he descends in a bucket, no longer mindful of reality. His senses are restored as soon as he hits the bottom, but then he is trapped.

How can he become so foolish that he mistakes his echo and reflection for his wife? He is not Petrus Alphonsi's stupid wolf. Indeed, he is not just any fox. The prologue declares that he is the clever and wise Renart we have already come to know, and later references to events in *Branche* II-Va will certify that both he and Ysengrin are supposed to be the same figures portrayed by Pierre. The wolf is more the embodiment of appetite that we found in *Branche* III and *Ysengrimus*, however, while so far in *Branche* IV Renart is too naive to have an antecedent in any of the works we have seen. Pierre's fox is tricked by Chantecler, the titmouse, and Tibert, but divine justice is on their side and they can be crafty, whereas a well is always simple.

The author of the variant in Manuscript H (note 26 to this chapter) must also have been unhappy with the fox's romantic delusion. He eliminated it, sending Renart into the depths only because the fox needs a drink after eating. Unfortunately, this simplification is also infelicitous, for it necessitates an ignorance of buckets on a pulley that is unlikely in a chicken thief accustomed to farms. (Brer Rabbit's misadventure suffers from the same sort of flaw.) After puzzling over the arrangement, the fox jumps into the pail at the top of the well, thinking it full, and vanishes down the shaft.

Returning to *Branche* IV's initial version, we find that before long Ysengrin explores the abbey in his own search for victuals and happens by the well. As he peers into it like Renart ahead of him, lines 155-58, which described how the fox hung on the edge, staring pensively down, are duplicated (lines 203-206), so that the parallelism in both actions is stressed.[27] In the manner of Renart, the wolf sees his reflection and assumes his spouse to be sojourning under ground, yet because he perceives the fox there, too, he infers that he is being cuckolded again, as in Pierre's classic, a knowledge of which the author of *Branche* IV (like XV's author) presupposed on the part of his audience.

No sooner does Renart speak up than Ysengrin forgets about Hersent and his reflection, however, for the fox professes to be in heaven, having died not long ago. He describes paradise as such a happy hunting ground—full of cattle, sheep, goats, and hares[28]—that the wolf wants access to it also, but Renart asserts that Ysengrin has been too wicked, making false accusations at court. The fox plays further with the wolf by telling him he must beg God to forgive his sins before being weighed in the balance (the buckets), so his good deeds will be heavier than the bad ones. Ysengrin, who says that he has already confessed to (i.e., consumed) a rabbit and a nanny goat, consequently genuflects and howls at his Maker, uncouthly pointing his rear toward the east just as his spiritual mentor has reversed the directions of heaven and hell in this sneer at religion.[29] Renart then refers to what are probably the reflections of stars and calls them candles burning on the water as a miraculous sign of Christ's forgiveness. The wolf jumps into the empty bucket and plummets down, while the fox rockets up. As they pass, Renart shouts that

Ysengrin is really going to hell, not heaven. According to folklore, wells are indeed entrances to the underworld,[30] but the fox simply means that his foe is bound for bedevilment.

Some monks who attempt to draw water the next morning discover the bedraggled bather cowering in the lower bucket. They call for reinforcements, and every member of the fraternity arrives, armed with something.[31] Ysengrin is pummeled when hoisted aloft, though the abbot spares his life. In staggering away he meets one of his sons, who vows revenge not only for this atrocity but also for what Renart did previously in their home (during *Branche* II-Va). Ysengrin limps to the cave, where doctors restore him.

BRANCHE V

Much like the concluding lines of *Branche* III, the last three verses in IV state that the wolf will avenge himself if he comes upon the fox. Those verses form a nice transition to 246-line *Branche* V, which consists of two main parts without a prologue. The first section is an abbreviated version of Nivardus's ham episode, and the second is a basically similar but otherwise unknown encounter between Renart and a cricket, abruptly terminated by an incursion of dogs.

When Renart meets the wolf one day, Ysengrin threatens to swallow him, ripping up his fur with much more violence than in the Latin source. Because the fox lies still, the wolf becomes alarmed at the possibility of having killed his "counselor," as he says, acknowledging that his relationship to Renart is the same as Ysengrimus's to Reinardus. He also resembles Nivardus's wolf by being the fox's uncle rather than merely Renart's godfather, as in most *branches* (though he is that, too).

Descrying a peasant with a ham, the fox proposes that they trick the man out of it. With a pretense of lameness he causes the rustic to pursue him, discarding the ham and stumbling far afield. By the time Renart returns, Ysengrin has downed all the meat, saving only the rope by which it hung. Instead of reproaching his perfidious uncle, Renart excuses himself to insure his safety, alleging that he must visit Santiago Compostella.

For two weeks he wanders around dressed as a pilgrim,[32] yet without the attitude of one, because he desires revenge. He also wants something to eat as he arrives at a priest's house teeming with rats. He is unable to catch any of them, but with a detachable sleeve he manages to bag a cricket chanting near an oven. Just as Reinardus behaves like Ysengrimus in regard to Sprotinus, so Renart behaves like Ysengrin here. Whereas Ysengrin seems not to have been serious about devouring Renart, however, Renart is quite serious about devouring the cricket. When the cricket (named Frobert by the author of *Branche* I)[33] objects that murder misbecomes a pilgrim, Renart avers that he merely wanted to ingest the caroler's psalter in order to know

more hymns. Hoping to put his prey off guard with a pious pose, he pretends that he is about to expire and asks whether he might confess his sins to the cricket, since the priest at whose house they are is not around. "You're about to have plenty of 'priests,'" the cricket cries, hearing hunters with their dogs, which chase Renart until he eludes them by hiding atop the oven. As if God were heeding the fox's wish for vengeance, Ysengrin appears, and the dogs nip him much as he nipped Renart two weeks earlier.

Having flatly plagiarized Nivardus in his first episode, the author of *Branche* V was a less slavish imitator in his second incident, for it is essentially a recasting of the contest between Sprotinus and another would-be pilgrim who is also put to flight by dogs. Sprotinus's hounds are mere make-believe, but the effect is the same. (Although Foulet sees influence only from Pierre de Saint-Cloud in the second episode, he contends correctly that it manifests itself in the dogs' names.)[34] To tie the two incidents together, through a combination of elements from both, *Branche* V's author added the coda in which Ysengrin is punished by Renart's pursuers.

The cricket's ironic reference to hunters as "priests" (lines 200-201) resembles a joke by Tibert in lines 314-24 of *Branche* XV. Probably inspired by the Salaura episode of *Ysengrimus,* the cat speaks there of invading dogs as "a company . . . celebrating mass and matins." The similarity between that jest and the cricket's in *Branche* V could be coincidental, but both structurally and thematically V mirrors XV, which likewise consists of two related episodes concerned with greed. The artistic superiority of XV, which is more imaginative than V, suggests that it was V's model rather than vice versa. The author of V took his structure from XV, his contents from *Ysengrimus,* and his theme from both. Foulet misjudged V in affirming that its creator did not follow ham dupery with ice fishing like Nivardus simply because *Branche* III was already in existence.[35]

BRANCHE XIV

Like all preceding poems in the **Roman de Renart,** 1,088-line XIV opens with a hungry fox looking for food. The resemblance is greatest to III, for Renart is initially at his home (called Malpertuis), but the time is in May, near Ascension Day rather than Christmas. The action in XIV, as in IV, commences at night, though in neither work are we told so explicitly. Unlike IV, XIV has no prologue.

Near a farm belonging to a peasant named Gonbaut, Renart again meets Tibert, who wants some milk which Gonbaut's wife keeps in a bin. Together the cat and the fox find a hole in Gonbaut's palisade and proceed to the house, Renart agreeing to assist his companion before attacking any poultry, which might awaken Gonbaut's dogs. While Tibert laps contentedly, down inside the hutch, Renart obligingly strains to hold up its heavy lid. Not only does the cat take his time, but when he has drunk his fill he spills what is left of the milk to prevent the fox from enjoying any. In *Branches* XV and XIV together he therefore cheats Renart out of both food and drink, but in XIV the fox gets even, dropping the lid too soon and bobbing Tibert's tail when the cat finally jumps from the bin. By averring that the loss is really a gain, since Tibert will have less to lug around, Renart reminds us of Ysengrimus telling Corvigarus that the sacrifice of some flesh would help the horse to run faster.

At the chicken coop the fox accepts the cat's malicious advice to take the rooster rather than any of the hens because the latter are molting. When he has seized the cock, which is said to be perched next to Pinte, even though the flock belongs to Gonbaut instead of to Constant des Noes, Tibert asks him whether he is holding his prize securely. Renart repeats the old mistake of opening his mouth to reply. This time the cock not only escapes but also rouses Gonbaut by crowing. The farmer sets two dogs on the fox, who is roughed up and chased away. Tibert absconds ahead of him and will not be seen again in *Branche* XIV.

The enterprise of Renart and the cat to some extent resembles the fox's and Brun's as recounted by Pierre's bear at court. In each story Renart and a comrade sneak into a farm for their favorite food, but in *Branche* XIV the comrade succeeds, while the fox is attacked. Rather than exploit the cat like the bear, moreover, Renart is exploited himself, since he vainly props the lid.

Through the remaining 890 lines he plays a succession of five tricks on Ysengrin's brother Primaut, a character invented by XIV's author. Thus, as Foulet has pointed out,[36] the basic format of this poem seems to have been derived from Pierre's, where the fox warms up with several lightweight but agile sparring partners before his main bout with a ponderous wolf. There is no question of a single conflict between Primaut and Renart, however, and Primaut in his obtuse voracity apes the Ysengrin of *Branches* III, IV, and V or Nivardus's wolf much more than Pierre's. A fox giving a wolf misleading advice in a series of episodes is also reminiscent of *Ysengrimus.*

After outrunning Gonbaut's dogs, Renart discovers a box of hosts dropped by a tipsy priest. He eats all but two of them, and when he meets Primaut he gives the rest to the wolf, alleging that he found them in a nearby village church. Because Primaut wants more, Renart conducts him to that sanctuary, just as Reinardus lures Ysengrimus into Saint Peter's with cakes. By digging under the threshold, Renart and Primaut enter, finding not only more hosts but also meat, bread, and wine, hidden away by the same priest who lost the hosts outside and is therefore a gluttonous hamster as well as a drunk. In the course of banqueting, Primaut swills too much wine, like Ysengrimus in the monastery cellar, with the result that he wishes to hold a vesper service. The hour is not quite appropriate, but an alb, a chasuble, and a missal are lying on the altar. The author of *Branche* XIV was probably thinking of Ysengrimus's mock consecration as bishop, though Nivardus is less sacrilegious. The leering disrespect for religion in this episode also transcends what we found in *Branche* IV.

Foulet asserts that Ysengrin is replaced with Primaut primarily because he had become too well known as the fox's foe for Renart and him to consort as Renart and Primaut do here.[37] Being Reinardus's enemy does not prevent Ysengrimus from being duped repeatedly by Nivardus's fox, however. A better reason is that the author of XIV wanted a farcical tonsuring as a preliminary to burlesquing vespers, and Ysengrin had already received one in *Branche* III. He had no need for another. The depilation in XIV reflects that in III, where boiling water is poured over Ysengrin's head, because Renart shaves Primaut after dousing him with urine.

Feeling qualified to proceed with the service on account of his baldness, Primaut rings the church bells, dons the vestments, leafs through the missal, and howls, oblivious to danger and Renart, who slips out and packs shut their hole beneath the door. Awakened by the noise, the curé peeks through a crack and beholds the wolf, whose presence he announces to parishioners by shouting through the village streets. Everyone hops out of bed, arms himself, and batters the unwelcome worshiper, rather like Bovo's congregation in the fishing episode of *Ysengrimus.*

Renart has kept one herring for Primaut after fooling some merchants as in *Branche* III. Despite the feast in the church the wolf is still hungry enough to try the fox's ruse, when he rejoins Renart in the forest. Instead of being tossed aboard the fish cart, however, he is almost killed. Just in time to avoid being stabbed with a sword, he jumps up and reels back to Renart, aching from new blows.

His third unhappy adventure harks back ultimately to an ancient Greek fable, related in somewhat different form by Horace, which tells of a famished fox gorging itself to such an extent on bread and meat in a hollow tree that it cannot squeeze out through the opening.[38] Renart leads Primaut to a peasant's cabin where three hams await them on their entrance through a chink in the wall. The wolf eats till only his head will fit through the crack again. The fox pulls him by the ears and by a withe around his neck, forcing him to yelp and wake the master of the house, who advances in the dark with a club and a candle. In the first clash the candle is extinguished. The peasant bends down to relight it at the fireplace, and the wolf bites his rump, refusing to let go until the man's wife opens their door to call for help. Primaut then rips out a hunk of flesh and bolts into the woods, knocking the woman down. When he finds Renart he tells the fox to taste the peasant meat, but Renart disdains such unsavory fare. Geese are preferable, says the fox, and he recommends a gaggle of them close at hand.

Although the author does not say so, day has presumably dawned when the wolf invades the flock, only to meet two mastiffs which Renart has neglected to mention. Able to outrun them, Primaut furiously mauls the fox for giving bad advice. As he stomps on Renart's stomach, a whimper for mercy moves him to pity, and like Ysengrin in *Branche* V he stops short of murdering his counselor.[39] After insisting he knew nothing of the dogs, Renart threatens to complain at court about the beating he has suffered, so intimidating Primaut that the wolf proposes a sacred oath never to harm him again.

Like the fox in Nivardus's perjury episode, Renart takes the wolf to a place where a saint is supposedly buried but where in fact a trap is concealed. By kneeling there, the fox declares, Primaut can make his oath binding. He swears that he will never hurt Renart again and plops down on the iron teeth, which crush one foot. Ignoring his pleas for help, the fox skips home to a warm reception, like the one in *Branche* III.

It is curious that the author does not end XIV at this point but appends another five lines (1084-88), stating no fewer than three times that Renart repents of his wrongdoing. Stressing his contrition through mere reiteration (rather than presenting it elaborately, as in the first 164 lines of *Branche* VIII) is a lame attempt at persuading us to accept what is markedly out of character. The author appears to have felt that we might be scandalized at a sinner who was never sorry, whereas an apology to God would permit Renart to have devil's-food cake, so to speak, and eat it, too. The imp could make heinous mischief without giving offense. Though his remorse is an asinine tail pinned onto the poem, it nevertheless determines how his conduct toward Primaut should be interpreted. It implies that he has persecuted the wolf not because the wolf endangers him, as Ysengrimus menaces Reinardus, but only because he himself is a spiteful prankster, whose behavior is unjustified. The same motive can also be imputed to him vis-à-vis Ysengrin in *Branche* III.

BRANCHE I

In all of the French works so far considered, except the fifteenth *branche,* Renart gets the better of a wolf, like Nivardus's fox. Even V, where he loses a ham to Ysengrin, concludes triumphantly for him, thanks to happenstance. In these poems he is also a threat to little creatures, though the only ones he manages to kill are the hens at the outset of *Branche* IV. In 1620-line I, by contrast, his role becomes more sinister and significant because his prey is all of society. He graduates from being primarily a tormentor of wolves to the status of a subversive at war with the whole establishment, and satire on society again becomes important, as it was in II-Va. There, however, the fox was very much a part of the system being ridiculed—he shared in those faults to which Pierre objected—whereas in *Branche* I he is outside society and the unidentified author's censure of it. In fact, through Renart, who represents him, most of that minstrel's scorn for French leadership at the close of Louis VII's long, inglorious reign (1137-80) is expressed.

In a ten-line prologue he chides Pierre, whom he deprecatingly calls Perrot, for having forgotten to complete the fox's trial at King Noble's court. He implies that he will supply a denouement for Pierre's poem, and *Branche* I is

indeed conceived as a continuation of II-Va. Despite the fact that in his prologue the author of I cites only adultery with Hersent as the charge against Renart, it—along with Ysengrin's other indictments—is to be superseded by a more serious complaint.

When the story begins, some ten months must be presumed to have elapsed since the fox outran Roonel's pack at the end of II-Va, for the season is spring rather than summer. Ascension Day (mentioned at the opening of *Branche* XIV) has not yet come. In a cheerful setting of roses and hawthorn Noble summons the entire animal kingdom, and only Renart fails to respond, giving his enemies a splendid chance to blacken him, as in the sick-lion episode of *Ysengrimus.* Though the wolf is no longer said to be an official of any kind, he provides a transition from II-Va by out-shouting everyone else in a call for the vindication of his besmirched honor. He recounts how the fox raped Hersent, urinated on her cubs, and reneged on the oath of innocence imposed.

Again the monarch winks at illicit love, joking that nowadays even his own like are cuckolded, as Louis VII was rumored to have been by Eleanor of Aquitaine. Brun the bear, who is still Ysengrin's chief supporter, chides Noble for such indifference and requests a proper hearing, for which he would be willing to fetch the defendant. Bruyant the bull, a character we did not meet in II-Va, bellows that the disreputable fox's notorious affair needs no adjudication and that Ysengrin ought to dispense justice himself. Grimbert the badger, Renart's cousin, asserts that the fox's love for Hersent has done no damage and that a trial would compromise her even more than her husband's accusation. Swearing by the Virgin that she is chaste as a nun, she volunteers to prove her fidelity in an ordeal (essentially repeating her offer to Ysengrin after Renart's visit in II-Va). She so convinces Bernart of her sincerity that he wishes all women were as faithful, but Bernart is only an ass.

In general Noble's subjects feel that the fox must testify, while their king is more indulgent. So long as loyalty to the crown is maintained, he prefers to overlook a petty squabble between vassals. When the wolf threatens war against Renart, Noble vehemently objects, observing that the fox would probably beat him and reminding him that peace has been officially established throughout the land. It cannot be broken with impunity. The vengeance which Hersent back in II-Va suggested the court might provide is therefore to be conclusively withheld, so that a gloomy Ysengrin slumps to the ground, his tail between his legs. The end of hostilities, alleged to the titmouse in II-Va, has become fact rather than fiction in *Branche* I and is a precondition for Noble's eventual condemnation of Renart.

Scarcely has His Majesty informed us that the truce is in effect when Chantecler, Pinte, and three other hens bring proof that the fox has broken it. On a bier they carry the mutilated corpse of Pinte's sister Copee. To the court Pinte wails that after butchering her five brothers and her four other sisters Renart murdered Copee yesterday and fled before their master, Gonbert del Frenne (rather than Constant des Noes), could catch him. On completing her tale of woes, Pinte faints, together with the other female members of Copee's cortege, and solicitous knights sprinkle their faces with water. When they regain consciousness, they join Chantecler at the feet of the king in pleading for revenge. Noble, who has not been perturbed by Ysengrin's complaints, is furious over the chickens', thundering so loudly and thumping himself so viciously with his tail that everyone quakes. Couart the hare, an important new character in the ***Roman de Renart***,[40] comes down with a fever. Because the lion promises Pinte to have the fox punished in her sight, however, Ysengrin is thrilled. The crime against Copee even induces Noble to accept the rape charge now. On behalf of the plaintiffs he accuses Renart of both disturbing the peace and adultery.

Before summoning the fox, he orders a funeral service for Copee. Brun officiates, being a priest in *Branche* I (perhaps as a gibe at sacerdotal corpulence), while Bruyant digs a grave. When the second day of the story dawns, Copee is buried in a leaden casket, with an epitaph proclaiming that she was "martyred" by the fangs of Renart. Noble then dispatches an eager Brun to fetch the fox, and the bear jiggles off on a horse, it seems, because he is said to have one later (line 580).

In this poem, which set a regrettable precedent for subsequent *branches,* various animals appear to be actually mounted at times and not just described as if they were, or instead of merely pretending to be, like Pierre de Saint-Cloud's Tibert.[41] The cat really rides in *Branche* XV, of course, but he crouches atop the saddle and is transported passively to Rufrangier's abode. He is not sufficiently humanized to have feet in the stirrups and hands on the reins, controlling his palfrey.[42] It is also unfortunate that the author of I leaves us unsure whether figures are equestrian or not. His intentions may well have been inconsistent.

The pause in the action caused by Brun's journey is used for a burlesque of miracles, in which Couart is cured of his fever by lying on Copee's grave. Taking advantage of this opportunity to increase opposition to Renart, Ysengrin feigns relief from an earache, on Roonel's recommendation, after likewise reposing above the "martyr's" remains.[43]

When the scene shifts to Malpertuis (consistently a burrow in *Branche* I but often referred to as if it were a castle), we find big Brun, who cannot go in, calling Renart to come outside. The fox justifies his absence by modifying Reinardus's rationalization from the sick-lion episode of *Ysengrimus.* He implies that he has stayed at home because as a pauper he would not be fed well at court. While the rich dine sumptuously there, he pouts, the poor must eat from their lap, fending off dogs which snap at their meager fare.

Even if Renart really is impoverished, he would not be subjected to such indignities, because he is also a baron. His author, as a jongleur, might very well have suffered

them, however. The fox's complaint, which is bitterly expressed, reads like a statement of his author's own resentment. If indeed it is, as other critics have thought[44] then a grudge against the privileged helps explain why Renart is cast in the role of a left-wing radical. Through a rebel who snipes at the elite the author could revel in vicarious revenge for being demeaned as a mere entertainer.

The fox seduces Brun by fibbing that he has just enjoyed some honey. With an exclamation in broken Latin, reminiscent of Ysengrin's *nomini dame* in *Branche* III, the bear neglects his duty as emissary, galloping after Renart to the home of a woodsman named Lanfroi, A large split log, held open by wedges, has a honeycomb down inside, says the fox. When Brun sticks his snout and forepaws into the crack, Renart manages to pull the wedges out, clamping him fast. Until Lanfroi appears, the fox makes fun of the bear, scoffing that he wants to keep all the honey to himself. Renart then scoots away, leaving Brun for the fate which the forester prepares by soliciting help from a nearby village, like the priest in *Branche* XIV.

Soon peasants—some of whom are satirized by being named as floridly as gentry—swarm through the woods, armed with clubs, hoes, and flails. Lanfroi leads them, brandishing an ax. In order to escape, the bear must yank himself from the log, tearing the hide from his face and paws and leaving both ears behind. Evidently he is not able to mount up at once (if we assume that he does have a horse), for he is dealt many a blow, including one by the local priest, who has been spreading manure and nearly knocks him down with a pitchfork. Eventually Brun escapes, and as he passes Malpertuis Renart jeers at him again, wanting to know which order he belongs to, since he wears a scarlet "hood." We are reminded of Reinardus with the skinned wolf in the sick-lion episode of *Ysengrimus,* but even more similar is the fox mocking the flayed bear in *Aegrum Fama Fuit,* although that bear is the reverse of Brun—having lost hide everywhere except on his head and paws. When Brun reaches court, collapsing from loss of blood, the king bellows oaths and tears out mane in a tantrum. After vowing to avenge the bear, Noble orders the cat to bring Renart, and less for trial than for punishment.

Like the Tibert section of *Branche* XIV, Brun's calamity probably derives from his story in II-Va of how the fox used him as a stalking horse,[45] while the cat's mission now is patterned after the bear's. Tibert will also suffer because desire for a delicacy will make him incautious, even though he is apprehensive rather than complacent like Brun when he departs on what is termed his mule, praying for safety. As if anticipating the future, he addresses his prayers not only to God but also to Saint Leonard, "who liberates captives."

It is perhaps not for nothing that we are told he starts out "to the left,"[46] and upon his arrival at Malpertuis in the evening a "Saint-Martin's bird" flies ominously to his left instead of to his right. Fearing the worst from Renart, whom he considers an atheist, Tibert does not venture into the den but halloos in Brun's manner. Since words cost nothing, as the author remarks, Renart croons back an amicable welcome and offers to face Noble obediently. Put off guard, the travel-weary cat requests something to eat. He is promised his fill of mice and conducted to the house of the priest who hit Brun with a pitchfork. Like his colleague in *Branche* V, this curé has a problem with rodents, or at least the fox says he does. At Renart's urging Tibert springs through a hole in the wall, only to be caught by a snare which the priest's illegitimate son Martin (heralded by the "Saint-Martin's bird") laid for the chicken-stealing fox. Renart's designs on the cat, which failed in both II-Va and XV, finally succeed.

As Tibert is strangled, Martin awakens his parents. The clergyman rises naked from his bed, holding his genitals, while the concubine lights a candle, wielding her distaff. The scene calls to mind Primaut's skirmish with the peasant couple in *Branche* XIV, and just as the wolf bit out a chunk of buttock under duress, so pummeled Tibert claws out one of his unchaste assailant's testicles. The author of I may also have been influenced by *Branche* XV, where the cat rends Rufrangier. The suitably punished lover is incapacitated in I, his mistress swoons, and Martin tries to revive her, so that Tibert can escape. Since Renart has disappeared, the cat returns to court alone, bitter at being so cruelly deceived but partially consoled by thinking that the amorous priest can henceforth "ring" with only one "clapper."

When, on the third day of the action, Tibert informs the king of what has happened, Noble does not again fly into a rage but, feeling rather helpless, simply commands Grimbert to fetch the renegade. The badger requests an official warrant stamped with a royal seal to certify his authority. Armed with it, he reaches his destination at dusk, after passing through a meadow, a forest, and a clearing, but no mention is made of a valley which both Brun and Tibert traverse. Since Grimbert is Renart's cousin, he is not afraid to enter the den, though he does creep in backwards. He is cordially received and dined at home instead of being led off to a trap in the mere expectation of food.

Only after supper does he broach the reason for his visit. In a funk portrayed by the author as genuine, however much it seems out of character for such a wanton spirit, Renart reads the summons, which threatens him with torture if he fails to be present on the following day to hear his death sentence pronounced. He asks his cousin for advice, and Grimbert recommends that he unburden himself of his sins. In the absence of a priest the badger can serve as father confessor (like the cricket in *Branche* V).

The fox consents, perhaps to amuse himself with a recollection of his fondest capers but surely not to save his soul as he claims. He really did commit adultery with Hersent, he admits, and he hurt Ysengrin in many more direct ways. For example, he says, he caused the wolf to fall into a pit trap and be thrashed after seizing a lamb (reminiscent of the eleventh-century Latin poem *Sacerdos et Lupus*);[47] to be caught again and beaten by three shepherds; to devour hams and be prevented by a bloated belly from escaping (as in *Branche* XIV); to be frozen into the ice while fishing (*Ysengrimus* and *Branche* III); to descend into a well at night, thinking the full moon's reflection was a big cheese (*Branche* IV and *Disciplina Clericalis*); to try deceiving fish merchants (*Branche* XIV); and to become a monk yet profess to be a canon when discovered eating meat (according to a Latin poem, *De Lupo*, from around 1100).[48] Whereas it is Pierre de Saint-Cloud's wolf who sets the plot of *Branche* I in motion, the wolf of Renart's confession is once more Nivardus's, as in *Branches* III, IV, V, and XIV.

The fox acknowledges further that he has sinned not only against Ysengrin but also against every other beast in the king's court. Specifically he mentions the previous night's hoodwinking of Tibert, the decimation of Pinte's clan, and (otherwise unknown) a trick he played on an army hired by Ysengrin: after defeating the wolf's mercenaries, he stole their pay, he concludes in contrite tones. Admonishing him not to backslide should God prolong his life, Grimbert absolves him from his sins.

The next morning, early in the fourth and last day of *Branche* I, Renart kisses his family good-bye and bids his sons to defend his "castle" by "raising its bridges." Because it is impregnable, as he says and the end of the poem will confirm, he has no need either to obey the summons or to be afraid. He even has plenty of food now, in contrast to his situation in every one of the previous *branches,* where hunger is his motive for embarking on adventures. In lines 1121-22 he asserts that Malpertuis is sufficiently stocked to withstand a siege of "seven years." Why, under these circumstances, does he risk his life at court, except that the poem's plot depends on his compliance?[49] Be that as it may, he indulges in more religiosity (comparable to his confession) by praying for acquittal and revenge,[50] by falling prostrate to pronounce himself three times a sinner, and by warding off devils with a sign of the cross. Such hypocrisy will later save him from the gallows.

After crossing a stream, mountains, and a plain, he and the badger lose their way in a forest and chance upon a prosperous farm run by nuns. The author states that the travelers err on account of the fox's grief, yet at the cloister Renart is not too distraught to allege that the direction they need to take is past the chicken coop. Grimbert scolds him vigorously for relapsing, whereupon the fox meekly yields, but as they journey on he repeatedly turns a wistful gaze toward the nunnery, evidencing his hopelessly vulpine nature. If his head were cut off, the author comments, it would fly to that poultry.

We are told that Renart is again afraid of what will befall him at court and that his horse expresses this fear by stumbling, while Grimbert's mule trots smoothly along. At their arrival, nevertheless, the tardy delinquent addresses

King Noble in a self-assured manner. With his head held high he asserts that he is the most valuable of barons and declares that he has been slandered by jealous, egotistic flatterers who would ruin the realm if heeded. Brun and Tibert have only themselves to blame for being caught, he continues, and he has not mistreated Hersent because she and he have been in love. Copee and the other butchered fowl he wisely forbears to mention. He concludes his speech with an appeal for pity, averring that he is too old and weak—the hair on his chest is turning white[51]—to argue with the sovereign, who may dispose of him at will but ought to be fair.

Undeterred by this rhetoric, Noble snarls that Renart will not be spared unless he can clear himself. Grimbert warns that the fox, according to law, must be allowed to refute in public any accusation against him. Instead of granting due process, however, Noble is swayed by Renart's many enemies, who protest the badger's call for a fair trial. Without permitting any defense whatsoever, the arbitrary king requests a sentence from the mob, which clamors for a hanging. Hastily a gallows is erected, for Noble wants the fox strung up before he can escape.

As the crowd torments Renart, Couart casts stones from a safe distance, but a menacing shake of the prisoner's head still sends that poltroon scampering to a hedge, where Renart will later seize him. In *Branche* V the fox excuses himself from Ysengrin with the pretext of a pilgrimage to Santiago Compostella. Here he tells the king that he wishes to atone for his sins by going to the Holy Land. Noble's initial fondness for the colorful cavalier is rekindled, making the king most fickle, though he accedes to Renart's request only on condition that the dangerous adventurer remain permanently in exile. To the dismay of the multitude, Renart is therefore dressed as a pilgrim, pardoned, and released. The author states that the charlatan feels contempt for everyone but the royal couple, yet that observation must be ironic. Renart will soon insult Noble, and he swindles Noble's consort Fere[52] out of a ring by promising to pay for it a hundred times over with prayers in her behalf.

By three in the afternoon he is able to depart, but the author states that he does so on his horse rather than on foot, and instead of heading for Jerusalem he contents himself with the hedge where the hare, a nice dinner for his pups at home, is lurking. When Couart tries to gallop away (for suddenly a mount is credited even to him), Renart grabs his reins (perhaps only metaphorically) and pierces him with the staff that is part of a pilgrim's accoutrement. Dangling the hare from his own saddle, if indeed he has one, Renart appears on the tallest of four rocks that tower above the court. After wiping his rear with his borrowed gear, he hurls it at Noble, shouting that the sultan of Syria and Egypt, Nur-ud-din,[53] sends greetings and that all heathens tremble before the Christian king.

Such is his scorn for the leader of that social system on which he has preyed (a scorn no doubt reflecting the author's attitude toward Louis VII, who was humiliated in the Second Crusade, 1147-49), but the establishment finally gains a modicum of revenge. Renart's indignity and an entreaty from wounded Couart, who is said to free himself from the fox's horse and ride his own to the court, move Noble to order a chase, vainly threatening death to the whole assembly if Renart escapes. An army of knights (led by Tardif the snail!)[54] pursues the obnoxious fox all the way to Malpertuis, "where he fears neither host nor assault," nipping his fur and stabbing his flanks in a climactic scene obviously inspired by the close of Pierre de Saint-Cloud's epic.[55] More like *Branche* XIV, however, I concludes with a vignette of the hero ensconced at home amidst his doting family, although he does not repent of his misdeeds here. Instead, Hermeline, Percehaie, Malebranche, and Rovel, "more beautiful than the others" (perhaps because the author of I created the third son), lavish attention on their master until he recuperates.

Branche I presents a series of outrages perpetrated by the fox against his fellow animals. Ysengrin's grievances against him are taken over from II-Va, and Pinte's also result from wrongs committed before the story begins, while we see his abuse of Brun, Tibert, Couart, and Noble. Those whom he afflicts in this work range from the weakest to the strongest among the nobility and comprise a kind of cross section through that social class which is Renart's actual enemy, even though he belongs to it himself. The poem is unified by the fact that each individual conflict between the fox and another creature (or a family, in Pinte's case) is an aspect of his conflict with the establishment as a whole. Appropriately, all the knights—except Grimbert, of course—take part in the grand pursuit at the end.

Renart is a rogue, as the author repeatedly recognizes,[56] but he is still heroic, like all great villains, while his victims are gullible (Brun and Tibert), effete (Couart and the chickens), cuckolded (Ysengrin), or derelict (Noble), thus becoming contemptible. Because they represent the power structure, it is ultimately that bastion of authority and privilege which is satirized. The author longed to punish the feudal order he knew for its failings and apparently also for its disdain of him, but the court's superiority en masse constitutes an admission that the system was too strong for him, no matter how much he disliked it. What chafed could not be changed. Besides expressing his dissatisfaction with the state, he also wished to make fun of religion and the peasantry (especially as combined in the village curé), probably under the influence of *Branche* XIV.

Along with Pierre's original Reynard poem in French, *Branche* I was favored with unusual popularity, evidenced by the string of half a dozen works which it inspired. They are *Branches* Ia, VI, X, and XXIII, plus the Franco-Italian delight *Rainardo e Lesengrino* and the Flemish masterpiece *Van den Vos Reynaerde*. We will have occasion to deal with *Branche* VI in Chapter Four, but *Van den Vos Reynaerde* is our immediate concern.

Notes

1. On both date and authorship see Foulet, *Roman de Renard,* pp. 217-37.

2. Ibid., pp. 100-19. See also John Flinn, *Le Roman de Renart dans la Littérature Française et dans les Littératures Étrangères au Moyen Age* (Toronto, 1963), pp. 16-18.

3. Ernst Martin, *Le Roman de Renart,* 3 vols. (Strasbourg, 1882-87).

4. See Foulet, *Roman de Renard,* pp. 239, 244-45, 251-52. It is doubtful that either XV or V was written for insertion into II-Va, since neither harmonizes with Pierre's epic and each is self-contained. Foulet's claim on p. 244 that Ysengrin would have no motive for attacking Renart in *Branche* V if V were not designed to succeed the rape scene in II-Va is invalidated not only by the author's possible presupposition of acquaintance with earlier *branches* but also by the fact that the wolf needs no motive, being *mauvais* (like Ysengrimus), as the fox states in line 8 of V.

5. See Martin, *Roman de Renart,* l:xxv.

6. Foulet, *Roman de Renard,* pp. 124-26, 143-56.

7. See Martin, *Roman de Renart,* 1:101, line 349; 104, line 472; 125, lines 1221-23; and 178, lines 641-42.

8. Warnke, *Fabeln der Marie de France,* pp. 154-55, fable 46.

9. Foulet, *Roman de Renard,* p. 153.

10. Warnke, *Fabeln der Marie de France,* pp. 47-49.

11. See Foulet, *Roman de Renard,* pp. 158-62.

12. Ibid., pp. 212-13. Pierre's audience did not need 1,000 lines to become acquainted with Renart.

13. See also Warnke, *Fabeln der Marie de France,* p. 40, fable 11, and Foulet, *Roman de Renard,* pp. 371-72, note 4.

14. See, however, Gunnar Tilander, "Notes sur le Texte du Roman de Renart," *Zeitschrift für romanische Philologie* 44 (1924):667, regarding line 1249.

15. See Foulet, *Roman de Renard,* pp. 218-26.

16. In Va, line 1075, Grimbert is said to be Renart's first cousin; in line 1154, his nephew. In *Branche* I they are consistently cousins. Although we will see much of Grimbert in subsequent epics, no badger figures in *Ysengrimus.* He is Pierre's invention.

17. See Martin, *Roman de Renart,* 1:187, line 954, and 3:174.

18. Pierre's contemporary Andreas Capellanus blames much warfare on love. See E. Trojel, ed., *Andreae Capellani Regii Francorum De Amore Libri Tres* (München: Fink, 1972), p. 330.

19. Juan Nogués, *Estudios sobre el Roman de Renard* (Salamanca, 1956), pp. 74-75, suggests that Pietro is derided as an exponent of Roman law.

20. Ysengrimus's cave and Ysengrin's in *Branche* II-Va also have a door that opens and closes.

21. Voigt, *Ysengrimus,* p. 301, line 742 of Book V. Reinardus is jesting, but he would not speak of his children if he had none. I disagree with Voigt, ibid., p. lxxix.

22. See Ernst Martin, *Observations sur le Roman de Renart* (Strasbourg: Trübner, 1887), p. 36.

23. Foulet, *Roman de Renard,* pp. 281-86.

24. See for example Krohn, *Bär (Wolf) und Fuchs,* pp. 46-54.

25. See Foulet, *Roman de Renard,* pp. 304-12.

26. MS H includes a different version of *Branche* IV after line 150, and in this variant the third chicken is remembered. See P. Chabaille, *Le Roman du Renart, Supplément* (Paris: Silvestre, 1835), pp. 113-21.

27. Lines 156 and 204 repeat line 439 of *Branche* II, where Renart wants Chantecler as badly as he wants water in IV.

28. It is surely meant to be incongruous that Renart also includes hawks and falcons (line 276), as if Ysengrin would have a bird catch his game in chivalric manner.

29. The author of the MS-H variant had more respect for Christianity. See Chabaille, *Supplément,* pp. 116-20. Note the change to *paradis terrestre,* which also occurs elsewhere—Martin, *Roman de Renart,* 1:214, line 616; 293, line 513, and 3:139, line 268.

In *Branche* XVII, when Noble's court believes that the fox has died and it is conducting his funeral service, Ferrant the horse describes his putative afterlife. His soul will enter heaven backwards, says Ferrant, and will be seated next to the she-ass on a bed composed of chickens, which he dare not harm: In that way he will atone for having been the bane of poultry on earth, the horse concludes (Martin, ibid., 2:224, lines 997-1012). Renart will therefore fare like a second Tantalus, the reward envisioned for him containing a bit of punishment. Ferrant's fantasy derives from the fox's in *Branche* IV. Paradise, which includes its opposite in XVII, becomes its opposite in IV, while in both works it is said to feature its prospective occupant's favorite food. Other examples of backward entrances in the *Roman de Renart* (*Branche* I, line 964; *Branche* VI, line 38; *Branche* XVII, line 1579) indicate that the fox's soul will be afraid on its arrival in Ferrant's version of the beyond, and it has good reason to be. Its juxtaposition with the *arnesse* is probably meant to suggest Renart's duplicity (even though the she-ass is not described as *fauve*). See *Branche* I, line 1291; *Branche* VI, lines 161-62; and Arthur Langfors, *Le Roman de Fauvel par Gervais du Bus* (Paris: Firmin-Didot, 1914-19), p. lxxxiv.

30. *Handwörterbuch des deutschen Aberglaubens* (Berlin: De Gruyter, 1927), 1:1677-80.

31. The scene may have been prompted by Nivardus's monastery episode, especially since the prior wields a candlestick (line 409).

32. This is the first time in the *Roman de Renart* (provided *Branche* V antedates XIV) that an animal really wears clothes of any kind.

33. The fact that the cricket lacks a name in *Branche* V (except for line 180 of MSS C, M, and H) indicates that V is older than I.

34. Foulet, *Roman de Renard,* pp. 250-51.

35. Ibid., pp. 249-50.

36. Ibid., pp. 314-15.

37. Ibid., p. 316.

38. Hausrath, *Corpus Fabularum Aesopicarum,* 1, pt. 1:36-37, and Horace's Epistles, 1:7, lines 29-33.

39. The similarity to *Branche* V could be coincidental but probably is not, justifying the assumption that V antedates XIV. See Foulet, *Roman de Renard,* p. 320.

40. Pierre mentions a *Dant Galopin . . . li levres* in line 1083 of *Branche* Va, Martin, *Roman de Renart,* 1:190.

41. For example, can Brun go all the way back to court *fuiant . . . plus que le trot* (line 702), having lost the hide from his front feet, if he is not indeed *esporonant* (line 705)?

42. Foulet, *Roman de Renard,* p. 256, is mistaken in saying that Tibert and Renart are mounted in the first half of XV. *A esperon* in line 182 is not meant literally.

43. Canterbury pilgrims were claiming in the 1170s that Thomas à Becket's tomb was thaumaturgic, and Louis VII visited it in 1179 (the year *Branche* I was probably written) to secure the recovery of his ill son Philip Augustus.

44. For example, Robert Bossuat, *Le Roman de Renart* (Paris: Hatier, 1967), pp. 113-14. The passage in question is Martin, *Roman de Renart,* 1:15-16, lines 505-30.

45. See Foulet, *Roman de Renard,* p. 333.

46. See Naoyuki Fukumoto, *Le Roman de Renart, Branches I et la* (Tokyo: Librairie France Tosho, 1974), pp. 202-203, regarding line 740 of that edition.

47. Jacob Grimm and Andreas Schmeller, *Lateinische Gedichte des X. und XI. Jh.* (Göttingen: Dieterich, 1838), pp. 340-42.

48. See Foulet, *Roman de Renard,* pp. 336-38. Cf. Voigt, *Egberts Fecunda Ratis,* pp. 195-96.

49. See for example Gaston Paris, *Mélanges de Littérature Française du Moyen Age* (Paris: Champion, 1912), pp. 413-14. Jauss (*Untersuchungen,* p. 264, note 1) maintains that Renart heeds Noble because he is a *Schelm,* yet even rogues avoid being hanged.

50. In lines 417-29 of *Ecbasis Captivi* the fox feeds the panther who has brought word of developments at court, and after leaving home he prays for pity, a safe return, and the wolf's defeat.

51. One is reminded here of the fox claiming senescence in lines 473-80 of *Ecbasis Captivi,* as mentioned in Chapter One, regarding the sick-lion episode of *Ysengrimus.*

52. Fere is not in evidence at court until the fox is about to leave (line 1440). At his arrival, for instance, he greets only the king.

53. The author did not know that Nur-ud-din had died in 1173.

54. Tardif's debut in the *Roman de Renart* occurs at Copee's funeral, in which he participates because *Branche* I's author needed *limacons* to rhyme with *lecons* (lines 409-10). Having created Tardif, the author could not resist the comic contrast which results from radically altering a snail's proverbial pace. That intentionally absurd anthropomorphism probably inspired the even better example of tongue-in-cheek topsy-turviness found in *Branche* XVII, where Couart rides a horse with a captured peasant around his neck (Martin, *Roman de Renart,* 2: 198-200, lines 61-108). Not only has the normally craven captor reversed his nature like the speedy snail; he has also switched roles with his catch. The peasant is a furrier, who customarily treats hares as the hare is treating him.

55. Whether the chase in *Branche* I is on horseback is ambiguous. Cf. *Branche* XVII's imitation, Martin, ibid., pp. 226-30. In both I and XVII Tardif carries a banner. Note the resemblance of Renart at the end of I to Walwein in lines 11741-78 of Wace's *Brut.*

56. Lines 9, 23, 480, 610-11, 833, 892, and 1499. Negative auctorial comments about Renart had become a tradition, begun by Pierre de Saint-Cloud, who was sincerely critical of the fox.

Josseline Bidard (essay date 1994)

SOURCE: "Reynard the Fox as Anti-Hero," in *Heroes and Heroines in Medieval English Literature,* edited by Leo Carruthers, D. S. Brewer, 1994, pp. 119-23.

[*In the following essay, Bidard details examples of how Reynard's character runs counter to that of the typical medieval hero.*]

I would like first to comment on the title of this paper. Reynard the Fox is of course a convenient name to refer to the different foxes appearing in medieval literature between the XIIIth and XVth centuries. It is the name used for instance by Caxton in his 1481 translation and printing. It is also the name most commonly used by modern critics, a name that underlines the link between the British works and the French tradition of the **Roman de Renart.** Yet, we can find our fox under other names: in *Of the Vox and Wolf,* written by the mid-XIIIth century, he is called Reneuard, which is quite close to the French name; in the *Nonnes Preestes Tale,* he becomes Russel, and in the *Fables* of Henryson, he turns into Lowrence. But in fact, as we shall see, he always remains the same and his different names can be seen as parts of his masks and disguises.

The second point I would like to insist on is the notion of anti-heroism. It may sound somewhat strange, even paradoxical, to speak of Reynard as anti-hero. Most of the time, he is considered as the hero of the fables and the tales in which he appears. Hero is then taken in its wider and weaker meaning, i.e. main protagonist, chief personage. Reynard is described as a manipulator, an instigator, a trickster, and, as such, he is very often called a hero. Moreover, the anti-hero is a modern notion, not to be applied to medieval literature. The anti-hero, in modern fiction, is characterized by absence: absence of heroic qualities, absence of reaction, sometimes even absence of personality. The anti-hero, more often than not, is a shadow, an outsider, a nobody, moving in a world full of absurdity he is quite incapable of either understanding or controlling. If we can say that Reynard is also characterized by a complete absence of heroic qualities, we cannot speak of his absence of reaction. He is no passive witness: on the contrary, he is the one who pulls the strings. Moreover, he perfectly understands and controls the world he lives in and that world is not full of absurdity but fraught with meaning. To draw a comparison between Reynard and modern anti-heroes would be a total absurdity. What I will try to show in this paper is that Reynard is an anti-hero in so far as he gives an inverted image of what a medieval hero was supposed to be. One could even call him a counter-hero.

First a medieval hero was a man and Reynard is an animal. We are always reminded of his animality. The authors constantly allude to his being a four-footed beast, easily recognizable thanks to his pointed ears and nose, his bushy tail and his thick red coat. He always moves in a natural setting: the forest, the field, the farm-yard. In *Of the Vox and Wolf,* he gets out of the forest. In the *Nonnes Preestes Tale,* he is lurking in a bed of cabbage. His motivation has nothing psychological or spiritual about it: he is mostly driven by hunger or thirst. In *Of the Vox and Wolf,* he gets out of the wood because he is hungry and, after eating three hens, he looks for water to quench his thirst.[1]

In the *Nonnes Preestes Tale*[2] he wants to grab Chauntecleer to have a good meal and it is exactly the same in Henryson's *Fables.*[3] Hunger is his first incentive and hens, ducks, lambs, etc. are his favourite victims. Moreover as an animal, he is supposed to be completely deprived of reason. Henryson, in 'The taill of Schir Chantecleir and the Foxe', explains that brutal beasts are irrational, that is to say wanting discretion (13/397-8). So this animality is completely alien to heroism: there can be neither identification with Reynard nor admiration for his feats! On the contrary the teller, and through him the reader, cannot help feeling superior to this irrational beast.

Yet, we should not dwell too much on Reynard's animality because it is partly obliterated on the one hand by his ability to speak and on the other hand by the moral vision of the authors. It is true that Reynard the Fox is presented as an irrational beast, deprived of reason; yet, he is endowed with the power of speech. Not only can he speak but he also knows how to use speech to further his aims. Most of his traps are set into words. The masks he puts on are very often verbal masks. Even in iconography it appears quite clearly. We see Reynard, disguised as a preacher, standing in a pulpit and talking his audience (mainly hens, ducks and geese) into blind submission. The end of his sermon will also be the end of these stupid fowls. Of course, this is just a convention and the other animals can speak too. But Reynard's mastery of words, the subtlety and cleverness of his arrangements tend to make us forget about his animality. This animality is also obliterated by the moral vision adopted by the authors. It is true that many details are given about his physical appearance but these details are just allusions, made in passing and quickly forgotten. They are conventional, based most of the time on the Bestiaries. They do not aim at giving a full-length description of a fox, based on direct observation. As always in medieval works, everything is man-centered and anthropomorphism is never very far. The physical portraits of Reynard are always counterbalanced by moral portraits.

Sometimes physical and moral features are intertwined, highlighting each other. When Russel appears at last in the *Nonnes Preestes Tale,* he is depicted as 'A col fox ful of sly iniquitee' (l. 3215). Sometimes physical features are given a moral significance: the fox neither walks nor runs, he sneaks, he lurks, he slinks, etc., revealing thus his false and treacherous nature. Henryson, in particular, piles up derogatory epithets. Lowrence is 'false', 'fenyeit', 'crafty', 'cautelous', etc. The fox is an animal but he is first and foremost an image of man. In the moralitas to the 'Tale of Schir Chantecleir and the Foxe', Henryson makes it clear. 'This fenyeit foxe may well be figurate To flateraris with plesand wordis quhyte With fals mening and mynd maist toxicate' (19/600-2).

Medieval authors did not start from an objective observation of animals, inferring their conclusions from these observations. They started from their beliefs and conceptions of man and the Universe and applied them to the animal word, trying to establish a network of cross references. They all shared Alan of Lille's opinion: 'Omnis mundi creatura, Quasi liber et pictura, Nobis est in speculum.'[4] All the physical, mental and spiritual phenomena are woven together into a huge web of connections. To study Reynard in himself has no interest whatsoever; what matters is to make out the links between the human and the animal world. So, what prevents Reynard from being a hero is not his being an animal, but rather his being false and treacherous. As an image of man, he represents sinful mankind and thus cannot but be condemned. He cannot be held up as an example, he is only exemplary in so far as he shows what must not be done. Of course, the emphasis on morality differs from one work to another, but in the British tradition morality is ever present.

Morality is ever present but morality does not preclude comedy. Even Henryson insists on the necessity of mingling 'merry' tales with a wise doctrine: too much seriousness leads to boredom and dullness, but the reader will accept the moral lesson more easily if he is entertained by the story (1-2). This 'comic' aspect of the tales can be considered as the second reason preventing Reynard from being a hero in the medieval sense of the word. A comic character is neither a hero nor an anti-hero. All his characteristics are distorted, exaggerated, to be held up to ridicule. A medieval hero is handsome: tall, fair-haired, blue-eyed, broad-shouldered and narrow-hipped. He is clever, intelligent, brave, courageous, and courteous. On the contrary the comic character is often ugly or at least plain. Puny little chaps with hooked noses or nutcracker faces alternate with pot-bellied, big-footed fellows. They can be stupid, making blunders, mistaking one thing for another. They can be cowards, quaking with fear, hiding in case of danger. They appear all the more ridiculous as they are always plunged into ludicrous situations. So we could tend to think that Reynard is an anti-hero because his adventures make us laugh. Either in the fables or the tales, we are in the world of comedy, not in the world of romance and heroism. Once again, things are not so clearly divided.

The world in which he moves is a comic world but Reynard himself is seldom a comic character. Physically speaking, he is neither handsome nor ugly: he is a fox. Morally speaking, Reynard is full of defects: proud, selfish, ruthless, and hypocritical, but these defects cannot make us laugh. They are not mere weaknesses but vices and as such they are dangerous and threatening, all the more threatening as he is far from being stupid. He uses his intelligence to lure his victims into his traps. In fact the general tone is the tone of comedy, but Reynard himself rather belongs to the world of drama. He is the villain, the false traitor, cheating and lying to the others. The others: they are the ones who are comical. The comic essentially rises from the situations (the tricks played by Reynard) and the other characters (the victims of his tricks). The word 'victim' is somewhat misleading because we seldom feel any pity for these victims. On the contrary we laugh at them. They seem to deserve what they get because of their foolishness or stupidity.

In *Of the Vox and Wolf* for instance, Sigrim the wolf seems to be the perfect laughable victim. He finds the fox, for once, in an awkward predicament: trapped in a bucket at the bottom of a dark, damp and miry well. Sigrim could easily take revenge on Reneuard, but he is so stupid as to believe all the blatant lies made up by the fox. The latter manages to convince him that the bottom of the well is in fact the gate of Paradise: any person in the Middle Ages knew that Paradise must be on top of a high mountain or

in a golden island! Reneuard also convinces him of the necessity to confess himself and to cleanse his soul in order to reach this Paradise teeming with sheep and goats. Reneuard even persuades him that he can hear his confession and absolve him from his sins. When, finally, Sigrim takes the place of Reneuard at the bottom of the well, we cannot feel any pity for him (xx-xxiv). Too much is too much. So, once again, we come to a dead end: first we saw how Reynard's animality did not really account for his being an anti-hero; we have just seen how the comic aspect of the tales does not explain anything either. He is not an anti-hero because he is an animal or a comic character. To my mind, he is essentially an anti-hero because, as already said, he gives us an 'inverted' image of the hero.

We do not have space to examine all the qualities required of a medieval hero, but there is one which sums up and comprehends all the others, i.e. truth. As Arveragus, in the *Franklin's Tale,* says, 'Trouthe is the hyeste thyng that man may kepe' (l. 1479). Criseyde, in *Troilus and Criseyde,* said she found and loved in Troilus 'Moral vertu, grounded upon trouthe' (IV l. 1672). Truth had several meanings in the Middle Ages, as it still does. It could be a mere promise, a pledged word: to keep one's truth meant not to break a promise. It could stand for integrity (to be true to one's inmost self) or loyalty (the very bond of dependence that kept feudal society together). On a higher level of course, it could be synonymous with Christian truth. Whatever its meaning, it was in fact the root of all heroic virtues. All the qualities required from a good knight were grounded upon truth: courage, purity, and integrity. The hero had to be true to himself and his quest was not a mere physical adventure but very often a quest to discover his inner self. The hero had to be true to his community and the integrity of the Round Table rests on the truthfulness of its members.

With Reynard truth no longer exists. Reynard is such a manipulator that he succeeds in giving reality to his lies and in building up a false image of truth. I will take two examples which are quite significant. At the beginning of *Of the Vox and Wolf,* Reneuard eats three hens and tries to catch Chauntecleer who has flown away onto a percher. The fox cannot hide the blood he has shed: this blood is the tangible proof of his crime. So the fox attempts to transform the reality of this blood, trying to convince the cock that he is a charitable and kind-hearted person. The hens were sick and he has let their bad blood in order to cure them. He feigns concern about Chauntecleer's health and is ready to do the same for his sake (xvii, 27-31). The second example is to be found in one of Henryson's Fables: 'the Taill how this foirsaid Tod maid his Confessioun to Freir Wolf Waitskaith'. Lowrence has just confessed to the wolf and has been condemned not to eat meat before Easter. No sooner has he left the wolf than he meets a kid. The temptation is too great. He takes the kid, plunges it into water and gives it a new name: 'Ga doun Schir Kid, cum up Schir Salmon agane!' (23, l. 751). In both examples truth is completely falsified. For Reynard truth means what is more profitable for him. He constantly pretends to be the opposite of what he is. He is selfish, but pretends to be charitable and generous. He is ruthless, but pretends to be kind-hearted. He is a liar, but pretends to be sincere and pure.

In all the tales and fables we have two antagonistic movements: on the one hand, the authors try to cast off the veil of appearances to reveal true reality and they invite us to find the sweet kernel of truth under the fiction of the story;[5] on the other hand, Reynard is eager to disguise reality under as many wrappings as possible. This is the very reason why he cannot be a hero. As Guy Bourquin points out in his article in the present volume, the hero is a person who shows himself, who reveals something to others; Reynard, on the contrary, conceals everything including himself. He is an anti-hero in so far as he represents a disruptive force, the force of darkness, whereas the hero stands in glorious light.

Notes

1. 'Of the Vox and Wolf', in *A Selection of Latin Stories of the XIIIth and XIVth centuries,* ed. T. Wright, London, 1842 (subsequent quotes refer to this edition).

2. *The Riverside Chaucer,* ed. Larry Benson, New York: Houghton Mifflin, 1987, Oxford: OUP Paperbacks, 1988.

3. Robert Henryson, *Poems,* ed. Ch. Elliot, Oxford: Clarendon, 1963 (subsequent quotes refer to this edition).

4. Alan of Lille quoted by F.J.E. Raby, *Christian-Latin Poetry,* 2nd ed. 1953, 355.

5. Jacques Le Goff, *La Civilisation de l'Occident Médiéval* (Paris, 1964), 420.

FURTHER READING

Criticism

Blake, N. F. "A Possible Seventh Copy of Caxton's *Reynard the Fox* (1481)?" *Notes and Queries* 10, No. 8 (August 1963): 287-88.
    Presents evidence that a conjectured seventh Caxton copy is actually a Pynson edition.

———. "The Epilogue in William Caxton's Second Edition of *Reynard the Fox.*" *Notes and Queries* 11, No. 2 (February 1964): 50-51.
    Presents evidence that the epilogue found in the Pepysian Library, Cambridge, copy of Caxton's edition is not the work of Caxton and may date from the seventeenth century.

Gravdal, Kathryn. "Law and Literature in the French Middle Ages: Rape Law on Trial in *Le Roman de Renart.*" *Romanic Review* LXXXII, No. 1 (January 1991): 1-24.
    Explores the relationship between medieval literature and law, particularly in regard to rape. A later version of this essay is excerpted above.

Speer, Mary B. "Comments on the Text of the γ-Redaction of the *Roman de Renart.*" *Romance Philology* XXXVII, No. 1 (August 1983): 63-71.
    Critiques the works of Noboru Harano and Naoyuki Fukumoto and discusses the editing problem of whether or not, when creating a new edition, to correct mistakes which appear in previous transcriptions.

Varty, Kenneth. "Reynard the Fox and the Smithfield Decretals." *Journal of the Warburg and Courtauld Institutes* 26 (1963): 347-54.
    Describes and comments on the many fox illustrations found in a medieval English volume of glossed decretals of Gregory IX.

———. "The Death and Resurrection of Reynard in Mediaeval Literature and Art." *Nottingham Medieval Studies* 10 (1966): 70-93.
    Analyzes the seventeenth branch of the *Roman de Renart* and describes and categorizes related iconographic material from various insular and continental sources.

———. "The Earliest Illustrated English Editions of *Reynard the Fox*; and Their Links with the Earliest Illustrated Continental Editions." In *Reynaert Reynard Reynke: Studien zu Einem Mittelalterlichen Tierepos,* edited by Jan Goossens and Timothy Sodmann, pp. 160-95. Köln, Germany: Böhlau, 1980.
    Focusing on new discoveries, provides a history of early illustrated editions of *Reynard the Fox*, and describes and compares their woodcuts.

———. *The "Roman de Renart": A Guide to Scholarly Work.* Lanham, Md.: The Scarecrow Press, 1998, 179p.
    Provides a wealth of information on manuscripts, editions, translations, adaptations, and critical studies.

How to Use This Index

Literary Criticism Series
Cumulative Author Index

A/C Cross
See Lawrence, T(homas) E(dward)

Abasiyanik, Sait Faik 1906-1954
See Sait Faik
See also CA 123

Abbey, Edward 1927-1989 .... **CLC 36, 59**
See also CA 45-48; 128; CANR 2, 41; DA3; MTCW 2

Abbott, Lee K(ittredge) 1947- .... **CLC 48**
See also CA 124; CANR 51; DLB 130

Abe, Kobo 1924-1993 ...... **CLC 8, 22, 53, 81; DAM NOV**
See also CA 65-68; 140; CANR 24, 60; DLB 182; MTCW 1, 2

Abelard, Peter c. 1079-c. 1142 ...... **CMLC 11**
See also DLB 115, 208

Abell, Kjeld 1901-1961 .... **CLC 15**
See also CA 111; DLB 214

Abish, Walter 1931- .... **CLC 22**
See also CA 101; CANR 37; DLB 130, 227

Abrahams, Peter (Henry) 1919- .... **CLC 4**
See also BW 1; CA 57-60; CANR 26; DLB 117, 225; MTCW 1, 2

Abrams, M(eyer) H(oward) 1912- ... **CLC 24**
See also CA 57-60; CANR 13, 33; DLB 67

Abse, Dannie 1923- .... **CLC 7, 29; DAB; DAM POET**
See also CA 53-56; CAAS 1; CANR 4, 46, 74; DLB 27; MTCW 1

Achebe, (Albert) Chinua(lumogu) 1930- ...... **CLC 1, 3, 5, 7, 11, 26, 51, 75, 127; BLC 1; DA; DAB; DAC; DAM MST, MULT, NOV; WLC**
See also AAYA 15; BW 2, 3; CA 1-4R; CANR 6, 26, 47; CLR 20; DA3; DLB 117; MAICYA; MTCW 1, 2; SATA 38, 40; SATA-Brief 38

Acker, Kathy 1948-1997 .... **CLC 45, 111**
See also CA 117; 122; 162; CANR 55

Ackroyd, Peter 1949- .... **CLC 34, 52, 140**
See also CA 123; 127; CANR 51, 74; DLB 155, 231; INT 127; MTCW 1

Acorn, Milton 1923- .... **CLC 15; DAC**
See also CA 103; DLB 53; INT 103

Adamov, Arthur 1908-1970 .... **CLC 4, 25; DAM DRAM**
See also CA 17-18; 25-28R; CAP 2; MTCW 1

Adams, Alice (Boyd) 1926-1999 .. **CLC 6, 13, 46; SSC 24**
See also CA 81-84; 179; CANR 26, 53, 75, 88; DLB 234; DLBY 86; INT CANR-26; MTCW 1, 2

Adams, Andy 1859-1935 .... **TCLC 56**
See also YABC 1

Adams, Brooks 1848-1927 .... **TCLC 80**
See also CA 123; DLB 47

Adams, Douglas (Noel) 1952- .... **CLC 27, 60; DAM POP**
See also AAYA 4, 33; BEST 89:3; CA 106; CANR 34, 64; DA3; DLBY 83; JRDA; MTCW 1; SATA 116

Adams, Francis 1862-1893 .... **NCLC 33**

Adams, Henry (Brooks) 1838-1918 .... **TCLC 4, 52; DA; DAB; DAC; DAM MST**
See also CA 104; 133; CANR 77; DLB 12, 47, 189; MTCW 1

Adams, Richard (George) 1920- ... **CLC 4, 5, 18; DAM NOV**
See also AAYA 16; AITN 1, 2; CA 49-52; CANR 3, 35; CLR 20; JRDA; MAICYA; MTCW 1, 2; SATA 7, 69

Adamson, Joy(-Friederike Victoria) 1910-1980 .... **CLC 17**
See also CA 69-72; 93-96; CANR 22; MTCW 1; SATA 11; SATA-Obit 22

Adcock, Fleur 1934- .... **CLC 41**
See also CA 25-28R, 182; CAAE 182; CAAS 23; CANR 11, 34, 69; DLB 40

Addams, Charles (Samuel) 1912-1988 .... **CLC 30**
See also CA 61-64; 126; CANR 12, 79

Addams, Jane 1860-1945 .... **TCLC 76**

Addison, Joseph 1672-1719 .... **LC 18**
See also CDBLB 1660-1789; DLB 101

Adler, Alfred (F.) 1870-1937 .... **TCLC 61**
See also CA 119; 159

Adler, C(arole) S(chwerdtfeger) 1932- .... **CLC 35**
See also AAYA 4; CA 89-92; CANR 19, 40; JRDA; MAICYA; SAAS 15; SATA 26, 63, 102

Adler, Renata 1938- .... **CLC 8, 31**
See also CA 49-52; CANR 5, 22, 52; MTCW 1

Ady, Endre 1877-1919 .... **TCLC 11**
See also CA 107

A.E. 1867-1935 .... **TCLC 3, 10**
See also Russell, George William

Aeschylus 525B.C.-456B.C. .. **CMLC 11; DA; DAB; DAC; DAM DRAM, MST; DC 8; WLCS**
See also DLB 176

Aesop 620(?)B.C.-(?)B.C. .... **CMLC 24**
See also CLR 14; MAICYA; SATA 64

Affable Hawk
See MacCarthy, Sir(Charles Otto) Desmond

Africa, Ben
See Bosman, Herman Charles

Afton, Effie
See Harper, Frances Ellen Watkins

Agapida, Fray Antonio
See Irving, Washington

Agee, James (Rufus) 1909-1955 ...... **TCLC 1, 19; DAM NOV**
See also AITN 1; CA 108; 148; CDALB 1941-1968; DLB 2, 26, 152; MTCW 1

Aghill, Gordon
See Silverberg, Robert

Agnon, S(hmuel) Y(osef Halevi) 1888-1970 .... **CLC 4, 8, 14; SSC 30**
See also CA 17-18; 25-28R; CANR 60; CAP 2; MTCW 1, 2

Agrippa von Nettesheim, Henry Cornelius 1486-1535 .... **LC 27**

Aguilera Malta, Demetrio 1909-1981
See also CA 111; 124; CANR 87; DAM MULT, NOV; DLB 145; HLCS 1; HW 1

Agustini, Delmira 1886-1914
See also CA 166; HLCS 1; HW 1, 2

Aherne, Owen
See Cassill, R(onald) V(erlin)

Ai 1947- .... **CLC 4, 14, 69**
See also CA 85-88; CAAS 13; CANR 70; DLB 120

Aickman, Robert (Fordyce) 1914-1981 .... **CLC 57**
See also CA 5-8R; CANR 3, 72

Aiken, Conrad (Potter) 1889-1973 .... **CLC 1, 3, 5, 10, 52; DAM NOV, POET; PC 26; SSC 9**
See also CA 5-8R; 45-48; CANR 4, 60; CDALB 1929-1941; DLB 9, 45, 102; MTCW 1, 2; SATA 3, 30

Aiken, Joan (Delano) 1924- .... **CLC 35**
See also AAYA 1, 25; CA 9-12R, 182; CAAE 182; CANR 4, 23, 34, 64; CLR 1, 19; DLB 161; JRDA; MAICYA; MTCW 1; SAAS 1; SATA 2, 30, 73; SATA-Essay 109

Ainsworth, William Harrison 1805-1882 .... **NCLC 13**
See also DLB 21; SATA 24

Aitmatov, Chingiz (Torekulovich) 1928- .... **CLC 71**
See also CA 103; CANR 38; MTCW 1; SATA 56

Akers, Floyd
See Baum, L(yman) Frank

Akhmadulina, Bella Akhatovna 1937- .... **CLC 53; DAM POET**
See also CA 65-68

Akhmatova, Anna 1888-1966 ..... **CLC 11, 25, 64, 126; DAM POET; PC 2**
See also CA 19-20; 25-28R; CANR 35; CAP 1; DA3; MTCW 1, 2

Aksakov, Sergei Timofeyvich 1791-1859 .... **NCLC 2**
See also DLB 198

Aksenov, Vassily
See Aksyonov, Vassily (Pavlovich)

Baker, Elliott 1922- .... **CLC 8**
See also CA 45-48; CANR 2, 63
Baker, Jean H. TCLC 3, 10
See also Russell, George William
Baker, Nicholson 1957- .... **CLC 61; DAM POP**
See also CA 135; CANR 63; DA3; DLB 227
Baker, Ray Stannard 1870-1946 .... **TCLC 47**
See also CA 118
Baker, Russell (Wayne) 1925- .... **CLC 31**
See also BEST 89:4; CA 57-60; CANR 11, 41, 59; MTCW 1, 2
Bakhtin, M.
See Bakhtin, Mikhail Mikhailovich
Bakhtin, M. M.
See Bakhtin, Mikhail Mikhailovich
Bakhtin, Mikhail
See Bakhtin, Mikhail Mikhailovich
Bakhtin, Mikhail Mikhailovich
1895-1975 .... **CLC 83**
See also CA 128; 113
Bakshi, Ralph 1938(?)- .... **CLC 26**
See also CA 112; 138
Bakunin, Mikhail (Alexandrovich)
1814-1876 .... **NCLC 25, 58**
Baldwin, James (Arthur) 1924-1987 . **CLC 1, 2, 3, 4, 5, 8, 13, 15, 17, 42, 50, 67, 90, 127; BLC 1; DA; DAB; DAC; DAM MST, MULT, NOV, POP; DC 1; SSC 10, 33; WLC**
See also AAYA 4, 34; BW 1; CA 1-4R; 124; CABS 1; CANR 3, 24; CDALB 1941-1968; DA3; DLB 2, 7, 33; DLBY 87; MTCW 1, 2; SATA 9; SATA-Obit 54
Bale, John 1495-1563 .... **LC 62**
See also DLB 132
Ball, Hugo 1886-1927 .... **TCLC 104**
Ballard, J(ames) G(raham) 1930- . **CLC 3, 6, 14, 36, 137; DAM NOV, POP; SSC 1**
See also AAYA 3; CA 5-8R; CANR 15, 39, 65; DA3; DLB 14, 207; MTCW 1, 2; SATA 93
Balmont, Konstantin (Dmitriyevich)
1867-1943 .... **TCLC 11**
See also CA 109; 155
Baltausis, Vincas
See Mikszath, Kalman
Balzac, Honore de 1799-1850 ... **NCLC 5, 35, 53; DA; DAB; DAC; DAM MST, NOV; SSC 5; WLC**
See also DA3; DLB 119
Bambara, Toni Cade 1939-1995 ...... **CLC 19, 88; BLC 1; DA; DAC; DAM MST, MULT; SSC 35; WLCS**
See also AAYA 5; BW 2, 3; CA 29-32R; 150; CANR 24, 49, 81; CDALBS; DA3; DLB 38; MTCW 1, 2; SATA 112
Bamdad, A.
See Shamlu, Ahmad
Banat, D. R.
See Bradbury, Ray (Douglas)
Bancroft, Laura
See Baum, L(yman) Frank
Banim, John 1798-1842 .... **NCLC 13**
See also DLB 116, 158, 159
Banim, Michael 1796-1874 .... **NCLC 13**
See also DLB 158, 159
Banjo, The
See Paterson, A(ndrew) B(arton)
Banks, Iain
See Banks, Iain M(enzies)
Banks, Iain M(enzies) 1954- .... **CLC 34**
See also CA 123; 128; CANR 61; DLB 194; INT 128
Banks, Lynne Reid CLC 23
See also Reid Banks, Lynne
See also AAYA 6

Banks, Russell 1940- .... **CLC 37, 72; SSC 42**
See also CA 65-68; CAAS 15; CANR 19, 52, 73; DLB 130
Banville, John 1945- .... **CLC 46, 118**
See also CA 117; 128; DLB 14; INT 128
Banville, Theodore (Faullain) de
1832-1891 .... **NCLC 9**
Baraka, Amiri 1934- . **CLC 1, 2, 3, 5, 10, 14, 33, 115; BLC 1; DA; DAC; DAM MST, MULT, POET, POP; DC 6; PC 4; WLCS**
See also Jones, LeRoi
See also BW 2, 3; CA 21-24R; CABS 3; CANR 27, 38, 61; CDALB 1941-1968; DA3; DLB 5, 7, 16, 38; DLBD 8; MTCW 1, 2
Barbauld, Anna Laetitia
1743-1825 .... **NCLC 50**
See also DLB 107, 109, 142, 158
Barbellion, W. N. P. TCLC 24
See also Cummings, Bruce F(rederick)
Barbera, Jack (Vincent) 1945- .... **CLC 44**
See also CA 110; CANR 45
Barbey d'Aurevilly, Jules Amedee
1808-1889 .... **NCLC 1; SSC 17**
See also DLB 119
Barbour, John c. 1316-1395 .... **CMLC 33**
See also DLB 146
Barbusse, Henri 1873-1935 .... **TCLC 5**
See also CA 105; 154; DLB 65
Barclay, Bill
See Moorcock, Michael (John)
Barclay, William Ewert
See Moorcock, Michael (John)
Barea, Arturo 1897-1957 .... **TCLC 14**
See also CA 111
Barfoot, Joan 1946- .... **CLC 18**
See also CA 105
Barham, Richard Harris
1788-1845 .... **NCLC 77**
See also DLB 159
Baring, Maurice 1874-1945 .... **TCLC 8**
See also CA 105; 168; DLB 34
Baring-Gould, Sabine 1834-1924 ... **TCLC 88**
See also DLB 156, 190
Barker, Clive 1952- .... **CLC 52; DAM POP**
See also AAYA 10; BEST 90:3; CA 121; 129; CANR 71; DA3; INT 129; MTCW 1, 2
Barker, George Granville
1913-1991 .... **CLC 8, 48; DAM POET**
See also CA 9-12R; 135; CANR 7, 38; DLB 20; MTCW 1
Barker, Harley Granville
See Granville-Barker, Harley
See also DLB 10
Barker, Howard 1946- .... **CLC 37**
See also CA 102; DLB 13, 233
Barker, Jane 1652-1732 .... **LC 42**
Barker, Pat(ricia) 1943- .... **CLC 32, 94**
See also CA 117; 122; CANR 50; INT 122
Barlach, Ernst (Heinrich)
1870-1938 .... **TCLC 84**
See also CA 178; DLB 56, 118
Barlow, Joel 1754-1812 .... **NCLC 23**
See also DLB 37
Barnard, Mary (Ethel) 1909- .... **CLC 48**
See also CA 21-22; CAP 2
Barnes, Djuna 1892-1982 .... **CLC 3, 4, 8, 11, 29, 127; SSC 3**
See also CA 9-12R; 107; CANR 16, 55; DLB 4, 9, 45; MTCW 1, 2
Barnes, Julian (Patrick) 1946- .... **CLC 42; DAB**
See also CA 102; CANR 19, 54; DLB 194; DLBY 93; MTCW 1
Barnes, Peter 1931- .... **CLC 5, 56**
See also CA 65-68; CAAS 12; CANR 33, 34, 64; DLB 13, 233; MTCW 1

Barnes, William 1801-1886 .... **NCLC 75**
See also DLB 32
Baroja (y Nessi), Pio 1872-1956 ..... **TCLC 8; HLC 1**
See also CA 104
Baron, David
See Pinter, Harold
Baron Corvo
See Rolfe, Frederick (William Serafino Austin Lewis Mary)
Barondess, Sue K(aufman)
1926-1977 .... **CLC 8**
See also Kaufman, Sue
See also CA 1-4R; 69-72; CANR 1
Baron de Teive
See Pessoa, Fernando (Antonio Nogueira)
Baroness Von S.
See Zangwill, Israel
Barres, (Auguste-) Maurice
1862-1923 .... **TCLC 47**
See also CA 164; DLB 123
Barreto, Afonso Henrique de Lima
See Lima Barreto, Afonso Henrique de
Barrett, (Roger) Syd 1946- .... **CLC 35**
Barrett, William (Christopher)
1913-1992 .... **CLC 27**
See also CA 13-16R; 139; CANR 11, 67; INT CANR-11
Barrie, J(ames) M(atthew)
1860-1937 .... **TCLC 2; DAB; DAM DRAM**
See also CA 104; 136; CANR 77; CDBLB 1890-1914; CLR 16; DA3; DLB 10, 141, 156; MAICYA; MTCW 1; SATA 100; YABC 1
Barrington, Michael
See Moorcock, Michael (John)
Barrol, Grady
See Bograd, Larry
Barry, Mike
See Malzberg, Barry N(athaniel)
Barry, Philip 1896-1949 .... **TCLC 11**
See also CA 109; DLB 7, 228
Bart, Andre Schwarz
See Schwarz-Bart, Andre
Barth, John (Simmons) 1930- ... **CLC 1, 2, 3, 5, 7, 9, 10, 14, 27, 51, 89; DAM NOV; SSC 10**
See also AITN 1, 2; CA 1-4R; CABS 1; CANR 5, 23, 49, 64; DLB 2, 227; MTCW 1
Barthelme, Donald 1931-1989 ... **CLC 1, 2, 3, 5, 6, 8, 13, 23, 46, 59, 115; DAM NOV; SSC 2**
See also CA 21-24R; 129; CANR 20, 58; DA3; DLB 2, 234; DLBY 80, 89; MTCW 1, 2; SATA 7; SATA-Obit 62
Barthelme, Frederick 1943- ...... **CLC 36, 117**
See also CA 114; 122; CANR 77; DLBY 85; INT 122
Barthes, Roland (Gerard)
1915-1980 .... **CLC 24, 83**
See also CA 130; 97-100; CANR 66; MTCW 1, 2
Barzun, Jacques (Martin) 1907- ..... **CLC 51**
See also CA 61-64; CANR 22
Bashevis, Isaac
See Singer, Isaac Bashevis
Bashkirtseff, Marie 1859-1884 .... **NCLC 27**
Basho
See Matsuo Basho
Basil of Caesaria c. 330-379 .... **CMLC 35**
Bass, Kingsley B., Jr.
See Bullins, Ed
Bass, Rick 1958- .... **CLC 79**
See also CA 126; CANR 53, 93; DLB 212
Bassani, Giorgio 1916- .... **CLC 9**
See also CA 65-68; CANR 33; DLB 128, 177; MTCW 1

Bastos, Augusto (Antonio) Roa
See Roa Bastos, Augusto (Antonio)

Bataille, Georges 1897-1962 .... **CLC 29**
See also CA 101; 89-92

Bates, H(erbert) E(rnest)
1905-1974 . **CLC 46; DAB; DAM POP; SSC 10**
See also CA 93-96; 45-48; CANR 34; DA3; DLB 162, 191; MTCW 1, 2

Bauchart
See Camus, Albert

Baudelaire, Charles 1821-1867 . **NCLC 6, 29, 55; DA; DAB; DAC; DAM MST, POET; PC 1; SSC 18; WLC**
See also DA3

Baudrillard, Jean 1929- .... **CLC 60**

Baum, L(yman) Frank 1856-1919 ... **TCLC 7**
See also CA 108; 133; CLR 15; DLB 22; JRDA; MAICYA; MTCW 1, 2; SATA 18, 100

Baum, Louis F.
See Baum, L(yman) Frank

Baumbach, Jonathan 1933- .... **CLC 6, 23**
See also CA 13-16R; CAAS 5; CANR 12, 66; DLBY 80; INT CANR-12; MTCW 1

Bausch, Richard (Carl) 1945- .... **CLC 51**
See also CA 101; CAAS 14; CANR 43, 61, 87; DLB 130

Baxter, Charles (Morley) 1947- .... **CLC 45, 78; DAM POP**
See also CA 57-60; CANR 40, 64; DLB 130; MTCW 2

Baxter, George Owen
See Faust, Frederick (Schiller)

Baxter, James K(eir) 1926-1972 .... **CLC 14**
See also CA 77-80

Baxter, John
See Hunt, E(verette) Howard, (Jr.)

Bayer, Sylvia
See Glassco, John

Baynton, Barbara 1857-1929 .... **TCLC 57**
See also DLB 230

Beagle, Peter S(oyer) 1939- .... **CLC 7, 104**
See also CA 9-12R; CANR 4, 51, 73; DA3; DLBY 80; INT CANR-4; MTCW 1; SATA 60

Bean, Normal
See Burroughs, Edgar Rice

Beard, Charles A(ustin)
1874-1948 .... **TCLC 15**
See also CA 115; DLB 17; SATA 18

Beardsley, Aubrey 1872-1898 .... **NCLC 6**

Beattie, Ann 1947- ..... **CLC 8, 13, 18, 40, 63; DAM NOV, POP; SSC 11**
See also BEST 90:2; CA 81-84; CANR 53, 73; DA3; DLBY 82; MTCW 1, 2

Beattie, James 1735-1803 .... **NCLC 25**
See also DLB 109

Beauchamp, Kathleen Mansfield 1888-1923
See Mansfield, Katherine
See also CA 104; 134; DA; DAC; DAM MST; DA3; MTCW 2

Beaumarchais, Pierre-Augustin Caron de 1732-1799 . **LC 61; DAM DRAM; DC 4**

Beaumont, Francis 1584(?)-1616 .... **LC 33; DC 6**
See also CDBLB Before 1660; DLB 58, 121

Beauvoir, Simone (Lucie Ernestine Marie Bertrand) de 1908-1986 .... **CLC 1, 2, 4, 8, 14, 31, 44, 50, 71, 124; DA; DAB; DAC; DAM MST, NOV; SSC 35; WLC**
See also CA 9-12R; 118; CANR 28, 61; DA3; DLB 72; DLBY 86; MTCW 1, 2

Becker, Carl (Lotus) 1873-1945 ..... **TCLC 63**
See also CA 157; DLB 17

Becker, Jurek 1937-1997 .... **CLC 7, 19**
See also CA 85-88; 157; CANR 60; DLB 75

Becker, Walter 1950- .... **CLC 26**

Beckett, Samuel (Barclay)
1906-1989 .. **CLC 1, 2, 3, 4, 6, 9, 10, 11, 14, 18, 29, 57, 59, 83; DA; DAB; DAC; DAM DRAM, MST, NOV; SSC 16; WLC**
See also CA 5-8R; 130; CANR 33, 61; CD-BLB 1945-1960; DA3; DLB 13, 15, 233; DLBY 90; MTCW 1, 2

Beckford, William 1760-1844 .... **NCLC 16**
See also DLB 39

Beckman, Gunnel 1910- .... **CLC 26**
See also CA 33-36R; CANR 15; CLR 25; MAICYA; SAAS 9; SATA 6

Becque, Henri 1837-1899 .... **NCLC 3**
See also DLB 192

Becquer, Gustavo Adolfo 1836-1870
See also DAM MULT; HLCS 1

Beddoes, Thomas Lovell
1803-1849 .... **NCLC 3**
See also DLB 96

Bede c. 673-735 .... **CMLC 20**
See also DLB 146

Bedford, Donald F.
See Fearing, Kenneth (Flexner)

Beecher, Catharine Esther
1800-1878 .... **NCLC 30**
See also DLB 1

Beecher, John 1904-1980 .... **CLC 6**
See also AITN 1; CA 5-8R; 105; CANR 8

Beer, Johann 1655-1700 .... **LC 5**
See also DLB 168

Beer, Patricia 1924- .... **CLC 58**
See also CA 61-64; 183; CANR 13, 46; DLB 40

Beerbohm, Max -1956
See Beerbohm, (Henry) Max(imilian)

Beerbohm, (Henry) Max(imilian)
1872-1956 .... **TCLC 1, 24**
See also CA 104; 154; CANR 79; DLB 34, 100

Beer-Hofmann, Richard
1866-1945 .... **TCLC 60**
See also CA 160; DLB 81

Begiebing, Robert J(ohn) 1946- .... **CLC 70**
See also CA 122; CANR 40, 88

Behan, Brendan 1923-1964 ...... **CLC 1, 8, 11, 15, 79; DAM DRAM**
See also CA 73-76; CANR 33; CDBLB 1945-1960; DLB 13, 233; MTCW 1, 2

Behn, Aphra 1640(?)-1689 .... **LC 1, 30, 42; DA; DAB; DAC; DAM DRAM, MST, NOV, POET; DC 4; PC 13; WLC**
See also DA3; DLB 39, 80, 131

Behrman, S(amuel) N(athaniel)
1893-1973 .... **CLC 40**
See also CA 13-16; 45-48; CAP 1; DLB 7, 44

Belasco, David 1853-1931 .... **TCLC 3**
See also CA 104; 168; DLB 7

Belcheva, Elisaveta 1893- .... **CLC 10**
See also Bagryana, Elisaveta

Beldone, Phil "Cheech"
See Ellison, Harlan (Jay)

Beleno
See Azuela, Mariano

Belinski, Vissarion Grigoryevich
1811-1848 .... **NCLC 5**
See also DLB 198

Belitt, Ben 1911- .... **CLC 22**
See also CA 13-16R; CAAS 4; CANR 7, 77; DLB 5

Bell, Gertrude (Margaret Lowthian)
1868-1926 .... **TCLC 67**
See also CA 167; DLB 174

Bell, J. Freeman
See Zangwill, Israel

Bell, James Madison 1826-1902 ... **TCLC 43; BLC 1; DAM MULT**
See also BW 1; CA 122; 124; DLB 50

Bell, Madison Smartt 1957- ...... **CLC 41, 102**
See also CA 111, 183; CAAE 183; CANR 28, 54, 73; MTCW 1

Bell, Marvin (Hartley) 1937- ...... **CLC 8, 31; DAM POET**
See also CA 21-24R; CAAS 14; CANR 59; DLB 5; MTCW 1

Bell, W. L. D.
See Mencken, H(enry) L(ouis)

Bellamy, Atwood C.
See Mencken, H(enry) L(ouis)

Bellamy, Edward 1850-1898 ...... **NCLC 4, 86**
See also DLB 12

Belli, Gioconda 1949-
See also CA 152; HLCS 1

Bellin, Edward J.
See Kuttner, Henry

Belloc, (Joseph) Hilaire (Pierre Sebastien Rene Swanton) 1870-1953 ...... **TCLC 7, 18; DAM POET; PC 24**
See also CA 106; 152; DLB 19, 100, 141, 174; MTCW 1; SATA 112; YABC 1

Belloc, Joseph Peter Rene Hilaire
See Belloc, (Joseph) Hilaire (Pierre Sebastien Rene Swanton)

Belloc, Joseph Pierre Hilaire
See Belloc, (Joseph) Hilaire (Pierre Sebastien Rene Swanton)

Belloc, M. A.
See Lowndes, Marie Adelaide (Belloc)

Bellow, Saul 1915- . **CLC 1, 2, 3, 6, 8, 10, 13, 15, 25, 33, 34, 63, 79; DA; DAB; DAC; DAM MST, NOV, POP; SSC 14; WLC**
See also AITN 2; BEST 89:3; CA 5-8R; CABS 1; CANR 29, 53; CDALB 1941-1968; DA3; DLB 2, 28; DLBD 3; DLBY 82; MTCW 1, 2

Belser, Reimond Karel Maria de 1929-
See Ruyslinck, Ward
See also CA 152

Bely, Andrey TCLC 7; PC 11
See also Bugayev, Boris Nikolayevich
See also MTCW 1

Belyi, Andrei
See Bugayev, Boris Nikolayevich

Benary, Margot
See Benary-Isbert, Margot

Benary-Isbert, Margot 1889-1979 .... **CLC 12**
See also CA 5-8R; 89-92; CANR 4, 72; CLR 12; MAICYA; SATA 2; SATA-Obit 21

Benavente (y Martinez), Jacinto
1866-1954 .... **TCLC 3; DAM DRAM, MULT; HLCS 1**
See also CA 106; 131; CANR 81; HW 1, 2; MTCW 1, 2

Benchley, Peter (Bradford) 1940- . **CLC 4, 8; DAM NOV, POP**
See also AAYA 14; AITN 2; CA 17-20R; CANR 12, 35, 66; MTCW 1, 2; SATA 3, 89

Benchley, Robert (Charles)
1889-1945 .... **TCLC 1, 55**
See also CA 105; 153; DLB 11

Benda, Julien 1867-1956 .... **TCLC 60**
See also CA 120; 154

Benedict, Ruth (Fulton)
1887-1948 .... **TCLC 60**
See also CA 158

Benedict, Saint c. 480-c. 547 .... **CMLC 29**

Benedikt, Michael 1935- .... **CLC 4, 14**
See also CA 13-16R; CANR 7; DLB 5

Benet, Juan 1927- .... **CLC 28**
See also CA 143

Buckler, Ernest 1908-1984 .... **CLC 13; DAC; DAM MST**
See also CA 11-12; 114; CAP 1; DLB 68; SATA 47

Buckley, Vincent (Thomas)
1925-1988 .... **CLC 57**
See also CA 101

Buckley, William F(rank), Jr. 1925- . **CLC 7, 18, 37; DAM POP**
See also AITN 1; CA 1-4R; CANR 1, 24, 53, 93; DA3; DLB 137; DLBY 80; INT CANR-24; MTCW 1, 2

Buechner, (Carl) Frederick 1926- . **CLC 2, 4, 6, 9; DAM NOV**
See also CA 13-16R; CANR 11, 39, 64; DLBY 80; INT CANR-11; MTCW 1, 2

Buell, John (Edward) 1927- .... **CLC 10**
See also CA 1-4R; CANR 71; DLB 53

Buero Vallejo, Antonio 1916-2000 ... **CLC 15, 46, 139**
See also CA 106; CANR 24, 49, 75; HW 1; MTCW 1, 2

Bufalino, Gesualdo 1920(?)- .... **CLC 74**
See also DLB 196

Bugayev, Boris Nikolayevich
1880-1934 .... **TCLC 7; PC 11**
See also Bely, Andrey
See also CA 104; 165; MTCW 1

Bukowski, Charles 1920-1994 ... **CLC 2, 5, 9, 41, 82, 108; DAM NOV, POET; PC 18**
See also CA 17-20R; 144; CANR 40, 62; DA3; DLB 5, 130, 169; MTCW 1, 2

Bulgakov, Mikhail (Afanas'evich)
1891-1940 . **TCLC 2, 16; DAM DRAM, NOV; SSC 18**
See also CA 105; 152

Bulgya, Alexander Alexandrovich
1901-1956 .... **TCLC 53**
See also Fadeyev, Alexander
See also CA 117; 181

Bullins, Ed 1935- .... **CLC 1, 5, 7; BLC 1; DAM DRAM, MULT; DC 6**
See also BW 2, 3; CA 49-52; CAAS 16; CANR 24, 46, 73; DLB 7, 38; MTCW 1, 2

Bulwer-Lytton, Edward (George Earle Lytton) 1803-1873 .... **NCLC 1, 45**
See also DLB 21

Bunin, Ivan Alexeyevich
1870-1953 .... **TCLC 6; SSC 5**
See also CA 104

Bunting, Basil 1900-1985 ..... **CLC 10, 39, 47; DAM POET**
See also CA 53-56; 115; CANR 7; DLB 20

Bunuel, Luis 1900-1983 .. **CLC 16, 80; DAM MULT; HLC 1**
See also CA 101; 110; CANR 32, 77; HW 1

Bunyan, John 1628-1688 ... **LC 4; DA; DAB; DAC; DAM MST; WLC**
See also CDBLB 1660-1789; DLB 39

Burckhardt, Jacob (Christoph)
1818-1897 .... **NCLC 49**

Burford, Eleanor
See Hibbert, Eleanor Alice Burford

Burgess, Anthony -1993 .... **CLC 1, 2, 4, 5, 8, 10, 13, 15, 22, 40, 62, 81, 94; DAB**
See also Wilson, John (Anthony) Burgess
See also AAYA 25; AITN 1; CDBLB 1960 to Present; DLB 14, 194; DLBY 98; MTCW 1

Burke, Edmund 1729(?)-1797 .... **LC 7, 36; DA; DAB; DAC; DAM MST; WLC**
See also DA3; DLB 104

Burke, Kenneth (Duva) 1897-1993 ... **CLC 2, 24**
See also CA 5-8R; 143; CANR 39, 74; DLB 45, 63; MTCW 1, 2

Burke, Leda
See Garnett, David

Burke, Ralph
See Silverberg, Robert

Burke, Thomas 1886-1945 .... **TCLC 63**
See also CA 113; 155; DLB 197

Burney, Fanny 1752-1840 .... **NCLC 12, 54**
See also DLB 39

Burns, Robert 1759-1796 . **LC 3, 29, 40; DA; DAB; DAC; DAM MST, POET; PC 6; WLC**
See also CDBLB 1789-1832; DA3; DLB 109

Burns, Tex
See L'Amour, Louis (Dearborn)

Burnshaw, Stanley 1906- .... **CLC 3, 13, 44**
See also CA 9-12R; DLB 48; DLBY 97

Burr, Anne 1937- .... **CLC 6**
See also CA 25-28R

Burroughs, Edgar Rice 1875-1950 . **TCLC 2, 32; DAM NOV**
See also AAYA 11; CA 104; 132; DA3; DLB 8; MTCW 1, 2; SATA 41

Burroughs, William S(eward)
1914-1997 .. **CLC 1, 2, 5, 15, 22, 42, 75, 109; DA; DAB; DAC; DAM MST, NOV, POP; WLC**
See also AITN 2; CA 9-12R; 160; CANR 20, 52; DA3; DLB 2, 8, 16, 152; DLBY 81, 97; MTCW 1, 2

Burton, SirRichard F(rancis)
1821-1890 .... **NCLC 42**
See also DLB 55, 166, 184

Busch, Frederick 1941- .... **CLC 7, 10, 18, 47**
See also CA 33-36R; CAAS 1; CANR 45, 73, 92; DLB 6

Bush, Ronald 1946- .... **CLC 34**
See also CA 136

Bustos, F(rancisco)
See Borges, Jorge Luis

Bustos Domecq, H(onorio)
See Bioy Casares, Adolfo; Borges, Jorge Luis

Butler, Octavia E(stelle) 1947- .... **CLC 38, 121; BLCS; DAM MULT, POP**
See also AAYA 18; BW 2, 3; CA 73-76; CANR 12, 24, 38, 73; CLR 65; DA3; DLB 33; MTCW 1, 2; SATA 84

Butler, Robert Olen (Jr.) 1945- .... **CLC 81; DAM POP**
See also CA 112; CANR 66; DLB 173; INT 112; MTCW 1

Butler, Samuel 1612-1680 .... **LC 16, 43**
See also DLB 101, 126

Butler, Samuel 1835-1902 . **TCLC 1, 33; DA; DAB; DAC; DAM MST, NOV; WLC**
See also CA 143; CDBLB 1890-1914; DA3; DLB 18, 57, 174

Butler, Walter C.
See Faust, Frederick (Schiller)

Butor, Michel (Marie Francois)
1926- .... **CLC 1, 3, 8, 11, 15**
See also CA 9-12R; CANR 33, 66; DLB 83; MTCW 1, 2

Butts, Mary 1892(?)-1937 .... **TCLC 77**
See also CA 148

Buzo, Alexander (John) 1944- .... **CLC 61**
See also CA 97-100; CANR 17, 39, 69

Buzzati, Dino 1906-1972 .... **CLC 36**
See also CA 160; 33-36R; DLB 177

Byars, Betsy (Cromer) 1928- .... **CLC 35**
See also AAYA 19; CA 33-36R, 183; CAAE 183; CANR 18, 36, 57; CLR 1, 16; DLB 52; INT CANR-18; JRDA; MAICYA; MTCW 1; SAAS 1; SATA 4, 46, 80; SATA-Essay 108

Byatt, A(ntonia) S(usan Drabble)
1936- ...... **CLC 19, 65, 136; DAM NOV, POP**
See also CA 13-16R; CANR 13, 33, 50, 75; DA3; DLB 14, 194; MTCW 1, 2

Byrne, David 1952- .... **CLC 26**
See also CA 127

Byrne, John Keyes 1926-
See Leonard, Hugh
See also CA 102; CANR 78; INT 102

Byron, George Gordon (Noel)
1788-1824 .... **NCLC 2, 12; DA; DAB; DAC; DAM MST, POET; PC 16; WLC**
See also CDBLB 1789-1832; DA3; DLB 96, 110

Byron, Robert 1905-1941 .... **TCLC 67**
See also CA 160; DLB 195

C. 3. 3.
See Wilde, Oscar (Fingal O'Flahertie Wills)

Caballero, Fernan 1796-1877 .... **NCLC 10**

Cabell, Branch
See Cabell, James Branch

Cabell, James Branch 1879-1958 .... **TCLC 6**
See also CA 105; 152; DLB 9, 78; MTCW 1

Cabeza de Vaca, Alvar Nunez
1490-1557(?) .... **LC 61**

Cable, George Washington
1844-1925 .... **TCLC 4; SSC 4**
See also CA 104; 155; DLB 12, 74; DLBD 13

Cabral de Melo Neto, Joao 1920- ... **CLC 76; DAM MULT**
See also CA 151

Cabrera Infante, G(uillermo) 1929- . **CLC 5, 25, 45, 120; DAM MULT; HLC 1; SSC 39**
See also CA 85-88; CANR 29, 65; DA3; DLB 113; HW 1, 2; MTCW 1, 2

Cade, Toni
See Bambara, Toni Cade

Cadmus and Harmonia
See Buchan, John

Caedmon fl. 658-680 .... **CMLC 7**
See also DLB 146

Caeiro, Alberto
See Pessoa, Fernando (Antonio Nogueira)

Cage, John (Milton, Jr.) 1912-1992 . **CLC 41**
See also CA 13-16R; 169; CANR 9, 78; DLB 193; INT CANR-9

Cahan, Abraham 1860-1951 .... **TCLC 71**
See also CA 108; 154; DLB 9, 25, 28

Cain, G.
See Cabrera Infante, G(uillermo)

Cain, Guillermo
See Cabrera Infante, G(uillermo)

Cain, James M(allahan) 1892-1977 .. **CLC 3, 11, 28**
See also AITN 1; CA 17-20R; 73-76; CANR 8, 34, 61; DLB 226; MTCW 1

Caine, Hall 1853-1931 .... **TCLC 97**

Caine, Mark
See Raphael, Frederic (Michael)

Calasso, Roberto 1941- .... **CLC 81**
See also CA 143; CANR 89

Calderon de la Barca, Pedro
1600-1681 .... **LC 23; DC 3; HLCS 1**

Caldwell, Erskine (Preston)
1903-1987 .. **CLC 1, 8, 14, 50, 60; DAM NOV; SSC 19**
See also AITN 1; CA 1-4R; 121; CAAS 1; CANR 2, 33; DA3; DLB 9, 86; MTCW 1, 2

Caldwell, (Janet Miriam) Taylor (Holland)
1900-1985 .. **CLC 2, 28, 39; DAM NOV, POP**
See also CA 5-8R; 116; CANR 5; DA3; DLBD 17

Cheever, John 1912-1982 ..... **CLC 3, 7, 8, 11, 15, 25, 64; DA; DAB; DAC; DAM MST, NOV, POP; SSC 1, 38; WLC**
See also CA 5-8R; 106; CABS 1; CANR 5, 27, 76; CDALB 1941-1968; DA3; DLB 2, 102, 227; DLBY 80, 82; INT CANR-5; MTCW 1, 2

Cheever, Susan 1943- .... **CLC 18, 48**
See also CA 103; CANR 27, 51, 92; DLBY 82; INT CANR-27

Chekhonte, Antosha
See Chekhov, Anton (Pavlovich)

Chekhov, Anton (Pavlovich) 1860-1904 .... **TCLC 3, 10, 31, 55, 96; DA; DAB; DAC; DAM DRAM, MST; DC 9; SSC 2, 28, 41; WLC**
See also CA 104; 124; DA3; SATA 90

Chernyshevsky, Nikolay Gavrilovich 1828-1889 .... **NCLC 1**

Cherry, Carolyn Janice 1942-
See Cherryh, C. J.
See also CA 65-68; CANR 10

Cherryh, C. J. CLC 35
See also Cherry, Carolyn Janice
See also AAYA 24; DLBY 80; SATA 93

Chesnutt, Charles W(addell) 1858-1932 .. **TCLC 5, 39; BLC 1; DAM MULT; SSC 7**
See also BW 1, 3; CA 106; 125; CANR 76; DLB 12, 50, 78; MTCW 1, 2

Chester, Alfred 1929(?)-1971 .... **CLC 49**
See also CA 33-36R; DLB 130

Chesterton, G(ilbert) K(eith) 1874-1936 . **TCLC 1, 6, 64; DAM NOV, POET; PC 28; SSC 1**
See also CA 104; 132; CANR 73; CDBLB 1914-1945; DLB 10, 19, 34, 70, 98, 149, 178; MTCW 1, 2; SATA 27

Chiang, Pin-chin 1904-1986
See Ding Ling
See also CA 118

Ch'ien Chung-shu 1910- .... **CLC 22**
See also CA 130; CANR 73; MTCW 1, 2

Child, L. Maria
See Child, Lydia Maria

Child, Lydia Maria 1802-1880 .. **NCLC 6, 73**
See also DLB 1, 74; SATA 67

Child, Mrs.
See Child, Lydia Maria

Child, Philip 1898-1978 .... **CLC 19, 68**
See also CA 13-14; CAP 1; SATA 47

Childers, (Robert) Erskine 1870-1922 .... **TCLC 65**
See also CA 113; 153; DLB 70

Childress, Alice 1920-1994 .. **CLC 12, 15, 86, 96; BLC 1; DAM DRAM, MULT, NOV; DC 4**
See also AAYA 8; BW 2, 3; CA 45-48; 146; CANR 3, 27, 50, 74; CLR 14; DA3; DLB 7, 38; JRDA; MAICYA; MTCW 1, 2; SATA 7, 48, 81

Chin, Frank (Chew, Jr.) 1940- ...... **CLC 135; DAM MULT; DC 7**
See also CA 33-36R; CANR 71; DLB 206

Chislett, (Margaret) Anne 1943- ...... **CLC 34**
See also CA 151

Chitty, Thomas Willes 1926- .... **CLC 11**
See also Hinde, Thomas
See also CA 5-8R

Chivers, Thomas Holley 1809-1858 .... **NCLC 49**
See also DLB 3

Choi, Susan CLC 119

Chomette, Rene Lucien 1898-1981
See Clair, Rene
See also CA 103

Chomsky, (Avram) Noam 1928- ..... **CLC 132**
See also CA 17-20R; CANR 28, 62; DA3; MTCW 1, 2

Chopin, Kate TCLC 5, 14; DA; DAB; SSC 8; WLCS
See also Chopin, Katherine
See also AAYA 33; CDALB 1865-1917; DLB 12, 78

Chopin, Katherine 1851-1904
See Chopin, Kate
See also CA 104; 122; DAC; DAM MST, NOV; DA3

Chretien de Troyes c. 12th cent. - . **CMLC 10**
See also DLB 208

Christie
See Ichikawa, Kon

Christie, Agatha (Mary Clarissa) 1890-1976 .... **CLC 1, 6, 8, 12, 39, 48, 110; DAB; DAC; DAM NOV**
See also AAYA 9; AITN 1, 2; CA 17-20R; 61-64; CANR 10, 37; CDBLB 1914-1945; DA3; DLB 13, 77; MTCW 1, 2; SATA 36

Christie, (Ann) Philippa
See Pearce, Philippa
See also CA 5-8R; CANR 4

Christine de Pizan 1365(?)-1431(?) .... **LC 9**
See also DLB 208

Chubb, Elmer
See Masters, Edgar Lee

Chulkov, Mikhail Dmitrievich 1743-1792 .... **LC 2**
See also DLB 150

Churchill, Caryl 1938- .... **CLC 31, 55; DC 5**
See also CA 102; CANR 22, 46; DLB 13; MTCW 1

Churchill, Charles 1731-1764 .... **LC 3**
See also DLB 109

Chute, Carolyn 1947- .... **CLC 39**
See also CA 123

Ciardi, John (Anthony) 1916-1986 . **CLC 10, 40, 44, 129; DAM POET**
See also CA 5-8R; 118; CAAS 2; CANR 5, 33; CLR 19; DLB 5; DLBY 86; INT CANR-5; MAICYA; MTCW 1, 2; SAAS 26; SATA 1, 65; SATA-Obit 46

Cicero, Marcus Tullius 106B.C.-43B.C. .... **CMLC 3**
See also DLB 211

Cimino, Michael 1943- .... **CLC 16**
See also CA 105

Cioran, E(mil) M. 1911-1995 .... **CLC 64**
See also CA 25-28R; 149; CANR 91; DLB 220

Cisneros, Sandra 1954- . **CLC 69, 118; DAM MULT; HLC 1; SSC 32**
See also AAYA 9; CA 131; CANR 64; DA3; DLB 122, 152; HW 1, 2; MTCW 2

Cixous, Helene 1937- .... **CLC 92**
See also CA 126; CANR 55; DLB 83; MTCW 1, 2

Clair, Rene CLC 20
See also Chomette, Rene Lucien

Clampitt, Amy 1920-1994 .... **CLC 32; PC 19**
See also CA 110; 146; CANR 29, 79; DLB 105

Clancy, Thomas L., Jr. 1947-
See Clancy, Tom
See also CA 125; 131; CANR 62; DA3; DLB 227; INT 131; MTCW 1, 2

Clancy, Tom CLC 45, 112; DAM NOV, POP
See also Clancy, Thomas L., Jr.
See also AAYA 9; BEST 89:1, 90:1; MTCW 2

Clare, John 1793-1864 ... **NCLC 9, 86; DAB; DAM POET; PC 23**
See also DLB 55, 96

Clarin
See Alas (y Urena), Leopoldo (Enrique Garcia)

Clark, Al C.
See Goines, Donald

Clark, (Robert) Brian 1932- .... **CLC 29**
See also CA 41-44R; CANR 67

Clark, Curt
See Westlake, Donald E(dwin)

Clark, Eleanor 1913-1996 .... **CLC 5, 19**
See also CA 9-12R; 151; CANR 41; DLB 6

Clark, J. P.
See Clark Bekederemo, J(ohnson) P(epper)
See also DLB 117

Clark, John Pepper
See Clark Bekederemo, J(ohnson) P(epper)

Clark, M. R.
See Clark, Mavis Thorpe

Clark, Mavis Thorpe 1909- .... **CLC 12**
See also CA 57-60; CANR 8, 37; CLR 30; MAICYA; SAAS 5; SATA 8, 74

Clark, Walter Van Tilburg 1909-1971 .... **CLC 28**
See also CA 9-12R; 33-36R; CANR 63; DLB 9, 206; SATA 8

Clark Bekederemo, J(ohnson) P(epper) 1935- .. **CLC 38; BLC 1; DAM DRAM, MULT; DC 5**
See also Clark, J. P.; Clark, John Pepper
See also BW 1; CA 65-68; CANR 16, 72; MTCW 1

Clarke, Arthur C(harles) 1917- .... **CLC 1, 4, 13, 18, 35, 136; DAM POP; SSC 3**
See also AAYA 4, 33; CA 1-4R; CANR 2, 28, 55, 74; DA3; JRDA; MAICYA; MTCW 1, 2; SATA 13, 70, 115

Clarke, Austin 1896-1974 ... **CLC 6, 9; DAM POET**
See also CA 29-32; 49-52; CAP 2; DLB 10, 20

Clarke, Austin C(hesterfield) 1934- .. **CLC 8, 53; BLC 1; DAC; DAM MULT**
See also BW 1; CA 25-28R; CAAS 16; CANR 14, 32, 68; DLB 53, 125

Clarke, Gillian 1937- .... **CLC 61**
See also CA 106; DLB 40

Clarke, Marcus (Andrew Hislop) 1846-1881 .... **NCLC 19**
See also DLB 230

Clarke, Shirley 1925- .... **CLC 16**

Clash, The
See Headon, (Nicky) Topper; Jones, Mick; Simonon, Paul; Strummer, Joe

Claudel, Paul (Louis Charles Marie) 1868-1955 .... **TCLC 2, 10**
See also CA 104; 165; DLB 192

Claudius, Matthias 1740-1815 .... **NCLC 75**
See also DLB 97

Clavell, James (duMaresq) 1925-1994 .. **CLC 6, 25, 87; DAM NOV, POP**
See also CA 25-28R; 146; CANR 26, 48; DA3; MTCW 1, 2

Cleaver, (Leroy) Eldridge 1935-1998 . **CLC 30, 119; BLC 1; DAM MULT**
See also BW 1, 3; CA 21-24R; 167; CANR 16, 75; DA3; MTCW 2

Cleese, John (Marwood) 1939- .... **CLC 21**
See also Monty Python
See also CA 112; 116; CANR 35; MTCW 1

Cleishbotham, Jebediah
See Scott, Walter

Cleland, John 1710-1789 .... **LC 2, 48**
See also DLB 39

Clemens, Samuel Langhorne 1835-1910
See Twain, Mark
See also CA 104; 135; CDALB 1865-1917; DA; DAB; DAC; DAM MST, NOV; DA3; DLB 11, 12, 23, 64, 74, 186, 189; JRDA; MAICYA; SATA 100; YABC 2

Clement of Alexandria
150(?)-215(?) .... **CMLC 41**
Cleophil
See Congreve, William
Clerihew, E.
See Bentley, E(dmund) C(lerihew)
Clerk, N. W.
See Lewis, C(live) S(taples)
Cliff, Jimmy CLC 21
See also Chambers, James
Cliff, Michelle 1946- .... **CLC 120; BLCS**
See also BW 2; CA 116; CANR 39, 72;
DLB 157
Clifton, (Thelma) Lucille 1936- .... **CLC 19,
66; BLC 1; DAM MULT, POET; PC
17**
See also BW 2, 3; CA 49-52; CANR 2, 24,
42, 76; CLR 5; DA3; DLB 5, 41; MAI-
CYA; MTCW 1, 2; SATA 20, 69
Clinton, Dirk
See Silverberg, Robert
Clough, Arthur Hugh 1819-1861 ... **NCLC 27**
See also DLB 32
Clutha, Janet Paterson Frame 1924-
See Frame, Janet
See also CA 1-4R; CANR 2, 36, 76; MTCW
1, 2; SATA 119
Clyne, Terence
See Blatty, William Peter
Cobalt, Martin
See Mayne, William (James Carter)
Cobb, Irvin S(hrewsbury)
1876-1944 .... **TCLC 77**
See also CA 175; DLB 11, 25, 86
Cobbett, William 1763-1835 .... **NCLC 49**
See also DLB 43, 107, 158
Coburn, D(onald) L(ee) 1938- .... **CLC 10**
See also CA 89-92
Cocteau, Jean (Maurice Eugene Clement)
1889-1963 .... **CLC 1, 8, 15, 16, 43; DA;
DAB; DAC; DAM DRAM, MST, NOV;
WLC**
See also CA 25-28; CANR 40; CAP 2;
DA3; DLB 65; MTCW 1, 2
Codrescu, Andrei 1946- .... **CLC 46, 121;
DAM POET**
See also CA 33-36R; CAAS 19; CANR 13,
34, 53, 76; DA3; MTCW 2
Coe, Max
See Bourne, Randolph S(illiman)
Coe, Tucker
See Westlake, Donald E(dwin)
Coen, Ethan 1958- .... **CLC 108**
See also CA 126; CANR 85
Coen, Joel 1955- .... **CLC 108**
See also CA 126
The Coen Brothers
See Coen, Ethan; Coen, Joel
Coetzee, J(ohn) M(ichael) 1940- ...... **CLC 23,
33, 66, 117; DAM NOV**
See also AAYA 37; CA 77-80; CANR 41,
54, 74; DA3; DLB 225; MTCW 1, 2
Coffey, Brian
See Koontz, Dean R(ay)
Coffin, Robert P(eter) Tristram
1892-1955 .... **TCLC 95**
See also CA 123; 169; DLB 45
Cohan, George M(ichael)
1878-1942 .... **TCLC 60**
See also CA 157
Cohen, Arthur A(llen) 1928-1986 ...... **CLC 7,
31**
See also CA 1-4R; 120; CANR 1, 17, 42;
DLB 28
Cohen, Leonard (Norman) 1934- ...... **CLC 3,
38; DAC; DAM MST**
See also CA 21-24R; CANR 14, 69; DLB
53; MTCW 1

Cohen, Matt(hew) 1942-1999 .... **CLC 19;
DAC**
See also CA 61-64; 187; CAAS 18; CANR
40; DLB 53
Cohen-Solal, Annie 19(?)- .... **CLC 50**
Colegate, Isabel 1931- .... **CLC 36**
See also CA 17-20R; CANR 8, 22, 74; DLB
14, 231; INT CANR-22; MTCW 1
Coleman, Emmett
See Reed, Ishmael
Coleridge, Hartley 1796-1849 .... **NCLC 90**
See also DLB 96
Coleridge, M. E.
See Coleridge, Mary E(lizabeth)
Coleridge, Mary E(lizabeth)
1861-1907 .... **TCLC 73**
See also CA 116; 166; DLB 19, 98
Coleridge, Samuel Taylor
1772-1834 .... **NCLC 9, 54; DA; DAB;
DAC; DAM MST, POET; PC 11; WLC**
See also CDBLB 1789-1832; DA3; DLB
93, 107
Coleridge, Sara 1802-1852 .... **NCLC 31**
See also DLB 199
Coles, Don 1928- .... **CLC 46**
See also CA 115; CANR 38
Coles, Robert (Martin) 1929- .... **CLC 108**
See also CA 45-48; CANR 3, 32, 66, 70;
INT CANR-32; SATA 23
Colette, (Sidonie-Gabrielle)
1873-1954 . **TCLC 1, 5, 16; DAM NOV;
SSC 10** .
See also CA 104; 131; DA3; DLB 65;
MTCW 1, 2
Collett, (Jacobine) Camilla (Wergeland)
1813-1895 .... **NCLC 22**
Collier, Christopher 1930- .... **CLC 30**
See also AAYA 13; CA 33-36R; CANR 13,
33; JRDA; MAICYA; SATA 16, 70
Collier, James L(incoln) 1928- .... **CLC 30;
DAM POP**
See also AAYA 13; CA 9-12R; CANR 4,
33, 60; CLR 3; JRDA; MAICYA; SAAS
21; SATA 8, 70
Collier, Jeremy 1650-1726 .... **LC 6**
Collier, John 1901-1980 .... **SSC 19**
See also CA 65-68; 97-100; CANR 10;
DLB 77
Collingwood, R(obin) G(eorge)
1889(?)-1943 .... **TCLC 67**
See also CA 117; 155
Collins, Hunt
See Hunter, Evan
Collins, Linda 1931- .... **CLC 44**
See also CA 125
Collins, (William) Wilkie
1824-1889 .... **NCLC 1, 18, 93**
See also CDBLB 1832-1890; DLB 18, 70,
159
Collins, William 1721-1759 . **LC 4, 40; DAM
POET**
See also DLB 109
Collodi, Carlo 1826-1890 .... **NCLC 54**
See also Lorenzini, Carlo
See also CLR 5
Colman, George 1732-1794
See Glassco, John
Colt, Winchester Remington
See Hubbard, L(afayette) Ron(ald)
Colter, Cyrus 1910- .... **CLC 58**
See also BW 1; CA 65-68; CANR 10, 66;
DLB 33
Colton, James
See Hansen, Joseph
Colum, Padraic 1881-1972 .... **CLC 28**
See also CA 73-76; 33-36R; CANR 35;
CLR 36; MAICYA; MTCW 1; SATA 15
Colvin, James
See Moorcock, Michael (John)

Colwin, Laurie (E.) 1944-1992 .... **CLC 5, 13,
23, 84**
See also CA 89-92; 139; CANR 20, 46;
DLBY 80; MTCW 1
Comfort, Alex(ander) 1920- .... **CLC 7; DAM
POP**
See also CA 1-4R; CANR 1, 45; MTCW 1
Comfort, Montgomery
See Campbell, (John) Ramsey
Compton-Burnett, I(vy)
1884(?)-1969 .... **CLC 1, 3, 10, 15, 34;
DAM NOV**
See also CA 1-4R; 25-28R; CANR 4; DLB
36; MTCW 1
Comstock, Anthony 1844-1915 ...... **TCLC 13**
See also CA 110; 169
Comte, Auguste 1798-1857 .... **NCLC 54**
Conan Doyle, Arthur
See Doyle, Arthur Conan
Conde (Abellan), Carmen 1901-
See also CA 177; DLB 108; HLCS 1; HW
2
Conde, Maryse 1937- .... **CLC 52, 92; BLCS;
DAM MULT**
See also BW 2, 3; CA 110; CANR 30, 53,
76; MTCW 1
Condillac, Etienne Bonnot de
1714-1780 .... **LC 26**
Condon, Richard (Thomas)
1915-1996 ...... **CLC 4, 6, 8, 10, 45, 100;
DAM NOV**
See also BEST 90:3; CA 1-4R; 151; CAAS
1; CANR 2, 23; INT CANR-23; MTCW
1, 2
Confucius 551B.C.-479B.C. .. **CMLC 19; DA;
DAB; DAC; DAM MST; WLCS**
See also DA3
Congreve, William 1670-1729 .... **LC 5, 21;
DA; DAB; DAC; DAM DRAM, MST,
POET; DC 2; WLC**
See also CDBLB 1660-1789; DLB 39, 84
Connell, Evan S(helby), Jr. 1924- . **CLC 4, 6,
45; DAM NOV**
See also AAYA 7; CA 1-4R; CAAS 2;
CANR 2, 39, 76; DLB 2; DLBY 81;
MTCW 1, 2
Connelly, Marc(us Cook) 1890-1980 . **CLC 7**
See also CA 85-88; 102; CANR 30; DLB
7; DLBY 80; SATA-Obit 25
Connor, Ralph TCLC 31
See also Gordon, Charles William
See also DLB 92
Conrad, Joseph 1857-1924 .... **TCLC 1, 6, 13,
25, 43, 57; DA; DAB; DAC; DAM
MST, NOV; SSC 9; WLC**
See also AAYA 26; CA 104; 131; CANR
60; CDBLB 1890-1914; DA3; DLB 10,
34, 98, 156; MTCW 1, 2; SATA 27
Conrad, Robert Arnold
See Hart, Moss
Conroy, Pat
See Conroy, (Donald) Pat(rick)
See also MTCW 2
Conroy, (Donald) Pat(rick) 1945- ... **CLC 30,
74; DAM NOV, POP**
See also Conroy, Pat
See also AAYA 8; AITN 1; CA 85-88;
CANR 24, 53; DA3; DLB 6; MTCW 1
Constant (de Rebecque), (Henri) Benjamin
1767-1830 .... **NCLC 6**
See also DLB 119
Conybeare, Charles Augustus
See Eliot, T(homas) S(tearns)
Cook, Michael 1933- .... **CLC 58**
See also CA 93-96; CANR 68; DLB 53
Cook, Robin 1940- .... **CLC 14; DAM POP**
See also AAYA 32; BEST 90:2; CA 108;
111; CANR 41, 90; DA3; INT 111

Duncan, Robert (Edward)
1919-1988 .... **CLC 1, 2, 4, 7, 15, 41, 55;**
DAM POET; PC 2
See also CA 9-12R; 124; CANR 28, 62;
DLB 5, 16, 193; MTCW 1, 2

Duncan, Sara Jeannette
1861-1922 .... **TCLC 60**
See also CA 157; DLB 92

Dunlap, William 1766-1839 .... **NCLC 2**
See also DLB 30, 37, 59

Dunn, Douglas (Eaglesham) 1942- .... **CLC 6,**
40
See also CA 45-48; CANR 2, 33; DLB 40;
MTCW 1

Dunn, Katherine (Karen) 1945- .... **CLC 71**
See also CA 33-36R; CANR 72; MTCW 1

Dunn, Stephen 1939- .... **CLC 36**
See also CA 33-36R; CANR 12, 48, 53;
DLB 105

Dunne, Finley Peter 1867-1936 ...... **TCLC 28**
See also CA 108; 178; DLB 11, 23

Dunne, John Gregory 1932- .... **CLC 28**
See also CA 25-28R; CANR 14, 50; DLBY
80

Dunsany, Edward John Moreton Drax
Plunkett 1878-1957
See Dunsany, Lord
See also CA 104; 148; DLB 10; MTCW 1

Dunsany, Lord -1957 .... **TCLC 2, 59**
See also Dunsany, Edward John Moreton
Drax Plunkett
See also DLB 77, 153, 156

du Perry, Jean
See Simenon, Georges (Jacques Christian)

Durang, Christopher (Ferdinand)
1949- .... **CLC 27, 38**
See also CA 105; CANR 50, 76; MTCW 1

Duras, Marguerite 1914-1996 . **CLC 3, 6, 11,**
20, 34, 40, 68, 100; SSC 40
See also CA 25-28R; 151; CANR 50; DLB
83; MTCW 1, 2

Durban, (Rosa) Pam 1947- .... **CLC 39**
See also CA 123

Durcan, Paul 1944- .... **CLC 43, 70; DAM**
POET
See also CA 134

Durkheim, Emile 1858-1917 .... **TCLC 55**

Durrell, Lawrence (George)
1912-1990 .... **CLC 1, 4, 6, 8, 13, 27, 41;**
DAM NOV
See also CA 9-12R; 132; CANR 40, 77;
CDBLB 1945-1960; DLB 15, 27, 204;
DLBY 90; MTCW 1, 2

Durrenmatt, Friedrich
See Duerrenmatt, Friedrich

DuRrenmatt, Friedrich
See Duerrenmatt, Friedrich

Dutt, Toru 1856-1877 .... **NCLC 29**

Dwight, Timothy 1752-1817 .... **NCLC 13**
See also DLB 37

Dworkin, Andrea 1946- .... **CLC 43, 123**
See also CA 77-80; CAAS 21; CANR 16,
39, 76; INT CANR-16; MTCW 1, 2

Dwyer, Deanna
See Koontz, Dean R(ay)

Dwyer, K. R.
See Koontz, Dean R(ay)

Dwyer, Thomas A. 1923- .... **CLC 114**
See also CA 115

Dybek, Stuart 1942- .... **CLC 114**
See also CA 97-100; CANR 39; DLB 130

Dye, Richard
See De Voto, Bernard (Augustine)

Dylan, Bob 1941- .... **CLC 3, 4, 6, 12, 77**
See also CA 41-44R; DLB 16

E. V. L.
See Lucas, E(dward) V(errall)

Eagleton, Terence (Francis) 1943- .. **CLC 63,**
132
See also CA 57-60; CANR 7, 23, 68;
MTCW 1, 2

Eagleton, Terry
See Eagleton, Terence (Francis)

Early, Jack
See Scoppettone, Sandra

East, Michael
See West, Morris L(anglo)

Eastaway, Edward
See Thomas, (Philip) Edward

Eastlake, William (Derry)
1917-1997 .... **CLC 8**
See also CA 5-8R; 158; CAAS 1; CANR 5,
63; DLB 6, 206; INT CANR-5

Eastman, Charles A(lexander)
1858-1939 .... **TCLC 55; DAM MULT**
See also CA 179; CANR 91; DLB 175;
NNAL; YABC 1

Eberhart, Richard (Ghormley)
1904- .. **CLC 3, 11, 19, 56; DAM POET**
See also CA 1-4R; CANR 2; CDALB 1941-
1968; DLB 48; MTCW 1

Eberstadt, Fernanda 1960- .... **CLC 39**
See also CA 136; CANR 69

Echegaray (y Eizaguirre), Jose (Maria
Waldo) 1832-1916 ..... **TCLC 4; HLCS 1**
See also CA 104; CANR 32; HW 1; MTCW
1

Echeverria, (Jose) Esteban (Antonino)
1805-1851 .... **NCLC 18**

Echo
See Proust, (Valentin-Louis-George-
Eugene-) Marcel

Eckert, Allan W. 1931- .... **CLC 17**
See also AAYA 18; CA 13-16R; CANR 14,
45; INT CANR-14; SAAS 21; SATA 29,
91; SATA-Brief 27

Eckhart, Meister 1260(?)-1328(?) ... **CMLC 9**
See also DLB 115

Eckmar, F. R.
See de Hartog, Jan

Eco, Umberto 1932- .... **CLC 28, 60; DAM**
NOV, POP
See also BEST 90:1; CA 77-80; CANR 12,
33, 55; DA3; DLB 196; MTCW 1, 2

Eddison, E(ric) R(ucker)
1882-1945 .... **TCLC 15**
See also CA 109; 156

Eddy, Mary (Ann Morse) Baker
1821-1910 .... **TCLC 71**
See also CA 113; 174

Edel, (Joseph) Leon 1907-1997 .. **CLC 29, 34**
See also CA 1-4R; 161; CANR 1, 22; DLB
103; INT CANR-22

Eden, Emily 1797-1869 .... **NCLC 10**

Edgar, David 1948- .. **CLC 42; DAM DRAM**
See also CA 57-60; CANR 12, 61; DLB 13,
233; MTCW 1

Edgerton, Clyde (Carlyle) 1944- ...... **CLC 39**
See also AAYA 17; CA 118; 134; CANR
64; INT 134

Edgeworth, Maria 1768-1849 .... **NCLC 1, 51**
See also DLB 116, 159, 163; SATA 21

Edmonds, Paul
See Kuttner, Henry

Edmonds, Walter D(umaux)
1903-1998 .... **CLC 35**
See also CA 5-8R; CANR 2; DLB 9; MAI-
CYA; SAAS 4; SATA 1, 27; SATA-Obit
99

Edmondson, Wallace
See Ellison, Harlan (Jay)

Edson, Russell CLC 13
See also CA 33-36R

Edwards, Bronwen Elizabeth
See Rose, Wendy

Edwards, G(erald) B(asil)
1899-1976 .... **CLC 25**
See also CA 110

Edwards, Gus 1939- .... **CLC 43**
See also CA 108; INT 108

Edwards, Jonathan 1703-1758 .... **LC 7, 54;**
DA; DAC; DAM MST
See also DLB 24

Efron, Marina Ivanovna Tsvetaeva
See Tsvetaeva (Efron), Marina (Ivanovna)

Ehle, John (Marsden, Jr.) 1925- ...... **CLC 27**
See also CA 9-12R

Ehrenbourg, Ilya (Grigoryevich)
See Ehrenburg, Ilya (Grigoryevich)

Ehrenburg, Ilya (Grigoryevich)
1891-1967 .... **CLC 18, 34, 62**
See also CA 102; 25-28R

Ehrenburg, Ilyo (Grigoryevich)
See Ehrenburg, Ilya (Grigoryevich)

Ehrenreich, Barbara 1941- .... **CLC 110**
See also BEST 90:4; CA 73-76; CANR 16,
37, 62; MTCW 1, 2

Eich, Guenter 1907-1972 .... **CLC 15**
See also CA 111; 93-96; DLB 69, 124

Eichendorff, Joseph Freiherr von
1788-1857 .... **NCLC 8**
See also DLB 90

Eigner, Larry CLC 9
See Eigner, Laurence (Joel)
See also CAAS 23; DLB 5

Eigner, Laurence (Joel) 1927-1996
See Eigner, Larry
See also CA 9-12R; 151; CANR 6, 84; DLB
193

Einstein, Albert 1879-1955 .... **TCLC 65**
See also CA 121; 133; MTCW 1, 2

Eiseley, Loren Corey 1907-1977 .... **CLC 7**
See also AAYA 5; CA 1-4R; 73-76; CANR
6; DLBD 17

Eisenstadt, Jill 1963- .... **CLC 50**
See also CA 140

Eisenstein, Sergei (Mikhailovich)
1898-1948 .... **TCLC 57**
See also CA 114; 149

Eisner, Simon
See Kornbluth, C(yril) M.

Ekeloef, (Bengt) Gunnar
1907-1968 ... **CLC 27; DAM POET; PC**
23
See also CA 123; 25-28R

Ekelof, (Bengt) Gunnar
See Ekeloef, (Bengt) Gunnar

Ekelund, Vilhelm 1880-1949 .... **TCLC 75**

Ekwensi, C. O. D.
See Ekwensi, Cyprian (Odiatu Duaka)

Ekwensi, Cyprian (Odiatu Duaka)
1921- ...... **CLC 4; BLC 1; DAM MULT**
See also BW 2, 3; CA 29-32R; CANR 18,
42, 74; DLB 117; MTCW 1, 2; SATA 66

Elaine TCLC 18
See also Leverson, Ada

El Crummo
See Crumb, R(obert)

Elder, Lonne III 1931-1996 .... **DC 8**
See also BLC 1; BW 1, 3; CA 81-84; 152;
CANR 25; DAM MULT; DLB 7, 38, 44

Eleanor of Aquitaine 1122-1204 ... **CMLC 39**

Elia
See Lamb, Charles

Eliade, Mircea 1907-1986 .... **CLC 19**
See also CA 65-68; 119; CANR 30, 62;
DLB 220; MTCW 1

Eliot, A. D.
See Jewett, (Theodora) Sarah Orne

Eliot, Alice
See Jewett, (Theodora) Sarah Orne

Eliot, Dan
See Silverberg, Robert

Ewart, Gavin (Buchanan)
1916-1995 .... **CLC 13, 46**
See also CA 89-92; 150; CANR 17, 46;
DLB 40; MTCW 1

Ewers, Hanns Heinz 1871-1943 ..... **TCLC 12**
See also CA 109; 149

Ewing, Frederick R.
See Sturgeon, Theodore (Hamilton)

Exley, Frederick (Earl) 1929-1992 .... **CLC 6, 11**
See also AITN 2; CA 81-84; 138; DLB 143;
DLBY 81

Eynhardt, Guillermo
See Quiroga, Horacio (Sylvestre)

Ezekiel, Nissim 1924- .... **CLC 61**
See also CA 61-64

Ezekiel, Tish O'Dowd 1943- .... **CLC 34**
See also CA 129

Fadeyev, A.
See Bulgya, Alexander Alexandrovich

Fadeyev, Alexander .... **TCLC 53**
See also Bulgya, Alexander Alexandrovich

Fagen, Donald 1948- .... **CLC 26**

Fainzilberg, Ilya Arnoldovich 1897-1937
See Ilf, Ilya
See also CA 120; 165

Fair, Ronald L. 1932- .... **CLC 18**
See also BW 1; CA 69-72; CANR 25; DLB 33

Fairbairn, Roger
See Carr, John Dickson

Fairbairns, Zoe (Ann) 1948- .... **CLC 32**
See also CA 103; CANR 21, 85

Fairman, Paul W. 1916-1977
See Queen, Ellery
See also CA 114

Falco, Gian
See Papini, Giovanni

Falconer, James
See Kirkup, James

Falconer, Kenneth
See Kornbluth, C(yril) M.

Falkland, Samuel
See Heijermans, Herman

Fallaci, Oriana 1930- .... **CLC 11, 110**
See also CA 77-80; CANR 15, 58; MTCW 1

Faludi, Susan 1959- .... **CLC 140**
See also CA 138; MTCW 1

Faludy, George 1913- .... **CLC 42**
See also CA 21-24R

Faludy, Gyoergy
See Faludy, George

Fanon, Frantz 1925-1961 ... **CLC 74; BLC 2; DAM MULT**
See also BW 1; CA 116; 89-92

Fanshawe, Ann 1625-1680 .... **LC 11**

Fante, John (Thomas) 1911-1983 ..... **CLC 60**
See also CA 69-72; 109; CANR 23; DLB 130; DLBY 83

Farah, Nuruddin 1945- .. **CLC 53, 137; BLC 2; DAM MULT**
See also BW 2, 3; CA 106; CANR 81; DLB 125

Fargue, Leon-Paul 1876(?)-1947 .... **TCLC 11**
See also CA 109

Farigoule, Louis
See Romains, Jules

Farina, Richard 1936(?)-1966 .... **CLC 9**
See also CA 81-84; 25-28R

Farley, Walter (Lorimer)
1915-1989 .... **CLC 17**
See also CA 17-20R; CANR 8, 29, 84; DLB 22; JRDA; MAICYA; SATA 2, 43

Farmer, Philip Jose 1918- .... **CLC 1, 19**
See also AAYA 28; CA 1-4R; CANR 4, 35; DLB 8; MTCW 1; SATA 93

Farquhar, George 1677-1707 ... **LC 21; DAM DRAM**
See also DLB 84

Farrell, J(ames) G(ordon)
1935-1979 .... **CLC 6**
See also CA 73-76; 89-92; CANR 36; DLB 14; MTCW 1

Farrell, James T(homas) 1904-1979 . **CLC 1, 4, 8, 11, 66; SSC 28**
See also CA 5-8R; 89-92; CANR 9, 61; DLB 4, 9, 86; DLBD 2; MTCW 1, 2

Farren, Richard J.
See Betjeman, John

Farren, Richard M.
See Betjeman, John

Fassbinder, Rainer Werner
1946-1982 .... **CLC 20**
See also CA 93-96; 106; CANR 31

Fast, Howard (Melvin) 1914- .. **CLC 23, 131; DAM NOV**
See also AAYA 16; CA 1-4R, 181; CAAE 181; CAAS 18; CANR 1, 33, 54, 75; DLB 9; INT CANR-33; MTCW 1; SATA 7; SATA-Essay 107

Faulcon, Robert
See Holdstock, Robert P.

Faulkner, William (Cuthbert)
1897-1962 .... **CLC 1, 3, 6, 8, 9, 11, 14, 18, 28, 52, 68; DA; DAB; DAC; DAM MST, NOV; SSC 1, 35, 42; WLC**
See also AAYA 7; CA 81-84; CANR 33; CDALB 1929-1941; DA3; DLB 9, 11, 44, 102; DLBD 2; DLBY 86, 97; MTCW 1, 2

Fauset, Jessie Redmon
1884(?)-1961 .... **CLC 19, 54; BLC 2; DAM MULT**
See also BW 1; CA 109; CANR 83; DLB 51

Faust, Frederick (Schiller)
1892-1944(?) .... **TCLC 49; DAM POP**
See also CA 108; 152

Faust, Irvin 1924- .... **CLC 8**
See also CA 33-36R; CANR 28, 67; DLB 2, 28; DLBY 80

Fawkes, Guy
See Benchley, Robert (Charles)

Fearing, Kenneth (Flexner)
1902-1961 .... **CLC 51**
See also CA 93-96; CANR 59; DLB 9

Fecamps, Elise
See Creasey, John

Federman, Raymond 1928- .... **CLC 6, 47**
See also CA 17-20R; CAAS 8; CANR 10, 43, 83; DLBY 80

Federspiel, J(uerg) F. 1931- .... **CLC 42**
See also CA 146

Feiffer, Jules (Ralph) 1929- ..... **CLC 2, 8, 64; DAM DRAM**
See also AAYA 3; CA 17-20R; CANR 30, 59; DLB 7, 44; INT CANR-30; MTCW 1; SATA 8, 61, 111

Feige, Hermann Albert Otto Maximilian
See Traven, B.

Feinberg, David B. 1956-1994 .... **CLC 59**
See also CA 135; 147

Feinstein, Elaine 1930- .... **CLC 36**
See also CA 69-72; CAAS 1; CANR 31, 68; DLB 14, 40; MTCW 1

Feldman, Irving (Mordecai) 1928- ..... **CLC 7**
See also CA 1-4R; CANR 1; DLB 169

Felix-Tchicaya, Gerald
See Tchicaya, Gerald Felix

Fellini, Federico 1920-1993 .... **CLC 16, 85**
See also CA 65-68; 143; CANR 33

Felsen, Henry Gregor 1916-1995 ..... **CLC 17**
See also CA 1-4R; 180; CANR 1; SAAS 2; SATA 1

Fenno, Jack
See Calisher, Hortense

Fenollosa, Ernest (Francisco)
1853-1908 .... **TCLC 91**

Fenton, James Martin 1949- .... **CLC 32**
See also CA 102; DLB 40

Ferber, Edna 1887-1968 .... **CLC 18, 93**
See also AITN 1; CA 5-8R; 25-28R; CANR 68; DLB 9, 28, 86; MTCW 1, 2; SATA 7

Ferdowsi, Abu'l Qasem 940-1020 . **CMLC 43**

Ferguson, Helen
See Kavan, Anna

Ferguson, Niall 1967- .... **CLC 134**

Ferguson, Samuel 1810-1886 .... **NCLC 33**
See also DLB 32

Fergusson, Robert 1750-1774 .... **LC 29**
See also DLB 109

Ferling, Lawrence
See Ferlinghetti, Lawrence (Monsanto)

Ferlinghetti, Lawrence (Monsanto)
1919(?)- ... **CLC 2, 6, 10, 27, 111; DAM POET; PC 1**
See also CA 5-8R; CANR 3, 41, 73; CDALB 1941-1968; DA3; DLB 5, 16; MTCW 1, 2

Fern, Fanny 1811-1872
See Parton, Sara Payson Willis

Fernandez, Vicente Garcia Huidobro
See Huidobro Fernandez, Vicente Garcia

Ferre, Rosario 1942- ...... **CLC 139; HLCS 1; SSC 36**
See also CA 131; CANR 55, 81; DLB 145; HW 1, 2; MTCW 1

Ferrer, Gabriel (Francisco Victor) Miro
See Miro (Ferrer), Gabriel (Francisco Victor)

Ferrier, Susan (Edmonstone)
1782-1854 .... **NCLC 8**
See also DLB 116

Ferrigno, Robert 1948(?)- .... **CLC 65**
See also CA 140

Ferron, Jacques 1921-1985 .... **CLC 94; DAC**
See also CA 117; 129; DLB 60

Feuchtwanger, Lion 1884-1958 .... **TCLC 3**
See also CA 104; 187; DLB 66

Feuillet, Octave 1821-1890 .... **NCLC 45**
See also DLB 192

Feydeau, Georges (Leon Jules Marie)
1862-1921 .... **TCLC 22; DAM DRAM**
See also CA 113; 152; CANR 84; DLB 192

Fichte, Johann Gottlieb
1762-1814 .... **NCLC 62**
See also DLB 90

Ficino, Marsilio 1433-1499 .... **LC 12**

Fiedeler, Hans
See Doeblin, Alfred

Fiedler, Leslie A(aron) 1917- .. **CLC 4, 13, 24**
See also CA 9-12R; CANR 7, 63; DLB 28, 67; MTCW 1, 2

Field, Andrew 1938- .... **CLC 44**
See also CA 97-100; CANR 25

Field, Eugene 1850-1895 .... **NCLC 3**
See also DLB 23, 42, 140; DLBD 13; MAICYA; SATA 16

Field, Gans T.
See Wellman, Manly Wade

Field, Michael 1915-1971 .... **TCLC 43**
See also CA 29-32R

Field, Peter
See Hobson, Laura Z(ametkin)

Fielding, Henry 1707-1754 ..... **LC 1, 46; DA; DAB; DAC; DAM DRAM, MST, NOV; WLC**
See also CDBLB 1660-1789; DA3; DLB 39, 84, 101

Fielding, Sarah 1710-1768 .... **LC 1, 44**
See also DLB 39

Fields, W. C. 1880-1946 .... **TCLC 80**
See also DLB 44

Francis, Claude 19(?)- .... **CLC 50**

Francis, Dick 1920- .... **CLC 2, 22, 42, 102;
DAM POP**
See also AAYA 5, 21; BEST 89:3; CA 5-8R;
CANR 9, 42, 68; CDBLB 1960 to Present;
DA3; DLB 87; INT CANR-9; MTCW 1,
2

Francis, Robert (Churchill)
1901-1987 .... **CLC 15**
See also CA 1-4R; 123; CANR 1

Frank, Anne(lies Marie)
1929-1945 . **TCLC 17; DA; DAB; DAC;
DAM MST; WLC**
See also AAYA 12; CA 113; 133; CANR
68; DA3; MTCW 1, 2; SATA 87; SATA-
Brief 42

Frank, Bruno 1887-1945 .... **TCLC 81**
See also DLB 118

Frank, Elizabeth 1945- .... **CLC 39**
See also CA 121; 126; CANR 78; INT 126

Frankl, Viktor E(mil) 1905-1997 ...... **CLC 93**
See also CA 65-68; 161

Franklin, Benjamin
See Hasek, Jaroslav (Matej Frantisek)

Franklin, Benjamin 1706-1790 .. **LC 25; DA;
DAB; DAC; DAM MST; WLCS**
See also CDALB 1640-1865; DA3; DLB
24, 43, 73

Franklin, (Stella Maria Sarah) Miles
(Lampe) 1879-1954 .... **TCLC 7**
See also CA 104; 164; DLB 230; MTCW 2

Fraser, (Lady) Antonia (Pakenham)
1932- .... **CLC 32, 107**
See also CA 85-88; CANR 44, 65; MTCW
1, 2; SATA-Brief 32

Fraser, George MacDonald 1925- ...... **CLC 7**
See also CA 45-48, 180; CAAE 180; CANR
2, 48, 74; MTCW 1

Fraser, Sylvia 1935- .... **CLC 64**
See also CA 45-48; CANR 1, 16, 60

Frayn, Michael 1933- .... **CLC 3, 7, 31, 47;
DAM DRAM, NOV**
See also CA 5-8R; CANR 30, 69; DLB 13,
14, 194; MTCW 1, 2

Fraze, Candida (Merrill) 1945- .... **CLC 50**
See also CA 126

Frazer, J(ames) G(eorge)
1854-1941 .... **TCLC 32**
See also CA 118

Frazer, Robert Caine
See Creasey, John

Frazer, Sir James George
See Frazer, J(ames) G(eorge)

Frazier, Charles 1950- .... **CLC 109**
See also AAYA 34; CA 161

Frazier, Ian 1951- .... **CLC 46**
See also CA 130; CANR 54, 93

Frederic, Harold 1856-1898 .... **NCLC 10**
See also DLB 12, 23; DLBD 13

Frederick, John
See Faust, Frederick (Schiller)

Frederick the Great 1712-1786 .... **LC 14**

Fredro, Aleksander 1793-1876 .... **NCLC 8**

Freeling, Nicolas 1927- .... **CLC 38**
See also CA 49-52; CAAS 12; CANR 1,
17, 50, 84; DLB 87

Freeman, Douglas Southall
1886-1953 .... **TCLC 11**
See also CA 109; DLB 17; DLBD 17

Freeman, Judith 1946- .... **CLC 55**
See also CA 148

Freeman, Mary E(leanor) Wilkins
1852-1930 .... **TCLC 9; SSC 1**
See also CA 106; 177; DLB 12, 78, 221

Freeman, R(ichard) Austin
1862-1943 .... **TCLC 21**
See also CA 113; CANR 84; DLB 70

French, Albert 1943- .... **CLC 86**
See also BW 3; CA 167

French, Marilyn 1929- .... **CLC 10, 18, 60;
DAM DRAM, NOV, POP**
See also CA 69-72; CANR 3, 31; INT
CANR-31; MTCW 1, 2

French, Paul
See Asimov, Isaac

Freneau, Philip Morin 1752-1832 ... **NCLC 1**
See also DLB 37, 43

Freud, Sigmund 1856-1939 .... **TCLC 52**
See also CA 115; 133; CANR 69; MTCW
1, 2

Friedan, Betty (Naomi) 1921- .... **CLC 74**
See also CA 65-68; CANR 18, 45, 74;
MTCW 1, 2

Friedlander, Saul 1932- .... **CLC 90**
See also CA 117; 130; CANR 72

Friedman, B(ernard) H(arper)
1926- .... **CLC 7**
See also CA 1-4R; CANR 3, 48

Friedman, Bruce Jay 1930- ...... **CLC 3, 5, 56**
See also CA 9-12R; CANR 25, 52; DLB 2,
28; INT CANR-25

Friel, Brian 1929- .... **CLC 5, 42, 59, 115; DC
8**
See also CA 21-24R; CANR 33, 69; DLB
13; MTCW 1

Friis-Baastad, Babbis Ellinor
1921-1970 .... **CLC 12**
See also CA 17-20R; 134; SATA 7

Frisch, Max (Rudolf) 1911-1991 ... **CLC 3, 9,
14, 18, 32, 44; DAM DRAM, NOV**
See also CA 85-88; 134; CANR 32, 74;
DLB 69, 124; MTCW 1, 2

Fromentin, Eugene (Samuel Auguste)
1820-1876 .... **NCLC 10**
See also DLB 123

Frost, Frederick
See Faust, Frederick (Schiller)

Frost, Robert (Lee) 1874-1963 .. **CLC 1, 3, 4,
9, 10, 13, 15, 26, 34, 44; DA; DAB;
DAC; DAM MST, POET; PC 1; WLC**
See also AAYA 21; CA 89-92; CANR 33;
CDALB 1917-1929; CLR 67; DA3; DLB
54; DLBD 7; MTCW 1, 2; SATA 14

Froude, James Anthony
1818-1894 .... **NCLC 43**
See also DLB 18, 57, 144

Froy, Herald
See Waterhouse, Keith (Spencer)

Fry, Christopher 1907- .... **CLC 2, 10, 14;
DAM DRAM**
See also CA 17-20R; CAAS 23; CANR 9,
30, 74; DLB 13; MTCW 1, 2; SATA 66

Frye, (Herman) Northrop
1912-1991 .... **CLC 24, 70**
See also CA 5-8R; 133; CANR 8, 37; DLB
67, 68; MTCW 1, 2

Fuchs, Daniel 1909-1993 .... **CLC 8, 22**
See also CA 81-84; 142; CAAS 5; CANR
40; DLB 9, 26, 28; DLBY 93

Fuchs, Daniel 1934- .... **CLC 34**
See also CA 37-40R; CANR 14, 48

Fuentes, Carlos 1928- .. **CLC 3, 8, 10, 13, 22,
41, 60, 113; DA; DAB; DAC; DAM
MST, MULT, NOV; HLC 1; SSC 24;
WLC**
See also AAYA 4; AITN 2; CA 69-72;
CANR 10, 32, 68; DA3; DLB 113; HW
1, 2; MTCW 1, 2

Fuentes, Gregorio Lopez y
See Lopez y Fuentes, Gregorio

Fuertes, Gloria 1918- .... **PC 27**
See also CA 178, 180; DLB 108; HW 2;
SATA 115

Fugard, (Harold) Athol 1932- . **CLC 5, 9, 14,
25, 40, 80; DAM DRAM; DC 3**
See also AAYA 17; CA 85-88; CANR 32,
54; DLB 225; MTCW 1

Fugard, Sheila 1932- .... **CLC 48**
See also CA 125

Fukuyama, Francis 1952- .... **CLC 131**
See also CA 140; CANR 72

Fuller, Charles (H., Jr.) 1939- .... **CLC 25;
BLC 2; DAM DRAM, MULT; DC 1**
See also BW 2; CA 108; 112; CANR 87;
DLB 38; INT 112; MTCW 1

Fuller, Henry Blake 1857-1929 .... **TCLC 103**
See also CA 108; 177; DLB 12

Fuller, John (Leopold) 1937- .... **CLC 62**
See also CA 21-24R; CANR 9, 44; DLB 40

Fuller, Margaret
See Ossoli, Sarah Margaret (Fuller marchesa
d')

Fuller, Roy (Broadbent) 1912-1991 ... **CLC 4,
28**
See also CA 5-8R; 135; CAAS 10; CANR
53, 83; DLB 15, 20; SATA 87

Fuller, Sarah Margaret 1810-1850
See Ossoli, Sarah Margaret (Fuller marchesa
d')

Fulton, Alice 1952- .... **CLC 52**
See also CA 116; CANR 57, 88; DLB 193

Furphy, Joseph 1843-1912 .... **TCLC 25**
See also CA 163; DLB 230

Fussell, Paul 1924- .... **CLC 74**
See also BEST 90:1; CA 17-20R; CANR 8,
21, 35, 69; INT CANR-21; MTCW 1, 2

Futabatei, Shimei 1864-1909 .... **TCLC 44**
See also CA 162; DLB 180

Futrelle, Jacques 1875-1912 .... **TCLC 19**
See also CA 113; 155

Gaboriau, Emile 1835-1873 .... **NCLC 14**

Gadda, Carlo Emilio 1893-1973 .... **CLC 11**
See also CA 89-92; DLB 177

Gaddis, William 1922-1998 ... **CLC 1, 3, 6, 8,
10, 19, 43, 86**
See also CA 17-20R; 172; CANR 21, 48;
DLB 2; MTCW 1, 2

Gage, Walter
See Inge, William (Motter)

Gaines, Ernest J(ames) 1933- ...... **CLC 3, 11,
18, 86; BLC 2; DAM MULT**
See also AAYA 18; AITN 1; BW 2, 3; CA
9-12R; CANR 6, 24, 42, 75; CDALB
1968-1988; CLR 62; DA3; DLB 2, 33,
152; DLBY 80; MTCW 1, 2; SATA 86

Gaitskill, Mary 1954- .... **CLC 69**
See also CA 128; CANR 61

Galdos, Benito Perez
See Perez Galdos, Benito

Gale, Zona 1874-1938 .... **TCLC 7; DAM
DRAM**
See also CA 105; 153; CANR 84; DLB 9,
78, 228

Galeano, Eduardo (Hughes) 1940- . **CLC 72;
HLCS 1**
See also CA 29-32R; CANR 13, 32; HW 1

Galiano, Juan Valera y Alcala
See Valera y Alcala-Galiano, Juan

Galilei, Galileo 1546-1642 .... **LC 45**

Gallagher, Tess 1943- ...... **CLC 18, 63; DAM
POET; PC 9**
See also CA 106; DLB 212

Gallant, Mavis 1922- .. **CLC 7, 18, 38; DAC;
DAM MST; SSC 5**
See also CA 69-72; CANR 29, 69; DLB 53;
MTCW 1, 2

Gallant, Roy A(rthur) 1924- .... **CLC 17**
See also CA 5-8R; CANR 4, 29, 54; CLR
30; MAICYA; SATA 4, 68, 110

Gallico, Paul (William) 1897-1976 ..... **CLC 2**
See also AITN 1; CA 5-8R; 69-72; CANR
23; DLB 9, 171; MAICYA; SATA 13

Gibran, Kahlil 1883-1931 .... **TCLC 1, 9;**
DAM POET, POP; PC 9
  See also CA 104; 150; DA3; MTCW 2
Gibran, Khalil
  See Gibran, Kahlil
Gibson, William 1914- .. **CLC 23; DA; DAB;**
DAC; DAM DRAM, MST
  See also CA 9-12R; CANR 9, 42, 75; DLB
  7; MTCW 1; SATA 66
Gibson, William (Ford) 1948- ... **CLC 39, 63;**
DAM POP
  See also AAYA 12; CA 126; 133; CANR
  52, 90; DA3; MTCW 1
Gide, Andre (Paul Guillaume)
  1869-1951 . **TCLC 5, 12, 36; DA; DAB;**
DAC; DAM MST, NOV; SSC 13; WLC
  See also CA 104; 124; DA3; DLB 65;
  MTCW 1, 2
Gifford, Barry (Colby) 1946- .... **CLC 34**
  See also CA 65-68; CANR 9, 30, 40, 90
Gilbert, Frank
  See De Voto, Bernard (Augustine)
Gilbert, W(illiam) S(chwenck)
  1836-1911 .... **TCLC 3; DAM DRAM,**
POET
  See also CA 104; 173; SATA 36
Gilbreth, Frank B., Jr. 1911- .... **CLC 17**
  See also CA 9-12R; SATA 2
Gilchrist, Ellen 1935- ...... **CLC 34, 48; DAM**
POP; SSC 14
  See also CA 113; 116; CANR 41, 61; DLB
  130; MTCW 1, 2
Giles, Molly 1942- .... **CLC 39**
  See also CA 126
Gill, Eric 1882-1940 .... **TCLC 85**
Gill, Patrick
  See Creasey, John
Gilliam, Terry (Vance) 1940- .... **CLC 21**
  See also Monty Python
  See also AAYA 19; CA 108; 113; CANR
  35; INT 113
Gillian, Jerry
  See Gilliam, Terry (Vance)
Gilliatt, Penelope (Ann Douglass)
  1932-1993 .... **CLC 2, 10, 13, 53**
  See also AITN 2; CA 13-16R; 141; CANR
  49; DLB 14
Gilman, Charlotte (Anna) Perkins (Stetson)
  1860-1935 .... **TCLC 9, 37; SSC 13**
  See also CA 106; 150; DLB 221; MTCW 1
Gilmour, David 1949- .... **CLC 35**
  See also CA 138, 147
Gilpin, William 1724-1804 .... **NCLC 30**
Gilray, J. D.
  See Mencken, H(enry) L(ouis)
Gilroy, Frank D(aniel) 1925- .... **CLC 2**
  See also CA 81-84; CANR 32, 64, 86; DLB
  7
Gilstrap, John 1957(?)- .... **CLC 99**
  See also CA 160
Ginsberg, Allen 1926-1997 .... **CLC 1, 2, 3, 4,**
6, 13, 36, 69, 109; DA; DAB; DAC;
DAM MST, POET; PC 4; WLC
  See also AAYA 33; AITN 1; CA 1-4R; 157;
  CANR 2, 41, 63; CDALB 1941-1968;
  DA3; DLB 5, 16, 169; MTCW 1, 2
Ginzburg, Natalia 1916-1991 .... **CLC 5, 11,**
54, 70
  See also CA 85-88; 135; CANR 33; DLB
  177; MTCW 1, 2
Giono, Jean 1895-1970 .... **CLC 4, 11**
  See also CA 45-48; 29-32R; CANR 2, 35;
  DLB 72; MTCW 1
Giovanni, Nikki 1943- .... **CLC 2, 4, 19, 64,**
117; BLC 2; DA; DAB; DAC; DAM
MST, MULT, POET; PC 19; WLCS
  See also AAYA 22; AITN 1; BW 2, 3; CA
  29-32R; CAAS 6; CANR 18, 41, 60, 91;
  CDALBS; CLR 6; DA3; DLB 5, 41; INT
  CANR-18; MAICYA; MTCW 1, 2; SATA
  24, 107

Giovene, Andrea 1904- .... **CLC 7**
  See also CA 85-88
Gippius, Zinaida (Nikolayevna) 1869-1945
  See Hippius, Zinaida
  See also CA 106
Giraudoux, (Hippolyte) Jean
  1882-1944 .... **TCLC 2, 7; DAM DRAM**
  See also CA 104; DLB 65
Gironella, Jose Maria 1917- .... **CLC 11**
  See also CA 101
Gissing, George (Robert)
  1857-1903 .... **TCLC 3, 24, 47; SSC 37**
  See also CA 105; 167; DLB 18, 135, 184
Giurlani, Aldo
  See Palazzeschi, Aldo
Gladkov, Fyodor (Vasilyevich)
  1883-1958 .... **TCLC 27**
  See also CA 170
Glanville, Brian (Lester) 1931- .... **CLC 6**
  See also CA 5-8R; CAAS 9; CANR 3, 70;
  DLB 15, 139; SATA 42
Glasgow, Ellen (Anderson Gholson)
  1873-1945 .... **TCLC 2, 7; SSC 34**
  See also CA 104; 164; DLB 9, 12; MTCW
  2
Glaspell, Susan 1882(?)-1948 . **TCLC 55; DC**
10; SSC 41
  See also CA 110; 154; DLB 7, 9, 78, 228;
  YABC 2
Glassco, John 1909-1981 .... **CLC 9**
  See also CA 13-16R; 102; CANR 15; DLB
  68
Glasscock, Amnesia
  See Steinbeck, John (Ernst)
Glasser, Ronald J. 1940(?)- .... **CLC 37**
Glassman, Joyce
  See Johnson, Joyce
Glendinning, Victoria 1937- .... **CLC 50**
  See also CA 120; 127; CANR 59, 89; DLB
  155
Glissant, Edouard 1928- . **CLC 10, 68; DAM**
MULT
  See also CA 153
Gloag, Julian 1930- .... **CLC 40**
  See also AITN 1; CA 65-68; CANR 10, 70
Glowacki, Aleksander
  See Prus, Boleslaw
Gluck, Louise (Elisabeth) 1943- .. **CLC 7, 22,**
44, 81; DAM POET; PC 16
  See also CA 33-36R; CANR 40, 69; DA3;
  DLB 5; MTCW 2
Glyn, Elinor 1864-1943 .... **TCLC 72**
  See also DLB 153
Gobineau, Joseph Arthur (Comte) de
  1816-1882 .... **NCLC 17**
  See also DLB 123
Godard, Jean-Luc 1930- .... **CLC 20**
  See also CA 93-96
Godden, (Margaret) Rumer
  1907-1998 .... **CLC 53**
  See also AAYA 6; CA 5-8R; 172; CANR 4,
  27, 36, 55, 80; CLR 20; DLB 161; MAI-
  CYA; SAAS 12; SATA 3, 36; SATA-Obit
  109
Godoy Alcayaga, Lucila
  1889-1957 .... **TCLC 2; DAM MULT;**
HLC 2; PC 32
  See also BW 2; CA 104; 131; CANR 81;
  HW 1, 2; MTCW 1, 2
Godwin, Gail (Kathleen) 1937- ..... **CLC 5, 8,**
22, 31, 69, 125; DAM POP
  See also CA 29-32R; CANR 15, 43, 69;
  DA3; DLB 6, 234; INT CANR-15;
  MTCW 1, 2
Godwin, William 1756-1836 .... **NCLC 14**
  See also CDBLB 1789-1832; DLB 39, 104,
  142, 158, 163
Goebbels, Josef
  See Goebbels, (Paul) Joseph

Goebbels, (Paul) Joseph
  1897-1945 .... **TCLC 68**
  See also CA 115; 148
Goebbels, Joseph Paul
  See Goebbels, (Paul) Joseph
Goethe, Johann Wolfgang von
  1749-1832 ...... **NCLC 4, 22, 34, 90; DA;**
DAB; DAC; DAM DRAM, MST,
POET; PC 5; SSC 38; WLC
  See also DA3; DLB 94
Gogarty, Oliver St. John
  1878-1957 .... **TCLC 15**
  See also CA 109; 150; DLB 15, 19
Gogol, Nikolai (Vasilyevich)
  1809-1852 . **NCLC 5, 15, 31; DA; DAB;**
DAC; DAM DRAM, MST; DC 1; SSC
4, 29; WLC
  See also DLB 198
Goines, Donald 1937(?)-1974 . **CLC 80; BLC**
2; DAM MULT, POP
  See also AITN 1; BW 1, 3; CA 124; 114;
  CANR 82; DA3; DLB 33
Gold, Herbert 1924- .... **CLC 4, 7, 14, 42**
  See also CA 9-12R; CANR 17, 45; DLB 2;
  DLBY 81
Goldbarth, Albert 1948- .... **CLC 5, 38**
  See also CA 53-56; CANR 6, 40; DLB 120
Goldberg, Anatol 1910-1982 .... **CLC 34**
  See also CA 131; 117
Goldemberg, Isaac 1945- .... **CLC 52**
  See also CA 69-72; CAAS 12; CANR 11,
  32; HW 1
Golding, William (Gerald)
  1911-1993 ..... **CLC 1, 2, 3, 8, 10, 17, 27,**
58, 81; DA; DAB; DAC; DAM MST,
NOV; WLC
  See also AAYA 5; CA 5-8R; 141; CANR
  13, 33, 54; CDBLB 1945-1960; DA3;
  DLB 15, 100; MTCW 1, 2
Goldman, Emma 1869-1940 .... **TCLC 13**
  See also CA 110; 150; DLB 221
Goldman, Francisco 1954- .... **CLC 76**
  See also CA 162
Goldman, William (W.) 1931- ...... **CLC 1, 48**
  See also CA 9-12R; CANR 29, 69; DLB 44
Goldmann, Lucien 1913-1970 .... **CLC 24**
  See also CA 25-28; CAP 2
Goldoni, Carlo 1707-1793 .... **LC 4; DAM**
DRAM
Goldsberry, Steven 1949- .... **CLC 34**
  See also CA 131
Goldsmith, Oliver 1728-1774 . **LC 2, 48; DA;**
DAB; DAC; DAM DRAM, MST, NOV,
POET; DC 8; WLC
  See also CDBLB 1660-1789; DLB 39, 89,
  104, 109, 142; SATA 26
Goldsmith, Peter
  See Priestley, J(ohn) B(oynton)
Gombrowicz, Witold 1904-1969 .... **CLC 4, 7,**
11, 49; DAM DRAM
  See also CA 19-20; 25-28R; CAP 2
Gomez de la Serna, Ramon
  1888-1963 .... **CLC 9**
  See also CA 153; 116; CANR 79; HW 1, 2
Goncharov, Ivan Alexandrovich
  1812-1891 .... **NCLC 1, 63**
Goncourt, Edmond (Louis Antoine Huot) de
  1822-1896 .... **NCLC 7**
  See also DLB 123
Goncourt, Jules (Alfred Huot) de
  1830-1870 .... **NCLC 7**
  See also DLB 123
Gontier, Fernande 19(?)- .... **CLC 50**
Gonzalez Martinez, Enrique
  1871-1952 .... **TCLC 72**
  See also CA 166; CANR 81; HW 1, 2
Goodman, Paul 1911-1972 ..... **CLC 1, 2, 4, 7**
  See also CA 19-20; 37-40R; CANR 34;
  CAP 2; DLB 130; MTCW 1

Gregory, Isabella Augusta (Persse)
1852-1932 .... **TCLC 1**
See also CA 104; 184; DLB 10
Gregory, J. Dennis
See Williams, John A(lfred)
Grendon, Stephen
See Derleth, August (William)
Grenville, Kate 1950- .... **CLC 61**
See also CA 118; CANR 53, 93
Grenville, Pelham
See Wodehouse, P(elham) G(renville)
Greve, Felix Paul (Berthold Friedrich)
1879-1948
See Grove, Frederick Philip
See also CA 104; 141, 175; CANR 79;
DAC; DAM MST
Grey, Zane 1872-1939 . **TCLC 6; DAM POP**
See also CA 104; 132; DA3; DLB 212;
MTCW 1, 2
Grieg, (Johan) Nordahl (Brun)
1902-1943 .... **TCLC 10**
See also CA 107
Grieve, C(hristopher) M(urray)
1892-1978 ..... **CLC 11, 19; DAM POET**
See also MacDiarmid, Hugh; Pteleon
See also CA 5-8R; 85-88; CANR 33;
MTCW 1
Griffin, Gerald 1803-1840 .... **NCLC 7**
See also DLB 159
Griffin, John Howard 1920-1980 ..... **CLC 68**
See also AITN 1; CA 1-4R; 101; CANR 2
Griffin, Peter 1942- .... **CLC 39**
See also CA 136
Griffith, D(avid Lewelyn) W(ark)
1875(?)-1948 .... **TCLC 68**
See also CA 119; 150; CANR 80
Griffith, Lawrence
See Griffith, D(avid Lewelyn) W(ark)
Griffiths, Trevor 1935- .... **CLC 13, 52**
See also CA 97-100; CANR 45; DLB 13
Griggs, Sutton (Elbert)
1872-1930 .... **TCLC 77**
See also CA 123; 186; DLB 50
Grigson, Geoffrey (Edward Harvey)
1905-1985 .... **CLC 7, 39**
See also CA 25-28R; 118; CANR 20, 33;
DLB 27; MTCW 1, 2
Grillparzer, Franz 1791-1872 .. **NCLC 1; DC
14; SSC 37**
See also DLB 133
Grimble, Reverend Charles James
See Eliot, T(homas) S(tearns)
Grimke, Charlotte L(ottie) Forten
1837(?)-1914
See Forten, Charlotte L.
See also BW 1; CA 117; 124; DAM MULT,
POET
Grimm, Jacob Ludwig Karl
1785-1863 .... **NCLC 3, 77; SSC 36**
See also DLB 90; MAICYA; SATA 22
Grimm, Wilhelm Karl 1786-1859 .. **NCLC 3,
77; SSC 36**
See also DLB 90; MAICYA; SATA 22
**Grimmelshausen, Johann Jakob Christoffel
von** 1621-1676 .... **LC 6**
See also DLB 168
Grindel, Eugene 1895-1952
See Eluard, Paul
See also CA 104
Grisham, John 1955- .... **CLC 84; DAM POP**
See also AAYA 14; CA 138; CANR 47, 69;
DA3; MTCW 2
Grossman, David 1954- .... **CLC 67**
See also CA 138

Grossman, Vasily (Semenovich)
1905-1964 .... **CLC 41**
See also CA 124; 130; MTCW 1
Grove, Frederick Philip TCLC 4
See also Greve, Felix Paul (Berthold
Friedrich)
See also DLB 92
Grubb
See Crumb, R(obert)
Grumbach, Doris (Isaac) 1918- . **CLC 13, 22,
64**
See also CA 5-8R; CAAS 2; CANR 9, 42,
70; INT CANR-9; MTCW 2
Grundtvig, Nicolai Frederik Severin
1783-1872 .... **NCLC 1**
Grunge
See Crumb, R(obert)
Grunwald, Lisa 1959- .... **CLC 44**
See also CA 120
Guare, John 1938- .... **CLC 8, 14, 29, 67;
DAM DRAM**
See also CA 73-76; CANR 21, 69; DLB 7;
MTCW 1, 2
Gudjonsson, Halldor Kiljan 1902-1998
See Laxness, Halldor
See also CA 103; 164
Guenter, Erich
See Eich, Guenter
Guest, Barbara 1920- .... **CLC 34**
See also CA 25-28R; CANR 11, 44, 84;
DLB 5, 193
Guest, Edgar A(lbert) 1881-1959 ... **TCLC 95**
See also CA 112; 168
Guest, Judith (Ann) 1936- .... **CLC 8, 30;
DAM NOV, POP**
See also AAYA 7; CA 77-80; CANR 15,
75; DA3; INT CANR-15; MTCW 1, 2
Guevara, Che CLC 87; HLC 1
See also Guevara (Serna), Ernesto
Guevara (Serna), Ernesto
1928-1967 .... **CLC 87; DAM MULT;
HLC 1**
See also Guevara, Che
See also CA 127; 111; CANR 56; HW 1
Guicciardini, Francesco 1483-1540 ..... **LC 49**
Guild, Nicholas M. 1944- .... **CLC 33**
See also CA 93-96
Guillemin, Jacques
See Sartre, Jean-Paul
Guillen, Jorge 1893-1984 .... **CLC 11; DAM
MULT, POET; HLCS 1**
See also CA 89-92; 112; DLB 108; HW 1
Guillen, Nicolas (Cristobal)
1902-1989 ... **CLC 48, 79; BLC 2; DAM
MST, MULT, POET; HLC 1; PC 23**
See also BW 2; CA 116; 125; 129; CANR
84; HW 1
Guillevic, (Eugene) 1907- .... **CLC 33**
See also CA 93-96
Guillois
See Desnos, Robert
Guillois, Valentin
See Desnos, Robert
Guimaraes Rosa, Joao 1908-1967
See also CA 175; HLCS 2
Guiney, Louise Imogen
1861-1920 .... **TCLC 41**
See also CA 160; DLB 54
Guiraldes, Ricardo (Guillermo)
1886-1927 .... **TCLC 39**
See also CA 131; HW 1; MTCW 1
Gumilev, Nikolai (Stepanovich)
1886-1921 .... **TCLC 60**
See also CA 165
Gunesekera, Romesh 1954- .... **CLC 91**
See also CA 159
Gunn, Bill CLC 5
See also Gunn, William Harrison
See also DLB 38

Gunn, Thom(son William) 1929- .. **CLC 3, 6,
18, 32, 81; DAM POET; PC 26**
See also CA 17-20R; CANR 9, 33; CDBLB
1960 to Present; DLB 27; INT CANR-33;
MTCW 1
Gunn, William Harrison 1934(?)-1989
See Gunn, Bill
See also AITN 1; BW 1, 3; CA 13-16R;
128; CANR 12, 25, 76
Gunnars, Kristjana 1948- .... **CLC 69**
See also CA 113; DLB 60
Gurdjieff, G(eorgei) I(vanovich)
1877(?)-1949 .... **TCLC 71**
See also CA 157
Gurganus, Allan 1947- . **CLC 70; DAM POP**
See also BEST 90:1; CA 135
Gurney, A(lbert) R(amsdell), Jr.
1930- ..... **CLC 32, 50, 54; DAM DRAM**
See also CA 77-80; CANR 32, 64
Gurney, Ivor (Bertie) 1890-1937 ... **TCLC 33**
See also CA 167
Gurney, Peter
See Gurney, A(lbert) R(amsdell), Jr.
Guro, Elena 1877-1913 .... **TCLC 56**
Gustafson, James M(oody) 1925- ... **CLC 100**
See also CA 25-28R; CANR 37
Gustafson, Ralph (Barker) 1909- ..... **CLC 36**
See also CA 21-24R; CANR 8, 45, 84; DLB
88
Gut, Gom
See Simenon, Georges (Jacques Christian)
Guterson, David 1956- .... **CLC 91**
See also CA 132; CANR 73; MTCW 2
Guthrie, A(lfred) B(ertram), Jr.
1901-1991 .... **CLC 23**
See also CA 57-60; 134; CANR 24; DLB
212; SATA 62; SATA-Obit 67
Guthrie, Isobel
See Grieve, C(hristopher) M(urray)
Guthrie, Woodrow Wilson 1912-1967
See Guthrie, Woody
See also CA 113; 93-96
Guthrie, Woody CLC 35
See also Guthrie, Woodrow Wilson
Gutierrez Najera, Manuel 1859-1895
See also HLCS 2
Guy, Rosa (Cuthbert) 1928- .... **CLC 26**
See also AAYA 4, 37; BW 2; CA 17-20R;
CANR 14, 34, 83; CLR 13; DLB 33;
JRDA; MAICYA; SATA 14, 62
Gwendolyn
See Bennett, (Enoch) Arnold
H. D. CLC 3, 8, 14, 31, 34, 73; PC 5
See also Doolittle, Hilda
H. de V.
See Buchan, John
Haavikko, Paavo Juhani 1931- .. **CLC 18, 34**
See also CA 106
Habbema, Koos
See Heijermans, Herman
Habermas, Juergen 1929- .... **CLC 104**
See also CA 109; CANR 85
Habermas, Jurgen
See Habermas, Juergen
Hacker, Marilyn 1942- ...... **CLC 5, 9, 23, 72,
91; DAM POET**
See also CA 77-80; CANR 68; DLB 120
Haeckel, Ernst Heinrich (Philipp August)
1834-1919 .... **TCLC 83**
See also CA 157
Hafiz c. 1326-1389 .... **CMLC 34**
Hafiz c. 1326-1389(?) .... **CMLC 34**
Haggard, H(enry) Rider
1856-1925 .... **TCLC 11**
See also CA 108; 148; DLB 70, 156, 174,
178; MTCW 2; SATA 16
Hagiosy, L.
See Larbaud, Valery (Nicolas)

Harson, Sley
See Ellison, Harlan (Jay)
Hart, Ellis
See Ellison, Harlan (Jay)
Hart, Josephine 1942(?)- .... **CLC 70; DAM POP**
See also CA 138; CANR 70
Hart, Moss 1904-1961 .... **CLC 66; DAM DRAM**
See also CA 109; 89-92; CANR 84; DLB 7
Harte, (Francis) Bret(t) 1836(?)-1902 .. **TCLC 1, 25; DA; DAC; DAM MST; SSC 8; WLC**
See also CA 104; 140; CANR 80; CDALB 1865-1917; DA3; DLB 12, 64, 74, 79, 186; SATA 26
Hartley, L(eslie) P(oles) 1895-1972 ... **CLC 2, 22**
See also CA 45-48; 37-40R; CANR 33; DLB 15, 139; MTCW 1, 2
Hartman, Geoffrey H. 1929- .... **CLC 27**
See also CA 117; 125; CANR 79; DLB 67
Hartmann, Sadakichi 1867-1944 ... **TCLC 73**
See also CA 157; DLB 54
Hartmann von Aue c. 1160-c. 1205 .... **CMLC 15**
See also DLB 138
Hartmann von Aue 1170-1210 ...... **CMLC 15**
Haruf, Kent 1943- .... **CLC 34**
See also CA 149; CANR 91
Harwood, Ronald 1934- .... **CLC 32; DAM DRAM, MST**
See also CA 1-4R; CANR 4, 55; DLB 13
Hasegawa Tatsunosuke
See Futabatei, Shimei
Hasek, Jaroslav (Matej Frantisek) 1883-1923 .... **TCLC 4**
See also CA 104; 129; MTCW 1, 2
Hass, Robert 1941- ... **CLC 18, 39, 99; PC 16**
See also CA 111; CANR 30, 50, 71; DLB 105, 206; SATA 94
Hastings, Hudson
See Kuttner, Henry
Hastings, Selina **CLC 44**
Hathorne, John 1641-1717 .... **LC 38**
Hatteras, Amelia
See Mencken, H(enry) L(ouis)
Hatteras, Owen **TCLC 18**
See also Mencken, H(enry) L(ouis); Nathan, George Jean
Hauptmann, Gerhart (Johann Robert) 1862-1946 .... **TCLC 4; DAM DRAM; SSC 37**
See also CA 104; 153; DLB 66, 118
Havel, Vaclav 1936- ..... **CLC 25, 58, 65, 123; DAM DRAM; DC 6**
See also CA 104; CANR 36, 63; DA3; DLB 232; MTCW 1, 2
Haviaras, Stratis **CLC 33**
See also Chaviaras, Strates
Hawes, Stephen 1475(?)-1523(?) .... **LC 17**
See also DLB 132
Hawkes, John (Clendennin Burne, Jr.) 1925-1998 .. **CLC 1, 2, 3, 4, 7, 9, 14, 15, 27, 49**
See also CA 1-4R; 167; CANR 2, 47, 64; DLB 2, 7, 227; DLBY 80, 98; MTCW 1, 2
Hawking, S. W.
See Hawking, Stephen W(illiam)
Hawking, Stephen W(illiam) 1942- . **CLC 63, 105**
See also AAYA 13; BEST 89:1; CA 126; 129; CANR 48; DA3; MTCW 2
Hawkins, Anthony Hope
See Hope, Anthony
Hawthorne, Julian 1846-1934 .... **TCLC 25**
See also CA 165

Hawthorne, Nathaniel 1804-1864 ... **NCLC 2, 10, 17, 23, 39, 79, 95; DA; DAB; DAC; DAM MST, NOV; SSC 3, 29, 39; WLC**
See also AAYA 18; CDALB 1640-1865; DA3; DLB 1, 74, 223; YABC 2
Haxton, Josephine Ayres 1921-
See Douglas, Ellen
See also CA 115; CANR 41, 83
Hayaseca y Eizaguirre, Jorge
See Echegaray (y Eizaguirre), Jose (Maria Waldo)
Hayashi, Fumiko 1904-1951 .... **TCLC 27**
See also CA 161; DLB 180
Haycraft, Anna (Margaret) 1932-
See Ellis, Alice Thomas
See also CA 122; CANR 85, 90; MTCW 2
Hayden, Robert E(arl) 1913-1980 . **CLC 5, 9, 14, 37; BLC 2; DA; DAC; DAM MST, MULT, POET; PC 6**
See also BW 1, 3; CA 69-72; 97-100; CABS 2; CANR 24, 75, 82; CDALB 1941-1968; DLB 5, 76; MTCW 1, 2; SATA 19; SATA-Obit 26
Hayford, J(oseph) E(phraim) Casely
See Casely-Hayford, J(oseph) E(phraim)
Hayman, Ronald 1932- .... **CLC 44**
See also CA 25-28R; CANR 18, 50, 88; DLB 155
Hayne, Paul Hamilton 1830-1886 . **NCLC 94**
See also DLB 3, 64, 79
Haywood, Eliza (Fowler) 1693(?)-1756 .... **LC 1, 44**
See also DLB 39
Hazlitt, William 1778-1830 ...... **NCLC 29, 82**
See also DLB 110, 158
Hazzard, Shirley 1931- .... **CLC 18**
See also CA 9-12R; CANR 4, 70; DLBY 82; MTCW 1
Head, Bessie 1937-1986 .... **CLC 25, 67; BLC 2; DAM MULT**
See also BW 2, 3; CA 29-32R; 119; CANR 25, 82; DA3; DLB 117, 225; MTCW 1, 2
Headon, (Nicky) Topper 1956(?)- ..... **CLC 30**
Heaney, Seamus (Justin) 1939- ... **CLC 5, 7, 14, 25, 37, 74, 91; DAB; DAM POET; PC 18; WLCS**
See also CA 85-88; CANR 25, 48, 75, 91; CDBLB 1960 to Present; DA3; DLB 40; DLBY 95; MTCW 1, 2
Hearn, (Patricio) Lafcadio (Tessima Carlos) 1850-1904 .... **TCLC 9**
See also CA 105; 166; DLB 12, 78, 189
Hearne, Vicki 1946- .... **CLC 56**
See also CA 139
Hearon, Shelby 1931- .... **CLC 63**
See also AITN 2; CA 25-28R; CANR 18, 48
Heat-Moon, William Least **CLC 29**
See also Trogdon, William (Lewis)
See also AAYA 9
Hebbel, Friedrich 1813-1863 .... **NCLC 43; DAM DRAM**
See also DLB 129
Hebert, Anne 1916-2000 .... **CLC 4, 13, 29; DAC; DAM MST, POET**
See also CA 85-88; 187; CANR 69; DA3; DLB 68; MTCW 1, 2
Hecht, Anthony (Evan) 1923- ...... **CLC 8, 13, 19; DAM POET**
See also CA 9-12R; CANR 6; DLB 5, 169
Hecht, Ben 1894-1964 .... **CLC 8**
See also CA 85-88; DLB 7, 9, 25, 26, 28, 86; TCLC 101
Hedayat, Sadeq 1903-1951 .... **TCLC 21**
See also CA 120
Hegel, Georg Wilhelm Friedrich 1770-1831 .... **NCLC 46**
See also DLB 90

Heidegger, Martin 1889-1976 .... **CLC 24**
See also CA 81-84; 65-68; CANR 34; MTCW 1, 2
Heidenstam, (Carl Gustaf) Verner von 1859-1940 .... **TCLC 5**
See also CA 104
Heifner, Jack 1946- .... **CLC 11**
See also CA 105; CANR 47
Heijermans, Herman 1864-1924 .... **TCLC 24**
See also CA 123
Heilbrun, Carolyn G(old) 1926- .... **CLC 25**
See also CA 45-48; CANR 1, 28, 58, 94
Heine, Heinrich 1797-1856 .... **NCLC 4, 54; PC 25**
See also DLB 90
Heinemann, Larry (Curtiss) 1944- .. **CLC 50**
See also CA 110; CAAS 21; CANR 31, 81; DLBD 9; INT CANR-31
Heiney, Donald (William) 1921-1993
See Harris, MacDonald
See also CA 1-4R; 142; CANR 3, 58
Heinlein, Robert A(nson) 1907-1988 . **CLC 1, 3, 8, 14, 26, 55; DAM POP**
See also AAYA 17; CA 1-4R; 125; CANR 1, 20, 53; DA3; DLB 8; JRDA; MAICYA; MTCW 1, 2; SATA 9, 69; SATA-Obit 56
Helforth, John
See Doolittle, Hilda
Hellenhofferu, Vojtech Kapristian z
See Hasek, Jaroslav (Matej Frantisek)
Heller, Joseph 1923-1999 . **CLC 1, 3, 5, 8, 11, 36, 63; DA; DAB; DAC; DAM MST, NOV, POP; WLC**
See also AAYA 24; AITN 1; CA 5-8R; 187; CABS 1; CANR 8, 42, 66; DA3; DLB 2, 28, 227; DLBY 80; INT CANR-8; MTCW 1, 2
Hellman, Lillian (Florence) 1906-1984 .. **CLC 2, 4, 8, 14, 18, 34, 44, 52; DAM DRAM; DC 1**
See also AITN 1, 2; CA 13-16R; 112; CANR 33; DA3; DLB 7, 228; DLBY 84; MTCW 1, 2
Helprin, Mark 1947- .... **CLC 7, 10, 22, 32; DAM NOV, POP**
See also CA 81-84; CANR 47, 64; CDALBS; DA3; DLBY 85; MTCW 1, 2
Helvetius, Claude-Adrien 1715-1771 .. **LC 26**
Helyar, Jane Penelope Josephine 1933-
See Poole, Josephine
See also CA 21-24R; CANR 10, 26; SATA 82
Hemans, Felicia 1793-1835 ...... **NCLC 29, 71**
See also DLB 96
Hemingway, Ernest (Miller) 1899-1961 .... **CLC 1, 3, 6, 8, 10, 13, 19, 30, 34, 39, 41, 44, 50, 61, 80; DA; DAB; DAC; DAM MST, NOV; SSC 1, 25, 36, 40; WLC**
See also AAYA 19; CA 77-80; CANR 34; CDALB 1917-1929; DA3; DLB 4, 9, 102, 210; DLBD 1, 15, 16; DLBY 81, 87, 96, 98; MTCW 1, 2
Hempel, Amy 1951- .... **CLC 39**
See also CA 118; 137; CANR 70; DA3; MTCW 2
Henderson, F. C.
See Mencken, H(enry) L(ouis)
Henderson, Sylvia
See Ashton-Warner, Sylvia (Constance)
Henderson, Zenna (Chlarson) 1917-1983 .... **SSC 29**
See also CA 1-4R; 133; CANR 1, 84; DLB 8; SATA 5
Henkin, Joshua **CLC 119**
See also CA 161
Henley, Beth **CLC 23; DC 6, 14**
See also Henley, Elizabeth Becker
See also CABS 3; DLBY 86

Just, Ward (Swift) 1935- .... **CLC 4, 27**
See also CA 25-28R; CANR 32, 87; INT
CANR-32

Justice, Donald (Rodney) 1925- .. **CLC 6, 19, 102; DAM POET**
See also CA 5-8R; CANR 26, 54, 74;
DLBY 83; INT CANR-26; MTCW 2

Juvenal c. 60-c. 13 .... **CMLC 8**
See also Juvenalis, Decimus Junius
See also DLB 211

Juvenalis, Decimus Junius 55(?)-c. 127(?)
See Juvenal

Juvenis
See Bourne, Randolph S(illiman)

Kacew, Romain 1914-1980
See Gary, Romain
See also CA 108; 102

Kadare, Ismail 1936- .... **CLC 52**
See also CA 161

Kadohata, Cynthia **CLC 59, 122**
See also CA 140

Kafka, Franz 1883-1924 . **TCLC 2, 6, 13, 29, 47, 53; DA; DAB; DAC; DAM MST, NOV; SSC 5, 29, 35; WLC**
See also AAYA 31; CA 105; 126; DA3;
DLB 81; MTCW 1, 2

Kahanovitsch, Pinkhes
See Der Nister

Kahn, Roger 1927- .... **CLC 30**
See also CA 25-28R; CANR 44, 69; DLB
171; SATA 37

Kain, Saul
See Sassoon, Siegfried (Lorraine)

Kaiser, Georg 1878-1945 .... **TCLC 9**
See also CA 106; DLB 124

Kaletski, Alexander 1946- .... **CLC 39**
See also CA 118; 143

Kalidasa fl. c. 400- .... **CMLC 9; PC 22**

Kallman, Chester (Simon)
1921-1975 .... **CLC 2**
See also CA 45-48; 53-56; CANR 3

Kaminsky, Melvin 1926-
See Brooks, Mel
See also CA 65-68; CANR 16

Kaminsky, Stuart M(elvin) 1934- ..... **CLC 59**
See also CA 73-76; CANR 29, 53, 89

Kandinsky, Wassily 1866-1944 .... **TCLC 92**
See also CA 118; 155

Kane, Francis
See Robbins, Harold

Kane, Henry 1918-
See Queen, Ellery
See also CA 156

Kane, Paul
See Simon, Paul (Frederick)

Kanin, Garson 1912-1999 .... **CLC 22**
See also AITN 1; CA 5-8R; 177; CANR 7,
78; DLB 7

Kaniuk, Yoram 1930- .... **CLC 19**
See also CA 134

Kant, Immanuel 1724-1804 ..... **NCLC 27, 67**
See also DLB 94

Kantor, MacKinlay 1904-1977 .... **CLC 7**
See also CA 61-64; 73-76; CANR 60, 63;
DLB 9, 102; MTCW 1

Kaplan, David Michael 1946- .... **CLC 50**
See also CA 187

Kaplan, James 1951- .... **CLC 59**
See also CA 135

Karageorge, Michael
See Anderson, Poul (William)

Karamzin, Nikolai Mikhailovich
1766-1826 .... **NCLC 3**
See also DLB 150

Karapanou, Margarita 1946- .... **CLC 13**
See also CA 101

Karinthy, Frigyes 1887-1938 .... **TCLC 47**
See also CA 170

Karl, Frederick R(obert) 1927- .... **CLC 34**
See also CA 5-8R; CANR 3, 44

Kastel, Warren
See Silverberg, Robert

Kataev, Evgeny Petrovich 1903-1942
See Petrov, Evgeny
See also CA 120

Kataphusin
See Ruskin, John

Katz, Steve 1935- .... **CLC 47**
See also CA 25-28R; CAAS 14, 64; CANR
12; DLBY 83

Kauffman, Janet 1945- .... **CLC 42**
See also CA 117; CANR 43, 84; DLBY 86

Kaufman, Bob (Garnell) 1925-1986 . **CLC 49**
See also BW 1; CA 41-44R; 118; CANR
22; DLB 16, 41

Kaufman, George S. 1889-1961 ...... **CLC 38; DAM DRAM**
See also CA 108; 93-96; DLB 7; INT 108;
MTCW 2

Kaufman, Sue **CLC 3, 8**
See also Barondess, Sue K(aufman)

Kavafis, Konstantinos Petrou 1863-1933
See Cavafy, C(onstantine) P(eter)
See also CA 104

Kavan, Anna 1901-1968 .... **CLC 5, 13, 82**
See also CA 5-8R; CANR 6, 57; MTCW 1

Kavanagh, Dan
See Barnes, Julian (Patrick)

Kavanagh, Julie 1952- .... **CLC 119**
See also CA 163

Kavanagh, Patrick (Joseph)
1904-1967 .... **CLC 22; PC 33**
See also CA 123; 25-28R; DLB 15, 20;
MTCW 1

Kawabata, Yasunari 1899-1972 ..... **CLC 2, 5, 9, 18, 107; DAM MULT; SSC 17**
See also CA 93-96; 33-36R; CANR 88;
DLB 180; MTCW 2

Kaye, M(ary) M(argaret) 1909- .... **CLC 28**
See also CA 89-92; CANR 24, 60; MTCW
1, 2; SATA 62

Kaye, Mollie
See Kaye, M(ary) M(argaret)

Kaye-Smith, Sheila 1887-1956 .... **TCLC 20**
See also CA 118; DLB 36

Kaymor, Patrice Maguilene
See Senghor, Leopold Sedar

Kazakov, Yuri Pavlovich 1927-1982 . **SSC 43**
See also CA 5-8R; CANR 36; MTCW 1

Kazan, Elia 1909- .... **CLC 6, 16, 63**
See also CA 21-24R; CANR 32, 78

Kazantzakis, Nikos 1883(?)-1957 .... **TCLC 2, 5, 33**
See also CA 105; 132; DA3; MTCW 1, 2

Kazin, Alfred 1915-1998 ..... **CLC 34, 38, 119**
See also CA 1-4R; CAAS 7; CANR 1, 45,
79; DLB 67

Keane, Mary Nesta (Skrine) 1904-1996
See Keane, Molly
See also CA 108; 114; 151

Keane, Molly **CLC 31**
See also Keane, Mary Nesta (Skrine)
See also INT 114

Keates, Jonathan 1946(?)- .... **CLC 34**
See also CA 163

Keaton, Buster 1895-1966 .... **CLC 20**

Keats, John 1795-1821 ...... **NCLC 8, 73; DA; DAB; DAC; DAM MST, POET; PC 1; WLC**
See also CDBLB 1789-1832; DA3; DLB
96, 110

Keble, John 1792-1866 .... **NCLC 87**
See also DLB 32, 55

Keene, Donald 1922- .... **CLC 34**
See also CA 1-4R; CANR 5

Keillor, Garrison **CLC 40, 115**
See also Keillor, Gary (Edward)
See also AAYA 2; BEST 89:3; DLBY 87;
SATA 58

Keillor, Gary (Edward) 1942-
See Keillor, Garrison
See also CA 111; 117; CANR 36, 59; DAM
POP; DA3; MTCW 1, 2

Keith, Michael
See Hubbard, L(afayette) Ron(ald)

Keller, Gottfried 1819-1890 .... **NCLC 2; SSC 26**
See also DLB 129

Keller, Nora Okja 1965- .... **CLC 109**
See also CA 187

Kellerman, Jonathan 1949- .. **CLC 44; DAM POP**
See also AAYA 35; BEST 90:1; CA 106;
CANR 29, 51; DA3; INT CANR-29

Kelley, William Melvin 1937- .... **CLC 22**
See also BW 1; CA 77-80; CANR 27, 83;
DLB 33

Kellogg, Marjorie 1922- .... **CLC 2**
See also CA 81-84

Kellow, Kathleen
See Hibbert, Eleanor Alice Burford

Kelly, M(ilton) T(errence) 1947- ...... **CLC 55**
See also CA 97-100; CAAS 22; CANR 19,
43, 84

Kelman, James 1946- .... **CLC 58, 86**
See also CA 148; CANR 85; DLB 194

Kemal, Yashar 1923- .... **CLC 14, 29**
See also CA 89-92; CANR 44

Kemble, Fanny 1809-1893 .... **NCLC 18**
See also DLB 32

Kemelman, Harry 1908-1996 .... **CLC 2**
See also AITN 1; CA 9-12R; 155; CANR 6,
71; DLB 28

Kempe, Margery 1373(?)-1440(?) ... **LC 6, 56**
See also DLB 146

Kempis, Thomas a 1380-1471 .... **LC 11**

Kendall, Henry 1839-1882 .... **NCLC 12**
See also DLB 230

Keneally, Thomas (Michael) 1935- ... **CLC 5, 8, 10, 14, 19, 27, 43, 117; DAM NOV**
See also CA 85-88; CANR 10, 50, 74; DA3;
MTCW 1, 2

Kennedy, Adrienne (Lita) 1931- ..... **CLC 66; BLC 2; DAM MULT; DC 5**
See also BW 2, 3; CA 103; CAAS 20;
CABS 3; CANR 26, 53, 82; DLB 38

Kennedy, John Pendleton
1795-1870 .... **NCLC 2**
See also DLB 3

Kennedy, Joseph Charles 1929-
See Kennedy, X. J.
See also CA 1-4R; CANR 4, 30, 40; SATA
14, 86

Kennedy, William 1928- .. **CLC 6, 28, 34, 53; DAM NOV**
See also AAYA 1; CA 85-88; CANR 14,
31, 76; DA3; DLB 143; DLBY 85; INT
CANR-31; MTCW 1, 2; SATA 57

Kennedy, X. J. **CLC 8, 42**
See also Kennedy, Joseph Charles
See also CAAS 9; CLR 27; DLB 5; SAAS
22

Kenny, Maurice (Francis) 1929- ..... **CLC 87; DAM MULT**
See also CA 144; CAAS 22; DLB 175;
NNAL

Kent, Kelvin
See Kuttner, Henry

Kenton, Maxwell
See Southern, Terry

Kenyon, Robert O.
See Kuttner, Henry

Lagerkvist, Par SSC 12
See also Lagerkvist, Paer (Fabian)
See also MTCW 2
Lagerloef, Selma (Ottiliana Lovisa)
1858-1940 .... **TCLC 4, 36**
See also Lagerlof, Selma (Ottiliana Lovisa)
See also CA 108; MTCW 2; SATA 15
Lagerlof, Selma (Ottiliana Lovisa)
See Lagerloef, Selma (Ottiliana Lovisa)
See also CLR 7; SATA 15
La Guma, (Justin) Alex(ander)
1925-1985 .... **CLC 19; BLCS; DAM NOV**
See also BW 1, 3; CA 49-52; 118; CANR 25, 81; DLB 117, 225; MTCW 1, 2
Laidlaw, A. K.
See Grieve, C(hristopher) M(urray)
Lainez, Manuel Mujica
See Mujica Lainez, Manuel
See also HW 1
Laing, R(onald) D(avid) 1927-1989 . **CLC 95**
See also CA 107; 129; CANR 34; MTCW 1
Lamartine, Alphonse (Marie Louis Prat) de
1790-1869 . **NCLC 11; DAM POET; PC 16**
Lamb, Charles 1775-1834 ..... **NCLC 10; DA; DAB; DAC; DAM MST; WLC**
See also CDBLB 1789-1832; DLB 93, 107, 163; SATA 17
Lamb, Lady Caroline 1785-1828 ... **NCLC 38**
See also DLB 116
Lamming, George (William) 1927- ... **CLC 2, 4, 66; BLC 2; DAM MULT**
See also BW 2, 3; CA 85-88; CANR 26, 76; DLB 125; MTCW 1, 2
L'Amour, Louis (Dearborn)
1908-1988 ...... **CLC 25, 55; DAM NOV, POP**
See also AAYA 16; AITN 2; BEST 89:2; CA 1-4R; 125; CANR 3, 25, 40; DA3; DLB 206; DLBY 80; MTCW 1, 2
Lampedusa, Giuseppe (Tomasi) di
1896-1957 .... **TCLC 13**
See also Tomasi di Lampedusa, Giuseppe
See also CA 164; DLB 177; MTCW 2
Lampman, Archibald 1861-1899 ... **NCLC 25**
See also DLB 92
Lancaster, Bruce 1896-1963 .... **CLC 36**
See also CA 9-10; CANR 70; CAP 1; SATA 9
Lanchester, John CLC 99
Landau, Mark Alexandrovich
See Aldanov, Mark (Alexandrovich)
Landau-Aldanov, Mark Alexandrovich
See Aldanov, Mark (Alexandrovich)
Landis, Jerry
See Simon, Paul (Frederick)
Landis, John 1950- .... **CLC 26**
See also CA 112; 122
Landolfi, Tommaso 1908-1979 .... **CLC 11, 49**
See also CA 127; 117; DLB 177
Landon, Letitia Elizabeth
1802-1838 .... **NCLC 15**
See also DLB 96
Landor, Walter Savage
1775-1864 .... **NCLC 14**
See also DLB 93, 107
Landwirth, Heinz 1927-
See Lind, Jakov
See also CA 9-12R; CANR 7
Lane, Patrick 1939- ... **CLC 25; DAM POET**
See also CA 97-100; CANR 54; DLB 53; INT 97-100
Lang, Andrew 1844-1912 .... **TCLC 16**
See also CA 114; 137; CANR 85; DLB 98, 141, 184; MAICYA; SATA 16
Lang, Fritz 1890-1976 .... **CLC 20, 103**
See also CA 77-80; 69-72; CANR 30

Lange, John
See Crichton, (John) Michael
Langer, Elinor 1939- .... **CLC 34**
See also CA 121
Langland, William 1330(?)-1400(?) ... **LC 19; DA; DAB; DAC; DAM MST, POET**
See also DLB 146
Langstaff, Launcelot
See Irving, Washington
Lanier, Sidney 1842-1881 ..... **NCLC 6; DAM POET**
See also DLB 64; DLBD 13; MAICYA; SATA 18
Lanyer, Aemilia 1569-1645 .... **LC 10, 30**
See also DLB 121
Lao-Tzu
See Lao Tzu
Lao Tzu fl. 6th cent. B.C.- .... **CMLC 7**
Lapine, James (Elliot) 1949- .... **CLC 39**
See also CA 123; 130; CANR 54; INT 130
Larbaud, Valery (Nicolas)
1881-1957 .... **TCLC 9**
See also CA 106; 152
Lardner, Ring
See Lardner, Ring(gold) W(ilmer)
Lardner, Ring W., Jr.
See Lardner, Ring(gold) W(ilmer)
Lardner, Ring(gold) W(ilmer)
1885-1933 .... **TCLC 2, 14; SSC 32**
See also CA 104; 131; CDALB 1917-1929; DLB 11, 25, 86; DLBD 16; MTCW 1, 2
Laredo, Betty
See Codrescu, Andrei
Larkin, Maia
See Wojciechowska, Maia (Teresa)
Larkin, Philip (Arthur) 1922-1985 ... **CLC 3, 5, 8, 9, 13, 18, 33, 39, 64; DAB; DAM MST, POET; PC 21**
See also CA 5-8R; 117; CANR 24, 62; CD-BLB 1960 to Present; DA3; DLB 27; MTCW 1, 2
Larra (y Sanchez de Castro), Mariano Jose de 1809-1837 .... **NCLC 17**
Larsen, Eric 1941- .... **CLC 55**
See also CA 132
Larsen, Nella 1891-1964 .... **CLC 37; BLC 2; DAM MULT**
See also BW 1; CA 125; CANR 83; DLB 51
Larson, Charles R(aymond) 1938- ... **CLC 31**
See also CA 53-56; CANR 4
Larson, Jonathan 1961-1996 .... **CLC 99**
See also AAYA 28; CA 156
Las Casas, Bartolome de 1474-1566 ... **LC 31**
Lasch, Christopher 1932-1994 .... **CLC 102**
See also CA 73-76; 144; CANR 25; MTCW 1, 2
Lasker-Schueler, Else 1869-1945 ... **TCLC 57**
See also CA 183; DLB 66, 124
Laski, Harold J(oseph) 1893-1950 . **TCLC 79**
Latham, Jean Lee 1902-1995 .... **CLC 12**
See also AITN 1; CA 5-8R; CANR 7, 84; CLR 50; MAICYA; SATA 2, 68
Latham, Mavis
See Clark, Mavis Thorpe
Lathen, Emma CLC 2
See also Hennissart, Martha; Latsis, Mary J(ane)
Lathrop, Francis
See Leiber, Fritz (Reuter, Jr.)
Latsis, Mary J(ane) 1927(?)-1997
See Lathen, Emma
See also CA 85-88; 162
Lattimore, Richmond (Alexander)
1906-1984 .... **CLC 3**
See also CA 1-4R; 112; CANR 1

Laughlin, James 1914-1997 .... **CLC 49**
See also CA 21-24R; 162; CAAS 22; CANR 9, 47; DLB 48; DLBY 96, 97
Laurence, (Jean) Margaret (Wemyss)
1926-1987 . **CLC 3, 6, 13, 50, 62; DAC; DAM MST; SSC 7**
See also CA 5-8R; 121; CANR 33; DLB 53; MTCW 1, 2; SATA-Obit 50
Laurent, Antoine 1952- .... **CLC 50**
Lauscher, Hermann
See Hesse, Hermann
Lautreamont, Comte de
1846-1870 .... **NCLC 12; SSC 14**
Laverty, Donald
See Blish, James (Benjamin)
Lavin, Mary 1912-1996 . **CLC 4, 18, 99; SSC 4**
See also CA 9-12R; 151; CANR 33; DLB 15; MTCW 1
Lavond, Paul Dennis
See Kornbluth, C(yril) M.; Pohl, Frederik
Lawler, Raymond Evenor 1922- .... **CLC 58**
See also CA 103
Lawrence, D(avid) H(erbert Richards)
1885-1930 .... **TCLC 2, 9, 16, 33, 48, 61, 93; DA; DAB; DAC; DAM MST, NOV, POET; SSC 4, 19; WLC**
See also CA 104; 121; CDBLB 1914-1945; DA3; DLB 10, 19, 36, 98, 162, 195; MTCW 1, 2
Lawrence, T(homas) E(dward)
1888-1935 .... **TCLC 18**
See also Dale, Colin
See also CA 115; 167; DLB 195
Lawrence of Arabia
See Lawrence, T(homas) E(dward)
Lawson, Henry (Archibald Hertzberg)
1867-1922 .... **TCLC 27; SSC 18**
See also CA 120; 181; DLB 230
Lawton, Dennis
See Faust, Frederick (Schiller)
Laxness, Halldor CLC 25
See also Gudjonsson, Halldor Kiljan
Layamon fl. c. 1200- .... **CMLC 10**
See also DLB 146
Laye, Camara 1928-1980 ... **CLC 4, 38; BLC 2; DAM MULT**
See also BW 1; CA 85-88; 97-100; CANR 25; MTCW 1, 2
Layton, Irving (Peter) 1912- .... **CLC 2, 15; DAC; DAM MST, POET**
See also CA 1-4R; CANR 2, 33, 43, 66; DLB 88; MTCW 1, 2
Lazarus, Emma 1849-1887 .... **NCLC 8**
Lazarus, Felix
See Cable, George Washington
Lazarus, Henry
See Slavitt, David R(ytman)
Lea, Joan
See Neufeld, John (Arthur)
Leacock, Stephen (Butler)
1869-1944 .... **TCLC 2; DAC; DAM MST; SSC 39**
See also CA 104; 141; CANR 80; DLB 92; MTCW 2
Lear, Edward 1812-1888 .... **NCLC 3**
See also CLR 1; DLB 32, 163, 166; MAICYA; SATA 18, 100
Lear, Norman (Milton) 1922- .... **CLC 12**
See also CA 73-76
Leautaud, Paul 1872-1956 .... **TCLC 83**
See also DLB 65
Leavis, F(rank) R(aymond)
1895-1978 .... **CLC 24**
See also CA 21-24R; 77-80; CANR 44; MTCW 1, 2
Leavitt, David 1961- ..... **CLC 34; DAM POP**
See also CA 116; 122; CANR 50, 62; DA3; DLB 130; INT 122; MTCW 2

MacDougal, John
See Blish, James (Benjamin)
MacDougal, John
See Blish, James (Benjamin)
MacEwen, Gwendolyn (Margaret)
1941-1987 .... **CLC 13, 55**
See also CA 9-12R; 124; CANR 7, 22; DLB
53; SATA 50; SATA-Obit 55
Macha, Karel Hynek 1810-1846 .... **NCLC 46**
Machado (y Ruiz), Antonio
1875-1939 .... **TCLC 3**
See also CA 104; 174; DLB 108; HW 2
Machado de Assis, Joaquim Maria
1839-1908 ..... **TCLC 10; BLC 2; HLCS
2; SSC 24**
See also CA 107; 153; CANR 91
Machen, Arthur TCLC 4; SSC 20
See also Jones, Arthur Llewellyn
See also CA 179; DLB 36, 156, 178
Machiavelli, Niccolo 1469-1527 ..... **LC 8, 36;
DA; DAB; DAC; DAM MST; WLCS**
MacInnes, Colin 1914-1976 .... **CLC 4, 23**
See also CA 69-72; 65-68; CANR 21; DLB
14; MTCW 1, 2
MacInnes, Helen (Clark)
1907-1985 .... **CLC 27, 39; DAM POP**
See also CA 1-4R; 117; CANR 1, 28, 58;
DLB 87; MTCW 1, 2; SATA 22; SATA-
Obit 44
Mackenzie, Compton (Edward Montague)
1883-1972 .... **CLC 18**
See also CA 21-22; 37-40R; CAP 2; DLB
34, 100
Mackenzie, Henry 1745-1831 .... **NCLC 41**
See also DLB 39
Mackintosh, Elizabeth 1896(?)-1952
See Tey, Josephine
See also CA 110
MacLaren, James
See Grieve, C(hristopher) M(urray)
Mac Laverty, Bernard 1942- .... **CLC 31**
See also CA 116; 118; CANR 43, 88; INT
118
MacLean, Alistair (Stuart)
1922(?)-1987 .. **CLC 3, 13, 50, 63; DAM
POP**
See also CA 57-60; 121; CANR 28, 61;
MTCW 1; SATA 23; SATA-Obit 50
Maclean, Norman (Fitzroy)
1902-1990 .... **CLC 78; DAM POP; SSC
13**
See also CA 102; 132; CANR 49; DLB 206
MacLeish, Archibald 1892-1982 ... **CLC 3, 8,
14, 68; DAM POET**
See also CA 9-12R; 106; CANR 33, 63;
CDALBS; DLB 4, 7, 45; DLBY 82;
MTCW 1, 2
MacLennan, (John) Hugh
1907-1990 . **CLC 2, 14, 92; DAC; DAM
MST**
See also CA 5-8R; 142; CANR 33; DLB
68; MTCW 1, 2
MacLeod, Alistair 1936- .... **CLC 56; DAC;
DAM MST**
See also CA 123; DLB 60; MTCW 2
Macleod, Fiona
See Sharp, William
MacNeice, (Frederick) Louis
1907-1963 .... **CLC 1, 4, 10, 53; DAB;
DAM POET**
See also CA 85-88; CANR 61; DLB 10, 20;
MTCW 1, 2
MacNeill, Dand
See Fraser, George MacDonald
Macpherson, James 1736-1796 .... **LC 29**
See also Ossian
See also DLB 109
Macpherson, (Jean) Jay 1931- .... **CLC 14**
See also CA 5-8R; CANR 90; DLB 53

MacShane, Frank 1927-1999 .... **CLC 39**
See also CA 9-12R; 186; CANR 3, 33; DLB
111
Macumber, Mari
See Sandoz, Mari(e Susette)
Madach, Imre 1823-1864 .... **NCLC 19**
Madden, (Jerry) David 1933- .... **CLC 5, 15**
See also CA 1-4R; CAAS 3; CANR 4, 45;
DLB 6; MTCW 1
Maddern, Al(an)
See Ellison, Harlan (Jay)
Madhubuti, Haki R. 1942- . **CLC 6, 73; BLC
2; DAM MULT, POET; PC 5**
See also Lee, Don L.
See also BW 2, 3; CA 73-76; CANR 24,
51, 73; DLB 5, 41; DLBD 8; MTCW 2
Maepenn, Hugh
See Kuttner, Henry
Maepenn, K. H.
See Kuttner, Henry
Maeterlinck, Maurice 1862-1949 ... **TCLC 3;
DAM DRAM**
See also CA 104; 136; CANR 80; DLB 192;
SATA 66
Maginn, William 1794-1842 .... **NCLC 8**
See also DLB 110, 159
Mahapatra, Jayanta 1928- .... **CLC 33; DAM
MULT**
See also CA 73-76; CAAS 9; CANR 15,
33, 66, 87
Mahfouz, Naguib (Abdel Aziz Al-Sabilgi)
1911(?)-
See Mahfuz, Najib
See also BEST 89:2; CA 128; CANR 55;
DAM NOV; DA3; MTCW 1, 2
Mahfuz, Najib CLC 52, 55
See also Mahfouz, Naguib (Abdel Aziz Al-
Sabilgi)
See also DLBY 88
Mahon, Derek 1941- .... **CLC 27**
See also CA 113; 128; CANR 88; DLB 40
Mailer, Norman 1923- ... **CLC 1, 2, 3, 4, 5, 8,
11, 14, 28, 39, 74, 111; DA; DAB;
DAC; DAM MST, NOV, POP**
See also AAYA 31; AITN 2; CA 9-12R;
CABS 1; CANR 28, 74, 77; CDALB
1968-1988; DA3; DLB 2, 16, 28, 185;
DLBD 3; DLBY 80, 83; MTCW 1, 2
Maillet, Antonine 1929- .. **CLC 54, 118; DAC**
See also CA 115; 120; CANR 46, 74, 77;
DLB 60; INT 120; MTCW 2
Mais, Roger 1905-1955 .... **TCLC 8**
See also BW 1, 3; CA 105; 124; CANR 82;
DLB 125; MTCW 1
Maistre, Joseph de 1753-1821 .... **NCLC 37**
Maitland, Frederic William
1850-1906 .... **TCLC 65**
Maitland, Sara (Louise) 1950- .... **CLC 49**
See also CA 69-72; CANR 13, 59
Major, Clarence 1936- .... **CLC 3, 19, 48; BLC
2; DAM MULT**
See also BW 2, 3; CA 21-24R; CAAS 6;
CANR 13, 25, 53, 82; DLB 33
Major, Kevin (Gerald) 1949- . **CLC 26; DAC**
See also AAYA 16; CA 97-100; CANR 21,
38; CLR 11; DLB 60; INT CANR-21;
JRDA; MAICYA; SATA 32, 82
Maki, James
See Ozu, Yasujiro
Malabaila, Damiano
See Levi, Primo
Malamud, Bernard 1914-1986 .. **CLC 1, 2, 3,
5, 8, 9, 11, 18, 27, 44, 78, 85; DA;
DAB; DAC; DAM MST, NOV, POP;
SSC 15; WLC**
See also AAYA 16; CA 5-8R; 118; CABS
1; CANR 28, 62; CDALB 1941-1968;
DA3; DLB 2, 28, 152; DLBY 80, 86;
MTCW 1, 2

Malan, Herman
See Bosman, Herman Charles; Bosman,
Herman Charles
Malaparte, Curzio 1898-1957 .... **TCLC 52**
Malcolm, Dan
See Silverberg, Robert
Malcolm X CLC 82, 117; BLC 2; WLCS
See also Little, Malcolm
Malherbe, Francois de 1555-1628 .... **LC 5**
Mallarme, Stephane 1842-1898 ...... **NCLC 4,
41; DAM POET; PC 4**
Mallet-Joris, Francoise 1930- .... **CLC 11**
See also CA 65-68; CANR 17; DLB 83
Malley, Ern
See McAuley, James Phillip
Mallowan, Agatha Christie
See Christie, Agatha (Mary Clarissa)
Maloff, Saul 1922- .... **CLC 5**
See also CA 33-36R
Malone, Louis
See MacNeice, (Frederick) Louis
Malone, Michael (Christopher)
1942- .... **CLC 43**
See also CA 77-80; CANR 14, 32, 57
Malory, (Sir) Thomas
1410(?)-1471(?) .... **LC 11; DA; DAB;
DAC; DAM MST; WLCS**
See also CDBLB Before 1660; DLB 146;
SATA 59; SATA-Brief 33
Malouf, (George Joseph) David
1934- .... **CLC 28, 86**
See also CA 124; CANR 50, 76; MTCW 2
Malraux, (Georges-)Andre
1901-1976 .... **CLC 1, 4, 9, 13, 15, 57;
DAM NOV**
See also CA 21-22; 69-72; CANR 34, 58;
CAP 2; DA3; DLB 72; MTCW 1, 2
Malzberg, Barry N(athaniel) 1939- ... **CLC 7**
See also CA 61-64; CAAS 4; CANR 16;
DLB 8
Mamet, David (Alan) 1947- .. **CLC 9, 15, 34,
46, 91; DAM DRAM; DC 4**
See also AAYA 3; CA 81-84; CABS 3;
CANR 15, 41, 67, 72; DA3; DLB 7;
MTCW 1, 2
Mamoulian, Rouben (Zachary)
1897-1987 .... **CLC 16**
See also CA 25-28R; 124; CANR 85
Mandelstam, Osip (Emilievich)
1891(?)-1938(?) .... **TCLC 2, 6; PC 14**
See also CA 104; 150; MTCW 2
Mander, (Mary) Jane 1877-1949 ... **TCLC 31**
See also CA 162
Mandeville, John fl. 1350- .... **CMLC 19**
See also DLB 146
Mandiargues, Andre Pieyre de CLC 41
See also Pieyre de Mandiargues, Andre
See also DLB 83
Mandrake, Ethel Belle
See Thurman, Wallace (Henry)
Mangan, James Clarence
1803-1849 .... **NCLC 27**
Maniere, J.-E.
See Giraudoux, (Hippolyte) Jean
Mankiewicz, Herman (Jacob)
1897-1953 .... **TCLC 85**
See also CA 120; 169; DLB 26
Manley, (Mary) Delariviere
1672(?)-1724 .... **LC 1, 42**
See also DLB 39, 80
Mann, Abel
See Creasey, John
Mann, Emily 1952- .... **DC 7**
See also CA 130; CANR 55
Mann, (Luiz) Heinrich 1871-1950 ... **TCLC 9**
See also CA 106; 164, 181; DLB 66, 118

Mann, (Paul) Thomas 1875-1955 ... **TCLC 2, 8, 14, 21, 35, 44, 60; DA; DAB; DAC; DAM MST, NOV; SSC 5; WLC**
See also CA 104; 128; DA3; DLB 66; MTCW 1, 2

Mannheim, Karl 1893-1947 .... **TCLC 65**

Manning, David
See Faust, Frederick (Schiller)

Manning, Frederic 1887(?)-1935 ... **TCLC 25**
See also CA 124

Manning, Olivia 1915-1980 .... **CLC 5, 19**
See also CA 5-8R; 101; CANR 29; MTCW 1

Mano, D. Keith 1942- .... **CLC 2, 10**
See also CA 25-28R; CAAS 6; CANR 26, 57; DLB 6

Mansfield, Katherine -1923 .. **TCLC 2, 8, 39; DAB; SSC 9, 23, 38; WLC**
See also Beauchamp, Kathleen Mansfield
See also DLB 162

Manso, Peter 1940- .... **CLC 39**
See also CA 29-32R; CANR 44

Mantecon, Juan Jimenez
See Jimenez (Mantecon), Juan Ramon

Manton, Peter
See Creasey, John

Man Without a Spleen, A
See Chekhov, Anton (Pavlovich)

Manzoni, Alessandro 1785-1873 .... **NCLC 29**

Map, Walter 1140-1209 .... **CMLC 32**

Mapu, Abraham (ben Jekutiel)
1808-1867 .... **NCLC 18**

Mara, Sally
See Queneau, Raymond

Marat, Jean Paul 1743-1793 .... **LC 10**

Marcel, Gabriel Honore 1889-1973 . **CLC 15**
See also CA 102; 45-48; MTCW 1, 2

March, William 1893-1954 .... **TCLC 96**

Marchbanks, Samuel
See Davies, (William) Robertson

Marchi, Giacomo
See Bassani, Giorgio

Margulies, Donald CLC 76
See also DLB 228

Marie de France c. 12th cent. - ..... **CMLC 8; PC 22**
See also DLB 208

Marie de l'Incarnation 1599-1672 ...... **LC 10**

Marier, Captain Victor
See Griffith, D(avid Lewelyn) W(ark)

Mariner, Scott
See Pohl, Frederik

Marinetti, Filippo Tommaso
1876-1944 .... **TCLC 10**
See also CA 107; DLB 114

Marivaux, Pierre Carlet de Chamblain de
1688-1763 .... **LC 4; DC 7**

Markandaya, Kamala CLC 8, 38
See also Taylor, Kamala (Purnaiya)

Markfield, Wallace 1926- .... **CLC 8**
See also CA 69-72; CAAS 3; DLB 2, 28

Markham, Edwin 1852-1940 .... **TCLC 47**
See also CA 160; DLB 54, 186

Markham, Robert
See Amis, Kingsley (William)

Marks, J
See Highwater, Jamake (Mamake)

Marks-Highwater, J
See Highwater, Jamake (Mamake)

Markson, David M(errill) 1927- .... **CLC 67**
See also CA 49-52; CANR 1, 91

Marley, Bob CLC 17
See also Marley, Robert Nesta

Marley, Robert Nesta 1945-1981
See Marley, Bob
See also CA 107; 103

Marlowe, Christopher 1564-1593 ...... **LC 22, 47; DA; DAB; DAC; DAM DRAM, MST; DC 1; WLC**
See also CDBLB Before 1660; DA3; DLB 62

Marlowe, Stephen 1928-
See Queen, Ellery
See also CA 13-16R; CANR 6, 55

Marmontel, Jean-Francois 1723-1799 .. **LC 2**

Marquand, John P(hillips)
1893-1960 .... **CLC 2, 10**
See also CA 85-88; CANR 73; DLB 9, 102; MTCW 2

Marques, Rene 1919-1979 ..... **CLC 96; DAM MULT; HLC 2**
See also CA 97-100; 85-88; CANR 78; DLB 113; HW 1, 2

Marquez, Gabriel (Jose) Garcia
See Garcia Marquez, Gabriel (Jose)

Marquis, Don(ald Robert Perry)
1878-1937 .... **TCLC 7**
See also CA 104; 166; DLB 11, 25

Marric, J. J.
See Creasey, John

Marryat, Frederick 1792-1848 .... **NCLC 3**
See also DLB 21, 163

Marsden, James
See Creasey, John

Marsh, Edward 1872-1953 .... **TCLC 99**

Marsh, (Edith) Ngaio 1899-1982 .... **CLC 7, 53; DAM POP**
See also CA 9-12R; CANR 6, 58; DLB 77; MTCW 1, 2

Marshall, Garry 1934- .... **CLC 17**
See also AAYA 3; CA 111; SATA 60

Marshall, Paule 1929- .. **CLC 27, 72; BLC 3; DAM MULT; SSC 3**
See also BW 2, 3; CA 77-80; CANR 25, 73; DA3; DLB 33, 157, 227; MTCW 1, 2

Marshallik
See Zangwill, Israel

Marsten, Richard
See Hunter, Evan

Marston, John 1576-1634 .... **LC 33; DAM DRAM**
See also DLB 58, 172

Martha, Henry
See Harris, Mark

Marti (y Perez), Jose (Julian)
1853-1895 ...... **NCLC 63; DAM MULT; HLC 2**
See also HW 2

Martial c. 40-c. 104 .... **CMLC 35; PC 10**
See also DLB 211

Martin, Ken
See Hubbard, L(afayette) Ron(ald)

Martin, Richard
See Creasey, John

Martin, Steve 1945- .... **CLC 30**
See also CA 97-100; CANR 30; MTCW 1

Martin, Valerie 1948- .... **CLC 89**
See also BEST 90:2; CA 85-88; CANR 49, 89

Martin, Violet Florence
1862-1915 .... **TCLC 51**

Martin, Webber
See Silverberg, Robert

Martindale, Patrick Victor
See White, Patrick (Victor Martindale)

Martin du Gard, Roger
1881-1958 .... **TCLC 24**
See also CA 118; CANR 94; DLB 65

Martineau, Harriet 1802-1876 .... **NCLC 26**
See also DLB 21, 55, 159, 163, 166, 190; YABC 2

Martines, Julia
See O'Faolain, Julia

Martinez, Enrique Gonzalez
See Gonzalez Martinez, Enrique

Martinez, Jacinto Benavente y
See Benavente (y Martinez), Jacinto

Martinez Ruiz, Jose 1873-1967
See Azorin; Ruiz, Jose Martinez
See also CA 93-96; HW 1

Martinez Sierra, Gregorio
1881-1947 .... **TCLC 6**
See also CA 115

Martinez Sierra, Maria (de la O'LeJarraga)
1874-1974 .... **TCLC 6**
See also CA 115

Martinsen, Martin
See Follett, Ken(neth Martin)

Martinson, Harry (Edmund)
1904-1978 .... **CLC 14**
See also CA 77-80; CANR 34

Marut, Ret
See Traven, B.

Marut, Robert
See Traven, B.

Marvell, Andrew 1621-1678 .. **LC 4, 43; DA; DAB; DAC; DAM MST, POET; PC 10; WLC**
See also CDBLB 1660-1789; DLB 131

Marx, Karl (Heinrich) 1818-1883 . **NCLC 17**
See also DLB 129

Masaoka Shiki TCLC 18
See also Masaoka Tsunenori

Masaoka Tsunenori 1867-1902
See Masaoka Shiki
See also CA 117

Masefield, John (Edward)
1878-1967 ..... **CLC 11, 47; DAM POET**
See also CA 19-20; 25-28R; CANR 33; CAP 2; CDBLB 1890-1914; DLB 10, 19, 153, 160; MTCW 1, 2; SATA 19

Maso, Carole 19(?)- .... **CLC 44**
See also CA 170

Mason, Bobbie Ann 1940- ... **CLC 28, 43, 82; SSC 4**
See also AAYA 5; CA 53-56; CANR 11, 31, 58, 83; CDALBS; DA3; DLB 173; DLBY 87; INT CANR-31; MTCW 1, 2

Mason, Ernst
See Pohl, Frederik

Mason, Lee W.
See Malzberg, Barry N(athaniel)

Mason, Nick 1945- .... **CLC 35**

Mason, Tally
See Derleth, August (William)

Mass, William
See Gibson, William

Master Lao
See Lao Tzu

Masters, Edgar Lee 1868-1950 .... **TCLC 2, 25; DA; DAC; DAM MST, POET; PC 1; WLCS**
See also CA 104; 133; CDALB 1865-1917; DLB 54; MTCW 1, 2

Masters, Hilary 1928- .... **CLC 48**
See also CA 25-28R; CANR 13, 47

Mastrosimone, William 19(?)- .... **CLC 36**
See also CA 186

Mathe, Albert
See Camus, Albert

Mather, Cotton 1663-1728 .... **LC 38**
See also CDALB 1640-1865; DLB 24, 30, 140

Mather, Increase 1639-1723 .... **LC 38**
See also DLB 24

Matheson, Richard Burton 1926- .... **CLC 37**
See also AAYA 31; CA 97-100; CANR 88; DLB 8, 44; INT 97-100

Mathews, Harry 1930- .... **CLC 6, 52**
See also CA 21-24R; CAAS 6; CANR 18, 40

McKuen, Rod 1933- .... **CLC 1, 3**
  See also AITN 1; CA 41-44R; CANR 40
McLoughlin, R. B.
  See Mencken, H(enry) L(ouis)
McLuhan, (Herbert) Marshall
  1911-1980 .... **CLC 37, 83**
  See also CA 9-12R; 102; CANR 12, 34, 61;
  DLB 88; INT CANR-12; MTCW 1, 2
McMillan, Terry (L.) 1951- .... **CLC 50, 61,**
  112; BLCS; DAM MULT, NOV, POP
  See also AAYA 21; BW 2, 3; CA 140;
  CANR 60; DA3; MTCW 2
McMurtry, Larry (Jeff) 1936- .. **CLC 2, 3, 7,**
  11, 27, 44, 127; DAM NOV, POP
  See also AAYA 15; AITN 2; BEST 89:2;
  CA 5-8R; CANR 19, 43, 64; CDALB
  1968-1988; DA3; DLB 2, 143; DLBY 80,
  87; MTCW 1, 2
McNally, T. M. 1961- .... **CLC 82**
McNally, Terrence 1939- ... **CLC 4, 7, 41, 91;**
  DAM DRAM
  See also CA 45-48; CANR 2, 56; DA3;
  DLB 7; MTCW 2
McNamer, Deirdre 1950- .... **CLC 70**
McNeal, Tom CLC 119
McNeile, Herman Cyril 1888-1937
  See Sapper
  See also CA 184; DLB 77
McNickle, (William) D'Arcy
  1904-1977 .... **CLC 89; DAM MULT**
  See also CA 9-12R; 85-88; CANR 5, 45;
  DLB 175, 212; NNAL; SATA-Obit 22
McPhee, John (Angus) 1931- .... **CLC 36**
  See also BEST 90:1; CA 65-68; CANR 20,
  46, 64, 69; DLB 185; MTCW 1, 2
McPherson, James Alan 1943- .. **CLC 19, 77;**
  BLCS
  See also BW 1, 3; CA 25-28R; CAAS 17;
  CANR 24, 74; DLB 38; MTCW 1, 2
McPherson, William (Alexander)
  1933- .... **CLC 34**
  See also CA 69-72; CANR 28; INT
  CANR-28
McTaggart, J. McT. Ellis
  See McTaggart, John McTaggart Ellis
McTaggart, John McTaggart Ellis
  1866-1925 .... **TCLC 105**
  See also CA 120
Mead, George Herbert 1873-1958 . **TCLC 89**
Mead, Margaret 1901-1978 .... **CLC 37**
  See also AITN 1; CA 1-4R; 81-84; CANR
  4; DA3; MTCW 1, 2; SATA-Obit 20
Meaker, Marijane (Agnes) 1927-
  See Kerr, M. E.
  See also CA 107; CANR 37, 63; INT 107;
  JRDA; MAICYA; MTCW 1; SATA 20,
  61, 99; SATA-Essay 111
Medoff, Mark (Howard) 1940- ... **CLC 6, 23;**
  DAM DRAM
  See also AITN 1; CA 53-56; CANR 5; DLB
  7; INT CANR-5
Medvedev, P. N.
  See Bakhtin, Mikhail Mikhailovich
Meged, Aharon
  See Megged, Aharon
Meged, Aron
  See Megged, Aharon
Megged, Aharon 1920- .... **CLC 9**
  See also CA 49-52; CAAS 13; CANR 1
Mehta, Ved (Parkash) 1934- .... **CLC 37**
  See also CA 1-4R; CANR 2, 23, 69; MTCW
  1
Melanter
  See Blackmore, R(ichard) D(oddridge)
Melies, Georges 1861-1938 .... **TCLC 81**
Melikow, Loris
  See Hofmannsthal, Hugo von
Melmoth, Sebastian
  See Wilde, Oscar (Fingal O'Flahertie Wills)

Meltzer, Milton 1915- .... **CLC 26**
  See also AAYA 8; CA 13-16R; CANR 38,
  92; CLR 13; DLB 61; JRDA; MAICYA;
  SAAS 1; SATA 1, 50, 80
Melville, Herman 1819-1891 ..... **NCLC 3, 12,**
  29, 45, 49, 91, 93; DA; DAB; DAC;
  DAM MST, NOV; SSC 1, 17; WLC
  See also AAYA 25; CDALB 1640-1865;
  DA3; DLB 3, 74; SATA 59
Menander c. 342B.C.-c. 292B.C. ... **CMLC 9;**
  DAM DRAM; DC 3
  See also DLB 176
Menchu, Rigoberta 1959-
  See also CA 175; HLCS 2
Mencken, H(enry) L(ouis)
  1880-1956 .... **TCLC 13**
  See also CA 105; 125; CDALB 1917-1929;
  DLB 11, 29, 63, 137, 222; MTCW 1, 2
Mendelsohn, Jane 1965- .... **CLC 99**
  See also CA 154; CANR 94
Mercer, David 1928-1980 .... **CLC 5; DAM**
  DRAM
  See also CA 9-12R; 102; CANR 23; DLB
  13; MTCW 1
Merchant, Paul
  See Ellison, Harlan (Jay)
Meredith, George 1828-1909 .. **TCLC 17, 43;**
  DAM POET
  See also CA 117; 153; CANR 80; CDBLB
  1832-1890; DLB 18, 35, 57, 159
Meredith, William (Morris) 1919- .... **CLC 4,**
  13, 22, 55; DAM POET; PC 28
  See also CA 9-12R; CAAS 14; CANR 6,
  40; DLB 5
Merezhkovsky, Dmitry Sergeyevich
  1865-1941 .... **TCLC 29**
  See also CA 169
Merimee, Prosper 1803-1870 ... **NCLC 6, 65;**
  SSC 7
  See also DLB 119, 192
Merkin, Daphne 1954- .... **CLC 44**
  See also CA 123
Merlin, Arthur
  See Blish, James (Benjamin)
Merrill, James (Ingram) 1926-1995 .. **CLC 2,**
  3, 6, 8, 13, 18, 34, 91; DAM POET; PC
  28
  See also CA 13-16R; 147; CANR 10, 49,
  63; DA3; DLB 5, 165; DLBY 85; INT
  CANR-10; MTCW 1, 2
Merriman, Alex
  See Silverberg, Robert
Merriman, Brian 1747-1805 .... **NCLC 70**
Merritt, E. B.
  See Waddington, Miriam
Merton, Thomas 1915-1968 ..... **CLC 1, 3, 11,**
  34, 83; PC 10
  See also CA 5-8R; 25-28R; CANR 22, 53;
  DA3; DLB 48; DLBY 81; MTCW 1, 2
Merwin, W(illiam) S(tanley) 1927- ... **CLC 1,**
  2, 3, 5, 8, 13, 18, 45, 88; DAM POET
  See also CA 13-16R; CANR 15, 51; DA3;
  DLB 5, 169; INT CANR-15; MTCW 1, 2
Metcalf, John 1938- .... **CLC 37; SSC 43**
  See also CA 113; DLB 60
Metcalf, Suzanne
  See Baum, L(yman) Frank
Mew, Charlotte (Mary) 1869-1928 .. **TCLC 8**
  See also CA 105; DLB 19, 135
Mewshaw, Michael 1943- .... **CLC 9**
  See also CA 53-56; CANR 7, 47; DLBY 80
Meyer, Conrad Ferdinand
  1825-1905 .... **NCLC 81**
  See also DLB 129
Meyer, June
  See Jordan, June
Meyer, Lynn
  See Slavitt, David R(ytman)

Meyer-Meyrink, Gustav 1868-1932
  See Meyrink, Gustav
  See also CA 117
Meyers, Jeffrey 1939- .... **CLC 39**
  See also CA 73-76; CAAE 186; CANR 54;
  DLB 111
Meynell, Alice (Christina Gertrude
  Thompson) 1847-1922 .... **TCLC 6**
  See also CA 104; 177; DLB 19, 98
Meyrink, Gustav TCLC 21
  See also Meyer-Meyrink, Gustav
  See also DLB 81
Michaels, Leonard 1933- .... **CLC 6, 25; SSC**
  16
  See also CA 61-64; CANR 21, 62; DLB
  130; MTCW 1
Michaux, Henri 1899-1984 .... **CLC 8, 19**
  See also CA 85-88; 114
Micheaux, Oscar (Devereaux)
  1884-1951 .... **TCLC 76**
  See also BW 3; CA 174; DLB 50
Michelangelo 1475-1564 .... **LC 12**
Michelet, Jules 1798-1874 .... **NCLC 31**
Michels, Robert 1876-1936 .... **TCLC 88**
Michener, James A(lbert)
  1907(?)-1997 .... **CLC 1, 5, 11, 29, 60,**
  109; DAM NOV, POP
  See also AAYA 27; AITN 1; BEST 90:1;
  CA 5-8R; 161; CANR 21, 45, 68; DA3;
  DLB 6; MTCW 1, 2
Mickiewicz, Adam 1798-1855 .... **NCLC 3**
Middleton, Christopher 1926- .... **CLC 13**
  See also CA 13-16R; CANR 29, 54; DLB
  40
Middleton, Richard (Barham)
  1882-1911 .... **TCLC 56**
  See also CA 187; DLB 156
Middleton, Stanley 1919- .... **CLC 7, 38**
  See also CA 25-28R; CAAS 23; CANR 21,
  46, 81; DLB 14
Middleton, Thomas 1580-1627 .... **LC 33;**
  DAM DRAM, MST; DC 5
  See also DLB 58
Migueis, Jose Rodrigues 1901- .... **CLC 10**
Mikszath, Kalman 1847-1910 .... **TCLC 31**
  See also CA 170
Miles, Jack CLC 100
Miles, Josephine (Louise)
  1911-1985 .. **CLC 1, 2, 14, 34, 39; DAM**
  POET
  See also CA 1-4R; 116; CANR 2, 55; DLB
  48
Militant
  See Sandburg, Carl (August)
Mill, John Stuart 1806-1873 .... **NCLC 11, 58**
  See also CDBLB 1832-1890; DLB 55, 190
Millar, Kenneth 1915-1983 ... **CLC 14; DAM**
  POP
  See also Macdonald, Ross
  See also CA 9-12R; 110; CANR 16, 63;
  DA3; DLB 2, 226; DLBD 6; DLBY 83;
  MTCW 1, 2
Millay, E. Vincent
  See Millay, Edna St. Vincent
Millay, Edna St. Vincent
  1892-1950 .... **TCLC 4, 49; DA; DAB;**
  DAC; DAM MST, POET; PC 6;
  WLCS
  See also CA 104; 130; CDALB 1917-1929;
  DA3; DLB 45; MTCW 1, 2
Miller, Arthur 1915- ...... **CLC 1, 2, 6, 10, 15,**
  26, 47, 78; DA; DAB; DAC; DAM
  DRAM, MST; DC 1; WLC
  See also AAYA 15; AITN 1; CA 1-4R;
  CABS 3; CANR 2, 30, 54, 76; CDALB
  1941-1968; DA3; DLB 7; MTCW 1, 2

Moore, Marianne (Craig)
1887-1972 .... **CLC 1, 2, 4, 8, 10, 13, 19, 47; DA; DAB; DAC; DAM MST, POET; PC 4; WLCS**
See also CA 1-4R; 33-36R; CANR 3, 61; CDALB 1929-1941; DA3; DLB 45; DLBD 7; MTCW 1, 2; SATA 20

Moore, Marie Lorena 1957-
See Moore, Lorrie
See also CA 116; CANR 39, 83; DLB 234

Moore, Thomas 1779-1852 .... **NCLC 6**
See also DLB 96, 144

Moorhouse, Frank 1938- .... **SSC 40**
See also CA 118; CANR 92

Mora, Pat(ricia) 1942-
See also CA 129; CANR 57, 81; CLR 58; DAM MULT; DLB 209; HLC 2; HW 1, 2; SATA 92

Moraga, Cherrie 1952- .... **CLC 126; DAM MULT**
See also CA 131; CANR 66; DLB 82; HW 1, 2

Morand, Paul 1888-1976 .... **CLC 41; SSC 22**
See also CA 184; 69-72; DLB 65

Morante, Elsa 1918-1985 .... **CLC 8, 47**
See also CA 85-88; 117; CANR 35; DLB 177; MTCW 1, 2

Moravia, Alberto 1907-1990 .... **CLC 2, 7, 11, 27, 46; SSC 26**
See also Pincherle, Alberto
See also DLB 177; MTCW 2

More, Hannah 1745-1833 .... **NCLC 27**
See also DLB 107, 109, 116, 158

More, Henry 1614-1687 .... **LC 9**
See also DLB 126

More, Sir Thomas 1478-1535 .... **LC 10, 32**

Moreas, Jean TCLC 18
See also Papadiamantopoulos, Johannes

Morgan, Berry 1919- .... **CLC 6**
See also CA 49-52; DLB 6

Morgan, Claire
See Highsmith, (Mary) Patricia

Morgan, Edwin (George) 1920- .... **CLC 31**
See also CA 5-8R; CANR 3, 43, 90; DLB 27

Morgan, (George) Frederick 1922- .. **CLC 23**
See also CA 17-20R; CANR 21

Morgan, Harriet
See Mencken, H(enry) L(ouis)

Morgan, Jane
See Cooper, James Fenimore

Morgan, Janet 1945- .... **CLC 39**
See also CA 65-68

Morgan, Lady 1776(?)-1859 .... **NCLC 29**
See also DLB 116, 158

Morgan, Robin (Evonne) 1941- .... **CLC 2**
See also CA 69-72; CANR 29, 68; MTCW 1; SATA 80

Morgan, Scott
See Kuttner, Henry

Morgan, Seth 1949(?)-1990 .... **CLC 65**
See also CA 185; 132

Morgenstern, Christian 1871-1914 .. **TCLC 8**
See also CA 105

Morgenstern, S.
See Goldman, William (W.)

Moricz, Zsigmond 1879-1942 .... **TCLC 33**
See also CA 165

Morike, Eduard (Friedrich)
1804-1875 .... **NCLC 10**
See also DLB 133

Moritz, Karl Philipp 1756-1793 .... **LC 2**
See also DLB 94

Morland, Peter Henry
See Faust, Frederick (Schiller)

Morley, Christopher (Darlington)
1890-1957 .... **TCLC 87**
See also CA 112; DLB 9

Morren, Theophil
See Hofmannsthal, Hugo von

Morris, Bill 1952- .... **CLC 76**

Morris, Julian
See West, Morris L(anglo)

Morris, Steveland Judkins 1950(?)-
See Wonder, Stevie
See also CA 111

Morris, William 1834-1896 .... **NCLC 4**
See also CDBLB 1832-1890; DLB 18, 35, 57, 156, 178, 184

Morris, Wright 1910-1998 .. **CLC 1, 3, 7, 18, 37**
See also CA 9-12R; 167; CANR 21, 81; DLB 2, 206; DLBY 81; MTCW 1, 2

Morrison, Arthur 1863-1945 .... **TCLC 72; SSC 40**
See also CA 120; 157; DLB 70, 135, 197

Morrison, Chloe Anthony Wofford
See Morrison, Toni

Morrison, James Douglas 1943-1971
See Morrison, Jim
See also CA 73-76; CANR 40

Morrison, Jim CLC 17
See also Morrison, James Douglas

Morrison, Toni 1931- . **CLC 4, 10, 22, 55, 81, 87; BLC 3; DA; DAB; DAC; DAM MST, MULT, NOV, POP**
See also AAYA 1, 22; BW 2, 3; CA 29-32R; CANR 27, 42, 67; CDALB 1968-1988; DA3; DLB 6, 33, 143; DLBY 81; MTCW 1, 2; SATA 57

Morrison, Van 1945- .... **CLC 21**
See also CA 116; 168

Morrissy, Mary 1958- .... **CLC 99**

Mortimer, John (Clifford) 1923- ..... **CLC 28, 43; DAM DRAM, POP**
See also CA 13-16R; CANR 21, 69; CD-BLB 1960 to Present; DA3; DLB 13; INT CANR-21; MTCW 1, 2

Mortimer, Penelope (Ruth)
1918-1999 .... **CLC 5**
See also CA 57-60; 187; CANR 45, 88

Morton, Anthony
See Creasey, John

Mosca, Gaetano 1858-1941 .... **TCLC 75**

Mosher, Howard Frank 1943- .... **CLC 62**
See also CA 139; CANR 65

Mosley, Nicholas 1923- .... **CLC 43, 70**
See also CA 69-72; CANR 41, 60; DLB 14, 207

Mosley, Walter 1952- .... **CLC 97; BLCS; DAM MULT, POP**
See also AAYA 17; BW 2; CA 142; CANR 57, 92; DA3; MTCW 2

Moss, Howard 1922-1987 ...... **CLC 7, 14, 45, 50; DAM POET**
See also CA 1-4R; 123; CANR 1, 44; DLB 5

Mossgiel, Rab
See Burns, Robert

Motion, Andrew (Peter) 1952- .... **CLC 47**
See also CA 146; CANR 90; DLB 40

Motley, Willard (Francis)
1909-1965 .... **CLC 18**
See also BW 1; CA 117; 106; CANR 88; DLB 76, 143

Motoori, Norinaga 1730-1801 .... **NCLC 45**

Mott, Michael (Charles Alston)
1930- .... **CLC 15, 34**
See also CA 5-8R; CAAS 7; CANR 7, 29

Mountain Wolf Woman 1884-1960 .. **CLC 92**
See also CA 144; CANR 90; NNAL

Moure, Erin 1955- .... **CLC 88**
See also CA 113; DLB 60

Mowat, Farley (McGill) 1921- .... **CLC 26; DAC; DAM MST**
See also AAYA 1; CA 1-4R; CANR 4, 24, 42, 68; CLR 20; DLB 68; INT CANR-24; JRDA; MAICYA; MTCW 1, 2; SATA 3, 55

Mowatt, Anna Cora 1819-1870 ..... **NCLC 74**

Moyers, Bill 1934- .... **CLC 74**
See also AITN 2; CA 61-64; CANR 31, 52

Mphahlele, Es'kia
See Mphahlele, Ezekiel
See also DLB 125, 225

Mphahlele, Ezekiel 1919- .... **CLC 25, 133; BLC 3; DAM MULT**
See also Mphahlele, Es'kia
See also BW 2, 3; CA 81-84; CANR 26, 76; DA3; DLB 225; MTCW 2; SATA 119

Mqhayi, S(amuel) E(dward) K(rune Loliwe)
1875-1945 ...... **TCLC 25; BLC 3; DAM MULT**
See also CA 153; CANR 87

Mrozek, Slawomir 1930- .... **CLC 3, 13**
See also CA 13-16R; CAAS 10; CANR 29; DLB 232; MTCW 1

Mrs. Belloc-Lowndes
See Lowndes, Marie Adelaide (Belloc)

M'Taggart, John M'Taggart Ellis
See McTaggart, John McTaggart Ellis

Mtwa, Percy (?)- .... **CLC 47**

Mueller, Lisel 1924- .... **CLC 13, 51; PC 33**
See also CA 93-96; DLB 105

Muir, Edwin 1887-1959 .... **TCLC 2, 87**
See also CA 104; DLB 20, 100, 191

Muir, John 1838-1914 .... **TCLC 28**
See also CA 165; DLB 186

Mujica Lainez, Manuel 1910-1984 ... **CLC 31**
See also Lainez, Manuel Mujica
See also CA 81-84; 112; CANR 32; HW 1

Mukherjee, Bharati 1940- .... **CLC 53, 115; DAM NOV; SSC 38**
See also BEST 89:2; CA 107; CANR 45, 72; DLB 60; MTCW 1, 2

Muldoon, Paul 1951- .... **CLC 32, 72; DAM POET**
See also CA 113; 129; CANR 52, 91; DLB 40; INT 129

Mulisch, Harry 1927- .... **CLC 42**
See also CA 9-12R; CANR 6, 26, 56

Mull, Martin 1943- .... **CLC 17**
See also CA 105

Muller, Wilhelm NCLC 73

Mulock, Dinah Maria
See Craik, Dinah Maria (Mulock)

Munford, Robert 1737(?)-1783 .... **LC 5**
See also DLB 31

Mungo, Raymond 1946- .... **CLC 72**
See also CA 49-52; CANR 2

Munro, Alice 1931- .... **CLC 6, 10, 19, 50, 95; DAC; DAM MST, NOV; SSC 3; WLCS**
See also AITN 2; CA 33-36R; CANR 33, 53, 75; DA3; DLB 53; MTCW 1, 2; SATA 29

Munro, H(ector) H(ugh) 1870-1916
See Saki
See also CA 104; 130; CDBLB 1890-1914; DA; DAB; DAC; DAM MST, NOV; DA3; DLB 34, 162; MTCW 1, 2; WLC

Murdoch, (Jean) Iris 1919-1999 ... **CLC 1, 2, 3, 4, 6, 8, 11, 15, 22, 31, 51; DAB; DAC; DAM MST, NOV**
See also CA 13-16R; 179; CANR 8, 43, 68; CDBLB 1960 to Present; DA3; DLB 14, 194, 233; INT CANR-8; MTCW 1, 2

Murfree, Mary Noailles 1850-1922 ... **SSC 22**
See also CA 122; 176; DLB 12, 74

Murnau, Friedrich Wilhelm
See Plumpe, Friedrich Wilhelm

Papadiamantopoulos, Johannes 1856-1910
See Moreas, Jean
See also CA 117

Papini, Giovanni 1881-1956 .... **TCLC 22**
See also CA 121; 180

Paracelsus 1493-1541 .... **LC 14**
See also DLB 179

Parasol, Peter
See Stevens, Wallace

Pardo Bazan, Emilia 1851-1921 .... **SSC 30**

Pareto, Vilfredo 1848-1923 .... **TCLC 69**
See also CA 175

Paretsky, Sara 1947- .. **CLC 135; DAM POP**
See also AAYA 30; BEST 90:3; CA 125; 129; CANR 59; DA3; INT 129

Parfenie, Maria
See Codrescu, Andrei

Parini, Jay (Lee) 1948- .... **CLC 54, 133**
See also CA 97-100; CAAS 16; CANR 32, 87

Park, Jordan
See Kornbluth, C(yril) M.; Pohl, Frederik

Park, Robert E(zra) 1864-1944 ..... **TCLC 73**
See also CA 122; 165

Parker, Bert
See Ellison, Harlan (Jay)

Parker, Dorothy (Rothschild)
1893-1967 .... **CLC 15, 68; DAM POET; PC 28; SSC 2**
See also CA 19-20; 25-28R; CAP 2; DA3; DLB 11, 45, 86; MTCW 1, 2

Parker, Robert B(rown) 1932- .... **CLC 27; DAM NOV, POP**
See also AAYA 28; BEST 89:4; CA 49-52; CANR 1, 26, 52, 89; INT CANR-26; MTCW 1

Parkin, Frank 1940- .... **CLC 43**
See also CA 147

Parkman, Francis Jr., Jr.
1823-1893 .... **NCLC 12**
See also DLB 1, 30, 186, 235

Parks, Gordon (Alexander Buchanan)
1912- .... **CLC 1, 16; BLC 3; DAM MULT**
See also AAYA 36; AITN 2; BW 2, 3; CA 41-44R; CANR 26, 66; DA3; DLB 33; MTCW 2; SATA 8, 108

Parmenides c. 515B.C.-c.
450B.C. .... **CMLC 22**
See also DLB 176

Parnell, Thomas 1679-1718 .... **LC 3**
See also DLB 94

Parra, Nicanor 1914- ...... **CLC 2, 102; DAM MULT; HLC 2**
See also CA 85-88; CANR 32; HW 1; MTCW 1

Parra Sanojo, Ana Teresa de la 1890-1936
See also HLCS 2

Parrish, Mary Frances
See Fisher, M(ary) F(rances) K(ennedy)

Parson
See Coleridge, Samuel Taylor

Parson Lot
See Kingsley, Charles

Parton, Sara Payson Willis
1811-1872 .... **NCLC 86**
See also DLB 43, 74

Partridge, Anthony
See Oppenheim, E(dward) Phillips

Pascal, Blaise 1623-1662 .... **LC 35**

Pascoli, Giovanni 1855-1912 .... **TCLC 45**
See also CA 170

Pasolini, Pier Paolo 1922-1975 .. **CLC 20, 37, 106; PC 17**
See also CA 93-96; 61-64; CANR 63; DLB 128, 177; MTCW 1

Pasquini
See Silone, Ignazio

Pastan, Linda (Olenik) 1932- .... **CLC 27; DAM POET**
See also CA 61-64; CANR 18, 40, 61; DLB 5

Pasternak, Boris (Leonidovich)
1890-1960 .... **CLC 7, 10, 18, 63; DA; DAB; DAC; DAM MST, NOV, POET; PC 6; SSC 31; WLC**
See also CA 127; 116; DA3; MTCW 1, 2

Patchen, Kenneth 1911-1972 .. **CLC 1, 2, 18; DAM POET**
See also CA 1-4R; 33-36R; CANR 3, 35; DLB 16, 48; MTCW 1

Pater, Walter (Horatio) 1839-1894 . **NCLC 7, 90**
See also CDBLB 1832-1890; DLB 57, 156

Paterson, A(ndrew) B(arton)
1864-1941 .... **TCLC 32**
See also CA 155; DLB 230; SATA 97

Paterson, Katherine (Womeldorf)
1932- .... **CLC 12, 30**
See also AAYA 1, 31; CA 21-24R; CANR 28, 59; CLR 7, 50; DLB 52; JRDA; MAI-CYA; MTCW 1; SATA 13, 53, 92

Patmore, Coventry Kersey Dighton
1823-1896 .... **NCLC 9**
See also DLB 35, 98

Paton, Alan (Stewart) 1903-1988 ...... **CLC 4, 10, 25, 55, 106; DA; DAB; DAC; DAM MST, NOV; WLC**
See also AAYA 26; CA 13-16; 125; CANR 22; CAP 1; DA3; DLB 225; DLBD 17; MTCW 1, 2; SATA 11; SATA-Obit 56

Paton Walsh, Gillian 1937- .... **CLC 35**
See also Walsh, Jill Paton
See also AAYA 11; CANR 38, 83; CLR 2, 65; DLB 161; JRDA; MAICYA; SAAS 3; SATA 4, 72, 109

Paton Walsh, Jill
See Paton Walsh, Gillian

Patton, George S. 1885-1945 .... **TCLC 79**

Paulding, James Kirke 1778-1860 ... **NCLC 2**
See also DLB 3, 59, 74

Paulin, Thomas Neilson 1949-
See Paulin, Tom
See also CA 123; 128

Paulin, Tom **CLC 37**
See also Paulin, Thomas Neilson
See also DLB 40

Pausanias c. 1st cent. - .... **CMLC 36**

Paustovsky, Konstantin (Georgievich)
1892-1968 .... **CLC 40**
See also CA 93-96; 25-28R

Pavese, Cesare 1908-1950 .. **TCLC 3; PC 13; SSC 19**
See also CA 104; 169; DLB 128, 177

Pavic, Milorad 1929- .... **CLC 60**
See also CA 136; DLB 181

Pavlov, Ivan Petrovich 1849-1936 . **TCLC 91**
See also CA 118; 180

Payne, Alan
See Jakes, John (William)

Paz, Gil
See Lugones, Leopoldo

Paz, Octavio 1914-1998 . **CLC 3, 4, 6, 10, 19, 51, 65, 119; DA; DAB; DAC; DAM MST, MULT, POET; HLC 2; PC 1; WLC**
See also CA 73-76; 165; CANR 32, 65; DA3; DLBY 90, 98; HW 1, 2; MTCW 1, 2

p'Bitek, Okot 1931-1982 .... **CLC 96; BLC 3; DAM MULT**
See also BW 2, 3; CA 124; 107; CANR 82; DLB 125; MTCW 1, 2

Peacock, Molly 1947- .... **CLC 60**
See also CA 103; CAAS 21; CANR 52, 84; DLB 120

Peacock, Thomas Love
1785-1866 .... **NCLC 22**
See also DLB 96, 116

Peake, Mervyn 1911-1968 .... **CLC 7, 54**
See also CA 5-8R; 25-28R; CANR 3; DLB 15, 160; MTCW 1; SATA 23

Pearce, Philippa **CLC 21**
See also Christie, (Ann) Philippa
See also CLR 9; DLB 161; MAICYA; SATA 1, 67

Pearl, Eric
See Elman, Richard (Martin)

Pearson, T(homas) R(eid) 1956- .... **CLC 39**
See also CA 120; 130; INT 130

Peck, Dale 1967- .... **CLC 81**
See also CA 146; CANR 72

Peck, John 1941- .... **CLC 3**
See also CA 49-52; CANR 3

Peck, Richard (Wayne) 1934- .... **CLC 21**
See also AAYA 1, 24; CA 85-88; CANR 19, 38; CLR 15; INT CANR-19; JRDA; MAICYA; SAAS 2; SATA 18, 55, 97; SATA-Essay 110

Peck, Robert Newton 1928- .... **CLC 17; DA; DAC; DAM MST**
See also AAYA 3; CA 81-84; 182; CAAE 182; CANR 31, 63; CLR 45; JRDA; MAI-CYA; SAAS 1; SATA 21, 62, 111; SATA-Essay 108

Peckinpah, (David) Sam(uel)
1925-1984 .... **CLC 20**
See also CA 109; 114; CANR 82

Pedersen, Knut 1859-1952
See Hamsun, Knut
See also CA 104; 119; CANR 63; MTCW 1, 2

Peeslake, Gaffer
See Durrell, Lawrence (George)

Peguy, Charles Pierre 1873-1914 ... **TCLC 10**
See also CA 107

Peirce, Charles Sanders
1839-1914 .... **TCLC 81**

Pellicer, Carlos 1900(?)-1977
See also CA 153; 69-72; HLCS 2; HW 1

Pena, Ramon del Valle y
See Valle-Inclan, Ramon (Maria) del

Pendennis, Arthur Esquir
See Thackeray, William Makepeace

Penn, William 1644-1718 .... **LC 25**
See also DLB 24

PEPECE
See Prado (Calvo), Pedro

Pepys, Samuel 1633-1703 ..... **LC 11, 58; DA; DAB; DAC; DAM MST; WLC**
See also CDBLB 1660-1789; DA3; DLB 101

Percy, Thomas 1729-1811 .... **NCLC 95**
See also DLB 104

Percy, Walker 1916-1990 .... **CLC 2, 3, 6, 8, 14, 18, 47, 65; DAM NOV, POP**
See also CA 1-4R; 131; CANR 1, 23, 64; DA3; DLB 2; DLBY 80, 90; MTCW 1, 2

Percy, William Alexander
1885-1942 .... **TCLC 84**
See also CA 163; MTCW 2

Perec, Georges 1936-1982 .... **CLC 56, 116**
See also CA 141; DLB 83

Pereda (y Sanchez de Porrua), Jose Maria de 1833-1906 .... **TCLC 16**
See also CA 117

Pereda y Porrua, Jose Maria de
See Pereda (y Sanchez de Porrua), Jose Maria de

Peregoy, George Weems
See Mencken, H(enry) L(ouis)

Rawlings, Marjorie Kinnan
1896-1953 .... **TCLC 4**
See also AAYA 20; CA 104; 137; CANR
74; CLR 63; DLB 9, 22, 102; DLBD 17;
JRDA; MAICYA; MTCW 2; SATA 100;
YABC 1

Ray, Satyajit 1921-1992 .. **CLC 16, 76; DAM
MULT**
See also CA 114; 137

Read, Herbert Edward 1893-1968 ..... **CLC 4**
See also CA 85-88; 25-28R; DLB 20, 149

Read, Piers Paul 1941- .... **CLC 4, 10, 25**
See also CA 21-24R; CANR 38, 86; DLB
14; SATA 21

Reade, Charles 1814-1884 .... **NCLC 2, 74**
See also DLB 21

Reade, Hamish
See Gray, Simon (James Holliday)

Reading, Peter 1946- .... **CLC 47**
See also CA 103; CANR 46; DLB 40

Reaney, James 1926- .. **CLC 13; DAC; DAM
MST**
See also CA 41-44R; CAAS 15; CANR 42;
DLB 68; SATA 43

Rebreanu, Liviu 1885-1944 .... **TCLC 28**
See also CA 165; DLB 220

Rechy, John (Francisco) 1934- ...... **CLC 1, 7,
14, 18, 107; DAM MULT; HLC 2**
See also CA 5-8R; CAAS 4; CANR 6, 32,
64; DLB 122; DLBY 82; HW 1, 2; INT
CANR-6

Redcam, Tom 1870-1933 .... **TCLC 25**

Reddin, Keith CLC 67

Redgrove, Peter (William) 1932- . **CLC 6, 41**
See also CA 1-4R; CANR 3, 39, 77; DLB
40

Redmon, Anne CLC 22
See also Nightingale, Anne Redmon
See also DLBY 86

Reed, Eliot
See Ambler, Eric

Reed, Ishmael 1938- .. **CLC 2, 3, 5, 6, 13, 32,
60; BLC 3; DAM MULT**
See also BW 2, 3; CA 21-24R; CANR 25,
48, 74; DLB 2, 5, 33, 169, 227;
DLBD 8; MTCW 1, 2

Reed, John (Silas) 1887-1920 .... **TCLC 9**
See also CA 106

Reed, Lou CLC 21
See also Firbank, Louis

Reese, Lizette Woodworth 1856-1935 . **PC 29**
See also CA 180; DLB 54

Reeve, Clara 1729-1807 .... **NCLC 19**
See also DLB 39

Reich, Wilhelm 1897-1957 .... **TCLC 57**

Reid, Christopher (John) 1949- .... **CLC 33**
See also CA 140; CANR 89; DLB 40

Reid, Desmond
See Moorcock, Michael (John)

Reid Banks, Lynne 1929-
See Banks, Lynne Reid
See also CA 1-4R; CANR 6, 22, 38, 87;
CLR 24; JRDA; MAICYA; SATA 22, 75,
111

Reilly, William K.
See Creasey, John

Reiner, Max
See Caldwell, (Janet Miriam) Taylor
(Holland)

Reis, Ricardo
See Pessoa, Fernando (Antonio Nogueira)

Remarque, Erich Maria
1898-1970 ... **CLC 21; DA; DAB; DAC;
DAM MST, NOV**
See also AAYA 27; CA 77-80; 29-32R;
DA3; DLB 56; MTCW 1, 2

Remington, Frederic 1861-1909 ..... **TCLC 89**
See also CA 108; 169; DLB 12, 186, 188;
SATA 41

Remizov, A.
See Remizov, Aleksei (Mikhailovich)

Remizov, A. M.
See Remizov, Aleksei (Mikhailovich)

Remizov, Aleksei (Mikhailovich)
1877-1957 .... **TCLC 27**
See also CA 125; 133

Renan, Joseph Ernest 1823-1892 .. **NCLC 26**

Renard, Jules 1864-1910 .... **TCLC 17**
See also CA 117

Renault, Mary -1983 .... **CLC 3, 11, 17**
See also Challans, Mary
See also DLBY 83; MTCW 2

Rendell, Ruth (Barbara) 1930- . **CLC 28, 48;
DAM POP**
See also Vine, Barbara
See also CA 109; CANR 32, 52, 74; DLB
87; INT CANR-32; MTCW 1, 2

Renoir, Jean 1894-1979 .... **CLC 20**
See also CA 129; 85-88

Resnais, Alain 1922- .... **CLC 16**

Reverdy, Pierre 1889-1960 .... **CLC 53**
See also CA 97-100; 89-92

Rexroth, Kenneth 1905-1982 .... **CLC 1, 2, 6,
11, 22, 49, 112; DAM POET; PC 20**
See also CA 5-8R; 107; CANR 14, 34, 63;
CDALB 1941-1968; DLB 16, 48, 165,
212; DLBY 82; INT CANR-14; MTCW
1, 2

Reyes, Alfonso 1889-1959 .. **TCLC 33; HLCS
2**
See also CA 131; HW 1

Reyes y Basoalto, Ricardo Eliecer Neftali
See Neruda, Pablo

Reymont, Wladyslaw (Stanislaw)
1868(?)-1925 .... **TCLC 5**
See also CA 104

Reynolds, Jonathan 1942- .... **CLC 6, 38**
See also CA 65-68; CANR 28

Reynolds, Joshua 1723-1792 .... **LC 15**
See also DLB 104

Reynolds, Michael S(hane) 1937- ..... **CLC 44**
See also CA 65-68; CANR 9, 89

Reznikoff, Charles 1894-1976 .... **CLC 9**
See also CA 33-36; 61-64; CAP 2; DLB 28,
45

Rezzori (d'Arezzo), Gregor von
1914-1998 .... **CLC 25**
See also CA 122; 136; 167

Rhine, Richard
See Silverstein, Alvin

Rhodes, Eugene Manlove
1869-1934 .... **TCLC 53**

Rhodius, Apollonius c. 3rd cent.
B.C.- .... **CMLC 28**
See also DLB 176

R'hoone
See Balzac, Honore de

Rhys, Jean 1890(?)-1979 ...... **CLC 2, 4, 6, 14,
19, 51, 124; DAM NOV; SSC 21**
See also CA 25-28R; 85-88; CANR 35, 62;
CDBLB 1945-1960; DA3; DLB 36, 117,
162; MTCW 1, 2

Ribeiro, Darcy 1922-1997 .... **CLC 34**
See also CA 33-36R; 156

Ribeiro, Joao Ubaldo (Osorio Pimentel)
1941- .... **CLC 10, 67**
See also CA 81-84

Ribman, Ronald (Burt) 1932- .... **CLC 7**
See also CA 21-24R; CANR 46, 80

Ricci, Nino 1959- .... **CLC 70**
See also CA 137

Rice, Anne 1941- .. **CLC 41, 128; DAM POP**
See also AAYA 9; BEST 89:2; CA 65-68;
CANR 12, 36, 53, 74; DA3; MTCW 2

Rice, Elmer (Leopold) 1892-1967 ...... **CLC 7,
49; DAM DRAM**
See also CA 21-22; 25-28R; CAP 2; DLB
4, 7; MTCW 1, 2

Rice, Tim(othy Miles Bindon)
1944- .... **CLC 21**
See also CA 103; CANR 46

Rich, Adrienne (Cecile) 1929- ... **CLC 3, 6, 7,
11, 18, 36, 73, 76, 125; DAM POET;
PC 5**
See also CA 9-12R; CANR 20, 53, 74;
CDALBS; DA3; DLB 5, 67; MTCW 1, 2

Rich, Barbara
See Graves, Robert (von Ranke)

Rich, Robert
See Trumbo, Dalton

Richard, Keith CLC 17
See also Richards, Keith

Richards, David Adams 1950- .... **CLC 59;
DAC**
See also CA 93-96; CANR 60; DLB 53

Richards, I(vor) A(rmstrong)
1893-1979 .... **CLC 14, 24**
See also CA 41-44R; 89-92; CANR 34, 74;
DLB 27; MTCW 2

Richards, Keith 1943-
See Richard, Keith
See also CA 107; CANR 77

Richardson, Anne
See Roiphe, Anne (Richardson)

Richardson, Dorothy Miller
1873-1957 .... **TCLC 3**
See also CA 104; DLB 36

**Richardson (Robertson), Ethel Florence
Lindesay** 1870-1946
See Richardson, Henry Handel
See also CA 105; DLB 230

Richardson, Henry Handel TCLC 4
See also Richardson (Robertson), Ethel Flo-
rence Lindesay
See also DLB 197

Richardson, John 1796-1852 .... **NCLC 55;
DAC**
See also DLB 99

Richardson, Samuel 1689-1761 ...... **LC 1, 44;
DA; DAB; DAC; DAM MST, NOV;
WLC**
See also CDBLB 1660-1789; DLB 39

Richler, Mordecai 1931- ...... **CLC 3, 5, 9, 13,
18, 46, 70; DAC; DAM MST, NOV**
See also AITN 1; CA 65-68; CANR 31, 62;
CLR 17; DLB 53; MAICYA; MTCW 1,
2; SATA 44, 98; SATA-Brief 27

Richter, Conrad (Michael)
1890-1968 .... **CLC 30**
See also AAYA 21; CA 5-8R; 25-28R;
CANR 23; DLB 9, 212; MTCW 1, 2;
SATA 3

Ricostranza, Tom
See Ellis, Trey

Riddell, Charlotte 1832-1906 .... **TCLC 40**
See also CA 165; DLB 156

Ridge, John Rollin 1827-1867 ...... **NCLC 82;
DAM MULT**
See also CA 144; DLB 175; NNAL

Ridgway, Keith 1965- .... **CLC 119**
See also CA 172

Riding, Laura CLC 3, 7
See also Jackson, Laura (Riding)

Riefenstahl, Berta Helene Amalia 1902-
See Riefenstahl, Leni
See also CA 108

Riefenstahl, Leni CLC 16
See also Riefenstahl, Berta Helene Amalia

Riffe, Ernest
See Bergman, (Ernst) Ingmar

Riggs, (Rolla) Lynn 1899-1954 ..... **TCLC 56;
DAM MULT**
See also CA 144; DLB 175; NNAL

St. John, David
    See Hunt, E(verette) Howard, (Jr.)
Saint-John Perse
    See Leger, (Marie-Rene Auguste) Alexis
    Saint-Leger
Saintsbury, George (Edward Bateman)
    1845-1933 .... TCLC 31
    See also CA 160; DLB 57, 149
Sait Faik TCLC 23
    See also Abasiyanik, Sait Faik
Saki TCLC 3; SSC 12
    See also Munro, H(ector) H(ugh)
    See also MTCW 2
Sala, George Augustus NCLC 46
Saladin 1138-1193 .... CMLC 38
Salama, Hannu 1936- .... CLC 18
Salamanca, J(ack) R(ichard) 1922- .. CLC 4,
    15
    See also CA 25-28R
Salas, Floyd Francis 1931-
    See also CA 119; CAAS 27; CANR 44, 75,
    93; DAM MULT; DLB 82; HLC 2; HW
    1, 2; MTCW 2
Sale, J. Kirkpatrick
    See Sale, Kirkpatrick
Sale, Kirkpatrick 1937- .... CLC 68
    See also CA 13-16R; CANR 10
Salinas, Luis Omar 1937- ..... CLC 90; DAM
    MULT; HLC 2
    See also CA 131; CANR 81; DLB 82; HW
    1, 2
Salinas (y Serrano), Pedro
    1891(?)-1951 .... TCLC 17
    See also CA 117; DLB 134
Salinger, J(erome) D(avid) 1919- .. CLC 1, 3,
    8, 12, 55, 56, 138; DA; DAB; DAC;
    DAM MST, NOV, POP; SSC 2, 28;
    WLC
    See also AAYA 2, 36; CA 5-8R; CANR 39;
    CDALB 1941-1968; CLR 18; DA3; DLB
    2, 102, 173; MAICYA; MTCW 1, 2;
    SATA 67
Salisbury, John
    See Caute, (John) David
Salter, James 1925- .... CLC 7, 52, 59
    See also CA 73-76; DLB 130
Saltus, Edgar (Everton) 1855-1921 . TCLC 8
    See also CA 105; DLB 202
Saltykov, Mikhail Evgrafovich
    1826-1889 .... NCLC 16
Samarakis, Antonis 1919- .... CLC 5
    See also CA 25-28R; CAAS 16; CANR 36
Sanchez, Florencio 1875-1910 .... TCLC 37
    See also CA 153; HW 1
Sanchez, Luis Rafael 1936- .... CLC 23
    See also CA 128; DLB 145; HW 1
Sanchez, Sonia 1934- .... CLC 5, 116; BLC 3;
    DAM MULT; PC 9
    See also BW 2, 3; CA 33-36R; CANR 24,
    49, 74; CLR 18; DA3; DLB 41; DLBD 8;
    MAICYA; MTCW 1, 2; SATA 22
Sand, George 1804-1876 ..... NCLC 2, 42, 57;
    DA; DAB; DAC; DAM MST, NOV;
    WLC
    See also DA3; DLB 119, 192
Sandburg, Carl (August) 1878-1967 . CLC 1,
    4, 10, 15, 35; DA; DAB; DAC; DAM
    MST, POET; PC 2; WLC
    See also AAYA 24; CA 5-8R; 25-28R;
    CANR 35; CDALB 1865-1917; CLR 67;
    DA3; DLB 17, 54; MAICYA; MTCW 1,
    2; SATA 8
Sandburg, Charles
    See Sandburg, Carl (August)
Sandburg, Charles A.
    See Sandburg, Carl (August)

Sanders, (James) Ed(ward) 1939- ... CLC 53;
    DAM POET
    See also CA 13-16R; CAAS 21; CANR 13,
    44, 78; DLB 16
Sanders, Lawrence 1920-1998 .... CLC 41;
    DAM POP
    See also BEST 89:4; CA 81-84; 165; CANR
    33, 62; DA3; MTCW 1
Sanders, Noah
    See Blount, Roy (Alton), Jr.
Sanders, Winston P.
    See Anderson, Poul (William)
Sandoz, Mari(e Susette) 1896-1966 .. CLC 28
    See also CA 1-4R; 25-28R; CANR 17, 64;
    DLB 9, 212; MTCW 1, 2; SATA 5
Saner, Reg(inald Anthony) 1931- .... CLC 9
    See also CA 65-68
Sankara 788-820 .... CMLC 32
Sannazaro, Jacopo 1456(?)-1530 .... LC 8
Sansom, William 1912-1976 .... CLC 2, 6;
    DAM NOV; SSC 21
    See also CA 5-8R; 65-68; CANR 42; DLB
    139; MTCW 1
Santayana, George 1863-1952 .... TCLC 40
    See also CA 115; DLB 54, 71; DLBD 13
Santiago, Danny CLC 33
    See also James, Daniel (Lewis)
    See also DLB 122
Santmyer, Helen Hoover 1895-1986 . CLC 33
    See also CA 1-4R; 118; CANR 15, 33;
    DLBY 84; MTCW 1
Santoka, Taneda 1882-1940 .... TCLC 72
Santos, Bienvenido N(uqui)
    1911-1996 .... CLC 22; DAM MULT
    See also CA 101; 151; CANR 19, 46
Sapper TCLC 44
    See also McNeile, Herman Cyril
Sapphire
    See Sapphire, Brenda
Sapphire, Brenda 1950- .... CLC 99
Sappho fl. 6th cent. B.C.- ..... CMLC 3; DAM
    POET; PC 5
    See also DA3; DLB 176
Saramago, Jose 1922- ..... CLC 119; HLCS 1
    See also CA 153
Sarduy, Severo 1937-1993 .... CLC 6, 97;
    HLCS 1
    See also CA 89-92; 142; CANR 58, 81;
    DLB 113; HW 1, 2
Sargeson, Frank 1903-1982 .... CLC 31
    See also CA 25-28R; 106; CANR 38, 79
Sarmiento, Domingo Faustino 1811-1888
    See also HLCS 2
Sarmiento, Felix Ruben Garcia
    See Dario, Ruben
Saro-Wiwa, Ken(ule Beeson)
    1941-1995 .... CLC 114
    See also BW 2; CA 142; 150; CANR 60;
    DLB 157
Saroyan, William 1908-1981 ... CLC 1, 8, 10,
    29, 34, 56; DA; DAB; DAC; DAM
    DRAM, MST, NOV; SSC 21; WLC
    See also CA 5-8R; 103; CANR 30;
    CDALBS; DA3; DLB 7, 9, 86; DLBY 81;
    MTCW 1, 2; SATA 23; SATA-Obit 24
Sarraute, Nathalie 1900-1999 .... CLC 1, 2, 4,
    8, 10, 31, 80
    See also CA 9-12R; 187; CANR 23, 66;
    DLB 83; MTCW 1, 2
Sarton, (Eleanor) May 1912-1995 ..... CLC 4,
    14, 49, 91; DAM POET
    See also CA 1-4R; 149; CANR 1, 34, 55;
    DLB 48; DLBY 81; INT CANR-34;
    MTCW 1, 2; SATA 36; SATA-Obit 86

Sartre, Jean-Paul 1905-1980 . CLC 1, 4, 7, 9,
    13, 18, 24, 44, 50, 52; DA; DAB; DAC;
    DAM DRAM, MST, NOV; DC 3; SSC
    32; WLC
    See also CA 9-12R; 97-100; CANR 21;
    DA3; DLB 72; MTCW 1, 2
Sassoon, Siegfried (Lorraine)
    1886-1967 .... CLC 36, 130; DAB; DAM
    MST, NOV, POET; PC 12
    See also CA 104; 25-28R; CANR 36; DLB
    20, 191; DLBD 18; MTCW 1, 2
Satterfield, Charles
    See Pohl, Frederik
Satyremont
    See Peret, Benjamin
Saul, John (W. III) 1942- ...... CLC 46; DAM
    NOV, POP
    See also AAYA 10; BEST 90:4; CA 81-84;
    CANR 16, 40, 81; SATA 98
Saunders, Caleb
    See Heinlein, Robert A(nson)
Saura (Atares), Carlos 1932- .... CLC 20
    See also CA 114; 131; CANR 79; HW 1
Sauser-Hall, Frederic 1887-1961 ...... CLC 18
    See also Cendrars, Blaise
    See also CA 102; 93-96; CANR 36, 62;
    MTCW 1
Saussure, Ferdinand de
    1857-1913 .... TCLC 49
Savage, Catharine
    See Brosman, Catharine Savage
Savage, Thomas 1915- .... CLC 40
    See also CA 126; 132; CAAS 15; INT 132
Savan, Glenn 19(?)- .... CLC 50
Sayers, Dorothy L(eigh)
    1893-1957 .... TCLC 2, 15; DAM POP
    See also CA 104; 119; CANR 60; CDBLB
    1914-1945; DLB 10, 36, 77, 100; MTCW
    1, 2
Sayers, Valerie 1952- .... CLC 50, 122
    See also CA 134; CANR 61
Sayles, John (Thomas) 1950- . CLC 7, 10, 14
    See also CA 57-60; CANR 41, 84; DLB 44
Scammell, Michael 1935- .... CLC 34
    See also CA 156
Scannell, Vernon 1922- .... CLC 49
    See also CA 5-8R; CANR 8, 24, 57; DLB
    27; SATA 59
Scarlett, Susan
    See Streatfeild, (Mary) Noel
Scarron
    See Mikszath, Kalman
Schaeffer, Susan Fromberg 1941- ..... CLC 6,
    11, 22
    See also CA 49-52; CANR 18, 65; DLB 28;
    MTCW 1, 2; SATA 22
Schary, Jill
    See Robinson, Jill
Schell, Jonathan 1943- .... CLC 35
    See also CA 73-76; CANR 12
Schelling, Friedrich Wilhelm Joseph von
    1775-1854 .... NCLC 30
    See also DLB 90
Schendel, Arthur van 1874-1946 ... TCLC 56
Scherer, Jean-Marie Maurice 1920-
    See Rohmer, Eric
    See also CA 110
Schevill, James (Erwin) 1920- .... CLC 7
    See also CA 5-8R; CAAS 12
Schiller, Friedrich 1759-1805 . NCLC 39, 69;
    DAM DRAM; DC 12
    See also DLB 94
Schisgal, Murray (Joseph) 1926- .... CLC 6
    See also CA 21-24R; CANR 48, 86
Schlee, Ann 1934- .... CLC 35
    See also CA 101; CANR 29, 88; SATA 44;
    SATA-Brief 36

Straub, Peter (Francis) 1943- . **CLC 28, 107; DAM POP**
See also BEST 89:1; CA 85-88; CANR 28, 65; DLBY 84; MTCW 1, 2

Strauss, Botho 1944- .... **CLC 22**
See also CA 157; DLB 124

Streatfeild, (Mary) Noel
1895(?)-1986 .... **CLC 21**
See also CA 81-84; 120; CANR 31; CLR 17; DLB 160; MAICYA; SATA 20; SATA-Obit 48

Stribling, T(homas) S(igismund)
1881-1965 .... **CLC 23**
See also CA 107; DLB 9

Strindberg, (Johan) August
1849-1912 .... **TCLC 1, 8, 21, 47; DA; DAB; DAC; DAM DRAM, MST; WLC**
See also CA 104; 135; DA3; MTCW 2

Stringer, Arthur 1874-1950 .... **TCLC 37**
See also CA 161; DLB 92

Stringer, David
See Roberts, Keith (John Kingston)

Stroheim, Erich von 1885-1957 ..... **TCLC 71**

Strugatskii, Arkadii (Natanovich)
1925-1991 .... **CLC 27**
See also CA 106; 135

Strugatskii, Boris (Natanovich)
1933- .... **CLC 27**
See also CA 106

Strummer, Joe 1953(?)- .... **CLC 30**

Strunk, William, Jr. 1869-1946 ...... **TCLC 92**
See also CA 118; 164

Stryk, Lucien 1924- .... **PC 27**
See also CA 13-16R; CANR 10, 28, 55

Stuart, Don A.
See Campbell, John W(ood, Jr.)

Stuart, Ian
See MacLean, Alistair (Stuart)

Stuart, Jesse (Hilton) 1906-1984 ... **CLC 1, 8, 11, 14, 34; SSC 31**
See also CA 5-8R; 112; CANR 31; DLB 9, 48, 102; DLBY 84; SATA 2; SATA-Obit 36

Sturgeon, Theodore (Hamilton)
1918-1985 .... **CLC 22, 39**
See also Queen, Ellery
See also CA 81-84; 116; CANR 32; DLB 8; DLBY 85; MTCW 1, 2

Sturges, Preston 1898-1959 .... **TCLC 48**
See also CA 114; 149; DLB 26

Styron, William 1925- .... **CLC 1, 3, 5, 11, 15, 60; DAM NOV, POP; SSC 25**
See also BEST 90:4; CA 5-8R; CANR 6, 33, 74; CDALB 1968-1988; DA3; DLB 2, 143; DLBY 80; INT CANR-6; MTCW 1, 2

Su, Chien 1884-1918
See Su Man-shu
See also CA 123

Suarez Lynch, B.
See Bioy Casares, Adolfo; Borges, Jorge Luis

Suassuna, Ariano Vilar 1927-
See also CA 178; HLCS 1; HW 2

Suckling, John 1609-1641 .... **PC 30**
See also DAM POET; DLB 58, 126

Suckow, Ruth 1892-1960 .... **SSC 18**
See also CA 113; DLB 9, 102

Sudermann, Hermann 1857-1928 .. **TCLC 15**
See also CA 107; DLB 118

Sue, Eugene 1804-1857 .... **NCLC 1**
See also DLB 119

Sueskind, Patrick 1949- .... **CLC 44**
See also Suskind, Patrick

Sukenick, Ronald 1932- .... **CLC 3, 4, 6, 48**
See also CA 25-28R; CAAS 8; CANR 32, 89; DLB 173; DLBY 81

Suknaski, Andrew 1942- .... **CLC 19**
See also CA 101; DLB 53

Sullivan, Vernon
See Vian, Boris

Sully Prudhomme 1839-1907 .... **TCLC 31**

Su Man-shu **TCLC 24**
See also Su, Chien

Summerforest, Ivy B.
See Kirkup, James

Summers, Andrew James 1942- .... **CLC 26**

Summers, Andy
See Summers, Andrew James

Summers, Hollis (Spurgeon, Jr.)
1916- .... **CLC 10**
See also CA 5-8R; CANR 3; DLB 6

Summers, (Alphonsus Joseph-Mary Augustus) Montague
1880-1948 .... **TCLC 16**
See also CA 118; 163

Sumner, Gordon Matthew **CLC 26**
See also Sting

Surtees, Robert Smith 1803-1864 .. **NCLC 14**
See also DLB 21

Susann, Jacqueline 1921-1974 .... **CLC 3**
See also AITN 1; CA 65-68; 53-56; MTCW 1, 2

Su Shih 1036-1101 .... **CMLC 15**

Suskind, Patrick
See Sueskind, Patrick
See also CA 145

Sutcliff, Rosemary 1920-1992 .... **CLC 26; DAB; DAC; DAM MST, POP**
See also AAYA 10; CA 5-8R; 139; CANR 37; CLR 1, 37; JRDA; MAICYA; SATA 6, 44, 78; SATA-Obit 73

Sutro, Alfred 1863-1933 .... **TCLC 6**
See also CA 105; 185; DLB 10

Sutton, Henry
See Slavitt, David R(ytman)

Svevo, Italo 1861-1928 ...... **TCLC 2, 35; SSC 25**
See also Schmitz, Aron Hector

Swados, Elizabeth (A.) 1951- .... **CLC 12**
See also CA 97-100; CANR 49; INT 97-100

Swados, Harvey 1920-1972 .... **CLC 5**
See also CA 5-8R; 37-40R; CANR 6; DLB 2

Swan, Gladys 1934- .... **CLC 69**
See also CA 101; CANR 17, 39

Swanson, Logan
See Matheson, Richard Burton

Swarthout, Glendon (Fred)
1918-1992 .... **CLC 35**
See also CA 1-4R; 139; CANR 1, 47; SATA 26

Sweet, Sarah C.
See Jewett, (Theodora) Sarah Orne

Swenson, May 1919-1989 ...... **CLC 4, 14, 61, 106; DA; DAB; DAC; DAM MST, POET; PC 14**
See also CA 5-8R; 130; CANR 36, 61; DLB 5; MTCW 1, 2; SATA 15

Swift, Augustus
See Lovecraft, H(oward) P(hillips)

Swift, Graham (Colin) 1949- ...... **CLC 41, 88**
See also CA 117; 122; CANR 46, 71; DLB 194; MTCW 2

Swift, Jonathan 1667-1745 ..... **LC 1, 42; DA; DAB; DAC; DAM MST, NOV, POET; PC 9; WLC**
See also CDBLB 1660-1789; CLR 53; DA3; DLB 39, 95, 101; SATA 19

Swinburne, Algernon Charles
1837-1909 .... **TCLC 8, 36; DA; DAB; DAC; DAM MST, POET; PC 24; WLC**
See also CA 105; 140; CDBLB 1832-1890; DA3; DLB 35, 57

Swinfen, Ann **CLC 34**

Swinnerton, Frank Arthur
1884-1982 .... **CLC 31**
See also CA 108; DLB 34

Swithen, John
See King, Stephen (Edwin)

Sylvia
See Ashton-Warner, Sylvia (Constance)

Symmes, Robert Edward
See Duncan, Robert (Edward)

Symonds, John Addington
1840-1893 .... **NCLC 34**
See also DLB 57, 144

Symons, Arthur 1865-1945 .... **TCLC 11**
See also CA 107; DLB 19, 57, 149

Symons, Julian (Gustave)
1912-1994 .... **CLC 2, 14, 32**
See also CA 49-52; 147; CAAS 3; CANR 3, 33, 59; DLB 87, 155; DLBY 92; MTCW 1

Synge, (Edmund) J(ohn) M(illington)
1871-1909 . **TCLC 6, 37; DAM DRAM; DC 2**
See also CA 104; 141; CDBLB 1890-1914; DLB 10, 19

Syruc, J.
See Milosz, Czeslaw

Szirtes, George 1948- .... **CLC 46**
See also CA 109; CANR 27, 61

Szymborska, Wislawa 1923- .... **CLC 99**
See also CA 154; CANR 91; DA3; DLB 232; DLBY 96; MTCW 2

T. O., Nik
See Annensky, Innokenty (Fyodorovich)

Tabori, George 1914- .... **CLC 19**
See also CA 49-52; CANR 4, 69

Tagore, Rabindranath 1861-1941 ... **TCLC 3, 53; DAM DRAM, POET; PC 8**
See also CA 104; 120; DA3; MTCW 1, 2

Taine, Hippolyte Adolphe
1828-1893 .... **NCLC 15**

Talese, Gay 1932- .... **CLC 37**
See also AITN 1; CA 1-4R; CANR 9, 58; DLB 185; INT CANR-9; MTCW 1, 2

Tallent, Elizabeth (Ann) 1954- .... **CLC 45**
See also CA 117; CANR 72; DLB 130

Tally, Ted 1952- .... **CLC 42**
See also CA 120; 124; INT 124

Talvik, Heiti 1904-1947 .... **TCLC 87**

Tamayo y Baus, Manuel
1829-1898 .... **NCLC 1**

Tammsaare, A(nton) H(ansen)
1878-1940 .... **TCLC 27**
See also CA 164; DLB 220

Tam'si, Tchicaya U
See Tchicaya, Gerald Felix

Tan, Amy (Ruth) 1952- . **CLC 59, 120; DAM MULT, NOV, POP**
See also AAYA 9; BEST 89:3; CA 136; CANR 54; CDALBS; DA3; DLB 173; MTCW 2; SATA 75

Tandem, Felix
See Spitteler, Carl (Friedrich Georg)

Tanizaki, Jun'ichiro 1886-1965 ... **CLC 8, 14, 28; SSC 21**
See also CA 93-96; 25-28R; DLB 180; MTCW 2

Tanner, William
See Amis, Kingsley (William)

Tao Lao
See Storni, Alfonsina

Tarantino, Quentin (Jerome)
1963- .... **CLC 125**
See also CA 171

Tarassoff, Lev
See Troyat, Henri

Tarbell, Ida M(inerva) 1857-1944 . **TCLC 40**
See also CA 122; 181; DLB 47

Tarkington, (Newton) Booth
1869-1946 .... **TCLC 9**
See also CA 110; 143; DLB 9, 102; MTCW
2; SATA 17

Tarkovsky, Andrei (Arsenyevich)
1932-1986 .... **CLC 75**
See also CA 127

Tartt, Donna 1964(?)- .... **CLC 76**
See also CA 142

Tasso, Torquato 1544-1595 .... **LC 5**

Tate, (John Orley) Allen 1899-1979 .. **CLC 2,
4, 6, 9, 11, 14, 24**
See also CA 5-8R; 85-88; CANR 32; DLB
4, 45, 63; DLBD 17; MTCW 1, 2

Tate, Ellalice
See Hibbert, Eleanor Alice Burford

Tate, James (Vincent) 1943- ..... **CLC 2, 6, 25**
See also CA 21-24R; CANR 29, 57; DLB
5, 169

Tauler, Johannes c. 1300-1361 ...... **CMLC 37**
See also DLB 179

Tavel, Ronald 1940- .... **CLC 6**
See also CA 21-24R; CANR 33

Taylor, Bayard 1825-1878 .... **NCLC 89**
See also DLB 3, 189

Taylor, C(ecil) P(hilip) 1929-1981 .... **CLC 27**
See also CA 25-28R; 105; CANR 47

Taylor, Edward 1642(?)-1729 ..... **LC 11; DA;
DAB; DAC; DAM MST, POET**
See also DLB 24

Taylor, Eleanor Ross 1920- .... **CLC 5**
See also CA 81-84; CANR 70

Taylor, Elizabeth 1912-1975 ..... **CLC 2, 4, 29**
See also CA 13-16R; CANR 9, 70; DLB
139; MTCW 1; SATA 13

Taylor, Frederick Winslow
1856-1915 .... **TCLC 76**

Taylor, Henry (Splawn) 1942- .... **CLC 44**
See also CA 33-36R; CAAS 7; CANR 31;
DLB 5

Taylor, Kamala (Purnaiya) 1924-
See Markandaya, Kamala
See also CA 77-80

Taylor, Mildred D. CLC 21
See also AAYA 10; BW 1; CA 85-88;
CANR 25; CLR 9, 59; DLB 52; JRDA;
MAICYA; SAAS 5; SATA 15, 70

Taylor, Peter (Hillsman) 1917-1994 .. **CLC 1,
4, 18, 37, 44, 50, 71; SSC 10**
See also CA 13-16R; 147; CANR 9, 50;
DLBY 81, 94; INT CANR-9; MTCW 1, 2

Taylor, Robert Lewis 1912-1998 .... **CLC 14**
See also CA 1-4R; 170; CANR 3, 64; SATA
10

Tchekhov, Anton
See Chekhov, Anton (Pavlovich)

Tchicaya, Gerald Felix 1931-1988 .. **CLC 101**
See also CA 129; 125; CANR 81

Tchicaya U Tam'si
See Tchicaya, Gerald Felix

Teasdale, Sara 1884-1933 .... **TCLC 4; PC 31**
See also CA 104; 163; DLB 45; SATA 32

Tegner, Esaias 1782-1846 .... **NCLC 2**

Teilhard de Chardin, (Marie Joseph) Pierre
1881-1955 .... **TCLC 9**
See also CA 105

Temple, Ann
See Mortimer, Penelope (Ruth)

Tennant, Emma (Christina) 1937- .. **CLC 13,
52**
See also CA 65-68; CAAS 9; CANR 10,
38, 59, 88; DLB 14

Tenneshaw, S. M.
See Silverberg, Robert

Tennyson, Alfred 1809-1892 ... **NCLC 30, 65;
DA; DAB; DAC; DAM MST, POET;
PC 6; WLC**
See also CDBLB 1832-1890; DA3; DLB
32

Teran, Lisa St. Aubin de CLC 36
See also St. Aubin de Teran, Lisa

Terence c. 184B.C.-c. 159B.C. ...... **CMLC 14;
DC 7**
See also DLB 211

Teresa de Jesus, St. 1515-1582 .... **LC 18**

Terkel, Louis 1912-
See Terkel, Studs
See also CA 57-60; CANR 18, 45, 67; DA3;
MTCW 1, 2

Terkel, Studs CLC 38
See also Terkel, Louis
See also AAYA 32; AITN 1; MTCW 2

Terry, C. V.
See Slaughter, Frank G(ill)

Terry, Megan 1932- .... **CLC 19; DC 13**
See also CA 77-80; CABS 3; CANR 43;
DLB 7

Tertullian c. 155-c. 245 .... **CMLC 29**

Tertz, Abram
See Sinyavsky, Andrei (Donatevich)

Tesich, Steve 1943(?)-1996 .... **CLC 40, 69**
See also CA 105; 152; DLBY 83

Tesla, Nikola 1856-1943 .... **TCLC 88**

Teternikov, Fyodor Kuzmich 1863-1927
See Sologub, Fyodor
See also CA 104

Tevis, Walter 1928-1984 .... **CLC 42**
See also CA 113

Tey, Josephine TCLC 14
See also Mackintosh, Elizabeth
See also DLB 77

Thackeray, William Makepeace
1811-1863 ...... **NCLC 5, 14, 22, 43; DA;
DAB; DAC; DAM MST, NOV; WLC**
See also CDBLB 1832-1890; DA3; DLB
21, 55, 159, 163; SATA 23

Thakura, Ravindranatha
See Tagore, Rabindranath

Tharoor, Shashi 1956- .... **CLC 70**
See also CA 141; CANR 91

Thelwell, Michael Miles 1939- .... **CLC 22**
See also BW 2; CA 101

Theobald, Lewis, Jr.
See Lovecraft, H(oward) P(hillips)

Theodorescu, Ion N. 1880-1967
See Arghezi, Tudor
See also CA 116; DLB 220

Theriault, Yves 1915-1983 .... **CLC 79; DAC;
DAM MST**
See also CA 102; DLB 88

Theroux, Alexander (Louis) 1939- .... **CLC 2,
25**
See also CA 85-88; CANR 20, 63

Theroux, Paul (Edward) 1941- ..... **CLC 5, 8,
11, 15, 28, 46; DAM POP**
See also AAYA 28; BEST 89:4; CA 33-36R;
CANR 20, 45, 74; CDALBS; DA3; DLB
2; MTCW 1, 2; SATA 44, 109

Thesen, Sharon 1946- .... **CLC 56**
See also CA 163

Thevenin, Denis
See Duhamel, Georges

Thibault, Jacques Anatole Francois
1844-1924
See France, Anatole
See also CA 106; 127; DAM NOV; DA3;
MTCW 1, 2

Thiele, Colin (Milton) 1920- .... **CLC 17**
See also CA 29-32R; CANR 12, 28, 53;
CLR 27; MAICYA; SAAS 2; SATA 14,
72

Thomas, Audrey (Callahan) 1935- .... **CLC 7,
13, 37, 107; SSC 20**
See also AITN 2; CA 21-24R; CAAS 19;
CANR 36, 58; DLB 60; MTCW 1

Thomas, Augustus 1857-1934 .... **TCLC 97**

Thomas, D(onald) M(ichael) 1935- . **CLC 13,
22, 31, 132**
See also CA 61-64; CAAS 11; CANR 17,
45, 75; CDBLB 1960 to Present; DA3;
DLB 40, 207; INT CANR-17; MTCW 1,
2

Thomas, Dylan (Marlais)
1914-1953 ...... **TCLC 1, 8, 45, 105; DA;
DAB; DAC; DAM DRAM, MST,
POET; PC 2; SSC 3; WLC**
See also CA 104; 120; CANR 65; CDBLB
1945-1960; DA3; DLB 13, 20, 139;
MTCW 1, 2; SATA 60

Thomas, (Philip) Edward
1878-1917 .... **TCLC 10; DAM POET**
See also CA 106; 153; DLB 98

Thomas, Joyce Carol 1938- .... **CLC 35**
See also AAYA 12; BW 2, 3; CA 113; 116;
CANR 48; CLR 19; DLB 33; INT 116;
JRDA; MAICYA; MTCW 1, 2; SAAS 7;
SATA 40, 78

Thomas, Lewis 1913-1993 .... **CLC 35**
See also CA 85-88; 143; CANR 38, 60;
MTCW 1, 2

Thomas, M. Carey 1857-1935 .... **TCLC 89**

Thomas, Paul
See Mann, (Paul) Thomas

Thomas, Piri 1928- .... **CLC 17; HLCS 2**
See also CA 73-76; HW 1

Thomas, R(onald) S(tuart) 1913- ...... **CLC 6,
13, 48; DAB; DAM POET**
See also CA 89-92; CAAS 4; CANR 30;
CDBLB 1960 to Present; DLB 27; MTCW
1

Thomas, Ross (Elmore) 1926-1995 .. **CLC 39**
See also CA 33-36R; 150; CANR 22, 63

Thompson, Francis Clegg
See Mencken, H(enry) L(ouis)

Thompson, Francis Joseph
1859-1907 .... **TCLC 4**
See also CA 104; CDBLB 1890-1914; DLB
19

Thompson, Hunter S(tockton)
1939- ... **CLC 9, 17, 40, 104; DAM POP**
See also BEST 89:1; CA 17-20R; CANR
23, 46, 74, 77; DA3; DLB 185; MTCW
1, 2

Thompson, James Myers
See Thompson, Jim (Myers)

Thompson, Jim (Myers)
1906-1977(?) .... **CLC 69**
See also CA 140; DLB 226

Thompson, Judith CLC 39

Thomson, James 1700-1748 ... **LC 16, 29, 40;
DAM POET**
See also DLB 95

Thomson, James 1834-1882 .... **NCLC 18;
DAM POET**
See also DLB 35

Thoreau, Henry David 1817-1862 .. **NCLC 7,
21, 61; DA; DAB; DAC; DAM MST;
PC 30; WLC**
See also CDALB 1640-1865; DA3; DLB 1,
223

Thornton, Hall
See Silverberg, Robert

Thucydides c. 455B.C.-399B.C. ..... **CMLC 17**
See also DLB 176

Thumboo, Edwin 1933- .... **PC 30**

Thurber, James (Grover)
1894-1961 .... **CLC 5, 11, 25, 125; DA;
DAB; DAC; DAM DRAM, MST, NOV;
SSC 1**
See also CA 73-76; CANR 17, 39; CDALB
1929-1941; DA3; DLB 4, 11, 22, 102;
MAICYA; MTCW 1, 2; SATA 13

Tryon, Tom
See Tryon, Thomas

Ts'ao Hsueh-ch'in 1715(?)-1763 .... **LC 1**

Tsushima, Shuji 1909-1948
See Dazai Osamu
See also CA 107

Tsvetaeva (Efron), Marina (Ivanovna)
1892-1941 .... **TCLC 7, 35; PC 14**
See also CA 104; 128; CANR 73; MTCW 1, 2

Tuck, Lily 1938- .... **CLC 70**
See also CA 139; CANR 90

Tu Fu 712-770 .... **PC 9**
See also DAM MULT

Tunis, John R(oberts) 1889-1975 ..... **CLC 12**
See also CA 61-64; CANR 62; DLB 22, 171; JRDA; MAICYA; SATA 37; SATA-Brief 30

Tuohy, Frank CLC 37
See also Tuohy, John Francis
See also DLB 14, 139

Tuohy, John Francis 1925-
See Tuohy, Frank
See also CA 5-8R; 178; CANR 3, 47

Turco, Lewis (Putnam) 1934- ..... **CLC 11, 63**
See also CA 13-16R; CAAS 22; CANR 24, 51; DLBY 84

Turgenev, Ivan 1818-1883 .... **NCLC 21, 37; DA; DAB; DAC; DAM MST, NOV; DC 7; SSC 7; WLC**

Turgot, Anne-Robert-Jacques
1727-1781 .... **LC 26**

Turner, Frederick 1943- .... **CLC 48**
See also CA 73-76; CAAS 10; CANR 12, 30, 56; DLB 40

Tutu, Desmond M(pilo) 1931- .... **CLC 80; BLC 3; DAM MULT**
See also BW 1, 3; CA 125; CANR 67, 81

Tutuola, Amos 1920-1997 ...... **CLC 5, 14, 29; BLC 3; DAM MULT**
See also BW 2, 3; CA 9-12R; 159; CANR 27, 66; DA3; DLB 125; MTCW 1, 2

Twain, Mark 1835-1910 ...... **TCLC 6, 12, 19, 36, 48, 59; SSC 34; WLC**
See also Clemens, Samuel Langhorne
See also AAYA 20; CLR 58, 60, 66; DLB 11, 12, 23, 64, 74

20/1631
See Upward, Allen

Tyler, Anne 1941- . **CLC 7, 11, 18, 28, 44, 59, 103; DAM NOV, POP**
See also AAYA 18; BEST 89:1; CA 9-12R; CANR 11, 33, 53; CDALBS; DLB 6, 143; DLBY 82; MTCW 1, 2; SATA 7, 90

Tyler, Royall 1757-1826 .... **NCLC 3**
See also DLB 37

Tynan, Katharine 1861-1931 .... **TCLC 3**
See also CA 104; 167; DLB 153

Tyutchev, Fyodor 1803-1873 .... **NCLC 34**

Tzara, Tristan 1896-1963 ...... **CLC 47; DAM POET; PC 27**
See also CA 153; 89-92; MTCW 2

Uhry, Alfred 1936- .. **CLC 55; DAM DRAM, POP**
See also CA 127; 133; DA3; INT 133

Ulf, Haerved
See Strindberg, (Johan) August

Ulf, Harved
See Strindberg, (Johan) August

Ulibarri, Sabine R(eyes) 1919- .... **CLC 83; DAM MULT; HLCS 2**
See also CA 131; CANR 81; DLB 82; HW 1, 2

Unamuno (y Jugo), Miguel de
1864-1936 ..... **TCLC 2, 9; DAM MULT, NOV; HLC 2; SSC 11**
See also CA 104; 131; CANR 81; DLB 108; HW 1, 2; MTCW 1, 2

Undercliffe, Errol
See Campbell, (John) Ramsey

Underwood, Miles
See Glassco, John

Undset, Sigrid 1882-1949 .... **TCLC 3; DA; DAB; DAC; DAM MST, NOV; WLC**
See also CA 104; 129; DA3; MTCW 1, 2

Ungaretti, Giuseppe 1888-1970 ... **CLC 7, 11, 15**
See also CA 19-20; 25-28R; CAP 2; DLB 114

Unger, Douglas 1952- .... **CLC 34**
See also CA 130; CANR 94

Unsworth, Barry (Forster) 1930- .... **CLC 76, 127**
See also CA 25-28R; CANR 30, 54; DLB 194

Updike, John (Hoyer) 1932- . **CLC 1, 2, 3, 5, 7, 9, 13, 15, 23, 34, 43, 70, 139; DA; DAB; DAC; DAM MST, NOV, POET, POP; SSC 13, 27; WLC**
See also AAYA 36; CA 1-4R; CABS 1; CANR 4, 33, 51, 94; CDALB 1968-1988; DA3; DLB 2, 5, 143, 227; DLBD 3; DLBY 80, 82, 97; MTCW 1, 2

Upshaw, Margaret Mitchell
See Mitchell, Margaret (Munnerlyn)

Upton, Mark
See Sanders, Lawrence

Upward, Allen 1863-1926 .... **TCLC 85**
See also CA 117; 187; DLB 36

Urdang, Constance (Henriette)
1922- .... **CLC 47**
See also CA 21-24R; CANR 9, 24

Uriel, Henry
See Faust, Frederick (Schiller)

Uris, Leon (Marcus) 1924- .... **CLC 7, 32; DAM NOV, POP**
See also AITN 1, 2; BEST 89:2; CA 1-4R; CANR 1, 40, 65; DA3; MTCW 1, 2; SATA 49

Urista, Alberto H. 1947-
See Alurista
See also CA 45-48, 182; CANR 2, 32; HLCS 1; HW 1

Urmuz
See Codrescu, Andrei

Urquhart, Guy
See McAlmon, Robert (Menzies)

Urquhart, Jane 1949- .... **CLC 90; DAC**
See also CA 113; CANR 32, 68

Usigli, Rodolfo 1905-1979
See also CA 131; HLCS 1; HW 1

Ustinov, Peter (Alexander) 1921- .... **CLC 1**
See also AITN 1; CA 13-16R; CANR 25, 51; DLB 13; MTCW 2

U Tam'si, Gerald Felix Tchicaya
See Tchicaya, Gerald Felix

U Tam'si, Tchicaya
See Tchicaya, Gerald Felix

Vachss, Andrew (Henry) 1942- .... **CLC 106**
See also CA 118; CANR 44

Vachss, Andrew H.
See Vachss, Andrew (Henry)

Vaculik, Ludvik 1926- .... **CLC 7**
See also CA 53-56; CANR 72; DLB 232

Vaihinger, Hans 1852-1933 .... **TCLC 71**
See also CA 116; 166

Valdez, Luis (Miguel) 1940- .. **CLC 84; DAM MULT; DC 10; HLC 2**
See also CA 101; CANR 32, 81; DLB 122; HW 1

Valenzuela, Luisa 1938- .... **CLC 31, 104; DAM MULT; HLCS 2; SSC 14**
See also CA 101; CANR 32, 65; DLB 113; HW 1, 2

Valera y Alcala-Galiano, Juan
1824-1905 .... **TCLC 10**
See also CA 106

Valery, (Ambroise) Paul (Toussaint Jules)
1871-1945 ... **TCLC 4, 15; DAM POET; PC 9**
See also CA 104; 122; DA3; MTCW 1, 2

Valle-Inclan, Ramon (Maria) del
1866-1936 .... **TCLC 5; DAM MULT; HLC 2**
See also CA 106; 153; CANR 80; DLB 134; HW 2

Vallejo, Antonio Buero
See Buero Vallejo, Antonio

Vallejo, Cesar (Abraham)
1892-1938 .. **TCLC 3, 56; DAM MULT; HLC 2**
See also CA 105; 153; HW 1

Valles, Jules 1832-1885 .... **NCLC 71**
See also DLB 123

Vallette, Marguerite Eymery
1860-1953 .... **TCLC 67**
See also CA 182; DLB 123, 192

Valle Y Pena, Ramon del
See Valle-Inclan, Ramon (Maria) del

Van Ash, Cay 1918- .... **CLC 34**

Vanbrugh, Sir John 1664-1726 .... **LC 21; DAM DRAM**
See also DLB 80

Van Campen, Karl
See Campbell, John W(ood, Jr.)

Vance, Gerald
See Silverberg, Robert

Vance, Jack CLC 35
See also Vance, John Holbrook
See also DLB 8

Vance, John Holbrook 1916-
See Queen, Ellery; Vance, Jack
See also CA 29-32R; CANR 17, 65; MTCW 1

Van Den Bogarde, Derek Jules Gaspard
Ulric Niven 1921-1999 .... **CLC 14**
See also CA 77-80; 179; DLB 19

Vandenburgh, Jane CLC 59
See also CA 168

Vanderhaeghe, Guy 1951- .... **CLC 41**
See also CA 113; CANR 72

van der Post, Laurens (Jan)
1906-1996 .... **CLC 5**
See also CA 5-8R; 155; CANR 35; DLB 204

van de Wetering, Janwillem 1931- ... **CLC 47**
See also CA 49-52; CANR 4, 62, 90

Van Dine, S. S. TCLC 23
See also Wright, Willard Huntington

Van Doren, Carl (Clinton)
1885-1950 .... **TCLC 18**
See also CA 111; 168

Van Doren, Mark 1894-1972 .... **CLC 6, 10**
See also CA 1-4R; 37-40R; CANR 3; DLB 45; MTCW 1, 2

Van Druten, John (William)
1901-1957 .... **TCLC 2**
See also CA 104; 161; DLB 10

Van Duyn, Mona (Jane) 1921- ...... **CLC 3, 7, 63, 116; DAM POET**
See also CA 9-12R; CANR 7, 38, 60; DLB 5

Van Dyne, Edith
See Baum, L(yman) Frank

van Itallie, Jean-Claude 1936- .... **CLC 3**
See also CA 45-48; CAAS 2; CANR 1, 48; DLB 7

van Ostaijen, Paul 1896-1928 .... **TCLC 33**
See also CA 163

Van Peebles, Melvin 1932- .... **CLC 2, 20; DAM MULT**
See also BW 2, 3; CA 85-88; CANR 27, 67, 82

Vansittart, Peter 1920- .... **CLC 42**
See also CA 1-4R; CANR 3, 49, 90

Wakefield, Dan 1932- .... **CLC 7**
See also CA 21-24R; CAAS 7

Wakoski, Diane 1937- ...... **CLC 2, 4, 7, 9, 11, 40; DAM POET; PC 15**
See also CA 13-16R; CAAS 1; CANR 9, 60; DLB 5; INT CANR-9; MTCW 2

Wakoski-Sherbell, Diane
See Wakoski, Diane

Walcott, Derek (Alton) 1930- ... **CLC 2, 4, 9, 14, 25, 42, 67, 76; BLC 3; DAB; DAC; DAM MST, MULT, POET; DC 7**
See also BW 2; CA 89-92; CANR 26, 47, 75, 80; DA3; DLB 117; DLBY 81; MTCW 1, 2

Waldman, Anne (Lesley) 1945- .... **CLC 7**
See also CA 37-40R; CAAS 17; CANR 34, 69; DLB 16

Waldo, E. Hunter
See Sturgeon, Theodore (Hamilton)

Waldo, Edward Hamilton
See Sturgeon, Theodore (Hamilton)

Walker, Alice (Malsenior) 1944- ... **CLC 5, 6, 9, 19, 27, 46, 58, 103; BLC 3; DA; DAB; DAC; DAM MST, MULT, NOV, POET, POP; PC 30; SSC 5; WLCS**
See also AAYA 3, 33; BEST 89:4; BW 2, 3; CA 37-40R; CANR 9, 27, 49, 66, 82; CDALB 1968-1988; DA3; DLB 6, 33, 143; INT CANR-27; MTCW 1, 2; SATA 31

Walker, David Harry 1911-1992 ...... **CLC 14**
See also CA 1-4R; 137; CANR 1; SATA 8; SATA-Obit 71

Walker, Edward Joseph 1934-
See Walker, Ted
See also CA 21-24R; CANR 12, 28, 53

Walker, George F. 1947- . **CLC 44, 61; DAB; DAC; DAM MST**
See also CA 103; CANR 21, 43, 59; DLB 60

Walker, Joseph A. 1935- .... **CLC 19; DAM DRAM, MST**
See also BW 1, 3; CA 89-92; CANR 26; DLB 38

Walker, Margaret (Abigail) 1915-1998 .... **CLC 1, 6; BLC; DAM MULT; PC 20**
See also BW 2, 3; CA 73-76; 172; CANR 26, 54, 76; DLB 76, 152; MTCW 1, 2

Walker, Ted **CLC 13**
See also Walker, Edward Joseph
See also DLB 40

Wallace, David Foster 1962- ..... **CLC 50, 114**
See also CA 132; CANR 59; DA3; MTCW 2

Wallace, Dexter
See Masters, Edgar Lee

Wallace, (Richard Horatio) Edgar 1875-1932 .... **TCLC 57**
See also CA 115; DLB 70

Wallace, Irving 1916-1990 .... **CLC 7, 13; DAM NOV, POP**
See also AITN 1; CA 1-4R; 132; CAAS 1; CANR 1, 27; INT CANR-27; MTCW 1, 2

Wallant, Edward Lewis 1926-1962 ... **CLC 5, 10**
See also CA 1-4R; CANR 22; DLB 2, 28, 143; MTCW 1, 2

Wallas, Graham 1858-1932 .... **TCLC 91**

Walley, Byron
See Card, Orson Scott

Walpole, Horace 1717-1797 .... **LC 49**
See also DLB 39, 104

Walpole, Hugh (Seymour) 1884-1941 .... **TCLC 5**
See also CA 104; 165; DLB 34; MTCW 2

Walser, Martin 1927- .... **CLC 27**
See also CA 57-60; CANR 8, 46; DLB 75, 124

Walser, Robert 1878-1956 .... **TCLC 18; SSC 20**
See also CA 118; 165; DLB 66

Walsh, Gillian Paton
See Paton Walsh, Gillian

Walsh, Jill Paton **CLC 35**
See also Paton Walsh, Gillian
See also CLR 2, 65

Walter, Villiam Christian
See Andersen, Hans Christian

Wambaugh, Joseph (Aloysius, Jr.) 1937- .... **CLC 3, 18; DAM NOV, POP**
See also AITN 1; BEST 89:3; CA 33-36R; CANR 42, 65; DA3; DLB 6; DLBY 83; MTCW 1, 2

Wang Wei 699(?)-761(?) .... **PC 18**

Ward, Arthur Henry Sarsfield 1883-1959
See Rohmer, Sax
See also CA 108; 173

Ward, Douglas Turner 1930- .... **CLC 19**
See also BW 1; CA 81-84; CANR 27; DLB 7, 38

Ward, E. D.
See Lucas, E(dward) V(errall)

Ward, Mary Augusta 1851-1920 ... **TCLC 55**
See also DLB 18

Ward, Peter
See Faust, Frederick (Schiller)

Warhol, Andy 1928(?)-1987 .... **CLC 20**
See also AAYA 12; BEST 89:4; CA 89-92; 121; CANR 34

Warner, Francis (Robert le Plastrier) 1937- .... **CLC 14**
See also CA 53-56; CANR 11

Warner, Marina 1946- .... **CLC 59**
See also CA 65-68; CANR 21, 55; DLB 194

Warner, Rex (Ernest) 1905-1986 ...... **CLC 45**
See also CA 89-92; 119; DLB 15

Warner, Susan (Bogert) 1819-1885 .... **NCLC 31**
See also DLB 3, 42

Warner, Sylvia (Constance) Ashton
See Ashton-Warner, Sylvia (Constance)

Warner, Sylvia Townsend 1893-1978 .... **CLC 7, 19; SSC 23**
See also CA 61-64; 77-80; CANR 16, 60; DLB 34, 139; MTCW 1, 2

Warren, Mercy Otis 1728-1814 ..... **NCLC 13**
See also DLB 31, 200

Warren, Robert Penn 1905-1989 .. **CLC 1, 4, 6, 8, 10, 13, 18, 39, 53, 59; DA; DAB; DAC; DAM MST, NOV, POET; SSC 4; WLC**
See also AITN 1; CA 13-16R; 129; CANR 10, 47; CDALB 1968-1988; DA3; DLB 2, 48, 152; DLBY 80, 89; INT CANR-10; MTCW 1, 2; SATA 46; SATA-Obit 63

Warshofsky, Isaac
See Singer, Isaac Bashevis

Warton, Thomas 1728-1790 ..... **LC 15; DAM POET**
See also DLB 104, 109

Waruk, Kona
See Harris, (Theodore) Wilson

Warung, Price 1855-1911 .... **TCLC 45**
See also Astley, William

Warwick, Jarvis
See Garner, Hugh

Washington, Alex
See Harris, Mark

Washington, Booker T(aliaferro) 1856-1915 ...... **TCLC 10; BLC 3; DAM MULT**
See also BW 1; CA 114; 125; DA3; SATA 28

Washington, George 1732-1799 .... **LC 25**
See also DLB 31

Wassermann, (Karl) Jakob 1873-1934 .... **TCLC 6**
See also CA 104; 163; DLB 66

Wasserstein, Wendy 1950- .. **CLC 32, 59, 90; DAM DRAM; DC 4**
See also CA 121; 129; CABS 3; CANR 53, 75; DA3; DLB 228; INT 129; MTCW 2; SATA 94

Waterhouse, Keith (Spencer) 1929- . **CLC 47**
See also CA 5-8R; CANR 38, 67; DLB 13, 15; MTCW 1, 2

Waters, Frank (Joseph) 1902-1995 .. **CLC 88**
See also CA 5-8R; 149; CAAS 13; CANR 3, 18, 63; DLB 212; DLBY 86

Waters, Roger 1944- .... **CLC 35**

Watkins, Frances Ellen
See Harper, Frances Ellen Watkins

Watkins, Gerrold
See Malzberg, Barry N(athaniel)

Watkins, Gloria Jean 1952(?)-
See hooks, bell
See also BW 2; CA 143; CANR 87; MTCW 2; SATA 115

Watkins, Paul 1964- .... **CLC 55**
See also CA 132; CANR 62

Watkins, Vernon Phillips 1906-1967 .... **CLC 43**
See also CA 9-10; 25-28R; CAP 1; DLB 20

Watson, Irving S.
See Mencken, H(enry) L(ouis)

Watson, John H.
See Farmer, Philip Jose

Watson, Richard F.
See Silverberg, Robert

Waugh, Auberon (Alexander) 1939- .. **CLC 7**
See also CA 45-48; CANR 6, 22, 92; DLB 14, 194

Waugh, Evelyn (Arthur St. John) 1903-1966 .. **CLC 1, 3, 8, 13, 19, 27, 44, 107; DA; DAB; DAC; DAM MST, NOV, POP; SSC 41; WLC**
See also CA 85-88; 25-28R; CANR 22; CD-BLB 1914-1945; DA3; DLB 15, 162, 195; MTCW 1, 2

Waugh, Harriet 1944- .... **CLC 6**
See also CA 85-88; CANR 22

Ways, C. R.
See Blount, Roy (Alton), Jr.

Waystaff, Simon
See Swift, Jonathan

Webb, Beatrice (Martha Potter) 1858-1943 .... **TCLC 22**
See also CA 117; 162; DLB 190

Webb, Charles (Richard) 1939- .... **CLC 7**
See also CA 25-28R

Webb, James H(enry), Jr. 1946- ...... **CLC 22**
See also CA 81-84

Webb, Mary Gladys (Meredith) 1881-1927 .... **TCLC 24**
See also CA 182; 123; DLB 34

Webb, Mrs. Sidney
See Webb, Beatrice (Martha Potter)

Webb, Phyllis 1927- .... **CLC 18**
See also CA 104; CANR 23; DLB 53

Webb, Sidney (James) 1859-1947 .. **TCLC 22**
See also CA 117; 163; DLB 190

Webber, Andrew Lloyd **CLC 21**
See also Lloyd Webber, Andrew

Weber, Lenora Mattingly 1895-1971 .... **CLC 12**
See also CA 19-20; 29-32R; CAP 1; SATA 2; SATA-Obit 26

Weber, Max 1864-1920 .... **TCLC 69**
See also CA 109

Webster, John 1579(?)-1634(?) ... **LC 33; DA; DAB; DAC; DAM DRAM, MST; DC 2; WLC**
See also CDBLB Before 1660; DLB 58

Webster, Noah 1758-1843 .... **NCLC 30**
See also DLB 1, 37, 42, 43, 73

Wedekind, (Benjamin) Frank(lin) 1864-1918 .... **TCLC 7; DAM DRAM**
See also CA 104; 153; DLB 118

Weidman, Jerome 1913-1998 .... **CLC 7**
See also AITN 2; CA 1-4R; 171; CANR 1; DLB 28

Weil, Simone (Adolphine) 1909-1943 .... **TCLC 23**
See also CA 117; 159; MTCW 2

Weininger, Otto 1880-1903 .... **TCLC 84**

Weinstein, Nathan
See West, Nathanael

Weinstein, Nathan von Wallenstein
See West, Nathanael

Weir, Peter (Lindsay) 1944- .... **CLC 20**
See also CA 113; 123

Weiss, Peter (Ulrich) 1916-1982 .. **CLC 3, 15, 51; DAM DRAM**
See also CA 45-48; 106; CANR 3; DLB 69, 124

Weiss, Theodore (Russell) 1916- ... **CLC 3, 8, 14**
See also CA 9-12R; CAAS 2; CANR 46, 94; DLB 5

Welch, (Maurice) Denton 1915-1948 .... **TCLC 22**
See also CA 121; 148

Welch, James 1940- ..... **CLC 6, 14, 52; DAM MULT, POP**
See also CA 85-88; CANR 42, 66; DLB 175; NNAL

Weldon, Fay 1931- . **CLC 6, 9, 11, 19, 36, 59, 122; DAM POP**
See also CA 21-24R; CANR 16, 46, 63; CDBLB 1960 to Present; DLB 14, 194; INT CANR-16; MTCW 1, 2

Wellek, Rene 1903-1995 .... **CLC 28**
See also CA 5-8R; 150; CAAS 7; CANR 8; DLB 63; INT CANR-8

Weller, Michael 1942- .... **CLC 10, 53**
See also CA 85-88

Weller, Paul 1958- .... **CLC 26**

Wellershoff, Dieter 1925- .... **CLC 46**
See also CA 89-92; CANR 16, 37

Welles, (George) Orson 1915-1985 .. **CLC 20, 80**
See also CA 93-96; 117

Wellman, John McDowell 1945-
See Wellman, Mac
See also CA 166

Wellman, Mac 1945- .... **CLC 65**
See also Wellman, John McDowell; Wellman, John McDowell

Wellman, Manly Wade 1903-1986 ... **CLC 49**
See also CA 1-4R; 118; CANR 6, 16, 44; SATA 6; SATA-Obit 47

Wells, Carolyn 1869(?)-1942 .... **TCLC 35**
See also CA 113; 185; DLB 11

Wells, H(erbert) G(eorge) 1866-1946 . **TCLC 6, 12, 19; DA; DAB; DAC; DAM MST, NOV; SSC 6; WLC**
See also AAYA 18; CA 110; 121; CDBLB 1914-1945; CLR 64; DA3; DLB 34, 70, 156, 178; MTCW 1, 2; SATA 20

Wells, Rosemary 1943- .... **CLC 12**
See also AAYA 13; CA 85-88; CANR 48; CLR 16, 69; MAICYA; SAAS 1; SATA 18, 69, 114

Welty, Eudora 1909- ...... **CLC 1, 2, 5, 14, 22, 33, 105; DA; DAB; DAC; DAM MST, NOV; SSC 1, 27; WLC**
See also CA 9-12R; CABS 1; CANR 32, 65; CDALB 1941-1968; DA3; DLB 2, 102, 143; DLBD 12; DLBY 87; MTCW 1, 2

Wen I-to 1899-1946 .... **TCLC 28**

Wentworth, Robert
See Hamilton, Edmond

Werfel, Franz (Viktor) 1890-1945 ... **TCLC 8**
See also CA 104; 161; DLB 81, 124

Wergeland, Henrik Arnold 1808-1845 .... **NCLC 5**

Wersba, Barbara 1932- .... **CLC 30**
See also AAYA 2, 30; CA 29-32R; 182; CAAE 182; CANR 16, 38; CLR 3; DLB 52; JRDA; MAICYA; SAAS 2; SATA 1, 58; SATA-Essay 103

Wertmueller, Lina 1928- .... **CLC 16**
See also CA 97-100; CANR 39, 78

Wescott, Glenway 1901-1987 .. **CLC 13; SSC 35**
See also CA 13-16R; 121; CANR 23, 70; DLB 4, 9, 102

Wesker, Arnold 1932- ... **CLC 3, 5, 42; DAB; DAM DRAM**
See also CA 1-4R; CAAS 7; CANR 1, 33; CDBLB 1960 to Present; DLB 13; MTCW 1

Wesley, Richard (Errol) 1945- .... **CLC 7**
See also BW 1; CA 57-60; CANR 27; DLB 38

Wessel, Johan Herman 1742-1785 .... **LC 7**

West, Anthony (Panther) 1914-1987 .... **CLC 50**
See also CA 45-48; 124; CANR 3, 19; DLB 15

West, C. P.
See Wodehouse, P(elham) G(renville)

West, Cornel (Ronald) 1953- .... **CLC 134; BLCS**
See also CA 144; CANR 91

West, (Mary) Jessamyn 1902-1984 ... **CLC 7, 17**
See also CA 9-12R; 112; CANR 27; DLB 6; DLBY 84; MTCW 1, 2; SATA-Obit 37

West, Morris L(anglo) 1916-1999 ..... **CLC 6, 33**
See also CA 5-8R; 187; CANR 24, 49, 64; MTCW 1, 2

West, Nathanael 1903-1940 .... **TCLC 1, 14, 44; SSC 16**
See also CA 104; 125; CDALB 1929-1941; DA3; DLB 4, 9, 28; MTCW 1, 2

West, Owen
See Koontz, Dean R(ay)

West, Paul 1930- .... **CLC 7, 14, 96**
See also CA 13-16R; CAAS 7; CANR 22, 53, 76, 89; DLB 14; INT CANR-22; MTCW 2

West, Rebecca 1892-1983 ... **CLC 7, 9, 31, 50**
See also CA 5-8R; 109; CANR 19; DLB 36; DLBY 83; MTCW 1, 2

Westall, Robert (Atkinson) 1929-1993 .... **CLC 17**
See also AAYA 12; CA 69-72; 141; CANR 18, 68; CLR 13; JRDA; MAICYA; SAAS 2; SATA 23, 69; SATA-Obit 75

Westermarck, Edward 1862-1939 . **TCLC 87**

Westlake, Donald E(dwin) 1933- .... **CLC 7, 33; DAM POP**
See also CA 17-20R; CAAS 13; CANR 16, 44, 65, 94; INT CANR-16; MTCW 2

Westmacott, Mary
See Christie, Agatha (Mary Clarissa)

Weston, Allen
See Norton, Andre

Wetcheek, J. L.
See Feuchtwanger, Lion

Wetering, Janwillem van de
See van de Wetering, Janwillem

Wetherald, Agnes Ethelwyn 1857-1940 .... **TCLC 81**
See also DLB 99

Wetherell, Elizabeth
See Warner, Susan (Bogert)

Whale, James 1889-1957 .... **TCLC 63**

Whalen, Philip 1923- .... **CLC 6, 29**
See also CA 9-12R; CANR 5, 39; DLB 16

Wharton, Edith (Newbold Jones) 1862-1937 .... **TCLC 3, 9, 27, 53; DA; DAB; DAC; DAM MST, NOV; SSC 6; WLC**
See also AAYA 25; CA 104; 132; CDALB 1865-1917; DA3; DLB 4, 9, 12, 78, 189; DLBD 13; MTCW 1, 2

Wharton, James
See Mencken, H(enry) L(ouis)

Wharton, William (a pseudonym) CLC 18, 37
See also CA 93-96; DLBY 80; INT 93-96

Wheatley (Peters), Phillis 1754(?)-1784 ...... **LC 3, 50; BLC 3; DA; DAC; DAM MST, MULT, POET; PC 3; WLC**
See also CDALB 1640-1865; DA3; DLB 31, 50

Wheelock, John Hall 1886-1978 .... **CLC 14**
See also CA 13-16R; 77-80; CANR 14; DLB 45

White, E(lwyn) B(rooks) 1899-1985 . **CLC 10, 34, 39; DAM POP**
See also AITN 2; CA 13-16R; 116; CANR 16, 37; CDALBS; CLR 1, 21; DA3; DLB 11, 22; MAICYA; MTCW 1, 2; SATA 2, 29, 100; SATA-Obit 44

White, Edmund (Valentine III) 1940- .... **CLC 27, 110; DAM POP**
See also AAYA 7; CA 45-48; CANR 3, 19, 36, 62; DA3; DLB 227; MTCW 1, 2

White, Patrick (Victor Martindale) 1912-1990 ...... **CLC 3, 4, 5, 7, 9, 18, 65, 69; SSC 39**
See also CA 81-84; 132; CANR 43; MTCW 1

White, Phyllis Dorothy James 1920-
See James, P. D.
See also CA 21-24R; CANR 17, 43, 65; DAM POP; DA3; MTCW 1, 2

White, T(erence) H(anbury) 1906-1964 .... **CLC 30**
See also AAYA 22; CA 73-76; CANR 37; DLB 160; JRDA; MAICYA; SATA 12

White, Terence de Vere 1912-1994 ... **CLC 49**
See also CA 49-52; 145; CANR 3

White, Walter
See White, Walter F(rancis)
See also BLC; DAM MULT

White, Walter F(rancis) 1893-1955 .... **TCLC 15**
See also White, Walter
See also BW 1; CA 115; 124; DLB 51

White, William Hale 1831-1913
See Rutherford, Mark
See also CA 121

Whitehead, Alfred North 1861-1947 .... **TCLC 97**
See also CA 117; 165; DLB 100

Whitehead, E(dward) A(nthony) 1933- .... **CLC 5**
See also CA 65-68; CANR 58

Whitemore, Hugh (John) 1936- .... **CLC 37**
See also CA 132; CANR 77; INT 132

Whitman, Sarah Helen (Power) 1803-1878 .... **NCLC 19**
See also DLB 1

Whitman, Walt(er) 1819-1892 .. **NCLC 4, 31, 81; DA; DAB; DAC; DAM MST, POET; PC 3; WLC**
See also CDALB 1640-1865; DA3; DLB 3, 64, 224; SATA 20

Whitney, Phyllis A(yame) 1903- ...... **CLC 42; DAM POP**
See also AAYA 36; AITN 2; BEST 90:3; CA 1-4R; CANR 3, 25, 38, 60; CLR 59; DA3; JRDA; MAICYA; MTCW 2; SATA 1, 30

Whittemore, (Edward) Reed (Jr.)
1919- .... **CLC 4**
See also CA 9-12R; CAAS 8; CANR 4; DLB 5

Whittier, John Greenleaf
1807-1892 .... **NCLC 8, 59**
See also DLB 1

Whittlebot, Hernia
See Coward, Noel (Peirce)

Wicker, Thomas Grey 1926-
See Wicker, Tom
See also CA 65-68; CANR 21, 46

Wicker, Tom CLC 7
See also Wicker, Thomas Grey

Wideman, John Edgar 1941- ...... **CLC 5, 34, 36, 67, 122; BLC 3; DAM MULT**
See also BW 2, 3; CA 85-88; CANR 14, 42, 67; DLB 33, 143; MTCW 2

Wiebe, Rudy (Henry) 1934- .. **CLC 6, 11, 14, 138; DAC; DAM MST**
See also CA 37-40R; CANR 42, 67; DLB 60

Wieland, Christoph Martin
1733-1813 .... **NCLC 17**
See also DLB 97

Wiene, Robert 1881-1938 .... **TCLC 56**

Wieners, John 1934- .... **CLC 7**
See also CA 13-16R; DLB 16

Wiesel, Elie(zer) 1928- .... **CLC 3, 5, 11, 37; DA; DAB; DAC; DAM MST, NOV; WLCS**
See also AAYA 7; AITN 1; CA 5-8R; CAAS 4; CANR 8, 40, 65; CDALBS; DA3; DLB 83; DLBY 87; INT CANR-8; MTCW 1, 2; SATA 56

Wiggins, Marianne 1947- .... **CLC 57**
See also BEST 89:3; CA 130; CANR 60

Wight, James Alfred 1916-1995
See Herriot, James
See also CA 77-80; SATA 55; SATA-Brief 44

Wilbur, Richard (Purdy) 1921- ..... **CLC 3, 6, 9, 14, 53, 110; DA; DAB; DAC; DAM MST, POET**
See also CA 1-4R; CABS 2; CANR 2, 29, 76, 93; CDALBS; DLB 5, 169; INT CANR-29; MTCW 1, 2; SATA 9, 108

Wild, Peter 1940- .... **CLC 14**
See also CA 37-40R; DLB 5

Wilde, Oscar (Fingal O'Flahertie Wills)
1854(?)-1900 .... **TCLC 1, 8, 23, 41; DA; DAB; DAC; DAM DRAM, MST, NOV; SSC 11; WLC**
See also CA 104; 119; CDBLB 1890-1914; DA3; DLB 10, 19, 34, 57, 141, 156, 190; SATA 24

Wilder, Billy CLC 20
See also Wilder, Samuel
See also DLB 26

Wilder, Samuel 1906-
See Wilder, Billy
See also CA 89-92

Wilder, Thornton (Niven)
1897-1975 .. **CLC 1, 5, 6, 10, 15, 35, 82; DA; DAB; DAC; DAM DRAM, MST, NOV; DC 1; WLC**
See also AAYA 29; AITN 2; CA 13-16R; 61-64; CANR 40; CDALBS; DA3; DLB 4, 7, 9, 228; DLBY 97; MTCW 1, 2

Wilding, Michael 1942- .... **CLC 73**
See also CA 104; CANR 24, 49

Wiley, Richard 1944- .... **CLC 44**
See also CA 121; 129; CANR 71

Wilhelm, Kate CLC 7
See also Wilhelm, Katie (Gertrude)
See also AAYA 20; CAAS 5; DLB 8; INT CANR-17

Wilhelm, Katie (Gertrude) 1928-
See Wilhelm, Kate
See also CA 37-40R; CANR 17, 36, 60, 94; MTCW 1

Wilkins, Mary
See Freeman, Mary E(leanor) Wilkins

Willard, Nancy 1936- .... **CLC 7, 37**
See also CA 89-92; CANR 10, 39, 68; CLR 5; DLB 5, 52; MAICYA; MTCW 1; SATA 37, 71; SATA-Brief 30

William of Ockham 1285-1347 ..... **CMLC 32**

Williams, Ben Ames 1889-1953 ..... **TCLC 89**
See also CA 183; DLB 102

Williams, C(harles) K(enneth)
1936- .... **CLC 33, 56; DAM POET**
See also CA 37-40R; CAAS 26; CANR 57; DLB 5

Williams, Charles
See Collier, James L(incoln)

Williams, Charles (Walter Stansby)
1886-1945 .... **TCLC 1, 11**
See also CA 104; 163; DLB 100, 153

Williams, (George) Emlyn
1905-1987 .... **CLC 15; DAM DRAM**
See also CA 104; 123; CANR 36; DLB 10, 77; MTCW 1

Williams, Hank 1923-1953 .... **TCLC 81**

Williams, Hugo 1942- .... **CLC 42**
See also CA 17-20R; CANR 45; DLB 40

Williams, J. Walker
See Wodehouse, P(elham) G(renville)

Williams, John A(lfred) 1925- ..... **CLC 5, 13; BLC 3; DAM MULT**
See also BW 2, 3; CA 53-56; CAAS 3; CANR 6, 26, 51; DLB 2, 33; INT CANR-6

Williams, Jonathan (Chamberlain)
1929- .... **CLC 13**
See also CA 9-12R; CAAS 12; CANR 8; DLB 5

Williams, Joy 1944- .... **CLC 31**
See also CA 41-44R; CANR 22, 48

Williams, Norman 1952- .... **CLC 39**
See also CA 118

Williams, Sherley Anne 1944-1999 . **CLC 89; BLC 3; DAM MULT, POET**
See also BW 2, 3; CA 73-76; 185; CANR 25, 82; DLB 41; INT CANR-25; SATA 78; SATA-Obit 116

Williams, Shirley
See Williams, Sherley Anne

Williams, Tennessee 1911-1983 . **CLC 1, 2, 5, 7, 8, 11, 15, 19, 30, 39, 45, 71, 111; DA; DAB; DAC; DAM DRAM, MST; DC 4; WLC**
See also AAYA 31; AITN 1, 2; CA 5-8R; 108; CABS 3; CANR 31; CDALB 1941-1968; DA3; DLB 7; DLBD 4; DLBY 83; MTCW 1, 2

Williams, Thomas (Alonzo)
1926-1990 .... **CLC 14**
See also CA 1-4R; 132; CANR 2

Williams, William C.
See Williams, William Carlos

Williams, William Carlos
1883-1963 .... **CLC 1, 2, 5, 9, 13, 22, 42, 67; DA; DAB; DAC; DAM MST, POET; PC 7; SSC 31**
See also CA 89-92; CANR 34; CDALB 1917-1929; DA3; DLB 4, 16, 54, 86; MTCW 1, 2

Williamson, David (Keith) 1942- ..... **CLC 56**
See also CA 103; CANR 41

Williamson, Ellen Douglas 1905-1984
See Douglas, Ellen
See also CA 17-20R; 114; CANR 39

Williamson, Jack CLC 29
See also Williamson, John Stewart
See also CAAS 8; DLB 8

Williamson, John Stewart 1908-
See Williamson, Jack
See also CA 17-20R; CANR 23, 70

Willie, Frederick
See Lovecraft, H(oward) P(hillips)

Willingham, Calder (Baynard, Jr.)
1922-1995 .... **CLC 5, 51**
See also CA 5-8R; 147; CANR 3; DLB 2, 44; MTCW 1

Willis, Charles
See Clarke, Arthur C(harles)

Willy
See Colette, (Sidonie-Gabrielle)

Willy, Colette
See Colette, (Sidonie-Gabrielle)

Wilson, A(ndrew) N(orman) 1950- .. **CLC 33**
See also CA 112; 122; DLB 14, 155, 194; MTCW 2

Wilson, Angus (Frank Johnstone)
1913-1991 . **CLC 2, 3, 5, 25, 34; SSC 21**
See also CA 5-8R; 134; CANR 21; DLB 15, 139, 155; MTCW 1, 2

Wilson, August 1945- ... **CLC 39, 50, 63, 118; BLC 3; DA; DAB; DAC; DAM DRAM, MST, MULT; DC 2; WLCS**
See also AAYA 16; BW 2, 3; CA 115; 122; CANR 42, 54, 76; DA3; DLB 228; MTCW 1, 2

Wilson, Brian 1942- .... **CLC 12**

Wilson, Colin 1931- .... **CLC 3, 14**
See also CA 1-4R; CAAS 5; CANR 1, 22, 33, 77; DLB 14, 194; MTCW 1

Wilson, Dirk
See Pohl, Frederik

Wilson, Edmund 1895-1972 .. **CLC 1, 2, 3, 8, 24**
See also CA 1-4R; 37-40R; CANR 1, 46; DLB 63; MTCW 1, 2

Wilson, Ethel Davis (Bryant)
1888(?)-1980 .... **CLC 13; DAC; DAM POET**
See also CA 102; DLB 68; MTCW 1

Wilson, Harriet E. Adams
1828(?)-1863(?) .... **NCLC 78; BLC 3; DAM MULT**
See also DLB 50

Wilson, John 1785-1854 .... **NCLC 5**

Wilson, John (Anthony) Burgess 1917-1993
See Burgess, Anthony
See also CA 1-4R; 143; CANR 2, 46; DAC; DAM NOV; DA3; MTCW 1, 2

Wilson, Lanford 1937- .... **CLC 7, 14, 36; DAM DRAM**
See also CA 17-20R; CABS 3; CANR 45; DLB 7

Wilson, Robert M. 1944- .... **CLC 7, 9**
See also CA 49-52; CANR 2, 41; MTCW 1

Wilson, Robert McLiam 1964- .... **CLC 59**
See also CA 132

Wilson, Sloan 1920- .... **CLC 32**
See also CA 1-4R; CANR 1, 44

Wilson, Snoo 1948- .... **CLC 33**
See also CA 69-72

Wilson, William S(mith) 1932- .... **CLC 49**
See also CA 81-84

Wilson, (Thomas) Woodrow
1856-1924 .... **TCLC 79**
See also CA 166; DLB 47

Winchilsea, Anne (Kingsmill) Finch Counte
1661-1720
See Finch, Anne

Literary Criticism Series
Cumulative Topic Index

This index lists all topic entries in the Gale Group's *Classical and Medieval Literature Criticism, Contemporary Literary Criticism, Literature Criticism from 1400 to 1800, Nineteenth-Century Literature Criticism,* and *Twentieth-Century Literary Criticism.*

Topic Index

Topic Index

CMLC Cumulative Nationality Index

CMLC Cumulative Title Index

Title Index

Title Index

Title Index

Title Index

Title Index

Title Index